Encyclopedia *of*
Recorded Sound

Encyclopedia *of* Recorded Sound

Second Edition

Volume 2
M–Z
Index

Frank Hoffmann, Editor
Howard Ferstler, Technical Editor

ROUTLEDGE

NEW YORK AND LONDON

Published in 2005 by

Routledge
270 Madison Avenue
New York, NY 10016
www.routledge-ny.com

Published in Great Britain by Routledge
2 Park Square
Milton Park, Abingdon
Oxon OX14 4RN
www.routledge.co.uk

10 9 8 7 6 5 4 3 2 1

Library of Congress Cataloging-in-Publication Data
Encyclopedia of recorded sound / edited by Frank Hoffmann.— 2nd ed.
    p. cm.
  Rev. ed. of: Encyclopedia of recorded sound in the United States. 1993.
  Includes bibliographical references (p.   ) and index.
  ISBN 0-415-93835-X (hb: alk.paper)
  1. Sound recordings—Dictionaries. 2 Sound recording industry
  —Dictionaries. I. Hoffmann, Frank W., 1949— II. Encyclopedia
  of recorded sound in the United States.
  ML102.S67E5 2004
  384—dc22

                                    2003026491

Contents

M

MAAZEL, LORIN (6 MAR 1930–)

Conductor, born of American parents in Neuilly, France. He was taken to the U.S. as an infant and studied violin and piano in Los Angeles. At age eight he conducted a performance of the visiting orchestra from the University of Idaho, and in 1939 he conducted the National Music Camp Orchestra (Interlochen, Michigan) at the New York World's Fair. At age 11 he conducted the NBC Symphony Orchestra, and a year later the New York Philharmonic Orchestra. Then he modestly left conducting and played as a violinist with the Pittsburgh Symphony Orchestra. With a Fulbright Grant to Italy, he conducted various groups there in 1953–1955, then toured Europe and South America. He was the first American to conduct at Bayreuth (1960). In 1962 he conducted at the Metropolitan Opera and returned to Europe to direct various ensembles. Maazel succeeded Georg Szell as music director of the Cleveland Orchestra in 1972, remaining until 1982. He took the post of artistic director of the Vienna State Opera in 1982, but resigned amid some controversy two years later. From 1984–1986, he was music consultant for the Pittsburgh Symphony Orchestra, and then its music director through 1996. Until 2002, he was music director for the Bavarian Radio Symphony Orchestra.

Among Maazel's distinguished recordings are Beethoven's Ninth Symphony with the Cleveland Orchestra (CBS MK #76999), the Mahler symphonies with the Vienna Philharmonic Orchestra, also for CBS, and complete operas *Carmen* (Erato #880373) and *Luisa Miller* (DGG #415 366-2GH). He has two Grammys, one for Best Opera Recording for his recording of *Porgy & Bess* with the Cleveland Orchestra awarded in 1976, and a second from 1984 for the soundtrack of the opera-film, Bizet's *Carmen*, with Placdio Domingo and Ruggero Raimondi.

MACCOLL, EWAN (25 JAN 1915–22 OCT 1989)

British folklorist, radio producer, and performer, MacColl recorded prolifically from the 1950s through the 1980s. Born in Salford, Lancashire, to Scottish parents, MacColl quit school at age 15 to work as an actor/singer. He was hired by the BBC in the 1950s to produce a series of "radio plays," incorporating traditional music recordings. He also recorded a series of albums of traditional English and Scottish ballads and folksongs for a variety of labels, including Riverside, Folkways, Topic, Tradition, and many others. He was often accompanied by his wife, folksinger Peggy Seeger. Besides his work as a folksong performer, MacColl composed the pop ballad "The First Time Ever I Saw Your Face," a major hit for Roberta Flack in 1972. Because of his left-wing political sympathies, MacColl never toured the U.S. as a performer, but was long active on the London folk scene, where he ran the famous Singer's Club.

CARL BENSON

MACDONALD, THOMAS HOOD (1859–3 DEC 1911)

American inventor, born in Marysville, California. He was a research scientist at the Bridgeport, Connecticut, plant of the American Graphophone Co. and developed many key devices in the cylinder and disc fields. Macdonald was granted 54 individual patents and two as joint inventor with Frank L. Capps. His most important ones were for the Graphophone, Type N — the "Bijou"; it was U.S. patent #569,290 (filed 2 Nov 1895; granted 13 Oct 1896). Later he filed for the double-spring "Eagle" Graphophone (16 Sep 1897; patent #680,794 granted 20 Aug 1901). A toy Graphophone, marketed 1899, had patent #683,130 (filed 21 Feb 1899; granted 24 Sep 1901). An invention of special interest was the Multiple Graphophone, marketed as the Multiplex Grand; Macdonald received patent #711,706 for it (filed 11 June 1898; granted 21 Oct 1902). This was the first attempt at stereo recording, using three separately recorded tracks on the same cylinder. As all the records have been lost, it cannot be ascertained how well the process worked, but it was shown at *the* Paris Exposition of 1900. Macdonald went to England to organize Columbia's British factory at Earlsfield, Surrey, in 1905; cylinder and disc records were produced there. [Koenigsberg 1990.]

See also **Columbia Record Players**

MACDONOUGH, HARRY
(30 MAY 1871– 26 SEP 1931)

Canadian tenor, born as John Scantlebury MacDonald, in Windsor, Ontario. He was one of the most popular early recording artists, having made cylinders before 1900 for the Michigan Electric Co. (to be played in coin-ops) and for Edison. His surname was misspelled as Macdonough on his first cylinder label, and he decided to leave it that way; then he deliberately changed the first name. Ralph Raymond was another performing name he used. His first Edison record was "Good-Bye, Sweet Dream, Good-Bye" (#6500; 1898); he made 105 Edison cylinders by 1912, all popular ballads of the day. He began working with Victor in 1903, making "No One to Love" (#2183), and made some 350 records by 1908. "The Holy City" was his greatest Victor hit (#94; 1903). Macdonough was a member of the Schubert Trio and of the Edison Quartet (also known as the Haydn Quartet) until it disbanded in 1914. Then he sang with the Orpheus Quartet and the Lyric Quartet. He made duets with Grace Spencer and many other star performers. The "Miserere" duet from *Trovatore*, with Olive Kline, was long one of the most popular Victor offerings. There were still 77 titles in the 1917 Victor catalog, but the number had dropped to four ("Miserere" one of them) by 1927.

Macdonough was also active in the Victor business office as assistant recording director. He carried on with both executive and performing work from the early 1900s to 1920, then quit recording but remained as an executive until 1925, at which time he moved to Columbia as director of recording studios. He died six years later in New York City. [Walsh 1943/11-12; 1952/5.]

MACERO, TEO (30 OCT 1925–)

A noted jazz record producer, Macero was born Attilio Joseph Macero in Glen Falls, New York. After service in the Navy, Macero came to New York to study composition at Juilliard, which he attended from 1948–1953. During this period, he met avant-garde composer Edgard Varèse, became interested in tape composition, and also gigged around New York as a jazz saxophonist. In 1953, Macero joined jazz bass player Charles Mingus's Jazz Composer's Workshop; he also cut his first album as a leader for Mingus's Debut label, a recording that featured an unusual quintet of alto and soprano sax (played by Macero), accordion, two basses, and drums. He also recorded for Prestige and smaller labels as a leader and was invited to record half an album for Columbia in 1955 called *What's New?* (Columbia C #842), which featured tape experimentations as well as live performances. Macero's work impressed Columbia's jazz producer, George Avakian, who hired him to work for the label in 1957. Beginning in the late 1950s, Macero worked on all of Miles Davis's recordings and is best known for his assembling and editing of Davis's late 1960s and early 1970s jazz-rock albums, notably *Bitches Brew* (Columbia #40577) and *In a Silent Way* (Columbia #40580). Macero continued to work for Columbia through the early 1980s. After his retirement, he returned occasionally to performing on the saxophone and recording. Beginning in the late 1990s, Macero reissued a number of his recordings through his own Teo label.

CARL BENSON

MACKIE, GREG[ORY CLARK]
(22 SEP 1949–)

Professional audio designer. Mackie was a frustrated rock musician who took to making his own amps and PA systems because he was unhappy with the quality of what was commercially available. Mackie formed his first company in 1969 as cofounder of Technical Audio Products (TAPCO) with partner Martin Schneider, operating out of a house in the Pacific Northwest. The company introduced the first six-channel mixer designed to handle the heavy demands of rock bands. The mixers became very popular because of their heavy-duty construction. In 1977 Mackie left the firm to form another company, AudioControl, to manufacture home stereo equipment, particularly equalizers and analyzers. In 1989 he returned to the mixer business, recognizing the needs of contemporary bands that utilized banks of synthesizers as well as conventional instruments. Today the company produces highly regarded recording mixers, digital recording products, studio consoles, studio loudspeaker monitors, and professional amplifiers. In 1993 the company produced the first reasonably priced, eight-bus analog console.

CARL BENSON AND HOWARD FERSTLER

MACON, "UNCLE" DAVE (7 OCT 1870– 22 MAR 1952)

Star of the *Grand Ole Opry* from its inception and major recording artist of the 1920s and early 1930s, Macon was a fine banjo player and songster. Born David Harrison Macon in Smart Station, Tennessee, Macon worked as a wagon driver professionally while entertaining nights and on weekends. After the invention of the automobile ended his business, he became a full-time performer. He recorded hundreds of 78s, often accompanied by the talented McGee brothers (guitarists Sam and Kirk) and fiddler Sid Harkreader, going under the name The Fruit Jar Drinkers (illegal moonshine liquor was often dispensed in used fruit jars, hence the name). In the 1940s and early 1950s, he was often accompanied by his son, Dorris, in *Opry* appearances. Macon's last commercial recordings were cut for Bluebird in 1935. He died in Nashville, Tennessee.

CARL BENSON

MADISON (LABEL)

An American record issued from about 1926 to 1931; it was an affiliate of Grey Gull. Although "Madison Record Co." appears on the labels, "the firm had no corporate existence" (Rust). It was the Woolworth stores that distributed them for $.10 each. A few interesting jazz numbers are found, but nearly all the material is standard dance and popular song. [Barr 1982; Rust 1978.]

MADONNA [LOUISE VERONICA CICCONE] (16 AUG 1958–)

It is easy to dismiss Madonna's superstar status as the product of her considerable flair for self-promotion. Beyond her physical allure, seemingly never-ending repertoire of fashion statements, and effective career

moves, Madonna's success owed much to the irresistible pull of her dance-oriented rock recordings. In her best music, the elements — somewhat pedestrian arrangements, synthesizer lines, and programmed drum beats; competent, though not particularly distinguished singing; and hook-laden, if not profound compositions — add up to a much more impressive whole, with emphasis on personality — an ingredient best showcased via the video medium. Madonna burst into the public consciousness with "Jellybean" Benitez-produced eponymous LP (Sire #23867; 1983; #8), which heralded the return of the disco ethic (sans that outré label) to the pop music scene. The follow-up, *Like a Virgin* (Sire #25157; 1984; #1) — produced by former Chic guitarist Nile Rodgers and featuring the breakthrough hits, "Like a Virgin" (Sire #29210; 1984; #1) and "Material Girl" (Sire #29083; 1984; #2) — elevated her (at this juncture, in her "boy toy" manifestation) to iconic status. Her place in the pop culture pantheon now ensured, she embarked upon a series of ambitious artistic statements — the eclectic tour de force, *True Blue* (Sire #25442; 1986; #1), best remembered for the anti-abortion plea in "Papa Don't Preach" (Sire #20492; 1986; #1); the remix collection, *U Can Dance* (Sire #25535; 1987; #14), featuring material first appearing on the three earlier albums); socially conscious *Like a Prayer* (Sire #25844; 1989; #1), and hits compilation, *The Immaculate Collection* (Sire #26440; 1990; #5), which included considerable studio editing of the originals (e.g., Q-sound remastering, faster tempos, earlier fade-outs, seguing of tracks) — punctuated by

Madonna during her "boy toy" era. Courtesy Frank Hoffmann

forays into film acting and book production. Madonna's recorded output (and the public reception) was more uneven in the 1990s. *Erotica* (Maverick #18782; 1992; #3) was a sensual, pulsating workout; its comparatively poor commercial showing seems to have influenced her decision to produce a more intimate, low-key LP, *Bedtime Stories* (Maverick #45767; 1994; #3). Following her success in the movie adaptation of Andrew Lloyd Webber's *Evita* — *Selections from Evita* (Warner Brothers; 1997) which featured highlights from the original two-disc soundtrack — she attempted to update her sound by enlisting techno producer William Orbit for *Ray of Light* (Maverick #46847; 1998; #2). She perfected her electronica-inspired approach in *Music* (Maverick #47598; 2000), darting effortlessly from club grooves to trip-hop and synth-based ambient textures. Newly committed to a more domestic lifestyle in the 21st century, it appears likely that future recordings will continue to incorporate contemporary trends within a seamless, beat-inflected framework, emphasizing production values over the image making.

FRANK HOFFMANN

MAGNAVOX CORPORATION

Electronics manufacturing firm founded in 1917 by Peter Jensen and Edwin Pridham when they merged their own Commercial Wireless and Development Co. with the Sonora Phonograph Corp. The company began by manufacturing loudspeaker systems but could not compete with the bigger AT&T so they moved into making radios and phonographs. Jensen left the firm in 1925. After World War II, Magnavox became a prominent manufacturer of television sets, and then in the 1970s video recorders. In the late 1970s, Magnavox developed the video game Odyssey², which became a classic of its type. In the 1980s and 1990s, the company has made televisions, video recorders and players, DVD players, and portable camcorders, among other products. The Magnavox name is owned by Philips NV.

See also **Jensen, Peter Laurits**

MAGNEPAN LOUDSPEAKERS

Pioneered in 1969 by Jim Winey, the flat-panel magnetic-driven loudspeaker design has been intriguing audiophiles for more than 30 years. Winey had previously owned flat-panel electrostatic systems and admired their dipolar-radiation signature. However, he wanted to create something that worked similarly in terms of acoustic output and radiation pattern but that would not require an external power source and present a friendlier load to amplifiers. The result was the thin-film magnetic equivalent to the electrostatic design, and the company he created to produce and market the systems was called Magnepan. Corporate and manufacturing facilities are located in White Bear Lake, Minnesota, a small community north of St. Paul and Minneapolis. Having outgrown its original facilities, Magnepan's current plant is over 50,000 square feet, in addition to corporate and engineering offices, with over 40 people employed. Magnepan manufactures two different kinds of proprietary drivers for its systems: true ribbon tweeters with response beyond 20 kHz and planar-magnetic/quasi-ribbon midrange and bass drivers. The latter driver is the one upon which Winey built his company, and it operates without an electrostatic driver's transformer, essentially behaving like a very large, very light dynamic driver, although the design is more like a series of dynamic drivers that fire along a vertical axis. Each and every model is still designed by Winey, and to this date over 200,000 pairs of his Magneplanar speakers have found their way into the homes of panel-speaker enthusiasts.

See also **Loudspeaker**

HOWARD FERSTLER

MAGNETIC RECORDING

Varying magnetic patterns, which correspond to sound waves, can be imposed on a moving magnetizable surface. Such patterns can be played back and the magnetic patterns can be read and transduced to sound waves. This principle, which underlies all modern tape recording systems, was discovered independently by several 19th-century inventors. Thomas Edison, while working on the cylinder phonograph in the late 1870s, observed that it would be possible to magnetize indented tracks on a tinfoil cylinder, then to record in the tracks and read the deformations in the foil with an electromagnet. He did not develop that idea, but Charles Sumner Tainter did some experiments in the Volta Laboratory. Tainter's approach was to propose a fountain pen attached to the recording diaphragm, the pen carrying ink that contained bits of iron; the pen would then write on a paper-covered cylinder in response to the sound signal. He filed on 29 Aug 1885 for a patent, which was granted (U.S. #341,287; 4 May 1886), but decided to concentrate on mechanical cylinder recording instead of pursuing the electromagnetic trail.

An article by Oberlin Smith, "Some Possible Form of Phonograph," appeared in *Electrical World* on 8 Sep 1888; in it Smith proposed that particles of steel, carried by cotton or silk thread, could serve as the magnetized medium for recording telephone speech. Those particles could be scanned by an electromagnet. But Smith did not develop the notion into a patent.

The first working magnetic recorder was the Telegraphone of the Danish engineer Valdemar Poulsen, dating from 1898. That device looked something like a cylinder phonograph, with its cylinder grooved to hold a carbon steel wire. An electric motor rotated the cylinder at 84 inches per second, running the wire past the poles of an electromagnet. Signals were indeed inscribed on that wire; one message remains playable to this day. But there was a lack of amplification and it had a major obstacle of short playing time — limited to no more than a minute per length of wire. One of Paulsen's patents suggested variant media, such as a band (steel tape) machine, and a paper strip coated with magnetizable metal dust. Later he and Oscar Pedersen did construct a usable wire machine for dictation, with 20 minutes playing time. Both the British Post Office and War Office — and the U.S. Navy — bought these devices before and during World War I.

Lee De Forest suggested in 1924 the possible application of his amplifier to the wire recording process, thus allowing music reproduction, but he did not follow up on the concept. A year later Henry C. Bullis got a U.S. patent (#1,213,150) for the application of magnetic recording in motion pictures; this concept was not immediately developed either. A strong deterrent to all magnetic systems designers was the success of the talking machine in both its cylinder and disc formats. In the years before World War I, improvements in recording machines and media poured in from hundreds of thriving manufacturers, and the public in America and Europe was apparently insatiable for the products.

Nevertheless, research continued. W.L. Carlson and G.W. Carpenter patented their substitution of high-frequency bias in place of direct-current bias applied to the recording head in 1921 (U.S. #1,640,881). And in Germany, Kurt Stille made diverse ameliorations and innovations. He developed a finer wire, capable of longer duration; and a steel-tape recording machine with sprocket holes in the tape, the purpose being synchronization with motion picture film. His wire machine had a cartridge containing supply and take-up reels, on the order of today's cassette. It was patented in the U.K. (#331,859; 1928). He described it in a 1930 article, under the name of Dailygraph, and saw it receive some commercial production: rights were acquired by the International Telephone and Telegraph Co. in 1932, who redesigned it and produced it in Germany as the Textophone (1933).

Stille's steel tape machine was noisy and erratic and ran too fast (six feet per second) to be practical. A demonstration in London in 1929, by film producer Ludwig Blattner, it was not successful in blending film and speech. Blattner — who had acquired the rights from Stille by license — persisted with this sound carrier and sold some devices to the British Broadcasting Corp. (BBC) in 1930. New models were devised with playing time up to 30 minutes per spool, and a British Blattnerphone Co. was chartered. Later the rights passed to Guglielmo Marconi's Wireless Telegraph Co., where further improvements were forthcoming, sufficient to make the machines usable at the BBC into the 1950s. A comparable machine was developed by the C. Lorenz AG in Germany and adopted by the German radio system.

Military research in World War II led to American wire recorder models with 0.1 millimeter stainless steel wire moving at 30 inches/second; one spool could run 60 minutes. Commercially available recorders were made by the Brush Development Co. and Western Electric Co., both with steel tapes. Marvin Camras, of Armour Research Foundation (Chicago), received many patents in the early 1940s and saw production of steel wire machines by General Electric Co. Wire recording reached high quality in the late 1940s, notably with an Armour Research model and the Magnecorder in the U.S. and a Boosey & Hawkes device in Britain. However, the rapid improvements in plastic tape recording soon eclipsed the wire machines.

Fritz Pfleumer, of Dresden, brought to a practical stage the idea of a paper or plastic base for a recording tape. He began experiments in 1927, using soft iron powder as the magnetic coat, attaching it to the base with sugar or other organic binders. Pfleumer received German patents #500,900 and #544,302, then U.K. patent #333,154 (1928). Various improvements in the tape were made in Germany through the 1930s. By 1934 the Badische Anilin und Soda Fabrik was producing cellulose acetate tapes coated with ferric oxide. The Allgemeine Elektrizitäts Gesellschaft (AEG) was able to record a symphonic concert on their Magnetophon in 1936, albeit not very satisfactorily. It took another two years of research by AEG before a machine suitable for broadcasting was available, and music could at last be presented in decent rendition, with a frequency response of 50–6,000 Hz.

In the postwar period tape recording spread throughout the world. The introduction of Mylar as a thinner, durable base accompanied numerous technical refinements. The Ampex Corp. was the first to market high quality tape equipment in the U.S. (1948). Sales of prerecorded reel to reel tape began around 1954, but the medium was not commercially successful because of the clumsy manual process required to thread a tape onto the take-up reel. Quality did reach high levels, and tapes were soon utilized by record companies as the original recording media, with the signal later transferred to disc.

A monumental stride was taken by Philips in 1963, with the introduction of the audiocassette and its compact portable recorder. Improvements in fidelity followed. Then in 1986 Sony introduced the DAT (Digital Audio Tape), transforming the field. [Hoover 1971 has illustrations of reel-to-reel and cassette formats, p. 125; Jansen 1983.]

See also **Cassette; Tape; Tape Recording**

MAGNETOPHON

The magnetic tape recorder first made by Allgemeine Elektrizitäts Gesellschaft (AEG) in 1935. It was demonstrated at the Berlin Radio Fair, showing the new cellulose acetate base tapes coated with ferric oxide. Although intended for business dictation, the machine was also used for musical recording. When Thomas Beecham and the London Philharmonic Orchestra performed in Germany in 1936 the Magnetophon recorded the concert. In 1938 AEG produced an improved version, type K4. It had a frequency response of 50–6,000 Hz, adequate for radio use. In 1942 another improved version, type HTS, was put into service; it carried the frequency range of 50–9,000 Hz, while reducing distortion characteristics and signal to noise ratio. During World War II the machine was used for broadcasting taped concerts, with a fidelity that puzzled listeners outside Germany; when the Allies captured Radio Luxembourg on 11 Sep 1944 they found the Magnetophon, in the last version, type K7. It ran the tape at 30.31 inches/second (77 centimeters/second), and gave up to 10,000 Hz in response. It had facilities for editing, a time clock, and a means of running two or more machines in synchronization for continuous play. One tape reel ran 22 minutes. Manufacture of high quality machines based on the Magnetophon began outside Germany in 1947 — one of the first was the EMI's BTR1. In America the design was modified by Jack Mullin and Ampex Corp.

MAGNOLA TALKING MACHINE CO.

A Chicago firm, active from 1916–1923. It made the Magnola line of record players, with five models advertised in *TMW* of January 1917. An advertisement in the January 1923 *TMW* reported the "7th year of steady success."

MAHAVISHNU ORCHESTRA

The Mahavishnu Orchestra was a primary recording and performing outlet for guitar virtuoso John McLaughlin. Born 4 Jan 1942, in Yorkshire, England, McLaughlin initially made his name performing in area blues bands, most notably units headed by Graham Bond and Brian Auger. Matriculating to the U.S. after recording the highly regarded *Extrapolation* (Verve/Polydor #PD-5510; 1969), he recorded six jazz-rock albums with Miles Davis and the Tony Williams' Lifetime between 1969–1971. McLaughlin experimented with various fusion lineups in his early U.S. solo releases: *Devotion* (Douglas #4; 1971) featured Jimi Hendrix's Band of Gypsys rhythm section Lifetime organist Larry Young, and *My Goal's Beyond* (Douglas #30766; 1972) included drummer Billy Cobham, violinist Jerry Goodman, and Indian tabla player Badal Roy. He then formed the Mahavishnu Orchestra by adding two European jazz-oriented musicians, bassist Rick Laird and keyboardist Jan Hammer, while retaining Cobham and Goodman. Choosing a name provided by his guru Sri Chimnoy, McLaughlin further refined the fusion formula by adding his own East-West synthesis, melding the stop-and-start melodies and rhythms of Indian ragas with the rock's power and the improvisational options of jazz. Despite its unprecedented success — the second album, *Birds of Fire* (Columbia #31996; 1973) reached number 15 on the pop charts — he disbanded the group after the release of the third LP, the live *Between Nothingness & Eternity* (Columbia #32766; 1973), due to conflicts over composer credits (generally claimed by him). McLaughlin retained the Mahavishnu Orchestra moniker for various recording projects; releases included *Apocalypse* (Columbia #32957; 1974), *Visions of the Emerald Beyond* (Columbia #33411; 1975), and *Inner Worlds* (Columbia #33908; 1976). In 1976, however, he gave up the name after renouncing Sri Chimnoy; he briefly formed a group as the Mahavishnu Orchestra from 1984–1986, featuring drummer Danny Gottlieb, keyboardist Mitch Foreman, and saxophonist Bill Evans. Throughout, McLaughlin has continued to explore new musical directions both as a solo artist and in a number of group settings, most notably Shakti and Free Spirits. His charting albums have included *Love Devotion Surrender* (with Carlos Santana) (Columbia #32034; 1973), *Electric Guitarist* (Columbia #35785; 1979), and *Friday Night in San Francisco* (Columbia #37152; 1981). [Romanowski and George-Warren 1995.]

FRANK HOFFMANN

MAIN AMPLIFIER

See Power Amplifier

MAJESTIC (LABEL) (I)

A seven-inch vertical-cut record offered for $.25 by the Majestic Phonograph Co., Inc., of New York, in 1916–1917. Advertising in *TMW* for October 1916 gave the firm's name as Majestic Record Corp. Playing time was said to be "as long as any 10-inch record," and a nine-inch disc to play 4 1/2 minutes was announced for November 1916 at $.50. Thirty new titles were marketed each month in 1916: classical, popular and dance, humor, and sacred numbers. There were 100 titles in the catalog by November 1916. A bankruptcy petition was filed on 27 Aug 1917, and the stock of 700 titles was offered at a bargain sale. A rare disc today, Majestic had an etched design instead of a paper label. [Rust 1978.]

MAJESTIC (LABEL) (II)

A record produced ca. 1923 by the Olympic Disc Record Corp. for sale in Ross Stores, Inc. The catalog series is the same as that of the Olympic label, suggesting an affiliation between Olympic and Majestic, but they did not entirely duplicate each other. [Rust 1978.]

Budget label produced by the Olympic Disc Record Corp. for sale in the Ross chain of stores, c. early '20s. Courtesy Kurt Nauck/Nauck's Vintage Records

MAJESTIC (LABEL) (III)

A record issued by Majestic Records, Inc., of New York, a subsidiary of the Majestic Radio and Television Co. (St. Charles, Illinois), from 1945 to 1947. The output consisted of pop, jazz, country and western, and gospel material. Majestic bought the Hit label (the Classic Record Co.) from Eli Oberstein and continued issuing Hit concurrently with the new Majestic, while also reissuing Hit material on Majestic. The new label was immediately successful, sparked by the Eddy Howard recording of "To Each His Own" (#1070; 1946). Other artists on Majestic included Louis Prima, Ray McKinley, Jimmie Lunceford, Jack Leonard, Ella Logan, and Jimmie Durante. Former New York Mayor Jimmy Walker was president of Majestic Records, Inc.; John Hammond was recording director from 1946. Around 1949 Mercury Records acquired the Majestic catalog. [Porter 1978/12 is a label listing.]

MAJESTIC PHONOGRAPH CO.

A Chicago firm established in 1916, maker of the Majestic line of record players in five models. Shortly thereafter, the firm appears to have moved to New York City, where it launched a record label. The firm seems to have ceased operation after 1917.

See also **Majestic (Label) (I)**

MALACO MUSIC (LABEL)

Leading independent R&B label of the last third of the 20th century. College friends Tommy Couch and Wolf Stephenson began their careers in music booking fraternity concerts; after graduation, along with Couch's brother-in-law Mitchell Malouf (MALouf + COuch = Malaco), they formed a booking agency called Malaco Attractions. In 1967, they expanded by opening a recording studio. They began by licensing material to major labels. However, when a recording by King Floyd called "Groove Me" was rejected by the majors in 1970, Malaco decided to issue it themselves on the Chimneyville label, resulting in a number one R&B and number six pop hit. For the next five years, Malaco both issued its own recordings on Chimneyville and continued to work as a studio for hire, including sessions for the Pointer Sisters for Atlantic and Paul Simon for Columbia. In 1975, the first release was made under the Malaco name, "Misty Blue" by Dorothy Moore, which reached number two R&B and number three pop. Moore would remain a main hitmaker for the label through 1980. Also during the 1970s and 1980s the label became very active in gospel music, scoring major hits with the Jackson Southernaires (the group's Frank Williams became the label's gospel A&R man, producing most gospel sessions through his death in 1993), the Soul Stirrers, and several others. A brief flirtation with disco in the later 1970s led to hits with "Get Up and Dance" by Freedom. From the 1980s forward, the label focused on blues and R&B artists whose records, while rarely charting, sold steadily in large enough number to support the enterprise. Among the label's 1980s signings were ZZ Hill, Denise LaSalle, Johnnie Taylor, and Bobby "Blue" Bland. In 1985, Malaco purchased the famous Muscle Shoals Sound Studio and its related label and music-publishing operations, and then a year later the gospel division of Savoy Records. During the 1990s, Malaco continued to grow by purchasing other labels, launching new subsidiaries and signing new artists. Couch's son started Waldoxy Records to release more contemporary sounding groups, while J-Town was started for pop-R&B releases. Malaco Jazz was formed to release vintage concert recordings from Europe made in the 1950s and 1960s, as well as a distribution arm for other smaller jazz labels. [website: www.shop-malaco.com.]

CARL BENSON

MALE QUARTETS

The early use of the talking machine for reproducing music coincided with the peak of America's male quartet movement. The first quartet to record (1891) was the Manhasset Quartet. Many of the earliest male recording artists were not only vocal soloists, but also members of quartets. Henry Burr, Albert Campbell, Billy Murray, Arthur Collins, Steve Porter, and William Hooley were some of the better known artists who doubled as soloists and harmony singers. The songs of the times as recorded by the male quartets stimulated the art of singing in harmony around the country because many of these tunes could be readily harmonized by average singers applying "ear harmonies" to the recorded songs.

Early recording artists were sturdy, intrepid vocalists. Singing into the horns was vocally demanding, since the master records they made around 1900 would only produce 25 to 50 cylinder pressings before wearing out. If a particular recording was selling well, the artists would have to make further masters. Even multiple horns, which cut up to seven masters per take, did not relieve the tedium. There was no crooning in the premicrophone days prior to 1925, and singers had to possess durable voices to sustain the rigors of the recording session. The quartet men were also versatile, often singing more than one part as they went from session to session: here a duet, there a trio; then a quartet, maybe a quintet; yesterday a soloist, tomorrow a choralist.

Victor had the finest catalog of male ensembles, notably the Hayden Quartet, Peerless Quartet, and the American Quartet. Quartets often used different names when recording for different companies. Thus the American Quartet became the Premier Quartet for Edison; the Shannon Four became the Singing Sophomores when doing college songs for Columbia, and then became the Revelers for modern cabaret-style songs on Victor.

The Peerless Quartet was an offshoot of the Columbia Quartet, which can be traced to the Invincible Quartet, also known as the Invincible Four. It was one of the more stable groups, in a time when the genealogy of quartets was a tangled web of personnel changes, with singers moving frequently from group to group. Henry Burr provided continuity for Peerless, as well as management, for almost 20 years.

Between them, Burr and Murray, lead singers for the Peerless and American Quartets, recorded about 16,000 songs through the years, including solos, duets, trios, and other combinations. (By comparison, Bing Crosby and Frank Sinatra recorded about 3,600 songs between them.)

A dramatic change in vocal style arrived with the microphone in the mid-1920s. Where the horn had required singers to push their voices, the electric recording process allowed them to croon softly. Gene Austin, Rudy Vallee, and Bing Crosby replaced the old-time singers like Burr and Murray. By the end of the 1920s most of the recording quartets of the acoustic era had broken up; a few like the Maple City Four and some vaudeville foursomes survived. (There were still 10 sides by Peerless and eight sides by Shannon in the 1940 Victor catalog.) In the 1940s there were only a few significant ensembles, such as the Ink Spots, the Mills Brothers, The Sportsmen, and the Golden Gate Quartet.

VAL HICKS

MALNECK, MATTY
(9 DEC 1903–25 FEB 1981)

American jazz violinist, Big Band leader, and composer, born in Newark, New Jersey. He played violin and made arrangements for the Paul Whiteman orchestra in 1926–1937. Later he had his own orchestra, which was on the Dick Powell radio program and other shows in 1942–1943. Malneck's most popular composition was "Stairway to the Stars" (1939). Among his more interesting recordings were "Londonderry Air"/"Listen to the Mocking Bird"

(Brunswick #8413; 1939) and "Carnival of Venice"/"William Tell Overture" (Columbia #35299; 1939). Malneck also wrote some pop hits during the 1930s, including "Goody Goody." His last recordings were made for Decca in 1938–1939. He died in Hollywood, California.

MAMAS AND THE PAPAS

American rock group of the mid-1960s, consisting of John Phillips, Dennis Doherty, (Ms.) Cass Elliott, and Michelle Gilliam Phillips. Discovered by producer Lou Phillips, the group helped promote the California folk-rock sound during the mid- to late 1960s. The group made 14 chart singles in 1966–1967, beginning with "California Dreamin'" (Dunhill #4020; 1966). "Monday, Monday" (Dunhill #4026; 1966) was said to have sold 160,000 copies the day it appeared in the shops. There were seven chart albums in the 1960s, of which the most popular were *If You Can Believe Your Eyes and Ears* (Dunhill #50006; 1966) and *The Mamas and the Papas* (Dunhill #D 500010). The group broke up in 1968, but several successful albums of their 1960s material appeared later, the last in 1973. John Phillips brought together a new ensemble under the name Mamas and the Papas — featuring his daughter Mackenzie and Spanky MacFarlane (formerly of Spanky and Our Gang) — in 1982 and achieved modest popularity but had no chart records. Another one of Phillips's daughters, Chyna, had some success with the group Wilson Phillips (featuring Carnie and Wendy Wilson, daughters of eccentric rock legend Brian Wilson) in the early 1990s. MCA has reissued their back catalog in numerous forms on CD over the past decade.

MANC SOUND, THE

The "Manc Sound" — based in Manchester, England — grew out of the onslaught of rave culture. Its audience — drawn from postdisco regulars, soccer thugs, and hippies — was most likely to congregate at the Factory Records–run Hacienda Club. Ecstasy constituted the drug of choice. The performers — most notably The Farm, Happy Mondays, Inspiral Carpets, the Soup Dragons, and Stone Roses (whose eponymous debut, Silvertone #1184; 1989, was called "a contender for album of the decade" by British discographer Martin Strong) — were drawn from the British indie band movement. They sported baggy trousers, flowery T-shirts, and bowl haircuts. Their music consisted of hook-laden pop-rock accented by rich vocal harmonies and druggy dance beats. In the fad-driven British trade and fan publications, the Manc Sound

(also dubbed "Madchester") was quickly deemed passé. In response, bands such as James (whose improvisational experimentation made them an arena attraction by the time *Seven*, Mercury #510952, 1992, #2 U.K., was released) and Primal Scream — whose best LP was the Stones-influenced *Screamadelica* (Sire #26714; 1991; #8 U.K.) — toned down the more stylized retro elements (e.g., Los Angeles psychedelia of the Strawberry Alarm Clock and Yellow Payges ca. 1967) of this music and joined the alternative mainstream.

FRANK HOFFMANN

MANCINI, HENRY
(16 APR 1924–14 JUNE 1994)

American composer and orchestra leader, born in Cleveland. After study at the Juilliard School he played piano in dance bands. In the late 1940s he was arranging for Tex Beneke's band. He was in Hollywood writing movie scores in the 1950s, and also composed music for television programs. In 1961 he wrote "Moon River" and in 1962 "Days of Wine and Roses"; both songs won Academy awards. As a conductor he made 14 chart singles of his own compositions and other works and 30 chart albums. *Peter Gunn* (RCA #1956; winner of a Grammy for Album of the Year at the first annual awards ceremony in 1958) and *The Pink Panther* (RCA #2795; 1964) were the greatest sellers of his many successful LPs. In 2000, RCA released a 20-track *Greatest Hits* collection that featured his best-loved themes, digitally remastered, that supersedes earlier collections (#67997). Mancini won 18 Grammys between 1958–1970. He died in Beverly Hills, California.

MANDEL MANUFACTURING CO./
MANDEL (LABEL)

A Chicago firm, established in 1915. Louis Mandel was one of the owners. Joseph F. Grossman was president, J.H. Hupp was secretary, and Raymond T. Bell works superintendent. The Mandel line of disc players was on sale in 1916 in four models. The firm introduced a lateral-cut record under the Mandel label beginning in January 1921. Masters came from Arto, Lyric, and other sources supplied by the Standard Records brokering agency of New York. The material was popular vocal and dance numbers. Mandel was only advertised once, in April 1921, with a selling price of $1. However, in June 1921, liquidation proceedings were reported. Louis and Nathan Mandel were listed as proprietors of the Mandel Phono Parts Co., in the Chicago 1923 directory. However, that firm was not listed in subsequent directories. [Rust 1978; a label list appeared in *RR* #88 (January 1968).]

MANDOLIN RECORDINGS

In July 1899 there was an anonymous rendition of "D'amor passaggero" on Gramophone Co. (#57351) made in Naples. Two Neapolitan mandolinists made 11 Gramophone discs in Naples in 1900: Professor Giandolfi and Professor Pallavicini; among the latter's performances were "Polka con variazioni" (#57358) and "Trionfo mandolinistico" (#57361). Guido Volpe recorded one side for G & T in London, "Sylvia Ballet: Pizzicato" (#37350; 1902).

Edison cylinders presented mandolin playing as early as 1899, the earliest number being #7233: "Pixies," performed by W.C. Townsend. The same artist was heard on another four cylinders, and Samuel S. Siegel was heard on 10, one a duet with guitarist M.L. Wolf, "Autumn Evening" (#9014; 1905). There were six mandolin solos in the Victor 1917 catalog, performed by Clarence Penney or William Place, Jr. Mandolins in groups of guitars were featured on 11 other Victor discs, with Samuel S. Siegel performing on several of them. In the 1922 Victor catalog there were only four solos and five records of mandolins with guitar(s). By 1927 the category had disappeared from the Victor catalog. Nonetheless, the mandolin remained popular, particularly among country acts, duos like the popular Blue Sky Boys and the Monroe Brothers. In the popular music arena, Dave Apollon was a popular stage performer, although he made only a handful of recordings during his heyday in 1929 and 1932; he recorded for Decca in 1940 and again after World War II. However, solo mandolin records were not listed in the later Victor catalogs, nor in the Columbia catalogs of the 1940s.

The mandolin enjoyed a renaissance after World War II thanks to the playing of Bill Monroe, credited as the founder of bluegrass music. Monroe's high-energy playing inspired a new generation of players, first in bluegrass, and then in the related genres of new-grass and jazz-grass. Another popular postwar mandolinist was Jethro Burns, half of the popular country comedy team of Homer & Jethro. The instrument was widely used by roots-oriented rock bands in the late 1960s such as Kaleidoscope and Earth Opera. Since the mid-1970s, David Grisman has been the key popularizer of the mandolin, performing in a jazz-styled ensemble. The mandolin also remains a strong presence on mainstream country recordings.

REV. CARL BENSON

MANDRELL, BARBARA [ANN] (25 DEC 1948–)

Born in Houston but raised in Southern California, Mandrell came from a musical family. She began playing with the family band at a young age and was adept at a number of instruments, particularly the pedal steel guitar. When Mandrell was 11, she was already playing the instrument in Las Vegas shows, and two years later she toured with Johnny Cash performing for military shows in Vietnam and Korea. After a minor hit as a vocalist on "Queen for a Day" released in 1966 by the small Mosrite label, Mandrell and family moved to Nashville, where she was signed by Columbia in 1969. Her first success was covering R&B standards, beginning with "I've Been Loving You Too Long" originally recorded by Otis Redding, followed with such chestnuts as "Do Right Woman — Do Right Man" through 1973s "Midnight Oil." In mid-decade, she signed with ABC/Dot, and her first period of major success occurred, including 1977s "Married (But Not to Each Other)" and the 1978 number one country hit, the cleverly titled "Sleeping Single in a Double Bed." Mandrell continued to be a major star in the early 1980s, thanks to increased exposure hosting a network variety program with her sisters, Irlene (b. 29 Jan 1956) and Louise (b. 13 July 1954). Mandrell continued to turn out solo hits, including 1981's "I Was Country When Country Wasn't Cool," 1983's "One of a Kind Pair of Fools," and 1984's duet with Lee Greenwood, "To Me." She won two Grammys, in 1982 and 1983, however both were for gospel recordings. In 1984, she was involved in a head-on collision with another car, leading to a long period of hospitalization and some doubts about her ability to recover. She came back full steam a year later, with the hit "Angels in Your Arms," although her popularity on the country charts was already eroding due to the influx of new country stars. In 1990, she published her autobiography, *Get to the Heart.* Mandrell continued to tour through 1997, but her chart-topping days were over. In 1997, she gave a well-publicized farewell show, stating she wished to focus on her acting career.

CARL BENSON

MANHASSET (MANHANSETT) QUARTETTE

A studio vocal group of the 1890s, formed expressly for recordings; "possibly the first vocal group to record under its own name" [Brooks]. Membership varied; the original group consisted of John Bieling, tenor; George Gaskin, second tenor; Joe Riley, baritone; and Jim Cherry, bass. Later Cherry was replaced by Walter Snow, and for a time by a bass named Evans. The quartet's first Edison recording was made on 27 Sep 1891: "Reception Medley." They made 19 other cylinders on that day. In 1892 they sang for the New Jersey Phonograph Co. and for Boswell; they also worked for Columbia, Berliner, Zonophone, and Leeds & Catlin. The group broke up in 1896, succeeded by the Edison Quartet. [Brooks 1979; Walsh 1962/10.]

MANHATTAN LADIES QUARTET

A vocal group that recorded for Edison after 1912. It consisted of Irene Cummings, Mabel Meade Davis, Annie Laurie McCorkle, and Anne Winkoop. [Walsh 1962/10.]

MANHATTAN QUARTET

A male vocal group that recorded chiefly for Edison and Victor from ca. 1912 to 1929. The singers identified were Henry Weiman, Arthur Hall, Nick Latterner, and Frank Schwarz. Victor's 1912 catalog was the first to list them, as singers of German language material. During World War I this was understandably an untenable specialty in the U.S., but the quartet was in the catalog again after the Armistice. "Deutschland über Alles" (Edison Diamond Disc #50187; 1914) was cut out of the Edison catalog on 12 July 1918 "for patriotic reasons." Of the 14 Diamond Discs by the Manhattan Quartet the "most amusing title" [Walsh] appeared in 1927; it was a dance-tempo version of "Studentenlieder"/"Volkslieder" (#57023). [Walsh 1962/10; Walsh 1972/12.]

MANILOW, BARRY (17 JUNE 1946–)

American vocalist, pianist, accordionist, arranger, and composer of popular songs; born in Brooklyn. He began as a performer, then made arrangements and composed television and radio commercials. His composition "Mandy" was a hit in 1974 (Bell #45613); he followed it with "It's a Miracle" (Arista #0108; 1975), "I Write the Songs" (Arista #0157; 1975), "Looks Like We Made It" (Arista #244; 1977), and "Can't Smile without You" (Arista #0305; 1978). Manilow had 18 albums on the charts between 1975 and 1985; those with the longest chart life were *Tryin' to Get the Feeling* (Arista #AB4060; 1975), 93 weeks; *This One's for You* (Arista #AB4090; 1976), 92 weeks; and *Live* (Arista #AL8050), 87 weeks. Manilow's career as a pop hitmaker has been in eclipse since the mid-1980s. Nonetheless, from time to time, he enjoys renewed popularity. In 2001, a

greatest hits package of his earlier recordings sold unexpectedly well, leading him to hit the road once again in the following year.

REV. CARL BENSON

MANN, BARRY (9 FEB 1939–) AND CYNTHIA WEIL (18 OCT 1937–)

American songwriters. Mann, born in Brooklyn, and Weil, in New York, were one of the most successful songwriting teams of the Brill Building in the early 1960s. (Mann was also a performer who reached the Top 10 in 1961 with "Who Put the Bomp.") The husband-and-wife duo had their biggest hit with "You've Lost that Lovin' Feelin'," recorded by the Righteous Brothers for a number one hit in 1965 (Philles #124), and also composed such teen pop classics as the Drifters' 1963 hit "On Broadway" (Atlantic #2182) and The Animals' "We Gotta Get Out of This Place" (MGM #13382; 1965). The duo left the Brill Building scene in the later 1960s, relocating to Hollywood. Subsequently, the duo continued to work together, as well as with other partners, and Mann continued to record on occasion as a solo artist. During the 1980s and 1990s, the duo primarily scored animated features, including *An American Tail*.

WILLIAM RUHLMANN

MANN, ESTELLA LOUISE (1 NOV 1871– 24 AUG 1947)

American soprano, born in Nashville, Tennessee. She was the first woman to make a career of recording, doing grand opera to coon songs. Mann's solo and ensemble records came from Columbia in the late 1890s. She also made discs for Berliner and at least one Zonophone, "Prince of Peace" (#9461; 1900). She also sang with the Lyric Trio. Mann was also the first woman to own a share of a record company, the Lyric Phonograph Co. She died in Evansville, Indiana. [Brooks 1979; Walsh 1952/4. A photograph of her making a record in 1898 appears in Hoover 1971.]

MANN, HERBIE (16 APR 1930–1 JULY 2003)

American jazz flutist, born Herbert Jay Solomon in New York. He studied at the Manhattan School of Music and performed with major symphony orchestras. He made popular records in 1968 "Unchain My Heart" (A&M #896) and 1969 "Memphis Underground" (Atlantic #2621), then was less prominent until the mid-1970s. The single "Hi Jack"

(Atlantic #3246; 1975) was on the charts 14 weeks. Mann had four chart albums between 1975 and 1979, and another with Fire Island. *Discotheque* was the album with the longest chart life, 17 weeks. Mann left Atlantic at the end of the 1970s. Although he never equaled his chart success of the 1970s, he returned to playing jazz in the 1980s and recorded and performed until a few months before his death. He also ran his own label, Kokopelli, from 1988–1990, and then during the later 1990s Lightyear/Herbie Mann Music. Mann's last album, released in 2000, drew on traditional eastern European melodies; he said he made it to acknowledge his Jewish background. Mann died in Pecos, New Mexico, of prostate cancer.

MANN, JOHNNY (30 AUG 1928–)

Johnny Mann was born in Baltimore and went to school there. At the age of five, he sang in a church children's choir, and from age eight to 12 he was in Baltimore's St. Paul Episcopal Choir and then in his teen years was an active member of school choruses and choirs. His mother insisted that he learn to play the piano and at the age of 15 he publicly performed Gershwin's "Rhapsody in Blue." He also learned to play the trombone and the bass. After serving in the U.S. Army, Mann went to Los Angeles and met film composer Paul Sawtell, who guided his musical talents. Soon, Mann was writing music for seven Warner Brothers films. He became the choral director of the *NBC Comedy Hour*, which led to the formation of the Johnny Mann Singers. The Johnny Mann Singers were signed to Liberty Records in 1956, and eventually did 39 albums, with five receiving Grammy nominations and winning two Grammys. He was known for swinging arrangements in numbers like "Sing Along with Singing Twenties," "Sing Along with the Singin' Thirties," and a charted single of Jimmy Webb's "Up, Up and Away," which made it into the U.S. Top 10. He has continued to maintain an active schedule. In the 1980s he created a Johnny Mann National Choral Festival that had eight regional competitions leading up to a contest of regional choral winners, which culminated in the selection of a national champion choral group. Mann has won numerous awards and medals for his loyalty and love of country and emceed many charity events including the year 2000 Senior Olympic event, "Let the Games Begin."

VAL HICKS

MANNE, SHELLY
(11 JUNE 1920–26 SEP 1984)

American jazz drummer, born Sheldon Manne in New York. As a young man he played saxophone in New York clubs and on transatlantic ships. At age 18 he changed from saxophone to drums. He was with the Raymond Scott and Will Bradley bands in 1941–1942, then with Les Brown in 1942. There were important records with Coleman Hawkins and Woody Herman in 1948–1949. "The Man I Love" (Signature #9001) with Hawkins, Eddie Heywood, and Oscar Pettiford showed his skills to great advantage. After military service he joined Stan Kenton (1946–1947, and at intervals to 1952), then worked with various bands and combos. He recorded for Decca, Capitol, and several other labels. Manne absorbed the new bebop style, teaming with Dizzy Gillespie in 1945, but he preferred a cooler approach and became one of the forces behind West Coast jazz. He played in trios with André Previn and with Ornette Coleman. Manne's Capitol records with Stan Kenton were popular (notably "Artistry in Percussion," #289; 1946), and his LPs for Contemporary (*Shelly Manne and His Friends*, *My Fair Lady*, made with Previn in 1956, and *My Son the Drummer*) presented some of his best work. In 1984 he backed Barry Manilow in the chart album *2:00 AM Paradise Cafe* (Arista #AL8-8245. Manne won the *Downbeat* and *Metronome* polls many times during 1947–1960 as the favorite jazz drummer. He operated a popular club in Hollywood, Shelly's Manne-Hole, from 1960 to 1974. Manne died in Los Angeles.

MANNHEIM STEAMROLLER

Headquartered in Omaha, Nebraska, and founded in 1974 by Chip Davis, this performing group's name was derived from an 18th-century orchestra known for building intensity by adding layers of sound, color, texture, other instruments, and volume. Davis, a classically trained musician and composer who had already created and recorded a number of best-selling and innovative country and western hits, had gone on to compose, produce, and record, in state-of-the-art sound, an innovative and new form of music that he called 18th-century rock and roll. He named his first production *Fresh Aire* and approached several record companies about a contract. Politely rebuffed by all of them because the music defied being pigeonholed into a specific musical category, Davis went together with Don Sears to create American Gramaphone, a record company that was specifically oriented toward producing his new style of music, which has since come to be called New Age. Rather than market through record stores, the recordings were sold to stereo showrooms and audio salons that were demonstrating home hi-fi equipment to serious audio enthusiasts. The result was a hit, followed by a run of remarkable sales successes from an entire series of top-selling *Fresh Aire* releases, in addition to a number of Mannheim Steamroller Christmas albums that both serious audio enthusiasts and the general public found very listenable. Davis has made a point of using cutting-edge electronic-music forms, combined with equally cutting-edge recording technologies. Today, having produced three multi-platinum, two platinum, and 14 gold recordings, with consistently high positions on sales charts, the group continues to successfully tour and also produce best-selling albums in both compact disc and DVD music formats, with innovations that even include educational videos in DVD video form.

HOWARD FERSTLER

MANOIL (JAMES) CO., INC.

A firm established in Newburgh, New York, in 1916. It made the Manophone, a disc player, in six models.

MANONE, WINGY
(13 FEB 1904–9 JULY 1982)

American jazz trumpeter and vocalist, born Joseph Mannone in New Orleans. He lost his right arm in an accident as a child and learned to play the trumpet with the left. He played in riverboats as a teenager, moved to Mobile, Alabama, and then to St. Louis. He had his own band by 1926, performing in the South and in the early 1930s in Chicago and New York. In 1935 he made a hit record, singing a spoof on "Isle of Capri" (Vocalion #2913). He was featured in the Bing Crosby motion picture *Rhythm on the River* in 1940 and recorded the title song for Bluebird (#10844; 1940); later he appeared frequently with Crosby. Manone's Big Band of 1941 had Mel Powell at piano and Zutty Singleton on drums; they made some fine sides for Bluebird, like "The Boogie Beat'll Getcha" (#11298). His later work, based in Las Vegas, tended to be more comical than jazzy. He continued performing into the 1970s. The Danish jazz reissue label, Collector's Classics, has reissued Manone's complete recordings on a series of CDs. Manone died in Las Vegas.

MANSON, MARILYN (5 JAN 1969–)

Marilyn Manson (born Brian Hugh Warner) was the most censored musician of the 1990s. The concerted efforts of parental groups, religious leaders, politicians, and other authority figures to suppress him have focused more on his alleged stage behavior and public statements than his recordings per se (although detractors would argue that they contain material that is equally unpleasant). Manson has emerged from the controversies surrounding him as a savvy media manipulator and outspoken martyr for First Amendment rights.

Inspired by lectures about the subliminal messages allegedly embedded in rock albums he received while attending a private Christian school, Warner formed the band, Marilyn Manson and the Spooky Kids, in 1989. Each member adopted a stage name based on both a female icon and storied murderer (in Warner's case, Marilyn Monroe crossed with Charles Manson). Releasing a series of self-produced cassettes, the band impressed Trent Reznor, who signed them to his own label, Nothing Records, in 1993. Touring with Reznor's group, Nine Inch Nails, in support of his debut LP, the industrial-hardcore Portrait of an American Family (Nothing/Interscope #92344; 1994), Manson made headlines over alleged sexually lewd behavior and self-mutilations onstage as well as for being named a "reverend" of the Church of Satan. His notoriety, combined with the success of the band's revved-up version of the Eurythmics's "Sweet Dreams (Are Made of This)" (Nothing/Interscope #95504; 1995), helped the Smells Like Children EP (Nothing/Interscope #92641; 1995; #31) go platinum. Manson's next album, Antichrist Superstar (Nothing/Interscope #90006; 1996; #3), represented the first part of a "pseudoautobiographical trilogy"; its aggressive edge effectively framed the concept about a nihilistic rock god.

Later installments, the David Bowie–influenced, glam-rock *Mechanical Animals* (Nothing/Interscope #98273; 1998; #1) and goth rock–oriented *Holy Wood (In the Shadow of the Valley of Death)* (Nothing/Interscope #490790; 2000; #13), further reinforced his status as a shock-rock American institution. Having written (with Neil Strauss) an autobiography, *The Long Hard Road out of Hell* (1997), Manson would go on to form his own label, Post Human Records, in 2000.

FRANK HOFFMANN

MANTELLI, EUGENIA
(1860–3 MAR 1926)

Italian soprano, also mezzo-soprano. Her debut was at Lisbon in 1883. In 1894 she sang at the Bolshoi Opera, as Mantelli-Mantovani, then toured Russia with Francesco Tamagno. She was at the Metropolitan Opera in 1894–1900 and in 1902–1903. Bettini recorded four numbers by her in 1899. She also worked for Zonophone ca. 1905. IRCC reissued four of the arias made at that time on a seven-inch LP (#7007; 1955); "Una voce poco fa" is perhaps the most distinguished of that group.

MANTOVANI, ANNUNZIO PAOLO (15 NOV 1905–29 MAR 1980)

Italian/British conductor, born in Venice. He went to London as a youth and attended Trinity College of Music. At 18 he formed an orchestra in Birmingham. He became a British subject in 1933, and died in Tunbridge Wells, England. Mantovani recorded first in the 1920s as a violinist, often under the name Signor Gandini. He was heard on Columbia, Crystalate, British Homophone, and Decca records with various orchestras. He had major U.S. hits in 1935–1936 with "Red Sails in the Sunset" and "Serenade in the Night." It was with Decca in the 1940s that he developed the lush orchestral sound that made him famous. He went on to make 51 chart albums, all for the London label, between 1955 and 1971, of which the most popular was *Exodus* (London #3321; 1960), on the album charts 43 weeks, which sold over 7 million copies. There are numerous CD reissues, mostly on budget-oriented labels.

MANUAL SEQUENCE (ALSO KNOWN AS STANDARD SEQUENCE)

The recording sequence of 78-rpm or LP discs in an album in which the material flows from disc one, side one, to disc one, side two; thence to disc two, side one, etc. With the advent of automatic record changers, manufacturers provided alternative sequencing that would keep the material in order when the discs dropped one after the other onto the turntable; in that "automatic sequence" the material flowed from disc one, side one, to disc two, side one, etc. Album numbers showed the distinction: e.g., for Columbia Masterworks, M or X prefixes denoted manual sequence and MM or MX denoted automatic sequence.

MAPLESHADE (LABEL)

Begun in 1986 by Pierre Sprey (an ex-aeronautical engineer and statistician by training, who was one of the principal designers of the A-10 and F-16 fighter jets), and located in a large mansion in Upper Marlboro, Maryland, the label emphasizes minimalist microphone and recording techniques (only two to four microphones, short cables, and no mixing, filtering, noise-reduction, compression, or added equalization), in order to deliver the least sonically compromised transcriptions possible. The company specializes in jazz releases and has recorded a number of music notables, including Shirley Horn, Clifford Jordan, Randy Weston, Walter Davis, Jr., Chris Anderson, David Murray, Hamiet Bluiett, Larry Willis, and many others. [website: www.mapleshaderecords.com]

HOWARD FERSTLER

MAPLESON CYLINDERS

Lionel S. Mapleson (1865–1937), nephew of impresario "Colonel" James Henry Mapleson, was librarian of the Metropolitan Opera Co. in 1889–1937. On 20 Mar 1900 he purchased an Edison "Home" Model A phonograph, for $30, and on 21 Mar he made a cylinder of Suzanne Adams singing "Valse" by her husband Leo Stern. On 30 or 31 Mar 1900 he recorded the voice of Marcella Sembrich. During the opera seasons of 1901–1902 and 1902–1903, Mapleson recorded on 120 cylinders segments of live performances at the Metropolitan Opera, at first not too successfully from the prompter's box, then with better results with a six-foot horn from a vantage point over the stage. More than 60 records from the 1902–1903 season survive: "remarkably consistent in quality and often genuinely impressive" [Hall].

The cylinders remained in the Mapleson family until 1937, when William H. Seltsam acquired 124 of them. Through the initiative of Seltsam and his International Record Collectors' Club, reissues of 64 cylinders were prepared and released on nineteen 78s and five LPs from 1939 to 1966. Other cylinders were discovered and reissued on LP: 10 through Aida Favia-Artsay came out under the name *Met Stars 1901–02* in 1959. Altogether 136 cylinders are extant today, 117 of them vocal operatic selections, four of nonoperatic vocal material, and 11 of instrumental music. These are the survivals of Mapleson's activity. He made many more records, which he took back to his family in London and which disappeared without a trace.

The principal artists heard on these cylinders include several for whom there are no surviving commercial recordings: Georg Anthes (tenor), Lucienne Bréval (soprano), Andreas Dippel (tenor), Luigi Mancinelli (conductor), Emilio de Marchi (tenor), Jean de Reszke (tenor), Luise Reuss-Belce (contralto), Albert Saléza (tenor), Thomas Salignac (tenor), Fritzi Scheff (soprano), and Milka Ternina (soprano). The other major artists are Suzanne Adams (soprano), Albert Alvarez (tenor), Alexander von Bandrowski (tenor), David Bispham (baritone), Robert Blass (bass), Alois Burgstaller (tenor), Emma Calvé (soprano), Giuseppe Campanari (baritone), Walter Damrosch (conductor), Carlo Dani (tenor), Emma Eames (soprano), Johanna Gadski (soprano), Emil Gerhäuser (tenor), Charles Gilbert (baritone), Alfred Hertz (conductor), Louise Homer (contralto), Marcel Journet (bass), Nellie Melba (soprano), Adolph Mühlmann (baritone), Lillian Nordica (soprano), Pol Plançon (bass), Edouard de Reszke (bass), Ernestine Schumann-Heink (contralto), Antonio Scotti (baritone), Marcella Sembrich (soprano), and Anton van Rooy (baritone).

Of all these luminaries, Jean de Reszke is of the greatest interest, for the legendary tenor cannot be heard elsewhere. He is very faint in airs from *L'africaine*, *Le Cid*, and *Huguenots*; more distinguishable in *Siegfried* Act I. (The IRCC reissue of "Schmiede, mein Hammer" is however wrongly attributed to De Reszke; it is sung by Anthes.)

Five excellent recordings were made of *Götterdämmerung* with Lillian Nordica, and five others give strong documentation of the *Tosca* of 3 Jan 1903, with Emilio de Marchi and Emma Eames. Two fine cylinders were made of *Fille du régiment*, with Sembrich, Thomas Salignac, and Charles Gilbert. After years of restoration and research work at the New York Public Library, an LP was issued in 1986 by the Library, distributed by the Metropolitan Opera Guild, of "all the known playable recordings and fragments" made by Mapleson. Credit for final transfer of the cylinder tapes to LP belongs to engineer Tom Owen and producer David Hamilton. David Hall, who retired as curator of the Rodgers and Hammerstein Archives in 1983, did the basic research and, with Owen, the initial transfer to tape. [Hall 1981/1; 1981/2; Hall 1982/1; Hall 1982/7; Hall 1984; Taylor Aug. 1987.]

MARANTZ, SAUL (1902–16 JAN 1997)

Marantz became fascinated by electronic devices when a boy in Brooklyn. In the early 1950s, in New York, he and Sidney Smith started the Marantz Co., with the idea being to make and market very high-quality audio equipment (mainly record players, amplifiers, and speakers) for the nascent hi-fi sound business. After several years of design research, his first commercial product, the Model 1 Audio Consolette Preamplifier, was released in 1953. Working with such audio engineers as Smith and Richard Sequerra, Marantz continued to produce vacuum-tube components that became synonymous with upscale audio. In the early 1960s, he and his people developed the first all-transistor hi-fi audio receiver (combination tuner, preamplifier, and amplifier) for consumer use.

After building the company to the point at which the Marantz name was almost synonymous with the high-end high fidelity, Marantz realized that he needed more capital with which to expand his research

and development, particularly after putting so much capital into the Model 10B tuner. This led to the purchase of Marantz by the Japanese company Superscope in 1964. Marantz continued to work with the new operation until 1968, after which he retired, but only for a short time. In 1972, along with John Dahlquist, he founded the Dahlquist Speaker Co., and Marantz served as president until 1978. He also helped to form two other audio businesses: the New Lineage Corp. and Eye Q Loudspeakers. (In 1991, Superscope sold the Marantz Co. to Philips Electronics in The Netherlands.)

HOWARD FERSTLER

MARATHON (LABEL) (I)

A British issue sold by the National Gramophone Co., Ltd. in 1912 and National Gramophone Co., Ltd., in 1913. It was a vertical-cut disc, offered in both 10-inch and 12-inch sizes. The grooves were narrow enough to produce "the first real long play record" [Walsh]: at 80 rpm, the discs played five minutes 40 seconds per 10-inch side, and eight minutes 12 seconds per 12-inch side. Marathon #2042 (December 1913) was advertised as "the longest record ever made"; it contained four songs by Tom Kinniburgh. There were "nearly 30 hits on one disc": #2050, a dance medley. A special soundbox was sold to give the records "a clearer tone, and greater volume." The 10-inch discs appeared with numbers #101 to #473, the 12-inch discs with numbers from #2001 to #2065. National Gramophone Co., Ltd., experienced a financial crisis in 1914, and went into receivership, and no new Marathon records were issued after March 1915. [Andrews 1987/4.]

MARATHON (LABEL) (II)

An American record marketed by the Nutmeg Record Corp. in November 1928 — a seven-inch disc that played as long as a standard 10-inch disc. Distortions in the output affected public interest in the record, which was accordingly discontinued in a few months. [Rust 1978.]

MARCONI, FRANCESCO
(14 MAY 1855– 5 FEB 1916)

Italian tenor, born in Rome. He made his debut in Madrid in the 1878–1879 season as Faust, then sang in Rome and (1880) at La Scala. He gained great popularity throughout Europe, notably in Russia, as well as in South America. His voice was said to be unequaled in Italy before the advent of Enrico Caruso. Unfortunately his recordings were made after his vocal prime. He worked for G & T in Milan, 1903–1904, beginning with #52016, "Dai campi, dai prati" from *Mefistofele*. Another group of records was made in Milan for the same label in 1908, including an outstanding "Tu che a Dio" from *Lucia*, "Invan, invan" from *Nerone*, and "Vieni fra queste braccia" from *Puritani*; these were reissued by Top Artists Platters in 1959–1961 (#303, #321, #326 respectively). Marconi died in Rome.

MARCONI, GUGLIELMO (25 APR 1874– 20 JULY 1937)

Born in Bologna, Italy, of an Italian mother and an Irish father, Marconi was educated first in Bologna and later in Florence. Then he went to the technical school in Leghorn, where he studied physics. In 1895, he built the equipment and transmitted electrical signals through the air from one end of his house to the other, and then from the house to the garden. A bit later he transmitted the Morse Code letter "S" for three miles, with the receiver located behind a hill, for good measure. These experiments were, in effect, the dawn of practical wireless telegraphy or radio. A couple of years later, he built a transmitter 100 times more powerful than any previous station at Poldhu, on the southwest tip of England, and in November 1901, he installed a receiving station at St. John's Newfoundland. On 12 Dec 1901, using those facilities, he received signals from across the ocean. News of this achievement spread around the world, and he was acclaimed for his accomplishment by outstanding scientists, including Edison. Marconi received many honors in his lifetime, including the Nobel Prize for Physics in 1909.

HOWARD FERSTLER

MARCONI VELVET TONE (LABEL)

In 1906 Guglielmo Marconi, the Italian scientist and developer of radio, visited the American Graphophone Co. plant in Bridgeport, Connecticut, and became a consultant for the firm. October 1907 saw his idea of a thin, flexible, laminated disc with a paper core and plastic surface produced as Columbia's Marconi Velvet Tone label. Although the disc was a "half century ahead of its time" [Rust] it had to be played with gold-plated needles, each one good for only 12 plays. The public bypassed the new

Marconi in a military uniform. From the Emile Berliner Collection, The Library of Congress

A special record, with less surface noise than a standard 78, developed by the Italian inventor and produced by Columbia briefly from 1906-07. Courtesy Kurt Nauck/Nauck's Vintage Records

silent surfaces of Velvet Tone because of this considerable cost increment over standard (noisy) discs they were used to. The record was also available in Britain, through an agent. [Rust 1978.]

MARDIN, ARIF (1932–)

Born in Istanbul, Turkey, Mardin has been a legendary producer of jazz, R&B, and pop recordings for over four decades. Born to a prominent Turkish family, Mardin became interested in jazz at the age of 10 when he heard his first Duke Ellington recording; he began playing piano and eventually arranging for a local band as a teenager, while also studying economics. In 1956, Quincy Jones and Dizzy Gillespie toured Turkey as part of a U.S. State Department–sponsored trip; Jones heard Mardin's arrangements and recommended him to be the first Quincy Jones Scholarship recipient at Boston's Berklee College of Music. Mardin arrived at the school in 1958 and, upon graduation, continued as an instructor until 1963, when he met Atlantic Records' executive Nesuhi Ertegun; Ertegun hired him as his assistant, and Mardin was quickly put in charge of arranging and running Atlantic's New York studio.

His first major pop hit was the Young Rascals's 1966 single, "Good Lovin'," which he coproduced with Jerry Wexler. Mardin worked with several key Atlantic acts through the decade, including landmark recordings by Aretha Franklin, leading him to be named vice president of the label in 1969. Mardin is credited with helping to revive the Bee Gees's career in the mid-1970s when he suggested that they try singing in falsetto, creating their characteristic disco-era vocal sound. He also oversaw the major hits of the rock duo Hall & Oates during that decade. In the 1980s he had major success with stars Chaka Khan ("I Feel for You") and Bette Midler's ballad hit "Wind Beneath My Wings." Mardin also worked closely with Phil Collins on his enormously successful 1980s era hits. In the 1990s, Mardin continued to work with new artists, like Jewel and Smashing Pumpkins.

He has been the recipient of numerous awards; he was placed in the National Academy of Recording Arts and Sciences Hall of Fame in 1990 and seven years later was given a NARAS HEROES award. He has been nominated for 16 Grammy awards as a producer and won six times. In 1993, he celebrated 30 years at Atlantic Records, with the title of senior vice president; by decade's end, he retired from the label, although he continued to work actively as a producer and arranger.

CARL BENSON

MARGIN CONTROL

Margin control is a disc recording technique developed in the early 1950s which controlled groove spacing one revolution ahead of the signal being recorded; it utilized an extra head on the tape reproducer.

MARLEY, BOB
(2 FEB 1945–11 MAY 1981)

Although Bob Marley enjoyed limited commercial success in the U.S., he remains the most important artist to come out of the reggae movement. He was not only a wonderfully expressive vocalist and competent guitarist, but a first-rate composer; songs like "Stir It Up" (Trojan #617; 1968), "Guava Jelly" (Tuff Gong #4025; 1972), and "I Shot the Sheriff" (Island #005; 1974) would be covered by Johnny Nash, Eric Clapton, and others, thereby facilitating the international acceptance of reggae. The uncompromising sociopolitical beliefs outlined in much of his later work — most notably, "Them Belly Full (But We Hungry)," "Revolution," and the title track from *Natty Dread* (Island #9281; 1975; #92), and his observations on the plight of Africa in *Survival* (Island #9542; 1979; #70) — continue to be instructive to listeners worldwide. Born in St. Ann's, Jamaica, Marley's earliest singles — "Judge Not (Unless You Judge Yourself)" (Island #088; 1962) and "One Cup of Coffee" (Island #128; 1963) — displayed a distinct preference for the emerging ska and bluebeat styles rather than the more established calypso.

By 1964 he had formed the first edition of the Wailers, then a vocal quintet (initially billed as the "Wailin' Wailers") including Peter Tosh, Bunny Livingston (aka Bunny Wailer), Junior Braithwaite, and Beverley Kelso. Teaming up with seminal Jamaican producer Coxsone Dodd, they issued a string of successful singles on the Studio One and Coxsone labels during the mid-1960s. In 1967, following a brief stay in the U.S., he reunited the Wailers (now a trio including Tosh and Livingston) and formed his own record company with the assistance of American soul singer Johnny Nash.

Strongly influenced by producer Lee "Scratch" Perry and Rastafarian doctrine, Marley and his cohorts (expanded in 1970 to include brothers Aston Barrett on bass and Carlton Barrett on drums) evolved from a ska/R&B vocal act to a pioneering reggae group over the course of several years. By 1971 the Wailers had founded a label, Tuff Gong, and were producing their own material. It was the group's affiliation with Chris Blackwell's Island label, however, that facilitated the distribution of their music worldwide. Although Island continued to issue their material on singles, albums became the band's creative focus. Although Tosh and Livingston would depart for solo careers in 1974, Marley continued producing work of uniformly high quality — including *Catch a Fire* (Island #9241; 1973), *Burnin'* (Island #9256; 1973), *Rastaman Vibration* (Island #9383; 1976; #8), *Exodus* (Island #9498; 1977; #20), *Kaya* (Island #9517; 1978; #50), and *Uprising* (Island #9596; 1980; #45) — until his death from lung cancer on 11 May 1981. Due to Marley's legendary status in parts of Europe, Africa, North America, and — of course — Jamaica, recordings spanning his entire career have been widely reissued, from the original Island LPs to varied anthologies.

FRANK HOFFMANN

MARRINER, NEVILLE, SIR
(15 APR 1924–)

British violinist and conductor, born in Lincoln. He studied at the Royal College of Music in London and at the Paris Conservatory. He was a violinist with the Martin String Quartet in 1946–1953, then with the London Symphony Orchestra in 1956–1968. In 1959 he formed a chamber orchestra in London with the name Academy of St. Martin-in-the-Fields (in the Trafalgar Square church), and achieved international stature with performances of music from the baroque to the 20th century. Successful recordings were made for Argo, Philips, and EMI. Marriner formed a similar orchestra in the U.S., the Los Angeles Chamber Orchestra, then another in Australia. Marriner served as the director of the original Academy ensemble until 1978, when he was appointed to the directorship of the Minnesota Orchestra, a position he held until 1985, the same year he was knighted. He directed the Academy group in the Mozart music of the motion picture *Amadeus* (1984) and later for the film *Valmont* (1989). From 1983–1989, he was the chief conductor of the Stuttgart Radio Orchestra. While continuing to conduct the Academy orchestra, Marriner has worked as a freelance conductor with opera and symphony orchestras around the world since the early 1990s.

MARSALIS, BRANFORD (26 AUG 1960–)

The Branford Marsalis legacy has always been problematic to the jazz purist. Although widely held to be one of most technically capable of the "new traditionalists" — i.e., the youthful vanguard in the contemporary scene dedicated to exploring the hard bop and modal jazz from the post–World War II era — he has also willingly immersed himself in the funk, rhythm and blues, and rock music currently in vogue with his peers. Following stints with the Lionel Hampton Orchestra, Clark Terry, and Art Blakey's Jazz Messengers, Branford joined brother Wynton Marsalis's band in 1981. He played tenor and soprano saxophones on Wynton's recordings until leaving to work with ex-Police vocalist Sting in 1985. He appeared on Sting's *The Dream of the Blue Turtles* (A&M #3750; 1985; #2) and … *Nothing Like the Sun* (A&M #6402; 1987; #9) before starting his own quartet. Utilizing his group as a vehicle for serious jazz as his brother had done, Branford has released a string of critically acclaimed LPs over the years, including *Scenes in the City* (Columbia #38951; 1984; #164), *Royal Garden Blues: Romances for Saxophone* (Columbia #40363; 1986), *Random Abstract* (Columbia #44055; 1988), and *Requiem* (Sony #69655; 1999), a tribute to his former keyboard associate, Kenny Kirkland.

Branford's collaborations with other artists, however, have spanned a wide range of popular music styles. He has contributed to recordings by Public Enemy (political rap), the Neville Brothers (R&B/funk), Tina Turner (Black contemporary), the Grateful Dead (progressive rock), and Bruce Hornsby (AOR), with whom he won a Grammy for Best Pop Instrumental Performance ("Barcelona Mona"). He has also supplied music to film soundtracks — most notably, Spike Lee's *Mo' Better Blues* (Columbia #46792; 1990; #63) — and has acted in *Bring on the Night*, *School Daze*, and *Throw Mama from the Train*. He was perhaps most criticized for serving as musical director of *The Tonight Show*, starring Jay Leno, between 1992–1995; he would eventually leave due to the creative limitations imposed upon him by the variety show format.

FRANK HOFFMANN

MARSALIS, WYNTON (18 OCT 1961–)

American trumpeter, born in New Orleans, son of jazz pianist Ellis Marsalis. At 14 he won a competition and played the Haydn Trumpet Concerto with the New Orleans Philharmonic Orchestra. He studied at Juilliard School, then played with Art Blakey's Jazz Messengers and toured with a quintet that included his brother Branford as saxophonist. He also worked with Miles Davis. Marsalis was signed to Columbia as a solo artist in both its jazz and classical divisions, amid much hoopla, in 1981. Two years later, he won Grammy awards in both jazz and classical categories, the first artist ever to do so, and repeated this feat in 1984. In 1987, Marsalis was cofounder of Jazz at Lincoln Center, and continues to serve as the program's artistic director. A tremendously prolific recording artist, Marsalis has recorded dozens of albums leading his own small groups as well as the Lincoln Center Jazz Orchestra. His long composition, *Blood on the Fields* (released on three CDs as Columbia #57694; 1997), won the Pulitzer Prize, the first jazz composition to do so. Marsalis has been an outspoken proponent of traditional jazz against the avant-garde and a critic of racism in jazz writing and music. His critics counter by citing him as old fashioned in his compositional style and too narrow in his programming at Lincoln Center.

REV. CARL BENSON

MARSH LABORATORIES, INC.

A Chicago firm established ca. 1921 by Orlando Marsh (1881–1938); successor to Cullen, Marsh & Co. T.B. Lambert — "almost certainly the same Lambert of celluloid record fame some two decades earlier" [Bryan] — was vice president, Marsh was president, though at first Marsh was listed as vice president, and Harve [*sic*] J. Badgerow was president and treasurer. The same advertisement states that "seventeen years ago Orlando R. Marsh instituted the first electrical recording laboratory in the world." If that is accurate, it would date the founding of the Marsh Laboratories (or perhaps Cullen, Marsh & Co.) at 1914, earlier than has been supposed. The principal claim to fame of the laboratories was the creation and production of the first electrical recordings, issued on the Autograph label in 1924. Marsh seems to have sold his interest to the New York Recording Laboratories around 1927. In 1931 the firm was engaged in "electrical transcription service," providing material for radio stations. While there is no terminal date available for the firm, Marsh himself was known to be active in the recording business until at least 1936. [Bryan 1990.]

MARSPEN (LABEL)

A British record of the mid-1920s, issued in two sizes: five and 3/8 inches and six inches in diameter. It was made by the Edison Bell Works of J. E Hough, Ltd., and also by the Crystalate Gramophone Record Manufacturing Co., Ltd., from the masters of both firms, for distribution by the Marks and Spencer chain of stores.

FRANK ANDREWS

MARSTON (LABEL)

Reissue label founded by noted audio engineer Ward Marston. Martson was born blind in 1952, and began collecting early and historic recordings as a teenager. He became well known for his skills in audio restoration beginning in 1979 when he restored the earliest known stereo recording, made at Bell Labs in 1932. He worked as a reissue engineer for all the major classical labels and was nominated for a Grammy for Best Historical Album for his work on BMG's Fritz Kreisler collection in 1997. That same year, he began his own label to issue historic recordings with complete liner notes and superior sound. The label has built an impressive catalog of early opera and classical performances. [website: www.marston.com]

MARTIN, DEAN
(7 JUNE 1917–25 DEC 1995)

Although something of an anachronism during his peak period of popularity as a recording artist — from the mid-1950s to the mid-1960s — Dean Martin managed to produce a lengthy string of hit ballads during the golden age of rock 'n' roll and, later, at the height of the "British Invasion" when American artists of every stripe had trouble getting their songs played on the radio. While his relaxed crooning style failed to generate much critical acclaim, he enjoyed widespread public support across a wide range of media, including the recordings, the cinema, radio, television, and live performing venues.

Born Dino Crocetti in Stuebenville, Ohio, Martin became interested in a singing career after finding

Dean Martin late '60s Reprise album. Courtesy Frank Hoffmann

little fulfillment working as a mill hand, gas-station attendant, and gambling casino croupier. In 1946, he teamed up with comedian Jerry Lewis; their popularity on the nightclub circuit led to a film contract with Paramount. The duo starred in 16 movies — including *My Friend Irma* (1949), *At War with the Army* (1952), and *The Caddy* (1953) — until their breakup in 1957. Although Martin continued to star in a wide range of film roles — in addition to being in great demand both as a host (the *Dean Martin Show* ran from 1965–1974) and guest performer on television — he was perhaps best known for his successful recordings, beginning with a comic duet with Lewis, "That Certain Party" (Capitol #15249; 1948; #22). By the time he recorded "That's Amore" (Capitol #2589; 1953; #2) his suave, urbane approach was in place.

Like Bing Crosby and Frank Sinatra, Martin was a master microphone singer, using the mike to establish an intimacy with his listeners both on stage and record. He continued to chart consistently through the 1950s, most notably with "Memories Are Made of This" (Capitol #3295; 1955; #1 for six weeks), "Return to Me" (Capitol #3894; 1958; #4), and "Volare" (Capitol #4028; 1958; #12; more popular versions were recorded by Domenico Modugno in 1958 and Bobby Rydell in 1960). Following an extended dry spell, Martin was signed by buddy Frank Sinatra's fledging Reprise label in 1962. While considering material in the studio, Martin's conductor and pianist, Ken Lane, suggested a song he'd cowritten more than 15 years earlier, "Everybody Loves Somebody" (Reprise #0281). Although Sinatra (the first to record it in 1948), Dinah Washington, Peggy Lee, and other prominent singers had failed to make it a hit, Martin's updated version reached number one on the *Billboard Hot 100* in August 1964 (it remained atop the adult contemporary charts for eight weeks). He produced 10 more top 40 hits in the 1960s, including "The Door Is Still Open to My Heart" (Reprise #0307; 1964; #6) and "I Will" (Reprise #0415; 1965; #10). Martin also became a highly successful albums artist with Reprise, placing 23 titles on the *Billboard* charts between 1963–1972, most notably, *Dream with Dean* (Reprise #6123; 1964; #15), *Everybody Loves Somebody* (Reprise #6130; 1964; #2), *The Door Is Still Open to My Heart* (Reprise #6140; 1964; #9), *Dean Martin Hits Again* (Reprise #6146; 1965; #13), *(Remember Me) I'm the One Who Loves You* (Reprise #6170; 1965; #12), *Houston* (Reprise #6181; 1965; #11), *Welcome to My World* (Reprise #6250; 1967; #20), and *Gentle on My Mind* (Reprise #6330; 1969; #14).

FRANK HOFFMANN

MARTIN, FREDDY
(9 DEC 1906–1 OCT 1983)

American dance band leader, born in Cleveland. He played tenor saxophone in his youth and formed a band while still in high school. In 1932 he organized a professional band and had early engagements at the Hotel Bossert in Brooklyn, the Hotel Roosevelt, Waldorf Astoria, and other major New York ballrooms. He was also popular in Chicago and became a fixture in the late 1930s at the Coconut Grove in Los Angeles. Martin's band was featured on radio shows in the 1930s. Success was greatly expanded in 1941 with a hit recording of "Tonight We Love," an adaptation of the first theme of Tchaikovsky's B-Flat Piano Concerto, arranged by Ray Austin and played by Jack Fina (Bluebird #11211). Martin followed that with an adaptation of a theme from the Grieg Concerto (Bluebird #11430). With vocalist Merv Griffin he had a 1948 hit record, "I've Got a Lovely Bunch of Coconuts" (Victor #20-3554). During the 1940s his band appeared in several motion pictures, and he remained active until his death in Newport Beach, California. Nostalgia CD labels Hindsight, Laserlight, and others have reissued some of Martin's hits on CD.

MARTIN, GEORGE (3 JAN 1926–)

Recognized as one of music's most versatile and imaginative talents, Martin entered the music industry in 1950, after studying at the Guildhall School of Music, and went on to play the oboe professionally in London. Somewhat later, he began recording classical music, specializing in the Baroque period. His later experience with jazz and pop led to his appointment as head of the Parlophone label in the EMI Group in 1955. As a producer, Martin has been responsible for bringing a host of artists into recording studios, particularly in the humorous field with brilliant performers such as Peter Sellers, Spike Milligan, Flanders and Swann, and the "Beyond the Fringe" team of Jonathan Miller, Peter Cook, Dudley Moore, and Alan Bennett. He has also worked with jazz artists Cleo Laine, John Dankworth, Humphrey Lyttelton, and the legendary Stan Getz. In 1962, Martin signed the Beatles to record for EMI, a decision that launched them on their remarkable career, with Martin producing every record they made until they disbanded in 1970. In 1965, he formed a production company with three other producers, and four years later began the design and construction of A.I.R. Studios, a recording complex in the center of London, which to this day is one of the most successful studio operations in the world.

HOWARD FERSTLER

MARTIN, RICCARDO
(18 NOV 1874–11 AUG 1952)

American tenor, born Hugh Whitfield Martin in Hopkinsville, Kentucky. He studied violin and piano as a child, then had some vocal training in Europe. Returning to America, he took up composition under Edward MacDowell at Columbia University (1896). But his singing attracted more notice than his compositions, and he returned to Europe to study in Paris, making his debut in October 1904 in Nantes, as Faust. After further study in Italy, he sang in Verona on 4 Nov 1905, took the name Riccardo Martin, and appeared in Milan, then joined the San Carlo Opera Co. In 1906–1907 he took part in a U.S. tour with the troupe, and on 20 Nov 1907 he made his debut at the Metropolitan Opera Co. as Faust. He remained nine seasons — missing 1916–1917 to sing with the Boston Grand Opera — doing 159 appearances in 17 roles, and was regarded as the first American-born tenor to achieve operatic eminence. After his years at the Metropolitan Martin sang with the Chicago Opera Co. in 1920–1922, then settled in New York as a teacher, where he later died. Martin recorded for Edison in 1908, making "Vesti la giubba" (#B-160) and four other arias, plus Francesco Tosti's "Goodbye." He sang for Victor from 24 Feb 1910 to 8 Dec 1910, doing eight numbers; the first was "Als die alte Mutter" ("Songs My Mother Taught Me") by Dvorák (#87051), and the last the "Addio alla madre" from *Cavalleria rusticana* (#88277). There was also one Operaphone record, on an eight-inch vertical cut disc, of "Amarella." [Bott 1980.]

MARTIN, TONY
(25 DEC 1912–9 NOV 1995)

American popular vocalist, born Alvin Morris in Oakland, California. He sang with various orchestras, including Ray Noble's, and appeared in motion pictures from 1936. He was prominent on radio in the 1940s, then on television, and was a well-known nightclub performer in the 1970s. He often appeared with his wife, singer/dancer Cyd Charisse. Martin recorded for Decca in the mid- to late 1930s, briefly for Mercury from 1946–1947, and then through the 1950s for RCA Victor. Among his notable discs were "Begin the Beguine"/"September Song" (Decca #2375; 1939), "All the Things You Are" (Decca #2932; 1939), and "I Get Ideas" (Victor #20-4141; 1950). His 1936–1968 Decca recordings are anthologized on Collectors Classics (#7465), and RCA issued a greatest hits collection in 2000 featuring 14 1950s-era recordings (#69397).

MARTIN-LOGAN LOUDSPEAKERS

Conceptualized in 1980, by high-end audio store manager Gayle Martin Sanders and engineer Ron Logan Sutherland, with production beginning in 1983, the Martin-Logan company is a noted producer of high-end, cutting-edge-design, electrostatic loudspeaker systems. The company struggled initially, and Sutherland left in 1985 to pursue other interests, even though sales were just beginning to climb. By the late 1980s, business was very good, indeed, and *Inc. Magazine* recognized Martin-Logan as one of the fastest growing privately owned enterprises in the country. Today, the company is known for its distinctive electrostatic system designs, which make use of a curved radiation panels, coupled with dynamic woofer systems for exemplary bass reproduction and a highly refined electrostatic sound in the midrange and treble.

See also **Loudspeaker**

HOWARD FERSTLER

MARTINELLI, GIOVANNI
(22 OCT 1885– 2 FEB 1969)

Italian tenor, born in Montagnana, near Padua. He played clarinet in the town band, then went to study voice in Milan and made his debut there on 3 Dec 1910 in the Rossini *Stabat Mater*, followed by his operatic debut as Ernani. Puccini heard him sing and gave him the role of Dick Johnson in the premiere of *Fanciulla del West* in Rome, on 12 June 1911. He sang at Covent Garden and in Philadelphia, then at the Metropolitan Opera as Rodolfo on 20 Nov 1913, remaining 30 years. His farewell concert was on 8 Mar 1945, but he sang on, making his final appearance in *Turandot* (Seattle, 1967) at age 82.

At the Metropolitan he sang Radames 126 times and Don José 75 times. Wagner was not in his regular repertoire, though he did sing Tristan in German in Chicago opposite Kirsten Flagstad in 1939.

Martinelli recorded prolifically from 1912 through 1968; the discography in Collins [1979] has 202 numbered entries, including broadcasts. In 1913 he made eight Edison Diamond Discs, singing the main tenor arias from *Aida, Boheme, Gioconda, Manon Lescaut, Martha, Rigoletto,* and *Tosca*. From 1913 to 1929 he worked with Victor, performing the Italian/French repertoire. The most elegant recordings of that period may be the *Aida* duets with Rosa Ponselle (1924–1926) and the *Carmen* duets with Geraldine Farrar (1915). He participated in outstanding ensemble recordings from *Forza del destino* with Ponselle, Giuseppe de Luca, and Ezio Pinza (1927–1928); and from *Faust* with Frances Alda and Marcel Journet in 1919. His "Miserere" (*Trovatore*) duet with Ponselle

(Victor #8097; 1928) is widely admired. "O muto asil" from *Guillaume Tell* (Victor #6212; 1923) and "Come rugiada al cespite" from *Ernani* (Victor #64514, 737; 1915) are highly regarded by collectors.

From 1935 to 1939 Martinelli made seven selections from *Otello* with the Metropolitan Opera, Helen Jepson, and Lawrence Tibbett. He made 12 Vitaphone soundtracks during 1926–1927, recorded on 16-inch discs. These were short subjects, lasting about eight minutes, filmed at the old Manhattan Opera House. With his voice in decline, Martinelli continued to record, and in 1948–1968 made LPs for various labels. On CD (Nimbus #7804) he presents the Verdi ensemble numbers mentioned above, the *Guillaume Tell* aria, and the tenor showpieces from *Pagliacci*, *Cavalleria rusticana*, *Fedora*, and *Eugene Onegin*. Pearl #30 is a two-CD set of 1925–1929 recordings focusing on his recordings of arias from Verdi's operas, while Pearl #9184 is a single disc overview of his recordings of Puccini arias. Martinelli died in New York. [Collins 1979; Wile 1971/2.]

MASCOT TALKING MACHINE CO.

A New York firm, established in 1916. It offered the "Mascot" line of record players in seven models.

MASKING

An audio phenomenon that involves the ability of louder or more complex sounds to obscure the sound of simultaneous sounds — usually at lower sound levels. Masking is very important with data-reduction recording and playback techniques, because it allows inaudible data to be ignored during the encoding process, thereby increasing the storage capacity of the medium.

HOWARD FERSTLER

MASSENBURG, GEORGE Y.
(18 AUG 1947–)

Born in Baltimore, Maryland, and raised between there and Macon, Georgia, Massenburg was interested in music, electronics, and sound recording at an early age. Indeed, he was working part time both in the recording studio and in an electronics laboratory at 15 years of age and worked on an engineering degree at Johns Hopkins University. In 1972 he presented a paper at the Audio Engineering Society convention on parametric equalization, and he is credited with being the first person to come up with a viable design for studio use. He was chief engineer of Europa Sonar Studios in Paris in 1973 and 1974, and also did freelance engineering and equipment design in Europe during those years.

In 1982 he began GML, Inc., to produce specialized equipment for recording applications, including parametric equalizers, dynamic gain controllers, mixing consoles, and microphone preamplifiers. GML also consults and provides independent design for several major audio electronics manufacturers. He has designed, built, and managed several recording studios, notably ITI Studios in Huntsville, Maryland, and The Complex in Los Angeles, and has contributed acoustical and architectural designs to many others, including Skywalker Sound and The Site in Marin County, California. .Individually or collaboratively, Massenburg has also participated in the production of over 200 record albums during the past 30 years. His engineering and producing credits include working with Billy Joel, Kenny Loggins, Journey, Madeleine Peyroux, James Taylor, Randy Newman, Lyle Lovett, Aaron Neville, Little Feat, Michael Ruff, Toto, and Linda Ronstadt.

He has been nominated many times for the non-classical engineering Grammy, for Record of the Year in several years, and has won a number of Grammys for his work as a producer. In 1998 he received the Grammy for Technical Achievement, one of only four such awards presented in the history of NARAS. He also won the Academy of Country Music award for Record of the Year in 1988. In 1989, he received the *Mix Magazine* TEC award for Producer and Engineer of the Year, as well as Engineer of the Year award in 1991 and 1992. Massenburg is currently adjunct professor of recording arts and sciences at McGill University in Montreal, Quebec, Canada, and visiting lecturer at UCLA and USC in Los Angeles and MTSU in Murfreesboro, Tennessee.

HOWARD FERSTLER

MASSIVE ATTACK

Massive Attack is widely credited with having created trip-hop, a trance-like rhythmic blend of hip-hop, DJ sampling, soulful singing, funk, and Jamaican dub music. A club-scene alternative to the hyperactive energy of techno in the 1990s, trip-hop became a fixture on film soundtracks and recordings of DJ remixes. Massive Attack evolved out of a Bristol, England–based group of DJs, rappers, singers, and sound engineers known as the Wild Bunch that began staging dance parties in 1983. The Wild Bunch's 1986 cover of Burt Bacharach's "The Look of Love" became a major hit in the European club circuit. Internal disputes and harassment by legal officials led to a breakup of the collective; graffiti artist/vocalist

3-D (Robert Del Naja), vocalist/keyboardist/producer Daddy G (Grant Marshall), and keyboardist/producer Andrew Vowles (better known as Mushroom) emerged out of its ashes to form Massive Attack in 1987.

Generating career momentum from the release of a string of popular club singles, Massive Attack released its debut album, *Blue Lines* (Virgin #91685; #13 U.K.), in 1991, featuring a varied array of vocalists, including DJ Tricky, Shara Nelson, and reggae artist Horace Andy. Although the group always viewed dance singles as the ultimate artform (according to discographer Martin Strong, their hypnotic "Unfinished Sympathy" (Circa #2; 1991; #13 U.K.; mixed by Paul Oakenfold) is often cited as one of the most perfect singles ever crafted; their LPs — *Protection* (Virgin #3847; 1994; #14 U.K.), which featured jazz-pop singer Tracey Thorn and Nigerian vocalist Nicolette, among others; *No Protection: Massive Attack vs. Mad Professor* (Circa/Virgin #3; 1995; #10 U.K.), a remix of *Protection* with the assistance of reggae producer, Mad Professor; *Mezzanine* (Virgin #45599; 1998; #1 U.K., #60 U.S.), augmented with vocals by Andy, Cocteau Twins alumnus Elizabeth Fraser, and Sara Jay; and the 11-CD box set of remixes, *Singles 90/98* (Virgin #95443; 1998) — represented important statements of past studio experiments. Massive Attack's future was somewhat in doubt following Mushroom's departure in mid-1999. Given public announcements of plans to continue as a duo, combined with the group's legacy of fruitful collaborations with outside talent, it appeared likely that new releases would eventually be forthcoming.

FRANK HOFFMANN

MASTER

The copper or nickel shell made from an original disc or tape recording, from which copies are made, leading to the final pressing. It is also known as a "metal master." It may also be a lacquer disc (in instantaneous recording). In the early days of recording, the master was usually of wax for cylinders and discs.

See also **Disc; Recording Practice**

MASTER (LABEL)

An American record issued from February 1937, lasting less than one year. It was marketed by the music publisher Irving Mills, who issued the Variety label at the same time. Jazz was the featured material, with artists like Duke Ellington, Cab Calloway, and the Raymond Scott Quintet included. [Rust 1978.]

Label begun by publisher Irving Mills in 1937 to feature acts he represented, including Duke Ellington. Courtesy Kurt Nauck/Nauck's Vintage Records

MASTERPHONE CO.

A New York firm, advertising in *TMW* for May 1914 the sale of a device to "clarify and amplify record tone."

MASTER-PHONE CORP.

A New York firm. In January 1915 there was advertising for the "red needle," a composition of improved fiber that promised five to 10 plays, with no wear and no "muffled sound." An announcement in *TMW* for 15 Sep 1915 stated that a patent for this needle had been acquired by the Phonograph Accessories Corp.

MASTER TAPE

The tape that is used to produce the final product after the recording and editing process. In some cases, it might be created live from two tracks during the recording session. Usually it is put together from multiple recorder tracks later on, during mixing and post-production work. A master tape may have two or more channels, depending on the playback medium required.

HOWARD FERSTLER

MASTER TONE (LABEL)

A department store label distributed by Kaufmann & Baer Co., Pittsburgh, in the early 1920s. The record was apparently produced by the Bridgeport Die and

Machine Co., Bridgeport, Connecticut. Material was popular dance and vocal. [Kendziora 1987/3.]

MASTERS, FRANKIE
(4 OCT 1904–13 FEB 1990)

American Big Band leader, born in St. Mary's, West Virginia. He attended Indiana University and played in a dance orchestra there, then moved to Chicago and worked in various theaters. He attracted attention in the later 1930s and had a radio show in 1937. His orchestra was of the sweet variety, in demand for hotel and ballroom engagements. He co-composed the hit song "Scatterbrain" in 1939 (Vocalion #4915). David Rose became the band's arranger in the 1940s; there were many radio shows and long engagements at Chicago hotels. Vocalist Phyllis Miles was featured on a number of fine discs, such as "Blue Champagne"/"Harbor of Dreams" (Okeh #6279; 1941). After the World War II, Masters briefly relocated the band to California and then returned to Chicago, retiring the band in the mid-1950s, but reviving the band for private parties and the like again in the late 1960s through the 1970s.

MASTERS, IAN (25 APR 1944–)

Born in Toronto, and earning a B.A. degree from the University of Toronto in 1968, Masters took a stab at the accounting business and decided that the work did not suit him. Consequently, he started writing about audio and video equipment and has continued to do so since 1972. He spent more than a decade as editor of *AudioScene Canada*, and for a further three years he was editor of *Inside Audio Video*. In 1984, he became a contributing editor for the Toronto-based magazine *Sound & Vision*, that country's leading consumer electronics magazine (not affiliated with the U.S. magazine of the same name). In May 1996 he was appointed editor of the magazine, although the publication ceased production some months later. During the same period, Masters had been a regular contributor to the U.S. magazine *Stereo Review*, and since the magazine merged with *Video* magazine in 1999 to form *Sound & Vision*, he has been a contributing technical editor and regular columnist. He also writes a weekly audio and video column for Canada's largest newspaper, the *Toronto Star*, and has contributed articles on audio and video topics to *Home Computing & Entertainment* magazine. Over the years, Masters has also been a regular contributor to such diverse publications as *Car Stereo Review*, *Audio*, Ottawa's *Canadian Consumer* magazine, Sydney's *Australian Hi-Fi*, and *Home Goods Retailing*, a national trade publication, as well as a

number of other publications, plus the *Journal of the Society of American Archivists*.

HOWARD FERSTLER

MASUR, KURT (18 JULY 1927–)

One of the 20th century's great conductors, Masur was born in the town of Brieg in Silesia. He studied piano and cello, first attending the Breslau Music School (1942–1944) and then the Leipzig Hochschule fur Musik (1946–1948). He is best known as the conductor of the Dresden Philharmonic (1955–1958; 1967–1972), the Gewandhaus Orchestra (1970–1998), and the New York Philharmonic (1991–2002). Masur lead these ensembles on dozens of recordings for various labels, including Deutsche Grammophon, Teldec, and Philips. He has conducted recordings of everything from opera to the standard classical repertory to contemporary classical compositions.

MATHIS, JOHNNY (30 SEP 1935–)

American popular singer, born in San Francisco. After training as a classical singer, he turned to nightclub work and became an international star. Although African-American, Mathis was known for his smooth pop vocalizing in the Nat King Cole tradition. Between 1957 and 1974 he made 39 chart singles, among them "It's Not for Me to Say" (Columbia #40851; 1957) and the late career hit "Too Much, Too Little, Too Late" (Columbia #10693; 1978), a duet with pop star Deniece Williams. He also had 54 chart albums by 1974, most from the late 1950s and early 1960s, notably *Heavenly* (Columbia #1251, 8152; 1959), on the lists 56 weeks. As of the turn of the 21st century, Mathis continued to record for Columbia, making him one of the label's longest active acts. Columbia has reissued a number of his original albums on CD, along with various hit packages on its Legacy label.

MATLOCK, MATTY
(27 APR 1909–14 JUNE 1978)

American jazz clarinetist, born Julian C. Matlock in Paducah, Kentucky. He grew up in Nashville and played there in the 1920s, then joined Ben Pollack's band in 1929, replacing Benny Goodman. He was one of the original members of the Bob Crosby band in 1935 and became its arranger; then he arranged for Red Nichols, Pee Wee Hunt, and others. He is heard on many Bob Crosby records, of which "March of the Bob Cats" (his composition) may be mentioned (Decca #1865; 1938). When he left Bob Crosby in

1942 he went to Hollywood, working in radio and television. Matlock made several LP albums with his own groups, including *Pete Kelly's Blues* (Columbia 1955, #690), inspired by the motion picture (directed by and starring Jack Webb in 1955) and the following 1959 television series, both of which featured Matlock. Inspired by this success, Matlock recorded a series of Dixieland-themed albums for Warner Bros. released in 1958–1959. He led successful groups in the 1960s, with a long run in Las Vegas and dates in Lake Tahoe, as well as a tour of the Far East. He died in Van Nuys, California.

MATRIX (I)

An alternative term for master.

MATRIX (II)

A circuit in an electrical system that mixes or separates signals.

MATRIX NUMBER

A serial number engraved or embossed on each side of a disc record by the manufacturer, usually near the center; or on the circumference of a cylinder record. This number is a guide to the date of the record; it may indicate which take or performance is on the record; and it may provide other data as well. The matrix number is sometimes useful in the case of reissues, as it suggests whether or not the reissue does in fact offer the identical take as the earlier record.

MATZENAUER, MARGARETE (1 JUNE 1881–19 MAY 1963)

Hungarian contralto/soprano, born in Temesvár. She grew up in a musical family and studied in Graz, Berlin, and Munich. On 15 Sept 1901 she joined the Strasbourg Opera, then in 1904–1911 she was with the Munich Court Opera. She sang in Bayreuth in 1911 and made her Metropolitan Opera debut on 13 Nov 1911 as Aida; she remained with the company until 1930, while singing also in Europe. Matzenauer had a remarkable vocal range and was able to sing both the soprano and contralto repertoires throughout her career. She retired in 1938 and died in Van Nuys, California. Matzenauer made relatively few records: 86 are enumerated in Miller [1976]. She recorded for G & T in Munich during 1906–1909. "Ach, mein Sohn" ("Ah, mon fils") and "O gebt, o gebt" ("Donnez, donnez") from *Prophète* (#043079 and #043080) are among her finest records of that period.

She was with Victor in the U.S. during 1912–1913, singing Verdi, Wagner, and other roles in German, Italian, and French; and again with Victor in 1924–1926. A favorite among collectors in "Nobles seigneurs, salut!" from *Huguenots* (Victor #6471). "Ah, mon fils" was recorded again in 1925 (#6531). She also made Edison Diamond Discs from 1919 to 1922, among them a *Lucia* sextette with an ensemble comprising Thomas Chalmers, Marie Rappold, Giovanni Zenatello, Enrico Baroni, and Arthur Middleton. Top Artists Platters and Collectors Guild reissued many of her arias on LP in 1959 and 1960; there are no CD reissues as of this writing. [Miller 1976.]

MAUREL, VICTOR (17 JUNE 1848–22 OCT 1923)

French baritone, born in Marseilles. He studied at the Paris Conservatory and made his debut at the Paris Opéra in 1868; then sang throughout Europe and the U.S. From 1879 to 1894 he was a member of the Opéra, after which he sang at the Metropolitan Opera from 3 Dec 1894 (debut as Iago) to 1896. He was back in Paris until 1904, then transferred permanently to America in 1909. Maurel was most distinguished in Wagnerian and Verdian roles. He created Iago (5 Feb 1887) and Falstaff (9 Feb 1893). He died in New York. Maurel recorded for G & T in Paris in 1903, doing "Sogno di Iago" (#2-32814) and an air from Gluck. In 1904 and again in 1907 he was with Fonotipia in Milan, singing the "Serenata" of *Don Giovanni* (#39041), "Era la notte" from *Otello*, and "Quand'ero paggio" from *Falstaff*. His few recordings were reissued by various labels, including IRCC, Scala, Olympus, Belcantodisc, and Top Artists Platters. Marston's complete recordings are available from Marston, along with Adelina Patti's output, on a two-CD set.

MAURO, PHILIP (1859–1952)

Legal counsel for the American Graphophone Co. in the 1890s and early 1900s. The graphophone patent #569,290, granted to Thomas A. Macdonald on 13 Oct 1896, was acquired in part because of the arguments of Mauro and his fellow attorney Pollok; the patent examiner had at first cited a German and an American patent as prior conceptions. Mauro became known for aggressive patent litigation and won injunctions against Hawthorne & Sheble, Frank Seaman, and Emile Berliner. American Graphophone Co. was enabled to produce disc records in 1901–1906 on the strength of Mauro's case for the validity of the Joseph Jones patent; he had to rewrite the claims several times to demonstrate their novelty to a skeptical patent examiner. On 31 Jan 1899 he gave a "brilliant paper" [Read & Welch] before the Washington Academy of Sciences, "Development of the Art of Recording and Reproducing of Sound," and repeated it for the Franklin Institute in Philadelphia; he credited Macdonald and American Graphophone scientists for the invention and improvement of the talking machine. [Read and Welch 1976.]

MAXFIELD, J[OSEPH]. P. (28 DEC 1887–1977)

Born in San Francisco, Maxfield had a Ph.D. in architecture, but his chosen field of interest was audio and acoustics. After World War I, while at Bell Laboratories, he and Henry Harrison devised the first recording and reproducing system using electricity. Using microphones and amplifiers, they extended the reproducible sound range by more than an octave and appreciably improved fidelity, resulting in the Orthophonic phonographic player of 1925. That same year, he also led the project that produced E.C. Wente's moving coil speaker, and pioneered the Vitaphone talking motion picture system in 1926. Maxfield also developed the 33 1/3 rpm rotational speed for electrical recordings. The chosen speed was based upon the need for disc systems to properly synchronize with motion-picture reel length during the early era of talking pictures, and a patent was granted for his work in 1927. Although it was more than 20 years before consumer versions of this design showed up for home-audio use, the 33 1/3 speed was chosen for precise mechanical and mathematical reasons that Maxfield had worked out. For his pioneering work, the Audio Engineering Society awarded him its Potts award in 1954.

HOWARD FERSTLER

See also **Disc; Surface Speed; Turntable**

MAXICUT PROCESS

A technique developed by EMI, Ltd., using an electronic logic circuit in the preview computer, to recognize frequencies and levels otherwise difficult for average record players to reproduce.

MAYALL, JOHN (29 NOV 1933–)

An early blues revivalist, Mayall is famous for leading his band, The Bluesbreakers, which featured on guitar at one time or another Eric Clapton, Peter Green, and Mick Taylor, as well as bassists Jack Bruce and John McVie and drummer Mick Fleetwood. Born in Macclesfield, England, Mayall formed his first band in Manchester, but then came to London to join the booming blues scene there in 1963. Signed to a contract with British Decca in 1964, Mayall led at least 15 different Bluesbreakers lineups through mid-1970. Perhaps his most famous album (at least in the U.S.) is *Bluesbreakers with Eric Clapton* (Deram #800086; 1965). Mayall also cut solo albums during this period with a more mainstream rock orientation than his blues outings. Although he has continued to record and perform over the following decades, Mayall's influence waned after 1970, at least among his fellow musicians.

CARL BENSON

MAYFAIR (LABEL)

A British record made from Edison Bell Winner, Panachord, or Piccadilly masters, offered in exchange for coupons found in Ardath cigarettes in 1931–1933. All artists used pseudonyms, including such American performers as Joe Venuti, Benny Goodman, and Red Nichols. [Rust 1978.]

FRANK ANDREWS

MCA, INC. (MUSIC CORPORATION OF AMERICA)

An entertainment industry conglomerate, established in Chicago in 1924 by Jules C. Stein; it is now located in Universal City, California. Originally the firm was a booking agency for jazz and swing bands; by 1927 it represented about 40 of them. Two-thirds of the active bands were MCA clients by the late 1930s. Moving to California in 1937, MCA expanded its interests to booking of movie actors and to acquisition of other talent agencies. Television booking and production was added to the firm's activities in 1949 with great success and profits. Universal Studios was acquired in 1959, and MCA, Inc. was organized to replace the Music Corporation of America. Decca Records, Inc. was purchased in 1962. Shortly after, the firm gave up its talent booking and concentrated on feature film production (Universal) as well as other entertainment production, including recordings. Other labels acquired were Coral, Kapp, and UNI; these were merged into the single MCA label. ABC-Dunhill was acquired in February 1979. In 1985 the Chess label was added to the catalog, and five years later Geffen and GRP were purchased and the company was renamed the MCA Music Entertainment Group. In 1991 Japanese electronics giant Matsushita purchased MCA's holdings, including its record labels. In 1995, Seagram purchased 80 percent of MCA, Inc., and a year later renamed the music division Universal Music Group (UMG). Also in 1996, UMG took a half ownership share in the rap label, Interscope Records. The late 1990s have seen MCA and its labels consolidated twice into larger groups. In 1998, Seagram acquired PolyGram and folded it into UMG, forming an enormous group of labels.

See also **Universal Music Group**

MCCARTNEY, PAUL (18 JUNE 1942–)

Perhaps the most successful of the Beatles in his solo career, McCartney achieved great popular, if not critical, success through the 1990s. He recorded his first solo album, the self-titled *McCartney* (Apple #3363), in his home studio, overtracking all the parts; the simple production value was a direct response to the agony of trying to complete the *Let It Be* album with the Beatles. His first solo hit came with "Uncle Albert/Admiral Halsey" (Apple #1837; 1971; #1), from his second solo album, *Ram* (Apple #3374). In 1971 McCartney formed the first version of the band Wings, with which he would perform through the balance of the decade. The band recorded prolifically and had many top 10 pop hits, including the 1973 number one hits "My Love" and "Live and Let Die" (Apple #1861 and #1863, respectively), 1974's "Band on the Run" (Apple #1873), 1975's "Listen to What the Man Said" (Capitol #4091), 1976's "Silly Love Songs" (Capitol #4256), 1979's "With a Little Luck" (Capitol #4559), and 1980's "Coming Up" (Columbia #11263). Critics regard their album, *Band on the Run* (Apple #3415), as their best work.

In the early 1980s, McCartney returned to a solo career. He had a number one hit with "Ebony and Ivory," a duet with Stevie Wonder, in 1982 (Columbia #02860), from his album *Tug of War* (Columbia #37462), which reunited him with producer George Martin and gained him renewed critical respect. He also had several major hits, including duets with Michael Jackson on 1982's "The Girl Is Mine" (Epic #03288; #2 pop, #1 R&B and adult contemporary) and "Say Say Say" from a year later (Columbia #04168; #1 pop). However, he followed this with the major flop movie, *Give My Regards to Broadstreet* (although it did produce the number six hit, "No More Lonely Nights" [Columbia #04581]), and several weaker albums. He returned to form in 1989's *Flowers in the Dirt* (Capitol #91653), featuring songs cowritten with Elvis Costello, including the top 25 hit, "My Brave Face" (Capitol #44367) A world tour followed.

During the 1990s, McCartney produced a wide variety of music, including the classical work *Liverpool Oratorio* (Angel #54371), as well as participated in the Beatles's *Anthology* project, which included recording two "new" tracks using demo recordings by John Lennon as their basis. He also collaborated with producer Youth on two albums of electronic/ambient music released by "The Fireman" in 1994 and 1998. His 1997 album *Flaming Pie* (Capitol #56500), gained warm reviews, but did not produce any solid hits. His most recent work is 2001's *Driving Rain* (Capitol #35510), featuring the post-9/11 anthem, "Freedom."

CARL BENSON

MCCORMACK, JOHN (14 JUNE 1884–16 SEP 1945)

Irish/American tenor, born in Athlone, Ireland. He sang in the St. Patrick's (Dublin) cathedral choir, won a national singing competition in 1903, studied voice in Milan (1905), and made his opera debut in 1906 in Savona. He then sang in Ireland, and at Covent Garden in October 1907 in *Cavalleria*. He was a great success with the San Carlo Co. in Naples, as Alfredo and the Duke. His American debut was at the Manhattan Opera Co. on 10 Nov 1909 in *Traviata*. He was with the Metropolitan Opera from 29 Nov 1910, singing in the 1912–1914 and 1917–1919 seasons. In 1910–1911 he was with the Chicago Opera. On the crest of world fame, he toured Australia with Nellie Melba in 1911 and appeared in Europe and South America. He became an American citizen in 1919. After 1920 McCormack devoted himself mostly to concertizing throughout the world. He did sing Wagner in Los Angeles in 1928, and starred in the motion picture *Song of My Heart* in 1930. His last tours were in the late 1930s and early 1940s, after which he made radio broadcasts for the BBC. He died near Dublin on 16 Sept 1945.

McCormack's pure light voice — representing "the last link with 18th century vocalism" [Johnston] — was ideally displayed in Mozartean roles and in Rossini, though he excelled also in the rest of the lyric repertoire. On the concert stage he presented a repertoire of Irish and British songs, as well as art songs of Europe and the United States.

His earliest records were made in London in 1904. He recorded Irish material for on seven-inch and 10-inch discs for G & T, on 19 September and again on the 23rd, 24th, and 26th of the month. At the same time (21–23 September) he was making cylinders for the National Phonograph Co., Ltd. "The Snowy Breasted Pearl" was the first cylinder (#13124); there were nine other Irish songs in that session. In November 1904 he made two-minute cylinders for Edison Bell (three sessions of Irish songs), then he worked with Sterling Records in July 1906, making more two-minute cylinders, and with Pathé. For the Odeon label in 1906–1909 he extended his repertoire to include Italian and French arias, making about 80 sides; they were issued by Sterling and Hunting, Ltd., and some were later reissued by the American Odeon Corp. of New York.

Victor signed McCormack in 1910, starting a long association on Red Seal records. He began with the *Lucia* Tomb Scene (C #8535-1). His most famous and most popular disc was "I Hear You Calling Me" (#64120; 1910). By 1917 he had 130 solo numbers in the Victor catalog, plus duets with various artists and the great recording of the *Rigoletto* Quartet with Lucrezia Bori, Josephine Jacoby, and Reinald Werrenrath (#89080; 1914). "Il mio tesoro" (Victor #74484; 1916) was voted the favorite tenor acoustic record by collectors, as reported in *Hobbies* magazine (March 1947). "Oh Sleep, Why Dost Thou Leave Me?" from *Semele*, is another perennial favorite (#66096; 1920) among numerous remarkable discs. McCormack recorded for HMV in 1924–1942, making 220 discs in Britain for that label, and for many smaller labels. He took part in the Hugo Wolf Society issues in 1932. There are numerous CD reissues on Pearl, ASV, RCA, Rego Irish, and other labels. [Johnston 1988.]

MCFERRIN, BOBBY (11 MAR 1950–)

A one-of-a-kind talent, McFerrin possesses the ability to reproduce vocally virtually any musical instrument as well as many other natural sounds. Born in New York City to opera singing parents, he studied piano rather than voice at Juilliard and Sacramento State College. Following stints playing piano with University of Utah dance workshops and singing in various journeyman bands, he was asked to join Jon Hendricks's jazz group. On the strength of highly acclaimed solo performances at the Playboy Jazz Festival (1980) and Kool Jazz Festival (1981), he was signed to a recording contract by Elektra. From the beginning, McFerrin's releases ran contrary to traditional notions of jazz vocalizing. He performed without instrumental backup, combining his multitextured voice with rhythmic body slaps to simulate full-band accompaniment. His material — a blend of original compositions and covers — spanned the classical, jazz, soul, funk, and, pop genres. After a series of moderately selling albums, he broke through with a chart-topping single, "Don't Worry Be Happy" (EMI-Manhattan #50146; 1988). By the late 1980s, he seemed to be everywhere, collaborating with jazz stars (Herbie Hancock, the Manhattan Transfer, Chick Corea), classical musicians (Yo-Yo Ma), film star narrators (Robin Williams, Jack Nicholson); recording

the theme to *The Cosby Show*; and providing the accompaniment to a number of television commercials. [Romanowski and George-Warren 1995.]

FRANK HOFFMANN

MCGILVRA, J.H.

American record industry executive. He was president of the Old Dominion Phonograph Co., Roanoke, Virginia; and an official of the Volta Graphophone Co. At the first convention of the National Phonograph Association, 1890, he was elected temporary chairman.

MCGREAL, LAWRENCE

American record industry jobber, doing business in Milwaukee, Wisconsin, from ca. 1911 to his bankruptcy in 1915. In July 1911 it was announced that he was the new president of the National Association of Talking Machine Jobbers.

M.C. HAMMER (30 MAR 1963–)

M.C. Hammer, born Stanley Kirk Burrell in Oakland, California's subsidized housing district, was the first rapper to cross over to pop superstardom. An ingenious songwriter/arranger whose material featured liberal samples of soul-funk hitmakers such as James Brown and Parliament/Funkadelic, his considerable dance skills and expertly choreographed performances played a major role in his success. Burrell was nicknamed "Little Hammer" while working as a batboy for the Oakland Athletics as a result of his resemblance to home run king, "Hammerin'" Hank Aaron. Baseball player friends lent him the money to establish his own record company; his Bay Area success led to a contract with Capitol Records. His second major label album, *Please Hammer Don't Hurt 'Em* (Capitol #92857; 1990; #1 for 21 weeks) — featuring "U Can't Touch This (Capitol #11571; 1990; #8), based on an unauthorized sample from the Rick James hit, "Super Freak (Part 1)" (Gordy #7205; 1981; #16); a rap update of the Chi-Lites' "Have You Seen Her" (Capitol #44573; 1990; #4) and "Pray" (Capitol #44609; 1990; #2), accompanied by a promotional video clip which melded religion, hip hop, and a West Side Story–influenced dance sequence — introduced him to the bigtime. High profile tours, a children's cartoon (*Hammerman*), and endorsement deals with Pepsi and Kentucky Fried Chicken followed. However, the rise of gangsta rap (which rendered his flashy, slick approach as dated), bad investments (e.g., horse breeding, real estate), and uneven follow-up LPs — *Too*

Legit to Quit (Capitol #98151; 1991; #2) and *The Funky Headhunter* (Giant #24545; 1994) — caused his career to stall. In 1996, he had to declare bankruptcy with $13.7 million in debts. Since then, Hammer has attempted to resurrect his career, while dividing time raising funds for his ministry.

FRANK HOFFMANN

MCINTOSH, FRANK
(12 JULY 1906– C. JAN 1990)

A notable manufacturer of consumer-audio amplifiers, preamplifiers, and tuners, McIntosh was born in Omaha, Nebraska. As a young man, he was an accomplished cellist, but he was more interested in engineering, and eventually became chief engineer at radio station WOAW. He also taught math and radio at a YMCA school, wrote columns on radio for various newspapers, and was radio editor for *Popular Mechanics*. In 1929, he went to work for Bell Telephone Laboratories. During his eight years there, he either installed or worked on the equipment for 235 radio stations. He joined the Radio and Radar Division of the War Production Board in early 1942. In 1945 he started his own consulting business.

While working for Frank Stanton, who was then president of CBS, he learned of the need for better quality audio amplifiers. He decided to build his own, employing a unity-coupling circuit, and he patented this in 1949 and set up his own manufacturing company, McIntosh Laboratories, in Silver Spring, Maryland. His company specialized in extremely high-quality amplifier, preamplifier, and tuner components, beginning in an era when high-end audio was almost unheard of. McIntosh retired in 1977, and sold his stock shares to top management and a few dedicated McIntosh investors, although he was retained with a salary on a consulting basis. He moved from his home in Endicott, New York, to Scottsdale, Arizona, where he lived until he passed away. [Information obtained from Roger Russell.]

HOWARD FERSTLER

MCINTOSH LABORATORIES

Founded in 1949 by Frank McIntosh, in Silver Spring, Maryland. McIntosh was awarded several patents for the unity coupled amplifier, which was able to deliver an unprecedented (for the era) 50 watts from 20–20 kHz with less than 1 percent distortion. In 1951, the company moved to Binghamton, New York, and later on the product line was expanded to preamplifiers, tuners, loudspeakers, and eventually car stereo and home theater. Gordon Gow, serving as executive vice president, became president in 1977 when McIntosh retired. Sidney Corderman was vice president of engineering and Morris Painchaud was vice president and treasurer. At that time, Larry Fish was chief electronics engineer and Roger Russell was company director of acoustic research. After Gordon Gow and Frank McIntosh passed away in 1989 and 1990 respectively, the company was sold to Clarion of Japan. Engineering and production remain in Binghamton and continues to produce top-quality products. [Thanks to Roger Russell for supplying information about both Frank McIntosh and the company.]

HOWARD FERSTLER

MCKENZIE, RED
(14 OCT 1899–7 FEB 1948)

American jazz bandleader and singer, born in St. Louis. He grew up in Washington, D.C., then returned to St. Louis and formed the Mound City Blue Blowers in 1923. This was a novel group, with McKenzie playing a comb, Dick Slevin playing the kazoo, and Jack Bland playing banjo; they got a Brunswick contract and began to record in 1924 with "Arkansaw [*sic*] Blues"/"Blue Blues" (#2581). Outstanding artists joined this bizarre ensemble in the next few years, including Frankie Trumbauer, Eddie Lang, Eddie Condon, Gene Krupa, Jack Teagarden, Glenn Miller, Pee Wee Russell, Coleman Hawkins, Muggsy Spanier, Jimmy Dorsey, Bunny Berigan, and Dave Tough — but through all that talent McKenzie (who did not play a regular instrument) performed on his comb. He also sang, as in "Georgia on My Mind"/"I Can't Believe that You're in Love with Me" (Okeh #41515; 1931). He was less active after the Blowers disbanded in the late 1930s. The mid-1940s Dixieland revival brought him briefly back to the public eye, and he made a few more recordings before his death in New York City. His early recordings from 1924–1930 have been reissued on two CDs on Sensation (#29, #30).

MCKINLEY, RAY
(18 JUNE 1910–7 MAY 1995)

American jazz drummer, vocalist, and Big Band leader, born in Fort Worth, Texas. After playing with various groups he joined the Dorsey Brothers band in 1934. From 1939–1942, he co-led the Will Bradley Orchestra, recording hits including the boogie-woogie flavored "Beat Me Daddy Eight to a Bar" (released 1939), featuring pianist Freddie Slack, for Decca. In 1942 he formed his own band and was quickly successful; he was featured in a motion picture in 1943, *Hit Parade*. During World War II he was with Glenn

Miller's Air Force Band, and became co-leader of that ensemble upon Miller's death. From 1946–1949 he led one of the more progressive of the postwar Big Bands, recording for Savoy from 1946–1947 (and reissued on CD on Storyville #2033). In 1956 he led Glenn Miller's orchestra, playing the old hits as well as new material on tour and on record for RCA Victor, continuing to lead the group for a decade. He was less active after the mid-1960s, although he returned to touring during the 1970s. He spent the mid-1980s hosting a British television show, and then returned to Florida in 1990, where he died five years later in the town of Largo.

MCKUEN, ROD (29 APR 1933–)

American singer, composer, poet, and actor, born in Oakland, California. Before he was 20 he was a disc jockey on Oakland radio and author of a syndicated newspaper column. During military service in Korea he appeared as a singer in a Tokyo supper club and in several motion pictures, and after leaving the Army he made several films for Universal in Hollywood. He wrote and sang songs in New York, Paris, London, and throughout the world; he gave command performances in U.K., Korea, and at the White House. His most successful album was *Rod McKuen at Carnegie Hall* (Warner #2WS 1794; 1969). Among his most popular compositions was "The World I Used to Know," which was a chart record by Jimmie Rodgers (Dot #16595; 1964). Suffering from depression, McKuen withdrew from public performance in 1982. His recordings are available on Laserlight, Delta, and other budget reissue labels.

MCLACHLAN, SARAH (28 JAN 1968–)

Best known as the founder of Lilith Fair, a tour providing a forum for female artists, Sarah McLachlan emerged from the 1990s as one of the highly regarded — and commercially successful — singer/songwriters on the music scene. Both her recordings and Lilith Fair have encouraged countless women to consider popular music as a viable career option. Born in Halifax, Nova Scotia, McLachlan took piano, guitar, and voice lessons as a youth. Attracting the interest of the Nettwerk label while performing with the new wave act, October Game, she recorded *Touch* (Nettwerk 30024; 1988; released in the U.S. by Arista #18594; 1989; #132), which went gold in Canada. The follow-up, *Solace* (Arista #18631; 1991; #167), showed McLachlan to be treading water. However, the next LP, *Fumbling Towards Ecstasy* (Arista #18725; 1993; #50), with its insightful song lyrics — most notably, adding a sociopolitical dimension to her prior concentration on

personal relationships — complementing her expressive singing, represented an artistic breakthrough. The momentum generated by its triple platinum sales extended to the next album of newly recorded material, *Surfacing* (Arista #18970; 1997; #2), which ultimately sold more than 7 million copies on the strength of three hit singles: "Adia" (Arista #13497; 1998; #3), "Angel" (Arista #13497/13621; 1997; #4), and "Building a Mystery" (Arista #13395; 1997; #13). The LP also won Grammy awards for Best Female Pop Vocal and Best Pop Instrumental Performance.

McLachlan was inspired to mount the 1997 edition of Lilith Fair when promoters stated that a tour featuring more than one women would not turn a profit. Also featuring Tracy Chapman, Paula Cole, Jewel, and Joan Osborne, it became the most successful tour of the summer. The progressively more diversified lineups of the 1998 and 1999 — spanning such genres as rap, R&B, the blues, world music, country, alternative rock, and adult contemporary — also did well; nevertheless, McLachlan kept to her plan of a three-year run, citing other musical challenges. The live album, *Mirrorball* (Arista #19049; 1999; #3), continued her string of successes, selling more than 3 million units. It also netted her a Grammy in 2000 for Best Female Pop Vocal Performance.

FRANK HOFFMANN

MCLAUGHLIN, JOHN

SEE MAHAVISHNU ORCHESTRA

MC LYTE (11 OCT 1971–)

Born Lana Moorer in Queens, New York, MC Lyte was one of the earliest female rap stars to project a hard-edged image. At age 12 she was trading rhymes with half-brother Milk and his Audio Two partner, Gizmo. They would achieve moderate success with "I Cram to Understand You (Sam)" (First Priority # ; 1987), an indictment of crack addiction, released on a label founded by her father Nat Robinson. Lyte made a substantial impact on the rap scene with her first two album releases, *Lyte as a Rock* (High Priority/Atlantic #90905; 1988) and *Eyes on This* (High Priority/ Atlantic #91304; 1989), dissing — among others — rival rapper Roxanne Shante, game-show hostess Vanna "Whyte," dope dealing hustlers, and sex-scamming homeboys. From 1991's *Act Like You Know* (First Priority/Atlantic #91731) onward, she experimented with her established formula, attempting to incorporate new influences and stay abreast of current fashions. Her "Ruff Neck" (First Priority #98401; 1993), gold single and only song to hit pop charts (albeit only #35). She remains an outspoken social and political activist, contributing public service announcements for the Rock the Vote movement and working tirelessly in the fight against AIDS. [Graff 1998.]

FRANK HOFFMANN

MCPARTLAND, JIMMY
(15 MAR 1907– 13 MAR 1991)

American jazz cornetist, born James Dougald McPartland in Chicago. He studied violin and cornet, then founded and played in the Austin High Gang, young, white, self-taught musicians who built on the Black New Orleans Dixieland style. He was soon performing with Bix Beiderbecke, whose style was similar to his own, and whom he replaced in the Wolverines when he was just 17 years old. McPartland was a key artist in the development of the Chicago jazz style. He was in the bands of Art Kassel and Ben Pollack during the late 1920s. In the 1930s he was with Horace Heidt, who led his own groups; he had a year with Jack Teagarden, 1941–1942, then went into military service. He met and married Marian Turner, a jazz pianist; later divorced and remarried her before he died. They played in Chicago groups together. He was active into the 1980s. He died in Port Washington, New York. McPartland was heard on the last Wolverine recordings, made in December 1924: "When My Sugar Walks down the Street" and "A Prince of Wails" (Gennett #5620). He recorded with McKenzie and Condon's Chicagoans in 1927, on four sides for Okeh. "Singapore Sorrows" was one of his discs with Ben Pollack (Victor #21437; 1928). With his own orchestra in 1939 he made "Jazz Me Blues"/"China Boy" (Decca #18042) and "The World Is Waiting for the Sunrise"/"Sugar" (Decca #18043). There were LP albums for a half dozen labels, of which the most notable was MCA #2-4110 (1956).

MCPARTLAND, MARIAN
(20 MAR 1920–)

British jazz pianist, born Margaret Marian Turner near Windsor, England. She studied violin, then piano at the Guildhall School of Music in London. Turning from classical to jazz piano, she performed in music halls. Having met and married Jimmy McPartland in 1945, she returned to the U.S. with him and worked with him in Chicago groups. In 1951 she began to perform with her own trio, developing a sophisticated style with classical elements, and became popular in quality jazz clubs. She remained active, and hosted a celebrated radio program for National Public Radio,

Piano_Jazz, from the late 1970s (many of these programs have been issued on CD by the Jazz Alliance label). She also recorded prolifically as a solo artist beginning in the early 1950s, including albums for Savoy (1951–1952), Capitol (1953–1958), and Argo (1958) early in her career, and then returning to record, beginning in 1969, on her own label, Halycon. In 1982, she signed with Concord Jazz, and continued to record for the label through the turn of the 21st century. She also recorded two albums with her husband in the mid-1950s, *The Middle Road* (Jazztone #J-1227) and *Dixieland Now and Then* (Jazztone #J-1241).

MCPROUD, C.G. (1904–16 APR 1986)

A graduate mechanical engineer, McProud joined Paramount pictures during the early talking-picture era and stayed with the company for over a decade. During World War II, he helped produce sonar manuals for the Navy, which triggered an interest in technical writing. Following the war, he got into freelance work, and ended up as managing editor of *Audio Engineering*, which eventually became *Audio* magazine. In 1949, he became the magazine's editor, and served in that capacity until 1971. He is credited with conceiving the audio show as a major element in popularizing high-fidelity music systems. A life member of the Institute of Electrical and Electronics Engineers, in 1953 the Audio Engineering Society presented him with an award for helping to advance the Society, and in 1954 he won a fellowship from the organization for his work in the recording and reproduction of sound, and for his work in transducer design, development, and production. In 1959, he also won a citation from the Society for his magazine's work in educating the audio community.

HOWARD FERSTLER

MD&G (LABEL)

Musikproduktion Dabringhaus und Grimm was founded 1978 by Werner Dabringhaus and Reimund Grimm. Specializing in recordings of the very highest quality, including DVD-A releases utilizing proprietary microphone and mixing techniques, the label mainly releases chamber works and modern and period classics, performed by ensembles such as the Camerata of the 18th Century, the Consortium Classicum, the Ensemble Villa Musica, the Ensemble Avantgarde, and the Calefax Reed Quintet, among many others. [website: www.mdg.de.]

HOWARD FERSTLER

MECHANICAL ELECTRICAL ANALOGIES

The properties that determine the passage of an electric current are analogous to properties concerning mechanical motion. The analogies are: (1) inductance = mass; (2) capacitance = compliance; (3) resistance = friction or viscosity. Thus for every mechanical situation there is an equivalent electric circuit situation, and the solution of a problem in one medium is equivalent to the solution in the other. This fortunate fact of nature makes possible, among other things, electrical recording of sound.

MECHANICAL RECORDING

SEE ACOUSTIC RECORDING

MECHANICAL RIGHTS

SEE PERFORMANCE RIGHTS

MEDALLION (LABEL)

An American record, trademarked in 1919 by the Baldwin Piano Co. of Cincinnati. Emerson masters were used for the issues, which were nearly all dance numbers. Some vocal pieces were released, such as "When You're Gone I Won't Forget" by the Shannon Four (#8245), and some sacred items. Emerson artists often used pseudonyms on Medallion. There were no issues after 1921. [Hinze 1977; Rust 1978.]

MEEKER, EDWARD WARREN (22 JAN 1874–19 APR 1937)

American comedian and singer, also animal imitator and announcer; born in Orange, New Jersey. He made cylinders for Edison from March 1906, beginning with "What's the Use of Knocking When a Man Is Down" (#9234); and made many coon songs and Irish dialect records. He was with Edison for 32 years. Meeker was the announcer for hundreds of records up to 1908, when announcements were dropped. His final Edison recordings were Diamond Discs "Mr. Gallagher and Mr. Shean" with Steve Porter (#50970; 1922) and "He's Living the Life of Reilly" (#51040; 1923). He also imitated animals and did background bits in assistance of other artists. Meeker died in Newark, New Jersey. [Koenigsberg 1987; Walsh 1946/2-4; 1971/4.]

MEEKLENS, BESSIE

Saxophonist, the first to record the instrument. She made 12 cylinders for Edison on 23 Apr 1892, with piano accompaniment, beginning with "Ave Maria." [Koenigsberg 1987.]

MEHTA, ZUBIN (29 APR 1936–)

Indian conductor, born in Bombay, India. He studied violin and piano; went to Vienna and played double bass as well. Then he took up conducting, and when he graduated from the Vienna Academy of Music in 1957 he made his debut directing the Tonkkünstler Orchestra in the Musikverein. In 1960 he became director of the Montreal Symphony Orchestra, then conducted the Los Angeles Philharmonic Orchestra concurrently, and was named director of the Israel Philharmonic Orchestra in 1977. In 1978 he became music director of the New York Philharmonic Orchestra, a position he held until 1991. In 1995 he was named music director of the Bavarian State Opera, although he did not take this position until three years later. Mehta's discs with the Los Angeles Philharmonic were rather numerous; they covered 20th-century composers like Ives and Varèse as well as the standard repertoire. With the New York Philharmonic for CBS Records he recorded *Symphonie fantastique* plus the Beethoven and Brahms symphonies. Mehta has conducted at the Metropolitan Opera, and recorded complete versions of *Turandot*, *Tosca*, *Aida*, and *Trovatore*.

MEISSELBACH (A.F.) AND BRO., INC.

A Newark, New Jersey, firm, established in 1887. In 1916, it sold sapphire and diamond point needles.

MELBA, NELLIE, DAME (19 MAY 1861–23 FEB 1931)

Australian soprano, born Helen Porter Mitchell near Richmond. She studied piano, violin, and harp; and she played organ in church. After her marriage in 1882 she took up singing, studying in London and Paris. Her operatic debut was as Gilda in Brussels on 13 Oct 1887; it created a sensation. Triumphs throughout Europe followed, and a Metropolitan Opera debut on 4 Dec 1893 as Lucia. She was widely regarded as the greatest of coloraturas. Melba sang her farewell concert at Covent Garden on 8 June 1926, and retired to Australia. She died in Sydney.

Melba had a long recording career. She was first recorded by Mapleson onstage at the Metropolitan in

1901, doing nine arias. Her earliest commercial discs were for the Gramophone Co. in London, March 1904, beginning with Francesco Tosti's "Mattinata" (#03015); she continued with that label to 1907, making 56 records altogether. Then she worked with Victor in New York and Camden, in 1907, making 23 sides. One of those was the "O soave fanciulla" duet from *Boheme* with Caruso (#95200); she also did two other arias from that opera. Melba recorded in Europe and America from 1908–1921, making 86 more records, some with John McCormack and Mario Sammarco.

Her Covent Garden farewell on 8 June 1926 was recorded live, including her speech; then she sang a final studio recording session on 17 Dec 1926, from which four records were made. A special label, lilac in color, was made for her by G & T; she also bargained for unusually high royalties. Her discs sold at premium prices, but very successfully. Among the most popular was "Caro nome" (Victor #88078 and #6213). An EMI Références CD (#761070; 1989) presents a good selection of her favorite arias. Naxos has reissued her complete Gramophone Co. recordings on CD (#8110738), and recordings made between 1906–1926 (primarily from 1910–1913) are available on a Nimbus CD (#7890). The National Library of Australia holds a collection of memorabilia associated with Melba, including theatrical programs. [website: http://www.nla.gov.au/collect/prompt/melba.html.] Moran 1984; Harvey 1949.]

MELCHIOR, LAURITZ (20 MAR 1890–18 MAR 1973)

Danish/American tenor, born in Copenhagen. His early singing was as a baritone, and it was in that aspect that he made his debut in 1913 at the Copenhagen Royal Opera. By 1918 he had changed focus and begun to sing the dramatic tenor repertoire, though his voice always retained a shading from the lower range. He was soon recognized as an outstanding interpreter of Wagner, and remains today the legendary Heldentenor. From 1924 to 1931 he was a regular performer in Bayreuth. On 17 Feb 1926 he made his Metropolitan Opera debut as Tannhäuser, and stayed with the company until 1950, missing only the 1927–1928 season. He took American citizenship in 1947 and settled in California, where he died (in Santa Monica). It was as a baritone (Germont, in Danish) that Melchior made his earliest record, for Odeon in Denmark during 1913. He was still making records 40 years later, on several labels. HMV recorded him in a few songs during 1913, then Polyphon recorded his tenor voice (*Lohengrin, Walküre,* and *Tosca*) in 1920–1921. In 1924 he sang in Germany for DGG, then for Parlophon in 1925–1926. After his arrival in America he made one record for Brunswick: *"Winterstürme" and the Prize Song* (#50085; 1926). Melchior's major block of recording was for HMV and Victor beginning in 1928, almost exclusively from the Wagner operas. (He was the consummate specialist: he did Tristan more than 200 times; at the Metropolitan, during 24 seasons, he sang only seven roles.) Pearl and Seraphim released LP versions of his major arias. On CD there is EMI Références (#69789; 1989), which selects from his releases of the early 1930s. Other CDs include RCA (#87914; 1990) of material from the later 1930s and 1940 — including outstanding duets with Kirsten Flagstad. Another RCA CD (#87915), of Wagnerian scenes, is mostly for Flagstad, but includes fine duets with Melchior.

MELLENCAMP, JOHN (7 OCT 1951–)

John Mellencamp has evolved from an AOR friendly hard rocker in the Bob Seger–Bruce Springsteen mold to a critically hailed exponent of country and R&B-flavored roots rock. Born in Seymour, Indiana, with a form of spina bifida, he started his first band at age 14. After attending community college and trying a series of blue-collar jobs, he relocated to New York City in the mid-1970s with a backlog of self-penned songs and hopes of establishing a music career. There, he signed with David Bowie's manager, Tony DeFries, who assigned him the moniker "Johnny Cougar" and helped secure a reported million-dollar deal with Main Man. The resulting album, *Chestnut Street Incident* (Main Man #601; 1976), was a commercial failure, and he was dropped by parent company MCA. Signing with Riva Records in the late 1970s (to his frustration, still billed as John Cougar), Mellencamp began building a following through well-crafted recordings — including the hit singles "I Need a Lover" (Riva #202; 1979), "This Time" (Riva #205; 1980), and "Ain't Even Done with the Night" (Riva #207; 1981) — and constant touring. His commercial breakthrough came with *American Fool* (Riva #7501; 1982; #1), driven by Grammy-winning "Hurts So Good" (Riva #209; 1982; #2), the ballad "Jack and Diane" (Riva #210; 1982; #1), and "Hand to Hold on To" (Riva #211; 1982), all of which were in heavy MTV rotation. The 1980s were a watershed decade for him, including several top 10 albums: *Un-Huh* (Riva #7504; 1983), *Scarecrow* (Riva/Mercury #824865; 1985), *The Lonesome Jubilee* (Mercury #832465; 1987) — which heralded Mellencamp's first notable foray into Americana-styled music, and *Big Daddy* (Mercury #838220; 1989). In addition to producing his own recordings, he was in demand to perform similar duties for other artists, including Mitch Ryder's *Never Kick a Sleeping Dog* (1983) and James McMurtry's *Too Long in the Wasteland* (1989). Mellencamp was a co-organizer of Farm Aid along with Willie Nelson and Neil Young in 1985; he would go on to appear at Farm Aid concerts I through VI. He has given more concerts over the years to bring attention to the problems of the American farmer, and, in 1987, he testified before a congressional subcommittee. His strong political activism also extended to criticism of beer- and cigarette company sponsorship of concert tours and the refusal to allow his music to be employed in commercials. By the 1990s, Mellencamp's recordings were less commercially successful, due in part to their more introspective tone and greater reliance on folk instrumentation. He was now moving into other fields, directing and acting in the film, *Falling From Grace* (1992; scripted by author Larry McMurtry), and mounting exhibitions of his paintings. He suffered a heart attack in 1994, but has continued to remain active as a performer and recording artist.

FRANK HOFFMANN

MELODISC RECORDS (LABEL)

An American disc marketed in 1921 by the Emerson Phonograph Co. of New York. The records were seven-inches in diameter, selling for $.35. Although advertising in *TMW* claimed great success for the Melodisc, it appeared at an infelicitous time, while the Emerson firm was in receivership and reorganization. The record was not advertised after 1921.

FRANK ANDREWS

MELODIYA (ALL-UNION GRAMOPHONE RECORD ENTERPRISE MELODIYA) (LABEL) (I)

Formed in 1964 by the Soviet Ministry of Culture by combining various earlier Soviet labels, Melodiya grew to be the sixth-largest record company in the world during the 1970s and 1980s (due to its monopoly as the sole producer in the former Soviet Union). The label primarily released classical and pop recordings by Soviet artists. Its classical list was enhanced by its ability to have exclusive arrangements with Soviet performers, as well as its own in-house orchestra. Many of these recordings were licensed and released in the West, initially by the Angel label (during the 1960s and 1970s) and later by Mobile Fidelity (from 1985–1992). Their best-selling pop artists were limited to a Soviet audience; during the 1970s and 1980s, Alla Pugachova was

their biggest seller, whose "A Millon Roses" was a tremendous hit. Pugachova sang traditional Slavic-sounding songs with a soft-rock accompaniment. Regional branches of Melodiya produced material for their native populations; the Tashkent office, for example, catered to the 10 million Uzbeks who craved everything from traditional music to disco performed in their language. Melodiya's production of LPs reached 200 million per year in the 1970s and early 1980s, and 8 million cassettes. Seventy percent of the sales (60–65 percent of the output) was in the popular field. The first Melodiya compact discs (65 items) appeared in April 1990, although the label continued to produce LPs beyond the fall of the Soviet Union. At the height of its growth, the company had pressing plants and facilities in Riga, Leningrad, Aprelevka, Moscow, Tbilsi, and Tashkent. However, after the fall of the Soviet Union, Melodiya closed many of these plants; its main headquarters remained in Aprelevka, but it reduced its one-time 3,600 employees down to 1/10 that number by 1998. [Bennett 1981; Gronow & Saunio 1998.]

REV. CARL BENSON

MELODIYA (LABEL) (II)

Small, independent punk-ska label operating out of a Calgary, Canada, record store of the same name and founded by Ben Falconer, named after the longtime Soviet label.

MELODOGRAPH CORP.

A New York firm established in 1916. The Melodograph disc player was advertised in *Cosmopolitan* for November 1916, selling for $10 by mail order. It was said to be made of a "secret process composition of metals" which cannot warp and will not rust. Using any kind of needle, it could play either vertical or lateral cut records (by turning the soundbox). The firm also issued some vertical-cut discs of their own, with the Melodograph label, in seven-inch size. The firm petitioned for bankruptcy on 5 Sep 1917. [*NAG* 36 (Spring 1981) reproduces the *Cosmopolitan* advertisement on p. 12; Rust 1978.]

MELODY (LABEL) (I)

A British record, 10-inch and 12-inch size, issued in December 1918 by Morgan, Scott & Co., Ltd., religious music publishers. The discs were made by the

Crystalate Record Manufacturing Co., Ltd., from Guardsman matrices of the Invicta Record Co., Ltd.

FRANK ANDREWS

MELODY (LABEL) (II)

An American label, issued briefly during 1923. Masters were from Olympic. [Rust 1978.]

MELODY THREE

A male trio, also known as the Men About Town, who recorded for various labels in the late 1920s. Members were Jack Parker, Will Donaldson, and Phil Duey (Dewey). Frank Luther took the place of Donaldson later. Among their three Victor records of 1928–1929 was "Remember Me to Mary"/"Pals, Just Pals" (#21754; 1928).

MELOGRAPH (LABEL)

A double-sided lateral-cut German record, of the Melograph Record Gmbh, sold from Liverpool by the Melograph Disc Record Co., Ltd., from October 1907. Both 10-inch and 12-inch records were offered, until World War I made it impossible to continue by making supplies unobtainable from an enemy country.

FRANK ANDREWS

MELOPHONE TALKING MACHINE CO.

A New York firm established in 1915. Advertising of 1916 offered the Melophone line of inexpensive disc players in four models, selling from $7.50 to $15.00.

MELOTO (LABEL)

A British issue of the Meloto Co., Ltd., London (controlled by Aeolian Co., Ltd.) on sale by March 1922 to about 1927. Distribution was not through shops, but through a system that required buyers to take an initial 12 records to qualify for the loan of a cabinet gramophone; the machine became the buyer's property following the purchase of another eight discs per month for a further 23 months. Nearly 700 records were released in 10-inch size (there were also 12-inch records), drawn from Aco material. While most of the output was dance music and popular vocals, there were some jazz items that had originated in the Gennett catalog. [Rust 1978.]

FRANK ANDREWS

MELOTONE (LABEL)

An American record, the inexpensive ($.50, later $.35) Brunswick (Warner Brothers) subsidiary, issued from 13 Nov 1930 to spring of 1938. Jazz reissues and originals are found, as well as music by good dance bands. The country repertoire was well covered by Tex Ritter, Gene Autry, Red Foley, and others. Artists as disparate as Leadbelly and Bing Crosby appeared on Melotone. Mexican, Cajun, and Hawaiian series were also offered. Many Melotone recordings appeared in Britain on the Panachord label. [Rust 1978.]

MELTON, JAMES
(2 JAN 1904–21 APR 1961)

American tenor, born in Moultrie, Georgia. He played saxophone in college groups, at the University of Georgia, then studied voice and sang on radio. His concert debut was on 22 Apr 1932 in New York; his opera debut in Cincinnati on 28 June 1938. From 7 Dec 1942 until 1950 he sang with the Metropolitan Opera. Although primarily a classical singer, he crossed over to popular styles where he achieved national renown. He was with the Revelers male quartet, and made solo records for Victor, Columbia, and others of love songs and show tunes. His first popular Victor was "There's Danger in Your Eyes, Cherie"/"A Year from Today" (#22335; 1930). He appeared on the *Voice of Firestone* and other radio programs, and was seen in several motion pictures. Melton introduced the song "September in the Rain" and recorded it for Decca (#1247; 1937). One of his favored operatic roles was Pinkerton; he is heard in the Flower Duet with Licia Albanese on Victor #VM-1068, three 12-inch discs. LP reissues included *James Melton Sings* (Mayfair #9609) and *James Melton Sings George Gershwin and Cole Porter Favorites* (Craftsman #8031); there are no CD reissues devoted solely to Melton as of this writing. He died in New York City.

MELVA (LABEL)

A disc issued by the Melva Record Co., Brooklyn, apparently in 1922. Only 20 records are known to have been released. [Rust 1978.]

MENDELSSOHN MIXED QUARTETTE

A vocal group that recorded for Edison in 1903 and 1904. Members were Edith Chapman, Corinne Morgan, George Morgan Stricklett, and Frank C. Stanley. Eight two-minute cylinders are listed by

Koenigsberg [1987], beginning with "Good Night, Good Night, Beloved" (#8321) and concluding with "What Shall the Harvest Be?" (#8834).

MENGELBERG, WILLEM
(28 MAR 1871–21 MAR 1951)

Dutch conductor, born in Utrecht, The Netherlands. He studied in Holland and in Cologne, and at age 20 was music director in Lucerne. From 1895 to 1945 he was conductor of the (Royal) Concertgebouw Orchestra in Amsterdam, bringing it to world acclaim. He specialized in the music of Beethoven, Mahler, and Strauss. CD reissues from Teldec and EMI have covered the principal Mengelberg recordings from 1926 to 1944, although many of them are technically unsatisfactory. Mengelberg was accused of being a Nazi sympathizer and exiled to Switzerland by his government, cutting off the possibility of high quality post–World War II recordings. He died in Chur, Switzerland.

MENUHIN, YEHUDI, LORD
(22 APR 1916–12 MAR 1999)

American violinist and conductor, born in New York. His family took him to San Francisco, where he studied for his debut, which took place in Oakland when he was seven years old. He played a New York recital at age nine, then studied in Paris with Georges Enesco. He made a sensational appearance in 1927 with the New York Symphony Orchestra, performing the Beethoven Concerto. Thereafter he made world tours, and also directed the Bath Festivals in 1959–1968, and the Windsor Festival in 1969–1972. He was awarded an honorary knighthood in 1965. In 1993, he was named a Life Peer with the title of Lord. Menuhin died in Berlin. Menuhin's first records were made for Victor while he was yet 11 years old, as two engineers crossed the continent to Oakland just for one session and four short pieces with the prodigy. By age 15 he was able to record the Bruch Concerto in G Minor with mature artistry (Victor DB#1611; 1932). Biddulph CD LAB #031 presents early recordings in *The Young Yehudi Menuhin* (1991). In 1932 he performed and recorded the Elgar Concerto with the composer conducting (Victor M#174). In the 1938 Victor catalog he has 11 concertos plus many shorter pieces, in addition to duets with his pianist-sister Hephzibah. He and Geroges Enesco also recorded, making the Bach Concerto for Two Violins (Victor #7732, 7733). Perhaps his finest recording was of the Beethoven Concerto with the Vienna Philharmonic Orchestra in

1960, reissued on CD by EMI in 1990. Over the years Menuhin has recorded virtually the entire standard repertoire for his instrument, and also works by modern composers such as Francis Poulenc, Paul Ben Haim, Lukas Foss, and Aram Khachaturian. And in a crossover spirit he recorded swing pieces with Stéphane Grappelli, and made an album with Ravi Shankar. As a conductor Menuhin appears on record with the Bath Festival Orchestra of the 1960s, the English Chamber Orchestra, the Royal Philharmonic Orchestra, and other ensembles.

MERCER, JOHNNY
(18 NOV 1909–25 JUNE 1976)

Composer, lyricist, singer, label executive. Johnny Mercer's songbook comprises a wealth of standards sung by every jazz singer. Though he got his start as an actor in New York, and published his first (co-written) song in 1930, Mercer's true career began with a job writing songs for RKO movies in 1935. He was a featured vocalist for Benny Goodman and Paul Whiteman, and hosted a radio show in the 1940s. In 1942, Johnny Mercer cofounded Capitol Records. Mercer's collaborations are legendary, including Hoagy Carmichael, Michel Legrand, Henry Mancini, Judy Garland, Bing Crosby, Billie Holiday, Peggy Lee, Glenn Miller, and Frank Sinatra. Mercer composed or wrote lyrics for over 1,000 songs, and he won four Academy awards for his film work.

BRAD HILL

MERCURY RECORDS (LABEL)

This entry is divided into two sections: 1. A general history of Mercury Records; and 2. A history of Mercury's classical music recordings.

1. *General History.* In the late summer of 1945, pressing plant owner Irving Green launched Mercury Records in partnership with artists manager, Berle Adams (who quickly sold his share to Green). Headquartered in Chicago, the label was named after Mercury automobiles. Initially an R&B and jazz label, Mercury quickly broadened into pop and country. The first major artists were Frankie Laine (whose 1947 recording of "That's My Desire" gave the label its first major hit) and Patti Page. Mitch Miller was among the label's early A&R directors. Mercury was the first label, in 1949, to arrange with Columbia for use of its LP technology. By the dawn of rock 'n' roll era, Mercury was a quasi-major label with a presence in all fields, including classical. In June 1961, Green sold the label to Philips Electric in The Netherlands,

Mercury 45 label, c. mid-'50s. Courtesy David A. Jasen.

Small Kansas City-based label active in the mid-'20s.
Courtesy Kurt Nauck/Nauck's Vintage Records

although he remained president until 1969. In 1971, it became part of the Dutch-German Polygram group. Green's former accountant, Irwin Steinberg, assumed the presidency of Mercury, moving it to New York in 1980. He signed Rod Stewart, Rush, and other artists that made Mercury a major presence in the rock market. The country division, under the leadership of Jerry Kennedy, was also successful (the Statler Brothers, Roger Miller, and Reba McEntire were among Kennedy's signees), and, under the stewardship of Luke Lewis, Mercury Nashville signed Shania Twain. In 1999, Polygram was sold to Universal, and the Mercury name was retired from all but the Nashville division.

COLIN ESCOTT

2. *Mercury's Classical Division.* Mercury's classical division began in 1948 with the takeover of John Hammond's Keynote Records. Hammond asked David Hall to lead the new division, to be based in New York. A catalog was built from both domestically produced chamber music and solo instrumental discs. Large-scale domestic symphony recording by Mercury began with the Louisville Orchestra, featuring the William Schuman dance scores *Judith* and *Undertow*. C. Robert Fine, the guiding engineering genius for Mercury's domestic program, produced the Louisville disc with a single Telefunken U47 microphone. Thus began a long line of distinguished recorded performances that included the Minneapolis Symphony under Antal Dorati and the Detroit Symphony under Paul Paray, plus an extensive American music program with the

Eastman-Rochester Symphony Orchestra under Howard Hanson and the Eastman Wind Ensemble under Frederick Fennell. Chamber music and solo instrumental recording continued as well, producing among other items a first integral recording of the Charles Ives violin sonatas (with Rafael Druian and John Simms). The Mercury New York staff had been joined by Wilma Cozart, who was eventually made vice president, the first woman to hold such a position with a major record firm. Mercury was taken over by Philips in June 1961, and by mid-1963 hard times in the record business forced cutbacks all along the line. The classical division was among the casualties. In 1990 Polygram resurrected the Living Presence line in the CD format.

MERITT (LABEL)
A short-lived American record issued by the Kansas City music store Winston Holmes from 1925–1929. Perhaps only a dozen or so issues appeared, some of them with interesting material such as blues numbers by local Black artists and sides by George E. Lee and his Orchestra. [Rust 1978.]

MERLI, FRANCESCO
(27 JAN 1887–12 DEC 1976)
Italian tenor, born in Milan. He sang as a youth in Italian provincial opera houses, finished second to

Beniamino Gigli in a competition in 1914, then began singing at La Scala in 1916, where he remained to 1946. He also appeared in Covent Garden, Teatro Colón in Buenos Aires, and the Metropolitan Opera (where he made his debut as Radames on 2 Mar 1932). He retired in 1950, and died in Milan a quarter of a century later. Merli sang the lyric roles in his early career, then more dramatic parts. He was distinguished for his Otello, Manrico, Des Grieux in *Manon Lescaut*, and Canio. His recording career, mostly with Columbia, began ca. 1924 in Milan, with duets from *Forza del destino*. His most important discs were the complete operas he recorded with the La Scala company: *Manon Lescaut*, *Pagliacci*, and *Trovatore*. LP reissues appeared on several labels, including Top Artists Platters; Preiser has reissued two CDs of his recordings (#89026, #89091).

MERRIMAN, HORACE OWEN
(21 NOV 1888–1972)

Canadian audio engineer, born in Hamilton, Ontario. He received a B.A. science from the University of Toronto. During World War I he and Guest were engaged in efforts to enhance air to ground communication via electric loudspeakers; with the Armistice they turned to other applications and decided to develop a method of making phonograph records electrically. After considerable experimentation, in later stages at the studio of Columbia Graphophone Co., Ltd., in London, they produced the moving coil recording head for electric disc recording (British patent #141,790; 1920). He and Guest recorded a part of the Ceremony of Burial of the Unknown Warrior, in Westminster Abbey (London), on 11 Nov 1920. Microphones and signal buttons were placed at three points in the Abbey, wired to a sound recording van located near the south transept entrance. Although an attempt to record the entire ceremony was made, only two hymns were well enough transcribed to be issued commercially (by Columbia Graphophone Co., Ltd.: Kipling's "Recessional" and "Abide with Me." These recordings were the first to be sold using any type of electrical process. Merriman later served as engineer in charge of the Interference Section, Radio Branch, Department of Transport, until his retirement in 1954. [*TMR* 40 (June 1976) carries Merriman's own account of the Westminster Abbey project.]

See also **Electrical Recording**

METAL BLADE (LABEL)

Metal Blade was founded in 1982 by Brian Slagel, who felt that Los Angeles metal scene was not receiving the attention it deserved from the record industry. Slagel — then employed at the metal emporium, Oz Records, and developing one of the earliest metal fanzines, *The New Heavy Metal Revue* — enlisted friends to distribute a recorded compilation of unsigned acts. The label's first release, *The New Heavy Metal Revue Presents Metal Massacre*, included Black 'N' Blue, Metallica, and Ratt. Although intended as a side project to promote his fanzine, favorable response spurred Slagel to release more Metal Blade compilations as well as separate LPs by bands such as Bitch, Dark Angel, Demon Seed, Destruction, Fates Warning, Flotsam and Jetsam, Hellhammer (aka Celtic Frost), Lizzy Borden, The Obsessed, Omen, Sacred Reich, Slayer, Sodom, Trouble, and Voivid. By the mid-1980s, the label was considered a linchpin of the New Wave of British Heavy Metal, providing an alternative to the AM-friendly hard rock of Def Leppard, Motley Crue, and Quiet Riot. Metal Blade's commercial potential was greatly enhanced by a distribution agreement with Enigma/Capitol Records in 1985. Not only was the label now able to better promote established artists, but its newly created subsidiary, Death Records, aggressively pursued cutting-edge talent, including Atheist, Cannibal Corpse, Corrosion of Conformity, Cryptic Slaughter, and The Mentors. In addition, the company broadened its roster to encompass alternative and AOR fare as exemplified by the likes of Armored Saint, Goo Goo Dolls, Junk Monkeys, Nevada Beach, and Princess Pang. In 1990 Metal Blade signed a multitiered distribution deal with Warner Bros. which freed the label to concentrate on artist development. Dissatisfaction with the arrangement, however, led Metal Blade to return to independent status with distribution by R.E.D. In the meantime, the company continued to cultivate new talent, most notably Amon Amarth, Cradle of Filth, Crisis, The Crown, Flesh Crawl, Galactic Cowboys, God Dethroned, Grip Inc., In Extremo, King Diamond, Memory Garden, The Quiet Room, Six Feet Under, and Tourniquet. It also helped facilitate the revival of powermetal by acquiring Destiny's End, Labyrinth, and Sacred Steel.

FRANK HOFFMANN

METALLICA

Since forming in 1981, Metallica has led the way in redefining the stylistic boundaries of heavy metal.

While incorporating elements of punk and hardcore, the band has brought a greater energy, sonic diversity (ranging from visceral thrash and riff-heavy grinders to roots-derived rockers and melodramatic ballads), and attention to songcraft, most notably appealing melodic hooks and strong lyrics, to what was perceived as a rather tired, moribund genre. Guided by drummer/composer Lars Ulrich and lead vocalist/rhythm guitarist/composer James Hetfield — the constants in the constantly shifting lineup of the early 1980s — Metallica emerged as one of the premier American bands on the strength of frenetically paced, loud albums such as *Kill 'Em All* (Megaforce #069; 1983), *Ride the Lightning* (Megaforce #769; 1984; #100), and *Master of Puppets* (Elektra #60439; 1986; #29). Following the flawed *... And Justice for All* (Elektra #60812; 1988; #6) — where cluttered arrangements and poor production values blunted the visceral intensity of the material. The band entered a creative watershed period with the release of *Metallica* (Elektra #61113; 1991; #1), *Load* (Elektra #61923; 1996; #1), and *Re-Load* (Elektra #62126; 1997; #1). Some observers have argued that Metallica's late 1990s work represented the musical equivalent of treading water. Nevertheless, the albums from this period — *Garage Inc.* (Elektra #62323; 1998; #2), an exploration of the work of seminal metal groups, and *S&M* (Elektra #62463; 1999; #2), a live greatest hits collaboration with the San Francisco Symphony Orchestra — reveal a continued commitment to innovation within a post-metal framework. It remains to be seen, however, whether Ulrich's high profile role in the music industry fight against Napster and other unauthorized downloading of MP3 files on the internet will ultimately erode the band's popularity.

FRANK HOFFMANN

METAPHONE

SEE ECHOPHONE

METEOR (LABEL)

An American record issued by an unidentified firm in Piqua, Ohio, in 1919 or 1920. It was affiliated with Arto. Some items by Earl Fuller's Novelty Orchestra are of interest, but most releases were of little musical value. [Kendziora 1987/10; Rust 1978.]

METHENY, PAT (12 AUG 1954–)

Metheny was the dominant jazz guitarist of the last two decades of the 20th century; the winner of 13 Grammys through 2000, he has enjoyed commercial success while never compromising his constantly evolving artistic vision. He was influential in freeing the guitar of the technical and stylistic limitations that kept it from becoming one of the genre's leading solo instruments. Emerging in the late 1970s, when fusion guitarists dominated the jazz field, Metheny has, from the start, embodied a blend of bop formalism and lyricism based on elements of contemporary pop music songcraft, including rich melodicism, harmonic sophistication, and country and rock embellishments. Working professionally in Kansas City by age 16, he was invited by vibist Gary Burton to teach at Boston's Berklee College of Music and play in his band. His earliest solo albums — *Bright Size Life* (ECM #1073; 1975) and *Watercolors* (ECM #1097; 1977) — which teamed him with bassist Jaco Pastorius and drummer Bob Moses, only hinted at his emerging talent. *Pat Metheny Group* (ECM #1114; 1978; #123) signaled the beginning of the highly arranged, synthesizer-based quartet sound that Metheny developed along with keyboardist Lyle Mays. Its breezy, engaging tone — which struck a responsive chord with the record-buying public — was continued with the solo outing, *New Chautauqua* (ECM #1131; 1979; #44), and collaborative efforts such as *American Garage* (ECM #1155; 1980; #53) and *As Falls Wichita, So Falls Wichita Falls* (ECM #1190; 1981; #50). In contrast to the rock-band format employed in these releases, Metheny also experimented with more traditional jazz approach; most notably, *80/81* (ECM #1180; 1980; #89), a wide-ranging set featuring bassist Charlie Haden, drummer Jack DeJohnette, and saxophonists Dewey Redman and Michael Brecker, and *Song X* (Geffen #24096; 1985), with avant-garde saxophonist Ornette Coleman. Metheny continued to excel in new venues during the 1980s, supplying the soundtrack to John Schlesinger's popular film, *The Falcon and the Snowman* (EMI America #17150; 1985; #54) and technological experimentation, including guitar effects and new instrument designs. He also explored world music, expanding his group to accommodate African-based polyrythms and sitting in on studio sessions by Brazilian singer/songwriter Milton Nascimento. Metheny has consolidated his growth in the 1990s and beyond. The poetically reflective *Beyond the Missouri Sky, A Map of the World* (Verve #537130; 1997), another collaboration with Haden, represented a triumphant return to film scoring. On the other hand, albums like *Question and Answer* (Geffen #24293; 1990; #154), featuring bassist Dave Holland and drummer Roy Haynes, and *Trio 99>00* (Warner Bros. #47632; 2000), with bassist Larry

Grenadier and drummer Bill Stewart, demonstrated his continued technical and improvisational prowess within a small jazz combo.

FRANK HOFFMANN

METRO (LABEL) (I)

An American record issued by the Metropolitan Record Co., New York, in the early 1920s. All the known releases are of Irish material, and the record itself bears an Irish label motif.

METRO (LABEL) (II)

An American record, like the preceding label devoted to Irish music, produced in the 1920s for Tom Ennis, an Irish pipes player. The two Metro labels were not connected. [Rust 1978.]

METRO-GOLDWYN-MAYER (LABEL)

An American record, produced by Columbia "exclusively for Loew's Theatres everywhere" — as the label reads — from ca. 1928. The material was drawn from M-G-M motion pictures. It was not connected to the later MGM label.

Label produced in the late '20s by Columbia drawing on MGM soundtracks. Courtesy Kurt Nauck/Nauck's Vintage Records

METROPOLE (LABEL)

A British record issued by the Metropole Gramophone Co., Ltd., of London; later by Metropole Industries, Ltd., from April 1928 to ca. 1930. Those two firms had taken over the former Hertford Town factory whose previous occupant had been the Parlophone Co., Ltd. (under Columbia's control). About 300 discs were released; some were offered free with the purchase of the firm's Metrophone portable and console record players. American material from Grey Gull was used on about 50 of the records, and much of the material was shared with the Piccadilly label, from the associated firm Piccadilly Records, Ltd. [Rust 1978.]

FRANK ANDREWS

METROPOLITAN BAND

A group directed by "Signor G. Pelaso" that made 179 brown wax cylinders for the Norcross Phonograph Co. in 1898.

METROPOLITAN ENTERTAINERS

A vocal trio that recorded one Edison Diamond Disc, "Too Many Parties and Too Many Pals" (#51681) in 1926. It consisted of Elizabeth Spencer, Charles Harrison, and Ernest Hare.

METROPOLITAN MIXED TRIO

A vocal group that recorded for Edison in 1903. Members were Corinne Morgan, George S. Lenox, and Frank C. Stanley. Later, on other labels, the members were Elise Stevenson, Henry Burr, and Stanley. The same singers were also identified on some Edison records as the Manhattan Trio.

METROPOLITAN OPERA COMPANY

A New York company that gave its first season in 1883–1884, and has achieved universal recognition as one of the world's superior ensembles. Nearly all the great singers and operatic conductors have appeared on its programs. Saturday afternoon broadcasts began on 7 Dec 1940 and continue today, constituting the longest running radio show in U.S. history. Since 1986, the artistic director of the company has been James Levine. Lionel Mapleson made the first recordings of the Metropolitan Opera on his famous cylinders of 1901–1903. These records were made without commercial intent, and were not marketed. A catalog from Leeds & Catlin, dated

1902, offered 19 recordings made by the "Metropolitan Opera House String Orchestra" directed by Nahan [misspelled Nathan] Franko, one of the conductors for that season. All these records, of instrumental parts from opera and some nonoperatic selections, have been lost. Apparently the earliest commercial record dates from 1906, a Victor issue that for some reason identified the Metropolitan chorus as the "New York Grand Opera Chorus" (Victor #64049; session of 8 June 1906). The number sung was "Scorrendo uniti" from *Rigoletto*. In other sessions of June 1906 another five chorus numbers were recorded, again with the name New York Grand Opera Chorus. Not until January 1910 was there a recording session with identified soloists: the "Miserere" sung by Frances Alda and Enrico Caruso (Victor #89030; 1910). By the end of 1916, 40 records had been made by Victor, but in the 1917 Victor catalog there is no specific entry in the artist's section for the company. From 1918 to 1920 Columbia recorded the Metropolitan Orchestra, without vocalists, since most of the singers had Victor contracts. The great period of records was 1927–1930, some 70 sides for Victor. Star performers offered much of the French/Italian repertoire, and in many cases made definitive interpretations (e.g., the "Miserere" by Rosa Ponselle and Giovanni Martinelli (#8097; 1928), the "Vergine degli angeli" duet from *Forza del destino*, by Ponselle and Ezio Pinza (#8097; 1928), *Rigoletto* duets by Amelita Galli-Curci and Giuseppe De Luca, and the *Rigoletto* Quartet by Galli-Curci, Louise Homer, Beniamino Gigli, and De Luca. From 1930 to 1938 only 11 recordings were made, but in 1939 there was renewed activity, notably with an *Otello* set, featuring Martinelli, Lawrence Tibbett, and Helen Jepson. In 1940 there was a set of *Tristan* discs, with Rose Bampton and Arthur Carron. A *Tannhäuser* set followed, and then a *Lohengrin*, with the same lead singers. Victor catalogs had begun listing the chorus and orchestra in the Red Seal artist section. In 1941 the company began to record for Columbia, and made the first complete opera recordings in the U.S., as well as several extended excerpt sets. Among these the *Carmen* set attracted special attention, featuring the new favorite interpreter of the role, Rise Stevens (Columbia #M-607; 1946). But it was *Hänsel und Gretel* that marked the beginning of complete recordings, a set made on 24 sides with Rise Stevens and Nadine Conner as the children (Columbia #MOP-26; 1947). *La Boheme* was next recorded in its entirety, with Richard Tucker, Bidu Sayao, Mimi Benzell, and Francesco Valentino (Columbia #OP-27; 1948). When *Madama Butterfly* was recorded complete, with Eleanor Steber and

Richard Tucker, it was released on LP (Columbia #SL 4; 1949) as well as 78 rpm (Columbia #MOP-30; 1949). Victor resumed recording of the Metropolitan in 1955, making a series of extended excerpts. Commercial recordings of the company ceased after the DG release of a complete *Carmen*, with Marilyn Horne, James McCracken, and Tom Krause (DG #2709 043; 1972). A special project of 1940 should be mentioned. More than 80 sides of popular opera numbers were sold through newspapers, with the artists and even the company shrouded in anonymity. Victor did the recording, in an arrangement with the Publishers Service Co., Inc., and the National Music Appreciation Committee. Nineteen recordings were made in 1956–1957 jointly with the Book-of-the-Month Club. These were extended excerpt sets, offered to the public through an organization named the Metropolitan Opera Record Club. The high costs involved in making records of the company were responsible for the suspension of that activity after 1972. A total of 477 commercial recordings issued by that time are listed by Fellers. Then in 1989 *Walküre* was recorded complete on four CDs, with Hildegard Behrens, Jessye Norman, Christa Ludwig, Gary Lakes, and James Morris, with James Levine conducting (DG #423389-2), winning a Grammy. In 1990, *Rheingold* was recorded complete on three CDs, with James Morris, Christa Ludwig, and Siegfried Jerusalem (conducted by James Levine); and this recording also won the Grammy award for Best Operatic Recording of the year (DG #427-607-2). Another Grammy came in 1991, with the recording of *Götterdämmerung* (Behrens, Reiner Goldberg, and Matti Salminen, with Levine conducting) on four CDs (#429-3852). However, after this three-year run, no further Grammys have been awarded to the company through the early 21st century. [Fellers 1984, a complete discography of the commercial issues; Hamilton 1984 is a useful review of Fellers; Gray 1975 is an account of the 1940 project.]

See also **Mapleson Cylinders**

METROPOLITAN PHONOGRAPH CO. (I)

One of the 33 companies affiliated with the North American Phonograph Co.; founded in 1888. Charles A. Cheever was president; Felix Gottschalk was secretary. At the 1890 convention of the National Phonograph Association, Cheever stated that Metropolitan had 325 (Edison) phonographs leased in the New York area, and about 50 or 60 graphophones. In fall 1890 the firm merged with the New York Phonograph Co. [Brooks 1979.]

METROPOLITAN PHONOGRAPH CO. (II)

A firm established on 5 Oct 1914 in New York. William S. Finberg was president.

METROPOLITAN QUARTETTE

A mixed vocal group that recorded for Edison cylinders in 1909–1911, and later on Diamond Discs. The original members were Florence Hinkle, Margaret Keyes, John Young, and Frederick Wheeler. Later members included Elizabeth Spencer, Thomas Chalmers, and Mary Jordan. "Darling Nellie Gray" was their first issue (#10053). [Koenigsberg 1987.]

MEYER, JOHN H. (12 JULY 1877–3 MAY 1949)

American bass singer, born in New York. He was also a pianist and arranger. His first record was a hymn for U-S Everlasting cylinder in 1908: "Why Do You Wait" (#217). Most of his recording was in groups. He succeeded Frank C. Stanley as bass in the Peerless Quartet in 1911; and he was a member of the Sterling Trio and the Eight Famous Victor Artists. Later he made duets for Grey Gull and Gennett discs. He should not be confused with his contemporary, John W. Myers. He died in Flushing, New York. [Walsh 1972/8.]

MGM RECORDS

Although Loew's Inc., the parent company of MGM, had been in business since 1924, it wasn't until 1945 that they hired industry veteran Frank Walker to start a record label. The label debuted in March 1947, headquartered in New York. Although planned as a full-line label, MGM depended on soundtracks from its parent company (*Gigi*, *Ben Hur*, etc.). EMI issued MGM recordings in the U.K. under exclusive license beginning in 1949. Walker's major acquisition was country singer Hank Williams. After Walker's retirement in 1956, his successor, Arnold Maxin, signed Connie Francis, Roy Orbison, and several British Invasion bands, including the Animals and Herman's Hermits. MGM also acquired Norman Granz's jazz label, Verve, in 1961; concluded a distribution pact with Germany's Deutsche Grammophon classical label; and opened a Nashville office in 1965. After the parent corporation ran into financial difficulties, MGM Records was sold to Deutsche Grammophon's Polydor division in April 1972, although the soundtracks were excluded from the purchase. Polydor ceased using the MGM Records trademark in 1976.

MGM 45 label, c. mid-'50s. Courtesy David A. Jasen

MGM's catalog is now controlled by the Universal Music Group.

COLIN ESCOTT

MICHIGAN PHONOGRAPH CO.

A Detroit firm, established in 1890 as one of the North American Phonograph Co. affiliates; it was located in the Opera House building. C.C. Bowen was president in 1890–1893. Charles Swift, who was secretary in 1890 and a member of the board of directors, was a "champion in the cause of unification among phonograph interests" [Read & Welch 1976].

MICKEL, GEORGE E.

American record industry executive, also in the bicycle business. He was elected vice president of the National Association of Talking Machine Jobbers in 1912 and reelected in 1913. In 1914 he was president of the Nebraska Cycle Co. of Omaha.

MICROCASSETTE

A small version of the audiocassette, using tape 1/8 inch wide and moving at a speed of 15/16 inches per second. Its case is 5.5 by 3.3 by 0.7 centimeters (two and 3/16 by one and 5/16 by 9/32 inches). It is used in telephone answering machines and for other business functions, and to a limited extent for musical programming.

Panasonic Micro Cassette Recorder RN-202. Courtesy Panasonic, Inc.

MICROGROOVE RECORD

SEE LONG PLAYING RECORD

MICROPHONE

This entry consists of seven sections: 1. Types of microphone. 2. First microphones: 1870s to 1920s. 3. The radio age. 4. The postwar boom. 5. The rock era: 1960s. 6. The golden era: 1970s. 7. Modern microphones.

1. *Types of Microphone.* A microphone converts sound energy into electrical energy, and the earliest microphones were of the pressure type. Over the years, there have been several basic microphone designs put to use. Carbon microphones use pellets, rods, or granules of carbon sandwiched between two electrodes. A DC current passes through the carbon, while a diaphragm vibrates, compressing the carbon, which causes a change in the electrical resistance of the carbon, creating an AC voltage component across the electrodes. Piezoelectric microphones rely on the properties of certain materials that create a voltage when they are mechanically distorted. A diaphragm vibrates, bending the piezoelectric material, creating an AC voltage. Crystal microphones use Rochelle salts, a naturally occurring piezoelectric substance. Ceramic microphones use a synthetic material which is more rugged. More recently, certain plastics, such as Kynar or PVDF, have been used. Piezoelectrics are inexpensive, but somewhat fragile. Dynamic microphones work much like an electrical generator, and essentially function as a dynamic loudspeaker in reverse. The diaphragm is attached to a coil of wire suspended between the poles of a magnet. As the diaphragm vibrates, the coil cuts the magnetic field, generating an AC voltage. Ribbon microphones work like dynamics, but use a pleated metal ribbon suspended between a horseshoe magnet's poles, essentially functioning as a ribbon-type loudspeaker in reverse. Ribbons are more frail than dynamics and have lower output voltages. Ribbon microphones are also called velocity microphones. Condenser microphones consist of a capacitor having one fixed electrode and one movable electrode serving as the diaphragm. A DC bias voltage is applied to both electrodes. As the diaphragm electrode vibrates, the change in capacitance caused by its movement creates an AC voltage. Modern electric microphones are permanently charged, but still require a supply of electricity, usually a penlight battery, to power a circuit used to convert their very high impedance to a lower impedance to minimize noise and loss of high frequencies. "Condenser" is an older name for a capacitor; most newer designs use the term capacitor microphone. Some microphones, called "omni" models, are sensitive to sound equally in all directions, while others exhibit directionality, especially at higher frequencies. Cardioid microphones are more sensitive to sound arriving from the front, less so from the sides, and lesser still from the rear. Cardioid means "heart shaped," and the term refers to the shape of a two-dimensional graph of its directional sensitivity. Supercardioid microphones are more directional cardioids. Bidirectional (sometimes called figure-8) microphones are sensitive mainly from the front and rear, and much less so from the sides. Ribbons are the most common bidirectional types, and Harry Olson did cardioid microphone experiments by "shading" one side of a ribbon. Single-tube line microphones (sometimes called rifle or shotgun microphones) use an interference tube in combination with a hypercardioid element for a highly directional pickup pattern. More directional still are parabolic microphones, which use a curved dish to focus sound energy onto the microphone diaphragm. Contact microphones use rubber discs or solid rods to sense vibrations in solid materials, such as walls or rock. Hydrophones are underwater microphones.

2. *The First Microphones: 1870s to 1920s.* The very first microphones were designed for use in tele-

phones. As such, they were called transmitters, not microphones. Alexander Graham Bell's design of April 1876 used a carbon rod suspended vertically in a pool of diluted sulfuric acid to cause a change in resistance to a DC voltage, creating what he called "undulating current." A diaphragm of sheepskin mounted horizontally at the bottom of a funnel vibrated the carbon rod. This "liquid" microphone was a meager success, and was quickly superseded because of the hazards involved with the open cup of acid. Later that year, Bell's improved design used a diaphragm that pressed a small platinum button against a carbon block to create the varying resistances. All the principal manufacturers of transmitters followed this pattern, including Ader, Berliner, and Edison. Batteries supplied the DC voltages. Another design used in many early Bell telephones was the "magnetic" transmitter. This design was the same as a telephone receiver: a coil of wire was wound around the end of a magnet. A steel diaphragm was placed at the end of the magnet by the coil. As it vibrated, it induced a weak AC voltage in the coil. Although this simplified telephone design allowed the same device to send and receive, it limited the telephone's range and usefulness, and the design was quickly superseded by battery-driven carbon microphones. Carbon microphones developed higher voltages in the era before electronic amplifiers existed. By 1880, carbon rods began to substitute for carbon blocks, improving reliability and sensitivity. It was with a rod-type carbon microphone that Bell demonstrated binaural sound, with a pair of transmitters placed on either side of a mannequin's head. In a separate room, "auditors" experienced "binaural audition" by listening to a pair of receivers, much like modern headphones. In 1881, Clement Ader placed pairs of his transmitters in the footlights of the Paris Opera. Visitors to the Electrical Exhibition Hall 10 miles away could hear the opera through pairs of receivers, connected by telephone circuits to the transmitters there. The year 1885 brought the Blake transmitter, which for the first time used carbon granules instead of rods or blocks. The White transmitter of 1890 placed the carbon microphone in its familiar, modern form. Called the "solid back" transmitter, it allowed vertical mounting for the first time, and greatly reduced the "packing" of the carbon granules that plagued earlier designs. Various improvements in materials, manufacturing, and power supply occurred up to the 1920s, but no major improvements in sound quality derived, because the sole application of microphones was in telephone systems.

3. *The Radio Age.* The advent of radio, talking movies, and electronic amplifiers in the 1920s gave impetus for better designs to meet the quality demands of these applications. Whereas telephones were concerned with speaking voice only, radio and the movies often included music. Although the very first radio microphones were still carbon types, new designs quickly arrived. The first condenser microphones were simultaneously developed by Bell Laboratories in the United States, Telefunken in Germany, and AKG in Austria, during 1923 and 1924. Bell Laboratories' Model 103 was used in their early experiments into "wide-range electrical recording," and the 1932 landmark stereophonic recording experiments in Philadelphia with Leopold Stokowski. The Radio Corporation of America (RCA) seven-inch square box condenser, and the Western Electric cathedral-shaped model became standards of film and broadcasting. The 1930s were an era of rapid improvements in microphone design and use. Bell Laboratories upgraded its condenser models, largely because of recording experiments begun in the late 1920s. In England, Alan Dower Blumlein used omni microphones and derived first-order directional patterns (at low frequencies) through a technique called "shuffling," ultimately leading to his pioneering successful stereo recordings. Other ribbon microphones gained rapid acceptance too, most visibly by the distinctive angular RCA Model 44, and models by Shure Brothers, Electro-Voice, and others. Huge cylindrical Telefunken microphones festooned the podium during rousing speeches by Adolf Hitler. Crystal microphones, such as those made by Astatic, Amperite, and Brush, adorned the podiums of less grandiose public address systems. Western Electric marketed the first cardioid microphone, their model 639 "birdcage," which used a ribbon and omnidirectional dynamic inside the same housing. A switch could select only the ribbon element for bidirectional pickup, only the dynamic element for omnidirectional pickup, or both to create a cardioid pickup. Their models 630 "8-ball" and 633 "saltshaker" also became mainstays. Dynamic microphones arrived with the discovery of better magnetic materials. Besides RCA, Shure, Electro-Voice, AKG, and Calrec, less costly models were marketed by companies such as Turner, Universal Microphone Co., and American Microphone Co.. Ben Bauer developed the classic Shure Unidyne in 1939. During World War II, microphone development continued. The huge Telefunken U-27 became a world standard following the war. RCA's innovative Model 77 ribbon became almost universal in film and radio, and later in television. Adjustable vanes inside the "time capsule"–shaped perforated metal housing allowed it to be bidirectional, cardioid, or nearly omnidirectional. RCA 77s are still sought after today.

4. *The Postwar Boom.* The arrival in America and Europe of German tape recording technology in the late 1940s brought fresh demand for even higher quality microphones. Electro-Voice created a cardioid dynamic that vented the rear of the diaphragm, creating partial cancellation of the sound resulting in a cardioid pickup pattern. This technique was quickly copied, and is still the most-used method for cardioid microphones. Radio, stereophonic movies, television, and home tape recording led to a proliferation of microphone designs. In 1956, court actions forced the divestiture of Western Electric's microphone division to speaker giant Altec. Telefunken introduced their classic U-47 (which was actually a relabled Neumann U-47), a condenser in which a pair of elements was electronically switched to create different pick-up patterns. (Some years later, Gotham Audio picked up the line directly.) Other models came into being: the Electro-Voice 635, 644, and 664; Shure 515, 545, and the 55, associated with the birth of rock and roll; and AKG C-12 brought back as "The Tube." The C-12 had also been marketed by Telefunken, relabled as the ELAM 251, until AKG made other foreign distribution arrangements. Many of these microphones are still made today.

5. *The Rock Era: 1960s.* Improved materials, lower manufacturing costs, and a proliferation of models characterized the 1960s. Neumann, Schoeps, AKG, Shure, Electro-Voice, Altec, Peavey, and Calrec marketed a wide range of successful models, primarily dynamic and condenser types. Carbon microphones remained in telephones, and crystal types became used only in the cheapest home models. Neumann updated the Telefunken U-47. B&K (Bruel & Kjaer), introducing what many claim is the best microphone ever created. Sennheiser and Electro-Voice marketed their very rugged designs. Nearly all quality microphones were dynamics or condensers. Pressure from the demands of television and movie sound brought the lavaliere microphone, inconspicuously worn around the speaker's neck.

6. *The Golden Era: 1970s.* New technologies arrived in the 1970s. Electro-Voice marketed the Mike Mouse, an innovative product based on research into boundary layer effects. An omnidirectional microphone was placed inside a specially shaped foam windscreen and laid on the floor. This eliminated the comb filter effect that occurs when sound from a nearby floor or wall arrives at the microphone, blends with direct sounds, and causes partial cancellations. Crown took this idea a step further with their Pressure Zone Microphone, or PZM. A PZM mounted a tiny condenser upside down a very short distance from a metal boundary plate. The unique configuration duplicated the Mike Mouse but gave greater freedom of place-

ment. The Electret microphone was introduced, in which the "bias" DC voltage was replaced by a permanent static charge. Nearly every recorder manufacturer could then offer quality condenser models. Studio and broadcast microphones dropped in cost. Electrets were built into portable cassette recorders. Lavaliere microphones using electrets became so small as to be nearly invisible. Electrets replaced crystals in low cost models, and were used in telephones. Piezoelectric models using conductive plastics, such as Kynar or PVDF, were introduced in operator's headsets, music instrument pickups, hydrophones, ultrasound microphones, and contact microphones. The direct-to-disc audiophile record craze brought a generation of transformerless condensers. Originally modifications of existing units, they improved transient response by eliminating losses caused by transformer core saturation. AKG C-414, C-451, and C-461 condensers became popular and the cosmetically distinctive D-190 dynamic became one of the most visible European models. AKG two-way dynamic models D-200 and D-202, with separate high/low frequency dynamic elements, gave condenser-like quality. Neumann updated the U-67, which became the U-87. (This was some time after the U-47 had been discontinued.) Shure SM-57 and SM-58 cardioids became arguably the two most visible public address microphones.

7. *Modern Microphones.* In the 1980s, rare-earth magnets led to a new generation of dynamic microphones. Electro-Voice marketed the N-Dym line, and Shure, the Beta line. Their neodymium magnets created such high magnetic flux that they exhibited a clarity normally associated with condensers, along with higher output. Digital microphones built the quantization circuits into condenser microphones to attain remarkable results. Great improvements in wireless microphone technology occurred. In the 1990s innovations were appearing quickly. One was B&K's "Ball" accessory for the 4000 series omnidirectional condensers. The seven-centimeter diameter solid plastic ball made the omnidirectional microphone into a somewhat cardioid pattern. Updated by Howard Ferstler [Borwick 1987/1, 1990; Ford Summer 1962; Olson 1947.] With thanks to John Eargle for some detail corrections.

KERMIT V. GRAY

See also **Electrical Recording; Orchestra Recordings; Recording Practice**

MICRO-PHONOGRAPH

The name given by Gianni Bettini to his cylinder recording/playing device, patented in 1889.

Shure Performance Gear Microphones, showing a variety of modern microphone designs. Courtesy Shure Inc.

MIDDLE-OF-THE-ROAD (MOR)

A popular music style said to be of interest primarily to women [Denisoff says "married women over the age of 24"], emphasizing nostalgic and romantic material. Among the favorite performers have been Michael Jackson, Barry Manilow, Kenny Rogers, and Dionne Warwick. [Denisoff 1975.]

MIDI (MUSICAL INSTRUMENT DIGITAL INTERFACE)

The industry standard bus and protocol (digital signal system, or system of number signals) used to communicate performance information to and from musical instruments making music. First utilized in 1983, it has been expanded to include both signal processing as well as lighting control.

HOWARD FERSTLER

MIDLER, BETTE (1 DEC 1946–)

Although Bette Midler possesses an extraordinary voice — capable of tackling Broadway fare, Big Band swing numbers, torch ballads, the blues, and straight-ahead rock in equally convincing fashion — her multifaceted talents tend to pull her in many directions, including club performing, film acting, television work (talk shows, specials, and a series), book writing (memoirs of her first world tour, *A View From a Broad*, 1980, and the children's book, *The Saga of Baby Divine*, 1983), and large-scale charity work for causes such as AIDS, restoring New York City highways and parks, and voter registration. Taken on their own merits, Midler's recordings often came across as pale facsimiles of the energy and excitement projected in her live shows. Although born in Paterson, New

Jersey, Midler was raised in Hawaii. She came to New York City as a teenager to pursue a Broadway career. After working musicals and other stage productions during the late 1960s, Midler decided to concentrate on singing. She developed a cult reputation doing camp comedy interspersed with a broad musical repertoire at the Continental Baths, a New York City–based gay men's club. Her accompanist in the early days was pianist Barry Manilow. A round of television talk show appearances greatly expanded her fan base, and a recording contract with Atlantic followed. Her debut album, *The Divine Miss M* (Atlantic #7238; 1973; #9), achieved platinum status in addition to yielding a hit single, a cover of the Andrews Sisters' "Boogie Woogie Bugle Boy" (Atlantic #2964; 1973; #8). It would also earn Midler the 1973 Grammy for Best New Artist. Although she retained her loyal concert, following LP releases — *Bette Midler* (Atlantic #7270; 1973; #6; earned gold record), *Songs for the New Depression* (Atlantic #18155; 1976; #27), *Live at Last* (Atlantic #9000; 1977; #49), *Broken Blossom* (Atlantic #19151; 1977; #51), and *Thighs and Whispers* (Atlantic #16004; 1979; #65) — she underwent a steady decline in both sales and critical favor. Midler's fortunes rebounded when her featured role in *The Rose* (1979), a film inspired by events from Janis Joplin's life, earned her an Oscar nomination for Best Actress. Her dramatic reading of the title song (Atlantic #3656; 1980) reached number three, and the soundtrack album (Atlantic #16010; 1979; #12) went platinum. Her next project, a concert film and soundtrack, *Divine Madness* (Atlantic #16022; 1980; #34), also achieved considerable success. The negative publicity ensuing from a poorly received film, *Jinxed* (1982), ushered in another dormant career phase. Revived by a series of comedies for the Disney-owned Touchstone Pictures (*Down and Out in Beverly Hills*, 1986; *Ruthless People*, 1986; *Outrageous Fortune*, 1987; and *Big Business*, 1988), she found chart success with the triple-platinum soundtrack to *Beaches* (Atlantic #81933; 1989; #2), which included the Grammy-winning hit, "Wind Beneath My Wings" (Atlantic #88972; 1989; #1). While Midler remained a top film draw in the 1990s (including a second Oscar nomination for her role in *For the Boys*), her recording career was considerably more erratic in nature. *Some People's Lives* (Atlantic #82129; 1990; #6) — assisted by the Grammy-winning ballad, "From a Distance" (Atlantic #87820; 1990; #2), which was heavily played during the Gulf War — achieved double-platinum status. Although Midler has failed to record a top 40 hit since that time, she has continued to release LPs — many of them film and television soundtracks — at regular intervals. In all of them, she seems content to reprise her earlier work; for example, *Bathhouse Betty* (Warner Bros.; 1998) represents a return to the bawdy, glam style of her early 1970s club sets.

FRANK HOFFMANN

MIGHTY MIGHTY BOSSTONES

The Mighty Mighty Bosstones coined the term "ska-core" to describe their sound, a blend of the 1980s hardcore movement and England's 2-Tone craze. Although initially unable to build a strong following within either the punk or ska cultures, the band's high-energy approach and willingness to experiment with the ska-core formula left them poised on the verge of superstardom by the late 1990s. The group, initially called the Bosstones, evolved out of a Boston-based ska revival band, the Cheap Skates, in the mid-1980s. Although the Bosstones contributed tracks to at least two different ska compilations in the late 1980s, their debut album, *Devil's Night Out* (Taang! #044; reissued May 1998) — comprised of ska music filtered through a postpunk perspective — was not released until 1990. With the major 2-Tone acts — most notably, Madness, the Specials, Selector, and the English Beat — having disbanded, the Mighty Mighty Bosstones (the group's name after they discovered that a 1950s Boston band been called the Bosstones) assumed leadership of the moribund ska scene almost by default. Not content to recycle time-worn bluebeat conventions, the band's early 1990s releases — *Where'd You Go EP* (Taang! #048; 1991; reissued May 1998), *More Noise and Other Disturbances* (Taang! #060; 1992; reissued May 1998), *Skacore, the Devil and More* (Mercury #514551; 1993), and *Don't Know How to Party* (Mercury #514836; 1993) — applied a hardcore-metal, rock-steady fusion to an inspired mix of new and old (e.g., Aerosmith, Bob Marley, Metallica, Minor Threat, Van Halen) material. Their next LP, *Question the Answers* (Mercury #522845; 1994; #138), represented an artistic breakthrough, featuring the production work of the Philadelphia-based Butcher Brothers (who'd previously worked with Aerosmith, Cypress Hill, and Urge Overkill), Kolderie (Hole, Radiohead), and Westwood One sound engineer, Ross Humphrey. MTV video clips, a guest spot in the hit film *Clueless* (1995), and headliner status for the 1995 Lollapalooza tour helped ensure the band's commercial success as well. *Let's Face It* (Mercury #534472; 1997; #27) was even better, due largely to improved songwriting, while *Live from the Middle East* (Big Rig/Mercury #558900; 1998; #144) revealed that the Bosstones were still capable of generating raw excitement in performance.

FRANK HOFFMANN

MIGNON (LABEL)

A British record of 1912, made by Beka Records division of Carl Lindström (London), Ltd. It was a 6-inch, double-sided disc, sold with a small record player to accommodate it. There was little promotion after the first advertisements, and then World War I stopped imports.

FRANK ANDREWS

MIL

One thousandth of an inch. A measure used to describe the thickness of the base in a magnetic tape, stylus dimensions, groove dimensions, etc.

MILANOV, ZINKA
(17 MAY 1906–30 MAY 1989)

Croatian soprano, born in Zagreb. After study in Zagreb, she made her professional debut with the Ljubljana Opera in 1927, then went to Hamburg and Vienna. In 1937 she was acclaimed for singing in the Verdi *Requiem* under Arturo Toscanini in Salzburg. Her Metropolitan Opera debut was on 17 Dec 1937, in *Trovatore*; she remained to 1966, but not without interruptions; and also appeared internationally. The role of Aida, her second at the Metropolitan (sung first on 2 Feb 1928) became one of her outstanding interpretations; she also excelled in *Gioconda* and *Cavalleria rusticana*. She retired in 1966, and died 23 years later in New York. Milanov was a Victor artist. Among her important recordings were many complete opera recordings: *Trovatore*, *Tosca*, *Cavalleria* (these with Jussi Björling); *Aida*, *Forza del destino*, and *Gioconda* (all with Giuseppe Di Stefano). "Voi lo sapete" (Victor #11-8927) represents her voice at its peak.

MILESTONE (LABEL)

The New York–based Milestone was founded in 1966 by jazz producer Orrin Keepnews. Like his earlier company, Riverside Records, it served as an alternative to the corporate policies of the major labels, which tended to ignore the needs of jazz artists. Its artist-friendly approach attracted the cream of the contemporary jazz scene, including Gary Bartz, Joe Henderson, and McCoy Tyner. Milestone relocated to Berkeley, California, in 1972 as part of the Fantasy Records group. Keepnews continued with the label as director of jazz A&R until the early 1980s, and was instrumental in developing the recording career of Brazilian vocalist Flora Purim. The company is still active; at the outset of the 21st century its roster included Hank

Crawford, Joe Locke, George Mraz, Arturo O'Farrill, and Manny Oquendo & Libre.

FRANK HOFFMANN

MILITARY BAND RECORDINGS

In Britain and in continental Europe, military bands of the various army regiments and some naval establishments formed the backbones of many record catalogs, from the earliest days of the industry until the end of World War I. Their repertoires, which covered a great range of popular and light classical material in addition to marches, was later undertaken by studio orchestras and then by established symphony and concert orchestras. The popularity of military bands in the U.S. during the latter 19th and early 20th centuries was immense. Such bands flourished in communities across the nation, playing all categories of popular music in addition to marches. The early record companies, cylinder and disc, gave high priority to band music. An Edison recording session of June 1889 brought forth six numbers by Duffy and Imgrund's Fifth Regiment Band, an ensemble that returned about 20 times to the Edison studio by 1892. The 12-piece band of Patrick S. Gilmore was recorded by Edison on 17 Dec 1891, doing 19 numbers of various types, some featuring cornetist Tom Clark. Voss' First Regiment Band was another Edison group of the period. The first Edison Diamond Discs made by military bands were done in 1913, by the National Promenade Band and the New York Military Band; later by the Edison Concert Band (the material recorded was dance and pop as well as march). Columbia signed John Philip Sousa and his United States Marine Band to an exclusive contract as soon as the firm began to make entertainment records in 1889. The 1891 Columbia sales list included 27 marches plus 23 other orchestral items. Sousa had a new ensemble in the 1895 catalog, the Grand Concert Band, featuring the famous trombonist Arthur Pryor. A list of Columbia brown-wax two-minute cylinders issued from 1896 to 1900 shows the United States Marine Band playing "Washington Post March" (#1; 1896), followed by close to 100 other numbers. Many were marches, e.g., "Columbia Phonograph March" (#58) and "Columbia Phonograph Co. March" (#63); others were waltzes, overtures, operatic potpourri, medleys of national airs, patriotic songs, and even "Safe in the Arms of Jesus" (#378). Sousa's Grand Concert Band made many Columbia cylinders from 1895 to 1900, including popular songs, marches, and two solo items by Arthur Pryor. The year 1896 also saw the beginning of a series by the Washington Military Concert Band, Gilmore's Band, The Old Guard Band (New York), and the Twenty-third Regiment Band (New York). Columbia continued to record military bands when it phased into the disc format (from 1902; Columbia cylinder sales ceased in 1912). A house group, the Columbia Band, made a series of overtures and operatic excerpts in 1904 and continued to 1909. Many other bands were recording for the label too: Prince's Military Band, Rena Military Band, British Grenadiers Band, etc. The interest in band music continued into the electrical recording era (1925–), with the Grenadier Guards Band and the Highland Military Band among others on Columbia. Berliner's earliest seven-inch discs included material by Sousa's Band, Victor Herbert's 22nd Regiment Band, the United States Marine Band, and various unnamed bands. More than 1,000 Berliner discs with bands or band members as soloists had appeared by 1900. Sousa's Band had six sessions for Victor in October 1900, making 167 takes, of which 84 were released. Their repertoire included marches, gallops, waltzes, polkas, musical show tunes, etc. "Hands across the Sea March" started the first session, released as number 300. By the end of 1902 another 375 releases were credited to the Sousa Band. Kendle's First Regiment Band was in the Victor studio 11 times in 1901 and 1902; other bands of the period on Victor were Kilties Band of Canada (with bagpipes), the American Band of Providence, Rhode Island (directed by cornetist Herbert L. Clarke), and Pryor's Band — a Victor house organization established in 1903. The Pryor Band output was unmatched by any group: more than 2,000 titles emerged from 5,000 takes. In Williams 1972 it is suggested "that the Pryor recordings began to represent the bread and butter sales of the company." Sousa's was more famous, but less active in recording. The Garde Republicaine Band, of France, made Victor records in New York in October 1904, producing 20 titles. After 1912 there was less work by the Pryor and Sousa bands, as Victor formed a new house organization, the Victor Band. This group ran into the dance craze of the pre–World War I period, and recorded mostly in that genre. The Marine Band was with Victor for two sessions, in one of which (15 Oct 1906) it recorded the first U.S. version of Scott Joplin's "Maple Leaf Rag." When the Original Dixieland Jass Band made its famous first disc on 26 Feb 1917 (Victor #18255), the realm of dance and pop music began to pass from military bands to jazz/pop/swing ensembles. Although the wartime interest in military matters sustained further recording of marches, there was a quick decline of public interest in the military band in the 1920s. Records by the Victor Band were fewer each year: down to four in 1930, and none in 1931. Only a few more discs came out in the 1930s from one band or another. There were still about 100 titles listed under

Band Music in the 1940 Victor catalog. In the late 1940s Columbia was listing fewer than 40 singles and four or five band music albums, mostly by the Goldman Band and the Band of H.M. Grenadier Guards. With the advent of LP, a new flowering of military band music appeared. During the 1950s around 90 military or marching bands made records; among them were old familiar groups like the Band of the Coldstream Guards, the Garde Republicaine, the Goldman Band, and the Grenadier Guards. Interesting new groups included German military ensembles, and others from Sweden, Spain, Austria, Wales, and Holland. Much of the LP repertoire has carried into CD fromat, and CD format has also brought reissues of early material such as Herbert L. Clarke directing the Sousa Band (1909–1921). [Smart 1970; Williams 1972.]

MILLER, EDDIE
(23 JUNE 1911–1 APR 1991)

American tenor saxophonist and clarinetist, born in New Orleans. He played locally until 1930, then went to New York. He spent four years with Ben Pollack, then joined the new Bob Crosby band, becoming its most featured soloist. Miller's style remained in a joyous Dixieland mode (although the sax was not a regular part of the traditional New Orleans groups), with lean, elegant improvisations, as in "Till We Meet Again" (Decca #2825; 1939) with Bob Crosby's Bob Cats. In "Milenberg Joys" he took part in a remarkable four-way improvisation (Decca #25293; 1942). In 1944 he played a memorable counterpoint for Martha Tilton's popular "Stranger in Town." He freelanced after military service, and played again with Crosby groups and with Bob Crosby on television. He made hundreds of records with many ensembles and for numerous labels. Miller continued playing, mostly in New Orleans, into the 1980s, then suffered a debilitating stroke in 1988. He died in Van Nuys, California.

MILLER, GLENN
(1 MAR 1904–15 DEC 1944)

American Big Band leader and trombonist, born Alton Glenn Miller in Clarinda, Iowa. He attended the University of Colorado, then left to pursue a musical career. After some time on the West Coast he joined Ben Pollack's band in Chicago in 1926. From 1928 he was a freelance trombonist in New York, then he was with Smith Ballew as arranger in 1932–1934. He was briefly with the Dorsey Brothers, then with Ray Noble's first American band in 1935. In 1937 he organized his own band, and began recording for Decca and Brunswick; financial difficulties led to dissolution of that group, but he founded another in 1938 and became recognized by 1939 for his splendid arrangements, gaining a Bluebird contract. "Moonlight Serenade," his composition and his theme song, was an early hit record (Bluebird #10214; 1939). Another was "In the Mood" (Bluebird #10416; 1939). Miller had a radio show in 1939–1942. Ray Eberle and Marion Hutton were the principal vocalists; Tex Beneke, Billy May, and Hal McIntyre were also utilized by the band. In 1941 the band acquired a stylish vocal quartet, the Modernaires. They made a motion picture that year, *Sun Valley Serenade*, and recorded a great hit from it, "Chattanooga Choo Choo" (Bluebird #11230; 1941). From 1941 to September 1942 the Miller band grew in stature and was widely judged to be the finest of its kind. "Elmer's Tune" (Bluebird #11274; 1941), "String of Pearls" (Bluebird #11382; 1941), and "Skylark" (Bluebird #11462; 1941) had great popularity. Other hit records — on the Victor label, as a prestige move — included "I've Got a Gal in Kalamazoo," Tex Beneke singing, with "At Last" (Victor #27935; 1942), and "Serenade in Blue" (Victor #27995; 1942); all these coming from his other film, *Orchestra Wives*; and the instrumental "American Patrol" (Victor #27873; 1942). Miller enlisted in the Army Air Force in September 1942, and was tasked with direction of the AAF Dance Band. That group made regular radio broadcasts and V-Discs; it included other militarized swing/jazz performers, such as Mel Powell and Ray McKinley. Miller was killed as his plane went down between Britain and France, and the AAF Band was taken over by McKinley and arranger Jerry Gray. In the postwar years various musicians led members of the old Miller band: among them Tex Beneke, Ralph Flanagan, Ray Anthony, Ray McKinley, and Buddy De Franco; it continued performing into the 1970s. There were many LP reissues of the Miller recordings, including *The Complete Glenn Miller* (1976). On CD many of the hits are on RCA's *Unforgettable Glenn Miller* (#PCD1-5459), made from the 78s with no remastering. Another important CD is *Glenn Miller in Hollywood* (Mercury #826 635-2), taken from soundtracks of his films. [Flower 1972; Polic 1989.]

MILLER, MITCH (4 JULY 1911–)

Recording artist and label executive. While Mitch Miller might forever (and unfairly) be remembered for his goatee, stiff baton style, and the bouncing ball projected on to early television screens, the man was a considerable force in the recording industry during the 1950s and 1960s. A classically trained musician who studied oboe at the Eastman School of Music, Miller graduated to become a soloist with the CBS Symphony. From 1947–1950, Miller worked for Mercury Records, where he produced excellence in the classical (Fine Arts Quartet) and pop (Frankie Lane) departments. He then joined Columbia, where he remained for 15 years. Miller brought Lane over to Columbia, and also broke Tony Bennett, Mahalia Jackson, Jerry Vale, Rosemary Clooney, and Johnny Ray. During the 1950s, Miller also recorded with "His Orchestra," enjoying several hits beginning in 1955 with his adaptation of "The Yellow Rose of Texas." In 1958, his first *Sing Along With Mitch* album (Columbia #1160; #1) was released, which became a phenomenal success. It spawned a television show in 1961, which helped promote further releases in a similar style. Miller left Columbia in 1965, and *Sing Along With Mitch* was canceled the following year. Miller is sometimes blamed for Columbia's backward-looking pop department of the early 1960s; he resisted signing rock and roll artists, continuing to focus on mainstream pop singers long after their hit-making days were over.

BRAD HILL

MILLER, POLK
(2 AUG 1844–20 OCT 1913)

American popular singer, born in Grape Lawn, Virginia. He served in the Civil War, then became a drugstore owner. Although himself white, Polk organized a quartet of Black singers around the turn of the 20th century, named the "Old South Quartette" (as the name was spelled on their recordings). This was probably due to the popularity of blackface minstrelsy and the craze for so-called "coon songs"; Miller was offering a more "authentic" group to appeal to those who enjoyed hearing the blackface "re-creations" of this music. Miller and his group made Edison cylinders in 1910; those listed in Koenigsberg [1987] are "Rise and Shine" (#10332), "Old Time Religion" (#10333), and "Jerusalem Mournin'" (#10334). Miller played banjo with the quartet, of which James L. Stamper, bass, and Randall Graves are the only identified members. Miller died in Richmond, Virginia. [Koenigsberg 1987; Walsh 1960/1; 1962/10.]

MILLER, REED
(29 FEB 1880–29 DEC 1943)

American tenor, born in Anderson, South Carolina. He was "the finest oratorio singer of his day" [Walsh 1958/3], with records for the major labels. Miller's earliest recordings were made in 1904 for Zonophone, under the name of James Reed; the first was "Teasing" (#6035). His first Edison cylinder was "Birds in Georgia Sing of Tennessee" (#9658; 1907). He went to Victor in 1910, and Columbia in 1914 (an excerpt from *Elijah*). Opera arias, in English, were among his 27 Edison Diamond Discs of 1913–1921: "Vesti la giubba"/"Siciliana" (#82031). He also made duets with Fred Wheeler, and sang with the Stellar Quartet and the Frank Croxton Quartet. His recording ceased after 1921. Miller's wife, Nevada Van der Veer, was a contralto who also made early records. He died in New York.

MILLER, ROGER
(2 JAN 1936–25 OCT 1992)

American country singer, instrumentalist, and songwriter, born in Fort Worth, Texas. He was a cowboy and rodeo performer as a youth, while learning to play the guitar, banjo, and piano. After military service in the 1950s and various odd jobs, he went to Nashville to concentrate on a musical career. He achieved great success in the 1960s and 1970s, with 43 chart singles and six chart albums. "When Two Worlds Collide" (Victor #7868; 1961) was his first national hit, with 22 weeks on the charts. "King of the Road" (Smash #1965; 1965), his own composition, was his signature song; and there were five other chart records in the same year. Smash, Victor, Mercury, and Columbia were the labels he worked with. Miller won 11 Grammys in 1965–1966. Miller enjoyed a comeback as a Broadway composer when he scored the musical, *Big River*, based on Mark Twain's *Huckleberry Finn*, in the mid-1980s. However, just as he was making a comeback, Miller succumbed cancer in 1992; he was inducted posthumously into the Country Music Hall of Fame in 1995.

MILLER, WALTER

American recording engineer and inventor, an associate of Thomas Edison from ca. 1888 to 1929. He had various duties, including direction of research, supervision of entertainment cylinder production, and general supervision of recording. Miller had 18 U.S. patents in the area of sound recording between 1898 and 1904, five of them in his name alone, and the others with Jonas W. Aylsworth or Alexander N. Pierman. His principal invention was the molding technology that made mass production of cylinders possible; it was covered in several patents with Pierman: #726,965 (filed 21 Nov 1902; granted 5 May 1903), and #785,510 (filed 26 Feb 1903; granted 21 March 1905), etc.

MILLS BROTHERS

A popular male vocal group, consisting of four Ohio-born brothers: Herbert, Harry, Donald, and John; they flourished in the 1930s and 1940s, and remained active into the 1970s. After local work in Cincinnati they went to New York for radio shows in 1930. Their smooth, relaxed style weathered the various style changes of their time. They first recorded for Brunswick in 1931, but quickly moved to Decca, where they scored hits, often with crooner Bing Crosby. They scored their initial success with their vocal imitations of musical instruments and their jazzy harmonies; then, after World War II, the group became best known for its smooth crooning. "Paper Doll" was their greatest hit (Decca #18318; 1943); "Lazy River" was another notable success (Decca #28458; 1952). "Glow Worm" was on the charts for 18 weeks in 1952 (Decca #28384). In 1968 they recorded their final chart song, "Cab Driver" (Dot #17041). There have been many LPs as well, at least seven on the Dot label; *Fortuosity* (Dot DLPS #25835; 1968) was on the charts 15 weeks, undoubtedly due to the success of "Cab Driver." In one form or another, the group performed until the last surviving brother, Donald, died in 1999. There are numerous CD reissues, including a series offering their complete recordings in chronological order on the British JSP/Storyville label (six CDs covering 1931–1939), and more manageable "best of" collections on MCA, which inherited the Decca and Dot recordings.

MILLS NOVELTY CO.

A Chicago firm, maker of slot machines and amusement devices, and the popular Violano-Virtuoso. This was an electric-powered violin-playing machine, representing both violin and piano accompaniment on paper music rolls. About 5,000 were made from 1909 to 1930, primarily for restaurants and taverns. There had been an earlier automatic violin advertised, the Virtuosa, in 1907. One version for theater use had four different rolls, allowing the projectionist to select the music. Mills also made a theater instrument called the Mills Melody Violin: it allowed violins to be played from a keyboard. It marketed the Dance Master, a disc coin-op with 12 selections, each on a separate turntable in a ferris wheel arrangement (similar to the cylinder Multiphone). Later the firm went into juke box manufacture; their postwar Constellation model had 20 records and 40 selections.

MILSAP, RONNIE (16 JAN 1943–)

Born in Robbinsville, North Carolina, Milsap was a major country music hitmaker from the mid-1970s through the early 1980s. He settled in Nashville in 1969 and began writing and performing in a mainstream country style. Although he had some minor hits, his career didn't really take off until he signed with RCA in 1973. His recordings were given the standard strings-and-choruses production, making them immediately popular not only on the country but also the mainstream pop charts. From 1975's "Day Dreams about Night Things" (RCA #10335), Milsap scored country chartbusters through the mid-1980s, primarily focusing on smooth ballads. His biggest crossover pop/country hits were 1977's "It Was Almost Like a Song" (RCA #10976; #1 country, #16 pop), 1981's "Smoky Mountain Rain" (RCA #12084; #1 country and adult contemporary; #24 pop), the million-selling "(There's) No Gettin' Over Me" (RCA #12264; #1 country, #5 pop) and "I Wouldn't Have Missed It for the World" (RCA #12342; #1 country, #20 pop), and his 1982 remake of Chuck Jackson's 1962 hit, "Any Day Now" (RCA #13216; 1982, #1 country and adult contemporary; #14 pop). However, Milsap's recording career pretty much petered out by the mid-1980s, although he continues to be a strong concert draw.

CARL BENSON

MILWAUKEE [WISCONSIN] TALKING MACHINE MANUFACTURING CO.

A firm established in 1915. In 1916 it offered the Perfectrola line of record players, in seven models.

MIMOSA (LABEL)

A British record, single-sided, five and 3/8 inches and six inches in size, made by Crystalate Gramophone Record Manufacturing Co., Ltd., and sold by Sound Recording Co., Ltd. and Woolworth's from 1921. Material was military music, dance music, and popular songs. Later the record was issued double-sided. Mimosa masters were used for other labels, e.g., Kiddyphone, Pigmy, Oliver, Marspen, Beacon, Butterfly, and Savana.

FRANK ANDREWS

MINGUS, CHARLES
(22 APR 1922–5 JAN 1979)

American jazz bass player and composer, born in Nogales, Arizona. He studied cello and bass while in his teens, and played with several bands: Lee Young, Louis Armstrong, and Lionel Hampton. His first recording was with the Russell Jacquet orchestra in 1945, for the Globe label. An important record, "Mingus Fingus," was made with Hampton in 1947 (Decca #24428). He

Charles Mingus Impulse album, from the mid-'60s. Courtesy Frank Hoffmann

First Sony MiniDisc player, moderl MZ-1, with discs, introduced November 1992. Courtesy Sony.

was a member of the Red Norvo Trio, recording for the Discovery label in 1950–1951. Mingus was peripatetic most of his career, never long with one group of colleagues. He formed a sextet in 1964, with Eric Dolphy (alto sax, bass clarinet, flute), Clifford Jordan (tenor sax), and Danny Richmond (drums), Johnny Coles (trumpet), and Jaki Byard (piano); and made the three-album set *The Great Concert* in Paris (America AM#003-05). His last records were done in January 1978, in three sessions for Atlantic. Appropriately his final number was "Farewell, Farewell" (Atlantic SD #8805). The CDs *Black Saint and the Sinner Lady* (MCA Impulse MCAD #5649) and *Mingus Revisited* (EmArcy #826 498, originally recorded in 1960) offer a wide selection of his work and the many musicians he teamed with. Mingus died in Cuernavaca, Mexico.

MINIDISC (MD)

A small disc (slightly larger than half the diameter of the compact disc), recording and playback format pioneered by Sony. By using 5-to-1 data reduction and data compression, a program that would just fit on a 5.25-inch compact disc can be installed on the MD surface with only minimal fidelity loss. The technology allows for both prerecorded programs and recording to blank discs, and allows for portable players of very small size. The format has never caught on in the U.S., although it remains popular in Japan.

HOWARD FERSTLER

MINIMALISM

Minimalism is, in a sense, a misleading term for an experimental musical form centered around a consistent pulse and the repetition of melodic fragments and samples. The style was brought to the fore in the 1970s by Philip Glass, although its roots can be traced back to a few decades before with John Cage's truly minimalist piece *4'33"*. Minimalist thinking in music has since reverberated through numerous genres and eras. In the 1970s, the theme was extended by pioneers such as Terry Riley and Steve Reich. The arrival of complete electronic artists such as Jarre and Kraftwerk further extended the possibilities of minimalism while in the 1980s dance field, acid house owed a lot to minimalist thinking. In the 1990s, electronica was a logical extension of Glass's minimalism which itself inspired a postminimalist movement in avant-garde classical circles. These many splinters stand as testament to the originality of Glass's concept, which – more than any piece of music — sent ripples across the surface of modern music which show no signs of stopping.

IAN PEEL

MINIMALIST RECORDING TECHNIQUES

SEE LIVE TO TWO TRACK

MINNESOTA MINING AND MANUFACTURING CO. (3M)

A diversified American firm, established in 1902, located in St. Paul. 3M is of interest in the sound recording field for its development of magnetic tape players and (1947) "Scotch" recording tapes. Research under direction of Wilfred W. Wetzel led to an improved magnetic tape with an iron oxide coating; this was the Scotch tape. It reached a high frequency of 15,000 Hz, moving at seven and 1/2 inches per second. When this tape went into production in 1947 it almost immediately replaced discs in professional work, such as making of radio transcriptions. The firm has also manufactured videotapes and CD media, and many other nonaudio products. [website: www.3m.com.]

MINNESOTA PHONOGRAPH CO.
A Minneapolis firm, established in 1890 as one of the North American Phonograph Co. affiliates; it was located at 108 Rochester Block. C.H. Chadbourne (or C.N. Chadbourn) was general manager in 1890 and president in 1892.

MINSTREL RECORDINGS
The minstrel show — variety dance/comedy/musical productions by white artists in blackface, later by Black artists — was a popular genre in America from the mid-19th century. The Virginia Minstrels, organized by Edwin Pearce Christy, were the first troupe of minstrels, appearing in New York in February 1843, and creating a sudden sensation. Renamed as Christy's Minstrels, they began a New York run on 27 Apr 1846 and performed every night until 13 July 1854. Stephen Foster songs were featured by the group. When E.P. Christy died in 1862, his son George kept the company going for some time, but it closed down finally in 1865. A characteristic element in the shows was the humor drawn from players who portrayed stupid Blacks and made absurd responses to questions posed by a player representing the superior white man. This curious format dominated American theater (with great success in Britain also) into the 1890s, when vaudeville, burlesque, and the Broadway revue took over much of its audience. Early recordings made much of the white person's image of the dim-witted, self-deprecating Black, as in coon songs and foolish dialogues. Minstrel recordings were made by white and Black artists; among them (in the 18 items of the Victor 1917 catalog) Billy Murray, the Peerless Quartet, and the American Quartet. On Edison cylinders there was the Billy Heins Ancient City Quartet recording in 1898; and there were the Edison Minstrels, recording from ca. 1899 on five-inch Concert cylinders. From 1903 there were two-minute cylinders by the same group, also known as the Edison Modern Minstrels. On Columbia Twentieth Century cylin-

ders there was a group named the Rambler Minstrels in 1907. Victor's Evening with the Minstrels series of eight discs began in 1902, and ran to 1909. A confusion of titles was attached to many of the early Victor releases, such as Olden Time Minstrels, Victor Minstrels, and Matinee Minstrels. were names given to the same ensembles. In 1907 a group taking the name of the long-defunct Christy Minstrels made four records. Victor's 1922 catalog still carried a section of 15 Minstrel Records, by the Victor Minstrel Co., Peerless Quartet, Murray, and a few others. But by 1927 the category had been dropped from the catalog. In Britain there were recordings by the Excelsior Minstrels on Edison Bell cylinders, and by the Black Diamonds Minstrels (formed by Russell Hunting, who took part) on Sterling, Pathé, and Odeon records. The Coontown Minstrels were on the Jumbo label. Popular minstrel troupes were heard on almost all makes of disc in Britain up until World War I. The Kentucky Minstrels recorded for HMV in the 1930s. After World War II the Black and White Minstrel Show recorded and gave live performances. [Andrews 1977/1 has a selective discography of British issues; Koenigsberg 1987; Leonard 1986; Fagan 1986.]

MISSOURI PHONOGRAPH CO.
A St. Louis firm, one of the North American Phonograph Co. affiliates, established in 1890. A.W. Clancy was vice president in 1890, and president in 1891–1893. J.C. Wood was general manager in 1891–1893, and vice president in 1892–1893. The firm had about 50 multiple-tube coin-ops on location in 1891, earning about $100 a week from each one.

MITCHELL, JONI (7 NOV 1943–)
Joni Mitchell is the quintessential singer-songwriter; although her songs have been widely recorded by other artists — Judy Collins reached number eight on the pop charts with "Both Sides Now" (Elektra #45639; 1968), Tom Rush made "The Circle Game" the title song of his third album (Elektra #74018), and three versions of "Woodstock" made the *Billboard Hot 100* — her own idiosyncratic renditions remain the definitive versions of her material. While her folk troubador origins and confessional lyrics conform to the conventions of this genre, she has avoided stylistic categorization in a recording career spanning five decades. Born Roberta Joan Anderson in rural Saskatchewan, Canada, she studied piano and displayed a talent for composing melodies at an early age. Despite battling polio at age nine, she continued

Self-portrait by Joni Mitchell which she painted for the cover of her second album, *Clouds,* released on Reprise in 1969.

playing music (learning guitar from a Pete Seeger do-it-yourself manual) prior to starting art school in Calgary. After a year of college, she matriculated to Toronto, working in a clothing store and trying to break into the Yorkville district's coffeehouse circuit. While there, she met and married Chuck Mitchell, a cabaret singer hailing from Detroit. Success as a songwriter, combined with the failure of her marriage, brought Mitchell to New York in 1967. There she met longtime manager, Elliot Roberts, and David Crosby, who produced her first album, *Joni Mitchell* (Reprise #6293; 1968). In 1968 she moved to Los Angeles, producing a series of folk-inflected LPs characterized by her unusual guitar tunings, the increasingly layered use of instrumentation, and poetic treatment of themes such as sexual liberation and the search for meaning in human relationships: *Clouds* (Reprise #6341; 1969), *Ladies of the Canyon* (Reprise #6376; 1970), *Blue* (Reprise #2038; 1971), *For the Roses* (Asylum #5057; 1972), and her pop breakthrough, *Court and Spark* (Asylum #1001; 1974). Following the live *Miles of Aisles* (recorded with the jazz-fusion group, the L.A. Express; Asylum #202; 1974), Mitchell's next five albums — *The Hissing of Summer Lawns* (Asylum #1051; 1975), *Hejira* (Asylum #1087; 1976), *Don Juan's Reckless Daughter* (Asylum #701; 1977), *Mingus* (Asylum #505; 1979), and *Shadows and Light* (Asylum #704; 1980) — were strongly grounded in jazz idioms. However, the abstract, detached flavor of her verses and virtual absence of traditional melodies led to a gradual decline in sales. *Wild Things Run Fast* (Geffen #2019; 1982), however, signaled a return to her earlier pop-rock style. Following a brief experiment with electronica and broader geopolitical themes in *Dog Eat Dog* (Geffen #24074; 1985), Mitchell has preferred to craft songs from familiar clay rather than take stylistic risks. Nevertheless, her releases continue to sell moderately well and *Turbulent Indigo* (Geffen #45786; 1994) was awarded two Grammys. Other notable honors include *Billboard* magazine's 1995 Century award and her 1997 induction into the Rock and Roll Hall of Fame.

FRANK HOFFMANN

MITCHELL, PETER (1942–30 DEC 1995)

Born in Quincy, Massachusetts, Mitchell graduated from Vermont Academy in 1960, and received a B.A. in physics and astronomy from Boston University in 1966. For a while, he worked for Avco Corp., studying ablative nose-cone materials, in preparation for future Apollo landings. Throughout the 1970s he and cohost Richard Goldwater had a weekly, audio-oriented talk show on WBUR-FM in Boston, called *Shop Talk*. Mitchell was also one of the founders of the Boston Audio Society. Mitchell was a gifted writer, and during the last 25 years of his life, he published several hundred articles on audio, many very influential, in *The Boston Phoenix*, *Stereo Review*, *High Fidelity*, *Stereophile*, *Atlantic Monthly*, and *db* magazine, among others. He also wrote a number of audio instruction manuals for Apt, NAD, and other companies. As a longtime member of the Audio Engineering Society, he presented papers, chaired workshops, and served on a working group of the Digital Standards Committee.

HOWARD FERSTLER

MITCHELL, WILLIE (1 MAR 1928–)

Born in Ashland, Mississippi, musician/producer Mitchell is best known for his work for Memphis's Hi label in the 1970s, particularly his production work for singer Al Green. Originally a trumpeter and keyboard player, Mitchell was raised in Memphis where, in 1959, he was hired to lead the houseband for the fledgling Hi label. He produced hits for the Bill Black Combo as well as Ace Cannon. Mitchell also released instrumental recordings under his own name, as well as leading the Bill Black Combo on record after Black's death in 1965. Original Hi owner Joe Cuoghi died in 1970, and Mitchell took over as vice president. Beginning that year, he oversaw sessions by Hi's most successful singers, Al Green, Ann Peebles, and Syl Johnson. Mitchell led the band on these recordings as well as arranging and producing them, and his band style was a classic update of the earlier Stax/Memphis sound. For Green, he oversaw a series of top 10 pop hits, beginning with the December 1971 pop and R&B number one song, "Let's Stay Together" (Hi #2002), and continuing through 1974; he also worked with Green again in 1985 and 1986 when Green returned to recording. Mitchell left Hi in 1979 and later worked briefly for Bearsville before going independent.

CARL BENSON

MITCHELL RECORDS (LABEL)

An American record issued in 1924–1926 by the Mitchell Phonograph Corp. of Detroit. Masters came first from the Emerson family of labels, then from Grey Gull. Production of Mitchell Records was effected by the Bridgeport Die and Machine Co. until it dissolved in 1925. [Rust 1978.]

MITROPOULOS, DIMITRI (1 MAR 1896–2 NOV 1960)

Greek/American conductor and pianist, born in Athens, Greece. He studied in Athens and Brussels, then piano with Ferruccio Busoni in Berlin. He was assistant conductor of the Berlin Opera from 1921 to 1924. His Paris debut in 1932 was a notable success; he then conducted in many cities, and made an American debut in 1937 with the Boston Symphony Orchestra. Mitropoulos was appointed director of the Minneapolis Symphony Orchestra, and held the post from 1937 to 1949. He became an American citizen in 1946. From 1950 to 1958 he directed the New York Philharmonic Orchestra, conducting also at the Metropolitan Opera and various other orchestras and opera companies. He died while rehearsing the La Scala Orchestra in Milan. Among his fine recordings the most famous was the Mahler First Symphony, with the New York Philharmonic (Columbia SL #118), which he had also done with the Minneapolis Symphony in 1941 (Columbia #469). His most acclaimed operatic recordings were *Boris Godunov* (Victor #LM-6063; 1956) and *Vanessa* (Victor #LM-6138; 1958) with the Metropolitan Opera Co.

MIXDOWN

A reduction in the number of channels from the original recording, as signals are transferred from a multi-

Studer Vista 6 Mixing Console. Courtesy Harman Kardon International

track reproducer to a two-track master record, or to a monaural master, etc.

See also **Mixer**

MIXER

A device that blends two or more recorded signals. In recording, the mixer permits a manipulation of outputs from several channels, so that they may be faded, selected, or combined in any combination and in any arrangement of volumes.

See also **Mixdown**

MOBILE FIDELITY SOUND LABS (LABEL)

A label founded in the early 1970s by enthusiasts Brad Miller and Gary Giorgi to issue audiophile quality LPs. The company specialized in licensing rock albums from major labels and then remastering them at half-speed, pressing on high-quality vinyl, and packaging them in the archival-grade materials. In 1980, Herbert Belkin, an ex-ABC Records executive, became president of the firm and the engine of its subsequent growth. In 1979, the company turned its attention to producing finer quality cassettes, and then in 1987 introduced the Ultradisc CD, also called a "gold" disc because of the use of gold in its substrate. Many of Mobile Fidelity's reissues not only featured superior sound but bonus material discovered on the original master tapes. From 1985–1992, the company issued material from the Soviet Union's Melodiya Records archives. In 1994, Mobile Fidelity opened its own pressing plant to make high-quality LP pressings on 200-gram vinyl, but the plant closed in 1996 due to the limited market for its products. The firm made its first DVD release in 1998, but a year later the label was forced to close due to overexpansion. Mobile Fidelity's issues of classic rock albums, notably Pink Floyd's *Dark Side of the Moon* and the Who's *Tommy*, are much sought after by collectors.

CARL BENSON

MOBLEY, EDWIN H

American inventor, holder of nine early patents in sound recording: diaphragms, soundboxes, a turntable for discs, and a phonograph-reproducer (patent #690,069; filed 3 July 1901; granted 31 Dec 1901) that improved stylus tracking and volume of the Edison Automatic Reproducer. Edison sued him successfully on the grounds that Mobley had no right to alter Edison's patented device. [Koenigsberg 1990.]

MOBY GRAPE

Moby Grape will always be identified with the worst excesses of record industry hype arising from the excitement engendered by the San Francisco Sound. With the Summer of Love (1967) gathering momentum and leading Bay Area bands such as the Jefferson Airplane and Grateful Dead already enjoying impressive record sales, the major labels rushed to sign any local bands displaying commercial potential. Columbia's signing of Moby Grape was widely viewed as a major coup; the group's popularity in the area was virtually unrivaled. The producer of the band's first two albums, David Rubinson, would later comment, "They were the closest thing to the Rolling Stones that America has produced."The Grape's strengths included a triple guitar lineup (Peter Lewis, Jerry Miller, and Skip Spence), seamless four-part harmonies, and mature songwriting capable of incorporating country, R&B, psychedelia, and other contemporary music styles. Columbia celebrated the release of the band's *Moby Grape* (Columbia #9498; 1967) by also issuing simultaneously five singles from the debut album. Although critics agree that the LP was a classic, the public appears to have been confused by this marketing ploy. Only one of the singles, "Omaha" (Columbia #44173; 1967), reached the *Billboard Hot 100*, stalling at number 88. Although the first album peaked at number 24, the media furor surrounding its release rendered this performance something of a disappointment. The label continued its grandiose promotional efforts with the Grape's next release, *Wow* (Columbia #9613;

1968), a double-album set including a psychedelic studio disc (including one track cut at 78 rpm) along with a bonus "Grape Jam" supersession featuring Mike Bloomfield, Al Kooper, and other famous guest musicians. In the face of general public indifference and declining sales, the band recorded two more albums before splitting up, *Moby Grape'69* (Columbia #9696; 1969) and *Truly Fine Citizen* (Columbia #9912; 1969). After 1970, the various band members attempted a number of reunions. Only one album ensuing from these projects, *20 Granite Creek* (Reprise #6460; 1971) entered the charts. [McDonough 1985.]

FRANK HOFFMANN

MODERN JAZZ QUARTET (MJQ)

A group formed by vibraphonist Milt Jackson in 1952, successor to his own Milt Jackson Quartet of 1947. Members were Jackson, pianist John Lewis, drummer Kenny Clarke, and bassist Percy Heath. Clarke was replaced by Connie Kay in 1955. They began to record for Blue Note in 1952, moving to Atlantic in 1956, and established a reputation for structured performance with a classical aspect. Lewis was the group's primary composer/arranger. A key player in the third-stream movement that sought to meld classical music and jazz, Lewis composed chamberlike pieces that were played note-for-note by the quartet. The group dressed like classical performers, and tended to perform in halls usually featuring classical ensembles. They even adapted classical music to jazzlike settings. Over the years, the group primarily recorded for Atlantic Records (1956–1974; 1992), but also for Savoy (1951), Prestige (1952–1955), Verve (1957), United Artists (1959), Apple (1967–1969), and Pablo (1981–1985). They have an extensive discography, with notable albums including *Django* (featuring the famous title cut by Lewis; Prestige #7057, 1953), 1959's *Pyramid* (Atlantic #1325), 1962's *Lonely Woman*, featuring the title cut by Ornette Coleman, showing Lewis's interest in contemporary jazz performers (Atlantic #1381), and *Blues on Bach* from 1973, featuring alternating original blues by Lewis with his arrangements of classical themes by Bach (Atlantic #1652). When Jackson departed in 1974 the quartet dissolved, but got together again in 1981 and continued to play occasional reunion tours and concerts over the next decade or so. A four-CD set on Atlantic was issued in 1991 as a career summary (*MJQ 40*; Atlantic #82330). Connie Kay died in 1995, and the group continued sporadically thereafter until Milt Jackson's death in 1999.

REV. CARL BENSON

MODULATION

The technique of varying a characteristic (i.e., amplitude) of a wave (the carrier) as a function of the instantaneous value of another wave (the modulator). Amplitude modulation (AM) and frequency modulation (FM) are basic to radio broadcasting. Modulation is also a factor in acoustic and electrical recording, telephony, etc.

MOMAN, CHIPS (1936–)

Born Lincoln Wayne Moman in LaGrange, Georgia, Moman was one of the leading producers of country, soul, and pop music in the 1960s and 1970s. As a teenager, Moman traveled to Memphis, beginning to play guitar locally, notably with Sun recording artist Warren Smith. With Memphis rockabilly stars Johnny and Dorsey Burnette, Moman traveled to Los Angeles in the late 1950s, where he worked as a session guitarist at the famed Gold Star Studios. By the early 1960s, he had returned to Memphis, where he was hired by Jim Stewart and Estelle Axton to work as an engineer for their new record label, then called Satellite but soon renamed Stax Records. At Stax, Moman oversaw classic recordings by artists like Rufus Thomas and Booker T and the MGs. Moman was promised an ownership role in the label, but when Stewart refused to honor this promise, he left the firm in 1964 and opened his own competing studio, American Sound Studio. Several Memphis hit-makers of the mid-1960s recorded there, notably The Box Tops and Joe Tex. Atlantic Records' producer Jerry Wexler also patronized Moman's studio in the later 1960s, including sessions for Dusty Springfield (the famous Dusty in Memphis album) and Wilson Pickett. In 1969, Moman produced Elvis Presley's classic From Elvis in Memphis album, and its follow-up in the next year, albums that relaunched Elvis as a major contender on the pop charts. In 1973, Moman relocated to Atlanta, and then by decade's end to Nashville. By 1985, he was back in Memphis, where he oversaw the Class of '55 album that brought together Sun Studio legends Johnny Cash, Jerry Lee Lewis, Carl Perkins, and Roy Orbison for a reunion album. Moman issued it on his own American Records label. In the 1990s, he returned to Georgia and was out of the music business for a while; in early 2000, he announced a new venture, a web-based label at www.chipsmoman.com, although as of this writing the site was inactive. Moman also coauthored several hits with Dan Penn in the late 1960s, notably "Do Right Woman" (a hit for Aretha Franklin) and "Dark End of the Street" (initially recorded by James Carr). Moman also played lead guitar on several of Aretha Franklin's classic recordings of this period. In the mid-1970s, he turned to writing country songs, notably 1975's "Hey Won't You Play Another Somebody Done Somebody Wrong Song" (with Larry Butler) and 1977's "Luckenbach, Texas" (with Bobby Emmons), a major hit for Waylon Jennings.

CARL BENSON

MONARCH RECORD (LABEL)

An American label of the Victor Talking Machine Co., also titled Victor Monarch Record; issued from 3 Jan 1901. These were the earliest 10-inch discs from any firm. Earlier Victors had been seven-inch size. Some 585 seven-inch Victors had already appeared before the Monarch 10-inch was introduced, and the name Victor was retained for the smaller records. Many of the same titles were duplicated in both series. Victors — phased out by 1906 — sold for $.50, Monarchs for $1. It was on the Victor Monarch Record that the Nipper trademark first appeared in the U.S. A special series of Monarch imports began with material originating in London, Milan, Paris, and St. Petersburg in 1901 and 1902, with a red label (announced as "imported Red Seal Records"). When Victor initiated its American-made Red Seals in 1903, the Monarch imports (they were in a 5000 series) were renumbered into the 91000 series. Monarch as a label name was carried into Victor's 1904 catalog, then dropped. The reason Victor abandoned the Monarch name was the associated G & T 12-inch discs, Gramophone Monarch Record, had been introduced in June 1903. [Fagan & Moran 1986.]

MONAURAL

Single-channel sound transmission or recording, another term for monophonic; it is often shortened to "mono."

MONITOR (LABEL)

A world-music record label founded in 1956 by Michael Stillman and Rose Rubin. Stillman was an amateur pianist who studied at NYU and then served in the military during World War II. After the war, he settled in New York and got a job working for music publisher Leeds Music, particularly working with their Soviet composers. In the early 1950s, he met Ruth Rubin, who had worked with Russian war relief agencies. Both lamented the unavailability of good Soviet recordings in the U.S. They founded Monitor initially to release Soviet classical recordings, but then quickly moved on to traditional music, including popular recordings by the Soviet Army Chorus. In the early 1960s, the label had its greatest success with a variety of traditional and popular world music recordings, most notably several albums of music for belly dancing performed by George Abdo (1937–2002), with his band The Flames of Araby, who performed a kitschy combination of Middle Eastern–sounding music with strong Western pop influences (a "best of" compilation CD was issued by Smithsonian/Folkways [#40458] in 2002). The label also issued a few recordings in the late 1950s/early 1960s aimed at the U.S. folk revival market, including albums by banjoist Billy Ed Wheeler and revivalists Logan English and Ramblin' Jack Elliott. In the later 1970s, the label moved into political music, issuing the recordings of murdered Chilean protest singer Victor Jara in the U.S. The label's production slowed during the 1980s, and finally Stillman and Rubin donated its master recordings to the Smithsonian Institution, which combined its 250 recordings with its archives based on the Folkways catalog.

CARL BENSON

MONK, THELONIOUS
(10 OCT 1917–17 FEB 1982)

American jazz pianist, born in Rocky Mount, North Carolina. His family moved to New York, where he learned to play the piano and worked at Minton's Playhouse ("the cradle of modern jazz"). In 1944 he made records with Coleman Hawkins, presenting his personal style that did not fit the current bebop phase. He worked for the Blue Note label, then Prestige, before moving to Riverside and a successful album, *Brilliant Corners* (1956; on Riverside CD #1526); this was followed by further Riverside discs that established his reputation for originality. Monk recorded for Columbia in the 1960s, and continued to record, tour, and compose until 1972, when he withdrew from all activities; his last recordings were issued on the British Black Lion label. He remained in seclusion until his death, refusing to see visitors or play music. Monk died in Englewood, New Jersey. Monk's music is available on numerous CD reissues, including reissues of original Prestige, Riverside, Columbia, and Black Lion albums. There are also three major sets of his recordings: *The Complete Blue Note Recordings* (#30363) offers four CDs of his 1947–1952 sessions for the label, along with a final 1957 session with Sonny Rollins; *The Complete Prestige Recordings* (#4428) is a three-CD set of his 1952–1954 recordings for that label; and *The Complete Riverside Recordings* (Riverside #022) is a 15-CD (originally 22-LP) set of 153 numbers, Monk's complete Riverside output from 1955–1961. *The Columbia Years* (#64887) is a three-CD set offering the best of his 1962–1968 recordings for that label.

MONKEES

The Monkees were a manufactured group — a revolutionary concept at the time — created by Columbia Pictures producer Don Kirshner. Their concept consisted of a television sitcom based on the adventures of a rock band. While the extraordinary success enjoyed by both the NBC-TV show between 1966–1969 and Monkees' recordings validated the prefab notion (and laid the groundwork for the bubblegum genre), the later problems ensuing from the independent thinking of band members led to the creation of cartoon rock stars and recordings cut by anonymous studio musicians for imaginary acts. Despite the fact that the foursome comprising the Monkees had a reasonable amount of experience as musicians — Mickey Dolenz had been a child actor, Peter Tork had been part of the 1960s Greenwich Village folk scene, Mike Nesmith was performing in Los Angeles folk clubs, and David Jones had sung in London musicals and television programs — their label insisted that session players provide the instrumental backing on the first couple of albums, *The Monkees* (Colgems #101; 1966; #1) and *More of the Monkees* (Colgems #102; 1967; #1). When the band, with Nesmith as spokesperson, rebelled against this policy, Colgems ceded them full musical control. Although lacking the polish of its predecessors, the

The Monkees in an early publicity photo, c. 1965.

first LP under the new arrangement, *Headquarters* (Colgems #103; 1967; #1), enjoyed a comparable chart run. The later albums — *Pisces, Aquarius, Caprisorn & Jones Ltd.* (Colgems #104; 1967; #1), *The Birds, the Bees & the Monkees* (Colgems #109; 1968; #3), the movie soundtrack, *Head* (Colgems #5008; 1968; #45), *Instant Replay* (Colgems #113; 1969; #32), *The Monkees Present* (Colgems #117; 1969; #100), and *Changes* (Colgems #119; 1970) — featured musical experimentation and songwriting contributions by band members. Tork departed in 1968 due to musical differences, and when NBC dropped the show and record sales slowed to a trickle the following year, the Monkees disbanded. While Nesmith found success both as a solo recording artist and in the production of conceptual videos (*Michael Nesmith in Elephant Parts* won the 1981 Grammy for Video of the Year), Dolenz and Jones — whose acting careers had lost momentum — formed a marginally popular Monkees revival band in the mid-1970s called (for legal reasons) Dolenz, Jones, Boyce and Hart (featuring the famous songwriting duo, Tommy Boyce and Bobby Hart, who had supplied many of the group's 1960s-era hits). In the mid-1980s, a resurgence of interest in the band due to cable television reruns of the NBC episodes inspired Dolenz, Jones, and Tork to re-form the Monkees. In addition to issuing CD editions of the original albums (six of which made the charts in 1986), Rhino began releasing new material by the band, including *Pool It!* (Rhino #70706; 1987; #72) and *20th Anniversary Concert Tour 1986* (Rhino #71110; 1987). The revival gained momentum in the new decade, with Nesmith coming aboard as a performer and producer for the LP, *Justus* (Rhino #72542; 1996), which coincided with Rhino's release of the television show episodes in a 21-volume video anthology. In 2000, VH1 broadcast a made-for-TV film of their career, *Daydream Believer*.

FRANK HOFFMANN

MONO; MONOPHONIC

SEE MONAURAL

MONROE, BILL
(13 SEP 1911–9 SEP 1996)

American country singer and "Father of Bluegrass Music," born in Rosine, Kentucky. He played fiddle tunes on the mandolin (the only instrument available to him) as a youth in a family group. In 1938 he organized the Blue Grass Boys, and developed the new blue-

Bill Monroe, c. early '50s. Courtesy David A. Jasen.

grass style; he was on *Grand Ole Opry* in October 1939, and became nationally acclaimed. The Blue Grass Boys had an unusual instrumentation for country music, including a plucked string bass as well as the Monroe mandolin. It had an up-tempo beat, bringing it close to jazz. He built the Bluegrass Hall of Fame and Museum in Nashville, later moving it to Hendersonville, Tennessee. After stardom in country music during the 1940s, Monroe was overshadowed by musicians he had trained: Lester Flatt and Earl Scruggs. But in the 1970s his innovative style was again recognized (he was elected to the Country Music Hall of Fame in 1970) and he remained in the vanguard of bluegrass performers. Monroe won the first Grammy for a bluegrass album in 1988; that same year, his song "Blue Moon of Kentucky" was made the official state song. He continued to perform and record until 1996, when he had a major stroke. He died soon after. Monroe's Decca/MCA recordings from 1950–1980 have been reissued on three boxed sets by Bear Family Records; his complete Columbia recordings are also available in a boxed set. His early recordings with his brother Charlie as the Monroe Brothers are being reissued on a series of CDs by Rounder Records.

REV. CARL BENSON

MONSTER CABLE

Began in 1979, by Noel Lee, the company is the world's leading producer and supplier of upscale cables for audio, video, home theater, car, computer, satellite, and custom installation. Monster has since grown to encompass several different new divisions that manufacture and market a variety of noncable products including Monster Game, Monster brand power conditioners, Entech audio and video components, and loudspeakers. The company also produces music through its record label, Monster Music. [website: www.monstercable.com.]

HOWARD FERSTLER

MONTANA, PATSY
(30 OCT 1914–3 MAY 1996)

American country singer, guitarist, and songwriter, born Ruby Blevins in Hot Springs, Arkansas. She began her singing career in her teens, and was lead vocalist with a group called the Prairie Ramblers from 1934 to 1948, touring widely, and appearing on the *National Barn Dance* radio show. Known as "The Cowboy's Sweetheart" or "The Yodeling Cowgirl,"

Patsy Montana in the '40s. Courtesy David A. Jasen.

she was one of the mainstays of the *Barn Dance* for about 25 years, and had her own radio program as well. She sang with the influential string band named The Prairie Ramblers (Chick Hurt, Jack Taylor, Tex Atchison, and Salty Holmes). Montana's radio appearances and recordings were instrumental in the establishing of country music as a prime force in American life. She recorded extensively from 1932 to 1959 on various labels, including Columbia, Decca, Surf, Victor, and Vocalion. An early Victor was typical of her enduring popular discs: "I Love My Daddy Too"/"When the Flowers of Montana Were Blooming" (#23760; 1932). Montana never retired; she has composed more than 200 songs, and continued making appearances, sometimes with her two daughters. In 1989 she released a new album, *The Cowboy's Sweetheart*, on the Flying Fish label, and she performed in the annual University of Chicago Folk Festival. She was elected to the Country Music Hall of Fame shortly after her death.

MONTANA PHONOGRAPH CO.

A firm established in 1890, one of the affiliates of the North American Phonograph Co.; location was Helena, Montana. The president in 1892 was E.D. Edgerton. The firm was still in business, as an Edison distributor, as late as October 1925.

MONTAUK TRIO

An instrumental group that made one Edison Diamond Disc in 1923: "You Wanted Someone to Play With"/"Somebody's Wrong" (#51228). Members were Walter Wooley, piano; Henry L. Taylor, banjo; and Stanley Brooks, saxophone.

MONTEUX, PIERRE
(4 APR 1875–1 JULY 1964)

French conductor, violinist, and violist, born in Paris. He played viola in various orchestras, then in 1911 became conductor for the Ballets Russes. He was on the podium during the riotous premiere of *Sacre du printemps* in 1913, calmly taken the piece to its final bar in the midst of pandemonium. He also directed the world premieres of *Petrouchka*, *Daphnis et Chloe*, and other works. From 1917 to 1919 he was a conductor at the Metropolitan Opera; then he conducted the Boston Symphony Orchestra from 1919 to 1924. He went to the Concertgebouw Orchestra as an associate conductor with Willem Mengelberg in 1924–1934, then was principal conductor of the Orchestre Symphonique de Paris during 1929–1938. Monteux was director of the

San Francisco Symphony Orchestra from 1936 to 1952, and of the London Symphony Orchestra from 1961 to 1964. He died in Hancock, Maine. His first discs were made with the Paris orchestra in the 1930s. With the San Francisco orchestra he recorded the standard symphonies, plus Stravinsky and Ravel, for RCA Victor. Thereafter he recorded for many labels with many orchestras. His most appreciated records have been those of Stravinsky and Ravel, notably *Sacre du printemps* with the Paris Conservatory Orchestra (on 78s as London #55-1538; LP as Decca #750; 1957) and *Daphnis et Chloe Suite* with the London Symphony Orchestra (on 78s as London #15090; LP as Decca #69; 1959). However, neither is currently available on CD.

MONTGOMERY, WES (6 MAR 1923 [SOME SOURCES GIVE 1925]– 15 JUNE 1968)

American jazz guitarist, born John Leslie Montgomery in Indianapolis, Indiana. He is regarded as the successor to Charlie Christian, achieving a "vocalized expression" with the instrument, playing with his thumb instead of a pick. He was with Lionel Hampton in 1948–1950, then returned to Indianapolis for local work. In 1959 he signed with the Riverside label and did his best jazz playing. Later albums for Verve and A&M show him in lush orchestral settings, with less jazz character. However, these later recordings were highly popular; seven were on the charts in 1966–1968, most notably *A Day in the Life* (A&M #3001; 1967), which had 30 chart weeks. Of the many fine CDs available, *Round Midnight* (Affinity #13; originally from 1965) and *Full House* (Riverside #1508; 1962) show him at his best. His full output for Riverside is available on a 12-CD set (#4408). Montgomery died in Indianapolis.

MONTGOMERY WARD AND CO., INC.

A Chicago-based retailer, beginning as a mail-order house in 1872. As early as 1898 the firm was offering Edison cylinder phonographs and Berliner gramophones, as well as records for them. In the 1930s the firm began to issue records under its own label, Montgomery Ward; at first these were pressed by Victor using Victor or Bluebird masters, offering good jazz and country material. They also sold phonographs under the Lakeside name. During 1939–1940 there was a series from the Varsity label. In 1988 the firm discontinued catalog sales and the use of house-brand products.

MONUMENT (LABEL)

Washington, D.C.–based promotion man Fred Foster, incorporated Monument Records (named for the Washington Monument) on 11 Mar 1958. The first release, Billy Grammer's "Gotta Travel On" (#400), reached number 4 on *Billboard*'s pop charts, but Foster's crucial signing came the following year when Roy Orbison was brought to the label. Orbison's third Monument record, "Only the Lonely" (#421) became a number two hit, inaugurating a five-year hit streak. Both Orbison and Foster moved to Nashville, and, from 1960, Monument was a Nashville label. Among the artists signed to Monument during the 1960s and early 1970s were Kris Kristofferson, Dolly Parton, Willie Nelson, the Gatlin Brothers, Ray Stevens, and Tony Joe White. Foster purchased a studio, opened a West Coast branch (which signed Robert Mitchum), and co-owned a music publishing company, Combine Music, which published Kristofferson and most of the Monument artists. Foster overcommitted himself, though, and relinquished the Monument presidency in August 1982 to Los Angeles–based Bob Fead. In 1986 Foster lost his 70 percent stake in Combine, and on 21 Apr 1987 Monument was purchased by CBS Special Products for $810,000. In October 1997, CBS's new owners, Sony, relaunched Monument as a Nashville-based boutique label. The Dixie Chicks have made it a very successful imprint.

78 produced for sale through the popular mail-order catalog. Courtesy Kurt Nauck/Nauck's Vintage Records

COLIN ESCOTT

MOODY BLUES

Although the bulk of their creative output appears frozen in a late 1960s progressive rock time-warp, the Moody Blues have retained a strong core of followers up to the present day. During the band's innovative years, they greatly influenced the development of the classical rock genre, the integration of both symphonic instruments and synthesizers into rock music arrangements, the refinement of the concept album, and the interpretive value of cover artwork and graphics. Like many British bands beginning in the early 1960s, the Birmingham, England-based Moody Blues — comprised of vocalist/guitarist Denny Laine, vocalist/pianist Mike Pinder, vocalist/bassist Clint Warwick, drummer Graham Edge, and Ray Thomas (flute, harmonica, vocals) — were initially committed to updating American blues music. After one notable hit, the Bessie Banks cover "Go Now" (London #9726; 1965; #10 U.S., #1 U.K.), and a string of minor successes, Laine and Warwick departed in late 1966. With replacements Justin Hayward (vocals, guitar) and John Lodge (vocals, bass, the group opted for a more ambitious hybrid of orchestral pop-rock and mind-expanding song lyrics. The first album with this revamped lineup, *Days of Future Passed* (London #18012; 1967; #3 U.S., #27 U.K.), was put together while the band was making demonstration discs for British Decca's new recording process. Featuring the London Festival Orchestra, the LP was conceived as a song cycle connected by poetic fragments and instrumental interludes; two of the tracks, "Nights in White Satin" (Deram #85023; 1967; #2 — 1972 reissue — U.S., #19 U.K.) and "Tuesday Afternoon" (Deram #85028; 1968; #24), would also score highly on the pop charts. Now recognized as pop-philosopher gurus much like the Beatles and Bob Dylan, the band's popular follow-up LPs — which featured the mellotron, a synthesizer derivative capable of providing thin, reedy approximation of a string choir — included *In Search of the Lost Chord* (Deram #18017; 1968; #23 U.S., #5 U.K.), *On the Threshold of a Dream* (Deram #18025; 1969; #20 U.S., #1 U.K.), *To Our Children's Children's Children* (Threshold #1; 1969; #14 U.S., #2 U.K.; the inaugural release of the band's designer label intended, like the Beatles' Apple, to foster artistic creativity), *A Question of Balance* (Threshold #3; 1970; #3 U.S., #1 U.K.), *Every Good Boy Deserves Favour* (Threshold #5; 1971; #2 U.S., #1 U.K.), and *Seventh Sojourn* (Threshold #7; 1972; #1 U.S., #5 U.K.). The group took a five-year hiatus beginning in early 1973 to explore solo avenues; all members (with the exception of Edge, who concentrated on a hard rock approach) achieved a modicum of commercial success releasing rather bland rehashes of the trademark Moodies sound. Reunited in 1978, the Moody Blues (with for-mer Yes keyboardist Patrick Moraz replacing Pinder, who'd tired of touring) continued producing lush, albeit retro, albums which — depending on the strength of singles releases and musical fashions — achieved varying degrees of popularity. *Octave* (London #708; 1978; #13 U.S., #6 U.K.), *Long Distance Voyager* (Threshold #2901; 1981; #1 U.S., #7 U.K.), and *The Other Side of Life* (Threshold #829179; 1986; #9 U.S., #24 U.K.), the latter featuring the autobiographical single (driven by an evocatively nostalgic MTV-friendly video clip) "Your Wildest Dreams" (Threshold #883906; 1986; #9), all earned gold or platinum awards for sales.

FRANK HOFFMANN

MOOG, ROBERT (1934–)

Born in Flushing, New York, Moog was interested in electronic musical instrument design even as a youngster, and following instructions in an electronics magazine, built a theremin when he was only 14 years of age, and published an article about building theremins when he was only 19. His academic degrees include a B.S. in physics from Queens College, a B.S. in electrical engineering from Columbia University, and a 1965 Ph.D. in engineering physics from Cornell University. In 1954, while still in school, Moog founded the R.A. Moog Co. as a part-time business to design and build electronic musical instruments, and between 1961 and 1963 he sold over 100 theremin kits, while working out of his three-room apartment. The company became a full-time business in 1964 (the year before he earned the Ph.D.), and that year it introduced a line of electronic music synthesis equipment. Significantly, Moog's was the first synthesizer to use attack-decay-sustain-release (ADSR) envelopes, set with four different knobs, which control the qualities of a sound's onset, intensity, and fade. Moog's synthesizers were designed in collaboration with composers Herbert A. Deutsch and Walter (later Wendy) Carlos, and after the success of Carlos's album *Switched on Bach*, entirely recorded using Moog synthesizers, Moog's instruments made the leap from the electronic avant-garde into commercially successful popular music. In 1971, after being sold to a private investor, the name of the company was changed to Moog Music, Inc., and in 1973 the company became a division of Norlin Music, Inc. Moog served as president of the Moog branch, mainly designing guitar effects and guitar amplifiers, until 1977. In 1978, he and his family moved to Asheville, North Carolina, and there he founded Big Briar, Inc., for the purpose of designing and building novel electronic music equipment, especially new types of performance control devices. At the

International Computer Music Conference in 1982, he introduced the multiple-touch-sensitive keyboard, developed with John Eaton of Indiana University. From 1984 to 1988, Moog was also a full-time consultant and vice president of new product research for Kurzweil Music Systems. At the present time, Big Briar's activities include building theremins, MIDI interfaces, and electronic musical instrument kits. Moog's awards include honorary doctorates from Polytechnic University and Lycoming College, as well as the Silver Medal of The Audio Engineering Society, the Trustee's award of the National Academy of Recording Arts and Sciences, *Billboard* magazine's Trendsetter award, and the SEAMUS award from the Society of Electroacoustic Music in the United States. He has written and spoken widely on topics related to music technology, and has contributed major articles to the *Encyclopaedia Britannica* and the *Encyclopedia of Applied Physics*. In 2002, Moog won a Grammy for technical achievement.

HOWARD FERSTLER

MOOGK, EDWARD B. (15 JULY 1914–18 DEC 1979)

Canadian librarian and discographer, born in Weston, Ontario. Moogk had a career as a drummer with dance bands. He founded and developed the recorded sound collection at the National Library of Canada. From 1945 to 1970 he had a radio show that featured old recordings. From the name of the show he took the title of his acclaimed book, *Roll Back the Years/En remontant les années* (1975), a detailed history of recorded sound in Canada up to 1930. He died in London, Ontario, before he could complete a second volume.

MOONLIGHT TRIO

A vocal group that recorded two Edison Diamond Discs in 1918. "Rose of No Man's Land" was one of them (#80434). Members were Gladys Rice, George Wilton Ballard, and Thomas Chalmers.

MOORER, JAMES A. (25 NOV 1925–)

Moorer earned an S.B. degree in applied mathematics from MIT in 1968, and had already picked up an S.B. degree in electrical engineering from the same university in 1967. He went on to earn a Ph.D. in computer science from Stanford University in 1975, and is a founder and director of advanced development at Sonic Solutions. He is an internationally known figure in digital audio and computer music, with over 40 technical

publications and two patents to his credit. He personally designed and wrote much of the SonicSystem and developed the advanced DSP algorithms for the NoNOISE process, which is used to restore vintage recordings for CD remastering. To date, NoNOISE has been used in the production of over 50,000 CDs. While vice president of research and development at Lucasfilm Droid Works between 1980 and 1987, he designed the Audio Signal Processor (ASP), which was used in the production of sound tracks for *Return of the Jedi*, *Indiana Jones and the Temple of Doom*, and other high-impact films. Between 1977 and 1979, he was a researcher and the scientific advisor to IRCAM in Paris. In the mid-1970s he was codirector and cofounder of the Stanford Center for Computer Research in Music and Acoustics. In 1990, he received the Audio Engineering Society (AES) Silver award for Lifetime Achievement and in 1999 he received the Academy of Motion Picture Arts and Sciences Scientific and Engineering award for his pioneering work in the design of digital signal processing and its application to audio editing for film. Moorer is currently working at Adobe Systems, Inc. as senior computer scientist in the DVD team.

HOWARD FERSTLER

MORGAN, CORINNE, CA. (1874–1945)

American contralto, singer of opera, operetta, and popular songs. She recorded for Edison in 1902, beginning with "Whisper and I Shall Hear" (#8223); by 1905 she had 20 other solos plus duets with Frank Stanley, all of these being popular songs. She also made 17 Columbia 10-inch discs during 1902–1906, and around 50 Victor discs between 1903 and 1908. Zonophone also recorded Morgan, with 17 discs in 1902–1905. There were two Busy Bee cylinders also, in 1904–1905. Her final records were for Emerson in 1921. On Victor she did opera and oratorio numbers as well as pop material. One of the best received Victors was "When You and I Were Young, Maggie" with Frank Stanley (#2533). She also recorded as a member of the Lyric Quartet in 1906–1910, and with the Peerless Quartet. [Walsh 1971/7–9.]

MORODER, GIORGIO (26 APR 1940–)

Known mainly for his musical accomplishments, but a modern Renaissance man if there ever was one, Moroder was born in Ortisei, Val Gardena, Italy, started playing guitar when he was 16 or 17, and left both school and home at 19 to play in a dance-group band, touring Europe with them for more than five years. In 1967, in Berlin, he quit touring and concentrated on songwriting, and also polished his recording/producing skills. Between 1967 and 1979 he produced a number of hits, including material by Michael Holm, Ricky Shane, and most famously, Donna Summer, and in 1979 he won an Oscar and a Golden Globe award for the theme song for the movie *Midnight Express*. In the 1980s, in addition to doing production work in New York and Los Angeles and writing songs for Summer, David Bowie, Kenny Loggins, Elton John, and Blondie, he produced neon sculptures and had several exhibitions of his works. He even helped to design an ultraexotic sports car with Claudio Zampolli, designed several pieces of architecture, and has helped produce recordings by Barbra Streisand, Janet Jackson, Roger Miller, Roger Daltry (of the Who), and Pat Benatar, among many others. In 1984 he won his second Oscar and two Golden Globes with the song *Flashdance* (*What a Feeling*), and in 1987 he took his third Oscar and fourth Golden Globe with the track *Take My Breath Away* from the movie *Top Gun*. In the 1990s, he continued to work as a songwriter, artist, and producer, and also experimented with computer art and film. In 1998 he won his third Grammy for a production of *Carry On*, with Summer. During his career, Moroder has produced over 100 golden and platinum discs.

HOWARD FERSTLER

MORRIS, DOUG (1939–)

Born in New York City, Morris has been a major record executive, first at the Warner music group and then at Universal. After graduating from Columbia University, Morris worked as a songwriter in the early 1960s, becoming a producer for the pop label Laurie Records in 1965. He left Laurie in 1970 to form his own Big Tree Records in partnership with Atlantic in 1970; Atlantic bought the label in 1978 and made Morris head of its Atco division. In 1980 he was named head of Atlantic, and in 1990 co-chair of Warner Elektra Atlantic (WEA). He became WEA's CEO in 1994. However, after a long run at Warner, Morris was summarily fired in June 1995 in a shakeup at the label; he subsequently sued for wrongful termination. By that November, he was hired by the newly formed Universal Music Group, then owned by Seagram. He oversaw the acquisition of PolyGram records, as well as the innovative Interscope label, and then the sale of Universal to Vivendi, the French conglomerate, in 2000.

MORRIS, ELIDA
(12 NOV 1886–25 DEC 1977)

American soprano and comedienne, born in Philadelphia. She started out in minstrel shows, then went on the Keith vaudeville circuit doing Black dialect songs; thence to the opera stage. In 1913 she scored a great success in a 10-week run in Britain, and for several years after that she divided her time between Britain and America; she also toured South Africa. Her first records were for Columbia in 1910, beginning with "You'll Come Back" (#A826). In August 1910 she recorded for Victor, "Angel Eyes" — a duet with Billy Murray (#5782). Her most famous record for Victor was "Stop! Stop! Stop!" (#16687; 1911); she did the same piece for Columbia (#A953; 1912). Morris left Victor in 1913, and worked for Pathé and Columbia. She had a hit record in 1914: "High Cost of Loving"/"I Want to Go Back to Michigan" (Columbia #A1592). Morris continued on stage into the 1960s. She died in Santa Barbara, California. [Walsh 1963/1–4.]

MORTON, EDDIE
(15 MAY 1870–11 APR 1938)

American comedian, born in Philadelphia. He was a policeman in Philadelphia, and was known as "the singing cop" in vaudeville. He recorded for Victor from 1907–1913, beginning with "Mariutch" (#5220) and "That's Gratitude" (#31661). "Don't Take Me Home" was a Morgan favorite that he offered on Edison (#9949; 1908) and for Columbia, Victor, and Zonophone. One of his funniest records was "If He Comes In I'm Goin' Out" (Victor #16650). His all-time best seller was "Oceana Roll" (#16908; 1911) — but much of the sales impetus came from the B-side, "Alexander's Ragtime Band" by Arthur Collins and Byron Harlan. Morton's last Victor record was one of the best: "Noodle Soup Rag"/"Isch ka bibble"; he made a final Columbia record in 1914, then some Emersons in 1916. He died in Wildwood, New Jersey.

MORTON, JELLY ROLL
(20 OCT 1890– 10 JULY 1941)

American jazz pianist, one of the pioneers of jazz composition and arrangement, born Ferdinand Joseph LaMothe (Morton was his stepfather's name) in Gulfport, Louisiana. He played in the brothels of New Orleans until around 1906, then moved up to New York by 1911 and Chicago by 1914. After further travel he settled in Chicago in 1923. Morton began to record in 1923, with an orchestra of his own, doing "Big Foot Ham" for Paramount (#12050) followed by "Muddy Water Blues"; and then appearing with the New Orleans Rhythm Kings in "Sobbin' Blues" (Gennett 5219; 1923), followed by "Clarinet Marmalade" and "Mr. Jelly Lord" on the same date.

He did more Gennett records in Richmond, Indiana, on the next day, then went on to work for various labels. Morton was one of the first artists to make electrical recordings for the Autograph label in 1924. From 1926 he was with Victor in Chicago with his Red Hot Peppers group and made his finest discs. "Black Bottom Stomp" has become legendary (Victor #20221; 1926), and most of his records of that period are classics. These and later somewhat less exciting records made in New York, are included on *Great Original Performances* (BBC #604). Alan Lomax recorded Morton's piano playing and reminiscences for the Library of Congress in 1938 (later issued in the 1950s on several LPs by Riverside, and then in the 1990s on CD by Rounder Records). This led to a small revival in interest in Morton and a few commercial recording sessions. Some of his best solo piano performances, made for the General label in 1939, are on Commodore #8-24062. However, his health was failing, and Morton died in Los Angeles two years later.

MOSAIC (LABEL)

An American record company founded in 1983 in Santa Monica, California, by record producer Michael Cuscuna and Blue Note executive Charlie Lourie. Currently located in Stamford, Connecticut, the label is devoted to re-releasing vintage jazz recordings in limited-edition boxed sets. Previously unissued and alternate takes are often included. Each set comes with a new artist biography, as well as photographs, discographical information, and reproduced jazz press on the artist. The label has issued sets of Mildred Bailey, Duke Ellington, Curtis Fuller, Woody Herman, Hank Mobley, Anita O'Day, Woody Shaw, and Lennie Tristano. It is now a part of Capitol/EMI Group, and has been combined with the Blue Note label. [website: www.mosaicrecords.com.] [Morgenstern 1983.]

JULIA SCOTT

MOST, MICKIE
(JUNE 1938–30 MAY 2003)

Born Michael Peter Hayes in Aldershot, England (a London suburb), Most was an important rock producer/impresario of the 1960s and 1970s. He began his career in the late 1950s singing in the British pop group, the Most Brothers, where he earned his new surname. In 1959, he relocated to South Africa, working there for four years leading his own group, the Playboys, who had hits with covers of U.S. rock songs like "Johnny B. Goode." On his return to England, he moved from performing to producing, signing a then-unknown Newcastle group, the Animals, to a production deal in late 1963. With their hit "House of the Rising Sun" in 1964, Most was launched, and he oversaw all of their mid-1960s hits, also supervising the first hits of Herman's Hermits and the Nashville Teens. In 1965, he signed a five-year production deal with the U.S. branch of Columbia Records, producing their British Invasion acts, including folk-turned-pop-star Donovan, guitar hero Jeff Beck, and actress/singer Lulu. In 1970, he established his own RAK studio and label, which for the next decade was consistently successful producing hits on the U.K. charts for acts including guitarist Chris Spedding, the teen-pop rocker Suzi Quatro, and the disco act Hot Chocolate ("You Sexy Thing"). Most achieved additional fame by appearing as a panelist on the popular BBC program, *New Faces*, through the 1970s. Most sold the RAK label catalog to EMI in 1983, and was semiretired thereafter, although he continued to operate his studio as an independent. In 1995, he was named one of "Britain's Richest 500" by the [London] *Sunday Times*. He died of cancer in London.

CARL BENSON

MOTEN, BENNIE
(13 NOV 1894–2 APR 1935)

American jazz pianist and bandleader, born in Kansas City, Missouri. His ensemble, established in 1923, was "progenitor of the black Swing-Era orchestras, as epitomized by the Basie band in the mid-to-late 1930s" [Schuller 1976]. Moten and Basie were the bands that carried on the Kansas City style. (Count Basie was pianist with Moten before setting up his own group.) Ben Webster, Walter Page, and Jimmy Rushing were among the artists in the Moten band of 1932, when they recorded their most remarkable sides, all for Victor on 13 Dec: "Toby" "Moten Swing" (#23384), "Blue Room" (#24381), and seven others. Moten died in Kansas City; following his death, Basie took over the ensemble, then formed his own band, using some of the Moten personnel. His complete recordings as a leader are collected on the Classics label on four individual CDs, and have been reissued in part by various other (primarily European reissue) labels.

MOTHER GOOSE BOOK

A children's book including two unbreakable six-inch discs, sold for $.50 in November 1921 by the Cabinet and Accessories Co. of New York. Oliver Goldsmith was president of the company.

FRANK ANDREWS

MOTHER GOOSE RECORDS

In 1920 the Talking Book Corp. of New York released sets of records with books for children. The records were pressed in Atlanta by the Southern States Phonograph Co. and distributed by the Emerson Phonograph Co. Imported to Britain and sold there by the Herman Darewski Publishing Co., they were still being marketed in 1922. [Andrews 1988/4.]

See also **Kiddy Record (Label)**

MOTION PICTURE MUSIC

There were various systems in the early days of the film that provided mood music related to action on the screen. The photoplayer arrived around 1912. It was an orchestrion with various special effects under operator control. These were made by the North Tonawanda Musical Instrument Co., Rudolph Wurlitzer Co., Justus Seeburg, American Photoplayer Co., The Operators Piano Co., Chicago, Lyon & Healy, and the Automatic Music Co. (later the Link Piano Co.). The photoplayer thrived until around 1923. Only a few of the thousands made have survived.

MOTION PICTURE SOUND RECORDING

The first motion pictures with any kind of sound added to them were shown in Thomas Edison's laboratory, in West Orange, New Jersey, on 6 Oct 1889. The system, developed by William Kennedy Dickson, used a cylinder synchronization device. Running about 12 seconds, at 46 frames per second, the resulting films included Dickson's own voice giving a greeting to Edison. That was the forerunner of Edison's Kinetophone, developed in a 1912 version to the point of making short subjects and selling the system to theaters. In 1897 George W. Brown claimed invention of a device to synchronize the projector with the phonograph; in 1900 Léon Gaumont made the first practical synchronizer, linking the projector and phonograph electrically. He presented a filmed speech to the Société Française de la Photographie in November 1902, with a type of Auxetophone amplifier. (His product was sold in America by the Gaumont Co., under the trade name Chronophone, in 1904.) Oskar Messter in Germany had similar success in 1903–1904. Other systems of synchronizers were Viviphone (1907), Cameraphone (1908), Synchronoscope (1908), and Cinephone (Britain, 1909). All of these early systems faced the same problems: (1) getting the synchronization exactly right and keeping it so throughout the showing, (2) coping with the short playing time of early records, (3) and finding ways to enhance the phono-

graphic volume to fill a theater. While these difficulties were being researched, the main use of the phonograph in the early theaters was to bring customers in as it played through large horns that projected through the wall into the street. In 1903 Eugen Lauste demonstrated a method of getting sound from film through photographed sound waves, with the light passing through the film onto a selenium cell. He gained British patents and gave successful demonstrations, but did not do well commercially. The soundtrack idea, with the sound inscribed on the film with the pictures, was patented in 1919 by Theodore W. Case. Lee De Forest joined in the research, acquiring the Case patent and improving the quality of voice and music reproduction. He made a stock of short films by comedians and musicians, under the name of Phonofilms, by 1925, including one by Al Jolson, *Sonny Boy*. The first Mickey Mouse cartoon with sound, *Steamboat Willie* (1928), used this method. William Fox used the system in Movietone News short subjects, shown first in 1927 in New York and London. The British Talking Picture Corp. used the De Forest system in early Pathé newsreels. The concept of the soundtrack (a strip on the film, 0.1-inch wide) replaced the idea of the synchronized disc by 1928. Ortofon, a Danish company was also working on a system for putting sound into motion picture presentations. By 1923 they were able to demonstrate a sound film, using the "variable area" method that required two films run simultaneously — one carrying the audio, the other the video. The method was licensed in Europe and America. Edison's sound film research had been detoured by a fire in the plant in 1914, plus there were difficulties with the unions and Edison's own multitude of other activities. Indeed, he had lost interest in the Kineteophone project by 1915. Meanwhile, Bell Telephone Laboratories made some improvements. One was the reduction of record speed from 78 rpm to 33 1/3 rpm to give more playing time in the synchronized system. They also developed amplifiers and large horns to extend the sound range. Bell's process was called Vitaphone, an inadvertent use of an old company name. Vitaphone discs were lateral cut, center-start items, 12 to 16 inches in diameter, and running 33 1/3 rpm. The Vitaphone Corp., under contract with Warner Bros., made a series of short subjects (four to 10 minutes each) between 1926 and 1932; they included work by Giovanni Martinelli, Mischa Elman, Harold Bauer, and Efrem Zimbalist. Vitaphones were shown in New York in February 1926, and on 5 Oct 1927 the famous Al Jolson film, *The Jazz Singer*, premiered. This feature-length motion picture, the first with speech, ushered in the era of talking pictures. When it was released there were about 100 theaters in the U.S. that were equipped to show sound films, out of about 7,500 Warner Bros.

Malcolm Arnold conducts the orchestra during the recording of the soundtrack for William Walton's film, *The Battle of Britain,* 1969. © Hulton-Deutsch Collection/CORBIS

houses. By the end of 1929 there were some 4,000 theaters with sound installation. During the 1930s there were many areas of progress. Reliable film-drive systems were developed, noise reduction was achieved, postsynchronizing in the studio rather than on location, and various improvements in theater installations and in sound reproducing apparatus. In 1940, Disney even released a sound film, *Fantasia,* in multichannel form. After World War II magnetic recording became operational for motion picture use. When wide-screen films were made in the early 1950s, soundtracks were made on a separate three-track magnetic coated film. Those soundtracks were then dubbed onto the film print itself. Cinemascope carried three tracks 63 mm wide and one track 29 mm wide. The Todd-A-O system used six magnetic tracks on 70 mm film. With most of these systems, there were three to five separate channels up front, with one surround channel feeding a multitude of speakers along the side walls of the theater. However, many theater owners could not afford to install systems elaborate enough to deal with such source material. In the late 1970s, Dolby introduced Dolby Surround Sound to the movie industry, which allowed theaters with more modest budgets to deliver

exemplary full-theater sound. The most famous film to make use of this new technology was *Star Wars,* released in 1977, but *A Star Is Born,* released in 1976, actually was the first widely released movie to make use of the technology. The sonic impressiveness of *Star Wars* did, however, allow the technology to grab people's attention, and after that action movies were not really action movies without surround sound. The Dolby system was carried over into video tapes and laser discs for home-theater use, which further enhanced the public's interest in surround sound. Somewhat later, Lucasfilm Corporation attempted to standardize theater-sound parameters by introducing the THX program. By allowing theaters to achieve THX "certification" after an appropriate upgrading of playback hardware and an inspection by THX officials (these were to be done at intervals, to ensure continuous adherence to the THX theater-sound standards), a theater was allowed to advertise its superior sound system, further whetting the public's appetite for superior theater sound. The THX program was later expanded to include home-theater hardware and software. Modern theater sound has for the most part become digital, with six-channel software technologies (five satellite channels, plus a subwoofer channel for low-frequency effects) available from several companies, including Dolby, Digital Theater Systems, Sony, and for a while, even Eastman Kodak. The Sony and DTS systems even allowed for as many as seven or even eight satellite channels. With these systems, there would continue to be three to five channels up front, with the surround feed split into two or even three separate channels, allowing for often stupendous theater surround effects. In the late 1990s, these digital systems also became available to the home theater industry as part of the DVD system. [Ferstler 1997; Ford Spring 1962, Autumn 1962; Geduld 1975; Shaman 1991.]

REV. HOWARD FERSTLER

MOTOWN (LABEL)

Perhaps the most successful label ever run by a Black entrepreneur, Motown defined a pop style and sound that, second to British Invasion groups like the Beatles, dominated the charts in the 1960s. The label was the brainchild of ex-boxer, automobile assembly-line worker, and sometime-songwriter Berry Gordy, Jr. Gordy began working with local singer/songwriter Jackie Wilson in the mid-1950s. Eager to strike out on his own, Gordy began producing a local singer, Marv Johnson (b. Detroit, Michigan, 15 Oct 1938–16 May 1993), first for the small independent Kudo label, and then, in 1959, for his newly formed Tamla label. Another aspiring songwriter and singer from Detroit, Smokey Robinson, became Gordy's right-hand man in his growing empire, which including Robinson's group, The Miracles, who produced Motown's first major hit, "Shop Around" (Tamla #54034; #1 R&B, #2 pop) in 1960. Other early signings included the Marvelettes (with the #1 pop and R&B hit, "Please Mr. Postman" [Tamla #54046] in 1961) and the Temptations. Besides Motown and Tamla, Gordy also issued records under the Gordy and Anna labels in the early days. From the start, Gordy aimed his product at the white pop charts, as well as the traditional R&B audience. He emulated the sound, makeup and costuming, and general presentation of the successful white pop groups of the day in the packaging of his performers, who were all carefully groomed, taught stage presence and dance routines, and even given speech and etiquette lessons, all in an effort to market Motown's offerings to the mainstream. Gordy discovered numerous important singers and songwriters through the mid-1960s, including vocal groups like the Supremes and the Four Tops (and later the Jackson 5) and performers like Stevie Wonder, Marvin Gaye, and Mary Wells. The label was a veritable hit-making

factory, dubbed "Hitsville U.S.A.," by Gordy. However, Gordy's empire was beginning to come apart by the early 1970s. His artists were insisting on more control over their product, and he was losing valuable staff musicians and producers. An attempt to form a rock label, Rare Earth, in 1970 fizzled, and in 1973 the label moved to Hollywood as Gordy turned his attention to films, beginning with the Diana Ross starring vehicle, *Lady Sings the Blues* (very loosely based on Billie Holiday's autobiography). Despite success in the 1970s with the Commodores, and early 1980s with Lionel Ritchie, the label survived basically through reissuing its back catalog. In 1988, Motown's holdings were sold to MCA; the catalog today is controlled by the Universal Music Group.

CARL BENSON

MOTTOLA, TOMMY (14 JULY 1949–)

Born in the Bronx, New York, Tommy Mottola headed Columbia Records (later Sony Music) in the U.S. from 1988–2002, fostering many major hitmakers for the label. Like many other teenagers, Mottola had dreams of becoming a rock star, beginning to play guitar in a local band, the Exotics, at the age of 14. In his early 20s, he recorded for Epic Records under the name of T.D. Valentine, while also taking jobs at various music companies. Hearing the new duo Hall & Oates, he signed on as their manager in 1974, securing them an unheard of 25 percent interest in their publishing, performing, and recording income. This lead to a career as a major manager. He moved on to manage other major acts, including Carly Simon and John Cougar Mellencamp. Recognized by Columbia Records president Walter Yetnikoff, Mottola is made head of Columbia in 1988, and helps arrange Sony's purchase of the label in that same year. Mottola's major discoveries at Columbia include pop chanteuse Mariah Carey, who he signed during his first year at the label, and then married in 1993 after overseeing her initial success (they divorced five years later). Mottola also brought Pearl Jam, Celine Dion, Lauryn Hill, and Jennifer Lopez to the label. Mottola has often been featured in the gossip columns because of his high-prolife social life. In summer 2002, Michael Jackson surprised the music industry and media commentators when he lashed out at Mottola, accusing him of racism because of the poor performance of his then-current album. He led a brief campaign against the label head, riding a bus around New York City following a press conference, leading a group in a chant of "Down with Tommy Mottola." Facing increasing pressure to cut costs, Mottola announced in early 2003 that he was stepping down as head of Sony Music to start his own label.

CARL BENSON

MOUTRIE (S.) AND CO., LTD.
According to a notice in *TMW* in 1906, a jobber with an office in Shanghai; he was an agent for Victor, and perhaps other firms.

MOXIE (LABEL)
An American record, known in just one issue. It was an advertising record for a soft drink named Moxie, made by Gennett in New York in late 1921. Arthur Fields sings on one side, and Harry Raderman's orchestra does a dance number on the flip side. A bottle of the beverage is shown on the label. [Rust 1978.]

MOYSE, MARCEL
(17 MAY 1889–1 NOV 1984)
French flutist and conductor, born in Saint Amour, one of the leading performers on the instrument in the 20th century. He studied at the Paris Conservatory from age 15, then — after playing in several orchestras — he returned there as a professor in 1932. Meanwhile, he was flutist for the Opéra-Comique in Paris in 1913–1938. In 1913 he accompanied Nellie Melba on a tour of the U.S. During the 1920s he gave the premieres of works by Ravel, Debussy, and Ibert. His earliest records were made in 1926. He and Adolph Busch revived several works by J.S. Bach in the 1930s and recorded them: the Second Orchestral Suite (Victor #11996; 1936) and the Fifth Brandenburg Concerto (Columbia #68442; 1935) among them. He performed in a trio with Busch and Rudolf Serkin. In 1949 he moved to the U.S. and helped organize the Marlboro Festival in Vermont. He was still conducting when in his 90s. He died in Brattleboro, Vermont. Moyse's major recordings were reissued on Seraphim (#60357 in America) and World Records (#SHB-68 in Britain).

MOZART TALKING MACHINE CO.
A St. Louis firm established in 1916. It made the Mozart line of record players in seven models, and a vertical-cut record with the label name Mozart.

MP3
MP3 or, in long-hand, layer 3 MPEG compression, is a protocol for compressing digital music files without

Apple IPOD MP3 player. Courtesy Apple Computers, Inc.

loss of sound quality. Music from a compact disc transferred to a computer in pure digital form is known as a wave (or in PC-speak a wav) file where one minute of music occupies approximately 10 megabytes of data and drive space. The advent of MP3 allowed such files to be compressed to 10 percent of their original size. Not only did this make them easier to play back on a computer (smaller files being quicker and easier to manage) but it also made them easier to transfer. Attaching an MP3 file to an e-mail for example made it possible to send an entire CD-quality music track around the world in seconds. The music industry was transformed as a result of this new file format. An underground consumer culture for "ripping" (the process of extracting audio from MPs as audio) and "burning" (recording received files on to normal audio CDs) took firm hold. New systems such as peer-to-peer networking (a famous example being Napster) also sprung up as illegal MP3 "sharing" (i.e., bootlegging) portals. With the seemingly impossible task of clamping down on MP3 music piracy, the music industry has been working frantically to develop its own fee-based, file-sharing services. Some switched-on record companies have embraced the concept by putting time and energy into promoting and talent scouting artists via MP3 files on public websites. The coexistence of this and established formats such as CD remains to be seen.

IAN PEEL

MS (MID/SIDE) STEREO RECORDING TECHNIQUE

SEE COINCIDENT STEREO RECORDING

MUCK, KARL
(22 OCT 1859–3 MAR 1940)

German conductor, born in Darmstadt. He pursued an academic course and took a doctorate in classical philology, also studying piano at Leipzig Conservatory. After conducting in several opera houses, he became the first conductor of the Berlin Opera in 1892. Muck was conductor of the Wagnerian repertoire at Covent Garden in 1899, and director of *Parsifal* at Bayreuth in 1901 (he directed most of the *Parsifal* performances there until 1930). From 1906 to 1908 he directed the Boston Symphony Orchestra, then returned to Germany, and returned to a permanent appointment in Boston in 1912. There was concern about his German sympathies, and he was interned as an enemy alien in 1918. After the World War I he returned to Germany, directing the Hamburg Philharmonic in 1922–1933. He also conducted at Bayreuth. Then he went to Stuttgart, where he died. Muck's fame onstage and in recordings rests with his Wagnerian interpretations. His finest records are the *Parsifal* excerpts made in Bayreuth in 1927 for Columbia (#L2007-2011), reissued on Pearl (OPALCDS #9843; 1990). But he had begun to record 10 years earlier, for Victor, with the Boston Symphony. His first disc was the Tchaikovsky Symphony No. 4 Finale (Victor #74553). From 1927 to 1929 Muck worked for HMV in Berlin. He recorded numbers from seven Wagner operas.

MULLIGAN, GERRY
(6 APR 1927–19 JAN 1996)

Gerald Joseph Mulligan, born in New York City, was a baritone saxophonist, composer, and bandleader. He began his career as an arranger, first for Gene Krupa and then with the experimental band of Claude Thornhill, in which he briefly played alto sax. Mulligan combined a very original style of composition and arranging with his playing, but it was in the Miles Davis *Birth of the Cool* (Capitol #762) seminal album of 1949–1950, with fellow arranger Gil Evans, that the two sides of Mulligan's work first found a suitable balance. As an arranger, Mulligan was among the first to attempt to adapt the language of bop for big band. He achieved a measure of success with both Krupa (who found Mulligan "a kind of temperamental guy who wanted to expound a lot of his ideas") and Thornhill, but for all the variety of his later work, as writer and as performer, Mulligan retains the colors and effects of his 1950s quartets in which he explored the possibilities of scoring and improvising jazz in a low-key, seemingly subdued manner with complex lines that always retained a rich, melodic approach. Mulligan fronted his own 10-piece band on disc in the early 1950s, then began a musical association with Chet Baker in 1952 (documented on *Best of the Gerry Mulligan Quartet with Chet Baker* [Pacific Jazz #95481, 1991]). When Baker quit (1953), Mulligan formed other quartets, notably with trombonist Bob Brookmeyer in the mid-1950s, and became a proponent of the California "cool jazz" movement. Although the quartet format dominated Mulligan's work during this part of his career, he occasionally formed larger groups, sometimes working with veteran saxophonist Ben Webster on recordings and in concert. Early in the 1960s, Mulligan formed his Concert Jazz Band, which was periodically revived. He interspersed this with directing groups of various sizes, working and recording with other leaders, including a long stint in Dave Brubeck's quartet, 1968–1972, and in frequently rewarding partnerships with musicians such as Paul Desmond, Stan Getz, Johnny Hodges, Zoot Sims, and Thelonious Monk. In the early 1970s, Mulligan led big bands, a series of jazz ensembles with Mulligan playing saxophones and piano, and small groups for worldwide concert tours, recording sessions, and radio and television appearances. The 1980s and early 1990s saw him following a similar pattern, sometimes expanding the size of the big band, sometimes content to work in the intimate setting of a quartet or a quintet. A highlight of this period was his performance at *All Star White House Tribute to Duke Ellington* (Blue Note #35249, 1969). In 1981, his album *Walk on the Water* (DRG #5194), a big-band recording, was awarded a Grammy for Best Jazz Large Ensemble Recording. After his death, several Mulligan discs were released, mostly containing reissues of previously recorded material. One that contained material from his last years is *Art of Gerry Mulligan: The Final Recordings* (Telarc Jazz #83517, 2000), consisting of previously released material recorded between 1993 and 1995. Mulligan was inducted into the Jazz Hall of Fame in 1991 and into the Down Beat Hall of Fame the next year. He died in Darien, Connecticut.

MARTIN. J. MANNING

MULLIN, JOHN, T. (JACK)
(5 OCT 1913– 24 JUNE 1999)

Born in San Francisco and growing up in Larkspur in Marin County, Mullin graduated from Santa Clara

University in what is today Silicon Valley, with a major in electrical engineering. He was a member of the U.S. Army Signal Corps during World War II, and during the postwar occupation in Germany he visited a studio near Frankfurt that was occupied by the Allies and was shown a small storehouse of magnetic quarter-inch tape and machines. He had already suspected that the Germans had some kind of superior recording device from his monitoring experiences when he was stationed in England, and the device he discovered that was most important was the high-fidelity version of the German AEG Magnetophon K-4 audio tape recorder, a machine with extremely low distortion and a frequency response, almost matching the human hearing range. Getting official permission to send home samples of what he felt was important, he shipped 50 reels of tape, head assemblies, and two of the tape transports back to America (in pieces in multiple mailbags), and later worked to improve the technology. In October 1946, at a meeting of studio executives, Mullin used his modified Magnetophone recorders to demonstrate how the new recording technology worked. Soon Bing Crosby, who hated the pressure of live broadcasting, started using the then revolutionary technology to pretape his radio show for ABC. The show included laugh tracks, which Mullin also invented. Previous to Mullin, prerecorded programs (usually done on 16-inch transcription discs) presented terrible sound quality. His new technology, which not only allowed for production during convenient time periods, but also allowed for scissors-and-tape editing that removed bloopers, revolutionized the industry and set a precedent in broadcast production that remains the norm to this day. Mullin's prototype machines proved the feasibility of the new tape technology to Ampex Corp., a small northern California company that then decided to become the first American manufacturer of the Mullin-enhanced German technology. The result was the Model 200A, and later the Model 300, tape recorders, which went on to revolutionize the entertainment and information industries. Mullin went on to work for Minicom, a division of 3M, and helped to formulate many recording industry standards, including the NAB equalization curve that is still in use for analog recording. He remained Minicom's chief engineer until his retirement in 1975. At that time, he began a second career of voluntary teaching, writing, and lecturing, in addition to helping to work out recording technology for the blind and dyslexic. He created over 2,000 hours of books on tape that now reside at the university library at Princeton and that are still nationally distributed to the reading-impaired. He also created one of the finest collections of historic entertainment technology available, including radios, recorders, microphones, tapes,

and discs. The Mullin Museum is now a part of the Pavek Museum of Broadcasting in St. Louis Park, Minnesota, near 3M in St. Paul. For his work in recording technology, the Audio Engineering Society presented him with numerous awards, including the organization's Silver Medal, in 1994.

HOWARD FERSTLER

MULTINOLA

An automatic record player, advertised in 1909 as capable of handling 16 four-minute cylinder records in succession. The user had a choice of hearing one of the cylinders, or a disc record. In 1911 The American Multinola Co., The Arcade [Euclid Ave.], Cleveland, was named as the manufacturer. It sold home models as well as coin-ops.

MULTIPHONE

The first selective coin-op phonograph, available in Britain from the late 1890s into the early 1900s, and in the U.S. from 1905. W. Mayer and Co., trading as the Multiphone Co., sold the machines in U.K. Multiphones had five-inch mandrels to accommodate six-inch long cylinders. The Multiphone Operating Co., New York, sold the machines in the U.S. They each held 24 cylinders on a ferris wheel device, in a cabinet around seven feet high. John C. Dunton was the inventor of the feed mechanism (U.S. patent #797,102; filed 28 Nov 1904; granted 15 Aug 1905). A patron could turn the wheel to the desired cylinder, crank up the spring motor, then insert a coin to hear the selection. The lack of an electric motor contributed to the failure of the enterprise in 1908 or 1909. [Hoover 1971 has illustrations; Koenigsberg 1990.]

MULTIPLEX GRAND

The earliest multitrack recording device was shown by Columbia at the Paris Exposition of June 1900. It was an invention of Thomas Hood Macdonald (U.S. patent #711,706; filed 11 June 1898; granted 21 Oct 1902), the "first attempt at single-record stereo recording" [Koenigsberg]. The machine "simultaneously recorded three separately spaced tracks and played them back on a five-inch diameter cylinder (14 inches long) through three 56-inch long brass horns" [Koenigsberg]. None of the records made are extant, and only parts of one machine are known to survive. The Shah of Iran bought one in 1901, for $1,000. [Koenigsberg 1990.]

MULTIPLEXER

A switching circuit in an audio system that makes possible the serial transfer of signals from various sources in a defined sequence intended for a single output.

MULTITRACK RECORDING

The use of two or more multiple tracks of recorded sound to create a composite audio recording from separately recorded parts. Prior to the introduction of multitrack recording, music performances were usually recorded as complete performances in real time. The introduction of two-track stereo recording in the early 1940s permitted two tracks to be recorded separately and then mixed to create a composite recording. This was the generally accepted practice by the late 1960s. Multitrack recording originated with the use of multiple track tape recorders and is currently emulated by digital studio recorders using magnetic, optical, and other computer media. Experiments in multiple track recording began soon after the magnetic tape recorder became available in the United States following World War II. Some notable achievements in the early history of multitrack recording included:

1931, England. Alan Blumlein of Columbia Graphophone Co. applied for a patent for a binaural or two-channel sound system, an early conception of stereophonic sound recording.

1936, United States. Unaware of Blumhein's earlier work in England, Arthur Keller of Bell Labs applies for a patent for single-groove stereo. A similar approach was used by Westrex in the 1950s when single-groove two-channel stereo recording and reproduction became widespread.

1940, United States. Earlier experiments by A.C. Keller and I.S. Rafuse of AT&T led to the first U.S. two-channel, single-groove stereo recording system. The first commercial use of stereo sound was in movie theaters when the Walt Disney Studios released the movie *Fantasia*.

1953, United States. Raymond Scott builds two multitrack tape recorders. His patented machines could record 7 and 14 parallel tracks on a single reel of tape.

1953, Germany. In the newly opened electronic music studio of West German Radio (WDR) in Cologne, founders Meyer-Eppler, Beyer, and Eimert equipped the studio of a four-track tape recorder.

1954, United States. Guitar player and instrument designer Les Paul built a prototype eight-track multitrack tape recorder.

1955, Canada. Hugh Le Caine invented the Special Purpose Tape Recorder that mixed six separate but synchronized tapes down to one track. The recording device was later improved and installed in the electronic music studios of the University of Toronto and McGill University in Montreal. Although inventors such as Scott and Le Caine had created sophisticated multitrack tape recorders during the 1950s, it was not until the mid-1960s that four-track machines were generally available. The Beatles' album *Sergeant Pepper's Lonely Hearts Club Band* (1967) was recorded using the painstaking process of connecting two four-track tape recorders to get eight tracks.

1956, United States. The Recording Industry Association of America (RIAA) formally adopted the Westrex system of single-groove stereo recording and reproduction as the industry standard. This made stereo records incompatible with monophonic record players, although mono records could still be played on stereophonic systems. The advent of multitrack recording spawned the related industry of noise reduction systems, most notably those made by Dolby. Dolby introduced its Type A noise reduction system in 1965. Noise reduction systems are used to reduce tape hiss associated with magnetic tape recording, a problem that is magnified by the use of multiple tape tracks. Multitrack recording using digital mixing panels can often use as many as 128 separately recorded tracks of sound.

THOM HOLMES

MUNCH, CHARLES
(26 SEP 1891–6 NOV 1968)

Alsatian conductor, born in Strasbourg. He studied violin, then conducting with Wilhelm Furtwängler. During World War I he was gassed and wounded, but resumed his career as concertmaster of the Strasbourg orchestra and of the Gewandhaus Orchestra in Leipzig. He went to Paris and organized and conducted an orchestra in 1935–1938. Then he directed the Paris Conservatory Orchestra in 1938–1946. His U.S. debut was with the Boston Symphony Orchestra in 1946; he became its permanent conductor in 1949. Munch left Boston in 1962 and became founding director of the Orchestre de Paris. He died during a tour with that ensemble in Richmond, Virginia. While he was with the Paris Conservatory Orchestra Munch made his first recordings, for HMV and Columbia. Over a period of 33 years he recorded more than 200 works by 64 composers. After World War II he worked for Decca, and made one disc that was particularly acclaimed: *Daphnis et Chloe Suite Number 2* (#K1585-1586). With the Boston orchestra he recorded extensively for RCA Victor, specializing in French composers. He made further discs of French music after leaving Boston, with several European orchestras. Several CDs have been released that cover outstanding Munch performances, including *Symphonie fantas-*

tique (RCA #7735-2-RV); *La mer* and *Nuages* (RCA #6719-2); and above all *Daphnis et Chloe* (RCA #60469-2-RG).

MURDER INC. (LABEL)

Label founded by producer/disc jockey Irv Gotti (b. Irving Lorenzo, Hollis, Queens, 1971) in 1997. The label was funded by Def Jam/Island Records, a division of the Universal Music Group. Gotti discovered and produced several rap hitmakers of the later 1990s, including DMX, Ja Rule, Jay-Z, and, in 2002, Ashanti, whose debut album broke all records for a new artist by selling 4.3 million copies. Gotti operates his own studio in New York known as The Crack House. Like many rap impresarios, Gotti has been associated with acts of violence, including a well-publicized assault in March 2000 on the rapper 50 Cent (a protégé of Eminem). He has also been linked with convicted drug dealer Supreme (b. Kenneth McGriff, Queens, New York, 1960), who has been associated with the label since his release from serving a 10-year sentence on federal narcotics charges in 1998.

CARL BENSON

MURDOCH (JOHN G.) AND CO., LTD.

A British wholesale distributor of various record labels, and also operator of a recording studio in the firm's main building in the Farringdon Road, London. The composer Albert W. Ketelbey was recording director. Columbia Indestructible (cylinder) Records were sold starting in July 1909, and Bel Canto was one of the disc labels handled. Murdoch supplemented the American repertoire coming to Indestructible by recording British artists. The early cylinders were two-minute, 100 threads/inch, but in September 1910 the new four-minute, 200 threads/inch records went on sale. An Argosy phonograph, imported from Germany by Murdoch, was sold as well, from January 1911; there were two models, each able to play both types of cylinder records. After May 1910, the Columbia name was dropped from Murdoch's advertising, but he continued to sell the indestructible records until at least 1913.

See also **Indestructible Phonographic Record Co. (III)**

FRANK ANDREWS

MURPHY, LAMBERT
(15 APR 1885–24 JULY 1954)

American tenor, born in Springfield, Massachusetts. He was a versatile artist, performing in popular quartets, church choirs, and opera. He made a debut at the Metropolitan Opera on 17 Nov 1911, and was with the company four years; his repertoire there included Wagner, and the new American operas *Mona* and *Cyrano de Bergerac*. Murphy was a leading tenor on Victor records for almost 20 years, from 1911. His first solo record was "Hmm, She Is the One Girl," sung under the name of Raymond Dixon; he made more than 200 other records for the label. Best sellers included "Mavourneen Roamin" and "Sunshine of Your Smile" (1916). In 1927 he was moved to the Red Seal series, but he was dropped from the catalog when Victor was sold to Seligman. He then sang with the American Singers on radio and records, into the early 1930s. Murphy died in Hancock, New Jersey.

MURRAY, BILLY
(25 MAY 1877–17 AUG 1954)

American singing comedian, born in Philadelphia. He is recognized as the greatest performer of his kind, having started out humbly enough in a road show based in Denver. In 1897 he made his earliest records, for Peter Bacigalupi in the Edison San Francisco office, doing duets with Matt Keefe. His first Edison solo was "I'm Thinkin' of You All the While" (#8452; 1903). He was with Field's Minstrels on the East Coast in 1903, doing ballads and coon songs, and making records for various labels. With Victor in 1904 he made the firm's all-time best seller (up to that time): "Yankee Doodle Boy" (#4229) — but he bested that sales feat in 1906 with "You're a Grand Old Flag" (#4634) and had a second great hit that year with "Cheyenne" (#4719). In 1907 he began making duets with Ada Jones. Another "all-time best seller" was recorded for Victor and Edison, "Casey Jones" with the American Quartet (Victor #16483; Edison #10499; 1911). Murray was one of the Eight Famous Victor Artists, and had a joint exclusive contract with Victor and Edison in 1909; he became a Victor exclusive in around 1922, remaining so until 1928. From 1914 to 1918 he made Edison Diamond Discs. In the 1917 Victor catalog there are over 100 titles by Murray. However, he did not adjust to electrical recording and the new crooning style, and his popularity waned after 1925. In his last years with Victor he formed Murray's Trio, with Carl Mathieu and Monroe Silver. His Victor contract was not renewed in 1928, he turned to Edison again, and Brunswick, Pathé, and others, and continued to make records until 1932. Later he was a radio actor. He made a brief comeback in 1940–1941 for Bluebird, singing "It's the Same Old Shillelagh" and a few more old favorites. He died in New York City.

MURRAY THE K
(14 FEB 1922–21 FEB 1982)

Radio personality and music promoter born Murray Kaufman, Murray the K was born to a show-business family and appeared as a child extra in several Hollywood movies of the 1930s. Beginning his radio career as a producer of live celebrity interview programs in New York City during the early 1950s, Murray moved to a show of his own, and quickly became the president of the National Conference of Disk Jockeys. As a ratings leader in New York, Murray the K worked at AM stations WMCA, WMGM, and WINS. Often known as "the fifth Beatle," Murray dominated the New York airwaves when the Beatles were embarking on the first American tour in 1964, and his work promoting and emceeing their concerts helped ensure the group's success. An innovative broadcaster, Murray the K conducted radio shows from flying airplanes and subways, and hosted a broad range of live events. Eventually moving from AM hit-radio to FM album-oriented programming, the veteran disc jockey worked at WOR-FM, and his last radio job was at WKTU, which he left to serve as a consultant for *Beatlemania*. He died after battling cancer.

BRAD HILL

MUSCLE SHOALS SOUND

SEE FAME STUDIO

MUSE (LABEL)

An American record produced by the American Record Manufacturing Co. of Framingham, Massachusetts, in 1922. It used masters from Cameo for about 100 issues, then from Plaza-Banner, Emerson, and Grey Gull. The highest Muse number was 429. Possibly the label changed name to Tremont after the Muse distributor, Kress Stores, dropped the line. [Rust 1978.]

MUSIC CORPORATION OF AMERICA

SEE MCA, INC. (MUSIC CORPORATION OF AMERICA)

MUSIC MINUS ONE (LABEL)

Music Minus One was begun in 1950 by Irv Kratka, who continues to own and operate the firm. As of 2002, its catalog includes over 700 titles, featuring all of the major concerti and chamber music selections in the classical world plus recordings of almost 80 Broadway shows in whole or part. The basic idea is simple: each recording gives a full rendition of a particular piece of music, "minus" one instrument — such as the piano or solo violin part. The student then can "play along" with a "real" ensemble, honing his or her skills.

Kratka also formed a related line, Pocket Songs, offering singers the same opportunity to practice with real accompaniments. This product line earned Kratka the nickname of "Father of Karaoke" by the National Association of Music Merchants (NAMM), the main industry organization. Pocket Songs offers over 14,000 popular songs, including pop, standards, jazz, rap, country, blues, and folk. The entire line is offered on CDG, the "G" standing for graphics, a projection of the lyrics on a television screen in the home, utilizing a CDG player. [websites: www.musicminusone.com; www.pocketsongs.com.]

MUSIC ON THE NET

Music has provided content on the internet since it was invented. When the usenet discussion groups system started in the 1980s, several were set aside for the discussion of genres and artists; now there are thousands. In the late 1980s, well before the dawn of the World Wide Web (WWW), "talkers," internet relay chat (IRC), mail exploders (e-mail forums) and Multi User Dungeons (MUDs) all had thriving music communities. In 1990 when Tim Berners-Lee of the European Particle Physics Laboratory unveiled his new system for moving intuitively between data and computers, aka WWW, it is unlikely that he foresaw the revolutionary ripples this would send across the music industry. Record companies and artists (both signed and unsigned) used the Web to promote their work. Magazines set up online versions and, like the labels and artists, reached a global audience for the first time. The WWW also revolutionized fanzine culture. Idiosyncratic publications with small print run by fans of particular artists were transformed into multimedia centers accessible worldwide. Many of the earliest and best examples were adopted by the artists and given an official seal of approval. With the arrival of the MP3 format for saving and transferring music digitally, the internet became a hotbed to hear both new, unsigned music from around the world, and for sharing and bootlegging pirate recordings. The latter reached a head with the Napster file sharing system court case in 2000.

IAN PEEL

MUSICAL HERITAGE SOCIETY

An American organization established in 1963 to market records by mail. Material came from Europe and

U.S. labels under license arrangements. At first the specialty was early music, but the repertoire expanded to cover all periods and even jazz and folk music. More than 3,000 titles have appeared. Among the major projects completed were the issue of all 107 Haydn symphonies on 49 LPs (MHS 201–249; 1968–1970), and all the Bach organ works on 25 discs. In the 1980s a label presenting original material (classical and jazz) was made available in retail stores, named Musicmasters. At the same time, the Jazz Heritage Society was launched to offer a similar service to jazz fans by the company.

MUSICAL THEATER RECORDINGS

Edison's commercial recording and manufacture of cylinders began in 1889, and the dominant format of the 78-rpm disc was introduced by Berliner in 1894. Theatrical recordings only became popular in the first decade of the 20th century. Songs composed for the musical theater were written to be performed live, and no thought was given to preserving theater performance materials that were quickly discarded. The earliest catalogs for cylinders and 78-rpm discs contain a broad selection of classical instrumentals and vocals, marches, comedy, band, sacred, and minstrel recordings; but theatrical music has but a small presence. Jack Raymond, noted discographer, collector, and authority on American Theatre Music, in his *Show Music on Record* [Smithsonian Institution Press, 1992, rev. 1998], presents as comprehensive a theatrical discography as can be found in print. The Library of Congress offers access to this information on its website. Its logical companion may be found in a four-volume set of 12 compact discs *Music from the New York Stage (1890–1920)* comprising 297 early original cast recordings, issued on the Pearl label, and produced under his supervision.

The history of recorded songs performed by the original cast for the American musical stage can arguably be said to have begun in 1890 with DeWolf Hopper's brown wax Columbia three-inch cylinder recording of "You Can Always Explain Things Away" from the comic opera *Castles in the Air* (5 May 1890, Broadway Theatre, 105 performances). Hopper was one of the reigning stars of comic opera between 1884–1928, and his recording of one of the hit songs from composer Gustave Kerker's score stands up as a representative of indigenous American theater music of its era. This early cylinder may have never been for sale to the public, but in 1898 Jessie Bartlett Davis recorded "O Promise Me" from Reginald DeKoven and Harry B. Smith's comic opera *Robin Hood* (1891); for the next century, the song would retain its unique reputation as the quintessential wedding march. The previous year Edward M. Favor recorded "The King's Song" (and several others no longer extant) from the Carl Pflueger/R.A. Barnet 1893 musical farce *1492*. The sound of many stage performers' speaking and singing voices were often ill-suited to the primitive technology of early acoustic recordings, and many were reportedly loathe to preserve their voices in a way they deemed unflattering.

Today we are left with a sparse and uneven selection of American stage performances from 1890–1920. In March and May 1898, original cast members from the Bostonians' production of Victor Herbert's early comic opera *The Serenade* were reassembled to record four songs released as Berliner discs. Later that year, James T. Powers recorded his comic tour de force of Chinese malapropisms "Chin Chin Chinaman" from the British comic opera *The Geisha* for the same firm. Victor Herbert was further represented by four more original cast Berliners from *The Fortune Teller* in late 1898. Published sheet music or piano-vocal arrangements of songs for the stage had only begun to reach a wider public with the increasing popularity of piano music in homes at the turn of the century. Charles K. Harris's "After the Ball" from *A Trip to Chinatown* (1891) sold over 5 million copies in sheet music, and thereby awakened publishers to the potential fortune to be made from theater music. Neither the publishers of music sheets nor the early manufacturers of sound recordings could have imagined the public's future appetite for theater music, or the extent to which each could be used to promote, educate, and cross-market the other's product.

Meanwhile in Great Britain, an altogether different theater culture combined with the recording industry to preserve theatrical stage performance in far greater depth and number than in the U.S. In London, the Gramophone (& Typewriter) Co. licensed Berliner's technology, and in 1898 H. Scott Russell was the first to record two vocal selections from Sidney Jones's *The Geisha*, "Jack's the Boy" and "A Geisha's Life," respectively. Russell also recorded "Take a Pair of Sparkling Eyes" from *The Yeoman of the Guard*, thus inaugurating a century's love and loyalty to the hugely popular oeuvre of Gilbert & Sullivan, whose works were recorded again and again by D'Oyly Carte performers and many other willing interpreters.

Popular stage works such as *The Runaway Girl* (1898), *A Greek Slave* (1898), *San Toy* (1899), *Florodora* (1899), *The Messenger Boy* (1900), *The Silver Slipper* (1901), *A Country Girl* (1902), and *Three Little Maids* (1902) all received three or more "Original Cast" recordings in U.K. and dozens more studio cast recordings. Although all of these works were later presented in New York, there existed no comparable commitment to record works for the stage in the United States. The playful or raucous style of such early stage comediennes, from the lyrical Lillian Russell ("Come Down, Ma' Evenin' Star" from *Twirly Whirly*), virtuoso coon-shouter May Irwin ("The Bully" from *The Widow Jones*), the rambunctious Marie Cahill ("Under the Bamboo Tree" from *Sally in Our Alley*), the Irish comedy of Nora Bayes ("Has Anybody Here Seen Kelly?" from *The Jolly Bachelors*), Blanche Ring ("Yip-I-Addy-I-Ay" from *"The Merry Widow" Burlesque*), and the pseudo-Parisienne Eva Tanguay ("I Don't Care" from *Ziegfeld Follies of 1909*) afford a vivid picture of the Broadway stage prior to World War I. Equally popular were the comic light operas of Gilbert & Sullivan, and the romantic light operas of Victor Herbert and Franz Lehàr, whose lyric ballads and love duets were widely recorded more often not by their stage performers but by studio singers such as Billy Murray, Ada Jones, Henry Burr, and Arthur Fields for Victor or Columbia, among many others. Although musical numbers in theatrical performance may have been from three to 10 minutes in length, the 10-inch 78-rpm disc necessitated that songs be truncated to fit a three-minute limit. Out went the introductory verse and the repeated choruses. Even a 12-inch 78 rpm disc was limited to less than five minutes playing time, and few theater songs, apart from the instrumental or vocal gem medleys, were issued on 12-inch discs. Joe Weber and Lew Fields, whose knockabout comedy was more visual than verbal, made a curious selection of early comedy routines written for their musical burlesques, revised and re-created late in their careers in 1912 for Columbia Records.

Thomas Q. Seabrooke (recording from 1895–1903), Raymond Hitchcock (1910–1916), Jack Norworth (1910–1922), and George M. Cohan (1911) rank among the earliest male interpreters of recorded theatrical song, principally for Columbia and Victor. Bert Williams, initially known as half of Williams & Walker, became the first major Black American star to be top-billed alongside a white cast; he recorded more than 50 sides for Columbia, many from his early Black musicals, revues, and the *Ziegfeld Follies*. His earliest tracks for Victor and Monarch are among the rarest theatrical recordings extant. The Irish tenor ballad was also a staple of the American musical theater from 1880–1920; its foremost proponent was undoubtedly Chauncey Olcott, whose "My Wild Irish Rose" (from *A Romance of Athlone*) typifies such work. Olcott, like Andrew Mack, Walter Scanlan, George MacFarlane, Colin O'Moore, and many others, toured the United States with one-week or one-night stands of their trademark Irish melodramas, laced with their own romantic ballads.

The Goliath of popular song for the stage was Al Jolson, whose recordings (principally for Columbia, Brunswick, with a few early Victors, and a late career with Decca) sold millions of discs, long after his stage career from 1911–1940. Jolson worked almost exclusively for the Messr. Shubert who tailored lavish musical spectacles around his talents (*Vera Violetta*, *The Whirl of Society*, *Robinson Crusoe Jr.*, *Sinbad*, *Bombo*, *Big Boy*, etc.). Curiously the hit songs that emerged from these Jolson vehicles were not those written for the shows themselves, but rather those Jolson interpolated into his specialty solo scenes ("You Made Me Love You," "Swanee," "Rock-a-bye Your Baby," "Toot Toot Tootsie," "California Here I Come," etc.). Early theater music was often recorded in five-minute vocal medley form and marketed as "Vocal Gems"; the often anonymous vocalists and conductors were seldom identified except in modern discographies. Victor, and to a lesser degree Columbia, Brunswick, Vocalion, and other labels, recorded such medleys of the standard Gilbert & Sullivan repertoire, *Girofle/Girofla*, *The Merry Widow*, *Chimes of Normandy*, as well as popular stage hits 1900–1932, and these sold widely. So what if the ensemble lyrics were hardly discernible!

Following World War I, what is widely regarded as the Golden Era of American musical theater and American popular song began with the careers of songwriters Irving Berlin, Jerome Kern, George Gershwin, Richard Rodgers and Lorenz Hart, Cole Porter, Oscar Hammerstein II, and then later E.Y. Harburg, Harold Arlen, Alan Jay Lerner and Frederick Loewe, and Frank Loesser. Theater music would dominate popular music for roughly 1915–1965 until the emergence and ultimate supremacy of rock 'n' roll and R&B.

With the introduction of jazz into popular music in the 1910s and 1920s and electronic recording techniques in 1925, recordings of theater music both proliferated and changed. Dance band instrumentals and vocals popularized theater music to a wider audience than had attended stage shows ever before. Theater music could be heard in a style approximating the stage performance (recorded by Arden and Ohman, Roger Wolfe Kahn, etc.), in a dance band style (Paul Whiteman, Ben Bernie, etc.), and in popular vocal styles (Ruth Etting, Marion Harris, Libby Holman, etc.). While most composers and performers welcomed the chance to record their theatrical successes, some rebelled! Jerome Kern stipulated that no recordings be made of his score to *Sitting Pretty* (1924) so that theater goers might experience his score for the first time in the theater. This unfortunately doomed the score to oblivion until John McGlinn and company revived and recorded the score complete in 1989.

At first ragtime and jazz became staple elements of the Broadway revues of Ziegfeld, George White, Earl Carroll, and Irving Berlin's Music Box series. With the success of Black musicals and revues such as *Shuffle*

Along, *Runnin' Wild*, *Blackbirds of 1928*, and *Hot Chocolates*, Black composers, writers, and performers were increasingly integrated into revues in the 1920–1930s. Even Irving Berlin wrote a theater blues song for Ethel Waters (the radical "Suppertime" in Berlin's *As Thousands Cheer*). Bill Robinson, Florence Mills, Ethel Waters, and Josephine Baker expanded upon the roles previously available to Blacks, introducing Broadway audiences to the idioms of Black dance, jazz, and R&B. Audiences had begun flocking north to Harlem to the Cotton Club, Connie's Inn, and other Harlem clubs offering live jazz and revue entertainment, and Broadway rallied to compete.

While American record labels continued to record Broadway theatrical performers with individual 78 rpm sides only sporadically, in Great Britain HMV and Columbia systematically recorded six to eight sides for most major musical theater successes. For example, the extant eight "original cast" recordings for Gershwin's *Funny Face* with Fred and Adele Astaire were recorded in London, not New York; only Victor Arden and Phil Ohman's duo piano version from the Broadway production was recorded in New York, with Johnny Marvin providing a studio cast vocal. Similarly, *Watch Your Step* (8 sides), *Lady Be Good* (5), *The Desert Song* (8), *Wildflower* (7), *Hit the Deck* (8), *The New Moon* (9), *Rio Rita* (7), *Irene* (10), *Tip-Toes* (8), *No No Nanette* (8), and *The Student Prince* (8), all American successes, were recorded in England with their original English stage performers and conductors intact. HMV and Columbia would continue to record generously from the musical theater with original cast artists and dance bands until the advent of World War II. Even France and Germany recorded its indigenous theater artists prolifically up until the late 1930s. With the exception of Al Jolson, Eddie Cantor, Fred Astaire, Sophie Tucker, and Ethel Merman, few Broadway theater performers achieved enduring national or international fame as recording artists.

The introduction of new competition from film talkies, beginning with Jolson's *The Jazz Singer* in 1927, threatened Broadway's creative and economic monopoly for musical theater; with the Great Depression of 1929, the vast defection of performing and writing talent for Hollywood had a further devastating impact. As paying audiences shrank with the Depression and flocked to musical films, the number of new stage musicals produced in 1929 plummeted from 40 to 25 in 1932. Most were failures. Suddenly Berlin, Kern, Rodgers and Hart, Arlen, Gershwin, Porter, and many new or untried songwriters were writing Hollywood movie musicals; in creative dismay or disgust, most returned to writing for the stage late in the 1930s, even if they did the occasional film for the easy financial rewards they offered.

In the late 1920s through the early 1940s, an unexpected confluence of great writing talents combined with the economic threat to the musical theater stage, resulting in the creation of many of its greatest works, including *Show Boat*, *Of Thee I Sing*, *Porgy and Bess*, *On Your Toes*, *The Cradle Will Rock*, *Pal Joey*, *Oklahoma!*, *Carousel*, to name but a few. Earlier ambitious attempts to record "complete" works, principally Brunswick's 1932 reconstituted *Show Boat* and *Blackbirds of 1928*, were undoubtedly victims of the economic problems ensuing from the Depression, given their hefty retail price. One of the earliest original cast albums arose from the unlikeliest of shows, *The Cradle Will Rock*, the fabled labor protest opera of Marc Blitzstein. Originally produced and nearly suppressed by the Works Project Administration (WPA), a small label Musicraft assembled the cast and recorded its complete musical score in a set of 12-inch discs, which received limited distribution.

In 1943 it was the unprecedented success of Rodgers and Hammerstein's *Oklahoma!* that inspired Jack Kapp at the upstart Decca label to assemble the Broadway cast and record 12 sides combined for sale as an album of six 10-inch discs at $4.85. His immense success defined what has ever since been known as the Original Broadway Cast album. Other labels were slow to respond to the challenge and compete with Decca to record new shows. Decca continued to record almost everything (*One Touch of Venus*, *Bloomer Girl*, *Carousel*, *Call Me Mister*, etc.), while Columbia recorded only the 1946 revival of *Show Boat*. Capitol recorded *St. Louis Woman*, coauthored by the label's founder Johnny Mercer in 1946. Only in 1947 did Columbia record *Finian's Rainbow* and *Street Scene*, and RCA Victor produce *Brigadoon*. These labels also discovered the strategic advantage of promoting their cast albums by releasing alternate "cover" versions of stage hits by popular artists already under contract. Alternative formats such as the Columbia's 33 rpm seven-inch and 12-inch LP and RCA's 45 rpm seven-inch EP were introduced in the late 1940s to supplant and then replace the dominant 78 rpm format by the mid-1950s. The advantage of the LP was that up to 27–28 minutes of playing time per side allowed 55-minute cast albums to be issued. The competition to secure the recording rights to promising new musicals reached a fevered pitch; in 1956 Goddard Lieberson's Columbia Records committed much of the $350,000 capitalization for Herman Levin's forthcoming musical production of *My Fair Lady*. As an investment and also as a recording, this investment paid back handsomely. Unlike popular recordings wherein an individual singer received royalties for the number of discs sold (apart from the mechanical royalties paid to the songwriters), actors and musicians were initially paid session fees for recording cast albums. Once Original Cast Albums became big business for the record labels, Actors Equity negotiated a minimum fee of one week's performance salary per recording day, plus pension and welfare for all members of the company, including stage managers, company managers, and press agents, for the right to record a currently running show.

In the 1950s–1960s, Original Cast Albums (such as *My Fair Lady, West Side Story, The Music Man, The Sound of Music, Camelot, Funny Girl, Hello Dolly!, Fiddler on the Roof*) continued to be big sellers, frequently reaching the number one position on the *Billboard* or *Variety* charts. Less costly Studio Cast, pop vocal, jazz, or instrumental "crossover" recordings flourished as well to support the public's appetite for theater music in all forms. Beginning with *My Fair Lady*, the Original Cast Album became not only a historical record of a unique performance and a home souvenir, but also an indispensable marketing tool for producers and authors seeking new productions in far-flung venues around the country and around the world. *Oklahoma!* had opened that door somewhat in 1943, but the impact of World War II and *Oklahoma's* uniquely American story was no match for the international appeal of *My Fair Lady*. Not only was *My Fair Lady* produced and/or recorded in Great Britain, Australia, New Zealand, Canada, South Africa, but also in Germany, Netherlands, Sweden, Norway, Denmark, Russia, Italy, Japan, Spain, Mexico, Israel, Austria, France, to name but a few. Suddenly a universe of opportunity was opened for the American musical, the likes of which hadn't been seen since Offenbach and then Gilbert and Sullivan took the world by storm in the 19th century.

Beginning with the emergence of rock 'n' roll music in the 1950s, its explosive growth and then cultural dominance in the protest era of the 1960s, theater music ceased to be a dominant force in popular music. At first Broadway all but ignored or else ridiculed rock 'n' roll. *West Side Story* (1957) was musical theater's most ambitious work by authors Arthur Laurents, Stephen Sondheim, and Jerome Robbins. They incorporate teenage culture and language into a contemporary and relevant story, with composer Leonard Bernstein using jazz idioms and orchestration. It became an instant classic both onstage and on film. But more often Broadway was happier to satirize youth and rock 'n' roll as in *Bye Bye Birdie* (1960), *Grease* (1972), and London's *The Rocky Horror Show* (1974). Popular and rock composers increasingly saw the theater, and especially Broadway, as irrelevant and unwelcoming. A few breakout wild card successes such as *Hair* (1968), *Jesus Christ Superstar* (1971), and a couple of off-Broadway musicals such as

Godspell (1971) attempted to give musical theater a contemporary edge and relevance, but in revival their librettos have grown ludicrous with age, leaving us with a handful of hit songs, much as the musicals of the 1920s and 1930s once did. Except for generic compilation revues or biomusicals, rock 'n' roll, R&B, and pop music in general became increasingly irreconcilable with the coherent and audible lyrics, character development, and storytelling that musical theater demanded. Surprisingly, the reintegration of popular music into the theater can be credited to the British with Andrew Lloyd Webber and Tim Rice, beginning with *Jesus Christ Superstar* (1971) and *Evita* (1979). *Superstar* became a successful pop concept album prior to any staging, thereby reinventing the traditional path to theatrical production. Here for the first time an audience came to a new musical's opening night knowing the songs! *Evita*, too, was introduced first to the public as a pop concept album, though the authors never concealed their intent to stage it. Written first as a through-sung pop opera or cantata, as were their previous hits *Jesus Christ Superstar* and *Joseph and the Amazing Technicolor Dreamcoat*, Webber and Rice wisely chose veteran Broadway stager Harold Prince to translate *Evita* to the stage. Here was a serious theatrical work that incorporated contemporary music and fluid cinematic staging, and it became an international success. *Evita* launched a British musical theater juggernaut worldwide, and under the aegis of producer Cameron Mackintosh, *Cats, Les Miserables, Phantom of the Opera*, and *Miss Saigon* would dominate the world musical theater scene for almost 20 years. While none of these works would ever claim to be pure rock music, they nonetheless fused pop music instrumentation and rock concert visual techniques and staging into a modern popular music theater form.

Meanwhile American hits looked backward with *42nd Street, Ain't Misbehavin', Sugar Babies, Sophisticated Ladies, My One and Only, Crazy for You*, and *Black and Blue*, plus a steady diet of safe revivals. The principal American voice of challenge and experimentation through this era from 1970 to the present continued to be Stephen Sondheim. Apart from a nod to contemporary pop orchestration with *Company* (1970), Sondheim decided that rock 'n' roll was largely irrelevant and inhospitable to intelligent musical theater. With the help of his librettists (Hugh Wheeler, John Weidman, James Goldman, George Furth, James Lapine) and directors (Harold Prince, Michael Bennett, James Lapine), Sondheim forged a thinking-man's musical theater with such seminal works as *Company* (1970), *Follies* (1971), *A Little Night Music* (1973), *Pacific Overtures* (1976), *Sweeney Todd* (1979), *Merrily We Roll Along* (1981), *Sunday in the Park With George* (1984), *Into the*

Woods (1987), and *Passion* (1994). Unlike the 15-plus-year runs enjoyed by *Cats* or *A Chorus Line*, critical praise and limited audiences have seldom propelled Sondheim's work beyond a Broadway run of two years, but with time each of these works has attained the status of a modern classic. Belatedly, they are finally being translated and performed in other languages, *Company* (Brazil, Amsterdam), *Follies* (Berlin), *A Little Night Music* (Vienna,1975), *Pacific Overtures* (Japan, 2001), *Into the Woods* (Denmark), and *Sweeney Todd* (Barcelona, Amsterdam).

The concept of the Original Cast Recording has proven over time to be an indispensable strategic tool to promote and secure future stage productions. Tams-Witmark, Music Theatre International, Samuel French, and Rodgers and Hammerstein, as licensors of performance rights for stock and amateur productions, recognize the tangible importance of a well-recorded cast album as a prerequisite to attracting new productions. Works such as *Where's Charley?*, *As the Girls Go*, and *Love Life* went unrecorded in 1948 because of a recording industry strike, an oblivion the latter two shows have never recovered from. Conversely, because of their Original Cast Albums, the failures *Candide* (71 performances), *Anyone Can Whistle* (9 performances), *The Baker's Wife* (closed before New York), *Working* (25 performances), *Rags* (4 performances), *Baby* (241 performances), and *Merrily We Roll Along* (16 performances) have all discovered a future performance life so brief that their New York runs would never have been anticipated. Without judging their artistic or commercial merits, had Lerner and Loewe's *The Day Before Spring* (165 performances), Jerry Bock and Sheldon Harnick's *The Body Beautiful* (60 performances), Richard Adler's *Music Is* (8 performances), Mercer and Dolan's *Foxy* (72 erformances), or the critically reviled cult favorite *Carrie* (1 performance) been recorded, what future life beyond New York might have been born? Thus Bernstein and Lerner's maligned *1600 Pennsylvania Avenue* and Villa Lobos/Wright and Forrest's forgotten *Magdalena* have been now reprieved. Even the Moross-Latouche through-sung masterpiece *The Golden Apple*, severely truncated to less than 50 minutes and, saddled with inept narration in its 1954 RCA Victor release, would welcome a complete new recording.

Musical comedy all but ceased on film by 1970, with the exception of Disney's successful series of animated musicals (*The Little Mermaid*, *Beauty and the Beast*, *Aladdin*, *The Lion King*, *Pocahontas*) or the rare studio film (*Cabaret*, *Annie*, *Evita*, *Chicago*). Original rock musicals created for film became movie studio fodder, and many have found their way back to the stage in inferior re-creations, such as *Footloose*, *Fame*, *Sgt. Pepper's Lonely Hearts Club Band*, and *Saturday Night Fever*. Recent television remakes of traditional musicals such as *Gypsy*, *Cinderella*, *Annie*, and *South Pacific* have reached vast new audiences with surprising success, and new versions of *The Music Man* and *Fiddler on the Roof* are being planned. As these classic works age in copyright, the heirs and rights holders are devising yet new ways of extending the income-producing life for such works, with new librettos, revised lyrics, new CDs, new DVDS, etc. From the unlikely world of animated film, Disney has emerged as a major creative producer of new works for the musical theater.

Whereas their first transfer of a musical comedy from animated screen to live stage musical with *Beauty and the Beast* was initially ridiculed by the critical press and theatrical community, the New York production's run of more than eight years and 3,200 performances has vindicated Disney's measure of popular taste. *The Lion King* was a riskier but successful transfer to the live stage, and their pop version of *Aida* was conceived for the stage without a prior animated film version. Disney recognizes that the market value of a proven title is an immense advantage in attracting an audience. Musical theater enjoys a peculiar love-hate relationship with popular music not written for the theater. As far back as *The Beggar's Opera* in 1750, there has been a long-standing tradition of interpolating popular music and harnessing its proven appeal to narrative purpose in the theater. Beginning in the 1880s, farce comedies, comic operas, and later musical comedies routinely interpolated recognized popular songs into productions whose integral scores lacked "hits." Stars such as Bert Williams, Blanche Ring, Al Jolson, and Eddie Cantor frequently performed their favorite song hits by popular demand in specialty or solo spots in musicals and revues, without regard for the narrative content of the show. Conversely composers such as Victor Herbert and Jerome Kern contractually protected the integrity of their scores by forbidding producers to interpolate the work of outside writers, no matter what the star's demands. Ironically, Kern's introduction to musical theater arose through producer Charles Frohman and other's interpolating Kern songs into imported English musicals during 1904–1914, such as *The Catch of the Season*, *An English Daisy*, *The Earl and the Girl*, *The Marriage Market*, and *The Girl from Utah*. Kern himself was not above making shrewd use of popular interpolations. The most famous of all is Charles K. Harris's "After the Ball" that Kern interpolated into *Show Boat* for Magnolia's onstage solo at the Trocadero, along with Joe Howard's 1904 chestnut "Goodbye, My Lady Love." Kern deployed this device in 1929 with

Irene Franklin's songs in *Sweet Adeline*. More often the interpolation of popular hit songs into musicals and revues proved to be a blatant, facile, and manipulative bid to win audience approval lazy with the satisfaction of hearing the familiar. How pleasing and much less challenging it is for an audience to walk into the theater humming the hits, than it is to hear and remember new music on a first hearing!

In the past 20 years or so, librettists, directors, and producers have grown more devious or ambitious, wedding old Cole Porter songs to Philip Barry's "Holiday" to yield the now-forgotten *Happy New Year* (1980), or all new librettos fashioned around Gershwin scores in *Crazy for You* (1991) loosely adapted from *Girl Crazy* (1930), and *My One and Only* (1983) fashioned from *Funny Face* (1927). If there is any consolation to musical theater purists, at least these songs were written to be performed in the theater! With *Mamma Mia!*, however, musical theater now has a simple story to which an existing catalog of pop songs has been shoe-horned, and its success has prodded producers to launch a series of book musicals to which the songs of the Beatles (*All You Need Is Love*), Queen (*We Will Rock You*), and Billy Joel (*Movin' Out*) have been force-fitted. This cultural "strip-mining" of our pop-music catalog stifles the creativity of new composers and lyricists struggling to write new work for the theater. Fortunately, certain renowned pop/rock writers have courageously created new works for the theater, notably ABBA's *Chess*, Paul Simon's *The Capeman*, or Elton John's *Aida*.

The advent of the compact disc has also ushered in a quiet revolution in the recording of musical theater. No longer constrained by the limitations of a two-sided LP to 50 minutes' playing time, newer cast albums may contain more introductory dialogue and lyrics, dance music, and reprises than were heretofore possible, up to 79 minutes per CD. The reissue of earlier musical theater classics has not only allowed these historic recordings to be remastered with the latest audio techniques, but additional bonus tracks, including unreleased songs, composer's demos, pop versions, and interviews, have been added to entice buyers to replace discs they may have bought before in other formats. Prior to the introduction of the CD, it was rare that any musical might be recorded complete; Columbia Masterworks recorded *The Most Happy Fella*, *Regina*, and *Porgy and Bess*, presumably because these works had operatic credentials and crossover appeal. Now John Yap's That's Entertainment Records (TER) in U.K. has recorded the complete musical scores of *My Fair Lady*, *Cabaret*, *The King and I*, *Annie Get Your Gun*, *West Side Story*, and many other classics, including every note of music, underscoring, and supporting dialogue,

with a seriousness previously reserved only for operatic repertoire. Conductor John McGlinn created a legendary archival reconstruction of *Show Boat* which filled 3 CDs for EMI, and has performed a similar service for the original 1934 *Anything Goes* and other titles.

Concomitant with these new studio recordings of established musical theater titles comes an unprecedented commitment to recording neglected scores from the theatrical Golden Age. In the 1950s, Columbia Records' producer Goddard Lieberson teamed with conductor Lehman Engel to produce a series of studio cast recordings of early classics, usually with "updated" orchestrations. Among the best-known Columbia titles were *Pal Joey* (which prompted its 1952 revival), *On Your Toes*, *Oh, Kay!*, *Roberta*, *The Merry Widow*, *Girl Crazy*, *Show Boat*, and *The Bandwagon/Anything Goes*. Few other labels attempted such retrospective recordings, although RCA Victor's *The Chocolate Soldier* and *Rose Marie* spring to mind. Beginning in the early 1990s, the Gershwin estate funded, at no small expense, restored orchestrations, recovery of lost music and lyrics, and produced completely new recordings of *Lady Be Good*, *Tell Me More*, *Tip Toes*, *Oh, Kay!*, *Funny Face*, *Strike Up the Band*, *Girl Crazy*, and *Pardon My English*.

The welcome visibility and availability of such recordings and restored performance materials have made possible new stagings and concert revivals of these works that would have been unimaginable decades ago. Similar projects to record lesser-known works by Kurt Weill, Jerome Kern, Victor Herbert, and John Philip Sousa have begun. Newly restored performance versions, broadcasts, and recordings of titles such as Berlin's long-neglected *Louisiana Purchase* (DRG, Carnegie Recital Hall, 1996), Arlen and Mercer's *St. Louis Woman* (Mercury, Encores revival of 1998), Vernon Duke and Ira Gershwin's *Ziegfeld Follies of 1936* (Decca Broadway, Encores revival of 1999), Vincent Youmans' *Through the Years* (PS Classics, 2001), Cole Porter's *Jubilee*, *Gay Divorce*, and *Dubarry Was a Lady*, and Kurt Weill's *A Kingdom for a Cow* (BBC Radio) are testimony to the collective willingness of historians, scholars, heirs, music publishers, and dedicated conductors, actors, and singers to revive the unique wealth of our musical theater heritage.

RICHARD C. NORTON

MUSICASSETTE

The enclosed cassette launched by Philips in a compact cassette portable recorder in 1963.

MUSICRAFT (LABEL)

An American record issued from 1937 to 1948 by the Musicraft Corp. of New York, and founded by entrepreneur Oliver Sabin. It offered pop, jazz, classical, country, Latin, folk, children's, and gospel material. An important series of organ music, performed by Carl Weinrich, was released beginning in 1937. In 1938 Musicraft issued the first original cast album of a Broadway musical, *The Cradle Will Rock* (#1075/81 in album 18). After World War II, the label made a serious attempt at expansion, signing major jazz artists including Artie Shaw, Teddy Wilson, Sarah Vaughan, and, in May 1946, a generous contract with Duke Ellington. However, the company was soon overextended and by June 1947 Ellington had left. New management temporarily stabilized the label's situation, but by 1948 it was bankrupt.

MUSIKPRODUKTION DABRINGHAUS UND GRIMM

See MD&G (Label)

MUSIQUE CONCRÈTE

Preempting sampling and DJ culture by almost 50 years, musique concrète was first theorized in the 1940s by French composer Pierre Schaeffer. Schaeffer was convinced that music of the future would be created from recycled recordings of the past. He was a mainstay of Club d'Essai, the experimental studio at Radio France, recording tracks that were "concrete" (i.e., of the future) as opposed to "symbolic" (i.e., of the past). Other collaborators and regulars at the Club d'Essai included Boulez and Henry, both key figures in France's input into early, experimental musical thinking. In the post–hip-hop era of dance music, where the majority of records are created from fragments of others, extending musique concrète into the mainstream, Schaeffer is marked out as an early visionary. John Cage's "William's Mix" was perhaps the most ambitious tape composition ever conceived, randomly assembled from thousands of pieces of tape over a period of nine months, to create a 4.25-minute work; the "score" for the work runs 192 pages.

See also **Electronic Music; Tape Composition**

IAN PEEL

MUTE

To silence, to reduce, to soften the output of an audio instrument.

See also **Muting Circuit**

MUTE (LABEL)

The largest independent label in U.K. After 10 years without affiliation, it merged with the U.S. Enigma in 1988.

MUTI, RICCARDO (28 JULY 1941–)

Italian conductor, born in Naples. He studied violin and piano, then composition at the Naples Conservatory; went to Milan to take up conducting. In 1967 he won the Guido Cantelli competition and had several important engagements with Italian orchestras. He was named principal conductor of the Teatro Comunale, Florence, in 1970; performances in Salzburg followed, and with both the Berlin Philharmonic Orchestra and the Vienna Philharmonic Orchestra (he remains a regular guest conductor with both orchestras). Muti's American debut was with the Philadelphia Orchestra on 27 Oct 1972. He was named principal conductor of the Philharmonia Orchestra, London, and remained 10 years (1973–1982). Then he succeeded Eugene Ormandy as conductor of the Philadelphia Orchestra in 1982. He also became music director at La Scala in 1986. In 1990 his retirement from Philadelphia was announced, effective 1992; he has since held the title of laureate conductor. From 1999–2000, he was actively courted to be the next music director of the New York Philharmonic, but he subsequently turned it down because of the considerable time commitment involved. Muti has been an exclusive EMI artist from 1975, although as a conductor he has also recorded for other labels. His most acclaimed records with the Philadelphia Orchestra have been of Beethoven, Mahler, Stravinsky, Scriabin, and Tchaikovsky. In 2001, on the occasion of Muti's 60th birthday, EMI issued boxed sets of the complete Scriabin symphonies (with the Philadelphia Orchestra) and the complete Schubert symphones (with the Vienna Orchestra).

REV. CARL BENSON

MUTING CIRCUIT

In an audio system, the circuit that silences audible sound during the change cycle of a record player, or in a tape deck when the tape is rewinding or fast-forwarding, or in a radio receiver when it is tuned across the band.

MUTUAL TALKING MACHINE CO.

A New York firm, established in 1916. The Mutual line of record players was offered.

MUZAK

An American firm, with headquarters in South Carolina. It provides recorded music as a background sound to public places and work environments. The service was founded by General George Squier in 1920, who patented a system of providing background music from phonograph records played over telephone lines. The Muzak system became popular particularly in urban centers, where large buildings piped in its soothing sounds to quell anxious riders of a new technological innovation, the elevator; hence, Muzak is often called elevator music. Muzak selections are all soothingly arranged and recorded by house musicians, who present songs with the lyrics removed and the overall effect softened. The concept underlying Muzak dates back to the 1906 Ampliphone. The service was purchased by film studio Warner Bros. in 1938, who sold it the next year to *Encyclopaedia Britannica* publisher Senator William Benton. By the 1950s, Muzak had developed a new programming strategy called "stimulus progression," designed to motivate the worker through each hour of the business day. By the mid-1950s, the service had switched to audiotape from the more cumbersome phonograph records, and had 150 franchises. Ownership of Muzak changed hands several times over the next few decades, from Wrather Corp. in 1957 to TelePrompter Corp. in 1972, to large electronics giant the Westinghouse Corp. in 1981. By then, Muzak had abandoned phone lines for satellite delivery of its programming, with 16 different choices (by 2000, the satellite offered 60 channels of Muzak). In the mid-1980s, Muzak partnered with Yesco Corp., a provider of "foreground music," so it could provide current hit recordings. Also, video programming for nightclubs and restaurants was introduced. In 1997, former Muzak franchise owner Bill Boyd became the CEO of the new Muzak LLC. He has directed the company to return to its original mission of providing background music for businesses big and small. By 1998, Muzak was being piped in to 250,000 U.S. locations, and was heard by an estimated 80 million persons daily. Revenue for the first six months of the 2002 fiscal year was $105 million, with Muzak holding about 60 percent of the market for background music in the U.S. [website: www.muzak.com.]

REV. CARL BENSON

MUZIO, CLAUDIA (7 FEB 1889–24 MAY 1936)

Italian soprano, born Claudina Muzzio in Pavia. She studied in Milan and made her debut in Arezzo in *Manon Lescaut* on 15 Jan 1910. Her Metropolitan Opera debut was in a *Tosca* of 4 Dec 1916, with Enrico Caruso and Antonio Scotti. She stayed with the Metropolitan to spring 1922, then sang in Chicago to 1932. The Metropolitan saw her for one more season, 1933–1934, then she returned to Italy. Muzio died in Rome. Among her first recordings, for HMV in Milan, 1911 and 1914, were several fine examples of her art: "La mamma morta" from *Andrea Chenier* (#82224), "Sorgi, o padre" from Bellini's *Bianca e Fernando* (#82267), and "Spiagge amate" from Gluck's *Paride ed Elena* (#82267). IRCC reissued the Bellini and Gluck arias on #192. She auditioned for an Edison representative in London, but was not accepted, so went to Pathé; for that label she recorded 40 sides during World War I. Edison then decided to engage her for a fine series of Diamond Discs between 1920 and 1925. Selections from the 1920–1921 Diamond Discs appear on Odyssey (#Y33793); one is the "Mamma morta" aria she had done for HMV. Some of her greatest singing is Tatiana's aria from *Eugene Onegin* (Diamond Disc #82224; 1921) and the Bird Song from *Pagliacci* (Diamond Disc #82232; 1921). The Edisons are reissued on CD on Cantabile/Harmonia Mundi (#705). Muzio's Columbia electrical recordings of 1934–1935 have been reissued on EMI Références (#H7 69790-2). One of the most remarkable is Stefano Donaudy's song "O del mio amato ben" (BX #1376; 1935).

MYERS, JOHN W. (CA. 1864–CA. 1919)

Welsh baritone, also a theater manager. He came to the U.S. at age 12, and became a successful singer. He began recording ca. 1892 for the New Jersey Phonograph Co., then for Columbia and other labels, and was one of the most popular recording artists at the turn of the century. There were 22 Edison cylinders, the first being "Light of the Sea" (#7820; 1901). For Columbia two-minute cylinders, ca. 1896–1900, Myers sang such numbers as "Beer, Beer, Glorious Beer" (#6012), "The Star Spangled Banner" (#6015), and "Sweet Rosie O'Grady" (#6036). Myers founded the Globe Phonograph Record Co. in 1897, a maker of brown wax cylinders. He was usually identified on records as J.W. Myers; he should not be confused with his contemporary, John H. Meyer. Myers recorded over 100 titles for Victor from 1901–1906. He quit recording in 1907, except for a few discs about 10 years after. [Brooks 1979; Walsh 1944/7.]

N

NADSCO (LABEL)

An American record, one of the Grey Gull affiliates, issued from around 1922 to sometime after 1925. Material was dance music and popular vocals. [Barr 1982; Rust 1978.]

NAGATA, MINORU (26 APR 1925–)

An internationally known expert on architectural acoustics, Nagata was born in Fukuoka, Japan, and graduated from Tokyo University in 1949. Between 1949 and 1971, he was employed by NHK, in the company's technical research laboratories. In 1962, while still working for NHK, he received his doctorate from Tohoku University, and during 1963 and 1964, he engaged in further studies at Goettinngen University, Germany. In June 1971, he left NHK to establish his own company, Minoru Nagata Acoustic Engineer & Associates Co., Ltd. (later renamed Nagata Acoustics Inc.). During his career, he has acoustically engineered a large number of fine concert halls including Suntory Hall, Casals Hall, and Tokyou Metropolitan Art Space Concert Hall in Tokyo, as well as Kyoto Concert Hall and Sapporo Concert Hall in other parts of Japan, and Walt Disney Concert Hall in Los Angeles. Nagata is a member of the Acoustical Society of America, the Audio Engineering Society, the Acoustical Society of Japan, and the Japan Organ Society. He has won the Sato prize from the Acoustical Society of Japan, a Best Technical Paper prize from the Acoustical Society of America, and won the prestigious Prize of the Architectural Institute of Japan.

HOWARD FERSTLER

NAGRA

Since Swiss Federal Institute of Technology physics student Stefan Kudelski built the Nagra I portable audio recorder, the firm's equipment has been widely utilized by audio professionals because of its sound quality and mechanical reliability in the fields of scientific research, radio broadcasting, cinema, journalism, and the record industry. With the introduction of the Nagra III, a transistorized tape recorder with electronic speed control, for the first time a unit weighing only five kilograms could be relied on to produce recordings the equal of those achieved by the best nonportable studio recorders. Models such as the Nagra 4.2 and Nagra IV-S Time Code were pivotal developments within the film industry. The company's products have garnered three Oscars and an Emmy (for development of digital : pay-per-view television in the U.S.) as well as many electronics-related awards. In 1997 the firm entered the high-end audiophile market with the PL-P preamplifier and the C-PP (a recorder/editor/CODEC, a companion of the Academy award-winning ARES-C). The VPA — Vacuum Tube Power Amplifier — appeared the following year. February 2002 saw the introduction of the Nagra V — a two-channel, 24-bit portable digital audio recorder offering all of the features required by contemporary sound recording engineers — which has signaled the demise of analog and DAT recorders then in use within the film, television, and music industries. Nagra products fall within the Kudelski Group, a combine encompassing digital television and broadband network applications, pay-per-view television systems, professional and prestige hi-fi hardware, physical access and ticketing solutions, health sector applications, and the e-voting and cyber-administration sector.

See also **Kudelski, Stefan**

HOWARD FERSTLER

NAKAJIMA, HEITARO (1921–)

Interested from childhood in math and physics, Nakajima was one of the first individuals responsible for actually recording digitally processed sound, and is considered by many to be the father of the compact disc, along with Johannes (Joop) Sinjou of Philips, and Toshitada Doi of Sony. Nakajima earned a degree in electrical engineering from the Tokyo Institute of Technology in 1944, with a concentration in telecommunications, because the school had no degree program in math and physics at that time. Shortly thereafter, he earned a master's degree at Kyushu University, and in 1947 he went to work for NHK Industries, doing research in acoustics and microphone design. In 1958 he got his doctorate from Kyushu, continued to advance in the NHK hierarchy, and from 1965 through 1968 he was the general manager of the Acoustic Research Division, later on being promoted to head of the Science Research Laboratory. During this time, he began to experiment with prototype digital recording systems. In 1971, he left NHK and joined Sony, working at first on analog recording systems but eventually working on the digital technology that resulted in DAT, and later, in consort with engineers at Philips, the compact disc. He is past president of the Japan Audio Society, and for his pioneering work in digital recording systems he was awarded the Audio Engineering Society Gold Medal in 1989.

HOWARD FERSTLER

NAKAMICHI

Founded by Etsuro Nakamichi in 1948, the Tokyo-based Nakamichi Corp. is known worldwide for the manufacture of high performance audio-visual and multimedia electronic hardware. The firm originally designed and developed portable radios, speakers, phonograph tone arms, and communications equipment. By 1951 the company was manufacturing open reel tape decks for the "Magic Tone" line. Nakamichi created proprietary magnetic tape heads in 1957; with the appearance of the cassette configuration, the firm assumed a leadership role in the development of a tape head capable of reproducing sound ranging from 20 Hz to 20 kHz. In 1967, the company began supplying cassette and open-reel decks on an OEM basis to many

of the top hi-fi brands. By 1972, the first products bearing the Nakamichi name — geared toward the audiophile — entered the marketplace; the premium item was the first ever three-head cassette deck, thereby enabling the audiocassette to became a high quality music medium. Shifting its research and development emphasis to the digital domain, Nakamichi introduced its widely acclaimed MusicBank CD changer mechanism in 1990. The device would also provide the impetus for the company's entrance into the computer peripheral market. By the 21st century, Nakamichi had emerged as the foremost manufacturer within the "design-driven" category of audio and home theater systems. Seven SoundSpace systems — the 1, 2, 3, 5, 8, 9, and 21 — received the Consumer Electronics Association Innovations award (overseen by the Industrial Designers Association of America) in 2000, 2001, and 2002. A 24-bit CD player/tuner for mobile applications was introduced in 2000, claiming to have the best sound quality of any in-automobile system available. The E. Nakamichi Foundation was established in 1982. The nonprofit, philanthropic organization advances the musical arts through subsidizing competitions, public concerts, and public radio programming. [website: www.nakamichi.com.]

HOWARD FERSTLER

NANES ART FURNITURE CO.

A New York firm established in 1915. Disc players in five models were sold under the tradename Savoy.

NAPOLEON, PHIL
(2 SEP 1901–30 SEP 1990)

American jazz trumpet player, born Filippo Napoli in Boston. He began performing in public as a young child, and in 1916 recorded as a cornet soloist. Napoleon and Frank Signorelli founded the Original Memphis Five, one of the earliest Dixieland groups, in 1917. He also had his own band, recording for Pathé, Edison, and Victor in 1926–1927. Napoleon's Emperors was the name of his ensemble that recorded for Victor in 1929; it included Jimmy Dorsey, Tommy Dorsey, Joe Venuti, and Eddie Lang. "Mean to Me" (Victor V #38057) and "Anything" (V #38069) were two notable discs. He had another band in 1937, and made four sides for the Victory label. With the Dixieland revival, Napoleon reformed the Original Memphis Five in 1949. The group worked in New York until 1956, when Napoleon moved to Miami Beach, Florida, where he opened his own club. He made several Dixieland-styled recordings in the 1950s, with his last sessions coming in 1959–1960 for

Capitol Records, producing three albums (not reissued on CD). He continued to lead a band there through the 1980s. He died in Miami. A CD of live concert recordings from 1949–1950 (*Live at Nick's*; Jazzology #30) is the only current reissue of his later recordings.

NAPSTER INC.

In August 1999, Napster, Inc. was launched as an internet file swapping service. It helped internet users locate files, particularly music files in MP3 format, available for uploading from other users. The Napster software sorted files by type, artist, title, and speed of user connection. Users selected the file they wanted and the Napster software would tell the two computers to connect to each other and begin the transfer of the designated file. Within months transfers of music files using Napster reached into the millions per day. In December 1999, record labels and artists sued to shut Napster down for copyright infringement. The record labels were largely victorious in their suit, *A & M Records, Inc. v. Napster, Inc.* A federal court of appeals ruled that it was likely that (1) Napster users were copyright infringers, engaging in unauthorized copying and distribution of recordings and songs, (2) Napster, Inc. was liable for this infringement either as a vicarious or contributory infringer, (3) Napster, Inc. was not sheltered by the Digital Millennium Copyright Act because it was not a "service provider" as defined in the statute, and (4) that Napster must take positive steps to screen out infringing files and transfers. By July 2001, BMG Music had bought a share of Napster to turn the service into a licensed digital music distribution company. In January 2002 Napster launched a subscription version in competition with other pay services, MusicNet, PressPlay, and Rhapsody; in May 2002, Bertelsmann purchased Napster completely, hoping to realize this goal. However, it closed the operation in September 2002, and subsequently Napster's assets were purchased by Roxio, Inc., a maker of CD-burning software. A pay service, Napster II, was launched by the company in 2003. [website: www.napster.com.]

See also **MP3**

G.P. HULL

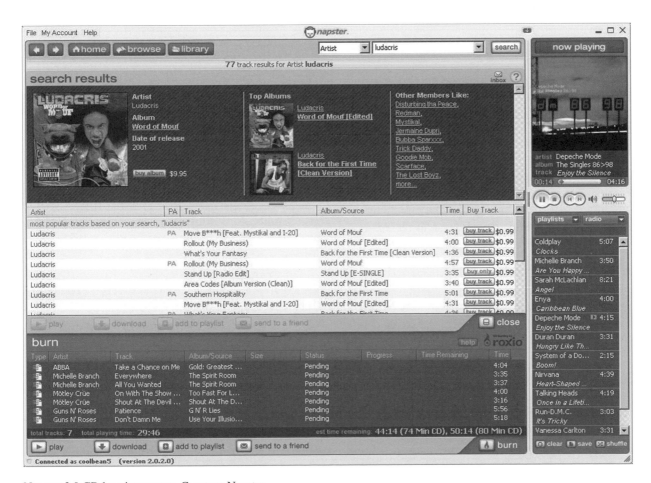

Napster 2.0 CD burning screen. Courtesy Napster

Marie Narelle. From the Collections of the Library of Congress

NARELLE, MARIE (1870–26 JAN 1941)

Australian soprano, born Catherine Mary ("Molly") Ryan in Combanning Station. She studied in Australia, London, and Paris. Her acclaimed debut was in London in 1902, sharing the program with Adelina Patti. She gave a command performance. Then she sang in concerts with John McCormack; both made their U.S. debuts at the St. Louis Exposition in 1904, and they toured the U.S. in 1909–1911. Narelle became known as the "Queen of Irish Song." She began to record for Edison in September 1905, with "Killarney" (#9081; later as Amberol #495), making cylinders and Diamond Discs until 1914. Later she worked for Pathé, singing "Dear Old Honolulu" (#20134; 1916); she may have also recorded under the name Marie Ryan. Her last stage appearances were in 1931. Narelle died in Chipping Norton, England. [Walsh 1964/2–3.]

NASHVILLE SOUND

SEE COUNTRY MUSIC RECORDINGS

NASSAU (LABEL)

An American record of 1906, masters from Imperial, pressed by the Leeds and Catlin Co., sold by Macy's department store. A record player named Nassau was also available through Macy's. [Andrews 1984/12.]

NATHAN, SYD

SEE KING RECORDS

NATIONAL (LABEL) (I)

A record issued by the National Certificate Co., New York, in the early 1920s. Pressing was done by the Bridgeport Die and Machine Co. [Rust 1978.]

NATIONAL (LABEL) (II)

A record produced in the early 1920s by the National Record Exchange Co., Iowa City, Iowa. It was linked with Paramount. Some good jazz material was included, but most of the output was dance music and popular vocals. [Rust 1978.]

NATIONAL (LABEL) (III)

A record credited to the National Record Co., New York, issued in 1925; it was one of the Emerson-Consolidated group, with matrix numbers paralleling those on the Clover label. [Kendziora 1988/11; Rust 1978.]

NATIONAL (LABEL) (IV)

A Paramount subsidiary record, issued from October 1944. National Disc Sales, Inc., 1841 Broadway, New York, was the distributor. Material was pop, race, and hillbilly. Among the artists were Raymond Scott, Vincent Lopez, Al Trace, Pete Johnson, Billy Eckstine, Kate Smith, Red McKenzie, and Charlie Ventura. Savoy acquired the label in 1957. [Porter 1978/7.]

NATIONAL ACADEMY OF RECORDING ARTS AND SCIENCES (NARAS)

An organization established in 1957 to promote creative and technical progress in the sound recording field. The first chapter office was opened in Los Angeles in 1957, followed by 11 more offices, including New York (1958), Chicago (1961), Nashville (1964), Atlanta (1969), Memphis (1972), San Francisco (1974), Austin (1998), Philadelphia (1999), Florida (2000), and Washington, D.C. (2000). The membership consists of performers, producers, engineers, and others engaged in the industry; as of 2002, there were over 20,000 members. A Producers and Engineers Wing was also established in early 2000 as a means of representing members in special areas of the recording profession; other wings are planned. From 1958 NARAS has presented the annual Grammy awards for outstanding recordings. The NARAS Hall of Fame was established to honor records issued before the Grammys began. NARAS has also established several charitable and advocacy organizations, including MusiCares Foundation, established in 1989 to provide health care and other services to musicians; the Grammy Foundation, supporting education in music; and the National Coalition for Music Education. In 1997, NARAS founded the Latin Academy of Recording Arts & Sciences (the Latin Recording Academy, with offices in Miami and Santa Monica, California, as its first international membership organization, representing Spanish-speaking artists. The First Latin Grammy awards were held in September 2000. [website: www. grammy.com.]

REVISED BY CARL BENSON

NATIONAL ANTHROPOLOGICAL ARCHIVES AND HUMAN STUDIES FILM ARCHIVE (SMITHSONIAN INSTITUTION)

The National Anthropological Archives, part of the Department of Anthropology, in the National Museum of Natural History, Smithsonian Institution, collects and preserves historical and contemporary anthropological materials that document the world's cultures and the history of the discipline. Its collections represent the four fields of anthropology: ethnology, linguistics, archaeology, and physical anthropology. Materials include manuscripts, field notes, correspondence, photographs, maps, sound recordings, and film and video created by Smithsonian anthropologists and other preeminent scholars. The collections document the Smithsonian's earliest attempts to record North American Indian cultures, which began in 1846 under Joseph Henry, and they include the research reports and records of the Bureau of American Ethnology (1879–1964), the U.S. National Museum's Division of Ethnology, its Division of Physical Anthropology, and River Basin Survey archaeology. The NAA also maintains the records of the Smithsonian's Department of Anthropology and of dozens of professional organizations, such as the American Anthropological Association, the American Ethnological Society, and the Society for American Archaeology. Among the earliest ethnographic collections are the diaries of John Wesley Powell, which recount his exploration of Colorado and study of the region's Indians, and the pictographic histories of Plains Indians collected by

U.S. military officers and BAE ethnographers. Other significant manuscript collections include the ethnographic and linguistic research of Franz Boas, Frances Densmore, Albert S. Gatschet, John Peabody Harrington, and J.N.B. Hewitt, as well as the expedition logs, photographs, and film record produced on Matthew Stirling's explorations in New Guinea (1926–1929). The NAA's holdings include nearly 400,000 ethnological and archaeological photographs, including some of the earliest images of indigenous people worldwide, and 20,000 works of Indian art (North American, Asian, and Oceanic). The archives's audio collections have 1,200 aluminum discs recorded by J.P. Harrington during his extensive work in California, the Northwest Coast, and Alaska. With the recent addition of the Human Studies Film Archives, NAA added more than 8 million feet of original film and video materials to its collections. The Smithsonian's broad collection policy and support of anthropological research for over 150 years have made the NAA an unparalleled resource for scholars interested in the cultures of Latin America, Oceania, Africa, and Asia. [website: http://www.nmnh. si.edu/naa/.]

MARTIN J. MANNING

NATIONAL ASSOCIATION OF BROADCASTERS

Formed in 1922, initially to work for rational rules related to spectrum allocation for U.S. radio broadcasting, the NAB was crucial in bringing about the Radio Act of 1927. This created legislation for station licensing and frequency allotment, while avoiding government control of station's business operations and programming. A second major concern of the organization's founders focused on demands made by the American Society of Composers, Authors and Publishers (ASCAP) that broadcasters license and pay for all music played over the air. In working out relations with ASCAP, and later with other licensing organizations, the NAB became the chief business representative as well as the governmental lobby representing the broadcasting industry. With headquarters in Washington, D.C., the NAB is one of the most active lobbies in the U.S. It represents more than 900 television stations and almost 5,000 radio stations, as well as 7,500 members from the radio and television industry. It monitors FCC activities and legislation, as well as economic, legal, social, and technical trends that might affect the industry, and holds yearly conferences and conventions that deal with the radio and television business and technology, including aspects related to recording. [website: www.nab.org.]

NATIONAL ASSOCIATION OF TALKING MACHINE JOBBERS

A U.S. trade organization established in 1907 (originally the Talking Machine Jobbers National Association; new name first cited in *TMW* of 15 June 1908). W.D. Andrews was the first vice president. The officers in 1908–1909 were James Bowers, president; W.D. Andrews, vice president; Louis Buehn, treasurer; and Perry B. Whitsit, secretary. New officers elected at the third convention of the association, July 1909, were Whitsit, president; J. Newcomb Blackman, vice president; Buehn, treasurer; and Joseph C. Roush, secretary. The fourth convention was held in Atlantic City, New Jersey, in July 1910, with all the officers reelected. A new president, Lawrence McGreal, was elected at the fifth convention, in Milwaukee, Wisconsin, in July 1911; E.F. Taft became vice president; Roush, treasurer, and William F. Miller, treasurer. At the sixth convention, Atlantic City, July 1912, Blackman was elected president; George E. Mickel, vice president; Buehn, secretary; John B. Miller, treasurer. Roush was the new president in July 1913, elected at the seventh convention in Niagara Falls, New York. Mickel became vice president; W.H. Reynalds [*sic*], treasurer; Whitsit, secretary. In July 1914, at the eighth convention in Atlantic City, Mickel was president, E. F. Taft, vice president; E. C. Rauth, secretary; and W. H. Reynalds, treasurer. Andrew G. McCarthy was the new president in 1915, elected at the ninth convention, in San Francisco. H.F. Miller was vice president; Reynalds, treasurer; Rauth, secretary. At the 10th convention, in July 1916 in Atlantic City, Rauth was president, H. A. Winkelman, vice president; L.C. Wiswell, secretary; and Reynalds, treasurer. The 11th convention was in Atlantic City in July 1917. Blackman became president; I Son Cohen [*sic*], vice president; Arthur A. Trostler, treasurer; and Roush, secretary. There was no convention in 1918, but the executive committee met in Philadelphia. The *TMW* story of the 12th convention, Atlantic City, 1919, refers to the group for the first time as "Victor jobbers." Mickel was elected president; Thomas H. Green, vice president; Trostler, secretary; and Reynalds, treasurer. At the 14th convention, Atlantic City, 1920, Wiswell became president; Buehn, vice president; Trostler, secretary; and Reynalds, treasurer. The organization met in Colorado Springs, Colorado, in July 1921, for its 15th convention; Buehn was elected president; Trostler, vice president; Charles K. Bennett, secretary; and George A. Mairs, treasurer. At the 16th convention, Atlantic City, June 1922, Trostler was elected president; Thomas Green, vice president; W.F. Davidson, secretary; and Mairs, treasurer. The executive committee met in July 1922 and voted to dissolve the association.

NATIONAL AUTOMATIC MUSIC CO.

An American firm, affiliated with the Automatic Musical Instrument Co. It provided coin-op pianos to places of entertainment, 4,200 were on location in 1925.

NATIONAL BARN DANCE

A country music radio show broadcast from WLS, Chicago, in 1924–1960, and from WGN, Chicago, in 1960–1970. Under director George D. Hay (who later went to Nashville to form the Grand Ole Opry), the *Barn Dance* became the first nationally known program of its type, and was a major force in the acceptance of the country genre in mainstream America. Among the artists who began great careers in the Eighth Street Theatre (venue of the WLS program) were Gene Autry, Bob Atcher, Patsy Montana, Lulu Belle and Scotty, and Red Foley. Over the years nearly every significant country artist appeared on the program. Sears, Roebuck and Co., the first sponsor, promoted recordings by the country stars in its mail order catalogs.

NATIONAL GRAMOPHONE CO.

A firm established on 19 Oct 1896 by Frank Seaman, in New York, succeeding his New York Gramophone Co.; in advertising it was styled the National Gram-o-phone Co. It was eventually succeeded by the National Gramophone Corp., another Seaman firm established in March 1899. Seaman had contracted personally with Berliner Gramophone Co. for U.S. sales rights — except for Washington, D.C. — to Berliner products, and he set up the National Gramophone Co. to handle sales. After an unsuccessful first year, business improved greatly. In 1897 the firm was advertising the "Gram-o-phone Zon-o-phone" — in fact a Berliner gramophone — and the "Improved Gram-o-phone Zon-o-phone." Sherman, Clay & Co., San Francisco, was the Pacific Coast agent. Sale price of the record player in an October 1898 advertisement was $25.00. Records were selling at $0.50 each. The April 1899 catalog of the firm included material by the Sousa Band, the Banda Rossa, Cal Stewart, Albert C. Campbell, Vess L. Ossman (banjo), W. Paris Chambers (cornet), Henry A. Higgins (cornet), and George Graham (humorist). F.M. Prescott was noted as the "sole export agent." However, there were legal problems, as American Graphophone Co., led by Philip Mauro, brought litigation over alleged infringement of its Bell-Tainter patents. There was also a dispute between Seaman and Berliner, based on Seaman's failed effort to have Berliner take on more cheaply made gramophones. Seaman finally stopped ordering gramophones in October 1899. Berliner refused to supply Seaman with discs, so National Gramophone Co. had no Berliner products to sell and was phased out of business. Seaman's second firm, National Gramophone Corp., was left to deal with the American Graphophone Co. litigation. [Wile 1991.]

FRANK ANDREWS

NATIONAL GRAMOPHONE CO., LTD.

A British firm established in London, in 1911, certificated to do business as of 3 Aug. Directors were P.J. Packman, James Albert Corey, Walter Amelius Cloud, Robert Crawford Lees, and Walter Hansen Rawles. After some litigation brought by the National Phonograph Co., Ltd., over the prior use of the name "National" in Britain, the plaintiff firm determined to withdraw its complaint and change its own name to Thomas A. Edison, Ltd. (August 1912). Nevertheless the National Gramophone Co., Ltd., decided not to go ahead with plans to issue a disc labeled "National," and advertised (for the first time in July 1912) one named Marathon Record. This was a narrow-grooved vertical cut record with longer playing time than typical discs of the time. A new company was created on 2 Jan 1913, named the National Gramophone Co. (1913), Ltd. It took over Marathon Records and Marathon record players. Business was excellent in 1913, but there was a financial crisis in early 1914, and the firm went into receivership in March 1915. The last additions to the Marathon Records catalog came in March 1915. Apparently the Orchestrelle Co., Ltd., of London, acquired some or all of the national assets. [Andrews 1987/4.]

NATIONAL GRAMOPHONE CORP.

Frank Seaman, who had been operating the National Gramophone Co. since 19 Oct 1896, established a second firm on 10 Mar 1899. The purpose of the National Gramophone Corp. was to be the sales agency of the new distinctive Zonophone disc players being developed by L.P. Valiquet and manufactured by the Universal Talking Machine Co. The first Zonophones were merely clones of the Berliner Gramophone, and Seaman knew that he could not carry on indefinitely with that product. As it happened, problems developed with Berliner in 1899 and came to a head just at the time (late 1899) when the new Zonophone products — record players and discs — were ready. The early firm, National Gramophone Co., was phased out, and Seaman concentrated his plans on the new corporation. Frank J. Dunham was its president, Orville La Dow its secretary; Seaman was treasurer. The patent conflict with the Columbia interests (American

Graphophone) remained to hinder sales of the new Zonophones. Seaman's strategy was to admit infringement of the Columbia patents, but to devise a cross-licensing agreement whereby he could continue to make and sell the new Zonophones, and Columbia (which did not yet have its own disc machines) could also handle them. With the cross-licensing agreement in effect, from May 1900, Columbia was able to drop the Vitaphone line of machines and discs that had been operating under Columbia protective licensing. Advertising by the National Gramophone Corp. in November 1900 promoted the "Zon-o-phone (substituted for our Gram-o-phone which is abandoned)." All these machinations came to a dismal end for Seaman, for the Zonophone venture did not prosper, and by March 1901 the National Gramophone Corp. was in difficulties from which it could not recover; it was put into liquidation in September 1901. In 1903 the Zonophone tradename and the Universal Talking Machine Co. assets passed to the Victor Talking Machine Co. [Wile 1991.]

FRANK ANDREWS

NATIONAL MALE QUARTET

A vocal group that recorded for Edison Diamond Discs in 1924–1927. Members were Clarence da Silva, tenor (replaced in 1926 by Arthur Hall); Lloyd Wiley, tenor (replaced in 1926 by John Ryan); Harry Jockin, baritone; and Harry Donaghy, bass. The group's best record was "Yankee Rose" (#51967; 1927). Another popular disc was "Bye, Bye, Blackbird"/"Honey Bunch" (#51758; 1926).

NATIONAL MUSIC LOVERS, INC. (LABEL)

An American record label of 1922–ca. 1927 issued by an organization of that name in New York. Material came from Paramount, Emerson, Olympic, and Plaza-Banner; it included dance music, novelty items, band and concert music, sacred music, Irish numbers, songs, and operatic items. Some well-known artists appeared under pseudonyms, such as the California Ramblers and Fletcher Henderson. These records were available by mail order, with a money-back guarantee of satisfaction. [Cotter 1975–1988 is a complete label list.]

NATIONAL PHONOGRAPH ASSOC.

A trade organization formed by the 33 regional affiliates of the North American Phonograph Co. A convention was held in Chicago on 28–29 May 1890, chaired by J.H. McGilvra of the Volta Graphophone Co. Edward Easton called the convention to order. R.F. Cromelin was secretary. Among the issues discussed were the poor performance of graphophones, and the need for a single standardized instrument (association members were selling both the Graphophone and the Edison phonograph); and the problem of hostility between the interests of Charles Sumner Tainter and Thomas Edison. The principal business of the regional affiliates at the time was in leasing instruments for business use. But a number of the members were also involved with musical cylinders placed on location in coin-operated machines. At the second convention, New York, June 1891, only 19 companies were represented. A.W. Clancy was elected president, and Easton, vice president. There were 22 firms represented at the third convention, held in Detroit in 1893. Clancy was reelected president. In 1894, as Edison liquidated the North American Phonograph Co., the National Phonograph Assoc. ceased to function. Then there was a new assembly, in Cincinnati on 25 Sep 1900; Henry D. Goodwin was chairman, and James L. Andem the secretary at that meeting. [Proceedings 1974.]

NATIONAL PHONOGRAPH CO.

The firm established by Thomas Edison in Orange, New Jersey, in January 1896 to manufacture and distribute spring-driven cylinder phonographs for home use. This firm also held the relevant Edison patents. The first products were the Edison Home Phonograph, sold for $40, and the Edison Standard Phonograph, sold for $20. Manufacturing of the machines was carried out in Orange, in the Edison Phonograph Works. Concentrating on mail order sales to the rural market, the enterprise provided the first successful competition for the graphophone. By 1901 there were offices in New York (83 Chambers St.), Chicago (144 Wabash Ave.), and San Francisco (933 Market St.). A European headquarters was set up in Antwerp (it moved to London in 1904). Branch offices were established in Paris, Berlin, Brussels, Vienna, and Milan. These overseas activities were coordinated by Will Hayes. Recording began in London in May 1903, at 52 Grays Inn Road, then in new premises in the Clerkenwell Road in January 1904. The European factories had closed by 1908, but recording studios and sales agencies remained open. Machines and records were manufactured in the U.S. after 1911. Production figures for Edison cylinders show a steady increase from 1896 to 1904. For the year ending 28 Feb, the total records manufactured were:

1897	None
1898	87,690
1899	428,310
1900	1,886,137
1901	2,080,132
1902	1,976,645
1903	4,382,802
1904	7,663,142

In 1905–1907 there were about 12,000 Edison dealers in the U.S. When Edison established Thomas A. Edison, Inc. in 1910, the National Phonograph Co. was absorbed into it, along with the Edison Phonograph Works. [*APM* 1–10 (December 1973): 3, gives the production figures.]

NATIONAL PHONOGRAPH CO., LTD.

The only British firm authorized to distribute genuine Edison goods wholesale; established in London in March 1902 by J.L. Young and E. Sinclair. It was independent of the Edison business at first, but was engaged by Edison's attorney in July 1902 to handle the Edison interests in Britain. It had its own record pressing plant, also in London. In August 1912, the company was absorbed into the new firm, Thomas A. Edison, Ltd.

FRANK ANDREWS

NATIONAL SOUND ARCHIVE (NSA)

A unit in the British Library since 1983, originally (1947) the British Institute of Recorded Sound. The Archive holds over 1 million discs of all kinds, over 185,000 recorded tapes, and CD, DVD, and minidisc recordings. Member companies of the British Phonographic Industry send two copies of about 75 percent of their releases for deposit to NSA. The collections illustrate the development of recorded sound in all formats, and in all categories. There are important holdings in Western art music (including BBC broadcast material not otherwise available); traditional music from most countries of the world (including hundreds of hours of field recordings, some dating back to the late 1890s, as part of the International Music Collections); the Library of Wildlife Sounds; drama (including the repertoires of the Royal Shakespeare Co. and other national groups, as well as radio plays); spoken literature; jazz and popular music, British and imported (including live sessions and concerts broadcast by the BBC). A free listening service is provided by appointment to any member of the public, and reference service through a comprehensive library. NSA is very concerned with restoration and transfer of materials from temporary media like acetate tapes to more permanent sound carriers. During the 1980s, a development of that effort was the Computer Enhanced Digital Audio Restoration (CEDAR) system. [Borwick 1989/7; website: www. bl.uk/collections/sound-archive/nsa.html.]

NATIONAL TALKING MACHINE CO.

A New York firm, established in 1916. It marketed the Bluebird line of record players, in four models.

NATIONAL VOICE LIBRARY

See Vincent Voice Library

NATION'S FORUM (LABEL)

An American record, produced by Columbia for Nation's Forum, an historical society founded in 1918 by St. Louis attorney Guy Golterman, with cooperation of the U.S. State Department, to preserve the voices of statesmen and prominent leaders. In 1918 the first series of discs appeared, 10-inch records, not sold commercially. The second series, 12-inch records, appeared in 1919–1920. Among the voices heard were Calvin Coolidge, General George Pershing, Eamon de Valera, and Samuel Gompers. As radio became available in 1920 (presidential election results were broadcast in November), the public interest in such records — slight as it had been — disappeared, and the project ceased. [Rust 1978.]

FRANK ANDREWS

Label devoted to issuing political speeches, active in the early '20s. Courtesy Kurt Nauck/Nauck's Vintage Records

NATUS, JOE (1 MAR 1860–21 APR 1917)

American singer and comedian, born in Detroit. He performed alone and with minstrel groups, and made cylinders in 1896, followed by discs for Berliner. In about 1900, he began recording for Edison, making 36 vaudeville numbers and solo ballads, plus 19 duets with Arthur Collins. He also worked for Lambert, Zonophone, Victor (and Monarch), and Columbia (to 1907). Among his Columbia two-minute cylinders were "Sweet Annie Moore" (#31584) and "Wrap Me in the Stars and Stripes" (#31587). He died in Rome, New York.

NAXOS (LABEL)

A budget-priced, classical CD label established in 1987 by Klaus Heymann, headquartered in Hong Kong. Heymann began his career as a journalist, and then launched a mail-order electronics firm in Hong Kong during the Vietnam War. In the early 1970s, he became exclusive distributor for a number of audio companies in Hong Kong, and began organizing classical music concerts to promote high-end audio equipment. He also became distributor for several budget classical labels, including Vox, Hungaroton, Opus, and others. In 1978, he issued his first recording, made by his wife, Takako Nishizaki, a classical violinist, of the Chinese violin concerto, *The Butterfly Lovers*. The success of this recording led him to form his first label, HK Records, eventually incorporated into Pacific Music, which both released its own recordings and distributed many other Western classical labels throughout the region. After specializing in Asian music written in a classical style, Heymann decided to begin recording the standard Western repertoire with local orchestras, including the Hong Kong Philharmonic (he was a key supporter of this orchestra as a board member and fundraiser) and the Singapore Symphony Orchestra, among others. He founded a new label, Marco Polo, for these recordings. By the mid-1980s, Heymann was producing most of his recordings out of Eastern Europe, where he had well-established contacts with several classical labels. In 1987 he founded a budget CD classical label, Naxos, originally marketing only in the Pacific Rim region. The label soon grew strongly in Europe and the U.S., where a branch office was opened in 1990. By the year 2000, the label had released more than 1,700 CDs, with 200 new releases planned per year. The label specialized in recording entire repertories by individual composers or by instrument, such as the complete Vivaldi concertos, a planned 150–200 CD set of organ music, 100 CDs of piano music, as well as the complete standard orchestral and chamber repertories. [website: www.naxos.com.]

CARL BENSON

NEBRASKA PHONOGRAPH CO.

One of the 33 affiliates of the North American Phonograph Co., established in 1890 in Omaha, Nebraska. E.A. Benson was president in 1890 and 1892; H.E. Cary was vice president and general manager in 1891–1892. The company continued to 1893. Leon F. Douglass began his career with the firm; he went on to success as an inventor and joined Eldridge Johnson's Consolidated Talking Machine Co.

NEEDLE CHATTER

Vibration of the pickup in a disc player, caused by insufficient vertical compliance of its moving parts.

NEEDLE CUT

See Lateral Recording

NEEDLES

Replaceable needles were a hallmark of the 78-rpm period. They were made of various materials: steel, chrome, fibers, thorn, cactus, sapphire, and diamond. Some needles were designed for a single play only (e.g., the Beltona), others played as many as 10 records (e.g., the Petmecky), and some went on to 20 or more performances (e.g., the Euphonic). With the popularity of the juke box in the 1930s there was improved needle design: alloy tipped shockproof needles came into use, capable of many plays. The diamond needle was theoretically nonwearable. And some sapphires, such as the one marketed by Neophone in 1905, were also "permanent" — advertised to play from 500–800 times. As early as 1906 there were nine types of needle available: three to play quietly, three to play at medium volume, and three types for loud playback. (These were sold by Universal Talking Machine Co. of New York.) Loud needles had rounded tips, and softer-sound needles had sharper tips. The problem with all metal and jewel needles was that they chewed up the record grooves. Fiber, thorn, and cactus needles were popular with collectors in the 1930s and 1940s because they produced minimal record wear, but of course the needles themselves wore out instead. They could be shaved for replay, and shaving devices something like pencil sharpeners were sold for the purpose. Victor sold a fiber "needle cutter" in 1909 that used a plunger action, "enabling you to use each fiber needle at least 10 times." Major manufacturers offered a choice of materials; for example in 1924 HMV was advertising steel, fiber, and "tungstyle" — said to be semipermanent — varieties. The Petmecky Co. had the favorite

brand-name needles of the acoustic period, made by the W.H. Bagshaw Co., of Lowell, Massachusetts. In the electric era the Recoton brand was among the most popular in America.

With the arrival of LP records, the light-weight stylus took the place of the needle.

NEEDLE TINS

During the 78-rpm era, phonograph needles were sold in tin boxes, often bearing colorful designs; they have become collectors' items. Many of the needles were made by record manufacturers, and carry the same logo as the disc labels of those companies. For example, Nipper appears on HMV needle tins, and the two-note Columbia trademark on its tins. Not all needles were sold in tins; there were also various kinds of paper boxes and even aluminum boxes. [Lambert 1985 gives numerous illustrations.]

NEGATIVE FEEDBACK

The inversion and return of a portion of an amplifier's output to its input. It is used intentionally to reduce distortion and to provide more predictable amplification and response. Since negative feedback also reduces gain, the amplifier must have a greater open-loop gain to compensate for this factor. But the considerable improvement in many other characteristics often outweighs the reduction in gain.

See also **Acoustic Feedback**

NELSON, BILL (18 DEC 1948–)

Although he has flirted with major commercial success on a number of occasions, Yorkshire, England, native Bill Nelson appears content to remain a cult artist, releasing experimental albums at unpredictable intervals. The singer/multi-instrumentalist/composer's recorded work covers a wide range of styles, from dynamic progressive rock built on the interplay of guitar pyrotechnics and keyboards to ambient synthesizer-based landscapes. Nelson's debut LP, the limited edition *Northern Dream* (Smile #2182; 1971), attracted attention in the British underground scene through airplay on BBC Radio 1 (England's main radio outlet). He went on to form Be-Bop Deluxe, a band whose art-rock inclinations were tempered by audience-pleasing glam/power-pop accents. Despite frequent personnel changes, Be-Bop Deluxe issued a succession of critically acclaimed albums — *Axe Victim* (Harvest #11689; 1974), *Futurama* (Harvest #11432; 1975), *Sunburst Finish* (Harvest #11478; 1976; #17 U.K., #96 U.S.), *Modern Music* (Harvest

#11575; 1976; #12 U.K., #88 U.S.), *Live in the Air Age* (Harvest #11666; 1977; #10 U.K., #65 U.S.), and *Drastic Plastic* (Harvest #11750; 1978; #23 U.K., #95 U.S.) — and appeared to be on the verge of superstardom when Nelson dissolved the band to form the more experimental Red Noise. Apparently recognizing the creative limitations of the band format, Nelson went solo after issuing only one LP. Since 1980, Nelson's prolific body of work has ranged across the full spectrum of the avant-garde. His more notable ambient releases included *Quit Dreaming and Get on the Beam* (Mercury #7557 010; 1981; #7 U.K.), *The Love that Whirls* (Mercury WHIRL/CURL #3; 1982; #28 U.K.), *Chimera* (Mercury MERB #19; 1983; #30 U.K.), *On a Blue Wing* (Portrait #40146; 1986; #91 U.K.), *Chamber of Dreams* (Cocteau JC #7; 1986), and *Map of Dreams* (Cocteau CCD #19; 1987). Nelson attempted to get closer to the mainstream in the 1990s, as reflected in LPs like *Practically Wired* (All Saints/Gyroscope #022; 1995), a more energetic collection — the opening track, "Roses and Rocketships," could easily be mistaken for techno — utilizing keyboards and samples to spice up its atmospheric guitar work. Nelson's acknowledged ability to produce lush soundscapes has also led to collaborations with postpunk acts such as the Associates, the Skids, David Sylvian, and Yellow Magic Orchestra, as well as the new age duo Roger Eno/Kate St. John.

FRANK HOFFMANN

NELSON, KEN (19 JAN 1911–)

Born in Caledonia, Minnesota, Kenneth F. Nelson was raised in a midwest orphanage and became a classical music disc jockey on WJJD, Chicago. He was placed in charge of auditioning country performers for the station's *Suppertime Frolics* show, and was recruited by Capitol Records A&R man Lee Gillette in 1948. In 1951, he assumed Gillette's role as head of country music A&R at Capitol, a role he held until retirement in 1976. Based in Los Angeles, he drew most of his artists from the California country scene, resisting the industry's Nashville centrism. Among his signees were Faron Young, Ferlin Huskey, Sonny James, Buck Owens, and Merle Haggard, as well as rock 'n' roll singers like Gene Vincent. He also launched (and surreptitiously owned) a music publishing company, Central Songs, which boasted a rich catalog of country copyrights, and was eventually sold to Capitol's parent company, EMI. Nelson was inducted into the Country Music Hall of Fame in 2002.

COLIN ESCOTT

NELSON, RICK (8 MAY 1940–31 DEC 1985)

American rock singer, born Eric Hilliard Nelson in Teaneck, New Jersey. At age 12 he began to take part (as Ricky) in his parents' television show, the *Adventures of Ozzie and Harriet*. In 1957 he started singing on the program, and made his first hit records, "Be-Bop Baby"/"Have I Told You Lately that I Love You" (Imperial #5463) and "I'm Walking" (Verve #10047). Nelson was able to promote his records by presenting the material on the television show, and had a series of 45 chart singles by 1965. Following a dip in popularity, as the Ozzie and Harriet program went off the air, he moved to a country rock style and achieved new successes. "Garden Party," with his country group the Stone Canyon Band, was a gold single of 1972, 18 weeks on the charts (Decca #32980). Nelson was again out of public favor in the later 1970s, but made another comeback in 1981, with the chart album *Playing to Win* (Capitol #12109). He was killed in a Texas plane crash on New Year's Eve in 1985.

NELSON, WILLIE (30 APR 1933–)

American country singer, guitarist, and songwriter, born in Abbott, Texas. He was a disc jockey in Texas and on the West Coast, and sang in various locales before moving to Nashville in 1960. There he established himself as a composer, with such songs as "Crazy" — made into a hit record by Patsy Cline. He did not succeed as a singer in Nashville, and moved to

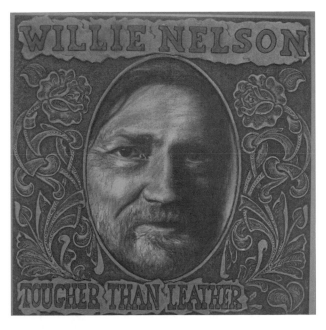

Willie Nelson album cover, c. mid-'70s. Courtesy Frank Hoffmann

Austin, Texas, where he adopted a more exuberant, rock-oriented style and in 1973 recorded a successful album, *Shotgun Willie* (Atlantic #7262; 1973). In 1975 his song "Blue Eyes Crying in the Rain" was the best-selling country record (Columbia #10176; also in the album *Red-headed Stranger* [Columbia KC #33482; 1975]). Between 1975 and 1985 Nelson had 25 chart albums on his own, plus others with Waylon Jennings, Kris Kristofferson, Johnny Cash, Ray Price, or Leon Russell. *Willie Nelson's Greatest Hits* (Columbia KC #2–37542; 1981) was on the charts 112 weeks. Nelson's career was spotty since the mid-1980s, although he continued to be a popular touring artist. In the late 1980s, dogged by the IRS, who claimed the singer owed them penalties for unpaid taxes, he issued two albums sold through direct-mail television offers called *Who'll Buy My Memories?*, with the proceeds going to pay off the government. In 1993, Nelson issued a 60th birthday album and television special, but it failed to move his career forward. In 1996, Nelson moved to Island Records, issuing albums of new material and covers of blues and earlier styles. He was awarded a "Lifetime Achievement" award at the 2000 Grammy ceremonies. In 2002, he released *The Great Divide on Lost Highway* (a division of Mercury Records), featuring duets with various other pop and country stars, including Kid Rock and Sheryl Crow. The first single, "Mendocino County Line," a duet with Lee Ann Womack, was his first charting record in some time.

REV. CARL BENSON

NEOPHONE CO., LTD.

A British manufacturer, located in London, incorporated 10 Oct 1904. William Michaelis was founder and general manager; E.J. Sabine was assistant manager. The new firm took over the business of a previous one operated by Michaelis, the Neophone Disc Phonograph Co. Vertical-cut discs (German-made at first) of various sizes were offered, some of 20-inch diameter with about 10 minutes playing time per side. Made of a material called Neolite, the large black records were playable on any machine; but the smaller nine-inch white discs (made of pressed paper with a white enamel surface) required a sapphire reproducer. The white discs were unbreakable, but the black ones were breakable. A line of Neophone record players was sold to accommodate the firm's discs, and in 1905 an attachment was sold that would make it possible to play the vertical-cut discs on regular talking machines. Another interesting product was a home disc recorder, the first in the industry, offered in 1905 (*TMR* #52–53, 6 June 1978, reproduced an advertisement for it).

Neophone was very successful, and in 1905 had established branches in France, Italy, Germany, Russia, Austria, and Belgium. Artists from La Scala were among those available on Neophone records. Nevertheless, it was decided to put the company into liquidation, and to replace it with one named Neophone (1905) Ltd., incorporated on 22 Sep 1905, at 22 Philpot Lane, London. William Michaelis was principal shareholder and a director of the new company. In February 1906 there were seven types of Neophone discs on sale, from nine inches to 20 inches in size, covering operatic works (some in a series that had labels autographed by the artists) and popular repertoire. "Neolite Disc Phonograph Records" — 12 inches, double sided — were first issued in June 1906, along with Neolite Universal Reproducers that could be adjusted to play vertical or lateral-cut records. Offices in New York, Toronto, Paris, Brussels, Berlin, Milan, Australia, and Japan were reported during 1906. On 4 Feb 1907 a subsidiary company was registered in Britain to handle sales everywhere except in the U.K.: International Neophone Co. (2 Tabernacle St., London). Then Neophone was acquired by the General Phonograph Co., Ltd., in July 1907. That firm resolved to wind up its affairs on 13 Apr 1908, and the Neophone trademark disappeared. The International Neophone Co., Ltd., was stricken from U.K. Companies Register on 21 Feb 1911. [Andrews 1978/3 is a history and label list.]

NEUMANN, GEORG (OCT 1898–30 AUG 1976)

Born in Chorin, near Berlin, during most of the 1920s, Neumann worked for Eugen Reisz, who was credited with developing the first decent-quality carbon microphone. Neumann went on to design a still better version, which was called the Reisz microphone, after the firm's owner. During this period, Neumann was also responsible for numerous phono pickups, the capacitive loudspeaker, and electro-mechanical cutter head designs. In 1928, in Berlin, Neumann, along with Erich Rickmann, started the company that still bears his name, and went on to design and build condenser microphones which became famous throughout the recording and radio industry for their quality. The company also produced some fine test equipment, the most notable of which was the linear motion, logarithmic pen recorder. After World War II, Neumann temporarily moved to Paris, where he worked to develop a new storage-battery design. The result was the gas-tight NiCad battery, which revolutionized the portable power industry. In 1947, the company was reorganized, and the result was Neumann's U-47 microphone, a device that changed what could be heard with recordings. After a long career of building innovative products for the audio and recording industries, Neumann won the Audio Engineering Society's Gold Medal in 1976. Years after his death, in 1999, the company that bears his name won a Grammy for technical achievement, and many of those achievements were a direct result of the genius of Georg Neumann.

See also **Microphone**

HOWARD FERSTLER

NEVE, RUPERT (1926–)

One of the most famous audio-recording console designers of all time, Neve was born in Newton Abbot, Devonshire, England. From the beginning he had been interested in electronics, and at age 13, he designed and built audio amplifiers and radio receivers. He was educated at Belgrano Day School and St. Alban's College, Lomas de Zamora, Buenos Aires. When World War II erupted, he returned to England to serve in His Majesty's Royal Signals. Peace time found him running a public address and disc recording business in England, and later he worked for several other companies, specializing in transformer design. During this time, he also designed one of the first ever bookshelf-oriented loudspeakers, and was invited to lecture on it at the Royal Society of Arts in London in 1958. For four additional years he designed and manufactured hi-fi equipment. In 1961, he started Rupert Neve & Co., located near Cambridge, specializing in custom equipment for the recording, television, film, and broadcasting industries. The enterprise, and his reputation as a designer, grew rapidly, and in 1969 the company moved to a new factory at Melbourne. In 1975 he sold control of the company, and by 1978 he had ceased to design equipment for them. With the later sale of the Neve companies to Siemens in 1985, the company was reorganized, although it ceased operations in 1992. Neve continued as an independent designer, and in 1985, Beatles producer George Martin commissioned Neve to build a no-compromise microphone-preamp and EQ circuit that he could add to the Neve console in his A.I.R. Montserrat studio. Neve is now a long-term design consultant to Amek (a Harman International company), whose expertise in the audio sound control and manufacturing fields is supported by Neve's innovative approach to the sound path. Recent designs include new analog rack-mount microphone preamps, equalizers, dynamic-control units, and consoles for live sound, film, and music recording. Neve won a Grammy for technical achievement in 1997.

HOWARD FERSTLER

NEVEU, GINETTE (11 AUG 1919–28 OCT 1949)

French violinist, born in Paris. She made her debut at age seven with the Colonne Orchestra of Paris, playing the Bruch First Concerto. Then she took first prize at the Paris Conservatory at age 14, and won the Wieniawski Grand Prize Competition in Warsaw (defeating, among others, David Oistrakh), in 1934. Carl Flesch and Georges Enesco were among her teachers. Neveu's U.S. debut was with the Boston Symphony Orchestra in 1947. She was a world success, at the peak of her career, when she died in an air disaster in the Azores. Her few recordings display a sensitive virtuosity, in particular with French composers. EMI Références CD #63493 (1990) includes her Debussy Violin Sonata (HMV ALP #1520; 1957), the Ravel *Tzigane* (HMV DB #6907/08; 1949), Chausson's "Poème" (HMV ALP #1520; 1957), and the Richard Strauss Violin Sonata in E-Flat (HMV #DB4663/6; 1948).

NEW AGE MUSIC

New age music evolved out of a shared consciousness among composers and performers. Their credo held that music should be based on harmony and consonance, rather than dissonance; minus the hooks and rhythmic pulse typifying popular music; employ soothing instrumental sounds (e.g., prominence of piano, harp, flute, bells, string ensembles); and elevate space to a key role (i.e., the electro-acoustic enhancement of instrumental tones through reverb and echo). New age music began taking form in the latter half of the 1970s as baby boomers, approaching middle age and facing the full effect of career and family pressures, began exploring softer forms of pop music. A pivotal development was William Ackerman's formation of the Windham Hill label in 1976; the label's first superstar was pianist George Winston, whose *December* (Windham Hill #1026; 1983) spent more than three-and-a-half years on the *Billboard* "Top Pop Albums" charts. Despite the preponderance of electronic/space and acoustic folk-flavored albums during the 1980s, the commercial success of Enya's *Watermark* (Geffen #24233; 1989) spurred a Celtic music fad within the genre. A broad, amorphous category, new age includes the following subgenres: 1. Electronic/computer music; 2. folk music; 3. jazz/fusion; 4. meditation music; 5. American Indian/indigenous music; 6. pop music; 7. progressive music; 8. solo instrumental music; 9. sound health music; 10. space music; 11. traditional music; 12. vocal music; and 13. world music.

1. *Electronic/Computer Music.* The rapidly evolving technology of modern society has placed the

resources of a small orchestra within the means of most artists. This has facilitated the creation of innovative sounds hitherto impossible to achieve with traditional acoustic instruments. The key tools here are synthesizers — a large, expanding class of dissimilar instruments that often combine tape recorders, computers, and specialized digital equipment — and samplers (enabling a musician/programmer to blend snippets of recorded acoustic sound — e.g., a violin passage or bird songs — with electronic tones to generate new music pieces). David Arkenstone's *Valley in the Clouds* (Mystique #62001; 1987) — built around shimmering textures set within a Third World ambience — elucidates these techniques in textbook fashion. Other leading practitioners include Wendy Carlos, Jean-Michel Jarre, Steve Roach, Klaus Schulze, Isao Tomita, Vangelis, and Yanni.

2. *Folk Music.* Based on influences derived from traditional folk and ethnic sources (e.g., Celtic, bluegrass), this style is usually acoustic and instrumental in orientation. Divided between original compositions and classic folk material in an upbeat mode, the sound is built around such instruments as six- and 12-string guitars, Celtic harp, flutes, and dulcimers. Notable exponents include William Ackerman — whose intimate vehicle for solo acoustic guitar, *Passage* (Windham Hill #1014; 1981) belies criticisms that new age lacks poignancy and soul — Checkfield, Malcolm Dalglish and Greg Larsen, Mark O'Connor, and Allan Stivell.

3. *Jazz/Fusion.* Representing a gentle rebellion against overly spacey new age music and frenetic jazz, this fusion style avoids the abstract dissonance typified by avant-garde jazz or classical compositions in favor of mood, texture, and flowing movement. Jazz crosses into new age territory when it avoids standard "swing" rhythms, its instrumentation is enhanced by synthesizers and the use of digital reverb, and it is not repetitious or inaccessibly intellectual. It is distinguished from other new age subgenres, especially space music, by its rhythm and identifiable melodies. Typical instrumentation includes woodwinds, horns, percussion, keyboards, and string instruments. Among the better known artists are Beaver and Krause, who virtually defined the genre with *Gandharva* (1971; now available on Warner Bros. CD #45663 coupled with the duo's 1970 release, *In a Wild Sanctuary*), which features ambient improvisations recorded in San Francisco's Grace Cathedral; synthesizer player Peter Davison; former Big Band-rock violinist (Flock) Jerry Goodman, perhaps best known for his collaborations with Jeff Beck; Hiroshima; guitarist Pat Metheny, whose recorded work alternates between frenetic fusion workouts and more impressionistic soundscapes; chamber music ensemble Oregon; electric vio-

lin virtuoso Jean-Luc Ponty; British guitarist John Renbourn, whose work includes elements of folk, jazz, and classical music modalities; and flutist Tim Weisberg.

4. *Meditation Music.* This style aims at expanding awareness into deeper and higher levels of consciousness. It removes negativity through careful arrangement of each note and one pattern. It isn't always serene and gentle in nature; more dynamic forms often combine drumming and pulsing music to stimulate an active response within the listener (e.g., dancing). Key practitioners include Aeoliah, Chazz, Steven Halpern, and Laraaji.

5. *American Indian/Indigenous Music.* The accompaniment is provided by rattles, drums, and group chorus, depending upon the context and form of the musical presentation. The types of songs, their placement in a ceremony, and the textural form — meaningful words or vocalized sounds — reflect the worldviews of various tribes. Duple meter (patterns of two drum beats throughout) percussion patterns, a wide variety of tempos, and dynamic accents contribute to the distinctive quality of tribal music. The genre includes three subdivisions: sacred/ceremonial songs; social songs; and personal vocal and instrumental music. Among the notable exponents are Kevin Locke, A. Paul Ortega, and R. Carlos Nakai, whose gentle string and woodwinds arrangements — e.g., *Winter Dreams* (Canyon #7007; 1990; with William Eaton) — frequently grace the new age charts.

6. *Pop Music.* Of all new age genres, this one is the most energetic and accessible. It tends to be very melodic, often weaving acoustic and electronic instruments into a sonic whole. It has depth, using harmony, melody, and simple key modulations rather than creating spacelike sounds. Leading artists include Bruce Becvar, Checkfield, David Darling, the Durutti Column, Michael Hedges, and Liz Story.

7. *Progressive Music.* This category mixes the excitement and vision of progressive and experimental music with the sensitivity and warmth of the new age genre. Largely created by state-of-the-art technology and a wide array of electronic instruments, it's cinematic in scope and imparts a feeling of momentum. Compositions deliver symphonic — sometimes psychedelic — crescendos intended to jar the listener's perception of reality. Michael Oldfield's hypnotic *Tubular Bells* (Virgin #105; 1973) created a sensation when placed within the soundtrack to *The Exorcist*. Mannheim Steamroller's popularity — particularly with respect to seasonal titles such as *Mannheim Steamroller Christmas* (American Grammaphone #1984; 1984) and *A Fresh Aire Christmas* (American Grammaphone #1988; 1988) — is substantial enough to regularly place the group (essentially a studio vehi-

cle for originator Chip Davis) high on the pop albums charts. Other notable practitioners Gavin Bryars, Cusco, Patrick Gleeson, Mark Isham, Daniel Lentz, and Patrick O'Hearn.

8. *Solo Instrumental Music.* The style serves to slow down the mind, thereby aiding in relaxation or meditation. The music often consists of long tones and is at times almost harmonically structureless. It acts as a blank canvas on which the listener can visualize personal "mind pictures." Key exponents include Philip Aaberg, Alex De Grassi, Paul Greaver, Daniel Hecht, Paul Horn, Peter Kater, Andreas Vollenweider, and George Winston, whose collection of introspective piano pieces, *December* (Windham Hill #1025; 1983) is often cited as the first true new age LP to achieve best-seller status.

9. *Sound Health Music.* Specifically created as a tool for health and wellness, the genre attempts to either facilitate brain activity for accelerated learning or take the listener to deep places in the consciousness for meditation (via slow brain wave patterns). Many releases deal with the relationship among keynotes, colors, and the chakras; others combine vowel sounds, rhythmic pulses, drones, and different scales to resonate and affect the physical body as well as the etheric energy field. Top artists include Roger Eno, Steven Halpern, Paul Temple, and Michael Uyttebroek.

10. *Space Music.* Concerned with both inner and outer space, this style opens and creates spatial relationships. Most composers use synthesizers (sometimes exclusively) which can sustain notes timelessly or produce wholly new sounds. The balance between the rhythm track and melody line determines a great deal of the imagery and perspective of a particular piece. Constance Demby's electronic-choral masterpiece, *Novus Magnificat: Through the Stargate* (Hearts of Space HS #003; 1986), remains a genre classic. Other leading exponents include Kevin Braheny, Mychael Danna, Peter Davison, Edgar Froese, Kitaro, David Lange, Ray Lynch, Steve Roach, Michael Stearns, and Stomu Yamashta.

11. *Traditional Music.* Contemplative rather than entertaining by nature, it is typically instrumental and incorporates sacred, meditative, and healing properties. Utilizing a structure based on ancient traditions such a Pythagorean harmonics, it transforms the vibrational level of any environment into a relaxing, inspiring, and healing atmosphere. Key practitioners include Dean Evenson, Steve and David Gordon, Bob Kindler, Steve Kindler, Daniel Kobialka, Mike Rowland, Nancy Rumbel, Ira Stein and Russell Walder, Tim Story, Eric Tingstad, and Paul Winter.

12. *Vocal Music.* A broad-based category encompassing folk, pop, jazz, and rock. Themes covered include (a) an expanded sense of personal identity; (b) a recognition of connection with the global family; (c) a holistic awareness of the planet; (d) an awakened responsibility for one's thoughts, words, and actions; (e) an acknowledgment of the wisdom or divinity in everyone; (f) an emphasis on the healing power in relationships; (g) a recognition of the wholeness of body, mind, and spirit; and (h) an admission that there is an underlying power and intelligence called God, Love, Universal Spirit, etc., with an absence of spiritual elitism. Among the notable artists are Clannad, Eliza Gilkyson, David Hykes, Ian Matthews, Kim Robertson, Michael Stillwater, and Michael Tomlinson.

13. *World Music.* The genre spans music (a) derived solely from one culture and accepted by others; (b) created when the indigenous material of one culture is combined with the material of other cultures (e.g., melodic structures and rhythms of India fused with the impovisation of European pop music); and (c) drawn from or uniting both ancient and contemporary styles (e.g., South American flutes mixed with Spanish guitar and modern synthesizers). Key exponents include Spencer Brewer, Stephan Grossman, Jan Hassell, Inti-Illimani, Stephan Micus, Popol Vuh, and Tri Atma. [Birosik 1989.]

FRANK HOFFMANN

NEW CHRISTY MINSTRELS

American folk and popular singing group, formed in 1961 by Randy Sparks, named for the 19th-century troupe of E.P. Christy. Much of their material was composed for them but in a folk-styled idiom. The group disbanded in the mid-1970s, having sold more than 13 million albums. Their greatest hits were made in 1962–1964, among them *Ramblin* (Columbia CL #2055; 1963), 41 weeks on the charts; and *Today* (Columbia CL #2159; 1964), 32 weeks.

NEW COMFORT RECORDS (LABEL)

A disc issued by New Comfort Talking Machine Co., Cedar Rapids, Iowa, in 1921. The firm advertised its discs and phonographs in *TMW*, and announced its incorporation in June 1921, but there is no further information about its products. Rust says the record was "a rare member of the Grey Gull complex" about which little is known other than its numbering in a 5000 series. [Rust 1978.]

FRANK ANDREWS

NEW EDITION (1983–1988)

While New Edition had a relatively short run as a hit-making entity, the vocal quintet nurtured some of the leading R&B artists of the 1990s. The group's original members — Bobby Brown, Ralph Tresvant, Ricky Bell, Michael Bivins, and Ronnie DeVoe — met in the early 1980s as junior high school students in Boston's Roxbury district. Promoter Maurice Starr, who discovered them performing at a local talent show, secured them a recording contract with the hip-hop label, Streetwise. Following the release of two top 10 R&B singles — "Candy Girl" (Streetwise #1108; 1983) and "Is This the End" (Streetwise #1111; 1983), New Edition parted ways with Starr (who would form New Kids on the Block) and signed with MCA Records. Their next album, *New Edition* (MCA #5515; 1984) crossed over to number six on the *Billboard Hot 100*, propelled by the hit singles, "Cool It Now" (MCA #52455; 1984) and "Mr. Telephone Man" (MCA #52484; 1984–1985). Their follow-up albums — *All for Love* (MCA #5679; 1985), *Under the Blue Moon* (MCA #5912. 1986), and *Heart Break* (MCA #42207; 1988) — enjoyed moderate success, but the group's singles did not perform well on the pop charts.

New Edition was ultimately torn apart by the loss of key personnel to solo careers, beginning with Brown in 1986. His replacement, Johnny Gill, also struck out on his own in the late 1980s, as did Tresvant. In 1988, the remaining members formed the hip-hop trio, Bell Biv DeVoe. The group members have remained close, however, often working together in the 1990s as well as considering the possibility of reuniting to produce an album. [Romanowski and George-Warren 1995.]

FRANK HOFFMANN

NEW ENGLAND PHONOGRAPH CO.
An affiliate of the North American Phonograph Co., established in 1890 in the Boylston Building, Boston. General A.P. Martin was president in 1892; Charles A. Cheever and Jesse Lippincott were among the directors. Russell Hunting and W.F. Denny were the leading artists.

NEW FLEXO (LABEL)
A record issued from early 1925 to autumn of the same year, by the Warner Record Co. of Kansas City; Missouri. Flexible discs without paper labels, many survive in illegible form. No well-known artists have been identified as performers. [Rust 1978.]

NEW GRAMOPHONE
A disc player marketed in 1925 by the Gramophone Co. in the U.K., for use with the new electric recordings. It replaced the standard pre-electric instruments, as the Victor Orthophonic did in America. [There is a photo in Andrews 1985/6.]

NEW JERSEY PHONOGRAPH CO.
One of the affiliates of the North American Phonograph Co., established in 1890 in Newark. George Frelinghuysen was president in 1892, and Nicholas Murray Butler was vice president. General manager was Victor H. Emerson. Frank L. Capps was an employee when he invented the three-spring motor that was used on the Edison Concert Phonograph and other machines. A catalog issued before November 1891 offered 499 brown wax cylinders. The repertoire included band selections, "parlor orchestra" works, instrumental solos with piano accompaniment (piccolo, clarinet, cornet, xylophone), vocal solos (comic, coon songs, sentimental, and so forth), and vocal ensembles. There were also bird imitations and some anecdotes. George W. Johnson made his earliest appearance for this label, singing "Whistling Coon" (#423) and "Laughing Song" (#424). In 1893 the firm was succeeded by the U.S. Phonograph Co. of New Jersey. [*TMR* #10 (June 1971) reprinted the catalog cited above; *TMR* #20–21 (February–April 1973) printed date information supplied by Raymond Wile.]

NEW JERSEY SHEET METAL CO.
A firm located in, Newark, New Jersey. In 1907 it marketed the Ajax horn of "rust proof sheet steel" and the collapsible Kompakt horn.

NEW KIDS ON THE BLOCK
New Kids on the Block are widely viewed within the record industry as white clones of the youthful pop-soul phenoms, New Edition. After parting with the latter act over a record-contract dispute, composer/ producer/ promoter Maurice Starr enlisted a Boston talent agency to locate talented white singers, rappers, and dancers. The resulting group — comprised of Donnie Wahlberg, break dancer Danny Wood, Joe McIntyre, and brothers Jonathan and Jordan Knight — released an eponymous debut album, *New Kids on the Block* (Columbia #40475; 1986), which sold poorly. However, the follow-up, *Hangin' Tough* (Columbia #40985; 40985), topped the charts, propelled by the hit singles, "Please Don't Go Girl" (Columbia #38-07700; 1988) and "You Got It" (Columbia #38-08062; 1988). Although their R&B-inflected bubblegum was generally panned by rock journalists, a string of top 10 singles followed: "I'll Be Loving You (Forever)" (Columbia #38-68671; 1989), "Hangin' Tough" (Columbia #38-68960; 1989), "Didn't I (Blow Your Mind)" (Columbia #38-68960; 1989), "Cover Girl" (Columbia #38-69088; 1989), "This One's for the Children" (Columbia #38-73064; 1989), "Step by Step" (Columbia #73443; 1990), and "Tonight" (Columbia #73461; 1990). In 1991, the unit topped *Forbes* magazine's list of top-grossing American enter-

tainers. Professional and legal problems (e.g., allegations of brawling and arson, a lawsuit disclosing that members had lip-synched performances of their recordings) served to diminish the group's popularity. In 1992, they resurfaced as NKOTB; the recordings revealed a more musically ambitious approach. Although a modest seller by past standards, *Face the Music* (Columbia #52569; 1994) — produced by Wahlberg, Teddy Riley, and Narada Michael Walden (known for his work with Whitney Houston and Marian Carey), among others — earned uniformly high marks from critics. By the late 1990s, however, the group had been eclipsed by newer acts catering to the youth market such as the Backstreet Boys and 'N Sync. Wahlberg turned increasingly to production work (among his clients was younger brother, Marky Mark) and Jordan Knight attempted to mount a solo career. [Romanowski and George-Warren 1995.]

FRANK HOFFMANN

NEW LOST CITY RAMBLERS, THE

Old-time string-band revival group, featuring Mike Seeger, John Cohen, Tom Paley (1958–1962); Paley was replaced by Tracy Schwartz in 1963. Seeger, the son of folklorist Charles Seeger and half-brother of folk revivalist Pete Seeger, was enamored of bluegrass and country music in the Washington, D.C., area where he grew up. Yale-educated Cohen was active in the New York folk scene in the 1950s, while Paley, a mathematician, was from the Boston area. The trio's academic background is reflected in their approach to the music, in which they strove to accurately re-create the 78-era recordings that they used as their source material. They often focused on a single theme — on albums such as *Songs from the Depression* (Folkways FH #5264; 1959) and *American Moonshine and Prohibition Songs* (Folkways FH #5263; 1962) — and presented the music with meticulous documentation, including information on their sources. Their appearance at the 1959 Newport Folk Festival introduced them to the folk-revival audience, and led to many years of popularity on the college and small folk-club circuit. Paley left the group in 1963, and Seeger brought in his friend Tracy Schwartz, who brought a more modern sound to the group. Schwartz's background in bluegrass widened the group's repertoire to include recreations of 1950s-era country recordings as well as the older styles they had previously performed. The band recorded an all-instrumental album, perhaps the first to emphasize this side of the old-time music tradition, as well as accompanying legendary country performer Cousin Emmy on a 1967 recording. The concept album, *Modern Times* (Folkways FTS #30027; 1968), was perhaps one of their best recordings; while still centering on a general theme (country folk's reaction to the changes in their lives brought about by industrialization),

the band took a freer approach to the music, bringing their own personal musical stamp to it. By the early 1970s, the Ramblers were performing only sporadically together. Although they never officially "disbanded," they have only performed together on and off for over two decades, mostly for special occasions such as reunions or at festivals. They issued their first new album of studio recordings in over a decade in 1998 for the Smithsonian/Folkways label (*There Ain't No Way Out*; #40098). That label also issued two career overview CDs of the Ramblers's recordings, *The Early Years* (Smithsonian/Folkways #40036) and *The Later Years* (Smithsonian/Folkways #40040).

CARL BENSON

NEW MUSIC QUARTERLY RECORDINGS (LABEL)

A record issued in 1933–1948 by *New Music Quarterly*, a publication devoted to contemporary American music. After 1940 the label was renamed New Music Recordings. There were 64 sides in toto, offering 62 titles by 38 composers; all were first recordings. In 1978 eight sides were reissued on LP by Composers Recordings, Inc. Orion issued an LP in 1971, with works of Charles Ives and Carl Ruggles; and New World Records issued Ives's *General William Booth Enters into Heaven* in 1976 as part of a large anthology. Among the 83 artists on the NMQR records were flutist Georges Barrère, pianists Leonard Bernstein and Aaron Copland, violist/composer Quincy Porter, harpist Carlos Salzédo, conductor Nicolas Slonimsky presenting the earliest Ives orchestral music on record — and violinist Joseph Szigeti in the initial recording of the Ives Violin Sonata No. 4. Before the NMQR records appeared, there had been virtually no commercial recording of contemporary American music; the available repertoire had included major works by George Gershwin, Ferde Grofé, John Alden Carpenter, and a few others. Composers Henry Cowell, Charles Ives, and Otto Luening were principal supporters of the enterprise. When it folded, the matrices found their way through Theodore Presser Music Co. to (1977) Composers Recordings, Inc. of New York. [Hall 1984/1 is a history and label list.]

NEW ORDER

New Order's dark synthesis of postpunk and dance music gained a substantial following during the 1980s, particularly in Great Britain. They achieved success in uncompromising fashion, avoiding virtually all forms of publicity, including band photos on album covers and promotional materials. New Order arose out of the ashes of Joy Division, a band formed in 1976 after guitarist

Bernard Sumner and bassist Peter Hook saw the Sex Pistols perform in their hometown of Manchester. The later additions of singer Ian Curtis and drummer Stephen Morris completed the lineup. The band first performed as Warsaw, later adopting the moniker Joy Division, a reference to Nazi military prostitute compounds. Their debut recording, a four-track EP titled *Ideal for Living* (Enigma #139), was issued in late 1977. The band's debut album, *Unknown Pleasures* (Factory #10; 1979), anticipated the goth movement of the 1980s with its message of alienation and existential angst framed by a propulsive drone. With Joy Division on the verge of superstardom, Curtis committed suicide shortly before the release of their follow-up LP, *Closer* (Factory #25; 1980; #6 U.K.). Changing their name again, this time to New Order, the band — now built around Sumner's understated vocals and more pronounced keyboard textures, supplied by new band member, Gillian Gilbert — continued producing infectious club hits, including "Everything Gone Green" (Factory #53; 1981; #38 U.K.), "Temptation" (Factory #63; 1982; #29 U.K.), and "Blue Monday" (Factory #73; 1983; #9 U.K.), the latter of which was produced by American hip-hop producer Arthur Baker. New Order released a string of best-selling albums — *Movement* (Factory #50; 1981; #30 U.K.), *Power, Corruption and Lies* (Factory/Streetwide #25308; 1983; #4 U.K.), *Low-Life* (Qwest #25289; 1985; #7 U.K., #94 U.S.), *Substance* (*1980–1987*) (Qwest #25621; 1987; #3 U.K., #36 U.S.), and *Technique* (Qwest #25845; 1989; #1 U.K., #32 U.S.) — before its members opted to pursue solo activities. Following several years of silence, the band re-formed to record *Republic* (Qwest #45250; 1993; #1 U.K., #11 U.S.). With the exception of a 1998 reunion show in Manchester and the inclusion of a new recording, "Bruta" in the Leonardo DiCaprio film, *The Beach* (1999), members have remained active in outside projects. Sumner has collaborated with ex-Smiths guitarist Johnny Marr and vocalist Neil Tennant, formerly of the Pet Shop Boys, in Electronic; Hook forming Monaco; and Gilbert and Morris recording as the Other Two.

FRANK HOFFMANN

NEW ORLEANS RHYTHM KINGS (NORK)

An ensemble established in Chicago in the early 1920s by trumpeter Paul Mares, trombonist Georg Brunis, and clarinetist Leon Roppolo [spelling usually seen as Rappolo], white men from New Orleans. Their group, which included seven or eight other musicians, performed 17 months at Friar's Inn, and was at first known as the Friar's Society Orchestra. They were quickly famous, rivaling the older great white group, the Original Dixieland Jazz Band. In 1923, they made two sessions with pianist Jelly Roll Morton, among the first interracial sessions in jazz. They disbanded in 1924, revived a year later, then broke up permanently. NORK recorded for Gennett in 1922, beginning with "Eccentric" (#5009). "Panama"/"Tiger Rag" was a showpiece for Roppolo (Gennett #4968; 1922), who was also brilliant in "Wolverine Blues" (Gennett #5102; 1923). In 1925 NORK recorded for Okeh and Bluebird. Altogether they only recorded 28 titles. This group should not be confused with two later ones of the same name, headed by Wingy Manone and Muggsy Spanier. Milestone #40720 reissues all of their recordings on CD (which is itself a reissue of an earlier Milestone two-LP set). Classics has also reissued all of their 1922–1923 recordings (#1129) and additionally offers later versions of the band, recorded from 1925–1935, on a second CD (#1150).

NEW PHONIC (LABEL)

A record issued by Carl Henry, Inc., of New York, in 1927–1928. Matrices came from the Plaza/Banner labels, with the artists disguised by pseudonyms. It is a rare label, with only a few copies known. [Kendziora 1989/4; Rust 1978.]

NEW ROMANTICS, THE

The New Romantic movement, also termed blitz, combined techno-pop elements with a glitzy fashion sense originating from the disco club scene. The popularity of dance-oriented rock styles in England following the disco era of the mid-1970s, combined with the heightened fashion consciousness exhibited by British youth, contributed to the birth of the blitz movement. While the genre had its origins in the late 1970s, it didn't move out of the underground until late 1982. The pivotal factor proved to be MTV's receptiveness to broadcasting video clips of blitz bands. Established in the fall of 1981, the pioneering cable channel suffered from a dearth of quality product to program round the clock. The New Romantics — telegenic, sexy, and exuding a careful, fun-loving approach to life — soon dominated MTV playlists and, ultimately, radio programming and industry sales charts. Key acts included ABC, Adam and the Ants, Culture Club, Duran Duran, Spandau Ballet, and the Thompson Twins. The movement had lost its momentum by the mid-1980s, however, due to competition from a wide array of postpunk styles as well as the tendency of many blitz bands to implode from within. While a considerable number of solo performers — most notably, Adam Ant, Boy George, and Simon Le

Bon — emerged from the fragmentation of these groups, none of them were able to achieve anything approaching the success they'd enjoyed the first time around.

NEW WAVE

The new wave was a product of the stagnating British pop music scene in the mid-1970s. Heavy metal and the progressive rock hybrids then dominating sales had turned off many listeners, exuding pretentious self-consciousness, art for art's sake, and a profit orientation that favored arena-sized audiences. At the same time, pubs had nurtured an alternative style featuring a rollicking mixture of old-style rock and roll, careening honky-tonk, and good-timey skiffle music. The "pub-rock" movement was assisted further by the formation of small labels such as Stiff Records (1976). Its prime exponents reflected the genre's eclectism: Graham Parker was one of the most passionate — and angriest — rock poets ever; Brinsley Schwarz exhibited a preference for bucolic, country-inflected material; Dr. Feelgood attempted to re-create the sweaty ambience of 1950s R&B clubs; and Rockpile (featuring Dave Edmunds and Nick Lowe) was a classic rock 'n' roll band. The new wave, in essence, represented a refinement of the American punk scene then undergoing a renaissance in New York City spearheaded by the Ramones, Blondie, Television, and the Talking Heads. It was appropriated by British tastemakers, who neutralized the genre's destructive tendencies, utilizing punk's energy to revitalize traditional rock conventions. Leading artists — including Joe Jackson, the

Jonathan Richman's Modern Lovers, one of the first new wave groups. Courtesy Frank Hoffmann

Pretenders, Police, Wreckless Eric, Elvis Costello, and the Tom Robinson Band — also displayed a receptiveness to a wide array of stylistic influences such as reggae and jazz. Like the pub rock and punk movements, the new wave represented a conscious reaction against the American rock industry innovations of the late 1960s, including (1) Woodstock-styled rock fests and stadium venues; (2) a dependence on mega-corporations to disseminate recordings; and (3) the view of the rock audience as a community with the artist functioning as a unifying agent (in contrast, new wave artists projected themselves as alienated loners reaching out to the loner in each listener). In contrast, the U.S. scene lacked any kind of socioeconomic core. It was largely the product of youthful middle-class eccentrics motivated by the desire to leave a mark on rock history. It is notable that many of them were located far from major urban centers. Ohio — particularly Akron and Cleveland — became a focal point for the emerging new wave ethic. These artists tended to fall into one of the following categories: (1) the arty (Pere Ubu, Tin Huey, the Human Switchboard), (2) the profane (the Bizarros, Teacher's Pet, the Dead Boys, the Rubber City Rebels); and (3) the poppy (Rachel Sweet). Lacking the media resources available in the larger cities, local fans provided the initiative and insights necessary to generate a full-fledged movement. Where major labels weren't interested, fans managed and signed up local talent for small regional outfits. Further support was provided by mimeographed manifestos, homemade rock magazines, and an ad-hoc network for the distribution of records. By the late 1970s, the genre had finally made a substantial commercial impact at the national level when American bands such as the Cars and the Knack placed records in the upper reaches of the charts. This coincided with the first stateside breakthrough of a British new wave band, the Police. The movement remained successful into the early 1980s, fragmenting into a wide array of spin-offs, including techno-pop, the new romantics, neo-rockabilly, neo-psychedelia, goth rock, thrash, alternative dance, the ska/bluebeat revival, and indie rock. The latter style, known as "alternative" or "modern" rock by the early 1990s, took on many of the brash, rebellious tendencies of the new wave. [Miller 1980.]

FRANK HOFFMANN

NEW WORLD RECORDS (LABEL)

An American record of 1975, founded with a grant from the Rockefeller Foundation, and officially known as Recorded Anthology of American Music, Inc. The Rockefeller grant was intended to produce a representative collection of recordings of American music for presentation to libraries and schools. In 1978 the

New World Records label. Courtesy Frank Hoffmann

Wilhelm Furtwängler (1925–1927), Arturo Toscanini (1927–1936), John Barbirolli (1936–1943), Artur Rodzinski (1943–1947), Bruno Walter (1947–1949), Dimitri Mitropoulos (1949–1957), Leonard Bernstein (1958–1969), Pierre Boulez (1971–1978), Zubin Mehta (1978–1990), and Kurt Masur (1990–2002), and Lorin Maazel (2002–). There were also a number of regular conductors who shared principal duties, and prominent guest conductors; e.g., George Szell was music advisor and senior guest conductor from 1969 to 1971. In 1928 the Philharmonic merged with Damrosch's Symphony Society orchestra, and took the name Philharmonic-Symphony Society Orchestra. The orchestra now gives more than 200 concerts per year. It is recognized as one of the premier ensembles of the nation. The orchestra has made over 2,000 recordings as of the beginning of the 21st century, with 500 or so still in print. It was honored with a Trustee's award from the Grammy organization in 2003, the first classical orchestra to be so honored; its recordings had previously won nine Grammys over the years.

Anthology was completed and distributed free of charge to almost 7,000 educational and cultural institutions throughout the world; an additional 2,000 Anthologies were sold at cost to other similar institution. The label has continued to produce about 25 new recordings a year beyond the original "anthology," supported by grants from various government and private foundations. [website: www.newworldrecords.org.]

NEW YORK GRAMOPHONE CO.
The firm operated by Frank Seaman from 7 Feb 1896, prior to the formation of his National Gramophone Co. on 19 Oct 1896. It implemented Seaman's sales rights for Berliner Gramophone Co. products in New York and New Jersey.

NEW YORK PHILHARMONIC ORCHESTRA
Founded in 1842 as the Philharmonic Symphony Society of New York, this is the oldest continuous major orchestra in the U.S. There were various conductors at first, with no permanent director. Then Theodore Eisfeld was appointed director in 1852, remaining until 1865. He was followed by Carl Bergmann (1855–1876), Theodore Thomas (1877–1891), Anton Seidl (1891–1898), Emil Paur (1898–1902), Walter Damrosch (1902–1903), Vasily Safonov (1906–1909), Gustav Mahler (1909–1911), Josef Stransky (1911–1922), Willem Mengelberg (1921–1930), Willem van Hoogstraten (1923–1925),

NEW YORK PHONOGRAPH CO.
An affiliate of the North American Phonograph Co., established in 1890 John P. Haines was president in 1890–1892. Recording studios were set up around 1890 to make brown wax cylinders. Coin-op machines were a major enterprise; there were 175 of them leased in 1891. In 1906 the firm brought an action against the National Phonograph Co., with a successful outcome in 1908.

NEW YORK PRO MUSICA
An ensemble established in New York by Noah Greenberg in 1952; it was originally named the Pro Musica Antiqua, suggesting its focus on music of the Middle Ages, Renaissance, and baroque periods. Great acclaim followed its performance in 1957–1958 of the medieval *Play of Daniel*, performed in the appropriate surroundings of the Cloisters (a monastery that is part of the Metropolitan Museum of Art). When Greenberg died in 1966, J.R. White became director (1966–1970), followed by Paul Maynard (1970–1972), and George Houle (1972–1974). The group disbanded in 1974. Recordings of the Pro Musica were important in creating audiences for early music, and for the acceptance of authentic instruments in modern performance. As their work coincided with the emergence of the LP record, they achieved popularity through that medium. Among their outstanding recordings were the *Play of Daniel* (MCA #2504) and the *Play of Herod* (MCA #2–10008).

NEW YORK RECORDING LABORATORIES

A record manufacturer established in 1916, with an executive office not in New York but in Port Washington, Wisconsin. Studios were in New York City; and the pressing plant was in Grafton, Wisconsin. Much recording was done in Chicago, and from late 1929 also in Grafton. Paramount was the principal label produced (1916–1932), along with its various affiliate labels such as Broadway, Famous, and Puritan. [Rust 1978.]

NEW YORK TALKING MACHINE CO.

A firm established as a successor to the Victor Distributing and Export Co. in 1910. A 1911 advertisement described the company as an exclusive Victor wholesaler. H.D. Geissler was president in 1920.

NEW YORK TRIO

An chamber ensemble that recorded for Edison Diamond Discs in 1928. It consisted of Louis Edlin, violin; Cornelius Van Vliet, cello; and Clarence Adler, piano.

NEW YORKERS

A vocal quintet that recorded three Edison Diamond Discs in 1929. Members were Ed Smalle, Colin O'More, Harry Donaghy, and two men known only by their last names: Mr. Shope and Mr. Preston.

NEW ZEALAND

The history of sound recording in New Zealand is inevitably of a more modest nature than that of Australia, largely due to the substantial difference in the size of population (approximately one-fifth that of Australia). During the 19th and early 20th centuries mechanical instruments played a part in New Zealand musical life, just as they did in that of Australia. There are a number of accounts of pianolas in the hands of private persons, and various forms of musical automata were in existence. Advertisements from around 1905 show that companies like Charles Begg & Co., Ltd. and the Dresden Piano Co. stocked a wide range of talking machines and records, primarily from Gramophone and Typewriter Ltd., in England. An advertisement for HMV, with the familiar Nipper photograph, appeared in the *N.Z. Free Lance* (Wellington) in November 1905. Despite the appearance of discs, Edison phonographs and cylinders were still imported, and in 1910 were still extensively promoted in New

Zealand. The Cecil Zonophone, from America, appeared in 1910. His Master's Voice (N.Z.), Ltd., was incorporated on 10 May 1926, although recordings and equipment were still imported. Only occasionally were records actually made in New Zealand. Such was the case in June 1930 when recordings of the Rotorua Maori Choir were made in the Tunihopua Meeting House at the suggestion of W.A. Donner, of the Columbia Graphophone Co., Australia, after he had visited Rotorua. The discs were subsequently given worldwide distribution. In the 78 era New Zealand artists frequently recorded at the Australian HMV studios at Homebush. Until the late 1980s the industry was dominated by six firms who accounted for over 90 percent of record sales. These were CBS, EMI, Festival, Polygram, RCA, and WEA. EMI and Polygram owned record clubs. Several local companies produced and distributed records by New Zealand artists, among them Viking and Kiwi Pacific. More than 90 percent of records sold were made from imported masters, pressed locally at the plants of EMI and Polygram. In 1978 sales of records and tapes in the country amounted to about NZ$34.5 million. Over 5 million LPs were produced, and about 1.6 million cassettes. National economic conditions forced EMI to close its pressing plant in 1988. No CDs are currently produced in New Zealand. Works by New Zealand composers and artists are recorded locally and master tapes are sent overseas for processing. There are many independent labels in the main cities. A special role in sound recording history has been played by the New Zealand Broad-casting Corp. (now Radio New Zealand), established in 1936, and by the National Orchestra (1946). An important repository is the Radio New Zealand Sound Archive (1956), with rare recordings of Polynesian and Pacific music, complementing holdings of the Archive of Maori and Pacific Music at the University of Auckland. There are also important materials in the Sound and Music Centre, and in the Alexander Turnbull Library, both units of the National Library; and in the Hocken Library, Dunedin. [Acknowledgments: Beverley Anscombe, Music Librarian, University of Auckland; Auckland Public Library; Tony Chance, Recording Industry Association of New Zealand, Inc.; Roger Flury, Librarian, Sound and Music Centre; Hocken Library; Radio New Zealand; Jill Palmer, Music Librarian, Alexander Turnbull Library.]

GERALD R. SEAMAN

NEWPORT CLASSIC (LABEL)

Begun in 1985, by Larry Kraman, this Newport, Rhode Island–based company's first releases involved keyboardist Anthony Newman in all manner of standard early keyboard repertoire. The company has grown into a provocative and eclectic record label that has released everything from Bach, Beethoven, and Victor Herbert to Feldman, Cage, Luening, Amram, Rorem, Menotti, and Mollicone. Newport has debuted such offbeat pieces as the *Concerto for Orchestra, Chainsaw and Cow*, and even released a recording from the Newport Music Festival the day after it was recorded. The label's album *Hornsmoke*, written by Peter Schickele, and performed by the Chestnut Brass Ensemble and the composer, won the Grammy for Crossover Record of the Year in 1999. [website: www.newport-cd.com/.]

HOWARD FERSTLER

NEWTON-JOHN, OLIVIA (26 SEP 1947–)

Olivia Newton-John was one of the leading pop-rock recording artists from the early 1970s to the mid-1980s. Due to her photogenic good looks, she also made a substantial impact in the visual media. She released a number of best-selling video titles in the early 1980s, made regular appearances on television, and had starring roles in a string of films, including *Grease* (1978), *Xanadu* (1980), and *Two of a Kind* (1984). Born in Cambridge, England, Newton-John grew up in Australia singing folk material. Shifting to mainstream pop styles, she had become an established recording star in England by the early 1970s. Her manager, John Farrar — who had teamed with ex-Shadows guitarists Hank Marvin and Bruce Welch to form a Crosby, Stills & Nash–styled trio earlier in the decade — steered her in the direction of country pop. Several major hits — "Let Me Be There" (MCA #40101; 1973–1974; #6 pop, #7 c&w), "If You Love Me (Let Me Know)" (MCA #40209; 1974; #5 pop, #2 c&w), and "I Honestly Love You" (MCA #40280; 1974; #1 pop, #1 AC, #6 c&w) — resulted in her controversial selection as the Country Music Association's Entertainer of the Year in 1974. Her albums — comprised for the most part of soft rock — also sold well; *If You Love Me, Let Me Know* (MCA #411; 1974) and *Have You Ever Been Mellow* (MCA #2133; 1975) both topped the charts. While she continued to place high on the country charts for most of the decade, her music took on an increasingly smooth, middle-of-the-road feel. In fact, "Have You Ever Been Mellow" (MCA #40249; 1975; #1), "Please Mr. Please" (MCA #40418; 1975; #3), "Something Better to Do" (MCA #40459; 1975; #13), "Let It Shine" (MCA #40495; 1976; #30), "Come on Over" (MCA #40525; 1976; #23), "Don't Stop Believin'" (MCA #40600; 1976), and "Sam" (MCA #40670; 1977; #20) were all number one adult

contemporary hits, thereby helping broaden the appeal of that genre. By the late 1970s, her releases — most notably, "You're the One that I Want" (RSO #891; 1978; #1; with John Travolta), "Summer Nights" (RSO #906; 1978; #5; with Travolta), "Magic" (MCA #41247; 1980; #1 pop 4 weeks, #1 AC), and "Physical" (MCA #51182; 1981; #1 10 weeks) — had incorporated a stronger rock feel. She signed with Geffen in 1989; her first LP for the label, *Warm And Tender* (#24257; 1989; #124), a collection of lullabies, appears to have been influenced by the recent birth of her daughter. Although Newton-John had ceased being a chart fixture by the mid-1980s and oversees a retail clothing chain, she continues to intermittently tour and make new recordings.

FRANK HOFFMANN

NEWARK TINWARE AND METAL WORKS

A manufacturer of talking machine horns, advertising in 1907 a line made of simulated wood. Location was in Newark, New Jersey.

NEWMAN, RANDY (28 NOV 1944–)

At first glance, Randy Newman would not seem a likely candidate for popular success. As a composer, his work is saturated with dark humor and irony — the lyrics often portray bigoted rednecks, perverts, and other assorted losers — backed by chromatic flourishes more typical of George Gershwin than top 40 songs. He sings with a lazy drawl accompanied by simple piano chords and subtle, impressionistic orchestra arrangements. Nevertheless, his material is widely covered by other artists and his own recordings generally sell well. Born in New Orleans, he grew up in a musical family; his uncles, Alfred and Lionel, were major Hollywood film composers during the post–World War II era. He became a staff writer for a California-based publishing company as a 17-year-old, dropping out of UCLA one semester short of earning a B.A. in music. A friend and staff producer at Warner Bros., Lenny Waronker, helped him secure a recording contract with the label. Newman first gained fame as a songwriter; his songs were recorded by Judy Collins, Peggy Lee, and Three Dog Night, whose rendition of "Mama Told Me (Not to Come)" (Dunhill #4239; 1970) reached number one on the pop charts. Harry Nilsson would record an entire LP with Newman at the piano, *Nilsson Sings Newman* (RCA #4289; 1970). Touring with Nilsson helped him develop a cult following on college campuses. His early albums — including *Randy Newman* (Reprise #6286;

1968), *12 Songs* (Reprise #6373; 1970), *Randy Newman/Live* (Reprise #6459; 1971), *Sail Away* (Reprise #2064; 1972), *Good Old Boys* (Reprise #2193; 1974), and *Little Criminals* (Warner Bros. #3079; 1977) — were all critical successes; as a result, each release sold a bit better than its predecessor. The furor created by his first hit single, "Short People" (Warner Bros. #8492; 1977; #2) — which attacked bigotry, but was taken literally by an offended minority — made him a popular culture phenomenon. While his albums continued to sell well, he began receiving offers to compose movie soundtracks, most notably *Ragtime* (Elektra/Asylum #565; 1979) — nominated for two Oscars (Best Song, Best Score) — *The Natural* (Warner Bros #1161.; 1984), *Three Amigos* (Warner Bros #25558.; 1987), *Parenthood* (Reprise #26001; 1990), *Avalon* (Reprise #26437; 1990), *Awakenings* (Reprise #26466; 1991), *The Paper* (Reprise #45616; 1994), and *Meet the Parents* (Reprise #450286; 2000). Although much of his time was now taken by film projects, he returned to the singles charts with "I Love L.A." (Warner Bros. #29687; 1983) — which achieved anthem status largely due to an iconic video clip directed by his cousin, Tim Newman — and "It's Money that Matters" (Reprise #7-27709; 1988).

FRANK HOFFMANN

NHT CORP.

The letters stand for "Now Hear This." First established in 1986, in San Francisco, by Ken Kantor and Chris Byrne, the company's inaugural product, the Model 1 (possibly the first speaker produced by anybody that included video shielding) appeared in 1987. In 1988 all operations were moved to a new plant in Benicia, California, and during the period between 1988 and 1990, the company experienced notable success. In 1990 NHT was purchased by International Jensen, three months after Jensen had also purchased Acoustic Research. The post-1990 period showed accelerated growth, due to the influx of Jensen capital, with Kantor working as Jensen's corporate head of technology and Byrne in charge of the NHT branch as its managing director. In 1992 NHT was put in charge of the acoustic research branch, and both companies were more tightly consolidated under Jensen control. Its expanding and diverse product line (the company produced one of the first genuinely workable and affordable sub-woofer/satellite speaker packages) began to earn an even stronger reputation for very high quality, both in terms of bang-for-buck quality and cost-is-no-object performance, with its Model 3.3 being a good example of the latter. In 1996 Jensen sold its several branded activities (but not the industrial hardware facilities) to

Recoton Corp., thereby changing the ownership of NHT. Shortly thereafter, Recoton installed a new leadership team, made up mainly of past Harman International executives, with the mandate being to consolidate all the branded operations of Acoustic Research, Advent, NHT, and Jensen. Kantor and Byrne both left the company in 1998, although Byrne eventually returned to work directly for Recoton. NHT continues to produce and market full-range speaker systems and subwoofers of very high quality for home use (many having been designed by Bill Bush, who had been with the company over a decade, but left in 2001), and the company's NHT Pro branch is noted for its powered studio monitor systems.

HOWARD FERSTLER

NICHOLS, RED
(8 MAY 1905–28 JUNE 1965)

American jazz cornetist, born Ernest Loring Nichols in Ogden, Utah. His father taught him cornet and gave him a place in his brass band; from there Nichols went on to play in theater orchestras and, at age 17, with a dance band in Ohio named the Syncopating Five. In 1923 he was playing in the New York area with various groups. During the 1920s he was with Vincent Lopez, Sam Lanin, Harry Reser, the California Ramblers, and Paul Whiteman. He formed his own group, Red Nichols and His Five Pennies, in 1926. This ensemble varied in number and membership; it included — in recording sessions of December 1926 and January 1927 — such luminaries as Jimmy Dorsey, Eddie Lang, Miff Mole, and Joe Venuti. Later on Pee Wee Russell, Benny Goodman, Glenn Miller, Jack Teagarden, Bud Freeman, Dave Tough, Red McKenzie, Tommy Dorsey, Gene Krupa, Ray McKinley, and Will Bradley were in the Pennies; and there were vocalists such as Dick Robertson, Smith Ballew, and the Boswell Sisters. As the size of the group grew to as many as 14 artists, it was in fact a big band, and was identified as an orchestra on some recordings. Nichols was popular on radio through the 1930s. After World War II he led another group in long engagements at California venues. A 1959 motion picture based on his life, *The Five Pennies*, with Danny Kaye playing Nichols, gave him a late career boost. He died in Las Vegas. Nichols recorded prolifically, beginning as a sideman with Sam Lanin in 1924, and continuing with various Lanin groups to 1931. He recorded for Edison Diamond Discs from 1924–1927, including four sides with Red and Miff's Stompers (the Miff being Miff Mole) in October 1926. With the Pennies he recorded from December 1926 to October 1963, mostly on Brunswick, Victor, Bluebird, and

Capitol. "Sometimes I'm Happy"/"Hallelujah!" (Brunswick #4701; 1930) was a typical disc of the smaller ensemble (with both the Dorseys and Gene Krupa). The larger group is well displayed in "Love Is Like That" (Brunswick #6118; 1931), with a Ballew vocal. Capitol released several other LP albums, covering work of the 1950s. There are numerous CD reissues, including his complete Edison recordings (nine regular and nine alternate takes; Jazz Oracle #8007); radio transcriptions recorded in 1929–1930 (IARJC #1011); various "complete" chronological sets from Swaggie, Classics, and others, covering the 1924–1939 period; and many reissues of his 1950s Dixieland revival recordings for a variety of labels. [Backensto 1969 is a memorial issue of *RR*, with the Lanin-Nichols discography and a list of the Nichols records after 1956.]

NICHOLS, ROGER (22 SEP 1944–)

One of America's most notable recording engineers and producers, Nichols was born in Oakland, California, and was interested in astronomy as a child. Indeed, when he was in the seventh grade he constructed a hand-ground telescope lens, built a reflecting telescope, and used it to discover a comet in 1957. After graduating from high school, he won an appointment to the Air Force Academy, but declined and went to Oregon State University instead, and later completed nuclear engineering course through Capitol Radio Engineering Institute, in Washington, D.C. After earning his degree, he initially worked as a nuclear engineer at the San Onofre Nuclear Generating Station in Southern California. While at San Onofre, he and two other sound-recording enthusiasts built a studio in Torrance, and worked there on weekends. Plans were canceled for other nuclear plants, and Nichols, who was becoming more interested in expert recording technologies than nuclear reactions, left for full-time recording in late 1969. Nichols has recorded and produced recordings in a number of musical styles. Those he has collaborated with read like a veritable performing who's who, including John Denver (producer for 17 years), Steely Dan (engineering for 30 years, winning four engineering Grammys in the process), Donald Fagan (independently from Steely Dan), Frank Sinatra, Motorhead, Rosanne Cash, Reba McIntyre, Natalie Cole, Jim Messina, Gloria Estefan, The Beach Boys, Placido Domingo, Bela Fleck, Yo Yo Ma, Walter Becker, Michael Franks, Rickie Lee Jones, Lee Greenwood, John Klemmer, Crosby, Stills & Nash, Diana Ross, Flora Purim, Rodney Crowell, Sly Stone, Michael Bloomfield, Mark Knopfler, Frank Zappa, Patti Austin, John Lee Hooker, and numerous others. In addition, he has mixed soundtracks for a number of television shows and films. The material he has produced or recorded has been nominated for 11 Grammys, with seven of them winning, and he has had several TEK award nominations and wins. Nichols has been deeply involved in digital recording technology since 1977, and as part of his engineering work, he designed and built WENDELjr, a high-fidelity digital audio percussion replacement device used by many major artists, including Pink Floyd, Heart, Donald Fagan, and Paul Simon, as well as sound companies like Clair Brothers in the production of their albums and live shows. He has worked on a technique involving tape restoration process, as well as a completely new kind of microphone, with patents for three of his designs pending. He serves on the Board of Governors for the Miami chapter of the National Academy of Recording Arts & Sciences (NARAS), gives master's class lectures at the Berklee School of Music, the Musicians Institute, the Recording Workshop, Full Sail, and University of Miami. A sought after guest speaker, he has also given seminars on digital audio and recording techniques in Hong Kong, Buenos Aires, Singapore, Sweden, and at various AES and NARAS functions in the U.S. He also serves as a consultant on digital audio technology for the Culpepper Archiving Facility at the Library of Congress. Starting in 1984, he archived and restored digital/analog tapes for *The Big Chill* soundtrack (Motown), all the Steely Dan original master tapes, the entire Roy Orbison catalog, early Blue Thumb catalog tapes for re-release, the JVC Jazz catalog, and many more. He also designed the recording curriculum for the Musicians Institute in Hollywood, and is a regular columnist and equipment reviewer for *EQ* magazine.

HOWARD FERSTLER

NICOLE (LABEL)

A cylinder and disc record issued by Nicole Frères, Ltd., a firm that can be traced back to a family of music box makers in Switzerland. The business passed from family hands and was established in Britain in the late 19th century. Music boxes were replaced by Gramophones and Edison phonographs in the London manifestation. In 1901 the firm switched from Gramophone Co. products to those of International Zonophone Co., Berlin. Because of lack of supplies from Germany, Nicole Frères, Ltd., began to make its own records, unbreakable paper-based discs, in seven- and 10-inch sizes. The Nicole Record Co., Ltd., was formed to manufacture the discs. At the close of 1905 cylinder records were made. Nicole had an international repertoire of material, much of it acquired by recording engineer Steve Porter, who journeyed as far as India to make records. In 1906 the Disc Record Co., Ltd., of Stockport, Cheshire, acquired all the Nicole masters, which it used to press shellac records for clients, later on the clients' own labels. [*Catalogue 1971.*]

FRANK ANDREWS

NIELSEN, ALICE
(7 JUNE 1868?–8 MAR 1943)

American soprano, born in Nashville, Tennessee; her birthdate is usually given as 7 June 1876, but her death record shows age 74, which would place the birthdate ca. 1868. (*Encyclopaedia Britannica* guesses 1870 as the year of her birth.) She sang in church choirs, then toured for two years with a light opera company. Two of Victor Herbert's operettas were composed for her, *Fortune Teller* (1898), and *Singing Girl* (1899). Her grand opera debut was in Naples as Marguerite, on 6 Dec 1903. She sang Mimi opposite Enrico Caruso at Covent Garden. Her first American appearance was in New York in November 1905, then she toured with the San Carlo Opera Co. From 1909 to 1913 Nielsen sang with the Boston Opera Co. and from time to time with the Metropolitan Opera. Norina in *Don Pasquale* and Mimi were two Metropolitan roles; but she was overshadowed there by Emmy Destinn, Lucrezia Bori, Frances Alda, and Frida Hempel. She retired from the stage and taught voice in New York, where she died. Nielsen sang with the Alice Nielsen Quartet on Berliner records in the 1890s, and for other labels. She made landmark Berliners in 1898, participating in the first U.S. cast recordings of a musical (*Fortune Teller*). Her first Victor was "Addio del passato" (#64068; 1907); she had five solos and five duets with tenor Florencio Constantino in the Victor 1917 catalog. A favorite record with collectors is her "Last Rose of Summer" which appeared on Victor #74121 and Columbia #A5283.

NIKISCH, ARTHUR
(12 OCT 1855–23 JAN 1922)

Hungarian conductor, born in Szentmiklós. He studied violin at the Vienna Conservatory; after graduating in 1874 he played in orchestras in Vienna and Leipzig. From 1882 to 1889 he was first conductor at the Leipzig Theater. Appointed to conduct the Boston Symphony Orchestra, he served in that post from 1889 to 1893. Then he returned to conduct in Budapest, and to lead the Gewandhaus Concerts in Leipzig. He was a visiting conductor with the Berlin Philharmonic Orchestra and the London Symphony Orchestra.

Nikisch was greatly influential in establishing the primary role of the conductor. He died in Leipzig. In the history of recorded sound, Nikisch occupies a significant place as the first great conductor of the first (almost) complete symphony played by a major orchestra. This was the Beethoven Fifth Symphony, performed by the Berlin Philharmonic Orchestra in 1909, issued on eight single-sided discs by the Gramophone Co. during 1914. These discs (HMV #040784/91) were greatly popular, despite the alterations in the scoring necessitated by acoustic recording limitations, and led to a flow of symphony records from U.K., Germany, and America. (This was not, however, the earliest symphonic recording.) Symposium has issued a set of two compact discs (#1087/8) including all the Nikisch recordings with the Berlin Philharmonic and London Symphony of 1913–1921, in works by Beethoven, Berlioz, Liszt, Mozart, and Weber. [Shawe-Taylor and Hughes 1961.]

See also **Orchestra Recordings**

NILES, JOHN JACOB
(28 APR 1892–1 MAR 1980)

American folksong collector, singer, and composer, born in Louisville, Kentucky. He studied at the Cincinnati Conservatory of Music, and collected folksongs in the Southern Appalachian region. He arranged songs for publication, and also wrote songs in folk style. During the 1930s he was popular as a singer; he made an album for Victor in 1939 titled *Early American Ballads*. Many singles and albums followed, into the 1960s. In 1965 Victor issued an LP, *John Jacob Niles: Folk Balladeer*. Niles died on his farm near Lexington, Kentucky.

NIMBUS (LABEL)

A British record, issued by Nimbus Records, Ltd., Monmouth; the label was founded by Frances Baskerville, Michael and Gerald Reynolds, and Jonathan Halliday. A speciality is CD reissues of early material, primarily vocal. The Prima Voce series has included material by Enrico Caruso, Giovanni Martinelli, and Rosa Ponselle; plus anthology records like *Divas 1906–1935*. There is also an extensive catalog of current recordings. In the 1990s, the label branched out into producing world music recordings. The Nimbus company developed the Ambisonics technique of recording. An Ambisonic microphone is also used in transferring acoustic material to contemporary formats. The company grew into a large distributor of classical recordings in U.K., but subsequently both label and distribution firm went bankrupt in 2001. In

2002, the original owners purchased the assets of the label and resumed its operation. [website: http://www.nimbus.ltd.uk/nrl/.]

FRANK ANDREWS

NIPPER (1884–1895)

A white fox terrier with black markings, the dog in the painting "His Master's Voice" by Francis Barraud, famous as the Victor/Gramophone Co. trademark. Born in Bristol, Nipper was owned first by the painter's brother, Mark Henry Barraud. When Mark Henry died in 1887, Nipper moved in with Francis, in Liverpool, and the painting followed at some uncertain date. He was seen in advertising by Emile Berliner, who registered the trademark with the U.S. Patent Office in July 1900; and by Eldridge Johnson's Consolidated Talking Machine Co., in 1900. The dog was next seen on Victor Monarch record labels from January 1902, and on Gramophone Co. labels from February 1909. He appeared in other countries as well, wherever Gramophone affiliates were found, with the text translated appropriately into "Die Stimme seines Herrn," "La Voce del Padrone," etc. In Germany the dog trademark was used by the affiliate until 1949, while the Gramophone Co. branch, Electrola (established 1926) used it only on products sold outside Germany until 1949, when EMI gained control of the trademark and used it on early LPs in Germany. In 1949 a plaque was placed (according to undocumented reports) over Nipper's supposed grave, near a mulberry tree on Eden St., Kingston-on-Thames. That was the place of employment of Mark Barraud, nephew of the painter and son of Nipper's first owner; he took the dog to work with him each day. However, later developments in that location have resulted in a parking lot, under which Nipper apparently lies. The property, now addressed as 83 Clarence St., belongs to Lloyds Bank. A marker was laid in the parking area on 15 Aug 1984, by David Johnson, chairman of HMV Shops, Ltd., and a memorial plaque was placed in the foyer of the bank. Nipper's birth and death years as given above, are taken from the memorial plaque and marker, which are illustrated in *TMR #70* (December 1985): pp. 1948–1949 .As for the current use of the trademark, a letter from J.P.D. Patrick, vice president for international marketing for EMI Classics, stated that "Nipper is alive and well and to be found in all the territories where EMI have the right to use the trademark. This right does not, however, apply worldwide (not in the USA and the Far East, for instance). … Nipper will continue to grace tape and LP releases in the relevant territories … and is also appearing on CDs conceived for, and distributed by, specific territories: an example is West German EMI Electrola's current Meisterwerk series" [*Gramophone*, November 1989, p. 822]. In late 1990 RCA began to use two "Nippers" — a grown dog and a puppy — in advertising its new line of television models and camcorders. RCA was acquired from General Electric by Thomson Consumer Electronics, a French company, in 1987. Thomson has the right to use the Nipper symbol and so does General Electric. The latter firm owns the four green stained glass windows — circular, 14 1/2 feet in diameter — now in the nine-story tower in Camden, New Jersey, which was for years the centerpiece of Victor's vast establishment there. Eldridge Johnson commissioned Nicola D'Ascenzo Studios of Philadelphia to make the windows in 1915. They remained in place until the late 1960s, when RCA changed its logo and donated three of the windows to the Smithsonian Institution, Widener College, and Pennsylvania State University. The fourth window was stored by RCA until 1988, when it was given to Camden County Historical Society. A revival of interest in Nipper resulted in a fresh commission by RCA to D'Ascenzo in 1979, and four new windows, copies of the originals, were installed. [Berliner 1977; Hoover 1971 has full-page photographs of the 1915 windows, on pp. 48–49; Petts 1983.]

See also **Deutsche Grammophon Gesellschaft (DGG); Victor**

Original Nipper logo for "His Master's Voice" (HMV) label

NIPPON COLUMBIA CO., LTD.

A Japanese firm, located in Tokyo, maker of Denon products and other audio items. In U.K. the distributor is Hayden Laboratories.

NIPPONOPHONE CO., LTD.

A Japanese firm, the pioneer of the talking machine industry in that country, established in 1911. The head office was at 1 Chome, Ginza, Tokyo; there were branches all over Japan. In June 1912 the company published the fourth edition of its machine catalog; this was reprinted in *TMR #75* (Autumn 1988). Records made in Tokyo were marketed, as well as American and European imported material. In 1921 it was noted in *TMW* that Russell Hunting, Jr., was head of recording. In May 1927, *TMW* announced that the Columbia Phonograph Co. had acquired control of Nipponophone.

NIRVANA

Nirvana is widely recognized as the most important band to emerge from the Seattle-based grunge scene in the late 1980s. Whereas many of its compatriots — most notably, Soundgarden, Mudhoney, and Alice in Chains — concentrated on postpunk hardcore with heavy metal accents, this group also brought a melodic subtlety and strong sense of pop songcraft to the genre. Singer/songwriter/guitarist Kurt Cobain and bassist Krist Novoselic recruited drummer Chad Channing to form Nirvana in 1987. Although based in Aberdeen, Washington, the excitement generated by their live shows soon led to a record contract with the indie label, Sub Pop, in nearby Seattle. Following the release of a highly collectible single, "Love Buzz" (Sub Pop #23; 1988), written by the 1960s Dutch group, Shocking Blue, Nirvana released the critically acclaimed *Bleach* (Sub Pop #34; 1989). A brooding, angry collection built around throbbing bass and distorted guitar, it showcased Cobain's raging vocals and rapidly maturing compositional skills. Signing with a major label, the next *Nevermind* (Geffen #24425; 1991; #1), created a sensation. Driven by the radio-friendly, power pop-punk of "Smells Like Teen Spirit" (Geffen #19050; 1991; #6), Nirvana's success caused a scramble on the part of domestic record companies to sign alternative bands. Hailed as the Bob Dylan of his generation, Cobain exhibited increasing psychological problems in coping with his success. Although follow-up albums — an anthology of older, previously unavailable tracks, *Incesticide* (Geffen #24504; 2992; #39), and the uncompromisingly raw *in utero* (Geffen #24536; 1993; #1) — represented something of a creative drop-off, Nirvana remained on the cutting edge of the indie rock revolution until Cobain committed suicide on 4 Mar 1994. Posthumous releases — particularly the live compilations, *Unplugged in New York* (Geffen #24727; 1994; #1) and *From the Muddy Banks of the Wishkah* (Geffen #25105; 1996; #1) —

have found a wide audience, while the band's legacy, albeit in a more musically conservative, polished edition, has been carried on by Dave Grohl (who'd joined Nirvana as a drummer prior to the recording of *Nevermind*), who went on to found Foo Fighters and take on the lead vocalist/guitarist/songwriting roles. The Yugoslavian-born Novoselic has been less visible, doing occasional session work and releasing an obscure band project, the eponymous *Sweet 75* (Geffen #25140; 1997).

FRANK HOFFMANN

NITTY GRITTY DIRT BAND, THE

California country-rock band that crossed over into being a pure country band in the mid-1970s. Formed out of the California folk-rock community, the original band wed the sensibilities of a traditional jugband with a electric-folk sound. They disbanded in the late 1960s only to re-form in the early 1970s, scoring their biggest pop hits with Jerry Jeff Walker's "Mr. Bojangles" (Liberty #56197). In 1973 the band organized sessions in Nashville that brought together traditional country stars (Earl Scruggs, Maybelle Carter, Jimmy Martin, Merle Travis, and Doc Watson) to perform a set of country standards. The result was the landmark three-LP set, *Will the Circle Be Unbroken?* (United Artists #9801; CD reissue as Capitol #46589), which helped popularize these country stars among rock audiences, as well as elevating the band into hero status of both the country and rock communities. There were two follow-ups in 1989 (with a cast of new country stars) and in 2002. By the mid-1970s, the band was performing country-rock material under the name the Dirt Band. They were down to a quartet (Thompson had left the group), but they continued to try to appeal to both their rock and country constituencies. By the 1980s, the "Nitty Gritty" was back in their name, and they were recording as a pure, new country act. They scored a number of hits performing a combination of original songs and Nashville songwriters' products, with just a hint of traditional flavorings. In 1984, they had their first country number one with Rodney Crowell's "Long Hard Road (The Sharecropper's Dream)." In 1985–1986, in time for their 20th anniversary, they hit number one again with "Modern Day Romance," a pure new country song cowritten by Kix Brooks (later of Brooks and Dunn). Founder-member John McEuen left in 1987 to pursue a career as a solo banjo performer, further pulling the band in the "new country" direction. In 1989, the band produced a streak of top-10 country singles, solidifying their position as more consistent hitmakers than in the past. The band's final decade saw them touring and producing a handful of albums, although without the success they had enjoyed on the country charts in the 1980s. They disbanded in 1999 although have reunited from time to time for concerts and recordings.

CARL BENSON

NITZSCHE, JACK (22 APR 1937–)

Chicago-born Nitzsche gained fame as a producer/ arranger beginning in the early 1960s for pop-rock acts. Although born in the city, he was raised in rural Michigan, where he showed early talented on piano, saxophone, and clarinet. After graduating high school, he began working in a steel factory in Muskegon, Michigan, as a dance-band sax player at night. At the same time, Nitzsche took a correspondence course in orchestration, dreaming of working as a film composer. In pursuit of this dream he moved to Los Angeles in the early 1960s, where he began working with various small labels. He met Sonny Bono (later of Sonny & Cher) who was then working for the small Specialty label, and the duo wrote a pop song, "Needles and Pins," that was later a top hit for the British Invasion group the Searchers. Through Bono, he met the master producer Phil Spector, and Nitzsche quickly found work on Spector's many famous "Wall of Sound" productions as a musician and arranger. Nitzsche also produced several of the Rolling Stones' classic mid-1960s singles, including "Satisfaction" and "The Last Time." In 1966 he worked for the first time with Neil Young, then a member of Buffalo Springfield, on Young's miniopus "Expecting to Fly." This led to work on Young's first solo albums as an arranger and producer. His last major pop music production was on Graham Parker's album *Squeezing Out Sparks*. Nitzsche has focused since the mid-1970s on his career as a film composer, having scored over 45 films to date.

CARL BENSON

NOBLE, RAY (17 DEC 1903–3 APR 1978)

British Big Band leader and composer, born in Brighton, England. He studied music at Cambridge University, then formed a dance band in London. In 1929–1934 he was musical director for HMV in London. He transferred to the U.S. in 1934, and with Glenn Miller's assistance he established a band in New York. On 1 June 1935 he opened at the Rainbow Room, atop Rockefeller Center, and was highly successful there with a sweet-swing style; he also began regular appearances on radio. The 1935 ensemble included outstanding artists, e.g., Charlie Spivak, Pee Wee Ervin, Glenn Miller, Will Bradley, Bud Freeman, Claude Thornhill, and vocalist Al Bowlly. They began recording in February 1935 for Victor, remaining with

that label until 1937. Noble's composition, "The Touch of Your Lips," with vocal by Bowlly, was a great success in 1936 (Victor #25277). With Bowlly's return to England in 1936 Noble's stellar assemblage had begun to dissolve; he broke up the band in early 1937, then reorganized and switched to Brunswick records (from January 1938), with new vocalist Tony Martin making a fine disc of the Noble song "I Hadn't Anyone Till You" (Brunswick #8079; 1938). In October 1938 the group recorded another Noble hit, "Cherokee" (Brunswick #8247). Other songs by Ray Noble became popular records by his band, on the Columbia label from 1939: "The Very Though of You"/"Goodnight, Sweetheart" (Columbia #36546, vocals by the composer). The Noble orchestra was featured in four motion pictures between 1935 and 1945, and was frequently on radio. In the mid-1950s Noble retired. He died in London. Noble's recordings have been reissued on a number of nostalgia/jazz CD labels, mostly out of Europe, including Dutton, Parade/Koch, and Soundies.

NO DEPRESSION MOVEMENT

"No Depression" — drawn from a vintage Carter Family song ("No Depression in Heaven"), and later the name of an Uncle Tupelo album — represents an extension of the alternative country rock genre that originated at the end of the 1960s with the Byrds and the Flying Burrito Brothers and was revived in the 1980s through the work of Jason and the Scorchers, Uncle Tupelo, and others. It drew upon Woody Guthrie's dust bowl balladry and melded country (particularly the twangy, honky-tonk style exemplified by Hank Williams, Sr.) and punk. Steve Earle's seminal albums, *Guitar Town* (MCA #5713; 1986) and *Copperhead Road* (Uni #7; 1988) played a key role in attracting greater attention to the genre. By the time Uncle Tupelo (a band whose influence on the scene was far greater than mere sales might suggest) split off into two new groups in 1993, Wilco and Son Volt, the No Depression movement had acquired a clear-cut identity, inspiring the publication of numerous fanzines, the establishment of countless websites throughout the world, and a new type of radio programming known as "Americana." Other prime exponents of the sound include the Old 97's, Whiskeytown, and the Jayhawks.

See also **Country Music Recordings**

FRANK HOFFMANN

NOISE (I)

Any undesired signal in a recording or transmission system; an interfering disturbance.

See also **Distortion**

NOISE (II)

In acoustics, noise is a sound with a large number of frequencies outside the harmonic series of the fundamental.

NOISE (III)

White noise is a random signal, having the same energy level at all frequencies, sometime used as a mask to conceal disagreeable sounds.

NOISE (IV)

Pink noise is a band-limited random signal with the same amount of energy in each octave.

NOISE (V)

Ambient noise is the total of the undesired signals in the listening environment. It renders inaudible the desired portion of a received signal that falls below a certain decibel level; in an average home situation, it is estimated that signals of volume below 30 dB are not actually heard because of ambient noise.

NOISE (VI)

Surface noise is the result of friction between a record surface and the playback stylus, friction that is enhanced and more audible when the surface is scratched or damaged or when the stylus is worn. But even with all elements in perfect condition, there was an audible hissing noise in playback of 78-rpm records. LP records in fine condition, played with proper lightweight styli, were for practical purposes free of surface noise. Some cylinder records had extremely quiet surfaces when new.

See also **Noise Reduction; Signal-to-Noise Ratio (S/N Ratio)**

NOISE FILTER

SEE SCRATCH FILTER

NOISE REDUCTION

In recording technology, any number of electronic processes that are designed to reduce background noise and increase dynamic-range potential. Surface noise was a nuisance from the beginning of the sound recording industry. Early discs were so noisy from the contact of hard needles with gritty grooves that the desired performance signals could nearly disappear into the background. Improvements in materials lessened the seriousness of this problem, which in any case appeared to have been solved in the advertising of the manufacturers — who promoted "silent surfaces" long before such things were practical; and indeed the audience for 78s did learn to listen through the surface noises to a certain extent, ignoring them somewhat like white noise. The best Edison Diamond Discs possessed nearly silent surfaces, and other good discs could be rendered almost free of noise when played with fiber, thorn, or cactus needles. Tape recording brought its own noise, tape hiss. Real work on noise reduction through technical means began in the 1950s. D.T.N. Williamson gave a lecture in Britain in 1953 on "Suppression of Surface Noise," using a capacitor/ inductor delay line and valve equipment. His ideas were employed by the Garrard MRM/101 of 1978, intended to cancel clicks on stereo LPs. Essentially the system analyzed waveforms as they occurred, delayed those with frequencies that matched click frequencies, shunted them out of the signal, and returned the entire cleaned signal to its place in the audio stream. This approach to noise reduction, the "dynamic noise filter," has been used in most of the popular modern systems: Burwen, SAE, SEA, Dolby, MicMix, dbx, and Packburn. Another approach, the "static filter," was adapted by Owl, Orban, UREI, and Pultec. Digital processing has opened a new pathway to noise reduction. A computer with appropriate instructions can translate a sound signal into digital (numerical) form, sample it for specific patterns named in its program, eliminate those patterns that have been designated as unwanted, and replace them with the average of neighboring number patterns. CEDAR is a functioning digital system that operates along the line just described. It is also able to compare several records of similar content, to find the points where there is least noise, and to produce a new combined recording with the best characteristics of all of them and the fewest intrusive sounds. [Tuddenham & Copeland 1988.]

See also **Cedar; DBX Corporation; Dolby Noise Reduction Systems; Noise (III); Packburn Audio Noise Suppressor; Sonic Restoration of Historical Recordings**

NOISE SHAPING

In digital recording systems a technique that reduces subjectively important, in-band noise levels by moving the more audible parts of the background-noise spectrum to areas where the ear is less sensitive.

HOWARD FERSTLER

See also **HDCD (High Definition Compatible Digital)**

NONESUCH (LABEL)

Budget classical label launched by Jac Holzman of Elektra Records in 1964. The label made available mostly European recordings licensed for U.S. sale at a price of about half the ordinary retail price for LPs. A related "Explorer" line was launched soon after for world music recordings. Theresa Sterne ran the label for several decades, championing new American music, electronic music, and experimental recordings. Nonesuch was absorbed with Elektra into Warner-Elektra-Atlantic in 1971, and has had various homes in the Warner empire since. From 2000, the label has been a division of the Atlantic group, and has offered recordings by pop (Joni Mitchell), alt-rock (Wilco), and country (Emmylou Harris) performers in addition to classical material. In 2002, it launched a CD reissue series of its famous Explorer series, beginning with African recordings. [website: www.nonesuch.com.]

CARL BENSON

NONMAGNETIC TAPE RECORDING

The idea of cutting a groove into a ribbon of some kind, by acoustical means, is an old one. Thomas Edison's first reproduction of sound in fact took place on a paper ribbon, and he alluded to this kind of medium, and other sound carrier formats, in his British patent #1644. U.S. patent #944,608 was granted to Franklin C. Goodale on 28 Dec 1909; it was for a talking machine based on a celluloid tape instead of a cylinder. Frank E. Holman had a U.S. patent granted on 9 Nov 1909 for a talking machine with a belt for a

Nonesuch label, c. mid-'70s. Courtesy Frank Hoffmann

carrier; it was claimed to play for 50 minutes. Optical (photographic) sound recording on film was another nonmagnetic approach; it was developed by Frenchmen Eugene Lauste and Eugene Boyer before 1913. These early systems failed to replace the short-playing noisy discs because they lacked amplification devices, and their unamplified playback was very weak. With the development of electron tubes by Lee de Forest optical systems became significant, especially in motion picture sound. In U.K., British Ozaphane, Ltd. used sound films without pictures, offering an eight-millimeter film soundtrack with playing time up to 90 minutes. The Dutch Gramofilm of 1934 was similar in concept; and there were comparable devices in other countries. The many promising features of the nonmagnetic systems were eclipsed by the arrival of magnetic recording, first on wire, then in its several tape manifestations. [Jansen 1983.]

NOONE, JIMMIE
(23 APR 1895–19 APR 1944)

American jazz clarinetist and saxophonist, born in Cut-Off, Louisiana. He played guitar first, then went to the clarinet, perhaps studying with Sidney Bechet in New Orleans and playing there with his group. He then performed in Chicago with various bands, and was successful at the Apex Club there from 1926 with his own Apex Club Orchestra, which included Earl Hines at the piano. Noone made his first records — an important series — with that ensemble, for Vocalion in 1928: "I Know that You Know"/"Sweet Sue" (#1184), and continued with the label to January 1931. "Apex Blues" (Vocalion #1207; 1928) and "Four or Five Times" (Vocalion #1185; 1928) were outstanding numbers. Mildred Bailey was vocalist on the final Vocalion cuts, "He's Not Worth Your Tears"/"Trav'lin' All Alone" (#1580). His later records were for Brunswick, Vocalion again, Decca, and Bluebird. Noone's records demonstrate his place as a link between the New Orleans jazz style and the Chicago swing style of clarinet playing. He died suddenly in 1944 while touring with Kid Ory's New Orleans revival band in Los Angeles. *Apex Blues* reissued his 1928–1930 recordings for Vocalion (GRP #633). The European Classics label has reissued his complete recordings in chronological order on a series of five individual CDs, taking him through the 1930s.

NORDICA, LILLIAN
(12 DEC 1857–10 MAY 1914)

American soprano, born Lillian Norton in Farmington, Maine. She studied in Boston and made her debut there in 1876. She was a soloist with Gilmore's Band in 1878. Then she studied in Milan, and took the name Nordica for her debut there as Elvira, on 8 Mar 1879. Tours of Europe, including Russia, followed; and on 18 Dec 1891 she appeared as Valentine in *Huguenots* at the Metropolitan Opera. Subsequently she specialized in Wagnerian roles, remaining at the Metropolitan intermittently to 1909. She died in Batavia, Java. Nordica's recordings were few. Mapleson cylinders of 1901–1903 display her voice in Wagner fragments. She then worked for Columbia in 1906–1911, making a fine "Liebestod" (#30652; 1911) and a collector's favorite, Elisabeth's aria from *Hunyadi László* by Erkel, sung in Hungarian. There were also arias from *Mignon, Madama Butterfly, Tannhäuser,* and *Gioconda.* A selection of Nordica's commercial recordings from 1906–1911 and the Mapleson cylinders are available on *Three American Sopranos: Lillian Nordica, Olive Fremstad and Ada Adini* (Marston). [Dennis 1951/9; Moran 1963.]

NORDSKOG (LABEL)

An American record, claimed to be the first from the Pacific Coast, issued from 1921 to ca. 1923 by the Nordskog Phonograph Recording Co., main office in Santa Monica, California. Andrae Nordskog was founder and head of the firm. Only 27 issues are known, but they have interesting material. Abe Lyman recorded first for Nordskog, and Eva Tanguay made her only record for the label. Kid Ory's Jazz Band

One of the first West Coast labels, c. early '20s. Courtesy Kurt Nauck/Nauck's Vintage Records

made six sides. Ory's discs — issued with the Sunshine label pasted over the Nordskog label — were the first made by a Black New Orleans jazz group. In addition to original recordings, Nordskog released material from Arto masters; this was done as part of an exchange agreement with Arto, which did the Nordskog pressing at first, and which also distributed Nordskog material under its own label. Some artists lost their names in these transcontinental trips; for example, the Original Memphis Five on Arto became the Hollywood Syncopators on Nordskog 3013. [Kendziora 1968/7; Rust 1978.]

NORMAN, JESSYE (15 SEP 1945–)

Jesse Norman, opera singer and concert artist, was born in Augusta, Georgia, the daughter of Silas Norman, an insurance broker, and Janine King Norman, a teacher. The soprano started her singing in church when she was four years old. Norman received a B.A., Music, Howard University, 1967; studied further at Peabody Conservatory, 1967; and took a master's degree in music, University of Michigan, 1968. She made her operatic debut at the Deutsche Oper, Berlin, as Elisabeth in *Tannhaeuser* in 1969. Her American debut was at the Hollywood Bowl, 1972. Her distinguished association with Metropolitan Opera began with her debut on the opening night of the company's centennial season in 1983. Norman's operatic performances include *Die Walkure* by Richard Wagner; *Idomeneo* by Wolfgang Amadeus Mozart; *L'Africaine* by Giacomo Meyerbeer; the Countess in *Le Nozze de Figaro* (Marriage of Figaro) by Wolfgang Amadeus Mozart; *Oedipus Rex*, a modern version of the Greek tragedy, by Igor Stravinsky; and *Salome* by Richard Strauss. Norman has also concentrated on concert music, performing in recital with the Los Angeles Philharmonic, Boston Symphony Orchestra, New York Philharmonic, Vienna Philharmonic, Stockholm Philharmonic, and the Chicago Symphony Orchestra, and television viewers saw her performances at the inauguration of President Bill Clinton and at the 1996 Olympics in Atlanta. In recent seasons, she has premiered the song cycle, *woman.life.song*, by composer Judith Weir, commissioned for her by Carnegie Hall, with texts by Toni Morrison, Maya Angelou, and Clarissa Pinkola Estes, and performed the sacred music of Duke Ellington in a dramatic musical production. In 2000, she released her first jazz CD, *I Was Born in Love with You: Jessye Norman Sings Michel Legrand* (Philips #456654). Norman's remarkable catalog of recordings has won numerous international awards, including two Grammys. She became the youngest recipient of a Kennedy Center Honor in 1997. She has received some 30 honorary doctorates from colleges and universities, including her alma maters, Howard University (1982) and the University of Michigan (1987), and she has been awarded decorations and distinctions from governments around the world, including First Prize, Bavarian Radio Corporation International Music Competition (1968); Grand Prix Disque (1973, 1976, 1977); Deutsche Schallplatten Preis (1975); and an appointment in 1990 as an honorary U.N. ambassador. In Augusta, Georgia, her hometown, the Amphitheatre and Plaza overlooking the tranquil Savannah River were named for Jessye Norman in 1996 and she has an orchid named after her. Norman has been well represented on both video and records. She recorded many of her opera roles and recitals; they are available on CDs and include The Countess in *Le Nozze de Figaro* (1992) and Arminda in *Die Gartnerin aus Liebe* (1991), both for Philips in its Complete Mozart Edition series; Sieglinde in *Die Walkure*; and Kundry in *Parsifal*. Many of these performances were further taped for video and DVDs, including one of her most successful roles, Ariadne in the Richard Strauss opera, *Ariadne auf Naxos* (CD: Philips, 1988; DVD: Deutsche Grammophon, 2002), and a documentary, *Jessye Norman, Singer: Portrait of an Extraordinary Career* (1986). A sampling of the specialty albums includes: *Amazing Grace* (Philips #432526, 1991); *Jessye Norman at Notre Dame* (Philips #432731, 1992); *Lucky to Be Me* (Philips #422401, 1992); and *With a Song in My Heart* (Philips #412625, 1985).

MARTIN MANNING

NORMAN, JIM ED (16 OCT 1948–)

Born in Fort Edwards, Florida, Norman was one of the architects of the West Coast country-rock sound before becoming a mainstream country producer and music executive. Norman was raised in Texas, where as a teenager he hooked up with a group of local players, including drummer Don Henley, to form a group known as Felicity. By 1969, the group's name was Shiloh and they were working out of Los Angeles. They cut one album in 1970 before disbanding, but Norman remained friendly with Henley, and worked as an arranger/pianist on several of the early Eagles' recordings. In 1977, Norman produced his first mainstream hit, Jennifer Warnes's sultry "Right Time of the Night," and then two years later hooked up with country chanteuse Anne Murray. His next big break came in 1986 when he began coproducing Hank Williams Jr.'s recordings (with Barry Beckett), leading to a string of big hits. Other 1980s-era acts that Norman produced include Mickey Gilley, Crystal Gayle, Johnny Lee, and T.G. Sheppard. In 1989, he was appointed president of Warner Bros.'s Nashville

offices, a position he holds today. He continues to develop new talent and occasionally produce in his position as head of Warner Bros. Nashville.

CARL BENSON

NORTH AMERICAN PHONOGRAPH CO.

A firm established by Jesse H. Lippincott — originally named the American Phonograph Co. — on 14 July 1888 as the sole outlet for the Graphophone and sole sales agency for Edison phonograph products. Patents of the Edison Phonograph Co. were acquired, but not the Bell-Tainter Graphophone patents. Lippincott's associates were Thomas R. Lombard, George S. Evans, George H. Fitzwilson, and John Robinson. They capitalized the company at $4 million. Offices were in the Edison Building (44 Broad St.), New York, and the Masonic Temple, Chicago. North American engaged in leasing phonographs and "phonograph-graphophones" to business offices for dictation purposes, selling supplies, leasing coin-ops for entertainment, and selling entertainment cylinders for the home market. Thirty-three regional companies were appointed as franchises to handle all leases and sales in specific territories, under strict rules. The member companies bought their stock from North American at a discount of about 30 percent, and took the responsibility for their own marketing. There were 34 U.S. affiliates (two of them merged ca. 1890) and a Canadian agent. These were the member firms of the early 1890s: Alabama Phonograph Co., Central Nebraska Phonograph Co. (including the western part of the state), Chicago Central Phonograph Co. (covering Cook County), Colorado and Utah Phonograph Co., Columbia Phonograph Co., Eastern Pennsylvania Phonograph Co., Florida Phonograph Co., Georgia Phonograph Co., Holland Brothers (the Canadian agents), Iowa Phonograph Co., Kansas Phonograph Co. (including New Mexico), Kentucky Phonograph Co., Leeds and Co. (for Indiana), Louisiana Phonograph Co., Metropolitan Phonograph Co. (merged with New York Phonograph Co. ca. 1890), Michigan Phonograph Co., Minnesota Phonograph Co., Missouri Phonograph Co. (including Arkansas and Indian Territories), Montana Phonograph Co., Nebraska Phonograph Co. (for Eastern Nebraska), New England Phonograph Co., New Jersey Phonograph Co., New York Phonograph Co., Ohio Phonograph Co., Old Dominion Phonograph Co. (for Virginia, North Carolina, and South Carolina), Pacific Phonograph Co. (for Arizona, California, and Nevada), South Dakota Phonograph Co., Spokane Phonograph Co. (covering Oregon, Idaho, and eastern Washington), State Phonograph Co. of Illinois (covering the state except for Cook County), Tennessee

Phonograph Co., Texas Phonograph Co., West Coast Phonograph Co. (for western Oregon and western Washington), Western Pennsylvania Phonograph Co. (covering western Pennsylvania and West Virginia), Wisconsin Phonograph Co., and Wyoming Phonograph Co. (See individual articles on the firms for details of location, dates of operation, etc.) The companies deployed themselves in a trade organization called the National Phonograph Assoc. in 1890 and met for annual conventions. It should be noted that one of the member companies was in a unique position: Columbia Phonograph Co. had been established before North American, in 1888 (incorporated 1889). Its directors had arranged with American Graphophone Co. (licensee of the Volta Graphophone Co.) to have Graphophone sales rights to the territory of Washington, D.C., Maryland, and Delaware. Columbia was the only one of the regional franchises to survive unscathed the termination of North American. Several other companies limped along for a few years, some with new names. A trade journal, *Phonogram*, was published by North American from January 1891 to 1893. In April 1892 the company began to emphasize entertainment cylinders for the home market. The main problem faced was that not many homes were ready to spend $150 or more for a phonograph; another problem was the difficulty in making satisfactory duplicates from the original cylinders. Nevertheless, the first edition of the *Catalogue of Musical Phonograms* appeared in 1890, and more than 1,400 selections were available within two years. These were the Edison "2-minute" brown-wax cylinders. Some of the member companies began to compete with the parent firm by producing their own cylinders: Columbia, Louisiana, New England, Ohio, and the Canadian Holland Bros. Samuel Insull was president in 1892, and Thomas Lombard was president in 1893. Following early successes and later financial difficulties North American Phonograph Co. was bankrupt in August 1894, and its assets went into receivership in 1896. Lippincott died in 1894. The stock and assets were auctioned by court order, and Thomas Edison himself bought everything, "becoming for the first time sole proprietor of his phonographic enterprise" (Read & Welch). [Andrews 1976/2; Koenigsberg 1987; Read & Welch 1976; Wile 1972/2.]

NORVO, RED (31 MAR 1908–6 APR 1999)

American jazz xylophonist, pianist, and Big Band leader, born Kenneth Norville in Beardstown, Illinois. He studied at the University of Missouri during 1926–1927, and played locally; was with Paul Ash's group at the Oriental Theater in Chicago; had a band in Milwaukee, Wisconsin, in 1928. In the early 1930s he joined Paul Whiteman (and married feature singer Mildred Bailey). He put together a band in 1935, with Bailey as vocalist, and was successful in New York. Eddie Sauter did arrangements, George Wettling was the drummer. Later he was with the Benny Goodman Quintet and Sextet (1944–1945), and with Woody Herman (1945–1946). He was pioneer on the xylophone in jazz context, and also performed on the vibraphone. Norvo made numerous world tours, and was seen on television; during the 1960s, and 1970s. After suffering a stroke in 1986, he ceased performing. He died in Santa Monica, California. He had been most popular on the West Coast and in Las Vegas. Norvo's early recordings, in small groups that included Jimmy Dorsey and Benny Goodman, were made in New York for Brunswick in 1933. "Knockin' on Wood"/"Hole in the Wall" (#6652) was his first record, and also the first jazz xylophone solo to appear on disc. Then he recorded with his own septet, octet, and, from January 1936, with his orchestra. Among the fine records made by the orchestra, those with Mildred Bailey's vocals stand out, e.g., "I've Got My Love to Keep Me Warm" (Brunswick #7813; 1937) and "Love Is Here to Stay" (Brunswick #8068; 1938). Norvo's band also recorded for Vocalion and Columbia. Norvo's recordings have been reissued on various CD labels, from the 1930s through his second career in the 1950s; these have appeared on Jazzology, Classics, HEP, Stash, and many others.

NOS RECORDING TECHNIQUE (NEDERLANDSCHE OMROEP STICHTING)

A microphone-positioning technique that involves two, directional cardioid microphones placed 30 cm (11.8 inches) apart, with them angled outward at approximately 90 degrees to each other. The spacing is somewhat further apart than what is used with the ORTF system, and the result is coincident microphone behavior at lower frequencies, combined with some pronounced time-delay–related clues at higher frequencies that add a degree of spaciousness to the sound.

HOWARD FERSTLER

NOTCH FILTER

A way to electronically null out certain, potentially obnoxious frequency-related anomalies in a recording during the mixing/editing phase of the production process. The better filters can simultaneously adjust frequency, bandwidth, and depth, while cheaper versions have fixed bandwidth and depth settings, with only the frequency being adjustable.

HOWARD FERSTLER

NOUSAINE, TOM (15 OCT 1944–)

A major audio writer and journalist, Nousaine was born in Brainerd, Minnesota, and went on to receive an M.B.A. from Michigan State University in 1971. He retired in 1996 from Ameritech, where he had managed a staff of graduate analysts investigating economic and technology obsolescence, and has since been a regular contributor to *Audio* magazine (until it folded), *Car Stereo Review*, *Stereo Review*, *The Sensible Sound*, *Sound & Vision*, *Mobile Entertainment*, and *The Audio Critic*. He was cofounder and president of the Society of Depreciation Professionals, has been central region USA vice president of the Audio Engineering Society, and was the founder of the Prairie State Audio Construction Society. In addition to his regular journalistic and product-reviewing work, Nousaine has designed, conducted, analyzed, and published the results of an extensive series of controlled listening tests, as well as in-room low frequency and surround-speaker placement experiments.

HOWARD FERSTLER

NOVOTNA, JARMILA (23 SEP 1907–9 FEB 1994)

Czech soprano, born in Prague. She studied with Emmy Destinn, and made her debut in Prague as Violetta on 27 June 1926. Then she joined the Berlin State Opera. Her American debut was in San Francisco in 1939. She was heard first at the Metropolitan Opera as Mimi on 5 Jan 1940, remaining to 1951, and returning for the 1952–1956 seasons. She appeared in dramatic and vocal roles in a number of films, notably the 1951 biopic, *The Great Caruso*, starring Mario Lanza. In the later 1950s, Novotna retired to Vienna. She died in New York. Her best roles were Cherubino, Mimi, Elvira, Euridice, Pamina, Violetta, Marenka in *Bartered Bride*, and Octavian. She began recording for Columbia in 1925, doing "Caro nome" and three other arias, all in Czech. Two HMV acoustics, not issued until 1926, presented her in two Czech arias. In April 1931 she was recording for HMV in Germany, singing in German or Czech four numbers from *Traviata*. She did more German and Czech pieces for Electrola in June 1931, and for Odeon; then sang Czech folk songs for Victor in 1942 with Jan Masaryk at the piano (three-disc album #M-936; later on LP as #1383, 1969). A selection of her operatic and popular recordings is available on CD on the Czech Music Vars label (*The World of Fair Music*; #0066). [Frankenstein & Dennis 1979.]

NO WAVE

The no wave movement grew out of the coalescence of lower Manhattan's avant-garde art and music scenes (most notably, punk rock) in the late 1970s. Its exponents were primarily unschooled musicians alienated by rock's inherent conservatism. Although appropriating punk's nihilism and raw, minimal (often using noise for noise's sake) approach, they remained wary of the genre's increasing institutionalization. The deconstructivist inclinations of no wave were best exemplified by DNA (featuring guitarist Arto Lindsey), whose only brush with mass acceptance came through a collaboration with Suzanne Vega on the 12-inch EP, "Tom's Diner" (A&M #75021-2342-1, 1990); Mars; and Teenage Jesus and the Jerks, featuring underground poet Lydia Lunch. The Contortions were perhaps the most "musically developed" no wave group, melding atonality, free jazz, and Captain Beefheart–influenced guitar sonorities with revved-up funk rhythms. The band's greatest success, *Buy the Contortions* (ZE/Arista ZEA #33-002; 1979), was a brief cult novelty. Lacking any self-perpetuating mechanism, the genre rapidly lost momentum in the early 1980s. Its most enduring performers included former Theoretical Girls member, Glenn Branca, who went on to create layered, hyper-amped guitar music with pronounced heavy metal leanings — best exemplified in his *Symphony No. 1: Tonal Plexus* (ROIR A #125; 1981), and ex-Branca associates, Thurston Moore and Lee Ranaldo, who would found white noise pioneers, Sonic Youth.

FRANK HOFFMANN

'N SYNC

'N Sync represents the late 1990s variant of the bubblegum phenomenon. Like their antecedents — the Monkees, the Partridge Family, the New Kids on the Block, the Spice Girls, and the Backstreet Boys — 'N Sync has combined slick record production values with intensive multimedia marketing and promotion. Two members of the group — JC Chasez and Justin Timberlake — worked together on the Disney Channel's *The Mickey Mouse Club*. Both were temporarily relocated to Nashville, where they pursued solo careers while sharing the same vocal coach and songwriters. When things failed to click, Timberlake hooked up with Joey Fatone and Chris Kirkpatrick back in Orlando; they contacted Chasez, who agreed to join the proposed band in 1996. James Lance Bass was recruited later to fill out the lineup. Their debut album, *'N Sync*, originally released in Germany on BMG Ariola Munich, became hugely popular across Europe, largely on the strength of two hit singles, "I Want You Back: (RCA #65348; 1997) and "Tearing Up My Heart" (RCA, 1997). Released in the U.S. on RCA (#67613) in spring 1998, and promoted by a nationwide tour of roller rinks, the LP duplicated its overseas success.

Intended to capitalize on their career momentum, *Home for Christmas* (RCA #67726; 1998) was issued later that same year. The third album, *No Strings Attached* (Jive #41702), parlayed a buoyant pop sound to exceed even the most optimistic expectations, selling almost two-and-a-half million copies during its first week of release in spring 2000 and lingering for months in the top-10 pop charts. A DVD concert (also available in the video-tape configuration), *Live at Madison Square Garden* (Jive #41739), was issued in December 2000. Their next LP, *Celebrity* (Jive #41758; 2001) reinforced their hold on adult contemporary, dance, and top-40 playlists.

FRANK HOFFMANN

NUGENT, TED (13 DEC 1948–)

Ted Nugent was one of the more dynamic performers within the hard rock field during the 1970s. Born in Detroit, Michigan, Nugent played in a succession of rock bands in the early 1960s before forming the Chicago-based Amboy Dukes in 1966. Three releases on the Mainstream label — *The Amboy Dukes* (#6104; 1967; #183); *Journey to the Center of the Mind* (#6112; 1968; #74), featuring the title single (#684; 1968; #16); and *Migration* (#6118; 1969) — cemented their national reputation as a premier acid rock band. Later albums — *Marriage on the Rocks/Rock Bottom* (Polydor #4012; 1970; #191) and *Survival of the Fittest/Live* (Polydor #4035; 1971; #129) — suffered from internal differences as to the stylistic direction the band should take in the face of changing fashions within the music scene. Interested in taking greater control of his career, Nugent went solo in 1975. A key ingredient in his future success was the decision to sign with Epic Records; supporting his contention that top-40 radio did not represent a viable promotional vehicle, the Columbia subsidiary supported an exhaustive touring schedule aimed at reaching the potential record-buying audience. As a result, Nugent's high-energy, guitar-driven recordings sold consistently at platinum levels, including *Ted Nugent* (Epic #33692; 1975; #28), *Free-For-All* (Epic #34121; 1976; #24), *Cat Scratch Fever* (Epic #34700; #17), Double *Live Gonzo!* (Epic #35069; 1978; #13), and *Weekend Warriors* (Epic #35551; 1978; #24). Two more albums — *State of Shock* (Epic #36000; 1979; #18) and *Scream Dream* (Epic #36404; 1980; #13) — achieved gold status. Despite the success of these albums, Nugent's style did not translate well to records. Well aware of the differences between the two forms of communication, the singer/guitarist/songwriter explained to *Circus* magazine how he used this situation to further the creative process in the studio: "There's no way anyone will ever capture a live performance on record because you just don't have all the elements. You don't

have the face-to-face, body-to-body, flesh-to-flesh, volume-to-skull; but seeing how my entire inspiration comes from the stage and the intensity thereon, I secure that whole desire for that intensity in the studio and that's where [my] songs come from" (March 16, 1978). Personal problems (the disruption of his strong family orientation by a late 1970s divorce) and major shifts in the lineup of his backing band contributed to the declining success of Nugent's 1980s albums: the live *Intensities in 10 Cities* (Epic #37084; 1981; #51), *Nugent* (Atlantic #19365; 1982; #51), *Penetrator* (Atlantic #80125; 1984; #56), *Little Miss Dangerous* (Atlantic #81632; 1986; #76), and *If You Can't Lick 'Em … Lick 'Em* (Atlantic #81812; 1988; #11). Later in the decade, he was further distracted by celebrity appearances on television programs and other public events and car racing activities. In 1989 he linked up with former Styx vocalist/guitarist Tommy Shaw to form Damn Yankees, an attempt at refining his blunt metallic attack with the polished AOR melodicism then dominating the charts. After a measure of success with the group — *Damn Yankees* (Warner Bros. #26159; 1990; #13), featuring the single, "High Enough" (Warner Bros. #19595; 1990; #3); *Don't Tread* (Warner Bros. #45025; 1992; #22) — he returned to a solo career. Unable to secure major label support, his commerical viability remains tied to the recycling of his classic 1970s material.

FRANK HOFFMANN

N.W.A.

A loose combine of rappers based in the Compton section of Los Angeles, N.W.A. (an acronym for the commercially indigestible moniker, Niggaz With Attitude) pioneered the gansta rap movement. Although the group fragmented shortly after the release of their third album, individual members would continue to exert an influence on the evolution of hip-hop throughout the 1990s. N.W.A. was formed in the mid-1980s when vocalist Eazy-E — aka Eric Wright, son of soul/funk artist Charles Wright, and founder of the seminal West Coast rap label, Ruthless — combined forces with ex-C.I.A. vocalist Ice Cube (O'Shea Jackson), vocalist M.C. Ren (Lorenzo Patterson), and former World Class Wreckin' Drew members, producer Dr. Dre (Andre Young) and turntable maestro DJ Yella (Antoine Carraby). Along with Arabian Prince, The Doc, and other hip-hop artists, the group recorded *N.W.A. And The Posse* (Macola; 1987; reissued Ruthless CD 57119), which featured Eazy-E's harsh proto-gangsta diatribe, "Boyz 'N' the Hood." The next LP, *Straight Outta Compton* (Ruthless #57102; 1989; #37), all but defined the gansta rap genre, most notably in the biting social commentaries of "Gangsta Gangsta" (Ruthless

#191; 1990; #70 U.K.) and widely censored "F Tha Police" (Ruthless; 1991; also issued in the 12-inch and CD singles formats). Although the heavily anticipated follow-up, *Efil4zaggin'* (Ruthless #57126; 1991; #1), was a smash hit (extremely popular with rebellious middle-class white youth), internal dissention caused group members to go their separate ways. Dr. Dre would find success with his G-funk innovations and the creation of the Death Row label (funded in part by Interscope Records). Ice Cube enjoyed even greater commercial popularity both as a recording artist — his angry solo album, *The Predator* (Priority #57185; 1992), which widely sampled Black music innovators like George Clinton and James Brown, would debut at number one on the pop charts — and Hollywood film star. M.C. Ren and Eazy-E also produced best-selling singles and LPs; the latter's career was cut short, however, when he died of AIDS in March 1995.

FRANK HOFFMANN

NYQUIST FREQUENCY

The digital sampling rate required to obtain an undistorted signal at half that frequency and all lower frequencies. To obtain accurate wave form reproduction out to 20 kHz (the upper hearing limit for those with excellent hearing), the Nyquist theorem determines that it is necessary to have a sampling rate of 40 kHz. In practice, a guard band is necessary between the upper program frequency and the Nyquist frequency, and so a sampling rate of 44.1 kHz is utilized for the compact disc. Modern digital recording systems often have sampling rates substantially higher than this. Although this allows for more flexibility with digital recording procedures, it is not really necessary for adequate sound reproduction in final-product, digital playback systems.

HOWARD FERSTLER

See also **Oversampling**

O

OAKLAND, WILL (15 JAN 1880 or 1883–15 MAY 1956)

American countertenor, born Herman Hinrichs in Jersey City, New Jersey. Rust observes that he had the highest male voice ever heard on stage [Rust 1989]. His specialties were the sentimental song and the Civil War ballad. Oakland first recorded in 1904, and in 1908 released his first Edison recording, "When the Autumn Moon Is Creeping Thro' the Woodlands" (#9902), and, a year later, made his first Victor disc, "When You and I Were Young, Maggie" (#5682). He had 13 solo items in the Victor 1917 catalog, plus numbers with the Heidelberg Quintette. He recorded many solos and quartet numbers for Edison, Columbia, U-S Everlasting, and other labels until 1926. His final issue was "Let's Grow Old Together"/"Gone" (Harmony #162–H; 1926). Oakland went into radio and became famous; he was voted the most popular radio singer in a 1926 poll. He also appeared in vaudeville and operated a nightclub. He died on a bus going to Newark, New Jersey. [Walsh 1949/11.]

OAKLEY, OLLY

British banjoist, a pioneer recording artist for that instrument; real name James Sharpe. He recorded for G & T beginning in 1901, with "Rugby Parade March" (#6334), again in 1902 (11 numbers) and then to 1904. Rust identifies "Whistling Rufus" (#6374; 1903) as "early ragtime." The disc is of further interest for its piano accompaniment, by Landon Ronald. Oakley went on to record prolifically for many cylinder and disc labels. [Rust 1989.]

OBERLIN, RUSSELL (11 OCT 1928–)

American countertenor, born in Akron, Ohio. He studied at Juilliard School in New York, graduating in 1951. He was a founding member, with Noah Greenberg, of the New York Pro Musica, and did much to popularize the countertenor voice in America along with its repertoire. Oberlin was a popular recording artist from the mid-1950s through the 1960s. He was the first to record the complete *Cantigas de Santa Maria* (Experiences Anonymes/Lyrichord #0023, 1958), as part of a 10-LP set of *Music of the Middle Ages*. He also recorded for Columbia, Decca, and other smaller labels. He taught at Hunter College from 1966 until his retirement in 1994.

OBERSTEIN, ELI (13 DEC 1901–13 JUNE 1960)

American record industry executive, born Elliott Everett Oberstein. Some sources report that he began his career working as an accountant for Victor in 1922, although his name does not appear on the Victor ledgers until 1930, when he oversaw a jazz session for the company. In the early years of the Depression, Oberstein pushed Victor to introduce budget labels, including Bluebird (which he directed from 1936–1939) and the cheaper-still Electradisk. Oberstein oversaw sessions by many jazz musicians, including Benny Goodman who he signed to Bluebird, as well as country artists. In 1939 he set up the United States Record Co., establishing the budget Varsity and Royale labels, taking many of the Big Band artists with him from Bluebird.

Additionally, masters came from Crown, Gennett, and others. However, he was soon embroiled in problems with creditors, including his record pressing plant, and Oberstein formed the short-lived Tophat label to issue risque "party"records. However, United States Record Co. was soon in bankruptcy. In 1940 Oberstein was back in business under the new name of Imperial. Record Co., issuing records under the budget Elite label. Oberstein then merged his label with the Classic Record Co. of Pittsburgh, Pennsylvania. During the recording ban of 1942, Oberstein continued to issue new material, on the midpriced Hit label; he gained the reputation of "pirate" and was ousted from the American Federation of Musicians, which had imposed the ban. Dogged by legal problems, Oberstein sold his various label holdings in early 1945 to Majestic Records. In July 1945, he returned to RCA, where he turned his attention to singers like Perry Como. However, by 1948, he was back in business on his own, although he briefly worked as a consultant to Columbia in 1949 when they started their budget Harmony label. In the 1950s, he expanded into budget LP production under various labels, including Allegro (a classical label he bought from Paul Pruner around 1952), and his old monikers Royale, Varsity, and Elite. By the late 1950s, Oberstein sold all of these holdings to Pickwick International. When he died, in Westport, Connecticut, he held the presidency of Rondo Record Corp., New York. His son, Maurice, took over the label's operation and later worked for CBS/Sony.

See also **Crown (Label) (IV); Harmony (Label) (III)**

REV. CARL BENSON

OCARINA RECORDINGS (HISTORIC)

A globe-shaped flute, invented by Giuseppe Donati, made of various materials and in various sizes. It is also known as a sweet potato because of its shape. A Berliner record of 29 Aug 1898, "Whistling Coon," offered an ocarina with banjo, by performers identified as Mays and Hunter. In February 1906 Edison issued an ocarina solo by Eugene C. Rose, "Genevieve Waltz Medley" (#9197). The celebrated ocarina player on British and European records was Mose Tapiero of Italy. He recorded classical and semiclassical works for many labels.

OCHS, PHIL (19 DEC 1940–9 APR 1976)

In many ways, Phil Ochs was a victim of Bob Dylan's critical and commercial success in the 1960s. He gained little solace from the fact that many considered him second only to Dylan as a writer of political

polemics within the New York City folk scene. After all, Dylan had applied his prodigious composing skills to virtually the entire spectrum of American popular song — including love laments, talking blues, protest anthems, surrealistic free verse, country ballads, and straight-ahead rockers — whereas Ochs had chosen to specialize in antiestablishment diatribes framed within an urban folk vernacular. Furthermore, as Dylan reached far beyond his localized counterculture roots to achieve the status of a popular culture icon, Ochs would become increasingly marginalized by the new musical trends he seemed unable to adapt to. Ochs attended military school in Virginia and pursued a journalism degree at Ohio State University before deciding to pursue a career as a singer/songwriter. After a brief stint with the Singing Socialists (later known as the Sundowners), he ended up in New York City as a solo performer. His first album, *All the News That's Fit to Sing* (Elektra #7/269; 1964), caused a sensation within the East Coast folk scene. His strident commentaries on topical issues, most notably his criticism of the Vietnam War effort (e.g., "Draft Dodger Rag"), in the next LP, *I Ain't a' Marchin' Anymore* (Elektra #7/287; 1965), further advanced his celebrity. The failure to produce a mass anthem with universally appealing imagery such as Dylan's "Blowin' in the Wind" considerably slowed the upward trajectory of Ochs's career. Following a couple of uneven albums — *Phil Ochs in Concert* (Elektra #7/310; 1966) and *Pleasures of the Harbor* (A&M #4133; 1967) — he shifted his base of operations to Los Angeles. The

Phil Ochs's *I Ain't Marching Anymore* album, from the mid-'60s. Courtesy Frank Hoffmann

recordings produced there — *Tape from California* (A&M #4148; 1968), *Rehearsals for Retirement* (A&M #4181; 1969), *Greatest Hits* (not in fact a compilation of previous "hits," but an ironically titled collection of all new recordings; A&M #4253; 1970), and *Gunfight at Carnegie Hall* (A&M #9010; recorded April 1970; released 1975 only in Canada) — featured session musicians in order to achieve a slicker, more rock-oriented sound (including orchestral arrangements). The last album was particularly interesting; it documented Ochs's appearance before a largely folk crowd at New York's Carnegie Hall. For some reason, he decided to perform in a gold lamé suit, and refused to perform his better-known material. The resulting audience reaction was captured in this live recording that has achieved legendary status. After living in Africa and London during the early 1970s, Ochs returned to New York in 1974 to record the protest song "Here's to the State of Richard Nixon" (A&M #1509) and to organize a concert protesting the U.S.-instigated military junta in Chile. However, Ochs became increasingly depressed by his lack of success and turned to heavy drinking. He committed suicide by hanging himself while staying at a relative's home on Long Island. Brother Michael Ochs compiled an anthology release, *Chords of Fame* (A&M #4599; 1976), following Ochs's death. Now remembered primarily for his seminal mid-1960s protest recordings, Ochs is well represented by CD compilations (many featuring previously unavailable material) and reissues of his original albums.

FRANK HOFFMANN

O'CONNELL, CHARLES
(22 APR 1900–1 SEP 1962)

American recording industry executive, and conductor, born in Chicopee, Massachusetts. He studied organ in Paris with Charles-Marie Widor, and was A&R head for Victor, with responsibility for Red Seal records, 1930–1944. From 1944 to 1947 he headed the masterworks division of Columbia Records. He was conductor of studio orchestras for both labels. O'Connell wrote the *Victor Book of the Symphony* (1934) and contributed to revisions of the *Victor Book of the Opera.* He died in New York.

O'CONNOR, GEORGE H. JR.
(20 AUG 1874–28 SEP 1946)

American tenor/baritone, born in Washington, D.C. He studied voice and dancing as a child, and appeared in *Pirates of Penzance*; then sang in the Georgetown University Glee Club. His local fame reached the White House, and he became known as the favorite entertainer there, singing for Presidents McKinley, Theodore Roosevelt, Taft, Wilson, Harding, and Coolidge. While his specialty was the coon song and other dialect numbers, he also sang ballads. O'Connor was a lawyer, admitted to the D.C. bar in 1895. His first Columbia record, which O'Connor considered his finest, was "Mississippi Barbecue"/"Alabama Jamboree" (#A1669; 1915). In 1916 Columbia released what proved to be the most popular of his discs, "Nigger Blues" (#A2064). Another great hit was the humorous "I Ain't Prepared for That" of 1917. Many of his discs had flip sides by Al Jolson, which helped the sales. His final release was "Jazzin' the Cotton Town Blues"/"There's Always Something Doin' Down in Dixie" (Columbia #A2507; 1918). [Walsh 1955/1–2–3.]

O'DAY, ANITA (18 DEC 1919–)

American popular singer, born Anita Belle Colton in Kansas City, Missouri. She began singing professionally in Chicago as a teen, and joined Gene Krupa's band in 1941, remaining to 1943. Then she was with Stan Kenton in 1944–1945, returned to Krupa (1945–1946), and then went freelance. O'Day became famous as a singer of jazz, with improvisation and scat singing that were comparable to instrumental performance. She was a sensation at the Newport Festival of 1958, and sang throughout America and Europe. In 1985 she gave a Carnegie Hall concert, to observe her 50th year as a performer. O'Day's records with Krupa include "Let Me Off Uptown" — her biggest hit, with Roy Eldridge's trumpet in counterpoint — (Okeh #6210; 1941), "Skylark" (Okeh #6607; 1941), and "Side by Side" (Columbia #36726; 1942). O'Day's first album, *Anita* (Verve #2000; 1955, re-released on CD as Verve #829261) — also the first LP released by Verve — was an immediate success and launched her pop career. She would go on to release 20 albums for the label through the 1960s, establishing herself as a leading pop-jazz vocalist. However, a growing addiction to heroin took its toll, and in 1967 the singer's health failed and she was forced to retire. She returned to be a cabaret star in the mid-1970s, forming her own label, Emily, to release her new recordings. She published her autobiography, *High Times, Hard Times*, in 1981. Her 1941–1942 and 1945 recordings for Okeh/Columbia as a band singer with Gene Krupa are collected on *The Big Band Years* (President #547), which also includes four tracks with Stan Kenton recorded in 1944–1945 for Capitol; a similar selection is *And Her Tears Flowed Like Wine* (ASV/Living Era #5369), while the Columbia/Krupa material is also anthologized on *Let Me Off Uptown* (Columbia/

Legacy #65625). Her 1942–1950 Signature/London label recordings are collected on a two-CD set from the Japanese Jazz Factory label (#22824). Many of O'Days original Verve albums have been reissued in their original format on CD, and Verve and related Universal labels have issued many "best of" selections on CD as well. In 2000, the completist label Mosaic issued O'Day's complete Clef/Verve recordings on a 198-track set (Mosaic #188).

ODEON RECORD (LABEL)

A record first issued in Germany by the International Talking Machine Co. mbH, the firm organized by Frederick M. Prescott to replace his lost control over the International Zonophone Co. The label name Odeon was taken from the name of a famous theater in Paris. Odeon was assiduous in seeking out European opera stars (Lilli Lehmann, Emmy Destinn, John McCormack) to record. Odeon discs were recorded and marketed in many countries; and marketed briefly by Columbia in the U.S. from 1908 to 1910. Odeon Records were made in several metric sizes: 19 centimeters (7 1/2 inches), 27 centimeters (10 3/4 inches), 30 centimeters (12 inches), and 35 centimeters (13 1/2 inches), all but the latter being double-sided. Those were the first double-faced records marketed in Europe (Zonophone had marketed double-faced records in South America in 1902). When the patent claim for double-sided records, by Prescott and Ademor Petit, was defeated in an

Austrian court on a challenge from the Favorite Schallplatten Fabrik (1907), Odeon was deprived of a desirable monopoly. Before Fonotipia, Ltd., of England, acquired a controlling interest in Odeon Records (International Talking Machine Co.) during 1906, the American Record Co. issued blue discs with the American label, showing an American Indian on the label. The firm carried out special 27-centimeter pressings for Prescott's business in Europe, the discs being labeled American Odeon Record. The export records were also blue and carried the Indian picture. In 1908 there was another Odeon subsidiary, the Jumbo Record Fabrik, which marketed Jumbo and Jumbola Records. Many were later converted to "Blue-labelled Odeon Records." Otto Heinemann, a founder-director of International Talking Machine, was involved. From July 1911, the business of Fonotipia, Ltd., was acquired by Carl Lindström AG (Beka and Parlophon records), giving Lindström the Odeon, Jumbo, Jumbola, and Fonotipia labels. In 1925 the Odeon label became a part of the Columbia business in Europe (not in the U.S.), which eventually passed to EMI, Ltd., in 1931. Today the label remains one of the EMI trademarks. In the U.S. the Columbia Phonograph Co. concession for Odeon discs terminated in 1910, and the label was no longer generally available in America until January 1921. At that time an American agency of Lindström, the American Odeon Corp. began selling Odeon and Fonotipia discs with American and international repertoires in 21 languages. Newly recorded American Odeon Records (10 inches, $0.85) appeared in March 1921. In June 1921 the firm had either changed its name to the American Odeon Phonograph Corp., or the business had passed into new management; the address was unchanged: 100 W. 21st St., New York. Records of such stars as John McCormack, Emmy Destinn, and Lilli Lehmann became available in America from the Odeon European backlog catalogs. Another name change was reported in July 1921, to American Odeon Record Corp.; but the trading name was American Odeon Corp. by September 1921. All "the latest popular hits" were then available on the label, with some foreign language catalogs. On 31 Dec 1921 the firm decided to go out of business. Meanwhile, Otto Heinemann's General Phonograph Corp. had announced (November 1920) that it had secured access to Lindström's catalogs, including Dacapo, Beka, Favorite, Fonotipia, Lyrophon, Parlophon, and Odeon. That material was issued on the Okeh label until January 1922, when the Odeon name began to appear (with the takeover by General of the American Odeon Corp. business). Upon the acquisition by the British-controlled Columbia Phonograph Co., Inc. of

Label of the American Odeon Record company, c. 1920.
Courtesy Kurt Nauck/Nauck's Vintage Records

the disc business of General Phonograph, the enterprise was renamed Okeh Phonograph Record Corp. Odeon Records seem to have vanished from the U.S. with the Columbia takeover, although the name was revived with a label circulating to the West Coast trade in 1929 as Odeon Electric Records.

FRANK ANDREWS

ODETTA (31 DEC 1930–)

American folk singer and guitarist, born Odetta Holmes Felious Gordon in Birmingham, Alabama. She studied music at Los Angeles City College, and began performing in California in her teens. She sang Black work songs, spirituals, and blues, becoming a key figure in the folksong revival of the 1950s, with acclaimed appearances at such venues as the Blue Angel in New York and the Gate of Horn in Chicago. Odetta toured widely and gave recitals at Town Hall and Carnegie Hall. She was one of the performers at the Newport Folk Festival of 1959. Her first album, on the Tradition label, was *Odetta Sings Ballads and Blues* (#1010; 1956). Among her favorite songs were "He's Got the Whole Wide World in His Hands" and "Take This Hammer," both of which were included in a 1957 LP, *Odetta at the Gate of Horn* (Tradition #1025). *Odetta at Town Hall* (Vanguard #9103; 1961), and *One Grain of Sand* (Vanguard #9137; 1963) were two other successful albums. She continued performing into the 1990s, on television, stage, and in motion pictures. In 1999, she was awarded the Medal of the Arts by President Bill Clinton. Many of her original albums are available on CD, and Vanguard has issued a "Best Of" compilation CD (#79522) as well.

O'DOWD RECORD (LABEL)

An American disc advertised in February 1922, featuring Irish material, sold by Thomas O'Dowd. Artists included O'Dowd himself and James O'Neill.

FRANK ANDREWS

OFFSET (I)

The slight inward slant of the mounting of the headshell on a phonograph pivoted tone arm. Its purpose is to minimize the angle of the stylus in the groove.

OFFSET (II)

In a CD system, the difference between access time and start time.

O'HARA, GEOFFREY (2 FEB 1882–31 JAN 1967)

Canadian/American tenor and composer, born in Chatham, Ontario. He transferred to the U.S. in 1904 and became a citizen in 1922. O'Hara was highly versatile, appearing in minstrel shows and vaudeville, as well as operettas. He was also a church organist. He composed "Your Eyes Have Told Me," recorded by Enrico Caruso; and he sang American Indian songs. "K-K-K-Katy" was the most popular of his 300 songs. His first record was an Edison cylinder in 1905, "The Rosary" with the Knickerbocker Quintet (#9052). Then he sang for Zonophone in 1906–1907 as a member of the Criterion Quartet. He went to Victor in 1916. Victor #17635 (also on Edison Blue Amberol #2451) presented O'Hara in Indian songs with tom-tom accompaniment. His best-selling record was "They Made It Twice as Nice as Paradise and They Called It Dixieland" (Victor #18051; 1916). O'Hara died in St. Petersburg, Florida. [Walsh 1960/2.]

OHIO PHONOGRAPH CO.

One of the affiliates of the North American Phonograph Co., situated in Cincinnati, from 1890 to 1897. James Andem, a pioneer in the entertainment use of the phonograph, was president in 1890–1893. The firm was one that produced its own records, in addition to selling those from the parent company. Dan Kelly was a leading artist, maker of the "Pat Brady" series of records. In May 1897 the company was succeeded by the Edison Phonograph Co., with Andem as general manager. Calvin Child gained his early experience with the company.

OHIO PLAYERS

Like most other notable funk acts, the Ohio Players kinetic mix of percussion, loping bass lines, and stabbing horn flourishes owed much to Sly and the Family Stone's progressive rock-soul fusion of the late 1960s. In terms of both recording productivity and career longevity, the group was unrivaled within the funk genre. The band was formed in 1959, in Dayton, as Greg Webster and the Ohio Untouchables. Early on, they played behind the R&B vocal group, the Falcons, appearing on recordings such as the hit, "I Found a Love" (Lupine #1003; 1962; #6 R&B). With the addition of three members from an area band, they became known as the Ohio Players. Although they had first recorded on their own for Lupine in 1963, their stint as the studio group for Compass Records in 1967–1968 proved to be something of a breakthrough. In addition to releasing singles under their own name, they produced a number of demo tapes, one of which was released as *Observations in Time* (Capitol #192; 1969). Moving on to Westbound Records in the early 1970s, the band enjoyed one big hit, "Funky Worm" (Westbound #214; 1973; #1 R&B, #15 pop), which revealed their penchant for tongue-in-cheek humor. They also established another tradition during this period: marketing their work through provocative album covers typically featuring scantily clad women in sexually suggestive poses. Signing with the Mercury label in 1974, the Players began a highly successful commercial run: *Skin Tight* (Mercury #705; 1974; #11; featuring the title cut, #2 R&B, #13 pop), *Fire* (Mercury #1013; 1974; #1; featuring the title cut, #1 R&B, #1 pop), *Honey* (Mercury #1038; 1975; #2; featuring "Love Rollercoaster," #1 R&B, #1 pop), *Contradiction* (Mercury #1088; 1976; #12), *Ohio Players Gold* (Mercury #1122; 1976; #31), and *Angel* (Mercury #3701; 1977; #41). By the time the group had switched to Arista Records in 1979, their popularity had dropped off considerably. They continued to record for a variety of labels in the 1980s — including Accord, Boardwalk, Air City, and Track — with only intermittent success. With the advent of compact discs, many of the band's classic albums were reissued (along with assorted hit collections such as PolyGram's *Funk on Fire: The Mercury Anthology*, released in 1995). Despite the death of two longtime members — saxophonist "Satch" Mitchell and trumpeter "Pee Wee" Middlebrooks — in the 1990s, the band has continued to tour up to the present day.

FRANK HOFFMANN

OHM ACOUSTICS

Started by Marty Gersten in 1971, presided over by John Strohbeen since 1978, and still located in Brooklyn, New York, Ohm has earned a reputation as an innovative producer of both reasonably priced and high-end speaker systems. The company's most notable models, first exemplified with the monumental Model A, later on the Model F, and currently with the MK-2 series, have employed a coherent line-source driver design first conceived by the late Lincoln Walsh. This driver is a cone unit, with the cone itself being much greater in depth than usual, vertically oriented at the top of the tower-style speaker cabinet, and with the sound thereby radiating uniformly from the backside of the cone area in a 360-degree radiation pattern. Some versions make use of multiple materials in the cone, and the result is a wave front that behaves as if it were radiated from a pulsating, vertically oriented cylinder. Later versions employed damping materials over part of the circumference around the cone, to shape the radiation pattern for better soundstaging and imaging, and some also employed a conventional tweeter at the very top to extend the extreme treble. Today, the company not only produces the Walsh systems, but also markets home-theater speaker packages, affordable conventional systems, and subwoofers. They also have a policy that allows owners of older Ohm Walsh systems to upgrade them to current-product standards. Unlike most other audio companies, Ohm sells factory direct to consumers, eliminating middleman costs. [website: www.OhmSpeakers.com.]

HOWARD FERSTLER

L'OISEAU-LYRE (LABEL)

A French record, established in 1933 in Paris. Louise Dyer, an Australian, founded the company for the issue of early music. Printed scores and recordings (made at the Pathé studios) were offered. The catalog is a small one, but of great interest for music by lesser-known composers. Interesting LPs were made by Christopher Hogwood and the Academy of Ancient Music. The label focuses on early music releases, and has both issued new recordings and reissues of its key back catalog releases on CD. It is part of the Universal Classics, a division of the Universal Music Group.

FRANK ANDREWS

L'Oiseau-Lyre label. Courtesy Frank Hoffmann

OISTRAKH, DAVID
(30 SEP 1908–24 OCT 1974)

Russian violinist, born in Odessa, Ukraine. He studied in Odessa and made his debut in Kiev, playing the Glazunov Concerto under the composer's baton. In 1928 he went to Moscow, and in 1934 was appointed to the faculty of the Moscow Conservatory. He won a major competition in Brussels in 1937, leading to appearances in European capitals (1955) and in the U.S. He died in Amsterdam. His son Igor also achieved international fame. Oistrakh's recordings, with many great orchestras, span the concerto repertoire. Among the notable albums (reissued on CD) are those made with the Philadelphia Orchestra under Eugene Ormandy, including the Sibelius Concerto (Odyssey #30489; 1961) and the Tchaikovsky Concerto (Odyssey #30312). He also recorded a brilliant Brahms Concerto (Angel #36033; 1970) and Brahms Double Concerto with Mstislav Rostropovich (Angel #36032; 1970), both with the Cleveland Orchestra under George Szell. Igor Oistrakh recorded several works with his father, including the J.S. Bach Concerto for Two Violins.

OKEH (LABEL)

An American record first produced by the Otto Heinemann Phonograph Supply Co., Inc., of New York. Heinemann had resigned in December 1915 from his post as managing director of Carl Lindström AG, and set up this new firm; it had a factory in Elyria, Ohio, and an office in Chicago. In May 1916 he was

Okeh label from the early '20s. Courtesy David A. Jasen

Early Okeh Record Lateral Cut disc label with "Indian head" logo. Courtesy David A. Jasen.

selling talking machines with the tradename Vanophone. By October 1917 the company declared itself to be the world's largest manufacturer of talking machine supplies. Okeh records were on sale in May 1918, 10-inch, vertical-cut discs for $.75 each. The label was written in various ways, commencing as "OkeH" then going to all capitals with the middle letters smaller. By 1921 the form was Okeh, with only the initial capitalized; "OKeh" is also seen. The name supposedly came from Otto Heinemann's initials combined with an Indian word meaning "It is so." Material on the label included outstanding jazz and blues items, and folk music of various nations. "Ja Da" (#1155) and "Ole Miss" (#1156), issued in 1919, are described by Rust as "the only genuine New Orleans jazz on records at the time other than the music of the Original Dixieland Jazz Band." Jimmy Durante led a group named the New Orleans Jazz Band. Mamie Smith made her first record for Okeh in 1920, "You Can't Keep a Good Man Down" (#4113), leading to the Okeh race series that started in 1921. Louis Armstrong's earliest discs under his own name were Okeh. Later there were great popular artists of all kinds, including Duke Ellington, Smith Ballew, and Vernon Dalhart. A complete Okeh catalog appeared in October 1918. The price of records went up to $0.85 by December 1918. During 1919 about 25 new records came out each month. Agents in London were appointed in April 1919, and Okeh records were sold there from 1920. After 1 Oct 1919 the Heinemann company came to be known as the General Phonograph Corp., with Heinemann as president and general manager. The first lateral-cut Okeh records were advertised in December 1919. The General Phonograph Corp. of Canada, Ltd., was organized in Toronto. General announced in November 1920 that it had secured access to the recorded repertoire of Carl Lindström AG, including the catalogs of Beka, Dacapo, Favorite, Fonotipia, Lyrophon, Odeon, and Parlophone. These were to become the Okeh "Foreign Records" series. American Odeon Corp. issued its last two lists in November 1921, of Odeon and Fonotipia releases; from January 1922 General issued Odeon and Fonotipia with their label names. Okeh material was used in Britain by the Parlophone Co., Ltd. from 1923. Some Okeh masters were used by Parlophone to press Ariel Grand Records for the mail order house of John G. Graves, Ltd. A new "red label" record using the "Truetone process" — evidently electric — was announced in February 1926, and the word Truetone appeared on labels. Columbia Phonograph Co. acquired Okeh in October 1926 and Heinemann was made president of a new Columbia subsidiary, the Okeh Phonograph Corp., in November 1926. Many label designs followed, in numerous colors, but the same jazz and swing repertoire continued. From 1935 to 1940 there was no Okeh label, but then CBS revived the Columbia label and Columbia changed its old subsidiary Vocalion into a new Okeh. It carried pop, jazz, gospel, country, sacred, and R&B material. Okeh remains in the CBS group, now owned by Sony. In Britain Parlophone has been the Okeh outlet. [Rust 1989.]

FRANK ANDREWS

OKUN, MILT[ON] (23 DEC 1923–)

Folk-pop producer/arranger Okun was born in Brooklyn. A child prodigy pianist, Okun seemed destined for a career as a classical performer until a case of nephritis left him bedridden and unable to play when he was 16 years old. Two years later, he decided to pursue a career in music education, studying at NYU and Oberlin. A fan of traditional folk music, Okun began composing orchestral arrangements of songs to perform around the country. He also recorded as a singer-guitarist for several small folk labels, including Stinson and Riverside. In 1957, Okun was hired by Harry Belafonte to play piano for his summer tour; he subsequently became a full-time employee, conducting and arranging for Belafonte as well as performing as a pianist and backup vocalist for the singer's many performances. This led to work as an arranger for Vanguard Records, for artists like Leon Bibb and Paul Robeson. A key figure on the Greenwich Village folk scene, Okun heard a new group called the Chad Mitchell Trio performing one night and got them a record deal, producing their first albums. In 1960 Okun left Belafonte's employment and went out on his own. He was quickly hired by folk promoter Albert Grossman to work with a new act he was forming to be called Peter, Paul, and Mary. Okun trained the group and made all of their arrangements, leading to a series of number one successes through the 1960s. Through his connection with the Chad Mitchell Trio, he brought to Peter, Paul, and Mary the work of a young songwriter named John Deutschendorf, who had replaced Mitchell as the lead singer in 1965. The song "Leaving on a Jet Plane" was a major hit under the songwriter's new name (suggested by Okun), John Denver. Okun got Denver a solo contract with RCA and produced all of his initial hits including "Take Me Home Country Roads," "Annie's Song," and "Thank God I'm a Country Boy." Okun's last production work was in the 1980s in partnership with Plácido Domingo. He provided full orchestral arrangements for Domingo's performances of pop songs and standards, leading to several successful albums beginning with *Perhaps Love*. Besides his production work, Okun founded Cherry Lane Music in 1960, now a major music publisher.

CARL BENSON

OLCOTT, CHAUNCEY (21 JULY 1858–18 MAR 1932)

American composer and tenor, born in Buffalo, New York. He was probably the most popular stage performer in Irish background plays and musical shows, and the most renowned Irish tenor of his day. He composed the songs "When Irish Eyes Are Smiling," "My Wild Irish Rose," and "Mother Machree," all of which became staples of the Irish song repertoire. Olcott recorded first for Columbia in June 1913, singing "My Wild Irish Rose" (#A1308). He also recorded his other compositions, and many other songs, until his last issues in March 1922. Olcott died in Monte Carlo.

OLD DOMINION PHONOGRAPH CO.

One of the North American Phonograph Co. affiliates, located in Roanoke, Virginia (Masonic Temple Building). It was established in 1890, with J.H. McGilvra as president. In June 1891 the firm had 142 coin-op machines leased to customers.

OLD GUARD BAND

A New York ensemble, one of the early instrumental groups to record. They were heard on Columbia two-minute cylinders in 1896, playing eight numbers.

"Rastus on Parade March" was the first (#1801). Operatic medleys were performed also, from *Lohengrin, Prophete,* and *Tannhäuser.*

OLDEST PERSON TO RECORD

By this is meant the person with the earliest birthdate, not the person of most advanced age at the time of recording. The *Phonogram* reported that the manager of the Ohio Phonograph Co., Arthur Smith, had visited the home of Horatio Perry, a Cleveland centenarian, and made a record of his voice. Perry was born in 1790 — so for a year he was a contemporary of Mozart. An even earlier birthdate is ascribed to one Peggy O'Leary, who sang an Irish melody into a phonograph in 1900; she was said to be 112 years old at the time, placing her birthdate in 1787 or 1788 (this was reported in *HN* #131, April 1983, by John S. Dales, who quoted a contemporary magazine account of the O'Leary rendition). Ms. O'Leary would almost surely be the earliest-born person to make a record. It seems that among professional singers, the earliest birthdate belongs to Peter Schram, a Danish baritone born in 1819. As reported in *Recorded Sound* 85 (January 1984) he made a private record in Copenhagen in 1889. Among well-known persons to record (noncommercially), the oldest was Cardinal John Henry Newman (born 1801), who is known to have made a cylinder in the late 1880s (reported by Peter Martland in *HN* #131, April 1983). The earliest born national leader to make a record was Lajos Kossuth (1802–1894) of Hungary. His address in Turin, Italy, on 20 Oct 1890, was recorded and a broken cylinder remains in the National Library in Budapest. Fragments of the speech are discernible. In 1977 a 45-rpm disc containing the fragment, plus the full speech read by an actor, was issued by Hungaroton. On commercial recordings, the recording artist with the earliest birthdate seems to be J.G. Tollemache Sinclair, who did recitations for G & T, Columbia (in London), and for Odeon. His declamation of "La jeune fille mourante" (G & T #1333) dates from November 1906. His birth took place in Edinburgh on 11 Aug 1825. Josef Joachim (born 1831) seems to have been the instrumentalist with earliest birthdate to record commercially, for G & T. Gustave Walter and Charles Santley (both born 1834) were apparently the earliest-born singers on commercial discs, recording for G & T in the 1900s. Santley's rendition of "Non piu andrai" (G & T #05200; 1903) marked him as the earliest born singer to record an opera aria. Walter was the earliest born signer to record an aria in German: "Leb' wohl, Mignon" ("Adieu, Mignon") from *Mignon* (G & T #3–42154; 1905). [Johnson 1983.]

OLDEST RECORDS

The oldest known record in existence today is one made in 1878 by Augustus Stroh (inventor of the Stroh violin). Still on the mandrel of his machine and never played, it was reported in *Sound Box*, November 1990, and *ARSC Journal* 22–1 (Spring 1991). Among extant records that have been played, the oldest may be an engraved metal cylinder made by Frank Lambert in 1878 or 1879. It was intended to be the sound track in a talking clock, and offers the hours: "One o'clock, two o'clock, three o'clock …" through twelve o'clock, with ten o'clock for some reason omitted. Another venerable record is the white wax cylinder made by composer Arthur Sullivan, praising Thomas Edison for inventing the phonograph, but saying he shudders to think how much horrible music it will cause to be recorded. Jim Walsh (*Hobbies* April 1965) gives the date of that record as 5 Oct 1888. Another group of cylinders from 1888 was reported to be at the Edison National Historic Site, West Orange, New Jersey, in 1988 (*NAG* #65, July 1988). It consists of 22 records, 21 in white wax, made by Colonel Gouraud in London, during August 1888. They include a whistling number by "Mrs. Shaw," a "letter from Col. Gouraud to Mr. Edison," three live recordings of a Handel Festival at the Crystal Palace, and an "organ solo played on the grand organ at Westminster Abbey by Prof. Bridge." There was no announced plan by officials at the Historic Site to play or reissue the cylinders, and it was not stated when (if ever) the records had been played in the past.

OLDFIELD, MIKE (15 MAY 1953–)

One of the most successful progressive rock artists of the 1970s, Mike Oldfield is best remembered for the inclusion of an excerpt from his first LP, *Tubular Bells* (Virgin #105; 1973; #1 U.K., #3 U.S.), in the hugely popular horror film, *The Exorcist.* Despite the appeal of this work, it would be grossly unfair to characterize his career (as some have done) as an extended rehash of *Tubular Bells.* His experimentation with extended musical forms, Third World styles, and eclectic instrumentation significantly influenced a generation of rock musicians, many of whom would help bring these devices closer to the pop mainstream. Born in Reading, England, Oldfield formed the folk-pop duo, Sallyangie, with his sister Sally, in the late 1960s, later performing with Kevin Ayers's band and doing session work for the Edgar Broughton Band and David Bedford. His first solo release, *Tubular Bells,* helped Richard Branson's fledging Virgin label become viable. Provided ample studio time, Oldfield recorded every instrumental track for the work, thereby earning the moniker, "wizard of 1,000 overdubs." He would follow *Tubular Bells* with a succession of ambitious albums, including *Hergest Ridge* (Virgin #109; 1974; #1 U.K., #87 U.S.; his last release to chart stateside), *The Orchestral Tubular Bells* (Virgin #2026; 1975; #17 U.K.), *Ommadawn* (Virgin #33913; 1975; #4 U.K.), *Incantations* (Virgin #101; 1978; #14 U.K.), and *Exposed* (Virgin #2511; 1979; #16 U.K.). His work took on more of a pop-rock feel in the 1980s, highlighted by his score to the critically acclaimed film, *The Killing Fields* (Virgin #2328; 1984; #97 U.K.). By the 1990s, Oldfield seemed more content to capitalize on the by-then legendary debut album; his releases included *Tubular Bells II* (Reprise #2002; 1992; #1 U.K.), *Tubular III* (Reprise #24349; 1998; #4 U.K.), and *The Millennium Bell* (Reprise #80885; 1999).

FRANK HOFFMANN

OLDHAM, ANDREW LOOG (1944–)

Born in Hampstead, London, England, Oldham became a well-known pop-music impresario during the British Invasion years thanks to his association with the Rolling Stones. He began his career as an assistant in the fashion industry, and then moved on to music publicity and promotion; working for pop-music manager Brian Epstein, he helped promote a new group called the Beatles in 1963. Hearing the early Rolling Stones performing at a club, he became the group's manager and encouraged the singers to build their "bad boy" image (to distinguish them from the loveable Beatles). He got the group their recording contract with Decca Records and produced their recordings through 1967. Oldham also led his own "Orchestra" on four albums of instrumental versions of pop music during this period. In 1965, he formed the Immediate label (and the subsidiary label, Instant) with fellow publicist/manager Tony Calder, which signed the Small Faces, among other groups. Oldham broke with the Stones in 1967 and Immediate closed in 1970. Oldham moved to New York in the mid-1970s, producing new groups on occasion. In the 1980s, he moved to Bogota, Colombia, where he continues to live. In Argentina, he produced Los Ratones Paranoicos from the late 1980s through 1996, a group that achieved considerable success in the Latin music market. He has written two volumes of his autobiography, *Stoned* (St. Martin's Press, 2001) and *2 Stoned* (2002); a third volume is planned to complete the story.

CARL BENSON

OLIVE, SEAN (10 SEP 1959–)

Born in Brockville, Ontario, Canada, Olive received a bachelors degree in music from the University of Toronto in 1982 and a master's degree in sound recording from McGill University in 1986. From 1986–1993, he was a research scientist in the Acoustics & Signal Processing Group at the National Research Council in Ottawa, Canada. During that time, he was a member of the research team of the ATHENA project, that developed one the first room-adaptive loudspeakers. Since 1993 he has been the manager of subjective evaluation for the R&D Group of Harman International Industries, Northridge, California. He is a fellow of the Audio Engineering Society, past-governor, and past-chair of the Los Angeles AES section, and has authored and co-authored over 25 papers and preprints in the *AES Journal*, for which he received AES publications awards in 1990 and 1995. Olive is a member of two AES Technical Councils and the AES Working Group for listening tests. For nine weeks each year, he teaches a critical listening course to recording engineering students at UCLA. He recently coauthored a chapter on "Subjective Evaluation" with Dr. Floyd Toole in John Borwick's third edition of the *Loudspeaker and Headphone Handbook*.

HOWARD FERSTLER

OLIVER, KING
(11 MAY 1885–8 APR 1938)

American jazz cornetist and band leader, born Joseph Oliver on a plantation near Abend, Louisiana. He played in New Orleans brothels, and formed a group that became the Creole Jazz Band. In 1918 he moved to Chicago and in 1922 invited Louis Armstrong to join his Creoles. Historic recordings followed in 1923 (discussed in the article on Armstrong), showing Oliver at his peak, especially in two-cornet work with Armstrong. After Armstrong left in 1924, Oliver's group moved toward a smoother style, featuring Barney Bigard, Albert Nicholas, Kid Ory, and Omer Simeon. Fine recordings were made in 1926–1927 in Chicago, including "Someday, Sweetheart" (Vocalion #1059; 1926) and "Black Snake Blues" (Vocalion #1112; 1927). The ensemble was then titled King Oliver and His Dixie Syncopators. A sophisticated sound developed in the next few years, in part because of the arrival of trombonist J.C. Higginbotham who replaced Kid Ory. "Speakeasy Blues" (Vocalion #1225; 1928) is a good example. Oliver recorded for Victor in 1929–1930, then for Brunswick and again for Vocalion (his final recordings) in 1931. Oliver died in Savannah, Georgia. Oliver's recordings are available on various European and U.S. label CDs; Classics has issued his complete recordings in chronological order on a series of CDs, and other labels have reissued selections, including Milestone,

King Oliver's Creole Jazz Band in Chicago, c. 1923. L to r: Honore Dutrey (trombone), Baby Dodds (drums), King Oliver (trumpet), Louis Armstrong (slide trumpet), Lil Hardin (piano), Johnny St. Cyr (banjo), and Johnny Dodds (clarinet). Courtesy BenCar Archives

ASV/Living Era, JSP, and Music Memoria, to name a few. [Allen 1955.]

OLIVER, SY (17 DEC 1910–28 MAY 1988)

American trumpeter, arranger, and composer, born Melvin James Oliver in Battle Creek, Michigan. He played with various bands in his teens, and was with Jimmie Lunceford in 1933 as performer and arranger. Oliver's arrangements for Lunceford were outstanding, giving that ensemble a unique and sophisticated timbre. "The magical way in which Sy Oliver could blend harmony and instrumental color with his own unique brand of relaxed swing is shown to perfect effect on 'Dream of You'" [Schuller]. Oliver arranged for Tommy Dorsey in 1939–1943, doing his most famous work ("Yes Indeed," "Opus No. 1," "Well, Git It," etc.). In a "dramatic overnight impact" [Schuller] he produced a jazz-based sound for Dorsey. Oliver was a music director and producer for Decca Records, breaking the color line in the music industry. He led his own band at times, notably in the late 1970s when

he was installed at the Rainbow Room in New York. He also composed for Hollywood and for television programs. He died in New York. [Schuller 1989.]

OLNEY, BENJAMIN

See Loudspeaker

OLSON, HARRY (1901–1 APR 1982)

Born in Mt. Pleasant, Iowa, Olson was a pioneer in musical sound reproduction and one of the most important researchers and designers in the history of audio. He received his B.E. degree from the University of Iowa in 1924, continued his graduate studies at the same institution, and was awarded a master's in solid mechanical wave filters in 1925 and went on to obtain a Ph.D. in atomic physics in 1928. He joined RCA in 1928 and stayed with the company for 40 years. Some of the primary things Olson tackled at RCA were the development of the RCA magnetic tape recorder for television and the music synthesizer. Another problem was the poor quality sound in the new talking pictures that had recently been introduced. Part of the solution Olson came up with involved the development of the velocity microphone, and he was also instrumental in work done on RCA's second-order gradient microphone. In 1932 he patented the first cardioid ribbon microphone using a field coil instead of a permanent magnet. In 1934 he was placed in charge of acoustical research for the RCA Manufacturing Co., at the company's Camden acoustic laboratory, where he went on to develop the electronic synthesizer with Herbert Millar. Subsequently, he became director of the acoustical and Electromechanical laboratory at RCA Laboratories, in Princeton, New Jersey. In 1938, under his supervision, Leslie J. Anderson came up with the design for the RCA 44B ribbon bi-directional microphone and the 77B ribbon unidirectional, and in 1942, Olson patented a single-ribbon cardioid microphone and a phased-array directional microphone. Apart from microphone design, he worked to develop high-directivity horn speaker systems for theater and sound-reinforcement use, and also designed a loudspeaker woofer system that was a precursor to the acoustic suspension design further developed by Edgar Villchur some years later. Between 1958 and 1963, Olson, drawing on profits from Elvis Presley's record sales for RCA, developed what became known as the Dynagroove record. This was actually a system of recording and reproducing music that retained the phase relationships while compressing the 70- to 90-decibel dynamic range of live classical music to the 60-decibel limit of LP phonograph records. In the 1960s, Olson also experimented with surround sound, and in 1966, he was appointed staff vice president of acoustical and electromechanical research for the entire company. During his long career, Dr. Olson was granted more than 100 patents, published more than 130 technical articles, and wrote a number of important books, including *Applied Acoustics*; *Acoustical Engineering*; *Modern Sound Reproduction*; *Music, Physics, and Engineering*; and *Musical Engineering*. Elected to the National Academy of Science in 1959, and later becoming a fellow of the American Physical Society and Society of Motion Picture and Television Engineers, Olson received numerous additional awards in the field of audio engineering, among them being the Audio Engineering Society's John H. Potts award, in 1949 (later to become the Gold Medal), an Honorary Membership, in 1957, and the AES award, in 1965. A past president of the organization, he was editor of the Society's journal from 1966 until 1969, and was editor emeritus for 13 years. He also received three awards from the Institute of Electrical and Electronics Engineers, including a fellowship, and was awarded the first Silver Medal in Engineering Acoustics ever offered by the Acoustical Society of America, in 1974, and the Society's first Gold Medal, in 1981.

See also **Loudspeaker; Microphone**

HOWARD FERSTLER

OLYMPIC (LABEL)

An American record issued from April or May 1921 by the Olympic Disc Record Corp., a subsidiary of the Remington Phonograph Corp. Phil E. Remington was president of Olympic, J.S. Holmes was vice president, Everett H. Holmes was treasurer, and John Fletcher was secretary. Matrices and equipment acquired from the Operaphone Co. formed the basis of the business, which had its main offices in New York; there was also a recording studio in Brooklyn. Material included dance and popular vocal numbers, plus Hawaiian, operatic, and sacred items. Issues ceased after December 1921, when Remington and Olympic went bankrupt. A revival of the label took place in 1922–1923, by the Fletcher Record Co., Inc., of New York. John Fletcher — once vice president of Operaphone and secretary of Olympic Disc Record Corp. — and Harry Pace of the Pace Phonograph Co. were the men who formed that company, through purchase of the Olympic plant. The new company was located in Long Island City. Pace was president of the Pace Phonograph Record Corp., from which Black Swan discs emanated. The Fletcher Co. pressed Black Swan records, and the two labels shared many of the same matrices (contrary to Black Swan's avowed intention of publishing records only by Black artists). The firm announced bankruptcy in December 1923. The Capitol Roll and Record Co., Chicago, revived the label briefly in 1924. Matrices were brought from Long Island by John Fletcher. One hundred selections were available in November 1924. [Kendziora 1986/4; Kunstadt 1987; Rust 1978.]

FRANK ANDREWS

OLYMPIC RECORD (LABEL)

A British issue, not connected with the American Olympic label, registered as a trademark by the Sound Recording Co., Ltd., in 1912. Exclusive use of the label was taken by Levy's of Whitechapel, London, which enjoyed rights in the label even after the trademark passed to the Crystalate Manufacturing Co., Ltd., and then to the Crystalate Gramophone Record Manufacturing Co., Ltd. Masters came from Grammavox, Popular, and Imperial. Some Olympics had stuck-on labels over Grammavox and Popular labels. There were 10-inch and 10 1/4-inch sizes, double-faced.

FRANK ANDREWS

ONEGIN, SIGRID (1 JUNE 1889–16 JUNE 1943)

Swedish contralto, born in Stockholm as Elizabeth Elfriede Emile Sigrid Onegin. She studied in Frankfurt, Munich, and Milan, and made her debut in recital (using the name Lily Hoffmann) in Wiesbaden on 10 Sep 1911. Her first operatic role was Carmen, in Stuttgart on 4 Oct 1912. She made her Metropolitan Opera debut as Amneris on 22 Nov 1922. In 1931 she retired to Switzerland, and died there on 16 June 1943, in Magliaso. Onegin recorded for Polydor in Germany in 1921–1925, singing Carmen, Delilah, and several Verdi and Wagner roles, all in German. She was also recording a similar repertoire in English for Brunswick, in the U.S. During the electric era she was with Brunswick, Victor, and HMV. Among her outstanding discs are three *Carmen* numbers on Brunswick (#15128 and #50077; 1927), "Mon coeur s'ouvre à ta voix" in German (HMV DB #1420; 1929), and "Ah! mon fils" from *Prophète* (HMV DB #1190; 1929). These and several other arias are included on the Harmonia Mundi CD (#89027; 1991). In a review of this disc, John B. Steane observed that "there is probably no more beautiful contralto voice on record than Onegin's" [*Gramophone*, February 1991]. [Dennis 1950/10.]

O'NEILL, ARTHUR J. (1868–OCT 1916)

American record industry executive, one of the founders of the O'Neill-James Co. of Chicago in 1904. He gained a U.S. patent (#874,985) for a talking machine with a three-inch diameter turntable spindle (filed 11 Apr 1907, granted 31 Dec 1907), and developed discs with large center holes to play on them. He also started another firm, Aretino Co., Inc., then merged the two companies in 1910. He continued in the business until 1915, then became the first Pathé representative in Chicago, trading under the name of State Street Pathéphone Co. He died in Chicago. [Fabrizio 1979; Koenigsberg 1990.]

O'NEILL-JAMES CO.

A Chicago firm, established on 22 Apr 1904 by Arthur J. O'Neill, Winifred B. James, and Sherwin N. Bisbee. It dealt in various products, but soon came to specialize in talking machines and discs. Its record label was Busy Bee, the name taken from Bisbee's surname. A partner firm was set up in 1907, Aretino Co., Inc., to trade in talking machines of a sort invented by Arthur O'Neill, with a large spindle, manufactured by Columbia and by Hawthorne & Sheble. Indeed the spindle was large enough (three inches) to accommodate the various large-holed discs on sale (Standard and Diamond, 9/16 inch; Harmony, 3/4 inch; United, 1 1/2 inch), and even normal discs (with an adaptor ring). Thus, the firm had a universal talking machine, and it was that product upon which attention became concentrated. But Victor forced Hawthorne & Sheble out of business in 1909, requiring Aretino to turn to Columbia for its machines and adding to the cost of operations. O'Neill merged his two firms, but was unable to stay in business beyond 1915. [Fabrizio 1979, 1980.]

ONE-STOP OUTLET

The name given to a record wholesaler who handles all labels.

OPEN LOOP GAIN

The added gain before feedback, required of an amplifier to compensate for negative feedback amplification loss.

OPEN REEL TAPE

SEE REEL-TO-REEL TAPE

OPERA DISC MUSICA (LABEL)

An unauthorized record, using Gramophone Co. masters that had been held by Deutsche Grammophon AG when World War I broke out. After the war the records were issued in Germany until stopped by legal action. The Opera Disc Distributing Co., of New York, issued in 1921 a 32-page catalog of about 1,000 items by about 500 star singers. Victor litigation put an end to the business in March 1923. [*Hobbies* lists the offerings, in 1943/4–5, 1944/3–4.]

OPERA RECORDINGS

This article is in two parts: 1. Single numbers; 2. Complete sets.

1. *Single Numbers*. Before 1900 the cylinder manufacturers took three approaches to operatic material. They offered instrumental selections (overtures and arrangements of the vocal numbers), arias translated

Shortlived label of the early '20s. Courtesy Kurt
Nauck/Nauck's Vintage Records

into English, and (occasionally) arias in their original
languages. In most cases truncations were required to
fit the numbers into the typical two-minute time of the
brown wax cylinders. On 25 May 1889 Alfred
Amrhein recorded a violin solo version of the overture
to *Fra diavolo* on a cylinder for Thomas Edison's
North American Phonograph Co. A few days later, on
28 May 1889, cornetist John Mittauer performed
"Rigoletto." Selections from *Faust* were recorded on
29 May 1889 by flutist C. Aug. Joepel and clarinetist
Henry Giese. Similar performances followed, by vari-
ous instrumentalists. Among the first renditions by
Issler's Orchestra was "Selection" from *Mikado*, made
for Edison on 13 Nov 1889. A "Polka" from *Paul et
Virginie* (by Victor Massé) was inscribed by the Fifth
Regiment Band in an Edison session on 29 July 1891.
Nineteenth-century vocal cylinders by the major labels
were few. Thomas Bottsang "Song of the Toreador" on
Edison (#353), announced in September 1898. Frank
C. Stanley sang the "Armorer's Song" from Reginald
De Koven's *Robin Hood* on a five-inch Concert cylin-
der for Edison (#B97; 1898). Bernard Bégué made 10
Columbia cylinders in 1898 and several Edison
records ca. 1899. Henri Weber was active for Pathé in
Paris from 1897, making at least 42 records by 1900.
Fifteen of those cylinders were French opera arias.
The cylinders made by Gianni Bettini in New York in
the late 1890s included an extensive selection of arias
by recognized opera singers. Bettini's May 1897 catalog listed baritone numbers by Alberto de Bassini,
from *Carmen, Nozze di Figaro, Traviata, Pagliacci,*

*Rigoletto, Ballo in maschera, Favorite, Barbiere di
Siviglia, Lucia di Lamermoor, Ernani,* and *Trovatore.*
Soprano Gertrude Sylva had 12 arias listed in that catalog; contralto Carlotta Desvignes had three arias;
tenor Dante del Papa had 19 arias. Other major voices
included baritone Mario Ancona (four arias), bass Pol
Plançon (two arias), soprano Rosalia Chalia (five
arias), baritone Giuseppe Campanari (five arias),
soprano Frances Saville (two arias), and soprano
Marie Engle (one aria). Later American catalogs
issued by Bettini (1898, 1899) offered more material
by those artists, and a few new ones. The most interesting addition in the 1899 was baritone Anton van
Rooy, the first Wagnerian singer to record. Soprano
Marcella Sembrich appeared in the 1900 catalog.
When Bettini moved to Paris in 1901 he continued
making opera cylinders (and discs dubbed from them),
engaging prominent artists from the Paris Opéra and
Opéra-Comique. By that time there were also discs
from the two firms that were to become the leaders of
operatic recording, the Gramophone Co. in Britain and
the Victor Talking Machine Co. (and its predecessors,
Berliner Gramophone Co., and the Consolidated
Talking Machine Co.). Fred Gaisberg, as a young
employee of Emile Berliner, heard tenor Ferruccio
Giannini singing in Atlantic City, and brought him to
the Berliner studio to record. The result was "La donna
è mobile," apparently the earliest aria on disc (#967;
21 Jan 1896). Giannini made at least 21 other discs by
1899, and also recorded for Columbia, Victor, and
Zonophone. The Berliner, Gramophone, and
Zonophone seven-inch discs made in Britain from
August 1898 included various operatic items. The
Hotel Cecil Orchestra played the *Trovatore* "Miserere"
(#504; 2 Sep 1898) and the *Mignon* "Polonaise"
(#513; 8 Sep 1898). James Norrie sang "Then You'll
Remember Me" from *Bohemian Girl* (#2031; 8 Sep
1898), and Tom Bryce sang an English version of the
"Drinking Song" (Brindisi) from *Cavalleria rusticana*
(#2058; 22 Sep 1898). Montague Borwell sang the
"Toreador Song" (#2080; 4 Oct 1898). As a result of
Fred Gaisberg's recruiting, G & T recorded the
world's leading operatic artists. By the time of its
February 1903 catalog, the firm was offering arias by
such luminaries as Emma Albani, Suzanne Adams,
Mattia Battistini, Emma Calvé, Enrico Caruso, Feodor
Chaliapin, Giuseppe De Luca, Fernando De Lucia,
Victor Maurel, Pol Plançon, Maurice Renaud, Mario
Sammarco, Antonio Scotti, Francesco Tamagno, and
Anton Van Rooy. Red Label records made by those
artists were later available in America as Victor Red
Seal records. Victor's earliest opera recordings came
before the firm was established, on the labels of the
predecessor Eldridge Johnson firms. On 14 July 1900,
Johnson's Improved Gramophone Record label

recorded the Voss' First Regiment Band performing the *Zampa* overture; on 18 Oct 1900 violinist Charles D'Almaine playing the "Miserere." The first opera vocals on a Johnson label were made in June and July 1900. They were "Mephisto Serenade" from *Faust* and "Who Treads the Path of Duty" from *Magic Flute*, sung by George Broderick. Emilio de Gogorza, one of the most recorded baritones of the early years, sang the Drinking Song from *Martha* in July 1900, and "Di provenza il mar" with "Dio possente" from *Faust* in October 1900. The first female opera singers on the Johnson label were Marie Romaine, interpreting "Then You'll Remember Me" from *Bohemian Girl* (2 July 1900), and Rosalia Chalia, who sang three arias on 30 Oct 1900: "Ah fors è lui," Addio del passato," and "Una voce poco fa." Victor began recording its counterpart to the Gramophone Red Labels in May 1903. They were the Red Seals, of which the first to represent opera were "Connais tu le pays?" and "Habanera" sung by Zélie de Lussan (#M-2188; 17 May 1903). The Red Seal catalog grew to encompass all the great names of the operatic universe. Victor's 1917 catalog included interpretations by the artists already mentioned, plus sopranos Frances Alda, Blanche Arral, Celestina Boninsegna, Lucrezia Bori, Emmy Destinn, Emma Eames, Geraldine Farrar, Johanna Gadski, Amelita Galli-Curci, Alma Gluck, Nellie Melba, Alice Nielsen, Adelina Patti, Marcella Sembrich, and Luisa Tetrazzini. Among the contraltos were Clara Butt, Julia Culp, Maria Galvany, Jeanne Gerville-Réache, Louise Homer, Margarete Matzenauer, and Ernestine Schumann-Heink. Tenors included Enrico Caruso, Edmond Clément, Hipolito Lazaro, Fernando de Lucia, Francesco Marconi, Riccardo Martin, Giovanni Martinelli, John McCormack, Leo Slezak, and Evan Williams. The principal baritones were Pasquale Amato, Emilio de Gogorza, Giuseppe de Luca, and Titta Ruffo. Marcel Journet was among the bass voices. Through the acoustic era and the pre-LP electrical era, Victor and the Gramophone Co. (EMI from 1931) remained dominant in opera. The list of great singers recruited by 1940 is too long to give here; only a few of the most important names will be mentioned. Sopranos: Kirsten Flagstad, Lotte Lehmann, Lily Pons, Rosa Ponselle, Elisabeth Rethberg, Bidú Sayão, and Helen Traubel. Mezzo-sopranos and contraltos: Gladys Swarthout, Kerstin Thorberg. Tenors: Jussi Björling, Beniamino Gigli, Giacomo Lauri-Volpi, Giovanni Martinelli, Lauritz Melchior, Aureliano Pertile, Tito Schipa. Baritones: Friedrich Schorr, Lawrence Tibbett, Leonard Warren. Basses: Alexander Kipnis, Ezio Pinza. The Columbia Phonograph Co. also recruited noted singers, albeit never so many as Victor, and issued a catalog in spring 1903 of "Columbia Grand Opera Disc" records — that was the style of the labels. Those discs were made in New York in late 1902 or early 1903, and marketed the first time in March 1903. Artists in the series included Suzanne Adams, Antonio Scotti, Edouard de Reszke, Giuseppe Campanari, Marcella Sembrich, and Ernestine Schumann-Heink. Edison Diamond Discs did not feature opera, but did include some fine recordings (from 1913) by Alessandro Bonci, Lucrezia Bori, Anna Case, Emmy Destinn, Charles Hackett, Frieda Hempel, Maria Labia, Giovanni Martinelli, Margarete Matzenauer, Claudia Muzio, Marie Narelle, Marie Rappold, Jacques Urlus, Alice Verlet, and Giovanni Zenatello. With the introduction of the larger size discs, 10-inch (1901) and 12-inch discs (1903, with perhaps a few earlier), longer numbers were recorded and more complete versions of arias that had appeared in cut form were presented. It is of interest that "star albums" were not made for individual singers during the 78-rpm era. Victor did produce *Stars of the Metroplitan*, a two-volume set that included arias and duets by many of their famous artists. The LP brought a sudden profusion of new performers, and of individual albums for them. Among the outstanding names of the 1950s and 1960s were Carlo Bergonzi, Montserrat Caballé, Maria Callas, Franco Corelli, Mario del Monaco, Victoria de los Angeles, Giuseppe di Stefano, Placido Domingo, Dietrich Fischer-Dieskau, Mirella Freni, Nicolai Gedda, Nicolai Ghiaurov, Tito Gobbi, Marilyn Horne, Sena Jurinac, Alfredo Kraus, Erich Kunz, George London, Christa Ludwig, Cornell MacNeil, James McCracken, Robert Merrill, Sherill Milnes, Anna Moffo, Birgit Nilsson, Luciano Pavarotti, Jan Peerce, Leontyne Price, Elisabeth Schwarzkopf, Renata Scotto, Cesare Siepi, Beverly Sills, Giulietta Simionato, Joan Sutherland, Renata Tebaldi, Giorgio Tozzi, Richard Tucker, Jon Vickers, Ljuba Welitsch, Wolfgang Windgassen, and Fritz Wunderlich. Victor no longer controlled the world opera scene, as the labels brought forward by the LP contracted many leading singers. Callas and Schwartzkopf, for example, were on Angel; Del Monaco, Pavarotti, Sutherland, and Tebaldi on London; Fischer-Dieskau on Deutsche Grammophon. Most of the LP artists had albums of their favorite arias. The 1970s and 1980s saw the rise of such individuals as Thomas Allen, Agnes Baltsa, Kathleen Battle, Hildegard Behrens, José Carreras, Edita Gruberova, Siegfried Jerusalem, Tom Krause, Eva Martón, Kurt Moll, Jessye Norman, Leo Nucci, Elena Obraztsova, Lucia Popp, Herman Prey, Samuel Ramey, Katia Ricciarelli, Matti Salminen, Martti Talvela, Kiri Te Kanawa, and Frederica von Stade. In this group also, a variety of record labels are found. There are separate entries in this Encyclopedia for many of the artists cited above.

2. *Complete Sets.* One of the earliest efforts, perhaps the first, to record a substantial portion of an opera was an *Aida* on the Zonophone label (#12664/78, #24017, #24019/25) recorded in Milan in 1906 and 1907. The cast included no names of international stature: Teresa Chelotti and Elvira Magliuolo shared the role of Aida (the former participated only in Aida's two arias and the duet with Amonasro); Virginia Colombati (Amneris), Orazio Cosentino (Rhadames), Giovanni Novelli (Amonasro), and Alfredo Brondi (Ramfis) are the other named participants. That this recording contained substantial cuts is revealed by the absence of the Preludio and by the limitation of both "Ritorna, vincitor" and "O cieli azzurri" to one side each. The chorus in the "Gloria all'Egitto" is identified as that of La Scala, an ascription not to be taken too literally, while the single orchestral excerpt, the "Marcia trionfale," is performed by what is called the Banda di Milano. In 1907 there was also the more plausible choice (because of its brevity) of *Pagliacci* (G & T #54338/39, #052163/63, #052166/68, #053150, #054146/55) as a step in the direction of recording complete operas. This version had the marked advantage of Leoncavallo's personal supervision, although the conductor in charge was Carlo Sabajno. The cast for this effort included more notable singers than the *Aida* mentioned above: Giuseppina (Josefina) Huguet (Nedda), Antonio Paoli (Canio), Francesco Cigada (Tonio), Gaetano Pini-Corsi (Beppe), and Ernesto Badini (Silvio). The project had originally started out using the tenor Augusto Barbaini as Canio, but the five sides he recorded with the other cast members listed above were shortly remade with Paoli. Because this attempt at a complete recording was not issued as a separately packaged set, it would be theoretically possible to compile some parts of it with alternate leading tenors. After these first Italian efforts, endeavors began in Berlin from 1907 with Johann Strauss's *Fledermaus* (G & T #41971/74 (dialogue), #2–40543 (overture), #043074, #2–44213/22, #44624, #044059/61, #3–42789; 1907) on 21 sides, including four devoted to dialogue. The cast contained some popular local figures in this repertoire: Emilie Herzog (Rosalinde), Marie Dietrich (Adele), Robert Philipp (Eisenstein), and Julius Lieban (doubling the roles of Alfred and Dr. Blind). The following year two French operas were recorded complete in German translations: *Carmen* (Gramophone Co. Pre-Dog #2–40829/31, #4–42181/82, #2–43199/201, #042180, #053109, #44690, #2–44464/74, #044093/104, #044505/06; 1908–36 sides) and *Faust* (Gramophone Co. Pre-Dog #4–42075/79, #2–43095/96, #040521/23, #042163/64, #043101/02, #2–44366/80, #044081/85; 1908–34 sides). These sets offer the fascination of

Emmy Destinn months before her Metropolitan Opera debut in two roles (Carmen and Margarethe) which she never performed in the U.S. Her tenor partner in both works was Carl Jörn, who sang at the Metropolitan in 1909–1914. Other notable singers in these casts were Minnie Nast (who would create Sophie in *Rosenkavalier*) as Micaela, and Paul Knupfer as Mephistopheles. Besides the relative celebrity of the major participants, these sets have much to reveal about the German-language performing traditions of these two works in the first decade of the century (e.g., many high notes were added). The impetus of these German recordings led in 1909 to the first major attempt upon the Wagnerian repertory: the complete second act of *Tannhäuser* (Odeon #50699/710, #76125/26, #80046/48, #80051/53) in the Dresden version, performed by Anny Krull (in her only known recordings; she created the role of Elektra in the same year), the tenors Fritz Vogelstrom and Walter Kirchhoff (as Walter von der Vogelweide), the baritone Hermann Weil, and the American bass Leon Rains. Many years would elapse before a Wagnerian opera was preserved complete. Even more enterprising than these German discs was a series of full-length operas undertaken by the French firm of Pathé Frères starting in 1912, carried out under the generic title of *Le théatre chez soi.* This collection would by 1923 include relatively complete recordings of *Romeo et Juliette* (Pathé #1501/27; 1912), *Rigoletto* (Pathé #1536/50; 1912), *Favorite* (Pathé #1551/71; 1912), *Galathée* (Pathé #1572/86; 1912) of Victor Massé, *Traviata* (Pathé #1587/1602; 1912), *Trouvére* [*Trovatore*] (Pathé #1603/21; 1912), *Faust* (Pathé #1622/49; 1912), *Carmen* (Pathé #1650/67; 1912), *Noces de Jeannette* (Pathé #1708/17; 1921) of Massé, and *Manon* (Pathé #1718/41; 1923). Although they are sonically unappealing, particularly the earlier sets, these contain much of interest. Outside of France Donizetti's *Favorite* is almost always performed in an inaccurate Italian version. The work was originally written for the Paris Opéra (2 Dec 1840) and remained on both Parisian and French provincial stages for more than 70 years. The Pathé *Favorite* preserves that performing tradition, as nearly as we have come to understand it today. The *Trouvère* sequence (36 sides) documents the version that Verdi arranged for the Paris Opéra in 1857, which contains some fascinating changes as well as an expanded ending to the final scene. *Traviata* presents us with the French adaptation made for the Théâtre-Lyrique and introduced there in 1864 as *Violetta*, with the 21-year-old Christine Nilsson making her operatic debut, singing a French translation by Edouard Duprez, the brother of the famous tenor. *Romeo*, dating from 1912, comes from a time when the influence of Gounod still made itself felt only 19 years after his death. The two opéras-comiques of Massé, although they have disappeared from the international repertoire, provide fascinating souvenirs of a performance style that would otherwise have disappeared. Today, when anything approaching authentic French style is rarely to be encountered, this Pathé series offers much information to the serious student. The singers who participate in these performances are largely unfamiliar today, as relatively few appeared on other than French-language stages, but there are some notable examples of adroit, stylish singing to be found here. The *Romeo*, for instance, offers the 27-year-old Yvonne Gall as Juliette, the robust tenor of Agustarello Affre as Romeo, the great Marcel Journet as Frère Laurent, Henri Albers as Capulet, Alexis Boyer as Mercutio, and even the veteran Hippolyte Belhomme in the small role of Gregorio. The Manon is Fanny Heldy, and the title role in *Noces de Jeannette* is sung by the much-recorded Ninon Vallin. The role of Pygmalion in the other Massé work was originally written for mezzo-soprano, but later adapted by the composer for bass; in this series that part is assigned to the sonorous voice of André Gresse, who also sings Mephisto in the *Faust* set. The firm foundation of this series is provided by two baritones: Henri Albers and Jean Noté; the former contributes an aristocratic Alphonse (*Favorite*), d'Orbel (i.e., Germont), and a vigorous Escamillo; the latter, Rigoletto, di Luna, and Valentin. The historical value of this series far outweighs its sonic deficiencies. In Italy in 1916 and 1917 there appeared two *Rigolettos*, with traditional cuts and others as well, featuring two prominent baritones in their youthful heydays, Cesare Formichi on the earlier (Columbia #D16346/362; 1916) and Giuseppe Danise on the later (HMV #7–254023/34, #2–0252004/05, #2–0254014/28, #2–254511; 1917), but the casts are otherwise ordinary. Another complete *Rigoletto* (Phonotype #1566/67, #1592, #1777, #1795/96, and also #1795/take 3, #1875, #1883/87, #1910/23, #1929/36, #1939, #2299; 1918), most of which was recorded in Naples in 1918, but using some material from earlier sessions, features the 52-year-old Fernando De Lucia as the Duke, availing himself of convenient transpositions, and surrounded by a local cast. In the summer of that same 1918, De Lucia, who had made his debut in 1884, incised his Count Almaviva in a full-length *Barbiere* (Phonotype #1924, #1942/50, #1962/70, #1983/91, #1996/99, #2015, #2067/69, #2297/98, #2337, #2000/02; 1918) again with largely nondescript partners. These two De Lucia sets, idiosyncratic and uneven as they are, preserve in complete roles the highly individual art of one of the first generation of recorded singers and are of indubitable historic interest. The immediate post–World War I acoustic era saw

the major Italian companies returning to a limited number of complete sets. From 1918, there is a *Traviata* on 22 sides (HMV #5620/41; 1918); from 1919 another *Barbiere*, this one with Ernesto Badini as Figaro standing out from a generally lackluster entourage. In 1920 there was a single-cast *Aida* (HMV #S5150/80; 1920) from Voce del Padrone that superseded a 1912 version from Columbia (Columbia Zonophone #12664/678, #24017/25; 1912) that had been patched together with four Aidas while four mezzo-sopranos shared the role of Amneris, and two tenors sang Rhadames. Columbia issued an Italian *Carmen* (Columbia #D4620/43; 1920) with Fanny Anitua in the title role and Luigi Bolis as José. The first full-length Puccini recordings are another feature of this period: *Boheme* (HMV #S5056/78; 1918) and *Tosca* in two versions (Columbia; 1918) and Voce del Padrone (HMV #S5701–24; 1920). One other phenomenon of the later acoustic and early electric period deserves mention. This was a series of semicomplete operas in English. Among them is to be found the first recorded *Madama Butterfly* (HMV #D893/906), with British artists Rosina Buckman, Nellie Walker, Tudor Davies, and Frederick Ranalow in the leading parts, and Eugene Goossens at the musical helm. This tradition was carried on with an English *Pagliacci* (Columbia #4347/58; 1927) with Frank Mullings singing "On with the Motley," and a restrained *Cavalleria* (Columbia #5127/36; 1927). The most interesting one of this group is an abridged *Faust* (Columbia #DX 88–103; 1929–30), conducted by Thomas Beecham, with a cast headed by Miriam Licette and Heddle Nash. That more complete sets were not made in the period 1918–1925 may be explained in part by the rumors of the improved electric recording method then under development. Certainly, once the new technique became established, there was a rush both in Italy and France to replace older sets with modern ones and to explore some new territory. Both Columbia and Voce del Padrone produced rival sets of the standard works, and in the then more rarified field of the final Verdi, they divided the honors: Columbia with *Falstaff* (Columbia GQX #10563/576; 1930) and Voce del Padrone producing *Otello* (HMV S #10350/65; 1931). These sets reflect the performing practices of the period: e.g., the regulation cuts and traditional *oppure*. Unlike some recent complete recordings, they present seasoned (if not invariably pleasing) performers of their parts. Particular highpoints are the Rhadames (HMV AW #23/41; 1928) and Manrico (HMV AW #224/38; 1930) of Aureliano Pertile, the *Barbiere* Figaro (Columbia D #14565/79; 1929) and Rigoletto (Columbia GQX #10028/42; 1930) of Riccardo Stracciari, and the Tonio (Columbia QCX #10016/24; 1930) and Germont

(Columbia D #14479/93; 1928) of Carlo Galeffi. There are also agreeable surprises: the Azucena of Irene Minghini-Cattaneo, and the Count di Luna and Iago of Apollo Granforte. In Italy this was not merely a period of recapitulating what had already been done. There was also the treasurable *Don Pasquale* (HMV #1410/24; 1932) which contains Tito Schipa's only complete, commercially recorded role, as Ernesto. Columbia was even more venturesome, producing *Gioconda* (Columbia GQX #10600/18; 1928) with Giannina Arangi-Lombardi in the title role, and Boito's *Mefistofele* (Columbia GQX #10619/35; 1932) with Nazzareno De Angelis as the devil and a youthful Mafalda Favero as Margherita. There is even a *Fedora* (Columbia GQX #10496/506; 1931), blemished for some tastes by the damaged voice of Gilda Dalla Rizza in the title role, but redeemed from another point of view by being recorded when the *verismo* tradition still maintained some echoes of its original vitality. The French studios were also active. From 1928 there is a *Carmen* (Columbia #9527/41; 1928) with an almost impeccable José from Georges Thill. From 1931 came the famous version of *Faust* (HMV #C2122/41; 1931), with Cesar Vezzani in the title role, the veteran Journet as Mephisto, Mirielle Berthon as Marguerite, and the eloquent Louis Musy as Valentin, conducted by Henri Busser. One of the finest recordings of any period is the complete *Werther* (Columbia LFX #151/65; 1933) that boasts Ninon Vallin and Thill in leading parts. More than a bit of memorable stylishness is to be found in *Manon* (Columbia D #15156/73; 1932) with Germaine Feraldy as Manon and the poetic Rogatchewsky as Des Grieux. Besides these sets, there are some abridged versions of the same period that should not be overlooked; the *Mignon* (Columbia CM-Op #19) from the Monnaie that preserves most of the mellifluous Wilhelm of André d'Arkor, and the *Louise* (Columbia CM-Op #12; 1934), abridged by the composer, Gustave Charpentier, with Vallin and Thill. Far more enjoyable to listen to than the ground-breaking Pathé series of 20 years earlier, these sets as a whole are required listening for anyone wanting to understand the French style. There was no comparable spurt of activity in German studios. Although there were a number of versions of highlights, the sheer length of the Wagner operas made them a financial risk. Two important examples, however, deserve mention. One is the 1928 set of *Meistersinger* (IGI #298; 1928) from Berlin, with Leo Blech conducting and Friedrich Schorr as Hans Sachs. The other is the famous *Rosenkavalier* from Vienna (Victor #VM-196; 1933), presenting about two-thirds of the whole score. Lotte Lehmann was the Marschallin, Maria Olszewka was Octavian, Elisabeth

Schumann was Sophie, and Richard Mayr was Ochs. Nor should it be overlooked that in these years around 1930 from Bayreuth there appeared two historic recordings, the first festival recordings since the piano-accompanied excerpts from 1904. An abridged *Tristan* (Columbia #L2187/206) from 1928 contained only about half the score; it had an experienced Isolde in rather impersonal Nanny Larsen-Todsen. It was followed by a nearly complete *Tannhäuser*, Paris version (Columbia LFX #102/119; 1930). The first move toward a substantial recording of the *Ring* had been in England, with scenes from *Götterdämmerung* (HMV #D1572/87; 1928) sung in English. In a project divided between Berlin and London, with mixed casts and two conductors, about two-thirds of *Siegfried* was recorded (Victor #VM-83, 20 sides; #VM-161, 12 sides; #VM-167, eight sides; 1928–1933), dominated by Melchior's heroic Siegfried. A project to record *Walküre* (Victor #VM-298; 1935) began in Vienna in 1935, with Bruno Walter leading Lehmann, Melchior, and Emanuel List. A healthy start was made on Act II (Victor #VM-582; 1937–1938) by the same forces, but World War II intervened and the missing sections were filled in from Berlin. The war prevented the completion of the project from its original source, but U.S. Columbia produced Act III (Columbia CBS #32260018E; 1945) with a vintage Metropolitan Opera cast (Helen Traubel as Brünnhilde, Herbert Janssen as Wotan, and Irene Jessner as Sieglinde), under Artur Rodzinski's leadership. Probably the most significant and influential series of 78-rpm electric recordings of complete operas were the three Mozart recordings from the Glyndebourne Festival directed by Fritz Busch. That there were serious questions about the viability of such a project in mid-Depression is revealed by the form in which the first of them, the *Figaro* (HMV DB #2474/79, DB #2583/93) of 1934 was produced. It appeared in three volumes, one devoted to the larger ensembles, the other two containing arias and duets, but without any of the *recitativo secco*. Even without any sense of dramatic continuity, the music rather than the drab singing of it seemed like rain in mid-Sahara. The following year saw a *Così fan tutte* (Victor #VM-812/813/814; 1935) and the year after that a *Don Giovanni* (Victor #VM-423/424/425; 1936), both produced in correct sequence. It is no exaggeration to claim that these three recordings, plus Beecham's Berlin *Zauberflöte* (Victor #VM-541/542; 1937) — even without the dialogue — played a key part in preparing the ground for the general appreciation of Mozart's primacy as an opera composer. Contemporary with these Mozart recordings, there were important recordings in Italy of Beniamino Gigli. He was heard in *Pagliacci* (HMV

DB #2229/307; 1934), and Puccini's three masterworks *Boheme* (HMV DB #3448/60; 1938); *Tosca* (HMV DB #3562/75; 1938); and *Madama Butterfly* (HMV DB #3859/74; 1939). In the following year, he sang Turridu in the 50th anniversary *Cavalleria* (HMV DB #3960/70; 1940), plus a Verdi *Requiem, Andrea Chenier* (HMV DB #5423/35; 1940), and *Aida* (HMV DB #6392/411; 1942). Finally there was a *Ballo in maschera* (HMV DM #0100/16; 1943). Cetra began its important series of full-length operas with the first recordings of *Norma* (1937) and *Turandot* (1938), both featuring Gina Cigna in the title roles. By that time the notion of recording operas with international celebrities was fairly established. The LP record of 1948 and the change from acetate discs to magnetic tapes for the original recording media changed and simplified the process of recording complete operas. Cetra exploited the technological advances with a stream of firsts. Among them were *Sonnambula* with Lina Pagliughi, Ferruccio Tagliavini, and Cesare Siepi; *Ernani, Nabucco, Forza del destino, Simon Boccanegra, Don Carlos, L'amico Fritz, Adriana Lecouvreur, Fanciulla del West,* and *L'amore dei tre re.* After recording a few sets for Cetra, Maria Callas was signed by the company known in the U.S. as Angel, while London embarked upon a rival series starring Renata Tebaldi. The famous Toscanini series of opera broadcasts with the NBC Symphony from the 1940s was released by RCA in the 1950s. In the years since, there has been a proliferation of sets of an ever-widening repertory that extends from Jacopo Peri, Claudio Monteverdi, and Pier Cavalli to Benjamin Britten, Hans Werner Henze, and Karlheinz Stockhausen. The ever-widening range of available material is enriched by the choice between studio and live recordings, the latter promulgated by both commercial and private enterprises. Now, in the CD period, a great deal of out-of-print material is emerging. VCR and the DVD are providing access to the visible aspects of opera (section 2) [Blyth 1979.]

See also **La Scala; Metropolitan Opera Company**

WILLIAM ASHBROOK

OPERAPHONE (LABEL)

An American vertical-cut (with some lateral cuts) record made by the Operaphone Manufacturing Corp., New York, in 1916 and 1917, then by the Operaphone Co., Inc., from April 1918 to December 1920. John Fletcher was the organizer and vice president of the firm, which was established in 1914. When the company filed for trademark registration,

New York–based label of the early '20s. Courtesy Kurt Nauck/Nauck's Vintage Records

for the Operaphone name, on 13 Sep 1919, it was identified as the Operaphone Co., Inc., of Queens, New York City. That application stated that the corporation had been using the trademark continuously since 1 Mar 1915. The earliest advertisement for Operaphone records appeared in January 1916, announcing eight-inch double-sided discs, said to play as long as 12-inch discs, at $0.35 each. By April 1916 there were 144 titles available on 72 discs, and 12 new discs (24 selections) were being released each month. There were 200 titles issued by September 1916, but advertising in *TMW* ceased after February 1917. In April 1918 the label was again mentioned, as coming from the Operaphone Co., Inc. By July 1918 there were 300 selections in the catalog. A series of 10-inch lateral-cut records was released from September 1919 to December 1920. Advertising in July 1920 gave the price per disc as $1. The repertoire at that time was popular vocal, dance, and light orchestral material; there were no opera numbers on Operaphone. Among the artists in 1920 were Sam Ash, the Harmonizers, Ernest Hare, Lewis James, Billy Jones, Billy Murray, Al Bernard, and the Orpheus Trio. Al Ofman's Dance Orchestra and the Novelty Dance Orchestra provided the dance items. "Music for Everybody" was the slogan seen on the record labels. It was reported in March 1921 that the company was going to withdraw from the record field. The business was acquired by the Remington

Phonograph Corp., which reorganized it as the Olympic Disc Record Co. [Kunstadt 1986/4.]

FRANK ANDREWS

OPTICAL RECORDING (I)

A system of recording sound on film through a photographic process. The sound signal activates a light valve, causing variations in the light that falls upon and exposes the film as it moves past the valve. The changes in density that result are analogs to the frequency and amplitude of the original signal. Playback is achieved by drawing the film between a photoelectric cell and a light source, producing a fluctuation that is converted back into sound. Because the fidelity of this kind of recording is inferior to that of other processes, magnetic recording is used on film sound tracks for improved reproduction. The idea of recording with light beams is an old one, traceable to the Photophone of 1879. *TMW* described such a process in May 1912.

See also **Motion Picture Sound Recording**

OPTICAL RECORDING (II)

In CD systems, optical recording has a wide application, meaning any kind of medium using laser light to convey data to or from the disc.

OPTICAL SOUND TRACK

On a motion picture film, the narrow band that carries a photographic record of sound.

See also **Optical Recording (I)**

ORB

Borrowing from a wide range of sources, including psychedelia, progressive rock, German techno, disco, and reggae dub music, the Orb are generally acknowledged as originators of the ambient dance genre. Despite copyright litigation over their heavy use of samples — most notably, Minnie Riperton's "Loving You" and Rickie Lee Jones's voice in "Fluffy Little Clouds" — they were one of the most in-demand producers/remixers of the 1990s. The Orb — a name derived from Woody Allen's sci-fi film, *Sleepers* — was formed in South London, 1989, by synth/keyboardist Alex Paterson, then handling A&R duties for EG Records, and KLF's Jimmy Cauty. Utilizing samples from the New York radio station, KISS FM, the duo released a 12-inch EP, *Kiss*, on the British WAU! Mr. Modo label (#0107; 1989). Catering primarily to ambient dance clubs, they next issued the pioneering 12-inch EP, *A Huge Ever Growing Pulsating Brain that Rules from the Centre of the Ultraworld: Lovin' You* (WAU! Mr. Moto #0177; 1989) — blending trancelike rhythms and spacey dub effects — and the ethereal single, "Fluffy Little Clouds" (Big Life #33; 1990). Prior to the release of Orb's epic set, *Adventures Beyond the Ultraworld* (Big Life #5; #29 U.K.; issued 11/91 on Mercury #511034 in U.S.), in April 1991, Cauty was replaced by ex-Gong guitarist Steve Hillage, Miquette Giraudy, and Andy Falconer. Combining older singles and new material, the double album almost single-handedly created a vogue for ambient club nights that nurtured artists such as Aphex Twin and Mixmaster Morris. Collaborating with a wide array of artists, Paterson — while strictly an underground phenomenon stateside — became a hot commercial property in England. Continuing to explore the stretched-out beats of ambient dance, his best-selling releases have included the 12-inch EP, "The Blue Room" (Big Life #75; 1992; #8 U. K.), *U.F. Orb* (Big Life #18/Mercury #513749; 1992; #1 U.K.), *Live 93* (Island #8022/Mercury #535004; 1993; #23 U.K.), the harder-edged *Pommefritz* (Island ORB #1/Mercury #535007; 1994; #6 U.K.), *Orbus Terrarum* (Island #8037/Mercury #524099; 1995; #20 U.K.), *Oblivion* (Island #8055/Mercury #524347; 1997; #19 U.K.), and *U.F.Off – The Best Of* (Island #8078; 1998; #38 U.K.).

FRANK HOFFMANN

ORBISON, ROY
(23 APR 1936–6 DEC 1988)

Although Roy Orbison's musical roots were in country and rockabilly, he is remembered as perhaps the greatest rock ballad singer of all time. During Orbison's induction to the Rock and Roll Hall of Fame in January 1987, Bruce Springsteen provided the following tribute: "When I went in to the studio to make *Born to Run*, I wanted to write words like Bob Dylan that sounded like Phil Spector, but with singing like Roy Orbison. But nobody sings like Roy Orbison." Born in Vernon, Texas, Orbison began learning how to play guitar from his father at age six. He headed his own country band, the Wink Westerners, and had a radio show on Vernon's KVWC while still attending high school. While attending North Texas State College in Denton, he organized a new group and began performing on television and at local venues. One of the new rockabilly artists passing through the area, Johnny Cash, recommended that Orbison send a demo tape of his material to Sun

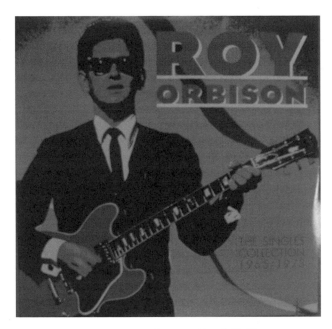

Roy Orbison reissue album. Courtesy Frank Hoffmann

Records owner, Sam Phillips. He included the song, "Oooby Dooby," realizing that it was similar to what Sun was releasing in the mid-1950s. The single (Sun #242; 1956) reached number 59 on the pop charts. Although now typecast as a rock 'n' roll artist, Orbison still aspired to sing country-flavored ballads. As a result, he jumped at the opportunity to become a staff songwriter with Nashville-based music publisher, Acuff-Rose, in 1957. Among his earliest compositions with the company was "Claudette" (Cadence #1348; 1958; #30), recorded by the Everly Brothers. Firm co-owner, Wesley Rose, became his manager, securing a recording contract with Monument Records in 1959. One of the earliest exponents of orchestrated country-pop, his success would have considerable impact on Chet Atkins's Nashville Sound. Orbison placed 20 Monument singles on the charts during the early 1960s, including "Only the Lonely" (#412; 1960; #2), "Blue Angel" (#421; 1960; #9), "Running Scared" (#438; 1961; #1), "Crying" (#447; 1961; #2), "Dream Baby" (#456; 1962; #4), "In Dreams" (#806; 1963; #7), "Mean Woman Blues" (#824; 1963; #5), "It's Over" (#837; 1964; #9), and "Pretty Woman" (#851; 1964; #1). In 1965 Orbison signed with MGM Records in order to have greater access to film and television work. Although record sales declined noticeably, he got to act and sing in his first movie, *Fastest Guitar Alive* (1966); however, the production was both a critical and box office failure. Before he could recover his hit-making touch, however, he suffered two personal tragedies: the death of his wife in a 1966 motorcycle accident, followed by the loss of two children when his Nashville home caught fire in 1967. Because his recording suc-

cess had involved his input at all levels of the process — including songwriting, arranging, and recording — Orbison retreated into the routine of live performing. Administrative turmoil within the MGM hierarchy further complicated efforts to resurrect his recording career. Orbison's popularity in Europe, Australia, and other parts of the world led him to concentrate on international tours during the 1970s. While his records sold well abroad, stateside releases — including Mercury recordings in the mid-1970s after he left MGM — met with public indifference. Other artists, however, began enjoying success with new renditions of his classics by the end of the decade, most notably Linda Ronstadt with "Blue Bayou" (1978) and Don McLean with "Crying" (1981). Orbison's own recording career also showed signs of revival by the late 1970s. Signing with Elektra in 1978, his debut album, *Laminar Flow* (Asylum #198; 1979), was widely praised by the rock press. A duet with Emmylou Harris, "That Lovin' You Feelin' Again" (Warner Bros. #49262; 1980), which appeared on the soundtrack of the film *Roadie*, won a Grammy for Best Country Performance by a Duo or Group with Vocal, his first such award. Orbison's career was provided an additional boost when director David Lynch included "In Dreams" in his film, *Blue Velvet* (1986). The following year his new label, Virgin, released *In Dreams: The Greatest Hits* (Virgin #90604), which consisted of new interpretations of his 1960s hits. Shortly thereafter, a September 1987 Coconut Grove tribute concert, "A Black and White Night," featuring stars such as Springsteen, Elvis Costello, Jackson Browne, and Bonnie Raitt in backup roles, was widely broadcast on both Showtime and PBS-TV. In 1988, an encounter with Dylan, George Harrison, Jeff Lynne, and Tom Petty led to the formation of laid-back supergroup, the Traveling Wilburys; the resulting LP, *Traveling Wilburys, Volume One* (Wilbury #25796; 1988), achieved double-platinum sales. In the meantime, he finished work on *Mystery Girl* (Virgin #91058; 1989; #5), which became his highest-charting album, due in part to the success of the single, "You Got It" (Virgin #99245; 1989; #9), his first top 10 hit in 25 years. Although his artistic rebirth was disrupted by a fatal heart attack, the 1990s saw the release of most of his recorded legacy on CD, including hitherto unavailable live and studio material. *King of Hearts* (Virgin #86520), a compilation of unissued and posthumously completed tracks, charted in late 1992.

FRANK HOFFMANN

ORBITAL

Orbital is best known for pioneering multimedia presentations within a dance environment, spontaneously restructuring music tracks preset into sequencers to the accompaniment of a state-of-the-art light show. Their recorded music — spatial electronic soundscapes tempered by an emotional warmth — likewise engaged the mind as well as the feet. The group has remained commercially viable despite a strong experimental orientation that has embraced innovative sampling and early forays into the drum 'n' bass genre. Orbital was formed in 1989 by the London-based Hartnoll brothers, Phil and Paul, who shared a desire to incorporate electronic and postpunk elements into the British rave party scene. Following the release of several dance-oriented singles, the duo issued a full-length album, *Orbital I* (Ffrr/London #350001; #71 U.K.), in September 1991. The follow-up LP, *Orbital II* (Ffrr/London #351026; 1993; #28 U.K.) further refined their techno-ambient wash, but *Snivilisation* (Ffrr/London #124027; 1994; #4 U.K.) possessed a strongly critical tone regarding a wide array of concerns, including governmental efforts to control Britain's dance culture. Now possessing a substantial body of loyal fans who all but ensured the commercial success of their recordings, Orbital seemingly could do no wrong. Despite the group's reputation for blazing new sonic trails, *In Sides* (Ffrr/London #124087; 1996; #5 U.K.) featured an even greater inclination to take risks in the studio. The CD — also packaged as three 12-inch LPs — refined Orbital's early experiments with drum 'n' bass and laid the groundwork for the future electronica vogue. Its pivotal cut, the half-hour-long single "The Box" (Internal LIECD #30; 1996; #11 U.K.), blended club beats with an encyclopedic array of exotic samples and other sonic effects. They have somewhat moderated the impulse to experiment in subsequent releases, including the hit singles "Satan" (Ffrr/London #850990; 1997; #3 U.K.; recorded live in New York) and "The Saint" (FFRR/London #296; 1997; #3 U.K.; recorded live in Belfast) as well as the relatively upbeat album, *The Middle of Nowhere* (FFRR/London #31065; 1999; #4 U.K.). Although thus far unable to crease the charts in the U.S., the duo's work has consistently sold well to dance and electronica audiences.

FRANK HOFFMANN

ORCHESTRA RECORDINGS

The history of orchestral recording is discussed here in six periods on the basis of the medium used to preserve sound: 1. Beginning (1877–1900). The era of the two-minute cylinder and the five- to seven-inch disc; 2. No longer a toy (1901–1924). The period of the first "long-playing" records (from the 10-inch disc of 1901 to Edison's genuine LPs of 1926) and of the first multidisc album sets of longer works; 3. The microphone

(1925–1947). The period that saw the introduction of electrical recording bring the gramophone to something like maturity as a means for the transmission of serious music; 4. Tape and the rebirth of LP record (1948–1981). The flowering of half a century of experiment that freed the record listener from "maddening interruptions [imposed] upon the continuity of an extended piece of music" [Sackville-West & Shaw-Taylor 1951]; 5. The compact disc (1982–1997); 6. The DVD (1998–).

1. *Beginning.* Commercial recording of orchestral music began in the final decade of the 19th century, but little remains with which to document the earliest period, apart from lists and catalogs published by the fledgling companies then active. On the evidence of these paper survivals, selections seem to have been drawn from programs of contemporary theater and restaurant ensembles: dance music by the Strauss family and others, *morceaux de salon* and potpourris from current operettas, a repertoire of light classics that was to remain popular (and hence salable) for the next 50 years. Sound recording might have been "the wonder of the age," but it was still a carnival wonder, a toy dismissed by most musicians and music lovers. It was not until the turn of the century that the names of established orchestras (from St. Petersburg, Warsaw and New York) began to appear in catalogs. Of these, only one series was wholly devoted to music from the standard repertoire: the Leeds & Catlin cylinders of the "Metropolitan Opera House String Orchestra" under its concertmaster, Nahan Franko. These were made during the period of Lionel Mapleson's experiments with live recording of actual performances in the Metropolitan Opera House itself. Played on modern equipment, some orchestrals that have survived from this period can sound remarkably vivid; but acoustical reproduction could distort orchestral sound far more than did the initial acoustical recording process, and at the time technology agreed with public taste. Despite occasional and short-lived exceptions, "orchestra" was synonymous with "wind band."

2. *No Longer a Toy.* Although the earliest technological advances had little immediate influence on the kind of music recorded, the development of records that were more durable, less cumbersome, and with a longer playing time than the two-minute wax cylinder and the seven-inch disc laid the foundations for a gradual revolution. Up to 1898, the longest orchestral work to have been issued was a suite of dances from Edward German's incidental music for Shakespeare's Henry VIII (on three seven-inch Berliners, #570-X and #573/74). By 1903 the Victor Co. had managed to get all three dances onto one 14-inch side, playing at 60 rpm (De Luxe #2036) and had attempted Beethoven's Egmont Overture (De Luxe #2010). Victor also issued

the "William Tell Overture" that year. It was not until 1905 that a more ambitious project was undertaken: the recording of the entire Overture to Rossini's William Tell, by the Orchestra of La Scala, Milan (G & T #50516, #50500/02). It was operatic celebrities, such as Mattia Battistini, Enrico Caruso, Feodor Chaliapin, Nellie Melba, and Adelina Patti, who brought artistic respectability and commercial viability to the recording industry. However, it was operatic routiniers — reliable artists of less than stellar rank — who initiated the trend that was to establish the gramophone as transmitter of the musical culture of an age. Costly celebrities could be engaged only "to do star turns," isolated arias requiring only one record side (at most, two); but less expensive singers were available to exploit the appetite for more extensive operatic recordings whetted by the hearing of a single aria. By 1903 Gramophone and Typewriter had begun to assemble generous abridgments (10 to 15 sides) of popular Italian operas, all recorded by La Scala forces. Discs could always be purchased singly, but the abridgments were marketed as sets. In 1906 Handel's *Messiah* was issued in London on 25 single-sided discs; by 1907 when Leoncavallo's *Pagliacci* (supervised by the composer) appeared in Milan on 21 sides and Lehár's *Lustige Witwe* in Berlin on 32 sides, such sets of compositions presented as "complete" and in their own albums were becoming a gramophonic commonplace. The immediate result of these operatic ventures was the publication, beginning in 1905, of the first musically significant recordings of orchestral music. The Scala Symphony Orchestra, playing under Carlo Sabajno, the conductor who usually led them in operatic accompaniments, demonstrated that recordings could provide a passable echo of what was to be heard in the theater and the concert hall — even of music by Wagner and Richard Strauss. What Caruso's 1902 series had done to encourage the finest voices of the day to appear before the recording horn, these La Scala performances seem to have accomplished (on a far more modest scale) for the orchestra. In 1907 the Gramophone Co. in Paris issued a group of Emil Waldteufel's waltzes conducted by the composer and Pathé Frères recorded Edouard Colonne and his orchestra (so well that the discs were still available 15 years after the conductor's death). The next year, Odeon published records conducted by Léon Jéhin in Monte Carlo. By the end of 1909, Victor Herbert's Orchestra had begun to appear on Edison cylinders (the orchestra, possibly conducted by Herbert, had made Victor records in 1903, the year of its formation, and returned to Victor in 1911). Landon Ronald, with the New Symphony Orchestra he had just been appointed to conduct, began their uniquely important association with the gramophone with two movements from the Grieg Concerto; the soloist was Wilhelm Backhaus (Gramophone #05523/24, December 1909); and the International Talking Machine Company (Odeon) had made history by issuing Tchaikovsky's *Nutcracker Suite*, the first extended work recorded by an orchestra (the London Palace Orchestra, under Herman Finck) and presented in an album (#0475/78, April 1909). A year later, Mendelssohn's music for *Midsummer Night's Dream* was issued under the same auspices and in the same format (#0641/44). And by the autumn of 1911 (two and one-half years before Arthur Nikisch's more famous recording appeared in February 1914 [HMV #040784/91]), the "Grosses Odeon-Streichorchester" could be heard playing Beethoven's Fifth Symphony (#XX76147/53). Within two years, Beethoven's Sixth Symphony (#XX76292/301), Haydn's "Surprise Symphony" (#XX76312/17), and the 39th and 40th symphonies of Mozart (#XX76331/36, #XX76325/30) could all be had, anonymously conducted but complete, on Odeon records. From this point onward, hardly a month was to pass without the announcement in London or Berlin of a first recording of a standard orchestral work. Riga and St. Petersburg supplemented those vocal offerings with orchestral music by Russian composers-years (in some cases, decades) before any of these works appeared in Western lists. Many performances were truncated and most were rescored. Except in Germany, a market for long orchestral works occupying several discs was slow to develop; even the attempts made to lengthen the playing time of record sides (such as the short-lived experiments sponsored in U.K. by the National Gramophone Company in 1912–1915, and World Records, 1922–1923) proved unsuccessful. The small size of recording orchestras (50 players constituted a large band, and most records were made with half that number), and the readiness of recording companies to employ "house conductors" and sponsor "house orchestras" (composed of musicians experienced in coping with the intricacies of the recording process), help to explain the reedy, brassy characteristic of many records made acoustically. The acoustical process could accommodate an orchestra only with difficulty. Since the distal diameter of the recording horns was limited, a wide arc of players was impossible, so there was inevitable overcrowding toward the center of the horn face. Low frequencies from stringed instruments and those of soft attack — such as the bass drum at anything less than fortissimo — were particularly difficult to record, as were large numbers of middle and upper strings. Cellos and basses might be replaced by bassoons, perhaps supported by one cello. No more than six violins would be needed, boosted by a couple of Stroh violins, and the violas could be replaced by the Stroh viola and a clarinet or two. The woodwinds — particularly the oboes — would be pressed up behind the strings seated immediately before the recording horns, while the bass sounding instruments would often be beneath these horns and facing the strings. Mirrors provided the only means of some performers seeing the conductor placed high above and behind them. Similarly the orchestral horns were elevated farther back with the rest of the brass, perhaps five or six feet above the rest of the players, but, since their bells point behind them, they had to face away from the recording horns so that their bells were directed at those horns. Here came into operation another set of mirrors so that they too could see the conductor [Melville-Mason 1977]. What remains astonishing in light of the problems involved is the fact that nearly all of the major orchestras and conductors of reputation active in Germany, U.K., and the U.S. in the period from 1910 to 1925 did in fact make records. The contribution of American companies was primarily technological. Recordings made in the U.S., especially from 1916 on, were often characterized by excellent sound: the Columbias full and resonant, the Victors and Brunswicks admirable in detail. There were some abbreviated firsts in the U.S.: Columbia's Schubert "Unfinished Symphony" (Prince's Symphony Orchestra #A5267, April 1911); and a Victor series: two symphonies by the Victor Concert Orchestra (Haydn's "Military Symphony" #35311; April 1913 and #35520; May 1916 and Mozart's "Jupiter Symphony" #17707 and #35430; March-April 1915) and two works of Bach: the Double Concerto (Fritz Kreisler and Efrem Zimbalist (#76028/30, March 1915) and the Suite No. 3 (Josef Pasternack and the Victor Concert Orchestra (#35656, #35669; November–December 1917). But only four extended works were recorded complete in the U.S. during the acoustic period, all by Victor: Beethoven's Symphony No. 5, with Josef Pasternack and the Victor Concert Orchestra (#18124, October 1916; #35580, November 1916; #18278, September 1917; #35637, October 1917), Liszt's Les préludes with Willem Mengelberg and the New York Philharmonic (#74780/82 and #66131; January–April 1923), Schubert's "Unfinished" and Stravinsky's Firebird Suite with Leopold Stokowski and the Philadelphia Orchestra (#6459/61, December 1924; and #6492/93, February 1925). Stokowski's first attempt to record Rachmaninoff's Concerto No. 2 with the composer as soloist was not satisfactory, and only two movements were published (#8064/66; May 1924). Apart from these (and Columbia's ground-breaking series with the modest Altschuler's Russian Symphony Orchestra, 1911–1912), most American recordings merely introduced to trans-Atlantic listeners short works and fragments already available in Europe. What was

accomplished in Europe, especially after 1916, was remarkable: Bach's Brandenburg Concerto No. 3, the keyboard Concerto in D Minor, BWV #1052; the solo Violin Concerto in E Major, BWV #1042; the Double Concerto and the Second Orchestral Suite; all of the symphonies of Beethoven (in 36 different sets, nine of them devoted to the Fifth), the Violin Concerto and four of the five piano concerti; Berlioz' Symphonie Fantastique; the first and second symphonies of Brahms; Bruch's Violin Concerto No. 1; Lalo's Symphonie Espagnole; three symphonic poems, the Hungarian Fantasy and both of the piano concerti of Liszt; Mahler's "Resurrection Symphony"; the Violin Concerto, first Piano Concerto and the "Italian Symphony" of Mendelssohn; three violin concerti (K. 216, K. 218, K. 219), two serenades (K. 375, K. 388) and three symphonies (K. 543, K. 550, K. 551) of Mozart; Ravel's Mamère l'oye and Tombeau de Couperin; Rimsky-Korsakov's Capriccio Espagnole, Russian Easter Overture, Scheherazade, and the suite from his Golden Cockerel; Saint-Saens' *Carnival of the Animals;* and Schubert's "Unfinished" (in a total of 17 recordings, eight of them complete, with Stokowski's American set making a ninth). There were also issues of Schumann's Piano Concerto and three of his four symphonies; Scriabin's *Poem of Ecstasy,* Smetana's *Moldau;* nine tone poems of Richard Strauss (of which only *Also Sprach Zarathustra* was abbreviated); Stravinsky's Petrushka and two versions of his Firebird Suite in addition to Stokowski's; and Tchaikovsky's *Francesca da Rimini,* first Piano Concerto and Fifth and Sixth symphonies (the Violin Concerto was recorded but remained unpublished). The preludes and orchestral interludes from Wagner's music dramas appeared, together with his *Siegfried Idyll* (two recordings of the original version for chamber orchestra and six of the version for large orchestra). Many of these works (and more than this partial list suggests) were available in a number of alternative versions, and many of the most important sets date from the years immediately preceding the introduction of electrical recording. That momentous development did not enforce radically new decisions about what to record but rather confirmed decisions already made.

3. *The Microphone.* The first electrical orchestral records were issued in the U.S. in July 1925 (Columbia #50014-D and Victor #6505); the first such issue in Europe (August 1925) was also an American recording (HMV #C1210, an experimental Victor published only in the U.K.). By the following October, the Gramophone Co. was able to issue selections from La Boutique Fantasque (#D1018), an electrical remake of a record (#D572) issued exactly four years earlier. In December HMV #D1037/41 appeared: Tchaikovsky's Symphony No. 4, a work never before issued in

complete form, and the first electrical recording of a symphony to be published. In March 1926 Columbia announced Berlioz's Symphonie Fantastique conducted by Felix Weingartner, a work that Weingartner had already recorded acoustically for Columbia (unpublished) and which had only recently become available in complete (but acoustical) versions conducted by Rhené-Baton (HMV #W608/13; April 1925) and Frieder Weissmann (Parlophon #P1934/39; May 1925), and the slightly abridged version by Oskar Fried (Polydor #69808/11; September 1925). Fried's recording was reissued, with the missing movement supplied (Polydor #66356/60), four months after the Weingartner set went on sale, for during this transitional period acoustical recordings continued to be issued side-by-side with the electricals: Alfred Hertz's Fra diavolo overture (Victor #6506; July 1925) with Stokowski's Danse macabre (#6505); Elgar's first recording of his Symphony No. 2 (HMV #D1012/17; September 1925) with the first electricals by Vladimir de Pachmann (HMV #DB861) and Albert Coates (HMV #E397); Dan Godfrey's set of the Vaughan Williams London Symphony (Columbia #1717/22; April 1926) a month after Weingartner's Symphonie Fantastique (#L1708/13); Oskar Fried's first electrical Eine kleine Nachtmusik (Polydor #69826/27; January 1926) two months before Hans Pfitzner's acoustical version of Schumann's Symphony No. 2 (#69828/32). The foregoing survey encapsulates roughly the first decade of the "age of the microphone." Some "old process" recordings intended for publication remained in the vaults while others continued to be issued until the end of 1926, only to yield to "new process" replacements as these became available. In the case of the Tchaikovsky Piano Concerto, this happened only seven months after the initial acoustical issue; Bruckner's Symphony No. 7 had to wait four years. By the time new versions had been prepared of Mahler's "Resurrection Symphony" (1935), Strauss's *Also Sprach Zarathustra* (1935), "Alpine Symphony" (1941), and *Macbeth* (1950), the acoustical sets had long since disappeared. Initial reaction to the new technology was mixed. An early review could praise one disc for reproducing "the different tone colors with astonishing truth" while dismissing another for its "coarse and distorted" tone despite its great volume and "very clear" definition [H. Wild, in *Sound Wave*, November 1925]. But the ultimate verdict was expressed by Ernest Newman: "It is now [1926] possible, by virtue of the new methods of recording that have come into use, for the gramophone listener to get the thrill of the real thing as he knows it in the concert-room. … At last an orchestra really sounds like an orchestra. Those records bring with them the very blood and nerves of the orchestra and the theater"

[quoted by Lawrence Gilman in his "Foreword" to Darrell 1936]. Such statements could be made because the microphone had freed the recording process from the constraints of the past half a century and enabled it to be undertaken in the theater and concert room, capturing the sound of an orchestra playing with its full complement music as scored by the composer. One of the more significant consequences of this liberation was the virtual disappearance of the "house orchestra" and "house conductor" except for the recording of "light music." The first decades of the century saw the emergence of the "star" conductor. Now technology enabled record producers to offer maestros the kind of prominence they had previously accorded the diva. Many names already familiar continued to appear in the catalogs — Leo Blech, Adrain Boult, Albert Coates, Hamilton Harty, Alfred Hertz, Landon Ronald, Frederick Stock, Frieder Weissman, Henry Wood — but the new age belonged to Thomas Beecham, Wilhelm Furtwängler, Serge Koussevitzky, Willem Mengelberg, Stokowski, Arturo Toscanini, Bruno Walter, and Weingartner, to whom the most important projects were committed. All (save Furtwängler and Koussevitzky) had recorded before; but it was the microphone (more through discs, arguably, than through radio broadcasting) that gave a more flattering display to their talents, made them international celebrities, and established their performances as formative for the taste of an international audience. The presence of some of them (Koussevitzky, Stokowski, and Toscanini, primarily, supervising orchestras of unsurpassed technical proficiency) helped the U.S. emerge as an important source of recordings, even before the outbreak of war in 1939 — the event which forced the American market, largely supplied from Europe in the lean years after 1930, to depend on domestic sources. This wholesale involvement of celebrities produced an expansion of repertoire at once vast and restricted. The gramophone became a close monitor of the careers of the great, as virtually every work they performed in public concerts found their way onto discs. Multiple versions of the classics from Beethoven onward came to abound as younger artists established themselves and technological advances rendered earlier recordings obsolete. Some of the "new music" was recorded as it began to find an audience; Stravinsky and Hindemith were invited to join Elgar and Richard Strauss in conducting their own music; a society was formed (by the Gramophone Co.) to issue the works of Sibelius by subscription after the Finnish government sponsored recordings of his first two symphonies; in Beechman Frederick Delius found a champion, as did Prokofiev in Koussevitzky and Shostakovich in Stokowski. Yet among composers before 1800, only Bach, Handel, and Haydn were even comparatively well represented in catalogs, and only Mozart could boast a discography that included most of his major works. Twentieth-century composers suffered from a similarly selective representation. Undoubtedly these omissions would have been supplied in time. However, until the mid-1940s, the large, established companies (Deutsche Grammophon, and EMI with its American affiliates) tended to give only cursory attention to works of any period which lay outside the mainstream of concert programming, and for which there was no ensured market. Apart from subscription issues of the kind already mentioned, it was left to small companies (the National Gramophonic Society and Decca in the U.K., Éditions de l'Oiseau–Lyre in France, and to a lesser extent Musicraft in the U.S.) to record material deemed more esoteric. Then in the midst of the postwar revival, a technological innovation as dramatic as the microphone intervened to transform the medium.

4. *Tape and the Rebirth of LP.* Although "long-playing" discs were used successfully as early as 1926 to provide sound for motion pictures and for radio broadcasting, Thomas Edison's attempts to introduce the record-buying public to the microgroove LP in 1926 failed as did RCA Victor's 33 1/3 rpm "program transcriptions" in 1931. However, the microgroove record that American Columbia introduced in June 1948 — a time of prosperity and unprecedented interest in recordings — was greatly successful. In many cases the LPs even sounded better than the 78s which they were intended to supersede: Columbia's LPs were not obvious patchups from noisy four-minute shellac pressings. Many years before, in anticipation of LP, the Columbia engineers had started recording a duplicate set of masters at each session in large acetate transcription blanks; by 1948 there existed a valuable backlog of high-quality, noise-free recordings readily transferable to LP [Gelatt 1955]. Each company had its own backlog; and as one after another committed themselves to the new medium (Decca/London and Vox in 1949, RCA Victor in 1950, EMI in 1952), a significant portion of the postwar orchestral catalogs were transferred to LP. Stereophonic recording, introduced in the middle 1950s, gradually drove virtually all monophonic issues into the cut-out bin or onto budget status, a category that some companies (notably CBS, Deutsche Grammophon, EMI, and RCA) augmented with transcriptions of much earlier material. Thus prewar recordings by Furtwängler, Hamilton Harty, Koussevitzky, Mengelberg, Frederick Stock, Stokowski, Toscanini, Bruno Walter, and Weingartner all returned to circulation during the 1950s and 1960s. While many of these restorations were sonic failures, some gave "new bloom" (in that favorite phrase of the critics) to what had seemed still

salable but faded performances. Interest in historical reissues began to spread from the legacies of famous singers to include the orchestra, especially when a composer's own interpretation (or that of an eminent soloist in a concerto) could be rescued; and so Elgar, Holst, and Richard Strauss all reappeared to join the company of Pablo Casals, Emanuel Feuermann, Jascha Heifetz, Bronislaw Hubermann, Fritz Kreisler, Rachmaninoff, Albert Sammons, and Joseph Szigeti. By the end of the 1960s, improvements in sound reproduction had drawn engineers to experiment with pre-electrical recordings; composers again (Elgar, German, and Stanford), conductors (Beecham, Fried, Otto Klemperer, Nikisch, and Toscanini); and a concerto performance of outstanding merit (Kreisler and Eugene Goossens in a previously unpublished version of Bruch's Opus 26). When the centenary of Edison's phonograph was celebrated in 1977, the gramophone could claim to have presented to contemporary listeners the broad spectrum of its own past. Of far greater significance, however, was the attention that could then be paid to the present, and to the past before the 19th century in which sound recording began. The expansion of repertoire on electrical 78s, which had seemed "vast" when compared with the products of the acoustical era, was dwarfed by the LP explosion. Integral recordings of the symphonies of Bruckner and Mahler became more numerous than integral recordings of the Beethoven symphonies had been on 78s; and the Beethoven cycle threatened to become a test piece for every ambitious conductor to record and re-record. By the 1970s one could expect to find the works of most of the major composers since the time of Bach available in complete or nearly complete editions. In addition, the widest conceivable variety of new music was being committed to discs, together with works unheard for centuries. The musical culture of the 19th century was ceasing to be the center of interest; and the deaths of Furtwängler (1954), Toscanini (1957), Beecham (1961), and Walter (1963) marked the passing of an era that ended with the autumnal careers of Otto Klemperer and Adrian Boult. None of the new generation of conductors — not even Von Karajan or Leonard Bernstein — won the esteem accorded their predecessors. Paradoxically, the very technology that enabled recordings to do something like justice to gargantuan forces under the control of a virtuoso conductor was helping to bring the "age of the conductor" to a close. That technology was at the same time changing the relation between recordings and music heard in public concerts. The substitution of one late 19th-century invention for another in the initial recording process, namely magnetized tape for wax blanks, meant that wherever music could be played and heard, recordings of it could be made. This simplification, felt especially in the preservation of live performances, meant also that works known only to musicologists and accessible only to a specialized audience could be modestly profitable ventures for even a small company to sponsor. Baroque music, whether performed on modern or "authentic" instruments, owed much of its popularity to the record player. The use of tape also made it possible to edit recorded material, eliminating passages imperfectly registered and splicing in improvements. What ultimately emerged from the loudspeakers might thus be an amalgam of several different performances, one more perfect than any of its sources. Although misgivings eventually prompted experiments with direct to disc recording and digital computerization, the fact remained that recordings had become (and would remain), not an echo of the public concert, but a quite distinct medium of musical communication.

5. *The Compact Disc.* The reappearance of the single-sided disc approximately five inches in diameter indicates how far sound recording has come in a century. Playing time has been extended from just over 90 seconds to over 75 minutes, the full audible range has been captured, and, through computer technology, most extraneous noise has been eliminated and distortion levels are but a fraction of what was encountered with the LP. The weakest link in the recording chain, the needle connecting the disc to the play-back unit, has been replaced by a laser beam promising accurate and wear-free reproduction. The LP with its turntable has joined the 78 with its gramophone and the cylinder with its phonograph in the museum of the outmoded. The CD revolution has followed the pattern of its microphone and LP predecessors. As in the late 1920s an entire catalog was replaced; as in the early 1950s previously available performances, transferred to the new format, formed a large part of the new issues. And as in the case of both earlier renewals, the breadth of the repertoire recorded was increased. A comment on the modestly priced Maxos label, made by critic William Little of the *Toronto Star* could be applied to the offerings of all companies combined: "just about everything" of musical significance has proved to be recordable. "Complete Editions," sometimes of gigantic size, have become common. Some comprised modern recordings, especially assembled, such as the Phillips Mozart Edition (182 CDs in 45 volumes); many were retrospective, such as RCA's Rubinstein and Heifetz collections (94 and 65 CDs, respectively). Complete Editions devoted to conductors tended to be of the latter kind: Edouard Colonne (recorded in 1906; Tahra, 1 CD), Weingartner (EMI Japan, 25 CDs), Toscanini (RCA, 82 CDs), Leonard Bernstein (3 sets, totaling 141 CDs: Sony's "Royal Edition," Deutsche Grammophon's "Bernstein Conducts Bernstein," and the New York Philharmonic box "Bernstein Live!"). A number of specialized labels devoted to archival reissues — Beulah, Biddulph, Dante LYS, Music & Arts, Pearl, Tahra — have offered a wide range of orchestral material. A number of symphony orchestras — those in Boston, Chicago, Cleveland, New York (the Philharmonic), Philadelphia, Vienna (the Philharmonic) — have sponsored collections of their own recordings under various conductors, usually published in 10 CD boxed sets. Recordings of live performances, drawn from radio archives, have become increasingly important, not only to add to studio recordings already issued, but to preserve material never recorded otherwise. For example, the art of Sergiu Celibidache, who came to regard recording as "a treason to music" [quoted in Holmes 1982, p. 166], has been preserved almost entirely through recordings of live performances. The first group of "New York Philharmonic Historic Broadcasts" actually included fragments of two Carnegie Hall concerts in December 1923 and April 1924, recorded electrically by the Bell Laboratories.

6. *The DVD.* In the late 1990s the already successful home theater industry was given a further shot in the arm by the introduction of the multichannel DVD recording. While mainly used for motion-picture playback in home theater systems, this new technology is in a position to supersede the CD as the playback medium of choice for those who want the very best in recorded orchestra sound in home-listening environments. The DVD not only allows an individual to hear an orchestral performance and be surrounded by the environmental acoustic where the performance took place, but also may allow the listener the option of actually seeing that performance. The format offers up five channels of discrete audio (three up front, with two surround "ambiance" channels), with a subwoofer channel thrown in if low-frequency effects (cannon shots in the *1812 Overture*, for instance) are required. Video-oriented DVD orchestral programs are recorded with either Dolby Digital or Digital Theater Systems technology, which offer up sound quality that is as subjectively clean on a per-channel basis as the two-channel CD ever was. Further developments include the DVD-A and SACD formats, which promise sound reproduction at a very high technical level, indeed, although these latter two technologies offer surround-sound audio only, without moving pictures. When hooked to a video monitor, the music DVD may also contain multiple bonus tracks that include interviews, visual stills of orchestral scores, and rehearsals, meaning that it can be an educational, as well as musically entertaining medium.

CLAUDE G. ARNOLD
With technology updates by HOWARD FERSTLER

ORCHESTRELLE CO., LTD.

A British firm established 1 July 1912, superseding the London branch of the American firm Orchestrelle Co. It took control of several other companies that had been subsidiaries of the American firm. It was the business of the Orchestrelle companies to market musical instruments, including Aeolian organs, pianos, pianolas, harps, etc., and piano rolls. In 1915 the company advertised the new Aeolian Vocalion talking machine, with the innovative Graduola control; possibly the machines were assembled in Britain from American components. Musola and Phoneto record labels were introduced in October 1916, and exported to Australia by Orchestrelle Co., Ltd. The firm opened its own recording laboratories in February 1917. Later that year the Aeolian Co., Ltd., absorbed Orchestrelle. [Andrews 1980/10.]

See also **Aeolian Co.**

ORCHESTROPE

A coin-op disc player made by the Capehart Co. in 1928. It offered 56 titles, but was not selective.

ORGAN RECORDINGS

Until the introduction of electrical recording in the mid-1920s there was very little recording of the solo pipe organ. The earliest known is a cylinder made by Colonel Gouraud at Westminster Abbey in 1888, the organist being "Prof. Bridge." There was organ accompaniment for a series of 15 sacred songs on Columbia two-minute cylinders made in early 1901. S.C. Porter was the singer, but the organist is not named. The first of the series was "Nearer My God, to Thee" (#31356). Apparently the earliest solo organ record was an Edison cylinder of August 1909, Albert Benzler playing "Abide with Me" (#10180). J.J. McClellan was recorded at the Salt Lake City (Utah) Mormon Tabernacle organ by Columbia in 1911, both as soloist and accompanying a violinist. In 1912–1913 Welte-Mignon made organ rolls in Freiburg, Germany, including 20 compositions of organist Eugène Gigout and his contemporaries; these were released on two LP records by Fulton Productions of Tulare, California (#UF-4 and #UF-5). In 1913 Easthope Martin, the composer, recorded on a grand organ at least 10 sides for HMV. The 1917 Victor catalog announced that efforts to record the organ had "met with little success until the recent series of experiments by the Victor"; but only one disc was offered, #35547, presenting the Chopin "Funeral March" played by Richard K. Biggs, and the "Hallelujah Chorus" played by Reginald L. McAll, both on an Estey pipe organ. The 1922 catalog carried the same lone example of the King of Instruments, and even the 1927 catalog had just one organ disc, albeit a different one. Before World War I Pathé, in England, had installed an instrument from the Positive Organ Co. and recorded it with Reginald Goss Custard, organist of St. Margaret's in Westminster. William Ditcham and F.R. Kinkee also recorded organ solos before the war. Albert W. Ketelbey performed solo items for Columbia in 1909, and Omar Letorey of Paris recorded for Odeon well before 1914. Electrical recording involved the organ from its inception. The first electric to be released was Columbia Graphophone's live inscription of the Westminster Abbey ceremony in November 1920, engineered by H.O. Merriman and Lionel Guest. When Autograph initiated commercial electrics in Chicago, in 1924, organ music was a specialty. Milton Charles and Jesse Crawford performed on instruments in two Chicago movie houses. In the succeeding decade a considerable assemblage of organ recordings was issued in America and Britain, and the problem became less technical and more one of repertoire. A writer in *Gramophone* of August 1932 grumbled that "a glance at the bulky but heterogeneous lists of organ records shows clearly that instead of a coherent and carefully planned repertoire of legitimate organ music, a mere jumble of assorted musical confectionery has come, bit by bit, into being." He noted the lack of recording of major composers like Rheinberger and Vierne, and even English composers like Parry and Stanford. Vierne had in fact recorded some of his pieces, at Notre Dame in December 1928, but for Odeon (#166149 and #171074), presumably not available in the U.K. It was in the 1930s that the organ took its rightful place among other instruments on record. Charles Widor recorded his own works in 1932 at St. Sulpice (HMV DB #4856). Performers like Marcel Dupré (nine titles in the 1938 Victor catalog, most of them by J.S. Bach), Albert Schweitzer (one Bach Prelude and Fugue in the Victor 1938 catalog, and four albums for Columbia by 1943), Alfred Sittard, and Mark Andrews — the most recorded artist in the 1938 Victor list, with 33 items, mostly hymns — began to make up for the long neglect of the organ by the record companies. There were 24 "grand organists" listed in the HMV catalog for 1937–1938; four in the Columbia catalog, eight in the Parlophone catalog, and five in the 1941 Decca catalog; not to mention numerous theater organists on all labels. Nevertheless, it was a slow march. David Hall wrote in the 1940 edition of *The Record Book* that "prior to 1937 ... there was not an organ recording in the domestic catalogues worth having." He mentioned the twin technical challenges: the need to make records in vast echoing churches, and the trouble with capturing the sweeping dynamic range of the instruments without distortion. In addition, there was the very real problem that the grooved analog record could not comfortably handle the deep-bass requirements of some organ music. For example, fine performances of Albert Schweitzer were "badly over-amplified, resulting in tremendous tonal blurs." But the young Musicraft label began in 1937 to get good technical results, and they had the outstanding organist Carl Weinrich. Then Technichord recorded E. Power Biggs on the baroque organ in Harvard's Germanic Museum, with splendid success. Use of smaller instruments was rare in this period, when the grand organs of great churches were preferred. The 33 1/3 rpm LP record introduced a complete change in the types of music recorded and the styles of instruments used. Small tracker-action instruments became popular, and sometimes the record jackets gave their actual specifications and lists of the stops used in the performance. Chorale preludes, hitherto conspicuously absent, suddenly became important. Recording techniques advanced to permit even the loudest passages to be recognizably recorded. There came also a vogue for recording on old instruments that existed at the time of the composition being played; for example a number of Bach works were rendered on a Silbermann organ. Another plan was to take a single organist and record him in different cities and churches, often in different countries (Biggs was the major exponent of this approach, while an English organist, Peter Hurford, recorded in Canada and Australia). With advantages of improved techniques, organ concerti joined the record lists. Handel had been standard for years; now other composers such as contemporary Malcolm Williamson were included in the catalogs. There were also recordings of the pipe organ with other solo instruments. Electronic organs have not found much favor on record, except in popular music. Compact discs, which for the first time allow the full bandwidth and dynamic range of even large organs to be reproduced cleanly, have already built a respectable repertoire of organ music. Artists like Carlo Curley, Michael Murray, Simon Preston, Peter Hurford, Alan Morrison, Frederick Swann, David Higgs, Joan Lippincott, and John Rose have presented the instrument in all its infinite variety and splendor. A fine series of CDs titled "Historic American Organs" provides the sounds of old instruments in various regions. "Great European Organs" is a colossal series of compact discs from the Priory label, with 23 volumes released by summer 1991. Gothic Records has earned a notable reputation for recording a variety of instruments and performers with state-of-the-art compact disc technology. New technologies include the DVD, which has the potential to not only equal the CD in terms of sonic purity and per-channel subjective accuracy, but with multichannel technologies like Dolby Digital, DTS, and DVD-A and SACD, is also able to re-create the acoustics of a church out in the listening area, instead of just from the front. [Carreck 1960.]

REV. E.T. BRYANT
Further updated by HOWARD FERSTLER

ORIGINAL DIXIELAND JAZZ BAND

A pioneer ensemble of white performers, responsible for much of the early interest in jazz and for the first commercial recordings. Members were Nick La Rocca, cornet; Larry Shields, clarinet; Eddie Edwards, trombone; Henry Ragas, piano; and Tony Sbarbaro [laterSpargo], drums. The spelling "jass" is found in early issues. The ODJB originated in New Orleans, played in Chicago in 1916, then went on to great success in New York at Reisenweber's Restaurant in January 1917. They made the first jazz recordings in jazz style, "LiveryStable Blues" and "Dixie Jass Band One-Step" on 26 Feb 1917 (Victor #18255). On 31 May 1917 the group recorded "Darktown Strutters' Ball"/"Indiana" for Columbia

Sheet cover for "Barnyard Blues" aka "Livery Stable Blues," a major record hit for the Original Dixieland Jazz Band. Courtesy David A. Jasen

(#A-2297). They went on to record prolifically, with personnel changes, for Victor and finally with Bluebird in 1938. Records were made in London also, for Columbia, in April, May, and August 1919, and again in January and May 1920. The group disbanded after 1938. It was at its best in vigorous spirited numbers like "Tiger Rag" (Victor #18483; 1918). In the LP era, Riverside helped reintroduce the group through its rerelease of some of these classic recordings (Riverside #156; 1962). There are countless reissues on European and American jazz labels of this material. All of their Victor recordings are reissued on a two-CD set, *The Complete* (RCA #66608), covering their 1917–1921 recordings and their 1936 "comeback" for the Victor budget label, Bluebird. [Enderman 1989 is a complete discography.]

ORIGINAL INSTRUMENT RECORDING

A musical recording that involves instruments similar to those used to perform the same works during the era when the music was composed. A number of modern orchestras specialize in performing and recording with instruments of this kind, with the primary emphasis being on material written during the Baroque and Classical periods.

HOWARD FERSTLER

ORIGINAL LYRIC TRIO

SEE LYRIC TRIO

ORIGINAL MEMPHIS FIVE

A group consisting of Phil Napoleon, trumpet; Miff Mole, trombone; Jimmy Lytell, clarinet; Frank Signorelli, piano; and Jack Roth, drums. Napoleon and Signorelli were the founders of the band (in 1917) and its chief performers. OMF was the most prolific of the ensembles working in the mode of the Original Dixieland Jazz Band, and even took that name for a period and used it on their first recordings: "Gypsy Blues"/"My Honey's Lovin' Arms" (Arto #9140; 1922). They went on with Arto, and also Pathé Actuelle, Vocalion, Victor, Edison, and many other labels. Before they stopped recording in 1931, the group had included a number of other performers, among them Red Nichols, Tommy Dorsey, and Jimmy Dorsey. Collector's Classics has issued an excellent CD (*Collection 1922–23*; #16) covering Napoleon's early band recordings, released under the names of the Jazzbo Carolina Serenaders and Southland Six as well as the Original Memphis Five (the two earlier groups

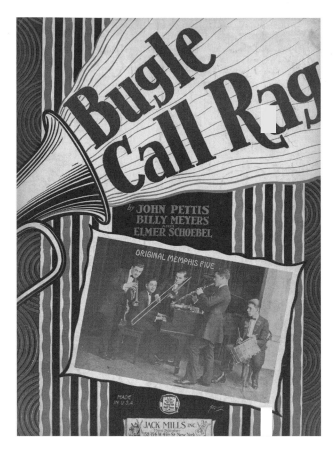

Original Memphis Five's "Bugle Call Rag" sheet music. Courtesy David A. Jasen

had slightly different personnel). Recordings made in 1922–1931 by the band with various personnel are collected on the French CD, *Great White Way Blues* (Jazz Archives #159542).

ORIGINAL NEW ORLEANS JAZZ BAND

A group consisting of Frank Christian, cornet; Frank Lhotak, trombone; Achille Baquet, clarinet; Jimmy Durante, piano; and Arnold Loyacano, drums. In 1918 they cut two sides for Okeh, then they went to Gennett for four sides in 1919. "Ja Da," recorded for both labels, was a popular number (Okeh #1156; Gennett #4508). They were obviously named to take advantage of the popularity of other "Original" groups.

ORIGINAL PIANO TRIO

A group that recorded two sides for Edison Diamond Discs in 1922. Members were George Dilworth, Edgar Fairchild, and Herbert Clair. Their record contained "Apache Love" and "Bimini Bay" (#50888).

Oriole label (I). Courtesy David A. Jasen

ORIOLE (LABEL) (I)

An American record, sold for $0.25 in McCrory's dime stores from 1921 to 1938. Matrices came from several sources: Grey Gull, Emerson, Plaza-Banner, and American Record Corp. Material was dance and popular vocal, with some race and hillbilly items. Many recordings were identical to issues from the Jewel label. [Rust 1978.]

ORIOLE (LABEL) (II)

A British record issued by Levy's of London, in 1927, featuring important blues and jazz material, mostly from the American Vocalion catalog. Levy's Sound Studios, Ltd. was opened in Regent St. in the 1930s by Jack Levy. Trading as Levy's Public Phono & Cycle Stores, the firm made Levaphone and Oriole records. In a series started in 1931, Oriole included material by the new Quintette of the Hot Club of France, and by Duke Ellington. That second series from Levy's ended in 1935. [Rust 1978.]

ORIOLE (LABEL) (III)

In 1949 there was another series of Levy's Orioles, including London-made pressings as well as American imports. Jack Levy, whose sound studios were used to record the earlier British Oriole, also made that label. These Orioles were mentioned in *Gramophone* in September 1949, and continued to be sold, as 78s, into early 1961. In 1954, Oriole was registered with Embassy and Allegro labels. Oriole was taken over by

CBS Records, which used the name for low-cost line in Australia. CBS also took Oriole's registered trademarks Plaza, Time Oriole, Realm, and Senator.

FRANK ANDREWS

ORLANDO, TONY, AND DAWN

Forerunners of the adult contemporary genre, Tony Orlando and Dawn recorded a string of easy listening hits during the early 1970s. The group is best remembered for the anthem depicting an ex-convict's homecoming, "Tie a Yellow Ribbon Round the Ol' Oak Tree"; it would be associated with the return of the Iranian hostages in 1981, while the yellow ribbon became symbolic of a homecoming, whether of a personal nature or national in scope (e.g., war). A protégé of Aldon Music executive Don Kirshner while still in his teens, Orlando — born Michael Anthony Orlando Cassavitis, 3 Apr 1944, in New York City — enjoyed a brief run as a teen idol with such Carole King–penned songs as "Halfway to Paradise" (Epic #9441; 1961; #39) and "Bless You" (Epic #9452; 1961; #15). When the hits stopped coming he worked both as a song promoter and manager of April-Blackwood Music, the publishing division for Columbia Records. Orlando's recording career was resurrected when Bell Records selected him to provide the lead vocal for a demo submitted by two Detroit-based backup singers, Telma Louise Hopkins and Joyce Elaine Vincent, who had worked with Freda Payne, Edwin Starr, Johnnie Taylor, and others. The song, "Candida" (Bell #903; 1970; #3), and a follow-up, "Knock Three Times" (Bell #938; 1970; #1) — both of which possessed a lilting, sing-a-long groove — became major hits. (Bell staff would claim that the two songs were recorded by Orlando with session singers.) At this point Orlando, along with Hopkins and Vincent, signed with Bell as "Dawn, featuring Tony Orlando." For the next six years, the group became a household name with best-selling singles like "Tie a Yellow Ribbon Round the Ol' Oak Tree" (Bell #45318; 1973; #1), "Say, Has Anybody Seen My Sweet Gypsy Rose" (Bell #45374; 1973; #3), "Steppin' Out" (Bell #45601; 1974; #7), and "He Don't Love You (Like I Love You)" (Elektra #45240; 1975; #1), and as hosts of a CBS-TV musical-variety show. Dawn was never an important album act; their finest chart showing came with *Greatest Hits* (Arista #4045; 1975; #16). When Orlando unexpectedly announced his retirement from show business in July 1977, Hopkins and Vincent attempted — without much success — to continue as Dawn. The threesome reunited briefly in 1988 without any recording activity of note.

FRANK HOFFMANN

ORMANDY, EUGENE
(18 NOV 1899–12 MAR 1985)

Hungarian/American conductor and violinist, born in Budapest, as Eugene Blau. He studied at the Royal Academy of Music in Budapest at age five, and with Jenö Hubay at age nine. He was 15 when he received his diploma and began recitals and orchestra playing. He transferred to the U.S. in 1921, taking a post as concertmaster, then conductor, of the Capitol Theater Orchestra in New York. In 1927 he became a U.S. citizen. He was appointed music director of the Minneapolis Symphony Orchestra in 1931, then left to become associate director of the Philadelphia Orchestra (with Leopold Stokowski) in 1936. He succeeded Stokowski to the directorship in 1938, and remained with the orchestra until 1980. Under his baton the Philadelphia Orchestra developed further the magnificently unique sound created by Stokowski, and was recognized as one of the preeminent ensembles of the world. Ormandy specialized in works of the 19th century. Ormandy's earliest recordings were two violin solos with piano accompaniment for Cameo (#465; 1923), made while he was with the Capitol Theater Orchestra. He played "Hymn to the Sun" and "Song of India" by Rimsky-Korsakoff. From 1924 to 1930 Ormandy recorded as a violin soloist in the popular repertoire for Okeh, with the Capitol Orchestra, with the Dorsey Brothers Orchestra (1928), and with his own salon orchestra. Ormandy seems to have been the earliest crossover conductor, making a remarkable transition from directing Phil Napoleon, Tommy Dorsey, Glenn Miller, Jimmy Dorsey, Eddie Lang, and Smith Ballew to the Minneapolis Symphony Orchestra. His classical recording career began in Minneapolis, where Victor discs brought him a national reputation in such works as Mahler's Second Symphony, the Sibelius First Symphony, and Schoenberg's *Verklärte Nacht*. With the Philadelphia Orchestra, for Victor and Columbia, he inscribed a huge repertoire from 1936 to 1986. Among the Philadelphia records reissued on CD are Tchaikovsky's Sixth Symphony; the Sibelius Violin Concerto, with Dylana Jenson; Bartók's *Music for Strings, Percussion and Celeste*; and Benjamin Britten's *Young Person's Guide to the Orchestra* with narration by David Bowie. [Williams, F. 1985.]

ORPHEUS QUARTET

A vocal group that recorded for Victor from 1911–1918; they were also known as the Victor Male Quartet. Members were Lambert Murphy, Harry Macdonough, Reinald Werrenrath, and William F. Hooley. In Britain there was a group named Orpheus Quartette, which recorded on Twin Double Sided Disc Records in 1908, but this was a different foursome whose membership is not known.

FRANK ANDREWS

ORTF RECORDING TECHNIQUE (*OFFICE DE RADIODIFFUSION- TELEVISION FRANCAISE*)

A microphone-positioning technique developed by the French broadcasting system, but now used worldwide, that spaces two, directional cardioid microphones 17 centimeters (6.7 inches) apart (roughly the same distance as between human ears) and angles them outward at approximately 110 degrees to each other. The angle may be varied, depending upon the needs of the recording engineer. The result is coincident microphone behavior at lower frequencies, combined with some time-delay–related clues at higher frequencies that add a degree of spaciousness to the sound.

See also **Nos Recording Technique**

HOWARD FERSTLER

ORTHOPHONIC

The Victor gramophone introduced in 1925 to play the new electric records.

See also **Victrola**

ORTOFON

A Danish firm established in 1918 in Copenhagen, by Axel Petersen and Arnold Poulsen, to develop sound motion pictures. By 1923 they were able to demonstrate a sound film, using what they called a "variable area" method that required two separate film strips to run simultaneously, with one carrying the audio and the other the video. The method was accepted and licensed in Europe and America. Later the firm developed new disc cutter heads and amplifying systems, with records issued by Tono. Improvements were also made in tape recording and in recording long-playing microgroove discs. Ortofon moving-coil and moving-magnet pickup cartridges became universally praised, and during the heyday of the LP record the company was one of the world's leading manufacturers. The firm's stereo cutterhead was also widely used. The company is also known for rugged, disco-oriented pickups that are admired by disc jockeys. High-quality audio equipment is still being produced and is marketed around the world.

REV. HOWARD FERSTLER

ORY, KID (25 DEC 1886–23 JAN 1973)

American jazz trumpeter and band leader, born as Edward Ory in La Place, Louisiana. His birth year is variously reported as 1881, 1886, or 1890. He played banjo, then turned to the trombone (developing the so-called tailgate style), but also played alto saxophone, cornet, and string bass. In 1912–1919 he led bands in New Orleans, with sidemen including at times King Oliver, Louis Armstrong, Johnny Dodds, Sidney Bechet, and Jimmie Noone. He was on the West Coast from 1919 to 1925, and there made one of the first jazz records to be cut by Black artists ("Ory's Creole Trombone"/"Society Blues"); then went to Chicago and recorded with Louis Armstrong's Hot Five and Hot Seven. Ory was with King Oliver's group during 1925–1927, then toured widely and freelanced. In 1926 he composed the jazz standard "Muskrat Ramble." From 1933 to 1942 he left music to be a chicken farmer and office worker, but returned in a combo with Barney Bigard in Los Angeles in 1942. Again he formed his own group, the Creole Jazz Band, making outstanding records in 1944–1945, such as "Do What Ory Say"/"Careless Love" (Cres #5; 1945) and "Blues for Jimmy Noone" featuring clarinetist Omer Simeon (Cres #2; 1944). The band signed with Verve in 1956, recording for the label through 1962. Ory toured Europe in 1956–1959 and made an important series of recordings with Red Allen in 1959, but then Ory was less active, finally retiring to Hawaii in 1966. He died in Honolulu. CD reissues of Ory's work abound, on European and domestic jazz-nostalgia labels. Classics has a single CD covering his output from 1922–1945 (#1069); this material is also available in different formats on various other labels. Mosaic has reissued his complete, 116 tracks recorded for Verve from 1956–1962 (#189).

OSBOURNE, OZZY (3 DEC 1948–)

One of the heavy metal genre's true survivors, John Michael "Ozzy" Osbourne has been a magnet for controversy since Black Sabbath first emerged into the public eye in the late 1960s. He has produced a solid body of recordings over the years, although they have taken a back seat to the publicity surrounding lawsuits alleging that his song, "Suicide Solution," caused the death of three teenage fans, as well as antics such as relieving himself on a wall of the Alamo and biting the head off a bat during a Des Moines, Iowa, concert. Dismissed from Black Sabbath after 11 years as lead vocalist, Osbourne went to assemble his own support band (known as the Blizzard of Ozz), featuring Quiet Riot alumnus Randy Rhoads on guitar, ex-Uriah Heep drummer Lee Kerslake, bassist Bob Daisley (formerly with Chicken Shack and Rainbow), and keyboardist

Ozzy Osbourne, in his high Satanic splendor. Courtesy Frank Hoffmann

Don Avery. His debut release, *Ozzy Osbourne's Blizzard of Oz* (Jet/CBS #36812; 1980; #21; platinum record) — which included the pulsating "Crazy Train" (Jet/CBS #02079; 1981) and the extended live track, "Mr. Crowley" (Jet/CBS #37640; 1980), augmented by Rhoads' tour de force guitar work — exhibited more energy and a darker vision than anything produced by Black Sabbath in nearly a decade. The next LP, *Diary of a Madman* (Jet/CBS #37492; 1981; #16; platinum record), made it clear that Osbourne's comeback was no fluke. However, the loss of Rhoads in a plane crash, followed by a succession of band personnel changes, halted his momentum for a time. He was content to recycle Black Sabbath material in live performance with *Talk of the Devil* (Jet/CBS #38350; 1982; #14; platinum record), while his studio albums — *Bark at the Moon* (CBS #38987; 1983; #19), *The Ultimate Sin* (CBS #40026; 1986; #6), and *No Rest for the Wicked* (CBS #44245; 1988; #13) — were lackluster efforts despite platinum sales. Although Osbourne would surface with new releases on occasion — *No More Tears* (CBS #46795; 1991; #7) and *Ozzmosis* (CBS #67091; 1995; #4) earned faint praise at a time when heavy metal in general had entered a moribund phase — the bulk of his releases — *Tribute* (CBS #40714; 1987; #6), consisting of 1981 live recordings with Rhoads; *Just Say Ozzy* (CBS #45451; 1990; #58), *Live & Loud* (CBS #46795; 1993; #22), and *The Ozzman Cometh – The Best of Ozzy Osbourne* (CBS #487260; 1997; #13), all of which included ample helpings of classic Black Sabbath material — consisted of concert performances and compilations. In the early 21st century, he received a career boost from the unlikeliest of sources, as a cable television sitcom star. *The Osbournes* would earn an Emmy award and become MTV's highest-rated program. The first season also achieved best-selling status as a DVD compilation (Miramax #29165; 2003).

FRANK HOFFMANN

OSSMAN, VESS L.
(21 AUG 1868–8 DEC 1923)

American banjoist, born Sylvester Louis Ossman in Hudson, New York. He started playing at 12 years of age, and by 1898 was an established international artist (with a command performance for King Edward VII in 1903), doing Black songs, ragtime, marches, etc. Ossman, "the banjo king," was "probably the leading instrumental soloist on record in the 1890s and early 1900s" [Brooks]. He started with Edison around 1893, then played for all the labels, disc and cylinder, mostly before 1911. He had 15 records in the Columbia 1896 catalog and was an exclusive for the label for a few years. He also worked for Bettini and Berliner (making his first recording for that label, "Rag Time Medley," on 19 Aug 1897), and was one of the first Victor artists. In 1899 he began to accompany Len Spencer and Arthur Collins in their Black songs. Ossman's best seller was "Turkey in the Straw Medley"/"Dixie" (Victor #4424; 1905; also on other labels). In 1906 he organized the Ossman-Dudley Trio (with Audley Dudley,

Vess L. Ossman from an early Victor Record catalog. Courtesy David A. Jasen

mandolin; and George F. Dudley, harp and guitar) and made a hit ragtime record for Victor, "St. Louis Tickle" (#4624). Between 1911 and 1916 Ossman made only a few records, among them numbers for the U-S Phonograph Co. on indestructible cylinders. Back in action in 1916, he had another Victor hit in "Good Scout — One Step," then established a Banjo Orchestra (really two banjos, with piano, saxophone, and drums). Later he was one of the Eight Famous Victor Artists. "Buffalo Rag" was the last of his records, kept in the Victor catalog until 1924. After Ossman died, in Minneapolis, many of his numbers were re-recorded by Fred Van Epps. [Brooks 1979; Walsh 1948/9–10–11, 1949/1–2, corrections in 1952/5.]

OSTIN, MO (27 MAR 1927–)

Born in New York City, Ostin served as an accountant at Verve (1954) and administrative vice president for Reprise (1960) prior to being named chairman of Warner Bros. Records in 1970. Responsible for bringing Jimi Hendrix, Joni Mitchell, the Kinks, and Neil Young to Warner-Reprise in the 1960s, as he continued the company's increasing involvement with rock artists in the 1970s and 1980s, signing James Taylor, Paul Simon, R.E.M., and the Red Hot Chili Peppers, among others. He was largely responsible for Warner's reputation as a label committed to free artistic expression. Since the death of WEA CEO Steve Ross in 1995, he has been in charge of SKG/Dreamworks.

FRANK HOFFMANN

OTALA, MATTI

SEE AMPLIFIER

OTIS, JOHNNY (28 DEC 1921–)

Born Johnny Veliotes to a Greek immigrant family in Vallejo, California, Otis became a leading performer, composer, producer, and talent scout for R&B acts from the mid-1940s through the 1950s. His father operated a grocery store in a Black neighborhood in Berkeley. Otis began performing as a teenager on the drums, and was recommended for a job with Harlan Leonard's Los Angeles–based Kansas City Rockets in 1943. Within two years, he was leading his own band at the city's Club Alabam, and in 1950 founded the Barrelhouse Club, the first club to exclusively feature R&B music in Los Angeles. His big band had its first hit with "Harlem Nocturne." He also began his long career as a disc jockey, broadcasting his "Johnny Otis

Show," and led several successful R&B touring shows. Other hits in this era include a series of so-called "blues" numbers, including "Double Crossing Blues" and "Mistrustin' Blues" (both #1, R&B), "Deceivin' Blues" (#4, R&B), and culminating in "Rockin' Blues" (#21 pop; #2 R&B). In 1951, Jackie Wilson covered Otis's song "Every Beat of My Heart," which was his first foray into composing R&B; the song was later a hit for Gladys Knight. During this period, he discovered two major singers, Etta James and Willie Mae "Big Mama" Thornton, producing James's hit "The Wallflower" (aka "Roll with Me, Henry") and producing and accompanying Thornton on "Hound Dog" (later covered by Elvis Presley). Another major hit for Otis as a performer and writer was 1958's "Willie and the Hand Jive" (Capitol #3966; #9 pop), a raplike lyric set over a Bo Diddley style beat. The song has been covered count-less times, notably by Eric Clapton. Otis moved into state politics in the 1960s while continuing to host his radio show. He also has had a career as an author and artist. He was inducted into the Rock and Roll Hall of Fame in 1994 and holds many other honors. Also in 1994, he recorded his first album in some time, *Spirit of the Black Territory Bands*, for Arhoolie (#384). His son, guitarist Johnny Jr., known as "Shuggie," has toured with his father since his early teen years, and had a novelty hit himself at age 13 with "Country Girl"; he later sessioned for a variety of artists, including Frank Zappa's jazz album *Hot Rats*. Another son, Nick, plays drums.

CARL BENSON

OUT OF PHASE

The term given to the situation when the moving ele-ments of two loudspeaker systems, in response to simultaneous identical signals, move in opposite direc-tions. The sonic effect, if the listener is seated an equal distance from each speaker, will be for normally cen-tered images to take on a vague and directionless char-acteristic. Bass response will also be reduced in strength. It is therefore important to have all speaker systems in an audio installation, including those in multispeaker surround-sound setups, wired as much in phase as possible. If the speaker models are different from each other (the center and surrounds are typical-ly different from the left and right mains), this can be tricky to pull off effectively.

REV. HOWARD FERSTLER

OUTPUT

In an audio system, any signal leaving any component.

OUT-TAKE

Material that is recorded (or filmed) but not retained in the final master.

OVERDUBBING

SEE MULTITRACK RECORDING

OVERLOAD

SEE DISTORTION

OVERSAMPLING

A better term might be "resampling." In a digital play-back system, it is one of several ways to enhance the performance. It involves sampling at a rate higher than the sampling Nyquist theorem (which states that a band-limited, continuous waveform may be represent-ed by a series of discrete samples if the sampling fre-quency is at least twice the highest frequency contained in the waveform), meaning that each sample from the data converter at the playback end is sampled more than once, i.e., oversampled. This multiplication of samples permits digital filtering of the signal, there-by reducing the need for sharp analog filters to control aliasing (unwanted frequencies created when sampling a signal of a frequency higher than half the sampling rate). The result is a more effective way to eliminate problems at frequencies above the audible range.

See also **Compact Disc; Nyquist Frequency; Sam-pling Frequency**

REV. HOWARD FERSTLER

OWEN, WILLIAM BARRY
(?–19 MAR 1914)

American record company executive, born in New Bedford, Massachusetts. He was a director of the National Gramophone Co. from October 1896, and was sent to London in 1897 by Emile Berliner to demonstrate the Improved Gramophone and to sell rights. He established the Gramophone Co. in April 1898 to import Gramophones and make recordings. He served as managing director of the new enterprise, located in London's Maiden Lane. In 1899 he pur-chased the Nipper painting from Francis Barraud. Owen made an unfortunate decision to diversify in 1900, and began to deal in typewriters; the company name was changed to the Gramophone and Typewriter, Ltd. With the market failure of his type-writer, Owen resigned and was succeeded by

Theodore Birnbaum in 1904. He then retired to Martha's Vineyard, Massachusetts, to raise chickens.

OXFORD (LABEL)

An American record, marketed by mail order by Sears, Roebuck and Co., from ca. 1900 to ca. 1918. There were only a few issues before 1911, when the main series began. Masters came from Zonophone, Victor, Leeds & Catlin, and Columbia. Major artists were included, such as Emilio de Gogorza and Bert Williams, but frequently the artists' names were omitted from the label. In 1911, 10-inch discs were selling at $0.30. In 1915, 12-inch discs were also sold at $0.50. Sears replaced the Oxford label with the new Silvertone records in 1912, but in fall 1917 there was a resurgence of Oxford when the supply of Silvertone paper labels was temporarily exhausted. [Bryan 1975 is a complete list.]

OZAWA, SEIJI (1 SEPT 1935–)

Japanese conductor, born in Fenytien (now Shenyang, Liaoning, China). His Japanese parents were living in China during the Japanese occupation of Manchuria, when Seiji was born; they moved the family back to Japan in 1944. He studied piano, composition, and conducting in Tokyo, then went to Europe to seek his fortune. He supported himself at first by selling motor scooters in France and Italy. He won a major competition for conductors in 1959 and was given a scholarship to study with Herbert von Karajan and the Berlin Philharmonic Orchestra. Leonard Bernstein engaged him as assistant conductor of the New York Philharmonic Orchestra in 1961. From 1970 to 1976 he directed the San Francisco Symphony Orchestra; in 1973 he was named music director of the Boston Symphony Orchestra, holding the position for 29 years, a record. He made his debut conducting at the Metropolitan Opera on 4 Dec 1992, leading the orchestra for the production of *Eugene Onegin*. In 1994, the orchestra's new concert hall at Tanglewood was named for him. In 2002, he was scheduled to leave Boston to conduct the Vienna State Opera Orchestra. Ozawa has a wide, eclectic repertoire and has recorded (for many labels) major works from all periods. An outstanding series was the Beethoven piano concertos with Rudolf Serkin (Telarc #10062). Another acclaimed disc presented the Berg and Stravinsky violin concertos with Itzhak Perlman (DGG #413725–2). These have been reissued on CD.

P

P CHANNEL

On a compact disc, a subcode (inaudible) channel used for carrying information on lead-in, lead-out, and playing areas.

PACE PHONOGRAPH RECORD CORP.

See Black Swan (label)

PACIFIC PHONOGRAPH CO.

One of the affiliated firms that comprised the North American Phonograph Co., later independent; it was established 7 Jan 1889 in San Francisco. In 1890, Louis Glass was general manager. Glass developed the coin-op cylinder phonograph, and a prime occupation of the company was leasing models. The first coin-op on location seems to have been at the Palais Royal saloon, in San Francisco, on 23 Nov 1889. After the breakup of North American, the Pacific Phonograph Co. continued in business. A notice in *TMW* for June 1915 states the "head" was A.R. Pommer at that time.

PACKAGED SYSTEM

A complete audio playback system, also known as a rack system, including all components with necessary connections. During the early hi-fi period of the 1950s, enthusiasts preferred to have separate components. But modern packaged systems demonstrate quality equivalent to that of assembled sets of compo-nents, and they may be harmoniously clustered as well as less costly.

PACKARD MANUFACTURING CO.

A firm established in 1932 by Homer Capehart, in Indianapolis, Indiana. It made coin-op phonographs for a few years after World War II, including the Manhattan jukebox.

PACKBURN AUDIO NOISE SUPPRESSOR

A device designed to suppress transient noises (ticks, pops, clicks, crackle, scratch, etc.) in phonograph records, mono or stereo, wherever or however made, as well as the audible hiss characteristic of all audio media prior to the development of successful encode/decode noise suppression systems, and more recently, digital audio. This article describes Model 323A, which has three principal components: a switcher, a blanker, and a continuous noise suppressor.

The switcher is designed specifically for the reduction of transient noises in monophonic disc and cylin-der records by taking advantage of the circumstance that, whereas the same signal is engraved on each side of the groove wall, the noises caused by dirt, mildew, scratches, cracks, particulate matter in the record material, etc., are not the same on each side of the groove wall.

Prior to the development of the Packburn switcher, a monophonic disc or cylinder was best reproduced for stereo by summing (in the appropriate polarity) the signals from the left and right channels. The switcher also does this, in the rest position. However, at any moment when the reproduction from the left or right channel is more noise-free than the sum signal (by a user-adjustable threshold amount), the switcher can reproduce from the quieter groove wall only. At frequencies lower than 300 Hz, where switching would not accomplish anything, the two channels are mixed to minimize rumble.

The switching process is applicable to vertical-cut recordings as well as to lateral-cut records, as a correct playback stylus rides on the side walls of the groove; it is, however, more effective with lateral records. The switching process is the least compromising mode of noise reduction, as it has no effect on the fidelity of reproduction and does not introduce distortion or have any other undesirable side effect. In fact, its audible effect is one of decreased distortion in the reproduction of records that have any substantial amount of transient noises. The output of the process is a monophonic signal in which the noise content consists of the residual noise that has survived the switcher's three-way choice.

Stereo records, monophonic tape recordings, and broadcasts cannot be processed with the switcher. For these the blanker is used. The blanker is designed to cope with transient noises from any source: the output of the switcher, a stereo disc, a tape, compact disc, or broadcasts. It will usually be most effective in dealing with an original record, as copying and broadcasting processes, which typically employ filtering, compression, and limiting, tend to dull the leading edge of a noise transient and thus lower its detectability by the blanker circuitry. Transient noise suppression is achieved by clipping the amplitude of each individual positive-going and negative-going pulsation of a noise transient whenever the amplitude of the transient exceeds a threshold value determined by the peak program level in the vicinity of the transient and by the setting of the "blanker rate" control. The blanker does not attempt to eliminate the totality of the transient, which would require momentarily reducing the signal level to zero. Therefore, a slight ghost of lower frequency components of certain noise transients will sometimes remain. Cracks, pits, gouges, dents, or bumps may still be audibly detectable but as low frequency thumps which normally will not be painful to listen to.

Once the switcher and blanker have completed their tasks — to cope with transient noise — there remains the need to reduce audible hiss. This is accomplished by the continuous noise suppressor. In the case of recordings containing no transient noises, such as master tapes or copies thereof, the continuous noise suppressor will be the only processor needed.

The Packburn continuous noise suppressor is classified as a dynamic noise suppressor. In such devices the cutoff frequency of a variable low-pass filter varies with the dynamics of the program material in such a way that audible noise is minimized with a zero or minimal degradation of the perceived fidelity of reproduction and without introducing extraneous noises as a result of the dynamics of the filter operation.

The success of such a device is crucially dependent on the design of its sensing and control circuits and on the user-operated controls that are provided. The operation of the filter in the Packburn continuous noise suppressor is controlled as follows:

1. The signal amplitude in the frequency range of 1.7 kHz to 3.4 kHz is employed as an index of the high frequency content of the signal in the audible range;
2. The time rate of change of the total signal-plus-noise is employed as an index of the audible surface noise;
3. A voltage derived from the ratio of measurements (1) and (2) is employed to control the width of the pass band;
4. Separate user-adjustable controls are provided to select the minimum cutoff frequency in quiet passages and the maximum cutoff frequency in loud passages;
5. User-adjustable means are provided for a rapid increase of the pass band width at the onset of signal transients.

As the continuous noise suppressor functions best if it "hears" the program material with the same treble equalization that one chooses for listening, the Packburn unit provides a treble equalization switch that allows one to select the Recording Industries Association of America (RIAA) curve or one of five other equalization curves that match those historically used in cutting records prior to the standardization of the RIAA curve by the record industry in 1953.

Other controls are provided in the Packburn 323A to assist in obtaining optimum results. Meters ensure proper adjustment of the input level, and a frequency meter reads the fluctuating value of the cutoff frequency as the continuous noise suppressor operates. The user can audition the separate groove walls of a record, which can be of assistance in selecting the optimum size stylus for record playing, and vertical component of lateral-cut records as well as the lateral component of vertical-cut records.

The channel balance control, which is important in adjusting the switching process, also serves as a canting control for vertical-cut records.

To accommodate stereo recordings, Model 323A is provided with two blankers, two treble equalization networks, and two continuous noise processors. It is designed to interface with contemporary stereo playback systems. It can be inserted in a tape loop of a preamplifier, amplifier, or receiver, or it can be interposed after the preamplifier.

In professional installations, the Packburn Audio Noise Suppressor is used immediately after the stereo preamplifier and prior to such devices as equalizers, filters, volume expanders, reverberation synthesizers, etc., save that, in record restoration work, one may prefer to utilize the continuous noise suppressor in the final stage of processing. (Packburn is registered with U.S. Patent and Trademark Office.)

See also **Noise Reduction**

RICHARD C. BURN

PADEREWSKI, IGNACE [JAN] (18 NOV 1860–29 JUNE 1941)

Polish pianist and composer, born in Kurylowka, Podolia (Russian Poland). He performed in public as a child and was sent to Warsaw Conservatory by wealthy patrons. On graduation in 1878 he joined the piano faculty. After further study with Theodor Leschetizky he gave recitals in Paris and Vienna (1888), then London (1890) and New York (1891). His playing and his personality brought him great adulation in America.

Paderewski was also an assiduous composer, though only one minor piece, the "Minuet in G," remains in the repertoire. And he was the first celebrated musician to occupy a high political post, being prime minister of the Polish Republic in 1919, and later his country's delegate to the League of Nations. He published his memoirs in 1938. In 1940 he was named president of the Polish parliament in exile. He died in New York.

His earliest records were made in Switzerland for HMV in 1911: seven numbers including his own "Minuet" (#045530), "Hark! Hark! The Lark" by Schubert/Liszt (#045532), and five Chopin pieces. All were reissued by Victor. Another group was made in Paris in 1912, for HMV (not issued with Victor numbers); six Chopin items, and pieces by Mendelssohn, Debussy, Paderewski, and Liszt, along with another "Hark! Hark! The Lark." There were another 13 HMV recordings, then Paderewski recorded for Victor, a series of his works from his usual limited repertoire. The 1917 Victor catalog carried five sides by him. He continued recording Chopin and other romantics through the acoustic period and into the electric era, becoming somewhat more adventurous in the 1930s with Wagner transcriptions, Brahms, Mozart, and Beethoven. His final session was on 15 Nov 1938. There are numerous compilation CDs that feature performances by Paderewski, including *The Polish Virtuosi* (Nimbus #8802; recordings from 1919–1932). *Ignaz Jan Paderewski Plays Schubert, Beethoven, Schumann, Mendelssohn, Wagner, and Schelling* and *Plays Chopin* (Nimbus #8812, #8816) are compiled from piano roll recordings made for Aeolian Duo Art in the early 1920s. Philips issued a two-CD set of his work as part of its "Great Pianists of the 20th Century" series (#456919), derived from 1930s-era recordings. [Methuen-Campbell 1984.]

PADGHAM, HUGH (15 FEB 1955–)

One of the industry's top recording engineers, producers, and mixers, Padgham's youth involved being educated at St. Edwards School, in Oxford, England. After graduation, he started out working for Advision Studios, in 1974, where he began learning his future trade. He moved on to Lansdowne Studios between 1975 and 1978, and then got a house-engineer job with the studios of Virgin Records (the Townhouse and the Manor Studios), which lasted from 1978 until 1981. Since 1981, he has been self-employed and has gone on to record a number of music-industry notables, with one of his credits being the "inventor" of Phil Collins's big-drum sound and another being his work to develop the early SSL mixing computer systems.

A member of NARAS, Padgham has won numerous awards and acknowledgments for his producing, engineering, and mixing work, including BPI Best Producer nominations, in both 1985 and 1986; a Grammy award for Producer of the Year and also a Grammy for Album of the Year in 1985 (Phil Collins's *No Jacket Required*); a Music Week Award for Best British Producer in 1985, plus Top Album Producer in 1990; a U.K. Award for Best Single in 1989, as well as the Grammy for Record of the Year in 1990 (both for Phil Collins's "Another Day in Paradise"); an acknowledgment as one of the top 10 most influential producers of the Mix magazine *Era* in 1992; the TEC Award for Outstanding Creative Achievement by a Recording Engineer in 1993; a Grammy award for engineering in 1994 (Sting's *Ten Summoner's Tales*); and a tribute for achievement from *Billboard* magazine in 1997. During the 1980s, the multifaceted Padgham was also co-owner of a private sports car racing team that took second place at the Le Mans 24-hour race in 1985.

HOWARD FERSTLER

PAGE, PATTI (8 NOV 1927–)

American popular singer, born Clara Ann Fowler in Claremore, Oklahoma. She grew up in Tulsa, Oklahoma, singing in church and on local radio.

Moving to Chicago, she did club and radio engagements, and began to record for Mercury in the late 1940s, continuing through 1964. She had a long series of hit records, beginning with her most enduring favorite, "Tennessee Waltz" (Mercury #5534; 1950). Among her 35 other chart songs through the 1960s were "I Went to Your Wedding" (Mercury #5899; 1952) and "How Much Is that Doggie in the Window" (Mercury #70070; 1953). Page had three best-selling LP albums in the 1960s, notably *Hush, Hush, Sweet Charlotte* (Columbia #2353; 1965). In the early 1970s, after an inactive period, she entered the country field and enjoyed another string of hit records, including "Make Me Your Kind of Woman" (Mercury #73199; 1971). After that, she faded from the scene, although she has continued to appear at clubs through the 1990s.

Mercury has done a two-CD anthology of her recordings, one focusing on the earlier years (through 1952) and another on her 1952–early 1960s recordings (#510433, #510434). Columbia has anthologized her mid-1960s recordings for its label on *16 Most Requested Songs* (#44401). There are various budget compilations on European and American labels as well.

PAGLIUGHI, LINA
(27 MAY 1907–2 OCT 1980)

American soprano, born in New York of Italian parents. At age six she gave a recital in San Francisco. Encouraged by Luisa Tetrazzini, she studied in Milan, and made her debut there as Gilda in 1927. From 1930 to 1947 she appeared at La Scala, then with Italian Radio. Her light childlike voice was best suited to delicate roles like Gilda, Rosina, and Lucia. She retired in 1956, and died in Rubicone, Italy.

Pagliughi recorded in Milan during 1928–1930 for HMV, for Parlophone (Italy) in 1932–1934, and then for Cetra in 1935–1943, standard coloratura numbers and several arias from Rossini and Bellini. She made four sides for Victor in 1940, the most popular being "Carnival of Venice," in which she sang a duet with a flute (Victor #2061). Her finest recording was the complete *Rigoletto* (Victor #M-32; 1928), with the La Scala company. She also recorded a complete *Lucia*. The Austrian reissue label Preiser Records has issued a CD sampler of her recordings (*Arias and Duets*, #89155). [Di Cave 1973.]

PALACE TRIO

An instrumental group that recorded for Victor and other labels in the 1920s. Members were Rudy Wiedoeft, saxophone; Mario Perry, accordion; and J. Russell Robinson, piano.

PALEY, WILLIAM SAMUEL
(28 SEP 1901–26 OCT 1990)

American radio and television executive, born in Chicago. He graduated in 1922 from the Wharton School of Finance, University of Pennsylvania, and went into his father's cigar business. Attracted to the new radio field, in 1928 he acquired a small chain of stations that had been set up in 1927 by Arthur Judson as the United Independent Broadcasters, Inc. (UIB). UIB had been in immediate financial difficulty, and had sold its operating rights to the Columbia Phonograph Co., which had renamed it the Columbia Phonograph Broadcasting System. In 1928 Columbia Phonograph sold UIB's operating rights back to it, and it changed itself to the Columbia Broadcasting System (CBS) in time for Paley to invest $400,000 in it and take over as president. By 1930 CBS had expanded from 16 to 70 stations across the U.S. CBS began its weekly broadcasts of the New York Philharmonic-Symphony Orchestra concerts in 1930. Important popular artists like Kate Smith and Bing Crosby were also featured.

Columbia Phonograph Co. was acquired when CBS bought the American Record Corp. in 1938. The Columbia Recording Co. was then the manufacturing arm; later the name of the enterprise became Columbia Records, Inc. Paley wished to revive the famous Columbia label, which had barely survived a decade of being passed among indifferent owners, and hired Edward Wallerstein to manage the unit. The result was a grand renaissance for the label, including a triumph with the new microgroove LP record in 1948. It was after Laurence A. Tisch became CEO of CBS that the Columbia label (changed to CBS Records in 1979) was sold to Sony Corp. (1986).

Paley had a distinguished military career in World War II as a civilian assigned to reconstruct the Italian radio network, then as a colonel in the Psychological Warfare Division. He earned decorations from several nations. After the war, CBS pioneered in regularly scheduled television broadcasting and in the development of color television. Paley turned over the presidency to Frank Stanton in 1946, remaining as chairman of the board. He died in New York.

PALLATROPE

The 1925 Brunswick system for making discs, adapted from Charles A. Hoxie's Photophone idea. It was a "light ray" recording process, using a microphone, a crystal mirror, a light source, and a photo-electric cell. The spellings Pallotrope and Palatrope are also seen.

PALMER, OLIVE

SEE REA, VIRGINIA

PALOMA QUARTET

The first women's group to record. They had three titles in the Victor catalog of February 1903: "La Paloma" (#1887), "Medley" (#1889), and "The Waterfall" (#1900). Walsh says he never heard any of these, nor had anyone else he knew of; and that they "must be among the rarest records." [Walsh 1965/5.]

PAN (LABEL)

An American record issued ca. 1920, of which only nine examples are known. The material includes Sousa marches, operatic arias, and violin solos (by Vera Barstow). Labels were triangular. The Pan Phonograph Co. is identified as the source. Lyric seems to have supplied the masters. [Rust 1978.]

Rare record label of the early '20s. Courtesy Kurt Nauck/Nauck's Vintage Records

PAN POTTING (OR PANNING)

The pan pot itself is an electrical device that distributes one audio signal to two or more channels or speakers. As used on recording mixers, pan potting involves moving or panning the apparent position of a single channel between two outputs — usually left and right for stereo outputs, but also with a center feed for three-channel soundstaging. At one extreme of travel the sound source is heard from only one output. At the other extreme it is heard from the other output. In the middle, the sound is heard equally from each output, but is reduced in level by 3 dB relative to its original value. With multitrack inputs, pan potting allows the mixing technician to properly lay out a soundstage with only two or three front channels.

HOWARD FERSTLER

PANACHORD (LABEL)

A British record issued by Warner-Brunswick, Ltd., of London, from May 1931 to December 1939. Masters were from Melotone, Decca, and Brunswick in the U.S.; from Broadcast, Decca, Brunswick, and Imperial in Britain; and also from Polydor in Germany. In 1933 Decca Record Co., Ltd., took over the label. Material was varied, lying primarily in the popular, dance, and country fields. Tex Ritter, Chick Webb, Woody Herman, and Ted Weems were among the artists represented. The most important releases were of Joe Venuti and Eddie Lang with their All Star Orchestra (#25151 and #25168; 1931), issued in the U.S. on Vocalion and Melotone. [Rust 1978.]

PANAMA-PACIFIC EXPOSITION, SAN FRANCISCO, 1915

A world's fair with important exhibits of talking machines. Victor had its own "Temple" for displays. John Gabel's Automatic Entertainer was shown. Thomas Edison had a Panama Canal display with special recorded narration. Awards won by the Columbia Graphophone Co. led to its issue of special "banner" discs, which were Columbia Records with a simulated award ribbon across the label.

PANASONIC

One of the world's largest electronic companies, Panasonic was founded in 1918 by Konosuke Matsushita as a vehicle to exploit his invention of a two-socket light fixture. Originally known as the Matsushita Electric Industrial Co., Ltd., the firm established a major share of the U.S. videocassette hardware market in the 1980s with its VHS line, ranging from basic playback machines to high-end recorders.

Panasonic presently manufactures dozens of consumer electronics products (e.g., CD and DVD players, televisions) as well as electronic components such as semiconductors, DVD-ROM drives for PCs, and flat screen plasma television displays. The company received a technical Emmy award for its development of many of the technologies relating to the DVD format. A leading producer of DVD entertainment software, it was the first to introduce the recordable DVD for the PC and led the way in developing recordable DVD players for the video marketplace at the outset of the 21st century.

With the establishment of the Panasonic Foundation in 1984, the firm began its long-term commitment to public education in North America. Since then it has implemented programs such as Kid Witness News — providing video resources to more than 200 schools as a means of stimulating student cognitive, communication, and organizational skills — and the Creative Design Challenge, which introduces high schoolers to real-world engineering problems.

HOWARD FERSTLER

PANATROPE

The all-electric record playback machine marketed by Brunswick in 1925. Developed in cooperation with RCA, General Electric, and Westinghouse engineers, it provided an extended frequency range (hence the name "pan" meaning all, "trope" meaning scale) — said to reach 16,000 Hz. The system used a horseshoe magnetic pickup, a vacuum-tube amplifier, and a dynamic loudspeaker (the first available for domestic use). The reproducer was modeled on the Victor Orthophonic. Records were made by a light-ray system.

See also **Pallatrope**

PANHELLENION PHONOGRAPH RECORD (LABEL)

A New York disc issued around 1922. The specialty was Greek language material, plus opera and songs performed by Greek artists.

FRANK ANDREWS

PANORAMIC POTENTIOMETER

A device used in multichannel recording to locate the signal from each channel into the stereo field. It is also called a Panpot.

PARABOLIC REFLECTOR

A curved sound reflector, intended to direct signals to a microphone.

PARADIGM LOUDSPEAKER COMPANY

Founded in 1982, by Jerry VanderMarel and Scott Bagby, and located in Mississauga, Ontario, Canada, Paradigm has earned a reputation as a maker of reasonably priced, precision loudspeaker systems. Initially, VanderMarel managed Paradigm's sales, marketing, and advertising, while Bagby looked after design and manufacturing. From modest beginnings, the company grew into a significant player in the Canadian speaker market. In 1986 Bill VanderMarel joined the company and formed AudioStream to market Paradigm speakers in the U.S. Paradigm now has cutting-edge research and design facilities, including both a controlled, double-blind listening room and one of the world's largest and most advanced anechoic chambers; the company also has made extensive use of the speaker-evaluating facilities at the Canadian National Research Council. At the turn of the century, Paradigm was one of the fastest-growing speaker companies in the world. [website: www.paradigm.ca.]

HOWARD FERSTLER

PARAMETRIC EQUALIZER

A type of equalizer that allows a boost or cutout of any frequency or any bandwidth.

PARAMOUNT (LABEL)

An American record issued by New York Recording Laboratories, Inc., first reported in *TMW* in March 1918. The firm had offices in Port Washington, Wisconsin, studios in New York, and a pressing plant in Grafton, Wisconsin. Early discs were vertical cut, but by the end of 1919 all issues were lateral cut. A. J. Baum was in charge of the New York Recording Laboratories in May 1921. Charles A. Prince was musical director there in December 1922, with Al Housman as his assistant; in February 1923 Housman was reported to be the recorder.

Important material appeared on the label, notably blues and jazz. Artists included Big Bill Broonzy, Alberta Hunter, Blind Blake, Fletcher Henderson, Jelly Roll Morton, Trixie Smith, King Oliver, Ethel Waters, Ida Cox, Elmo Tanner, Blind Lemon Jefferson (with a special label of his own once, #12650; 1928), and Ma Rainey (also with a personalized label for one release, #12098; 1924).

In April 1924 Paramount took over the Black Swan label, and in June issued a joint catalog of the two labels (reprinted in *Record Changer* of June 1950). Race records became the predominant category in the Paramount output. Paramount masters were used for Broadway, Famous, and Puritan records.

Paramount is credited with the first live recording of a sports event, namely the Jack Dempsey/Gene Tunney boxing championship bout from Soldier Field, Chicago, on 22 Sept 1927. It occupied 10 sides (#12534–12538), selling for $3.75. This was the regular price for Paramounts, $0.75 each (after an initial price of $0.85). The final Paramounts came out in summer 1932. [Rust 1978; Vreede 1971 gives label list of the 12000/13000 race series.]

FRANK ANDREWS

PARENTS MUSIC RESOURCE CENTER

A social/political action organization, the Parents Music Resource Center was founded in 1985 by Mary Elizabeth "Tipper" Gore, wife of then senator and later vice president Albert Gore, Jr., and other "Washington wives." The group campaigned against sexually explicit and violent lyrics in recordings and arranged congressional hearings on the matter. As a result, record companies agreed to self-regulate by placing a "Parental Advisory: Explicit Lyrics" label on recordings that might be objectionable. Some recordings with the label sold more copies because of its presence. Several state laws attempting to regulate the sale of "stickered" albums to minors were held unconstitutional. By the early 1990s, the group was more or less inactive.

G.P. HULL

PARIS EXPOSITION, 1889

The world's fair named Exposition Universelle ran only six months, from 6 May 1889 to 6 Nov 1889, but attracted some 25 million visitors. Thomas Edison had a major 9,000 square foot exhibit there, displaying 45 phonographs. Sarah Bernhardt and other celebrities were featured making records. The public could hear recordings through ear tubes. Edison presented a phonograph to Gustave Eiffel, who installed it in his apartment on the third level of the Tower. There was also an exhibit of the graphophone by Charles Tainter, but it was a less elaborate display. Henri Lioret had an exhibit of his clocks at the fair, and became interested in the talking machine; it is believed that the stimulus of meeting Thomas Edison

and hearing the phonograph inspired his own work in the field. Valdemar Poulsen's Telegraphone was also exhibited.

PARKER, CHARLIE
(29 AUG 1920–12 MAR 1955)

American jazz saxophonist, born Charles Christopher Parker in Kansas City, Kansas. He is known also as "Bird" or "Yardbird." He played both alto and tenor saxophone and composed; Parker was one of the pioneer figures of the bebop style. A self-taught musician, he left school at age 15 to make his way. He first recorded in 1940 in Wichita, Kansas, with the Jay McShann orchestra. "Coquette" was the most interesting number, suggestive of Parker's emerging mode. In 1943 he made a few more sides with McShann, notably "Jump the Blues" (Decca #4418). His innovative improvisations received national attention after the end of the U.S. record industry recording ban in November 1944, when he recorded 37 titles. "Ko-Ko" was one of the outstanding pieces of that period (Savoy #597; 1945). Later he recorded for Dial, Mercury, Clef, and Verve. For Jazz at the Philharmonic he did an outstanding version of "Lady Be Good" (Disc #2005). Between 1947 and 1951 he was often in the studio, recording his own quintet as well as other groups. Parker's physical and mental condition deteriorated beginning in 1954, particularly following the death of his daughter. He died in New York a year later.

Most of the Parker recorded output has been reissued, in everything from "greatest hits" compilations to massive complete sets. *Yardbird Suite* (Rhino #72260), a two-CD set, gives a good career overview for the beginning listener, beginning with his Musicraft recordings, through the Savoy/Dial sessions, and then key items from Norman Granz's Clef/Verve labels. For deeper listening, there are: *Best of the Complete Savoy and Dial Recordings* which offers 20 essential tracks from these labels (Savoy Jazz #17120); Mosaic's seven-CD boxed set of Parker solos by his disciple Dean Benedetti (#7-129), which were made on a wire recorder between 1947–1948 and feature live performances focusing on Parker's solos (often, Benedetti stopped the machine after Parker played, making much of this difficult listening for the uninitiated); and a range of Verve recordings made from 1949–1954, including *Bird: The Complete Charlie Parke*, a set of 10 CDs (#837141), as well as various CD compilations and reissues of albums drawn from this period. Many audience-made recordings on bootleg and official releases have also been released on CD, making

Parker's catalog one of the most extensive among any jazz performer.

In 1988 the film *Bird* appeared, directed by Clint Eastwood. The soundtrack was created using an approach that had previously been attempted with early vocal stars, such as Caruso. Parker's solos were extracted from their old discs and set into the context of new performances overdubbed by different sidemen. Sound quality was enhanced in comparison with the original records, but the result was, according to one critic "hopelessly anachronistic, because these present-day boppers are playing in a now somewhat dated style that Parker was still in the process of defining" [Koster & Bakker]. The soundtrack record of the film (Columbia) was criticized for its artificiality. [Koster and Bakker 1974.]

See also **Charlie Parker (Label)**

PARLIAMENT (LABEL)

A low-price American record, issued from 1959 by Parliament Records, New York. Material issued was classical. Artia was the parent label.

PARLIAMENT/FUNKADELIC

SEE CLINTON, GEORGE

PARLOPHONE (LABEL) (I)

A British record issued from 1923, by the Parlophone Co., Ltd., of London. Its origin was Parlophon, used by the Carl Lindström workshop as a model name for one of its manufactured phonographs. After the Lindström business was taken over and Carl Lindström AG formed, the Beka Record business was absorbed. The 12-inch Beka Meister Records were renamed Parlophon in Germany, and the name spread throughout a number of European catalogs. In Britain, "Parlophone" had been registered to some other concern, so Lindström continued (from 1910) with the Beka Meister name for its 12-inch discs. That label continued in the U.K., with fresh imports from Germany, after World War I.

A Dutch subsidiary of Carl Lindström AG was given control of the Lindström overseas enterprises, and it was through that company that Lindström was able to regain a foothold in Britain, in 1923, with the formation of the Parlophone Co., Ltd. That firm produced Parlophone record players and discs in 10- and 12-inch sizes. Parlophone was the initial label; later

Extended play label and sleeve for a Parlophone release from the late '50s. Courtesy David A. Jasen

there was also a label styled Parlophone Odeon Series.

In October 1925 Columbia Graphophone Co., Ltd., took a controlling interest in Carl Lindström AG, the Dutch company (Trans-Oceanic Trading Co.) and the Columbia Phonograph Co., Inc., of the U.S., and formed Columbia (International), Ltd. Parlophone was then controlled by Columbia in Britain, and Parlophon elsewhere. When British-owned Columbia Phonograph Co., Inc., acquired the Okeh label from Otto Heinemann, the Okeh repertoire was allowed to continue coming on Parlophone and Parlophon records. In 1931 Parlophone became part of EMI after Columbia merged with several other British labels.

Material on Parlophone included interesting jazz and blues from Okeh, with artists' names changed and even some of the titles altered to avoid possible offense. Unusual offerings included a "Laughing Record" (#E-5500; 1925) and a best-selling Hawaiian number by Kanui and Lula (#R-1614).

During the 1950s, producer George Martin began to reshape the label. He was responsible for signing a number of comedy acts, including Peter Sellers; he also began licensing pop music from the U.S. However, Martin's biggest coup was signing the Beatles in 1962, and he followed that with other 1960s' pop groups, including the Hollies and Billy J. Kramer. Martin left the label in 1965, and by the early 1970s it was more or less dormant. In 1979 EMI revived the Parlophone name, and through the 1980s and 1990s it featured contemporary pop acts, including Queen and the Pet Shop Boys. [Rust 1978; website: www.parlophone.co.uk/.]

FRANK ANDREWS

PARLOPHONE (LABEL) (II)

An American record issued from 1929 to 1931. It was a Columbia-Okeh affiliate, distinguished by smooth surfaces. Material was dance and jazz, much of it by pseudonymous artists. [Rust 1978.]

PAR-O-KET (LABEL)

An American record made by the Paroquette Manufacturing Co., Inc., New York, in 1916–1917. The firm was incorporated in 1915 by James A. Clancy, Frank J. O'Brien, and Arthur P. O'Brien. Henry Burr, the famous tenor, organized the company, which was said to be owned and operated by the recording artists themselves. The first discs were announced in October 1916. They were seven-inch and 10-inch vertical-cut records, which sold for $0.25 and $0.35 respectively. Paroquette was not successful, and in May 1918 the complete plant was sold at public auction for the benefit of its creditors. In January 1919 all the seven-inch masters were advertised for sale in *TMW*. [Rust 1978.]

FRANK ANDREWS

Shortlived label of the mid-teens. Courtesy Kurt Nauck/Nauck's Vintage Records

PARSONS, ALAN (20 DEC 1948–)

Widely recognized in the music and audio community, not only for his legendary hit records, exciting live performances, and 11 Grammy award nominations, but also as an engineering and producing pioneer. Parsons learned piano, guitar, and flute as a child. However, after early promise as a performing musician, he decided to begin a new career as a recording engineer and took a job as an assistant recording engineer at EMI Studios. There he worked with George Martin and Phil Spector, and participated in the last works recorded by the Beatles, being an assistant engineer on the *Let It Be* and *Abbey Road* albums. At EMI, he also earned his first Grammy award nomination for his engineering work on Pink Floyd's legendary *Dark Side of the Moon*. He went on to produce three hit recordings for Al Stewart, and also worked with the American band Ambrosia on their first two hit albums. When the Beatles broke up, Parsons continued to work with Paul McCartney on a number of albums.

In 1976 Parsons joined with Eric Woolfson to form the Alan Parsons Project, and over the next decade a succession of hit albums resulted, gaining Parsons 10 Grammy nominations, with many of the releases receiving gold and platinum sales awards worldwide. During this time, he also set up a company at Abbey Road that was devoted to improving the sound quality of films and video, and went on to direct a number of music-based television programs. His London Calling, made through EMI's video team, developed into a major series on MTV, and Parsons was instrumental in the creation of Music Box, the first European music cable service.

In 1994 he prepared to tour his music in concert for the first time ever, demanding the ultimate in sound production and presentation. Recordings of these shows resulted in *The Very Best Live* (RCA #68229), released in November of that year. In 1995, Parsons ventured into multimedia production to produce a ground-breaking CD-ROM, *On Air*. The CD-ROM delivered technical sophistication, exclusive graphics, and a wealth of information and interactive originality. In addition, Parsons also mixed a surround-sound version of the album which won the "Innovators 1998 Design and Engineering Showcase Award" at the Consumer Electronics Show in 1997. He also has produced a Sound Check compact disc that has become an industry standard technical testing tool. Since 1998, Parsons has been devoting more of his time to live concerts and recording projects, and in February 2002, he signed a production and artist deal with 5.1 Entertainment.

Parsons has been widely featured in, and written for, a number of pro-audio–related publications and the music press. He was the keynote speaker at the

1998 International Audio Engineering Society convention, and is a founding member of the British Music Producers Guild. He also lectures regularly at audio training institutions and at sound recording conventions all over the world.

HOWARD FERSTLER

PARSONS, CHARLES ALGERNON, SIR (13 JUNE 1854–11 FEB 1931)

British engineer and inventor, born in London. He studied at Cambridge University, then apprenticed in Newcastle-upon-Tyne. He set up a turbine generator business, and worked also with marine equipment. As a diversion, he experimented with sound amplification, and developed the Auxetophone, gaining three British patents for it: #10468 (1903), #10469 (1903), and #20892 (1904). He demonstrated the device for the Royal Society in May 1904, and sold the Gramophone rights to G & T sometime before 21 Mar 1905. He died at sea in 1931.

PARTON, DOLLY (19 JAN 1946–)

American country singer, songwriter, and guitarist, born Rebecca Parton in Locust Ridge, Tennessee. Living with an uncle in Nashville, she sang locally and played guitar as a child, and signed a contract with the Monument label at age 20. "Dumb Blonde" was an early chart single (Monument #982, 1967), followed by another "Why, Why, Why" (Monument #1032; 1967). Parton began a 10-year association with Port Wagoner in 1967, producing 22 chart songs, among them "Lost Forever in Your Kiss" (RCA #0675; 1972) and "Please Don't Stop Loving Me" (RCA #10010; 1974). Parton's greatest solo hits of this era were "Coat of Many Colors" (RCA #0538; 1971) — which covered the poverty her family endured when she was a child — and "Jolene" (RCA #0145; 1973). The Country Music Association voted Parton female vocalist of the year in 1975 and 1976.

She reached a wide audience in the motion picture, *9 to 5* (1980), composing the title song and winning a Grammy for it; the single was on the charts 13 weeks (RCA #12133; 1980). She subsequently had other starring film roles. Although less popular on the charts, Parton has continued to record and tour through the 1990s. In 1987, she recorded the well-received *Trio* album with Linda Ronstadt and Emmylou Harris; the three had been discussing making a record together for years. (A follow-up album appeared in 1998.) In 1999 Parton signed with the folk-bluegrass label, Sugar Hill, and released her first album with an all-acoustic, bluegrass-styled accompaniment, and was

Dolly Parton's first PR Photo, c. 1964. Courtesy Goldband Records

inducted into the Country Music Hall of Fame. A second bluegrass album followed in 2001. Parton won six Grammy awards between 1978–2001.

Besides recording, Parton is a talented songwriter. Her song "I Will Always Love You" was used as the theme song for Whitney Houston's film debut, *The Bodyguard* (1992), producing a number-one pop and R&B hit that topped the charts for a record-breaking 14 weeks and achieving quadruple platinum status (Arista #12490; 1992).

PARTRIDGE FAMILY

The Partridge Family, modeled after the real-life Cowsills, represented a marketing concept more than true performing unit. Based on actors in the television series, *The Partridge Family* — which premiered on ABC 25 Sep 1970 and ran until 1974 — depicted the adventures of a family functioning as a touring pop band. The only actors singing on the Partridge Family recordings were David Cassidy (who also played guitar) and his stepmother, Shirley Jones, whose resumé included lead roles in many musicals. The television family members also included Danny Bonaduce, model Susan Dey, Brian Foster, and Suzanne Crough.

Shortly after the show's debut, the group's first record, "I Think I Love You" (Bell #910; 1970), topped the charts, eventually selling 4 million copies. A string of hit singles — most notably, "Doesn't Somebody Want to Be Wanted" (Bell #963; 1971) and "I'll Meet You Halfway" (Bell #996; 1971) — and gold LPs — *The Partridge Family Album* (Bell #6050; 1970), *Up to Date* (Bell #6059; 1971), *The Partridge Family Sound Magazine* (Bell #6064; 1971), *The Partridge Family Shopping Bag* (Bell #6072; 1972), and *The Partridge Family at Home with Their Greatest Hits* (Bell #1107; 1972) — followed.

Like the Monkees before them, the group's music was drawn from pop-rock songs crafted by professional tunesmiths. Producer Wes Farrell — who previously cowrote songs for the Shirelles, signed Neil Diamond to his first songwriting contract, and provided pop hits for Jay and the Americans — was the brains behind the operation. He had previously produced the Cowsills, and would go on to greater production fame as the ear behind 1970s' middle-of-the-road popsters Tony Orlando and Dawn.

When the program ended, Cassidy attempted, with limited success, to build a solo career begun in 1971 with the release of the Top 10 disc "Cherish" (Bell #45150). Dey achieved a degree of distinction as an actress, and Bonaduce's stints as a disc jockey and celebrity has-been have been tainted by various legal problems.

FRANK HOFFMANN

PARVIS, TAURINO
(15 SEP 1879–9 MAY 1957)
Italian baritone, born in Torino, Italy. He sang at La Scala, and was with the Metropolitan Opera in 1904–1906. Parvis recorded on single-faced Zonophones, in the U.S., during 1904–1906, including an outstanding "La ci darem la mano" with Eugenia Mantelli (#12573). He went to Columbia cylinders and discs, from 1905 to 1914, and worked also for Pathé in Milan in 1913, making about 25 arias and duets. In 1918 he recorded for Edison Diamond Discs. He died in Barcelona, Spain.

PASTERNACK, JOSEF ALEXANDER
(1 JULY 1881–29 APR 1940)
Polish/American conductor, born in Czestochowa, Poland. He entered the Warsaw Conservatory at age 10, studying piano and composition, and learned to play virtually every orchestral instrument. At age 15 he transferred to the U.S., touring as a pianist; then played viola in the Metropolitan Opera Orchestra from 1900 to 1909, and served as assistant conductor of the orchestra in 1910–1912. He then returned to

Europe and conducted both opera and symphony concerts. Back in the U.S., he conducted the Century Opera Co. in New York, and various orchestras. In 1916 Pasternack became musical director of the Victor Talking Machine Co., a position that including conducting house orchestras. He remained with Victor until 1927. From 1928 until his death he was in demand as a conductor on the radio and as a composer for motion pictures. Pasternack died in Chicago.

PATCH
To patch is to connect items of equipment, as in an audio system, with cords and plugs. Such connections are usually controlled by break-jacks. The cord used for patching is the patch cord.

PATCH BAY
A rack-mounted, recording-studio component containing at least two rows of connectors used to "patch in" or insert into the signal path a piece of external equipment, usually console sections and tape machines. The two rows consist of send and receive jacks, with the better designs configured for balanced interconnection, rather than unbalanced. The two rows are tied together by shorting contacts, meaning that during normal operation the send and receive points will be connected, maintaining the signal path until something is plugged in. Patch bays are popular in recording studios where it is common to change the units in the signal path for each new session or client.

HOWARD FERSTLER

PATENTS
Millions of patents of all kinds have been issued since the birth of the U.S. patent system in 1790 (over 5 million since the Patent Office began its current consecutive system of numbering). Originally, working models of each invention were required by the examiners, but this condition was cancelled by Congressional Statute on 8 July 1870 and by Office Rule on 1 Mar 1889, saving the potential inventors some precious funds and lessening massive storage problems for the Patent Office and the National Archives. Many of the wood and metal models were destroyed by neglect and fire, especially in 1836 and 1877. Others were sold off and dispersed in 1925–1926, but a number still exist today in private collections and institutions.

After six days of intensive labor, John Kruesi completed the first working cylinder phonograph — invented by Thomas Edison — on 6 Dec 1877; on the seventh day, he constructed the then still-required model for submission to the Patent Office. It was returned to Edison on 22 June 1926, and is preserved today at the Henry Ford restoration of Menlo Park in Greenfield Village, Dearborn, Michigan. The model had been sent to Washington, D.C., with the formal application less than three months after the devastating Patent Office fire of 24 Sept 1877, in which over 76,000 models were destroyed (about one-third of the total then existing).

Between 1877 and 1912 (when the external horn machines lost their popularity) the U.S. Patent Office granted over 2,000 Utility (invention) Patents to about 1,000 inventors in the sound recording field, and more than 70 Design Patents. A patent remained in force for 17 years from the date of the grant and could not be extended, except under extraordinary circumstances. In the patent titles the word "phonograph" outnumbered "graphophone" five to one, although the subclass headings themselves used the latter term more often. "Talking machine" was a distant third. Although the "paper average" was about two phonograph patents per inventor, the reality was quite different. Thirty-two inventors received — either singly or jointly — 10 or more patents apiece. Although numbering only about 3 percent of the inventors surveyed, they received more than 33 percent of the patents. In that sense, the field became dominated by relatively few inventors, financed by the larger companies. Yet others who received only one or two patents — Charles Batchelor, John B. Browning, Heinrich Klenk, Henri Lioret, William F. Messer, Stanislaus Moss, and Werner Suess, for example — still managed to make a substantial impact.

These were the most prolific U.S. phonograph invention/design patentees, from 1877 to 1912, with the number of patents they received:

Thomas A. Edison, 134
Thomas H. Macdonald, 56
Eldridge R. Johnson, 54
Jonas W. Aylsworth, 38
Louis Valiquet, 33
John C. English, 31
Peter Weber, 27
Charles S. Tainter, 25
Ademor N. Petit, 23
Alexander N. Pierman, 22
Edward L. Aiken, 18
Walter H. Miller, 18
Thomas Kraemer, 15
Gianni Bettini, 14
Frank L. Capps, 14
George K. Cheney, 14
Victor H. Emerson, 14
Isidor Kitsee, 14
Horace Sheble, 14
Leon F. Douglass, 13
Emile Berliner, 12
Edward D. Gleason, 12
Edward H. Amet, 11
Robert L. Gibson, 11
Joseph W. Jones, 11
Wilburn N. Dennison, 10
Alexander Fischer, 10
George W. Gomber, 10
Luther T. Haile, 10
Frederick Myers, 10
John F. Ott, 10
William W. Young, 10

Edison's personal involvement with the field was the longest of any inventor, spanning 1877 to 1930. Ironically, his first U.S. phonograph patent, which established the industry, had little importance in the subsequent commercial development because of an unfortunate choice of words. Although Edison was aware that his first recorder would engrave paraffined paper in 1877, he had difficulties with wax clogging the stylus, and his lawyer failed to mention this detail in the original U.S. application, specifying "indentation" rather than "engraving." This lack of foresight would cost Edison dearly in the later struggles with Columbia.

Although millions of dollars were invested on the strength of a handful of major patents, other entrepreneurs gambled smaller sums — but frequently everything they had — on a single clever idea. For example, Louis Glass built and applied for a patent on the first U.S. coin-operated phonograph in 1889. Edward Amet constructed the first spring-wound motor for phonographs by 1891 (probably brought to market in mid-1894), and Thomas Lambert developed the first standard-size, unbreakable (celluloid) cylinder record by mid-1900.

A number of patentees were known in other, though allied, fields. Recording artist Steve Porter (Stephen C. Porter) had already been a founder of the American Phonograph Record Co. in 1901 when he later received a phonograph patent himself (#1,012,910). The only other singer with a patent was Berliner artist James K. Reynard (#666,819 and #776,941), but Hulbert A. Yerkes, Columbia's later jazz band director and vice president, received a design patent on a Grafonola (#41,902) and two other invention patents after 1912. Byron G. Harlan was the one-fifth assignee of Rudolph Klein's double-volute disc (#814,053), and the famed Victor recording engineer (and Berliner alumnus) William Sinkler Darby also managed to obtain one: #786,347. The keeper of Edison's musical accounts book from 1889 to 1892 and the world's first recording director, Adelbert Theo Wangemann later received two patents (#872,592 and #913,930) — but both posthumously.

Patents and the suits fought over them often changed the form of competing products. The early Echophones of Edward Amet had deeply indented mandrels, thus to avoid Edison's patent on the continuously tapered interior of a cylinder record. Thomas Lambert had to remove the little angular guide blocks from the title end of his first (hollow) white and pink celluloid cylinders. Columbia's Type AZ Graphophone with its fixed frame and Lyre Reproducer was only permitted on the market in late 1904 when Edison's patent #430,278 was held invalid. U-S Phonograph's unusual coiled-tube tone arm cylinder phonographs, developed by Harry McNulty and Thomas Towell with a double feedscrew, successfully avoided Victor's patent on the solid tapering tone arm and Edison's two-minute to four-minute gear-shifting devices. Some inventions and ideas that later became important in the industry were buried in earlier applications. For example, although Ademor Petit received a patent for a two-sided disc record in 1904 (#749,092), this very feature was mentioned as early as 1891 in the U.S., by Joseph Wassenich (#505,910), and also indicated by Edison in his British Patent #1644 of 1878, not to mention the 1878 abandoned patent application of William Hollingshead which fortuitously survived. Even the concept of a cabinet-styled phonograph with concealed horn slowly emerged in 1899 with a music box mechanism (J. Philips #632,925), but eventually, after years of litigation (and assistance from Keen-O-Phone and Brunswick) it was John Bailey Browning in 1927 who finally received credit for his prior conception of the Victrola. Other ideas, such as tapered tone arms, radial tracking, antiskating devices, magnetic recording, tone-modifiers, disc-changing mechanisms, and the ideal horn weave their way through the work of many inventors.

Extended litigation over patents marked the early years of the industry; much of it was brought on by brazen, unauthorized imitations. After the Victor Talking Machine Co. had spent of $1 million buying and defending Emile Berliner's pivotal patents (especially for the groove-driven reproducer), Eldridge Johnson (in the May 1909 issue of *TMW*) reacted to his own Supreme Court victory on this issue over Leeds & Catlin on April 19 by commenting on patent infringers: "Injunctions, fines, and even danger of imprisonment do not stop them. People infected with this curious spell seem more like the followers of some strenuous religious belief than simple business men who are working for a livelihood."

Research into the formative decades of the phonograph is greatly facilitated by use of Patent Office documents. Copies of the original applications are still available on request from the U.S. Patent and Trademark Office, Washington, DC 20231, at a cost of $1.50 each.

Patents issued by European countries followed various principles, bringing about a number of challenges for American inventors and firms. Foreign patents had varying terms, and many were subject to renewal. U.S. Statutes limited the American patent to the term of the inventor's shortest-running foreign counterpart (a practice not ended until the implementation of the Treaty of Brussels). The situation became so complex that some patents filed before 1898 expired before they were granted! American practice demanded that a U.S. citizen apply for a patent simultaneously in the U.S. and in any foreign country chosen. Edison's failure to file a U.S. application in 1878 (or promptly convert his March caveat) at the same time as his second English phonograph patent (Series 1878, 24 Apr and 22 Oct 1878, #1644) led to denial of the American patent application filed 15 Dec 1878 on the grounds of prior publication. Edison tried to repair the damage by reapplying, to no avail. Partly as a result, American Graphophone Co. was able to negotiate a royalty of $10 for every Edison machine sold until 1894.

Some of the pivotal names in European recorded sound had their patent histories. Léon Scott's important phonautographic patent was registered in France on 25 Mar 1857 (#17.897/31.470), with illustrations showing a flat recording surface; the 29 July 1859 amendment displayed the familiar travelling drum inspired by Young, Duhamel, and Wertheim. Charles Cros did not register a formal patent on his sealed Paleophone description of 16 Apr 1877 (opened 3 December) until 28 Apr–1 May and 2–3 Aug 1878 (French patent #124.313) and as far as is known never "reduced the idea to practice," built a model, nor even made a drawing. His explicator, Abbé Lenoir, did use the word "phonograph" in the 10 Oct 1877 issue of *La semaine du clergé*. However, the word had been previously used by Edison in August, and long before — in the 1840s — by Isaac and Benn Pitman to describe their newly invented system of shorthand transcription.

ALLEN KOENIGSBERG

A number of significant patents were granted after 1912. Electrical recording systems were made possible by the prior invention of the Audion — British patent #1427, issued in 1908 — and the single-stage amplifier — U.S. #841,387; 1907 — by Lee De

Forest. Among the great innovations of the 1920s was the pioneer moving coil recording head for disc recording, patented by Horace Owen Merriman and Lionel Guest (British patent #141,790; 1920).

Alan Dower Blumlein and H.E. Holman developed the moving coil microphone in the 1930s, gaining a patent from Britain (#350,998). They also patented a single turn moving coil cutting head (British patents #350,954 and #350,998).

At Bell Telephone Laboratories in the U.S. the research of Joseph P. Maxfield and Henry C. Harrison led to several related patents in 1923: U.S. #1,562,165; #1,663,884; #1,663,885; #1,678,116; and #1,709,571; plus British patent #262,839. Microphone research at Bell led to the patents for several instruments (U.S. #1,333,744; #1,456,538; #1,603,300; #1,611, 870; #1,675,853; British #134,872). The so-called rubber-line electrical recorder, designed to give a flat, extended range frequency response, also came from Bell Laboratories, in 1923 (U.S. #1,562,165; #1,663,884; #1,663,885; #1,678,116; #1,709,571; British #262,839). Advances in microphone design came from RCA in 1931, with the ribbon microphone (U.S. #1,885,001; British #386,478); there were numerous further developments of microphone design.

Full frequency range records (FFRR), introduced by Decca Record Co., Ltd., around 1945, was the result of Arthur Haddy's research; it ushered in the age of high fidelity.

In magnetic recording, based on the early work of Valdemar Poulsen (first British patent #8,961; 1899), progress was slow. Among the key patents of the 1920s were one for applying bias by W.L. Carlson and G.W. Carpenter in 1921 (U.S. #1,640,881), and Curt Stille's steel tape recorder (British #331,859; 1928). The Blattnerphone of the late 1920s was improved and patented by Guglielmo Marconi (British #458,255 and #467,105). Wire recording developments in the 1940s were largely credited to Marvin Camras of the Armour Research Foundation in Chicago. Among his patents were U.S. #2,351,003 and #2,351,007, filed in 1942. The use of coated tape as the magnetic medium was first patented in Germany in 1928 (#500,900 and #544,302; then British #333,154) by Fritz Pfleumer.

Stereophonic recording began with the work of W. Bartlett Jones, who patented in 1928 his idea of putting two channels into a single groove (U.S. #1,855,150), but he did not develop the concept into production. Alan Blumlein was researching the subject also, and put many basic ideas into his patent applications of December 1931 (British #394,325; U.S. #2,095,540). He laid the foundations of the modern stereo disc. Blumlein thought of spacing pressure microphones to provide the listener with localizing ability (British #394,325; U.S. #429,022).

Peter Maxfield's successful long-playing record, issued by Columbia in 1948, was based on a combination of ideas and processes previously patented, as well as some new ones. For example W.S. Bachman's U.S. patent #2,738,385, for a variable-pitch system of recording, allowed the extension of recording time to 30 minutes per side of the 12-inch LP.

PATHÉ FRÈRES COMPAGNIE

A firm established by Charles Pathé and Emile Pathé in Paris in 1896. It succeeded their earlier company, Les Phonographes Pathé (1894). The Pathé brothers had seen an Edison phonograph demonstration and had begun to put on exhibitions themselves. They went on to wholesale Edison machines, and to market their own cylinders for it. They also became interested in motion pictures. The Compagnie Général des Cinématographes, Phonographes et Pellicules was registered in December 1897; four years later the name was elaborated to Compagnie Général de Phonographes, Cinématographes et Appareils de Précision. In 1898 the Pathé brothers issued a catalog of their cylinders, offering nearly 800 recordings. "Celeste Aida" was number one in the catalog; like most of the records, it bore no artist's name; however announcements on the records did reveal the identity of the performers. The cylinders were made of perishable light-brown wax compounds, and only a few have survived.

Pathé's second catalog, 1899, continued with the same repertoire, which was basically classical and largely operatic. There were also popular songs, religious items, spoken records, children's songs, national anthems, and material in Italian, Spanish, German, and Russian.

Deluxe cylinders with prominent artists were offered from late 1901 or 1902, in competition with G & T's Red Label records. However the composition of the cylinder was unchanged. The "Céleste" five-minute cylinder was issued in 1903–1905, to counter G & T's new 12-inch discs. Because it required a new playback machine, the innovation was not a market success. In about 1903 Pathé abandoned its brown wax formula for the more durable black wax. In November 1906 the firm introduced its disc records, vertical cut, with shallow, wide grooves. They started at the center and played outward, using a sapphire stylus. Because the wide grooves reduced playing time, the disc diameter was larger than the conventional discs of G & T and other firms: up to 14 inches at first, then to 20 inches by 1909. All discs were in fact made to metric dimensions, although in Britain the sizes were expressed in Imperial measures, and later there were 10-inch and 12-inch discs there.

Pathé gave up its cylinders in Britain in 1906 (carrying on with them a few more years in France) and concentrated on disc production.

Pathé was also active in the sale of record players, cylinder at first, then (from 1906) both disc players (Pathéphones) and cylinder players. It sold Edison machines and Columbia Graphophones, at one time relabeling the Graphophone Eagle as their own Le Coq. The firm also produced its own brand of players, and in time discontinued the import of American machines. A line of office dictating machines, named Ronéophone, was available as well. The Pathé cylinder machines were of high quality, but the disc players were prevented from attaining the standard of Victor machines because of the Victor patent on the tapered tone arm.

This is a list of Pathé cylinder phonographs:

Model	Year	Illustrated in:
0	1904	Marty 1979, p. 94
1	1904	Marty 1979, p. 88
2	1904	Marty 1979, p. 88
3	1904	Marty 1979, p. 88
4	1904	Marty 1979, p. 94

The above were also identified as Nouveau Phonographe Pathé. They all played standard cylinders and 9.5-centimeter "Inter" cylinders. Model 4 also played the larger Stentor records.

Aiglon — before 1903 [Marty 1979, p. 89]
An adaptation of the Graphophone.

Céleste — ca. 1900 [Marty 1979, p. 91]
The largest Pathé phonograph, an adaptation of the Graphophone; it played cylinders of 8.2 inches by 4.1 inches (21 centimeters by 10.5 centimeters). Selling price was 1,000 francs. A lighter model came out in 1903 for 600 francs.

Chant-Clair — ca. 1905 [Marty 1979, pp. 86–87]
For concert-size cylinders. Some models had cardboard horns, others aluminum horns.

Coq — before 1899 [Marty 1979, p. 94]
Packaged for travel; it was a copy of the Graphophone Eagle. The cock was the Pathé trademark.

Coquet — before 1903 [Marty 1979, p. 94]
A smaller Coq, with an aluminum horn.

Français — before 1903
An adaptation of the Graphophone.

Gaulois — before 1903 [Marty 1979, pp. 92–93]
Discontinued after 1903.

Stentor — ca. 1900
These are Pathé gramophones (all with internal horn unless noted):

A 1905   [Marty 1979, p. 95]

Actuelle — 1920 [TMR #60–61, cover]
A console with lid and doors.

Aida — 1912 [TMR #19]
The top-of-the-line deluxe console, of mahogany, inlaid; could play discs up to 20 inches in diameter; spring motor ran 20 minutes. Sold in Britain for 60 guineas.

Carmen — 1912 [TMR #19]
A console, with 10-minute spring motor; made of mahogany, inlaid. Sold in Britain for 20 guineas.

Cert — 1912 [TMR #18]
A table model without a lid, with 10-minute spring motor. Sold in Britain for £2/5/0.

Concert — [Marty 1979, p. 102]
A large instrument for public entertainment, coin operated. Electric motor. Could play the large 20-inch diameter records.

Coronet — 1912 [TMR #18]
An external brass horn table model, in oak or mahogany, with 12-minute spring motor. Sold in Britain for £6/10/0.

Diamond — [Marty 1979, p. 103]
A portable that folded into a box.

Difusor — ca. 1922 [TMR #60–61, p. 1610]
Table model and console, with a large conical diaphragm at the rear of the apparatus to diffuse the sound. Sold in France for 575 and 650 francs.

Duplex — 1912 [TMR #19]
A double table model, with two complete turntable-motor-reproducer mechanisms. The purpose was to permit playing album sets, such as "Complete Opera at Home," without interruption. With a 12-inch turntable, it sold in Britain for £13/10/0. A cheaper model with a 10-inch turntable cost £9/10/0.

Elf — 1912 [TMR #18]
A table model with lid, 10-minute spring motor. Sold in Britain for £1/17/6.

Gioconda — 1912 [TMR #19]
An elegant console in mahogany, inlaid, with 20-minute spring motor. Sold in Britain for 45 guineas.

Hamlet — 1912 [TMR #19]
A console, with 12-minute spring motor. Sold in Britain for 35 guineas.

Ideal — 1912 [TMR #18]
A table model with carrying case. Sold in Britain for £2/15/0.

Jeunesse — 1910 [Marty 1979, p. 100]
Smallest of the table models, without lid; it played only the 21- and 24-centimeter records. Sold in France for 25 francs.

Leader — 1912 [TMR #18]
The least expensive external horn table model; sold in Britain for £2/2/0.

Louise — 1912 [TMR #19]

A table model with cover, made of mahogany, inlaid. Sold in Britain for £12/12/0.

Martha — 1912 [*TMR* #19]

A console, of mahogany, with 25-minute spring motor. Sold in Britain for 30 guineas. Described in the 1912 catalog as being in "Hettelwhite" style.

Omnibus — 1908 [Marty 1979, p. 97]

A table model with exterior horn. Sold in France for 35 francs.

Onward — 1912 [*TMR* #18]

A table model with interior horn, said to have a hinged lid (not shown in the illustration). Sold in Britain for £3/15/0.

Orpheus — 1912 [*TMR* #18]

A table model with lid, and two front doors for volume control. Sold in Britain for £7/15/0.

Oxford — 1912 [*TMR* #18]

An interior horn table model, with two front doors. Sold in Britain for £7/15/0.

Pathéphone: the generic name for Pathé disc players.

Romeo — 1912 [*TMR* #19]

A console in mahogany, with 12-minute spring motor. Sold in Britain for 40 guineas.

Ronéophone

A disc dictating machine for business use. A large wax disc was provided, which could be shaved for reuse. Spring motor and electric motor versions were available. The name came from the Ronéo firm, makers of office equipment, which joined with Pathé in this effort.

Scout — 1912 [*TMR* #18]

An external horn table model, available with brass or wood horn. Sold in Britain for £3/13/0 (brass) or £3/15/0 (wood).

Success — 1912 [*TMR* #18]

An internal horn table model, in oak. Sold in Britain for £5/5/0.

Tosca — 1912 [*TMR* #19]

A deluxe console in mahogany, with 12-minute spring motor. Sold in Britain for 20 guineas.

Zampa — 1912 [*TMR* #19]

A console, in oak, with 10-minute spring motor. Sold in Britain for 18 guineas.

The company was highly successful throughout Europe, and had branch offices in many countries before 1910. Pathé Frères (London) Ltd. was established in 1902; it issued a catalog of cylinders in 1904 and a catalog of record players on sale in 1906. Hurteau and Co. of Montreal were the agents for Pathé goods in Quebec. There were other factories elsewhere in Canada. There were also U.S. offices in New York (Pathé Frères Phonograph Co., Inc.). Rights for France and the colonies (not the U.S.) were acquired by Columbia Graphophone Co., Ltd., in October 1928.

Discs with the Pathé label were still made in France until 1932, although the company had been absorbed by the Société Pathé Marconi, which brought together the French interests of the Gramophone Co., Columbia, and Pathé. All became part of EMI, Ltd., in 1931. –FRANK ANDREWS [the company's history in the cylinder period is chronicled in Girard 1964. *TMR* #58 (June 1979) reproduced a 1904 cylinder catalog.]

PATHÉ FRÈRES PHONOGRAPH CO., INC.

A New York firm established in late 1911 or January 1912, incorporated in Delaware. The arrangement with the French firm, Pathé Frères Compagnie, allowed the American company to buy and market Pathé goods. Emile Pathé was consulting engineer for the American firm. In March 1913 Pathé products were demonstrated in New York, including Pathéphones, Pathégraphs, twin-turntabled Duplex Pathéphones, and a Pathé Reflex machine, along with Pathé discs. In May 1914 it was reported that the firm had leased the entire second floor of a newly erected building. Russell Hunting was named director of recording at a new pressing plant to be constructed.

Record sizes and prices in September 1914 were 11 1/2-inch ($2), 14-inch ($2.50), and 20-inch ($4). In subsequent months, as shipments continued to arrive from Europe despite World War I, dealers were named in several American cities. The O'Neill-James Co.

U.S. release on the Pathé Frères label. Courtesy David A. Jasen

assumed responsibility for Chicago and the West. The State Street Pathéphone Co. was established in Chicago by Arthur J. O'Neill. In New York, Eugene A. Widmann was reported to be general manager and treasurer. A $200 record player was marketed, with gold-plated parts and a four-spring motor. Later there was a Sheraton Pathéphone, with an electric (battery) motor, selling for $300. An extensive factory was occupied in Belleville, New Jersey, responding to great demand for Pathé discs. In July 1915 the American firm claimed to command the largest record catalog in the world, with over 96,000 selections.

Frank L. Capps became production manager in October 1915, in charge of all experimental, mechanical, and development work. The Pathé Pathéphone Shop opened opposite the New York Public Library on Fifth Ave. at 42nd St.

The center-start records were replaced by standard outside-start records in February 1916. Record labels bore the characteristic rooster trademark. The Pathé Frères Pathéphone Co., Ltd., of Canada was established, with a factory in Toronto. An agreement was made with Brunswick-Balke-Collender in 1916; Brunswick to make record players for Pathé, and Pathé to supply discs to be sold through Brunswick dealers. In February 1917 the New York office moved to Brooklyn. George W. Lyle, for many years vice president and general manager of Columbia Graphophone Co., was appointed assistant manager to Widmann. Walter L. Eckert, late chief of Thomas Edison's financial department, joined Pathé as general auditor and office manager. Pathé's output in 1917 was reported to have increased 500 percent over the previous year.

A revolutionary new record player, the Actuelle, was demonstrated. It had a cone-shaped parchment diaphragm fitted into a gold-plated aluminum frame and attached to the needle holder by a wire. It could play either vertical-cut or lateral discs with a twist of the needle. Two doors on one side of the cabinet and a device with a wire (a remote) were used to control the volume.

In November 1918 the Pathé Military Band marched on Fifth Ave. as part of Peace Day celebrations, joined by the office staff and administration; Widmann acted as parade marshall. One of the Pathé artists, Kathleen Howard, sang the national anthem on the public library steps. *Pathé News*, a house organ, was published from June 1919.

Widmann announced that from July 1919 the American firm would control the stock, plant, and policy of the British Pathé company, as well as other companies in the Western Hemisphere. (The British firm was sold in 1921 to the Compagnie Général des Machines Parlantes, Pathé Frères, Paris.)

Among the star artists on the Pathé label in 1919 were Eddie Cantor, Rudolf Ganz, Claudia Muzio, Tito Schipa, and Jacques Thibaud. The Actuelle (label), lateral cut, was introduced in the U.S. and U.K. There were popular series, including dance records, race records, comedy songs, Hawaiian, sacred, and standard vocal material. Pathé jazz and pop artists included Red Nichols, Duke Ellington, Annette Hanshaw, the California Ramblers (as the Golden Gate Orchestra), Lee Morse, and Cliff Edwards. Maurice Chevalier and other French performers were available from masters cut in Paris.

Eugene A. Widmann became chairman of the board, succeeded as president by W.W. Chase. Financial difficulties arose in 1921, due to the popularity of radio. Widmann resigned as chairman of the board in December. Receivers in equity were appointed to take charge of the firm and deal with the claims of its creditors. A reorganization emerged, and a name change took place in August 1922, to Pathé Sound Wave Corp. In November 1922 the name was changed to Pathé Frères Phonograph and Radio Corp. Emile Pathé was director of the new entity, and Widmann returned to the presidency. Actuelle discs were still selling well, at $0.55 each. And a new subsidiary was set up, called Perfect Record Co. Perfect lateral discs were issued around September 1922, at $0.50 each. Vertical-cut discs were no longer advertised.

The New York offices returned to midtown Manhattan in August 1923. A radio division was created, headed by James Watters. Throughout 1924 the company advertised Pathéphones, Pathé radios, and lateral-cut discs.

Widmann announced in September 1925 a new process of recording, based on extensive research in electrical and photoelectrical soundwave reproducing methods — a system differing from any other. It was not an electric process, but by 1927 a new Pathéphonic electrical method was in use. James E. Macpherson was president of the firm in 1928, and of the associated Pathé Record Corp. In 1928 Pathé and Cameo Record Corp. merged. Many records were then issued on both labels simultaneously.

The record industry was in economic crisis in 1929. Pathé was among the companies that were merged into the new American Record Corp. in August. Actuelle records were no longer produced, but Perfect continued, pressed from Cameo masters until 1938. Pathé and Perfect masters were used in Britain to produce some of the Pathé discs there, and for Actuelles and Pathé Perfect; and also for subcontracted work to Homochord, Grafton High Grade Record, Scala Record (7000 series), and Scala Ideal Record. Through further subcontracting, it was also used for Gamage and Vox Humana records.

FRANK ANDREWS

PATRIA RECORDS (LABEL)

An American 10-inch disc issued in 1917 by the Patria Records Corp. of New York. Phillip Waldman was general manager. A war message by President Woodrow Wilson was advertised in May.

FRANK ANDREWS

PATTI, ADELINA
(19 FEB 1843–27 SEP 1919)

Spanish soprano, born in Madrid as Adela Juana Maria Patti. She was the daughter of two Italian singers, who took her to New York as a child. She began singing in recitals there in 1851, and made a formal debut as Lucia in 1859. A juvenile sensation, she was acclaimed in Covent Garden and Paris. In 1877 she sang Violetta at La Scala, and in 1892 was heard at the Metropolitan Opera. She retired in 1895, to Craig Y Nos, a Welsh castle, but returned to sing a farewell concert in 1906 and a Red Cross benefit in 1914. She died in Brecknock, Wales.

Patti's sensational career, featuring 30 roles, was not marked by a flow of great recordings, as she was reluctant to make records. She was finally persuaded in 1905 by the Gramophone Co. to have recording equipment installed in her castle, and made 14 sides — accompanied by Landon Ronald — that were issued on a special pink Patti label. In 1906 she added a few more sides, bringing her total number of different pieces recorded on disc to 21. Her records were sold at premium prices in Britain (one guinea) and in America ($5 each by Victor). As a woman of 62 to 63 years when she made these records, following a 50-year public career, she did not sound at her greatest on them. EMI issued the Patti material on LP in 1974, and Pearl presented a CD of all her disc recordings in 1990 (#9312). More recently, Marston issued a new remastering of these same discs. [Williams & Moran 1956 is a complete discography.]

PATTON, CHARLEY
(c. APR/MAY 1891– 28 APR 1934)

Born in rural Hinds County near Edwards, Mississippi, Patton was one of the first and greatest of the Delta Blues recording artists. He was raised on the famous Dockery Plantation, where Alan Lomax would later discover Muddy Waters in the late 1930s (and record Patton cohort Henry "Son" Sims). Patton first recorded for Paramount on 14 June 1929, and he quickly became their best-selling blues artist. He recorded over 60 sides during his five-year career, and also recommended other blues singers to Paramount for recording, including Son House. His later sessions were for Vocalion. Patton often recorded with Willie Brown, and he also appears on at least seven other releases as an accompanist. Unfortunately, Paramount's pressings are notoriously bad, and Patton's records were enormously popular, meaning that they were heavily played, so most reissues suffer from poor sound quality. Nonetheless, Patton had an enormous influence on his contemporaries and the next generation of country blues pickers, notably Howlin' Wolf. Among his better-known recordings are "Pony Blues," "A Spoonful Blues," and "High Water Everywhere." Some of his religious recordings were released under the name of Elder J.J. Hadley, and some of the blues numbers under the Masked Marvel name. Patton died in Indianola, Mississippi; he apparently suffered from a weak heart exacerbated by alcoholism. Patton's recordings have been reissued many times, notably on two Yazoo releases, *Founder of the Delta Blues* (#1020; 1969) and *King of the Delta Blues* (#2001; 1999), and the lavish boxed set *Screamin' and Hollerin' the Blues* (Revenant #212; 2001).

CARL BENSON

PAUL, LES (9 JUNE 1916–)

American guitarist, born Lester William Polfuss in Waukesha, Wisconsin. He was on radio from the early 1930s, and was featured on the Fred Waring show in 1938–1941. After World War I he led his own trio, then found success in the 1950s using a multichannel recording process to present himself playing several guitar parts in backup to the vocals of his wife, Mary Ford. "How High the Moon" (Capitol #1451; 1951) and "Mocking Bird Hill" (Capitol #1373; 1951) were early chart singles. There were a dozen others in the next 10 years, notably "Vaya con Dios" (Capitol #2486; 1953) which was on the charts 22 weeks. The couple also had a pair of best-selling LP albums, in 1955 and 1959, and appeared on television. Paul "retired" in the late 1960s, after divorcing Ford. He returned with two albums of duets with Chet Atkins made in the 1976 and 1978, and returned to a regular club gig in New York in 1984, which continued through the 1990s (and sporadically thereafter). Paul is also famous for designing one of the first solid-body electric guitars, which has been manufactured by the Gibson company since 1952. His contributions to popular music have recognized through his induction into the Rock and Roll Hall of Fame.

There are numerous CD issues of Paul's recordings, both new and old. *The Complete Decca Trios — Plus (1936–1947)* presents his complete output for that label, including unreleased material, along with tracks where he served as a backup musician (two-CD set; MCA #11708). *The Best of the Capitol Masters*

Les Paul and Mary Ford hits collection, c. late '50s. Courtesy Frank Hoffmann

(Capitol #99617) offers a sampling of his best recordings with Mary Paul made for that label between 1948–1957 (the complete sessions for Capitol are also available on a four-CD set [#97654]), while *16 Most Requested Songs* (Columbia #64993), similarly anthologizes their 1958–1961 recordings for Columbia.

PAVAROTTI, LUCIANO (12 OCT 1935–)

Italian tenor, born in Modena, Italy. He taught school and sold insurance while taking voice lessons, and made his debut in Reggio Emilia in 1961 as Rodolfo. His success was immediate, and soon he was singing in all the major houses of Europe. In 1968 he appeared at the Metropolitan Opera as Rodolfo; by then he was already recognized as one of the preeminent singers of the century. Pavarotti has recorded extensively, covering the Italian/French repertoire, most notably in complete Verdi operas for Decca with Joan Sutherland and in numerous recital records. By 1985 he had placed eight albums on the best-seller charts, all on the London label. He received Grammys for three albums (1978, 1979, 1988). The 1990 album *Carreras, Domingo, Pavarotti in Concert* (London #430433; with José Carreras and Placido Domingo) sold nearly 6 million copies. The trio continued to record and perform on occasion throughout the mid-1990s. In 1998, the Met held a gala concert to celebrate Pavarotti's 30th year of performing there. Pavarotti was scheduled to give a farewell performance at the Met in a complete opera in May 2002, but cancelled it (along with other planned appearances), at the last minute. A year later, a new "farewell" performance at the Met was announced to be given in March 2004 as the beginning of a farewell tour. [Pavarotti 1981 contains a complete discography up to time of this publication.]

PAYOLA SCANDAL OF THE 1950S

Payola — narrowly defined as payment (i.e., cash or gifts) for radio airplay — has been a radio fixture since the medium's inception. The practice flourished among disc jockeys playing Tin Pan Alley pop, country, R&B, and rock 'n' roll. Payola helped augment the income of a poorly paid profession; furthermore, it enabled the new music reach its intended audience, no matter how small the label on which it appeared. By the late 1950s, the proliferation of independent labels recording rock had broken the stranglehold of the majors — in particular, Columbia, RCA, and Decca — on the sales and airplay of popular records.

The American Society of Composers, Authors and Publishers (ASCAP) also had reason to be unhappy with the state of affairs at that time. The society had become a dominant force in the music business through its licensing agreements regarding the sales of sheet music, piano rolls, and the recordings of Tin Pan Alley songs for its membership. A battle between ASCAP and the radio stations — whose programming had become increasingly committed to airing recorded music during the latter 1930s and early 1940s — spurred the latter to boycott ASCAP material and establish their own publishing firm, Broadcast Music Inc. (BMI). ASCAP's history of ignoring Black and country music compositions, combined with the tendency of many radio stations to target regional tastes overlooked by the major networks (ABC, NBC, and CBS) enabled BMI to secure a near monopoly on this new music. The advent of rock 'n' roll, itself largely a product of the marriage of R&B and country, ensured the continued dominance of BMI within the youth music market.

Therefore, it appeared to be a case of protecting vested interests when ASCAP pushed for the House Legislative Oversight subcommittee to broaden its inquiry into corrupt broadcasting practices — centered up to 1959 on television quiz programs — to cover payola practices within radio. According to the perspective held by many within the record industry, the payola investigation would assist in stamping out rock 'n' roll — already reeling from the loss of many of its top stars and faced with an onslaught of media friendly teen idols — altogether.

The music business quickly closed ranks in the face of outside political interference. ABC-TV forced *American Bandstand* host Dick Clark to unload his holdings in other music-related activities, ranging from record companies to publishing houses. In response to Federal Trade Commission directives, a number of independent record labels and distributors filed consent orders agreeing to eliminate payola. Such moves enabled the industry to withstand formal House hearings in early 1960. Clark, whose deportment under interrogation was that of a model citizen, was not found guilty of directly engaging in payola practices.

On the other hand, Alan Freed, the disc jockey most clearly identified with the rise of rock 'n' roll, refused to testify despite an offer of immunity. A pariah within the field he'd helped so much to nurture, he was ultimately found guilty on two counts of commercial bribery. In the end, the committee recommended antipayola amendments to the Federal Communications Acts that prohibited the payment of cash or gifts in exchange for airplay, and required radio stations to police such activities. These amendments formally became law on 13 Sep 1960.

While the overall impact of the hearings remains unclear, it is clear that the general media circus surrounding them far overshadowed whatever concrete results might have taken place. The smaller independent labels had been forced to compete on more equal terms with the majors and their superior publicity and distribution networks. As a result, many of the former went out of business during the early 1960s. Nevertheless, new labels continued to surface — and sometimes achieve great success — in the upcoming years. Within a few years AM pop music stations had adopted strict playlists, most notably the Drake format, leaving free-form programming largely to the newly emerging FM disc jockeys.

Payola itself continued to be employed within the industry, giving rise to yet another scandal in the early 1970s centered around Columbia Records president Clive Davis and allegations of bribes involving money, sex, and drugs. Columnist Jack Anderson coined the term "drugola" to describe payments made in drugs to disc jockeys; although he wrote widely on the practice in the early 1970s, no one was actually indicted for the practice at the time.

Beginning in the 1980s, major labels hired outside "consultants" and marketing experts to promote their recordings to radio station program directors. In this way, they could disclaim any direct responsibility for utilizing gifts, drugs, or other forms of payment to influence radio placement. [Miller 1980.]

FRANK HOFFMANN

PCM (PULSE CODE MODULATION)

A conversion method used in recording, in which digital words in a bit stream (actually, amplitude pulses encoded onto magnetic tape or disc) represent samples of analog information. Invented by Alec Reeves in 1937, it remains the basis of most digital audio recording and playback systems.

See also **Compact Disc; Dat (Digital Audio Tape); Digital Recording**

HOWARD FERSTLER

PEACOCK (LABEL) (I)

A British record issued in the mid-1930s, through Peacock Stores. British Homophone and Decca/Panachord masters were used. Repertoire was light popular, and the artists were pseudonymous. Peacock Stores, Ltd., is in business today, but does not issue records. [Rust 1978.]

FRANK ANDREWS

PEACOCK (LABEL) (II)

Houston-based R&B label founded in 1949 by promoter/night club owner, Don Robey (1902-16 June 1975), one of the few African-Americans to own a label at this time. Peacock's first artist was Clarence "Gatemouth" Brown, who Robey managed.

Other early signings include Memphis Slim, Floyd Dixon, and "Big" Mama Thornton (her Peacock release of "That's Alright [Mama]" was later copied by Elvis Presley on his first Sun single). Robey also signed an impressive number of gospel artists, including The Dixie Hummingbirds and The Mighty Clouds of Joy. In 1952, the holdings of Nashville's Duke Records were merged with Peacock, and within a year Robey had full ownership of both labels. Robey continued to run the Duke/Peacock labels and subsidiaries through May 23, 1973, when the company's assets were sold to ABC-Dunhill (now part of the Universal Music Group).

CARL BENSON

PEAK

The maximum numerical value for any given event; in audio systems usually applied to the maximum instantaneous output (peak output) of a given component. Usually the peak is occasioned by a musical fortissimo.

PEARL (LABEL)

A British record of Pavilion Records, Ltd., distributed by Harmonia Mundi and H.R. Taylor, Ltd., in the U.K., by Koch International in the U.S., and by other distributors worldwide. The firm specializes in reissues, many from Columbia and HMV/Victor matrices. Important material by such artists as Enrico Caruso, Pablo Casals, Fritz Kreisler, and Artur Schnabel has appeared. CD transfers are widely acclaimed for their technical excellence. Flapper and Opal are associated labels.

PEARL JAM

Although not a particularly innovative band, Pearl Jam played a key role in popularizing the grunge experiments of Seattle acts such as Mudhoney and Soundgarden. Their early work was indispensable in transforming grunge into the alternative rock mainstream.

Pearl Jam evolved out of the various configurations put together by guitarist Stone Gossard and bassist Jeff Ament. Originally with the proto-grunge band, Green River, which pioneered a distortion-heavy blend of punk rock and heavy metal, they helped form Mother Love Bone. A tribute project arising out of the death of the group's lead vocalist, Andrew Wood, brought the twosome into contact with lead guitarist Mike McReady. The additions of vocalist Eddie Vedder and drummer Dave Abbruzzese in 1991 would complete Pearl Jam's lineup. The debut, *Ten* (Epic #47857; 1991; #2), instantly elevated the band to superstar status on the strength of melodic hard rock material penned by Gossard and Ament and the soulful singing of Vedder (who also contributed the song lyrics). Their success unwittingly spawned a school of lumbering, submetal imitators and, consequently, considerable criticism from the rock press. Pearl Jam's political activism for a wide range of causes — most notably, the support of concert taping and an aborted attempt to undercut Ticketmaster's monopoly on the arena concert circuit — and willingness to collaborate with rock legends such as the Doors (sans Jim Morrison), Bob Dylan, and Neil Young helped expand their steadfastly loyal fan base. Follow-up LPs — *Vs* (Epic #53136; 1993; #1), *Vitalogy* (Epic #66900; 1994; #1; originally released in vinyl only format), *No Code* (Epic #67500; 1996; #1), and *Yield* (Epic #68164; 1998; #2) — have veered little from the band's basic formula, revealing a commitment to social consciousness verve and power rock basics.

Always a major touring attraction — in this regard, their popularity has surpassed only a few dinosaurs such as the Grateful Dead and the Rolling Stones — fans had to search out Internet files and the underground exchange of bootleg tapes and CDs until the release of *Live on Two Legs* (Epic #69752; 1998; #15), which belied the conventional wisdom that concert recordings don't sell well. In recognition of the demand for live material in the commercial marketplace, the band issued a complete collection (48 songs in all) of their 2000 tour dates the following year; the

first series consisting of European venues, the second, their American concerts.

FRANK HOFFMANN

PEARLMAN, LOU (1955–)

Born in Queens, New York, Pearlman became a major promoter of teen pop bands in the late 1990s, launching groups the Backstreet Boys and 'N Sync, among others. A cousin of singer Art Garfunkel, Pearlman had dreams of being a rock guitarist as a teenager, but settled for a more prosaic business venture, leasing commercial aircraft and blimps; some of his clients included pop groups, including boy band phenomenon New Kids on the Block. Impressed by the size of their audience — and income — Pearlman decided to launch his own boy group. Because his business was located in Orlando, Florida, he had access to young performers who were attracted to the area by employment opportunities at Disney World. In 1995, he successfully launched the group the Backstreet Boys, carefully selecting the singers to appeal to teenage girls, the main consumers of this style of music. He followed the Boys with 'N Sync, another hugely successful act. In 2001, he appeared in the television program *Making the Band*, which documented his attempt to form a new boy group, called O-Town. Meanwhile, Pearlman was embroiled in lawsuits when his earlier discoveries balked at continuing working with him under the terms of their original contracts.

In the late 1990s, Pearlman formed a company, Trans Continental Entertainment, to promote his acts. In 2002, the company merged with Options Talent agency, which was itself the subject of significant controversy; its ex-clients, mostly young people who dreamed of careers as actors and models, claimed to have been ripped off by its staff who were eager to take their money, but did little to promote their careers. Late in 2002, the Archie Comic book group announced that it had hired Pearlman to form "real" groups under the Archies and Josie and the Pussycats names.

CARL BENSON

PEER, RALPH [SYLVESTER]
(22 MAY 1892–19 JAN 1960)

Born in Kansas City, Missouri, Peer was one of the first great producers of country music as well as the founder of Peer-Southern Music. Peer's father sold phonographs and had a link with the Columbia company, for whom Peer worked in his native Kansas City from 1911 to 1919. He was hired by a rival firm, the General Phonograph Co., in 1920 to run their Okeh division. His first job was to oversee the recordings of blues singer Mamie Smith, recording her "Crazy Blues" in 1920, said to be the first blues recording by a Black singer. In 1923, he was contacted by an Atlanta furniture dealer who wanted him to record a local fiddler named Fiddlin' John Carson. The resulting record is generally credited as the first successful country music recording.

In 1925, Peer moved to Victor records, who offered him a unique arrangement: instead of paying him a salary, they gave him the publishing rights to any of the material he recorded. In 1928 Victor and Peer cofounded Southern Music, which became a leading publisher of blues and country material. In the summer of 1927, Peer made a field trip to Bristol, Tennessee, which has become legendary in recording circles. He "discovered" at this session both Jimmie Rodgers and the Carter Family, overseeing their first recordings. His music publishing arm would naturally become the outlet for both of these acts' prolific compositions.

In 1932, foreseeing the change in musical tastes, Peer branched out in his publishing business to sign popular songsmiths like Hoagy Carmichael, while he also explored the international market. He was central in the founding of Broadcast Music, Inc. (or BMI) in 1940, which challenged the more conservative ASCAP (American Society of Composers, Artists, and Performers) in its dominance of the music licensing field. In the later 1940s and 1950s, Peer left the day-to-day operations of his company increasingly to his son, while he pursued a lifelong interest in raising camelias.

CARL BENSON

PEERCE, JAN (3 JUNE 1904–15 DEC 1984)

American tenor, born Jacob Pincus Perelmuth in New York. He played violin and sang with dance bands in New York, and appeared in Radio City Music Hall from 1933 to 1941. He made his opera debut in Philadelphia, as the Duke, in 1938. His Metropolitan Opera career extended form 1941 to 1968. Arturo Toscanini chose him to sing in the NBC broadcast of the Beethoven Ninth Symphony in 1938; Toscanini referred to Peerce as his "favorite tenor." Peerce appeared with major opera companies and in recital worldwide. He suffered a stroke in 1982, and died in New York two years later.

It is uncertain whether Peerce is the unidentified singer on Grey Gull disc 1505 of ca. 1927: "My Ohio Home"/"There Never Was a Gal Like My Daddy's Gal." His first definite recordings were under the names Pinkie, Pinky, or Jack Pearl, for the Perfect label in 1931. (Another pseudonym used was Randolph Joyce.) He was then heard on various labels,

singing the light repertoire and operatic numbers. "Bluebird of Happiness" was a favorite with his fans (W.B. transcription 500-622; ca. 1934; it was first issued under the pseudonym Paul Robinson). He recorded the Toscanini-Beethoven symphony cited above in 1938 for ATRA (#3007). Peerce made 24 LP albums. He died in New York City. [Pinta 1987.]

PEERLESS (LABEL)

An American record, pressed by the Starr Piano Co. from Gennett masters. Only a few issues are known, from 1922. [Rust 1978.]

PEERLESS ORCHESTRA

An ensemble that recorded about 150 numbers for Edison cylinders before 1912. It also made many records, from overtures to ragtime, for Zonophone in Britain, in 1910–1922. [Koenigsberg 1987.]

PEERLESS PHONOGRAPH CO.

A New York firm, established in 1915 to handle Pathé products. Ben H. Janssen was president.

PEERLESS QUARTET

A male vocal ensemble active from 1906 to 1928. It was organized by Frank C. Stanley, who sang bass until his death in December 1910. The other members were Albert Campbell, tenor; Henry Burr, lead tenor; and Steve Porter, baritone. In 1910 Burr became manager, John H. Meyers took the bass line (also acting as arranger), and Arthur Collins replaced Porter as baritone. Having begun as an offshoot of the Columbia Quartet (which came from the Invincible Quartet or Invincible Four), they retained that name for Columbia records until 1912, when they became the Peerless on that label also. They made thousands of records for all labels, including eight Edison cylinders in 1909–1910, four Edison Diamond Discs in 1914–1915, and a great quantity of discs for Victor (125 titles in the 1917 catalog), with whom they signed as exclusive artists in 1920.

In 1917 the members were Campbell, Burr, Meyers, and Frank Croxton; this was the peak period for the group. Another personnel change took place in 1926, as Carl Mathieu replaced Campbell, Stanley Baughman replaced Meyers, and James Stanley replaced Croxton; this left Henry Burr as the only original member to remain with the quartet until it disbanded, in 1928. Their final Victor was made on 11 Sept 1927: "Old Names of Old Flames" (#21079). In 1940 Victor still carried nine of their sides in the catalog, including

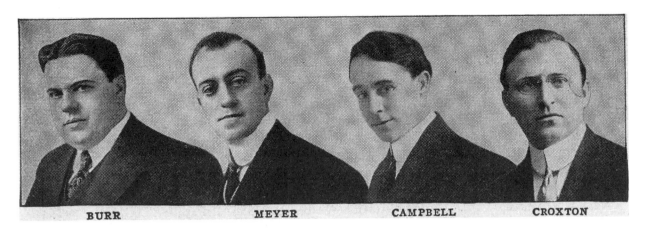

BURR   MEYER   CAMPBELL   CROXTON

The Peerless Quartet in the 1917 Victor catalog. Courtesy Jerald Kalstein

"Darling Nellie Gray" (#19887) and the ever popular "Sweet Adeline" (#20055). [Walsh 1969/12.]

PEERLESS RECORD (LABEL)

An American disc supplied by Leeds & Catlin in the first decade of the century. It was a double-sided record, 10-inch size.

FRANK ANDREWS

PEERLESS TRIO

A male vocal ensemble that recorded for Indestructible Records in 1907–1908, and for Victor. Members were Billy Murray, Byron C. Harlan, and Steve Porter. They were known as the Victor Vaudeville Co. on Victor discs, of which there were three in the 1917 catalog, two 10-inch and one 12-inch ("Court Scene in Carolina"/"Darktown Campmeetin' Experiences"; #35609).

PELLOWE, JOHN (21 SEP 1955–)

With an educational background mainly involving telecommunications, Pellowe joined Decca Records in 1974, and trained for a recording engineer career under the direction of one of the great engineering masters, Kenneth Wilkinson. He started recording and mixing session tapes in 1978, and went on to develop a successful partnership with James Lock, who had succeeded Wilkinson as chief engineer at Decca. In addition to working with opera and classical music, Pellowe also has mixed a number of pop-music albums, and has become adept at mixing multichannel surround sound.

In addition to his recording and mixing work, Pellowe started engineering for live-sound production with Luciano Pavarotti's concerts in 1986, and as a live-concert engineer he has mixed the "front of house"

sound for over 200 concerts in some of the world's largest and most prestigious venues. He now has over 180 albums to his credit, including recording, live broadcast, and postproduction work done on the 1990, 1994, and 1998 Three Tenors World Cup albums from Rome, Los Angeles, and Paris. Pellowe has recorded a substantial number of Grammy-nominated albums, with many of them winning, including his 1992 recording of Richard Strauss's *Die Frau Ohne Schatten* effort, which gained him a Grammy for engineering.

HOWARD FERSTLER

PENNINGTON (LABEL)

An American record issued by the Bridgeport Die and Machine Co. in 1924 and 1925, marketed by the L. Bamberger & Co. department stores. Masters came mostly from Paramount, Emerson, Olympic, and Blu-Disc. Releases ceased when Bridgeport Die and Machine went bankrupt in 1925. [Kendziora 1991/1; Rust 1978.]

PENTANGLE

Pentangle was widely perceived as being later than the British folk-rock movement of the latter half of the 1960s. However, the group was far more eclectic than the leading exponents of the genre — most notably, Fairport Convention, Steeleye Span, and Lindisfarne — with a recorded repertoire that spanned jazz, blues, Indian ragas, traditional English folk music, and self-penned pop-rock material.

This eclecticism was largely the result of the diversified backgrounds of the group members. Pentangle's music featured the interplay of two acoustic guitar virtuosos, Bert Jansch and John Renbourne. Jacqui McShee's unadorned vocals possessed a crystalline purity that effectively conveyed the emotional depth of traditional folk ballads; the fact that Jansch and Renbourne were also very capable singers made possible the inclusion of additional colors and textures. Bassist Danny Thompson and drummer Terry Cox provided a jazz-inflected underbelly to the overall group synergy. The dynamic blend of these sometimes disparate elements in *The Pentangle* (Reprise #6315; 1968; #21 U.K., #192 U.S.) opened a new direction for the U.K. folk scene.

Although later releases failed to measure up to the promise of the debut LP, Pentangle's sheer musicality and inherent good taste ultimately redeem them all. The double album, *Sweet Child* (Reprise #6334; 1969), employs a half-studio/half-live format. The solo segments provide insights into the individual contributions of each member. The jazzy, improvisational feel of these early works is largely absent from *Basket of Light* (Reprise #6372; 1970; #5 U.K., #200 U.S.); a more standardized folk-rock approach tends to dominate most of the tracks.

The group's best-known recording, *Cruel Sister* (Reprise #6430; 1970; #51 U.K., #193 U.S.), revealed the encroachment of progressive rock values. Side two of the original disc consisted of an extended suitelike treatment of the traditional ballad, "Jack Orion." Despite fine musicianship and the use of varied instrumentation (including wind instruments and muted electric guitars), the critical consensus held that the piece failed to sustain interest. Later albums — *Reflection* (Reprise #6463; 1971; #183), *Solomon's Seal* (Reprise #2100; 1972; #184), and *Pentangling* (Transatlantic #29; 1973; compilation of earlier material; not issued in U.S. until 1977) — saw the group revert to a more predictable song set format. Although more original material began to appear, most of it lacked the distinctiveness of the classic folk material.

Since Pentangle's breakup in 1973, individual members remained active in the music business. Jansch and Renbourne, in particular, issued a considerable number of critically acclaimed solo albums. The original group members got back together to record *Open the Door* (Varrick #017; 1985). Jansch and McShee — along with a shifting lineup of supporting players — kept Pentangle going until the mid-1990s. McShee has continued to use the name within the context of what is essentially a solo career.

FRANK HOFFMANN

PERCUSSION INSTRUMENT RECORDINGS (HISTORIC)

The only known drum solo on acoustic records is "Ragtime Drummer," played by James I. Lent. It was issued on G & T, and on Victor (#17092), Indestructible Cylinders (#689), and Emerson (#779), in 1904.

PERFECT (LABEL)

An American record issued by Pathé (but shown as coming from the Perfect Record Co., Brooklyn) from sometime between July and September 1922; the final releases were in April 1938, when the label belonged to the American Record Corp., which had taken over Pathé Frères Phonograph Co, Inc. in 1929. Much of the early output (until 1929) corresponded to the material on Pathé's Actuelle label. Perfect was a low-price record, selling for $0.50 at first, then dropping as low as $0.25; the regular price of standard labels in the 1920s was $0.75. Like other cut-rate labels from major companies, Perfect kept its artist names secret, using pseudonyms. Thus the California Ramblers appeared as the Golden Gate Orchestra, Fletcher Henderson as the Lenox Dance Orchestra or the Southampton Society Orchestra, etc. Some real names were given in the later years of the label.

Series issued on Perfect were race, standard vocal and standard instrumental, opera-classical, star series, popular vocal, and dance music. Discs were made at Pathé's New York studio. The label itself had several designs, of which the most striking featured two nude women apparently worshipping a perfect sunrise.

In the U.K. (1928) the Perfect label was an outwardly Pathé product, using mostly American Pathé matrices. It terminated with the takeover of Pathé in Europe by Columbia (International), Ltd. [Kendziora 1963/5–6 is a label list of the dance and race series; Rust 1978.]

FRANK ANDREWS

Perfect label. Courtesy David A. Jasen

PERFORMANCE RIGHTS

In January 1851, the Société des Auteurs, Compositeurs et Editeurs de Musique (SACEM) was established in Paris to work for the recognition of rights and to assist in the prosecution of infringers. Similar organizations were founded in other countries. France had the first laws (1905) to protect the producers of recordings against unwarranted reproductions. The Société demanded royalties on all records sold, and despite some setbacks, like the 1906 decision in Belgium against copyright holders, the movement took hold. In Italy in 1906 a composer society won a suit for royalties on record sales. In the U.S. the Copyright Act of 1909 included coverage of recordings, calling for a $0.02 royalty. These became known as "mechanical rights," while performance rights was defined as any "public performance," including live or broadcast performances. The major publishers' associations enforcing these rights in the U.S. are ASCAP (American Society of Composers, Artists, and Performers), founded in 1914 (which employs the Harry Fox Agency to represent its member publishers for mechanical rights), and BMI, a rival organization that arose in 1940. The American Mechanical Rights Association (AMRA) is one among several agencies that represents publishers, composers, and record companies in licensing mechanical rights.

See also **Copyright; Sound Recording Periodicals**

PERLMAN, ITZHAK (31 AUG 1945–)

Born in Israel, Perlman contracted polio at age four, leaving his legs paralyzed. Nonetheless, he became a prodigy on the violin, "discovered" by television personality Ed Sullivan who presented him on his popular Sunday night variety show in 1959, which brought him to New York. Perlman subsequently studied at Julliard and made his American professional debut in 1963. He has become one of the most popular performing and recording violinists in the world, playing not only classical, but also jazz, ragtime, pop, and Klezmer music. He has also become well known through his many appearances on PBS as a performer and host. In 1986 he was awarded the U.S. Medal of Freedom. He has primarily recorded for Columbia/Sony Classical and Angel. Among his more popular recordings are 1981's *A Different Kind of Blues* (Angel #37780), a collaboration with pianist/composer Andre Previn, his foray into playing Klezmer music, titled *In the Fiddler's House* (Angel #55555; 1995), and collaborations with John Williams on a series of albums of popular film scores.

PERKINS, CARL
(9 APR 1932–19 JAN 1998)

Although he had comparatively few hit recordings, Carl Perkins is regarded to be one of the trailblazers of rock 'n' roll. Perkins's reputation is built largely on his songwriting skills; however, it is also a product of a lengthy career as a performer and recording artist.

Born to a sharecropping family in Tiptonville, Tennessee, Perkins was one of the many young rockabilly performers (others included Johnny Cash, Roy Orbison, Jerry Lee Lewis, Billy Lee Riley, and Charlie Rich) drawn to Sam Phillips's Sun Records studio following Elvis Presley's early success there. Playing a dance one night, Perkins was inspired by the sight of a young man's pride in his footwear to write the song, "Blue Suede Shoes" (Sun #234). Recorded 19 Dec 1955, the song rose high on the pop (number two), country (number one), and R&B (number 2) charts early the following year. However, a serious car crash en route to appear on television's *Perry Como Show* in late March 1956 sidelined him for many months, significantly dampening his career momentum.

When recovered, Perkins creased the charts a few more times with "Boppin' the Blues" (Sun #243; 1956; #7 C&W, #60 pop), "Dixie Fried" (Sun #249; 1956; #10 C&W), "Your True Love" (Sun #261; 195; #13 C&W, #67 pop), "Pink Pedal Pushers" (Columbia #41131; 1958; #17 C&W, #91 pop), and "Pointed Toe Shoes" (Columbia; 1959). When the hits stopped, he continued performing live; an English tour in 1963 spurred the Beatles to record three songs from his repertoire: "Everybody's Trying to Be My Baby," "Honey Don't," and "Matchbox." After overcoming chronic drug and alcohol abuse, he played with Johnny Cash's road show for 10 years beginning in the mid-1960s. His solo spots on Cash's 1969–1971 network television run led to another Columbia recording contract. Two album releases — *On Top* (Columbia #9931; 1969) and *Boppin' the Blues* (with NRBQ; Columbia #9981; 1970) were modest sellers in the rock market — while nine of his singles made the country charts between 1966–1987 (for the Dollie, Columbia, Mercury, and America labels).

In 1976, Perkins formed his own band, the C.P. Express, featuring sons Stan on drums and Greg on bass guitar. By the late 1980s, they were calling themselves the Imarocker band (augmented by sax great Ace Cannon). Although he would record new material on occasion, much of it tended to be imbued with nostalgia, including *Ol' Blue Suede's Back* (Jet #208; 1978) — comprised of updated country-rock versions of classic 1950s songs, it sold more than 100,000 copies in England — and *The Class of '55* (American #83002; 1985), which also featured Cash, Lewis, and Orbison augmented by admirers such as John Fogerty and Rick Nelson. These releases, however, were overwhelmed by the glut of reissues devoted to his Sun tracks, including *Lil' Bit of Gold* (Rhino #373015; 1988), *The Carl Perkins CD Box Set* (Charly #2; 1990), and *The Classic Carl Perkins* (Bear Family #15494; 1990).

Perkins received many tributes during the later years of his life, most notably induction into the Rock and Roll Hall of Fame in 1987. An authorized biography, David McGee's *Go, Cat, Go! The Life and Times of Carl Perkins, the King of Rockabilly*, appeared in 1994.

FRANK HOFFMANN

PERLS, NICK (4 APR 1942–22 JULY 1987)

Devoting his professional life to the preservation, promotion, and distribution of blues from the 1920s and 1930s, Nick Perls founded Yazoo Records in the late 1960s primarily to re-release out-of-print recordings. The work of singers and guitarists such as Charlie Patton, Blind Willie McTell, Memphis Jug Band, Blind Blake, and Blind Lemon Jefferson was reborn on Yazoo. While a catalog heavy with 40-year-old rarities is not bound for high profits, Perls operated from the safety net of a prosperous family (owner of the Perls art gallery in New York), and thus could indulge his musical passions with light regard for the bottom line. Perls was noted for his skill in remastering often worn copies of scarce 78-rpm recordings, and his label distinguished itself for the quality of its sound reproduction, excellent liner notes, and creative packaging. In 1973, he founded the associated Blue Goose label to release new recordings of blues and ragtime performers, including Larry Johnson, R. Crumb and His Cheap Suit Serenaders, and David A. Jasen. After Perls's death at age 45, Yazoo was acquired by the slightly more mainstream label Shanachie Records.

BRAD HILL

PERMANENT NEEDLE SALES CO.

A Chicago firm, active around 1910. Advertising in *TMW* offered the first permanent jewel disc needle, which required no changing and no sharpening. It was available in loud, medium, and soft volume designs.

PERRY, LEE "SCRATCH" (28 MAR 1936–)

Influential dub producer and performer Perry was born Rainford Hugh Perry in Hanover, Jamaica. Perry got his first experience as a producer/talent scout working for legendary Jamaican ska producer Coxsone Dodd in the late 1950s and early 1960s. Dodd operated a record shop/label in Kingston, and was revolutionary in producing Jamaican acts. Perry produced sessions for various acts and also released recordings under his own name, introducing his characteristic combination of social/political commentary, personal attacks, and lewd, sometimes bawdy lyrics (forecasting the major concerns of rap music some 25 years before the style became popular).

In 1966, Perry broke free of Coxsone and began working on his own; two years later, he established Upsetter Records as an outlet for the many acts he produced and his own recordings. (He also took the nickname "The Upsetter" from a song he released that year.) A deal with the U.K. Trojan label for distribution in England led to several U.K. hits, beginning with the campy instrumental "Return of Django" in 1969. Through 1974 when the label folded, Perry oversaw sessions by many major Jamaican performers, most notably the early sessions of Bob Marley and the Wailers. He also first worked with legendary mixer/producer Osbourne "King Tubby" Ruddock during this period, who would be a great influence on his subsequent productions.

In 1974, Perry set up his own studio called Black Ark. There he began early experiments with sampling, using complex mixes of sound effects, echoes, snatches of dialogue recorded from television, baby's cries, and other effects in his mixes. Meanwhile, Perry's behavior became increasingly erratic, culminating in his setting fire to his own studio in 1980. Over the next two decades, he made sporadic recordings, featuring his own stream-of-consciousness lyrics, eventually settling in Switzerland where he married a wealthy heiress. Meanwhile, his early recordings have become legendary as prime examples of the dub style.

PERRY, RICHARD (18 JUNE 1942–)

Influential pop producer of the 1970s and 1980s, Perry was born in Brooklyn, New York, and began singing as a teenager with a local group known as the Legends. He began experimenting with songwriting and also picked up some production work with Leiber and Stoller's Red Bird label and Kama Sutra. He moved to Los Angeles in 1967, where he produced Captain Beefheart's first album, and then was hired as a staff producer for Warner Bros., where he oversaw sessions by a wide variety of artists, including Tiny Tim, Ella Fitzgerald, and Theodore Bikel. His "big break" came when Columbia Records asked him to produce Barbra Streisand's first rock-flavored album, 1970's *Stoney End*. He scored a major hit in 1972 with Carly Simon on her number-one smash, "You're So Vain," and then worked with Ringo Starr on his 1973 "comeback" album, *Ringo*, producing the number-one hit, "You're Sixteen"; he continued to work with Starr through much of the 1970s. In 1978, he found his own label, Planet Records, which five years later he sold to RCA. His big signing for the label was the Pointer Sisters, whose career he revitalized through a series of hits beginning with 1978's "Fire" (number-two pop). However, the Pointers career faded after the mid-1980s, as did Perry's.

PERSONICS
The practice of making customized tapes for clients.

PERSPECTA SOUND
The system premiered with the movie *White Christmas*, in 1954, as part of Paramount's VistaVision, horizontal 35mm widescreen format. Perspecta Sound employed a single, conventional monophonic soundtrack, onto which were encoded subaudible control signals. Tones of 30, 35, and 40 Hz were detected by an integrator unit connected to the projector's sound head and used to turn up the gain on center, left-, and right-hand speaker channels. Although this did not provide true stereo, it did create directional effects, with the additional advantage that mixing for Perspecta was considerably quicker than mixing for a CinemaScope magnetic soundtrack, because it only required that the sound to be panned between the three channels to follow the action on screen.

HOWARD FERSTLER

PERTILE, AURELIANO (9 NOV 1885–11 JAN 1952)
Italian tenor, born in Montagnana, Italy. He made his debut in *Martha* in Vicenza in 1911, sang in various Italian houses, and appeared at La Scala in 1916. His one season at the Metropolitan was 1921–1922, after which he settled at La Scala until 1937. He performed the Italian/French dramatic tenor repertoire, plus Lohengrin, and was acknowledged to be among the finest interpreters of his time. He died in Milan.

Pertile recorded for Pathé in Milan in 1923–1926, beginning with "Donna non vidi mai" from *Manon Lescaut* (#10371). "Cielo e mar" (#74949), and "Una vergine" from *Favorita* (#10411) were outstanding among these early numbers. Later he went to Fonotipia (1927), Columbia (1927–1931), and HMV (1928–1932). "Quando le sere" from *Luisa Miller* (HMV DB #1111; 1928) was one of his highly praised early electrics. He was heard in the complete recordings of *Aida* and *Carmen*. There were many LP reissues, and a CD of 1990 carried material from HMV, including the above-cited arias (the Pathés in

later re-recordings), from the 1928–1932 period. Historic recordings by Pertile have been reissued by Pearl (#9209, #9229) and in Italy on Clama CD (#23), *The Voice and Art*. [Morby 1952 is a complete discography.]

PETER, PAUL, AND MARY
An American folk-styled pop group, consisting of Peter Yarrow, Noel Paul Stookey, and Mary Ellin Travers. They began to perform together in New York in 1962, and were successful on a national tour. Having signed a Warner label contract, their debut album remained on the charts for two years, *Peter, Paul and Mary* (Warner W #1449; 1962), and followed it a few months later with *Movin'* (Warner W #1473; 1963); it remained on the charts for 76 weeks.

Their outstanding singles of the period were Grammy-award–winning "Blowin' in the Wind" (Warner #5268; 1963), and "Puff the Magic Dragon" — written by Yarrow — (Warner #5348; 1963). "Leaving on a Jet Plane" (Warner #7340; 1969) was one of the many later hit singles by the group. They appeared on major television shows in the 1960s and also in clubs and in concert. In the 1970s they were less active, but made one more chart album, *Reunion* (Warner BSK #3212; 1978). Several "reunion" tours, television specials, and recordings have appeared since the early 1980s.

PETERSON, OSCAR (15 AUG 1925–)
Canadian jazz pianist, born in Montreal, Canada. He performed on Canadian radio, then went to New York in 1949. He gained a reputation as a soloist and for his tasteful accompaniments; and formed an outstanding trio, with Ray Brown, bass, and Herb Ellis, guitar; in 1958 replacing Ellis with a drummer, Ed Thigpen. Norman Granz championed Peterson during the 1950s, releasing many albums of his work on his Verve label. The biggest hit of the trio's many albums came in the early 1960s, *Oscar Peterson Trio + 1* (Mercury #20975; 1964). Brown and Thigpen left in 1965. (In 1990 the original threesome came back together, and recorded *The Legendary Oscar Peterson Trio* for the Telarc Jazz label.) In 1972, Granz signed Peterson to his new Pablo label, and recorded the pianist extensively through the 1980s. In 1988, he signed with Telarc Jazz, a division of the classical music label. A stroke in 1993 put him out of action for two years, but he has since returned to recording and performing, although he no longer has the same command of the keyboards that he once did.

REV. CARL BENSON

PETMECKY CO.

A firm located in Kansas City, Missouri, and in 1907 in New York. They manufactured MultiTone needles, which played loudly or softly depending on their placement in the reproducer. Petmecky needles were claimed to "improve the record."

PETMECKY SUPPLY CO., INC.

A Texas firm, incorporated in Austin in December 1909, licensed to distribute Victor products in Texas and Oklahoma. Fred Petmecky was president; B.F. Reeves was vice president and general manager.

PETTY, NORMAN
(25 MAY 1927–15 AUG 1984)

Born in Clovis, New Mexico, Petty was a musician who became the owner/operator of an important recording studio. After serving in World War II, Petty worked as a radio announcer in Clovis, and then in 1948 formed a trio with his wife as vocalist, himself on piano, and a guitarist, which achieved some success in the early 1950s through mid-1950s. He opened his own studio, NorVaJak, in the mid-1950s to record his group, and soon began offering his services to outside clients. His recording of Buddy Knox's "Party Doll" was a major hit when he leased it to Roulette Records in 1957 (Roulette #4002; #1 pop). His most famous client was Buddy Holly; Petty became Holly's manager as well as producer, and took co-songwriting credit on several of Holly's hits. After Holly's death, work slowed for Petty, although he oversaw a few more pop hits in the early 1960s and also continued to rework his Holly recordings to create new versions for release. In the early 1970s, he sold his publishing rights to Holly's songs to Paul McCartney's MPL company. Petty died in Lubbock, Texas, from leukemia.

CARL BENSON

PETTY, TOM (20 OCT 1953–)

Petty is a rarity: a pop artist confident enough to work within a style without worrying about commercial success. His platform has always been meat-and-potatoes, FM-radio friendly rock. What separates Petty from many of the genre's practitioners — besides career longevity — is his refined sense of songcraft, intelligent lyrics, and distinctive (thin and reedy, yet passionately soulful) vocals.

Emerging at the height of the progressive rock vogue exemplified by the likes of Pink Floyd and King Crimson, Gainesville, Florida–native Petty favored a sound directly descendant from 1960s garage bands

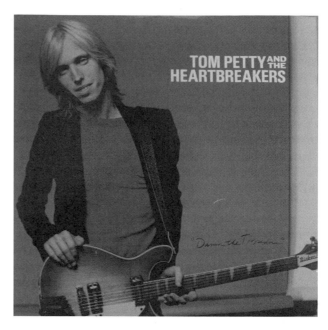

Tom Petty on the *Damn the Torpedos* album cover. Courtesy Frank Hoffmann

leavened with Byrds-influenced folk rock. After obtaining a contract from Shelter in the mid-1970s, he and his band — the Mudcrutches — struggled in the studio. Taking time to regroup, Petty and a new backing ensemble — consisting of keyboardist Benmont Tench, lead guitarist Mike Campbell, bassist/cellist Ron Blair, and drummer/keyboardist Stan Lynch — recorded *Tom Petty and the Heartbreakers* (Shelter #52006; 1976; #55). While the lack of label support hurt sales in the U.S., favorable reviews (the U.K. music magazine *Sounds* named them Best New American Band) and a 1977 U.K. tour propelled the LP to number 24 in the U.K. Band momentum was further facilitated by the release of *You're Gonna Get It* (Shelter #52029; 1977; #23), and by late 1978 both albums were certified gold.

MCA's purchase of Shelter's distributor, ABC, led to protracted litigation regarding Petty's contractual status. When MCA finally agreed to let the band record for another subsidiary label, the richly textured *Damn the Torpedoes* (Backstreet #5105; 1979; #2) — which had been financed largely by Petty himself — was released to virtually universal acclaim. However, by 1981, Petty was back in court due to MCA's stated intention of charging $9.98 (rather than the normal $8.98) for the next LP, *Hard Promises* (Backstreet #5160; 1981; #5). Petty justified his stance in the 1 Feb 1981 issue of the *Los Angeles Times*: "It's just not fair to the kids who buy records. It all comes down to greed — MCA doesn't need a new [office] tower. And if we don't take a stand, one of these days records are going to be $20."

Hard Promises and the band's fifth album, *Long After Dark* (Backstreet #5360; 1982; #9), continued to mine familiar territory with great success. However, Petty, feeling the need to map out new directions, took more than two years off while band members engaged themselves in outside projects. The resulting release, *Southern Accents* (Backstreet #5486; 1985; #7), focused on his regional roots, augmented by the liberal use of horns and a female chorus. The promotional video for the track, "Don't Come Around Here No More" (Backstreet #52496; 1985; #13), also attracted considerable attention, winning the MTV award for Best Special Effects and the Grand Prix for Best Video Clip at the Montreaux Golden Rose Television Festival. *Pack Up the Plantation* (Backstreet #8021; 1985; #22), the band's first live LP (also issued in various video configurations), retained the gospel/R&B touches of *Southern Accents*, even in the performance of older material.

Petty began expending more and more of his creative energy collaborating with other artists. After touring with Bob Dylan in 1986, he recorded an album, *Traveling Wilburys Volume 1* (Warner Bros. #25796; 1988; #3), with Dylan, George Harrison, Roy Orbison, and Jeff Lynne; its success inspired a follow-up (sans the deceased Orbison), *Volume 3* (Warner Bros. #26324; 1990; #11). He issued a couple of highly regarded solo LPs — *Full Moon Fever* (MCA #6253; 1989; #3) and *Wildflowers* (Warner Bros. #45792; 1994; #8) — both of which revealed greater stylistic diversity than his work with the Heartbreakers, ranging from acoustic-flavored ballads to no depression-influenced roots rockers. He also joined with the Heartbreakers to provide the backup to Johnny Cash's *Unchained* (American #39742; 1996). Through all this, Petty and the band released first-rate albums at periodic intervals, including *Let Me Up (I've Had Enough)* (Backstreet #5836; 1987; #20), *Into the Great Wide Open* (MCA #10317; 1991; #13), *Playback* (MCA #611375; 1995; a six-CD anthology including many previously unreleased tracks), *She's the One* (Warner Bros. #46285; 1996; #15; film soundtrack), and *Echo* (Warner Bros. #47294; 1999; #10).

FRANK HOFFMANN

PHANTASIE CONCERT RECORD (LABEL)

A rare American record of 1921, and perhaps early 1922. Material (dance, blues, and novelty items) came from Lyric, Olympic, or Criterion. Issues by a singer named Josephine Baker were not by the famous artist of that name. [Kendziora 1984/6; Rust 1978.]

Rare label of the early '20s. Courtesy Kurt Nauck/Nauck's Vintage Records

PHANTOM CENTER IMAGE

With traditional two-channel, stereophonic sound reproduction, this involves the ability of a pair of speakers to simulate a real performer in the middle of the array. A proper phantom image requires that the listener be located out in front of the speakers, and equidistant from both, and a good recording should be able to create additional phantom images all the way across the soundstage. Aside from the need for a sweet spot listening position, a major problem with a phantom image with two-channel stereo is that the center image is formed by four arrival clues: one for each ear from each of the two speakers. What's more, two of those clues are delayed in time, because the ears are not equidistant from each speaker. A true center channel, such as what exists not only with DSP steering systems, but also with Dolby Digital, DTS, SACD, and DVD-A (at least potentially, since not all engineers take full advantage of the technologies), overcomes this problem. It can do so because it simulates a genuine performer at center stage, with the image being formed by only two arrival clues: one from the centered source for each ear.

See also **Center Channel; Head-Related Transfer Function (HRTF)**

HOWARD FERSTLER

PHASE INVERTER

A circuit in an amplifier that derives the opposing voltage polarity required to drive the push-pull output stage.

PHASE LINEAR CORP.

Founded by Bob Carver in 1970, the company's first product was the Model 700, a power amplifier that offered unprecedented power and value for money. Along with his financial backers, Carver set up a small factory behind a grocery store in Edmonds, Washington. There the product line grew to include the Model 400 power amplifier and the remarkable Model 4000 preamplifier. In 1974, a new factory was built in nearby Lynnwood. The company continued to prosper, and its success and growth led to the introduction of other amplifiers, pre-amps, speakers, and an FM tuner.

Carver left the company in 1977 (moving on to begin Carver Corp. and still later on Sunfire), and Phase Linear was sold to Pioneer Electronics in 1979. Pioneer then marketed a high-end turntable, cassette deck, digital synthesized tuner, and speakers under the Phase Linear name. Pioneer sold the company to International Jensen in 1982, and P-L manufacturing was moved to Laredo, Texas, in December of that same year. The company continued to build products there through 1983. However, the venture was not altogether successful. Production ceased and Jensen put the Phase Linear name on a range of high-end car stereo components. Recoton Corporation acquired the Phase Linear brand when they acquired International Jensen in 1996.

HOWARD FERSTLER

PHASE SHIFT

A distortion in an audio system produced when signals, originally simultaneous, are heard with a small delay between them. This delay, often occasioned by ultrasonic filters in modern systems, may be as tiny as a thousandth of a second, but it will result in a mismatch of the signal peaks. If the signal peaks are at exact opposite stages of their cycles, they are 180 degrees out of phase and cancel each other out. Out-of-phase program material is a particular problem in stereo playback, as it may cause loudspeakers to vibrate out of step with each other. However, some out-of-phase programming is fundamental to the stereo effect: when signals are separately reproduced through different loudspeakers it is phase shift (at very low frequencies) that suggests to the listener that the sound is coming from somewhere between the two speakers. It seems that among audio components it is the loudspeakers that have the potential to create sufficient phase shift to be audible.

See also **Phasing (I); Phasing Switch**

PHASING (I)

The correlation between cone movement in one loudspeaker with respect to that in another loudspeaker.

See also **Phase Shift; Phasing Switch**

PHASING (II)

A special effect obtained in the sound studio by dividing a signal between two tape machines or networks, and subjecting one to a minuscule time delay.

See also **Flanging**

PHASING SWITCH

A control on an amplifier, also known as the phase reversal switch, that reverses the leads to one loudspeaker, thereby changing its relative phase.

See also **Phase Shift**

PHILADELPHIA INTERNATIONAL (LABEL)

R&B/soul label founded in Philadelphia by noted producers (Kenny) Gamble and (Leon) Huff in 1971, in association with Columbia Records, who marketed and distributed their product. Their artists included the O'Jays, Harold Melvin and the Blue Notes, the Spinners, and the Stylistics. They scored big in 1974 when they released Van McCoy's "The Hustle" on their Avco label #4653; (#1 pop & R&B) essentially launching the craze for disco music. The producers formed a house band that helped them achieve a signature sound on their recordings, much as Motown had done in the 1960s. Dogged by accusations of participating payola and other illegal activities, the label struggled in the later 1970s. In the early 1980s, the label had stars Patti LaBelle and Teddy Pendergrass, but had difficulty keeping up with new trends in popular music, and the label folded by mid-decade. In 2002, Sony/Legacy announced a series of reissues under the *Philly Soul Classics* name drawing on the label's recordings.

CARL BENSON

PHILADELPHIA ORCHESTRA

An ensemble established in 1900, succeeding an amateur orchestra that had played under the conductor W.W. Gilchrist. Fritz Scheel was the director until he died in 1907. Carl Pohlig headed the orchestra until 1912, when he resigned and was succeeded by Leopold Stokowski. Under Stokowski the resonant, glowing "Philadelphia sound" was developed, and with it world eminence. Eugene Ormandy was conductor from 1938 to 1980, further perfecting the ensemble timbre, when Riccardo Muti took the podium. Muti's resignation, effective in 1992, brought an unexpected successor in Wolfgang Sawallisch. Sawallisch remained at the helm through winter 2003; he is planned to be succeeded in fall 2003 by Chrisoph Eschenbach, and will become conductor laureate.

The orchestra made its first Victor records in 1917, and became a mainstay of the label. By the time of the 1940 catalog there were about 360 titles recorded. A number of events in recording history were centered on the orchestra. Victor's first orchestral electric recording was "Danse Macabre" (#6505; 1925). And Victor's 1931 initiative with long-playing records included the Philadelphians playing the first complete symphony for LP (albeit 78 rpm, not microgroove 33 1/3), Beethoven's Fifth. In 1932 Bell Laboratories conducted experiments in the Academy of Music, leading to recording the orchestra under Stokowski with two microphones; the signals were etched into parallel grooves on 78-rpm discs, giving a stereophonic effect that was demonstrated successfully at the Chicago Century of Progress Exposition in 1933. In 1940 the Disney film *Fantasia* featured the orchestra in a multiple-track recording that gave theater-goers a preview of surround sound.

In 1996, Victor (now part of the BMG empire) dropped its longtime exclusive contract with the orchestra, sending shock waves through the classical world. The cost of recording could not be recovered through sales. The orchestra has since marketed individual recordings to different labels. The orchestra's radio broadcast and archival recordings are currently available through Andante.

PHILHARMONIA (LABEL)
An American disc issued during 1951–1954 from Philharmonia Records Corp. of Brooklyn. The material was classical.

PHILHARMONIC (LABEL) (I)
A British disc issued in 1913–1914 from a company of the same name, pressed from Favorite Record matrices.

FRANK ANDREWS

PHILHARMONIC (LABEL) (II)
An American record, produced by Varsity for Firestone Tires in 1939–1940. Masters came from Columbia, Victor, and HMV. Material included some good jazz items, e.g., by W.C. Handy and Jack Teagarden. [Rust 1978.]

PHILHARMONIC STRING QUARTET
An ensemble that recorded for Edison in 1928. Members were Scipione Guidi and Arthur Lichstein, violins; Leon E. Barzin, viola; and Oswaldo Mazzucchi, cello. Ensembles of the same name recorded for Columbia and HMV in Britain in the 1920s.

PHILIPS (LABEL)
One of the record brands controlled by Universal Music Group. Recording under this label name began in the Netherlands in 1950, and branched out into Germany, Austria, Belgium, and (upon acquisition of the French Polydor Co.) in France. Reciprocal agreements were made with Columbia in the U.S. in 1951, and Philips repertoire appeared in America on the Epic label (a Columbia subsidiary) from 1955. Repertoire from Columbia was provided to Philips, rather than EMI, Ltd. In 1961 there was an exchange of material between Philips and Mercury Records.

In 1962, Philips Phonographic Industries (PPI) and Deutsche Grammophon Gesellschaft (DGG) merged interests, each taking 50 percent of the other's shares. On 3 Jan 1972, PPI was renamed Phonogram International, becoming a subsidiary of the new conglomerate PolyGram International, which acquired Decca in England on 17 Jan 1980. The entire group was sold to Seagram in 1998, which merged it with MCA. After MCA was purchased by the French conglomerate Viviendi, its music holdings were renamed the Universal Music Group.

FRANK ANDREWS

Philips label. Courtesy Frank Hoffmann

PHILLIPS, JOSEPH A.
(CA. 1880–15 JULY 1958)

American baritone, born in Buffalo, New York. He sang in Europe as well as the U.S., doing a repertoire of ballads, popular material, and operetta. He began to record for Victor in 1911, with "All that I Ask Is Love" (#5806). Then he worked for Edison from 1912 to 1923. "Mary Was My Mother's Name" (Edison #988; 1912) was a notable success. He made a number of well-received duet records with Helen Clark. On Pathé records he was "Justice Lewis"; on Okeh he was sometimes "Franklyn Kent." Phillips died in Buffalo. [Walsh 1972/10–11.]

PHILLIPS, SAM (5 JAN 1923–)

American record producer, record company owner, born in Florence, Alabama. Phillips originally worked as a disc jockey out of Muscle Shoals, Alabama, in 1942, moving in 1946 to a local station in Memphis. In 1950, he opened the Memphis Recording Service, mostly to record weddings and other local events for a fee. He began recording local blues musicians, initially licensing his recordings to Chess, RPM, and other labels; in 1952, he founded Sun Records to release his own recordings, releasing discs by local R&B singer Rufus Thomas and "Little Junior Parker," among others. In 1954, Elvis Presley walked in the door of his studio, and Phillips guided the young singer to national success before selling his contract to RCA Victor in late 1955. Phillips's recordings of Elvis were noteworthy for his use of slap-back echo, a recording technique that he pioneered and that became a signature for rockabilly recordings of the later 1950s. After Elvis left Sun, Phillips oversaw the early careers of Johnny Cash, Jerry Lee Lewis, Carl Perkins, and others. Phillips formed the Phillips International label as a subsidiary of Sun in the later 1950s, and opened a studio in Nashville in the early 1960s. He sold Sun Records to music industry entrepreneur Shelby Singleton in 1969.

WILLIAM RUHLMANN

PHILO RECORDS

Bill Schubart and Michael Couture founded Philo Records in 1973 in North Ferrisburg, Vermont, expanding from a recording studio they ran. The label was intended to support the work of folksingers/songwriters, especially those based in New England, and it has featured recordings by Mimi Fariña, Nanci Griffith, Patty Larkin, Christine Lavin, Mary McCaslin, Katy Moffatt, Bill Morrissey, Utah Phillips, Jean Redpath, and Dave Van Ronk. French Canadian traditional dance music was a second specialty of the label, including noted fiddlers Jean Carignan and Louis Beaudoin. The label originally made a point of emphasizing that all records were packaged and recorded in consultation with the artist, as opposed to some labels that sought to control how an artist was presented to the marketplace. A subsidiary label, Fretless, was formed for artists who wished to underwrite the recording costs of their records. Philo Records was purchased by Rounder Records in 1984.

WILLIAM RUHLMANN

PHISH

With the dissolution of the Grateful Dead following the death of guitarist Jerry Garcia, Phish have assumed the spiritual leadership of the jam-band movement, a staunchly noncommercial offshoot of progressive rock dedicated to improvisational interplay within typically extended musical pieces. Like Blues Traveler, the Dave Matthews Band, and other acts belonging to this genre, they employ an eclectic approach, melding jazz, blues, country, funk, Tin Pan Alley pop, rock, and classical music influences.

Phish formed in 1983 as part of the University of Vermont, Burlington, music scene. The members — guitarist/vocalist Trey Anastasio, bassist/vocalist Mike Gordon, drummer/vocalist Jon Fishman, and keyboardist/vocalist Page McConnell — focused on building a grassroots constituency largely through steady performing and word-of-mouth publicity. Interest was piqued by two independently released LPs, *Junta* (private label, 1988; reissued 1997 on Elektra #61413) and *Lawn Boy* (Absolute A-Go-Go #1992; 1990; reissued 1997 on Elektra #61273). The band's ability to sell out major live venues led to a recording contract with Elektra; the album releases — including *A Picture of Nectar* (Elektra #61274; 1992), *Rift* (Elektra #61433; 1993; #51), *(Hoist)* (Elektra #61628; 1994; #34), *A Live One* (Elektra #61772; 1995; #18), *Billy Breathes* (Elektra #61971; 1997; #7), *Slip Stitch and Pass* (Elektra #62121; 1997; #17), *The Story of the Ghost* (Elektra #62297; #8) — have been increasingly successful despite minimal marketing hype and only one single, the laid-back, AOR-friendly "Free" (Elektra #4205C; 1997). Phish took a two-year sabbatical beginning in 2000, but has released a flood of multi-disc vintage concert performances (six sets alone documenting past Halloween live re-creations of classic albums by the likes of Creedence Clearwater Revival, the Velvet Underground, Pink Floyd, the Talking Heads, the Who, and the Beatles appeared in late 2002) aimed primarily at their rapidly expanding cult following.

FRANK HOFFMANN

PHONADISC (LABEL)

A British record issued by Edison Bell in 1908 and 1909. It was 8 1/2 inches in size, vertical cut.

PHONAUTOGRAPH

The device invented by Léon Scott in 1857 to record (but not reproduce) sound signals on a lampblack-covered cylinder. Emile Berliner adapted the principle in his Gramophone.

PHONET

In Thomas Edison's early terminology, the stylus/diaphragm assembly of the phonograph.

PHONO-CUT

Another name for vertical cut, the process of inscribing sound signals on record surfaces through an up and down movement of the cutting stylus.

PHONO-CUT (LABEL) (I)

A vertical-cut record issued by the Phono-Cut Record Co. of Boston, a subsidiary of the Boston Talking Machine Co., ca. 1912. The label was sold to a Mr. Keen in 1913, and became Keen-o-phone.

PHONO-CUT (LABEL) (II)

An American record of the Phono-Cut Record Co., offered in 1916. It was a 10-inch disc, selling at first for $0.65, then for $0.25. In April 1916 the record was available from the Wonder Talking Machine Co. of New York.

FRANK ANDREWS

PHONOGRAM (I)

The original name given by Thomas Edison to his cylinder records, suggesting their intended use for business purposes. Later, musical cylinders were called "records."

PHONOGRAM (II)

The name of an early trade periodical.

See also **Sound Recording Periodicals**

PHONOGRAM INTERNATIONAL

SEE POLYGRAM INTERNATIONAL

PHONOGRAPH

In current terminology, any disc or cylinder record player. Originally it meant only the cylinder player, while the disc player was a gramophone, but that distinction faded early in the U.S. In the U.K. the specific terminology was retained through the 78-rpm era and lingers today in some contexts, e.g., the name of the principal sound recording journal, *Gramophone*.

See also **Cylinder; Edison, Thomas Alva; Graphophone**

PHONOGRAPH ACCESSORIES CORP.

A New York firm. In 1915 it announced the acquisition of the patent for the "red needle" from the Master-Phone Corp.

PHONOGRAPH AND RECORDING CO.

A New York firm, advertising in November 1921. It made records to order, for customers' own labels.

FRANK ANDREWS

PHONOGRAPH MANUFACTURERS NATIONAL ASSOC.

A trade organization established in Chicago on 19 Feb 1925. President was M.C. Schaff (or Schiff); vice president was Otto Heinemann.

PHONOGRAPH PARLORS

Establishments that provided coin-op phonographs for public listening, popular in the U.S. after 1889 and then worldwide. Notable parlors were the Pathé Salon de Phonographes in Paris and a similar establishment in London; and the lobby of the Vitascope Hall motion picture theater in Buffalo, New York (the first deluxe movie house in the U.S.), where 28 Edison phonographs were deployed. In Italy, the parlor was known as the Bar Automatico. Parlors declined in popularity with the introduction of automatic pianos and music boxes, but they persisted for years, often grouped with other coin machines in penny arcades.

PHONOGRAPH RECORDING CO. OF SAN FRANCISCO

A firm that made disc records to order; it was active in ca. 1926–1927. Only one example has been noticed in the literature. [Kendziora 1990/5–6; Rust 1978.]

PHONOGRAPH-GRAPHOPHONE

The commercial designation first given to the instrument of Chichester Bell and Charles Tainter when it was leased by the North American Phonograph Co. Later it was simply the Graphophone, the name they had given to their original experimental models, and later still it was the Columbia Graphophone.

PHONOGRAPHIC MUSIC CO.
A Brooklyn, New York, firm that advertised the Phonometer, a speed meter for disc players, in 1907.

PHONOLAMP
A device invented by George E. Emerson, marketed in the U.S. in 1916 by the Electric Phonograph Corp. of New York. It was an electric lamp with an electric motor phonograph in the lamp base. Doors in the base opened to give access to the turntable and reproducer, from which "the tone is carried upwards through the stem of the lamp, which acts as a concealed horn, and at the top is reflected downward by means of a globe and thereby producing a tone of unusual clarity" — this according to a *TMW* advertisement of 15 June 1916. The apparatus appeared in at least five models, selling from $75 to $200. A record with the same label name was produced by the Grey Gull organization and given to purchasers of the lamp. [Kendziora 1988/2.]

PHONOMETER

See Phonographic Music Co.

PHONOTHÈQUE NATIONALE (FRANCE)

See French National Sound Archives/Bibliothèque Nationale

PHONOTHÈQUE NATIONALE SUISSE
The Swiss national sound archive, part of its Bibliothèque Nationale, and founded in 1987. [website: http://www.fonoteca.ch/fr/presentation/welcome.htm.]

PHONOTYPE RECORDS (LABEL)
A record made in Italy, trademarked by the Italian Book Co. of New York. It was later known as Fonotype. *TMW* advertising from January 1922 to September 1925 offered Italian language comic material and Italian popular music, on 10-inch discs for $0.65 (later $0.75) and 12-inch discs for $1.25. Matrices were put on sale in October 1926.

FRANK ANDREWS

PHOTOPHONE
A light-ray system of sound recording, invented by Charles A. Hoxie, based on experiments of Alexander Graham Bell in 1879. The Bell concept was not practical at the time, because electronic amplification was not yet available. The principle was later adapted by General Electric for the Brunswick Pallatrope system of 1925.

PIAF, EDITH (19 DEC 1915–11 OCT 1963)
French popular singer, born Giovanna Gassion in Paris. Her first name, Edith, was inspired from Edith Cavell, and she was nicknamed Piaf ("swallow") by people who saw her singing in the streets — her first musical venue. She went on to become a highly praised nightclub singer, noted for sad, sentimental ballads. She was discovered by Polydor in 1936 and signed to a contract. Her first record was made in Paris, "La java de Cezique" (Polydor #2203; 1936), a song with accordion accompaniment. She stayed with Polydor until 1944, when Philips took over the label. Polydor leased U.S. rights to Vox, which then issued her earliest American records on 78-rpm format in the early 1940s, then on LP and EP. "L'accordioniste" (Polydor #5360; 1940) was one of her great hits; it appears on a CD reissue by EMI in 1990 (#315) with 19 other numbers. She also worked for Columbia, producing her greatest hit, her own composition, "La vie en rose" (Columbia #4014-F). There are numerous CD reissues of both the Polydor/Philips and Columbia material, both "official" and on various budget reissue labels, here and abroad. Angel issued a 10 CD set in 1984 (#79064) featuring her recordings for Polydor and Philips, 210 tracks in all. Piaf continued singing in Paris until her health failed in 1963; she died that year in Paris. [Rotante 1983.]

PIANO RECORDINGS (HISTORIC)
This article, generally limited to acoustic recordings, has five sections: 1. Technical problems; 2. Cylinders; 3. Discs; 4. Performance practice; 5. Historical reissues.

1. Technical Problems. Popular as the piano was in the home and in public recitals around 1900, it appeared as a solo instrument in very few recordings. Cylinders and discs of the time emphasized the vocal repertory and utilized the piano as an accompaniment only. Although there were gradual improvements in recording techniques, a pianist had problems in making acoustic recordings, whether as accompanist or soloist. Placement of the recording horn relative to the piano was critical to prevent loud playing from "blasting" and soft passages from vanishing in the surface noise. Even with ideal horn placement — which required the piano to be mounted on a platform — the pianist was normally constrained to a narrow dynamic range that obstructed musical expression. Furthermore, speed control of the recording was often irregular, resulting in a noticeably wavering piano tone.

Other inhibiting factors were the necessity to fit a composition (or part of one) on to a disc or cylinder with no more than four minutes playing time; the lack of an audience to induce spur-of-the-moment inspiration; and the concern that any slip or artistic flaw would be preserved for posterity. Many pianists found making records under such conditions to be a repugnant and difficult task, while some artists demanded perfection by repeating the same piece over and over; Artur Schnabel once did 29 takes before he was satisfied with a recording. Vladimir de Pachmann often demanded that the piano be moved, the lights be turned off, and an audience be found. The versatile and accessible piano was the accompaniment on early recordings for most of the solo instrumentalists (especially violinists) and numerous vocalists in popular and art song. It also served as an economical orchestra substitute in opera and oratorio arias. The earliest commercial recordings in the 1890s often presented local accompanists who were not famous or even well enough known in many cases to be named in the cylinder catalogs, or on the etched disc label; or accompanists might be designated only by a surname, like the "Mr. Guttinguer" on an early Pathé cylinder. Many pianists of great ability recorded accompaniments on prominent labels like Victor, Columbia, and HMV; e.g., Landon Ronald, André Benoist, Frank La Forge (1879–1953), and conductor Arthur Nikisch. The great HMV executive Fred Gaisberg is heard accompanying singers on many early records.

2. *Cylinders.* The first significant recordings of a famous musician were noncommercial private two-minute wax cylinders (mentioned in letters but unfortunately lost or destroyed) recorded by the 12-year-old prodigy pianist Josef Hofmann during a visit to Edison's laboratory in 1888. In 1889, Johannes Brahms became the first major composer known to have made a cylinder, recorded during a visit to Vienna by an agent of Edison. Although the fidelity of this important historical document of a fragment of his *Hungarian Dance No. 5* (preserved only in a 1935 dubbing) was exceedingly poor, the announcement "Herr Brahms" is plainly audible. It was issued on LP by the International Piano Archive (IPA #117).

Before mass production of cylinders was possible they had to be individually inscribed; thus multiple copies could only be made by setting up a row of recording machines, into which the performer played the same piece over and over. Thus not all copies made at the same session were identical, though they carried the same catalog number. Pianists listed in Bettini catalogs who each made a dozen such cylinders around 1898 in New York were Aimé Lachaume (playing pieces of Beethoven, Chopin, Godard, Debussy, Liszt, and the pianist's own works) and Joseph Pizzarello (playing Chopin, Godard, Grieg, Hofmann, Liszt, Moszkowski, Paderewski, Schumann and the pianist's "Gavotte"). Because of limited production, fragile construction, and the destruction of stock during World War I, few of these Bettini cylinders are known to still exist even as unique copies. [Moran 1965/2.]

Edison cylinders were manufactured over a longer period than any others (1889–1929) and many have survived. Pianists in the Edison catalogs included Frank Banta, Sr.; Frank Banta, Jr.; André Benoist; Albert Benzler; Karee Bondam, Walter Chapman, Zez Confrey, Ferdinand Himmelreich, Henry W. Lange, Constance Mering, Ernest L. Stevens, Donald Voorhees, and Victor Young.

Except for a few classical favorites such as Chopin Mazurkas and Liszt's "Liebestraum" played by Walter Chapman, almost all of the repertoire consisted of accompaniments and/or popular music. Some piano cylinders were also produced by other companies, such as the Pathé recordings of Lucien Lambert (1858–1945), made around 1905.

See also **Cylinder**

3. *Discs.* Few piano solo recordings were available at the turn of the century. Eldridge Johnson's "Improved Gram-o-phone" catalog (the predecessor of Victor) listed only three, all recorded in 1900: "A Cork Dance" (#A407), composed and played by Arthur Pryor (famous as a trombonist and bandmaster rather than as a pianist); "Hello Ma Baby" (#A402), an original fantasie by Frank P. Banta, Sr.; and "Variations on the Mariner's Hymn," played by the composer C.H.H. Booth (#A434).

The earliest significant commercial solo piano records were about 100 discs made by the Gramophone Co. (from 12 Dec 1900 to 18 Nov 1907 the Gramophone & Typewriter Co., Ltd.) in major European cities from about 1900 to 1909. The repertoire consisted almost exclusively of works by such 19th-century composers as Brahms, Chabrier, Chopin, Godard, Grieg, Liszt, Massenet, Mendelssohn, Rachmaninoff, Raff, Schubert, Schumann, and Volkmann. There were arrangements of J. Strauss and Wagner, and a few examples of 18th-century favorites (Handel and Scarlatti) originally for harpsichord. Most of the pioneering performances listed in Gramophone Co. catalogs were made in London by Wilhelm Backhaus (eight discs in 1908), Ilona Eibenschütz (1873–1967, three discs), Percy Grainger (three discs), Nathalie Janotha (1856–1932, four discs, including

Chopin's "Fugue in A minor," from the manuscript then owned by the pianist), Vladimir de Pachmann (six discs, of which five were by Chopin), Landon Ronald (two discs), and Lillian Bryant — the first female solo pianist to record commercially. Raoul Pugno (1852–1914) made 17 discs in Paris in 1903, Louis Diémer (1843–1919) made five, and Franz Rummel (1853–1901) made one. Alfred Grünfeld (1852–1924) made 23 discs in Vienna; Josef Hofmann recorded four numbers in Berlin; Alexander Michalowski (1851–1938) made one in Warsaw. One disc was known to come from St. Petersburg, by a pianist named P.P. Gross.

Of particular importance on G & T were pianist-composers who recorded only their own compositions: Camille Saint-Saëns (1835–1921, considered the earliest-born major pianist to make commercial discs in 1904); Edvard Grieg, on five and later nine discs, all recorded in Paris in April 1903; and Cécile Chaminade on six discs made in London in November 1901.

Fonotipia issued about 10 discs recorded ca. 1905 in Paris by Maria Roger-Miclos (1860?–?) of compositions by Chopin, Godard, Liszt, Mendelssohn, and Schumann.

The heavy predominance of 19th-century romantic repertoire in these earliest discs, with special emphasis on Chopin and Liszt and assorted salon-type offerings, continued throughout the entire acoustic era.

Only a few world-renowned pianists made solo Edison Diamond Discs, the most significant being (in 1919) the first recordings by Sergei Rachmaninoff: Liszt's "Hungarian Rhapsody No. 2" on three sides of Edison #82169/70; Scarlatti-Tausig's "Pastorale" as a filler on Edison #82170; the first movement of Mozart's Sonata in A major, K. #331; two Chopin waltzes, and the composer's own "Polka de W.R.," "Barcarolle, op. 10," and the renowned "Prelude in C Sharp Minor, op. 3." Rachmaninoff, soon lured over to Victor, made numerous records documenting his art until just before his death.

Other well known Edison keyboard artists were E. Robert Schmitz (1889–1949) in a 1914 disc of Chopin's "Valse Posthume" and the great Moriz Rosenthal (1862–1946) in several 1929 experimental electric lateral-cut discs (issued on LP, Mark #56 723 and 725) of Chopin compositions inscribed just before Edison ceased recording. Particularly well known as an accompanist, André Benoist also recorded a few solos for Edison around 1918–1920. However, Edison's catalog included mostly lesser-known pianists. The great inventor's personal prolific staff-pianist-arranger, Ernest L. Stevens, claimed to have made over 600 records (including experimental discs) most of them as an accompanist or ensemble pianist, many under pseudonyms.

Famous pianists who recorded in Europe often appeared on Victor, Columbia, and Brunswick American releases from ca. 1910 to 1925. Victor's most prestigious artists, issued on the Red Seal label series, included Wilhelm Backhaus, Harold Bauer (1873–1951), Alfred Cortot, De Pachmann, Ossip Gabrilowitsch (1878–1936), Guiomar Novaes (1895–1979), Ignace Jan Paderewski, Rachmaninoff, and Olga Samaroff (1882–1948). Less-celebrated pianists on the less expensive blue, purple, and black labels included Frank La Forge, Ferdinand Himmelreich, Alfred Grünfeld, Charles Gilbert Spross (1874–1961, who also recorded accompaniments), Julius L. Schendel, Benno Moiseiwitsch (1890–1963, who later advanced to Red Seal status), and "Master" Shura Cherkassky (1911–); "recorded at the age of eleven" according to the labels on 10-inch blue-label Victor #45394 which included the prodigy's own "Prelude Pathetique".

Although some of the repertoire seems rather frivolous by today's standards (e.g., transcriptions of popular songs like "Listen to the Mocking Bird," and "Silver Threads Among the Gold," or "Carnival of Venice Variations," or a piano transcription of the *Lucia* Sextette — all played by Himmelreich), concert miniatures composed by Beethoven, Moszkowski, Chaminade, Chopin, Gottschalk, Godard, Mendelssohn, Sinding, Liszt, Rachmaninoff, and Poldini were issued. The first piano record of a work by Debussy, "En Bateau" played by Spross, appeared about 1911. Pianists playing popular music also appeared on the non-red labels, such as Felix Arndt (1889–1918, famous for the song "Nola").

Columbia's impressive but somewhat smaller roster included Arthur Friedheim (1859–1932), Ignaz Friedman, Leopold Godowsky, Percy Grainger, Josef Hofmann, Mischa Levitski (1898–1941), and Xaver Scharwenka (1850–1924).

In the early 1920s, Brunswick acoustics presented important performances by Godowsky and Hofmann, and issues by Elly Ney (1882–1968). Other companies also offered major pianists, such as the Russian Vassily Sapelnikoff (1868–1941) on Vocalion.

Although most discs were lateral-cut, Pathé issued vertical-cut piano records. Among the most important were those of Bernhard Stavenhagen (1862–1914), performing Chopin's "Nocturne in D-Flat, op. 27, no. 2." Other Pathé pianists were Edouard Risler (1873–1929, Paris, 1917), Josef Lhévinne (U.S.A., 1921), and Rudolf Ganz (1877–1972, U.S.A., 1916–1918, who made some Pathé cylinders that were transcribed onto disc on the Actuelle label).

The piano concerto repertory was even more limited than solo piano in the acoustic era, the first piano concerto recording having been made by Wilhelm

Backhaus of the Grieg Concerto by HMV in 1910. In the Victor catalog, there were just a few favorites, all in truncated form, such as the "Adagio" from the Grieg Concerto (#70043) and "Adagio" from the Beethoven "Emperor Concerto" (#55030), both played by La Forge; the Grieg (Victor #55154/5) and Saint-Saëns Second Concerto (Victor #55160/1) both played by De Greef. These were on non red labels; however, Rachmaninoff's first recording of a concerto, his own second, the second and third movements only (Victor #8064/6; 1924) did appear on Red Seal. And the composer's authoritative performances of his other three concertos, and the *Rhapsody on a Theme of Paganini* were subsequently issued. Sapelnikoff, who had played the Tchaikovsky First Concerto under the composer, recorded it on an abbreviated late acoustic Vocalion in London in February 1926.

After 1925, the rapidly expanding electrically recorded piano catalogs of Victor, Columbia, and other companies provided a relatively generous choice of artists, genre (solo, chamber, and concerto), repertory, multiple versions, and multirecord sets. Although the Victor Red Seal catalog tended to predominate in the U.S. (with some acoustic period artists such as Rachmaninoff, Paderewski, and Cortot for Victor and Godowsky for both Columbia and Brunswick continuing to be active), some important artists were heard on the non-red labels, such as Hans Barth (1897–1956), a student of Reinecke, Hoagy Carmichael (1899–1981), and Fats Waller. European labels such as HMV (which exchanged some releases with its American affiliate Victor), Parlophone, Odeon (some licensed to American Decca), Polydor (some licensed to Brunswick), Homocord, and others brought out important releases. Smaller companies such as Musicraft, Concert Hall, and Vox presented innovative material, often by artists who later became world famous. The exponential expansion of postwar piano records on LPs and CDs is for the most part beyond the limited scope of this brief overview. Duet performances appeared rarely in the early period. One example was the Berliner disc recorded on 14 Apr 1899 by Jeanne Douste (ca. 1870–ca. 1936) and her sister Irene Douste playing an arrangement from *Cosi fan tutte* and Rubinstein's "Toreador." Two-piano acoustic recordings were also very few in number, examples being by Schnabel students Guy Maier (1891–1956) and Lee Pattison (1890–1966) on Blue Label Victor. Two-piano teams that later became well known on electric 78s included: Ethel Bartlett (1896–1978, a Matthay student) and Rae Robertson (1893–1956); Pierre Luboschutz (1891–1971, an Edouard Risler student) and Genia Nemenoff (1905–); and Vitya Vronsky (1909–) and her husband Victor Babin (1908–1972), especially remembered for several superb recordings of the two Rachmaninoff Suites.

4. *Performance Practice.* Time constraints of acoustic 78-rpm sides posed a major limitation to piano (and other) early recordings; longer works (if recorded at all) were often truncated. That repeats were seldom observed (except "da capo" repeats) would thus not provide a reliable clue as to whether repeats were observed in concert. Relatively few of the late acoustics (after about 1920) even devoted both sides of a double-sided disc to one composition, since most were couplings of different works issued earlier as a single-sided disc. Truncations did not merely consist of omitting repetitions. Beethoven's "32 Variations in C-Minor," as recorded in 1925 by Rachmaninoff, utilized two sides but was still truncated since six variations were omitted. Three early acoustics of Mendelssohn's "Rondo Capriccio op. 14," as recorded by Maria Roger-Miclos (Fonotipia #39256; ca. 1905), Josef Hofmann (Columbia #A6078; ca. 1915), as well as the early 1920s recording by Alfred Cortot (Victor #74810), all omit the 26-measure lyrical "andante" introduction. Roger-Miclos also omits 30 measures just before the broken octave coda. In comparison, Hofmann's 1913 Welte-Mignon roll (#3031) is uncut. Tempos, especially if fast and scrambled, were as likely dictated by time limits as by artistic conception. Most truncations were well planned to sound as inconspicuous as possible, but the Louis Diémer disc of Chopin's "Nocturne op. 27 no. 2 in D-Flat" (G & T #35544; ca. 1903) finishes before the piece finishes, with the last measures conspicuously missing. Conversely, a composition was occasionally expanded or markedly varied. Because Goossens's "Casperle Theatre" ("The Punch and Judy Show, op. 18 no. 6" from *Kaleidoscope*), a sprightly half-minute work, did not fill a side, Eugène d'Albert's recording (Deutsche Grammophon #B27045, reissued on LP Veritas VM #110) repeated the piece after the recording technicians (and perhaps the pianist?) provided some applause and laughter. When Harold Bauer recorded two of the Brahms Waltzes op. 39 he played No. 15, followed by No. 16 (Schirmer Records #2004, reissued on LP Veritas VM #108), and then repeated No. 15 to create the effect of an ABA structure.

Performances from the 78 era may provide reliable clues to the performance practices of the late 19th century because mature artists tended to reflect approaches taught to them, or performances heard while their own personal styles were being formed. This residue from the previous generation may often raise questions about the borderlines between artistic imagination and grotesque distortion. Early 20th-century piano recordings frequently present aspects of style and execution that stand out as striking or eccentric to modern listeners. These include modifications and variants from the score, such as playing single notes as octaves; adding ornamentation, scales, and parallel scales (especially in thirds); interpolating extra measures and cadenzas; spreading or arpeggiating chords and adding arpeggios and chords; playing the left-hand bass slightly before the right or letting the right hand be slightly delayed; pedaling in extremes — from little or none for clear counterpoint to blurred for sonorous effect; producing tone (difficult to describe) that is singing, ringing (bell-like), bright, brittle, or ethereal; phrasing and articulating imaginatively; bringing out inner voices; introducing unmarked tempo changes, retards, or accelerandos; and altering rhythm with exaggerated rubato.

Although most of the surprising, fascinating, and distinctive traits heard in early piano recordings are not easily described, the following examples will try to document the observations noted above. Multiple versions of a work by one performer often vary appreciably. Alexander Michalowski's paraphrase on Chopin's "Minute Waltz" (Polish Columbia DMX #258) and a quite different longer version (Polish Syrena #6578; ca. 1930) — both reissued on LP Veritas VM #115 — expand and elaborate the short work with intricate introductory, developmental, and coda material. Fortunately for comparison, Michalowski also recorded a relatively straightforward version (G & T #25601; ca. 1904–1905). Vladimir de Pachmann's first disc of the "Minute Waltz" (G & T #5566; ca. 1907) adds a quick ascending and descending D-flat scale run between the trio and the return of section A, but Pachmann's reproducing roll made about the same time lacks this added flourish, ending instead with several extra cadential chords. Ignaz Friedman's Duo-Art reproducing roll (#67220) adds a rapid brusquely rolled chord in the left hand before the return of the first theme, and delightfully varies the downward scale at the end by playing it in thirds. Outdoing all other minute waltzes, Josef Hofmann's concert performance (Casimir Hall concert of 7 Apr 1938, on LP IPA #5007-5008) surpasses Friedman by playing the entire return of the first section in thirds.

Chopin's "Waltz op. 42 in A-Flat" performed by Rachmaninoff (Edison Diamond Disc #82197; 1919) adds ritardandos at the ends of phrases, stretches or lengthens the A-flat trill on the upbeat to the next phrase, and adds parallel notes to an upward right-hand scale leading to the coda. Busoni linked two Chopin works together by playing at a fast tempo the "Prelude Opus 28 No. 7 in A Major" with a repeat (not in the score) followed by a short bridge passage leading directly into the "Etude Op. 10, No. 5 in G-Flat Major" ("Black Key Etude") which concludes with two extra measures of echo-effect figuration inserted just before the concluding downward double octaves (British Columbia L #1476, reissued on IPL #104).

Chopin's "Nocturne Op. 9 No. 2 in E-Flat" played by Raoul Koczalski (1885–1948) uses variant right-hand ornamentation learned from annotations reportedly written by Chopin in the score of Karol Mikuli (1821–1897), a student of Chopin and the teacher of Koczalski. [Methuen-Campbell, 1981, p. 75.] Chopin's "Etude Op. 25 No. 2 in F Minor" played by Francis Planté at age 90 in 1928 (French Columbia D #13060, reissued on LP IPL #101) has the closing downward run starting an octave higher than written so as to be executed twice as fast with twice as many notes as are in the score (giving a stretto effect).

Liszt's étude "La leggierezza" interpreted by Paderewski (reissued on LP Camden #310) adds a little-known elaborate Leschetizky cadenza that blends into the style of the work. Liszt's "Hungarian Rhapsody No. 2" recorded by Rachmaninoff in 1919 (Edison Diamond Disc #82169) incorporates an apparently improvised (unpublished) two-minute cadenza.

Arthur Friedheim's performance of Liszt's "La campanella" (Columbia #517; 1913) adds an upward glissando, an extra measure of the "bell" figuration (the title means "the bell"), and a sudden accelerando and ritardando in a measure of right-hand tremolo octaves. Schubert's "Impromptu in F-Minor Op. 142 No. 4" was played by Eugène d'Albert (Deutsche Grammophon #65516; ca. 1916; on LP Veritas VM #110) at an extremely fast tempo to fit the disc's time limit. The pianist omitted several whole note (i.e., whole measure) rests with fermatas.

5. *Historical Reissues.* Numerous LP and CD reissues and first issues have been made of historical piano recordings. For example, RCA and its budget subsidiaries RCA Camden and RCA Victrola have provided a significant sampling of the vast Victor heritage, the most monumental single release having been the complete known extant recorded performances by Sergei Rachmaninoff in five volumes (15 LPs issued ca. 1973) which included some test pressings released for the first time. Other commercial labels, particularly Veritas, Rococo, Pearl, Opal, and Music and Arts have made available significant historical materials. The International Piano Archives at Maryland (IPAM), previously known as the International Piano Archive (IPA) and the International Piano Library (IPL), has produced important material. Sources other than early commercial cylinders and discs include private recordings (made at concerts, social gatherings, etc.) and off-the-air broadcasts that allowed significant piano recordings to be issued for the first time on LP and CD.

Examples of such important historical offerings include the cylinder by Brahms already mentioned and one by Isaac Albéniz (1860–1909) of two improvisations recorded in 1903 — both issued on IPA #109. Privately recorded concert performances have also seen the first light of day on LP and CD, such as Josef Hofmann's Golden Jubilee concert on 28 Nov 1937 on the 50th anniversary of his American debut (IPA #5001–5002). Two versions of the Grieg Concerto in A-Minor played by Percy Grainger (from 1945 and 1956) filled out by the commercial 1908 cadenza excerpt (G & T #5570), made only a few years after Grieg coached the young performer in its interpretation, appeared on IPA #508. Paderewski's student Sigismund Stojowski (1870–1946) played Stojowski and Chopin (IPA #115) obtained from a 1944 broadcast. Previously unpublished commercial discs that were eventually issued include Josef Hofmann's 1935 RCA test pressings (LP Victrola VIC #1550). Such LPs and CDs provide a great service to pianists, musicologists, and others who wish to hear and study performance style and tradition of the past, and they ensure the preservation and survival for posterity of the valuable sonic information.

Pianists who recorded in the acoustic era rarely hesitated to infuse their playing with personal ideas and interpolated liberties in the grand 19th-century Romantic tradition. Later generations of pianists preferred to display virtuosity by demonstrating how precisely an artist could adhere to the printed score — though many older editions used by recording artists were overedited with misleading indications. Currently, pyrotechnical display has to be executed with precision to be considered acceptable. Expanded exposure to records, radio, and video formats has contributed significantly to homogenizing interpretative style (analogous to minimizing regional dialects and accents). [Basart 1985; Capes 1956; Crutchfield 1956; Dubal 1989; Edison 1987; Fagan 1983; Ferrara 1975; Holcman 1960, 1961/11, 1961/12, 1961/13, 1962; International 1983; Matthews 1977; Methuen-Campbell 1981, 1983, 1984; Perkins 1981; Sitsky 1985, 1990; Wodehouse 1977.]

STEVEN PERMUT

PIANOLA

The trade name of the inner player manufactured by the Aeolian Co. Weber was the most popular model; others were the Steck, the Wheelock, and the Stuyvesant. Dimensions of the Stuyvesant were typical of the inner player: 61 inches long, 29 1/2 inches deep, 56 1/2 inches tall; with a boxed weight of about 1,000 pounds. Pianola became widely used as a generic name for player pianos of all brands.

PIAZOLLA, ASTOR
(11 MAR 1921–5 JULY 1992)

Master of the Argentine tango, Piazolla was one of the 20th century's greatest artists on the bandoneon (a form

of accordion). Born in Mar del Plata, Argentina, Astor was brought to the U.S. at the age of three, where his family settled in New York City. He began studying bandoneon at age 9, along with studying the piano. The family returned to Argentina in 1936, where the teenage Piazolla began performing in tango bands. He moved to Buenos Aires in 1938, and a year later joined Anibal Troilo's band, a pioneering bandoneon player and orchestra leader. Piazolla remained with Troilo through 1944, performing as well as composing/arranging for the group. He was hired by rival bandleader Francisco Fiorentino in 1944, and then in 1946 formed the first band, which lasted three years. Meanwhile, he continued to work on his classical composing, premiering the piece "Buenos Aires" for bandoneon and orchestra in 1953; the piece gained international recognition and a scholarship for Piazolla to study in 1954 in Paris with famed music teacher Nadia Boulanger.

Piazolla returned to Argentina in 1955, and except for a two-year stint in New York City from 1958–1960, worked as a performer/composer there through 1973. He continued to meld his interest in tango with classical music, forming smaller groups, including his first legendary Quinteto Nuevo Tango in 1960. Through the 1960s and 1970s, he composed everything from songs to full-length operas and orchestral works. Facing a changing political scene in his home country, Piazolla settled in Italy in 1973, leading a jazz-fusion group from 1973–1978 known as the Conjunto Electronico. In 1978 he returned to performing with an acoustic quintet. He became an international star, recording and performing widely. His best work of this period is generally considered to be the 1986 album, *Tango: Zero Hour* (MCA #42138). That same year, a live collaboration with vibes master Gary Burton at the Montreux Jazz Festival resulted in an acclaimed album, *The New Tango* (Atlantic #81823). However, heart trouble that had plagued him since his first heart attack in 1973 flared up again in the late 1980s, and he suffered a debilitating stroke in 1990 that ended his performing career. His last major recording was a collaboration with the experimental Kronos Quartet on *Five Tango Sensations* (Elektra #79524; 1990). He died in Buenos Aires.

CARL BENSON

PICCADILLY (LABEL)

A U.K. record issued from 1928 to 1932 by Piccadilly Records, Ltd., a firm with commercial connections to Metropole Gramophone Co., Ltd. (later Metropole Industries, Ltd.). Metropole's English matrices and imported Emerson and Grey Gull matrices were used. There were low-cost records and "Celebrity" red-labeled records. The Piccadilly records continued after

Metropole went out of business. Piccadilly had gained ownership of the Hertford Town factory, which had belonged to the Hertford Record Co., Columbia Graphophone Co., Ltd., Parlophone Co., Ltd., and Metropole Gramophone Co.

FRANK ANDREWS

PICCOLO RECORDINGS (HISTORIC)

George Schweinfest was the first identified piccolo player on record, making 36 numbers for Columbia in 1897–1898; the earliest was "Golden Robin Polka" (#23500). Berliner recorded some piccolo solos and duets in September and October 1898, the players not identified, but Rust suggests that one of the artists was the flutist A. Fransella. [Rust 1981.]

PICKERING, NORMAN C. (1918–)

Born on Long Island, as a child Pickering wanted to be a musican. However, his father wanted him to study engineering, and so he went on to earn an E.E. degree at Newark College of Engineering in 1936. Having won a scholarship to the Juilliard School of Music, he enrolled with a concentration first in violin, and later in French horn. Music continued to dominate his interest (he eventually became an accomplished cellist), and in 1937, he joined the Indianapolis Symphony Orchestra and earned his living as a performer until 1940. While at Indianapolis, he also set up a small recording studio, and at that time he began to become interested in the design of phonograph playback cartridges. The war interrupted his new interest, however, and from 1942 until 1945 he worked on aircraft instrumentation. During that period, he continued to expand his interest in music by playing first horn with the South Bend Symphony, in Indiana, and then going on to conduct the Sperry Symphony. However, he also became even more interested in doing serious research in phonograph cartridge and stylus design, and in late 1945, after the war ended, he founded Pickering & Co., located in Oceanside, Long Island.

At first, his Pickering cartridges were sold only to professional users, but eventually the line was expanded to include the consumer market. The company also produced computer sensors and aircraft instruments, did research in magnetics, and also expanded into other areas in the audio marketplace, including equalizers and speaker systems. During this time, Pickering also hired Walter Stanton, who eventually became head of Pickering, and later on started his own company. In 1948 Pickering helped to found the Audio Engineering Society (in 1952 he earned the Society's Fellowship award and in 1955 went on to win the very prestigious

AES award), and between 1952 and 1955 he was also a visiting professor of acoustics at the City College of New York. In 1958 Pickering left the company and concentrated on consulting work in musical acoustics. For decades, he has also conducted research into violin design, and he is now considered one of the world's major authorities on the topic. In addition to building fine instruments of his own, he published *The Bowed String: Observations on the Design, Manufacture, Testing and Performance of Strings for Violins, Violas, and Cellos* (Amereon, 1991).

HOWARD FERSTLER

PICKETT, WILSON (18 MAR 1941–)

Although Wilson Pickett spent a comparatively brief amount of time as a hit-making force, for many, he was considered to be the classic soul singer. His rough, gritty voice was perfectly suited for uptempo material, melding a gospel fervor to a funky backbeat.

Pickett started out singing gospel music in church, first in his hometown of Prattville, Alabama, and then in Detroit between 1955–1959. In 1959 Willie Schofield invited him to join his R&B vocal group, the Falcons, best known for the recording, "You're So Fine" (Unart #2013; 1959; #2 R&B, #17 pop). He would go on to contribute many compositions to their repertoire, most notably "I Found a Love" (LuPine #1003; 1962; #6 R&B).

Pickett's dual talents as a singer/songwriter made a solo career inevitable. His departure from the Falcons followed a successful audition with Double-L Records, headed by R&B legend Lloyd Price, in 1963. He immediately scored two successive R&B hits with the self-composed "If You Need Me" (Double-L #713; 1963; #30) and "It's too Late" (Double-L #717; 1963; #7).

His breakthrough to a larger pop audience came shortly after his contract was purchased by Atlantic Records in 1964. Assisted by the label's marketing muscle and the decision to have him record with Stax — then affiliated with Atlantic in order to gain a wider market for its own artists — Pickett found immediate success with such hits as "In the Midnight Hour" (Atlantic#2289; 1965; #1 R&B, #21 pop), "634-5789" (Atlantic #2320; 1966; #1 R&B, #13 pop), "Land of 1,000 Dances" (Atlantic #2348; 1966; #1 R&B, #6 pop), "Mustang Sally" (Atlantic #2365; 1966; #6 R&B, #23 pop), "Funky Broadway" (Atlantic #2430; 1967; #1 R&B, #8 pop), "Sugar Sugar" (Atlantic #2722; 1970; #4 R&B, #25 pop), "Engine Number 9" (Atlantic #2765; 1970; #3 R&B, #14 pop), "Don't Let the Green Grass Fool You" (Atlantic #2781; 1971; #2 R&B, #17 pop), "Don't Knock My Love — Pt. 1" (Atlantic #2797; 1971; #1

R&B, #13 pop), and "Fire and Water" (Atlantic #2852; 1972; #2 R&B, #24 pop). The tight, stripped-down rhythm accompaniment provided by members of the Stax house band, Booker T. and the MGs (with production by their guitarist, Steve Cropper), proved to be the ideal foil for the dynamic tension communicated by Pickett's vocals. His albums also sold well in the later half of the 1960s, most notably *The Exciting Wilson Pickett* (Atlantic #8129; 1966; #21), *The Wicked Pickett* (Atlantic #8138; 1967; #42), and *The Best of Wilson Pickett* (Atlantic #8151; 1967; #35).

Pickett's sales dropped off considerably in the early 1970s as soul was superseded by new Black urban styles such as funk, disco, and reggae. He continued to tour extensively both stateside and abroad, although his new recordings — for RCA (1973–1975), Wicked (1975–1977), Big Tree (1977–1979), EMI America (1979–mid-1980s), and Motown (late 1980s) — had trouble competing with reissues of his vintage soul material. He attracted considerable publicity in the early 1980s by uniting with Joe Tex, Don Covay, and other 1960s Black singers as the Soul Clan. His legend receive added luster when the highly acclaimed film, *The Commitments* (1991), portrayed him as soul music's Holy Grail. Further recognition came with his induction into the Rock and Roll Hall of Fame in 1991.

FRANK HOFFMANN

PICKUP

SEE CARTRIDGE (II)

PICKWICK RECORDS (LABEL)

The largest budget and reissue label of its time, Pickwick Records was formed by Cy Leslie in 1950 in New York City. Leslie's first business was a prerecorded greeting card service, which in 1946 evolved into Voco Records, a label associated with inexpensive picture records for children. By 1953, Pickwick entered the LP market, offering customers a lower-priced record with the same or similar music to albums released by major companies.

In the late 1950s, Pickwick secured a licensing deal with Capitol Records, allowing Pickwick to distribute Capitol's secondary and noncurrent titles. This allowed customers to purchase low-priced albums by Frank Sinatra, Nat "King" Cole, Tennessee Ernie Ford (and later, the Beach Boys, Glen Campbell, and the Lettermen). Pickwick's records were often sold not in record stores, but in department stores and small "mom and pop" establishments where the company's bargain-priced records would be big sellers, and where the company would receive little sales

competition from other major labels. The success of the Capitol license gave other companies the impetus to allow Pickwick to license their secondary catalogs. In 1975 Pickwick acquired the rights to repress several of Elvis Presley's budget LPs that were originally issued on the RCA Camden label (those albums were still in the Pickwick catalog at the time of Presley's death).

Pickwick could also boast having reissued records by the Beatles (the "Star Club" Hamburg recordings) and Simon and Garfunkel (a compilation of pre-"Sounds of Silence" tracks under their duo's original name of "Tom and Jerry"). They also released albums with sound-alike recordings of popular songs, a trend that gave many aspiring singers and songwriters their first big break in the music business. One of those aspiring songwriters that benefited from his time at Pickwick was Lou Reed (later lead singer/songwriter for the Velvet Underground). In the early 1960s, Reed worked at the Pickwick studios in Queens as an in-house songwriter, composing songs like "The Ostrich" for the Primitives, and "I've Got a Tiger in My Tank" by the Intimates. Many of these songs were issued and reissued on Pickwick's Design imprint, on compilation albums like *Out of Sight* and *Soundsville*. Pickwick's first 45s (under the Pickwick City label) also contained songs either written by Reed or with him playing in the studio band.

Pickwick was also the largest independent record distributor in America; they also had successful reissue branches in both England and Canada. In 1977, the label and its operations were sold to American Can Corp. The distribution company ceased operations in 1983, when many of their accounts (Arista, Chrysalis, A&M, and Motown) opted for distribution through major labels.

CHUCK MILLER

PICTURE DISCS

Records with illustrations on their labels and/or playing surfaces, issued by many companies from 1905 as postcard records, then by Talk-O-Photo in 1920, and as Emerson children's records in 1922 (six inches in diameter, with color pictures on one side). In 1932–1933 there were 30 items by Victor, including sides with photos of Enrico Caruso and Jimmie Rodgers. Picture discs — along with colored vinyl — enjoyed a revival in popularity during the early 1980s as a result of record company efforts to boost sagging retail sales. A recent price guide listed about 6,000 picture discs worldwide. The most famous label in the picture field was Vogue, in 1946–1947.

Picture-disc label from c. 1919-20. Courtesy Kurt Nauck/Nauck's Vintage Records

PICTURIZED PHONOGRAPHS

Devices that showed illustrations as accompaniment to records played in coin-op phonographs during the early years of the 20th century. Some of the brand names were Illustraphone (Hawthorne & Sheble), Cailophone, and Scopephone (both by Caille Brothers), and the Illustrated Song Machine (Rosenfield Co., New York). The Discophone was the first in use with disc players in the U.S.; it was made by the Valiquet Novelty Co., Newark, New Jersey.

PIED PIPERS

American popular vocal group, formed in the 1930s, prominent in the early 1940s with the Tommy Dorsey orchestra. Members were John Huddleston, Chuck Lowry, Hal Hopper, Woody Newbury, Whit Whittinghill, Bud Hervey, and George Tait. Huddleston's wife, Jo Stafford, sang with them later. There were various other artists in the group from time to time. Having left Dorsey in 1942, the Pied Pipers appeared on many radio shows, including the *Lucky Strike Hit Parade*, and made motion pictures. They were active through the 1950s.

Most of the Pied Piper records were for Victor and Capitol. They backed up Frank Sinatra on his first hit solo with Tommy Dorsey, "I'll Never Smile Again" (Victor #26628; 1940), and in the fine arrangement of "There Are Such Things" (Victor #27974; 1942). Among their popular LP albums was Capitol #T-907, *Ac-cent-tchu-ate the Positive*, with Johnny Mercer.

PIERCE, DON (10 OCT 1915–)

A skilled marketer, Don Pierce (born in Ballard, Washington) ran one of the few truly successful independent country record labels, Starday. After his discharge from the Navy in 1945, Pierce worked in the sales department of 4-Star Records in Los Angeles until 1953. In September 1953, Pierce joined the fledgling Starday Records, eventually becoming president. He moved the label to Nashville in 1957, and assumed sole control in 1958. He signed artists jettisoned by the major labels, scored several big hits, and developed a thriving catalog business. He pioneered LPs and direct marketing in country music. He sold Starday in 1968 for $2 million, and became a real estate developer in Hendersonville, Tennessee.

COLIN ESCOTT

PIERCE, RICHARD (DICK) (1952–)

Involved in audio and technical software development professionally for over a quarter of a century, Pierce's activities have ranged from high-fidelity audio to radio astronomy to software development management. He has been the technical director of company — designing and manufacturing high-quality loudspeaker drivers for OEM customers — and senior development engineer for sophisticated CAD/CAM, data acquisition and process control, professional digital audio products, and more.

Since 1990, Pierce has been working as an independent consultant in the audio fields. For much of that period, he was the principal software engineer for the AKG DSE-7000 and Orban AUDICY digital audio editing workstations. As an offshoot of this work, he has proposed and developed (what will soon be) an AES standard for exchanging metadata along with audio between diverse professional audio applications. In addition to this, he has consulted with a wide range of loudspeaker manufacturers, providing technical assistance and advice in design, measurement, quality control, and manufacturing, and has acquired an extensive acoustics measurement and analysis facility that has allowed him to develop a comprehensive suite of loudspeaker-simulation and modeling tools. He has served on a number of technical review committees for organizations such as the Audio Engineering Society, and continues to write and present tutorials on subjects such as digital audio and loudspeaker operating principles.

Apart from his professional interests, Pierce has an active interest in fine-art photography, having had a number of photographs accepted in juried art shows, and will be teaching several upcoming course on the subject. Additionally, he has had a long-term involvement in Baroque keyboard instruments and music, having built a dozen instruments including harpsichords, clavichords, and small pipe organs.

HOWARD FERSTLER

PIERCE, WEBB (8 AUG 1926–24 FEB 1991)

American country singer, guitarist, songwriter, and publisher, born in West Monroe, Louisiana. After local performances, he appeared on the *Louisiana Hayride* radio program in 1950 and gained recording contracts with several labels, including Decca. He was successful with a nasal voice that helped to establish the so-called honky-tonk style. His first hit records were "Wondering" (Decca #46364; 1952) and "Back Street Affair" (Decca #28369; 1952). "Slowly" (Decca #28991; 1954) and "In the Jailhouse Now" (Decca #29391; 1955) were important records of the mid-1950s, when Pierce was featured on *Grand Ole Opry*. He established a Nashville publishing firm, Cedarwood Music, in 1953, and made a success of it while continuing his performances and recordings. By 1976 he had recorded 84 country chart songs. After the 1970s he was less active. He died in Nashville after being diagnosed with cancer.

Webb Pierce in the mid-'50s. Courtesy David A. Jasen

PIKE, ERNEST

British tenor, said to be King Edward's favorite; he was the son of one of the Royal bakers. For a time his popularity was as great as Peter Dawson's. As early as April 1904 Pike recorded for G & T, singing "Take a Pair of Sparkling Eyes" from *Gondoliers* (#2-2465; August 1904) and two other numbers in the same session. Pike also recorded for the Gramophone Co. Zonophone label and the Columbia Regal label. He made Edison two-minute cylinders in London in 1907, and four-minute cylinders later (to 1910), beginning with "When the Berry's on the Holly" (#13769). On some Edisons (#13769), he was identified as Herbert Payne. Among his other noms du disque were David Boyd, Arthur Brett, Eric Courtland, Alan Dale, Arthur Gray, Jack Henty, Sam Hovey, Herbert Payne, and Richard Pembroke. He was the Murray of "Murray and Denton." Pike remained popular in Britain into the 1920s.

PINCH EFFECT

In disc recording, the situation caused by the fact that the cutting stylus does not twist to face the groove direction, while the reproducing stylus does; thus points of contact between the one stylus and the groove are not identical to the points of contact of the other stylus and the groove. The result is tracing distortion. [Frederick 1932 gives illustrations.]

See also **Distortion**

PING-PONG EFFECT

A stereophonic separation of signals in which the sound output appears to come from one or the other of the loudspeakers, rather than from the space between or around them; the term coming from the alternating sounds of table tennis rackets striking the ball.

PINI-CORSI, ANTONIO (JUNE 1858–22 APR 1918)

Italian baritone, born in Zara. After a debut in Cremona in 1878, he sang in many Italian houses. Chosen by Verdi, he created the role of Ford in *Falstaff* at La Scala in 1893. He was with the Metropolitan Opera from 1899 to 1901 and from 1909 to 1914, recognized as one of the greatest portrayers of buffo roles like Leporello and Dr. Bartolo, as well as Ford. He died in Milan.

Pini-Corsi recorded for Pathé cylinders and discs in Paris, in 1905 and 1912. His first record was Pathé #4134, "Manca un foglio" from *Barbiere di Siviglia*. In 1912 he sang Ford's principal aria, "Quand'ero paggio" (#84542). He is also heard on Columbia records made in Milan in 1904, including his fine "Largo al factotum" (#10245); and on G & T from 1903 to 1909, including much material from *Don Pasquale*. There were numerous LP reissues, on Classic Edition, Belcantodisc, Top Artists Platters, Olympus, and Heritage labels. Most of the reissues are from *Barbiere di Siviglia*. Pini-Corsi's recordings are available on CD, mostly on anthologies of early opera cylinders.

PINK FLOYD

British rock and roll band active from 1965 until the present. Founding members were Syd Barrett, guitar and vocals; Roger Waters, bass and vocals; Rick Wright, keyboards; and Nick Mason, drums. Barrett named the band after two bluesmen, Pink Anderson and Floyd Council and the early band reflected this interest by performing experimental R&B mixed with the culture of psychedelics. Named from a poem by William Blake, *The Piper at the Gates of Dawn* (Columbia SCX #6157), the band's first album appeared in 1967. Barrett was the songwriter but he suffered a mental breakdown reportedly due to hallucinogens. He was replaced by David Gilmore in 1968. The band's second album, *A Saucerful of Secrets* (Columbia SCX #6258), was released the same year and ended rumors that the creative force in the band left with Barrett.

In the 1970s Pink Floyd achieved some of it most experimental work onstage and in the studio. Waters took over as lead songwriter and in 1973, the band released one of the most successful albums in rock his-

tory. *The Dark Side of the Moon* (Harvest SMAS #11163) stayed on the charts for over a decade and became legendary as the most popular concept album ever recorded. In 1975 the band released *Wish You Were Here* (Columbia PC #33453) which further reinforced their reputation as mixers of experimental rock and surrealism. Their concerts reflected this in the use of elaborate light shows and multimedia events, including the appearance of giant inflatable animals. The apex of the band's popularity coincided with the release of the double-sided epic concept album, *The Wall* (Columbia #PC2 36183) in 1979.

The film version of *The Wall* premiered in 1982. By the release of the band's final album with Roger Waters, *The Final Cut* (Columbia QC #38243), tensions in the group seemed to herald its demise. Waters left the band in 1987. Pink Floyd continued under the leadership of Gilmore to pack stadiums and release albums in spite of legal proceedings initiated by Waters.

The entire Pink Floyd catalog is available on CD. Notable albums include *Relics* (Harvest SW #759), *Meddle* (Harvest SMAS #832), *Animals* (Columbia JC #34474), *A Momentary Lapse of Reason* (Columbia OC #40599), and the extensive box set *Shine On* (Columbia CXK #53180).

JOHN ROCCO

PINK NOISE

Broadband noise whose energy content is inversely proportional to frequency. The rate of change as the frequency climbs is minus 3 dB per octave, which results in equal energy in each octave. Pink noise is often used as a sound source for testing audio components.

See also **White Noise**

HOWARD FERSTLER

Pink Floyd's first album. Courtesy Frank Hoffmann

PINNOCK, TREVOR (16 DEC 1946–)

English harpsichordist and conductor, born in Canterbury. He studied at the Royal College of Music in London, and toured with the Academy of St. Martin-in-the-Fields. In 1973 he established the English Concert, a group devoted to early music and authentic performance. He and the Concert have won many important awards, including the Grand Prix du Disque and the Gramophone award (for *The Messiah*). As soloist Pinnock has recorded the complete J.S. Bach toccatas, the "Goldberg Variations," and an album of popular harpsichord pieces named *The Harmonious Blacksmith*; all are on Deutsche Grammophon/Archiv label.

PINZA, EZIO (18 MAY 1892–9 MAY 1957)

Italian bass-baritone, born Fortunato Pinza in Rome. He studied engineering, then turned to singing and made his operatic debut in 1914 in Soncino, doing Oroveso in *Norma*. After military service with the Italian army he went to La Scala, and was heard in the world premiere of Boito's *Nerone*. His Metropolitan Opera debut was in *Vestale* on 1 Nov 1926; he remained with the company until 1947. Pinza's greatest roles, establishing him as the leading interpreter of the bass-baritone repertoire, were Mephistofeles, Don Giovanni, and Boris. But his most wonderful characterization was a crossover into the Broadway musical, as he sang opposite Mary Martin in *South Pacific* (1949). In 1954 he appeared in another Broadway show, *Fanny*. He died in Stamford, Connecticut.

Pinza recorded for HMV in 1923–1924, and again in 1929 and 1939. He was with Victor in 1927–1940, and 1950–1954; then with U.S. Columbia in 1944–1950. His first disc was one of his acclaimed arias, "Il lacerato spirito" (HMV #2-052240; 1923). Among his outstanding recordings were two of the Verdi *Requiem*, one made at La Scala for Victor (#V-9831-30; 1929), the other — with Beniamino Gigli and Maria Caniglia — at the Royal Opera House, Rome (Victor DB #6210-19; 1939). He was in the *Lucia* Sextette made for Victor, with Amelita Galli-Curci, Louise Homer, Gigli, Giuseppe De Luca, and Angelo Bada (#10012). His popular album *Falling in Love with Love* included selections from Hollywood musicals (Victor #10-3282). The original cast recording of *South Pacific* was released as a Columbia album (#850; 1949); its "Some Enchanted Evening," remarkably phrased by Pinza, was released on Columbia (#41190-1A). There are numerous CD reissues of his historical recordings, both on entire discs devoted to him (on Pearl, Presier, and other labels) as well as on anthologies of opera singers.

PIONEER ELECTRONICS (USA), INC.

A division of the Tokyo Pioneer Corp., which was founded in 1938 as a radio and speaker-repair company. The U.S. branch opened in 1972, and as of 2002 employs over 300 people at its Long Beach, California, headquarters. The firm is best known for its home and mobile (in-car) audio equipment, marketed under the Pioneer and Premier names. Pioneer introduced several new technologies, including the unsuccessful LaserDisc player, an early home-video format; however, it did serve as a model for the more successful DVD format, also introduced by Pioneer. In car audio, Pionner introduced the first in-dash CD player, and the first detachable face-plate car stereo. [website: www.pioneerelectronics.com.]

PIRATED RECORDINGS

Recordings copied and sold or used without authorization, and also sometimes known as bootlegged recordings. There are subtle differences between the two, however. Pirated music is the blatant and unauthorized copying and redistribution of copyrighted material. It directly takes money from the pockets of the musicians and producers, and although it's not exactly keeping most of them from eating, it is robbing them of income that is rightfully theirs. Bootlegging, on the other hand, involves the distribution of previously unreleased material. The bottom line is that both practices violate copyright laws and steal from producers and musicians.

The practice of making unauthorized copies began in the cylinder era, as the blanks were easily obtained and copying devices were available. The quality of copies was hard to distinguish at first from the quality of originals, neither being outstanding. However, by 1902 the superiority of factory-made cylinders was clear, and pirating diminished. It resumed in the analog disc era, as recording from radio ("air shots" or "air checks") became practical and flowered with the LP record and the tape master. Live concerts and operas were recorded surreptitiously on the scene and sold, often rather brazenly. Even American labels copied material from European socialist countries without payment (e.g., Coliseum label reissued many Russian, Czech, and Polish recordings). Jolly Roger and many other labels copied Victor and Columbia jazz performances. Among the most notorious pirated records were those made of Maria Callas in Traviata, a role she had not (for various odd reasons) recorded "legally" for EMI. In March 1966, her Covent Garden performance of 1958 materialized on LP, complete, thanks to an obscure label named FWR. Another bootleg Callas Violetta (from La Scala in 1955) appeared in 1972; and a Mexico City performance of 1952 came out in 1973, issued by the famous bootlegger, Edward J. Smith. EMI finally did issue a Callas Violetta, from 1958, the "Lisbon Traviata."

For years, analog cassette tapes proved the easiest format to copy and distribute illegally. There was already a $100 million market in the U.S. for bootleg cassettes by 1971, according to a story in *Business Week* magazine. The Recording Industry Association of America (RIAA) took steps to combat piracy through legislation, and succeeded in getting laws against it passed in several states. Then the U.S. Congress passed the revised Copyright Act (1978), giving legal protection to the original makers of recordings.

In 1981 and 1982 investigative reporting brought to light the pirating activities of the Aries Records firm in California. Uncommon modern works were recorded by the label from broadcasts or illegal tape copies, artists' names were changed (in most cases), and the records were boldly marketed along with those of legitimate producers. A report from the International Federation of the Phonographic Industry (IFPI) in 1991 pointed out that worldwide piracy is continuing on a massive scale. For 1989 bootlegs were said to have caused losses to the industry in the many millions of dollars. On the world map, the centers of illegality have been Southeast Asia, India, and Latin America. In Africa the legitimate music industry is said to be on the verge of collapse because of incursions by pirates; and IFPI reports greatly increasing problems in newly liberated Eastern Europe. In Western Europe the situation has stabilized, with losses of only a few million in dollars per year. However, the CD is proving to be another easy format to work with, and more than a third of the CD sales in Germany, for example, are attributed to illegal issues.

Modern digital technology is making pirating even more widespread than in the past and has dramatically changed the nature of the practice. The RIAA reported in 1999 that it confiscated 226,000 counterfeit CDs in the first half of that year alone. That was up sharply from the previous year, when the association removed 157,000 pirated recordings from circulation. Overseas, the pirating of CDs and cassette tapes has taken on almost epic proportions. In addition, the internet allows individuals to download titles and swap them to such an extent that one person can copy entire albums with impunity. The quality is not up to good CD standards, but those who do such pirating are often not connoisseurs of good sound anyway.

The original Napster service was an internet operation that allowed individuals to download MP3 copies from copyrighted albums for free without compensation to the musicians who performed the music. It was eventually shut down because the practice was costing producers and musicians money; a revived pay service was introduced in 2003. When the "free" Napster was in operation, it was a very simple program that "read" the MP3 music files on a correspondent's hard disk, and then published the list to a server somewhere out on the internet. Everyone using Napster published to a common database, which could then be searched to find any title an individual might be interested in. The program displayed a list of matches — nearly every popular song from the past 40 years could be found — and then the person wanting to download a music file simply clicked on an item, connected to another Napster user, and got the file directly from them. Napster was therefore a large-scale clearinghouse (or as one individual said, "a giant online pirate bazaar") that allowed individuals to pirate material directly, completely eliminating the middleman.

Even movie and music DVD releases, which supposedly have copy-code protections, have been pirated by intrepid hackers. Some intrepid types even market computer software that will allow you to copy both DVD and video cassette releases to a hard disc or recordable DVD blanks. [Gramophone report in April 1991, p. 1785; Wile 1985/1]

REV. HOWARD FERSTLER

PITCH (I)
The property of musical tone that is determined by the frequency of the sound wave that produces it. In order for musicians to play in ensemble, an agreement is necessary among them regarding the pitch to be sounded for each note of the score. Various standards for pitch have been in use, though none have found universal adoption. These agreements have gradually resulted in a raising of the pitch standard; it is believed now that musicians of the 18th century played any given note about a semitone lower than the same note would be played today. In the early 19th century, pitch in European opera houses was 425.5 cycles per second for the note A in the treble staff. A Paris agreement of 1859 established that the note A would be played at 435 cycles per second (435 Hz). In 1939 an international agreement set the pitch of A at 440 Hz, and this remains the most accepted norm.

Pitch in recording is affected by the speed at which the cylinder or disc rotates, the factor being applicable both in making the record and in playing it back. A 6 percent deviation in playing speed results in a change in pitch by a semitone: 6 percent faster, meaning the pitch rises a semitone, 6 percent slower that it falls a semitone. A 6 percent deviation is achieved on a 78-rpm disc by 4 1/2 revolutions per minute on either side of the correct rotation rate, and by only two rpm for an LP record. Early discs made to be played at speeds above 78 rpm (e.g., at 80 or 82 rpm) will result in a noticeably lower (flattened) pitch when the playback turntable is set for 78 rpm. These problems have been a prime concern to those who reissue acoustic discs in LP or CD format.

See also **Sonic Restoration of Historical Recordings; Stroboscopic Disc; Tuning Band**

PITCH (II)
The distance between tracks on a recording medium. For example, on a compact disc it is 1.6 microns.

PITCH (III)

The number of grooves (i.e., turns, or threads) per inch on a cylinder or disc record, expressed as a decimal; "0.1 inch pitch" refers to a configuration of 10 grooves per inch. Most cylinder records of the early 1890s had 1.0 pitch, or 100 grooves per inch. Standard 78 rpm discs have a pitch of 0.9 to 1.2. Microgroove LPs have a pitch of 2. 0 to 3.

See also **Cylinder; Disc**

PITS

The bumps on a compact disc, carriers of the signal. They are read by the laser pickup by diffracting the light they receive and decreasing the light returned to the pickup according to the characteristics of the signals they represent.

PITTS, EUGENE (3 AUG 1940–)

Awarded a B.A. in English literature from Northwestern University in 1962, Pitts was editor in chief of *Audio Magazine* from 1973 to 1995. During that time, he played a key roll in determining the magazine's style and the way it balanced the need for hard, engineering-style data as well as the important need to satisfy the reading requirements of a broad subscription base. Since he left *Audio* (which folded a few years after he left), Pitts has been manager/ owner/publisher of the *Audiophile Voice* (formerly the magazine of the Weschster Audiophile Society), an audio journal that stresses the analysis of recordings and performance aesthetics as much as equipment quality.

HOWARD FERSTLER

PIZZARELLO, JOSEPH

One of the earliest pianists identified on records, with 12 numbers in the Bettini catalog of May 1897, and 12 in Bettini's 1898 catalog.

PLANÇON, POL
(12 JUNE 1851–11 AUG 1914)

French bass, born Pol-Henri Plançon in Fumay. His opera debut was in Lyons in 1877. In 1883 he sang Mephistopheles at the Paris Opéra, the first of more than 100 times he would perform that role there in 10 seasons. He appeared first at the Metropolitan Opera in 1893, and remained until 1908. Plançon had more than 50 roles, including Wagnerian parts and the bass-baritone repertoire of the French/Italian composers. He died in Paris.

Pol Plançon in the 1917 Victor catalog. Courtesy Jerald Kalstein

His first records were for Bettini; there were listings in the three known catalogs from 1897 to 1898, a total of five songs and two arias. "Air du tambour-major" from *Le Caid* by Thomas was particularly notable, and he recorded it later for G & T (#2-2664; 1902) and Victor (#85019; 1903 and 1906). He made Zonophone discs in Paris in 1901–1902; and G & T's in London in 1902. Most of his output was in the U.S. for Victor during 1903–1908. There were 20 solos in the 1917 Victor catalog. Perhaps the finest of his discs is the "Serenade" from *Damnation du Faust* (Victor #81034; 1904 and 1906). There were many 78-rpm reissues, on IRCC, HMV Archive, and Historic Record Society; and numerous LP and CD reissues as well, on most of the reprint labels. [Hevingham-Root & Dennis 1953 is a complete discography.]

PLANET RECORDS (LABEL)

SEE PERRY, RICHARD

PLATE

The name given to the early hard rubber disc recordings made by Emile Berliner, issued by the U.S.

Gramophone Co. in 1894. Berliner continued referring to his discs as plates until 1896.

PLATE PHONOGRAPH

A tinfoil disc player, marketed in Paris in 1879 by Ducretet et Cie.

PLATTER

A phonograph disc record.

PLATTERS, THE

At the height of their career, the Platters were an anachronism, performing classic Tin Pan Alley material updated slightly to fit the rhythmic framework of the rock 'n' roll era. Founded by Herbert Reed in 1953, the group — which also included David Lynch, Paul Robi, and lead singer Tony Williams — initially recorded in a doo-wop style for the Federal label. Failing to achieve a hit record, members were working as parking lot attendants in Los Angeles when they met music business entrepreneur Buck Ram. Initially using them to make demonstration discs of his own compositions (that tended to fall within the crooning genre), Ram insisted that Mercury Records sign them

The Platters, c. mid-'50s. Courtesy David A. Jasen

as part of a package deal involving another of his clients, the Penguins, then on the verge of stardom with the recording, "Earth Angel" (Dootone #348; 1954–1955). In one of the supreme ironies in recording history, the Penguins faded from the public eye without another pop hit, while the Platters (adding Zola Taylor in late 1955) became the top-selling vocal group of the second half of the 1950s. Their Top 10 singles included "Only You" (Mercury #70633; 1955), "The Great Pretender" (Mercury #70753; 1955–1956; #1), "(You've Got) The Magic Touch" (Mercury #70819; 1956), "My Prayer" (Mercury #70893; 1956; #1), "Twilight Time" (Mercury #71289; 1958; #1), "Smoke Gets in Your Eyes" (Mercury #71383; 1958-1959; #1), and "Harbor Lights" (Mercury #71563; 1960).

The group's decline in the early 1960s has been attributed to a number of causes, most notably the morals arrest of the male members on 10 Aug 1959, the departure of Williams (one of the most gifted vocalists in pop) for a solo career in 1960, and changing consumer tastes. The Platters continued to enjoy steady album sales with the release of titles such as *Encore of Golden Hits* (Mercury #20472; 1960; 174 weeks on pop charts) and *More Encore of Golden Hits* (Mercury #20591; 1960). By the early 1970s, the group — by then recording for Musicor — was considered a nostalgia act, sometimes performing in promoter Richard Nader's rock 'n' roll revival shows. As copyright holder of the Platters's name, Ram continued to manage the official version of the group well into the 1980s. However, he was continuously forced to file lawsuits to keep pseudo groups from using the name. Greatest hits packages featuring the Mercury material have remained popular; Rhino issued a two-disc anthology and the German Bear Family label released a nine-CD box set in the late 1980s. [Stambler 1989.]

FRANK HOFFMANN

PLAUT, FRED (1907–1985)

Noted recording engineer for Columbia Records from the mid-1940s through the 1970s, Plaut specialized in classical music and broadway shows, and won two Grammy awards for engineering. During the years he worked as an engineer, he recorded notables such as Miles Davis, Virgil Thomson, Ned Rorem, Aaron Copland, Leonard Bernstein, John Williams (the guitarist), Robert Casadesus, Glenn Gould, Eugene Ormandy, Rudolf Serkin, and Igor Stravinsky. Plaut was also an avid photographer, and his photos of numerous musical personalities are housed in the

Archives at Yale University. Yale also has a recording facility named after him.

HOWARD FERSTLER

PLAYBACK CURVE

The reciprocal of the recording curve in an audio system; the degree of frequency compensation or equalization required in playback.

PLAYBACK HEAD

The element of a tape deck that generates electric currents from the recorded pattern on the tape passing by it; it may be the same head as the recording head.

PLAYBACK LOSS

The difference between recorded and reproduced levels at a given point on a disc record. It results from the variance in formation between the two walls of the modulated groove (one side being concave, the other convex).

PLAYBOY

A jukebox introduced by Seeburg in 1939; it was the first to have a wall box with selections in it, separated from the speaker apparatus.

PLAYBOY RECORDS (LABEL)

Record label founded by men's magazine mogul Hugh Hefner in 1972. The label recorded country (Mickey Gilley, Wynn Stewart), pop (including Playboy playmate Barbi Benton), disco, and R&B/soul music, releasing albums and singles through 1978, when it folded.

PLAYERPHONE TALKING MACHINE CO.

A Chicago firm, established in 1916. It advertised the Playerphone disc player, available in six models. The firm was reported bankrupt in February 1922. There was a vertical-cut record with the label name Playerphone for a time. [Rust 1978.]

PLAYING SPEEDS

SEE PITCH (I); SPEEDS

Disc made by the Playerphone company of Chicago, c. late teens. Courtesy Kurt Nauck/Nauck's Vintage Records

PLAYS

SEE LITERARY RECORDINGS

PLAYTIME (LABEL)

A children's record, in seven-inch diameter, issued by American Record Corp. and then by CBS in 1932 and 1941. [Rust 1978.]

Children's label issued by Columbia in the late '30s/early '40s. Courtesy Kurt Nauck/Nauck's Vintage Records

PLAZA (LABEL)

A British record issued from 1933 to 1935 by British Homophone Co., Ltd. It was an eight-inch disc, but had a long playing time equal to standard records; price was 6 pence.

PLAZA MUSIC CO.

A New York firm, established in 1911 as a music publisher. In September 1919 Plaza was advertising "Perfection" albums. Bankruptcy was announced in December 1920, but by April 1921 the firm was back in business. Discs with the Banner Record label were announced in January 1922. In March 1922 Plaza reported having acquired the Repeat-O-Voice business, with its six-inch, double-sided metal discs for home recording. Plaza continued dealing in sheet music, and sold phonographs and accessories.

Banner was the principal Plaza label for 14 years. At first Plaza drew on other firms for its matrices, e.g., Paramount and Emerson, but in 1923 began to record in its own studio. Among its own labels, there was considerable duplication of material, often with names of artists changed. The Plaza output was primarily dance music and popular vocals; there were also some light classical records, and miscellaneous ethnic and folk music. Noted artists like Vernon Dalhart, Billy Jones, Ernest Hare, Fletcher Henderson, and the Original Memphis Five appeared on the Banner label. Little Tots' Nursery Tunes was another Plaza label.

The Conqueror label was introduced in 1926, and was issued until 1942. It used Banner material, with the artists under pseudonyms. Domino was another label in the Plaza group, issued from 1924 to 1933. In the mid-1920s Plaza material was used for the Homestead label, distributed by the Chicago Mail Order Co. From 1927 to 1932 there was also the Jewel label. Lenox was a rare label with Plaza material. Oriole was issued from 1921 to 1938. Plaza masters were used by Regal from 1923 to 1931, Regal Record Co. being a Plaza subsidiary. The Regal Record Co. came under control of the Crystalate Gramophone Record Manufacturing Co., Ltd., of U.K. in 1929, as the first step in the formation of the American Record Corp. [*RR* carried a long series of lists from the Plaza 5000 series, beginning in the 36th issue (1961), and continuing to 1983; Rust 1980.]

FRANK ANDREWS

PLOTKIN, CHUCK

Born Charles Plotkin in Los Angeles, Plotkin played music as a hobby through his teen and college years, but trained to be a lawyer. However, a chance meeting with singer Wendy Waldman led him to open his own studio and produce her first album for Warner Bros. in 1973. That same year, he produced Steve Ferguson's first album for Geffen, which led to a long relationship with that label. Plotkin scored his first success with singer/guitarist Andrew Gold, and then hit it big with the folk-pop group, Orleans, and their hits "Dance with Me" in 1975 (Asylum #45261; #6) and "Still the One" from 1976 (Asylum #45336; #5). In 1976 he met Jon Landau, who asked for his assistance in mixing Bruce Springsteen's album *Darkness on the Edge of Town*; from that point forward, Plotkin became coproducer along with Springsteen and Landau on all of Springsteen's records (until 2002's *The Rising*). Plotkin also oversaw Bob Dylan's 1981 album, *Shot of Love*, which many Dylan fans feel ranks among his best later work. Plotkin is also a pianist who has performed on various albums that he produced.

CARL BENSON

POHLMANN, KEN C.

Pohlmann is a tenured full professor and director of the music engineering technology program in the School of Music at the University of Miami in Coral Gables. He holds B.S. and M.S. degrees in electrical engineering from the University of Illinois in Urbana–Champaign, and is the author of *Principles of Digital Audio* (4th edition, 2000, McGraw-Hill) and *The Compact Disc Handbook* (2nd ed., 1992, A-R Editions), coauthor of *Writing for New Media* (1st ed., 1997, Wiley), and editor and coauthor of *Advanced Digital Audio* (1st ed., 1991, Sams). He has written over 1,500 articles for audio magazines. He contributes to *Sound & Vision* and *Mobile Entertainment* magazines.

Pohlmann chaired the Audio Engineering Society's Conference on Digital Audio in 1989 and cochaired the Society's Conference on Internet Audio in 1997. He was presented two AES Board of Governor's awards (1989 and 1998) and an AES Fellowship award (1990) by the Audio Engineering Society for his work in the field of audio engineering. He is a nonboard member of the National Public Radio Distribution/ Interconnection Committee, and a member of the board of directors of the New World Symphony.

He serves as a consultant in the design of digital audio systems, for the development of mobile audio systems for automobile manufacturers, and as an expert witness in technology patent litigation. Some of his consulting clients include: Alpine, Baker & McKenzie, Bertlesmann, Blockbuster, Daimler Chrysler, Darby & Darby, Fish & Neave, Ford, Fujitsu Ten, Harman/Becker, Hyundai, IBM, Kia, Lexus, Microsoft, Motorola, Nippon Columbia, Onkyo,

RealNetworks, Sony, TDK, Time Warner, Toyota, and United Technologies.

HOWARD FERSTLER

POLAR RESPONSE: LOUDSPEAKERS

A graphic display of the speaker's dispersion at specific frequencies. Polar response will usually be quite wide if the driver diameter is small in relation to the frequencies being reproduced. Typical loudspeakers will therefore have variable polar response as the frequency varies, with it narrowing considerably in the top octave.

See also **Loudspeaker**

HOWARD FERSTLER

POLAR RESPONSE: MICROPHONES

A graphic display of the audio output levels of the microphone at different frequencies, caused by sound waves arriving at the diaphragm from different directions. Microphone polar response will vary from omni-directional to very narrow, with dispersion patterns also varying considerably as the signal frequencies change.

See also **Microphone**

HOWARD FERSTLER

POLE FACE ALIGNMENT

SEE GAP ALIGNMENT

POLICE, THE

The Police were one of many conventional rock acts allowing themselves to be marketed under the New Wave banner in order to enhance their chances for commercial acceptance. Although the band's savvy blend of stripped-down guitar-driven pop, smoothed-over reggae rhythms, and bleached-blond, poster-boy looks connected with the public from the start, an abundance of infectious compositions and clever video clips — programmed round-the-clock by MTV and other cable channels — elevated them to superstardom at the time of their breakup.

The original impetus for the Police was supplied by drummer Stewart Copeland, who provided its name and enlisted his brother, Miles, a talent agent and record executive, to manage their career. He added singer/bassist/composer Gordon Sumner (aka Sting) for his stage presence in 1976, and when the original lead guitarist left the following year, brought in Andy Summers, who was well known for session work and as a member of various U.K. rock groups.

The band's debut album, *Outlandos D'Amour* (A&M #4753; 1978; #23), failed to catch on immediately due to BBC censorship of the initial singles releases — "Roxanne" (A&M #2096; 1979; #32) and "Can't Stand Losing You" (A&M #2147; 1979; #42 U.K.) — and the music's failure to fit established radio playlist guidelines in the U.S. Music writers, however, were almost without exception enthusiastic; *New York Times'* John Rockwell wrote that "no other rock band in recent memory has been able to combine intellectuality, progressivism, and visceral excitement so well" (5 Apr 1979). When A&M decided to include "Roxanne" on the sampler LP, *No Wave*, the song entered the *Billboard Hot 100*.

With A&M providing greater studio and promotional support, the second album, *Regatta De Blanc* (A&M #4792; 1979; #25), earned a 1980 Grammy for Best Rock Instrumental Performance with the title track. The next release, *Zenyatta Mondatta* (A&M #4831; 1980; #5), did even better, going platinum and garnering two Grammys in 1981, Best Rock Performance by a Duo or Group with Vocal ("Don't Stand So Close to Me") and Best Rock Instrumental Performance ("Behind My Camel"). *Ghost in the Machine* (A&M #3730; 1981; #2), although receiving only lukewarm endorsements from the press (due in part to its darker thematic concerns), also achieved platinum sales.

The fifth LP, *Synchronicity* (A&M #3735; 1983; #1), commercially outstripped all of the Police's earlier work by a considerable margin, largely due to the widespread appeal of the Sting-composed ballad, "Every Breath You Take" (A&M #2542; 1983; #1). The work included many other gems as well, including three more hit singles: "King of Pain" (A&M #2569; 1983; #3), "Synchronicity" (A&M #2571; 1983; #16), and "Wrapped Around Your Finger" (A&M #2614; 1984; #8). *Synchronicity* pulled all of the band's earlier albums back onto the charts as well as earning two 1983 Grammys: Best Pop Vocal Performance by a Duo or Group with Vocal ("Every Breath You Take") and Best Rock Performance by a Duo or Group with Vocal.

At this point in time the band members split off to pursue various solo projects, only getting together to perform three benefit concerts for Amnesty International in summer 1986. Although demands for an official reunion have been repeatedly dashed, A&M has continued to market the Policy legacy via a steady stream of compilation releases, most notably *Every Breath You Take — The Singles* (A&M #3902; 1986; #7), *Message in a Box: The Complete Recordings* (A&M #0150; 1993; #79), and *The Police Live!* (A&M #0222; 1995; #86).

FRANK HOFFMANN

POLK AUDIO

Located in Baltimore, Maryland, Polk has been continuously in business since 1972, and has become a major player in the hi-fi loudspeaker business. The company's namesake, Matthew Polk, earned a degree in physics from Johns Hopkins in 1971, but got into the speaker-building business as a result of he and his future partner George Klopfer building custom systems for pop-music concerts. Although the company has been very successful and has produced some excellent upscale speaker systems, its basic orientation and the primary reason for its success involves the production of user-friendly, reliable, and affordable products (including audio-system packages that have everything but disc players) for mainstream Americans. [website: www.polkaudio.com.]

See also **Loudspeaker**

HOWARD FERSTLER

POLLACK, BEN
(22 JUNE 1903–7 JUNE 1971)

U.S. Big Band leader and drummer, born in Chicago. He played in various Dixieland combos, mainly the New Orleans Rhythm Kings in Chicago. He organized his first band in 1924, and began to attract star sidemen, many of whom went on to form their own orchestras: Benny Goodman, Glenn Miller, Charlie Spivak, Harry James, Jimmy McPartland, etc. In the 1920s he had one of the most outstanding white ensembles, with engagements at the Blackhawk Restaurant and Southmoor Hotel in Chicago and the Park Central Hotel in New York. After 1940 he was less active for a time, but returned to prominence in the 1950s on the West Coast, and appeared in a 1956 motion picture about Goodman. He died in Palm Springs, California.

Pollack's band recorded first for Victor, making "When I First Met Mary" (#20394) in December 1926; the group at that time was known as Ben Pollack and His Californians. As the Park Central Orchestra they recorded in 1928–1929, with Smith Ballew, Scrappy Lambert, and the popular tenor Franklyn Baur as vocalists (Ballew and Lambert under pseudonyms). After 1930 the band left Victor and worked with numerous labels, notably Banner and Columbia. They made their final discs in 1938 for Decca. The European reissue label, Jazz Oracle, has reissued his complete recordings in chronological order on a series of CDs, and there are several other compilations available on jazz-reissue labels.

POLONIA PHONOGRAPH CO.

A Milwaukee, Wisconsin, firm, active in 1921. It made machines and records, with a repertoire of interest to Polish immigrants. There was a recording laboratory in New York City, and a pressing plant at Grove St., Milwaukee.

FRANK ANDREWS

POLYDOR (LABEL)

A German record made by Deutsche Grammophon Gesellschaft, Berlin and Hanover, from 1921. The label was used only for exports, and although DGG originated as the German branch of the Gramophone Co., and had the right to use the Gramophone Co. trademarks in Germany, the export label did not carry the Nipper picture nor was it identified with "Die Stimme seines Herrn." Polydor was exported to the U.S., handled by Brunswick, and sold by them as Polydor/Brunswick records, included a roster of great artists (such as Wilhelm Furtwängler and the Berlin Philharmonic Orchestra). Polydor was also established in other countries and was greatly successful until the economic crisis of 1929. During the 1930s there was a Decca Polydor label marketed by British Decca, in the U.K. The French Polydor record was sold to Philips in 1950. U.S. Decca released Polydor recordings in America. Polydor was among the 11 labels listed in the first LP catalog (predecessor to *Schwann*), issued in October 1949. With the establishment of the new DGG label in 1952, Polydor was assigned to light music. After 1955 Polydor was marketed in the U.K. by Heliodor Record Co., Ltd. In 1962, Polydor/DGG merged with Philips in a 50-50 partnership to form Polydor International; a decade later, Polydor International was absorbed into Phonogram Records to form Polygram International.

POLYGRAM INTERNATIONAL

A firm established on 3 Jan 1972, owned by Philips NV, merging Polydor International and Phonogram The name was printed as PolyGram, better suggesting the roots of the enterprise in Polyphon Musikwerke (Leipzig, 1911) and the Gramophone Co. (although the suffix may have come from phono*gram*). The same year, Polygram acquired MGM and Verve Records, and would subsequently either purchase or distribute a large number of labels, including Atlanta Artists, Casablanca, Chocolate City, Compleat, Decca (U.K.), De-Lite, Deram, Emarcy, Enja, Gramavision, Lection, London, Mercury, Millenium, MPS, Oasis, Philips, Polydor, Riva, RSO, Threshold, Total Experience, 21, and Vertigo. The firm was also the first to widely promote the CD format, developed by Philips Electronics, introducing it worldwide in 1982; by 1990, over 60 percent of PolyGram's sales were in the new medium. In 1987

Philips took complete ownership of the group, and continued to add other labels to it, including Island in 1989, A&M in 1990, and Motown in 1993. In 1998, Seagram acquired PolyGram and combined it with their Universal/MCA holdings to form the Universal Music Group. Subsequently, Seagram sold its holdings to the French conglomerate Vivendi company.

POLYPHON (LABEL)

A lateral-cut, double-sided 10-inch disc on sale in Britain in 1908, presenting German repertoire. The first London agent was J.A. Williams, but by July 1910 the agency was Klingsor Works, London. With the September 1910 issues, the label name had been changed to Klingsor, but the Polyphon trademark remained. Polyphon Musikwerke AG established its own British branch and began selling Polyphon Records from January 1913 (the Klingsors having been discontinued). In June 1913 the label name changed again, to "Pilot Record — Formerly Polyphon Record." The label ceased with the outbreak of World War I in 1914.

FRANK ANDREWS

POLYPHON MUSIKWERKE AG

A German firm, established in Leipzig around 1890 as a music box maker. It began to issue disc records with the Polyphon label in 1905, and also made talking machines. By act of the German government, it took over the holdings of Deutsche Grammophon AG, the German branch of the Gramophone Co., on 24 Apr 1917. In 1924 the Anglo-German Arbitration Tribunal restored privileges to Deutsche Grammophon.

POLYPHONE

A phonograph with two sapphire-stylus reproducers, each tracking the same groove but 3/8 to 1/2 inch apart. Leon Douglass was the inventor. The manufacturer named in an 1899 *Phonoscope* advertisement was Polyphone Co., 107 Madison St., Chicago. It was marketed by H.B. Babson and the Talking Machine Co. of Chicago.

PONIATOFF, ALEXANDER MATHEW (25 MAR 1892–24 OCT 1980)

Russian-American electrical engineer responsible for the development of the professional tape recorder and the first commercially successful video tape recorder (VTR).

Poniatoff was born in Kazan District, Russia, and educated in Moscow and Karlsruhe, gaining degrees in mechanical and electrical engineering. In 1927 he immigrated to the U.S. and became a citizen. He was employed by the General Electric Co. and later by Dalmo Victor.

In 1944, taking his initials to form the title, Poniatoff founded the AMPEX Corp. By 1946 AMPEX had turned from the manufacture of airborne radar to the production of audio tape recorders developed from the German wartime Telefunken Magnetophon machine (the first tape recorder in the truest sense). In this, Poniatoff was supported by Bing Crosby, who needed high-quality replay facilities for broadcasting purposes. By 1947 Poniatoff was able to offer a professional-quality product and the business prospered.

With the rapid postwar boom in television broadcasting in the U.S., a need soon arose for a video recorder to provide "time-shifting" of live television programs between the different U.S. time zones. Many companies therefore endeavored to produce a video tape recorder (VTR) using the same single-track, fixed-head, longitudinal-scan system used for audio, but the very much higher bandwidth required involved an unacceptably high tape speed. AMPEX offered a machine with 12 parallel tracks, but it proved unsatisfactory. Next his development team, which included Charles Ginsburg and Ray Dolby, devised a four-head trasverse-scan system in which a quadruplex head rotating at 14,400 rpm was made to scan across the width of a 2-inch tape with a tape-to-head speed of 160 ft./sec. (about 110 mph) but with a longitudinal tape speed of only 15 in./sec. In this way, acceptable picture quality was obtained with a reasonable rate of tape consumption.

By April 1956, commercial production of studio-quality machines began to revolutionize the production and distribution of television programs, and the perfecting of time-base correctors, which could stabilize the signal timing to a few nanoseconds, made color VTRs a practical proposition. In the face of emerging competition from helical scan machines, where the tracks are laid diagonally on the tape, AMPEX developed its own helical machine in 1957. They also developed the Videofile system, in which 250,000 pages of facsimile could be recorded on a single tape, offering a new means of archiving information. Poniatoff was president and then chairman of AMPEX Corp. until 1970; he died a decade later. Although quadruplex VTRs were obsolete by 1986, Poniatoff's role in making television was decisive.

GEORGE BROCK-NANNESTAD

PONS, LILY (12 APR 1898–13 FEB 1976)

French/American soprano, born Alice Josephine Pons in Draguignan. She made her debut in Mulhouse in

1927, as Lakmé, a role that came to be associated with her. She sang elsewhere in France, then at the Metropolitan Opera on 3 Jan 1931 — singing another of her great roles, Lucia. Pons remained with the Metropolitan until 1958, in some 180 performances, appearing also in the major houses of Europe and Latin America. During the 1930s she made motion pictures as well. Her second marriage was to the conductor Andre Kostelanetz. She died in Dallas.

Pons recorded for Odeon in France, 1928–1929, notably with airs from *Lakmé* and "Una voce poco fa." She worked for HMV and Victor in 1930–1940, and for Columbia in the U.S. from 1941 to 1954. "Ardon gl'incensi," the Mad Scene from *Lucia*, was inscribed in 1930 (#7369) for Victor, and remained in the catalog into the 1940s; it was transferred to the LP album *Arias* (#1473). The Bell Song from *Lakmé* was one of her most famous records (Columbia #71640-D; 1944). Most of her other 78-rpm work was also reissued on LP.

She was Rosina in the complete Metropolitan Opera live recording of *Barbiere di Siviglia* of 1938, Lakmé in the 1940 performance, and Gilda in the 1939 performance; all these were issued on Golden Age of Opera records. Pons had the role of Adele in the complete recording of *Fledermaus* made in 1950 by the Metropolitan Opera under Eugene Ormandy (#78245). In 1954 she recorded a complete *Lucia* for Columbia (#127). There have been many compilations of Pons's recordings issued on CD. Her earliest recordings, made in 1928–1929 for the Odeon label, are collected on VAI #1125. Pearl #9415 is one of many CD reissues of a selection of her HMV and Victor material; an "official" compilation of her Victor material is on RCA #61411. *Coloratura Assoluta* (Sony #60655), is a two-CD set of her Columbia recordings, spanning opera to popular material. [Park 1960 is a complete discography.]

PONSELLE, ROSA
(22 JAN 1897–25 MAY 1981)

American soprano, born in Meriden, Connecticut. She sang in church, and then as a teen in a duo with her sister Carmela, "Italian Girls," or the Ponzillo Sisters (Ponzillo being the original family name). The sister act reached the New York Palace Theatre, performing material like "Kiss Me Again" and "Comin' thro' the Rye." She was brought to the attention of Enrico Caruso, who arranged an audition at the Metropolitan Opera, and was catapulted from vaudeville to the opera stage at age 21. Her debut was in *Forza del destino*, with Caruso and Giuseppe De Luca; it was a great success. Ponselle remained with the company until 1937, establishing herself as one of the leading dramatic sopranos in *Norma*, *Ernani*, *Trovatore*, *Aida*, etc.

She retired in 1937, to live in Maryland, and died in Green Spring Valley 44 years later.

Ponselle made Columbia records from 1919 to 1923, and Victors from 1923 to 1929. Her Columbias are best played at 80 rpm, to get the correct pitches; an 82-rpm playback is needed for "D'amor sull' ali rose" from *Trovatore* (Columbia #49559). Carmela and Rosa Ponselle made several records from their vaudeville repertoire on Columbia. For Victor her finest solo disc was probably "Pace, pace, mio Dio" (#6440; #74866). The *Forza del destino* trio, with Ezio Pinza and Giovanni Martinelli (Victor #8104) is another prized interpretation. Other notable offerings were the "Ave Maria" from *Otello* (Victor #6474; Columbia #98029) and "Casta diva" (Columbia #49720). Ponselle is heard on complete opera recordings taken from Metropolitan Opera performances of 1935–1936, in *Carmen* and *Traviata*; these came out on Golden Age of Opera records. LP releases appeared on all the reissue labels. Nimbus made a CD (#17805) of mostly Verdi numbers (including the *Forza* trio; plus "Casta diva" and "Mira, O Norma" with Marion Telva and several concert songs, and a three-CD set (*In Opera and Song*; #1777) covering both operatic and popular material. "Pace, pace" appeared on an RCA CD (#87810) in 1990, along with "Casta diva" and the familiar Verdi material. "Casta Diva" also appears on a CD of the same name from Pearl (#9210), drawn from her Victor recordings, and Pearl has also reissued her complete Columbia acoustic recordings on a two-CD set (#9964). [Park 1982 is a complete discography.]

PORT

A vent or auxiliary opening in a bass reflex baffle. It must be precisely located and of correct dimension to allow passage of rear sound waves through the enclosure while keeping them in phase with the front waves.

PORTABLE RECORD PLAYERS

The ability to carry music with you — today embodied in many ultra-minature playback devices — is almost as old as the phonograph itself. The Decca portable gramophone, introduced in 1912 and made popular at the front in World War I, was the first famous portable. But the Pigmy model of the Gramophone Co., introduced in 1909, was the earliest of the genre.

During the 1920s, portables became popular that were modeled after inexpensive box cameras; like these cameras, they would fold into a small, easy-to-carry box. These often featured folding leather-covered horns and took names like "Cameraphone" (from U.K.) and "Brownie" (from U.S.) in imitation of the popular folding cameras of the day. The Peter Pan Gramophone, made in England, is among the earliest

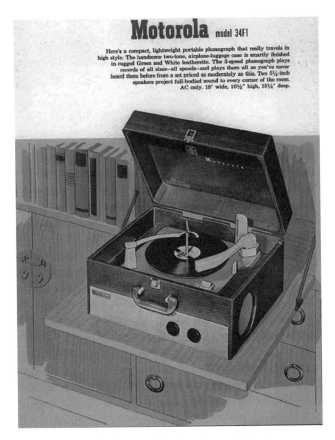

Motorola model 34F1

Here's a compact, lightweight portable phonograph that really travels in high style. The handsome two-tone, airplane-luggage case is smartly finished in rugged Green and White leatherette. The 3-speed phonograph plays records of all sizes—all speeds—and plays them all as you've never heard them before from a set priced as moderately as this. Two 5¼-inch speakers project full-bodied sound to every corner of the room. AC only. 18" wide, 10½" high, 15¼" deep.

Motorola portable phonograph advertisement. Courtesy BenCar Archives

in this style, introduced in August 1923; they even built a version that incorporated a clock, with the phonograph serving as the alarm (an early form of clock-radio!) During the mid-1920s, various models were made in U.K., Germany, and Switzerland, many using mechanical movements made by Thorens.

More conventional, suit-case–sized models were widely marketed by Victor during the later 1920s and into the 1930s. These all-in-one units lacked the novelty and extreme compactness of the box-camera models, but offered better sound without being too bulky to carry. These spring-driven models were also made by sewing machine manufacturers, such as Singer. They were ideal for door-to-door salesmen and even traveling preachers, particularly the Jehovah's Witnesses, whose leader, Joseph Franklin Rutherford, provided his troops with portable phonographs and recordings of Bible talks to carry with them during the 1930s. These phonographs became quite popular in rural areas of the U.S. and even Mexico, where electric floor models would have been impractical.

The introduction of the 45-rpm record after World War II launched a new era of portable phonographs, mostly aimed at young children and teenagers. "Singles" became the favorite method of selling pop songs to teens, and they could listen to them in their own rooms thanks to the introduction of small, self-contained, portable players. Spindles were developed so 45s could be stacked and played in sequence automatically. Portable toy phonographs were made by firms like Fischer-Price for use by younger children from the 1960s forward, often decorated with cartoon characters like Mickey Mouse.

Once cassettes and other media were introduced, an entire new generation of portable players not relying on discs were made possible. Of modern portable audio players, the most important has been the Sony Walkman, a cassette machine small enough to fit in the palm, used for headphone listening. Similar players have been introduced for the CD and MiniDisc formats. The introduction of the MP3 format in 1997 allowed music to be stored digitally in compressed files, leading to the development of several portable digital players, most notably Apple's iPod player, introduced in 2001.

REV. CARL BENSON

PORTER, STEVE (1862–3 JAN 1936)

American baritone, born Stephen Porter in Buffalo, New York. He sang in vaudeville, doing solo and ensemble work, appearing with Lillian Russell, the Diamond Comedy Four, and the American Quartet, all before or near the turn of the century. In 1906 he was one of the original members of the Peerless Quartet. His recording activities, from 1897 for Berliner, covered many labels and types of song. He did ballads, comic turns, sacred numbers, Irish monologs, and occasionally opera ("Toreador Song" is Columbia 4#538, ca. 1898). After 1900 he was heard mostly on ensemble records, with the Spencer Trio, American Quartet, Greater New York Quartet, etc. The 1917 Victor catalog had 21 titles by Porter, who continued to make records into the 1920s, some with a new group called the Harmonizers.

Porter and three colleagues established the American Phonograph Record Co. in 1901, to make cylinder records on demand. When that venture failed, Porter sailed for England and was engaged by Waterfield, Clifford and Co. of London as recording expert for their New Century Cylinder Record, for which he also performed. He moved to Nicole Records, Ltd., on formation of that company in 1903, as expert and performer. When Nicole Frères (India), Ltd., was established, Porter went to India as recording expert. By 1910 he was back in America, and remained until his death in New York. [Brooks 1979; Walsh 1943/7, 1943/10; 1952/5.]

FRANK ANDREWS

PORTLAND (LABEL)
A U.K. record of Curry's stores, issued in 1923–1924. Fewer than 100 releases are known, from matrices of Edison Bell. Some of the material was from Gennett. [Rust 1978.]

POST SYNC.
New audio material added in synchronization to a previously filmed motion picture.

POSTAGE STAMPS
The earliest stamps to illustrate a phonograph record were issued in Argentina in 1939 (*Scott Catalog* #470 and #472); they were promoting the use of flexible discs for mailing messages. A number of commemorative stamps that showed audio equipment or personalities of sound recording history were printed for the phonograph centenary year of 1977. The audio category is considered here to be separate from the much larger category of music and musicians on stamps.

Charles Cros appeared on a French stamp issued 3 Dec 1977 (Scott #B502). The U.S. issued a foolish stamp on 23 Mar 1977 (Scott #1705), showing a "phonograph unlike any ever seen before" [Brooks 1979/2]. Edison was also blasphemed by a 1977 stamp from Afars et Issas — a French territory in East Africa, now Djibouti — (Scott #C104 and #C105) that presented him listening to a lateral-cut disc, the format he fought nearly all his life. India #764 pictured an early Berliner gramophone. Surinam #476 and #477 showed a tinfoil phonograph in one denomination and a modern turntable in another.

Uruguay issued a stamp with a picture of Edison's 1878 phonograph in 1977 (#1003). An American stamp of 6 Oct 1977 honored *The Jazz Singer* with a correct illustration of a Vitaphone projector and disc playing mechanism (#1727).

It is also of interest that a postage stamp commemorating folk songs, playable on a standard LP phonograph, was issued by Bhutan in 1973; Scott did not give it a number.

POSTCARD RECORDS
Max Ettlinger & Co., of Long Acre, England, marketed Discal postcards in March 1905. In June of the same year Zonophone GmbH advertised singing postcards, and a few days later there was advertising from M. Taubert & Co. of Berlin for postcard records. Ettlinger was still selling the cards in May 1908. Such cards could be played on a standard turntable, but needed a clamp to keep them from slipping. Postcard records became common throughout the industry, and were issued in both 33 1/3– and 45-rpm speeds.

FRANK ANDREWS

POT
See PANORAMIC, *POTENTIOMETER*

POTENTIOMETER
In an amplifier, the variable attenuator, or potential divider, used to control volume; it is often referred to as a pot.

POULSEN, VALDEMAR (1869–1942)
Danish inventor and engineer, credited with the development of magnetic wire recording around 1898. His machine was named the Telegraphone, first patented in Britain (#8961) in 1899. He also invented a process for magnetic recording on iron discs and metal tape, but did not exploit it. Poulsen set up a corporation to hold his patents: A/S Telegraphonen Patent Poulsen; and a manufacturing firm: Dansk Telegraphone Fabrik A/S (1903). He showed his recorder at the Paris Exposition of 1900, and registered the voice of Emperor Franz Joseph. Later he recorded King Edward VII, and presented the wire to Queen Alexandra (its whereabouts are not known). In 1905 he sold those interests to the Telegraphone Corp. (U.S.A.) and the American Telegraphone Co. became the manufacturer. Among Poulsen's eight American patents, #661,619 (filed 8 July 1899, granted 13 Nov 1900) was most important as the bearer of his basic ideas for wire recording.

POWELL, MAUD
(22 AUG 1868–8 JAN 1920)
American violinist, born in Peru, Illinois. She studied in Leipzig and Paris, then returned to the U.S. and gave recitals. Female violinists were not often seen at that time, which was one reason she was a favorite with audiences; but she also played elegantly. Powell performed at the Columbian Exposition in Chicago in 1893. She recorded for Victor from 1904 to 1917, placing 50 solos in the 1917 catalog. Many of her recordings were arrangements, but among them were the Wieniawski "Polonaise" (#81052), Sarasate's "Zigeunerweisen" (Victor #64262) and two movements from the J.S. Bach Sonata in C-Minor (Victor #64618/19). She died in Uniontown, Pennsylvania. The Maud Powell Foundation has reissued her recordings on CD (website: http://music.acu.edu/www/

iawm/wimusic/mpf.html#anchor36525564), which are also available on Naxos #8.110961, 962, and 963.

POWELL, MEL
(12 FEB 1923–24 APR 1998)

American composers and jazz pianist, born Melvin Epstein in New York. He began as a jazz and swing player, with Benny Goodman; but also studied composition with Paul Hindemith, and took a music degree from Yale in 1952. He was on the Yale faculty from 1957 to 1969, and then went to the California Institute of Arts as Dean, remaining until his retirement. His piece Duplicates for two pianos and orchestra won the Pulitzer Prize in 1990. He has a long catalog of classical compositions, a number of which have been recorded on LP and CD.

Powell formed a jazz trio with Ruby Braff and drummer Bobby Donaldson, and made some brilliant recordings in 1954 for Vanguard, produced by John Hammond, bringing classical and jazz ideas together. For instance "Bouquet" and "You're My Thrill" are Debussian. Powell did not stay long in jazz, however, and did not record the genre after the mid-1950s. He died in Sherman Oaks, California. Powell's Vanguard recordings are anthologized on two CDs, *The Best Things in Life* (#79602) and *It's Been So Long* (#79605).

POWER AMPLIFIER

The main amplifier, or basic amplifier; the device that boosts the voltage supplied by the preamplifier to the level required to drive a loudspeaker.

See also **Amplifier**

PREAMPLIFIER

A device, commonly known as a preamp, added to an amplifier to accommodate the very low voltage output from pickups and tape recorders and to raise that voltage to a point that will drive the amplifier. For example the output level of a cartridge may be 1–5 millivolts; the preamplifier could raise it to 1–1.5 volts. The preamp may also provide frequency-response equalization and other functions as well. It may be built into the turntable or the amplifier, or may appear as a separate component.

See also **Amplifier; Controls**

PRECEDENCE EFFECT

The phenomenon of correctly identifying the direction of a sound source heard in both ears but arriving at different times. Due to the spacing of the ears, the direct sound from any source first enters the ear closest to the source, with the more distant ear getting a delayed signal. Research on this mechanism has shown that humans localize a sound source based upon the first-arrival sound, even if the subsequent arrivals are within 25–35 milliseconds. The phenomenon also describes how a stereophonic soundstage is possible from only two, up-front loudspeakers.

A practical example of the precedence effect working against realistic stereophonic sound reproduction can be seen when identical sounds come from two different speaker systems, forming a phantom center image if the listener is seated in the sweet spot out in front of but equidistant from the two speakers, and the listener then moves to the side, and therefore closer to one of the two speakers. The result is a tendency for the signal from the more distant speaker (for example, the phantom-center image) to collapse toward the nearer speaker.

See also **Franssen Effect**

HOWARD FERSTLER

PRE-EMPHASIS

A high-frequency boost used during the recording process. During playback, reciprocal deemphasis would be applied, and the result will be an improved signal-to-noise ratio.

HOWARD FERSTLER

PREISSER (LABEL)

Austrian classical label founded by Otto G. Preiser (1920–1996). Preiser was born in Vienna, but spent the war years in England. On his return to his hometown, he met musicologist H.C. Robbins Landon. The two decried the lack of recordings available of Haydn's works, so, in 1949, they formed the Haydn Society to remedy this situation. In 1952, Preiser formed his own label, primarily to release RCA and Westminster label recordings in the Austrian market. Beginning in the mid-1950s, the firm began releasing its own recordings, achieving great success with Vienesse cabaret singers, as well as classical recordings. In 1966, Preiser began a reissue program of historic recordings by opera singers; three years later, to celebrate the centennial of the Vienna State Opera, Preiser issued a five-disc set of recordings by its stars made between 1902–1937. The producer for the series, Jürgen Schmidt, has continued to oversee dozens of other reissues, moving to the CD format in 1987. After Preiser's death in 1996, Schmidt and Preiser's son Christoph took charge of the label. [website: www.presierrecords.at.]

PREMIER

The "Columbia Gold Moulded" cylinder records, six inches long, announced in April 1905. (There had been prior demonstrations.) Because of the enhanced volume produced — by the Higham mechanical amplifier built into the reproducer mechanism — the player marketed for these records was called the Loud Speaking Graphophone; it cost $100 minus horn; later the name Twentieth Century Graphophone was given to the machine, and to the records. The cylinders were issued until April 1909, despite poor sales. [Bryan 1982.]

PREMIER CABINET CO.

A firm located in 1916 in Williamsport, Pennsylvania. It offered the Premier line of disc players in 10 models.

PREMIER MANUFACTURING CO., LTD.

A U.K. firm, located in London; maker of the Clarion cylinder ca. 1907. They also made the Clarion disc from 1908, and Ebonoid discs from 1909. The Ebonoid discs, like the Ebonoid Gold Moulded Cylinders, played up to five minutes.

FRANK ANDREWS

PREMIER QUARTET

A vocal ensemble, also known (on Victor) as the American Quartet. Steve Porter, Thomas Chalmers, John Young, and Billy Murray were the original members. They made 40 Edison Diamond Discs between 1915 and 1918. Their material included items connected to World War I, such as " Bing! Bang! Bing 'Em on the Rhine" (Edison #50489; 1918) and "Submarine Attack" (Edison #50490; 1918). In 1925 the American Quartet had the same membership except for John Ryan, a tenor who replaced Young. One of their popular Victor discs was "That Certain Party"/"Tomorrow Morning."

PRESCOTT, FREDERICK MARION (1866–30 JULY 1923)

U.S. record company executive. He and his brothers began as general import/export traders in New York, emphasizing products of the Universal Talking Machine Co. They also stocked Graphophone Grands. In 1898 Prescott was trading as the Edison Phonograph Agency, and in 1899 was sole sales exporter for Frank Seaman's National Gramophone Co., getting Zonophones into the U.K. and Europe.

Prescott visited Britain in 1898, and returned to the New York business, handling machines and records from all companies. The firm issued more catalogs than any other in the trade. Prescott's 40-inch horns were used with Graphophone Grands in Koster and Bial's Music Hall, in New York. In addition to U.S., U.K., and Spanish phonographic materials, the firm handled motion pictures, bicycles, watches, and novelties. Prescott imported concert-size Pathé cylinders, and stocked all sizes of Pathé records.

Undertaking another European voyage, Prescott had contracts in Britain and agents in Germany, and Austria-Hungary for Zonophone Products. In March 1901 the International Zonophone Co. was established, with Prescott as managing director to 1903, when Gramophone Co. took over the firm. He then became founding president and general manager of the International Talking Machine Co. mbH in Berlin, marketing Odeon products.

The American Record Co. was set up in 1904 by International Talking Machine, through Hawthorne & Sheble with Frederick Prescott; the plant was in Springfield, Massachusetts. J.O. Prescott (one of Frederick's brothers) was manager.

In 1920 Frederick Prescott was living in Pompton Lakes, New Jersey, and advertising himself as a consultant to disc record manufacturers, promising to help any firm to increase record production.

FRANK ANDREWS

PRESENCE (I)

The impression given to the listener of an audio system that the original program source is actually present.

PRESENCE (II)

A boost given to frequencies in the region of 2,000–8,000 Hz, intended to enhance the forwardness of a recorded signal on playback, thus to give a greater impression of presence.

PRESERVATION OF SOUND RECORDINGS

This article has five sections: 1. General considerations; 2. Phonograph records; 3. Magnetic recordings; 4. Compact discs; 5. Archival work.

1. *General Considerations.* In the history of communication, the invention of sound recordings can be considered comparable to the invention of the printing press. It permitted people to preserve oral material so that it could be heard in aural form again and again, just as the printing press has enabled people to pre-

serve oral material in written form, available to those who can read. Today the sound recording is as important an information medium as the written word. Collections of sound recordings are a heavily used part of library and archival collections, yet less is known about the preservation of sound recordings than of printed materials.

Recorded materials come in a variety of formats, all of which are unstable and impermanent. The physical nature of each of these formats is discussed elsewhere in this encyclopedia, and will not be dwelt upon here. When establishing policies for the storage, handling, and use of sound recordings, it is important to determine whether the material is to be preserved for archival purposes or will be available for use by the general public.

Preservation is commonly defined as the maintenance of objects as closely as possible to their original condition through proper collection management, repair, and physical treatment. The goal of preserving sound recordings is to maintain the aural quality as closely as possible to the quality when the recording was made. Proper housing and storage in a stable environment will retard the deterioration of sound recordings. Proper handling will also preserve the physical recording and its sound quality. However, a library has no control over the conditions under which circulated material will be housed and played when it has left the building. Therefore, sound recordings in circulating collections should be considered impermanent. Rare and unique recordings should never be housed in collections that circulate to the public.

A clean, well-ventilated environment will extend the life of sound recordings and playback equipment. Discs and tapes are especially sensitive to the effects of heat, relative humidity, particulate matter, and light. Audio materials in circulating collections should be housed in an area with a constant temperature of approximately 68 degrees Fahrenheit, with a fluctuation of plus or minus five degrees, and a relative humidity range of 40 to 50 percent. The critical factor is the stability of temperature and relative humidity; rapid fluctuations in temperature and/or relative humidity can cause irreparable damage to most sound recordings within a short period of time. Sound recordings should be housed well removed from heat sources; direct exposure to heat will distort and destroy them. Discs and magnetic media are especially susceptible to damage from particulate matter, air pollution, and smoke; they must be protected from unnecessary exposure to these hazards. Smoking should never be permitted in a library or sound archive.

Archival collections should be stored in a controlled environment. Current research indicates that sound recordings are extremely sensitive to their environment, especially those that are paper-based, such as tapes and some discs. These materials should be stored under spe-cial conditions, with a cooler environment, as low as possible, and a relative humidity range of between 25 and 35 percent. If possible, rare and unique sound recordings, especially tapes, should be housed in a vault designed for the purpose. Recordings, on the rare occasion that originals are used, need to be acclimated for 24 to 36 hours before playback; the time for acclimation will depend upon the medium.

At present there is considerable research under way, in the U.S. and elsewhere, into the physical nature of sound recordings and the environmental requirements for their long-term preservation in original format. American sound archivists are active in their professional organization, the Association for Recorded Sound Collections (ARSC) and in international organizations, such as the International Council on Archives (ICA), concerned with the preservation of sound recordings. If collections of recorded sound are to be preserved, it is important that their custodians keep up with research in the field.

See also **Cylinder; Disc; Tape**

2. *Phonograph Records.* The earliest recorded sound was transcribed on cylinders made of a variety of compounds. These early recordings are rare and fragile. They must be stored in a secure, controlled environment with rigid temperature, humidity, and pollution controls. Cylinders, and other early recordings in a variety of unusual formats, are rarely, if ever, played.

The phonodisc (phonograph record) is a flat disc, made of a wide variety of materials. The physical nature of phonograph records is described elsewhere. What is important to understand when dealing with the preservation of these materials is that we do not know precisely what most of them are made of, nor how long they will last. Certainly many have lasted, in reasonably good condition, far longer than most specialists have expected. Research is under way to identify the processes used to manufacture discs, and the ingredients in them, to determine the optimum method, or methods, for the storage and preservation of original phonograph records in archives.

Discs, whether they be housed in archives or circulating collections, should be placed on baked enamel metal shelves in an upright position. Shelves should not be tightly packed, but discs should be placed close enough together so that each disc is upright. Phonodiscs that are askew on the shelves will warp within a short period of time. This will cause deterioration and sound distortion and will make the disc unplayable. Partitions placed every four to six inches along the shelf will help hold phonograph records in an upright position. Wooden shelves are not recommended for the housing of sound recordings, for the acids in wood may react adversely with the properties within the discs and accelerate deterioration. Metal shelves coated with baked enamel are recommended for the storage of library and archival materials, including sound recordings. If a new storage area is to be created, research on appropriate shelving will ensure that a collection survives for a long time.

Discs should be removed from the sleeves that contain them and placed in protective sleeves or envelopes. Most of the original envelopes for phonodiscs are made of acidic board, harmful to the recordings they house. (However, original envelopes often are preserved for their informational and artifactual value.) Protective sleeves can be obtained from suppliers of archival materials. The original plastic wrapping (shrink wrap) that surrounds the envelope and disc should be removed immediately and discarded. If it is not removed promptly, it will continue to shrink and can cause distortion of the disc. Also, this plastic, and the plastics used commercially for sleeves within the envelope, are chemically unstable and can damage the recording. Sound archivists do not agree on the most suitable protective sleeves for archival recordings. If an archival collection is to be rehoused, it is advisable to seek advice from the Library of Congress Motion Picture, Broadcasting and Recorded Sound Division, or, through the Association for Recorded Sound Collections, to hire a consultant to help set up a rehousing program. Discs should also be cleaned before each use. The study of sound recordings undertaken by A.G. Pickett and M.M. Lemcoe [1959] remains the most useful source of information on disc properties, stability, and longevity.

See also **Cleaning**

3. *Magnetic Recordings.* The development and physical nature of magnetic media are described elsewhere in this encyclopedia. Reel-to-reel tape recordings provide the best stability and fidelity, but they are not appropriate for circulating collections of recordings; they are more appropriately housed in research and/or archival collections. To prevent deterioration, magnetic recordings of archival value are often placed in cold storage with a controlled relative humidity to ensure their long-term preservation. Research is under way to determine the optimum storage conditions for magnetic tape; it is an extremely fragile medium. Surrogate copies should be made for general use.

The audiocassette is especially popular because each cassette is a contained unit, resistant to mishandling and simple to use, although its sound quality is inferior to that of reel-to-reel tape and it is not a stable or permanent medium. Cassette technology is also ephemeral, but this need not be a consideration in collections where the cassettes will wear out before they become obsolete and present playback problems. As users of circulating sound collections usually do not demand the finest quality of reproduction, the tape cassette is a convenient way to provide access to aural performances (information) while preserving original material in original format.

A major problem with cassette recordings is nonalignment of the tape within the cassette when the tape is wound too loosely on its spool or if the tension varies. Cassettes should be checked after each use to be sure that the tape is wound properly or soon distortion will become obvious. If the cassette is played on poorly maintained equipment, it can be damaged.

The print-through phenomenon is an effect caused by a combination of inferior tapes, improper rewinding, and improper storage. Proper storage of cassettes can somewhat lessen the risk of print-through.

It is important to house circulating collections of tape and video cassettes in an environmentally controlled area if they are to be preserved for any length of time. Fluctuations in temperature and relative humidity can quickly cause the tape and its sound quality to distort. High relative humidity will cause the stretching and warping of the tape. The binders will degenerate, ooze, and migrate, causing adjacent layers to stick together. Oxide coatings will come loose and can shed completely in playback. Affected tapes will leave a gummy residue on the tape transports and heads of the playback equipment, causing further distortion. Dust and particulate matter are especially harmful. Tape cassettes should be stored in plastic cases that offer support and protection from particulate matter. Paper-based archival storage boxes for cassettes are not recommended because the paper itself is a cause of particulate matter that can affect the tape. Appropriate storage containers are available from archival suppliers.

The careful maintenance of playback equipment in a sound collection is essential. Equipment should be checked and cleaned after each use. Unfortunately, librarians have no control over the playback equipment upon which circulating tapes will be played. However, tapes can and should be inspected for damage upon return to the library.

See also **Magnetic Recording; Tape Deck**

4. *Compact Discs.* Compact discs are easy to handle and are relatively impervious to damage by users and other hazards that threatened earlier discs. Originally, compact discs were advertised as "permanent." While they do offer considerable protection from the risks of rough handling and playback, their ingredients are not stable and will deteriorate over time. In addition to problems that are attributed to poor quality control in manufacture, sound archivists are beginning to recognize other problems with the medium. One

cause of deterioration is the ink used on the labels placed on some discs, which may react with the materials in the composition of the disc. This reaction appears to be accelerated when discs are stored in high relative humidity. Studies are under way to identify other causes of CD deterioration. Compact discs, and their playback equipment, are as sensitive as other media to fluctuations in temperature and relative humidity, and to dirt and air pollution. They require a controlled environment for storage and playback. Librarians should follow guidelines for the housing and storage of other sound media at this time.

Digital recording is a complex process, and many of the early compact discs were defective. Quality control in production is better today than it was a decade ago, but optical disc technology is constantly evolving. There are no standards for this medium. At present compact discs are suitable for circulating collections, but they present real and continuing problems for archival collections. The compact disc is considered a transitional medium. It is ideal for the transmission of information, but it is not the medium for storage of information. Compact discs will present serious challenges for the sound archivist in the not-too-distant future.

5. *Archival Work.* The curator of a collection of sound recordings needs to evaluate the use that the material will receive, then determine how it can best be preserved, through proper storage, handling, and use, for as long as possible. It is advisable to learn as much as possible about the media in the collections, from the professional literature of the sound archivist and that of the new technologies.

As the technology of sound recording is evolving at a rapid rate and there are few standards, a recording technology and its playback equipment can become obsolete within a short period of time. This problem plagues circulating collections as well as sound archives. Much early material has deteriorated so badly that it can no longer be used, and playback equipment is no longer available to retrieve the sound of some recordings. Maintaining playback equipment is a challenge that can be met by only a few sound archives in the world.

The re-recording (reformatting) of material is possible, but it is expensive and time-consuming. Re-recording the older sound recordings in a suitable format, without enhancements, for playback, is a preferred method for preservation and access in archival collections. Of concern is the fact that there are, at present, no standards for the re-recording of sound recordings into a newer medium for playback. When dealing with the preservation of aural materials, the goal is to retain the quality of the sound as closely as possible to the original, blips and all, not to enhance the quality of the sound. Sound archivists and audio librarians follow the same principle of preservation as curators of collections of printed materials.

Good housekeeping practices, a stable environment, and the proper maintenance of playback equipment will help extend the life of a collection, but an institution has no control over the conditions under which its material will be played once it leaves the library. Circulating collections must be considered impermanent. Printed guidelines for handling and playback of materials can be distributed with the recordings when they circulate; this can help to curtail abuses, and preserve materials for future users. [Association 1988; Brownstein 1990; Christopher Ann Paton, Popular Music Collection, Georgia State University, in the preparation of this article Day 1989; Geller 1983; Gibson 1991; McWilliams 1983; Pickett 1959; Smolian 1987; Swartzburg 1991; Vincent Pelote, Institute of Jazz Studies, Rutgers University and Ward 1990.] [The author wishes to acknowledge the assistance of Gerald Gibson, Motion Picture, Broadcasting, and Recorded Sound Division, Library of Congress]

See also **Sonic Restoration of Historical Recordings; Sound Recordings and the Library**

SUSAN SWARTZBURG

PRESIDENTS ON RECORD

The first U.S. president to make a record was Rutherford B. Hayes, when Thomas Edison took a tinfoil phonograph to the White House for a demonstration on 18 Apr 1878. Benjamin Harrison was the first to make a commercial record, for Bettini; but the record was never described or listed in a Bettini catalog; no copy is known to exist.

No live recording was made of William McKinley's last speech, 5 Sep 1901, just before his assassination, but many records were marketed with parts of the speech read by recording artists (Frank C. Stanley, William F. Hooley, Len Spencer, etc.).

William Howard Taft made a number of recordings while campaigning for the presidency in August 1908: 12 Edison cylinders, 13 Victor/HMV discs, and 15 Columbia discs, three of them repeated on cylinder. As president he made seven Victors, on 1 Oct 1912, speaking on issues of the day (peace, prosperity, tariff, etc.); these were the first commercially released records by a president in office. Earlier in 1912 ex-president Theodore Roosevelt and candidate Woodrow Wilson made records.

With the advent of radio, and then of talking motion picture newsreels in the 1920s, the magic of a president's voice was lessened, and only a few made commercial recordings. The most interesting was

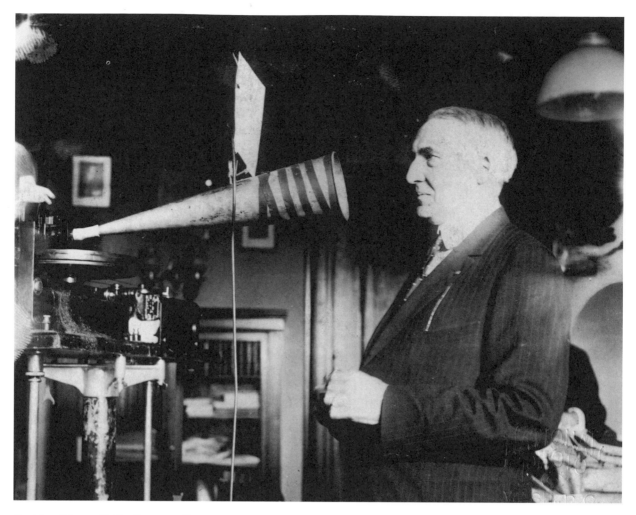

President Warren G. Harding recording a speech in 1922. © CORBIS

Franklin Roosevelt's "War Message to Congress and the Nation" of 8 Dec 1941, declaring war on Japan, and defining 7 December as a "day that will live in infamy" (Columbia #36516; 1941).

PRESLEY, ELVIS
(8 JAN 1935–16 AUG 1977)

Elvis Presley transcends categorization as the most important recording artist of the rock era; he may, in fact, be the most dominant cultural figure of the 20th century. Like the great heroes of Greek mythology, Presley's character has acquired a universality with which virtually all of us can identify. But it all began with his extraordinary voice, which fused gospel, Black rhythm and blues, and white country-pop sensibilities in a more convincing fashion than any performer up to that point in time.

Presley was born in Tupelo, Mississippi, the only child (a twin brother, Jesse, was stillborn) of working-class parents. He was raised in Memphis, Tennessee,

within a tightly knit household; indeed, strong family ties played a role in his decision to record a couple of pop ballads at the Memphis-based Sun Studios as a birthday present for his mother. Brought to the attention of owner Sam Phillips, he was encouraged to forge that synthesis of Black and white pop styles soon to be known as rockabilly and, in a broader stylistic context, as rock 'n' roll.

Following an apprenticeship period cutting demos for Sun, Presley was teamed with local session players, guitarist Scotty Moore and bassist Bill Black, and caught lightning in a bottle with a rave-up rendition of Arthur Crudup's R&B hit, "That's All Right, Mama," backed with Bill Monroe's bluegrass standard, "Blue Moon of Kentucky" (Sun #209; 1954). The A-side contains many of the features that made Presley, at least in an intuitive sense, deserving of the later appellation, "King of Rock 'n' Roll": his plaintive voice — literally dripping with teenage hormonal excitement — swoops and swoons over the spare accompaniment consisting of acoustic guitar chords (strummed by Presley himself),

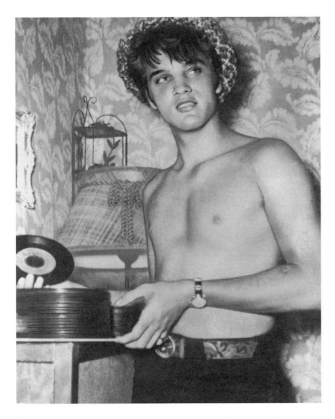

Elvis Presley admiring a stack of 45s and 78s of his first Sun Records release, "That's Alright, Mama," 1953.
© Bettmann/CORBIS

electric guitar flourishes, and propulsive upright bass. Phillips would retain the split R&B–C&W format on the four remaining Sun releases during 1954–1955, marketing Presley to a country audience (he became a regular on the *Louisiana Hayride* as well as appearing on WSM's *Grand Ole Opry*) because — as a southern white performer — no other viable options existed.

RCA's purchase of Presley's recording contract in late 1955 for the then princely sum of $35,000 can be attributed to two notable factors: (1) Sun's need for cash to pay off existing debts as well as to develop new talent (e.g., Johnny Cash, Carl Perkins, Roy Orbison), and (2) the management pact Presley signed with Colonel Tom Parker in mid-1955. Parker — whose business savvy would prove instrumental in advancing Presley's career (notwithstanding revisionist interpretations to the contrary) — had a long history of working with the label, most notably as Eddy Arnold's manager.

Boosted by a series of television appearances in early 1956 on the Dorsey Brothers, Milton Berle, and Ed Sullivan shows, Presley's first RCA single, "Heartbreak Hotel" (#47-6420) reached number one on the pop charts (remaining there for eight weeks beginning 21 Apr 1956), as did the follow-up, "I Want You, I Need You, I Love You" (RCA #47-6540; 1956).

The next single broke all existing precedents, with both sides — "Don't Be Cruel"/"Hound Dog" (RCA #47-6604; 1956) — ascending to the top position on the pop (11 weeks), country (10 weeks), and R&B (six weeks) charts. While the RCA recordings as a whole had thus far lacked the spontaneity and unadorned directness of the Sun material (featuring studied arrangements with his performing band augmented by professional session players — generally drummer D.J. Fontana, pianist Floyd Cramer, saxophonist Boots Randolph, and guitarists Chet Atkins and Hank Garland — and the ubiquitous harmonies of the Jordanaires), the 45-rpm disc culled from Presley's film debut, "Love Me Tender" (RCA #47-6643; 1956; #1 five weeks), introduced a maudlin element that would plague much of his future output. The problem seems to have been that Presley — unschooled in either musical technique or the concept of good taste — always mimicked — and integrated into his personal entertainment vocabulary — the influences to which he was exposed. Consequently, the boy who'd chosen to sing the sentimental boy-and-his-dog tear-jerker, "Old Shep" at the 1945 Mississippi–Alabama Fair (he placed second in the contest), grew up with the desire to reinterpret Engelbert Humperdinck, Tom Jones, and other singers diametrically opposed to the style that had made him famous in the first place.

Some popular music historians point to Presley's military stint from 24 Mar 1958–1 Mar 1960 as his pivotal career move. It is certainly true that the post-Army Elvis seemed more predisposed to record shlocky movie songs (e.g., "Viva Las Vegas," RCA #47-8360; 1964; #29 as well as the bulk of the tracks from countless soundtrack albums) and romantic ballads (e.g., "She's Not You," RCA #47-8041; 1962; #5) perhaps better suited to middle-of-the-road performers. It wasn't that Presley interpreted such mainstream material badly — gentler items like "Can't Help Falling Love" (RCA #47-7968; 1961; #2), "Good Luck Charm" (RCA #47-7992; 1962; #1), and "Return to Sender" (RCA #47-8100; #2) possessed a laid-back grace and charm that few popular artists of the period could have negotiated as convincingly. Because he was capable of so much more, however, the escapist fare he recorded for much of the 1960s gave the impression that he had sold out.

At the end of the decade, Presley provided a tantalizing glimpse as to what his recording career might have been. Motivated by criticism that he was out of touch with the tenor of the times — a politically mobilized era whose musical benchmarks included folk rock, psychedelia, and idiosyncratic singer-songwriters — and stabilized by his 1 May 1967 marriage and birth of a daughter early the following year, he opted out of the moviemaking rat-race and returned to live performing. Teamed with soulful session players from

Memphis, he produced a string of tougher, more socially relevant hit singles, including "In the Ghetto" (RCA #47-9741; 1969; #3), "Suspicious Minds" (RCA #47-9764; 1969; #1), and "Don't Cry Daddy" (RCA #47-9768; 1969; #6).

Although the quality of Presley's releases proved uneven in the 1970s — ranging from the spirited "Burning Love" (RCA #74-0769; 1972; #2) to the perfunctory, exaggerated reading of "The Wonder of You" (RCA #47-9835; 1970; #9) — he remained a major box office draw, with successes such as the 1972 Madison Square Garden concert and January 1973 Hawaii show telecast worldwide and documented on disc: *Elvis as Recorded at Madison Square Garden* (RCA #LSP-4776; 1972; #11) and *Aloha from Hawaii via Satellite* (#VPSX-6089; 1973; #1). The increasingly percentage of live and repackaged material among his album releases beginning in the 1970s owed much to his increasing tendency to avoid the studio. This aversion seems to have been related to his heavy drug use, from amphetamines to the recreational types then in vogue with many of his Hollywood associates. His physical deterioration was evident in the dramatic weight fluctuations and erratic behavior during concerts. Therefore, his sudden death — from a heart attack induced by a drug overdose — at his Memphis home, Graceland, didn't come as a complete surprise to well-informed observers.

Beyond trying to accommodate the immediate rush on his recordings in the aftermath of his passing, RCA (sometimes in conjunction with subsidiary imprints such as Camden and Pickwick) has continued to release new Presley titles — virtually all of which have consisted of repackagings of previously issued material. However, the comprehensive retrospectives — including *The King of Rock 'n' Roll — The Complete 50's Masters* (RCA #66050; 1992; five CDs), *Elvis: From Nashville to Memphis — The Essential 60's Masters I* (RCA #07863, 1993; five CDs), and *Walk a Mile in My Shoes — The Essential 70's Masters* (RCA #66670, 1995; five CDs) — aimed at collectors have earned universal raves from reviewers. Among the more dubious projects have been marketing gimmicks such as *The Elvis Presley Collection* (whose projected double-CD/cassette titles include "Country," "Rock 'n' Roll," "Love Songs," "Classics," and "Movie Magic" — each containing one "never-before-released bonus song"), leased to Time/Life Music in 2002. True rarities have surfaced over the years such as the *Louisiana Hayride* performances available on 10-inch open reel tape in the Louisiana State Library archives in addition to material from Presley's early career release on albums; e.g., *Elvis: The First Live Recordings* (Music Works #3601/JRCA 89387 102; 1984) and material culled from his legendary jam sessions with Jerry Lee Lewis and Carl Perkins at Sun Studios, the *Million Dollar Quartet* (RCA 2023) and *The Complete Million Dollar Session*

(Charly 102; 1988). But, more typically, the new material has tended to be of a documentary (or infotainment) nature, in which music is a secondary consideration; e.g., *Elvis: One Night With You* (HBO), *Elvis Presley's Graceland* (HBO), *Elvis on Tour* (MGM/UA #100153; 1984), and *Elvis Memories* (Vestron #1054; 1987).

Recent conservative estimates have placed the total number of legitimate Presley sound recordings sold worldwide at 500,000. Given his status as an "American Institution," with something to offer virtually every popular music enthusiast, it's likely that the selling of Elvis Presley recordings will continue unabated for many years to come.

FRANK HOFFMANN

PRESSING (I)
The final form of the disc, made from the stamper; it is the form that is sold to the end user.

See also **Disc**

PRESSING (II)
As a verb, the process of molding the biscuit as it is kneaded and squeezed flat between warmed bed plates.

See also **Disc**

PRESTIGE (LABEL)
An American record issued from 1949 to 1971; Bob Weinstock was the founder. The label was significant for its issues of the cool jazz school of the 1950s and 1960s. Sessions included such artists as Miles Davis, Stan Getz, Lee Konitz, the Modern Jazz Quartet, Thelonious Monk, and Lennie Tristano. John Coltrane, Barry Harris, and Pat Martino also appeared on Prestige. In addition to their original pressings, Prestige leased classic sessions from other labels for reissue. In May 1971 the label was sold to Fantasy Records, in San Francisco, which concentrated on LP (and later CD) reissues of the early Prestige material. [Ruppli & Porter 1980 is a complete label list.]

PRESTON, J

SEE LOUDSPEAKER

PREVIN, ANDRÉ, SIR (6 APR 1929–)
German/American pianist, composer, and conductor, born in Berlin. At age six he entered the Hochschule für Musik, Berlin; in 1938 his (Jewish) family had to leave Germany and took up residence in Paris. Previn

studied at the Conservatory there, and had lessons from Marcel Dupré. In 1939 the family transferred to Los Angeles, where Previn continued his studies and took American citizenship in 1943. He worked as an orchestrator and music director for MGM in Hollywood, and also performed as a jazz and concert pianist. He won Academy awards for scoring the films *Gigi* (1958), *Porgy and Bess* (1959), *Irma la douce* (1963), and *My Fair Lady* (1964).

Previn's conducting career began with a concert of the St. Louis Symphony Orchestra. In 1967–1969 he was conductor of the Houston Symphony Orchestra, then he directed the London Symphony Orchestra from 1968 to 1979. Previn also led the Pittsburgh Symphony Orchestra from 1976 to 1982, and both the Royal Philharmonic Orchestra and the Los Angeles Philharmonic Orchestra from 1982; he resigned from the Royal Philharmonic in 1986, and then left the Los Angeles Philharmonic following a dispute with its management in March 1989. He has since worked as a freelance conductor around the world.

Previn has a special affinity for English composers, and has made notable discs of several important works. Benjamin Britten's *Spring Symphony* (EMI #C747667-2) and the Vaughan Williams symphonies for RCA, all with the London Symphony, are fine examples. His most popular jazz recording was *My Fair Lady*, a 1964 album (Columbia CL #2195) with Shelly Manne that featured a remarkable version of "I Could Have Danced All Night." The single "Like Young" with the David Rose orchestra was on the charts 14 weeks in 1959 (MGM #12792), and won a Grammy as best popular orchestral record. Previn also received Grammys for two jazz albums on the Contemporary label — the 1960 *West Side Story* and the 1961 *André Previn Plays Harold Arlen*. Three other albums were chart successes between 1959 and 1964. He signed with Telarc Jazz in 1990, returning as a solo jazz pianist on record and in concert.

PRICE, LEONTYNE (10 FEB 1927–)

Famed Black soprano Price was born in Laurel, Mississippi. Her talents as a youngster brought her to the attention of the Juilliard School, which awarded her a scholarship in 1948. Four years later, Virgil Thomson chose her to star in the revival of his opera *4 Saints in 3 Acts*, and she spent the next two years touring the U.S. and Europe in a new production of Gershwin's *Porgy and Bess*. She made her concert debut in New York in autumn 1954, to wide renown, and then performed at major opera companies and as a soloist around the world. In 1961, she made her debut at the Metropolitan Opera, remaining with the company through 1985, after which she retired; that same year, she was awarded the National Medal of

the Arts. She has recorded for RCA/BMG Classics since the early 1960s, producing complete opera performances and the requisite holiday albums and recordings of popular material that all opera performers seem to be required to make. She has won 12 Grammy awards in the Best Classical Vocal Performance category, beginning with her 1960 album, *A Program of Song*; her most recent Grammy to date came in 1982.

PRIDE, CHARLEY (18 MAR 1938–)

American country singer and guitarist, born in Sledge, Mississippi. He taught himself guitar while engaged in miscellaneous occupations, and moved to Nashville in 1963. Signing with RCA Victor in 1964, he was the first Black country artist to be heard on a major label (although his race was at first concealed by Victor). His list of 51 country chart singles began with "Just Between You and Me" (Victor #9000; 1966). Other great successes came with "Afraid of Losing You Again" (Victor #0265; 1969), "All I Have to Offer You" (Victor #0167; 1969), "Is Anybody Goin' to San Antone?" (Victor #9806; 1970), and "Honky Tonk Blues" (Victor #11913; 1980). Pride semiretired from performing in the mid-1980s, although he continues to perform and record occasionally.

PRIMROSE, WILLIAM
(23 AUG 1903–1 MAY 1982)

Scottish violist, born in Glasgow. He studied violin in Glasgow, then took lessons in Belgium from Ysaye, who recommended a change to the viola. He played viola with the London String Quartet from 1930 to 1935. Settling in the U.S. in 1937, he became active as a soloist and ensemble player, then held the post of principal violist in the NBC Symphony Orchestra under Toscanini to 1942. Later, he taught in several universities while maintaining a concert schedule. His activities were valuable in bringing the viola to wide audiences; and he was the major exponent of the instrument on Victor records during the 1930s (appearing also on Columbia). He had five numbers in the 1940 Victor catalog, where he was described as *the* violist. Primrose also recorded the violin, for Columbia, Decca, and HMV, including the Bach Partita No. 3 and Sonata No. 2. His memoirs, *Walk on the North Side*, appeared in 1978. He died in Provo, Utah. Primrose's papers are held by the library of Brigham Young University (website: http://music.lib.byu.edu/piva/ WPintro.html). Pearl (#9453) and Grammofono 2000 (#78880) are two of several European reissue labels offering selections of his 1930s era recordings on CD.

PRINCE (7 JUNE 1958–)

American rock singer, born in Minneapolis. His full name is Prince Rogers Nelson, taken from the Prince Rogers Trio, a jazz group led by his father. As a child he learned to play all the instruments of a pop ensemble, and when he made his demo tape he sang and performed all the parts.

Between 1979 and 1985 he made six remarkably successful multichannel albums, in which he was composer, singer, and instrumentalist. The three most popular were on the Warner Bros. label: *Prince* (BSK #3366; 1979), 29 weeks on the charts; *1999* (#9-23720-1F; 1982), 162 weeks; and *Purple Rain* (#25110-1; 1984), more than 78 weeks. The album *Dirty Mind* (BSK #3478; 1980) aroused controversy over its "X-rated" lyrics, and many AOR stations refused to broadcast it. Among the most popular Prince singles were "I Wanna Be Your Lover" from the album *Prince*, "Little Red Corvette" from *1999*, and the 1986 hit "Kiss," from the *Parade* album. *Purple Rain*, the soundtrack album from a motion picture, is said to have sold more than 11 million copies, spending over 24 weeks at the top of the pop album charts. Prince continued to be successful through the early 1990s, but then entered into a long series of legal battles with his record label, Warner Bros. The very prolific artist was angered when the company tried to slow down the release of his product, and after several lawsuits, Prince left the label in 1995. During this period, Prince changed his name to a cryptic symbol, and so reviews of his work referred to him as "The Artist Formerly Known as Prince." In 1996, he established his own NPG label, distributed by EMI; a slew of CDs followed, but even devoted fans could not keep up with the product. In 2000, Prince returned to a major label, Arista, but was unable to duplicate his past success.

REV. CARL BENSON

PRINCE, ALEXANDER

British performer on the McCann-system duet concertina, among the earliest to record the instrument. He made five records with orchestral accompaniment for the Zonophone label (of G & T) in February 1906, beginning with "Life in Vienna" (#49106). Three more discs were dated from 4 Feb 1908 in the ledger of G & T (Zonophone #49110–49112); they were concertina solos. Prince recorded for Columbia in the teens, and continued to record for various labels through the 1920s. Prince was an active performer on the vaudeville circuit, and his recordings were so popular that they remained in print for years, particularly on budget labels like Gennett, Regal, and Winner in both the U.K. and U.S. [Walsh 1953/3.]

PRINCE, CHARLES ADAM (1869–10 OCT 1937)

American military band director, pianist, and organist; born in San Francisco. Prince's first recordings were made for the New York Phonograph Co. in 1891 as a pianist. He was the musical director for Columbia from the late 1890s, and conductor of the Columbia Orchestra/Columbia Band from about 1902–1903 until 1905, succeeding Fred Hager. After 1905 he directed Prince's Band and Prince's Orchestra. He retired to California in the late 1920s, and died in San Francisco.

In 1906 Prince's Band and Orchestra recorded extensively on the larger Columbia Twentieth-century cylinders, featuring the same popular repertoire as the Columbia Band. Columbia's first attempt at serious classical music was with Wagner's "Rienzi Overture," by the Columbia Orchestra conducted by Prince (#A6006; 1917), on a double-faced 12-inch disc. His last Columbia disc was made in 1922, after which he moved to the Puritan label briefly, then went to Victor in 1924, where he worked as associate music director for about a year. [Walsh 1952/12; 1953/1.]

PRINCESS SAPPHIRE RECORD (LABEL)

An American record issued by the Sapphire Record and Talking Machine Co., New York, probably between 1917 and 1920. "Little is known about them. They are very rare." [Rust 1978.]

Very rare label of the late teens. Courtesy Kurt Nauck/Nauck's Vintage Records

PRINT-THROUGH

The transferral of signal information from one portion of a magnetic tape to another portion, with the effect of simultaneous playback of the transferred signal and the signal already present. This is a major problem of the format, arising from the tight winding of tape on its reel, tape coercivity, or temperature aberrations. Thickness of the base is an important factor also.

Print-through is most likely to occur immediately after recording, and becomes less likely with the passage of time. It may be helpful to rewind a freshly recorded tape a few times before playback. Annual winding of little used tapes — fast forward and slow reverse — is recommended by some authorities as a means of reducing the tendency of tape layers to adhere to each other. However, "winding retightens the tape-pack and this freshly accumulated tension restarts the tape stretching cycle anew. Thus ritual rewinding may cause more ills than it cures" [Smolian]. There is no device or method that will remove print-through once it has occurred. [Smolian 1987.]

See also **Preservation of Sound Recordings**

PRO TOOLS

A computer-based multitrack recording hardware and software system, Pro Tools was first released in 1991. Over the next decade it became the top selling digital audio workstation. Some versions used only a computer's own CPU, while others required adding DSP cards to increase the number of available channels and effects. This created a platform that third-party companies could develop for, with hooks that allowed other pieces of software (plugins) to affect the audio stream. A number of control surfaces became available, providing buttons and sliders to ease access to and tactile feedback.

Pro Tools was developed by Digidesign, an innovative company begun in 1984 by Peter Gotcher and Evan Brooks, who started by producing sound replacement chips for drum machines. They went on to make the program Sound Designer, and then used its editing tools to create hard disc recording systems, capitalizing on the convergence of new technologies: programmable DSP chips, affordable 16-bit converters, computers with expansion slots, and the very rapid increase in hard drive storage capacity and chip processing power.

Computer-based systems revolutionized the recording industry by greatly lowering the cost of high quality systems. They began a trend away from tape-based facilities with expensive consoles and outboard gear and toward integrated systems that could handle recording, mixing, processing, editing, and playback.

ROBERT WILLEY

PROCOL HARUM

The roots of Procol Harum, one of leading exponents of the art-rock school, lie in the Paramounts, a London band that recorded five singles between October 1963 and September 1965 and included singer/pianist Gary Brooker, guitarist Robin Trower, bassist/organist Chris Copping, and drummer B.J. Wilson. In search of a new direction, Booker was introduced to lyricist Keith Reid sometime in 1966. The two began writing songs together; several demos led to a recording contract with Deram in early 1967. Procol's first single, "A Whiter Shade of Pale" (Deram #7507; 1967) — based on the melody from Johann Sebastian Bach's Suite No. 3 in D major — became an international smash, selling more than 4 million copies overall. In the face of heightened demand for concert engagements, the group broke up. Procol's revamped lineup — featuring Brooker, Trower, Wilson, organist Matthew Fisher, and bassist David Knights — produced three critically acclaimed albums: *Procol Harum* (Deram #18008; 1967), *Shine on Brightly* (A&M #4151; 1968), and *A Salty Dog* (A&M #4179; 1969).

Artistic differences within the band, combined with disappointing sales, led to the departure of Fisher and Knights. With the addition of Copping, Procol's next two albums — *Home* (A&M #4261; 1970) and *Broken Barricades* (A&M #4294; 1971) — reflected a transition from a thickly textured keyboard sound to a more guitar-based approach built around Trower's Jimi Hendrix–inspired virtuosity. Trower's decision to embark upon a solo career led to another change in personnel: David Ball was brought in as lead guitarist and Alan Cartwright on bass, thereby enabling Copping to concentrate on organ. An offer to perform in a classical music framework led to the release of the group's bestselling LP, *Procol Harum Live in Concert with the Edmonton Symphony Orchestra* (A&M #4335; 1972). The band failed, however, to capitalize on this revival in popularity, and their next four albums showed steadily declining sales.

Procol broke up in 1977, but Brooker, Fisher, Reid, and Trower reunited to record *The Prodigal Stranger* (Zoo #72445-11011-2; 1991). Brooker, Fisher, and hired hands have toured intermittently during the 1990s. [Stambler 1989.]

FRANK HOFFMANN

PRODUCTION MASTER

SEE MASTER

PROGRESSIVE RECORD LABELS

Progressive record labels — founded to promote left-wing or radical political agendas and mostly centered in New York City — have existed since the 1930s. Timely Records, launched by insurance salesman Leo Waldman, was the first company to specialize in left-wing/protest music, beginning in 1935 with an album by the New Singers performing "Rise Up," "The Soup Song," and "The Internationale." Two years later Timely issued an album by the Manhattan Chorus, with "Hold the Fort," "We Shall Not Be Moved," and "Solidarity Forever"; in 1939 and 1940 the label recorded Earl Robinson doing various folk songs, such as "John Brown," "John Henry," and "Drill Ye Tarriers," but mostly his own compositions. Other small companies also entered the field, such as Henry Cowell's New Music Quarterly Recordings, which released the single "Strange Funeral at Braddock" in 1936, although it was more involved in circulating avant-garde compositions; the left-wing musical theater "Cabaret T.A.C." also issued a few records in 1939.

More successful was Eric Bernay's Keynote Records, beginning in 1940, a major jazz label. Bernay issued Josh White's hard-hitting *Southern Exposure* album in 1941 featuring six songs about racial discrimination, as well as the Almanac Singers's albums, beginning with *Songs for John Doe* (although it came out on the Almanac Records label because of the songs controversial antiwar content), followed by *Talking Union and Other Union Songs* and *Dear Mr. President*, as well as the single "Boomtown Bill"/"Keep that Oil A-Rollin'" in 1942. Keynote also released two albums of songs about the Spanish Civil War recorded in Spain, *The Red Army Chorus of the U.S.S.R.*, and numerous other songs from the Soviet Union.

Herbert Harris launched Stinson Records in the late 1930s and began releasing songs from the Soviet Union. After joining with Moe Asch in early 1943, the Asch/Stinson label issued a steady stream of topical records, including *Songs of the Lincoln Brigade*, *Songs for Victory*, and *Citizen C.I.O.*, among others. Asch and Harris parted company at war's end, and soon Asch issued *Roll the Union On*, as an Asch Record before changing to the Disc label. Bernay sold Keynote in 1947 but quickly initiated the short-lived Theme label, which reissued four "Cabaret T.A.C. Songs," Paul Robeson's antiwar single of "Spring Song," and the original cast album of Marc Blitzstein's musical *No for an Answer*. Mario Casetta launched Charter Records in 1946, and until 1950 released various sides, including Sir Lancelot's *Walk in Peace* album, followed by Morry Goodson and Sonny Vale's satirical pop songs with a political slant, as well as the People's Songs Chorus and Pete Seeger. Charter was

connected with the People's Songs movement as well as the Henry Wallace Progressive Party presidential campaign in the 1948.

During the 1950s progressive labels were few, but did manage to produce a steady stream of records. Irwin Silber and Ernie Lieberman launched Hootenanny Records in 1949; their first record was the Weavers doing "The Hammer Song"/"Banks of Marble," followed over the next few years by single records from Jewish Young Folksingers, Betty Sanders, the People's Artists Quartet, and the album *Hootenanny Tonight!* issued in 1954. Joe Glazer recorded labor/political songs for the Labor Arts label, *Ballads for Sectarians* (1952) and *Songs of the Wobblies* (1954).

Meanwhile, Moe Asch continued to release a grab-bag of albums of music and sounds from the U.S. and throughout the world on his Folkways label. Not many were overtly political, although he did feature Woody Guthrie, Pete Seeger, Lead Belly, Earl Robinson, Joe Glazer's *Songs of Joe Hill*, and an expanded reissue of the Almanac Singers's *Talking Union*. Into the 1960s, as Folkways continued to release a steady stream of new records, including a series of southern recordings of the civil rights movement, it also marketed the topical Broadside label, an offshoot of *Broadside* magazine. Initiated in 1962 by Agnes "Sis" Cunningham, who had been a member of the Almanac Singers, and her husband Gordon Friesen, *Broadside* published hundreds of topical songs into the 1980s. There were well over a dozen albums, starting in 1963 with the Broadside Singers, and including Pete Seeger, Phil Ochs, and Sammy Walker.

Irwin Silber and Barbara Dane founded Paredon Records in 1969. Over the next two decades the label issued 50 albums of music, poetry, and speech relating to political and protest struggles from the U.S. and various Third World countries. The owners donated the label to the Smithsonian Institution in 1991. Joe Glazer launched Collector Records in 1970, specializing in labor and protest songs, mostly featuring Glazer and various accompanists. Numerous other albums of his were released by the CIO Education and Research Department, the UAW Education Department, and other union-affiliated labels. His own Collector Records albums ranged from *Down in a Coal Mine* (1974), to *Textile Voices* (1975) and *Union Train* (1975), up to *The Music of American Politics* (1996). Before the advent of CDs other labels issued an occasional protest/labor album since the 1970s, for example *Brown Lung Cotton Mills Blues* (June Appal), *Hard Times* and *Songs For Peace* (Rounder Records), and *Songs of the Working People* (Flying Fish). Holly Near launched Redwood Records in 1973, specializing in women's music, including her 1984 album with

Ronnie Gilbert, *Lifeline*. Her last Redwood album appeared in 1993. [Cohen and Samuelson, 1996; Glazer, 2001; Goldsmith, 1998; Place and Cohen, 2000; Reuss 2000.]

RONALD D. COHEN

PROGRESSIVE ROCK

Progressive rock implies a particular mindset in recording and performing music, a predisposition to test-established limits and boundaries. Often termed "art rock," the genre owed its exploratory nature largely to psychedelia. Stylistically speaking, though, progressive rock was all over the map. From the late 1960s onward, pioneering artists — typically coming from a middle, or upper middle, class background combined with considerably more education than working-class youths constituting the majority of early rock stars, and unfettered by preconceived notions of the status quo — could be found within all musical categories.

The means by which an artist would display "progressive" leanings varied according to the presence of one (or more) of the following features: complex — often lengthy, multisectional — compositions; virtuostic performances; exotic and/or eclectic instrumentation; frequent use of cosmic themes in the lyrics; and grandiosity, as opposed to earthy directness, in presentation.

The Beatles' release of *Sgt. Pepper's Lonely Heart Club Band* (Capitol #2653), represented a watershed development in the development of the genre. In retrospect, examples of progressive rock can be identified as existing prior to that album's appearance in June 1967, ranging from Elvis Presley's early rockabilly experiments to the Byrds' folk rock classics recorded between 1965–1967. However, post–*Sgt. Pepper* works tended to exude a seriousness of purpose (i.e., the consideration of aesthetics over the commercial marketplace) hitherto relegated to the jazz and classical music sectors. The emergence of rock journalism, largely built around young intellectuals who had grown up listening to rock 'n' roll and other popular music genres, helped to spread the gospel of highbrow rock art. The youth subculture, then preoccupied with weighty social matters such as civil rights and the anti–Vietnam War movement, wholeheartedly bought into the concept.

The concept album represented a notable subgenre within the progressive rock movement. In view of the increased profit-making potential of the long-playing 12-inch record (which generally included 10 to 14 songs and ranged in length from 30 to 50 minutes) over 45-rpm singles, record companies concentrated their promotional efforts toward establishing the LP as the primary mode of aesthetic expression within the rock scene. Accordingly, rock musicians began experimenting with ways of presenting a unified thematic message (both in the music and song lyrics) within the framework of a record album. Notable concept albums produced by rock artists included: Fairport Convention — *Babbacombe Lee* (A&M #4333; 1972); The Kinks — *Arthur* (Reprise #6217; 1968); The Moody Blues — *Days of Future Passed* (Deram #18012; 1967); *In Search of the Lost Chord* (Deram #16017; 1968); *On the Threshold of a Dream* (Deram #16025; 1969); Pink Floyd — *Animals* (Columbia #34474; 1977); *The Wall* (Columbia #36183; 1979); The Who — *Tommy* (Decca #7205; 1969); *Quadrophenia* (MCA #10004; 1973).

After a dazzlingly creative period in the late 1960s, which saw even mainstream pop artists incorporating progressive rock conventions into their work, the music business split off into an extensive array of stylistic fragments. While progressive rock was marginalized in the 1970s to the extent that its artists rarely achieved mainstream success, the genre could count on the support of a relatively substantial fan base, one that was at least the equal of funk and disco. However, the emergence of the punk movement, which viciously characterized corporate rock (many read this to mean "progressive rock") as a bloated guardian of the musical equivalent of dry rot, hastened the decline of the genre. By the 1980s, the term "new wave" was being loosely applied to all rock acts displaying progressive instincts.

FRANK HOFFMANN

PRT (LABEL)

SEE PYE RECORDS

PRYOR, ARTHUR
(22 SEP 1870–18 JUNE 1942)

American trombonist; a "youthful sensation of the band world in the 1890s" [Brooks], born in St. Joseph, Missouri. He played with the Liberati Band in 1889 and then with the Sousa Band from 1892. He became assistant conductor and directed most of the recordings made by the Sousa Band. In 1903 he left Sousa to form his own band, and toured extensively. Pryor is said to have made 1,000 recordings before 1930 with his band. A founding member of ASCAP, he is credited with nearly 300 works, ranging from operettas to novelty songs. His band flourished until he retired to Long Branch, New Jersey, in 1933, where he died.

Pryor recorded first for Columbia cylinders in 1895. He did solos with Sousa's Band on Columbia

Arthur Pryor from an early Victor Record catalog. Courtesy David A. Jasen

cylinders #516 and #517, "Say Au Revoir but Not Good-Bye," and "Little Marcia Marie Polka." In October 1900 he did his first Victor solo, again with Sousa's Band, playing his own arrangement of "Fanny Waltz" (#V-309). One of the four solos in the Victor 1917 catalog — reflecting Pryor's lifelong love of opera — was "Celeste Aida" (#35030). His band and his orchestra were also in the catalog, and he was identified as composer of 10 numbers. He recorded into the late 1920s, and was well represented (32 titles) in the 1940 catalog. Crystal Records (#451) offers a CD reissue of some of Pryor's recordings. [Brooks 1979.]

PSEUDONYMS

Recording artists have frequently used more than one stage name (nom du disque) in their studio work. One reason was to avoid contractual difficulties when they wished to work with one label while signed up as an exclusive to another. A second reason was that record companies wanted to simulate a long list of artists when they did not have such; if they gave each person

three names it quickly tripled the list without extra cost. Some of the invented names taken by the more prominent performers are given below. Where the real name in parentheses is marked with an asterisk, that name is itself a stage name. Pseudonyms for orchestras and large ensembles are not included here as they would be too numerous; for example Ben Selvin's orchestra recorded under at least 23 different names. [Principal sources: Bayly 1976/12; Lumpe 1990; Rust 1989, 1989; Sutton 1991 (the most exhaustive and well-researched list for U.S. records, with label names given for each pseudonym); Walsh 1944/5, 1952/5, 1962/11, 1970/6.]

Notable pseudonyms from 1900–1950 recordings:
Adams, Charles (Charles A. Prince)
Adams, Joe (Frank Luther*)
Adams and Clark (Frank Luther* and Carson Robison)
Ahern, James (Vernon Dalhart*)
Alexander, Alfred (Henry Burr*)
Alexander, George (Clifford Wiley)
Alix, May (Alberta Hunter)
Allen, Edward (Arthur Middleton)
Allen, Gary (Len Spencer)
Allen, Mack (Vernon Dalhart*)
Ames, Molly (Beulah Gaylord Young)
Anderson, Charles (Elliott Shaw)
Anderson, Ernie (Fred J. Bacon)
Andrew, Merry (Charles Penrose)
Andrews, Jim (Arthur Fields* or Irving Kaufman)
Anthony, Harry (John C. Young)
Astor, Paul (Easthope Martin)
Atkinson, George (Burt Shepard)
Aubrey, Charles (Wilfred Glenn)
Aunt Jemima (Tess Gardella)
Austin, Gene (Charles Keene or Gene Lucas)
Baker, Donald (Arthur Fields*)
Baldwin, Arthur (Arthur Fields*)
Ball, Ray (Frank Marvin)
Ballard, George Wilton (George Wilton)
Ballard, Wolfe (Vernon Dalhart*)
Balzer, Joseph (Gustav Görlich, Robert Heger, Artur Rother)
Barr, Harry (Henry Burr*)
Barrel House Pete (Art Gillham)
Barrett, Betty (Marie Tiffany)
Bartle, S. (Alexander Prince)
Beason, Kitty (Delores Valesco)
Beat Brothers (Beatles)
Beatty, Josephine (Alberta Hunter)
Beaver, George (Irving Kaufman)
Beaver, Harry (Irving Kaufman)
Bellwood and Burr (Albert Campbell and Henry Burr*)

Belmont, Joe (Joseph Walter Fulton)

Bennett, John (Al Bernard)

Bennett Brothers (Victor Arden and Wheeler Wadsworth)

Bergere, Bettina (Gladys Rice)

Bernie, D. Bud (Arthur Fields*)

Big Boy and Shorty (Phil Cook and Victor Fleming)

Billings, Bud (Frank Luther*)

Billings, Joe (Carson Robison)

Billings Brothers (Frank Luther* and Carson Robison)

Bingham, Ethel (Annette Hanshaw)

Birmingham Bud (Frank Luther*)

Black, Herbert (Frank Luther*, Charles Hart, Elliott Shaw, or Charles Harrison)

Black and White (Billy Jones and Ernest Hare)

Black Brothers (Frank Luther* and Carson Robison)

Blake, Harry (Billy Jones)

Blanchard, Dan (Frank Luther*)

Blue, Bob (Smith Ballew)

Blue, Buddy (Smith Ballew)

Bluebird Trio (Billy Jones, Ernest Hare, and piano)

Blue Ridge Duo (George Reneau and Gene Austin)

Bolton, Joe (Joe Batten)

Bonner, William (William A. Kennedy)

Boynton, Edward (Fred Van Eps)

Britt, Andy (Arthur Fields*)

Britten, Ford (Arthur Fields)

Bronson, George (Irving Kaufman, Arthur Fields*, or Lewis James)

Brown, Arthur (Irving Kaufman)

Brown, Betty (Vaughn De Leath)

Brown, Edna (Elsie Baker)

Brown, William (Scrappy Lambert)

Brown and Edwards (Boudini Brothers)

Bruce, Robert (Lewis James or Henry Burr*)

Buckley, Eugene (Arthur Fields*)

Burke, Edward (Elliott Shaw)

Burns, Arthur (Colin O'More)

Burr, Henry (Harry H. McClaskey)

Burton, Billy (Charles Harrison)

Burton, Howard (Arthur Hall*)

Burton, Sammy (Irving Kaufman, Billy Jones, or Ernest Hare)

Butler, Frank (George Baker)

Calhoun, Jeff (Vernon Dalhart*)

Calhoun, Jess (Vernon Dalhart*)

Calhoun and Leavitt (Frank Luther* and Carson Robison)

Cannon, Jimmy (Vernon Dalhart*)

Careau, Franklin (Frank Croxton?)

Carson, Cal (Carson Robison or Frank Luther*)

Casey, Michael (Russell Hunting)

Chappell, Miss (Edith Chapman)

Charles, Harold (Irving Kaufman)

Chester and Rollins (Frank Luther* and Carson Robison)

Christy, Frank (Irving Kaufman)

Christy Brothers (Irving Kaufman and Jack Kaufman, or Arthur Fields and Charles Harrison)

Cinway, Charles (Charles Hart)

Clare, Jack (Al Bernard)

Clare and Mann (Al Bernard and Ernest Hare)

Clark, James (Carson Robison)

Clark, Katherine (Grace Kerns)

Clark, Miriam (Grace Kerns?)

Clarke, Billy (Irving Kaufman)

Clarke, Catherine (Grace Kerns)

Clarke, Glory (Vaughn De Leath)

Clarke, Jane (Grace Kerns)

Clayton, Bob (Gene Autry)

Clifford, Arthur (George Alexander*)

Clifford, Ed (Cliff Edwards or Vernon Dalhart*)

Clifton, Edward (Cliff Edwards)

Collins, Bill (Gene Austin)

Collins, Charlie (Harry Fay)

Collins, Jane (Helen Clark)

Collins, Kitty (June Kirkby or Eleanor Jones-Hudson)

Collins, Sallie (Helen Clark)

Collins and Reynolds (Henry Burr* and Jack Kaufman)

Combs, Irving (Irving Kaufman)

Confidential Charley (Ernest Hare or Irving Kaufman)

Conrad, Louise (Louise Gaisberg)

Cook, Tom (Frank Luther*)

Courtland, Eric (Ernest Pike)

Craig, Al (Arthur Hall*)

Craig, Allen (Irving Kaufman)

Cramer, Al (Vernon Dalhart*)

Cramer Brothers (Vernon Dalhart* and Carson Robison)

Crane, Harry (Arthur Fields*)

Crange, George (Irving Kaufman)

Craver, Al (Vernon Dalhart*)

Craver and Wells (Vernon Dalhart* and Carson Robison)

Cummings, James (Vernon Dalhart*)

Curtis, Harry (Charles Hart or Charles Harrison)

Dale, Charles (Arthur Fields*, Lewis James, Franklyn Baur, Arthur Hall*, or Irving Kaufman)

Dale, Edward (Charles Hackett)

Dale, Edwin (Charles Hackett)

Dale, Walter H. (Arthur Fields*)

Dalhart, Vernon (Marion Try Slaughter)

Dalton, Charles (Vernon Dalhart*)

Dalton, Jack (Jack Kaufman)

Daniels, Wallace (Ernest Hare)

Daniels, Walter (Frank Luther*)
Dare, Dot (Annette Hanshaw)
Davies, Fred (Peter Dawson)
Dawson, Leonard (Peter Dawson)
De Kyzer, Marie (Marie Kaiser)
De Marco, Angelina (Vaughn De Leath)
De Rex, Billy (Billy Jones)
De Wees, George (Irving Kaufman)
Del Campo, A. (Alberto de Bassini)
Dell, Vernon (Vernon Dalhart*)
Destinova, Emmy (Emmy Destinn)
Dexter, Charles (Arthur Fields*)
Dickson, Charles (Irving Kaufman)
Dittman, Evans (Paul Althouse?)
Dixie Stars (Al Bernard and J. Russell Robinson)
Dixon, Charles (Irving Kaufman)
Dixon, Martin (Vernon Dalhart*)
Dixon, Raymond (Lambert Murphy)
Dixon and Andrews (Vernon Dalhart* and Carson Robison)
Donivetti, Hugo (Charles Harrison)
Donovan, Hugh (Charles Harrison, Arthur Fields*, or Ernest Hare)
Dooley and Shea (Billy Jones and Ernest Hare)
Dudley, S.H. (Samuel Holland Rous)
Duffy, Tom (Irving Kaufman)
Dwyer, Gertrude (Vaughn De Leath)
Edwards, A. (Ernest Pike)
Edwards, Billy (Arthur Fields*)
Edwards, Thomas (Billy Jones)
Edwards, Thomas (Elliott Shaw, or Arthur Fields*)
Edwards, Tom (Irving Kaufman)
Eide, Kaja (Eidé Norena)
Elliott, Joseph (Vernon Dalhart*, Arthur Fields*, Charles Harrison, Ernest Hare, Billy Jones, or Charles Hart)
Elliott, Joseph and Samuel Spencer (Billy Jones and Ernest Hare)
Elliott and Spencer (Ed Smalle and Gerald Underhill)
Ellis, Gay (Annette Hanshaw)
Ely, Carl (Walter Van Brunt?)
Epstein, George (Irving Kaufman)
Evans and Clarke (Vernon Dalhart* and Carson Robison)
Evans, Francis (Frank Luther*)
Evans, Frank (Vernon Dalhart*, Frank Luther*, Carson Robison, Arthur Fields*)
Evans, Franklin (Carson Robison)
Evans, Hal (Vernon Dalhart*)
Evans, Harry (Evan Williams)
Evans, Henry (Evan Williams)
Evans, William T. (Evan Williams)
Everett, Elliot (Wilhelm Kempff?)
Faber, Ed (Carson Robison)

Farkas, A. (Andor Földes)
Fernand, M. (Emilio de Gogorza)
Fields, Arthur (Abe Finkelstein)
Florio, Nino (Giuseppe di Stefano)
Flynn, Jimmy (Irving Kaufman)
Foster, Al (Sid Gary)
Foster, Charles (Fred Hillerbrand)
Francisco, Carlos (Emilio de Gogorza)
Francisco, E. (Emilio de Gogorza)
Francisco, Signor (Emilio de Gogorza)
Franklin, Ed (Emilio De Gogorza)
Frawley, Tom (Irving Kaufman)
Fredericks, William (Frank C. Stanley?)
French, George (Arthur Fields*)
Fuller, Jeff (Vernon Dalhart*)
Fuller, Jep (Vernon Dalhart*)
Gardiner, Arthur (Arthur Tracy)
Gargolo, Ugeso (Billy Jones)
Garland, Dorothy (Delores Valesco)
Geer, Georgia (Vaughn De Leath)
Geer, Gloria (Vaughn De Leath)
George, Arthur (George Baker)
Gilbert, Lawrence E. (Thomas Chalmers)
Gillette, Irving (Henry Burr*)
Goddard, Herbert (Emilio de Gogorza)
Gold Dust Twins (Earl Tuckerman and Harvey Hindermyer)
Gordon, Charles (Percy Hemus)
Gordon, George (Charles Hart)
Grant, Arthur (Arthur Hall* or Ernest Hare)
Grant, Hector (Peter Dawson)
Grant, Rachel (Gladys Rice)
Gray, Henry (Arthur Fields*)
Green, Alice (Olive Kline)
Green, Bert (Jack Kaufman)
Green, Marion (Wilfred Glenn)
Green, Rosa (Rosa Henderson)
Green, Sadie (Vaughn De Leath)
Grimes, Betty (Vaughn De Leath)
Guenther, Felix (John Bath)
Gunboat Billy and the Sparrow (Arthur Fields* and Fred Hall)
Haines, Ralph (Scrappy Lambert)
Haley, Harry (Henry Burr*)
Hall, Arthur (Adolph J. Hahl)
Hall, Edgar (Andrea Sarto)
Hall, Freddy (Billy Jones)
Hall, James (Andrea Sarto)
Hamilton, Edward (Reinald Werrenrath)
Hancock, Billy (Johnny Marvin)
Happiness Boys (Billy Jones and Ernest Hare)
Hardy, John (Gene Autry)
Hardy, Paul (William Wheeler)
Harmony Broadcasters (Billy Jones and Ernest Hare)

Harmony Brothers (Frank Luther* and Carson Robison)
Harold, Eugene (Billy Jones)
Harper, Billy (Irving Kaufman)
Harris, David (Billy Jones, Irving Kaufman, Vernon Dalhart*, Ernest Hare, Elliott Shaw, Walter Van Brunt, Charles Harrison)
Harris, Frank (Irving Kaufman)
Harris, Harry (Vernon Dalhart* or Cliff Edwards)
Harris, Henry (Vernon Dalhart*)
Harris, Mae (Rosa Henderson)
Harris and Smith (Charles Hart and Elliott Shaw)
Harrison, James F. (Frederick J. Wheeler)
Harrow, David and Thomas Edwards (Billy Jones and Ernest Hare)
Hartley, Lester (Franklyn Baur)
Harvey, Harold (Lewis James)
Hayes, Lou (Vernon Dalhart*)
Henry, Albert (Albert Benzler?)
Henty, Jack (Ernest Pike)
Herold, Francis (Arthur Fields*)
Hill, Murry K. (Joseph T. Pope, Jr.)
Hill, Sam (Gene Autry)
Hilly, Dan (Arthur Fields*)
Hilton, Charles (Charles Harrison)
Hobbs, Herb (Arthur Fields*)
Holland, Byron (Byron G. Harlan)
Holland, Charles (Stanley Kirkby)
Holmes, Dick (Jack Kaufman)
Holmes, John (Irving Kaufman)
Holt, Arthur (Irving Kaufman)
Holton, Larry (Arthur Fields* or Scrappy Lambert)
Hometowners (Arthur Fields* and Fred Hall)
Honey Duke and His Uke (Johnny Marvin)
Howard, Anna (Lucy Isabelle Marsh)
Howard, Frank (Albert Campbell or Arthur Hall*)
Hughes, Dan (Billy Murray)
Hunter, James (Arthur Fields*)
Hüttner, Maria (Margot Pinter)
Incognita, L' [Zonophone] (Violet Mount)
Ireland, S. (Stanley Kirkby)
Irving, Henry (Irving Kaufman)
Irving, John (Irving Kaufman)
Jack, Arizona (Alf Gordon)
Jackson, Happy (Frank Luther*)
James, Morton (Morton Downey)
Jamieson and Turner (Charles Hart and Elliott Shaw)
Jefferies, Walter (George Baker)
Jeffries, Jack (Harry Fay)
Jewel Trio (Vernon Dalhart*, Carson Robison, and Adelyn Hood)
Jimson Brothers (Frank Luther* and Carson Robison)

Johnson, Emma (Helen Clark)
Johnson, Gene (Gene Autry)
Johnson, Harold (John Harrison)
Johnson, Murray (Stanley Kirkby)
Johnson, Sara (Rosa Henderson)
Johnson, William (Billy Jones)
Jolly Jester (Charles Penrose/Billy Whitlock)
Jones, Duncan (Cal Stewart)
Jones, Harry (Carson Robison)
Jones, Henry (Ernest Hare)
Jones, Mamie (Aileen Stanley)
Jones, Mr. (Billy Jones)
Jones, Reese (Billy Jones)
Jones, Willy (Billy Jones)
Jones and White (Ernest Hare and Al Bernard)
Jones Brothers (Vernon Dalhart* and Carson Robison)
Jordan, Henry (Charles Hart)
Jordan, James (Elliott Shaw or Charles Hart)
Jordan Brothers (Charles Hart and Elliott Shaw)
Joyce, Randolph (Jan Peerce)
Judson, Robert (Ernest Hare)
Keene, Charles (Gene Austin)
Kelly, John (Billy Jones)
Kent, Franklyn (Joseph A. Phillips)
Kern, Jimmy (Arthur Fields*)
Kernell, Frank (S. H. Dudley*)
Killeen, Pete (Irving Kaufman)
Kimmble, John J. (John J. Kimmel)
Kincaid, Joe (Vernon Dalhart*)
King, Al (Henry Burr*)
King, Daisy (Vaughn De Leath)
King, Fred (Vernon Dalhart*)
King, Henry (Arthur Fields*)
King, Martin (Scrappy Lambert)
Kingston, Kathleen (Mary Carson)
Kirkby, Stanley (James Baker)
Knapp, Frank (Henry Burr*)
Lambert, Fred (Fred Duprez?)
Lance, Roland (Scrappy Lambert)
Lane, Jack (Johnny Marvin)
Latimer, Hugh (Vernon Dalhart*)
Lawrence, Harry (Joseph A. Phillips)
Lazy Larry (Frank Marvin)
Lee, Mabel (Annie Rees)
Lee, Mamie (Vaughn De Leath)
Lee, Marion (Annette Hanshaw)
Lee, Virginia (Vaughn De Leath)
Le Fevre, Edward (Edward M. Favor)
Lenox, Ruth (Helen Clark?)
Leon, Albert (Ernest Hare)
Leonard, Larry (Len Spencer)
Leslie, Walter (Ernest Hare)
Lewis, Howard (Arthur Hall*)
Lewis, Justice (Joseph A. Phillips)

Lewis, Robert (Lewis James)
Lewis, Rodman (Scrappy Lambert)
Lewis, William (Arthur Fields*)
Lewis and Scott (Billy Jones and Ernest Hare)
Lincoln, Chester (Byron G. Harlan)
List, Karl (Karl Böhm, Alfons Dressel, or Oswald Kabasta)
Litchfield, Ben (Franklyn Baur?)
Little, Tobe (Vernon Dalhart*)
Livingston (John Bieling)
Lloyd, Arthur (Burt Shepard)
Loew, Jack (Irving Kaufman or Jack Kaufman)
Lone Star Ranger (Vernon Dalhart* or Arthur Fields*)
Long, Tom (Gene Autry)
Lord, Jack (Scrappy Lambert)
Lorin, Burt (Scrappy Lambert)
Lumberjacks (Arthur Fields* and Fred Hall)
Luther, Francis (Frank Luther*)
Luther, Frank (Francis Luther Crow)
Luther and Faber (Frank Luther* and Carson Robison)
Luther Brothers (Frank Luther* and Carson Robison)
Lyons and Heilman (Billy Jones and Ernest Hare)
Lyons, Billy (Billy Jones)
MacDonough, Harry (John S. MacDonald)
MacFarland, Bob (Irving Kaufman)
Mack, Arthur (Arthur Fields*)
Mander, Ambrose (Arthur Fields*)
Mann, Frank (Ernest Hare)
Mark, Freddie (Irving Kaufman)
Marron, John (Ernest Hare)
Marsden, Victoria (Gladys Rice)
Martin, Happy (Jack Kaufman)
Martin, Jack (Arthur Fields*)
Massey, Bob (Vernon Dalhart*)
Massey, Guy (Vernon Dalhart*)
Matthew, J. (Henry Burr*)
Maxwell, P. (Harry Fay)
May, Jimmie (Johnny Marvin)
McAfee, Billy (Vernon Dalhart*)
McClaskey and Meyers (Henry Burr* and John H. Meyer)
McClaskey, Shamus (Henry Burr*)
McHugh, Martin (Walter Van Brunt)
McLaughlin, George (Vernon Dalhart*)
Meadows, Arthur (Arthur Fields*)
Meredith, May (Helen Clark)
Merritt, G. (Stewart Gardner)
Meyer, Saul (Monroe Silver)
Middlestadt, Edouard (Arthur Middleton)
Miller, Kenneth (Charles Harrison)
Miller, Walter (Stanley Kirkby)
Mitchell, Sidney (Irving Kaufman)

Mitchell, Warren (Vernon Dalhart*)
Mitchell and White (Vernon Dalhart* and Ed Smalle)
Mme. X [Pathé] (Alice Verlet)
Moore, Buddy (Al Bernard)
Moore, Harry A. (Vernon Dalhart* or Charles Harrison)
Moore, Tom (Billy Jones)
Moreley, Herbert (Morton Harvey)
Morgan, John (Stanley Kirkby)
Morley, Herbert (Harvey Morton)
Morris, William (Billy Jones)
Morse, Dick (Vernon Dalhart*)
Morton, James (Morton Downey)
Mr. X (Arthur Fields or Vernon Dalhart*)
Murphy and Shea (Albert Campbell and Jack Kaufman)
Myers, John (John H. Meyer)
Nash, Grace (Louise MacMahon)
Nelson, Gerald (Scrappy Lambert)
Nelson, Grace (Grace Hornby)
Nelson and Gwynne (George Ballard and William Wheeler)
Nesbit, Henry (Harvey N. Emmons)
Nevill, Tom (Irving Kaufman)
Nichols, Frank (Arthur Hall*)
Nielson, Varna (Aileen Stanley)
Noble, Harold (Scrappy Lambert)
Norton, Walter (Arthur Fields*)
Oakley, Olly (James Sharpe)
O'Brien, John (Walter Van Brunt)
O'Brien, Padric (Arthur Fields*)
Odde, Erik (Jussi Björling)
Old King Cole (Bob Pierce)
Old Pop Collins (Fred Hall)
Oliver, Paul (Frank Munn)
O'Malley, Dennis (Billy Jones)
Oriole Trio (Vernon Dalhart*, Carson Robison, and Adelyn Hood)
Osborne, James (Peter Dawson)
Palmer, Olive (Virginia Rea)
Palmer and Oliver (Virginia Rea and Frank Munn)
Pampini, Carlo (Guido Deiro)
Parker, H.C. (Frank C. Stanley)
Parsons, Happy Jim (Irving Kaufman)
Patterson, Lila (Ma Rainey)
Patti, Orville (Irving Kaufman)
Paula, Madame (Billy Whitlock)
Payne, Herbert (Ernest Pike)
Pearl, Jack (Jan Peerce)
Pearl, Pinky (Jan Peerce)
Perry, George (Arthur Hall*)
Peters, Sam (Vernon Dalhart*)
Peters and Jones (Vernon Dalhart* and Carson Robison)

Phillips, Curt (Ernest Hare)
Pietro (Pietro Deiro)
Pinckney, Henry (Reed Miller)
Pippins, Cyrus (Byron G. Harlan)
Pitkin, Cy (Billy Murray)
Post, Irving (Franklyn Baur or Irving Kaufman)
Price, Jimmy (Frank Marvin)
Prime, Alberta (Alberta Hunter)
Radio Aces (Gerald Underhill Macy and Ed Smalle)
Radio Boys (Arthur Hall* and John Ryan?)
Radio Franks (Frank Bessinger and Frank White)
Radio Girl (Vaughn De Leath)
Radio Imps (Gerald Underhill Macy and Ed Smalle)
Radio Joe (Ernest Hare)
Radio Kings (Billy Jones and Ernest Hare, or
    Frank Bessinger and   Frank Wright)
Radio Red (Wendell Hall)
Randall, Roy (Arthur Fields*)
Raymond, Harry (Vernon Dalhart*)
Raymond, Ralph (Harry Macdonough)
Red-Masked Baritone (Wendell Hall)
Reed, James (Reed Miller)
Reed and Griffin (Billy Jones and Ernest Hare)
Rees, William (Billy Jones)
Reese, William (Billy Jones)
Reeve, Arthur (Edgar Coyle)
Reeve, Floyd (Steve Porter)
Regal Rascals (Vernon Dalhart*, Carson Robison,
    and Adelyn Hood)
Rice, Robert (Henry Burr*)
Richards, Charles (Arthur Fields*)
Richards, Daisy (Vaughn De Leath)
Ritz, Sally (Rosa Henderson)
Roberts, Charles (Smith Ballew)
Roberts, Ed (Irving Kaufman)
Roberts, John (Scrappy Lambert)
Roberts, Roy (Ernest Hare)
Roberts, Victor (Billy Jones)
Roe, Turner (Elliott Shaw?)
Rogers, Gene (Harvey Morton)
Romeo Boys (Billy Jones and Ernest Hare)
Roy, Dudley (Billy Whitlock)
Rubahn, Gerd (Karl Böhm)
Rundle, William (Charles Harrison)
Russell, Al (Irving Kaufman)
Russell, Roy (Scrappy Lambert)
Ryan, Jimmy (Arthur Fields*)
Sampson, Sammy (Bill Broonzy)
Samuels, Claude (Carson Robison)
Sanborn, Dave (Al Bernard)
Sanders, Bessie (Alberta Jones)
Saunders and White (Billy Murray and Walter
    Scanlan*)
Scanlan, Walter (Walter Van Brunt)
Scott, Henry (Vernon Dalhart*)

Scott, Herbert (Walter Van Brunt)
Seelig, Arthur (Arthur Fields*)
Seward, Hatch (Meade Lux Lewis)
Shannon, Thomas (Charles Harrison or Walter Van
    Brunt)
Shaw, Janet (Annette Hanshaw)
Shea, Jack (Jack Kaufman)
Silver, Erik (Wilhelm Backhaus, Leonid Hambro,
    or Helmut Roloff)
Silver Masked Tenor (Joseph M. White)
Simpson, Al (Al Bernard)
Sims, Skeeter (Al Bernard)
Sloane, John (Arthur Fields*)
Smith, Anne (Ma Rainey)
Smith, Bertram (Billy Jones)
Smith, Harry (Irving Kaufman)
Smith, Josephus (Vernon Dalhart*)
Smith, Oliver (Frank Munn)
Sorano, Madame (E. Pett)
Southerners (Frank Luther* and Carson Robison)
Spence, Elton (Johnny Marvin)
Spencer and Harris (Billy Jones and Ernest Hare)
Spencer, Ernie (Ernest Hare)
Spencer, Samuel (Cliff Edwards, Arthur Fields*,
    or Billy Jones))
Stanley, Frank C. (William Stanley Grinsted)
Stebbins, Cy (Byron G. Harlan)
Stehl, George (George Steel)
Stein, Gerhard (Wilhelm Backhaus or Friedrich
    Wührer)
Stell, George (George Steel)
Stendahl, Mr. (Leon Beyle)
Sterling, Frank (Elliott Shaw)
Stewart, Cliff (Arthur Hall*, Vernon Dalhart*, or
    Arthur Fields*)
Stoddard, Edgar (Andrea Sarto)
Stone, Edward (Vernon Dalhart* or Charles Hart)
Stone, Fred (Arthur Fields*)
Street Singer (Arthur Tracy)
Strong, Arthur (Joseph A. Phillips)
Strong, Will (Peter Dawson)
Stuart, Billy (Vernon Dalhart*)
Sullivan, Walter (Charles Harrison)
Taylor, Harry (Burt Shepard?)
Taylor, Noel (Irving Kaufman)
Terrill, Norman (Charles Harrison)
Terry, Bert (Byron G. Harlan)
Terry, Will (Vernon Dalhart*)
Thomas, Bob (Arthur Fields* or Ernest Hare)
Thomas, Fred (Art Gillham)
Thomas, John (Ernest Hare)
Thomas, Josephine (Rosa Henderson)
Thomas and West (Billy Jones and Ernest Hare)
Thompson, Bob (Billy Jones)
Thompson, Bud (Frank Luther*)

Thompson, Madge (Vaughn De Leath)
Three Kaulfields (Arthur Fields*, Irving Kaufman, and Jack Kaufman)
Tillotson, Merle (Merle Alcock)
Topnotchers (Billy Jones and Ernest Hare)
Townson, Joe (Stanley Kirkby)
Treadway, Deacon (Byron G. Harlan)
Turner, Allen (Ernest Hare, Vernon Dalhart*, Charles Hart, or Elliott Shaw)
Turner, Fred (Olly Oakley*)
Turner, Hobo Jack (Ernest Hare)
Turner, Sid (Vernon Dalhart*)
Turney Brothers (Frank Luther* and Carson Robison)
Tuttle, Frank (Frank Luther* or Vernon Dalhart*)
Twitchell, Atwood (George Alexander*?)
Two Kaulfields (Arthur Fields* and either Jack Kaufman or Irving Kaufman)
Ukulele Ike (Cliff Edwards)
Uncle Billy (Billy Jones)
Uncle Ernest (Ernest Hare)
Uncle Ernie (Ernest Hare)
Uncle Joe (Al Bernard)
Uncle Josh (Cal Stewart)
Uncle Lewis (Lewis James)
Vaughn, Caroline (Beulah G. Young)
Vernon, Bill(y) (Vernon Dalhart*)
Vernon, Fred (Harry Fay)
Vernon, Herbert (Vernon Dalhart*)
Vernon, Walter (Billy Jones)
Vernon, Will (Vernon Dalhart*)
Veteran, Vel (Arthur Fields* and others)
Vincent, Sam (Fred Van Eps)
Wainwright Sisters (Brox Sisters)
Wallace, Frankie (Frankie Marvin)
Wallace, Ken (Johnny Marvin)
Walters, Nat (Ernest Hare)
Warfield, Lewis (Frank Marvin)
Warner, Florence (Aileen Stanley)
Warner, Yodlin' Jimmy (Frank Marvin)
Warren, Charles (Charles Hart)
Warren, G.P. (Fred Gaisberg)
Watson, Nora (Elsie Baker)
Watson, Tom (Vernon Dalhart*)
Watt, Brian (Irving Kaufman)
Weary Willie (Jack Kaufman, Frank Marvin, Frank Luther*, or Carson Robison)
Webster, Frank (Albert Campbell)
Webster Brothers (Billy Jones and Ernest Hare)
Wells, Charley (Carson Robison)
Wells, Lorenzo (Percy Hemus)
Welsh, Corinne (Corinne Morgan)
Welsh, George (Peter Dawson)
West, Billy (Billy Jones)
West, Jack (Frank Marvin)
West, Mabel (Elsie Baker)
West, William (Billy Jones)
Wheeler and Morse (Henry Burr* and Jack Kaufman)
Whispering Pianist (Art Gillham)
White, Bob (Vernon Dalhart*)
White, George (Frank Marvin, Vernon Dalhart*)
White, Gladys (Rosa Henderson)
White, Jerry (Jack Kaufman)
White, Joe (Billy Jones)
White, Robert (Vernon Dalhart*)
White, Slim (Al Bernard)
Whitlock, Walter (Vernon Dalhart*)
Wiggins, Pete (Frank Luther*?)
Wilbur, John (John H. Meyer)
Williams, Bessie (Rosa Henderson)
Williams, Carlton (Billy Jones)
Williams, Frank (Stanley Kirkby, Billy Jones, or Dan Quinn)
Williams, George S. (William Stanley Grinsted)
Williams Brothers (Frank Luther* and Carson Robison)
Wilmott, Leo (Fred Van Eps)
Wilson, Arthur (Charles Hart)
Wilson, Harvey (Harvey Hindermyer)
Wilton, George (George Wilton Ballard)
Windy City Duo (Vernon Dalhart* and Ed Smalle)
Winslow, Alice (Edith Clegg)
Winters, Horace (Irving Kaufman)
Wood, Robert (Arthur Fields*)
Woods, George (Vernon Dalhart*)
Woods, Gladys (Vaughn De Leath)
Woods, Grace (Helen Clark)
Woolf, Walter (Irving Kaufman)
X, Mr. (Vernon Dalhart* or Arthur Fields*)
Young, Blanche (Bessie Jones)
Young, Marvin (Irving Kaufman)
Young, Patsy (Annette Hanshaw)

PSYCHEDELIA

The psychedelic era evolved out of the social-consciousness movement engendered by a commitment to civil rights, antiwar protest, the legalization of recreational drugs, and other youth subculture concerns. These issues were frequently addressed in rock lyrics while the music itself often employed special effects geared to underscoring the song's message. For example, the Doors' "Unknown Soldier" (Elektra #45628; 1968) included a marching interlude accented by a drill sergeant's shrieked commands and the discharge of rifles. The Chicago Transit Authority's "Prologue, August 29, 1968" (*Chicago Transit*

Can, a psychedelic rock group. Courtesy Frank Hoffmann

Authority, Columbia #8; 1969) featured an actual recording from the 1968 Democratic National Convention that conveyed the following sequence: Black militants exhorting demonstrators, "God give us the blood to keep going"; the beginning of the march; police attempting to disperse marchers; and the demonstrators chanting, "The Whole World's Watching." Pearl Before Swine's polemic on the horrors of war, *Balaklava* (ESP #1075; 1968), began with a turn-of-the-century recording of the trumpet that was blown to commence the fabled charge of the British Light Brigade in 1856.

These spacey sound effects, however, paled in contrast to the mind-expanding techniques utilized to evoke the psychedelic drug experience. Guitarist Les Paul was the spiritual godfather of studio augmentation as a result of his experiments with overdubbing and multitracking; his seminal 1950s recordings with vocalist Mary Ford rivaled Big Band and orchestral productions for fullness of sound. The unique tones he was able to coax out of his guitar within a studio environment were not equaled until Jimi Hendrix's appearance on the scene. The infancy of stereo recording in the early 1960s had witnessed a succession of sonic experiments primarily within the light pops sector. Enoch Light and the Light Brigade pioneered the spatial left-right channel ping-pong effects later employed in a spectacular manner by Jimi Hendrix in his albums, *Axis: Bold as Love* (Reprise #6281; 1968) and *Electric Ladyland* (Reprise #6307; 1968). The introduction of synthesizers into the recording process by inventors such as Robert Moog in collaboration with Morton Subotnick, Walter (Wendy) Carlos, and other avant-garde artists, made available another key tool for rock production wizards.

As in so many other genres, the Beatles played a pioneering role in the evolution of psychedelic effects. The group's recording engineer, George Martin, proved extremely facile at reproducing the sounds that the Lennon-McCartney songwriting team professed to have in their heads. Martin's arsenal of studio effects included tapes run backward, filtered voices, and the inventive use of exotic instruments (e.g., the piccolo trumpet on "Penny Lane," Capitol #5810; 1967) and ambient sounds. The critical raves and commercial success of *Revolver* (Capitol #2576; 1966) and *Sgt. Pepper's Lonely Hearts Club Band* (Capitol #2653; 1967) — both of which reeked of psychedelic touches — spurred a tidal wave of imitators. The vast majority of rock acts insisted on (or were talked into) doing their own psychedelic projects. Even artists whose prior output appeared to be the antithesis of such studio excess — e.g., roots rocker Johnny Rivers, who was then enjoying a career revival with a series of soft ballads, and blues stylists, the Rolling Stones — were swept up by this new fad. Only Bob Dylan, who released a country-rock masterpiece, *John Wesley Harding* (Columbia #9604; 1968), at the peak of the psychedelic era, seemed able to run counter to prevailing fashion.

Psychedelia was sometimes referred to as "acid rock." The latter label was generally applied to a pounding, hard-rock variant that evolved out of the mid-1960s garage-punk movement. By late 1966, the Blues Magoos were calling their brand of wailing blues-rock "psychedelic" music. Although generally devoid of the studio gimmickry typifying the Beatles school of psychedelia, acid rock provided its own form of mind expansion by means of guitar pyrotechnics. Leading practitioners included Cream, Blue Cheer, and the Amboy Dukes. When rock began turning back to softer, roots-oriented sounds in late 1968, acid-rock bands mutated into heavy-metal acts. Traces of the psychedelic era can still be found in the stylistic excesses of many third-generation metal groups.

Successive refinements of the sound, generally referred to as "neo-psychedelia," have been appearing since the rise of the new-wave movement. Notable examples include the early 1980s British postpunk bands such as Echo and the Bunnymen (early 1980s), the Teardrop Explodes, and the Psychedelic Furs; proponents of the late 1980s rave scene (e.g., Stone Roses, Primal Scream, Inspiral Carpets); ambient experimentalists like Bill Nelson, Art of Noise, and Orbital; and talented eccentrics (the Lightning Seeds and XTC's side project, the Dukes of Stratosphear) positioned outside of prevailing pop music trends. [Miller 1980.]

FRANK HOFFMANN

PSYCHOACOUSTICS

The scientific study of the perception of sound, particularly important when we think of recorded musical or motion-picture-sound listening in home- or studio-listening environments. A knowledge of psychoacoustics will help the recording engineer produce recordings that have maximum realism and/or impact in home-playback situations. Those who design home-audio hardware, particularly speakers and surround processors, can use the same knowledge to produce superior products.

HOWARD FERSTLER

PUBLIC ENEMY

One of the most influential rap groups of all time. Public Enemy was formed by rapper Chuck D. (b. Carlton Ridenhour, 1 Aug 1960) when he was a student at Adelphi University. He'd been working as a disc jockey on the college radio station, where he befriended two other hip-hop fans, Bill Stephney and Hank Shocklee. The trio made a demo tape with Ridenhour rapping over a backing track assembled by Stepney and Shocklee called "Public Enemy No. 1"; it was heard by rap mogul Rick Rubin, who signed the rapper now known as "Chuckie D." for his fledgling Def Jam label. Chuck D. invited a second rapper-friend to join the group, Flavor Flav (b. William Drayton, 16 Mar 1959), who became a comic, higher-voiced foil to D.'s booming bass raps. The group was rounded out with DJ Terminator X (b. Norman Lee Rogers, 15 Aug 1966) and crew-dance leader Professor Griff (b. Richard Griff). The group issued their debut album in 1987, *Yo! Bum Rush the Show* (Def Jam #40658).

However, it was their second album, *It Takes a Nation of Millions to Hold Us Back* (Def Jam #44303; 1988), that gained wide critical acclaim for its combination of danceable grooves with powerful social protest lyrics. They followed with the single "Fight the Power," prominently featured in Spike Lee's film *Do the Right Thing* in 1989. During this period, Professor Griff was embroiled in controversy thanks to his support of Louis Farrakhan; following some antisemitic remarks made to reporters, he was forced out of the group. Their next two albums enjoyed great success, but then the group began to

lose momentum due to drugs and internal squabbling. In 1995, Chuck D. left Def Jam to form his own label and publishing company, and a year later published his autobiography. He has released a few albums since, but has failed to regain the popularity that the group initially enjoyed.

PUBLISHERS' SERVICE CO., INC.

An American firm that carried out a national campaign in the U.S. in 1939, involving a newspaper in each community. A record player was offered to buyers of 10 record albums at $3 each. The albums were titled *World's Greatest Music*. Performers were not named.

PUBLIX (LABEL)

An American record issued by Paramount Pictures to promote music from their films of the 1930s. Columbia did the pressings. [Rust 1978.]

PUCK

SEE CAPSTAN

PUENTE, TITO
(20 APR 1923–1 JUNE 2000)

Master Latin jazz bandleader and percussionist, Puente was born Ernesto Antonio Puente, Jr., in Spanish Harlem to a Puerto Rican family. He began working as a drummer at age 13, working with several local bands through 1941, when he was drafted into the Navy. After World War II, Puento studied composition and piano at Juilliard and the New York School of Music. He formed his first group, the Piccadilly Boys, in 1947, recording for the small Tico label. In 1955 he signed with major label RCA Victor, and his large band, combining Big-Band jazz harmonies with Latin rhythms, became widely recognized as a leader in the salsa community. He returned to recording for Tico through the 1960s and 1970s, and then signed in 1982 with Concord Picante. Amazingly prolific, by 1992 he had recorded 100 albums. Puente remained active through the year of his death. He won five Grammy awards and numerous other honors; after his death in 2000, his final album, *Mambo Birdland* (RMM #84047), was awarded Best Traditional Tropical Performance at the first Latin Grammy awards ceremony. Many famed musicians and vocalist performed with his band over the years, including Celia Cruz and Charlie Palmieri.

PULSE CODE MODULATION

SEE PCM (PULSE CODE MODULATION)

PUNK/GARAGE ROCK

The first wave of punk rock was not about virtuousity; indeed, its finest practitioners could barely play their instruments. Rather, it reflected "the utopian dream of everyman an artist." The origins of garage rock, the forerunner of mid-1960s punk, can be discerned in the instrumental groups based in California

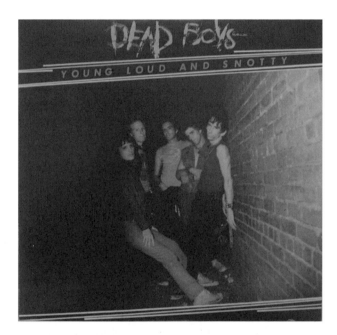

Punk Rockers Dead Boys and Nina Hagen album covers.
Courtesy Frank Hoffmann

and the Pacific Northwest during the early 1960s. Within a few years a number of Mexican-American bands in southern California had begun adding vocals, most notably the Premiers ("Farmer John," Warner Bros. #5443; 1964), Cannibal & the Headhunters ("Land of 1,000 Dances," Rampart #642; 1965), and Thee Midniters ("Land of 1,000 Dances, Part 1," Chattahoochee #666; 1965). By the middle of the decade, however, the creative center of the scene had shifted back to the northern Pacific coast, home base for groups such as the Sonics (Seattle), the Kingsmen, and Paul Revere & the Raiders (the latter two hailing from Portland).

The next phase, classic punk, coincided with the rise of psychedelia in 1966. New technical breakthroughs such as fuzztone and the electric 12-string guitar enabled young musicians possessing limited playing technique to experiment with an augmented sonic vocabulary. The genre also incorporated various fads of the moment including the drug subculture and Eastern music (e.g., ragas, sitars) and philosophy. Punk bands sprang up across the nation; those cited below (categorized by locale) all had at least one moderate hit:

Boston

The Standells — "Dirty Water" (Tower #185; 1966), "Sometimes Good Guys Don't Wear White" (Tower #257; 1966), "Why Pick on Me" (Tower #282; 1966); The Barbarians — "Are You a Boy of Are You a Girl" (Laurie #3308; 1965), "Moulty" (Laurie #3326; 1966).

Midwest

Terry Knight & the Pack — "I, Who Have Nothing" (Lucky Eleven #230; 1966); Cryan' Shames — "Sugar and Spice" (Destination #624; 1966); Shadows of Knight — "Gloria" (Dunwich #116; 1966), "Oh Yeah" (Dunwich #122; 1966); ? & the Mysterians — "96 Tears" (Cameo #428; 1966), "I Need Somebody" (Cameo #441; 1966), "Can't Get Enough of You, Baby" (Cameo #467; 1967).

South

John Fred & His Playboy Band — "Judy in Disguise" (Paula #282; 1967), "Hey Hey Bunny" (Paula #294; 1968); The Hombres — "Let It Out" (Verve Forecast #5058; 1967); The Gentrys — "Keep on Dancing" (MGM #13379; 1965), "Spread It on Thick" (MGM #13432; 1966); The Swingin' Medallions — "Double Shot of My Baby's Love" (Smash #2033; 1966), "She Drives Me Out of My Mind" (Smash #2050; 1966).

Los Angeles

Count Five — "Psychotic Reaction" (Double Shot #106; 1966); Syndicate of Sound — "Little Girl" (Bell #640; 1966), "Rumors" (Bell #646; 1966); The Music Machine — "Talk Talk" (Original Sound #61; 1966); The Leaves — "Hey Joe" (Mira #222; 1966); The Seeds — "Pushin' Too Hard" (GNP Crescendo #372;

1966), "Can't Seem to Make You Mine" (GNP Crescendo #354; 1967).

By 1968 punk had lost its momentum, with the more adventuresome bands evolving in the direction of acid rock. The remaining holdouts had no options other than heavy metal. For instance, in the Michigan area, the Amboy Dukes (fronted by gonzo guitarist Ted Nugent) took the former path, whereas Grand Funk Railroad (a spin-off of Terry Knight & the Pack), the MC5, and the Stooges (lead by Iggy Pop) opted for the latter. The rebellious element of punk attitude continued to be sustained in these stylistic offshoots, ultimately to be resurrected in the second punk wave of the mid-1970s. [Miller 1980.]

FRANK HOFFMANN

PURETONE (LABEL)

An American record issued by the Bridgeport Die and Machine Co., Bridgeport, Connecticut, in the mid-1920s. Matrices came from Paramount. [Rust 1978.]

PURITAN RECORD (LABEL)

An American vertical-cut (lateral-cut from December 1919) record made at United Phonographs Corp., Sheboygan, Wisconsin, from 1918 to February 1922, and at Bridgeport Die and Machine Co., Bridgeport, Connecticut, from March 1922 to 1925. Matrices, from Paramount and Plaza, included jazz and blues, by King Oliver, the Original Memphis Five, and other admired groups. The label continued to 1927. [Rust 1978.]

Puritan Records label. Courtesy David A. Jasen

PURITONE (LABEL)

An American record pressed from Columbia's Harmony masters for Strauss and Schram, Inc., a Chicago mail order house, in 1928–1929. Dance and popular vocals made up the repertoire. [Rust 1978.]

See also **Harmony (Label) (III)**

PUSH-UP PLAYER

The type of 1890s piano roll player that was mechanically independent of the piano, and had to be pushed up to it in order to function. Aeolian Co.'s Pianola was the most popular, and gave its name to the genre.

PUTNAM, MILTON T. (BILL) (1920–13 APR 1989)

A pioneer in recording studio acoustics, Putnam was born in Danville, Illinois. As a young man, he was influenced by his father, a businessman who also put on radio programs, including a number one country music show. By age 15, Putnam had passed the ham radio operator's exam and was constructing his own equipment. In high school, he worked repairing radios and renting out PA systems, while also singing on weekends with dance bands, developing his interest in the music business. Technical studies at the Illinois Institute of Technology were followed by work at radio stations, such as WDAN, in Chicago, and WDWS, in Champaign, and during World War II, Putnam did radio engineering work for the Army.

In 1946 he started his own recording studio, in Evanston, Illinois. His goals at the time, besides having a successful business, were the development of new recording techniques and the production of specialized equipment for recording studios. Putnam is acknowledged to be the first person to use artificial reverberation for commercial recordings, and the whole modern control-room concept in common use was his invention. He also developed the first multi-band equalizers, a specialized limiter, the first low-noise tube microphone preamplifier, and a half-speed mastering technique. His company, Universal Recording, was responsible for the development of classic equipment like the United Recording Electronics Industries (UREI) Time Align monitors, and he was also involved in the early development of stereophonic recording, at a time when other studios were afraid to fool with it. Putnam also published a number of articles on high-fidelity sound reproduction, and even conducted seminars and classes. During that time, he mentored upcoming engineers like Alan Sides and Bruce Swedien.

As success followed success, he founded additional facilities in Chicago, Hollywood, and San Francisco. A number of recording-industry firsts occurred at Universal: the first use of tape repeat, the first vocal booth, the first multiple voice recording, the first eight-track recording trials, and experiments with half-speed disc mastering. Universal was becoming famous, doing recordings for the Chicago-based labels VeeJay, Mercury, and Chess. The studio was a hub for R&B recordings, including cuts for Muddy Waters, Willie Dixon, Bo Diddley, Little Walter, and Chuck Berry. Jazz and more mainstream artists recorded by Putnam included Stan Kenton, Patti Page, Vic Damone, Dinah Washington, Tommy Dorsey, Count Basie, Dizzy Gillespie, Ella Fitzgerald, Sarah Vaughn, Nat King Cole, and the master, Duke Ellington, who considered Putnam his favorite recording engineer. During the 1960s and 1970s the studios were sometimes busy 24 hours a day, seven days a week with artists like Frank Sinatra (for many years, Putnam was the only engineer that Sinatra would allow into the recording booth), Bing Crosby, Dean Martin, Sammy Davis, Johnny Mercer, and Ray Charles. Putnam was also producing records for Decca, as well as writing songs and lyrics. Putnam was a member of the Audio Engineering Society, became a Fellow of the Society in 1959, and became an honorary member in 1983. In 2000, he won a posthumous Grammy for his technical accomplishments.

HOWARD FERSTLER

PYE RECORDS

In 1949, Alan Freeman, a Tasmanian disc jockey who had moved to England, set up an independent label called Polygon Records. Within a year he had signed up a ballad-singer named Johnny Brandon, and more successfully a teenage girl Petula Clark. The two of them provided a number of small chart hits, which was just at the time the *New Musical Express* (*NME*) was getting up and running, and introduced the first U.K. charts, which only had 10–12 entries at the time. A couple of years later, New Zealand businessman Hilton Nixon who was also living in the U.K. started up his own label Nixa, but found it a struggle after several business failures. Nixon approached Freeman to establish a distribution deal for their two labels, and they approached the electronics manufacturer, Pye of Cambridge, for a possible deal. In 1955 Pye bought a share in the two labels, and then moved Polygon's artists to Nixa, which then became Pye Nixa. The first artist to make a number one hit on the Pye Nixa label was influential skiffle comedian Lonnie Donegan who hit with "Rock Island Line" after being transferred from Decca. He became an influence on Liverpool guitar students Paul McCartney and John Lennon who belonged to a Liverpool band called the Quarrymen, and was also one of the few British artists to make the American Top 10 in the 1950s.

Pye was not slow to catch on to other trends in the market. Now that the label had the full backing of a top electrical distributor behind it, they invested in a division to distribute overseas products. In 1958 they formed the Pye International label, just as Decca had done with London, which was to primarily release records by American independent labels who were releasing rock and soul music when the likes of CBS, Decca, RCA Victor, and Capitol all felt sure that it was never going to be a lasting movement. Pye International bought the rights to Vanguard, A&M, Colpix, and King Records, and brought artists like Herb Alpert, the Marcels, James Brown, Dionne Warwick, and Chris Montez to the U.K. public. However Pye International did not turn out to be a prolific label, because in 1960 they were given the rights to use the Warner Bros. label in the U.K., and they used its American design on their records, which other U.K. major labels disliked doing. Three years later Frank Sinatra sold his Reprise label to Warner Bros. with the result that Pye also used its original design on the records.

With the British pop and rock market starting to soar in the 1960s, Pye made the mistake of rejecting the Beatles, as did Decca, Philips, Columbia, and HMV. They turned instead to another Liverpool band called the Searchers who hit number one with "Sweets for My Sweet" in 1963. With the newly appointed Tony Hatch as A&R leader, they developed a powerful marketing team to unearth U.K. talent. In a movement of favoritism they signed Tony Hatch's wife, Jackie Trent, who had one big hit followed by a string of much smaller ones. Next came the inventive London band, the Kinks, led by the charismatic Ray Davies; "You Really Got Me" is an all-time U.K. rock classic, which some argue was the groundwork for heavy metal. It was believed that the distorted guitar intro to that song was played by none other than Jimmy Page, who had also released some solo records on Pye before his work with the Yardbirds. Sandie Shaw won a contract with the label after being heard singing backstage at an Adam Faith concert, and she too hit the top with her first chart hit "Always Something There to Remind Me." She gained a degree of infamy by performing on television without any shoes on, but that didn't stop her from entering and winning the Eurovision Song Contest in 1967 with the nursery-rhyme song "Puppet on a String." Status Quo had their first hits with Pye, and their debut hit, the psychedelic cult classic "Pictures of Matchstick Men" showed very few hints of the hard working-class blues-rock band they were to evolve into the next decade, when they were signed with Phonogram's Vertigo label. Not all of the classic U.K. artists had a successful relationship with the label. David Bowie made three singles on Pye Records produced by Tony Hatch. Although they generated a lot of money, most record collectors agree that the records were very badly produced and did not show much promise for Bowie. As Pye had a reputation for being no-nonsense hit-makers, they were reluctant to keep artists who did not produce the goods after three attempts.

In the meantime while Pye was constantly delivering the hits, its ownership was about to change. As far back as 1959 half the company was sold to Lew Grade's ATV network, then in 1966 Pye Electrical sold its share of the record company to them too, although they still retained the massive distribution company. Pye did have some golden moments too; it was the first British label to have a single debut at number one with Lonnie Donegan's comedy song "My Old Man's a Dustman." They were the first British company to issue stereo records, and they also perfected fitting an hour's worth of music onto an LP for their Golden Hour label. Pye also contributed to the classical music market with the Marble Arch label, which released budget records by their pop artists too.

The one thing Pye was not competent at was setting up overseas subsidiaries, which could have given it a reputation as an international label. It did have an Australian subsidiary in the early 1960s, but it soon closed down and all artists were transferred to the Astor label. In France it had affiliations with Vogue records, and in America it licensed its artists to the Warner Bros. and Reprise labels. It also had some success in Scandinavia.

As with the other major labels in the 1970s, Pye wasted the fortunes it made in the 1960s on diversification. Now that its A&R people were starting to branch out into other styles of music, they wanted to finance their own satellite labels to release the artists. They set up Dawn Records in 1970, which hit the jackpot with mixed vocal group Brotherhood of Man, and country jug-band down homers Mungo Jerry who had a million seller with "In the Summertime." Other labels Pye invested in were BBC, Satril, Fly, DJM, and for dance club releases Disco Demand. Needless to say, none of these labels had a lasting appeal except for DJM which launched Elton John as a rock god after he had served an apprenticeship as a humble blues pianist in the late 1960s. Disco Demand did put out a few dance classics in the 1970s, including the innovative "Footsee," which could be regarded as one of the first industrial dance records, and Wayne Gibson's remake of "Under My Thumb." In 1976 the label hit an all-time high with Brotherhood of Man winning the Eurovision Song Contest with "Save Your Kisses for Me," which

was the biggest selling U.K. record that year, followed by Liverpool soul disco band the Real Thing with the classic "You to Me Are Everything." In the meantime other artists started to fade. Sandie Shaw retired from pop, the Kinks went to RCA and the hits stopped flowing, as did Petula Clark. Pye International came to a halt in 1977 after scoring a number one hit with Space's "Magic Fly" and Meri Wilson's jazz number "Telephone Man." Pye ignored the punk movement completely, preferring to concentrate on the disco scene and MOR music, virtually a reflection of its parent company who had also refused to bend with trends in the electronic market with the result that they were taken over by Philips. Pye's last number one hit was with Scottish country singer Lena Martell's slushy remake of the hymn "One Day at a Time."

The 1980s marked the death throes for Pye. Now that the label and distribution company were no longer a part of the electrical company, and under the guidance of ATV, the powers decided to give it a new name PRT (Precision Records & Tapes). They showed some promise in 1980 with Kelly Marie's disco anthem "Feels Like I'm in Love" written by Ray Dorset from Mungo Jerry for Elvis Presley. The following year they had another major hit with the holiday disco knees-up "The Birdie Song," which you should *only* do in the privacy of your own bedroom now! The label was losing a lot of its credibility, and they signed up a lot of dubious dance artists, as well as reissued their past artists' albums and compilations in budget packages, most notably in the "Spotlight On" series. They approached RCA for distribution that fell through, and then sold the company to Australian businessman Robert Holmes's A Court's Bell Group, as did ATV, which was renamed ACC. However, Bell defrauded its shareholders, which left the label virtually redundant, and now supported itself as an independent distributor, only to have labels like Jive, Numa, Carrere, Big Wave, and Supreme slip through its fingers after a couple of hits. Finally in 1988 PRT delivered its swan song, a remix of Petula Clark's "Downtown," which made the Top 10 and number one on the dance and indie charts, and by 1989 the company officially folded up, a pale shadow of its former self.

In 1990 PRT's valuable back catalog was sold to Castle Communications, who re-released Pye's past artists on CD, which was now becoming the music medium for the masses, and some also on the Knight Record's subsidiary. Others have also been released on other specialty indie labels, but hardly an improvement, either in quality or value. There have been a few dedications to Pye's artists, but nothing to do with the label itself, although there is a great compilation of its novelty records called "A Pye in the Face" with rib-tickling efforts from the likes of Arthur Mullard and

Hylda Baker, Dick Emery's "You Are Awful!," and Benny Hill's "Harvest of Love." If the jokes don't make you laugh now, then at least you'll have a giggle over the cover graphics.

Pye's electrical division was taken over by Philips in 1976, initially to launch CB radios, but unlike Philips, Sony, and Panasonic, it did little to advance itself in the world of technology, due to average product range and its inability to pioneer new inventions. In the mid-1990s, Philips finally decided to discontinue Pye's manufacturing line with the result that the company now lies dormant.

DARIO WESTERN

Q

Q CHANNEL

An inaudible subcode channel on a compact disc that carries information on tracks, index numbers, product codes, and the like.

QRS CO.

A Chicago firm established ca. 1903 to make piano rolls; it was still producing them on a limited scale in the early 21st century. QRS was a subsidiary or sister company of the Melville Clark Piano Co., maker of player pianos. Ernest G. Clark, brother of Melville Clark, was the first president, and Edwin F. Clark was secretary. In 1904 C.O. Baughman became secretary. Later the owners of the firm were Max Korlander and J. Lawrence Cook. In November 1926 the firm was at its peak of success, having acquired the U.S. Music Roll Co. The two manufacturers had a combined output of 8,700,000 rolls per year. Talking machines were produced for the first time in summer 1928. In April 1929 QRS merged with the DeVry Corp., an audio-visual equipment manufacturer.

QRS also marketed disc records for a time in 1923, using Gennett matrices. And a few years later they again entered the disc market, using Gennett-made records intended wholly for QRS use. A third series of discs, recorded and manufactured by the Cova Recording Corp. of New York, appeared around 1929 and was issued for about a year. Some were released on the Goodson label in U.K.

The most renowned artist on the QRS rolls was Fats Waller; he made 22 of them between 1923 and 1927, beginning with "Got to Cool My Doggies Now." In a biography of Waller by his son (1977), a solution is offered to the puzzle of what the letters QRS stand for: "Quality Reigns Supreme." Other speculations on the letters may be entertained, since "the factory has no notion today" of the original meaning [Ord-Hume] and the company archives contain no clues. In radio code QRS means "Shall I transmit more slowly?" or "Please transmit more slowly"; and the firm did make radio tubes. "Quality Real Special" has also been suggested, inelegant as it might be.

Label issued by the famed piano roll company briefly during the '20s. Courtesy Kurt Nauck/Nauck's Vintage Records

As of the early 21st century, the company was involved in manufacturing MIDI controllers and other computerized devices for self-playing pianos, continuing in new technologies its earlier involvement with player pianos. [Goslin 1983; Ord-Hume 1984; Rust 1978; Rust 1980; website: http://www.qrsmusic.com/.]

QUAD

SEE QUADRAPHONIC RECORDING

QUAD ELECTROACOUSTICAL LTD.

A British audio firm, established in the mid-1930s as Acoustical Manufacturing Co., Ltd. It pioneered in the production of electrostatic loudspeakers.

QUAD LOUDSPEAKER CO.

Founded in 1936 by Peter Walker, as the Quad Loudspeaker and Electronics Co. One of the oldest audio-product enterprises still in operation, Quad was founded by Peter Walker in 1936, under the name Acoustical Manufacturing Co. Although it originally specialized in producing public address systems and amplifiers, Walker was also interested in loudspeaker design and in 1949 he introduced the Corner Ribbon Loudspeaker, a system that was notable for its ability to reproduce very clean high frequencies. In the same year, the company name was changed to QUAD, which cryptically stood for "Quality Unit Amplified Domestic."

During this same period, Walker and Gilbert Briggs, founder of Warfedale, arranged a series of audio-system demonstrations at Royal Festival Hall in London and Carnegie Hall in New York. Briggs was trying to prove that recorded music could compete with live music. At one session, a capacity audience of 3,000 at Royal Festival Hall heard a demonstration of the clarity and quality of a well-designed hi-fi system. This technique presaged the live versus recorded demonstrations done by Acoustic Research in the 1960s.

In the late 1950s, Walker and David Williamson developed the world's first full-range electrostatic loudspeaker, which later came to be called the Quad ESL-57. (The technology was based in part on designs pioneered decades earlier by E.W. Kellog and Hans Vogt.) The ESL-57, for all of its maximum-output and low-bass limitations, was admired by a whole generation of direct-field listening audio enthusiasts, due to its very clean midrange performance.

In the early 1980s, Quad introduced the ESL-63, a more advanced electrostatic design that was unique, in that it used a concentric ring of sound-radiating electrodes fed through a calibrated delay line. The bulls-eye-styled radiating surface worked to create a simulated point source, even though the system was still at its best when precisely aimed at the listener. The ESL-63 was an immense success in high-end circles, with an entire year's production selling out within two months. Later iterations of this system, the ESL-88 and larger ESL-89, offered even more advanced performance. The current company produces both electrostatic and dynamic loudspeakers, in addition to electronic components.

See also **Loudspeaker**

QUADRAPHONIC RECORDING

Also known as Quadraphonic, Quadrasonic, or Quad. A four-channel sound reproduction system, promoted heavily in the 1970s, that was intended to reproduce or simulate concert hall, nightclub, studio, etc. ambiance. Four microphones were used in recording, and four loudspeakers — one in each corner — had to be set up in the listening room. Acoustic Research, Inc. made a number of experimental quad recordings in the late 1960s, but they never resulted in marketable products. Outfits like Sound Concepts, Advent, and Audio Pulse also made some ambiance simulators that delivered a quadraphonic effect.

There were marketing difficulties almost from the beginning. The cost of a four-channel amplifier and two additional speakers was sufficient to keep many audiophiles at bay, as was the problem of loudspeaker placement (even with small, bookshelf systems) in many home-listening environments. Then there was the nuisance of incompatible rival systems being offered by major firms. For example, EMI used the CBS matrix system, while Pye and others took the Sansui QS system, and RCA used still another. Record companies waited to see which system would prevail before investing in large-scale record production, although small quantities were produced in the various formats to test the market. The public also waited, and meanwhile sales were too small to form the basis for commercial viability. However, the biggest drawback was that the analog technology of the era simply could not deliver four discrete channels with any genuine fidelity, at least at a reasonable cost.

Nevertheless, the concept was at least educational. Experimentation on a practical level proved that a pair of speakers mounted up front cannot simulate the three-dimensional effect of a genuine performance environment in a typically small home-playback room. However, four-channel sound, at least if reasonably well executed, can be impressively realistic. In the late 1980s there was a rebirth of interest in quad, but with the addition of a center channel, as found in surround sound.

See also **Dolby Digital; Dolby Surround Sound; DTS (Digital Theater Systems); DVD-A (DVD-Audio); SACD (Super Audio Compact Disc); Surround Sound**

REV. HOWARD FERSTLER

QUALITON

In business since 1964, and based in New York City, Qualiton is the oldest independent distributor of imported classical recordings in the U.S. Begun by Hungarian refugee Otto Quittner, a prominent attorney in Budapest before the 1956 uprising, the company initially imported Hungarian LP recordings. Gradually, the distribution base expanded to include a large number of labels from other European nations. The company's distribution has expanded from classical titles to include world music, jazz, blues, nostalgia, rock-pop, country, films and shows, and new age. When the compact disc first appeared, Qualiton was one of the first suppliers (even before the major record labels) to make compact discs available to its accounts in sufficient quantities to satisfy the growing demand for that new format. The company eventually acquired distribution rights for a number of significant American labels, both classical and nonclassical, and in recent years, the company has added labels that originate from Asia Quadrasonic. [website: www.qualiton.com.]

See also **Quadraphonic Recording**

HOWARD FERSTLER

QUARTER TRACK

SEE TAPE

QUINN, DAN W. (CA. 1859–7 NOV 1938)

U.S. tenor and comedian, born in San Francisco. He sang in New York, and made his first records there in 1892, for the New York Phonograph Co.; he was among the earliest singers on record, and one of the three most prolific recording artists of the 1890s (with George Gaskin and Len Spencer). He did show tunes, coon songs, Irish songs, war songs, and standard popular numbers — about 2,500 titles in all. On record he was often accompanied by Frank Banta, Sr. Quinn appeared in the New Jersey Phonograph Co. catalog of 1893, and Columbia catalogs of 1895–1899, with hundreds of two-minute cylinders. He made about 250 items for Edison from before 1899 to December 1902, beginning with "All Coons Look Alike to Me" (#1001). Quinn was among the first artists on the Victor label, making the number nine matrix on 29 June 1900, "Strike Up the Band" and 11 other sides on that day and the following one. His final Victor was made in 1916, his last record (for Gennett) in 1918. Quinn's popularity faded after 1910; only one of his records remained in the 1917 Victor catalog: "At the Fountain of Youth"/"Hello Boys! I'm Back Again" (#17935). [Brooks 1979; Walsh 1945/3–5.]

QUINTET OF THE HOT CLUB OF FRANCE

A jazz ensemble formed in 1934 in Paris, the principal non-American group of its kind. Stéphane Grappelli, violinist, and Django Reinhardt, guitarist, were the star performers. The other members were Roger Chaput and Joseph Reinhardt, guitarists, and Louis Vola, bass. Various personnel changes took place later. The quintet made fine recordings for Ultraphon, HMV, Decca, and the Swing label. Its first issue, "Dinah" (Ultraphon #1422; 1934) and the second, "Tiger Rag" (Ultraphon #1423; 1934) were immediate sensations. Among the outstanding later discs were "Limehouse Blues" (HMV #K-7706; 1936), "Appel Direct" (Decca #F-6875; 1938), and "Billet doux" (Decca #F-7568; 1938). After Grappelli left the group in 1940, he was replaced by clarinetist Hubert Rostaing, and the quintet continued performing into the 1940s. There have been numerous reissues of the classic Quintet recordings on CD, notably a five-CD boxed set from JSP that includes the complete pre–World War II recordings.

QWEST RECORDS

SEE JONES, QUINCY DELIGHT JR.

R

R&B

SEE RHYTHM AND BLUES (R&B) RECORDINGS

RABBITT, EDDIE
(27 NOV 1944–7 MAY 1998)

Born in Brooklyn, New York, Rabbitt was raised in East Orange, New Jersey. As a teenager, he began working in local clubs in the New York City–New Jersey area. In the late 1960s, Rabbitt relocated to Nashville in search of a career as a performer. He initially found success as a songwriter, notably with "Kentucky Rain," which was covered by Elvis, earning Presley his 50th gold record (RCA #47-9791; 1970; #16 pop). In 1974, Eddie got his own recording contract with Elektra records.

Eddie had a couple of hits in the mid-1970s, mostly written or cowritten by him, and mostly in a neo–honky-tonk vein. In 1979, he was asked to perform the title song for Clint Eastwood's comic western, *Every Which Way But Loose*. This led to another movie job, singing the title song for *Roadie* in 1980, called "Driving My Life Away"; this was Rabbitt's first Top 10 crossover hit (Elektra #46656; #5 pop, #1 country). In the early 1980s, Rabbitt was rarely off the pop and country charts. He had a series of hits with the pop-rock songs "I Love a Rainy Night" (Elektra #47066; 1980; #1 pop, country, and adult contemporary), "Step by Step" (Elektra #47174; 1981; #5 pop, #1 country), and "Someone Could Lose a Heart Tonight" (Elektra #47239; 1981; #15 pop, #1 country). His last Top 10 country hit was a duet with Crystal Gayle on "You and I" (Elektra #69936; 1982, #7 pop,

#1 country). From the mid-1980s, Rabbitt's pop career faded, although he continued to tour and perform for his loyal country fans. His life was cut short by cancer.

CARL BENSON

RACE RECORDS

The term given by American record companies to recordings by Black performers intended for the Black market, in use from about 1921 until the early 1940s. Generally, these records were placed into a separate, numbered series, just as recordings aimed at various ethnic markets (Jewish, Italian, Irish, etc.) and other specialized markets (such as country music and jazz). Okeh was the first label to use the term in advertising: "All the greatest Race phonograph stars can be heard on Okeh records. ... Ask your neighborhood dealer for a complete list of Okeh race records" (*Chicago Defender*, January 1922). By the end of 1922 Okeh had issued 40 records in the 8000 series, featuring "The World's Greatest Race Artists on the World's Greatest Race Records." The material included blues songs, jazz instrumentals, and male quartet pieces. At first Black Swan and Arto were the only serious competitors to Okeh in the race area. Arto closed down in 1923. Then Paramount initiated a special series in 1923 for its Black talent, the 12000 series. Okeh described its 8000s as "The original race record" while Paramount called its 12000s "the popular race record." Columbia entered the field and had a hit with Bessie Smith's first recording, "Down Hearted Blues" (#A3844; 1923), but the company was in financial trouble and had difficulty sustaining its new 14000 race series.

Vocalion "Race" record sleeve and label. Courtesy BenCar Archives

In 1924 Paramount acquired Black Swan, a label that had intended to record Black artists exclusively, and was able to produce about one race disc a week in that year. Okeh was flourishing also, with around 100 new race records a year in the mid-1920s. Victor (19000 series, and — from 1929 — the V-38500 series) and Edison joined the race labels in 1923. Gennett (the only firm to print the words "race record" on the disc labels), Ajax (of Compo in Canada), and Vocalion introduced race series. Vocalion had the greatest success (1000 series), guided by Jack Kapp, head of the Race Division from March 1926. Ethel Waters sang for Vocalion; Blind Lemon Jefferson for Paramount; the Birmingham Jubilee Singers were a major boost for Columbia in 1926, which also scored with sermons by Rev. J.M. Gates (who then went on to Victor). The Black Patti label was active for a short time in 1927. Pathé's Perfect label had a race series that included Rev. Gates and Rosa Henderson. QRS had a race series in 1928–1929. In 1927 there were about 500 race records issued annually by all the labels.

During the 1930s, a disastrous period for the record industry, the flow of race records nearly stopped at the major labels. Paramount concluded its long-running 12000 race series, and the Gennett label was discontinued. Okeh went on, under its new owner, Grigsby-Grunow, but with only a record a month. Race records made up about 1 percent of industry sales in 1931, a drop from 5 percent in the mid-1920s. In this gloomy period, the American Record Corp. began to release race discs on several of the labels it had acquired: Oriole, Perfect,

Romeo, and Banner. With Big Bill Broonzy and the Famous Garland Jubilee Singers signed on, the ARC kept active and promised the only real competition to Vocalion; this competition became muted when Vocalion's parent firm, Brunswick, and ARC were both taken over by Consolidated Film Industries in 1930.

Bluebird entered the race field in 1933. At the end of 1934 there were just a few other companies still active in the race market: ARC/Vocalion, Columbia, and Victor. The new American firm, Decca, hired Jack Kapp (who had headed the Vocalion race series) and Mayo Williams, a prominent talent scout for race artists. Decca's 7000 series was soon established as a major force. All promoted the urban blues style, which had been replacing the traditional blues. Joe Pullum (Victor-Bluebird) and Leroy Carr (Vocalion) were stars of the mid-1930s. In 1937 there were revival signs in the industry, and race records began to emerge again in quantity: urban blues, gospel quartet music, and sermons. Washboard Sam (Robert Brown) enlivened the Bluebird list in the late 1930s.

World War II brought relief from the Depression, but also restrictions on the use of shellac — resulting in cutbacks of special severity in the race series. And the American Federation of Musicians recording ban of 1942 hurt the genre badly. Victor's December 1941 catalog had about 350 race items, a number that diminished to 75 in May 1943. Decca had no race category in its 1944 catalog, and by 1945 Victor had dropped the race section from its catalog. The term "race record" was generally abandoned, replaced to some extent by rhythm and blues; and the making of discs aimed at the Black buyer began to pass from the major companies to new independent labels like Chess.

Dixon and Godrich [1970] estimate that "between 1920 and 1942 about 5,500 blues and 1,250 gospel records had been issued, involving all told about 1,200 artists."

See also **Blues Recordings**

RACHMANINOFF, SERGEI VASILYEVICH (1 APR 1873–28 MAR 1943)

Russian pianist, conductor, and composer, born in Semyonovo, Russia. He studied at the St. Petersburg and Moscow conservatories, winning the composition prize for his opera *Aleko* (1892). At that time he also wrote his most famous work, the "Prelude in C-Sharp Minor" for piano. In 1891 he performed his second piano concerto.

From 1904 to 1906 he conducted the Bolshoi Opera; in 1909 he toured the U.S. During the Russian Revolution he lived in Sweden, then Denmark, and finally New York. Throughout the 1930s he toured widely, living most of the time in New York, and continuing to compose. In 1942 he retired to Beverly Hills, California, where he died.

Rachmaninoff's first recordings were 10 sides for Edison Diamond Discs in 1919–1920. Franz Liszt's three Hungarian Rhapsodies (opus 2) were the initial efforts, on discs #82169 and #82170. The artist had to use an upright piano in the studio, and the whole outcome was weak. Another of the Diamond Discs was the "Prelude in C-Sharp Minor" (#82202; 1920). He recorded for Ampico piano rolls in the same year, and worked with them intermittently for 10 years. In 1920 Rachmaninoff became a Victor artist, and stayed with the label until his death.

Among the principal Rachmaninoff recordings are those he made with the Philadelphia Orchestra, under Eugene Ormandy, of his own compositions. The Piano Concerto No. 2 was inscribed in April 1929 (Victor #8148-52, LP M-58), and the *Rhapsody on a Theme of Paganini* was done in December 1934 (Victor #8553-55, M-250). Several years later he recorded Concerto No. 1 (Victor #18374-76, LP M-865; 1939), and Concerto No. 4 (Victor #11-8611-14, LP M-972; 1941). In 1973 Victor issued *The Complete Rachmaninoff* in five albums holding 15 LPs. Melodiya produced an eight-record set, *The Art of Sergei Vasilevich Rachmaninov*, encompassing all the solo works. A CD of nearly all the solo electrical recordings that the composer made of his own music, plus works of seven other composers, appeared on RCA (GD #87766) in 1990. [Palmieri 1989 has a detailed discography.]

RACK JOBBER

In the American popular record industry, the person who provides a stock of current recordings to a discount store, drug store, supermarket, etc. Elliot Wexler of Philadelphia is believed to have been the first rack jobber, followed by David Handleman in Detroit. Although cutouts are basic to the inventory, the rack jobber will also acquire items on the charts — enjoying preferential terms from the major companies. Majors have also produced low-cost albums intended for the racks. In the early 1970s about 80 percent of all record sales were by these jobbers, who had moved into the department stores as well as smaller outlets, and who were in fact dominating pop/rock record distribution. [Denisoff 1986.]

See also **Dumping**

RADIEX (LABEL)

An American record of the 1920s, a subsidiary of Grey Gull. A *TMW* ad of 1924 gave the firm's location as Boston. The disc price was $0.25. Material was

popular vocals and dance music; matrices were from Emerson, Paramount, and Plaza. The final issues were in 1930. [Rust 1978.]

FRANK ANDREWS

RADIO FRANKS

A trio made up of Frank Wright, Frank Bessinger, and Frank White, who sang on the radio and recorded for Brunswick and other labels in the mid-1920s.

RADIO PHONOGRAPHS

The rise of radio in America from 1921 severely damaged the phonograph industry. The idea of combining the competing formats into one cabinet, a radio phonograph, was articulated first in advertising of August 1922, by Jewett Radio and Phonograph Co. of Detroit. The only other firm to advertise a combination in 1922 was George A. Long Cabinet Co., Hanover,

Advertisement for the Victor Radio with "Electrola," a combination radio-phonograph. Courtesy Jerald Kalstein

Pennsylvania. Emerson announced its new Phono Radio in January 1924. In all these early combinations it was necessary to remove the phonograph reproducer and attach a radio receiver in order to hear radio stations through the phonograph horn. But a *TMW* advertisement of February 1924 offered a model with a switch, by the Oro-Tone Co., of Chicago. Sonora then marketed its Sonoradio, also with a switch controlling the two functions.

It was the RCA 1924 product, Radiola, that dominated the combination market in the 1920s, and the model name became a convenient generic term for all radio phonographs. Brunswick announced a similar machine in July 1924. The Gramophone Co. marketed its table model Lumiere around that time, containing a crystal radio set and a folding external horn. Phonograph attachments for radio sets were a later approach; these were called Radiograms, a name also given to radio phonograph combinations.

See also **Disc**

RADIO PROGRAM RECORDINGS

This article has 12 parts spanning the medium's so-called "classic era.": 1. Overview; 2. Comedies; 3. Adventures and mysteries; 4. Detective stories; 5. Dramas; 6. Soap operas; 7. Music and variety shows; 8. Science fiction; 9. Children's programs; 10. Quiz shows; 11. Westerns; 12. Collectors and collections.

1. *Overview.* By the late 1930s almost all urban homes (and the majority of rural homes) in the U.S. had radio sets and played them an average of five or more hours a day. Yet radio's reign as the popular culture center of America was very brief. The "golden age of radio" lasted only about 20 years — from the emergence of Eddie Cantor as the first national radio figure in the fall of 1931, to Milton Berle as the first national television figure in the early 1950s.

The Bing Crosby Show was the first radio program broadcast from transcription discs, from fall 1946. Crosby refused to do a live show each week, and as a result almost all of his programs are available on tape today, along with more than 50,000 other shows from over 2,200 different series. Recordings range from a single 15-minute episode of *The Black Hood*, a program about a comic book super-hero whose adventures were broadcast over the Mutual Network in 1943–1945, to over 800 episodes — out of 7,000 broadcasts — of the comedy show *Fibber McGee & Molly* (NBC, 1935–1959).

Although thousands of radio shows have been lost, thousands of others are available — on reel-to-reel or cassette tape recordings, on long-playing records, or on CDs. In addition, compilation albums are for sale from several small firms that have been licensed by copyright owners. For example, *Radio Cliff Hangers*, offering episodes of Flash Gordon, Little Orphan Annie, Charlie Chan, etc., is offered by Radiola in a two-record set. About a dozen LPs each have been produced of radio performances of Bing Crosby, Judy Garland, and Al Jolson.

The most important radio programs for which recordings are available are mentioned below, by type of program. All shows were 30 minutes long, unless otherwise noted.

2. *Comedies.* The most consistently popular type of programming in radio was comedy. Many episodes from the following shows are available on records: *The Abbott and Costello Program* (NBC, 1942–1949), *The Adventures of Ozzie and Harriett* (CBS, 1944–1954), *The Alan Young Show* (ABC, 1944–1949), *The Aldrich Family* (NBC, 1939–1951), *Amos 'n' Andy* (NBC/CBS, 1928–1960), *The Baby Snooks Show* (CBS, 1937–1951), *Beulah* (CBS/ABC, 1945–1954), *Blondie* (CBS, 1939–1950), *The Bob Hope Show* (NBC, 1934–1953), *The Bob & Ray Show* (NBC/CBS, 1948–1960, 15 min.), *The Burns and Allen Show* (CBS, 1932–1958), *The Charlie McCarthy Show* (NBC, 1937–1956), *A Date with Judy* (NBC, 1943–1949), *Duffy's Tavern* (NBC/ABC, 1940–1951), *Easy Aces* (NBC/CBS, 1931–1945, 15 min.), *The Eddie Cantor Show*, (NBC, 1931–1954), *The Fred Allen Show* (CBS, 1932–1949), *The Great Gildersleeve* (NBC, 1941–1958), *The Halls of Ivy*, 1949–1952), *The Jack Benny Program* (CBS/NBC/CBS, 1932– 1955), *The Jack Carson Show* (CBS, 1943–1956), *The Judy Canova Show* (CBS/NBC, 1943–1953), *The Life of Riley* (NBC, 1944–1951), *Life with Luigi* (CBS, 1948–1952), *Lum and Abner* (NBC/CBS/ABC/Mutual, 1931–1953), *Meet Corliss Archer* (CBS/ABC, 1943–1955), *My Friend Irma* (CBS, 1947–1954), *Our Miss Brooks* (CBS, 1948–1957), *The Phil Harris–Alice Faye Show* (NBC, 1948–1954), and *The Red Skelton Show* (NBC, 1941–1953).

3. *Adventures and Mysteries.* Beginning with *Empire Builder* in 1928–1929, sponsored by the Great Northern Railroad, old-time radio abounded with thriller drama, and many people today remember radio most vividly for its many adventure and mystery series. Golden age radio was the era of the adventurer, the spy, and tales of crime, horror, and suspense. The best — and some of the most artistic — are available on tape: *The Big Story* (NBC, 1947–1955), *Big Town* (CBS/NBC, 1937–1954), *The Black Castle* (Mutual, 1943–1944, 15 min.), *The Black Museum* (Mutual, 1951–1952), *Bold Venture* (Syndicated, 1951–1952), *Box 13* (Syndicated, 1948–1949), *Casey, Crime Photographer* (CBS, 1946–1955), *The Clock* (ABC, 1946–1948), *Crime Club* (Mutual, 1935–1947),

Dangerous Assignment (NBC, 1950–1954), *David Harding, Counterspy* (ABC, 1942–1957), *Escape* (CBS, 1947–1954), *The Hermit's Cave* (Syndicated, 1940–1943), *I Love a Mystery* (NBC Red/Mutual/CBS, 1939–1952, 15–30 min.), *Inner Sanctum* (NBC Blue, 1941–1952), *Jason and the Golden Fleece* (NBC, 1952–1953), *Lights Out* (NBC, 1938–1946), *The Lone Wolf* (Mutual, 1948–1949), *The Man Called X* (ABC, 1944–1948), *Mr. District Attorney* (NBC, 1939–1954), *Mollé Mystery Theatre* (NBC, 1943–1948), *The Mysterious Traveler* (Mutual, 1943–1952), *Mystery in the Air* (NBC, 1945–1947), *Night Beat* (ABC, 1950–1952), *Quiet, Please* (Mutual/ABC, 1947–1949), *The Scarlet Pimpernel* (NBC, 1952–1953), *The Shadow* (CBS/NBC/Mutual, 1930–1954), *Suspense* (CBS, 1942–1962), *The Whistler* (CBS, 1942–1955), and *The Witch's Tale* (Mutual, 1931–1938).

4. *Detective Stories.* Inexpensive to produce and attractive to listeners, the radio detective story as a separate genre emerged around 1930 (*True Detective Mysteries* was broadcast during the 1929–1930 season). The detective program quickly became one of the most common types of evening radio broadcasting. Many episodes of the following programs are available: *The Adventures of Nero Wolfe* (ABC, 1943–1951), *Boston Blackie* (NBC, 1944–1948), *Broadway Is My Beat* (CBS, 1949–1954), *Candy Matson, Yukon 28209* (NBC, 1949–1951), *Dick Tracy* (ABC, 1943–1948, 15 min.), *Dragnet* (NBC, 1949–1956), *Ellery Queen* (CBS/NBC/ABC, 1939–1948), *The Falcon* (Mutual/NBC/Mutual, 1945–1954), *The Fat Man* (ABC, 1946–1951), *Hercule Poirot* (Mutual, 1945–1947), *Let George Do It* (CBS, 1946–1954), *The Green Hornet* (Mutual/ABC, 1936–1952), *The Line-Up* (CBS, 1950–1953), *Mr. and Mrs. North* (NBC/CBS, 1942–1955), *Mr. Chameleon* (CBS, 1948–1952), *Mr. Keen, Tracer of Lost Persons* (NBC, 1937–1954), *Nick Carter, Master Detective* (Mutual, 1943–1955), *Pat Novak for Hire* (ABC, 1946–1949), *Perry Mason* (CBS, 1943–1955, 15 min.), *Philip Marlowe* (NBC/CBS, 1947–1951), *Philo Vance* (NBC, 1945, 1948–1950), *Richard Diamond, Private Detective* (NBC, 1949–1953), *Rogue's Gallery* (ABC, 1945–1952), *The Saint* (NBC, 1945–1951), *Sam Spade* (ABC/CBS/NBC, 1946–1951), *The Thin Man* (NBC, 1941–1950), and *Yours Truly, Johnny Dollar* (CBS, 1949–1962).

5. *Dramas.* Of the various program types drama had the slowest start, but it came to embody the most artistic achievements of radio. Although the quality was uneven, there were prestige offerings each season. For example, in prime time each week *Cavalcade of America* (CBS/NBC, 1935–1953), entertained and educated listeners for 18 seasons (781 programs). With star performers and original scripts written by authors such as Maxwell Anderson, Stephen Vincent Benét, and Robert Sherwood, *Cavalcade of America* was radio at its finest. Of the 781 programs broadcast, more than 400 are available on cassettes. Other available dramatic programs include: *Academy Award Theatre* (CBS, 1946), *Brownstone Theatre* (Mutual, 1945–1946), *CBS Radio Workshop* (CBS, 1956–1957), *Campbell Playhouse* (CBS, 1938–1940), *Curtain Time* (Mutual/ABC/NBC, 1938–1950), *Damon Runyon Theater* (Syndicated, 1949–1950), *Family Theatre* (Mutual, 1947–1957), *Favorite Story* (Syndicated, 1946–1949), *The First Nighter* (NBC/CBS/Mutual/CBS, 1930–1949), *Ford Theatre* (NBC/CBS, 1947–1949, 60 min.), *Hallmark Playhouse* (CBS, 1948–1953), *Hollywood Theater of Stars* (NBC, 1946–1948), *Lux Radio Theater of the Air* (CBS/NBC, 1936–1955, 60 min.), *The Mercury Theatre of the Air* (CBS, 1938, 60 min.), *Screen Director's Playhouse* (NBC, 1949–1951), *Screen Guild Theater* (CBS/NBC/ABC, 1939–1951), *Studio One* (CBS, 1947–1948, 60 min.), *Theatre Guild of the Air/The U.S. Steel Hour* (ABC, 1945–1954, 60 min.), and *Whispering Streets* (ABC/CBS, 1952–1960).

6. *Soap Operas.* Often the object of contempt, daytime serial dramas were significant sources of revenue for the networks. Inexpensive to produce, they also allotted a greater percentage of time for advertising than the average comedy or drama program. Long runs of these programs are widely available, e.g., more than 350 episodes of *One Man's Family* (NBC, 1932–1959, 15 minutes), the popular and long-running serial, have been preserved. Other soap operas on record are: *Backstage Wife* (Mutual/NBC, 1935–1959, 15 min.), *Big Sister* (CBS, 1936–1952, 15 min.), *The Brighter Day* (NBC/CBS, 1948–1956, 15 min.), *David Harum* (NBC/CBS, 1936–1950, 15 min.), *Front Page Farrell* (Mutual/NBC, 1941–1954, 15 min.), *The Goldbergs* (NBC/Mutual/CBS, 1929–1950, 15–30 min.), *Guiding Light* (NBC/CBS, 1937–1956, 15 min.), *Just Plain Bill* (NBC/CBS, 1936–1955, 15 min.), *Life Can Be Beautiful* (CBS/NBC, 1938–1954, 15 min.), *Lorenzo Jones* (NBC, 1937–1955 15 min.), *Ma Perkins* (NBC/CBS, 1933–1960, 15 min.), *Our Gal Sunday* (CBS, 1937–1959, 15 min.), *Pepper Young's Family* (NBC, 1936–1959, 15 min.), *Portia Faces Life* (CBS/NBC, 1940–1951, 15 min.), *Right to Happiness* (NBC Blue/CBS, 1939–1960, 15 min.), *Road of Life* (CBS/NBC, 1937–1959, 15 min.), *The Romance of Helen Trent* (CBS, 1933–1960, 15 min.), *Scattergood Baines* (CBS/Mutual, 1937–1950, 15–30 min.), *Stella Dallas* (NBC, 1937–1955, 15 min.), *Vic and Sade* (NBC Blue/Mutual, 1932–1944, 15 min.), *When a Girl Marries* (CBS/NBC/ABC, 1939–1958, 15 min.), and *Young Widder Brown* (NBC, 1938–1956, 15 min.).

7. *Music and Variety Shows.* The bulk of broadcasting time was filled with music and variety offerings.

From the early 1920s music programs were the mainstay (with regard to hours aired per week) of both networks and independent stations, and variety shows grew in number during the late 1920s and early 1930s. Some of the most popular ones still available are: *Arthur Godfrey Talent Scouts* (CBS, 1946–1958), *The Bing Crosby Show* (ABC/CBS, 1946–1956), *Carnation Contented Hour* (NBC, 1932–1951), *The Fitch Bandwagon* (NBC, 1937–1948), *The Fleischmann's Hour* (NBC, 1929–1936, 60 min.), *The Frank Sinatra Old Gold Show* (CBS, 1945–1947), *The Fred Waring Show* (NBC/ CBS/NBC/ABC, 1931–1957, various formats), *Grand Ole Opry* (NBC, 1925–present, 30–60 min. segments), *House Party* (CBS, 1944– 1967), *The Kate Smith Show* (CBS, 1936– 1958), *Kraft Music Hall* (NBC, 1936–1948), *Manhattan Merry-Go-Round* (NBC, 1933– 1949), *NBC Bandstand* (NBC, 1956–1957, 60 min.), *The National Barn Dance* (NBC, 1933– 1950), *Philco Radio Time* (ABC, 1946–1949), *The Railroad Hour* (ABC/NBC, 1948–1954, various formats), *The Rudy Vallee Show* (NBC, 1944–1947), *Shell Chateau* (CBS, 1935–1937, 60 min.), and *Your Hit Parade* (NBC/CBS/NBC, 1935–1959, various formats).

8. *Science Fiction.* Originally a children's genre in the 1930s (Flash Gordon and Buck Rogers), science fiction shows for an adult audience did not appear until the early 1950s. On 8 Apr 1950 "The Outer Limit," by Graham Dorr, was presented on *Dimension X*, ushering in a new era in science fiction programming. With the presentation of stories by authors such as Isaac Asimov, Ray Bradbury, and Robert Heinlein, adult science fiction stories were introduced to the listening public. Episodes available today are from the following programs: *Beyond Tomorrow* (CBS, 1950), *Buck Rogers in the 25th Century* (Mutual, 1931–1947, 15 min.), *Destination Space* (NBC, 1947–1949), *Dimension X* (NBC, 1950–1951), *Exploring Tomorrow* (Mutual, 1957–1958), *Flash Gordon* (Mutual, 1935–1936, 15 min.), *Space Patrol* (ABC, 1950–1955), *Starr of Space* (ABC, 1953–1954), *Tales of Tomorrow* (ABC/ CBS, 1953), *Tom Corbett — Space Cadet* (NBC, 1952), *2000 Plus* (Mutual, 1950), and *X Minus One* (NBC, 1955–1958).

9. *Children's Programs.* Children's programs typically were aired in the afternoon hours after school, on Saturday mornings, and during the week in the early evening. *Little Orphan Annie*, based on the popular comic strip, began in 1931, the first of the adventure serial dramas for children. Others quickly followed. These programs were regular radio fare in the 1930s and 1940s. Some of the more popular ones available today include: *Abbott and Costello Children's Show* (ABC, 1947–1949), *Archie Andrews* (Mutual, 1943–1953), *Big Jon and Sparky/No School Today* (ABC, 1950–1958, 60 min.), *Captain Midnight* (Mutual, 1939–1949, 15 min.), *The Challenge of the Yukon/Sergeant Preston* (ABC/Mutual, 1947–1955; an earlier 15-minute version, 1938–1947, had been broadcast from WXYZ in Detroit), *Chick Carter, Boy Detective* (Mutual, 1943–1944, 15 min.), *Don Winslow of the Navy* (NBC Blue, 1942–1943), *Hop Harrigan* (ABC/Mutual, 1942–1948, 15 min.), *Jack Armstrong, the All-American Boy* (CBS, 1933–1950, 15 min.), *Jungle Jim* (Syndicated, 1935–1952), *Land of the Lost* (Mutual, 1943– 1948), *Lassie* (ABC, 1947– 1950, 15 min.), *Let's Pretend* (CBS, 1931– 1954), *Little Orphan Annie* (NBC Blue/Mutual, 1931–1943, 15 min.), *Mandrake the Magician* (Mutual, 1940–1942, 15 min.), *Mark Trail* (Mutual, 1950–1953), *The Sea Hound* (ABC, 1942–1948), *Sky King* (ABC/Mutual, 1946– 1954, 15–30 min.), *Smilin' Ed's Buster Brown Gang* (NBC, 1944–1952), *Superman* (Syndicated/ Mutual/ ABC, 1938– 1951, 15 min.), *Terry and the Pirates* (NBC/ ABC, 1937–1948, 15 min.), *Tom Mix* (NBC/ Mutual, 1933–1950, 15 min.), and *The Voyage of the Scarlet Queen* (Mutual, 1947–1948).

10. *Quiz Shows.* By 1938 network radio was filled with quiz shows adapted to every type of program: sports, news, mystery, and even parodies of quiz shows (e.g., *It Pays to Be Ignorant* (CBS, 1942–1949). Some of the programs were very popular. The success of *Stop the Music!* (ABC/CBS, 1948–1954, 60–75 min.) with a Hooper rating of 20.0 in its first season was a major factor in the demise of Fred Allen's career (Allen's show had a Hooper rating of 11.2 during the 1948–1949 season). Other quiz shows, currently available on cassette tape, are: *Beat the Band* (NBC, 1940– 1944), *Break the Bank* (Mutual/ABC/NBC, 1945–1955, 30 min.), *Can You Top This?* (Mutual/NBC/ABC, 1940–1954), *Dr. I.Q.* (NBC/ABC, 1939–1950), *Earn Your Vacation* (CBS, 1948–1949), *Information, Please!* (NBC/CBS/Mutual, 1938–1948, 60 min.), *Kay Kyser's Kollege of Musical Knowledge* (NBC/ABC, 1938–1949, 60 min.), *You Bet Your Life* (ABC/CBS/NBC, 1947–1959), and *Quiz Kids* (ABC/NBC/CBS, 1940–1953).

11. *Westerns.* The most underdeveloped popular genre in radio was the western. Although *Death Valley Days* began in 1930, until the 1950s only a few westerns were broadcast; and these were designed primarily for children. Some did appeal to adults, and one, *The Lone Ranger*, was instrumental in the formation of the Mutual Broadcasting System in 1934. When *Gunsmoke* and other more realistic radio shows were developed in the early 1950s, radio was already becoming secondary to television as a main entertainment medium. Indeed, competition from television is one of the reasons that westerns and other radio shows were improved so much in the early 1950s. Those available on record are: *The Cisco Kid* (Mutual,

1942–1943), *Fort Laramie* (CBS, 1956; starring Raymond Burr), *Frontier Gentlemen* (CBS, 1958), *Gene Autry's Melody Ranch* (CBS, 1940–1956), *Gunsmoke* (CBS,1952–1961), *Have Gun, Will Travel* (CBS, 1958– 1960), *Hopalong Cassidy* (Syndicated, 1950–1952; starring William Boyd), *The Lone Ranger* (Mutual/ABC, 1933– 1955), *Red Ryder* (Syndicated, 1942–1952), *The Roy Rogers Radio Show* (Mutual, 1944–1955), *The Six Shooter* (NBC, 1953–1954; starring James Stewart), *Straight Arrow* (Mutual, 1948– 1951), *Tales of the Texas Rangers* (NBC, 1950– 1952; starring Joel McCrea), *Tennessee Jed* (ABC, 1945–1947, 15 min.), and *Wild Bill Hickok* (ABC, 1951–1956; starring Guy Madison and Andy Devine).

12. *Collectors and Collections.* It has been estimated that there are about 1,500 serious collectors of old-time radio (OTR) in the U.S. In addition to collecting OTR, many of the serious collectors also compile logs (necessary for identifying the titles and airing dates of specific shows), produce newsletters that inform other collectors about the field, hold conventions, and trade (and sell) programs. One major collector, Jim Harmon, is a producer of radio programs and a writer/dealer in nostalgia and has authored several books, including *The Great Radio Comedians* and *The Great Radio Heroes.*

Other notable collectors include: Jay Hickerson, a musician/entertainer, who has over 8,000 general interest shows in his collection. He has published an OTR newsletter (*Hello Again*) since 1970, and since 1971 has helped run an annual OTR convention near his home. He has published *The Second, Revised Ultimate History of Network Radio Programming and Guide to ALL Circulating Shows* (2001) and other books on early radio. Terry Salomonson has a large general collection and has written logs on radio shows broadcast by WXYZ in Detroit: *The Lone Ranger*, *The Green Hornet*, and *Challenge of the Yukon,* among others. David S. Siegel describes his collection as consisting of over 100,000 shows (over 50,000 hours). By comparison, the Library of Congress has only about 500,000 shows in its collection. Raymond Stanich conducts research on OTR and has authored many logs. He wrote (with Francis M. Nevins, Jr.), *The Sound of Detection: Ellery Queen's Adventures in Radio* (1983).

Select major library collections of vintage radio programs include: Washington State University, with over 900 tape reels of various types of shows, donated by Paul C. Pitzer (http://www.wsulibs.wsu.edu/ MMR/pitzer.htm); the Museum of Television & Radio (www.mtr.org) with branches in Los Angeles and New York; Chicago's Museum of Broadcast Communications (http://www.museum.tv/archives/ index.shtml), with about 4,000 radio programs; the Stanford Archive of Recorded Sound, which among its other holdings houses the Pyror Collection of over 1,000 aluminum disc recordings of radio broadcasts from the mid-1930s through the early 1940s (http://www-sul.stanford.edu/depts/ars/pryor.html); the Rodgers and Hammerstein Archives of Recorded Sound housed at the New York Public Library, including several large radio collections, including WNEW's programming, and two long-running series, *The Bell Telephone Hour* and *Marian McPartland's Piano Jazz*; and the Library of Congress Recorded Sound Reference Center (http://www.loc.gov/rr/record/), which houses several radio archives, including material from NBC, National Public Radio, WOR, Voice of America, and the Armed Forces Radio and Television Services. [MacDonald 1982; Pitts 1986; Slide 1982; Smart 1982; Sterling 1978; Summers 1958.]

JON D. SWARTZ AND ROBERT C. REINEHR

RADIOGRAM/RADIOLA

SEE RADIO PHONOGRAPHS

RAGTIME RECORDINGS

The ragtime style of music was highly popular in the U.S. from the mid-1890s to the early 1920s. It was characterized by syncopated rhythm, and usually marked by improvisation; thus it was easily reshaped into jazz. Although there were ragtime vocals and ragtime instrumental ensembles, the main format for the style was the piano. Performers at the World's Columbian Exposition in Chicago, 1893, brought the style to wide attention, and the ragtime craze swept the country in the next few years.

"All Coons Look Alike to Me," an 1896 song popularized by Dan W. Quinn on Edison cylinder #1001, included a "rag accompaniment," a designation that appeared on other coon songs later. Composer-pianists Tom Turpin and Scott Joplin, based in St. Louis, brought the ragtime style to a height of ingenuity and sophistication. Joplin's "Maple Leaf Rag" was a great success in 1899. Gradually ragtime gave way to jazz, as ragtime pianists like Jelly Roll Morton expanded their stylistic repertoires.

A revival of interest in the early ragtime style began in the 1960s, through the work of Joshua Rifkin and Gunther Schuller, and through the impact of a motion picture that featured Scott Joplin's music, *The Sting* (1974). Modern composers like William Bolcom began to compose in ragtime, merging it with modern idioms.

Performances by the early ragtime piano artists were infrequently recorded. Scott Joplin made piano rolls from 1899–1914, reissued by Riverside on RLP #8815. The earliest disc of piano ragtime is "Creole

Belles" (Victor matrix #A-1079; 1901) played by Christopher H.H. Booth. It was the Columbia recordings of 1912 by Mike Bernard that initiated a more generous output by the record companies: there were about 100 titles under "ragtime" in the Victor 1917 catalog, for example, played by banjo, accordion, and Pryor's Band; sung by Al Jolson, Billy Murray, and the Peerless Quartet. But by then the classic ragtime had nearly run its course, soon to be replaced by so-called novelty rags and by jazz. The 1922 Victor catalog had just 25 ragtime titles, and the 1927 catalog listed none.

Early recordings were made by performers on many instruments: saxophone (Rudy Wiedoeft), accordion (Guido and Pietro Deiro), piccolo (George Schweinfest), flute (Frank Mazziotta), banjo (Vess Ossman, Olly Oakley, Fred Van Eps), and trombone (Arthur Pryor). Ossman is credited with the first ragtime disc record, for Berliner in 1897. Berliner then recorded the United States Marine Band in September 1899 playing "You Got to Play Ragtime" followed by banjoist Richard L. Weaver doing "Ragtime Dance" on 14 Dec 1899. In 1899 Fred Gaisberg recorded a guitar and mandolin performance by the Musical Avolos — a march from *Rice's Ragtime Opera* — which was the first European disc to bear any reference to ragtime. Victor made "Ragtime Skedaddle" by flutist Frank Mazziotta (#4033; 1904). Ossman's Victor record of "St. Louis Tickle" with the Ossman-Dudley Trio (#4624; 1906) was a best seller.

Ragtime was often played by military bands. A Berliner record of 1897 offered ragtime by a studio band, then by the Sousa Band. Arthur Pryor, who led the Sousa Band on records, was also the major composer of ragtime pieces for bands to play.

In the 1940s the piano finally took center stage, with such ragtime artists as Wally Rose and Joe "Fingers" Carr (Lou Busch) bringing about a renewed interest in the form through their recordings. Pee Wee Hunt's 1948 recording of "Twelfth Street Rag" was a great best seller, in the most frequently recorded of all rags. Joshua Rifkin, who endeavors to play the rags as written, offered a splendid album in 1969: *Piano Rags by Scott Joplin* (Nonesuch #H71248). *Pastimes and Piano Rags* was an important album by William Bolcom, including rags by James Scott and Artie Matthews (Nonesuch #H71299; 1973). Dick Hyman recorded all the Joplin rags in a five-disc set (Victor #ARL 5-1106). The soundtrack recording of *The Sting* (MCA #390; 1974) was on the charts for 47 weeks.

Although ragtime did not enjoy such a great level of success in the following decades, fans of the music kept it alive through newsletters and annual conventions. Meanwhile, further early ragtime recordings were reissued on LP (primarily compiled by producer Dave Jasen on the Folkways and Yazoo labels) and then on CD.

Gospel label of the teens and early '20s. Courtesy Kurt Nauck/Nauck's Vintage Records

RAINBOW (LABEL)

An American record devoted to sacred music, issued in the 1920s, by the Rodeheaver Record Co. (named for trombonist and gospel singer Homer Rodeheaver) of Chicago. The Rodeheaver firm was listed in the Chicago directory of 1915, and there was also a branch in Philadelphia. By June 1921, the firm had New York offices. It was reported in October 1921 that C.R. "Johnnie" Johnson, the recording expert who had inscribed the voices of Florence Nightingale and Alfred Tennyson in 1888, had joined Rainbow Records, and Thomas P. Ratcliff was the general manager. Ratcliff left Rainbow in April 1922 to join the Aeolian Co. L.E. Gillingham was reported to be general manager of the Rodeheaver Record Co. in July 1922. From 1923–1929, the firm continued to be listed in the Chicago directory, but no listing appeared in the 1929–1930 directory or thereafter. [Rust 1978.]

FRANK ANDREWS

RAINEY, MA (26 APR 1886–22 DEC 1939)

U.S. blues singer, born Gertrude Pridgett in Columbus, Georgia. She began singing in public at 12. In 1904 she married Will "Pa" Rainey and toured with him with the Rabbit Foot Minstrels, Tolliver's Circus, and other shows. She then established her Georgia Jazz Band. Rainey began to record in 1923 for Paramount, achieving great acclaim with "Bo-weavil Blues" (#12080) and "Moonshine Blues" (#12083). These early recordings convinced record executives that there was a market for blues music, and led to the signing of many other urban blues performers, many of them women, like Bessie Smith. Rainey was a mainstay of Paramount's 12000 series of "popular race records," with such hits as "Stormy Sea Blues"/"Levee Camp Moan" with the Georgia Jazz Band (#12295; 1925). Probably her greatest work on record was in "See See Rider" (#12252; 1924) and "Soon This Morning" (#12438; 1927). She was an influence on Bessie Smith and other later blues artists. Rainey retired in about 1933, and died in Rome, Georgia. The Austrian Document label has issued her complete recordings in chronological order on a series of CDs; other reissues have appeared on various blues specialty labels, including Yazoo, Biograph, and Milestone. [Lieb 1983 has a discography; Vreede 1971 is a Paramount discography with illustrations of Rainey advertisements.]

RAISA, ROSA (23 MAY 1893–29 SEP 1963)

Polish/American soprano, born Raisa Burschstein in Bialystok, Poland. She studied in Naples, and appeared in Rome in 1912. The next year she made her opera debut in Parma, singing in Verdi's *Oberto*. She then sang in Chicago, London, Paris, and Buenos Aires, and was for several seasons with La Scala. Her American performances were mostly in Chicago; when she retired in 1937 she remained in the city, opening a school for singers. Raisa died in Los Angeles.

Aida was her greatest role, and extracts from the opera are among her finest recordings; she did "La fatal pietra" and "O terra addio" for Vocalion, plus 13 other arias in the 1920–1924 period. She made five sides for Pathé in 1924, and then five for Brunswick in 1928–1930. Her last discs, for HMV in 1933, included "Vissi d'arte" (DB #2122) and "Voi lo sapete" (DB #2123). Marston has reissued her complete recordings on a three-CD set.

RAMBLER MINSTREL CO.

A male quartet that recorded ca. 1906–1907, also known as the Victor Minstrel Co. (in 1907), the Colonial Quartet, and the Zonophone Quartet. Members were Byron G. Harlan, Billy Murray, Arthur Collins, and Steve Porter.

RAMONE, PHIL (5 JAN 1940–)

One of the most respected and prolific music producers in the recording industry, Ramone was a child prodigy and began playing the violin at the age of three. He was so good that by the age of 10 he played a command performance for the Queen of England. As a student at the Julliard School of Music, the teenage Ramone put in grueling days studying and practicing classical violin while simultaneously attending regular high school classes. By the age of 18, he had worked as a performer and composer, traveling and appearing in clubs. Several talented recording engineers became his mentors, allowing him access to the behind-the-scenes world of pop recording. In 1961, he opened his own recording studio in New York City, the legendary A&R Recording, where his skills behind the board as an engineer led to production opportunities. As a result he became as comfortable with the intricacies of producing as he was with the creative process.

Ramone is associated with innovations that have changed the face of the recording industry. He was the first to use Dolby four-track discrete sound with the motion picture *A Star Is Born*, and was the first to use a satellite link between studios, specifically for that film. He was also the first to use Dolby Surround Sound for the motion picture *One Trick Pony*, and produced the first high definition television show *Liza Minnelli: Live from Radio City Music Hall*. He also produced digital live recordings for *Songs in the Attic*, paving the way for the widespread use of compact discs in the pop world. Finally, he was also the first to use a fiber optics system (EDNet) to record tracks in "real time" from different locations around the world for Frank Sinatra's *Duets I & II* recordings.

Over the years, Ramone has produced and engineered scores of film and television musical soundtracks, helped to produce numerous musical theater presentations and live concerts, and has worked with notables such as Tony Bennett, George Michael, Ray Charles, Harry Nilsson, James Taylor, Natalie Cole, Paul McCartney, Madonna, Luciano Pavarotti, Frank Sinatra, Dusty Springfield, Elton John, The Band, Judy Collins, Quincy Jones, B.B. King, Chicago, Kenny Loggins, Bob Dylan, Paul Simon, Dionne Warwick, Billy Joel, B.J. Thomas, and Stan Getz. With 29 Grammy nominations and nine Grammy wins, plus an Emmy and an honorary Ph.D. from Berklee and Five Towns College, Ramone's distinctive musical style and use of audio technology are unmatched among his peers.

HOWARD FERSTLER

RAMONES, THE

The first band emerging from 1970s New York punk scene to issue an album, the Ramones established the template for the movement: frenetic tempos, terse songs — often less than two minutes in length, stripped-down arrangements featuring buzz-saw guitars, humorously moronic lyrics, and a scruffy transmogrified hippie-greaser (torn blue jeans and leather

Ramones album cover. Courtesy Frank Hoffmann

jackets) fashion sense. After touring the U.K. in mid-1976, their bash-trash-pop sound and cartoonish attitude would be copied by countless new English punk acts — indeed, the Ramones' recordings would always find a more receptive audience in the U.K.

The Ramones' eponymous debut (Sire #7520; 1976) — released at a time when radio was ruled by corporate AOR rock, polished Top 40 singles, and the lush progressive rock of Pink Floyd, Genesis, and the like — was one of the most revolutionary albums in rock history. The band's studied primitivism would be maintained over a long string of critically lauded LPs, including *Leave Home* (Sire #7528; 1977; #45 U.K.), *Rocket to Russia* (Sire #6042; 1977; #60 U.K., #49 U.S.), *Road to Ruin* (Sire #6063; 1978; #32 U.K.), and *It's Alive* (Sire #26074; 1979; #27).

Following the band's first lineup change — with the departure of drummer Tommy Ramone (aka Tom Erdelyi), Marc Bell (aka Marky Ramone) joining mainstays lead vocalist Joey Ramone (aka Jeffrey Hyman), guitarist Johnny Ramone (aka John Cummings), and bassist Dee Dee Ramone (aka Douglas Colvin) — and a growing sense that the formula had grown stale, the Ramones enlisted wall-of-sound producer Phil Spector to assist in the making of the more polished *End of the Century* (Sire #6077; 1980; #14 U.K., #44 U.S.). Subsequent releases — *Pleasant Dreams* (Sire #3571; 1981; #58 U.S.), *Subterranean Jungle* (Sire #23800; 1983; #83 U.S.), *Too Tough to Die* (Sire #25187; 1984; #63 U.K.), *Animal Boy* (Sire #25433; 1986; #38 U.K.), *Halfway to Sanity* (Sire #25641; 1987; #78 U.K.), *Brain Drain* (Sire #25905; 1989; #73 U.K.), *Live Loco* (Sire #1901; 1991), and *Mondo Bizarro* (Radioactive #10615; 1992) — paled in comparison to the output of the leading hardcore groups of the 1980s.

Unable to capitalize on the punk revival of the early 1990s, the Ramones issued a tribute to the 1960s' songs that had inspired them in the first place, *Acid Eaters* (Radioactive #10913; 1993), followed by their farewell album, *Adios Amigos* (Radioactive #11273; 1995; #62 U.K.), and tour, documented by the live set, *We're Outta Here!* (Radioactive #11555; 1997). The group officially disbanded in 2000 following a final tour; a year later, Joey Ramone died of lymphoma, and in 2002 Dee Dee died.

FRANK HOFFMANN

RAMPAL, JEAN-PIERRE
(7 JAN 1922–20 MAY 2000)

French flutist, born in Marseilles on 7 Jan 1922. He studied at the Paris conservatory (and was a professor there from 1968), played in the orchestra of the Vichy Opéra, then at the Paris Opéra. To him and James Galway go the credit for bringing a wide flute repertoire to the attention of world audiences. He recorded first for the Boite à Musique label in the late 1940s, performing baroque and classical material. Rampal also performs in the popular vein, and had a Cash Box chart album (the first for any flutist) in 1976 with Claude Bolling, doing Bolling's *Suite for Flute and Jazz Piano* (Columbia #M33233). He died in Paris.

RAMSEY, FREDERIC, JR.
(1915–18 MAR 1995)

One of the first important jazz scholars, Frederic Ramsey greatly enriched the body of jazz history. In the late 1930s he edited, with Charles Edward Smith, *Jazzmen: The Story of Hot Jazz Told in the Lives of the Men Who Created It*. A notable feature of the work was his biographical survey of cornetist/band leader King Oliver.

Ramsey was introduced by record label owner Moses Asch in early 1943 when Asch was recording pianist James P. Johnson. The following winter, after Asch had started Disc Records to release jazz and popular music, Ramsey was hired to coordinate jazz sessions and write liner notes for the resulting albums. Ramsey produced sessions by blues guitarist Leadbelly, an entire album of jazz drum solos by legendary drummer Baby Dodds, white trad-jazz musicians like Joe Sullivan and Pee Wee Russell, and gospel recordings by the Two Keys and the Thrasher Wonders, among others, through the label's bankruptcy in 1946.

Around 1947 to early 1948, Asch founded a new label, Folkways, and again collaborated with Ramsey on a number of projects. Around 1950, the two decided to do a series of albums reissuing early jazz recordings under the name *The History of Jazz*. This was among the first — and most ambitious — 78 reissue programs, and it inspired others to reissue early recordings, beginning with Bill Grauer at Riverside Records in 1953. Ramsey had also made a series of taped interview/recordings with blues guitarist Leadbelly in 1948, and wished to see them issued commercially without any editing of the reminiscences. While major labels were interested in the material, they only wanted to issue part of it; Asch was happy to issue it all, cramming 30 minutes onto a single side of an LP to make the four-LP set affordable by doing away with most of the "bands" between tracks. The set, issued as *Leadbelly's Last Sessions* in 1953, was a milestone in blues scholarship.

In spring of 1953, Ramsey went on a field recording trip to the South after receiving a Guggenheim Fellowship. Eventually, the fruits of this trip were issued by Folkways on the 10–volume set, *Music from the South* (2650–2659). The breadth and variety of these recordings were astounding; this was also among the first "field trips" documented on LP, and it inspired many more to take tape recorders into the field.

After the mid-1950s, Ramsey was less active as a recording producer. However, he continued to write prolifically on music. Ramsey was affiliated with *The Saturday Review* between 1949–1961. In 1960, he authored *Been Here and Gone*, an analysis of Black culture. The book was the culmination of years spent photographing Black life in the South and recording the blues, country, folk, and church music in the field. Ramsey later worked in television in addition to serving as a consultant on educational programs for the Institute of Jazz Studies, Rutgers University, and for the William Ransom Hogan Jazz Archives, Tulane University. His final project of note, a series of interviews covering jazz topics, "Been Here and Gone: The Ramsey Chronicles," was broadcast on National Public Radio in 1988.

FRANK HOFFMANN

RANE CORP.

Founded and incorporated in 1981 in Washington State, the company specializes in the production of a variety of professional-grade and consumer-oriented equalizers, mixers, amplifiers, and other high-quality products. The five owners, all of whom are still with the company, previously worked together in middle management positions at Phase Linear Corp., a high-end consumer electronics company. Rane products, while not budget items by any means, are priced well below the top high-

end equipment, while yet outperforming and outlasting many of them. [website: www.rane.com.]

HOWARD FERSTLER

RAP/HIP-HOP

Rap — and its cut-and-paste backing music, hip-hop — might well be viewed as a form of musical piracy. The genre's live and recorded output is built upon the sampling of existing source material, with the record player and recording studio functioning as primary instruments. On the other hand, its emergence represents perhaps the most important cultural development within the popular-music scene over the past 20 years. Based largely on the urban Black experience, it is a form of populist poetry drawing on the street vernacular and set to funky rhythms suited to dance venues.

The genre incubated outside of the pop mainstream during the 1970s. Although commercial success eluded him, Kool DJ Herc is widely held to be the godfather of rap. His ideology would ultimately define hip-hop culture; he was a record collector, dedicated to finding jazz, rock, or reggae discs possessing a funky drum break ideal for dancing. Spinning records at Bronx venues, Kool DJ Herc attracted a Black audience largely from the Bronx and Harlem. These so-called b-boys dominated club dance contests until Puerto Rican youth developed a new vocabulary of power moves: windmills, backspins on one hand, flairs (dance-floor gymnastics), and turtle crawls. This new dancing became known as break dancing.

Grandmaster Flash provided the final impetus in making rap an art form; he specialized in playing breaks: the point when a DJ rapped or a b-boy displayed his flashiest moves. Flash was adept at extending breaks and then abruptly shifting records to the next break beat (the origin of "cutting"). He also perfected "scratching," the technique of taking the beginning of the beat, holding the record with your finger and making it go backward and forward with your finger. In this manner, he created a whole new rhythm, much like a musician.

In the meantime, rap culture had spread to other urban centers, with club or street dance disc jockeys providing the impetus by speaking over a seamless blend of recorded snippets. The Sugarhill Gang's "Rapper's Delight" (Sugar Hill #542; 1979), the first rap record to be a hit on the pop singles charts, brought the entire scene into the mainstream. Hip-hop pioneer, Kurtis Blow, followed shortly thereafter with "The Breaks (Part 1)" (Mercury #76075; 1980), the genre's first million-seller. Additional pop successes were slow to appear over the next few years, however, as many of the pioneer rap stars (e.g., Afrika Bambaataa,

Grandmaster Flash, Grandmaster Melle Mel) tended to focus on harsh social commentary.

Rap truly achieved crossover appeal when Run-DMC ushered in the "new school" with the release of its debut album, *Run-D.M.C.* (Profile #1202) in 1984. By incorporating rock rhythms and instrumentation into the genre — most fully realized in its triple platinum LP, *Raising Hell* (Profile #1217; 1986), which included the hit single collaboration with Aerosmith, "Walk This Way" (Profile #5112) — Run-DMC stimulated the appearance of a wide array of subgenres. These included (listed along with leading exponents):

Gangsta Rap (Dr. Dre, Ice Cube, Ice T, N.W.A., Snoop Doggy Dog, Tupac Shakur)

Bawdy Rap (Biz Markie, 2 Live Crew)

White Rap (Beastie Boys, Snow, 3rd Bass, Vanilla Ice)

Political Rap (Boogie Down Productions, KRS-One, Public Enemy)

Jazz Rap (Digable Planets, A Tribe Called Quest, UB3)

Pop Rap (DJ Jazzy Jeff and the Fresh Prince, De La Soul, Eric B. and Rakim, L.L. Cool J., M.C. Hammer, P.M. Dawn, Puff Daddy [Sean "Puffy" Combs], Salt-N-Pepa, Roxanne Shante)

Alternative Hip-Hop (Arrested Development, Basehead, Disposable Heroes of Hiphoprisy, Wu-Tang Clan)

"Screw Tape" Mixes (DJ Screw, other Big Time Recordz mix-masters).

Rap's diversity would seem to hold something for everyone. Nevertheless, the genre has continued to offend mainstream sensibilities due to its blatant sexuality, off-color language, spoken lyrics devoid of traditional singing, and glorification of misogyny, lawless behavior, the use of force to settle disputes, etc. In this sense, rap appears to have much in common with early rock 'n' roll, punk, heavy metal, and other styles that have taken a strong antiestablishment stance.

FRANK HOFFMANN

RAPKE (VICTOR H.) CO.

A New York firm, active in 1907. It advertised the Rapke horn and horn crane, said to be "free of foreign noises and rattle."

RAPPOLD, MARIE
(CA. 1873–12 MAY 1957)

U.K. soprano, born Marie Winterroth in London, of German parents. The family transferred to the U.S. when she was a child, settling in New York; she studied there and made her debut at the Metropolitan Opera on 22 Nov 1905. She sang with that company until 1920, then moved to Los Angeles. She died in North Hollywood.

Rappold began recording on two-minute Edison "gold moulded" cylinders in 1906–1907 with three numbers. "Ave Maria" (#B21), "Euch lüften die mein Klagen" from *Lohengrin* (#B33), and "Elisabeth's Prayer" from *Tannhäuser*. She was heard on four-minute cylinders from 1910 to 1912, in 11 arias and songs, then made Diamond Discs from 1915 to 1922. Among her later records were a *Lucia* sextet with Margaret Matzenauer and Giovanni Zenatello (#82266), and Wagner numbers with Jacques Urlus.

RARITIES

A "rarity" is a record that was either: 1. issued in extremely small quantities (and thus, hard to find); 2. an original pressing of a common recording (either on a smaller label or representing a first, smaller run); 3. a test pressing or some other unissued variant; 4. an unusual recording format; 5. a limited or special edition; 6. a record issued by a small or short-lived label; or 7. a misprint, mistake, or odditiy. Record collectors value rarity as one factor in determining the desirability (and thus value) of a recording (the other major factor is condition).

1. *Records Issued in Small Quantities.* Some recordings by well-known artists may be more valuable than others, because they occurred early in their careers or were issued in smaller numbers. Thus, Zonophone recordings by Enrico Caruso are more valuable than his later Victor discs; the Beatles's U.S. releases on Swan or Tally (if original pressings) are similarly more valuable than their Capitol releases. Elvis Presley's Sun singles in the 78 format are far rarer than his 45s of the same material, and thus more valuable to collectors.

2. *An Original Pressing of a Common Recording.* Original pressings — with the correct label and jacket — are more valuable than later repressings, particularly for major artists. Thus, again, *Introducing the Beatles*, their first U.S. album issued on VeeJay, was pressed many, many times; many people believe they own an "original" copy of this album, when in fact most copies do not represent the initial pressing. Only true first pressings are highly valuable.

3. *Test or Unreleased Pressings.* When an unissued test pressing of a Robert Johnson performance was discovered in Alan Lomax's collection, it was immediately hailed as an extremely valuable recording. If it were ever to be sold, it would fetch an extremely high price. (Johnson's released recordings are themselves rare, because they were not terribly successful during his life, and few copies in good condition have survived.) Test pressings of 78-era material usually have better sound

quality than discs that were sold commercially, because they may have been played only once or twice. Similarly, discs made for commercial use (such as radio broadcast or promotional use), because they were not generally available, are considered rare and valuable.

4. *Unusual Recording Formats.* Any recording representing a format that was not widely adopted could be rare. All white wax cylinders are rare. Original quadraphonic albums are collectible because few were issued. Early Berliner discs made for their toy machine of 1890 are collector's items, both because of their age and their unusual size. EPs (standing for "Extended Play"), usually seven-inch records that were made to be played at 33 1/3 rpm (as opposed to singles that played at 45 rpm), containing four songs (two to a side), were produced during the 1950s and 1960s and, depending on the artist and relative availability, are collectible. However, not all unusual formats are rare; Edison discs used a format unique to Edison equipment (so-called "hill-and-dale" recordings), but because they were issued in large numbers, they are not particularly rare.

5. *Limited or Special Editions.* Record companies have developed many different ways to market the same recordings. Limited editions manufactured using higher quality materials, picture discs, and anniversary or commemorative releases are just a few of these "special" issues. In some cases, the value of these special records is diluted by the fact that many copies were made. But if they are true limited editions, they can command high prices from collectors. Remixed versions, often released on 12-inch singles, are also usually released in small numbers, and thus collectible.

6. *Records Issued by Small or Short-Lived Labels.* Any label that issued only a few releases or only pressed small quantities of its releases has some value to collectors. From the 78 era, among the rarest and sought-after disc labels — with the fewest extant specimens — are Autograph and Black Patti. Collectors who specialize in one label — such as a jazz collector focusing on Riverside — would want to own all the recordings on the label, including early issues, issues on smaller imprints (Washington was a short-lived Riverside subsidiary issuing folk material), etc.

In the late 1960s and early 1970s, following the Beatles' introduction of the Apple label, many rock acts demanded their own labels, most of which were affiliated with a major record producer. Bill Graham's Fillmore, the Youngbloods' Raccoon, and Jefferson Airplane's Grunt are just a few of these labels that many collectors find highly desirable.

7 *Mistake, Misprint, or Oddity.* Any record featuring some deviation from the standard issue is bound to be collectible. Certain oddities, equivalent to postage stamps that are incorrectly printed, become rare for the mishaps they immortalize, such as Nellie Melba's "Sweet Bird" take on which she is heard to say "I'm sorry to be such a fool; we must begin it all over again." The Beatles' famous "butcher" cover from the album *Yesterday ... and Today*, which was quickly withdrawn by Capitol, is collectible. Highly obsessive collectors can recognize immediately when a label is printed in a different color than usual.

Record collecting has spawned many internet sites, newsletters, and societies. There are many published guidebooks to record values. The major publication aimed at record collectors is *Goldmine*.

See also **Collectors and Collecting**

REV. CARL BENSON

RASCALS/YOUNG RASCALS
Although best known as one of the most successful blue-eyed soul acts of the 1960s, the Rascals were also facile assimilators whose stylistic evolution mirrored the historical development of rock music. The individual band members cut their teeth on a wide range of genres, including jazz, rhythm and blues, doo-wop, pop, and rock 'n' roll. As the Rascals, they attempted to keep in step with changing fashions by veering from garage rock to soul, followed by psychedelia, progressive rock, and laid-back jazz fusion.

The band — originally called the Young Rascals — formed when drummer Dino Danelli then supporting R&B artists like Willie John, hooked up with three members of Joey Dee's Starlighters — keyboardist/vocalist Felix Cavaliere, vocalist/percussionist Eddie Brigati, and guitarist Gene Cornish — to create a repertoire of songs for performance during the winter of 1964–1965. Their exciting brand of dance-oriented rock led to a contract with Atlantic Records in late 1965.

The Young Rascals' first single, the up-tempo ballad "I Ain't Gonna Eat Out My Heart Anymore" (Atlantic #2312; 1965; #52), was only a moderate seller; however, the follow-up, a cover of the Vibrations' "Good Lovin'" (Atlantic #2321; 1966), topped the charts. The band's versatility — two strong lead singers, exceptional songwriting (often featuring Cavaliere's music and Brigati's lyrics) and arrangements, and equal command of slow and high-energy numbers — was largely responsible for the long string of hits that followed. The band moved easily between ballads, including "Groovin'" (Atlantic #2401; 1967; #1) and "A Beautiful Morning" (Atlantic #2493; 1968; #3), to rockers like "A Girl Like You" (Atlantic #2424; 1967; #10), to social-protest funk, in "People Got to Be Free" (Atlantic #2537; 1968; #1).

Unlike many rock bands in the 1960s, the Young Rascals' LPs sold nearly as well as their singles. Their first albums were simply collections of their singles and B-sides, a typical strategy employed by record labels in the mid-1960s. However, beginning with *Once Upon a Dream* (Atlantic #8169; 1968; #9), the group took the name "The Rascals" — perhaps to shed their teen-pop image — and focused on concept albums. Several more concept albums followed: *Freedom Suite* (Atlantic #901; 1969; #17), *See* (Atlantic #8246; 1970; #45), and *Search and Nearness* (Atlantic #8276; 1971; #198). When the hits slowed to a trickle by the 1970s, the Rascals regrouped, with Cavaliere and Danelli bringing in guitarist/pianist/vocalist/songwriter Buzzy Feiten, bassist Robert Popwell, and singer Ann Sutton to achieve a greater jazz orientation. The limited success of albums after the new configuration — *Peaceful World* (Columbia #30462; 1971; #122) and *The Island of Real* (Columbia #31103; 1972; #180) — led to a breakup in 1972.

The original members have continued to work within the music industry. Danelli, Cornish, and Cavaliere got together in 1988 for a U.S. tour. However, the threesome became embroiled in litigation shortly thereafter regarding use of the band name. In 1997 the Rascals were inducted into the Rock and Roll Hall of Fame.

FRANK HOFFMANN

RASPBERRIES

The Raspberries were one of the most highly regarded exponents of power-pop; however, they existed at a time when concise, melodic songs, jangly guitars, lush vocal harmonies, and mod-like dress were distinctly out of fashion. Formed in Cleveland in 1970 by drawing members from several local groups — including vocalist/bassist Eric Carmen, lead guitarist Wally Bryson, rhythm guitarist Jim Bonfanti, and drummer Dave Smalley — they signed a recording contract with Capitol in the following year after their demos made an impression on future producer Jimmy Ienner. The first album, *Raspberries* (Capitol #11036; 1972), which included a raspberry-scented, scratch-and-sniff sticker on the cover, contained the Top Five, million-selling single, "Go All the Way" (Capitol #3348; 1972). Following the release of two more moderately successful LPs — *Fresh* (Capitol #11123; 1972) and *Side 3* (Capitol #11220; 1973) — Bonfanti and Smalley (who were opposed to the band's teeny-bopper image) left to form Dynamite. Fortified with replacements Michael McBride and Scott McCarl, the group released *Starting Over* (Capitol #11329; 1974), a concept album about the pitfalls of stardom hailed by many critics as the album of the year. However, its flat sales led to the breakup of the band.

Eric Carmen is the only member of the Raspberries who has had any kind of solo success. In addition to recording hits such as "All by Myself" (Arista #0165;

1975), "Never Gonna Fall in Love Again" (Arista #0184; 1976), "Hungry Eyes" (RCA #5315; 1987), and "Make Me Lose Control" (Arista #1-9686; 1988), he has composed Top 10 songs for Shaun Cassidy — "That's Rock 'n' Roll" (Warner Bros. #8423; 1977) and "Hey Deanie" (Warner Bros. #8488; 1977) — and Mike Reno/Ann Wilson ("Almost Paradise," Columbia #38-04418; 1984).

RAWLS, LOU[IS ALLEN] (11 DEC 1935–)

Lou Rawls is living proof that popularizing blues, jazz, and gospel styled–music can be accomplished without sacrificing musical values and good taste. Despite the polish and sophistication characterizing his approach, he remains capable of displaying the hard, soulful edge that attracted his original audience. Many Black contemporary singers popular in the 1980s and 1990s — most notably, Peabo Bryson and Luther Vandross — were strongly influenced by his singing style.

Born in Chicago, he progressed for singing in church choirs as a youth to a stint with the famed gospel group, the Pilgrim Travellers, in the late 1950s. After the group broke up, Rawls sang the blues on the Chitlin' Circuit. He developed a unique performing style consisting of an introductory monologue that would segue into a blues song. These numbers — half soliloquy, half rap — effectively communicated the conditions faced by Blacks in the early 1960s.

His vocal interplay with Sam Cooke in "Bring It on Home to Me" (RCA #8036; 1962; #13) led a contract with Capitol. Rawls released a string of albums — 28 in all — over the next decade with the label. Although much of this output featured somewhat overpowering production values, the warmth of his vocals and flawless phrasing — particularly on the million-sellers *Lou Rawls Live!* (Capitol #2459; 1966; #4) and *Lou Rawls Soulin'* (Capitol #2566; 1966; #7), the latter of which included the hit single "Love Is a Hurtin' Thing" (Capitol #5709; 1966; #13) — kept things interesting while consistently making the charts.

Rawls moved to MGM in 1971, immediately scoring with the single, "A Natural Man" (#14262; #17). However, the company's insistence that he focus on middle-of-the-road material led to another label change, this time to Bell. When that association failed to click, Rawls asked Kenny Gamble and Leon Huff to add him to the roster of their Philadelphia International label. Their choice of material and arrangements reinvigorated his career. The up-tempo ballad, "You'll Never Find Another Love Like Mine" (Philadelphia International #3592; 1976; #2) became his biggest crossover hit, as well as providing the impetus for seven more best-selling albums over the next five years.

The hits stopped coming following a switch to Epic Records in the late 1970s. However, a shift to Blue Note led Rawls back to a blues-inflected approach — most notably, on the album *At Last* (Blue Note #91937; 1989) — although commercial success continued to elude him throughout the 1990s.

FRANK HOFFMANN

RAY, JOHNNY (10 JAN 1927–24 FEB 1990)

U.S. popular singer. He developed a style that blended R&B, country, and gospel idioms, adding to them some heartfelt sobbing; he earned the sobriquet "Prince of Wails." His first chart record, "Cry" (Okeh #6840; 1951) was an enormous success, and may have sold 25 million copies. "Little White Cloud that Cried" (1952) was featured in the film *There's No Business Like Show Business*; it was 14 weeks on the charts. Ray had 10 other chart singles in the 1950s. He continued performing until 1989, including tours of Britain and Australia, but never reached the recording heights again.

RCA (LABEL)

A record sold in U.K. by Decca Record Co., Ltd., from 1957, in 78-rpm, 45-rpm, and LP formats.

FRANK ANDREWS

RCA (RADIO CORPORATION OF AMERICA)

A American firm established on 17 Oct 1919 in New York. It had an early association with Victor Talking Machine Co. in 1925, through an arrangement for RCA radios to be included in certain Victrola record player models. Then, on 4 Jan 1929, RCA bought VTMC. The Victor label name was retained, with RCA added, and the record remained in the forefront of the industry. On 15 Apr 1986, RCA became part of the Bertelsmann conglomerate.

See also **Victor Talking Machine Co.**

RCA VICTOR (LABEL)

The name given to the Victor label after RCA acquired the Victor Talking Machine Co. in 1929. With the transfer of the RCA record business to Bertelsmann in 1986, several RCA label series remained distinct, within the BMG group. As of 2002, the RCA Victor group focused on classical (on the well-known Red Seal line) and Broadway cast albums.

78 label issued by RCA Victor. Courtesy Kurt Nauck/Nauck's Vintage Records

REA, VIRGINIA

American popular singer, born in Louisville, Kentucky. She studied in France, and is said to have successfully auditioned by telephone for the American Opera Co., New York. She sang with various companies in the 1920s, then turned to radio in 1925 and found her niche. Under the name Olive Palmer, she became one of the most acclaimed radio vocalists in the 1930s, as the "Olive Palmolive Girl" on the Palmolive soap program, then on the Goodyear and Buick programs. She dropped out of sight in 1937, however, and did not return to public performance.

Rea recorded for Edison, Brunswick, Columbia, and Victor. Her Brunswick work was the most extensive, covering six years and a wide repertoire. For both Columbia and Victor she was a studio artist, singing in diverse ensembles as needed. She worked for Edison Diamond Discs, as Virginia Rea, in 1920–1923, and again in 1929 as Olive Palmer. The early sessions produced three vocal waltzes in Italian — "Se saran rose," "La zingarella," and "La capinera" (#80731, #80524, #80705) — and "Goodbye, Beloved" with the Lyric Male Quartet (#80746). Only one disc was released from her 1929 sessions, "On the Beautiful Blue Danube" and "Indian Love Call" (#52633). [Ferrara 1988.]

REALAUDIO

Unlike traditional, stand-alone downloads, RealAudio is a system of listening to music "live" via the internet.

Harman Kardon DPR1001 Receiver. Courtesy Harman Kardon International

Launched in 1995 by Progressive Networks, the system spread like wildfire thanks in part to the fact that users di not need to install detailed software to start enjoying music "streamed" from websites. Seven years later an inordinate number of online radio stations are using RealAudio to broadcast with sound quality, which is constantly improving. The only drawbacks are those that were there at the beginning. RealAudio users still suffer from internet congestion and restrictions placed on playback due to their connection speed, both of which stagger and break up the audio that is heard.

IAN PEEL

REAL TIME SPECTRUM ANALYZER

An instrument that displays signal strength in the frequency domain, usually at specific one, one-third-, one-sixth-, or one-twelfth–octave intervals, plotting level versus frequency on an easy-to-read panel. One-octave versions have only limited use, but with a proper microphone, properly used, more refined one-third–octave and better versions can be especially useful for making accurate measurements of loudspeaker room response in home-listening environments. They can also help with calculating large room and hall acoustics, calibrating theater equalization, and determining background noise levels. Useful versions have been produced by Rane, AudioControl, Behringer, TerraSonde, Ivie, and dbx, and programs have been developed that allow personal computers to perform as RTAs.

HOWARD FERSTLER

REBEL RECORDS (LABEL)

Pioneering bluegrass record label, founded in 1959 by Washington, D.C., area, bluegrass promoters/fans Charles Freeland, Bill Carroll, and Sonny "Zap" Compton. They originally issued 45s of local bluegrass acts, and eventually signed some of the leading bands of the day, including Ralph Stanley, Larry Sparks, and the Seldom Scene. Freeland bought out his partners by the mid-1960s. The label was sold in 1979 to County Records, which has reissued earlier material on CD and continued to issue new recordings. Freeland formed his own self-named label to continue to issue bluegrass recordings after selling Rebel. [website: www.rebelrecords.com.]

CARL BENSON

RECEIVER

A unit in an audio or audio-video system that traditionally incorporates a tuner, a preamplifier control section, and the required number of amplifiers. Modern versions also include a Dolby Digital and often a DTS surround processor and video switching, and many current models include fairly powerful multichannel amplifier sections and DSP ambiance extraction or ambiance synthesis circuitry. The receiver has become the dominant control center and power source in modern audio and home-theater systems, and upscale versions can compete in terms of quality with many high-end separates.

HOWARD FERSTLER

RECKLINGHAUSEN, DANIEL R. VON (25 JAN 1925–)

Born in New York City, von Recklinghausen graduating from MIT with an engineering degree in 1951. He was employed for a while at Rohde & Schwartz, in Munich, Germany, but later joined Herman Scott at the H.H. Scott company in the U.S. as a project engineer. His tenure at Scott spanned more than 22 years and influenced nearly all the products the company produced, including amplifiers, tuners, turntables, loudspeakers, consoles, sound analyzers, and acoustic testing instruments, and he is also known for his pioneering efforts with FM stereo (Multiplex) broadcasting. After leaving Scott, he served as an in-house consultant for Electro Audio Dynamics, then parent of Eastern Air Devices, KLH, and Infinity. Recklinghausen is the designer of the first EMIT planar ribbon tweeter; he patented a system of dynamic equalization and he is the father of all processor-controlled loudspeaker systems. Since 1991, he has served as editor of the journal of the Audio Engineering Society. He is a fellow of the Institute of Electrical and Electronics Engineers and AES, was president of the AES in 1967, and won the AES Gold Medal in 1978. He holds 24 U.S. patents and has authored dozens of technical papers and actively supported and chaired many industry standards committees.

HOWARD FERSTLER

RECORD BOYS

A male ensemble that broadcast regularly on radio stations WJZ and WRC (New York) in 1926–1927. Members were Al Bernard, Frank Kamplain, and Sam Stept. A popular recording was "Hokum" (Vocalion #15308, and other labels). Kamplain, a yodeler and singer, started a new group of the same name when the original one dissolved in 1927. It included baritone Tom Ford and pianist Lew Cobey; they also recorded for Brunswick and made one Edison Diamond disc.

RECORD CATALOGS

Since the earliest years of the phonograph, catalogs have been used to promote recordings. The first printed catalog of a record company was that of the North American Phonograph Co. in 1890; Columbia's first catalog came out later in the same year. Victor became famous for its elaborate catalogs beginning in about 1905, along with regular monthly supplements. By the 1920s, the offerings of the major labels became so extensive that specialty catalogs were necessary directed to specific markets. These included the well-known Race, Old-Time, and Foreign (i.e., ethnic recordings) series. With the advent of LPs and the proliferation of many new labels, independent publishers attempted to develop comprehensive catalogs of new recordings, led by William Schwann who began his famous catalog in 1949. Complete printed catalogs from individual labels began to disappear, as it would be nearly impossible to list everything available, although smaller labels continued to use catalogs as marketing tools through the internet era of the mid-1980s when most listings of this type moved to electronic sites.

See also **Discography**

RECORD CHANGER

Traditionally, this involved a turntable and tone arm assembly that stacked records and played them in succession. It was also known as an automatic turntable. A disc changer was described in *Scientific American* in 1921, but none reached the market until 1927, then sold by Victor. A model of the Victor Orthophonic Victrola played 12 discs, on one side only, holding the stack at a 60-degree angle; it shut off after the last disc was played. The first British disc changer was made by Garrard; the same firm produced the first changer that could play both sides of each record in the stack, in 1938. Garrard machines (and their counterparts by the Capehart Co. in the U.S.) actually turned each record over; another approach was illustrated by the Sharp player of 1981, which held the disc vertically and played each side with its own tone-arm assembly.

In most record changers of the 78-rpm and LP eras, the stack of discs to be played was directly above the turntable and parallel to it. The records were held in a level position by a record leveler arm (or record support arm, or record balance arm). The same arm activated the shut-off mechanism after the final disc had been played. Breakage of 78s was avoided on the drop from the stack because there was a cushion of air that developed and provided a reasonably soft landing. Other formats existed: for example there were the machines that pushed each record off the turntable after playing it, into a hopper of some kind (the records awaiting play were stacked on the turntable).

Some record changers were able to handle only six records, but most could play 10 or more. It seemed that 12 was the maximum because as the fallen discs piled up on the turntable, the tone arm had to reach up to play the top one, creating an awkward playing (tracking) angle. Records also tended to slide around on each other, especially if any were warped. Finally there should be mention of the RCA novelty of 1949, the 45-rpm disc and its compact record changer. It was a high-speed operator, and reasonably quiet, but only in the wildest fancy could anyone have expected it to equal the speed of an LP moving from one band to the next. Good record changers were produced by outfits like Dual, GE, Garrard, Sony, and Pioneer.

As good as some of them might have been, record changers were not popular with many serious audio enthusiasts, because it was felt (with complete justification) that stacked records could not be properly cleaned just prior to being played, greatly increasing the chance of dust-related damage. Consequently, many changers were configured so that their changing mechanisms could be removed and replaced with a single spindle that allowed them to perform more like "audiophile" players. The advent and subsequent runaway success of the CD not only reduced the LP record to being a niche product, but practically put an end to the LP record changer. Only serious analog-sound enthusiasts remained loyal to the LP, and those individuals were not likely to be interested in playing their prized jewels on a changer.

Interestingly, the CD changer (and later on the DVD/CD changer) that first showed up as a somewhat novel item in the late 1980s has become the dominant CD playback device of the new century. Some early versions used a stacked cartridge system, but the most popular type now involves the use of a rotating carousel mechanism that makes it easy to play singles or up to five or even six discs at a session. [Hoover 1971, pp. 82–83, illustrates the Automatic Orthophonic; Kogen 1977.]

REV. HOWARD FERSTLER

RECORD CLUBS

Entities established by record manufacturers to promote mail order sales; they were introduced by Victor in 1934, in a plan that required participants to buy a record every month for one year. Other labels followed. Consumers were given certain bargains and bonuses to inspire participation. The clubs were affected by retailer objections, and by a 1962 Federal Trade Commission ruling that clubs must make available material from other labels as well as their own. There were also customer concerns about the practice of clubs that involved shipping records every month unless they were specifically rejected in advance by the club member. Yet club sales still accounted for about 9 percent of the American market in the mid-1980s. [Denisoff 1986.]

RECORD COLLECTING

SEE COLLECTORS AND COLLECTING

RECORD COLLECTOR SOCIETIES

Also known as Gramophone Societies, following British terminology; indeed they remain almost entirely a British phenomenon. Societies are simply groups of people who join together to listen to recorded concerts presented by one of their own members or by a visitor invited for the purpose; it is felt that listening in a sympathetic group is more enjoyable than listening alone. Although a church hall, schoolroom, etc., may be less comfortable than one's home, the acoustics may be better. And one can always discuss the program during the interval or at the end of the evening. In addition, one does not need to own playing equipment or any recordings to become a member.

The first society to be traced was formed before World War I by members of the Prudential Insurance Co. in Holborn, London — an organization that, unlike the society, still flourishes. Members met in a public house in Chancery Lane, bringing their own records and players. Competitions were held for the "best" records, but contemporary accounts give no indication of the criteria adopted.

In 1914 there were about a dozen such societies up and down the country, some of them "phonograph societies" and others "phonograph and gramophone societies." The war seems to have made little impact on meetings, partly because then — as now — members were usually middle-aged or elderly. But when import of phonograph records from the U.S. Edison factory was banned during the war, the interest in cylinder records declined, and did not revive at the end of the war.

The City of London Phonograph and Gramophone Society, founded in 1919, claims to be the oldest such group with a continuous existence. Thomas A. Edison became its first patron.

For some years the principal attraction in the clubs was equipment. Then with the introduction of electrical recording the situation was transformed. More orchestral and chamber music records were produced, bringing about a renewed concern for the music itself rather than for soundboxes and other technical components.

Brief reports of meetings were published in at least two periodicals, but there was no link among the societies until 1936. W.W. Johnson, a teacher who wrote in *Gramophone* about music in schools and was a member of a society in Gillingham (Kent), began to urge the idea of an association of societies and promoted a meeting at the EMI studios. At this inaugural event, 37 members of 14 societies attended, and the National Federation of Gramophone Societies was born with a highly ambitious list of intentions. During World War II the society movement reached a high point, as there was then less alternative recreation, and broadcasting was limited to a single national channel. About 350 societies were active, often meeting in public libraries. Because of air raids, evening meetings were shifted to Saturday afternoons (in some cases members were stranded in their meeting rooms until the all-clear sounded in the early hours of the morning).

With an increasing number of adverse factors in and after the late 1940s, it could be argued that the society movement should have foundered, but in fact it keeps afloat with nearly 300 affiliated societies in 1985. The National Federation officers and committee are all unpaid volunteers, and the group publishes a magazine twice a year. As noted above, the movement is almost entirely British. The nearest equivalents were to be found in New Zealand, usually formed by English expatriates, during the late 1940s and early 1950s. Most seem to have ceased operations, but this is not always clear, since the birth of a new group is often publicized, but rarely its demise. On occasion, societies have been formed in the U.S., a number of which appear to be actively operating today.

E.T. BRYANT

RECORD CONDITION

A topic primarily of interest to those who collect cylinders, 78 rpm, 45 rpm, and 33 1/3 rpm analog recordings. The term mint (M) or near mint (NM) describes records never played, in mint condition. A mint (M) rating is never a certainty, since the usual sign of an unplayed record is its factory packaging, but a record may have been removed from its package and resealed into it. Very good (VG) condition is the state of a record free from marks and scratches, although showing evidence of some playing; it is practically as good as new, but not NM. A good (G) record has been played but is not badly worn or damaged. A record in fair (F) condition has had heavy play but is usable. One in poor (P) condition is close to unplayable, and would be kept for historical reasons only.

Such designations have not been applied to open-reel or cassette tapes, or to compact discs, where noticeable wear or damage is not a factor of concern. Tapes do develop problems such as print-through or simple breakage. However, these are not gradual forms of decay; either they exist or they do not. Older tapes may exhibit oxide shedding, however, and when that happens the tape is usually no longer usable. For a while in the 1980s certain laser discs exhibited deterioration of the aluminum substrata. The problem was traced to impurities in the plastic coating, and later discs showed no sign of such chemical deterioration.

The compact disc, laser disc, and the DVD have not evidenced operational wearability, due to the lack of physical contact between the player and the laser pickup, and properly made versions should be very durable as long as they are not damaged by scratches or chemical blemishes. Although there have been fears that the aluminum substrata might deteriorate over time, it is likely that most discs will outlive their owners. Some deluxe CD releases produced by upscale smaller labels made use of gold, rather than aluminum, thereby ensuring a very long life, indeed. Minor scratches on the plastic-coated playing side should not bother some laser-pickup assemblies, although scratches on the label side of a CD or DVD could cause problems if they penetrate deep enough to make contact with the aluminum. The label side is actually the weak point with such discs, and some CD releases

did have problems with silk-screen printing damaging the lacquer coating, and ultimately the aluminum. However, such incidents are now nearly unheard of.

Another documented problem has involved the use of foam dividers in multiple-CD jewel box sets. Although a number of major labels — most notably, the PolyGram empire (including subsidiaries such as Deutsche Grammophone, Archiv, London, and Polydor) — have downplayed the negative effects of this 1980s practice, the plastic surface coming into contact with the dividers over long time periods would erode to the point where playback was impossible.

Some time back, when demand was outstripping supply, a Philips facility in the U.K. used a wet-process silver coating instead of vacuum-evaporated aluminum to form the layer that holds the digital data. While aluminum is fairly stable and protects itself with a self-generated coating when attacked by most airborne pollutants, silver does not self-protect and can tarnish. This is unlikely to happen if the plastic and lacquer coatings are properly applied. However, if they were not, particularly if the disc was stored in proximity to paper or cardboard materials containing sulfur by-products, the silver might gradually turn black, starting at the disc's outer edge and working inward. Fortunately, the wet process has been abandoned, but a number of discs produced by Hyperion, ASV, Unicorn, and a few other British labels that had "Made in the UK by PDO" printed around the center hole might still be exhibiting the problem.

REV. HOWARD FERSTLER

RECORD CORP. OF AMERICA

A firm located in Union City, New Jersey, from 1951 to ca. 1957, operated by Eli Oberstein. It issued licensed classical material on several labels: Allegro/Elite, Allegro/Royale, Concertone, Gramophone, Halo, King, Royale, and Varsity. Artists were given pseudonyms, or in some cases were incorrectly attributed. [Lumpe 1990.]

RECORD OUT SWITCH

A control in a recording system that permits the recording of one signal while listening to another signal.

RECORD PLAYER

A device consisting of components necessary to play and listen to a sound recording. For a cylinder record, it consists essentially of a mandrel to support and rotate the cylinder, a reproducer to track the grooves and produce vibrations, a motor or hand crank, and a horn to amplify the vibrations so they can be heard. For a disc record, an acoustic record player consists of a turntable to spin the record, a soundbox and needle to track the grooves and produce vibrations, a tone arm to hold the soundbox and carry the vibrations to the horn. An electric record player translates the vibrations to electrical impulses in a cartridge (pickup), enhances their volume in an amplifier, and then translates them back to audible sound vibrations in the loudspeaker(s).

In a CD record player a spindle drive rotates the disc, a laser beam pickup reads the pits on the record, and one or two D/A converters translate the digital signals into stereo analog signals that can be enhanced in the same kind of amplifier and loudspeaker that is used in an LP player.

RECORD REPEATER CO.
A New York firm. In January 1915 it advertised a "Rek-Rep" device for automatic stop or automatic replay in a disc record player.

RECORD SALES AGENCY
A New York firm that advertised in *TMW* in 1921. It had been pressing its own labeled discs, and discs for owners of other labels, for two years.

FRANK ANDREWS

Record Listening Booths at Magnamusic Shop, 1939, NYC. From the Collections of the Library of Congress

RECORD SHOPS
Cylinder records were sold by mail order as early as the 1890s, but were also available in record company offices and phonograph parlors. Columbia records had a first location at 5th St. and Louisiana Ave. in Washington, D.C. — which may have been the original record outlet. Their later phonograph parlor was at 919 Pennsylvania Ave. Affiliates of the North American Phonograph Co., throughout the U.S., had offices from which cylinder records and phonograph products could be purchased. The first retail store to sell disc records to the public was established by Emile Berliner in Philadelphia in 1895; Alfred Clark was the proprietor of the shop.

As the industry grew, the number of retail shops increased, as well as the number of record departments in larger stores. The practice of trying out records before purchase was common, but it was usually executed by shop personnel (a so-called record girl played the record for the customer). An innovation of 1921 was the notion of self-service trials in private listening booths; this was the American pattern through the 78-rpm era. (A secondary trend surfaced in 1924: listening stations with earphones instead of booths. These reappeared in the 1990s in many larger record shops.)

Certain shops gained attention for their enterprising activities beyond sales of records, such as the Commodore Music Shop (1924) and the Liberty Music Shop (1927) in New York, both of which issued recordings; the H. Royer Smith Co. in Philadelphia (1907), which issued a record review periodical from 1930–1987; and the Gramophone Shop in New York (1928), which published an early unified catalog of available recordings.

During the post–World War II era, several major chains developed that specialized in record selling. Smaller "mom-and-pop" stores had difficulty competing, unless they focused on a single area of specialization or built related mail-order businesses. From the 1950s through the 1970s, the Sam Goody chain, which originated in New York City, was a major dealer specializing in a wide selection of recordings of all types, often at a discount; the Goody chain was absorbed into the Musicland group, which has directed its energy to mass merchandiser popular music through mall stores. Tower Records, originating in San Francisco, became a major chain in the 1980s, modeled on the Goody strategy of offering a wide selection; Virgin's "Superstores" followed a similar model in the 1990s. Beginning in the

1990s, chain bookstores operated by Barnes & Noble and Borders also featured large departments to sell CDs in their larger outlets, and later in the decade electronics superstores like Best Buy followed suit.

Because CDs cannot be as easily damaged as LPs, used record stores blossomed during the 1990s, often also selling rarities. Some chains attempted to introduce used CDs, but when the major labels complained, most dropped this business and left it to the smaller stores. These stores often also stock hard-to-find, imported, or other specialized releases as a way of attracting customers, and usually operate mail-order and web-based businesses as well as retail stores.

REV. CARL BENSON

RECORDER

The soundbox and cutting stylus used to make cylinder records.

RECORDING CHARACTERISTIC

SEE RECORDING CURVE

RECORDING CURVE

Also known as recording characteristic. With analog recording systems, a plot of the relative emphasis given to the various frequencies in the audio spectrum in order to ensure low levels of distortion, reduced background noise, and reasonably long playing time. With analog disc systems, lower frequencies must be recorded at lower volume levels than higher frequencies to prevent cutting into adjacent grooves. Standards for the curve have been established by the Recording Industries Association of America. Such frequency balancing is not required with digital systems.

See also **Audio Frequency; Playback Curve**

REV. HOWARD FERSTLER

RECORDING HEAD

In a tape recorder, the electromagnetic device that impresses the signal, by means of a varying magnetic field, on the tape surface. It may be the same head as the playback head.

RECORDING INDUSTRIES ASSOCIATION OF AMERICA (RIAA)

A trade organization established in 1952. Its membership is open to "Legitimate record companies with main offices in the United States that are engaged in the production and sale, under their own brand label, of recordings of performances for home use." Its purpose is to promote the interests of the industry and to "foster good relations among all concerned" with it. Among its active concerns are record piracy, technical standards, freedom of speech, copyright, music and the web, licensing and royalties, audio technologies, and rewards for achievement.

On 14 Mar 1958, the RIAA awarded the first gold record award for sales of over $1 million to Perry Como's single "Catch a Falling Star," and four months later the cast album of *Oklahoma!* became the first gold album. In 1976, due to rising sales of albums, the platinum award was launched for sales of over 1 million records; Johnny Taylor's "Disco Lady" was the first platinum single, and the Eagles' *Greatest Hits* was the first platinum album. Multiplatinum was soon introduced to cover record sales of 2 million, 3 million, and so on. In 1999, a new award, the diamond award, was created for sales of over 10 million copies. A year later, to address the growing Latin/Spanish language market, the "Los Premios de Oro y Platino" awards were introduced, with Disco de Oro representing 100,000 copies sold; Disco de Platino, 200,000 copies; and Multi-Platino, 400,000 copies. The RIAA awards are based on total number of records shipped in the U.S., less returns, to all accounts. [website: www.riaa.com.]

RECORDING INDUSTRY CHARTS

The charting of sound recordings was inevitable in American society, where competition is a birthright and trivia—such as that included in countless best-selling "book of lists" publications—has become a national obsession. Charting appears to have begun shortly after Thomas Edison filed for a patent to his phonograph on 24 December 1877.

Its prime purposes then—as now—were to promote the recording industry (as associated business interests) by focusing interest on new releases, and to provide retailers a gauge of relative demand. The charts accomplish these ends by tracking the performance of a given entertainment unit through a number of distinguishing features:

- numbered position;
- time frame (generally expressed in weeks or the interval in which the chart is issued);
- special features: most notably, bullets, which designate fast upward movement, and outstanding performance within a specialized sector such as sales or radio plays; and
- supplementary charts, which delineate activity (in greater detail) within these specialized sectors.

For industry insiders and outsiders alike, the analysis and interpretation of charts can be problematical at best. The process of translating prior unit sales, airplay, online downloading, etc., into a present-day breakdown by positions represents a highly subjective process. Various elements must be weighted according to perceived consumer behavior and industry needs. The stakes for record companies are high enough to render chart tampering—whether consciously or subconsciously—an everyday fact of life. A major type of bribe consists of a record company buying expensive—often self-congratulatory—ads in the publication that reward its releases with favorable chart positions. For researchers and chartographers, any attempt to compare the chart performance of recordings from different eras is fraught with pitfalls. For example, the tabulation for any given chart edition does not measure intensity (i.e., specific unit sales, number of radio plays, etc.). Therefore, it is possible that a compact disc barely reaching the Top Ten in one period might actually outperform the top-rated title from another time frame by all quantitative measures employed by the chart compiler.

Phonogram, an early record industry periodical established in 1891, anticipated charting by including ongoing mention of top popular recordings. *The Phonoscope* featured monthly listings (though not in precise rank order) during the 1896-1899 period. Data on sheet music sales, and lists of popular song releases from ASCAP and the leading record labels served as early chart prototypes.

Billboard, the bible of the recording industry throughout most of the 20th century, instituted weekly lists of sheet music in 1913, and published lists of the most popular songs in vaudeville in 1913-1918. During 1914-1921, the major record companies provided *Talking Machine World* with monthly lists of their best-selling records. *Variety* advanced the practice to a considerable degree with ore systematic listings from late 1929.

By 1934, both *Billboard* and *Variety* were regularly charting the top songs in radio airplay and sheet music sales. From November 1934 through early 1938, *Billboard* carried the best-selling charts of the individual record labels, and in late 1938 instituted weekly surveys of the most popular records in jukeboxes. As a result, two separate weekly charts emerged within the industry at this time: best-selling records, and radio airplay-sheet music sales. As far as the general public was concerned, however, the long-running radi show, *Your Hit Parade*, provided the principal format for top hits; it continued to be influential on television during the 1950s. A similar top ten countdown was employed by Dick Clark on *American Bandstand*.

During the early 1940s, the pace-setting *Billboard* evolved the triad of charts that dominated the industry until the late 1950s: "Best Sellers in Stores" (20 July 1940-4 October 1958), the first comprehensive listing combining data from all labels; "Most Played By Disc Jockeys" (1945-19 July 1958); and the previously instituted "Most Played in Juke Boxes" (which ran until 12 June 1958). After World War II, *Billboard* began running supplementary charts to focus further the industry picture; for example, "Up & Coming Hits" (1947-1948), "Regional and Up & Coming Hits" (1952-1954), and the "Honor Roll of Hits" (which ran through 16 November 1963—a compilation of tunes rather than individual records).

With *Billboard*'s publication of the weekly "Hot 100" (of 45s) beginning on 18 August 1958, the industry could look to one chart for a combined factual account of a single's popularity. Similar listings soon appeared for other genres (country, rhythm & blues, classical, etc.) and formats (long-playing albums).

In the meantime, many radio stations and retail outlets began producing their own charts as a marketing tool (for example, to encourage listening to their local count-down programs). These proved particularly useful in spotting local talent and regional break-out hits. While initially available only by mail or pick-up at the local outlets, the industry trade publications began running selected charts of key markets in the 1960s based on such listings.

The late 1970s and 1980s saw the widespread proliferation of charts to include the important new genres and formats appearing at the time. These included disco/dance/12-inch singles, rap music, college/alternative rock, new age, easy listening, album-oriented radio, videotapes, videodiscs, video clips, computer software, video games, and compact discs (until subsumed by the mainstream pop album charts). One particular marketing stratagem, midline catalog albums (i.e., older classic releases still popular with buyers), proved sufficiently successful in the early 1980s to have its own chart for a time within the trade.

Industry trade journals, long the chief means of disseminating chart data, have included *Billboard*, *Cash Box* (which ceased publication in the mid-1990s), *Variety*, and *Record World* (ceased publication in 1981). By the late 1980s, a number of fanzines and serious music journals (e.g., *Rolling Stone*) have begun including their own listings as well. A decade later, the Internet had become a major player, both in terms of sound recording transactions and dissemination of the charts themselves. Notable web publications charting on-line music distribution include the EvO:R Street Journal (www.radioandrecords.com) and Radio & Records (www.evor.com). Literally thousands of other Net-based chart sites now exist, including many devoted to reprinting past editions of radio and trade listings.

Billboard's utilization of SoundScan (beginning with the "Hot 100" singles and "Top 200" albums in its 25 May 1991 issue) represented a concerted effort to counteract criticisms that industry charts were either falsified to reflect the interests of the highest bidder, or grossly inaccurate in reflecting actual performance (particularly sales). At the outset, SoundScan compiled computerized barcode information form store registers. The sudden rise of country recordings, and corresponding fall of alternative music titles, led many industry insiders to deride the system because it tended to be concentrated inlarge retail chains that catered more to middle-of-the-road/rural customers, rather than independent and specialty record stores. Adjustments in its sampling approach—combined with efforts gather data from an increasingly broader range of sources, all geared to assessing the relative popularity of various information and entertainment media—has assured the institutionalization of the SoundScan formula; it remains a key factor in the compilation of industry charts up to the present day.

The following charts were included in the 31 January 2004 issue of *Billboard*:

TOP ALBUMS—The Billboard 200, Bluegrass, Blues, Christian, Country, Electronic, Gospel, Heatseekers, Independent, Internet, Pop Catalog, Latin, R&B/Hip-Hop, Reggae, Soundtrack, World Music;

TOP SINGLES—Hot 100, Adult Top 40, Adult Contemporary, Country, Dance/Club Play, Dance/Radio Airplay, Dance/Singles Sales, Hot Digital Tracks, Hot Latin Tracks, Mainstream Top 40, Modern Rock, Hot R&B/Hip-Hop, Rap Tracks, Rhythmic Top 40;

VIDEOS—VHS Sales, DVD Sales, Health & Fitness, Kid Video, Music Video Sales, Recreational Sports, Video Rentals, Video Game Rentals;

UNPUBLISHED—Classical, Classical Crossover, Jazz, Jazz/Contemporary, Kid Audio, New Age.

FRANK HOFFMANN

RECORDING PRACTICE

The genesis of any commercial recording project is the careful selection of artist and repertoire. Once these artistic considerations have been determined, it is the task of the producer to make all the necessary musical, technical, physical, and monetary arrangements for the recording.

When searching for the proper venue to make the recording, the first decision the producer must make is where — in a studio, or on location — the session should be held. This prompts a fundamental question: Where will the music be performed to its best advantage? If the answer is that a recital or concert hall, a nightclub or cocktail lounge, or any other "real" environment is where the performers and their music are most comfortable, this is where the producer should consider scheduling the recording session — keeping in mind, however, that there are technical considerations which also influence the decision. For example, a noisy room, acceptable for a live performance with an audience, may not prove satisfactory for a recording because the other aural and visual stimuli of the live experience will not be present to "mask" the record listeners' awareness of the intruding noise. Recording studios, on the other hand, generally offer a very controlled acoustical environment — in most modern studios this usually means rather dry acoustics, so that any sense of "liveness" will need to be added artificially during recording.

Technical and other cost factors must be considered as well; on-location sessions often cost more than in-studio sessions because all of the equipment needs to be brought to the site, set up, calibrated, and tested prior to recording, and then it all must be removed at the end. In addition, risers, chairs, stands, and instruments (and sometimes even acoustical treatment) also need to be brought to the site. All these technical factors aside, sometimes the music will "just sound better" when recorded on location. These and numerous other tradeoffs between cost and result will be evaluated when making the decision.

Today, digital recording formats are readily available in both direct-to-stereo and multitrack processes (see below) and the costs are no longer so widely different as they were in the earlier days of digital recording. Since both formats can be used to produce analog or digital products (LPs, cassettes, CDs, DVDs, etc.) the primary factors involved in choosing the recording format will be based on the "sound" of the recording and the preferences of the producer.

For stereo release projects, the next decision the producer will need to make is whether to record direct-to-stereo (two-track) or to use a multitrack process. (Surround-sound recordings, by definition, require a multitrack process.) Both methods have their advantages as well as disadvantages. The decision between the two approaches will be determined primarily by the type of music being recorded and the capabilities of the performers and the recording facility. Traditionally, music intended to be played "live" (classical, folk, small jazz ensembles, and the like) has been recorded direct-to-stereo, and with the growth in popularity of home-theater systems, these styles are now being recorded in surround-sound formats as well.

Direct-to-stereo has been a time-proven method for recording music that can be performed in "real time," as in a live performance. The recording techniques are, generally, less complex than multitrack, and when properly implemented, will result in a realistic, lifelike sound. Similar "minimalist" microphone and recording techniques are employed even for surround-sound recordings. Contemporary recording practices generally tend toward multimicrophone, multitrack methods to avoid problems with musical balance. Thus, even if a direct-to-stereo mix is recorded, a multitrack "protection" tape will be made simultaneously.

Complex musical performances (Broadway musicals, opera, etc.), "popular" genres (rock, rap, etc.), electronic music, or other musical formats requiring "layering" or "over-dubs" will almost always be recorded via a multitrack process. Multitrack recording is employed whenever the artistic intent is to create a "new reality" that does not exist (either conveniently or at all) in real time or space. Multitracking becomes a necessity when overdubbing or layering parts, or where performance difficulties or the instrumentation dictate that a proper musical blend cannot easily be achieved in the actual performance.

Multitracking also affords the opportunity for electronic manipulation of existing sounds to create new sounds, or for the replacement of one voice or line with another. It gives the producer and performers, therefore, the ability to "bend reality" to suit their art. This is the primary benefit of, and reason for, multitrack recording: the ability to mix or remix the individual voices (tracks) after the initial recording session, to achieve the exact balance desired.

Cost factors always are of significant importance to the commercial success of any recording project, and since producers are always concerned with money, cost factors will also be considered when making the decision where and how to produce the recording. Direct-to-stereo recording sessions take much less time, and when they are finished, the basic recording is complete. Multitrack sessions not only take much more time during the initial recording (and usually at much higher hourly rates), but the result is not yet a finished recording. The producer must then spend additional time to mixdown the multitrack tape in order to produce the final stereo master tape. As a general rule, the total time required to complete a multitrack recording will be at least six to eight times that of a direct-to-stereo session. Surround-sound projects, as mentioned above, always require multitrack production.

During the recording sessions (except, of course, for "live concert" recordings) the performances are accomplished in a number of individual takes. Each take is a segment of the entire musical piece. With some forms of music — particularly classical music or short songs — a take of a complete movement or song will be made in order to provide an overall sense of continuity. Then, if needed, short segments ("pickups"

or "inserts") will be recorded to replace spots that did not go well during the full recording.

In modern recording practice, it has become commonplace for individual instruments, groups of instruments, or vocalists to be recorded separately sometimes at widely different times, or even in entirely different locations, depending on the availability of the performers or instruments. This process is called tracking, since each part is recorded to a separate track on the tape. A related process, called overdubbing, comes into play when one performer is required to record more than one part or line of the musical composition. In both processes, the original track is played back to the performer, via headphones, and the new part is performed and recorded onto another track in synchronization with the original. During the mixing process the two or more parts are mixed together to provide the complex texture so vital to modern musical performances.

Once the session master tape has been recorded, the next step in the process is postproduction. During editing, the first stage, the individual takes are selected and combined (spliced together) to produce a finished performance of each song or piece; these pieces are then sequenced to produce the complete recording as it will be released. Numerous artistic and technical processes are involved in this stage and are dictated by the musical genre, stylistic considerations, including the relationship of each piece to all of the others in the album, and technical matters, such as the final release format for the recording.

As mentioned earlier, multitrack recordings must be mixed-down to a stereo (and as appropriate also a surround-sound) master. This usually occurs after the editing, although some producers prefer to mix first, and then edit. In popular music, special signal processing (compression, equalization, reverberation, phasing, etc.) effects are frequently employed during the mixing process to augment or enhance the texture.

The days of the vinyl LP having passed, projects are now usually released as CDs, sometimes also with cassettes as a secondary format. The cost of CD production has fallen at the same time as the widespread adoption of CD players has grown, so that the CD is now more viable than the cassette for most recording projects today.

Editing and mixing a recording can be done in either the analog or the digital domain, and the decision as to how to proceed will usually follow the format of the original recording. With the growth and proliferation of digital "workstation" technology, however, most editing now is done digitally, even if the original recordings were analog. Once completed, this recording will then be the final edited master.

The total time available on the various release formats requires that different "duplication masters" be created for each. Cassette sides generally have a maximum running time of 45 minutes; two sides afford a total program length of 90 minutes. Compact discs provide a playing time of around 72 minutes (although up to 79 minutes can fit safely on a CD). Thus, the different program lengths will determine how the tapes are edited.

"Mastering" is the final stage in the creative process. Here, the edited masters will be reworked one more time to create the "duplication masters" for each release format required. Dynamic range of the release format will also play an important role in the mastering process; because cassettes have a more limited dynamic range than Compact Discs, the technical limitations of the different release formats will also be taken into consideration when producing these duplication masters. For cassettes, this master will be an equalized, often compressed, stereo master and may be either an analog or digital tape or CD-ROM. For compact discs and DVDs, the duplicating-master will be a digital tape, CD-ROM, or, as is becoming more common, a file on a computer drive, containing the musical program material or files, timecode, and all of the special data and codes necessary to indicate track numbers, timings, table of contents, surround-sound track formats and coding, etc.

During the preparation of these final duplicating masters the producer has a last chance to change the sound or order of the recording. Once the duplicating masters have been made, the remainder of the process is just mechanical replication.

See also **Disc**

RON STREICHER

RECORDING STUDIOS (HISTORIC)

Early American recording studios, often called laboratories, were those of Thomas Edison (1887), A.T.T. Wangemann (a New Jersey studio for Edison, opened May 1889), and the New York Phonograph Co. (1890). In Britain, the first studio was in Queen Victoria St., in the City of London, established by Colonel Gouraud's Edison Phonograph Co. in 1888; it moved to Edison House, Northumberland Ave., W.C., by 1890 when the company passed to the Edison United Phonograph Co. of Newark, New Jersey. (Clients paid to be recorded.) The next London studio was in Fore St., E.C., where J.L. Young, ex-manager of the Edison Phonograph Co., set up his own business in 1893, with a studio to record and sell items performed by British artists. J.E. Hough began recording his London label cylinders in 1894, from his Broad St. premises. Emile Berliner was making discs in the U.S. as early as June 1892, in a laboratory housed with his first American firm, the American Gramophone Co. The first British disc recording studio was opened by the Gramophone Co.,

in Maiden Lane, London (1898). Thereafter all major labels had their own studios, while most independent labels had their recording done for them.

FRANK ANDREWS

RECORDITE CO.

A New York firm, established in 1907. That year, they advertised a disc record cleaning fluid named Recordite.

RECORDOL CO.

A New York firm. In 1907 they marketed a cleaning fluid for cylinder records, named Recordol.

RECOTON CORP.

Begun in 1936, by F. Behrendt (as an American distributor of a preamp able to play 78-rpm records electronically, and also as a distributor of European phonograph styli), Recoton started off small, but has become a global leader in the development and marketing of more than 4,000 consumer electronic accessories, audio products, and video-gaming products. Several separate companies are now part of the Recoton group, including NHT, Acoustic Research, Advent, and Phase Linear (all four acquired in 1996 as part of a purchasing arrangement with the International Jensen group), as well as Diskwasher, Heco, MacAudio, Ambico, InterAct, Magnat, Road Gear, and several others. The varied product line includes specialized accessories for home audio, video, car audio, camcorder, multimedia/computer, home office, and cellular products, as well as accessories for standard and 900-MHz wireless technology. In addition, the above-noted subsidiary branches market home-, mobile-, and marine-audio products, home-theater speakers, car-audio speakers and components, and accessories for video and computer games. [website: www.recoton.com.]

HOWARD FERSTLER

RED BIRD (LABEL)

A partnership between industry veteran George Goldner and songwriters/producers Jerry Leiber and Mike Stoller, Red Bird Records was launched in April 1964. The first release, the Dixie Cups' "Chapel of Love" (Red Bird #001; 1964) became a number one pop hit, and Red Bird — along with subsidiary, Blue Cat — became a very successful, if short-lived venture. The partners assigned most of the production work to outsiders, including George "Shadow" Morton and the team of Jeff Barry and Ellie Greenwich. At least one side of one half of the first 40 Red Bird releases were Greenwich-Barry compositions and/or productions. Shadow Morton brought the Shangri-Las to the label, resulting in Sixties girl group classics such as "Leader of the Pack" (Red Bird 014; 1964; #1) and "Remember (Walkin' in the Sand)" (Red Bird #008; 1964; #5). In 1965 Greenwich and Barry wanted to set up Neil Diamond as an independent producer under the aegis of Red Bird, but Goldner, Leiber, and Stoller refused, so Greenwich and Barry left. In April the following year, amid artistic differences and concerns over Goldner's gambling debts, Leiber and Stoller sold their share of Red Bird to Goldner for $1. The label folded soon after, and most of the masters were sold to Shelby Singleton's SSS Records in Nashville.

COLIN ESCOTT

REDDING, OTIS
(9 SEP 1941–10 DEC 1967)

A one-of-a-kind soul stylist equally adept at rave-up houserockers and soft, caressing ballads, Otis Redding is remembered as much for his potential as for what he actually accomplished. Toiling for years on the R&B circuit before a breakthrough performance at the 1967 Monterey Pop Festival positioned him on the verge of mainstream stardom, he would die tragically in a small plane crash at age 26.

The Macon, Georgia, native did not seemed destined for a recording career until given an audition at Stax Records while serving as a chauffeur for an aspiring band headed by Johnny Jenkins. Redding's first release, "These Arms of Mine" (Volt #103; 1963), released on the Stax subsidiary label, Volt, reached the Top 20 on the national R&B charts. Stax immediately signed him to a long-term contract, and with Booker T and the M.G.s guitarist Steve Cropper serving as arranger/producer, Redding recorded a long string of R&B hits — many self-composed — including "Mr. Pitiful" (Volt #124; 1965; #41 pop, #10 R&B), "I've Been Loving You Too Long" (Volt #126; 1965; #21 pop, #2 R&B), "Respect" (Volt #128; 1965; #35 pop, #4 R&B), "Satisfaction" (Volt #132; 1966; #31 pop, #4 R&B), "My Lover's Prayer" (Volt #136; 1966; #61 pop, #10 R&B), "Try a Little Tenderness" (Volt #141; 1966; #4), "Tramp" (Stax #216; 1967; #26 pop, #2 R&B), and "Knock on Wood" (Stax #228; 1967; #30 pop, #8 R&B).

By the summer of 1967, when his Monterey appearance captured the imagination of white rock fans, Redding's singles were beginning to become fixtures on the pop charts. The widely acclaimed Queen of Soul, Aretha Franklin, took one of his compositions, "Respect" (Atlantic #2403; 1967), to the top of the pop charts. Furthermore, a mere two-and-a-half weeks before his death, he recorded a song that close associates felt would propel him to mainstream success, "(Sittin' on the) Dock of the Bay" (Volt #157; 1968; #1 pop, #1 R&B).

Although only moderate sellers during his lifetime, Redding's albums — all of which have been reissued as CDs — have remained in demand up to the present day. The material from his original LP releases — *Pain in My Heart* (Atco #161; 1964; #103), *The Great Otis Redding Sings Soul Ballads* (Volt #411; 1965; #147), *Otis Blue/Otis Redding Sings Soul* (Volt #412; 1965; #75), *The Soul Album* (Volt #413; 1966; #54), *Complete & Unbelievable ... The Otis Redding Dictionary of Soul* (Volt #415; 1966; #73), *King & Queen* (Stax #716; 1967; #36), *Otis Redding Live in Europe* (Volt #416; 1967; #32), *The Dock of the Bay* (Volt $419; 1968; #4), *The Immortal Otis Redding* (Atco #252; 1968; #59), and *Otis Redding in Person at the Whiskey A Go Go* (Atco #265; 1968; #52) — is also available through countless retrospective compilations.

FRANK HOFFMANN

REDDY, HELEN (25 OCT 1942–)

One of the most successful female recording artists of the 1970s, Reddy remains best known as the composer and singer of the feminist anthem, "I am Woman." Her style would provide the template for adult contemporary, a genre that would become a music industry fixture by the 1980s.

A native of Melbourne, Australia, Reddy moved to the U.S. in 1966 in order to further her singing career. The hallmarks of Reddy's future commercial success — the judicious choice of material, outstanding vocal technique, and an ingratiating delivery — were evident in her first hit, "I Don't Know How to Love Him" (Capitol #3027; 1971; #13), a selection from the then-popular rock musical, *Jesus Christ Superstar*. The ensuing LP of the same name (Capitol #762; 1971; #100; gold record), included a track that was to become her signature song, "I am Woman" (Capitol 3350; 1972; gold record). Released in May 1972 — well after the appearance of her second album, *Helen Reddy* (Capitol #857; 1971; #167) — it reached number one on the *Billboard Hot 100* the week of 9 Dec 1972, due in part to the support of women's liberation groups. The single earned a Grammy for Best Song of 1972, and lead to her own summer 1973 television program, *The Helen Reddy Show* (NBC).

Reddy's expanded media exposure provided an additional boost to her recording career. The Music Operators of America named her Artist of the Year on Jukeboxes for 1973. Her Top 10 singles included "Delta

Dawn" (Capitol #3645; 1973; #1; gold record), "Leave Me Alone (Ruby Red Dress)" (Capitol #3768; 1973; #3; gold record), "You and Me Against the World" (Capitol #3897; 1974; #9), "Angie Baby" (Capitol #3972; 1974; #1; gold record), and "Ain't No Way to Treat a Lady" (Capitol #4128; 1975; 1975; #8). Her albums also sold well, most notably *I am Woman* (Capitol #11068; 1972; #14; platinum record), *Long Hard Climb* (Capitol #11213; 1973; #8; gold record), *Love Song for Jeffrey* (Capitol #1284; 1974; #11; gold record), *Free and Easy* (Capitol #11348; 1974; #8; gold record), *No Way to Treat a Lady* (Capitol #11418; 1975; #11; gold record), *Helen Reddy's Greatest Hits* (Capitol #11467; 1975; #5; double-platinum record), and *Music, Music* (Capitol #11547; 1976; #16; gold record).

The popularity of Reddy's recordings dropped off considerably in the late 1970s, perhaps due to her increasing interest in acting; she appeared in films such as *Airport 75* (1974), *Pete's Dragon* (1977), and *Sgt. Pepper's Lonely Hearts Club Band* (1978). As a result, she signed with MCA Records in 1979. Her following LPs seemed out of touch with the MTV generation, and by the mid-1980s she was no longer affiliated with a major label. She began concentrating on theater; *Center Stage* (Varese #5962; 1998), comprised entirely of show music, represented her first album of new material since the early 1980s.

FRANK HOFFMANN

RED HOT CHILI PEPPERS

With a style based heavily on 1970s funk and Los Angeles hardcore, the Red Hot Chili Peppers have been one of the most lasting and commercially successful alternative rock bands. Although the band has composed many first-rate songs over the years — the antidrug "Knock Me Down" (EMI Manhattan #70; 1989), the searing ballad "Under the Bridge" (Warner Bros. #18978; 1992; #2), the ethereal album track "Walkabout" (from *One Hot Minute*, Warner Bros. #45733; 1995; #4), among others — the choice of cover material (spanning Robert Johnson, Hank Williams, Sly Stone, the Meters, Stevie Wonder, Jimi Hendrix, Bob Dylan, Frank Zappa, David Bowie, Iggy Pop, and Elton John) is a testament to their collective intelligence and encyclopedic taste.

Formed in 1983, the Hollywood-based band — originally comprised of vocalist Anthony Kiedis, guitarist Hillel Slovak, bassist Michael "Flea" Balzary, and drummer Jack Irons — gradually shifted from the funk-punk of *The Red Hot Chili Peppers* (EMI America #790616; 1984) and the George Clinton–produced *Freaky Stylie* (EMI America #790617; 1985) to the funk-metal of *The Uplift Mofo Party Plan*

(EMI Manhattan #48036; 1987) and *Mother's Milk* (EMI #92152; 1989; #52). Major label support, artistic video clips, and more pop-oriented songwriting helped catapult the Chili Peppers into the upper reaches of the album charts with *Blood Sugar Sex Magik* (Warner Bros. #26681; 1991; #3), *One Hot Minute* (Warner Bros. #45733; 1995; #4), and *Californication* (Warner Bros. #47386; 1999; #3). Despite personnel problems, the band appears posed to continue producing new music well into the 21st century.

FRANK HOFFMANN

RED LABEL RECORDS

Disc records with paper labels of red color have been intended to suggest high quality deluxe productions since the early years of the industry. G & T issued such discs in 1901, carrying voices of the Russian Imperial Opera (Chaliapin among them); they sold for $5. Red labels became a major series for G & T (the Gramophone Co.), carrying their great singers and instrumentalists, from 1902. Victor negotiated with G & T to issue the red labels in America, calling them Red Seals. Later Victor recorded its own Red Seals, but the two companies continued to share material. Victor's 10-inch Red Seals appeared in April 1903; the 12-inch Red Seals came out in September 1903. The public was receptive: 306,312 Red Seals were sold by the end of the year. Other companies later used red labels to present series of special interest, such as Decca's Personality Series; but in other cases the firms just had red or maroon-colored labels for all their discs (e.g., Nadsco or Romeo). Victor's Red Seal line continues to operate as its label for classical releases.

REDMAN, DON
(29 JULY 1900–30 NOV 1964)

American jazz saxophonist, Big Band leader, and arranger; born Donald Matthew Redman in Piedmont, West Virginia. He learned to play all the wind instruments, and to make outstanding jazz/swing arrangements. He worked with Fletcher Henderson, Louis Armstrong, Paul Whiteman, Jimmy Dorsey, Ben Pollack, and others. He had his own band from time to time in the 1930s and 1940s. Redman's group recorded for Brunswick in 1931–1933, then for various labels. (An LP selection of material from 1932–1937 appeared on CBS #E-52539.) But Redman's lasting value was as an arranger. He is generally credited with the concept of creating the standard Big Band sections, and creating rhythmic riffs that would be played in a "call-and-response" style between the groupings. He took the Henderson band from blandness to exciting complexity in just a year or two (1923–1924), and when he left in 1927 the group lost its focus. He led McKinney's Cotton Pickers in 1928–1931, then formed his own band. Notable examples of his work are heard in the Henderson records of "Copenhagen" (Vocalion #14926; 1924) and "Rocky Mountain Blues" (Columbia #970-D; 1927). His design of "Deep Purple" for Jimmy Dorsey and Bob Eberle (Decca #2295; 1939) was an outstanding specimen of his ballad style. Redman toured Europe with a band in 1946–1947, then was less active. He died in New York.

RED NEEDLE

A fiber needle made by the Master-Phone Corp. in 1915, and patented by them; the patent was sold in summer 1915 to the Phonograph Accessories Corp. The needle was said to give five to 10 plays without record wear and without "muffled tone."

RED SEAL RECORDS

See Red Label Records; Victor Talking Machine Co.

REDUCTION

The combining of tracks from a multitrack recording (often involving more than a dozen feeds) into a lesser number of tracks, such as for a two-channel stereophonic or five-channel surround-sound recording.

See also **Data Reduction**

REV. HOWARD FERSTLER

REED, DAWSON AND CO.

An American firm with offices in Newark, New Jersey, and New York, active in the late 1890s. They issued brown wax cylinders and catalogs. In 1899, issues of *Phonoscope* the firm advertised "the only successful violin records — loud, clear and distinct," played by T. Herbert Read. Other artists on their records — "strictly first class originals" — included Billy Golden, Dan Quinn, Vess Ossman, William Hooley, S.H. Dudley, Harry Macdonough, the Lyric Trio, Cal Stewart, the original American Quartet, and Estella Mann.

REED, PETER HUGH
(16 JUNE 1892–25 SEP 1969)

American record critic and journalist, born in Washington, D.C. He studied voice in Italy, but his career hopes were abandoned after he was gassed in World War I. He took up criticism and was a pioneer in radio reviews of recordings. In 1935 he was founder-editor of the *American Music Lover* (renamed *American Record Guide* in 1944), the only significant record review journal of its time in the U.S. He retired in 1957, succeeded as editor by James Lyons. Reed died in Wingdale, New York.

REEL-TO-REEL TAPE

A magnetic tape format, also known as open reel tape, popular in the 1950s and 1960s, in which the recorded tape is played back by attaching its end to an empty take-up reel and running it past the playback head. After play, the tape is rewound to its original feed reel. A reel seven inches in diameter contains about 1,200 feet of tape, and plays at 7 1/2 inches per second, for a total playing time of about 30 minutes. Although the running time of such a tape exceeded that of an LP record side, sales for prerecorded open reel tapes were poor. They were used in home recording and in making copies of disc material. Open reels were also used in professional studio work, to make the original recording from which the disc masters, stampers, etc. were prepared. With the introduction of cassettes in 1963, interest in reel-to-reel taping virtually vanished in the U.S.

See also **Magnetic Recording; Tape**

RE-ENTRANT GRAMOPHONE

The British version of the Victor Orthophonic record player, introduced in October 1927 by the Gramophone Co.

REEVES, AL (30 MAY 1865–26 FEB 1940)

American vaudeville and minstrel show performer, singer, and banjoist, known in the 1880s and 1890s as the "King of Burlesque." The only records he seems to have made were cylinders for Columbia in 1892. He died in Brooklyn, New York. [Brooks 1979.]

REEVES, JIM (20 AUG 1924–31 JULY 1964)

American country singer, guitarist, and composer, born in Panola County, Texas. He intended to make a career in professional baseball, but was injured in a game and did not recover properly. Turning to music, he performed on radio and made some records, one of which — "Mexican Joe" — brought him considerable attention. Reeves had success with singles on the

Fairways and Fabor labels, then was offered a contract with RCA where he became a superstar. After his death in July 1964, in a private plane crash, his wife arranged for posthumous issue of material not yet released. The *Cash Box* country singles charts included 64 of his discs between 1958 and 1980. "I Guess I'm Crazy" (RCA #8383; 1964) and "I Won't Come in While He's There" (RCA #9057; 1967) are among the most noteworthy of his successes. The album *Best of Jim Reeves* (RCA LPM #2980) was on the charts 23 weeks in 1964. He was elected to the Country Music Hall of Fame in 1967.

REFERENCE RECORDINGS (LABEL)

Begun in 1976, and currently headed up by Tamblyn Henderson (president) and Keith O. Johnson (technical director), the company specializes in very high-quality (audiophile standard) recordings of classical and jazz musical material. RR won its first Grammy award in 1986, and has been nominated for best engineering on a number of occasions; it has also won awards from the Association for Independent Music, the Academy for Advancing High Performance Audio and Video, and from various trade and consumer publications. The artists' roster features an assortment of musicians from the classical and jazz worlds, including Clark Terry, Joe Wilder, Red Norvo, Airto Moreira, Flora Purim, Dick Hyman, Mike Garson, Malcolm Arnold, Eugene Istomin, Ruggiero Ricci, Frederick Fennell, and Eileen Farrell. Ensembles include the Royal Philharmonic, Utah Symphony, Kronos Quartet, Turtle Creek Chorale, Dallas Wind Symphony, Czech State Philharmonic, Seattle Symphony, and Minnesota Orchestra, among others. [website: www.referencerecordings.com.]

HOWARD FERSTLER

REGAL (LABEL) (I)

A British low-price record issued by Columbia Phonograph Co., General–London, and then by the Columbia Graphophone Co., Ltd., from 1914 to 1931. Material was greatly varied: popular dance and vocals, John McCormack, sacred pieces, spoken records, and country/western numbers. Material came from the U.S., Britain, and the continent. With the EMI merger of 1931, Regal was attached to the HMV low-priced record, Zonophone, and the result was Regal-Zonophone, a label that continued to 1949, and was revived by EMI in the 1960s and again in 1980 for a few rock items.

FRANK ANDREWS

Regal label. Courtesy David A. Jasen

REGAL (LABEL) (II)

New York–based, low-priced record, not related to the British one above, made from Emerson and Plaza masters. At first (1921) it sold records, for $0.50 each, to department stores, but in 1922 the discs were offered to merchant dealers. Important artists appeared on Regal, including the Original Memphis Five, Noble Sissle, Eubie Blake, Cab Calloway, Duke Ellington, Ben Selvin, and Vincent Lopez. Little Tots Nursery Tunes was a series of seven-inch records, three in an album, sold in March 1923; at that time the claim was made that Regals were being made in the world's third-largest record factory.

It appears that sometime in 1924 the Plaza Music Co. acquired Regal Record Co. Regal's Playtime line was advertised by Plaza in December 1924. Then in January 1929 it was reported that the Crystalate Gramophone Record Manufacturing Co., Ltd., had purchased the Regal Record Co., Inc., from Plaza. Subsequently, Regal was combined with Cameo Records, Inc., and the Scranton Button Co. to form the American Record Corp. Production of the Regal label then ceased. [Rust 1978.]

FRANK ANDREWS

REGGAE

The genre was a product of a diverse array of influences, including African-derived children's games, the ecstatic Christian Pocomania cult, Garveyite Rastafarians, and New Orleans rhythm and blues, which was broadcast all over the Caribbean via clear-channel

Reggae star Jimmy Cliff's album *The Harder They Come.*
Courtesy Frank Hoffmann

radio stations in the late 1950s. These forces did not converge until the appearance of transistor radios revived Jamaican interest in popular-music recordings. Out of this state of affairs emerged the "sound system man," who operated a generator-powered, hi-fi rig mounted on the back of a flatbed truck that would be driven to rural areas for dances. These operators, utilizing catchy handles such as "Duke Reid," generated large audiences of fans.

In the early 1960s, the dearth of New Orleans talent (and corresponding drop-off of available imports) forced sound system men to make their own records. Primitive studios sprang up around Jamaica. The first recordings were bad copies of New Orleans music; the Jamaican musicians couldn't seem to get the New Orleans rhythm right. This "wrong" rhythm became standardized, and ska was born with its strict, mechanical emphasis on the offbeat (mm-cha! mm-cha!). One notable example of the ska style, Millie Small's "My Boy Lollipop" (Smash #1893; 1964) became a Top 10 hit in the U.S.

By 1965, ska had been superseded by the slow, even more rhythmic "rock steady" genre. Sound system men began employing disc jockeys who would "toast" or talk over the instrumental B-side of a record. The disc jockey — prime exponents included Prince Buster, Sir Collins, King Stitt, and U Roy — would improvise rhymes about his sexual prowess and the greatness of the sound system operator. This practice also became known as "dubbing"; some of it was "rude" (i.e., dirty — in Jamaican slang "dub" is equivalent to sexual intercourse).

Poppa-top was the next link in the evolutionary chain; bubblier than rock steady, it loosened up the beat to the point where greater rhythmic division was possible. The leading exponent of the style, Desmond Dekker, reached the U.S. Top 10 with his 1969 release, "Israelites" (Uni #55129).

The release of the Maytals's "Do the Reggay," in 1968, served notice that a new form had entered the marketplace. Jamaican music had been expanding the role of the bass for much of the 1960s; reggae brought the bass to the forefront, emphasizing the complex interrelationship between it, the trap drums, and the percussion instruments. The beat was interspersed with silences, and cross-rhythms abound. The bass appeared to be the lead instrument, with the guitar reduced to playing "change," mere scratching at a chord. Keyboard and horns were utilized to thicken the texture.

Despite the success of some reggae-styled material in the U.S. — e.g., Johnny Nash's "I Can See Clearly Now" (Epic #10902; 1972) and "Stir It Up" (Epic #10949; 1973), Eric Clapton's "I Shot the Sheriff" (RSO #409; 1974) — the genre remained relatively unknown to most Americans until the U.S. release of the film, *The Harder They Come*, starring Jimmy Cliff, in 1973. It became a cult favorite and opened the door to the American market for other reggae artists.

In contrast to its widespread acceptance in Europe, Africa, and South America, the genre's popularity in the U.S. was hampered by the scarcity of live reggae music. This was because (1) most of the records used the same pool of studio talent, and (2) most Jamaicans couldn't afford to go to night clubs or stage show performances. The most famous reggae performer was Bob Marley, whose recordings featured protest lyrics, first-rate melodies, high-quality production values, and seamless blend Jamaican roots and rock conventions (which enabled him to please both his original followers and U.S. fans). Marley's promising career was abruptly cut short by his death from lung cancer in 1981.

Nevertheless, reggae has left a substantial musical legacy, including hip-hop (a rap-inflected spin-off, "dancehall," was popular in urban clubs during the 1990s), disco dubs with a disc jockey rapping over the track, and an expansion of the rhythmic possibilities in rock (as realized by artists as diverse as Jimmy Buffett, the Grateful Dead, the Clash, Police, the Flying Lizards, the Selector, the English Beat, Public Image Ltd., and UB40). The genre continues to reflect the Jamaican lifestyle as well as support the world's most successful self-contained Third World record business. Home-grown artists such as Ziggy Marley, Musical Youth, Inner Circle, and Shabba Ranks managed to achieve international success in the 1990s within an updated reggae framework, which has incorporated dance clubs rhythms and techno-derived arrangements. [Bergman 1985.]

FRANK HOFFMANN

REGINA MUSIC BOX CO.

A firm established in 1892 in Rahway, New Jersey, with offices later in New York and Chicago. A German named Brachausen formed the company. He was one of the founders of the Polyphonmusikwerke in Germany a few years earlier, and had been employed by the German company that made the Symphonion brand of music boxes. Regina music boxes were essentially Polyphon music boxes at first. In 1898 Regina was marketing coin-op music boxes. The Regina Disc Changer of ca. 1900 played a dozen two-minute steel tune discs. The Reginaphone could play either Gramophone records or steel tune discs, and the Automatic Reginaphone of 1905 was able to play six cylinder records consecutively, one for each coin inserted. A selective coin-op, the Hexaphone, was offered in 1906. The Reginapiano (an inner player) was another product, vacuum cleaners still another.

In 1909 the firm name was shortened to the Regina Co. A contract with Columbia Phonograph Co. allowed the two firms to distribute each other's products, so Regina began to sell Columbia records. Regina was bankrupt in 1922. [Hoover 1971 has illustrations of the Hexaphone (pp. 36–37) and Reginaphone (pp. 40–41).]

FRANK ANDREWS

REID, ANTONIO "L.A." (7 JUNE 1957–)

Born Mark Rooney in Cincinnati, Ohio, producer Reid replaced Clive Davis as head of Arista Records in 2000. Reid began playing drums as a preteen in his hometown, and eventually performed locally as a musician and songwriter. He met Kenny "Babyface" Edmonds while working as a studio musician, and the duo began writing and producing together as members of the group Deale. They formed LaFace Records in Atlanta, Georgia, in 1989, in partnership with BMG/Arista, producing artists ranging from Bobby Brown to TLC and Toni Braxton; Braxton and TLC later sued the label over contract disputes. Reid and Babyface also produced artists for other labels, notably Pebbles (who was briefly married to Reid), Whitney Houston, and Boyz II Men. Reid was named the president of Arista in 2000, bringing Babyface with him, although Babyface soon took his label, NuAmerica, to Universal Music Group. New acts Avril Lavigne and Pink were Reid's greatest successes as of 2002–2003.

REINER, FRITZ
(19 DEC 1888–15 NOV 1963)

Hungarian conductor and pianist, born in Budapest. His professional debut was as a pianist, playing a Mozart concerto at age 13. He studied at the Budapest Academy of Music, coached and conducted opera in Budapest, then from 1914–1921 directed the Court Opera in Dresden. Reiner developed a close association with Richard Strauss in Dresden (where nine of his operas had their premieres). He also conducted as a guest in many European cities. He transferred to the U.S. in 1922 to conduct the Cincinnati Symphony Orchestra for nine years, teaching also at the Curtis Institute in Philadelphia (Leonard Bernstein among his pupils). From 1938–1948 he was music director of the Pittsburgh Symphony Orchestra. He then moved to the Metropolitan Opera for five years, beginning with an acclaimed performance of *Salome* with Ljuba Wellitsch. In 1953 he took the post of music director of the Chicago Symphony Orchestra, remaining until 1962 and raising that ensemble to world-class status. He died in New York while preparing a Metropolitan Opera performance of *Götterdämmerung.*

Many of Reiner's early recordings are not on commercial records. He did not record at all with the Cincinnati Orchestra. His first conducting discs were experimentals made by Western Electric in the Academy of Music, Philadelphia in 1931–1932. Although Leopold Stokowski was on the podium for most of the sessions, Reiner directed three performances, which remain in the Bell Laboratories archive. EMI recorded some Royal Opera performances in 1936–1937 at Covent Garden, but did not gain the approval of Reiner to release them; the sessions (segments of *Tristan, Fliegende Holländer,* and *Parsifal*) have been sold in the underground market. There are also air shots available from Reiner's broadcast operas from San Francisco, 1936–1938.

Finally in 1938 there were some authorized commercial records by Reiner, for the World's Greatest Music series — he directed the New York Philharmonic Symphony Orchestra in six discs — which were issued without artist identification. And while he was with the Pittsburgh Symphony Reiner at last conducted for the first time commercially with his name given on the discs: Columbia contracted with him in 1938. Important recordings emerged, as Reiner brought that ensemble to a high level of polish, notably in Strauss works, as well as Bartók, Mahler, Falla, and Shostakovich.

Reiner went to RCA Victor in 1950, and soon began his legendary series of records with the Chicago Symphony Orchestra. His first CSO recording was *Ein Heldenleben,* 6 Mar 1954. Among the great performances captured on disc are the Bartók *Concerto for*

Orchestra (1955), *La mer* and *Rapsodie espagnole* (1956–1957), the Rachmaninoff second concerto with Artur Rubinstein (1956), the Tchaikovsky violin concerto with Heifetz (1957), Prokofiev's *Alexander Nevsky* (1959), a wondrous group of Johann Strauss waltzes (1960), and the second concerto of Brahms, with Van Cliburn (1961). These have all been reissued on RCA CDs #60175, #60176, and #60179, in 1990. The only complete, approved, commercially issued opera recording by Reiner is *Carmen*, done at the Metropolitan Opera in 1952, with Rise Stevens, Jan Peerce, and Robert Merrill; it is regarded as the finest recorded version of the work (reissued on RCA #7981 in 1989). [Hart 1987; Helmbrecht 1981.]

REINHARDT, DJANGO
(23 JAN 1910–16 MAY 1953)

Belgian jazz guitarist, born Jean Baptiste Reinhardt in Liberchies. Reinhardt was born to a traveling gypsy family; as a child, he took up violin, then switched to banjo and guitar. In 1928 his left hand was severely damaged in a fire, and he lost the use of two fingers. Despite this injury, Reinhardt developed a lightning fast technique, playing streams of single notes and extended chords. He played in Paris from the late 1920s, accompanying popular singer Jean Sablon (1906–1994) in the early 1930s. In 1934 Reinhardt formed a group with violinist Stephane Grappelli, which became known as the Quintet of the Hot Club of France. Their first session was made in December 1934 for the Ultraphone label in Paris, and consisted of covers of American jazz favorites, including the pop song "Dinah." Over the next few years, the group cut several sessions in Paris and London for the European Ultraphone, Decca, and HMV labels, including several original Grappelli-Reinhardt compositions, notably "Clouds" (Nuages), first recorded in Paris in a July 1935 session, and "Minor Swing" (Paris, 25 Nov 1937). Reinhardt and Grappelli also played on sessions by American jazz players in Paris, notably Coleman Hawkins. The Quintet's recordings were hugely influential, not only in Europe but also in the U.S., particularly after World War II when servicemen brought home the Quintet's records they had acquired in France. The group was separated during the war, with Reinhardt remaining in Paris and Grappelli living in London. In 1946 Reinhardt was invited by Duke Ellington to join him on a tour of the U.S. as a featured soloist. After he played for the last time with Grappelli

Stephane Grappelli (violin) and Django Reinhardt (3rd from left on lead guitar) with the Quintet de Hot Club de France, c. 1934. © Bettmann/CORBIS

in 1949, Reinhardt embraced the electric guitar and experimented with new styles. His death in Fontainebleau, France, brought a great display of mourning and a lavish funeral in Paris. [Stroff 1988/5.]

REV. CARL BENSON

REISMAN, LEO
(11 OCT 1897–18 DEC 1961)

American dance band leader and violinist, born in Boston. He studied to be a concert violinist, then directed a salon orchestra and gained success with it, mostly in Boston during the 1920s. The Reisman orchestra was one of the finest in the "sweet band" category, playing without tricks or excess sentimentality. They first recorded for Columbia in 1921, and had an immediate hit with "Bright Eyes" (#A-3366). In the late 1920s the Reisman specialty had become Broadway and Hollywood show tunes. Fred and Adele Astaire were heard on 1931 Reisman recordings from *The Band Wagon*, as well as Noel Coward in a medley of his songs. Astaire returned to sing "Cheek to Cheek" in 1935 (Brunswick #7486). Among the men who played in the orchestra were Eddie Duchin (piano) and Adrian Rollini (saxophone); Smith Ballew, Frank Luther, Lee Wiley, Dick Robertson, Clifton Webb, and Anita Boyer were among the vocalists. Several of the early Victor long-playing records of the 1930s featured Reisman. In 1935 he left Victor for Brunswick, but did not carry his success with him; the swing bands were rising in public interest, and there was the general slump of the Depression to deal with. Reisman was back with Victor in the late 1930s and became identified with the "society orchestra" group, those that played for gatherings of the wealthy. In the mid-1940s Reisman moved to Decca, and was active until the early 1950s. He died in Miami, Florida.

REISSUES

A reissue is a new release of an earlier recording, often inspired by the introduction of a new recording format. During the 78 era, there were no "reissues" per se, although many labels would in effect reissue earlier recordings through acquiring the back catalog of defunct labels, or by licensing masters from other labels. The American Record Corp. specialized in issuing the same recordings on various different labels, often using different names for the artists.

After World War II, the new LP format inspired a new interest in reissues. The new medium was paralleled by consolidation in the record industry, with the development of the so-called major labels (RCA, Columbia, and Decca), who in most cases owned the back catalogs of dozens of smaller 78 labels. The majors focused on big-name artists, while putting much of their earlier more specialized recordings — primarily in jazz, blues, and country styles — out of print. Jazz enthusiasts were particularly dismayed by this trend; with an increasing sense of the importance of the history of earlier recordings, they took it upon themselves to begin reissuing earlier 78 recordings on LP. Bill Grauer of Riverside Records, formally a jazz record collector and journalist, started the label with this mission in mind. Others felt that the major labels had no right to "sit on" the older masters; folk and jazz producer Moses Asch took this position, reissuing early folk material (famously on the 1952 *Anthology of American Folk Music*, a six-LP set edited by eccentric record collector Harry Smith) and Fredric Ramsey's 11-LP set of early jazz recordings. The major labels were not happy, but eventually they too began to realize there was money to be made by reissuing earlier recordings. In 1961 Columbia issued an album of 12 songs recorded in 1937 by blues guitarist Robert Johnson, launching the blues revival. Victor also began reissuing earlier recordings, often in theme anthologies.

Meanwhile, pop albums of the 1950s and 1960s were often, in effect, reissues because they were often created simply by collecting a number of singles by a performer onto a single disc. The notion of a coherent "album," specifically recorded for the LP format, did not really develop until the 1960s and the tremendous growth of the rock audience. Even so, the so-called greatest hits packages were another way for companies to repackage earlier material and resell it to the same consumers. So-called budget lines were another way to reissue either entire albums or collections of tracks to attract a more cost-conscious buyer.

The arrival of CDs as the de facto medium for recorded sound in the mid-1980s turned reissues into a boom industry sector. The crystal clear sound offered by compact disc, to say nothing of the hype surrounding their "indestructibility," in the mid-1980s lead many labels to try reissuing out-of-print albums on this new format. They were a huge success thanks in no small way to the booming need for musical nostalgia from the 1960s baby boomer generation, who were also far more likely to buy the CD format in favor of vinyl given its (initially) higher price. Since then some artists and labels have turned reissuing into an art form in itself. The U.S. Rykodisc (for example, their 1990s reissues of John Lennon/Yoko Ono's *Two Virgins* and other early experimental albums) and See for Miles are prime examples. By the end of the 1990s the reissues market showed no sign of saturation. Quite the reverse. Artists such as Peter Gabriel, whose 1970s and 1980s albums had already been reissued on CD with the format's arrival, were planning to reissue the same albums again but this time with added artwork, bonus tracks, and remastered sound. The mid-1980s craze for boxed sets, launched by Eric Clapton's hugely successful *Crossroads* anthology, led to even more lavish productions, complete with full-color booklets and multiple CD collections featuring outtakes and alternate versions of well-known recordings.

For some artists, like Charlie Parker, seemingly every note that they ever played (that was recorded in any medium) is now available in massive collections (which themselves served as the basis for "best of" single CDs). Others, like Jimi Hendrix, have seen their original studio albums reissued several different times, as new technologies have allowed for better remastering or the rights to the material have changed hands. At the dawn of the 21st century, technologies such as DVD and other newer formats have led some to speculate that a new wave of reissues — this time of earlier CD reissues — is about to occur.

CARL BENSON AND IAN PEEL

R.E.M.

No American rock band has created a greater body of recorded work since 1980 than R.E.M. Although considered a guiding force in the indie rock movement, the group's jangly guitar-driven sound owed much to the Byrds and other mid-1960s folk rock artists.

The band members — lead singer Michael Stipe, guitarist Peter Buck, bassist/keyboardist Mike Mills, and drummer Bill Berry — initially performed together as the Twisted Kites in spring 1980 at an Athens, Georgia, party. Their debut single, "Radio Free Europe" (Hib-Tone #0001; 1981; reissued on I.R.S. #9916; 1983; #78), produced by Mitch Easter, attracted the attention of I.R.S.-head, Miles Copeland, who signed them to a long-term contract. The next release, the mini-LP, the Easter-produced *Chronic Town* (I.R.S. #70502; 1982), received widespread praise from the rock press. The debut album, *Murmur* (I.R.S. #70604; 1983; #36), co-produced by Easter and Don Dixon, continued to highlight Buck's chiming guitar and Stipe's laconic vocals. While follow-up releases — *Reckoning* (I.R.S. #70044; 1984; #27), *Fables of the Reconstruction — Reconstruction of the Fables* (I.R.S. #5592; 1985; #28), and *Life's Rich Pageant* (I.R.S. #5783; 1986; #21) — did not veer appreciably from this formula, R.E.M.'s melodic invention and intelligent, albeit often obscure, song lyrics attracted an increasingly larger audience.

Document (I.R.S. #42059; 1987; #10), driven by the band's first Top 40 single, the moody "The One I Love" (I.R.S. #53171; 1987; #9), and *Green* (Warner Bros. #25795-2; 1988; #12), which contained the uncharacteristically humorous single, "Stand" (Warner Bros.

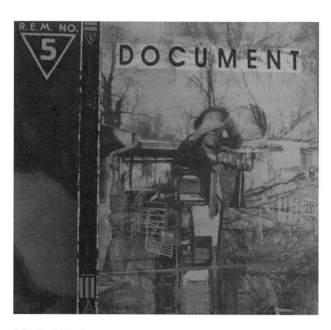

REM's fifth album, *Document*. Courtesy Frank Hoffmann

#27688; 1989; #6), lifted R.E.M. into the commercial mainstream. Exhibiting a penchant for subtle, insightful, yet catchy, material, they were able to accomplish this without losing their cult following. A nonstop touring schedule, combined with the marketing muscle of a major label, helped push the next album, *Out of Time* (Warner Bros. #26496-2; 1991; platinum record), to the top of the charts. It also included a couple of best-selling singles, the plaintive dirge, "Losing My Religion" (Warner Bros. #19392; 1991; #4), and unflinchingly upbeat "Shiny Happy People" (Warner Bros. #19242; 1991; #10). Now comfortably established as an American institution, the band produced yet another bittersweet masterpiece, *Automatic for the People* (Warner Bros. #45055; 1992; #2). Their patented idiosyncratic approach notwithstanding, *Monster* (Warner Bros. #45740; 1994; #1) revealed pronounced grunge influences. *New Adventures in Hi-Fi* (Warner Bros. #46320; 1996; #2) hailed a return to the group's classic 1980s sound, while *Up* (Warner Bros. #47112; 1998; #3) sold well despite its unrelentingly downbeat tone. With Berry having departed the band in the mid-1990s due to health problems and the other members active in side projects, the future of R.E.M. as an active recording and performing unit is unknown.

FRANK HOFFMANN

REMINGTON PHONOGRAPH CORP.
An American firm established in Philadelphia in 1919. It moved to New York in 1920, manufacturing phonographs and (by November 1920) disc records.

Remington operated the Olympic Disc Record Corp., which was formed in March 1921, issuing Olympic label records. Philo E. Remington was president of Olympic. With the bankruptcy of Remington and Olympic in December 1921, some of the assets passed to the Fletcher Record Co., which revived the Olympic label for a time in December 1922.

FRANK ANDREWS

REMOTE CONTROL

A small device that allows the user to turn on or off, adjust the volume, or perform other functions of an electronic device from a distance. The earliest example of a remote control for an audio system was a 1931 HMV device that had a 12-foot cord. Sophisticated remote control without a cord had to wait for the 1950s, when such features became available for television. Infrared LED remotes for television sets were introduced in the mid-1970s, and remotes for the video cassette player and the record player followed. Remotes in the early 2000s offered a full command of all audio and video functions, making it virtually unnecessary for the user ever to approach the sound source directly.

RENA MANUFACTURING CO., LTD.

A British firm established 12 Nov 1908 in London; Louis Sterling was general manager. Double-sided lateral-cut discs, from Columbia matrices, were sold in 10- and 12-inch sizes. In March 1909 the firm offered six models of its Rena record player; in July it also marketed Sonola machines. But in November 1909 the company was out of business. Columbia took over the disc assets and also the Rena offices and sales rooms. [Andrews 1985/1.]

RENAUD, MAURICE [ARNOLD] (24 JULY 1861–16 OCT 1933)

French bass-baritone, born in Bordeaux. He studied in Paris and Brussels, and sang at the Monnaie from 1883–1890. Then he was with the opéra-comique in Paris, 1890–1891, and the opéra in 1891–1902. He was a favorite at the Manhattan Opera from 1906 to 1909, then had a season in Chicago, and was at the Metropolitan Opera in 1910–1912. He was heard in about 60 operas. He died in Paris.

Renaud recorded nine titles for G & T in Paris in 1901, beginning with "Leonor viens" from *Favorite* (#32076). In the following year he appeared on the new Red Label series, with the Paris recordings reissued and five new items, notably "Evening Star" (#2-2704). He made another Red Label group of about 17 titles, in Paris in 1906; and a last set of 10 sides, on black label, in 1908. The black labels included "Voici des roses" from *Damnation de Faust* (#032041). Renaud was also on Pathé cylinders and discs, in 1903, beginning with the Toreador Song (master #3381). Marston records has reissued his complete Gramophone recordings made from 1901–1908 on a two-CD set. [De Cock 1957.]

RENNER, JACK (13 APR 1935–)

A major American recording engineer, Renner has a 1960 B.S. in music education from the Ohio State University School of Music, plus all the course work for a master's in music education from the same university. In 1998, he was awarded an honorary doctorate from the Cleveland Institute of Music, and is on that institution's faculty as adjunct professor of recording engineering. In October 1978, Renner engineered the first digitally recorded and commercially released recording of a major orchestra and conductor: the Cleveland Orchestra, conducted by Lorin Maazel, performing Mussorgsky's *Pictures at an Exhibition*. In 1977, along with Robert Woods, he began Telarc Records, and both men continue to run the company. Renner's technical acumen is legendary, and to date he has won a total of seven engineering Grammys.

See also **Stockham, Thomas**

HOWARD FERSTLER

REPRISE RECORDS (LABEL)

Unhappy with his association with Capitol Records, Frank Sinatra formed his own label in 1961, putting his business manager, Mo Ostin, in charge. Initially the label featured Sinatra's friends, including Dean Martin and Bing Crosby. As part of a deal to star in Warner Bros. films signed in 1963, Sinatra sold the label, with Ostin continuing to run it. The label made a deal with the British Pye label to license select acts for the U.S. markets, including the Kinks and Jimi Hendrix. Notable Reprise signings of the mid-1960s through early 1970s included Neil Young, Frank Zappa (as producer of his Straight/Bizarre labels), and Joni Mitchell. The label remained active until 1982, when Warners discontinued the name; however, it was revived in 1986 with the first release by country honky-tonk star Dwight Yoakam. Other notable late 1980s/1990s acts include Chris Isaak, Enya, and Neil Young (who left the label in 1982 and returned in the mid-1990s). [website: www.repriserec.com.]

CARL BENSON

REPROCESSED STEREO

Simulated stereophonic recordings made from monophonic masters; also known as electronically reprocessed stereo, electronic stereo, rechanneled stereo, simulated stereo, enhanced recordings, and enhanced stereo. Various techniques were used, mostly involving a slight delay between the left and right channels of the original recording, resulting in a distant, "echoy" sound quality that was less than satisfactory to many listeners. Nonetheless, from the mid-1960s through the early 1970s, many mono recordings were issued in this new format to appeal to owners of stereo playback equipment.

See also **Sonic Restoration of Historical Recordings**

REPRODUCER

The name given during the acoustic period to the pickup and its assembly; also known as the soundbox. Weight varied, always with the intent of achieving the lightest pickup that would track the grooves properly; in the Victor Orthophonic the reproducer weighed 142 grams (about five ounces). The reproducing piano differed from the music box and the player piano or pianola, being designed to play back the notes, rhythm, dynamics, and tonal characteristics captured in a pianist's performance. The pianist performed on a special reproducing piano, which marked a master roll to be punched later and replicated for distribution. In comparison to a standard player piano, the reproducing piano had additional pneumatics, activated by "expression holes" in the rolls.

The three famous major brands of reproducing pianos were Welte-Mignon (named after Edwin Welte) appearing about 1904, Duo-Art appearing about 1913, and Ampico (short for American Piano Co.) appearing about 1916, the most sophisticated and accurate system of its time. The rolls for one system were not compatible with the others, and Welte-Mignon produced three types of rolls which were not even compatible with each other. Smaller less widely known brands included Duca, Hupfeld, Artecho (also known as Celco or Apollo), Artrio-Angelus, Recordo, Pleyela, Empeco, and Stella. After a successful quarter century, the reproducing piano firms were nearly all out of business by 1930.

Reproduction mechanisms were pneumatic systems manufactured in two basic configurations: units built inside of the piano (mostly grands but sometimes in uprights) and units used outside the piano. The external system, called a Vorsetzer (German for "one who sits in front of") was a cabinet containing padded mechanical fingers for depressing each key.

Relatively few reproducing pianos were manufactured and very few survive in good condition. Since a reproducing piano needs to be finely tuned and painstakingly adjusted to provide a reasonable illusion of a live performance, an inadequately maintained instrument, containing many moving parts and intricate pneumatic tubing, could easily give a poor impression of what had been a nuanced performance.

Generally, virtuoso showpieces reproduced better than slow lyrical works in which any lack of subtle voicing and nuance became obvious, although mechanisms could not always adequately reproduce quick repeated notes. Like modern recordings mastered on magnetic tape, rolls could be edited to correct wrong notes, uneven passage work, and other technical shortcomings on the part of a pianist. Furthermore, the tempo of a performance could be accelerated (or retarded) without alteration of pitch; therefore, original performance tempos are suspect. Dynamics could also be unreliable. (Several Josef Hofmann rolls were advertised to have been directed and approved by the artist, who had notated the score to guide the dynamic-range manipulation of the engineers.)

Reproducing pianos utilizing recent scientific developments have been made in limited quantities in recent years. In the 1970s, an invention called the Pianorecorder used computer digital technology to provide the means to transfer piano rolls onto magnetic tape cassettes. In the 1980s, a computer-driven record/playback system producing extremely realistic results was available installed in Bösendorfer pianos.

The number of pianists and choice of repertoire was much greater for reproducing rolls than for acoustic discs. Many of the same pianists who made acoustic and electric recordings also made reproducing rolls. Significant pianists who are not known to have made cylinders or discs but left rolls as documents were Fanny Bloomfield-Zeisler (1863–1927), Teresa Carreño (1853–1917), Anna Essipoff (1851–1914), Theodor Leschetizky (1830–1915, best known as a teacher), Sophie Menter (1846–1918, who studied with Liszt and Tausig), Willy Rehberg (1863–1937), Alfred Reisenauer (1863–1907, a Liszt student), Alexander Siloti (1863–1945, disc test pressing rumored to exist), and Constantin Sternberg (1852–1924).

Recording-roll documents were made by numerous composers, listed here by nationality (some also made discs).

1. *American Composers*. Victor Herbert (1859–1924), Carrie Jacobs-Bond (1862–1946), Rudolf Friml (1879–1972), Charles Wakefield Cadman (1881–1946), Nathaniel Dett (1882–1943), John Powell (1882–1963), Charles Tomlinson Griffes (1884–1920), Ernst Toch (1887–1964), Ferde Grofé (1892–1972), George

Gershwin (1898–1937), Aaron Copland (1900–), Morton Gould (1913–).

2. *Austrian Composers.* Oscar Straus (1870–1954), Erich Wolfgang Korngold (1897–1957).

3. *British Composers.* John Ireland (1879–1962), Cyril Scott (1879–1970).

4. *French Composers.* Camille Saint-Saëns (1835–1921), Gabriel Fauré (1845–1924), Cécile Chaminade (1857–1944), Claude Debussy (1862–1918), Gabriel Pierne (1863–1937), Florent Schmitt (1870–1958), Reynaldo Hahn (1874–1947), Arthur Honegger (1892–1955), Darius Milhaud (1892–1974).

5. *German Composers.* Carl Reinecke (1824–1910, the earliest born significant composer to make any type of recording, although not known to have made commercial cylinders or discs), Max Bruch (1838–1920), Engelbert Humperdinck (1854–1921), Gustav Mahler (1860–1911), Richard Strauss (1864–1949), Ferruccio Busoni (1866–1924), Max Schillings (1868–1933), Hans Pfitzner (1869–1949), Max Reger (1873–1916).

6. *Hungarian Composers.* Ernö von Dohnányi (1877–1960), Béla Bartók.

7. *Italian Composers.* Ruggiero Leoncavallo (1857–1919), Pietro Mascagni (1863–1945), Alfredo Casella (1883–1947).

8. *Russian Composers.* Sergei Liapunov (1859–1924), Alexander Glazunov (1865–1936), Alexander Scriabin (1872–1915), Sergei Rachmaninoff, Nicolai Medtner (1880–1951), Igor Stravinsky (1882–1971), Serge Prokofiev (1891–1953).

9. *Spanish Composers.* Enrique Granados (1867–1916), Manuel de Falla (1876–1946).

Other significant composers on reproducing rolls include Ernesto Lecuona (Cuban, 1896–1963), Ludvig Schytte (Danish, 1848–1909), Manuel Ponce (Mexican, 1882–1948), Alexander Tansman (Polish, 1897–), Georges Enesco (Romanian, 1881–1955), and Wilhelm Stenhammer (Swedish, 1871–1927).

Most composers recorded primarily their own works, both original piano compositions and transcriptions of orchestral and vocal works. The composer's rendition, even if reduced to a piano version, provides valuable clues to performance practice.

Compositions were written expressly for player pianos (not meant to be interpreted or even playable by a human) by composers such as Paul Hindemith, Nikolai Lopatnikoff, Stravinsky, and Toch. Recently there have been numerous works by Conlon Nancarrow (1912–).

Conductors who made reproducing rolls (of interest but less significance since orchestral discs principally preserved their art) included Arthur Nikisch, Walter Damrosch (1862–1950), Felix Weingartner, Leo Blech (1871–1958), Ernest Schelling (1876–1939), Désiré Inghelbrecht (1880–1965), Eugene Goossens (1893–1962), Werner Janssen (1899–1990), and pianist-conductor Carlo Zecchi (1903–1984). Other celebrated musicians left some legacy on rolls, examples being Fritz Kreisler and musicologist Donald Francis Tovey (1875–1940, playing Chopin's Mazurka op. 50 no. 1).

Reproducing rolls were not exclusively solo performances, since some famous pianists performed duets. Examples listed in catalogs include Casella and Respighi playing a transcription of *Fountains of Rome*, and Bauer and Gabrilowitsch playing the Arensky Waltz from the Suite op. 15 (also recorded as an electric disc, Victor #8162).

Numerous rolls can be heard and studied from transfers onto commercial recordings. Although a few 78-rpm transfers were issued by American Decca, the first large sampling was a five-LP anthology (Welte-Mignon material recorded under adverse conditions just after World War II) by Columbia (#ML4291–ML4295). Several record labels devoted exclusively to such transfers were Distinguished, Welte Treasury, and Klavier. Major classical labels that issued important roll releases included Argo, Oiseau-Lyre, Telefunken, and Everest. Quality of the roll-to-disc transfers varied considerably, depending primarily on the variations among instruments and piano technicians.

Comparisons can be made of some pianists who recorded the same work on disc and roll, an example being Josef Lhévinne's magnificent performances of the Schulz-Evler paraphrase of Strauss's "Blue Danube" waltz. The electric disc (Victor #6840) compares very favorably to the Ampico roll (issued on Argo #DA 41), although it is a slightly different and longer version. Reproducing rolls and their recorded transfers, so readily available to students and scholars, should not be forgotten or summarily dismissed; they offer important information to be weighed in the study of historic performance practice. [Sitsky 1990.]

STEVEN PERMUT

RESONA (LABEL)

An American record of the early 1920s, pressed by the Bridgeport Die and Machine Co. from Paramount masters, then (1923) from Federal masters. The Charles Williams Stores are named on the later labels. After spring 1924 Emerson and Plaza supplied the masters, all of which were popular dance and vocal numbers. There were no issues after 1925. [Rust 1978.]

RESONANCE (I)

A vibration in a sound system that results from a relatively small periodic stimulus having the same or similar period as the natural vibration period of the system.

RESONANCE (II)

The intensification of a musical signal by supplementary vibration of the same frequency.

RESTORATION

SEE SONIC RESTORATION OF HISTORICAL RECORDINGS

RETHBERG, ELISABETH (22 SEP 1894–6 JUNE 1976)

German soprano, born in Schwarzenberg. A lyric and dramatic singer, she could also sing coloratura parts. She had been a piano prodigy, but decided to study voice. Fritz Reiner heard her in 1915 and arranged for a Dresden Opera audition; it resulted in her debut there on 22 June 1915 in *Zigeunerbaron*; she remained in Dresden until 1922, singing also in Berlin and Vienna. On 22 Nov 1922 she made her Metropolitan Opera debut as Aida, with Giovanni Martinelli, and remained with the company to 1942. Aida is considered to have been her finest role; she often sang it opposite Martinelli. Her repertoire encompassed Verdi, Mozart, Wagner, Puccini, and Weber. Rethberg was also a fine performer of the art song, with about 1,000 of them in her repertoire. Arturo Toscanini named her the "greatest living soprano" when she appeared under his direction at La Scala in 1929, and Willem Mengelberg said she had the most beautiful voice in the world. Though her prime was in the 1920s, she continued into the 1940s with no loss of strength. Her final public appearance was in Town Hall, New York, doing a lieder recital, on 20 Apr 1944. She died in Yorktown Heights, New York.

Rethberg's first recording was for Odeon in 1920, singing "Pastorale" by Bizet (#76215); she made 14 other Odeons, including five duets with Richard Tauber. In 1924–1925 she worked for Brunswick in Chicago, then she recorded for HMV and Odeon in Berlin. She became a Victor artist in 1929, beginning with six numbers from *Aida*, and principal airs from *Ballo in maschera*, *Meistersinger*, *Faust*, *Otello*, *Don Giovanni*, *Attila*, and *Lombardi*. Her final recordings were Mozart duets with Ezio Pinza, with whom she toured extensively in America, Europe, and Australia. She also made four sides for the Hugo Wolf Society ca. 1932, issued in 1935. Golden Age of Opera recorded her in complete operas from the stage of the Metropolitan: *Lohengrin* (#135; 1940 performance),

Nozze di Figaro (#118; 1940), *Otello* (#181, 1938; #106, 1940), and *Simon Boccanegra* (#177, 1935; #108; 1939). There are numerous CD reissues of recodings made throughout her career, including Nimbus (#7903) and Presier (#89051), and her work is also anthologized on various sampler CDs of early opera singers. [Richards, J. 1948/2, 1950/1.]

RETURN TO FOREVER

SEE COREA, CHICK

REVELERS

A male vocal quartet/quintet with piano, an outgrowth of the Shannon Four (established 1917), active from 1925 to ca. 1940. Original members were Franklyn Baur, first tenor; Lewis James, second tenor; Elliott Shaw, baritone; Wilfred Glenn, bass (also the organizer and manager); and Frank Banta, Jr., piano. Carson Robison sometimes whistled and played the guitar. Other artists in the Revelers at one time or another included James Melton, Charles Harrison, Sam Ash, Billy Jones, Frank Parker, and Robert Simmons (tenors); Phil Duey (baritone); Ed Smalle (tenor, pianist, arranger); and Frank Black (pianist). In response to changing musical tastes in America, the Revelers essayed a new quartet style, informal and swinging. They were highly popular on the radio in the U.S. and a great success on a European tour of 1926, particularly in London where a Command Performance was the highlight. They toured Europe annually into the 1930s.

The group was heard on many record labels, most prominently on Victor, where they began with "Just a Bundle of Sunshine"/"Every Sunday Afternoon" (#19731; 1925). In their next Victor session, there were five vocalists, as Smalle sang while playing the piano; "Dinah" — one of their great hits — and "I'm Gonna Charleston Back to Charleston" were recorded (#19778 and #19796; 1925). Other favorite records were "Birth of the Blues" (Victor #20111; 1926) and "Nola" with James Melton as first tenor (Victor #21100; 1927). They recorded extensively for Victor until 1934, finishing with "The Last Round-Up." The Revelers had a plethora of pseudonyms, including Acme Quartet, Aeolian Quartet, Cathedral Quartet, Gounod Quartet, Lyric Male Quartet, and Vocalion Quartet. On Columbia the group was named the Singing Sophomores; on Brunswick they were the Merrymakers. In addition they were the main voices in a number of choruses, such as the Victor Mixed Chorus and Trinity Choir. The group did not disband until 1954, when Glenn retired. [Riggs 1970.]

REVENANT RECORDS

Revenant Records was formed in 1996 by American primitivist guitarist John Fahey (1938–2001) and his manager Dean Blackwood. Guided by Fahey's vision, Revenant sought to release underappreciated, "raw musics," "undiluted stuff," that was languishing out of print. Meticulously remastered, reprocessed, and lavishly packaged, Revenant's output has brought Vol. 4 of the Harry Smith Anthology, the rural banjo of Dock Boggs, the hillbilly sound of the Stanley Brothers, and the sonic explorations of Captain Beefheart back to currency. The label's first release after Fahey's death, a seven-CD compilation of bedrock Delta bluesman Charley Patton's sides, led to a special Keeping Blues Alive award from the Blues Foundation, for historical work.

PAUL FISCHER

REVERBERANT FIELD

In home, studio, and live-music listening environments, it defines the sound field that exists when the reflected sound predominates over the direct sound coming directly from a source, be that source loudspeaker systems or live performers. Obviously, the strength of the reverberant field will depend upon the listening distance and the room's layout and reflectivity.

See also **Direct Field; Surround Sound**

HOWARD FERSTLER

REVERBERATION

Multiple reflections of sound waves within a closed space, resulting in echo effects that may be heard along with the original signals. The time taken up between the introduction of a sound wave to the closed space and the return of the reverberation to the point of introduction is the reverberation time. A room, or recording studio, is said to be "live" if it has a comparatively long reverberation time; "dead" if the reverberation time is comparatively slow. Reverberation can be created artificially with electromechanical devices or electronic circuits.

See also **Resonance; Room Acoustics**

REVERBERATION TIME

The interval required for the sound that remains after a primary signal stops to decay to a specific loudness level. It is normally quantified by measuring how long it takes the sound pressure level to decay to one-millionth of its original value. Since one-millionth equals

a 60 dB reduction, reverberation time is usually abbreviated RT60.

HOWARD FERSTLER

REVERSE EQUALIZATION

SEE EQUALIZATION (EQ)

REVIEWS

SEE CRITICISM

RE-VOICING

SEE DUBBING

REVOX

SEE STUDER/REVOX

REX (LABEL) (I)

A cylinder record sold in Britain by the Lambert Co., Ltd., after May 1904.

FRANK ANDREWS

REX (LABEL) (II)

A 10-inch disc sold in Britain ca. 1906 to 1914, pressed from matrices owned by the Disc Record Co., Ltd.

FRANK ANDREWS

REX (LABEL) (III)

Possibly the label of the New Rex Record Co., of London, which advertised in *TMW* from January 1907 to September 1907, stating that its records had preferential tariffs in the British colonies (probably directed to Canadian dealers).

FRANK ANDREWS

REX (LABEL) (IV)

An American vertical-cut disc record of 1914, based in Philadelphia. It was issued by the new Rex Talking Machine Co., which succeeded the liquidated Keen-O-Phone Co. Fred Hager, from Keen-O-Phone, and Charles L. Hibbard were in charge of recording. Apparently this was the first American firm to offer

Philadelphia based label that succeeded Keen-o-phone.
Courtesy Kurt Nauck/Nauck's Vintage Records

customers a record player under an agreement to purchase discs at given intervals.

Most of the material was dance music and popular songs, with light classics; but there was some good piano ragtime as well. Ferruccio Giannini and Ellen Beach Yaw were also heard on Rex.

A report of September 1916 stated that 1,200 titles were available, in 10-inch size for $0.75 and 12-inch size for $1.25, all vertical cut, to be played with a jewel stylus. Then the company went into liquidation, in October 1916, and was acquired by the Imperial Talking Machine Co. in May 1917. [Blacker 1975; Rust 1978.]

FRANK ANDREWS

REX (LABEL) (V)
A British disc record, registered to the Vocalion Gramophone Co., Ltd., then owned by the Crystalate Record Manufacturing Co., Ltd., when it acquired the Vocalion business. The first releases appeared in September 1933. In 1935 the record was priced at 1 shilling. "I'm Popeye the Sailor Man" was one of the 1935 discs (#8536). From April 1937 Rex records were issued by new owners, the Decca Record Co., Ltd., which had acquired the record side of Crystalate's business. American Brunswick and Vocalion matrices became available to the Rex label through the American Record Corp. Under Crystalate, Rex had access to Regal (of U.S.) matrices, as Crystalate owned Regal Record Co., Inc., then a part

of the American Record Corp. The final Rex issues were in March 1948. [Hayes 1974.]

FRANK ANDREWS

REYNALDS, W.H. (ALSO SPELLED REYNOLDS)
American record company owner. His Reynalds Music Co. was located in Mobile, Alabama. Reynalds was active in the National Association of Talking Machine Jobbers, serving as treasurer for most of the time between 1913 and 1920.

RHINO RECORDS
Rhino Records grew out of the Rhino record store opened by Richard Foos in west Los Angeles in October 1973. Foos and his partner Harold Bronson launched the label in January 1978 with the release of Wild Man Fischer's *Wildmania*. The label's first reissue album featured the West Coast band, the Turtles, also released in 1978. They found a niche reissuing 1960s rock music, becoming the paramount reissue label in the U.S. In 1984, the company issued its first CD reissues, and a year later launched a home video division. The company became well known for its large, thematic boxed sets and series, covering specific pop musical styles or eras (notably the "Have a Nice Day: Super Hits of the '70s" series begun in 1990). In 1991, Kid Rhino was launched to release music for children. In April 1992, Rhino announced a distribution deal with Atlantic Records that allowed access to a trove of vintage recordings. Other notable artists assigning their back catalogs to Rhino include Ray Charles (1997), and Elvis Cosetllo (2001). [website: www.rhino.com.]

WILLIAM RUHLMANN

RHYTHM AND BLUES (R&B) RECORDINGS
The term rhythm and blues (R&B) emerged as the most acceptable designation for the music that had developed out of pre–World War II blues styles, for the most distinctive new element in this genre was the addition of a dance beat. The expression first appeared in formal usage in the late 1940s as the name of RCA's division that served the Black audience; other alternatives at the time included "ebony" (MGM) and "sepia" (Decca and Capitol). Prior to the rise of rock 'n' roll, R&B had already evolved into a wide variety of subgenres, including:

(1) the self-confident, assertive dancehall blues which, in turn, encompassed (a) Big Band blues (e.g.,

Lucky Millinder, Tiny Bradshaw); (b) shout, scream, and cry blues (e.g., Wynonie Harris, Joe Turner, Big Maybelle, Ruth Brown, LaVern Baker, Roy Brown); and (c) combo blues or jump blues. The latter possessed a number of regional strains in addition to the cosmopolitan style exemplified by Louis Jordan: West Coast (e.g., Roy Milton, Amos Milburn, T-Bone Walker), Mississippi Delta (e.g., Ike Turner's Kings of Rhythm), New Orleans (e.g., Fats Domino, Professor Longhair, the Neville Brothers), and Eastern Coast (e.g., Chuck Willis, Wilbert Harrison);

(2) the more subdued club blues (e.g., Charles Brown, Cecil Gant, Ivory Joe Hunter);

(3) the country-tinged bar blues (usually centered in either the Mississippi Delta or Chicago) whose chief exponents included Muddy Waters, Howlin' Wolf, Elmore James, Lightnin' Hopkins, and John Lee Hooker;

(4) vocal group singing, which was subdivided into (a) the cool style (e.g., the Orioles, Cardinals, Spaniels); (b) the dramatic style (e.g., the Moonglows, Flamingos, Platters); (c) the romantics (e.g., the Harptones, Flamingos); (d) the cool style with a strong blues emphasis (e.g., the Clovers, Drifters); and (e) the sing-along novelty approach geared to mainstream pop acceptance (e.g., the Crows, Penguins, Frankie Lymon & the Teenagers); and

(5) gospel-based styles, which possessed three major strains: (a) spiritual singing, with the focus upon the quality of the voice (e.g., Mahalia Jackson); (b) gospel singing, with its concentration on the interplay between voices, which were often deliberately coarsened to stress the emotional conviction of the singers (e.g., Rosetta Tharpe, the Dixie Hummingbirds); and (c) preacher singing, with its tendency to speak the message in an urgent near-shout which often revealed the phrasing and timing of singing minus the melodic dimension.

It soon became evident, musically speaking, that "rhythm and blues" was a less than satisfactory name for at least two of the most important stylistic innovations of the 1950s, the various vocal group styles and the gospel-based styles, which were to become increasingly popular as rock 'n' roll began to siphon off the unique spirit of previous R&B forms. For instance, the new vocal groups invariably based their approach on the style of two Black ballad-singing aggregates who had proven to be successful with the easy listening audience, the Mills Brothers and the Ink Spots. Both groups sang in the close harmony "barbershop" style, accompanied by a light rhythm section. They were linked because of the ease with which they timed their harmonies and the purity of their voices.

Of course, these characteristics were a far cry from those comprising the classic R&B style. Therefore, the term rhythm and blues became most useful as a market designation; i.e., an indication that the performer was Black, recording for the Black audience. As noted by Gillett (1970), there was ample justification — at least until 1956 — for classifying the Black market separately. The Black audience was interested almost exclusively in Black performers; only five recordings by white acts reached the R&B Top 10 between 1950 and 1955, and three of those were rock 'n' roll records (Bill Haley's "Dim the Lights" and "Rock Around the Clock," and Boyd Bennett's "Seventeen"). Few white singers had either the interest of the cultural experience necessary to appeal to the Black audience's taste — until rock 'n' roll changed the equation, resulting in a new type of white performer.

Lacking the financial resources and industry connections of white pop acts, R&B artists displayed impressive persistence and creativity. The Harptones' doo-wop rendition of "The Shrine of St. Cecilia" (Rama #221; 1956) represents a case in point. Taking a well-known tune, the group overcame the shortage of studio resources by intoning the "tick-tocks" of a clock and "ding-dongs" of bells; the sincerity of the delivery managed to make dated lyrics sound relevant and meaningful.

Motown Records played the pivotal role in the development of R&B into a mainstream genre. The product of the vision of one man, owner and founder Berry Gordy, the label sculpted a mainstream pop sound out of gospel and blues roots which reflected the vision of upward mobility and wholesome fun held by young Blacks in the 1960s. Motown's stars were groomed to offend no one; the songs they sang had romantic lyrics that could appeal to practically anyone; and the music itself was rarely demanding, or even aggressive in the tradition of Southern soul. The closest thing to an overt political statement released by Motown in the mid-1960s was Stevie Wonder's "Blowin' in the Wind" (Tamla #54136; 1966).

Although the assembly-line approach employed by Motown led to criticism for monotony, the label released a remarkably diverse array of recordings, varying in sound, arrangement, and feel. This diversity — reinforced by Motown's mainstream commercial success — proved to be the launching pad for many of the Black music styles that evolved after the mid-1960s. Virtually all Black musicians were in some way influenced by the Motown Sound.

A host of regional independent labels producing soul music in the 1960s sought to control production values and nurture available talent with an eye to the long-term payoff, including Vee-Jay and Chess/Checker (Chicago), Stax/Volt/Enterprise, Goldwax and Hi (Memphis), Philadelphia International, Philly Groove, and Avco (Philadelphia), and Fame (Muscle

Shoals, Alabama). Funk, disco, and the dance-oriented styles of the 1980s such as go-go music also owed much to Motown (see "February 11, 1961" in the chronology at the end of this entry).

Hip-hop music — and its vocal offshoot, rap — represents the most significant innovation in Black popular music during the final decades of the 20th century. The genre — which drew heavily from both dance club culture, Black street poetry, and the dub music of reggae disc jockey toastmasters — remained a spontaneous underground phenomenon (largely centered in metropolitan New York City) throughout much of the 1970s. Although classic soul and disco records provided the core soundtrack for the pioneering MCs — who continually experimented with scratching and other rhythmic flourishes — much of what was preserved from hip-hop's gestation period was limited to rough audio cassette transfers. The release of "Rapper's Delight" (Sugar Hill #542; 1979; #36) — recorded by the Sugarhill Gang (a collection of session players gathered together by the record label expressly to capitalize on the street buzz being generated by hip-hop — proved to be a watershed development. While experimental work of hip-hop disc jockys has continued to elude mass-market acceptance, a wide array of rap styles — including the cartoon humor of the Fat Boys and DJ Jazzy Jeff with the Fresh Prince, the political diatribes of Grandmaster Flash and Public Enemy, the dance-inflected verse of Tone Loc and MC Hammer, and the gansta rap of N.W.A., Tupac Shakur, and Ice-T — have achieved crossover success.

Despite the continued cultural dominance of hip-hop at the onset of the 21st century, Black popular music — designated by the Black Contemporary moniker by some trade publications in the 1980s prior to the revival of the R&B designation — encompasses of wide range of styles, from the torch ballad tradition of Anita Baker and Whitney Houston to a kaleidoscopic succession of ambient and techno-infused dance genres. The latter forms include: (1) trip-hop, slow-motion breakbeat music melding rap, reggae dub, and film noire–influenced soundtrack samples, accented by audio loops and vinyl scratching; (2) jungle (or drum and bass), a fragmented, speeded-up blend of reggae afterbeats, hardcore techno, hip-hop, soul, and jazz; (3) house, featuring insistent bass figures, looping drums, and erotic vocals (although originating in Chicago, it would — by means of incessant cross-fertilization — give rise to acid house, disco house, deep house, ambient house, progressive house, power house, pop house, handbag house, and countless other subgenres); (4) techno, first identified with Detroit, an instrumental-based variant of electronica characterized by darting keyboards and impatient rat-

tling drums; and (5) trance — a late 1990s hybrid of techno, ambience, and house — consisting of processed, computer-generated extended compositions built around the repetition of keyboard arpeggios, octave-leaps, pitch-shifts, and lengthy drum breaks, and steadily rising crescendos.

The rich diversification of styles and comparatively rapid rate of change characteristic of Black popular music in the post–World War II era stands in bold contrast to the chief white-dominated genre indigenous to the U.S. country music. Gillett (1970) offers the following rationale for this situation:

This is partly because several white southern styles have never been widely popular with the national American audience, so that singers did not continually have to invent styles that would be special to their local audiences — those invented thirty or forty years ago were still special to a local area, or to the white south.

In contrast, almost every black southern style has proved to have universal qualities that attract national and international audiences, and this situation has placed continual pressure on singers to come up with new styles that are not already widely known and that the local audience can feel to be its own. And invariably, musicians and singers have responded positively to such pressure.

This predisposition for change has proven to be at once a strength and a weakness. It has enabled R&B to remain a dynamic genre, ever responsive to the needs and interests of its core audience. However, it has also discouraged participation on the part of the uninitiated, who are confused by the rapid succession of fads and fashions.

Key events in the history of R&B:

1946. *Billboard* begins charting the sale of records in the "Negro" market, employing the heading, "Harlem Hit Parade." The weekly listing is eventually renamed "Race Records."

1948. Atlantic Records is formed by Neshui and Ahmet Ertegun and Herb Abramson. The label has shown a flair for assessing performing styles and audience tastes that has been unmatched in the post–World War II era of popular music. Beginning with a roster of performers randomly collected from individuals without contracts, Atlantic acquired a succession of singers from various sources and with various styles. By the mid-1950s the company's artists included Joe Turner, Ruth Brown, LaVern Baker, Clyde McPhatter, Ray Charles, Ivory Joe Hunter, Chuck Willis, the Cardinals, the Clovers, the Drifters, the Coasters, and Bobby Darin. With these performers Atlantic's share of the R&B market grew from three Top 10 records in 1950 to 17 (out of 81) in 1956. Though no longer a true independent, Atlantic continues to thrive as part of the WEA family.

17 June 1949. *Billboard*, without any editorial comment, begins employing the term "rhythm and blues" in reference to the Black charts.

6 Mar 1959. "There Goes My Baby" is recorded by the Drifters (Atlantic #2025). It was one of the first rhythm and blues discs to use strings. Its combined artistic and commercial success inspired an upsurge in the development of sophisticated recording techniques for Black music, culminating in the "Golden Age of Soul" (1964–1968).

12 Mar 1960. *Cash Box* combines its pop and R&B charts. In an editorial appearing on the front page of that issue, the magazine justifies this decision by noting the similarity between the pop and R&B charts; i.e., the R&B listing was at that time almost 90 percent pop in nature. *Cash Box* evidently had second thoughts about this policy, and reinstated the separate R&B compilation on 17 Dec 1960 ("Top 50 in Locations"). *Billboard* used the same reasoning in deleting its R&B singles charts between 23 Nov 1963 and 30 Jan 1965. It, too, ultimately returned to the two-chart system.

16 Feb 1961. The Miracles' "Shop Around" (Tamla #54034) reaches number one, remaining three weeks. The song was the first major hit for Motown.

26 Aug 1961. The Mar-Keys' "Last Night" becomes the first Stax production to reach number one. Stax — and later in the decade, Fame, the Muscle Shoals, Alabama, studio headed by Rick Hall — offered a rawer, more spontaneous, gospel-influenced alternative to the Motown sound. The Mar-Keys (whose rhythm section also recorded as Booker T. & the M.G.'s) backed most of the label's artists, including Sam and Dave, Otis Redding, Eddie Floyd, Rufus Thomas, Carla Thomas, and Johnnie Taylor.

26 May 1962. Ray Charles's country-influenced "I Can't Stop Loving You" (ABC #10330) begins the first of its 11 consecutive weeks at the top of the R&B charts. The song typified — in dramatic fashion due to its incredible commercial success — the inclination of talented Black performers to favor sweet and sentimental sounds over personal expression in order to achieve mainstream pop impact. Similar career moves were taken by Sam Cooke, Jackie Wilson, Brook Benton, and others. Yet Black singers such as Wilson Pickett and Aretha Franklin were able to attain pop music success in the late 1960s while remaining true to their cultural roots.

12 Oct 1963. "Cry Baby," by Garnett Mimms & the Enchanters (United Artists #629) begins the first of two weeks at number one. "Cry Baby" was among the earliest — and certainly the most successful commercially — of the gospel-styled songs to have an accompaniment that was not slightly adapted from some other genre of music. Unlike most records, with their slow, gentle, lilting, "Cry Baby" offered an uncompromising expression of ecstasy. On other "gospel revivalist" records, the strong rhythms meant that the impact was absorbed physically by the listener and not on a purely emotional level as was the case with "Cry Baby." In short, the song possessed all the prime ingredients characterizing the classic soul genre.

11 Mar 1967. Dyke & the Blazers' "Funky Broadway" (Original Sound #64) enters the R&B charts, remaining there 27 weeks, peaking at number 11. The word "funk" didn't become part of the legitimate radio jargon until the song had "bubbled under" for so long that disc jockeys were forced to play it and say the word. Though nobody knows who coined the term, "funk" simply was not a word used in polite society. But "Funky Broadway" changed all that.

11 Mar 1967. Aretha Franklin's "I Never Loved a Man" (Atlantic #2386) reaches number one, remaining there for seven weeks. In a kind of soul-waltz time, the record built up from a quiet but dramatic opening organ figure into a hammering, screaming, but always firmly controlled yell of delight, as a brilliantly organized band fed more and more to support the singer's emotion. It was the first of Franklin's 18 number one songs on the R&B charts, more than any other artist between 1960 and 1985. Noteworthy commercial success combined with impeccable artistry earned her the sobriquet, "Queen of Soul."

10 Feb 1968. Sly & the Family Stone's first hit, "Dance to the Music" (Epic #10256) enters the R&B charts, eventually peaking at number three. The song shook off the assumptions about the separate roles of voices and instruments as sources of rhythm and harmony, alternating them and blending them yet never losing either melody or dance beat. The adventurousness of the sound was recognized by the white audience who had tended to deride soul arrangements as being overly simple. As Sly began employing increasingly personal lyrics, the social consciousness school of funk was created.

12 Oct 1968. "Say It Loud, I'm Black and I'm Proud" (King #12715) by "Soul Brother Number One," James Brown, tops the charts. "Say It Loud" was merely the most successful of the wave of political slogan songs exploiting Black pride.

23 Aug 1969. *Billboard* declares rhythm and blues officially dead by renaming its list of best-selling records for that market "Best-Selling Soul Singles." Ironically, there was every sign that the new euphemism for "Black" — which had been widely used during most of the 1960s — would soon be musically outdated, and its successor defied prophecy.

9 June 1973. Manu Dibango's "Soul Makossa" (Atlantic #2971) enters the R&B charts, eventually reaching the Top 20. Recorded by an African in Paris, "Soul Makossa" was imported into the U.S. when its

enormous popularity in discos made domestic release seem like a good business proposition. Thus, the first disco pop hit was born.

1977. Frankie Knuckles becomes a DJ at the Chicago-based club, the Warehouse. His innovations — e.g., incorporating a reel-to-reel tape machine into turntable grooves which mixed soul recordings with Donna Summer tracks and other contemporary disco fare.

29 July 1978. "Soft and Wet," the first hit by Prince (Warner #8619), enters the charts, eventually reaching number nine. Prince's combination of street-level hipness and musical inventiveness propelled him to the vanguard of Black music in the 1980s. His seemingly boundless energy spawned a new school of stars, including the Time, Vanity, Andre Cymone, and Sheila E.

10 Apr 1982. *Cash Box* first employs the term "Black contemporary" in the heading of its Black charts (i.e., "Top 100 Black Contemporary Singles"). For a time, the term gained nearly universal acceptance both inside and outside the music industry. Black contemporary encompassed the full range of Black pop music (dance music, easy listening, jazz fusions, etc.) as well as white releases that are expected to appeal to the Black audience. However, the rise of postpunk styles espounding a more color-blind ethic (e.g., House, electronica) helped bring rhythm and blues back into vogue as a term referring to classic Black pop music.

1986. Derrick May's "Strings of Life" (Kool Kat 12 under his moniker Rhythm Is Rhythm) becomes a huge British dance club hit. Featuring frenetic keyboard patterns, sampled orchestral strings, and a pounding drum track, it provided a launching pad for the spread of techno far beyond its Detroit roots.

1995. Tricky releases the album, *Maxinquaye*, a posthouse, trip-hop blend of rap, sampling, and rock that lays the groundwork for the rise of energetic club-based rhythms of drum and bass. [Albert & Hoffmann 1986; Gillett 1970; Hirshey 1994; Miller 1980; Whitburn 1988.]

See also **Blues Recordings; Race Records; Soul Music Recordings**

FRANK HOFFMANN

RIALTO (LABEL) (I)

An American record produced by the U.S. Record Manufacturing Corp. of Long Island City, New York, in 1921. It shared material with another record by the same firm, Hits. There was no connection with the later label of the same name. Only a few issues are known. [Kendziora 1962/11; Rust 1978.]

RIALTO (LABEL) (II)

A Chicago record sold by the Rialto Music House in 1924. Possibly the label and the store were named for the Rialto vaudeville-burlesque theater across the street. The records were made by Orlando Marsh, but whether the process was electric (like other Marsh issues of the time) or acoustic is not known. Rust has found only one specimen: "London Blues" played by Jelly Roll Morton, with a song by Frank Collins on the flip side; it has no number. The music store remained in business through at least 1929–1930. [Rust 1978.]

RICE, CHESTER W.

Rice was a pioneering researcher who, along with Edward Kellog, came up with the basic design of the modern, direct-radiator loudspeaker, which had a small coil-driven mass-controlled diaphragm in a baffle with a broad mid-frequency range and relatively uniform response. (Edward Wente at Bell Labs had independently discovered this same principle, and filed a patent for it in 1925, with the patent granted in 1931.) Kellog and Rice worked for GE, and together they published their "hornless loudspeaker" design in 1925, after five years of work. The Rice-Kellog paper also published an amplifier design that was important in boosting the power transmitted to loudspeakers. In 1926 RCA used this design in the Radiola line of AC-powered radios.

See also **Loudspeaker**

HOWARD FERSTLER

RICE, GLADYS (CA. 1890–17 SEP 1983)

American popular singer, born in Philadelphia. She sometimes used the names Rachel Grant and Bettina Bergere. Rice began to record for Edison in 1916, in a duet with Irving Kaufman, "My Hula Maid" (Edison Diamond Disc #50297; Blue Amberol cylinder #2759). Duets with various artists were a specialty; Billy Murray was her main partner after 1917. Her last Edison disc — of 59 in all — was a duet with Murray made in late summer 1929, a month before Edison ceased all recording activity ("That's You Baby"; #52642). She was also a member of the Homestead Trio from 1917–1921, and of the Moonlight Trio. Rice sang popular and comic songs for most of the labels into the early 1930s. [Wile 1976.]

RICH, CHARLIE (14 DEC 1932–25 JULY 1995)

Born in Colt, Arkansas, Rich was the son of a heavy drinking dirt farmer and a fundamentalist mother. He joined the Air Force and was stationed in Oklahoma, where he formed his first semiprofessional combo, the Velvetones, a jazz/blues combo in the Stan Kenton mold. Future wife Margaret was the group's lead vocalist. After leaving the Air Force, Rich returned to West Memphis. While performing with Bill Justis's band there, Rich was invited to audition with legendary producer Sam Phillips at Sun Records. Phillips encouraged him to listen to Jerry Lee Lewis's recordings and come back when he had absorbed Lewis's frantic keyboard pounding. Rich sessioned on many late 1950s' Sun recordings, and scored his first hit with 1959's "Lonely Weekends" (Phillips International #3552), a song very much influenced by the sound of the early Elvis Presley.

Rich struggled in the early to mid-1960s to find his sound, moving from the boogie-woogie influenced "Big Boss Man" of 1963 to the country novelty of "Mohair Sam," even recording a straight country/honky-tonk LP for Memphis's Hi Records, a label later better known for its soul acts. In 1968, he was signed by Epic Records' producer Billy Sherrill. It took five years for Rich and Sherrill to hit a winning formula, but they hit it big in 1973-1975 with songs like "Behind Closed Doors," "The Most Beautiful Girl in the World," "A Very Special Love Song," and "Every Time You Touch Me." However, after the mid-1970s, Rich's success faded; although he continued to have hits, most notably 1979's "I'll Wake You Up When I Get Home," his days of chart-topping success were over. Rich died from a blood clot in the lung at the age of 62.

CARL BENSON

RICH, DAVID (7 JAN 1958–)

A design engineer, Rich has B.S., M.S., and Ph.D. degrees in electrical engineering, with the latter earned from the Polytechnic University of New York, in 1991. Between 1981 and 1992, he worked for General Instruments and TLSI, moving on to Bell Labs from 1992 until 2001. In 1987, he cofounded Precision Audio, where he helped design an analog circuit to solve problems caused by slow-settling time in the current-to-voltage converter of early CD players. In 1995 he codiscovered tonal behavior in commercial delta-sigma analog-to-digital, and digital-to-analog converters, and demonstrated that the problem could be eliminated with proper architectural choices and appropriate levels of dither. As technical editor for *The Audio Critic* (1989–), he analyzed a number of amplifiers, preamps, tuners, and CD players, and developed a circuit analysis review method capable of demonstrating that topological differences in amplifiers do not correlate with sound quality. In addition to his

Audio Engineering Society (AES) presentations and preprints, Rich has published numerous papers in the Institute of Electrical and Electronic Engineering (IEEE) proceedings and journals. He is a member of the AES and IEEE, serving as a reviewer for the latter organization, and also for National Science Foundation proposals. He currently is associate professor of electrical and computer engineering at Lafayette College, in Pennsylvania.

HOWARD FERSTLER

RICHIE, LIONEL (20 JUNE 1949–)

One of the major forces in Black contemporary music in the 1970s and 1980s, Richie's diversified talents — he was a gifted songwriter and record producer, and played piano and saxophone as well as sang — enabled him to achieve industry success in a number of guises. His ability to appeal to a broad-based audience was a result of an upbringing that included formal training in the classics as well as exposure to the pop, rhythm and blues, and country genres then popular in his native Alabama.

While attending Tuskegee Institute, Richie joined a group that would become known as the Commodores. Signed by Motown in 1974, they negotiated funk and tender ballads with equal verve, releasing a string of hits that stretched well into the 1980s. By 1980 Richie was in great demand outside the group, writing and producing "Lady" (Liberty #1380; 1980; #1 pop six weeks, #1 AC four weeks, #1 c&w) for Kenny Rogers as well as the title song to the film, *Endless Love*. The latter work (Motown #1519; 1981; #1 pop nine weeks, #1 R&B seven weeks, #1 AC three weeks), recorded with Diana Ross, would become Motown's biggest-selling single ever as well as top duet recording of all time. These growing commitments spurred him to go solo. His smooth, easy listening style immediately clicked with "Truly" (Motown #1644; 1982; #1 pop two weeks, #1 AC four weeks), which won a Grammy for Best Pop Male Vocal Performance; the accompanying album, *Lionel Richie* (Motown #6007; 1982; #3) would achieve quadruple platinum sales. The eight singles drawn from it and his second LP, *Can't Slow Down* (Motown #6059; 1983; #1; 8+ million sales), would all reach the Top 10. The latter record also earned two 1984 Grammys, for Album of the Year and Producer of the Year. He would also be named Writer of the Year by the American Society of Composers, Authors and Publishers in both 1984 and 1985. While slow to appear due to Richie's full slate of activities, the third album, *Dancing on the Ceiling* (Motown #6158; 1986; #1), maintained his career momentum, selling more than 4 million copies.

Richie played a key role in the USA for Africa project, sharing writing credits with Michael Jackson and participating in the recording of both the record, "We Are the World" (Columbia #04839; 1985; #1 pop four weeks, #1 AC two weeks, #1 R&B two weeks) and accompanying video release. He would also contribute music to a number of high-profile films such as *White Nights* — most notably "Say You, Say Me" (Motown #1819; 1985; #1 pop four weeks, #1 AC five weeks, #1 R&B two weeks) — and *The Color Purple* (1985). Although perceived as dated — his last Top 10 single came in early 1987 with "Ballerina Girl" (Motown #1873; #7 pop, #1 AC four weeks) — he has continued to issue moderately successful recordings that appeal to mainstream pop, adult contemporary, and rhythm and blues audiences.

RICH-TONE (LABEL)

An American record sold in 1921 and 1922 by the Phonograph Record Exchange of America, Chicago. About 50 releases are known, sold for $0.85 (more costly by $0.10 than the discs of major firms at the time). Material was from Gennett masters, with artists using pseudonyms. [Kendziora 1988/6; Rust 1978.]

RICH-R-TONE RECORDS (LABEL)

Bluegrass, gospel, and country music label active mostly in the late 1940s through the early 1950s. It was established in Johnson City, Tennessee, sometime around 1946 by James Stanton. Most of its recordings were made at local radio stations. Name acts included the Stanley Brothers and Wilma Lee and Stoney Cooper. The Folk Star subsidiary label was used for vanity (performer-paid) releases. Stanton moved to Nashville in 1960, operating a studio for a while, but eventually his business petered out.

RIDDLE, NELSON
(1 JUNE 1921–6 OCT 1985)

Born Nelson Stock Riddle in Oradell, New Jersey, Riddle became one of the best-known arrangers, notably working with Nat "King" Cole, Frank Sinatra and other popular singers in the 1950s and 1960s. He played trombone in area bands in the early 1930s, and then worked as an arranger for various big bands. After serving in the Army, he settled in Southern California, signing on with NBC in the late 1940s. He soon joined the young Capitol label as a house arranger/conductor. He was responsible for the arrangements for Nat "King" Cole's biggest hits from 1955 to 1957. He also crafted the arrangement for Frank Sinatra's famous mid-1950s theme albums, including and *In the Wee Small Hours* (Capitol #581; 1954) and *Songs for Swingin' Lovers* (Capitol #653, 1955). He also arranged Ella Fitzgerald's *Songbook* series of albums for Verve Records. Riddle also led a studio orchestra on record, scoring a #1 pop hit in 1955 with the instrumental "Lisbon Antigua" (Capitol #3287). During the 1960s, Riddle mostly worked in television (notably scoring *Route 66* and *The Untouchables*) and films, but continued to arrange for old friends like Sinatra. In the early 1980s, pop singer Linda Ronstadt hired Riddle to conduct three hugely successful albums of covers of standards, beginning with *What's New?* (Asylum #60260; 1983), for which Nelson won a Best Arranging Grammy. Riddle died in Hollywood.

RIFKIN, JOSHUA (22 APR 1944–)

Born in New York City, Rifkin is a classical musician, scholar, and arranger who won his greatest fame in 1970 when he issued the album, *Piano Rags of Scott Joplin* (Nonesuch #71248). Rifkin studied at Juilliard and then did graduate work at NYU, Princeton, and Gottingen universities. He worked for Elektra Records in the mid-1960s as an arranger, notably on *The Baroque Beatles Book* (Elektra #71420), an album of classical-influenced arrangements of songs by the popular group. He also arranged the string parts for a series of Judy Collins albums, including the hit album *Wildflowers* (Elektra #74012; 1967). In 1970 he issued his first album of Joplin piano rags, which was hugely (and unexpectedly) successful and lead to concert tours and two follow-up albums. Since the mid-1970s, Rifkin has worked primarily as a classical performer.

RIGGS, MICHAEL (1951–)

Michael Riggs was born in Frankfort, Kentucky, and is a graduate of Washington University in St. Louis, where he studied physics and philosophy. He began writing professionally about audio and video in the mid-1970s, at a time when he was editing the Boston Audio Society's monthly newsletter. In 1980 he left *Mini-Micro Systems* (a Boston-based computer magazine) to join the staff of *High Fidelity* magazine in New York as a technical editor, and he served as that journal's chief editor from 1986 until its demise in 1989. Later that year he joined *Stereo Review* (now *Sound & Vision*), where he became executive editor. In 1995 he was appointed editor of the foundering *Audio* magazine, which ceased publication at the beginning of 1999. Currently a technology writer and consultant to the consumer electronics industry, Riggs is a member of the Audio Engineering Society and author of *Understanding Audio and Video* (Pioneer 1989).

HOWARD FERSTLER

RIGHTEOUS BROTHERS

The Righteous Brothers were the best known — and most commercially successful — exponents of blue-eyed soul (i.e., white performers displaying Black gospel/blues/R&B influences in their singing style). However, during their peak period of success, between 1963–1967, they were able to transcend stylistic categorization, appealing to teenage music consumers, an older mainstream pop audience, and Blacks alike. The duo's biggest hits — "You've Lost that Lovin' Feelin'" (Philles #124; 1964; #1), "Unchained Melody" (Philles #127; 1965; #4), and "Soul and Inspiration" (Verve #10383; 1966; #1) — continue to top polls tabulating all-time favorite recordings.

Tenor/lead vocalist Bill Medley and bass/harmony singer Bobby Hatfield — both of whom had sung in rock bands while attending high school in Southern California — met at an area club in 1962. Finding that their voices — and personalities — meshed, they decided to work together. Moonglow Records signed them to a contract shortly thereafter, releasing *Righteous Brothers Right Now!* (Moonglow #1001; 1964; #11), *Some Blue-Eyed Soul* (Moonglow #1002; 1964; #14), *This Is New* (Moonglow #1003; 1965; #39), and *Best of the Righteous Brothers* (Moonglow #1004; 1966; #130). While with Moonglow, the duo's work displayed a loose, funky edge highlighted by the call-and-response vocal interplay between Medley and Hatfield.

One of the leading record producers of the day, Phil Spector, was sufficiently impressed to bring them over to his Philles label. The singles featuring Spector's production work — "You've Lost that Lovin' Feelin'," "Just Once in My Life" (Philles #127; 1965; #9), "Unchained Melody," and "Ebb Tide" (Philles #130; 1965; #5) — instantly elevated the Righteous Brothers to the top of the music business (even their Moonglow albums charted for the first time). Although Spector considered singles to be the most important artform, their albums — *You've Lost that Lovin' Feelin'* (Philles #4007; 1965; #4), *Just Once in My Life* (Philles #4008; 1965; #9), and *Back to Back* (Philles #4009; 1965; #16) — also sold well. "You've Lost that Lovin' Feelin'"veered somewhat from the Righteous Brothers formula in that Hatfield took the lead voice. When Medley questioned Spector's judgment, asking, "What will I be doing?" Phil replied, "You'll be going to the bank!"

Aware of Spector's reputation for valuing the song over the artist, the Righteous Brothers signed with Verve Records. Their first hit for the label, "Soul and Inspiration," revealed a strong Spector influence. However, later album releases — most notably, *Soul & Inspiration* (Verve #5001; 1966; #7), *Go Ahead and Cry* (Verve #5004; 1966; #32), *Sayin' Somethin'* (Verve #5010; 1967; #155), *Souled Out* (Verve #5031;

1967; #198), and the live *One for the Road* (Verve #5058; 1968; #187) — attempted to showcase the duo's dynamic stage presence and affinity for pop standards.

Despite these efforts at creative growth, Medley felt the need to explore his options as a songwriter and solo performer. The decision to terminate the partnership was made public in early 1968, although Hatfield expressed a desire to continue the act with a new partner. When both floundered in their new career paths, they decided to get back together, allowing the official announcement to be made on a February 1974 broadcast of the "Sonny and Cher Comedy Hour." The Righteous Brothers enjoyed another major hit, "Rock and Roll Heaven" (Haven #7002; 1974; #3), but Medley retired for five years following the murder of his wife in 1976.

Medley and Hatfield have performed together intermittently over the years since appearing on an *American Bandstand* anniversary television special in 1981. Medley's top priority, however, continued to be his solo career. He signed with Planet Records in 1982, and would later have a number one hit, "(I've Had) The Time of My Life" (RCA #5224; 1987), a duet with Jennifer Warnes (the song also earned a Grammy for Best Pop Performance by a Duo or Group with Vocal), part of the soundtrack for the hit film *Dirty Dancing*. "Unchained Melody" returned to the charts (#13 pop, #1 AC) in 1990 as a result of its inclusion of the *Ghost* soundtrack. A newly recorded version of the song (Curb #76842; 1990; #19/#4 sales) achieved platinum status. The continued success of various compilations of the classic singles over the years — *Anthology (1962–1974)* (Rhino #71488; 1990) earned a gold record, while *Best of the Righteous Brothers* (Curb #77381; 1990) went platinum — have added further luster to the Righteous Brothers' legacy.

FRANK HOFFMANN

RIGLER AND DEUTSCH INDEX (RDI)

A compilation of information about 78-rpm recordings, the result of a project undertaken by the Associated Audio Archives, of the Association for Recorded Sound Collections, Inc. (ARSC). Planning for the project began in 1974, and work began in 1981 with support from the National Endowment for the Humanities, the Hewlett Foundation, and the Ledler Foundation. By 1984 a set of microfilm photographs and indexes were made available for purchase. Free consultation of the index is possible at the five participating libraries: Library of Congress, Rodgers and Hammerstein Archives of Recorded Sound at the New

York Public Library, Belfer Audio Laboratory and Archive of Syracuse University, the Archive of Recorded Sound of Stanford University, and the Yale Collection of Historical Sound Recordings of Yale University.

The Rigler and Deutsch Index consists of 1,230,000 microfilm photographs, on 946 reels, of the labels of 615,000 78-rpm records belonging to the member libraries. The index is computer accessible by title, composer, performer, label, record number, matrix number, and library. It is available online through the RLIN (Research Libraries Information Network) catalog. [website: www.riln.org.]

RILEY, TEDDY (8 OCT 1967–)

A Harlem-born-and-raised musical prodigy, Riley is a two-time Grammy winner and is renowned as one of the most influential figures in dance music, deserving much of the credit for inventing "Swingbeat" and "New Jack Swing." Indeed, he is probably one of the most successful producers in pop-music history and produced his first hit record at age 17. In 1988 Riley produced his first number one record, Keith Sweat's *I Want Her*. That same year, he produced the multiplatinum *Don't Be Cruel* for Bobby Brown, pioneering the New Jack Swing movement that would dominate the R&B scene for the next several years. In 1990, he founded his Future Records recording studios in Virginia Beach, Virginia. After establishing himself as one of the premier producers in urban music, Riley's career as an artist and songwriter expanded with his own hit-making groups Guy, Wreckx-N-Effect, and Blackstreet. As a writer, producer, arranger, and mixer, as well as a musician and vocalist, he has directly contributed to the success of many superstar artists, such as Mary J. Blige, Keith Sweat, the Winans, Hi-Five, Janet Jackson, Big Daddy Kane, Boy George, Bobby Brown, DJ Jazzy Jeff & the Fresh Prince, Father, Taral Hicks, and New Edition. Among his multiple additional credits in the 1990s were hits from Aretha Franklin, Whitney Houston, Michael Jackson, James Ingram, Tom Jones, Mariah Carey, 'N Sync, the Rolling Stones, Heavy D and the Boys, and Patti LaBelle.

FRANK HOFFMANN

RIMES, LEANN (28 AUG 1982–)

Country singer LeAnn Rimes, whose powerful, evocative vocals invited comparisons with Patsy Cline in the mid-1990s, has gone on to set her own benchmarks for pop crossover success. Still a teenager at the outset of the 21st century, she is on course to become one of the most successful recording artists in country music history.

Born in Jackson, Mississippi, but raised in Garland, Texas, Rimes cut her teeth singing in local talent contests. By age 11 she had recorded an album for the indie label, NorVaJak. She then caught the attention of Dallas disc jockey and record promoter Bill Mack, who took control of her career. On the strength of an active performing schedule and television appearances across Texas, Mack secured a record contract with the Curb label. The press release for her first single, "Blue" (Curb #76959; 1996; #26 pop), claimed that Mack had written it in the early 1960s for Cline; after the singer died in a plane crash, he'd waited 30 years to find the right vehicle for the song. (Although both Mack and Kenny Roberts had recorded "Blue" for Starday in the 1960s, and a rendition by Kathryn Pitt had been released in her native Australia in 1993, widespread dissemination of the story by music journalists fed the myth that Rimes was the anointed successor to Cline's tradition.)

"Blue" entered the *Billboard Hot 100* at number three, selling more than 123,000 copies in its first week of release, the highest amount ever measured up to that point by the SoundScan tracking system. Rimes became the youngest singer in the history of the Country Music Association awards to receive a nomination, both for the Horizon Award and Best Country Singer. She also won the 1996 Grammy for Best New Artist.

Since this auspicious beginning, her albums — *Blue* (Curb #77821; 1996), *Unchained Melody: The Early Years* (Curb #77856; 1997), *You Light Up My Life: Inspirational Songs* (Curb #77885; 1997), *Sittin' on Top of the World* (Curb #77901; 1998), *LeAnn Rimes* (Curb #77947; 1999) *I Need You* (Curb #77979; 2001) and *Twisted Angel* (Curb #78747; 2002) — and singles — "How Do I Live" (Curb #73022; 1997; #1 country, #2 pop), "You Light Up My Life" (Curb #73027; 1997; #34). "Looking Through Your Eyes" (Curb #73055; 1998; #18 pop), "Written in the Stars" (with Elton John; Rocket/Curb #566918; 1999; #29 pop), and "Big Deal" (Curb #73086; 1999; #23 pop) — have sold well on both the pop and country charts. "How Do I Live" was intended as the theme for the film *Con-Air*, but the producers ultimately selected Trisha Yearwood's version of the song, considering it a better fit. Nevertheless, the Rimes rendition held the record for *Billboard* pop chart longevity as of early 2002; 69 weeks in 1997–1998. In addition to its strong performance on the pop and country charts, it topped both the adult contemporary and dance charts, selling more than 3 million copies. Only time will tell, however, whether Rimes goes on to even greater success as an adult as did Stevie Wonder, or ultimately flames out like another youthful star, Brenda Lee.

FRANK HOFFMANN

RIMINI, GIACOMO
(22 MAR 1888–6 MAR 1952)

Italian baritone, born in Verona. He sang in various Italian houses, then in Rome as Scarpia and Germont in 1915. He won acclaim for his lively Falstaff, under Arturo Toscanini in Milan; and Falstaff became his signature role, sung throughout Europe and the U.S., as well as South America.

Rimini made four Pathé discs in 1917, beginning with "Invocazione" from *Faust*/"Brindisi" from *Otello* (#60052). He worked for Vocalion in 1918–1924, then for Brunswick to 1935. Columbia recorded him in a complete *Falstaff* album in 1932 (#10564/576, also released on LP in 1955).

RIOT GRRRL MOVEMENT

The riot grrrl revolution grew out of a loose network of female rock musicians based in Olympia, Washington and Washington, D.C. The latter was established as a leftist punk rock stronghold, while the former was the home of Evergreen College (long known for its strong women's studies programs) and K records, sponsor of the 1991 International Pop Underground convention, referred to as "Ground Zero for Revolution Girl Style."

Devoid of any guiding dogma, the movement served a wide range of needs: (1) a conduit for finding sister musicians; (2) a safe space for processing experiences such as rape and abuse; and (3) a forum for responding to society's conservative backlash through guerrilla art and film projects and shared resources (e.g., community meetings and fanzines like *Bikini Kill*, *Fantastic Magazine*, *Girl Germs*, *Jigsaw*, and *Riot Grrrl*).

The underground buzz gradually spread to the mass media; although publications (e.g., *Newsweek*, *USA Today*) misinterpreted its revolutionary leanings, the movement was nurtured by the support of mainstream artists such as Joan Jett and Sonic Youth. By the early 1990s, riot grrrl chapters had sprung up across the U.S. and abroad. Although many members have moved on to other political and social-consciousness movements, the core of the movement remains the raw, punk-oriented sound of bands comprised largely of female members, including Bikini Kill, Babes in Toyland, Fifth Column, Huggy Bear, Lunachicks, Sister George, Slant 6, Sleater-Kinney, and Tribe 8. [O'Dair 1997]

RISHELL PHONOGRAPH CO.

A firm established in 1867 as the Rishell Furniture Co., in Williamsport, Pennsylvania. In 1916 they offered the Rishell line of record players in eight models, all in the upper price range. At about the same time the firm produced records with the Rishell label, using material from Okeh and Imperial-Rex-Empire-Playerphone.

Bikini Kill album cover. Courtesy Frank Hoffmann

Label issued by the Rishell Phonograph Company, c. mid-to-late teens. Courtesy Kurt Nauck/Nauck's Vintage Records

931

As late as April 1924 Rishell was offering talking machines for sale. [Rust 1978.]

FRANK ANDREWS

RITTER, TEX (12 JAN 1907–2 JAN 1974)

American country singer, born in Panola County, Texas. He grew up as a cowboy, then studied law at the University of Texas, and later at Northwestern University near Chicago; but also sang and lectured on the cowboy traditions. He gained popularity in the 1930s in New York, as a stage actor and radio performer, then went to Hollywood to make many western films in the 1940s and 1950s. He was elected to the Country Music Hall of Fame in 1964. He died in Nashville, Tennessee.

After recording for Columbia (one disc in 1931) and Decca (11 issues in 1937–1939), Ritter became a Capitol artist, recording extensively from 1943 until he died. Among his chart singles the most popular was "Hillbilly Heaven" (Capitol #4567; 1961). [Toborg 1970 is a complete discography.]

RIVERS, JOHNNY (7 NOV 1942–)

Johnny Rivers was one of the top-selling pop-rock recording artists of the 1960s. His success owed much to the ability to discern new trends — folk rock, Motown Soul, psychedelia, the blues revival, the singer-songwriter tradition, and the rock 'n' roll revival, among others — and incorporate them into his own style. Many Rivers fans were not aware of the many facets of his talent other than the vocals and guitar work on the records; he was, in fact, a songwriter, record producer, record company executive, and music publisher of note.

A native of New York City born John Ramistella, Rivers moved to Baton Rouge, Louisiana, with his family at age three. Thanks largely to the assistance of disc jockey Alan Freed, he obtained a recording contract with the fabled doo-wop label Gone during a summer trip back to New York. He departed to Nashville after graduating from high school, recording demos while attempting to break into the music industry as a songwriter. After working as a staff writer for the New York–based music publisher Hill & Range, Rivers relocated to Los Angeles to build a performing career.

An acclaimed run as the star attraction at the Whiskey-A-Go-Go led to a contract with Imperial Records. His debut album, *Johnny Rivers Live at the Whiskey a Go Go* (Imperial #12264; 1964; #12) — and the Chuck Berry–penned single, "Memphis" (Imperial #66032; 1964; #2) — made him an overnight star. Rivers's engaging Southern drawl and the crowd noise (enhanced after the fact by his label) endowed his recordings with a sense of live excitement, resulting in

a string of hit singles, including "Mountain of Love" (Imperial #66075; 1964; #9), "Seventh Son" (Imperial #66112; 1965; #7), and "Secret Agent Man" (Imperial #66159; 1966; #3). His albums were equally successful: *Here We a Go Go Again!* (Imperial #12274; 1964; #38), *Johnny Rivers in Action!* (Imperial #12280; 1965; #42), *Meanwhile Back at the Whiskey a Go Go* (Imperial #12284; 1965; #21), *Johnny Rivers Rocks the Folk* (Imperial #12293; 1965; #91), *"… and I know you wanna dance"* (Imperial #12307; 1966; #52).

When his established formula began to wear thin, Rivers abruptly shifted from club and folk-blues–oriented rockers to pop-soul ballads. Singles such as "Poor Side of Town" (Imperial #66205; 1966; #1; cowritten with Lou Adler), "Baby I Need Your Lovin'" (Imperial #66227; 1967; #3), and "The Tracks of My Tears" (Imperial #66244; 1967; #10), followed by the hippie-flavored LP, *Realization* (Imperial #12372; 1968; #5), provided the momentum to keep him on the charts well into the 1970s. By then his greatest success came with laid-back versions of rock 'n' roll–era classics such as "Rockin' Pneumonia–Boogie Woogie Flu" (United Artists #50960; 1972; #6), "Blue Suede Shoes" (United Artists #198; 1973; #38), and "Help Me Rhonda" (Epic #50121; 1975; #22; including vocals by songwriter Brian Wilson). Although his last big hit was "Swayin' to the Music (Slow Dancin')" (Big Tree #16094; 1977; #10), Rivers has continued to record in addition to performing both stateside and abroad.

In 1966 Rivers began leaving his mark on other aspects of the record industry when Imperial permitted him to establish a subsidiary label, Soul City. His efforts to build the company included a pivotal role in the career of the 5th Dimension — providing their name, finding them first-rate material, and producing and playing on their early recordings. By the late 1960s, he also owned a music-publishing firm, Johnny Rivers Music. He would remain active in running these companies into the 21st century.

FRANK HOFFMANN

RIVERSIDE (LABEL)

SEE GRAUER, BILL, JR.

ROACH, MAX (10 JAN 1924–)

Max Roach, born in New Land, North Carolina, is an exceptionally important figure in jazz. While performing with Charlie Parker and Dizzy Gillespie in the 1940s, he helped define the bebop style of drumming. He also had an instrumental role in developing the cool jazz, hard-bop, and free-jazz styles.

Roach increased the rhythmic and textural complexity of jazz drumming and went on to expand the palette of percussion instruments that was heard in jazz. He contributed to Miles Davis's seminal recordings, *Birth of the Cool* (Capitol CDP #7243 4 94550 2 3; 1948–1950). In the mid-1950s, his musical partnership with Clifford Brown led to the release of *Study in Brown* (EmArcy #36037; 1956) and *At Basin Street* (EmArcy #36070; 1956). These two recordings helped to define the sound of hard-bop and featured excellent playing throughout.

On the ground-breaking recordings, *Roach Plus 4 at Newport* (EmArcy #80010; 1958) and *We Insist! Freedom Now Suite* (Candid #9002; 1960), Roach's compositions challenged the strictures of hard bop form and instrumentation. This successful experimentation continued with M'Boom, his ensemble of 10 percussionists founded in 1970 and lasted throughout his career. In 1986 he released *Bright Moments* (Soul Note #1159) that combined a jazz quartet with a string quartet. In the 1990s, Roach performed with symphony orchestras. He remains a powerful force in jazz to this day.

GARTH ALPER

ROBBINS, MARTY
(26 SEP 1925–8 DEC 1982)

Born Martin David Robinson, in Glendale, Arizona, Robbins was both a country and pop star in the late 1950s, but is best remembered for his country recordings. Robbins's family moved to Phoenix when he was

Martin Robbins album. Courtesy Frank Hoffmann

12, where he attended high school and began playing the guitar. After serving in the Navy in World War II, Robbins returned home and began performing locally. By the early 1950s, Marty was hosting a local radio station show, which led to his signing with Columbia Records. Robbins released his first single for Columbia in 1952, and a year later joined the *Grand Ole Opry*, where he remained a member for 29 years until his death.

Robbins's big break came in 1956 with "Singing the Blues" (Columbia #21545; #17 pop, #1 country) followed a year later by the teen-pop classic, "A White Sport Coat (and a Pink Carnation)" (Columbia #40864; #2 pop, #1 country). He continued in this pop-influenced vein through the 1950s, turning out 1958's "Just Married" (Columbia #41143; #26 pop #1 country) and "She Was Only Seventeen" (Columbia 41208; #27 pop).

Robbins's career took a Western swing with his appearance in the 1958 film *Buffalo Gun*. He recorded his classic album of Western story-songs, *Gunfighter Ballads and Trail Songs*, a year later, producing several hits, most notably "El Paso" (Columbia #41511), a song that would become closely associated with him. "El Paso" ran over four minutes, an amazingly long time for a hit single on radio of the day. It topped both country and pop charts, gaining the first Grammy ever given to a country song.

Robbins continued to be a force on the country charts through the 1960s. In 1969 he suffered the first in a series of massive heart attacks. Robbins continued to record and perform through the 1970s and turned out a few further hits, mostly under the hand of seasoned producer Billy Sherrill. In the 1970s, Robbins suffered many injuries pursuing his hobby of stock car racing. In 1981, he suffered a second heart attack, recovering to make a comeback a year later with his last release, "Some Memories Just Won't Die," which proved prophetic in 1982 when Robbins suffered a final major heart attack, dying six days later.

CARL BENSON

ROBE, THE

Released in 1953, *The Robe* had four-track stereo sound and was the first CinemaScope film. It was also the first of 33 stereo films to appear in 1953. However, stereo technology, due to the complexities involved, failed to transform motion picture soundtracks and would not reappear until 1975 with Dolby Surround Sound. *The Robe* used directional sound, footsteps of Roman legions marching from right to left, thunder and wind and rain at the crucifixion scene. For the first time off-screen voices were actually heard off-screen. With later stereo releases, only Fox and Todd-AO would record dialogue with directional sound. All other studios provided some music in stereo for magnetic soundtracks, but recorded voices and sound effects in mono.

HOWARD FERSTLER

ROBERTS, ROBERT
(27 APR 1879–21 JAN 1930)

American baritone and comedian, known as Bob Roberts or Ragtime Robert, born in Cincinnati, Ohio. He was a popular recording artist in the early years of the century, beginning with Columbia in 1902 with a hit rendition of "Ain't Dat a Shame?" He was successful also with "Woodchuck Song" on both Victor and Edison (1904). For Edison he made about 60 cylinders from 1904 to 1908. Roberts's greatest hit was "He Walked Right In, Turned Around and Walked Right Out Again," made for Victor in 1906. "Ragtime Cowboy Joe" (#17090; 1912) was one of two items still in the Victor catalog in 1917. Roberts dropped out of sight thereafter. He died in Cincinnati. [Walsh 1944/4.]

ROBESON, PAUL
(9 APR 1898–23 JAN 1976)

American bass singer, born in Princeton, New Jersey. He took a law degree from Columbia University in 1923, then turned to acting, on New York and London stages. He gave a song recital, of spirituals, in New York in 1925, then toured Europe as a singer. His acting career did not cease; he played Othello in London in 1930, for example. But neither the vocal nor dramatic paths were fully developed, because his Marxist politics — openly expressed — led to resistance in America and Western Europe during a period of communism phobia. He died in Philadelphia.

Robeson recorded in 1920 for Black Swan, two sides as a member of the Four Harmony Kings (#2016). Then he became a Victor/HMV artist, making remarkable discs of traditional and spiritual melodies. "Water Boy" (Victor #19824), "Swing Low, Sweet Chariot" (Victor #20068), and "Sometimes I Feel Like a Motherless Child" (HMV #B8604) exemplify his art. His "Ol Man River" from *Show Boat* remains definitive; it was coupled on Victor (#B8497) with a charming duet, "Ah Still Suits Me" — with Elizabeth Welch — from the same show, but often cut. His Stephen Foster songs are also exemplary, but he lacked the style for some of the pop/swing numbers he tried now and then. *Ballad for Americans* was a popular Victor album in 1940 (#P20), many times reissued. Columbia made a number of Robeson recordings too, notably his dramatic lead in *Othello* (complete set, #153) and the complete music to *Show Boat* (#C-55, reissue of Brunswick's 1932 cast

recording). After being blacklisted in the 1950s, Robeson turned to recording for the small folk label, Vanguard. Robeson did not record grand opera material.

CD reissues of Robeson's recordings include Pearl (#9356), a selection of his recordings from the 1920s and 1930s. EMI material from the 1930s has been reissued on a variety of labels, including various European affiliates of EMI and ASV/Living Era. *Songs of Free Man* (Sony #63233) collects recital material from the 1940s originally issued on 78 albums by Columbia and long unavailable. *Ballad for Americans* (Vanguard #117) includes a reissue of his legendary 1939 recording of the title track (originally issued by RCA Victor) and later 1950s-era recordings made for Vanguard.

ROBINSON, SMOKEY (19 FEB 1940–)

Born William Robinson in Detroit, Robinson was one of the creators of the Motown sound, thanks to his role as songwriter, producer, and performer for the label from its earliest days. He began performing with his vocal group, the Miracles, while still in high school in 1955; two years later, he met local boxing promoter and would-be songwriter Berry Gordy, who began producing Robinson's group. Gordy signed them to his new Motown label, and had Robinson oversee sessions for other Motown acts, including initially Mary Wells, scoring major hits like "My Guy"(Motown 1056; 1964; #1 pop and R&B) which Robinson both wrote and produced. In 1963, he began working with another Motown group, the Temptations, crafting their major hits between 1964–1965, including "The Way You Do the Things You Do" (Gordy 7028; 1964; #11 pop), "My Girl" (Gordy 7038; 1965, #1 pop and R&B), and "Get Ready" (Gordy 7049; 1966; #1 R&B, #29 pop). He also worked with Marvin Gaye on his early recordings.

At the same time, Robinson was a major hitmaker as lead singer, songwriter, and producer for the Miracles. The group had a string of hits, beginning with their break-through smash, "Shop Around" (Tamla #54034; 1960–1961; #2 pop and #1 R&B) and continuing through 1962's "You Really Got a Hold on Me" (Tamla #54073; #8 pop, #1 R&B), "Tracks of My Tears" (Tamla 54118; 1965; #16 pop), and "Tears of a Clown" (Tamla #54199, recorded 1967; released as single 1970; #1 pop, #1 R&B). Robinson's falsetto lead singing and his smooth delivery became a hallmark of the group's hit, and established the soft-soul/R&B ballad style that was widely imitated by other performers, notably Lionel Ritchie.

In 1971 Robinson announced he would be leaving the Miracles and, a year later, began a solo career. He continued to work for Motown, while his career had its ups and downs. Late career success included his 1981's "Being With You" (Tamla 54321; #2 pop, #1

Smokey Robinson and the Miracles album. Courtesy Frank Hoffmann

R&B) and 1987's "One Heartbeat" (Motown #1897; #10 pop). He published his autobiography in 1988, the same year he was inducted into the Rock and Roll Hall of Fame. He won a Grammy Living Legends award in 1990 and a Lifetime Achievement award in 1999.

CARL BENSON

ROBINSON, SYLVIA (6 MAR 1936–)

Born in New York City, Sylvia Robinson (maiden name Vanderpool) has left an indelible mark on the record industry in a variety of roles. In 1954 she teamed with session guitarist Mickey Baker to form the duo Mickey and Sylvia; their single, "Love Is Strange" (Groove #0175; 1956; #2 R&B, #11 pop) remains an early rock 'n' roll classic.

She married Joe Robinson in 1956; they would found a series of rhythm and blues labels, including All Platinum, Strong, Turbo, and Vibration. After splitting with Baker, she worked as a producer — her credits included Ike and Tina Turner's "It's Gonna Work Out Fine" (Sue #749; 1961; #14), the Moments' "Love on a Two-Way Street" (Stang #5012; 1970; #3), and Shirley and Company's "Shame, Shame, Shame" (Vibration #532; 1975; 12) — and as a session musician/songwriter. She continued to record intermittently as a solo artist, her greatest success coming with "Pillow Talk" (Vibration #521; 1973; #3).

With All Platinum (soon to be reorganized as Sugar Hill) involved in Chapter 11 proceedings, Robinson was introduced to the hip-hop scene by son Joey, Jr. She formed a studio group, the Sugarhill Gang, whose first release, "Rapper's Delight" (Sugar Hill #542; 1979; #4 R&B, #36 pop), became the first mainstream rap hit. Despite efforts to add legitimate hip-hop performers to its roster — most notably, Grandmaster Flash and Funky Four +1 — Sugar Hill Records was unable to keep pace with Tommy Boy, Def Jam, Profile, and other street-smart labels, going out of business in 1985.

FRANK HOFFMANN

ROBISON, CARSON J.
(4 AUG 1890–24 MAR 1957)

American country singer, guitarist, whistler, and composer, born in Chetopa, Kansas. He was singing professionally at age 15, and was an early radio performer (WDAF, Kansas City, 1922). He went to New York in 1924 and was signed by Victor. He specialized in duets, with either Wendell Hall or Vernon Dalhart as partners. "Song Birds of Georgia" was his first duet release, with Hall (Victor #19338; 1924). In 1926–1928 he also recorded Edison Diamond Discs, including four with Dalhart. Robison was a valuable

Sheet music cover for "The Mississippi Flood" showing both Carson J. Robison and Vernon Dalhart, and advertising their recordings of the song. Courtesy David A. Jasen

935

studio musician for Victor, contributing his guitar accompaniments and whistling obbligatos to the songs of artists like Gene Austin, Frank Crumit, Aileen Stanley, and the Revelers. He backed up Dalhart on the great hit record of the "Prisoner's Song" and "Wreck of the Old '97" in 1924.

In 1928 Robison broke off his association with Dalhart and formed the Carson Robison Trio; his partners were Frank Luther (recording as Bud Billings) and Phil Crow. They made a number of best sellers, notably "When the Bloom Is on the Sage" (Victor #V-40282; 1930). In 1932 and in 1939 he toured U.K. as Carson Robison and His Pioneers, and recorded there for many labels. He also broadcast from Radio Luxembourg, as Carson Robison and his Oxydol Pioneers.

As a composer, Robison wrote more than 300 songs. Among them were specimens of the popular genre, disaster chronicles. During World War II he contributed topical songs. A later group of his was the Pleasant Valley Boys, recorded on MGM. His Old Timers recorded for Columbia. Robison died in Poughkeepsie, New York. His 1928 through the early 1930s Victor recordings are anthologized on *Home, Sweet Home on the Prairie* (ASV/Living Era #5187), while *A Real Hillbilly Legend* (Cattle #265) gives a career overview based on originals from 1928–1951. [Morritt 1979.]

ROBISON, FABOR
(3 NOV 1911–SEP 1986)

Born in Beebe, Arkansas, Fabor Robison went to Hollywood after World War II. He signed rube comedian Carrot Top Anderson as a managerial client, then discovered Johnny Horton. Robison started Abbott Records in 1951 in partnership with drugstore owner Sid Abbott, and, in October 1953, started another label, Fabor Records, on his own. Among those discovered by Robison for Abbott and Fabor were Jim Reeves, the Browns, Floyd Cramer, the DeCastro Sisters, and, of course, Johnny Horton. In 1958, Robison launched a rock 'n' roll label, Radio Records, but sold his labels the following year to Jamie-Guyden Records. He relaunched Fabor Records in 1962, reissuing his 1957 recording of Ned Miller's "From a Jack to a King," which became a sizable hit. Robison lived in Brazil for a while and dabbled in the music business again on his return to the U.S. He died in Arkansas.

COLIN ESCOTT

ROBYN, WILLIAM (1894–12 APR 1996)

Latvian/American tenor. He recorded more than 300 sides for Victor, Columbia, Cameo, and around 50 other labels between 1919 and 1931. His repertoire of popular and ethnic songs was in great demand on the "dime store labels." Robyn had more than 50 noms du disque. On stage and radio he appeared as Wee Willie Robyn, a member of *Roxy's Gang* — one of the most successful variety shows of the period. Later he became a cantor. He died in Englewood, New Jersey.

ROCKFORD CORP.

Begun in 1970, by Jim Fosgate, as Fosgate Electronics, and now headquartered in Tempe, Arizona, as the much-expanded Rockford Corp., the company designs, manufactures, and distributes systems for the automotive, professional, and home-theater audio markets. Rockford's automotive-audio products are marketed under the Rockford Fosgate, Audio Innovations, and Lightning Audio brand names, while its professional and home-theater equipment is marketed under the Fosgate Audionics (where Jim Fosgate still does his design research), MB Quart, and Hafler brand names. As of 2001, the company was the number one producer of automotive audio amplifiers and the number four producer of car-audio speakers. Hafler amplifiers and speaker systems are used in a large number of recording studios around the country.

HOWARD FERSTLER

ROCK MUSIC RECORDINGS

If one had to pick the recording session at which rock 'n' roll was born, it would be the date of 12 Apr 1954, at Pythia Temple on Manhattan's West Side at which Bill Haley and the Comets cut "Rock Around the Clock." (Shaw #1974). Yet rock 'n' roll songs existed before Haley's disc (Decca #29124) topped the charts in 1955. Some historians have singled out the Crows, whose uptempo rhythm and blues recording, "Gee" (Rama #5) reached number 14 on the pop charts in early 1954. As early as 1951 Ike Turner (credited to his sideman Jackie Brenston for contractual reasons) had a number one R&B hit with "Rocket 88" (Chess #1458), which featured a wild saxophone solo, a boogie-woogie beat carried by an overamplified electric guitar, and lyrics celebrating the joys of the open road. Haley himself "covered" the song and by 1952 was recording full-fledged rock material like "Rock the Joint" (Essex #303). Still, the fact remains that these and other R&B prototypes appear in retrospect as oddities that were briefly popular and then disappeared. "Rock Around the Clock," in contrast to these hits, inspired a movement. (The fact that the song was featured in a popular movie was no small factor; *Blackboard Jungle* caused riots among youth worldwide, and its title song

Jerry Lee Lewis reissue album. Courtesy Frank Hoffmann

inspired countless imitations.) But Haley was a temporary phenomenon; he accumulated only three Top 10 hits during his long career. Not until the rise of Elvis Presley to superstar status, beginning with television appearances in 1956, was the commercial preeminence of rock 'n' roll was ensured.

The revolutionary nature of Presley's career cannot be fully appreciated without consideration of the countless disciples his success engendered. Artists like Jerry Lee Lewis, Buddy Holly, Eddie Cochran, Rick Nelson, Conway Twitty, Gene Vincent, Jack Scott, Roy Orbison, Johnny Cash, Frankie Avalon, Bobby Rydell, Fabian, Bobby Darin, and the Everly Brothers affected the structure of the American record industry. A&R men who had dominated the first half of the 20th century gave way to freelance songwriters who were close to their audience both in age and outlook. Often the singers themselves wrote and produced their own songs. Despite the resistance of the older record labels (whose control of the industry had been broken by the independent companies recording rock). The American Society of Composers, Authors, and Publishers (whose music sales were being eroded by Broadcast Music Inc.'s virtual monopoly of country and western, R&B, and rock 'n' roll material), and various conservative groups, the rock genre emerged intact.

Rock styles and developments are listed below, with the leading figures associated with them.

Gestation Period (pre-1956) — Drifters; Fats Domino; Hank Williams; Bill Haley and His Comets

The Beat Era (1956–1958) — Chuck Berry; Buddy Holly
Rockabilly (1954–1958) — Elvis Presley; Carl Perkins
Doo-Wop (1954–1957)/Neo-Doo-Wop (1958–1965) — Coasters; Penguins/Diamonds; Dion and the Belmonts
Brill Building Era (1959–1965)
Teen Idols/American Bandstand Phenomenon (1958–1963) — Frankie Avalon; Fabian; Rick Nelson
Dance Crazes (1960–1965) — Chubby Checker; Dee Dee Sharp
Instrumentals — Duane Eddy; the Ventures
Novelty Songs — Chipmunks; Ray Stevens
Payola Scandal — Dick Clark; Alan Freed
Commercial Folk (1958–1963) — Kingston Trio; Peter, Paul, and Mary
Calypso (1957–1958) — Harry Belafonte
Hootenanny (1963) — Rooftop Singers
Spector Sound (1958–1966) — Ronettes; Righteous Brothers; Crystals
Girl Groups — Shirelles; Chiffons
The British Invasion (1964–)
British Scene prior to 1964 — Cliff Richard; Shadows
First Wave (1964–1965) — Beatles; Dave Clark Five; Rolling Stones
Second Wave (1966–1970) — Bee Gees; Cream
Third Wave (1971–1975) — Elton John; 10cc
Commonwealth Contributions — Easybeats; Guess Who
American Renaissance (1965–1966)
California Sound
Surf Sound (1962–1964) — Beach Boys; Jan & Dean
Car Songs — Rip Chords; Ronnie & the Daytonas
Folk Rock (1965–1966) — Byrds; Turtles
Protest Movement — Bob Dylan; Phil Ochs
Urban Folk (1970s–) — Tracy Chapman; Washington Squares
Soul Music (early 1960s–1975)
Chicago Sound (1958–) — Jerry Butler; Impressions
Motown Sound (1960–) — Supremes; Temptations; Four Tops
Memphis Sound (1961–) — Booker T. & The MG's; Sam & Dave; Otis Redding
Muscle Shoals Sound (1966–) — Percy Sledge; Aretha Franklin
Philadelphia Sound (1968–) — O'Jays; Stylistics; Spinners
Blue-Eyed Soul — Rascals; Hall & Oates
Era of Specializaton
Other Regional Styles

Louisiana

New Orleans Sound (1954–) — Huey "Piano" Smith; Lee Dorsey

Cajun Rock — Doug Kershaw

Zydeco — Clifton Chenier

Tex-Mex (1956–) — Buddy Knox; Sir Douglas Quintet

Detroit Sound (1966–) — Mitch Ryder & the Detroit Wheels; MC5

San Francisco Sound (1966–) — Jefferson Airplane; Grateful Dead

Bosstown Sound (1967–1969) — Beacon Street Union; Earth Opera

Sounds of the South/Southern Rock (1970–) — Allman Brothers Band; Lynyrd Skynyrd; Marshall Tucker Band; Wet Willie

Ska (1964–)/Rock Steady (1966–)/Reggae (1970–)/Dub (1970s–) — Millie Small/Desmond Dekker/Bob Marley and the Wailers/Yellowman

Salsa/Merengue — Ray Barretto

Junkanoo — KC & the Sunshine Band

Hybrid Children of Rock

Punk Rock/Garage Rock (1966–1967) — Seeds; Standells; Barbarians

Acid Rock/Psychedelia (1966–1968) — Doors; Iron Butterfly; Jimi Hendrix

Classical Rock/Symphonic Rock (1967–) — Moody Blues; Electric Light Orchestra; Emerson, Lake and Palmer

Progressive Rock (1967–) — Pink Floyd; Traffic

Latin Rock (1969–) — Santana; Malo

Big Band Rock (1969–) — Blood, Sweat & Tears; Chicago

Heavy Metal (1969–) — Black Sabbath; Led Zeppelin; Blue Oyster Cult; UFO; Iron Maiden; Judas Priest

Pop Metal (late 1970s–) — Def Leppard

"Hair Bands" Movement (early 1980s–) — Motley Crue; Poison

Speed Metal (1982–) — Metallica; Megadeth

Grindcore (late 1980s–) — Godflesh; D.R.I.

Nu Metal (late 1990s–) — Queens of the Stone Age

Jazz-Rock (1970–) — Mahavishnu Orchestra; Weather Report

Pub Rock (1971–1975) — Graham Parker & the Rumour

Glitter Rock/Glam Rock (1972–1975) — Alice Cooper; Suzi Quatro

Afro-Rock (1972–) — Osibisa; Fela

Euro-Pop/Euro-Rock (1973–) — Abba/Focus; Golden Earring

Christian Rock/Christian Contemporary (late 1980s and early 1990s — Stryper; DC Talk/Amy Grant

Bubblegum (1967–) — Tommy James & the Shondells; Archies; Ohio Express; Bobby

Heavy Metal band Blue Oyster Cult album. Courtesy Frank Hoffmann

Sherman; David Cassidy/Partridge Family; Shaun Cassidy

Album-Oriented Rock (Radio) (1967–) — Aerosmith; Doobie Brothers

Contemporary Hits Radio (early 1980s–) — Madonna; Mariah Carey

Nostalgia (1963–)

Oldies But Goodies (1963–) — generally covers 1955–1974 hit singles

Rock and Roll Revival (1969–1974) — Sha Na Na; Flash Cadillac & the Continental Kids; Reunion

Blues Revival (1965–) — Paul Butterfield Blues Band; Blues Project

Rhythm and Blues Revival (1968–) — Creedence Clearwater Revival; J. Geils Band; Steve Miller Band

English R&B Revival (1960–) — Joe Cocker; Dr. Feelgood; Savoy Brown

Neo-Rockabilly (1980–1983) — Stray Cats; Cramps

Middle-of-the-Road (MOR)

Soft Rock (1966–1970) — The Mamas and the Papas; 5th Dimension

Pop-Rock (1971–1979) — Helen Reddy; Olivia Newton-John

Adult Contemporary (early 1980s–) — Lionel Richie; Laura Branigan; Celine Dion; Michael Bolton

Country Rock/Country Crossover Hits/Country Pop (1968–) — Eagles; Poco; Flying Burrito Brothers/Kenny Rogers; Eddie Rabbitt/Dixie Chicks

Fela's *Beasts of No Nation* album, an example of Afro-Rock. Courtesy Frank Hoffmann

Singer/Songwriter Tradition (1970–) — James Taylor; Carole King; Randy Newman; Cat Stevens

New Age (1973–) — Mike Oldfield; Enya; Yanni

Black Contemporary (1975–)

Funk (1975–) — Ohio Players; Earth, Wind & Fire

Disco (1974–1980) — Donna Summer; Chic; Bee Gees

Dance-Oriented Rock (1981–)

Go-Go (1980s; Washington, D.C. area) — E.U.; Trouble Funk

House (early 1980s) — Art of Noise; 808 State

Acid House (1989–) — Stone Roses; Primal Scream

Ambient House (early 1990s–) — Orb; William Orbit

Techno (late 1980s–) — Orbital; Aphex Twin; Chemical Brothers

Jungle/Drum and Bass (early 1990s–) — Goldie; LTJ Bukem; DJ Rap

Hip-Hop (1970s–) — Kurtis Blow

Garage/Electro (New York area) — Afrika Bambaataa; Grandmaster Flash

Rap (late 1970s–) — Run-D.M.C.; Public Enemy; M.C. Hammer

Gangsta Rap (late 1980s–) — N.W.A.; Ice-T

Crunk (early 2000s–) — Lil' Jon & the East Side Boyz; Chingy

New Wave (1975–)

Punk Revival (1975–1979) — Ramones; Sex Pistols

Power Pop (1973–) — Raspberries; Nick Lowe

Postpunk (1980–)

Hardcore (1980–) — Husker Du; Dead Kennedys

Thrash (early 1980s–) — JFA

DIY (1980s–) — Posies; Replacements

Low-Fi (late 1980s)

Funk-Punk (1978–) — Prince; Rick James

Oi (early 1980s) — Cockney Rejects; Rose Tattoo

Techno-Pop/Synth-Pop (1980–) — Kraftwerk; Human League

New Romantics/Blitz (1982–) — Duran Duran; Thompson Twins

Industrial/Material Music (early 1980s–) — Throbbing Gristle; Cabaret Voltaire; Ministry; Skinny Puppy; Nine Inch Nails

Ska/Bluebeat Revival (1979–) — Specials; Madness; Mighty Mighty Bosstones; Pietasters

Goth Rock (mid-1980s–) — Gene Loves Jezebel; Siouxsie & the Banshees

Neo-Psychedelia (early 1980s–) — Echo & the Bunnymen; the Cult

No Wave (early 1980s–; New York area) — Glenn Branca; Rys Chatham

White Noise (mid-1980s–) — Sonic Youth; Social Distortion; the Offspring

Ambient (1970s–) — Eno; Peter Namlook; Klaus Schulze

Electronica (1980s–) — Mannheim Steamroller

Indie Rock (early 1980s–) — R.E.M.; Beserkley label bands

Alternative Rock/Modern Rock (early 1990s–) — Stone Temple Pilots

The Replacements first album. Courtesy Frank Hoffmann

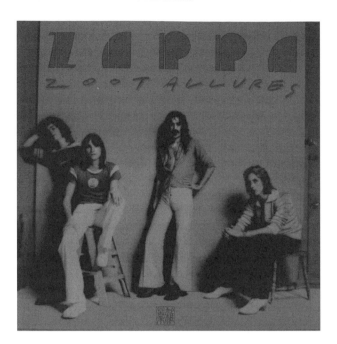

Frank Zappa, king of the avant-rockers. Courtesy Frank Hoffmann

Grunge (1991–) — Mudhoney; Nirvana
Jam Band Rock (early 1990s–) — Phish; Bela Fleck; Dave Matthews Band; Blues Traveler
Avant-Garde (1970s–) — Frank Zappa; Laurie Anderson

Rock 'n' roll has long been associated with adolescence. It has typically reflected themes such as the problems of young love, rebellion against the establishment (in the 1950s and early 1960s this usually meant parental authority), preoccupation with dress styles, and recreational pursuits (e.g., cars, surfing, dancing). However, as the teens who had experienced the early halcyon years of rock 'n' roll matured into adults, the music took on an increasingly sophisticated character. With the appearance of adult themes such as ecology, personal fulfillment, and the inhumanity of war, the essence of rock (the term that had gained widespread use by the mid-1960s) became clearer; that is, it represents a willingness by composers and performers to take chances artistically, and it contains a healthy dash of irreverence for established social mores.

The disinclination of the major record labels in the mid-1970s to sign fresh talent, particularly new wave acts, left the field open for the appearance of hundreds of independent labels dedicated to filling this gap (a situation roughly parallel to that of the early 1950s in which the "indies" took the lead in disseminating rock 'n' roll to the American consumer). The independents avoided mistakes made by established labels that had resulted in an industry-wide recession beginning in the late 1970s,

most notably the astronomical cash advances given to high status acts such as the Rolling Stones, Paul McCartney, and Stevie Wonder, whose most creative work was felt to be in the past. The practice of shipping quantities of record albums to retailers far in excess of projected demand was equally unenlightened. (While an announcement that a superstar's latest recording had been certified gold prior to its release date may have contributed to the general hype considered a necessary precondition to the enormous success sought by the majors, the losses resulting from the return of unsold products severely depleted profits throughout the industry.)

Forced to economize, and cognizant of the modest success enjoyed by the independents, the majors were attracted to acts that required minimal time and resources to produce a record. Those artists without sufficient material for an album were encouraged to release either a mini-LP (usually three to six songs on a 12-inch disc) or a 12-inch single. These new configurations, with enhanced sonic qualities and a lower price tag, helped to revitalize the industry. Disco, the dominant genre, became increasingly discredited by costly studio budget overruns and public reaction to its formulaic musical approach and show business excesses. New wave came to be seen by industry insiders as combining the best of two earlier eras: the raw energy and spontaneous excitement of the 1950s and the integrity and sense of purpose characterizing the 1960s. As the new wave's top artists matured musically and became adept at media manipulation, its hegemony — both in aesthetic and commercial terms — was ensured.

The development of rock was, as Chambers [1985] has noted, encouraged by technological possibilities that had become available inthe recording studio. The studio had rapidly become the privileged, if not unique, composition space for pop. Technological factors, due to their integral role as productive musical elements (echo, double-tracking, phasing, editing, etc.), have never been external but always "within" pop music's history; there at the "interface where the economics of capital and libido interlock." In fact, the full flowering of progressive rock at the end of the 1960s was directly involved in the second major turning point in the postwar history of sound recording. After the introduction of recording tape and the ensuing flexibilities that were increasingly exploited in pop through the 1950s and early 1960s, it was the introduction of multiple track recorders that led to a further revolution in recording in general, and producing pop music in particular. These new machines were initially four track, but there quickly followed in rapid succession eight-, 12-, 16-, and a little later, 24-track recording studios.

Balanced between increasingly sophisticated electronic hardware and a cultural impetus to establish the LP at the apex of pop music recording, the recording studio further advanced its importance in the making of the music. Record producers and engineers like Phil Spector, Jimmy Miller, Shel Talmy, and Glyn Johns rose to become the equivalent of recording stars in their own right. Even the peculiar sound characteristics of particular studios acquired their own individual fame and clientele. All this was deeply stimulated by the now widespread availability of relatively inexpensive hi-fi equipment and the universal adoption of the stereo LP record by the end of the 1960s.

Whereas the stereo process and the LP format were driven primarily by the classical and mainstream pop music genres, rock played a major role in ensuring the success of the compact disc. CDs — fueled by such mega-hits as Michael Jackson's *Thriller* (Epic #38112; 1983; #1 37 weeks), Prince and the Revolution's *Purple Rain* soundtrack (Warner Bros. #25110; 1984; #1 24 weeks), the *Dirty Dancing* soundtrack (RCA #6408; 1987; #1 18 weeks), Police's *Synchronicity* (A&M #3735; 1983; #1 17 weeks), and Dire Straits's sonic tour de force, *Brothers in Arms* (Warner Bros. #25264; 1985; #1 nine weeks) — helped lift the record industry out of its early Reagan-era economic doldrums. However, a number of forces — most notably, the decision of record companies to phase out the single in all physical configurations, inflated list prices for the CD (averaging $19 for a new release by the early years of the 21st century), and the proliferation of digital piracy on the part of consumers via online file downloading and the duplication of discs in computer drives — pushed the business into another recession.

Perhaps the most significant bond between rock and the recording establishment has resulted from the former's development as the first truly urban form of communal folk music. What started as the language of teenagers now embraces virtually all of Western society, reflecting its needs and aspirations. Its universal coinage is largely due to the dissemination of rock on sound recordings in an increasingly wide range of formats (e.g., CD, audio cassette, mini-disc, DAT, DVD, compressed digital files, online audio streaming). But while rock music remains a dominant cultural force — despite the inroads made by country, R&B/hip-hop, and Latin artists into the pop marketplace — record companies (along with traditional brick-and-mortar retailers) are faced with the risk of becoming increasingly marginalized entities. [Chambers 1985; Shaw 1974.]

ROCKOLA, DAVID C. (1897–26 JAN 1993)
Canadian business executive, born in Verden, Manitoba. Before the age of 20 he was in the food processing business, manufacturing coolers. In 1924 he began distributing vending machines and scales, and

patented a new scale mechanism. In 1932 he established the Rock-Ola Manufacturing Corp. in Chicago. (Address in 1945 was 800 N. Kedzie.) His firm acquired the patents of John Gabel, and began leasing the Entertainer instruments in 1934. A dial device for selection of tunes was added later, permitting a choice among 12 discs. Rock-Ola was one of the four successful juke box companies in the 1930s.

Rockola was one of those visionaries who believed that people would pay to telephone a central record center and request music to be played; he designed a "mystic music" service to accomplish this, but it failed to attract customers. He tried another remote system during World War II, which was also unsuccessful. After the war he developed the very popular Magic-Glo juke box. He had a 200-selection box in operation in 1958. [Hoover 1971, p. 113, illustrates a 1935 Rock-Ola juke box.]

ROCOCO (LABEL)
A Canadian LP record, based in Toronto, specializing in vocal reissues of early 78 material not otherwise available. The label was active from the early 1970s through the late 1980s, but is now defunct.

RODGERS, JIMMIE (8 SEP 1897–26 MAY 1933)
American country-western singer, known as "The Singing Brakeman," born in Mendoza, Mississippi. Rodgers is regarded as the "founding father of modern country and western patterns" [Stambler 1989]. His main work as a young man was not musical: he was a cowboy, then a railroad brakeman. In the mid-1920s, his health too poor to continue railroad work, he formed a group called the Jimmie Rodgers Entertainers and performed at rural fairs, not too successfully. When his financial situation had become desperate, in August 1927, he went to Bristol, Tennessee, for an audition with Victor; he — and the Carter Family, present at the same time — found success with the company. He cut "The Soldier's Sweetheart"/"Sleep, Baby, Sleep" on 4 August (#20864) and was on his way to stardom. A 15-minute film, *The Singing Brakeman* (1929), was probably the earliest country music motion picture.

By early 1933, he was said to have sold 20 million records. His nine "Blue Yodel" songs were among the most acclaimed of his discs. Victor issued one of its two picture discs depicting him, made in his session of 17 May 1933 ("Barefoot Blues"/"Cowhand's Last Ride"; #18-6000). He died of tuberculosis, in New York. Rodgers was the first person elected to the Country Music Hall of Fame, in 1961. The U.S. Postal

Reissue set of Jimmie Rodgers's classic 78s. Courtesy Frank Hoffmann

Service issued a commemorative stamp to observe his 80th birthday, in 1977.

Rodgers's recordings remained in print for decades, first reissued by Victor on 78 and LP, and more recently by numerous firms, foreign and domestic, on CD. Bear Family issued a lavish, six-CD boxed set (#15540), with a heavily illustrated book, of Rodgers's complete recordings, including the film soundtrack from the short *The Singing Brakeman*, for a total of 145 tracks, while the British JSP label followed with a far less-expensive six-CD box of 109 recordings from 1927–1933 (#7704); in the U.S., Rounder Records issued the complete recordings on a series of seven CDs at about the same time as the Bear Family box appeared. There are various anthologies of Rodgers's recordings available on RCA and other labels. The standard biography is by Nolan Porterfield. [Bond 1978; Porterfield 1992.]

RODGERS, NILE (19 SEP 1952–)

American guitarist, songwriter, record producer, born in New York. With his partner Bernard Edwards, Nile Rodgers founded the disco group Chic, which scored a series of hits in the late 1970s including the chart-toppers "Le Freak" (Atlantic #3519; 1978; #1) and "Good Times" (Atlantic #3584; 1979; #1). They also wrote and produced for other artists, such as Sister Sledge's "We Are Family" (Cotillion #44251; 1979; #2). After Chic disbanded, Rodgers mounted a solo career and became a producer, handling David

Bowie's *Let's Dance* (EMI #17093; 1983; #1 U.K., #4 U.S.) and other successful records.

WILLIAM RUHLMANN

ROGERS, KENNY (2 AUG 1939–)

American pop/rock singer, born Kenneth Roy Rogers in Houston, Texas. He sang with the Bobby Doyle Jazz Trio, then with the New Christy Minstrels and with the rock group First Edition. After 1975 he pursued a solo career, and in 10 years had produced 22 chart albums, plus others with Dolly Parton. The most durable of those records were *The Gambler* (United Artists UA-LA #934; 1978), 125 weeks on the charts; and *Greatest Hits* (Liberty LOO #1072; 1980), 164 weeks. "Lucille" (United Artists #929) was among his most noteworthy hit singles; it was on the charts 18 weeks, and won a Grammy for it in 1977. Rogers continued to perform through the 1980s and 1990s, however with less chart success.

ROGERS, ROY (5 NOV 1912–6 JULY 1998)

American country/western singer, born Leonard Slye in Cincinnati. He taught himself the guitar and began

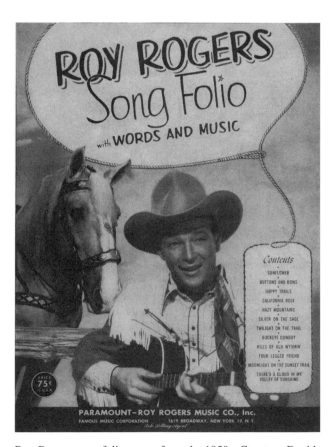

Roy Rogers song folio cover, from the 1950s. Courtesy David A. Jasen

to perform locally, then — having hitched a ride to California — organized a group called the Rocky Mountaineers, then another called the International Cowboys. When those failed, he joined the Sons of the Pioneers, which was beginning its climb to stardom. He auditioned for a movie part in Hollywood, and got the lead in *Under Western Stars*. Subsequently he (and often his wife, Dale Evans) was featured in more than 100 motion pictures. He was also prominent on radio and television. He died in Apple Valley, California.

Rogers had a long recording career, with many hits for Victor, Decca, Vocalion, and other labels. He was still on the charts in the 1970s, with four albums, and made a chart LP in 1980, *Ride Concrete Cowboy* (MCA #41294). One of his best singles was "Happy, Gene and Me" (1974), which was used as the title for an album in the following year; both single and LP were on the Twentieth Century label. He also recorded a duet with country star Clint Black in the 1990s.

ROGERS, WALTER BOWMAN
(14 OCT 1865–24 DEC 1939)

American cornetist and then musical director for Victor, born in Delphi, Indiana. He studied at the Cincinnati Conservatory of Music, then went to New York and became cornet soloist with Cappa's Seventh Regiment Band; in 1899 he joined the Sousa Band, remaining until 1904. At that time he accepted an invitation to be musical director for Victor Talking Machine Co. He also made records for the firm, beginning in 1902, as a cornetist accompanied by the Sousa Band or by a pianist. Rogers was one of the first artists to appear on 12-inch Victors, when that size was launched in 1903, playing "The Harp that Once through Tara's Halls" (#31110). He had two duets with Arthur Pryor, trombonist, in the Victor 1909 catalog; one of them, "Miserere," remained until the 1922 catalog (#16794).

As musical director he made arrangements and conducted dance records and organized the Victor Light Opera Co. and the Victor Opera Co. In 1916 he left Victor to be manager of Paroquette, and then went to Brunswick as recording director, remaining until about 1929. He died in Brooklyn. [Walsh 1959/2.]

RODGERS AND HAMMERSTEIN
ARCHIVES OF RECORDED SOUND

The research facility for sound recordings in the New York Public Library, located in the Library and Museum of the Performing Arts, Lincoln Center. It is a unit of the Music Division, but has holdings in non-musical fields as well, such as drama and documentation of special events. The archives have their roots in

a collection that began in the mid–1930s, when the Columbia label began donating each of its new releases to the library. The Archives opened to the public in November 1965, named for the Rodgers and Hammerstein Foundation that helped to support it. Jean Bowen was the first head of the Archives.

The collections of the Archives are second in size and importance only to those of the Library of Congress. There are about a half million discs, tapes, cylinders, and videotapes, in addition to printed research materials. Among the special collections are the Mapleson cylinders, Metropolitan Opera archives, WNEW radio programming, the *Toscanini Legacy*, documenting the conductor's long career, the *Bell Telephone Hour*, and *Marian McPartland's Piano Jazz* (two long-running radio series), and the Jan Holcman collection of recorded piano music. The Archives participated in the important Rigler and Deutsch Index project. [Hall 1974; website: http://www.nypl.org/research/lpa/rha/rha.html.]

ROLAND CORP.

In business since the early 1970s and located in Los Angeles, Roland is a leading manufacturer and distributor of electronic musical instruments including keyboards and synthesizers, guitar products, digital pianos, electronic percussion kits, digital recording equipment, amplifiers, and audio processing devices, such as digital mixers. The company also manufactures urban, dance, and techno-music production equipment, used by disc jockeys, rappers, and dance music producers worldwide. Roland's BOSS division produces a line of guitar and bass effects pedals, rhythm machines, personal digital studios, and other easy-to-use instruments for all musicians. [website: www.rolandus.com.]

HOWARD FERSTLER

ROLLING STONE (PERIODICAL)

Beginning in the modest manner of a fanzine in November 1967 — the first issue sold 6,000 of its 45,000 copy run — *Rolling Stone* became the primary journal of American pop/rock. Although the title seems connected with the Rolling Stones group, it was in fact drawn from the proverb "A rolling stone gathers no moss" (this from the announcement in the first issue; but the announcement also refers to the Muddy Waters song of the same name, and to the first record of Bob Dylan, and to the Stones group). Covering the entire youth culture as well as its music, the journal filled a niche in the publishing scene and was able to shed an early image of being a trade magazine for the music industry. Over the years the association with rock music faded, and the audience age level rose; content became generalized, but the reviews of new pop/rock records, a feature since the early days, remain influential.

ROLLING STONES

The Rolling Stones have been around for so long — they formed in mid-1962 — and have produced such a distinguished body of work that it is easy to forget their early — and greatest — music was produced in the shadow of other musicians: initially, the American electric blues masters of the 1950s (most notably, Chess artists such as Chuck Berry, Willie Dixon, and Muddy Waters) and, as Swinging London pop icons pursuing the latest fashion, that other, more innovative — and beloved — British band, the Beatles. The group was originally comprised of Mick Jagger, vocals and harmonica; Keith Richards, rhythm guitar; Brian Jones, lead guitar; Bill Wyman, bass; Charlie Watts, drums; and Ian Stewart, piano. Because he didn't look — and behave — much like a budding rock star, Stewart was soon relegated to shadowy session man status by their Barnum-styled manager, Andrew Loog Oldham. Oldham was a publicity genius, perhaps best known for the slogan, "Would you let your daughter marry a Rolling Stone?"

Oldham's maneuvering, combined with the Stones' propulsive early singles in 1963, had them poised to follow the Beatles, the Dave Clark Five, the Searchers, and others as the latest British beat group export stateside in early 1964. The early LPs — *The Rolling Stones* (London #375; 1964; #11), *12 x 5* (London #402; 1064; #3), and *The Rolling Stones, Now!* (London #420; 1965; #5) — were earthy and soulful (for white rock of that time), comprised largely of blues and R&B covers. Following several Top 20 hits, they became superstars with the release of "(I Can't Get No) Satisfaction" (London #9766; 1965; #1), which — with its proto-acid-rock riff and angry, rebellious lyrics — is still regarded by many pop historians as one of the two or three greatest rock songs ever.

While follow-up singles and albums continued to ascend to the upper reaches of the pop charts, the Stones — like most major groups of the late 1960s — felt compelled to match the Beatles' studio experiments. Consequently, the next few years saw the release of a series of flawed masterpieces, including *Aftermath* (London #476; 1966; #2), which featured extended song compositions (by now all authored by Jagger-Richards) and Jones's exotic instrumentation; *Between the Buttons* (London #499; 1967; #2), perhaps the most eclectic collection from the band, ranging from early 20th-century music hall to raga-rock; and *Their Satanic Majesties Request* (London #2; 1967; #2),

Cover of *Some Girls*. Courtesy Frank Hoffmann

a psychedelic tour de force that, unfortunately, comes across as a quaint relic of the flower power era.

Whether it was the example of artists like Bob Dylan and the Beatles — who released the retro recordings *John Wesley Harding* and "Get Back," respectively, in early 1968 — or simply the realization that the music had strayed far from what they did best, the next album, *Beggars Banquet* (London #539; 1968; #5), was the pivotal release in the Stones oeuvre, heralding a return-to-roots rock and incendiary lyrics (e.g., the raw sexuality of "Stray Cat Blues" and anti-establishment polemic, "Street Fighting Man," the malevolent anthem "Sympathy for the Devil"). The Stones remained on top of their game by producing four more classic records in a row: *Let It Bleed* (London #4; 1969; #3), featuring chilling songs of desperation that served as an apt coda for a year marked by the controversial death of Jones in July (immediately after being replaced by guitarist Mick Taylor) and the tragic violence marring their December Altamont concert; the group's seminal live effort, recorded in November 1969 at Madison Square Garden, *"Get Yer Ya-Ya's Out!"* (London #5; 1970; #6); the dynamic *Sticky Fingers* (Rolling Stones #59100; 1971; #1), accented by its titillating zipper cover; and *Exile on Main Street* (Rolling Stones #2900; 1972: #1), an inspired double-disc set of sloppy, debauched — albeit vital and evocative — of first-rate compositions (considered by some experts to be the finest LP of all time).

Widely recognized as the greatest rock band in the world by the 1970s, the Stones — despite further personnel changes — former Faces guitarist Ron Wood filling the slot vacated by Taylor, and the 1990s departures of Wyman (replaced by bassist Darryl Jones and keyboardist Chuck Leavell) and Watts — have remained a bankable entity up to the present day. Despite their commercial success — including the number one albums *Goats Head Soup* (#59101; 1973), *It's Only Rock 'n' Roll* (Rolling Stones #79101; 1974), *Black and Blue* (Rollong Stones #79104; 1976), *Some Girls* (Rolling Stones #39108; 1978), *Emotional Rescue* (Rolling Stones #16015; 1980), and *Tattoo You* (Rolling Stones #16052; 1981) — the group's output has been frequently criticized for its excessive posturing and lapses into self-parody. By the late 1970s, a new generation of punk musicians had came to the fore criticizing the Stones' bloated, corporate image. On occasion, however, they would tease their followers by shelving the tried-and-true formulaic approach, and releasing a truly inspired slice of rock 'n' roll such as "Start Me Up" (Rolling Stones #21003; 1981; #2), "Uncover of the Night" (Rolling Stones #99813; 1983; #9), and a reworking of the R&B classic, "Harlem Shuffle" (Rolling Stones #05802; 1986; #5).

By the 1990s, the tours and releases of newly recorded material were at least several years apart, and the individual members were devoting more attention to their solo projects. The group has operated as a quartet since the departure of bassist Bill Wyman early in the decade; the void has been filled by high-profile session men such as bassist Darryl Jones and pianist Chuck Leavell. Consequent studio releases — *Voodoo Lounge* (Virgin #39782; 1994; #2) and *Bridges to Babylon* (Virgin #2840; 1997; #3) — have been tentative and clichéd in approach. More recent live releases have presented the band in a better light, most notably *Stripped* (Virgin #41040; 1995; #9), which featured a no-frills, heavily acoustic format largely given over to their classic 1960s/1970s work, and *No Security* (Virgin #46740; 1998; #34), consisting of 1997 recordings spanning material representing all phases of their career.

In 2002, following the settlement of a long-running battle with Allen Klein and his ABCKO Records which owns the Stones 1964–1971 output, the Stones finally could release a true career spanning collection, the best-selling *40 Licks* (Virgin #13378). At the same time, ABCKO began reissuing the Stones' 1960s catalog on remastered CDs that were superior in quality to the original CD reissues.

FRANK HOFFMANN

ROLLINI, ADRIAN
(28 JUNE 1904–15 MAY 1956)

American jazz musician, performer on various instruments, born in New York. He was a piano prodigy, and made about 30 piano rolls for the Republic and Mel-O-Dee labels in 1920–1921; but became better known as a bass saxophonist. From 1924–1927 he was with the California Ramblers, then he performed for two years in the Savoy Hotel ballroom, in London. In the 1930s he was with Leo Reisman and Richard Himber, then led studio groups of major jazzmen. Rollini concentrated on vibes in the late 1930s, appearing frequently on radio. He settled in Florida and continued playing until 1955. He died in Homestead, Florida.

Many of Rollini's records were made with numerous orchestras and partners, including Bix Beiderbecke, Frankie Trumbauer, Joe Venuti, and Red Nichols. Working on his own, he recorded for several labels in greatly varied material. "Isle of Capri"/"Girl with the Light Blue Hair" (Okeh #5979; 1941) was a notable single. On LP, Mercury recorded the *Adrian Rollini Trio* (#20011). *Tap Room Swing* (ASV/Living Era #5424) pulls together 1927–1938 recordings issued under a variety of group names that feature Rollini's saxophone work; *Original 1938–40 Recordings* (Tax #8036) focuses on his later work on vibes. [Montgomery 1975 lists the piano rolls.]

ROLLINS, HENRY (13 FEB, 1961–)

Henry Rollins (aka Henry Garfield, born in Washington, D.C.) is easily the most versatile musician to have emerged from the 1980s postpunk movement. He remains active as the leader of a hardcore band, a songwriter, a spoken-word artist, author, publisher, and an actor in films and commercials.

Rollins's multimedia career owes much to his association with the pioneering hardcore band, Black Flag, originally founded by guitarist Greg Ginn in 1977. When lead singer Keith Morris departed to form the Circle Jerks, Black Flag tried several vocalists prior to recruiting Rollins in 1981. Ginn broke up the band in 1987 in order to concentrate on running his record label, SST. Rollins made an immediate impact as a frontman in his own right, releasing a string of solo and group albums — the uncompromisingly intense debut, *Hot Animal Machine* (Texas Hotel #001; 1987), *Drive By Shooting* (Texas Hotel #03; 1987; a mini-album released under the pseudonym Henrietta Collins and the Wife-Beating Child Haters), the incendiary *Life Time* (Texas Hotel #065; 1988), *Do It!* (Texas Hotel #013; 1989; a mixture of live and studio tracks), and *Hard Volume* (Texas Hotel #010; 1989) — all of which featured his overtly political lyrics and aggressive vocal posturing.

Rollins began achieving mainstream popularity after several years of constant touring capped by a headlining role in the 1991 Lollapalooza Tour (which led to a major label deal with Imago/RCA). The Rollins Band LP, *Weight* (Imago/RCA #21034; 1994; #22 U.K.,

#33 U.S.), was nominated for a Grammy. Thereafter, Rollins became increasingly involved in the production of spoken-word recordings and videos. In mid-1996, Rollins was the center of an eight-figure lawsuit instigated by Imago for allegedly signing with DreamWorks; he argued that BMG's major distributors refused to handle his works. His next album, *Come In and Burn* (DreamWorks #50011; 1997; #89), as well as subsequent releases, were in fact released by DreamWorks.

In the early 1990s, Rollins established his own press, 2.13.61, devoted to issuing his own books (most notably, the critically acclaimed collection of short stories, *Black Coffee Blues*) and those of underground writers such as Iggy Pop. He has also garnered acclaim as a versatile actor, narrating commericals for GMC trucks, the Gap, and Nike, and appearing in entertainment features ranging from gritty dramas like *Johnny Mnemonic* and *Heat*, to the family film, *Jack Frost*.

ROLLINS, SONNY (7 SEP 1930–)

A leading jazz saxophonist in the hard-bop school, Theodore Walter Rollins was born in New York City. Rollins first played piano, but then took up saxophone in high school. He made his first recordings accompanying singer Babs Gonzalez in 1948, and then began playing with bop musicians in the New York area, including pianist Bud Powell. Rollins first recorded for Prestige as a bandleader in 1951, remaining with the label for five years. He worked with Miles Davis in 1951 and Thelonious Monk in 1953; he recorded with Davis in 1954, before leaving New York for Chicago. He worked there with the Clifford Brown–Max Roach quintet, before going out on his own. Rollins recorded prolifically in the mid-1950s, including 1956's *Saxophone Colossus* (Prestige #7079) and *Tenor Madness* (Prestige #7047), the later featuring the famous title track duel between Rollins and John Coltrane. In 1957, he cut an album of jazz versions of country music titled *Way Out West* for the small Contemporary label (#7530), showing his adventurous spirit. In the later 1950s, Rollins recorded for Blue Note and Riverside, including the album *Freedom Suite* (Riverside #258; 1958), which showed him moving into more modern styles.

Rollins retired from music-making from 1959–1961 after hearing Ornette Coleman play; he returned playing in a freer style, continuing to lead various groups, recording for RCA and Impulse!, before again retiring from 1968–1971. In the 1970s, Rollins recorded in the then-popular jazz-rock style, primarily for the Milestone label, but by the 1980s had returned to playing a mix of styles, from hard bop to avant-garde to some electrified funk/jazz.

CARL BENSON

ROMAIN, MANUEL (1870–22 DEC 1926)

Spanish tenor and vaudeville artist. He was in the U.S. as a minstrel show performer and vaudeville singer by the early 1900s and began to record in 1907. He made about 40 Edison cylinders from 1907–1910, the first being "When the Blue Birds Nest Again" (#9628). He was the first singer on the Amberol records, singing "Roses Bring Dreams of You" (#2). In 1909 Romain made three discs for Victor, and in 1911 he was with Columbia, doing "Let's Grow Old Together, Honey" (#A1192). For Edison Diamond Discs he contributed two Irish songs (#50230; 1915). After working for Emerson in 1916–1917, he became an Edison exclusive artist. He died in Quincy, Massachussetts.

ROMEO (LABEL)

An American record issued from 1926 to 1939, originally a subsidiary of Cameo, sold through the S.H. Kress chain stores for $0.25. American Record Corp. absorbed Romeo in 1931, and kept it going for eight years, presenting some 2,300 issues. Many of the artists — popular and dance performers — used pseudonyms. [Rust 1978.]

RONALD, LANDON, SIR (7 JUNE 1873– 14 AUG 1938)

British pianist and conductor, born L.R. Russell in London. He studied composition and piano at the Royal College of Music in London, then began conducting light opera and summer concerts. In 1909 he became director of the New Symphony Orchestra. From 1910 to 1938 he was principal of the Guildhall School of Music. He was knighted in 1922. Ronald died in London.

Ronald had a long association with the Gramophone. He accompanied recording sessions of the musical show *Florodora* in 1900, in the Maiden Lane studios of the Gramophone Co., and in the same session made some piano solo records. The company then engaged him as musical advisor and accompanist. He was also a talent scout, and in that capacity persuaded Emma Calvè to record, and played the piano accompaniment for her. He also brought Nellie Melba into the studio in 1904. His triumph was to arrange for recording of Adelina Patti in her Welsh castle; she did so only on the condition that he would be her accompanist.

With the New Symphony Orchestra he achieved a significant recording first, making the earliest disc of a piano concerto — the Grieg work, with Wilhelm Backhaus as soloist (January 1910). He conducted the allegro movement from the Saint-Saens B-Minor Concerto, with pianist Irene Scharrer, on 13 Nov 1915 (HMV #E2-055500). In 1917 he negotiated a contract with the D'Oyly Carte Opera Co. He was also responsible for bringing Edward Elgar and the Gramophone Co. together, in a relationship fruitful for both over many years.

Ronald's orchestral records were highly acclaimed. Among them were important concertos with such soloists as Fritz Kreisler, Yehudi Menuhin, and Alfred Cortot. [Duckenfield 1990.]

RONETTES, THE

Classic exponents of producer Phil Spector's "Wall of Sound," the Ronettes parlayed massive beehive hairdos and an abundance of mascara to provide a tough, sultry accent to the girl-group genre. All three members — sisters Veronica and Estelle Bennett and cousin Nedra Talley — were born in New York City during the World War II years. They began singing together as the Darling Sisters and were performing a song-and-dance routine based on Chubby Checker's version of "The Twist" at the Peppermint Lounge by 1961. They went on to record for Colpix Records in 1961–1962 as Ronnie and the Relatives as well as performing with disc jockey Murray the K's rock shows and singing backup for the era's top pop stars.

Signed by Spector to his Philles label in 1963, the trio's first release, "Be My Baby" (Philles #116; 1963),

The Ronettes in a publicity photo from the early '60s; Ronnie Spector is in the center

reached number two on the *Billboard Hot 100*. Although their follow-up singles continued to feature Spector's production, none of them broke into the Top 20. By 1966 Spector had lost interest in making records and married Ronnie Bennett. After a couple of failed attempts at launching her solo career (A&M, 1969; Apple, 1971), the couple divorced in 1974.

With the other Ronettes now married, Ronnie Spector continued to work with other prominent musicians during the 1970s and 1980s, including Steven Van Zandt, Bruce Springsteen's E Street Band, and Genya Ravan. Her greatest success came with "Take Me Home Tonight" (Columbia #06231; 1986), a duet with Eddie Money that hit number four on the pop chart.

RONSTADT, LINDA (15 JULY 1946–)

American country and popular singer, born in Tucson, Arizona. She sang locally, then went to Los Angeles, forming a group called the Stone Poneys. She was successful in the country-western idiom, Motown, and New Wave, and in 1980 also in Gilbert and Sullivan (*Pirates of Penzance* on Broadway). She was invited to sing at the inauguration of Jimmy Carter, and had invitations from California governor Jerry Brown, her onetime boyfriend. Ronstadt had 14 chart albums between 1975 and 1985, of which the most popular were *Simple Dreams* (Asylum #6E-104; 1977) and *Greatest Hits* (Asylum #7E-1092; 1980). There was also a string of chart singles, beginning with the Stone Poneys's "Different Drum" (Capitol #2004; 1967; #13), and throughout a solo career that picked up momentum from 1970 onward. During the 1980s, Ronstadt collaborated with Nelson Riddle on a series of recordings of Big Band standards, and then returned to her "roots" by performing Mexican mariachi music. She has been less active as a recording artist or performer since the early 1990s.

ROOM ACOUSTICS

Room size, shape, furnishings, physical integrity, speaker locations, and listening position can all have a considerable impact upon the sound quality of an audio system. A large room requires greater acoustic output from the loudspeakers, particularly in the bass range. A room with lots of curtains, overstuffed couches, and dense carpeting tends to be "dead" (nonreverberating), and requires more acoustic output, particularly at midrange and higher frequencies, than a "live" room.

Room shape and size are both factors in the creation of standing waves, which are the result of the enhancement or weakening of signals at certain wavelengths that are submultiples of the distance between room surfaces. Obviously, then, an irregularly shaped room can do a lot to mitigate standing-wave problems (although it cannot remove them, and can sometimes make them worse) and it can also be seen that the least desirable room for audio listening would be a small one in the shape of a perfect cube. Rooms with dimensions that are multiples of each other will also cause problems. The larger the room, the less impact there is from these resonances, since the more problematic ones will be at lower frequencies. The stiffness of the room walls can have an impact on the strength of standing waves, and of course weak walls may also generate spurious sounds of their own. In some cases the effect of standing waves can be somewhat mitigated by shifting the location of the loudspeakers or by making use of a separate subwoofer speaker, preferably located in a corner to excite all room modes uniformly.

Reflective surfaces close to woofer systems will have an impact on speaker performance by reinforcing low frequency output, although they can also generate midbass suck-out effects that are independent from standing waves. Where these nulls and reinforcements occur on the frequency spectrum will depend upon the woofer-to-boundary distances, and their behavior was first analyzed by Roy Allison. Reflective surfaces can also have an impact on midrange and treble imaging and strength, and this can work against proper sound-staging if one speaker in a stereo pair is not the same distance from an adjacent wall as the other, or one boundary is damped with a drape and the other is hard surfaced.

Good quality equalization can sometimes correct for bass and midbass suck-out artifacts, and even for standing waves to an extent, but equalization may only slightly correct problems involving image-degrading midrange and high-frequency reflections. Speakers often sound better if located some distance from room walls, and smaller ones probably work better if they are placed on stands. However, placement of this kind will usually have a negative impact on midbass smoothness, meaning that designs that are built to work close to room boundaries may have an inherent advantage. Whatever is done about these matters, there will always remain good and bad places to sit while listening, and with two-channel stereo systems listeners should try to position themselves equidistant from both speakers, forming one tip of an equilateral triangle with them. With modern surround-sound systems that also employ a center channel, the listener position may be less critical, and other room-related artifacts may be better controlled.

HOWARD FERSTLER

ROSE, EUGENE C.
(26 JULY 1866–21 AUG 1961)
Flutist, born in Danzig. He played at the Paris Exposition of 1889, and with the Sousa Band. From 1911 to 1917 he played in the orchestra of the Metropolitan Opera. One of the earliest recording artists, he recorded for Edison cylinders in 1889, performing in a flute trio. Rose recorded later for many labels. His best seller was "Genevieve Waltz Medley, an ocarina solo (Edison #9197; 1906). He died in Freeport, New York. [Walsh 1947/10–11, 1952/5.]

ROSE, FRED (24 AUG 1898–1 DEC 1954)
A pioneer Nashville music publisher, Fred Rose was born in Evansville, Indiana. He became a Chicago-based pop songwriter ("Deed I Do" and "Red Hot Mama" were among his compositions), then began writing for western acts, including Gene Autry, Tex Ritter, and Roy Rogers. In 1942 Rose partnered with Roy Acuff to launch Nashville's first professional music publisher, Acuff-Rose Publications. Rose wrote for Acuff, his best-known songs including "Blue Eyes Crying in the Rain." He also discovered Hank Williams and brought songwriters Felice and Boudleaux Bryant to Nashville. As an A&R man, Rose produced Williams, Bob Wills, and the Louvin Brothers for MGM Records, before launching his own Hickory Records in January 1954. However, he died at year's end, and his son Wesley took over the business.

COLIN ESCOTT

ROSE, WESLEY
(11 FEB 1918–26 APR 1990)
American music publishing executive, born in Chicago. The son of Fred Rose, who cofounded Acuff-Rose Publishing, the prominent Nashville song publishing company, Wesley Rose joined the firm in 1945 and became president upon his father's death on 1 Dec 1954. The younger Rose was an influential figure in the development of country music. He cofounded the Country Music Assoc. in 1958 and served as its first chairman. He sold Acuff-Rose to Opryland USA in 1985.

WILLIAM RUHLMANN

ROSENTHAL, MORIZ
(17 DEC 1862–3 SEP 1946)
Polish pianist, born in Lwow. He studied with Karol Mikuli, a pupil of Chopin; later with Rafael Joseffy and Franz Liszt. He became one of the world's leading virtuosi, specializing in Chopin. He settled in the U.S. in 1938, and died in New York eight years later.

Rosenthal began to record in 1929 for Parlophone/Odeon, playing a Chopin mazurka and a Chopin/Liszt transcription. He remained with Parlophone into 1931, doing many Chopin works, including the first concerto with the Berlin State Opera (#38839/40; #21695/98; 1930). He worked for Edison in 1929, making two Chopin sides (Diamond Disc #82353), and for Victor in 1928, 1939, and 1942. His final record was of the same work with which he began his recording career, the Chopin/Liszt "My Joys" from "Chants polonais"; with it was the Chopin "Tarantelle in A-Flat" (Camden #377; released on LP). Several labels offer CD reissues of his 78 recordings, including Enterprise #316, a collection of Chopin recordings made between 1929–1937, and two CDS on Preiser (*Plays Chopin and Strauss*, #9339 and *Volume 2,* #9973). Pearl #9339 is a selection of recordings made when Rosenthal was over 65 years of age, but lacking nothing in technical command. [Methuen-Campbell 1984.]

ROSENTHAL, RICHARD S.

An early promoter of language instruction by phonograph; he spoke on the subject at the 1893 convention of the National Phonograph Assoc. Rosenthal's organization, the International College of Languages, sent out sets of prerecorded cylinders to students, with blanks for return of their recitations. Others followed this example — the "Languagephone Method" — in the cylinder era, but in the advanced technological age that followed instruction, ironically, became unilateral.

ROSS, DIANA (26 MAR 1944–)

Born in Detroit, Diana Ross first gained fame as the lead singer of the Supremes. Ross's sexy, malleable voice — combined with the group's charm school image and photogenic good looks — enabled them to cross over to the pop mainstream, a hitherto unprecedented achievement within the rhythm and blues/soul genre.

Her departure from the group seemed a foregone conclusion when, in 1967, they underwent a name change to "Diana Ross and the Supremes." Motown Records owner Berry Gordy had long felt Ross possessed sufficient star quality to warrant a solo in both the music business and motion pictures. Not only did her initial solo recordings — the singles "Reach Out and Touch (Somebody's Hand)" (Motown #1163; 1970; #20) and "Ain't No Mountain High Enough" (Motown #1169; 1970; #1) and eponymous album (Motown #711; 1970; #19) — sell well, but she garnered high Nielsen ratings for her 1971 television special (followed by a successful soundtrack LP) and an Oscar nomination playing singer Billie Holiday in the film, *Lady Sings the Blues*. Ross maintained her momentum throughout the decade, appearing in another big-budget movie, *Mahogany* (1975), and releasing a string of best-selling, if artistically uneven,

records, including *Lady Sings the Blues* (Motown #758; 1972; #1), *Touch Me in the Morning* (Motown ##771; 1973; #5), *Diana Ross* (Motown 861; 1976; #5), *Diana* (Motown #936; 1980; #2), and four number one singles — the bland ballads "Touch Me in the Morning" (Motown #1239; 1973) and "Theme from Mahogany" (Motown #1377; 1975) as well as the disco-flavored "Love Hangover" (Motown #1392; 1976) and "Upside Down" (Motown #1494; 1980).

By the time of her collaboration with Lionel Richie, the theme song to the film *Endless Love* (Motown #1519; 1981) had achieved a nine-week run at number one on the *Billboard Hot 100* charts, and Ross had signed a contract with RCA. Despite regular appearances on the charts over the next half-decade, she moved back to Motown (then owned by EMI London) in 1987. Despite her high visibility in the entertainment tabloids, Ross — who took a considerable amount of time off to raise a family — failed to place a recording on either the singles or albums charts during the 1990s.

ROSS (LABEL)

An American record issued through Ross Stores in 1924–1925; Bridgeport Die and Machine Co. made the discs. Matrices came from Paramount, Emerson, and probably Banner. Surviving specimens are rare. One item was "She Loves Me," sung by Arthur Hall with the Golden Gate Orchestra (#11410). [Rust 1978.]

ROSWAENGE, HELGE
(29 AUG 1897–19 JUNE 1972)

Danish tenor, born in Copenhagen. He studied engineering, then voice, and made successful concert tours of Europe. From 1929 to 1945 he was with the Berlin State Opera, and again from 1949. He also appeared with the Vienna State Opera in 1936–1958 and sang often in Bayreuth and Salzburg. Roswaenge was greatly acclaimed, and was compared favorably to Enrico Caruso. Among his hundred roles, Radames and Canio were outstanding, but he also gave remarkable interpretations in *Fidelio* and in lesser-known operas such as *Ivan Susanin* and Wille's *Königsballade*. He died in Munich.

Roswaenge recorded in 1927 for Grammophon/Polydor in Berlin, beginning with a German version of "Che gelida manina" (#B22434) and two arias from *Tosca*. He also recorded four sides for HMV/Electrola in 1927, then six sides for Parlophone/Odeon in 1928. During 1928–1932 Roswaenge was active for Polydor in Berlin, recording 131 numbers. Among eight arias he made for Telefunken (Berlin) in 1932, the "Preislied" (#018795) was particularly elegant. His German

"O paradiso" of 1933 (Telefunken #018978) was also noteworthy. He worked for Polydor and HMV/Electrola in 1935. The most enduring of his single discs was Sobinin's Aria from *Ivan Susanin* (HMV/Electrola #DB5563; 1940). His rendition of Tamino in the HMV *Zauberflöte* — with Thomas Beecham and the Berlin Philharmonic Orchestra — is regarded as the finest interpretation of the role on record.

A good selection of his favorite arias (including the numbers cited above) appears on a CD from Harmonia Mundi (#89018). Material from the 1920s and 1930s — Mozart, Puccini, Verdi, Bizet, Beethoven — appeared on CD on Pearl (#9394). [Dennis 1976.]

ROTATING HEAD RECORDER

A tape recorder that uses pickup and recording heads attached to a fast-spinning drum to increase the tape-read speed. This can be done because the slow-moving tape passes over the heads at an angle, and the fast rotation of the head allows it to put a succession of electronically controlled, short, angular scans down the length of the tape. This greatly increases the linear tape speed above what would be possible by simply having the tape itself speeded up and passed over stationary heads. The most common use is with standard, hi-fi video tape recorders, but the technology is also used with DAT recorders.

HOWARD FERSTLER

ROTATIONAL SPEED

SEE SURFACE SPEED

ROTHCHILD, PAUL
(18 APR 1935–30 MAR 1995)

Born in Brooklyn, New York, Rothchild is best-remembered for producing folk and rock albums in the 1960s and 1970s. The son of an opera singer mother and British businessman father, Rothchild was raised in arty Greenwich Village. By the early 1960s, he was working for a record distributor out of Cambridge, Massachusetts, where the folk boom was just beginning. In 1962, he was hired by Bob Weinstock of Prestige to start a folk division for the jazz label and recorded local Boston players including Geoff Muldaur and Tom Rush. Two years later, Jac Holzman of rival Elektra Records offered him a job. Rothchild produced Paul Butterfield's first albums for Elektra, and then discovered a new blues-rock group playing in Los Angeles called the Doors, and quickly signed them. Rothchild would produce all of their

classic recordings for Elektra. In 1970, he also oversaw Janis Joplin's solo album, *Pearl*, and ex-Lovin' Spoonful's head John Sebastian's first solo outing. Rothchild's final success came in 1979 with Bette Midler's hit album *The Rose*, although he continued to work as a producer through the early 1990s, when he was diagnosed with lung cancer, which eventually led to his death.

CARL BENSON

ROULETTE RECORDS (LABEL)

A successful independent label, Roulette was launched in January 1957 by George Goldner, Joe Kolsky, and Kolsky's brother, Phil Kahl. The first two records, Buddy Knox's "Party Doll" and Jimmy Bowen's "I'm Stickin' with You," were hits, but later in 1957, Goldner sold his share to club owner Morris Levy. Songwriters Hugo Peretti and Luigi Creatore bought a share of the company, and disc jockey Alan Freed also owned a share. By 1959, though, Levy was the sole owner. The label's most successful acts included Jimmie Rodgers, Ronnie Hawkins, Joey Dee ("Peppermint Twist"), the Essex ("Easier Said than Done"), and Tommy James and the Shondells. Levy also developed a jazz catalog, signing Count Basie, Dinah Washington, among others. By the time Levy ceased issuing new products on Roulette in 1978, the label's holdings included Goldner's earlier labels (Rama, Tico, Gee, Gone, and End) as well as Jubilee Records. In 1988 Roulette and its subsidiaries were sold to Rhino Records for the United States and EMI for the remainder of the world. By this point, several high-profile lawsuits had embroiled Roulette, Levy's subsequent labels, his music publishing ventures, and his record-jobbing business.

COLIN ESCOTT

ROUNDER RECORDS (LABEL)

Founded in 1971, by Bill Nowlin, Ken Irwin, and Marion Leighton, and still under the control of the three founders, the North Cambridge, Massachusetts, company started out as a way to produce an old-time banjo record for fun. The effort was a sales success, and the eventual result was the largest independent record label in the country. Over the years, the company's output has ranged from zydeco, cajun, and bluegrass to jazz, R&B, and reggae, with the thrust always in the direction of roots-based material. Much of what Rounder produces is contemporary, but it also releases a great deal of amateur and professionally recorded material originally made in the 1940s, 1950s, and 1960s. Rounder also

Rounder Records label, mid-'70s. Courtesy BenCar Archives

purchased other folk and bluegrass labels, including Philo and Flying Fish, and produces records under the Varrick and Bullseye Blues labels.

HOWARD FERSTLER

ROXY MUSIC

Roxy Music's decadent, densely textured variant of art rock appealed far more to a European, rather than an American, audience. Factors behind the group's limited appeal stateside included a complex image based as much on camp fashion (their early look blended futuristic costumes and 1950s hairstyles) and lifestyle concepts as music per se, rather arch, escapist lyrics not in tune with a society grappling with the very real issues of the Vietnam War and Watergate scandal, and the tendency of the rock press to portray them as a glitter-rock alternative to Alice Cooper, David Bowie, and others.

Roxy Music was founded by vocalist Bryan Ferry and keyboardist Brian Eno. With the addition of saxophonist Andy Mackay, lead guitarist Phil Manzanera, and drummer Paul Thompson (although this was the classic lineup, there would be frequent personnel changes over the years), the band recorded *Roxy Music* (Island #9200/Reprise #2114; 1972; #10 U.K.) prior to having ever performed live. The album cover — the first of many by Roxy to feature female models in provocative poses — attracted as much attention in the U.S. as the music in the grooves. Released on the heels

of extensive touring in Europe and North America, *For Your Pleasure* (Warner Bros. #2696; 1973; # 4 U.K., #193 U.S.) easily outsold the debut LP.

By 1973 it was clear that Roxy was Ferry's band due to the departure of Eno (to be replaced by Eddie Jobson) over artistic differences. Although remaining members devoted a considerable amount of time and energy over the few years to solo projects — Ferry producing *These Foolish Things* (Atlantic #7304; 1973; #5 U.K.), *Another Time, Another Place* (Atlantic #18113; 1974; #4 U.K.), and *Let's Stick Together* (Atlantic #18187; 1976; #160); Manzanera, *Diamond Head* (Atco #113; 1975) and *Mainstream* (Antilles #7008; 1975; with the band Quiet Sun); and Mackay, *In Search of Eddie Riff* (Island #9278; 1974) and *Rock Follies* (Island #9362; 1976) — the band gained increasing critical respect and commercial success, issuing *Stranded* (Atco #7045; 1974; #1 U.K., #186 U.S.), *Country Life* (Atco #106; 1975; #3 U.K., #37 U.S.), and *Siren* (Atco #127; 1975; #4 U.K., #50 U.S.).

Following a lackluster live LP, *Viva! Roxy Music* (Atco #139; 1076; #6 U.K., #81 U.S.), the band verified rumors that a breakup had taken place. When Ferry's solo career failed to gain momentum, however, he reformed Roxy along with Manzanera, Mackay, and Thompson. The ensuing releases — *Manifesto* (Atco #114; 1979; #7 U.K., #23 U.S.), *Flesh + Blood* (Atco #102; 1980; #1 U.K., #35 U.S.), the unabashedly romantic *Avalon* (Warner Bros. #23686; 1982. #1 U.K., #53 U.S.; achieved platinum status), and the live EP, *Musique/The High Road* (Warner Bros. #23808; 1983; #26 U.K., #67 U.S.) — all garnered critical acclaim and moderate sales in the U.S. Ferry's disinclination to tour in support of the band's releases led to another breakup in 1982. With the exception of Eno, who went on to father the ambient and electronica genres, Ferry has remained the most prominent ex-member of the band, periodically releasing a string of stylistic diverse solo albums.

ROYAL (LABEL) (I)
A lateral-cut, double-sided British record sold by the City Manufacturing Co., London, in 1908.

ROYAL (LABEL) (II)
An American record sold by the Royal Record Co. ca. 1921–1922. Material, which was popular and dance music, paralleled offerings on several other labels, but with artists' names changed. The matrices were shared with Cardinal, Clarion, Melva, Phantasie Concert Record, Symphony Concert Record, Cleartone, and others. [Kendziora 1988/11.]

ROYAL CONCERTGEBOUW ORCHESTRA AMSTERDAM

One of the premier orchestras of Europe, known as the Concertgebouw Orchestra until 1988, when it was renamed by royal decree in honor of its 100th anniversary. Willem Kes was the first conductor, succeeded in 1895 by Willem Mengelberg, who remained in the post until 1941, bringing the orchestra to world renown. Eduard van Beinum was conductor from 1941 to 1961, followed by Bernard Haitink (who shared the post with Eugen Jochum until 1964). Riccardo Chailly became conductor in the 1988–1989 season, and Haitink became conductor laureate. The orchestra's name comes from the hall in which it has played since its inception, the Amsterdam Concertgebouw.

Mengelberg conducted for the first Concertgebouw recording, of the *Tannhäuser Overture*, in May 1926 (Columbia #X-27), and recorded for Columbia until 1936; 11 works were listed in the 1943 Columbia catalog, including the Brahms third and fourth symphonies. Telefunken recorded the orchestra after that time until the 1940s, when DG/Polydor and Decca made some issues. Philips recorded the Concertgebouw in stereo from 1957. A 10-CD Teldec set of Mengelberg's Telefunken material has been issued, but because of engineering problems with it the older LP reissues on Past Masters label may be preferable. Several other CD releases have been criticized on sonic grounds as well. [Van Bart 1989 is a discography of the orchestra; in a review of the book, Bob Benson discusses the infelicities noted above in CD reissues (*ARSCJ* 20-2 [Fall 1989]: 198–201).]

ROYALE (LABEL)

An American record introduced in fall 1939 by Eli Oberstein. The issuing organization was the United States Record Corp. Original material on Royale — jazz, gospel, country, and classical — included cuts by Richard Himber and Johnny Green. Reissues included sides by the Quintet of the Hot Club of France. Jan Peerce and the Don Cossack Chorus were also heard on Royale.

In 1951 the United States Record Corp. was absorbed by the Record Corp. of America, which continued the Royale label name. An important series of operatic and symphonic material appeared, apparently made from radio broadcasts of the late 1940s in Germany and perhaps Italy. Artists were given pseudonyms. The label ceased around 1957. [Lumpe 1990.]

ROYAL TALKING MACHINE CO., INC.

A Chicago firm, established in 1918. Columbia disc players were sold, some with half-inch spindles like those on players of the Standard Talking Machine Co. Royal did not issue discs.

ROYALTIES AND FEES

Francesco Tamagno is believed to have been the first recording artist to insist on and receive royalties for discs sold, in 1903. Royalties to composers did not begin in U.K. until June 1912. Through the 78 era, however, it was not unusual to simply pay a performer a flat fee for each "side" recorded, with no royalties paid later. As these recordings have been reissued and recognized as increasingly valuable, many artists and their descendants have come forward to request royalty payments for the LP and CD reissues.

In the current American pop/rock field, artists usually receive about 7 percent of the list price of each record sold, though the percentage may reach twice that amount for star performers. Customarily the artist's income is reduced at the source by company deductions for promotion fees, costs of album graphics, and tour costs not made up by admission intake. The system makes it difficult for the pop performer to cull huge profits, even from a record on the charts. Many pioneering stars of the rock and R&B era of the 1950s were paid "in kind" with cars, loans, and other items, rather than receiving cash payments; in the 1990s, organizations like the R&B Foundation arose to put pressure on the recording industry to make up for these earlier practices by finally agreeing to pay royalties, at least on new issues of this classic material.

Records sent out to the media for promotion purposes do not earn royalties, nor do cutouts. Many record companies gave their favored customers extra free recordings, labeling them as "cutouts" to avoid paying royalties to their artists; major recording stars like the Beatles were able to challenge this practice, and successfully sued for nonpayment of royalties.

New artists who are anxious to be signed to a major label will often accept very low royalty payments on an initial contract. The record industry claims this practice facilitates signing many new acts, who otherwise might not have a chance, because so few actually end up earning money. However, major stars have become to object to be tied to their original contracts once they achieve success. In California, long-term recording contracts have been challenged under the state's labor laws. Successful groups like the Dixie Chicks have been able to renegotiate their original agreements with major labels after achieving chart success.

In addition to the performers, publishers and songwriters receive small royalties on records sold, based on the number of their songs in an album, around .3

percent each, per song, and the producer receives about 3 percent. [Denisoff 1986.]

FRANK ANDREWS

REV. CARL BENSON

ROYALTY RECORDINGS

It appears that the earliest surviving recording in any format made by a monarch was one made in Balmoral Castle, Scotland, in 1888, on a Bell-Tainter Graphophone carried there by a solicitor on behalf of Henry Edmunds, the American Graphophone Co. representative in the U.K. A broadcast of that recording — now in the Science Museum, London — was made on 10 Nov 1891. A few words in the queen's voice were heard, speaking about the tomatoes growing at Balmoral. It is reported that another record was made by Queen Victoria, in 1896; it was a cylinder sent by her with a message to the Emperor of Ethiopia, with instructions that it should be destroyed after he had heard it. There is no verification for the existence nor for the destruction of the record.

The earliest royalty recording on a magnetic medium was taken by the Poulsen Telegrafon in 1900, of Emperor Franz Joseph; that wire recording was transferred to an LP disc. King Edward VII also made a wire recording, but it has been lost.

Among disc recordings, the oldest survivor is HMV #1235 (1903), on which Queen Elizabeth of Romania recited five of her own poems, including one in English, titled "A Friend." Her name on the recording, which was made in Bucharest, was given as Carmen Sylva. Kaiser Wilhelm is said to have made a 1904 record.

Princess Peara Nene (Waiata Na Rangatira Peara Nene), a Maori princess of New Zealand, recorded two songs for Sound Recording Col, Ltd., on its Grammavox Record label (#D25), ca. 1911. Queen Kalakana of Hawaii made recordings for Edison (#11501 and #11504) sometime after 1912.

In 1923 King George V and Queen Mary recorded an "Empire Day Message to the Boys and Girls of the British Empire" for HMV (#19072).

ROYCROFT (LABEL)

An American record distributed in 1927–1928 by William H. Wise and Co. for the Roycrofters society. The material consists of English madrigals, carols, and folk songs, performed by a group identified as the English Singers. A 12-record set, the *Roycroft Album*, was apparently the first multi-disc nonoperatic album to be marketed in the U.S.; but the records were also sold singly. The labels carry the legend: Roycroft Living Tone Record; Microphone Recording; The Roycrofters, East Aurora, N.Y. [Blacker 1984.]

Label made for the Roycroft Society in the late '20s. Courtesy Kurt Nauck/Nauck's Vintage Records

RSO (LABEL)

SEE STIGWOOD, ROBERT

RUBIN, RICK (1963–)

Born Frederick Jay Rubin in Long Island, Rubin attended NYU university in the early 1980s, where he befriended Russell Simmons. In 1984 the two formed Def Jam Records out of a dorm room to promote rap and hip-hop music. A year later, they signed a distribution/production deal with Columbia. Rubin discovered and nurtured the talents of rap acts including the Beastie Boys and Public Enemy, both of which achieved great success in the late 1980s and early 1990s. Rubin broke with Simmons in 1989, renaming his company Def American. He began expanding his vision beyond rap in the early 1990s, producing the Red Hot Chili Peppers's hit album, *Blood Sugar Sex Majik* (Warner Bros. #26681) in 1991, and working with Mick Jagger in 1993. In 1994, he launched American Recordings, producing a new all-acoustic album with Johnny Cash, and working with Tom Petty. Rubin remained active as a producer through the 1990s, although the new acts he championed had less success in the second half of the decade.

RUBINSTEIN, ARTHUR
(28 JAN 1887–20 DEC 1982)

Polish/American pianist, born in Lodz. He was a piano prodigy born into a nonmusical family. After public performances at age seven, he was sent to Berlin for study and made a formal debut there at age 13. In 1903 he took lessons from Ignace Paderewski; but he was for the most part self-taught. Rubinstein played in Carnegie Hall on 8 Jan 1906 with the Philadelphia Orchestra, then toured Europe and South America, gaining recognition as one of the two premier pianists of his time. Chopin was the composer he performed most definitively, but he was renowned also for his Brahms, Beethoven, Spanish composers, and contemporaries. He made motion pictures in the 1940s, recorded and concertized widely, with intervals taken for intensive practice to correct his occasionally erratic technique. In 1946 he became an American citizen. He was given the U.S. Medal of Freedom in 1976, the year of his final recital. He died in Geneva, Switzerland.

Rubinstein's recordings, from the 1930s to the 1970s, span the repertoire of the instrument. After some work for Odeon, he became a Victor artist. His Chopin albums — mazurkas, nocturnes, scherzos, concertos, polonaises — remain the touchstone for pianists today. In addition to his solo work, he was distinguished in chamber music; a fine example is the Brahms Cello Sonata, with Gregor Piatigorsky (M-564). His performance of the Cesar Franck violin sonata with Jascha Heifetz, and his Tchaikovsky concerto no. 1 with Barbirolli, made in 1932 (Victor #7802-05) is still an unsurpassed rendition of that oft-recorded masterpiece.

There are abundant CD reissues of Rubinstein's recordings. He is perhaps the only artist with enough recordings in the RCA catalog who could be represented on a nearly 100-CD set, *The Rubinstein Collection* (retailing for over $1,500!); the set is also available as individual CDs and there's a *Highlights* disc (#63085) for those who wish to sample the range of material he recorded. Polygram issued three two-CD sets of Rubinstein's recordings in its "Great Pianists of the 20th Century" series (Vol. 2, #456958; Vol. 3 #456967; Vol. 1 is currently unlisted), also drawing from the massive Victor catalog. His earlier Odeon recordings are anthologized on various releases, including *The Legendary Rubinstein* (Angel #67007), drawn from 1928–1939 recordings of Chopin piano solos. *BBC Legends* (#4105) collects radio transcriptions made in England.

RUFFO, TITTA
(9 JUNE 1877–5 JULY 1953)

Italian baritone, born in Pisa as Ruffo Cafiero Titta (he later chose to reverse the elements of his name). He studied in Rome and Milan and made a debut in Rome as the Herald in *Lohengrin* (1898). Then he appeared throughout Italy, in Rio de Janeiro, Vienna, Paris, London, and Philadelphia. Finally he was heard at the

Titta Ruffo in the 1917 Victor catalog. Courtesy Jerald Kalstein

Metropolitan Opera on 19 Jan 1922, as Figaro in *Barbiere di Siviglia*; he remained with the company to 1928. He returned to Rome, and then settled in Florence, where he died.

Ruffo recorded first for Pathé cylinders in ca. 1904–1906, beginning with "Buona Zazà" from Leoncavallo's opera *Zazà* (#4200). He did 14 numbers, mostly standard baritone items. Thereafter he was a Victor/HMV artist, recording a wide French/Italian repertoire from 1907 to 1933. He had 40 solos in the Victor 1917 catalog, plus duets with Enrico Caruso (a Caruso duet, from *Otello* were still in the catalog of 1940, with Ruffo's final recording, "Nemico della patria"/"Adamastor" (#7153; 1929) and the *Otello* "Credo." The "Brindisi" from *Hamlet* (Victor #6266, #18140, #88619; first made for HMV #052188; 1907) is a favorite among collectors. There are numerous CD reissues, including Nimbus #7810, drawn from 1907–1922 recordings, and *The Early Recordings (1906/12)* (Preiser #89220), a two-CD set. [Moran 1984/2 has a complete discography.]

RUMBLE

A low-frequency noise, usually between 20 and 35 Hz, brought about in a phonograph by motor or transport vibrations. In some cases rumble originates in the recording mechanism, and is thus a part of the recorded signal. Aside from motor rumble there is the possibility of rumble caused by resonance in the springs which keep the idler wheel in contact with the turntable rim. Rumble also occurs in cylinder playback. A rumble filter is a control on an amplifier that may reduce audible rumble that originates in the turntable or record changer.

See also **Distortion**

RUNDGREN, TODD (22 JUNE 1948–)

Although Philadelphian Todd Rundgren has sold considerably fewer recordings than virtually any other high-profile artist with a career stretching back to the 1960s, he has been very active in a number of roles, including session playing, band leader, songwriting, studio engineering and production, and conceptual video work.

After a stint as the guiding force of the 1960s cult band, Nazz, Rundgren began recording a series of solo tour de force LPs — featuring only his vocal and instrumental performances — in a mildly psychedelic power-pop vein. His most successful album was 1972's *Something/Anything?* (Bearsville #2066; 1972; #29), which achieved gold status due in part to the hit singles "I Saw the Light" (Bearsville #0003; 1972; #16) and "Hello It's Me" (Bearsville 0009; 1973; #5), although he released many other solo albums through the early 1990s. In the mid-1970s, Rundgren founded a keyboard-based band, Utopia. Following the release of a series of avant-garde–oriented albums beginning with *Todd Rundgren's Utopia* (Bearsville #6954; 1974; #34), he opted for a more traditional lineup in the late 1970s featuring keyboardist Roger Powell, bassist Kasim Sulton, and drummer John Willie Wilcox. Although Rundgren's Spector-influenced production values and warped humor were acquired tastes, the reconstituted band enjoyed a measure of commercial success, most notably with *Adventures in Utopia* (Bearsville #6991; 1980; #32) and the Beatles homage-parody *Deface the Music* (Bearsville #3487; 1980; #65). Further albums through the mid-1980s failed to break the Top 100 album charts, however.

Beginning in the early 1970s, Rundgren served as engineer and producer for many notable artists, including Badfinger, the Band, Paul Butterfield, Rick Derringer, Grand Funk Railroad, Halfnelson (aka Sparks), Hall and Oates, Meatloaf, the New York Dolls, Patti Smith, the Tubes, Jesse Winchester, and XTC. With the rise of the MTV craze, he attempted to shift the focus of the video medium away from promotion in favor of conceptual art. His laser disc

release, *The Desktop Collection* (Rhino #ID2733RH; 1993), featured computer-enhanced interpretations of music compositions.

RUN-D.M.C.

Run-D.M.C. was a rare commodity when it first became successful in the mid-1980s; whereas early rap stars tended to come from economically repressed inner-city areas, Queens, New York rappers Joseph Simmons (Run) and Daryll McDaniels (D.M.C.) both grew up in a comfortable middle-class environment. Perhaps as a result of their background, Run-D.M.C.'s recorded material lacks the harsh, bitter edge (e.g., profanity, violent images, revolutionary dogma) typical of rank-and-file rap/hip-hop acts.

Simmons — a one-time protégé of hip-hop pioneer Kurtis Blow — and McDaniels became involved in the New York City by their early teens. By the early 1980s they had hooked up with a club disc jockey Jay Mizell, who adopted the moniker Jam Master Jay. Run-D.M.C.'s early records for the Profile label were popular in the New York area dance-rap scene; beginning with "It's Like That" (Profile #5019; 1983; #15 R&B), the group's singles consistently made the Black charts.

Their recordings — particularly the albums *Run-D.M.C.* (Profile #1202; 1984; #53; achieved gold status), *King of Rock* (Profile #1205; 1985; #52; achieved platinum status), *Raising Hell* (Profile #1217; 1986; #3; achieved triple-platinum status assisted in large part by hit single, "Walk This Way" [Profile #5112; #4 pop, #8 R&B; a collaboration with Aerosmith's Steve

Run DMC album cover. Courtesy Frank Hoffmann

Tyler and Joe Perry]), and the film soundtrack *Tougher Than Leather* (Profile #1265; 1988; #9; achieved platinum status) — often crossed over to the pop charts, still a comparatively rare occurrence in the mid-1980s. This broader appeal was based in part on positive lyrics that emphasized the importance of education and urged listeners to avoid drugs and violence.

Run-D.M.C.'s clean mainstream image created a credibility problem for the group by the late 1980s when changing public tastes seemed predisposed to prefer the political militancy and raw, street-smart message largely identified with gansta rappers. The group's commercial momentum was also blunted by a protracted legal battle with Profile and its publishing company, Protoons, beginning in 1987. They released only one hit single in the 1990s, "Down with the King" (Profile #5391; 1993; #21), while later albums — *Back from Hell* (Profile #1401; 1990; #81), *Greatest Hits 1983–1991* (Profile #1419; 1991; #199), and *Down with the King* (Profile #1440; 1993) — documented their rapid fall from favor. In 2002 DJ Mizell was murdered, and the group officially retired.

RUPE, ART

See Specialty (Label)

RUSH, TOM (8 FEB 1941–)

Born in Portsmouth, New Hampshire, Rush began working the Cambridge, Massachusetts, coffeehouse circuit in the early 1960s while earning his B.A. from Harvard. Although immediately categorized as a folksinger, his early albums — two with Prestige in 1963 and a 1965 Transatlantic release — reflected his career-long eclectic leanings, which included experimentation with blues, jazz, classical arrangements, and rock instrumentation. His recorded material was divided between self-penned songs, traditionals, and astutely chosen compositions by other singer-songwriters (e.g., Joni Mitchell, James Taylor).

After signing with Elektra Records at the height of the folk-rock boom, Rush's albums — *Take a Little Walk with Me* (Elektra #7308; 1966), *The Circle Game* (Elektra #74018; 1968), and *Classic Rush* (Elektra #74062; 1971) — began appearing on the pop charts. Although never achieving true stardom, his albums with Columbia — *Tom Rush* (Columbia #9972; 1970). *Wrong End of the Rainbow* (Columbia #30402; 1970), *Merimack County* (Columbia #31306; 1972), and *Ladies Love Outlaws* (Columbia #33054; 1974) — continued to sell moderately well in the early 1970s. Never comfortable as a mainstream label artist, he founded Maple Hill Productions in 1980 as well as his own mail-order record label, Night Light Recordings. He has been a longtime promoter of concerts featuring contemporary folk performers and the Wolf Fund, which is dedicated to wildlife causes. [Romanowski and George-Warren 1995.]

RUSHING, JIMMY (26 AUG 1902–8 JUNE 1972)

Born James Andrew Rushing in Oklahoma City, Oklahoma, Rushing became one of the great blues/Big Band jazz singers of the 1930s and 1940s. He began singing while still a teenager, first in his hometown and then in California. He worked with a band led by Walter Page (1927–1928) and then joined Bennie Moten in 1929; in 1935, after Moten's death, the band was taken over by Count Basie, and Rushing became the new band's lead singer. He remained with Basie for 13 years, establishing his fame. After 1948 he worked as a solo artist, often backed by a small jazz ensemble. He recorded for Vanguard during the mid-1950s (under the supervision of noted producer John Hammond), and during the 1960s for Columbia, Colpix, Impulse!, and Bluesway, among others. Rushing continued to record and perform until his death, although his later recordings were marred by the repetition of a small repertoire of material and the fading quality of his voice. He died of leukemia in New York City.

There are numerous CD reissues of Rushing's work. His work with Count Basie is included in reissues of Basie's classic recordings. His Vanguard work of the 1950s is anthologized on *Oh Love* (Vanguard #79606) and *Everyday* (#79607). His late 1960s ABC/Bluesway work is anthologized on Verve (#547967).

Carl Benson

RUSSELL, ANNA (27 DEC 1911–)

Russell was born Claudia-Anna Russell Brown in London. A great musical parodist, Russell is famed for her takeoffs of classic opera recordings. She had conventional classical training, she made her U.S. debut as a comic singer at New York's Town Hall in 1948. She became well-known for her mock lectures on musical topics, such as "How to Compose Your Own Gilbert and Sullivan Opera" and her explanation of Wagner's Ring Cycle. Her first album was recorded live at Town Hall in 1952–1953, and released by Columbia as *The Anna Russell Album?* Its success spawned several more albums from Columbia through the 1950s; they were sufficiently popular to be reissued several times on LP and then on CD. She continued to perform into the 1980s.

Carl Benson

RUSSELL, PEE WEE
(27 MAR 1906–15 FEB 1969)

American jazz clarinetist, born Charles Ellsworth Russell in Maplewood, Missouri. He played violin, piano, and drums as a youth, then turned to the clarinet. After some time at the University of Missouri he played in Texas with Jack Teagarden and in St. Louis with Bix Beiderbecke; in 1927 he went to New York, teaming with Red Nichols, Bobby Hackett, Eddie Condon, and others. Later he freelanced, concentrating first on the dixieland style, then experimenting with modern jazzmen like Thelonious Monk and John Coltrane. He was active into the 1960s — appearing at the 1963 Newport Jazz Festival — and died in Alexandria, Virginia.

An outstanding early recording was made with his group called the Rhythmakers (including James P. Johnson, piano, and Zutty Singleton, drums) for the Hot Record Society in 1938: "Dinah"/"Baby Won't You Please Come Home" (HRS #1000). "A Ghost of a Chance" with Buddy Hackett's band (Vocalion #4565; 1938) was a notable effort as sideman. He had a fine session on 29 Mar 1960 with Buck Clayton, trumpet; Tommy Flanagan, piano; Wendell Marshall, bass; and Osie Johnson, drums. Russell's lyrical gift is displayed in "The Very Thought of You," and his quick rhythmic manner in "Lulu's Back in Town"; issued on album *Swingin' with Pee Wee* (Swingville #2008; reissued as Milestone #24213). There are various CDs on European reissue labels drawn from his entire career.

RUSSELL, ROGER (13 SEP 1935–)

Earning a B.E.E. degree from Rensselaer Polytechnic Institute in 1959, Russell went on to work for Sonotone Corp., a maker of hearing aids, phonograph cartridges, ceramic microphones, nickel cadmium batteries, tubes, and tape heads, from 1959 to 1967, ending up as Senior Engineer. In 1967, he went to work for McIntosh Laboratory, as director of acoustic research, and stayed there until his retirement in 1992. While at McIntosh, he designed the highly regarded C26 preamplifier, and went on to set up the company's then new loudspeaker division. Over the years, he created 21 different speaker designs for the company, including column-type and equalized systems, winning patents for several of them. Russell has published audio-related articles in numerous consumer magazines and is a member of the Audio Engineering Society and the International Society for General Semantics.

HOWARD FERSTLER

RYKODISC (LABEL)

Founded in 1983, as the first CD-only music label, Rykodisc (Ryko is a Japanese word meaning "sound from a flash of light") remains one of the largest independent record companies in the U.S. While starting out as producer of only digital recordings, the company eventually began releasing CD-quality LP recordings and cassettes to satisfy a variety of consumer needs. While primarily concentrating on reissued material that has been carefully remastered, including transcriptions by Frank Zappa, Jimi Hendrix, Elvis Costello, and David Bowie, as well as the MGM soundtrack collection, the company also records original releases, including a number of world-music titles. In 1991 the company acquired the Hannibal label, and in 1994 it also purchased Gramavision, a label known for its catalog of contemporary jazz, funk, and new instrumental music. In 1996 the Tradition label, a folk label of the 1950s and 1960s founded by the Clancy Brothers, was purchased, with several of its original LPs appearing on budget-priced CDs. RykoLatino and Slow River are two other subsidiary labels. [website: www.rykodisc.com.]

HOWARD FERSTLER

S

SABINE, E. J.

Record industry executive. He was with the Columbia Phonograph Co., General — London, the new British branch of the Columbia Phonograph Co., in 1900; thence he went on to the Berlin branch. Later he was associated with the National Phonograph Co., Ltd. In 1904 he joined William Michaelis as assistant manager of the new Neophone business in London. After a turn in Brussels as manager of the Neophone office there, he returned to U.K. to manage the firm's wholesale depot in Manchester. When Neophone closed down in February 1907, Sabine went to the newly formed International Neophone Co., Ltd., as one of the directors. In July 1907 he joined Aldridge, Salmon and Co., Ltd. That firm opened a record department as the Universal Talking Machine Co.; it handled the Columbia, Pathé, and Favorite lines, and had its own Elephone Records (10-inch, double-sided discs).

SABINE, WALLACE C. (13 JUNE 1868–10 JAN 1919)

An American physicist and Harvard University professor who is credited with founding the systematic study of acoustics around 1895, Sabine is in particular regarded by many as the father of the science of architectural acoustics. One of the first notable things he accomplished as a 27-year-old assistant professor of physics at Harvard was to correct the acoustics in Harvard's Fogg Lecture Hall. During World War I, he became a staff member of the Bureau of Research for the Air Service of the American Expeditionary Forces and provided services for the British Munitions Inventions Bureau in England, for the French fleet at Toulon in the Mediterranean, and for Italy on the Italian front. After the war, in 1922, he came up with a formula for calculating the reverberation time of a room, although he may have been using it as early as 1911. He also helped to design Symphony Hall, in Boston, considered by many to be one of the finest concert halls in the world. The "sabin," a nonmetric unit of sound absorption used in acoustical engineering, was named in his honor.

HOWARD FERSTLER

SACD (SUPER AUDIO COMPACT DISC)

An extremely high-quality disc-playback system designed by Philips and Sony to surpass what was possible with the compact disc. The original technical proposal was for the disc to have a multichannel SACD program on a semitransparent middle layer, with a standard density, two-channel CD layer underneath. This would allow the disc to be played on conventional CD players as well as SACD players. The SACD tracks could also be done in high-quality two-channel format, for two-channel purists. For some reason, early SACD releases were done only in two channels, but surround versions followed somewhat later.

See also **DVD-A (DVD-Audio)**

HOWARD FERSTLER

SACHS, CURT (29 JUNE 1881–5 FEB 1959)

A Berlin native, Dr. Curt Sachs authored many seminal works on musicology, including *World History of the Dance* (1938), *The History of Musical Instruments* (1940), *The Rise of Music in the Ancient World East and West* (1943), *Our Musical Heritage* (1948), and *Rhythm and Tempo* (1953). Prior to leaving Nazi Germany in 1933, he prepared a series of phonograph records on world music, a culmination of his pioneering studies of musical instruments.

During the 1930s, Sachs won the French Grand Prix five times for his recordings of ancient music while serving as curator of the Ethnological Museum's instrument collection in Paris. In 1937 he was appointed visiting professor of music at New York University. He also served as music consultant for the New York Public Library, and restored the Metropolitan Museum of Art's Crosby-Brown collection of instruments. The general public knows him best for a series of lectures on the history of music given at the New York Public Library beginning in 1949.

FRANK HOFFMANN

SADLER, JOSIE

American vaudeville artist, participant in the Ziegfeld Follies of 1912. She recorded five two-minute cylinders for Edison in 1909–1910, beginning with "He Falls for the Ladies Every Time" (#10179; 1909) in German dialect. She tried Dutch dialect in "Come and Hear the Orchestra" (Amberol #184; 1909). Sadler also recorded for Victor, and the 1917 catalog carried her comic view of "Hilda Loses Her Job" (#16783).

SAFRANSKI, EDDIE (25 DEC 1918–10 JAN 1974)

American jazz bassist, born in Pittsburgh. He played with many bands, most prominently in the 1940s with Hal McIntyre and Stan Kenton. He won the *Downbeat* poll every year from 1946 to 1952 as the favorite bassist. In 1951 he was with the Benny Goodman Sextet. Later he was a freelancer with many radio and television appearances. He died in Los Angeles. Among his notable discs were "Safranski" (Capitol #20088; 1946) with Kenton, and "Farewell Blues" with the Goodman Sextet (Columbia #39564; 1951).

ST. LOUIS EXPOSITION (1904)

At this world's fair there was competition between Victor and Columbia products for the premium awards; both had large exhibits. Afterward Victor claimed to have won, and advertised accordingly. But it was Columbia who had won, so it sued Victor and the Exposition to prevent false claims of victory. Then Columbia added an award banner to its record label, naming the awards received. Read & Welch (1976) observes that the chairman of the talking machine competition at the fair was an official of the Columbia Phonograph Co. The Multiplex Grand cylinder and the Higham Amplifier were exhibited at the fair; and John McCormack was among the artists who performed.

ST. LOUIS TALKING MACHINE CO.

A firm active ca. 1907–1908. O.A. Gressing was reported to be the general manager in March 1908.

SALÉZA, ALBERT (18 OCT 1867–26 NOV 1916)

Belgian tenor, born in Bruges. He studied at the Paris Conservatory, and made his debut at the Opéra-Comique on 19 July 1888; then sang in Nice and Monte Carlo. He returned to Paris, and performed in Brussels, then at the Metropolitan Opera from 1898 to 1901, and again in 1904–1905. Among his roles at the Metropolitan were Radames, Rodolfo, Edgar, and Faust, the latter three sung opposite Nellie Melba. He became a professor at the Paris Conservatory in 1911. Saléza died in Paris.

He was recorded by Bettini in 1898 or 1899, producing six cylinders. "Morir si pura e bella" from *Aida* was the first. He was also heard on Mapleson cylinders made in 1901, doing the *Faust* finale with Melba and Edouard de Reszke; "Verranno a te sull'aure," a duet with Melba from *Lucia*; and "Che gelida manina." He made no regular commercial records.

SALON DU PHONOGRAPHE

A phonograph parlor located on Boulevard des Italiens, Paris, around the turn of the 20th century. It followed the practice of a century later in inviting customers to order selections through a speaking tube, upon which the record would be played in another room and heard by the customer through ear tubes. There were said to be 1,500 cylinders in the Salon collection. In a sense it was the earliest record library.

SALT-N-PEPA

The first female rappers of note, they were instrumental in paving the way for other female acts in a male-dominated genre. They provided an assertive, more grown-up vision of Black women — in contrast to the wise-cracking, arrogant young teens most visible among the female MCs — that helped rap cross-over to mainstream pop acceptance.

Salt-N-Pepa were the brainchild of Hurby "Luv Bug" Azor, who enlisted his girlfriend, Cheryl James (Salt), and Sandra Denton (Pepa) to provide an answer song to Doug E. Fresh and Slick Rick's hip-hop hit, "The Show." The ensuing single, "The Show Stoppa (Is Stupid Fresh)" (Pop Art; 1985) — with the duo billed as "Super Nature" — constructed around a sample from the *Revenge of the Nerds* soundtrack, had little trouble garnering massive airplay due to the limited number of rap releases then available for pop consumption. Its success led to a long-term deal with Next Plateau Records for the act, now known as Salt-N-Pepa from a line in "The Show Stoppa," where they referred to themselves as "the salt and pepper MCs."

The debut album, *Hot Cool & Vicious* (Next Plateau #1007; 1987; #26; platinum record) — with the DJ Spinderella (Pamela Greene) rounding out the group — was dominated by Azor's vision. He wrote their lyrics, was credited with the studio production, and created the b-girl-derived visual image — basketball warm-up gear, large gold bamboo earrings, rope chains, and asymmetrical haircuts — as seen on their first video, "Tramp." Ironically, the single's B-side, "Push It" (Next Plateau #315; 1987; #19) — built around innocuously suggestive lyrics and an engaging, go-go beat — proved to be the trio's commercial breakthrough, garnering a Grammy nomination and heavy MTV rotation. The popular follow-up LP, *A Salt With a Deadly Pepa* (Next Plateau #1011; 1988; #38; gold record), emphasized dance rhythms (best appreciated in the Salt-N-Pepa's video clips) at the expense of the verses, which contained little of literary or social import.

The third album, *Blacks' Magic* (Next Plateau #1019; 1990; #38; platinum record), featured greater creative control by the group, with four tracks produced by Salt and one by Spinderella. The music emphasized their rhythm and blues influences, including dead legends like Jimi Hendrix and Billie Holiday, while the verses covered mature themes such as self-esteem ("Expression"), predatory males ("Do You Want Me"), and loveless relationships ("Let's Talk About Sex"). *Very Necessary* (Next Plateau/London #828392; 1993; #4), which consolidated the artistic growth begun on the previous LP, elevated Salt-N-Pepa to the status of pop icons, selling more than 5 million copies on the strength of the hit singles "Shoop" (Next Plateau #857314; 1993; #4; gold record) and "Whatta Man" (Next Plateau #857390; 1994; #3; platinum record). Released in the wake of prolonged record label maneuvering punctuated by the trio's decision to cut ties with Azor, *Brand New* (Red Ant/London # 828959; 1997) sold poorly.

Much of problem appeared to rest with the act, which came across as tentative, perhaps due to the rise of more youthful imitators such as TLC. At this point in time, the act's future seemed in question, with the three members (including Deirdre Roper, who had replaced Greene as Spinderella) all expressing interest in solo careers.

FRANK HOFFMANN

SALVINI, TOMMASO (10 JAN 1829–1 JAN 1916)
Italian actor, famous for his Shakespearean roles. He toured the U.K. and U.S., and while in New York in 1897 recorded for Bettini, making a cylinder titled "A Dramatic Phrase."

SAM AND DAVE
Sam Moore, born 12 Oct 1935, in Miami, and David Prater, born 9 May 1937, in Ocilla, Georgia, were the most popular Black duo of the 1960s. Both were raised on gospel; their paths crossed on the Southern club circuit. After garnering attention within the Miami club scene, the pair signed with Roulette Records.

They switched to Atlantic in 1965, where executive Jerry Wexler loaned them out to the Stax label. Their gospel fervor was effectively captured on recordings by the Stax production/songwriting team of Isaac Hayes and David Porter. While most readily identified with the R&B market, the team known as "Double Dynamite" nevertheless crossed over to the pop charts with hits such as "Hold On, I'm Comin'" (Stax #189; 1966), "Soul Man" (Stax #231; 1967), and "I Thank You" (Stax #242; 1968).

At the peak of their success, Moore and Prater were barely speaking to each other. Although they broke up in 1970, there were several efforts at reunification. Following the Blues Brothers' hit remake of "Soul Man" (Atlantic #3545; 1978), the duo was besieged with bookings from clubs across the country. After touring for the balance of the year, Prater began performing with Sam Daniels. According to a 1983 *Los Angeles Herald Examiner* article, Moore's lack of respect for Prater, who'd shot his own wife during a 1968 domestic dispute, was the prime reason for their breakup. Prater's heavy drug use was also reputed to be a factor. Prater died 9 Apr 1988 in a Georgia automobile accident. Moore continued his career, singing on Bruce Springsteen's *Human Touch* (Columbia #53000; 1992). Later in 1992, Sam and Dave were inducted into the Rock and Roll Hall of Fame. [Romanowski and George-Warren 1995.]

FRANK HOFFMANN

SAM GOODY RECORD STORES

See Goody, Sam

SAMMARCO, MARIO
(13 DEC 1868–24 JAN 1930)

Italian baritone, born in Palermo. He made his debut in Palermo as Faust in 1888, then sang in many European houses including La Scala. A great success in Covent Garden, he appeared there every season from 1905 to 1913, and again in 1919. His American appearances were with the Manhattan Opera (1906–1910) and Chicago Opera (1910–1914). His repertoire encompassed the standard French/Italian works, plus English, Spanish, and Russian material. He retired in 1919, and died in Milan.

Sammarco recorded for G & T in Milan in 1902–1904, making 18 sides; the first was "Racconto" from Franchetti's *Germania* (#52371). Then he was with Fonotipia in 1905–1906, for about 40 sides. Victor and HMV recorded him in 1910–1911. Sammarco also recorded for Pathé discs, ca. 1912 in Milan. "Di provenza il mar" was the first record (#86398), followed by nine popular arias. Among his finest discs were "Ah Mimi! tu piu non torni," with John McCormack (Victor #89044; 1911), the *Rigoletto* quartet, with McCormack and Melba (HMV #2-054025; 1911) and "Numero quindici" from *Barbiere di Siviglia*, with McCormack (HMV #2-054021; 1911). These and many others were released on LP by the major reissue labels.

SAMPLING

In the mid-1980s the concepts, first theorized by John Cage 40 years before, of constructing music from details and samples of other recordings became a physical possibility with the launch of the Fairlight CMI combined computer/keyboard. The Fairlight took fragments of sound — recordings of anything from people talking to sections of records — and then replicated and transposed them across a full piano keyboard. Vastly expensive at the time, one of the first musicians able to afford a Fairlight was Trevor Horn who used it to create his wall of sound production style on records for Frankie Goes to Hollywood. As the leader of the group The Art of Noise, Horn pushed the Fairlight to create a whole new style of music based almost solely on "found" sounds.

Scratching and hip-hop culture took sampling to the streets and some of the earliest rap records are set to a backing track of music sampled from other singles from the time and cut-ups of 1950s' rock and roll. By the late 1980s sampling was a creative force pushing dance and pop music into a new dimension. It was also threatening the very nature of the music industry as record labels scrabbled to recoup royalties on the snatches of their recordings used in others. Sampling continues to this day — in a more visible way than ever — although now the rights of the "samplee" as well as the sampler are observed. Bringing the story almost full circle was "Firestarter" by Prodigy (Warner Bros. #43843). The worldwide dance hit from the late 1990s featured a single word sampled from the Art of Noise's first hit "Close to the Edit" (1984). This garnered all five members of the Art of Noise a cowriting credit for "Firestarter", alongside the Prodigy's single member Liam Howlett.

IAN PEEL

SAMPLING FREQUENCY

Also called the sampling rate. The frequency or rate at which an analog signal is sampled or converted into digital data for storage or eventual playback, with the reading expressed in Hertz (Hz). For example, the compact disc's sampling rate is 44,100 Hz (44.1 kHz). Since the earliest commercial digital audio recorders used a standard helical-scan video recorder for storage, it was necessary to have a fixed relationship between the sampling frequency and the horizontal video frequency. This allowed those frequencies to be derived from the same master clock by frequency division. For the NTSC 525-line television system used in the U.S., a sampling frequency of 44,055.94 Hz was selected, whereas for the European PAL 625-line system, a frequency of 44,100 Hz was chosen. The 0.1 percent difference shows up as an imperceptible shift in pitch. It is important to remember that there are other rates than those used by the compact disc, with common examples being 32 kHz, 48 kHz, and even 50 kHz. Those are mostly used by digital recording devices.

See also **DAT (Digital Audio Tape); Digital Recording**

HOWARD FERSTLER

SAMUEL (BARNETT) AND SONS LTD.

A U.K. musical instrument firm. Barnett Samuel was a wholesale merchant, dealing in musical items, among other things, from 1832. His firm was one of the first in London to take up phonographs and Gramophones, toward the end of the 19th century. It was announced in *TMN* during 1903 that the shop had 100,000 records in stock. Products of Columbia, Zonophone, and Edison were handled. In 1908 the firm was appointed sole agent in U.K. for Odeon, Fonotipia, and Jumbo Records of Fonotipia, Ltd. The most successful item marketed by Samuel was its own Dulcephone Decca portable (1914). The firm withdrew from the talking machine industry in summer 1928, its business converted into a public company called the Decca Gramophone Co. Ltd., after the brand name of its phonographs of that period. In 1929 the company was acquired by the new Decca Record Co., Ltd.

FRANK ANDREWS

SANDERS, GAYLE MARTIN

SEE MARTIN-LOGAN LOUDSPEAKERS

SANTANA

From Latin rock innovators in the late 1960s, the group — essentially guitarist Carlos Santana (b. Autlán de Navarro, Mexico, 20 July 1947) and a continually changing cast of rock journeymen, session players, and guest stars — has flirted with psychedelia, electric blues, jazz fusion, and pop influences within a broad progressive rock context. Relegated to commercial limbo for the better part of two decades, Santana revived his career in the late 1990s, receiving nine Grammys for the best-selling LP, *Supernatural* (Arista #19080; 1999; #1).

The Mexican-born Santana formed the Santana Blues Band in October 1966 amid the San Francisco flower-power movement. After a gestation period spent largely in the Bay Area (during which time their name was shortened), the group's distinctive sound —

Carlos Santana solo album cover. Courtesy Frank Hoffmann

built around Santana's fluid, lyrical guitar lines and an augmented rhythm section, originally including drummer Michael Shrieve, percussionist Jose "Chepito" Areas, and conga player Mike Carabello — captured the public's imagination during the August 1969 Woodstock Festival. The Latin-derived rhythms and psychedelic blues of the first three albums — *Santana* (Columbia #9781; 1969; #4), *Abraxas* (Columbia #30130; 1970; #1), and *Santana* (Columbia #30595; 1971; #1; commonly referred to as *Santana III*) — elevated Santana to superstar status. *Caravanserai* (Columbia #31610; 1972; #8), however, signaled a shift in the direction of jazz-inflected jamming. Much of the band's 1970s output — most notably, *Welcome* (Columbia #32445; 1973; #25), *Borboletta* (Columbia #33135; 1974; #20), *Moonflower* (Columbia #34914; 1977; #10; part live/part studio), and *Inner Secrets* (Columbia #35600; 1978; #27) — continued to explore the fusion genre.

The release of *Zebop!* (Columbia #37158; 1981; #9), featuring the single "Winning" (Columbia #01050; 1981; #17), and *Shango* (Columbia #38122; 1982; #22), which included "Hold On" (Columbia #03160; 1982; #15) and "Nowhere to Run" (Columbia #03376; 1982; #66), reflected a renewed commitment to the pop mainstream. While displaying competent musicianship and passionate social commentary, follow-up albums such as the Grammy-winning *Blues for Salvador* (Columbia #40875; 1987), *Spirits Dancing in the Flesh* (Columbia #46065; 1990; #85), and *Milagro* (Polydor #513197; 1992) experienced a sales drop-off in the face of mixed reviews. In 1998 the group was inducted into the Rock and Roll Hall of Fame, but Santana himself was in a career slump. The eclectic *Supernatural* (Arista #19080; 1999) — featuring studio contributions by the likes of Dave Matthews, Everlast, Lauren Hill, Wyclef Jean, Eric Clapton, and Matchbox 20's Rob Thomas, who sang on the number one single "Smooth" (Arista #13718; 1999; #1) — changed all that, lingering in the upper reaches of the *Billboard* LP charts for more than two years. A follow-up album using the same concept, *Shaman* (Arista #14737), was issued in 2002, initially scoring a hit with the single "The Game of Love" sung by Michelle Branch, a pleasant pop song featuring Santana's typical guitar work.

FRANK HOFFMANN

SANTLEY, CHARLES, *SIR*
(28 FEB 1834–22 SEP 1922)

U.K. baritone, born in Liverpool. He studied in Milan, and made his debut at Pavia in 1857, singing a minor role in *Traviata*. He sang mostly in oratorios and concerts for several years, then joined the Covent Garden company and stayed until 1863; thence he went to Mapleson's company. Valentine in *Faust* was a part which brought him much acclaim; indeed, Gounod wrote the famous aria "Avant du quitter ces yeux," for him as part of the 1864 London production. Subsequently, Santley toured the U.S. and joined the Carl Rosa Opera group. On 1 May 1907 he sang a jubilee concert and was knighted later that year. He died in London.

Santley was the second-earliest born singer to record an opera aria: "Non piu andrai" (G & T #052000; 1903); he was 69 years old at the time. At the same session (3 June 1903) he cut four other sides for G & T, all concert songs. All these discs are scarce today; he did not record again until 1913, when he had a final session for Columbia.

SAPPHIRE RECORD AND TALKING MACHINE CO.

A New York firm. It was acquired by the Indestructible Phonographic Record Co. in 1911.

SARGENT, MALCOLM, *SIR*
(25 APR 1895–3 OCT 1967)

British conductor, born Harold Malcolm Sargent in Stamford. He studied organ, then served in the infantry during World War I. In 1921 he began conducting and during the 1920s led the D'Oyly Carte Opera Co. and the Ballets Russes, plus the Royal Choral Society from 1928. Sargent directed the Halle Orchestra in 1939–1942, the Liverpool Philharmonic Orchestra in 1942–1948, and the BBC Symphony Orchestra in 1950–1957. He also directed the Promenade Concerts in London from 1948 to 1966. There were numerous world tours with his various orchestras. He died in London.

Sargent recorded across a wide repertoire, for Victor, HMV, and Columbia. Among his notable discs were the Beethoven Piano Concertos No. 1 and No. 5, with Artur Schnabel (Victor #M-158 and #M-155) and the London Symphony Orchestra; and the other three Beethoven concertos with Schnabel and the London Philharmonic Orchestra (Victor #295, #194, and #156). For Columbia he led the D'Oyly Carte Opera Co. in definitive recordings of many Gilbert and Sullivan operettas, made in the late 1920s and early 1930s. (These have been reissued on CD by Arabesque.) His support for English composers resulted in a few important discs, e.g., the Vaughan Williams "Lark Ascending" with the Liverpool Orchestra (Columbia #DX-1386/7) and "Fantasia on Greensleeves" with the Halle Orchestra (Columbia #DX 1087).

SARNOFF, DAVID
(27 FEB 1891–12 DEC 1971)

Inventor, programmer, network founder, futurist. While not technically the inventor of broadcast technology, David Sarnoff's visionary and hard-working influence on the double innovations of radio and television gave him the enduring reputation as the father of both media. Straddling the lines between profit-pouncing executive, patent-pursuing futurist, and artist-shmoozing programmer, Sarnoff was first to realize the consumer benefit of bringing both radio and television into the home. His vision of home radio began in 1915 and was scorned by the technology industry of the time. Not until after World War I, when Marconi (Sarnoff's employer) was absorbed by recently created General Electric subsidiary RCA, did the home-radio idea gain traction. Sarnoff swung into the role of programmer, arranging to broadcast a prizefight in 1921. Within a few years RCA's new product (the Radiola) was a success despite its hefty pre-Depression price of $75. With a media mogul's unerring sense of leverage, Sarnoff imagined the benefits of networking hundreds of local broadcast stations and formed the National Broadcasting Co. in 1926.

Television was next, and it was Sarnoff who saw its potential and began the first NBC television station in 1928. He demonstrated the technology at the 1939 World's Fair, but further progress was delayed by World War II, after which television was released upon the American public.

Sarnoff fought for controlling patents to develop the technology. NBC produced the first videotape telecast and the first made-for-television movie. Sarnoff became president of RCA in 1930, chairman of the board in 1947, and retired in 1970

BRAD HILL

SATHERLEY, ART
(19 OCT 1889–10 FEB 1986)

Born Arthur Edward Satherley in Bristol, England, Satherley came to the U.S. when he was 24, initially working in a lumber mill owned by the Wisconsin Chair Co. Like many other furniture manufacturers, the company expanded into producing phonographs in the late 1910s and then into making records on its house label, Paramount. Satherley worked his way up the ranks at the new label, developing the careers of bluesmen Blind Lemon Jefferson and Blind Blake and cabaret blues star Ma Rainey.

In 1929 Satheley joined with the Plaza label, which was mostly sold through Sears Roebuck and other catalog sources. Soon after, the label, along with other dime store outfits, was renamed American Record Co. or ARC. Satherley became the firm's Southern-music producer, traveling through the South setting up makeshift sessions to record whatever talent he could unearth. Among his country music finds were Roy Acuff, Bob Wills, and Gene Autry; he produced Autry's 1931 recording of "That Silver-Haired Daddy of Mine," a breakthrough hit for the cowboy star that also brought the company much-needed capital in the depths of the Depression.

In 1938 Columbia Records acquired ARC, and Satherley remained with that label until 1952. He established Columbia's presence in the new country music recording capital, Nashville, after World War II, overseeing sessions by Bill Monroe and Ray Price, among many others. His assistant, Don Law, was to become a leading country producer in the late 1950s and 1960s. Satherley lived happily in California following his retirement; he was elected into the Country Music Hall of Fame in 1971.

CARL BENSON

SAUTER, EDDIE
(2 DEC 1914–21 APR 1981)

American jazz trumpeter, Big Band leader, and arranger, born in Brooklyn. He studied at Columbia and the Juilliard School, and played in various dance bands. In 1935 he joined Charlie Barnet, then went to Red Norvo in 1936 as trumpeter and mellophone player. For Norvo he made outstanding arrangements, including those for Mildred Bailey, and gained fame for his original and resourceful orchestrations. Almost all of Norvo's records during 1936–1939 were Sauter designs. Then he became Benny Goodman's arranger in 1939, and continued to expand his instrumental colors. He made about 60 arrangements that Goodman recorded (many featuring vocals by Helen Forest) before the 1942 Petrillo ban, establishing the orchestra on a new sophisticated level. "How High the Moon" (Columbia #35391; 1940), "The Man I Love" (Columbia #55001; 1940), and "Cocoanut Grove" (Columbia #35527; 1940) exemplify his art. His setting of "My Old Flame" for Peggy Lee (Columbia #6379; 1941) was a "masterpiece of the genre" [Schuller 1989].

Sauter later worked with many top bands, including Artie Shaw, Tommy Dorsey, Woody Herman, and Ray McKinley; then he formed a new group with Bill Finegan: the Sauter-Finegan Band. When that ensemble dissolved in 1957, Sauter worked in German radio for two years, then went into television production in New York, and arranged for Broadway shows. He was active into the 1970s. He died in Nyack, New York.

SAVANA (LABEL)
A U.K. record, in five and 1/2-inch, six-inch, and 10-inch sizes, of the 1920s. Proprietors were the music retailers Rose, Morris and Co. (a firm still in business. Discs were pressed from Edision Bell and Crystalate masters, used on Bell, Imperial, and Mimosa discs; some matrices were American imports from Plaza Music Co. of New York. Material was dance music, popular vocals, and instrumentals. [Rust 1978.]

SAVILLE, FRANCES
(6 JAN 1863–8 NOV 1935)
American soprano, born in San Francisco. She sang oratorio in Australia, studied in Paris, and made her opera debut in Brussels; afterward Saville sang in many Eruopean houses. Her Metropolitan Opera debut was as Juliette, opposite Jean de Reszke, on 18 Nov 1895. She also sang Manon and Elisabeth in *Tannhäuser*. After the 1898–1899 season she went to sing in Vienna, then retired to California, where she died (in Burlingame).

Saville's only records were for Bettini. In his 1897 catalog she is listed singing "Caro nome" and an aria (not named but presumably Micaela's aria) from *Carmen*. Bettini's 1899 catalog carries the "Caro nome" but not the *Carmen* piece; it adds the Brahms "Wicgcnlicd."

SAVITT, JAN (4 SEP 1913–4 OCT 1948)
Russian/American violinist and Big Band leader, born in Petrograd, Russia. He grew up in Philadelphia and studied at the Curtis Institute, then played violin in the Philadelphia Orchestra. In the 1930s he was a musical director on a Philadelphia radio station, then formed a dance band for broadcasting. He took the band on tour, and gained a fine reputation for attractive swing and dance arrangements. He died in Sacramento, California.

Savitt made a few early records for the Variety label in 1937, then recorded for Bluebird (1937–1938), Decca (1939–1941), and Victor from 1941. "It's a Wonderful World," his own composition, was a popular disc (Decca #2836; 1939); "720 in the Books," another Savitt tune, was also successful (Decca #2771; 1939); both were sung by Johnny Watson. Gloria DeHaven was vocalist with Savitt for a time, and did a fine rendition of "If You Ever, Ever Loved Me" (Bluebird #B-11548; 1942).

SAVOY (LABEL)

An American record, issued from 1942 by the Savoy Record Co., Newark, New Jersey. Herman Lubinsky (30 Aug 1896–16 Mar 1974) was owner of the firm until his death. (In 1947, Lubinsky formed Regent Records to handle mainstream pop releases, but the label only lasted until the mid-1950s.) With the benefit of A&R man Tony Reig, Savoy signed important musicians of the bebop movement: Charlie Parker, Miles Davis, Stan Getz, Dexter Gordon, Ray Brown, Sonny Stitt, Fats Navarro, Kai Winding, and many others. Fred Mendelsohn joined the organization in the late 1940s and developed a great list of gospel singers. Rhythm and blues artists were recruited by Lee Magid, who also discovered Della Reese. Under A&R man Ozzier Cadena, Savoy produced the first records of Cannonball Adderley and Charlie Byrd and the outstanding work of Milt Jackson.

Savoy was one of the first jazz labels to release 12-inch LPs from 1955 in the MG 12000 series. However, the label lost momentum in the 1960s, and was acquired in 1975 by Arista Records. Over the next 25 years, the Savoy catalog changed hands several times, with distribution being held by Muse Records in the early 1990s, then Denon of Japan, and then, beginning in 1999, with Atlantic Records. In 1986, the label's gospel line was purchased by Malaco Music. [Ruppli & Porter 1980.]

See also **Modern Jazz Quartet (MJQ)**

REV. CARL BENSON

Savoy 78 from the mid-'40s. Courtesy Kurt Nauck/Nauck's Vintage Records

SAVOY BROWN

Formed in 1966, the London-based Savoy Brown has been a fixture in the U.S. rock scene for the better part of four decades without the benefit of hit singles or a strong following at home. Despite frequent personnel changes in which the only constant has been lead guitarist Kim Simmonds, the band built up a loyal following through incessant touring and the release of a string of consistency high-quality albums. Ever mindful of changing pop-music fashions, Simmonds has shifted stylistic gears from blues rock in the mid-1960s, to flirtations with acid rock by the end of the decade, to hard-rock boogie by the early 1970s.

Savoy Brown reached its zenith in popularity in the late 1960s and early 1970s; best-selling albums released during that period included *Blue Matter* (Parrot #71027; 1969), *A Step Further* (Parrot #71029; 1969), *Raw Sienna* (Parrot #71036; 1970), *Looking In* (Parrot #71042; 1970), *Street Corner Talking* (Parrot #71047; 1971), and *Hellbound Train* (Parrot #71052; 1972). However, Simmonds has soldiered on in the face of diminished record sales and the unprecedented success of ex-members Lonesome Dave Preverett, Tony Stevens, and Roger Earl as Foghat.

FRANK HOFFMANN

SAVOY GRAMOPHONE CO.

A subsidiary of the Nanes Art Furniture Co. of New York.

SAXOPHONE RECORDINGS (HISTORIC)

Evidently the earliest person to record the saxophone (sax) was a woman, Bessie Meeklens, who made 12 Edison wax cylinders with piano accompaniment on 23 Apr 1892. Her first number was "Ave Maria." Eugene Coffin was the earliest Columbia saxophonist, performing "Rocked in the Cradle of the Deep" and seven other pieces in 1896. Jean-Baptiste Moeremans, of the United States Marine Band, recorded ca. 1899 for Columbia cylinders, doing "The Heart Bowed Down" (#12700) and two other numbers. He was also with Victor from 1900 to 1911.

A saxophone quartet from Sousa's Band recorded three items for Victor discs in August 1902, and returned to the studio in September 1903. Other early artists included F. Wheeler Wadsworth, Nathan Glantz (of the Van Eps Trio), Duane Sawyer, the Six Brown Brothers (sextet), H. Benne Henton, and Steve Porpora.

The minuscule classical repertoire for the instrument inhibited the growth of that genre of recording, but there was no shortage of jazz performances. New Orleans dixieland bands did not use saxophones; but as this style expanded, the instrument appeared in ensembles of the 1920s. Don Redman played alto saxophone (and clarinet) with the Fletcher Henderson Dance Orchestra on their earliest recordings, for Brunswick in 1921. He was joined by Coleman Hawkins in the reed section in 1923, and Allie Ross in 1924. Paul Whiteman's 1920 lineup had three saxophone players, Ross Gorman, Don Clark, and Hale Byers, who doubled on altos and tenors when needed. By the mid-1920s Whiteman had a full choir of saxophones. Art Hickman's orchestra had three or four saxophones in 1919.

Harlan Leonard, alto saxophone (also soprano saxophone and clarinet), was one of the artists added when Bennie Moten increased the size of his orchestra in 1924. Otto Hardwick, a clarinetist who played alto and baritone saxophone as well, was with the Duke Ellington band of 1924; and Prince Robinson, clarinet and tenor sax, was added to the Ellington band in 1925. Don Redman was another alto (and clarinet) player with Ellington in 1926. The 1928 Ellington band included Barney Bigard and Johnny Hodges; both men played sax as well as clarinet — a combination that became standard in the swing bands.

Herschel Evans played a melodic and fluent tenor saxophone with Troy Floyd's Plaza Hotel Orchestra; he can be heard on "Dreamland Blues" (Okeh #8719; 1928). An early soprano saxophone solo by Siki Collins appeared on Floyd's only other record, "Shadowland Blues" (Okeh #8571; 1928). Walter Page, trumpet virtuoso, played a baritone saxophone on a recording of "Squabblin'" made by his Blue Devils (Vocalion #1463; 1929). From such initiatives it was the alto sax and tenor sax that entered the jazz/swing mainstream.

SAYAO, BIDU
(11 MAY 1902–12 MAR 1999)

Brazilian soprano, born Baluina de Oliveira Sayao near Rio de Janeiro. She studied in France with Jean de Reszke, returned to Brazil, and made a concert debut in 1925. A year later she appeared as Rosina in her opera debut and became a favorite in that and other coloratura and lyric roles. She sang throughout Europe opposite great artists like Beniamino Gigli, Aureliano Pertile, Titta Ruffo, and Jan Kiepura. In 1931 she sang Juliette with Georges Thill at the Paris Opéra. Arturo Toscanini invited her to sing with the New York Philharmonic Symphony, leading to a highly successful American debut. She began with the Metroplitan Opera on 14 Feb 1937, as Manon, and remained 15 seasons until she retired in 1952. Sayao was renowned

for her interpetations of Gilda, Mimi, Violetta, and Cio Cio San. In addition to opera, she was a brilliant concert artist, excelling in the French art song. She died in Rockport, Maine.

Sayao's recordings began with Victor, in Brazil, where she sang arias from *Guarany* and seven other numbers in 1935 (Victor #11561). She continued with Victor in the U.S., doing one side in 1938 and two others in 1940; then went to Columbia for her principal output from 1944 to ca. 1948. Ten records covered her outstanding arias; they were reissued on LP by Columbia, Philips, and several other labels. Air shots from Metropolitan Opera performances were released by Golden Age of Opera, displaying her art in the complete *Boheme*, *Don Giovanni*, *Don Pasquale*, *Nozze di Figaro*, and *Romeo et Juliette*; there was also a complete *Manon* from San Francisco, plus several extended excerpt albums. Odyssey issued an album (#Y33130) of her concert songs in 1977. [Léon 1960.]

SBK (LABEL)

Music business founded by record producer Charles Koppelman (b. 1940), along with Stephen Swid and Martin Bandler, in 1986, through the purchase of CBS's music-publishing holdings. Swid left the firm early in its existence, but Bandler and Koppelman built it into a large publishing house. Three years later, the duo sold its publishing business to EMI and used the proceeds to start a record label. Their greatest success came in the early 1990s with the teen-pop harmony group Wilson Phillips and the rapper Vanilla Ice. By 1992, Bandler and Koppelman sold out to EMI; Bandler is currently head of that firm's music-publishing business, and Koppelman remained at EMI running its pop labels until 1998, when he went into investment banking running CAK Entertainment in partnership with Prudential Securities.

CARL BENSON

SCALA (LABEL)

A British record issued from 1911 to 1927. In 1912 the source firm was Scala Record Co., Ltd., of London. Pressings were from Germany until World War I (masters from Beka and others), then made in London as well. A number of American masters were used, including Vocalion and Gennett, in producing a popular dance and vocal repertoire. [Rust 1978.]

SCANSPEAK

SEE LOUDSPEAKER

SCEPTER/WAND (LABELS)

Pop labels founded by Passaic, New Jersey, in the 1960s by housewife Florence Greenberg when her daughter introduced her to four of her classmates who had formed a singing group called the Poquellos. They sang a song they wrote called "I Met Him on a Sunday" which impressed Florence who issued the song under the group's new name, the Shirelles, on a new label, Tiara (#6112; 1958). The song hit big, and Greenberg sold the label and the group to Decca, but her husband continued as the group's manager. Decca didn't handle the group well, and soon dropped them, so Florence started a new label, Scepter, in 1959, out of New York. The first Scepter releases, by the Shirelles and other signings, saw little action, and the label struggled into 1960. A chance meeting by Florence with producer Luther Dixon led her to hire him to help revive the Shirelles's recording career; he became the head of A&R for the label and an important ingredient in creating its teen-pop sound. After achieving success with the Shirelles, Greenberg founded a related label, Wand, to focus on R&B acts, with its first signing being singer Chuck Jackson. Wand also briefly recorded the Isley Brothers in 1962, including their classic "Twist and Shout." Despite having been given his own label to run (Ludix), Dixon left the label in late 1963 after being wooed by Capitol Records.

In 1963 Greenberg purchased a master tape from a little-known Seattle record label, Jerden, of a local group singing a barely comprehensible song. The song was "Louie Louie" and the garage band who played it was the Kingsmen. After rumors spread that the song's lyrics were obscene, it hit #1 and has become a rock classic. It was issued as Wand #143 (1963; #2); the group had one follow-up Top 10 hit in 1965 with "The Jolly Green Giant" (Wand 172; #4).

Scepter's next big act came via songwriter Burt Bacharach, who discovered a young singer named Dionne Warwick. Her first hit came for the label in early 1964 with "Anyone Who Had a Heart" (Scepter #1262; #8 pop), and she would continue to be a hit-maker for the label through 1970. Thanks to Warwick's success, the label was able to move into grander offices in 1965 and open its own recording studio. They also launched a budget label, Pricewise, to reissue older hits on LP, but it quickly folded. Scepter's other big hitmaker of the late 1960s was B.J. Thomas, most famous for "Raindrops Keep Fallin' on My Head," featured in the 1970 film *Butch Cassidy and the Sundance Kid* (Scepter #12265; first issued as an album track and then re-recorded for the single; #1 pop), winning a Grammy and an Academy award for Best Song in 1970.

Scepter and Wand continued to have releases through 1976, but no major hitmakers. In 1976 Greenberg retired, selling her labels to Springboard International, who mined the back catalog on a series of (poorly produced) LPs on their Springboard, Trip, and Up Front labels. In 1991, Warner Bros. issued *The Scepter Records Story* (#42003), a superior-quality and well-documented three-CD set.

CARL BENSON

SCHEIBER, PETER

SEE AMBIANCE EXTRACTION; BAUER, BEN; FELDMAN, LEONARD; FOSGATE, JAMES

SCHEINER, ELLIOT (18 MAR 1947–)

One of America's premier recording engineers, Scheiner started out as a musician playing percussion in various bands, including Jimmy Buffett's s Coral Reefers, and began his recording career under the tutelage of Phil Ramone in 1967. By 1973 he had begun to freelance as an engineer and producer, becoming the first person ever to work as a freelance engineer for other artists. Since then, he has produced, recorded, and/or mixed for performers as diverse as Steely Dan, Toto, Boz Scaggs, Fleetwood Mac, Glenn Frey, Sting, Ricky Martin, Aretha Franklin, Natalie Cole, Barbra Streisand, Luciano Pavarotti, the Eagles, Van Morrison, Queen, the Doobie Brothers, Roy Orbison, and James Brown. He also recorded the soundtrack for *The Godfather*, parts I and II. His talents have been recognized with 16 Grammy nominations, five of which he has won, plus two Emmy nominations and three TEC award nominations.

HOWARD FERSTLER

SCHIØTZ, AKSEL
(1 SEP 1906–19 APR 1975)

Danish tenor, later a baritone, born in Roskilde. He studied languages at the University of Copenhagen, taking a master's degree in 1929; at the same time he pursued vocal studies. He made his opera debut in Copenhagen, in *Cosi fan tutte* (1939), commencing a career in which his Mozart roles were greatly admired. He specialized also in Lieder, and was instrumental in popularizing the Schubert cycles through his recordings with Gerald Moore. In the U.S. from 1948, he taught voice at several universities before retiring to Denmark in 1968. He died in Copenhagen.

The great Schiøtz/Moore interpetations of Schubert included the *Schîne Mâllerin* on HMV (#GM-407) plus individual songs from other cycles. Schiøtz also recorded several Mozart arias, e.g., "Dalla sua pace"

(HMV #DB-2564) and "Una aura amorosa" from *Cosi fan tutte* (HMV #DB-5265).

SCHIPA, TITO (2 JAN 1888–16 DEC 1965)

Italian tenor, born in Lecce as Raffaele Attilio Amadeo Schipa. He was a composer first, then took up singing; he made his debut in Vercelli as Alfredo in 1910. Then he sang throughout Europe, and with the Chicago Opera Co. from 1919 to 1932. His Metropolitan Opera debut was on 23 Nov 1932, as Nemorino; he remained with the company until 1935, achieving great success even in competition with Beniamino Gigli and Giovanni Martinelli, although his vocal prime had been in the 1920s. His lyric roles were the finest, not only in the usual Verdi, Rossini, and Mozart repertoire, but also in such operas as *Mignon*, *Werther*, and Cilea's *Arlesiana*. After world tours in the 1930s he settled in Italy, retired from opera in 1954, but continued giving recitals until 1963. He died in New York.

Schipa's earliest records were for HMV in Milan in 1913–1914. He first sang two airs from *Cavalleria rusticana* (#252127 and #252128), and numbers from *Gioconda*, *Lucia*, *Faust*, plus Verdi-Puccini material. In 1916–1919 he worked for Pathé in Milan, doing among other arias his greatly acclaimed "Questa o quella" (#10316; later also recorded for Victor) backed by "La donna ä mobile." Victor recorded Schipa in America during 1922–1926, including duets with Amelita Galli-Curci and Lucrezia Bori. A number of CD reissues have covered most of the Schipa output, including RCA GD #87969 (arias and Spanish songs, done in the 1920s and 1930s, Galli-Curci duets from *Lucia* and *Traviata* among them); EMI Références #H763200-2, on which one can hear the marvelous rendition of "Una furtiva lagrima" and the earliest Milan HMV's; and a complete *Don Pasquale* from 1933 at La Scala (EMI #CHS7 63241-2, in which Schipa displays "the very epitome of bel canto." [Steane, in his review of the set; Hutchinson 1960.]

SCHMITT, AL (17 APR 1938–)

One of America's top recording engineers, Schmitt gained his first recording studio experience at the early age of seven, while working for his uncle, Harry Smith, who was the owner of New York's first independent recording studio. Smith was a well-known engineer who had worked with the likes of Caruso, the Andrews Sisters, Art Tatum, Bing Crosby, and Orson Welles. Between the ages of 17 and 19 Schmitt served in the Navy and, when he came out, his uncle found him an apprenticeship at Apex Recording Studio in New York, where Schmitt was to meet and be strongly influenced by engineer Tom Dowd. He moved to Los Angeles in 1958, where he went to work at a studio called Radio Recorders. Soon after he was hired by RCA to become an engineer at RCA Studios in Los Angeles, and in 1963 he became staff producer. In 1967 he left RCA to become an independent producer, and in 1970 he returned to engineering work, realized that he thoroughly enjoyed that part of the trade, and went on to record many outstanding releases.

During his career, Schmitt has been involved in over 150 gold or platinum records. He has been honored with 25 Grammy award nominations and won 11 of them — more than any other recording engineer. In addition, he was a 1997 inductee into the Technical Excellence and Creativity Awards Hall of Fame. The list of people he has recorded reads like a who's who in contemporary music: Frank Sinatra, Barbra Streisand, Madonna, Steely Dan, Toto, Ray Charles, Dave Grusin, Joe Sample, Luther Vandross, Sam Cooke, Henry, Mancini, Jefferson Airplane, Brandy, David Benoit, Toni Braxton, Dr. John, Quincy Jones, Les Brown, Natalie Cole, Horace Silver, Robbie Robertson, Vanessa Williams, Greg Adams, Ruben Blades, Duke Ellington, Jackson Brown, George Benson, and Diana Krall, among others.

HOWARD FERSTLER

SCHNABEL, ARTUR (17 APR 1882–15 AUG 1951)

Austrian/American pianist, born in Lipnik. A child prodigy, he studied with Theodor Leschetitzky from 1891 to 1897, and then began public performances. He lived in Berlin and concertized there, playing recitals with violinist Carl Flesch, then teaching at the Hochschule fär Musik. His American debut was in 1921. Schnabel was universally acclaimed for his Beethoven interpretations and for his Mozart. He lived in New York from 1939, taking citizenship in 1944, but finally returned to Europe. He died in Morschach, Switzerland.

Schnabel did not like to record, and made no discs until he was 50 years old, slightly after his prime. He worked for Victor/HMV, doing the Beethoven concertos with Malcolm Sargent, Beethoven and Mozart sonatas, and works of Schubert and J.S. Bach.

Harmonia Mundi issued a CD in 1990 of Mozart works (#Z6590/93; later released by EMI Références #CHS7 63703-2) that offered some uneven technical results and infelicitous orchestral partnerships. Schnabel's superior Beethoven sonata interpetations appear on another EMI Références #CHS7 63765-2. [Bloesch 1986.]

SCHNEE, WILLIAM (4 JULY 1947–)

A major American recording engineer, Bill Schnee was born in Phoenix, Arizona, took keyboard lessons at age eight, started studying the trumpet when he was nine, and switched to the saxophone when he was 11. At age 13 he moved with his family to San Francisco, and in his 16th year the family moved again, this time to Los Angeles, where he spent his last year in high school. In Los Angeles, Schnee put his keyboard talents to good use and formed a band with the help of several of his friends. While he honed the band's sound and engineered their demos, the group's producer noticed his talents and encouraged Schnee to pursue the professional recording techniques that would later build his craft. Throughout college studies at California Polytechnic Institute (1965–1968) and Loyola Law School (1969–1970), Schnee continued to write songs and play music, but his natural gifts in sound engineering convinced him that recording work was what he wanted to do.

His natural engineering talents paid off, and one technical triumph followed another. In 1975 Schnee engineered the groundbreaking album from Thelma Houston on the Sheffield Labs label, *I've Got the Music in Me*, a live direct-to-disc recording that set new standards in sound engineering and still ranks as a favorite of audiophiles everywhere. In 1981 he opened his own recording facility, Schnee Studio. State-of-the-art in every way, it is equipped with a custom-made console, custom tube-microphone preamps, and an extensive collection of old tube microphones, and is regarded as one of the finest tracking rooms in Los Angeles. Since its opening, the studio has generated even more gold and platinum triumphs by hosting artists like Don Henley, Anita Baker, Aaron Neville, Cher, Natalie Cole, Bette Midler, Teddy Pendergrass, and Dionne Warwick.

Today, Schnee's musical background continues to help in communicating with artists and musicians in the studio as producer, engineer, and mix master. In a career that spans four decades, he has engineered gold or platinum releases with such artists as Three Dog Night, Barbra Streisand, Neil Diamond, Carly Simon, the Pointer Sisters, Whitney Houston, Michael Bolton, Amy Grant, and Chicago. Schnee has also mixed four projects for Mark Knopfler and engineered the last Dire Strait's album, *On Every Street*, one of the better-engineered rock recordings created by anybody, anywhere. Switching to his producer role, Schnee also has worked on multiple projects with Huey Lewis & the News, Boz Scaggs, and Pablo Cruise.

Schnee has been Grammy-nominated 10 times for Best Engineered Recording and has won twice for *Aja* and *Gaucho*, both from Steely Dan. Those two multi-platinum releases add to a list of hits that include over 60 gold records, 35 platinum projects, and 50 Top 20 singles. In 1992, he took an Emmy award for Best Sound Mixing for a Variety Special, Natalie Cole's live concert for PBS, and in 1996, he won a Dove award for *Raise the Standard*, a praise album for the Promise Keepers.

HOWARD FERSTLER

SCHOEPS

A microphone manufacturing company founded in 1948 by Karl Schoeps, as Schalltechnik Dr.-Ing. Schoeps. At the beginning, the company dealt with sound recording and reinforcement systems and engineered systems for use in motion-picture theaters, even manufacturing a tape recorder model for a short time. When it was started, the Schoeps "factory" was housed in private apartments; however, before long it moved to a rented house in Durlach, the oldest district of Karlsruhe. The company's current residence is one of the oldest houses preserved in Durlach, with its cellar and foundation walls dating back to 1662. The firm expanded into an adjacent building in 1965, doubling the available floor space, and in 1990 it expanded again into a former ballroom on the premises.

In the first 20 years of its history, Schoeps had practically no distribution network of its own. Nevertheless, its circle of customers steadily increased, thanks to the friendship between Dr. Schoeps and a French businessman, who had very good contacts at radio stations. As a consequence, Schoeps gained a strong market position in the French recording industry during the 1950s which it has managed to preserve to the present day. In the years that followed, Schoeps also developed contacts in German radio and television stations, making the name Schoeps well known in Germany. Throughout the years the company was known for its innovative small-capsule designs, and in 1973, the Colette series was launched, possibly the most extensive and versatile microphone system ever conceived. This series was used by a number of important American recording companies, including Telarc.

In 1980 the son of Dr. Schoeps, Ulrich Schoeps, joined the company, becoming second director in 1986, with his father remaining first director. At the end of 1993, Dr. Schoeps died, whereupon his son became head of the firm. In this position, the younger Schoeps has continued the tradition begun by his father. No doubt part of the company's success is due to the fact that, in a space of only 1,500 square meters, a total of 35 employees develop, manufacture, and distribute the whole range of Schoeps products. Today, Schoeps is one of the most innovative microphone manufacturers in the world, leading the way in many developments. Central to its design philosophy over the years is the company's insistence on absolute sound neutrality of the microphones, making them ideal for recording classical ensembles. [website: www.schoeps.de.]

HOWARD FERSTLER

SCHOETTEL (E.A. AND A.G.) CO.

A New York firm, located in 1907 in Queens. They marketed the Mega horn and other Gramophone horns made of papier-mâché.

SCHORR, FRIEDRICH
(2 SEP 1888–14 AUG 1953)

Hungarian/American baritone, born in Nagyvárád. He studied law in Vienna, and took voice lessons. He made his opera debut in Graz and remained with the company five seasons. He also appeared with the Chicago Opera in 1911–1912, then returned to Europe. He sang in Graz, Prague, and Cologne; then joined the Berlin State Opera and remained from 1923–1931. Schorr was with the Metropolitan Opera in 1924–1943, singing also in Bayreuth in 1925, 1927, 1928, and 1930. He was famed for his Wagnerian interpretations, notably Hans Sachs and Wotan, but was also distinguished as Amonasro and in the Richard Strauss operas. He later taught at the Manhattan School of Music. Schorr died in Farmington, Connecticut.

Schorr recorded for HMV, Brunswick, and Polydor (DG Schallplatte) in the 1920s. The earliest record was "Wotan's Abschied" from *Walkure* (Polydor #1108; 1921). Schorr made 26 sides, most of them Wagnerian, in 1921–1922. He went to Brunswick in 1924 and sang six numbers; the one of most interest to collectors was "Sonst spielt' ich" from Lortzing's *Zar und Zimmermann* (#15088). Electrola (the Berlin HMV branch) recorded Schorr in 1927–1929, 26 items plus 31 sides from a live performance of *Meistersinger* at the Berlin State Opera (Electrola EJ #277/86).

Outstanding discs were made by HMV in London in 1929–1931. Of the HMV items, the finest were 13 arias, duets, and the quintet from *Meistersinger*; Lauritz Melchior was his partner for "Abendlich gluhend" (#D2000; 1931). Melchior also sang with Schorr in a great scene from *Gîtterdämmerung*, "Hast du, Gunther, ein Weib?" (#D1700; 1929). In the 1930s Schorr was in Metropolitan performances that were recorded from radio broadcasts by the Golden Age of Opera label: *Siegfried* (EJS #173; 1937), *Rosenkavalier* (EJS #496; 1937), and *Walkure* (EJS #178; 1940). The same label also produced a *Meistersinger* (EJS #224; 1939). [Dennis 1971 is a complete discography.]

SCHROEDER, MANFRED
(12 JULY 1926–)

A major researcher in the fields of concert hall acoustics, the monaural phase sensitivity of human hearing, and computer graphics, among many other disciplines, Schroeder studied at the University of Göttingen in Germany, where he earned a B.S. in mathematics (1949), an M.S. in physics (1951), and a Ph.D., also in physics (1954), and spent time investigating the distribution of resonances in concert halls using microwave cavities as models. The chaotic distribution he discovered is now recognized as characteristic of complex dynamical systems. In 1954 Schroeder joined the research department of Bell Laboratories in Murray Hill, New Jersey. In the late 1950s he helped to formulate the U.S. standards for stereophonic broadcasting, which is now used worldwide. From 1958 to 1969 he directed research at Bell on speech compression, synthesis, and recognition.

Since 1969 he has served as professor of physics at the University of Göttingen, commuting between the University and Bell, and in 1991 he became a professor emeritus at the University. He is also a founding member of the Institut de Recherche et Coordination Acoustique/Musique of the Centre Pompidou in Paris. He is the author of over 150 papers and book chapters, as well as several complete books including: *Number Theory in Science and Communication*; *Fractals Chaos, Power Laws: Minutes from an Infinite Paradise*; and *Computer Speech: Recognition, Compression, Synthesis*. Schroeder also holds 45 U.S. patents in speech and signal processing and other fields, and has also been awarded gold medals from the Audio Engineering Society (1972) and the Acoustical Society of America (1991), the Lord Raleigh Medal of the British Institute of Acoustics, as well as the Helmholtz Medal of the German Acoustical Society. He is a fellow of the American Academy of Arts and Sciences and the New York Academy of Sciences, and is also a member of the National Academy of Engineering in Washington, D.C., and the Göttingen Academy of Sciences.

HOWARD FERSTLER

SCHUBERT RECORD (LABEL)

An American record, vertical cut, offered 1917 to ca. 1918 by the Bell Talking Machine Corp., New York. Twenty to 30 new selections were issued monthly, on

10-inch discs selling for $0.75 each. Franz Schubert's portrait graced the labels. The records were still on sale in December 1918, after which date there was no further advertising. [Rust 1978.]

FRANK ANDREWS

SCHUBERT TRIO

A mixed vocal group that recorded briefly for Victor. On 12 June 1906 they sang "Praise Ye" from Verdi's *Attila* (#4776). Members were Elise Stevenson, soprano; Harry Macdonough, tenor; and Frank C. Stanley, bass. There was no listing for the Trio in the Victor 1917 catalog.

SCHULZE, KLAUS (4 AUG 1947–)

Regarded in his native Germany as a composer/multi-instrumentalist within the classical music tradition, Klaus Schulze remains a cult figure in the U.S., where the bulk of his prolific output is available only through the import bins. Despite his marginal status stateside, he is widely considered an avant-garde mainstay as well as a founding father of both new age space music and the electronica genre.

Schulze first attracted attention as a member of the German progressive rock band, Tangerine Dream. Following the release of their debut LP, *Electronic Meditation* (Ohr #556 004; 1970), he departed for a solo career. His recorded work typically features extended pieces — sometimes filling an entire album — built around computer-generated synthesizers and other specially programmed electronic effects. The music itself — somewhat reminiscent of the oscillating sound loops pioneered by minimalist composers like Philip Glass — has been described as ethereal, surreal, spacey, dreamy, hypnotic, and relaxing. Since the release of the soundtrack *Body Love* (Brain #60.047; 1977), he has been in great demand as a composer/performer of European film music.

Schulze's recordings — many of which are complemented by engaging art work (e.g., the Daliesque paintings of some early 1970s titles) — include *Irrlicht* (Brain #1077; 1972), *Blackdance* (Virgin #2003; 1974), *Timewind* (Virgin #2006; 1975), *Moondawn* (Brain #1088; 1976), *Mirage* (Brain #60.040; 1977), *Dune* (Brain #0060.225; 1979), *Trancefer* (Innovative Communication #80014; 1981), *Audentity* (Brain #817-194-2; 1983; with keyboardist Rainer Bloss and percussionist Michael Schrieve), *Inter*Face* (Brain #827 673-2; 1985), *Cyborg* (A.V.I. #2002; 1986), *Mediterranean Pads* (Thunderbolt/Magnum Music Group #2027; 1990), *Beyond Recall* (Venture/Virgin #906; 1991), and *The Dome Event* (Virgin #918; 1993; recorded live at the Cologne Cathedral).

FRANK HOFFMANN

SCHUMANN, ELISABETH (13 JUNE 1888–23 APR 1952)

German/American soprano, born in Merseburg. She studied in Dresden, Berlin, and Hamburg; then made her debut in Hamburg on 2 Sep 1909 as the Shepherd in *Tannhäuser* and remained with the company there until 1919. She sang one season at the Metropolitan Opera (1914–1915), making her debut as Sophie, a role that brought her much acclaim. She was also noted for her Mozartian roles. Then Schumann spent 20 years with the Vienna State Opera before returning to the U.S. She became an American citizen in 1944. She taught at the Curtis Institute of Music, and gave outstanding Lieder recitals. She died in New York.

Schumann recorded for Favorite in Germany in 1913, then for Edison Diamond Discs in 1915 and 1922. Her other records were made in Europe in the early 1920s, for Polydor in Berlin and for HMV. "Vedrai, carino" (HMV DA #845) and "Batti, batti" (HMV DA #946) were among her fine Mozart selections (she also sang the arias in German, for Polydor); they were reissued by Top Artists Platters. *Rosenkavalier* was captured in a Sofia performance by HMV (DB #2060/72) and reissued on LP as HMV COLH #110/1 in 1962. Two compact discs covering her Schubert song cycles were released in 1990 by EMI (Références #CHS7 63040-2). Preiser issued a CD in 1991 that featured Mozart arias, plus several of Lieder by Richard Strauss, Mahler, and Robert Schumann (#89031). [Owen 1952 is a discography.]

SCHUMANN-HEINK, ERNESTINE (15 JUNE 1861–17 NOV 1936)

Czech contralto/mezzo-soprano, born in Ernestine Rîssler in Lieben, near Prague. She studied in Graz, and made her opera debut in Dresden, remaining with the company from 1878 to 1882. Then she appeared in Hamburg and Bayreuth, establishing herself as a Wagner specialist (Erda, Fricka, Brangaene) as well as in the Verdi repertoire and as Carmen. She was heard at the Metropolitan Opera on 9 Jan 1899 as Ortrud, in a cast that included the two De Reszke's, and quickly became an American favorite — not only in opera but as a concert singer. Schumann-Heink (whose stage name was a combination of the surnames of her first two husbands, both of whom died) sang until age 70 and gave a farewell Metropolitan appearance as Erda in *Siegfried* on 11 Mar 1932. She died in Hollywood.

Schumann-Heink began to record ca. 1899, with two Zonophone seven-inch discs, private recordings, one being a message to her children. She made her first commercial records for Columbia in 1903, five numbers beginning with "Ah mon fils" from *Prophete*. She was heard on Mapleson cylinders in the same year, in three Wagner fragments. Then she became a Victor artist, from 1906, beginning with "Mon coeur s'ouvre" in German (#85094), one of her most popular arias. In September 1906 she recorded an enduring hit, Brahms's "Wiegenlied" (#81085). In the 1917 Victor catalog she is represented by 40 solos, plus a duet with Enrico Caruso, "Ai nostri monti" (#89060; 1913), and a duet with Geraldine Farrar, "Wanderers Nachtlied," by Anton Rubinstein (#87504; 1913). "The Rosary" was perhaps her most appreciated solo record of that period (#87221 on 10-inch Red Seal, and #88108 on 12-inch; 1908). The Victor 1940 catalog still carried 15 of her Red Seals, including the acclaimed Christmas songs "Stille Nacht"/"Weihnachten" (#6723; 1926). Her final recording sessions were in January 1931. [McPherson 1967.]

SCHWANN CATALOGS

The earliest published catalog of long-playing records was issued by William Schwann in Boston, October 1949. Titled *Long Playing Record Catalog*, it consisted of 26 pages, typed out by Schwann himself, listing the LP output of 11 labels available in the U.S. Subsequently this modest publication grew into the respected Schwann catalog series, listing each month the records available in the U.S., with coverage of LP discs and tapes, and most recently of CDs. Name changes have been a frustrating characteristic of the series, which by the 1990s carried these titles: *Opus* (classical material; quarterly), *Spectrum* (pop material, spoken, children's; quarterly), and an annual *Artist Issue* (all formats arranged by performers), plus a monthly update service. Schwann was purchased by a record and video distributor, Valley Media, during the mid-1990s. An online version of the venerable catalog appeared in 2000, but by 2002 Valley was bankrupt, and its assets were sold to Alliance Entertainment, another distributor that also owns the *All Media Guide* (including the *All Music Guide*) databases. The company has discontinued the publication of the Schwann catalogs.

REV. CARL BENSON

SCHWARZKOPF, ELISABETH, DAME (9 DEC 1915–)

German soprano, born in Jarotschin. She studied in Berlin, and made her debut with the Deutsche Opera in 1938. Then she went to the Vienna State Opera, and Salzburg, becoming famous for her Mozartean roles. A great sensation at Covent Garden, she sang there from 1947 to 1951. She created the role of Anne Truelove in *Rake's Progress* in Venice in 1951. Schwarzkopf was immediately popular in the U.S. after her Carnegie Hall recital of 25 Oct 1953. She appeared with the San Francisco Opera and Chicago Lyric Opera, then from 1964 to 1966 at the Metropolitan Opera. The Marschallin was her Metropolitan debut role, and one that she made a favorite. She made a farewell tour of America in 1975 and settled in Switzerland. She edited her husband Walter Legge's book, *On and Off the Record* (1982). In 1992, she was made a Dame Commander of the British Empire.

Bridging the 78-LP eras, Schwarzkopf recorded for Columbia in London during 1946–1954, doing Mozart, Verdi, Puccini, Wagner, *Fidelio*, and *Hänsel und Gretel*. She continued with U.S. Columbia in the 1950s and early 1960s. The gems of her records are the complete operas, including Richard Strauss works and Mozart; also *Falstaff* (she sings Alice) and *Meistersinger* (Eva). In 1952 she was in a complete *Dido and Aeneas* made for HMV (#ALP 10026). She has an extensive CD discography, nearly all of it from EMI. [*Gramophone*, December 1990, listed her CDs.]

SCHWEINFEST, GEORGE (CA. 1860–8 JUNE 1949)

Pianist, flutist, and performer on nearly all the other instruments; one of the earliest and most prolific recording artists. He began with Edison on 28 Aug 1889, playing the piano in "Sea Breeze Polka" and six similar numbers. On 9 Sep 1889 he played the flute and piccolo in 11 numbers, beginning with "Etude de Concert" (flute); Edward Issler accompanied on the piano. The same duo returned for sessions on the next four days. On 8–10 October Schweinfest was piano accompanist for clarinetist William Tuson. In November he was pianist and also violinist; and he played flute for a recording by Issler's Orchestra. In 1890 he made more records on those instruments; in 1893 he was with the New Jersey Phonograph Co., playing the piccolo, then he worked for Berliner.

In 1897–1898 Schweinfest made a series of 37 piccolo cylinders for Columbia (#23500–23536); these were mostly polkas and similar dance numbers. On Victor records he confined himself to flute and piccolo, beginning with a series made in September 1900, repeating his dance repertoire. His final records were a Victor disc of 1902 (a remake of "Ben Bolt"), Columbia discs of ca. 1902, and a Columbia cylinder of 1906. He was also a member of Issler's Orchestra and the Columbia Orchestra. He died in Newark, New Jersey. [Brooks 1979.]

SCOTT, HERMON HOSMER
(28 MAR 1909–13 APR 1975)

Scott was born in Somerville, Massachusetts. A straight-A student at MIT, where he earned a master's degree, Scott went on to earn his doctorate at Lowell Technological Institute. In 1947, he founded the H.H. Scott Co. in Maynard, Massachusetts, with the idea being to provide high-quality products at reasonably affordable prices. In that respect, he was in direct competition with Avery Fisher's company. Indeed, for years the two equipment manufacturers practically defined the state of the moderately high-end audio market. Scott held more than 100 patents for innovations in the electronics field, including the first commercial noise-level meter, the RC oscillator (used in electronics laboratories all over the world), and the dynamic noise suppresser, which greatly reduced the sound of electronic and mechanical background noise in radio broadcast situations. The device worked so well that it allowed Paul Whiteman to prerecord his radio program for later broadcast. With the help of Daniel R. von Recklinghausen, the H.H. Scott Co. went on to earn an enviable reputation as one of the technically best in the business. Scott's reputation was such that he won the Audio Engineering Society's Potts Memorial award in 1951, and became a fellow of the organization in 1952. Unfortunately, Scott's unwillingness to master marketing issues, and his inability to match the cost-cutting techniques of his competitors, particularly Japanese companies that were able to use advanced design and construction skills, forced H.H. Scott into bankruptcy in 1972. Emerson Radio purchased the brand name in 1985, but the company has never regained the ironclad reputation it enjoyed in the 1950s and 1960s. He died in Newton, Massachusetts.

HOWARD FERSTLER

SCOTT, ROBERT FALCON
(6 JUNE 1868– CA. 29 MAR 1912)

British explorer. He is of interest in the history of recorded sound because the Gramophone Co. gave him two record players to take on his Antarctic expedition of 1910–1913, with several hundred discs. Accounts from expedition members indicate that the machines were in constant use. Among the artists heard by the explorers were Enrico Caruso, Nellie Melba, Luisa Tetrazzini, Geraldine Farrar, Clara Butt, and Harry Lauder. Scott and his crew froze to death after reaching the South Pole, caught in a brutal blizzard; their bodies were not found until the following November. The last entry in his diary was dated 29 Mar 1912.

SCOTT DE MARTINVILLE, EDOUARD-LÉON (25 APR 1817–29 APR 1879)

Scott de Martinville was a French amateur phonetician who developed a recorder for sound waves. Born in Paris, he became interested in making a permanent record of sounds in air. He constructed a phonautograph in collaboration with the leading scientific instrument maker in Paris at the time, Rudolph Koenig. The instrument was a success, and Koenig contracted Scott and published a collection of traces in 1864.

Although the membrane was parallel to the rotating surface, a primitive lever system generated lateral movements of a bristle that scratched curves in a thin layer of lampblack on the rotating surface. The curves were not necessarily representative of the vibrations in the air. Scott did not imagine the need for reproducing a recorded sound; rather, his intention was to obtain a trace that would lend itself to mathematical analysis and visual recognition of sounds. The contract with Koenig left Scott without influence over his instrument, and eventually he became convinced that everyone else, including Edison in the U.S., had stolen his invention. He died in Paris.

GEORGE BROCK-NANNESTAD

SCOTTI, ANTONIO
(25 JAN 1866–29 FEB 1936)

Italian baritone, born in Naples. He made his debut in Naples in 1889, then toured Europe and South America. In 1899 he was acclaimed for his Don Giovanni at Covent Garden, and repeated the success on 27 Dec 1899 at the Metropolitan Opera, where he remained on the roster for 33 years. His greatest roles were Don Giovanni, Scarpia, Iago, Rigoletto, and Falstaff. He died in his hometown.

Scotti was heard on Bettini cylinders, singing "Serenata" and "Fin ch' han del vino" from *Don Giovanni*, and "Bella siccome un angelo" from *Don Pasquale*. Mapleson recorded him on the Metropolitan stage, in fragments from *Ernani, Pagliacci* and *Tosca* (1901–1903). In 1902 Scotti made five sides for G & T in London. Then he made three Columbia records in 1903 before beginning a Victor career in 1903. He recorded six Edison two-minute cylinders in 1906–1908. One of them, "Vi ravviso" from *Sonnambula*, was a lifelong favorite, recorded later for

Victor (#87034). The best recording results came from his first U.S. issues of 1904, with piano accompaniment (the #81000–85000 series), although these were withdrawn when Scotti re-recorded the material with orchestral accompaniments beginning in 1906 (#87000–88000 series). There was a distinguished duet with Enrico Caruso, "Solenne in quest'ora" (#89001), and another outstanding duet, with Geraldine Farrar, "La ci darem la mano" (#89015). He was in two Victor recordings of the *Rigoletto* quartet, both with Caruso, and in the greatest version of the *Lucia* sextet, with Caruso, Marcella Sembrich, and Marcel Journet in the cast (#96200). There were 13 solos in the 1917 catalog, plus the ensemble pieces. Most of the 78-rpm and LP reissue labels offered Scotti material.

SCOTTISH GRAMOPHONE MANUFACTURING CO., LTD.

A Glasgow firm, established ca. 1917, incorporated 12 Apr 1919. At least two types of Gramophone were made, a table grand and an upright cabinet model. The firm was dissolved on 15 Feb 1943. [Hamilton, C. 1986.]

SCOTTO, RENATA (24 FEB 1933–)

One of the best-known sopranos of the second-half of the 20th century, Scotto was born in Savona, Italy. She made her debut in 1952, and sang with the famous La Scala opera company through the late 1950s, establishing her fame. In 1960, she made her U.S. debut in Chicago, and then five years later joined New York's famous Metropolitan Opera, where she remained through 1987. Like many contemporary opera stars, Scotto has recorded widely for many labels, notably EMI Classics and Sony. In addition to complete opera recordings, she has made various recordings of favorite arias, along with recording more popular material, such as traditional Christmas songs.

SCRANTON BUTTON WORKS

A Scranton, Pennsylvania, firm established in 1915. It pressed records for the dime store trade. Scranton combined with Cameo Records, Inc., and Regal Record Co., Inc. (owned by the Crystalate Gramophone Record Manufacturing Co., Ltd., of the U.K.; formerly belonging to the Plaza Music Co.) to form the American Record Corp. (ARC). Pressing for ARC labels was done by the Scranton Button Works.

FRANK ANDREWS

SCRATCH FILTER

A control on an audio preamplifier that serves to reduce the noise on an analog disc containing scratches or other surface defects. Scratch filters are rarely found on modern, consumer-grade equipment, because digital-audio software does not react to scratches the way analog systems do. However, there are now available computer systems that can nearly eliminate scratch sounds from analog recordings, allowing rare and valuable performances on such discs to be fairly cleanly transferred to digital storage for archiving or reproducing.

HOWARD FERSTLER

SCROLL

An inaudible segment of the groove on a recorded disc, used to separate and link the recorded bands. It would only be needed when a side carried more than one song or instrumental piece, so it was not much used in the acoustic era. The earliest example noted in the literature was Victor #16863 (1911), which has two songs by Henry Allan on side A, and five "Mother Goose Songs" by Elizabeth Wheeler on the flip side. Another Wheeler disc of Mother Goose songs, with separation scrolls, was #35225 (1912).

A French language set issued by HMV in 1927 (#C-1353+) had such dividers for lessons. The HMV *Instruments of the Orchestra* had scrolls that were "locked," so that the needle would not pass to the next band without human intervention; evidently the purpose was to give a teacher time to talk about the instruments as they were illustrated (HMV #C-1311+; 1927). In 1932 and 1933 the U.K. labels Durium and Broadcast Four-Tune used scroll separators. Scrolls became standard on LP records. [Copeland, P. 1990.]

SCRUGGS, EARL (6 JAN 1924–)

American country singer and banjo player, born in Flint Hill, North Carolina. He played banjo as a child, developing a three-finger style, and joined Bill Monroe's Blue Grass Boys, and in 1944 performed with them at the Grand Ole Opry. He then teamed with Lester Flatt, guitarist, and formed the Foggy Mountain Boys (1948). They became popular in the 1960s thanks to appearances on the *Beverly Hillbillies* television show and their soundtrack work for *Bonnie & Clyde*; the movie's theme, "Foggy Mountain Breakdown," became a bluegrass banjo-player's test piece. He remained with Flatt until 1969, then Scruggs set up another group, the Earl Scruggs Review, moving to a country-rock style. That ensemble made a chart album, *Earl Scruggs Revue Anniversary* in 1975

Earl Scruggs banjo instruction album. Courtesy Frank Hoffmann

(Columbia #33416) and another in 1976, *Earl Scruggs Revue* (Columbia #34090). Scruggs starred in the motion picture *Banjo Man* (1975). He retired in the mid-1970s, although he occasionally performs and records; a new album was released in 2001 produced by his son, Randy, featuring many leading stars of country and pop music.

REV. CARL BENSON

SDDS (SONY DYNAMIC DIGITAL SOUND)

Sony's competing format for the digital soundtrack system for motion picture playback. Unlike DTS and Dolby Digital, this format has never been used for home audio. For theater use, the signal is optically printed outside the film sprocket holes, along both sides of the print. The first movies to make use of the SDDS system in theaters were *In the Line of Fire* and *Last Action Hero*, in 1994.

HOWARD FERSTLER

SEAMAN, FRANK

American record company executive, one of the pioneer builders of the industry. He was owner of the New York Gramophone Co., which sold products made by Emile Berliner in New York and New Jersey up to 1896. Then he established and became president of the National Gramophone Co. in 1896. Seaman had personally contracted with Berliner for U.S. sales rights (except for Washington, D.C.), and did well after a slow first year. The Universal Talking Machine Co. was set up on 10 Feb 1898 to manufacture machines — which the Berliner Gramophone Co. refused to accept or allow Seaman to stock. Litigation ensued over Seaman's alleged infrignement of Bell-Tainter patents, both Seaman and his company being defendants in the proceedings. A new firm National Gramophone Corp., was set up in March 1899; through this firm and Universal, Seaman manufactured an unauthorized Berliner-clone machine named the Zonophone. The earlier National Gramophone Co. went into liquidation.

Berliner broke with Seaman, and Seaman replied with a petition to have the Berliner Gramophone Co. prohibited from using the name "gramophone" on the basis of Seaman's own exclusive contract to do so. This bizarre approach was successful: Berliner was enjoined not to use the name gramophone in June 1900, and Eldridge Johnson was similarly restricted on 1 Mar 1901. However Seaman was sued by the Graphophone interests for infringement of the Bell-Tainter patents, bringing about a consent agreement in which Columbia gained the assets of the Universal Talking Machine Co. and was able to market disc players with the Zonophone name.

Eldridge Johnson devised an improved recording process and record player, and marketed them over Seaman's claim that he was still sole sales agent for the Gramophone. The court supported Johnson, who removed the "gramophone" name from his record labels in favor of the "Improved Record." The National Gramophone Corp. folded in September 1901; Universal Talking Machine Co. held a sheriff's sale of patents and equipment on 28 Oct 1901. The Zonophone business was reorganized under the name Universal Talking Machine Manufacturing Co. on 19 Dec 1901. (The earlier Universal retained its corporate existence for a time, acting as a sales agent for the new one.) The new company made machines (claiming 700 per week) and discs (2,000 per day), but Seaman had lost the assets of his National Gramophone Corp. and Universal Talking Machine Co. and had to accept from Victor an out-of-court settlement of $25,000 in 1903 (from his suit against Eldridge Johnson and Berliner). He left the sound recording field in late 1903. He was not mentioned as an officer of either Universal company when G & T acquired the stock of both companies in June 1903.

FRANK ANDREWS

SEARCHERS, THE

Although overshadowed by fellow Liverpudlians, the Beatles, the Searchers was one of the most accomplished

British Invasion bands. Their close, four-part harmonies and rich, jangling guitar lines presaged the commercial ascendancy of folk-rock bands such as the Byrds.

The Searchers, named after John Ford's classic 1956 film starring John Wayne, were formed in 1961 to play behind U.K. vocalist Johnny Sandon. The group — originally comprised of guitarists John McNally and Mike Pender, bassist Tony Jackson, and drummer Chris Curtis — later struck out on their own, playing the Star Club (Hamburg, Germany) in the wake of the successful run there by the Beatles. A residency at Liverpool's Iron Door club led A&R man Tony Hatch to offer them a record contract. After charting in the U.K. with the Drifters' "Sweets for My Sweet" (Pye; released in U.S. as Mercury #72172) in 1963, the band achieved success on both sides of the Atlantic — number one in England, number 13 in the U.S. — with the million-selling "Needles and Pins" (Kapp #577; 1964). More hits — including "Don't Throw Your Love Away" (Kapp #593; 1964), "Love Potion Number Nine" (Kapp #27; 1964), "What Have They Done to the Rain" (Kapp #644; 1965), and "Bumble Bee" (Kapp #49; 1965) — and international tours followed.

When their recordings stopped charting, the Searchers continued to earn a living playing U.S. clubs and cabarets. Signing with Sire Records, the band returned briefly to the public eye with two album releases, *The Searchers* (Sire #6082; 1980) and *Love's Melodies* (Sire #3523; 1981). Always hampered by the absence of a talented composer within the group, the inclusion of high-quality material by contemporary songwriters on the Sire LPs elicited critical raves. Nevertheless, both discs sold poorly and the band returned to the touring circuit.

FRANK HOFFMANN

SEARCHLIGHT HORN CO.

A Brooklyn firm, active ca. 1906–1907. It advertised a horn designed "on the principle of the searchlight" that could play "louder and clearer than any other." Following that promotion in June 1906, there was a September advertisement claiming sales of 10,000 per month. A 1907 advertisement touted a "knock-down" model, "easily taken apart."

SEARS, ROEBUCK AND CO.

A Chicago firm, established with that name in 1893, succeeding a number of other companies. At first Sears was devoted entirely to mail order sales of a wide variety of products. In the mid-1920s retail stores were opened, and the sale of goods under several house tradenames (Allstate first; later Craftsman, Kenmore, etc.) began. The mail-order catalog business continued through the mid-1990s, but facing a changing market, it has since focused on its retail stores.

The 1897 mail order catalog (#104) offered cylinder phonographs and records. The Columbia Type A graphophone, sold for $25, or with a package of 12 records and a hearing tube for $35. The talking machine product line expanded in subsequent catalogs. Catalog #111, 1902, offered the Columbia Graphophone Model AB, under the name of "Gem Graphophone," for $10. An "exhibition outfit" was available with the machine, including a large horn, admission tickets, advertising posters, etc., all for $23.75. A Columbia Grand, with five-inch cylinders, was available in that catalog for $50. A large selection of cylinder records was also sold, at $0.50 each. In 1902 disc record players were offered as well, under the names "Regina Graphophone" and "Regal Graphophone Grand." Ten-inch Climax records were sold for $1, and seven-inch discs with the name Acme for $0.50.

In later catalogs Sears marketed discs under various names: Silvertone, Challenge, Conqueror, and Supertone labels; masters came from nearly every major record company in the 1920s. The firm was the first sponsor of the *National Barn Dance* radio program (1924), and subsequently featured recordings of country artists in its catalogs. In the mid-1920s the catalog offered dance and vocal records on the brown-label Silvertone Record, at $0.49 plus postage. Needles, phono parts, empty albums, etc. were sold as well. Phonographs cost $3.49 to $19.95.

In the catalog of fall–winter 1926–1927 the price of Silvertones was $0.39. "Selections by Negro Artists" included Alberta Jones and Jelly Roll Morton. The Challenge label was added to the catalog in fall 1927, at $0.24. Silvertone was discontinued in spring 1929, displaced by the Challenge (three for $0.65 postage paid; label discontinued in 1932) and a new one, Conqueror (three for $0.89 postage paid), and also new Supertone (at $0.43 each postage paid; discontinued in 1932). A successful race record of 1930 was Conqueror #7081 by Mandy Lee, "I Needs Plenty Grease in My Frying Pan"; it remained in the catalog until 1936. In spring 1934 the price of Conqueror was down to $0.19 in lots of 10, or $0.21 each. Josh White appeared on three country blues items in 1934. By 1938 the catalogs had dropped all country blues records and race records.

SEAS

SEE LOUDSPEAKER

SEDAKA, NEIL (13 MAR 1939–)

Neil Sedaka is an American institution, having achieved considerable success in two music fields — singing and songwriting — over an extended length of time. Despite widespread references to his limitations — a rather limited vocal technique and a tendency to graft the worst elements of formulaic Tin Pan Alley writing onto his pop-rock compositions — the sincerity and warmth communicated both by Sedaka's voice and material, further augmented in his own recordings by virtuoso production work, have resulted in an enviable recorded legacy.

Because both of his parents were accomplished pianists, it was inevitable that Sedaka's childhood would include musical training. Despite classical piano training at Juilliard, he displayed a pronounced preference for pop material. He began writing songs with fellow Lincoln High School (Brooklyn) student, Howard Greenfield. Their close proximity to the music publishers and record companies in Manhattan enabled them to eventually secure jobs as staff composers (Sedaka handling the music, Greenfield the lyrics) with Aldon Publishing Co. The firm's owners, Don Kirshner and Al Nevin, were successful in pitching the duo's material to emerging pop star Connie Francis. They first supplied her "Stupid Cupid" (MGM #12683; 1958; #14), followed by "Fallin'" (MGM #12713; 1958; #30), "Frankie" (MGM #12793; 1959; #9), and "Where the Boys Are" (MGM #12971; 1961; #4).

Aldon also pedaled Sedaka to the labels as a vocalist, securing a contract with RCA (he had recorded previously with the Tokens for Melba in 1956). He immediately scored with a string of successful singles — including the Top 10 recordings, "Oh! Carol" (supposedly written in honor of a young Carole King; RCA #7595; 1959), "Stairway to Heaven" (RCA #7709; 1960), "Calendar Girl" (RCA #7829; 1960), "Happy Birthday, Sweet Sixteen" (RCA #7957; 1961), "Breaking Up Is Hard to Do" (RCA #8046; 1962; #1), and "Next Door to an Angel" (RCA #8086; 1962) — which continued up to the British Invasion. Although Sedaka's singing career lost momentum, his songwriting partnership remained fruitful throughout the 1960s, resulting in hits like the 5th Dimension's "Workin' on a Groovy Thing" (Soul City #776; 1969) and "Puppet Man" (Bell #880; 1970), also a Top 30 single for Tom Jones (Parrot #40064; 1971).

Reunited with his old boss on Kirshner Records, Sedaka attempted to revive his recording career in the early 1970s. Discouraging sales led to the dissolution of his professional relationship with Greenfield; he began writing songs with lyricist Phil Cody, first testing them with the public during a concert tour of the U.K. His warm reception there led to the release of a couple of albums, *Solitaire* (Kirshner #117; 1972) and *The Tra-La Days Are Over* (1973) However, success eluded him in the U.S. until the release of *Sedaka's Back* (Rocket #483; 1974), driven by the number one single, "Laughter in the Rain" (Rocket #40313; 1974). More hit recordings followed, including "Bad Blood" (with Elton John; Rocket #40460; 1975; #1) and "Breaking Up Is Hard to Do" (Rocket #40500; 1975), a torch-style reworking of his 1962 up-tempo teen anthem.

Although his chart successes dropped off again — a notable exception being his duet with daughter Dara, "Should've Never Let You Go" (Elektra #46615; 1980) — Sedaka remains a highly visible entertainer, both live and on television variety programs.

FRANK HOFFMANN

SEEBURG, JUSTUS P. (1871–21 OCT 1958)

Swedish/American industrialist, born in Gothenburg. After technical training there, he transferred to the U.S. in 1886. He worked in a piano factory in Chicago, and became superintendent of Cable Piano; then he was co-founder of Kurz-Seeburg Co., Rockford, Illinois, which made piano actions. He sold his interest in 1902, and established the Seeburg Piano Co. in Chicago in 1907. That firm made coin-op pianos with electrically driven bellows and perforated paper rolls. A line of Orchestrions appeared in 1910, used in silent film theaters.

In 1927 Seeburg began to manufacture automatic electric coin-op phonographs. He discontinued the Orchestrion with the arrival of sound films. Two interesting products followed: the Audiophone, with eight turntables for selective play (1928), and the Melophone, allowing 12 selections (1930). In 1935 the Selectophone and the Symphonola were introdcued. A wall-mounted juke box, the Playboy, was introduced in 1939. The firm was in receivership during the 1930s, and diversified to other products. Finally the family sold out in 1956 to Fort Pitt Industries. Seeburg died in Stockholm, Sweden.

SEEGER, MIKE (15 AUG 1933–)

Mike Seeger, through his solo work and many collaborations with other artists, has dedicated his career to performing — both live and through recordings — the mountain string band music from the early 20th century in as authentic a fashion as possible. Utilizing primary source materials — oral history and the recordings made in the 1920s to 1950s by the major record labels and the Library of Congress — he willfully bucked the post–World War II folk revival trend in which most musicians interpreted traditional songs in a contemporary and commercial context.

Seeger comes from an illustrious musical family: his father, Charles Seeger, was one of the nation's leading ethnomusicologists, his mother, Ruth Crawford Seeger, a major classical music composer; sister Peggy Seeger has been an important folk music interpreter in her own right, and half-brother Pete Seeger helped father the rebirth of interest in the folk tradition. Mike spent his formative years in Washington, D.C., learning to play a wide array of acoustic string instruments, including the fiddle, autoharp, banjo, mandolin, dulcimer, and guitar as well as the jew's harp and harmonica.

Seeger is best known as a founding member (along with John Cohen and Tom Paley) of the New Lost City Ramblers. Formed in 1958, the trio acquired a cult following at the height of the commercial folk boom by steadfastly maintaining a traditional approach to old-time music. The group recorded 15 albums through the 1970s, including *New Lost City Ramblers, Volumes 1–5* (Folkways #2395/6/7/8/9), *The "New" New Lost City Ramblers* (Folkways #2491), and *Sing Songs of the New Lost City Ramblers* (Folkways #2494). The Ramblers' only personnel change — singer/fiddler Tracy Schwarz replaced Paley in 1962 — signaled an expansion both backward (to unaccompanied Anglo-Saxon balladry) and forward (classic bluegrass and Cajun music) in time. Their body of work has greatly influenced not only the new wave of folk musicians, but many important rock stars, including the late Jerry Garcia (Grateful Dead, Old and in the Way), the late Al Wilson (Canned Heat), Chris Hillman (Byrds, Flying Burrito Brothers, Desert Rose Band), Roger McGuinn (Byrds), and Clarence White (Byrds).

Seeger also served as the producer for several seminal albums in the old-time and bluegrass music revivals. He recorded and produced the first anthology of Scruggs's style banjo playing (*American Banjo Three-Finger and Scruggs Style*, Folkways #2314, 1956; reissued as Smithsonian/Folkways #40037, 1990), as well as one of the first bluegrass anthologies (*Mountain Music Bluegrass Style*, Folkways #2318, 1960; reissued as Smithsonian/Folkways #40038). His *Mountain Music Played on the Autoharp* (Folkways #2365, 1962) helped reintroduce this instrument to the folk revival audience. He also recorded albums of legendary musicians such as Dock Boggs (anthologized on *His Folkways Years, 1963-68*, Smithsonian/Folkways #40108, and Kilby Snow (*Country Songs and Tunes on Autoharp*, Folkways #3902, 1969). In 1997, the Smithsonian/Folkways archive celebrated the richness of his 30 years of fieldwork with the anthology album, *Close to Home* (Smithsonian/Folkways #40097).

By the early 1970s, the group's members took a break to explore other musical directions. Although Seeger had recorded solo albums before — most notably, a never-released 1957 project which relied heavily on overdubbing, and his official debut, *Old Time Country Music* (Folkways #2325; 1962) — the release of *Music from True Vine* (Mercury #627; 1972) signaled a new career phase. An artistic tour de force, Seeger supplied all of the vocals and instrumental work, ranging from square dances to Appalachian laments.

While some observers may have interpreted his signing with a large pop-oriented record company to represent a drive for more broad-based commercial acceptance, Seeger continued to reflect his lifelong dedication to collecting, researching, learning, performing, and recording authentic folk music styles. He has continued to release albums catering to his faithful, albeit small, audience.

FRANK HOFFMANN

SEEGER, PETE (3 MAY 1919–)

American folksinger and songwriter, born Peter R. Seeger in Patterson, New York. He was the son of musicologist Charles Louis Seeger. After two years at Harvard University he left academe to pursue a career playing banjo and singing folk music. He was in a group named the Almanac Singers in the early 1940s, and in 1949 joined the Weavers. He continued to perform solo as well, concentrating on songs of social content. As a composer, he had several successes, including "If I Had a Hammer," "Kisses Sweeter than Wine," and "Where Have All the Flowers Gone?" During the 1950s, when Seeger was blacklisted due to alleged communist activities, he recorded primarily for the small Folkways label. During the folk-revival years, Seeger recorded for Columbia. He could not appear on network television until 1966, when the Smothers Brothers broke the tacit blacklist and invited him to sing his antiwar song "The Big Muddy" on their program. His record of "Little Boxes" (Columbia #42940; 1964) was a chart hit. An album, *We Shall Overcome* (Columbia CL #2101; 1964) was on the charts 18 weeks. He and Arlo Guthrie made a successful album in 1975: *Together in Concert* (Warner #2R 2214). Seeger also wrote a standard instruction manual for the five-string banjo, and edited several song collections. He continued to perform through the 1990s, although he has been less active in the past decade.

SEGER, BOB (6 MAY 1945–)

Bob Seger exemplified the best in American hard rock during the 1970s: melodic, yet propulsive, guitar-dominated treatments of well-crafted songs sung with raw passion. Like others in this blue collar, heartland genre — including Bruce Springsteen, John Mellencamp, and Tom Petty — Seger eschewed hype and industry image-making, developing career momentum through touring and positive word-of-mouth to sell his recordings.

Michigan-native Seger first recorded for the Hideout and Cameo labels — five singles in all during the 1966–1967 period — as Bob Seger and the Last Heard. Signing with Capitol Records and changing the name of the band to the Bob Seger System, he issued *Ramblin' Gamblin' Man* (Capitol #172; 1969; #62), driven by the success of the title track (Capitol #2297; 1968; #17). When the follow-up LPs — *Noah* (Capitol #236; 1970) and *Mongrel* (Capitol #499; 1970) — achieved marginal sales, he shifted personnel, billing himself as a solo act. However, the album releases — including the oldies cover collection *Brand New Morning* (Capitol #3187; 1971), *Smokin' O.P.'s* (Capitol #2109; 1972), *Back in '72* (Capitol #2126), *Seven* (Capitol #2184; 1974), and *Beautiful Loser* (Capitol #11378; 1975) — continued to feature the same straight-ahead rock style.

Reorganizing his supporting musicians once more as the Silver Bullet Band in the mid-1970s, Seger began attracting critical raves for his mature compositions and precision performing, finding commercial success with releases such as *Live Bullet* (Capitol #11523; 1976; #34), *Night Moves* (Capitol #11557; 1977; #8), *Stranger in Town* (Capitol #11698; 1978; 4), and *Against the Wind* (Capitol #12041; 1980; #1). His later albums — the live *Nine Tonight* (Capitol #12182; 1981; #3), *The Distance* (Capitol #12254; 1982; #5), *Like a Rock* (Capitol #12398; 1986; #3), *The Fire Inside* (Capitol #91134; 1991; #7), and *It's a Mystery* (Capitol #99774; 1995; #27) — while lacking the intensity and innovative drive of his classic work, have all been workmanlike affairs that have retained his core audience.

FRANK HOFFMANN

SEGOVIA, ANDRÉS
(21 FEB 1893–2 JUNE 1987)

Spanish guitarist, born in Linares. He was self-taught, making a debut in Granada at age 16, then going on to play in Madrid, Barcelona, and South America. He was the first artist to elevate the Spanish guitar to the category of a concert instrument. Albert Roussel wrote a composition for him titled "Segovia," which he played in Paris in 1924. Segovia appeared in Carnegie Hall on 8 Jan 1928 and continued performing everywhere into the 1980s. He died in Madrid.

The earliest recordings date from 1927 on HMV. They include some of the J.S. Bach transcriptions for which Segovia was much admired. Much of his performing and recorded repertoire was made up of his arrangements. He remained with HMV to 1939, then recorded for Decca and Victor. Among the remarkable sides cut for HMV were "Recuerdos de la Alhambra" by Francisco Tárrega (#D1395; 1928), and "Theme varié" (#D1255) by Fernando Sor. Two works by Manuel Ponce — the "Theme, Variations, and Fugue" and the *Suite*, were brilliantly recorded in 1932 and 1941. A set of two CDs in the EMI Références series presents much of the 1927–1939material (#CHS 61047-2).

SELECTOPHONE

A Seeburg jukebox, 1935, developed by Wilcox. It had many turntables on a single revolving shaft.

SELENA (16 APR 1971–31 MAR 1995)

Selena, the musician, will be remembered for her ability to transform traditional Mexican musical styles such as cumbia dance-rhythms into a viable pop mainstream commodity. Selena, the personality has acquired a larger-than-life status, symbolizing tejano music's increasing profile within the record industry during the 1990s.

Born in Freeport, Texas, Selena Quintanilla — along with sister Suzette and brother A.B. — was encouraged to perform and record as a preteen. Beginning in 1989, the family band, Selena y Los Dinos (simply called "Selena" by 1991), graduated from generic synth-flavored, dance-pop released on indie labels to a more individualized sound via a succession of increasingly popular EMI recordings. Although Selena's photogenic image had much to do with the band's commercial success, the emotional depth of her singing — combined with A.B.'s clever songs and slick rhythmic arrangements — netted a Grammy for *Selena Live* (EMI Latin #42144 1993). The last album released prior to Selena's tragic shooting death at the hands of a former fan, *Amor Prohibido* (EMI Latin #28803 1994), demonstrated the band's wide range of styles, including reggae-inflected dance fare ("Bidi Bidi Bom Bom"), hard-edged rock ("Fotos y Recuerdos," a Spanish language version of the Pretenders's "Back in the Chain Gang"), and the torchy ballad, "No Me Queda Mas."

The media attention surrounding Selena's death appears to have encouraged EMI to go all-out for crossover success. In addition to dredging up every available English-language track, the producers of the posthumously released LP, *Dreaming of You* (EMI Latin #34123; 1995; album track "I Could Fall in Love" reached #8 on *Billboard Hot 100*), incorporated contemporary techno and hip-hop elements into the original recordings while smoothing out the ethnic features of her vocals. Since then, the company has attempted to promote remastered and/or remixed songs as "new" material. New compilations have also matched her existing vocals with different instrumental tracks.

FRANK HOFFMANN

SELTSAM, WILLIAM
(30 JUNE 1897–DEC 1968)

American writer on music and founder of the International Record Collectors Club (IRCC). He began a career as a musician, but was afflicted with hearing loss and went into office work. In 1932 he enlarged on a longtime interest in phonograph records by launching the IRCC, devoted to reissuing important vocal (and a few instrumental) recordings from the Golden Era. He was scrupulous in labeling and documentation of his records, giving exact recording dates and re-recording dates, and endeavored to determine proper record speed and pitch. From 1937 to 1939 Seltsam supervised the transfer of Mapleson cylinder material to IRCC discs. One of his discoveries was the first recording by Ernestine Schumann-Heink, a seven-inch privately made disc of ca. 1899; he reissued it on IRCC ("Wie ein Grüssen").

As an author, Seltsam is known for *Metropolitan Opera Annals* (New York: H.W. Wilson, 1947) and its two supplements. The three volumes cover all Metropolitan Opera New York performances from 1883 through 1966. He died in Fairfield, Connecticut.

SEMBRICH, MARCELLA
(15 FEB 1858–11 JAN 1935)

Polish soprano, born Prakseda Marcelina Kochanska in Wisniewczyk. Her father taught her violin and piano, and a friend of the family helped finance further instruction. She studied in Vienna, and turned to voice; made her debut in Athens on 3 June 1877 in *Puritani*, using her mother's maiden name then and thereafter. In 1878 she sang Lucia in Dresden and in 1880 at Covent Garden. Her Metropolitan Opera debut was on 24 Oct 1883, the second night of the company's first season. She was a great success as a singer, but showed her early training in a remarkable concert in which she played parts of a violin concerto and a Chopin mazurka, also singing some of Rosina's arias from *Barbiere di Siviglia*. She was a favorite with the Metropolitan until 1909; then gave song recitals until 1917. She also headed the voice department at the Curtis Institute of Music, Philadelphia. She died in New York.

Her main roles were Lucia, Violetta, Gilda, Rosina, Mimi (she was Puccini's personal favorite in the role), Zerlina, Susanna, and Queen of the Night. Unfortunately her voice did not record well. Her first records were three Bettini cylinders in 1900. She is heard on four Mapleson cylinders of 1902 and 1903, singing fragments of *Fille du régiment, Zauberflöte, Ernani*, and *Traviata*, plus Johann Strauss's "Voices of Spring." All of these were issued on IRCC discs. After three Columbia sides in 1903, Sembrich began recording for Victor in November 1904, singing "Ah! Fors' à lui" (#85035), and continued with the label. There were 25 solos in the 1917 Victor catalog, duets with Emma Eames and Antonio Scotti; a premium priced *Rigoletto* quartet with Enrico Caruso and Antonio Scotti (#96001, selling for $6) and a premium *Lucia* sextet, with Caruso, Scotti, and Marcel Journet among the cast (#96200; at $7). Her finest coloratura disc was "Ah non giunge" from *Sonnambula* (#81047; 1904 — reissued on IRCC #8). She made her last discs in 1919. Her recordings were reissued on 78 and LP and more recently on CD; among the CD reissues are *The Victor Recordings 1908–19* (Romophone #81027), a two-CD set, Nimbus #7901, *Rare Recordings, 1903–1919* (Minerva #40), and Queen of the Warsaw Opera House (Enterprise #1139). [Owen, H. 1969.]

SENNHEISER

Founded in 1945, by Dr. Fritz Sennheiser, near Hannover, Germany. The company has built its professional reputation on high-quality studio microphones and wireless microphone systems, and it also produces headphones that are used by both professionals and hi-fi enthusiasts, worldwide. One of its more notable consumer-product breakthroughs was the "open-aire" headphone design. An American branch of the company, SEC, was started in 1963, and it has since become Sennheiser's largest distributor. [website: www.seinheiser.com.]

HOWARD FERSTLER

SENSITIVITY

In an audio system, the response-signal ratio of a microphone or other transducer, taken under specified conditions.

SENSURROUND

A motion-picture, surround-sound recording/playback process developed by W.O. Watson and Richard Stumpf at Universal Pictures, which debuted with the movie *Earthquake* in 1974. Four large low-frequency horns were located behind the screen, two in each corner. The Model W horn in each corner was eight feet long, four feet wide, and four feet high. The Model C horn in each corner was a modular unit a foot wide and five feet high. Two additional horns were located on a platform in the rear of the theater. Each horn was driven by a 1,000-watt amplifier controlled by inaudible tones on a special optical control track along with the normal four-track magnetic soundtrack of the 35mm Panavision filmstrip. The tones turned the horns on and off at preset volumes, creating low-frequency vibrations of 5–40 cycles at sound pressures of 110–120 dB, causing the audience, chairs, and floor to feel the vibrations of the earthquake and dam-destruction scenes.

HOWARD FERSTLER

SEPARATION (I)

The ability of a microphone to accept signals from certain sources and not from other sources.

SEPARATION (II)

In elements of a stereo system, the degree to which individual channels are kept distinct.

SEPARATION RECORDING

A method of recording which assigns microphones to each performer or group of performers in an ensemble, inscribing their contributions independently of the other participants. The separate signals are mixed in the control room, not necessarily in a manner to duplicate the original event. Elements may also be recorded at different sessions and combined later in a mixdown.

SERIAL COPY MANAGEMENT SYSTEM (SCMS)

SEE DAT (DIGITAL AUDIO TAPE)

SERKIN, RUDOLF (28 MAR 1903–8 MAY 1991)

Bohemian pianist, born in Eger. He studied in Vienna, both piano and composition (with Arnold Schoenberg), and began a concert career in 1920. Many of his appearances were with violinist Adolf Busch, and it was with him that Serkin made his American debut in 1933. He was appointed to the faculty of the Curtis Institute of Music in Philadelphia in 1939, and served as director from 1968 to 1976. He was an active performer until the year of his death, widely acclaimed as one of the world's great interpreters of the Viennese repertoire. His son Peter is also a renowned pianist.

From the numerous recordings of highest quality that Serkin left, possibly the set of Beethoven's concertos, made with Eugene Ormandy and the Philadelphia Orchestra in 1966, stands out. (Four were reissued in 1991 on CD by CBS Masterworks, CD #42259, #42260.) He also recorded peerless renditions of the Beethoven sonatas, for Columbia; and of the Brahms and Schumann concertos, with the Cleveland and Philadelphia Orchestras, also for Columbia. The two Brahms concertos were reissued by CBS Masterworks on CD #42261 and #42262 in 1991. Serkin and Busch recorded the Beethoven "Kreutzer Sonata" for Columbia, as well as other chamber works.

SESSION

The event of actual recording, in a studio or on location. Sessions comprise a variable number of takes. The date of a session, which occupies no more than one day, is important in discography in order to establish precedence and the identification of personnel.

SESSION TAPE

The tape of all the material performed during a recording session, including both the accepted material that appears on the master, and the rejected (outtake) material.

78-RPM DISCS

Records revolving at 78 rpm, also known as standard or coarse groove discs, were the international industry norm from the 1920s until the introduction of the Columbia long-playing record (LP) in 1948. Earlier discs had displayed a variety of speeds, from 70 rpm to more than 90 rpm, although 78–80 was most common after 1900. By 1957 mass commercial manufacture of 78s had ceased. There were a few later releases: 15 are listed in Biel 1982/1, three others in Biel 1982/2. Not mentioned in those two lists was the 1962 Pickwick release in the U.K. of 36 children's records on seven-inch 78s. Sound effects records for professional use also continued to appear in 78-rpm format.

The 78 format has been the prime focus of record collectors. While no complete inventory of 78s exists, many useful lists have been published. Much attention has been given by audio experts to the best means of replaying 78s on modern equipment, to eliminating hiss and scratch noises, and to improving the sound on them. [Biel 1982/1; Biel 1982/2; Shipway 1983; Tuddenham and Copeland 1988; Williamson 1971.]

See also **Cleaning; Collectors and Collecting; Disc; Discography; Noise Reduction; Preservation of Sound Recordings; Reprocessed Stereo; Speeds**

SEX PISTOLS

One of the most revolutionary — and controversial — bands produced out of the rock subculture, the Sex Pistols are widely recognized as progenitors of the 1970s punk movement, merging a stripped-down, high-energy sound with incendiary lyrics born out of economic and social inequities of post–World War II U.K. Although they owed much to the mid-1960s garage bands such as the Seeds and the Standells, the antipop white noise of the Velvet Underground, the dumbed-down buzzsaw chording of the Ramones, and the glam-tinged, street-smart hard rock of the New York Dolls, the Pistols communicated a rage and political imperative missing in the music their antecedents.

The Sex Pistols were formed in London in summer 1975 when boutique owner and would-be pop music entrepreneur Malcolm paired former Swankers Steve Jones (guitar), Glen Matlock (bass), and Paul Cook (drums) with John Lydon (aka Johnny Rotten). Rotten's green spiky hair, snarling vocals, and ill-mannered behavior made him the center of the media's sensationalized coverage of the emerging group; however, raw excitement generated by the band in performance had much to do with their success in generating a strong grassroots following. Whether they were true to their nihilistic punk ethic or merely convincing poseurs, the Pistols proved to be too hot for a succession of corporate labels to handle. E.M.I. dropped the group after one widely censored single, "Anarchy in the U.K." (E.M.I. #2566; 1976; #38 U.K.) and the outrage ensuing from their behavior on the U.K. television program *Today*. A & M likewise bailed out in March 1977 after the antics of band members (now including Sid Vicious, who'd replaced Matlock) at the postsigning party with copies of the anticipated debut release, "God Save the Queen" (A & M #7284; 1977), becoming an instant

The Sex Pistols, c. late '70s, in a Warner Bros. publicity shot. Courtesy Warner/Reprise Records

collectors item. The seminal punk anthem was reissued a couple of months later by Virgin (#181; 1977), reaching number two on the U.K. charts, despite being banned by the BBC.

The equally vitriolic follow-ups, "Pretty Vacant" (Virgin #184; 1977; #6 U.K.) and "Holidays in the Sun" (Virgin #191; 1977; #8 U.K.), piqued interest in the long-awaited debut album, *Never Mind the Bollocks, Here's the Sex Pistols* (Warner Bros. #3147; 1977; #106 U.S., #1 U.K.). Now considered the classic statement of the British punk movement, the band — severely crippled by Rotten's departure following a brief American tour in early 1978 to form the postpunk experimental band, Public Image Ltd. — was nursed along by McLaren, releasing a string of Top 10 U.K. singles and recycled LPs, most notably the biopic soundtrack, *The Great Rock 'N' Roll Swindle* (Warner Bros. #45083; 1979; #7 U.K.) and the *Some Product: Carri On Sex Pistols* (Virgin #2; 1979; #6). The Pistols were effectively terminated by the death of Vicious on 2 Feb 1979 due to a heroin overdose. Nevertheless, interested in the band has remained high, in part as a result of the rise of alternative rock, specifically the grunge subgenre. As a result, all the group's recordings have been reissued on CD, and the original lineup reassembled for a live tour in 1996, documented in the recording *Filthy Lucre Live* (Virgin America #41926; 1996; #26 U.K.).

FRANK HOFFMANN

SEXUALLY ORIENTED LYRICS

During the 78-rpm era there were virtually no recorded songs with sexual content, except for "under the counter" party records. Love songs — the staple of the popular repertoire — contented themselves with talk about kisses. But in pop/rock songs of the 1960s lyrics tended to become sexually explicit, leading to consumer complaints and various levels of censorship. The very term "rock and roll" has a sexual connotation, although it has been interpreted simply as having a party or as dancing. Suggestive lyrics were found earlier, in the rhythm and blues period ("Roll All Night Long," "Work with Me, Annie"), but became more and more pervasive in the 1960s and 1970s. Such lyrics, especially when melded with the bump and grind mannerism popularized by Elvis Presley (whose lyrics were only mildly suggestive in themselves), resulted in public performances of plain eroticism. Noted representatives of this mode have been the Rolling Stones; The Fugs ("Wet Dream"); David Bowie; and the Doors, with Jim Morrison as the highly sensual lead singer ("Light My Fire"). Morrison was described by the *Miami Herald* as the "king of orgasmic rock." Protest movements arose in 1969–1970, as various "decency rallies" were held without great impact.

In the late 1980s the lyrics associated with rap music were preponderantly sexual. Recordings by the group 2 Live Crew were actually judged to be obscene by courts in some U.S. jurisdictions, but the performers were found innocent by higher courts. Their album *Nasty as You Wanna Be* appeared to break all earlier taboos for language and content. One shopkeeper in Florida was in fact convicted of selling obscene material, the same 2 Live Crew album that resulted in freedom for the performers who made it. In the mid-1980s the U.S. record industry responded to pressure from parent groups by affixing warning stickers on certain albums, reading "Parental Advisory — Explicit Lyrics." Another trend beginning in the late 1980s and continuing through the 1990s was to issue two versions of the same album or song, with the alternate being a "clean" version. This was common practice among rap singers, but spread also to others who used sexual or other inflammatory language in their music.

SHAD, BOB (12 FEB 1920–MAR 1985)

Jazz and R&B producer and record label owner, Shad had a long career beginning in the late 1940s. Shad produced Charlie Parker's legendary late 1940s sessions for Savoy, while also overseeing R&B albums for National. In 1948 he partnered with his brother Morty to form the Sittin' In With label, which had a five-year run featuring mostly Southern R&B performers, including Smokey Hogg, Elmore Nixon, and Lightnin' Hopkins (Hopkins's material was licensed from the Texas Gold Star label). In 1953 Mercury purchased the label and Bob went to work for them as director of A&R (brother Morty formed the Jax label). Shad remained at Mercury through most of the 1950s, overseeing jazz (Dinah Washington; Clifford Brown/Max Roach), doo-wop (the Diamonds, Platters), blues (Junior Wells), and rock (Conway Twitty) for the label and its Emarcy jazz division. In late 1958, he went independent again, forming the Time, Brent, and Shad group of labels. Shad continued to release his own recordings and licensed pop material through about 1962 on these labels. Returning to jazz, he then formed Mainstream, signing Dizzy Gillespie, Shelly Manne, Sarah Vaughn, among others, and — in 1966 — the new rock group Big Brother and the Holding Company, featuring lead singer Janis Joplin. (Columbia purchased their contract from Mainstream after their first album appeared.) By the mid-1970s, the company was struggling, and its back catalog went out of print by the decade's end. Shad's daughter, Tamara, reissued some of this material on CD in the early 1990s.

CARL BENSON

SHADOWS, THE

The Shadows have often been described, somewhat erroneously, as the "British Ventures." While each band established a standard within its own nation for producing consistently high quality guitar-dominated, instrumental recordings, the Shadows actually began producing hit singles one year before the Ventures. Furthermore, they doubled as a backing band for U.K.'s premier rock star of the day, Cliff Richard, and released a considerable number of their own recordings with vocals.

The two musicians with the Shadows from start to finish, guitarists Hank Marvin and Bruce Welch, met in school at Newcastle where they formed a skiffle group, the Railroaders. In April 1958, they began playing in a Soho (London) coffee bar, the Two I's. By summer, they'd met Richard, who invited them to join his back-up band, along with Jet Harris and Tony Meehan (who would remain members until the mid-1960s). While playing in London area clubs, Richard and his group, then known as the Drifters, submitted a demo disc to EMI. Securing a contract, they quickly became the most successful recording act in the U.K. on the strength of such hits as "Living Doll" (released in the U.S. as ABC-Paramount #10042; 1959; #1 U.K., #30 U.S.) and "Travellin' Light" (ABC-Paramount #10066; 1959; #1 U.K.). Marvin's dazzling technique would inspire a generation of U.K. rock guitarists, including Eric Clapton, Jeff Beck, and Pete Townsend.

By 1960, the band — now called the Shadows — was releasing its own records including "Kon-Tiki" (Atlantic #2135; 1961; #1 U.K.), "Wonderful Land" (Atlantic #2146; 1962; #1 U.K.), and "Dance On" (Atlantic #2177; 1962; #1 U.K.). Unlike other U.K. instrumental acts (e.g., Mr. Acker Bilk, the Tornadoes), the group was never able to make chart headway stateside. Their signature hit, "Apache" (Columbia; #1960; #1 U.K.), was successfully covered by Danish guitarist Jorgen Ingmann in the U.S. market (Atco #6184; 1961; #2). They also composed the music for a series of London Palladium pantomime shows — *Aladdin* (1964), *Babes in the Wood* (1965), and *Cinderella* (1965) — in addition to scoring and performing in the 1964 film, *Rhythm & Greens*. The group also continued to collaborate with Richard on stage, television, and the movies.

After the departure of bassist John Henry Rostill and drummer Brian Bennett (who'd joined the Shadows in the mid-1960s) in 1968, the band was officially dissolved. Marvin and Welch continued to work to Richard for a time. They then joined forces with Australian guitarist John Farrar to form the Crosby, Stills, and Nash–styled band, Marvin, Welch, and Farrar. The trio released two commercially unsuccessful LPs, *Marvin, Welch and Farrar* (Capitol #760;

1971) and *Second Opinion* (Sire #7403; 1972), that nevertheless featured an exquisite blend of accomplished songwriting, close-harmony singing, and acoustic guitar textures. A final project, *Marvin & Farrar* (EMI #11403; 1973), appeared while the group was in the process of disintegrating. Farrar would gain immediate fame for his production work with Olivia Newton-John in the early 1970s.

All ex-Shadows have remained active in the music business, with various members reforming many times over the years. Despite efforts to succeed with newly recorded material, fans both in the U.K. and abroad have shown a distinct preference for the classic 1960s tracks. Numerous anthologies have been released since the 1970s, the most comprehensive being the six-CD set, *The Early Years, 1959–1966* (EMI #7971712; 1991).

FRANK HOFFMANN

SHAMROCK STORE (LABEL)

An American record, issued between 1928 and 1936 by the Shamrock Store of New York. Material was of Irish interest; some of the masters came from Plaza. [Rust 1978.]

SHANACHIE (LABEL)

Originally an Irish music specialty label, Shanachie has grown to be a major independent releasing Irish, World, rock/pop, and jazz music. The label was founded in 1975 by Dan Collins, an Irish music enthusiast, and record collector Richard Nevins, who previously operated the Melodian and Morningstar labels. The initial releases included reissues of early 78 recordings along with new recordings primarily by U.S.–based Irish musicians. In the early 1980s, the label branched out into African music, licensing Ladysmith Black Mambazo's South African recordings for release in the U.S., and also into Jamaican reggae music. In 1987, following the death of its founder Nick Perls, Shanachie purchased Yazoo Records, which focused on blues reissues, expanding its list to cover reissues of a variety of music originally recorded on 78s, including old-time country, Jewish music, and other styles. Shanachie also ventured into cowboy-flavored country music and jazz during the 1990s, and formed a home-video division. [website: www.shanachie.com.]

CARL BENSON

SHA NA NA

Sha Na Na has often been dismissed as nothing more than an oldies revival act; however, the group blended dance routines, a period greaser look (greased-back haircuts, leather jackets, pegged jeans, and undershirts with cigarette packs inside the rolled-up sleeves), and seamless doo-wop harmonies to deftly satirize the 1950s teen lifestyle. Formed at Columbia University, New York, in the late 1960s, Sha Na Na gained national recognition during the height of the rock 'n' roll revival craze through a showstopping set at the Woodstock Festival (1969) and various television appearances. Although their albums — including *Rock & Roll Is Here to Stay!* (Kama Sutra #2010; 1969), *Sha Na Na* (Kama Sutra #2034; 1971), *The Night Is Still Young* (Kama Sutra #2050; 1972), *The Golden Age of Rock 'N' Roll* (Kama Sutra #2073; 1973), *From the Streets of New York* (Kama Sutra #2075; 1973–1974), *Hot Sox* (Kama Sutra #2600; 1964), and *Sha Na Now* (Kama Sutra #2605; 1975) — featured picture-perfect renditions of classic oldies such as "Teen Angel" and "Duke of Earl," they failed to convey the group's satire, which was inherently visual in nature.

In 1976 Sha Na Na gained a network television contract to produce a weekly variety program. No longer a commercially successful recording group, they continued in television syndication well into the 1980s and continue to perform (including an appearance at the 25th anniversary concert at Woodstock (1994). One member, lead guitarist Henry Gross, went on to solo fame, reaching number one the *Billboard Hot 100* with "Shannon" (Lifesong #45072; 1976), allegedly a elegy to Beach Boy Carl Wilson's deceased Irish setter. [Stambler 1989.]

FRANK HOFFMANN

SHANKAR, RAVI (7 APR 1920–)

Shankar was the force that fused Indian spiritual music into western pop and experimental genres. Born in Benares, India, Shankar was trained by his brother Uday in both music and dance. Shankar met American composer Philip Glass in Paris in the mid-1960s. This meeting inspired Glass to reject the traditional compositional techniques he had followed thus far, leading him on the journey that would start the minimalist movement. At the same time mainstream pop and rock musicians became interested in Shanker's unique approach to melody and structure displayed on his sitar recitals. The Beatles and the Byrds most notably were inspired by his appearances at the Monterey and Woodstock festivals, and Shankar's musical teachings and collaborations with George Harrison made him world famous. His autobiography *Raga Mala*, published in 1998, places his influence in the context of his own personal journey.

IAN PEEL

SHANNON FOUR

A male vocal quartet that recorded for Victor from 1917, and for various labels under various pseudonyms. Later they called themselves the Shannon Quartet, and made Victors until 1928. The original membership was Charles Hart and Harvey Hindermyer, tenors; Elliott Shaw, baritone; and Wilfred Glenn, bass, who organized the group. In 1918 Lewis James replaced Hindermyer. Hart was replaced by James Melton; others who sang tenor were Franklyn Baur, Charles Harrison, Frank Parker, and Robert Simmons. Ed Smalle joined the group at times, singing and/or playing the piano accompaniment. In 1925 the Victor recordings were made by Baur, James, Shaw, and Glenn. In that year the group took the name the Revelers, although they also continued with the Shannon name. The Shannon Four sang a more traditional quartet style; the Revelers a jazzy modern style.

Other names for the Shannon group were the Lyric Male Quartet (on Harmony, Edison Blue Amberol, and Edison Diamond Disc), Acme Male Quartet or Hudson Male Quartet (on Pathé), Campus Glee Club (on Cameo), Cathedral Quartet or Liberty Quartet (on Emerson), and the Peerless Four (on Okeh and Gennett).

SHAVERS

Cylinder record blanks had to be turned smooth for both initial use and for reuse, this task being accomplished by a shaver. Thomas Edison's British patent #17175 (1887) included such a device, attached to the carrier arm of the New Phonograph. Later the shaver (or planer, or parer) had a separate existence, which might have been powered by a treadle (1890s to ca. 1905; based on U.S. patent #375,579 by Charles S. Tainter) or by electricity (from ca. 1897). An electric drive could spin a cylinder under the planer at 1,500 rpm to 2,800 rpm. In March 1908 Edison marketed his Universal Shaving Machine, usable on both regular size and six-inch business cylinders. A simple hand-cranked machine was available in 1912, employing a steel blade that could smooth a cylinder with just a few turns. [Frow 1978.]

SHAW, ARTIE (23 MAY 1910–)

American jazz clarinetist and Big Band leader, born Arthur Jacob Arshawsky in New York. He began playing in a band in New Haven, Connecticut, his instrument being the alto saxophone. He turned to the clarinet, then played tenor sax in Irving Aaronson's band. He was freelancing in New York in 1931–1935, and formed a group in 1936 that had a string quartet in it — an unusual sound that was widely appreciated. He began recording for Brunswick, and performed at the Lexington Hotel in New York until 1937. He regrouped, forming a conventional swing band, engaged Helen Forrest as vocalist, and produced his first and perhaps greatest record, "Begin the Beguine" (Bluebird #7746; 1938), an arrangement by Jerry Gray. "All the Things You Are," sung by Forrest, was one of his finer ballad records (Bluebird #10492; 1939). Among the artist who played in his bands at this time were Billy Butterfield, trumpet; Johnny Guarnieri, piano and harpsichord; Ray Coniff, trombone; Tony Pastor, tenor sax; and Buddy Rich and Dave Tough, drums.

Shaw's second great hit was "Frenesi" (Victor #26542; 1940), again with an orchestra including a string section. Emulating Benny Goodman, Shaw formed a small hot group from his band, the Gramercy Five; they made an acclaimed record for Victor, "Summit Ridge Drive" (#26763; 1940). During World War II Shaw enlisted in the Navy and was asked to lead a band to entertain the troops in the Pacific. In 1944 he put together a strong jazz band, with Roy Eldridge; he also engaged the classical repertoire for clarinet, with a Carnegie Hall appearance and some recordings. He retired in 1954, then returned for another round of performances in 1983.

Among the LP reissues of earlier material there was a fine Sunbeam album (#SB207) that included sessions from 1936–1937, notably "Sweet Lorraine" and "Streamline." The Bluebird recordings were reissued by RCA; they cover 1938–1939, when Billie Holiday was briefly singing with the group, sparkling in "Any Old Time." Most of the Gramercy Five recordings reappeared on LP (RCA LSA #3087).

SHAW, ELLIOTT
(10 APR 1887–13 AUG 1973)

American baritone, known as a member of numerous male quartets in the 1920s. He began with the Shannon Four in 1918; continued with the same men as they formed the Revelers; and sang also with the Crescent Trio. On Pathé records he was known as Frank Sterling. Shaw retired to Sharon, Connecticut, and died in Bronxville, New York.

SHAW, ROBERT
(30 APR 1916–25 JAN 1999)

American choral and orchestra conductor, born in Red Bluff, California. He conducted his college glee club, and then the Fred Waring Glee Club (1938–1945). In 1948 he founded the Robert Shaw Chorale and conducted it for 20 years; it became recognized as one of the major choral groups of the world, making extended tours under the auspices of the U.S. Department of State. From 1956–1967, Shaw was associate conductor of the Cleveland Orchestra, and then he became director of the Atlanta (Georgia) Symphony Orchestra. Under his direction, the Atlanta Orchestra and its Chorus achieved a high level of excellence. Shaw won 10 Grammys (1961–1989) for performances with the Atlanta Symphony Orchestra and Chorus, including definitive renditions of the requiems of Berlioz, Verdi, and Britten.

SHEARING, GEORGE ALBERT
(13 AUG 1919–)

U.K./American jazz pianist, born in London. Blind from birth, he learned music from braille notation. Transferring to the U.S., he was greatly successful with an unusual piano style (locked hand, thick chords in parallel motion) and his gift for interpolating classical, contrapuntal elements into his improvisations. His George Shearing Quintet was highly popular from 1949 into the 1970s, featuring vibes and guitar blending with the piano line. He composed "Lullaby of Birdland," a major hit, and recorded it on MGM #11354. He had six chart albums for Capitol in the 1950s and 1960s, including *Shearing on Stage* (Capitol ST #1187; 1959). In the 1980s he made a remarkable series of appearances and recordings with Mel Tormé. In 1979, he signed with Concord Jazz, making a number of successful recordings for this label through the 1980s. In 1992, he moved to new label, Telarc Jazz. His 80th birthday was celebrated with a concert in 1999 at Carnegie Hall, and he has continued to record and perform into the 21st century.

REV. CARL BENSON

SHEBLE, HORACE

Philadelphia recording industry executive and inventor, a partner in Hawthorne & Sheble with Ellsworth A. Hawthorne. He held 14 patents in the audio field, notably U.S. #701,769 (filed 15 June 1901, granted 3 June 1902) for a talking machine cabinet in which the Gramophone was in a sliding drawer; and U.S. #872,586 (filed 21 Dec 1906; granted 3 Dec 1907) for a tone arm. The tone arm was Sheble's answer to the patented tapered tone arm of Eldridge Johnson; it was a "sound-conveying tube consisting of a plurality of sections of progressively increasing cross-sectional area." This configuration was used on the Hawthorne & Sheble Star Talking Machine. Sheble went to work for Columbia Phonograph Co. in 1911. [Koenigsberg 1990.]

SHEIP AND VANDEGRIFT INC.

A Philadelphia firm, stemming from the Henry Sheip Manufacturing Co., which had built cabinets for Berliner and Victor from 1900 to ca. 1906. When Victor began making its own cabinets in 1907, the firm made wooden horns; they were advertised in *TMW* of March 1910 as a maker of Musicmaster horns, in oak, mahogany or spruce.

SHELLAC

The name given to the compound that was used to make most disc records from about 1896 to about 1948. Shellac is also the name of the principal ingredient in the compound. Shellac is a resinous compound secreted by the lac, a tree insect native to India, Burma, and Thailand. The secretion is utilized to form a protective shell for the insect and for its unhatched eggs, such shells being about the size of a grain of wheat. This shell-lac is scraped from twigs and branches, and shipped in dry powder form. For the disc record application in its developed state, shellac itself formed 13.6 percent of the shellac compound. Other ingredients were vinsol (8.7 percent), Congo gum (0.92 percent), white filler (37.4 percent), red filler (37.4 percent), carbon black (1.3 percent), and zinc stearate (0.49 percent). It was Fred Gaisberg who discovered the utility of the shellac compound for discs, in 1896; he found it being used for button making by the Duranoid Co., of Newark, New Jersey.

Problems in the use of shellac for records included the uncertain quality of the shellac itself, which was often loaded with impurities; the variable inclusion of scrap (including, in times of shortage, old records returned for recycling) in the compound by different manufacturers; and the basic difficulty of getting enough of the material from India. During World War II the supply was virtually cut off. But even under the best conditions, shellac was subject to gross surface noise produced by the abrasive filler — most of it limestone. Another great problem was the brittleness of the record, requiring great care and cost in handling, packaging, and shipping.

Lamination of the final shellac disc, initiated and produced briefly by Columbia in 1906, reduced surface noise. Columbia returned to the laminated record in 1922, and presented a technically superior product that worked well later with jukeboxes, and which sustained the label through the shellac shortage of the war (since lamination reduced the need for so much shellac).

Shellac was finally replaced as a disc ingredient by vinyl, introduced in the 1930s, and rendered ubiquitous by the LP record. [Isom 1977.]

See also **Marconi Velvet Tone (Label)**

SHELTER (LABEL)

Rock label formed in 1969 by singer/performer/producer Leon Russell and producer Denny Cordell. The two had enjoyed great success in 1968 producing albums by Joe Cocker and Delaney and Bonnie. They formed the label in Tulsa, Oklahoma, Russell's hometown, and initially it featured Russell himself and his friends, notably singer/songwriter J.J. Cale and blues guitarist Freddy King. However, Russell split from the label in 1975. Cordell continued on his own, buoyed in 1976 by the success of a new act, Tom Petty and the Heartbreakers. Shelter was by then owned by ABC Records, which in turn was sold to MCA. Petty declared bankruptcy in 1979 because MCA refused to renegotiate his Shelter deal. The label did not survive beyond 1980.

CARL BENSON

SHEPARD, BURT

American born comedian and singer, especially popular on the U.K. stage. He was one of the Berliner recording artists, having recorded from November 1898. His first rendition was a "Parody on 'Home Sweet Home'" (#2151). As Berliner became the Gramophone Co. (and G & T), Shepard continued to make recordings in ever increasing numbers, often as Charles Foster. Rust speculates that another popular name on early HMV, Harry Taylor, was in fact Shepard. His "Laughing Song" — imitating the version of composer George Washington Johnson — was one of the greatest successes of the Gramophone Co., selling more than a million copies throughout the world. He worked for Victor from July 1901 to November 1906, beginning with "Limburger Cheese" (#V7); and he appeared in Pathé's 1904 catalog.

SHEPP, ARCHIE (24 MAY 1937–)

Shepp, one of the leaders of the 1960s' avant-garde jazz movement, has also delved into bop, R&B, and the blues during his career. He is a professor and playwright as well. He was raised in Philadelphia and received a B.A. in dramatic literature from Goddard College. He moved to New York and worked with Cecil Taylor, Don Cherry, and other avant-garde musicians in the early 1960s. He befriended John Coltrane, who subsequently introduced him to the record producer Bob Thiele of Impulse Records. His music and his plays were powerful vehicles for the expression of his impassioned views on the civil rights struggle.

One of Shepp's early recordings was *The New York Contemporary Five* (Sonet #36; 1963), a collaborative effort between some notable free jazz musicians. In 1964 he released *Four for Trane* (Impulse #71), his first recording as a leader. On it, Shepp approaches four of Coltrane's tunes while exploring his own artistic vision. The intensity and emotional turmoil of avant-garde jazz is evident throughout much of *Three for a Quarter, One for a Dime* (Impulse #9162; 1966), a recording that also features the great trombonist Roswell Rudd. Shepp released other highly regarded albums in the 1960s including *Mama Too Tight* (Impulse #9134; 1966) and *Live at the Donauesehingen Music Festival* (MPS #20651; 1967). In 1977 Shepp released an album that featured Black spirituals, accompanied only by pianist Horace Parlan, titled *Goin' Home* (Steeple Chase #31079). He explored different musical territory again with *Looking at Bird* (Steeple Chase #1139; 1980), on which he interpreted the music of Charlie Parker. After the mid-1980s, Shepp's career went into somewhat of a decline, at least in the eyes of some critics who faulted the quality of his later playing; nonetheless, he has continued to record for various labels and to perform.

GARTH ALPER

SHERMAN, CLAY AND CO.

A San Francisco firm, located in 1929 at Kearny and Sutter Streets. It sold Steinways and other pianos, phonographs, radios, and records.

SHERRILL, BILLY (5 NOV 1936–)

Born in Phil Campbell, Alabama, Sherrill was a legendary Nashville producer who nurtured the careers of Charlie Rich, Tanya Tucker, Tammy Wynette, and countless others as an A&R man at Epic records from the mid–1960s through the early 1980s. The son of an evangelist, Sherrill first took up the piano and then, as a teenager, switched to saxophone. After a brief career as a solo artist in the late 1950s and early 1960s, he hooked up with legendary producer Sam Phillips of Sun Records who hired him to operate his Nashville

studios. After Phillips's label collapsed, he joined Epic Records.

From the start, Sherrill worked not only molding artists' sound, but also selecting and often coauthoring their material, and carefully honing their image. Among his classic productions are "Stand By Your Man," Tammy Wynette's famous ode to marital fidelity, which he cowrote with her, all of Tanya Tucker's early hits, and Charlie Rich's megahits, "Behind Closed Doors" and "The Most Beautiful Girl." While Sherrill was the 1970s most successful producer, the new country movement of the 1980s made his style seem passé. During that decade, he focused more on administrative duties, although he continued to work occasionally as a producer. One of his last and most interesting projects was a collaboration with U.K. punk musician Elvis Costello in 1981 for a country homage album, *Almost Blue*.

CARL BENSON

SHIRELLES, THE

Probably most successful of the vintage girl groups other than the Supremes, the Shirelles — comprised of lead vocalist Shirley Owens, Addie Harris, Doris Kenner, and Beverly Lee — began singing together at school shows and parties. A classmate introduced them to her mother, music business executive Florence Greenberg. After the group-penned "I Met Him on a Sunday" (Decca #30588; 1958) reached number 49 on the pop chart, Greenberg formed Scepter Records. Spurred by the talents of writer-producer Luther Dixon, the Shirelles recorded a long string of pop/rhythm and blues hits, including "Tonight's the Night" (Scepter #1208; 1960; cowritten by Dixon and Shirley Owens; #14 R&B, #39 pop); "Will You Love Me Tomorrow" (Scepter #1211; 1960–1961; written by Gerry Goffin and Carole King; #1 pop), "Dedicated to the One I Love" (Scepter #1203; 1959, 1961), "Mama Said" (Scepter #1217; 1961), "Baby It's You" (Scepter #1227; written by Burt Bacharach, Hal David, and Barney Williams; 1961–1962), and "Soldier Boy" (Scepter #1228; 1962; #1 pop). Dixon's departure from the label slowed the group's momentum (although the first post-Dixon release, "Foolish Little Girl" [Scepter #1248; 1963] reached number four); however, the heightened competition provided by the British Invasion, folk rock, soul, and surf music artists ultimately had more to do with the disappearance of charting singles.

After breaking up in the late 1960s, the Shirelles reformed (often without the original lineup) to perform at rock 'n' roll revival concerts. In 1994 the three surviving members (Harris died of a heart attack in 1982) sang together for the first time in 19 years; they have reunited on occasion in the following years. [Betrock 1982.]

FRANK HOFFMANN

SHOEMAKER, KATHRYN (TRINA)
(14 JUNE 1965–)

Born in Illinois, and graduating from Joliet Central High School in 1983, Shoemaker has worked as an independent recording engineer for dozens of labels, and has had numerous articles published about her, her talent, and her work in professional journals, such as *EQ*, *Spin*, and *Mix*. In 1998 she won an engineering Grammy for the best nonclassical album, being the first woman ever to win that award.

HOWARD FERSTLER

SHOLES, STEVE
(12 FEB 1911–22 APR 1968)

Born in Washington, D.C., Stephen Sholes joined his father at RCA's Camden, New Jersey, plant in 1929 and remained with the label until his death in Nashville on 22 Apr 1968. Sholes trained as an A&R man under Eli Oberstein and Frank Walker, and produced jazz sessions during the late 1930s. In 1945 he was appointed head of Specialty Singles (which included country, R&B, gospel, and children's music). In 1954 he built the first major label studio in Nashville, but remained in New York, placing the studio in the hands of Chet Atkins (whom he'd signed as an artist in 1947). Other artists signed or produced by Steve Sholes included Eddy Arnold, Hank Snow, Jim Reeves, Neil Sedaka, Ann-Margret, Perry Como, and, of course, Elvis Presley, whom he signed from Sun Records in 1955. Presley's success ensured Sholes's elevation in 1957 to head of pop singles. He headed RCA's West Coast operation from 1961 until 1963. From 1963 until his death, he was vice president of pop A&R in New York.

COLIN ESCOTT

SHONK (CHARLES W.) CO.

A Chicago firm, established in 1877. It manufactured the Mag-Ni-Phone disc player in 1916.

SHORE, DINAH
(1 MAR 1917–24 FEB 1994)

American popular singer, born Frances Rose Shore in Winchester, Tennessee. She studied sociology at Vanderbilt University, Nashville (B.A., 1938), and sang on local radio. Moving to New York to pursue a musical career, she sang on WNEW and performed with the Xavier Cugat orchestra, taking the name Dinah from the title of a song she often sang. By 1940 she was well known, recording for Bluebird and appearing on the Eddie Cantor radio show. Soon she was the top female vocalist on radio and records. Shore had her own television shows after World War II, achieving the highest audience ratings. In the 1960s her popularity faded, but she remained active as a television special hostess and guest. She died in Los Angeles.

Shore's early records were made with Cugat; they included an evocative "Breeze and I" (Victor #26641; 1940). Her first independent recording was a great hit: "Yes, My Darling Daughter" (Bluebird #10920; 1940). Other important discs were "Blues in the Night" (Bluebird #B-11436; 1942), "Sleigh Ride in July"/"Like Someone in Love" (Victor #20-1617; 1945), and "Buttons and Bows" (Columbia #38284; 1948). Her last hit single was "Scene of the Crime" (Victor #7349; 1958). She made LPs for Victor, Columbia, and several other labels.

SHORTER, WAYNE (25 AUG 1933–)

Shorter has remained one of the major figures in jazz since his emergence in the late 1950s. At age 16, he began studying the clarinet but switched to tenor saxophone by the time he was a music education major at New York University in 1952. He met Joe Zawinul in 1958, with whom he would later colead the jazz-fusion group Weather Report. He was a member of Art Blakey's Jazz Messengers from 1959 to 1963 and was an important force in Miles Davis's group from 1964 to 1970. Shorter coled, performed, and recorded with Weather Report from 1970 to the mid-1980s. He is considered one of the most important jazz composers of his time.

Shorter began his recording career as a sideman for Art Blakey's Jazz Messengers. *Caravan* (Riverside #9438; 1962), which displays Shorter's wry saxophone work and the compositions, "Sweet 'n' Sour" and "This Is for Albert," is considered by many to be Blakey's finest album. In the mid-1960s, Shorter's compositions helped to define the sound of Miles Davis's group. In 1964 Shorter released *Night Dreamer* (Blue Note #84173) and *Juju* (Blue Note #84182), albums whose compositions displayed vague tonal centers and an expanded harmonic palette. Other essential Shorter albums from this period include *Speak No Evil* (Blue Note #84194; 1964) and *Adam's Apple* (Blue Note #84232; 1966). His playing and compositions were essential to the artistic success of the Miles Davis releases *E.S.P.* (Columbia #CS9150; 1965), *Miles Smiles* (Columbia #CS9401; 1966), and *Nefertiti* (Columbia #CS9594; 1967).

Shorter recorded at least 15 albums with Weather Report, a group that fused jazz, rock, and world music influences into a uniquely potent amalgam. It was here that Shorter began to favor the soprano saxophone, an instrument that could better be heard over Zawinul's thick keyboard textures. *Sweetnighter* (Columbia #KC32210; 1973) demonstrated the group's emerging groove-oriented style of jazz-fusion. *Mysterious Traveler* (Columbia #KC32494; 1974), *Black Market* (Columbia #PC34099; 1976), and *Heavy Weather* (Columbia #FC37616; 1977) find the group at the peak of its powers.

In 1985 Shorter recorded the Grammy-nominated Atlantis (Columbia #FC40055), an album with complex jazz-fusion rhythms and harmonies. He released some mediocre pop-jazz albums in the later 1980s, and then retired from performing until 1992. He signed with Verve in 1994, and continued to record with various groups, including his 1997 appearances on tour with the Rolling Stones and on recordings with Herbie Hancock during the later 1990s. He released Footprints Live in 2002 (Verve #314 589 679-2), a CD in which intense and masterful performances by Shorter and his sidemen earned it numerous awards and critical acclaim.

GARTH ALPER

SHURE, STANLEY N.
(27 MAR 1902–17 OCT 1996)

An Audio Engineering Society member, Shure was born in Chicago and earned a degree in geography from the University of Chicago. Known professionally as S.N. Shure, he started the Shure Radio Co. in 1925, which was a distributor of parts for home radio set builders. Eventually he was joined by his brother in the business, and the company was renamed Shure Bros. Shure was interested in technology as much as business enterprise, and it was not long until he became interested in microphone design. In 1938 he helped Ben Bauer invent the world's first single-element directional microphone, called the Unidyne, which was marketed in 1939 and later became the design foundation for the later, world-renowned SM57 and SM58 models.

Somewhat prior to that time, in 1935, Shure had begun to design and produce phonographc cartridges, and this diversification helped the company to expand into the growing and lucrative home-audio market. In 1954, he began doing research on stereophonic phonograph cartridges, and within a few years, at the dawn of the stereophonic era, he introduced the M3D stereophonic cartridge. Because of this and other design innovations, the company expanded into being one of the world's major phonograph cartridge enterprises.

Shure was also an avid photographer, an internationally recognized philatelist, and an expert on linguistics and languages. A portion of his extensive stamp collection has been donated to the Smithsonian Institution.

HOWARD FERSTLER

SHURE BROS.

American audio firm located in Evanston, Illinois. Established in 1925 by Stanley N. Shure, as Shure Radio Co., which specialized in selling radio parts kits. In 1926, the founder's brother, S.J. Shure joined the company and the name was changed to Shure Bros. The company branched out into the production of microphones in 1932, and one major product was a two-button carbon microphone. The first single-diaphragm unidirectional microphone, the Unidyne (invented by Ben Bauer), was introduced in 1939. Later designs, such as the SM57 and SM58 models, introduced in 1965, were very popular and are still used internationally for recording rock and pop concerts. In the world of live sound, the Beta series of microphones (1989) took the proven design philosophy of the SM58 and applied it to the special needs of the modern concert stage. Similarly, Shure's UHF wireless system (1996) has become an industry standard. Other sound recording and reinforcement products include a line of in-ear wireless stage monitoring systems that give performers control of how they hear themselves while aiding in hearing conservation. Recent product innovations for professional installations include digital feedback reducers and automatic mixers.

Among audiophiles, the company was probably best known for its innovative and often reasonably priced phonograph cartridges than for its microphones. Shure's important V15 series of cartridges were continually upgraded reference standards for years, and the latest version is still being produced. [Whyte 1986/4.]

REV. HOWARD FERSTLER

SIDES, ALAN (SEP 1951–)

After attending Pepperdine University, Sides, later to become one of the most respected producers and recording engineers in the industry, inched his way into the recording business, and got his first job working for United Western Recording, in Hollywood, in 1968. He later started a small studio, named Ocean Way, in Santa Monica, and after several years of honing his skills and building up the business, he went back and purchased United Western, in 1977, and changed its name to Ocean Way Studios. After still more recording successes, he went on to also found Record One Studios, in Los Angeles, as well as a second Ocean Way facility in Nashville.

With over 400 albums to his credit, Sides's engineering and mixing work includes releases by Eric Clapton, Alanis Morissette, the Goo Goo Dolls, David Benoit, Neil Diamond, John Lee Hooker, Barry Manilow, Olivia Newton-John, Oscar Peterson, Benny Carter, Andre Previn, Diane Schuur, Frank Sinatra, Mel Torme, Aerosmith, Patti Austin, Count Basie, Dolly Parton, Zoot Sims, Vanessa Williams, and Nancy Wilson, among many others. His engineering work also includes the film scores to *Primary Colors*, *Dead Man Walking*, *Phenomenon*, *Runaway Bride*, *City of Angels*, and *Last Man Standing*, among quite a few others. Other credits include Beck, Ry Cooder, Emmylou Harris, the Brian Setzer Big Band, Deana Carter, the GRP All Star Big Band, and *The Songs of West Side Story*, featuring Phil Collins, Natalie Cole, All for One, Trisha Yearwood, Wynonna Judd, Tevin Campbell, Kenny Loggins, Michael McDonald, Little Richard, and Aretha Franklin.

As a producer, Sides has completed several albums for Disney, featuring Linda Ronstadt, Etta James, the Pointer Sisters, Barenaked Ladies, Take 6, James Ingram, Brian McKnight, and Bobby McFerrin. He is a member of the RIAA, and during his career he has won numerous Tech awards, as well as an engineering Grammy for his work on the Joni Mitchell album *Both Sides Now*.

HOWARD FERSTLER

SIEGEL, SAMUEL

Mandolin player, among the first to record the instrument. He was heard on seven-inch Berliners, and on the Improved Record of Eldridge Johnson's Consolidated Talking Machine Co. ("Medley of Coon Songs"; #A-449). He made 10 Edison cylinders, one a duet with guitarist M.L. Wolf, "Autumn Evening" (#9014; 1905). As the mandolin faded from popularity in the 1920s, his records were deleted. There were two left in the 1922 Victor catalog, duets with a guitarist named Butin, but none remained in the 1927 catalog.

SIGNAL

In audio terminology, the complex of sound waves that is introduced to the recording system to be captured and reproduced.

SIGNAL-TO-NOISE RATIO (S/N RATIO)

Often arbitrarily assigned, in an audio system, it is the ratio between the desired signal level and the extraneous audible material, such as hum, surface scratches, vibrations from components, etc. It is usually expressed in decibels (dB). For instance, an S/N ratio of 50 dB means that the signal is 50 dB louder than the extraneous noise. Obviously the higher the ratio, the better the result, because an overlay of equipment-generated background noise is undesirable in audio recording and playback systems. The noise should be measured using a true RMS type voltmeter over a specified bandwidth, and sometimes weighting filters should be used to account for audibility differences at various frequencies. All these things must be stated for a S/N spec to have meaning, and simply saying a playback device or recorder has a S/N ratio of 70, 80, or 90 dB means nothing, without giving the reference level, measurement bandwidth, and any weighting filers. Note also that a system's maximum S/N should equal its dynamic range.

Early equipment and record materials yielded very low ratios. For example, it was said about Emile Berliner's hard-rubber discs that "in terms of signal-to-noise ratio, the best probably did not exceed 6 dB and the average was very near unity." The shellac record that came later was better, but "the best signal-to-noise ratio never exceeded 32 dB and 28 dB was a high average performance." With the vinyl record, 55 dB to 60 dB ratios were reached. A good CD player with 16 bit resolution has a S/N ratio of 96 dB (6 dB per bit, with the range expanded if noise shaping is employed), which is more than adequate for all but the most robust symphonic music. Ideally there should be no noise at all in a CD output, but the optimal situation is not achieved in practice because of noise in the analog circuitry. [Isom 1977, source of the quotations; Pohlmann 1989.]

REV. HOWARD FERSTLER

SIGNATURE (LABEL)

An American record issued from the mid-1940s, by the Signature Recording Corp. of New York. The firm was owned by Bob Thiele. Jazz and some boogie woogie appeared in early issues, then a wider repertoire of

Mid-'40s label owned by Bob Thiele. Courtesy Kurt Nauck/Nauck's Vintage Records

popular material. Artists in 1946 included Ray Bloch (who was also music director), Harry Cool, Hazel Scott, and Will Bradley. Releases continued through 1959.

SILLS, BEVERLY (25 MAY 1929–)

Born Belle Miriam Silverman in Brooklyn, New York, Sills became one of America's best-loved operatic sopranos and, following her performing career, a major figure in performing arts administration. Sills began performing locally on radio and at amateur talent shows from age three, earning the nickname "Bubbles." She made her operatic debut in 1947 with the Philadelphia Civic Opera, and toured for the next few years with a number of smaller companies. In 1955 she made her first appearance with the New York City Opera, and was soon a major star of the company. She made her first appearance with the Metropolitan Opera in 1966 at a Lewisohn Stadium performance; she did not make her "formal," Lincoln Center premiere with the company until nine years later. In 1979, she was named general director of the New York City Opera, and retired from performing the next year. She was elected chairman of the Lincoln Center for the Performing Arts in 1994, a position she held through spring 2002; six months later, it was announced that Sills would be the new chairwoman of the Metropolitan Opera.

Like many other opera stars, Sills recording career ranges from "serious" recordings of full operas to more light-hearted, popular fare. She has recorded for Angel/EMI and Deutsche Grammophon, among many other labels. Her labels have been slow to reissue major recordings on CD, and many critics feel that she was never adequately recorded, with her recordings failing to capture the full beauty of her vocal timbre. Besides audio recordings, DVDs are available of major performances filmed for television, along with noncommercial recordings of radio broadcasts.

SILVER, HORACE (2 SEP 1928–)

Silver, a pianist, composer, arranger, and bandleader, is largely credited with the creation of the hard-bop style of jazz that incorporated R&B and gospel styles. This funkier style was prevalent in the 1950s and Silver's recordings are some of the finest examples of the subgenre.

Silver was introduced to the piano in high school and lists pianists Bud Powell and Thelonious Monk as two of his major influences. He toured with Stan Getz in 1950, moved to New York in 1951, and began playing with some of the most important performers in the jazz world. In 1953, he and the drummer Art Blakey cofounded the Jazz Messengers, a group that Blakey would lead successfully for another 34 years after Silver left to lead his own group in 1956.

Horace Silver and the Jazz Messengers (Blue Note #5058; 1954) is an album that features the Silver compositions "The Preacher" and "Doodlin'." *Blowin' the Blues Away* (Blue Note #4017; 1959) contains the ballad "Peace" which has become a classic standard. *Horace-Scope* (Blue Note #84042; 1960) and *Song for My Father* (Blue Note #84185, 1964) are two more outstanding Silver recordings from this period.

Silver continued to record for Blue Note through most of the 1970s, although his work attracted less attention. In the 1980s, he formed his own Silveto label to release his works, but these albums were not widely reviewed. He returned to a major label, Columbia, in 1993, and then recorded for GRP/Impulse in the mid-1990s. In 1996 Silver released *Hard Bop Grandpop* (Impulse #MPD192), a CD that featured Michael Brecker on tenor saxophone and Ron Carter on bass, and received critical acclaim.

GARTH ALPER

SILVER, MONROE (21 DEC 1875–3 MAY 1947)

Yiddish dialect comedian, born in New York. He was a prolific recording artist, making Victor records from 1911 to 1926, and working for many other labels. He began with "Abie, Take an Example from You Fader" (Victor #16841; 1911), and ended with a two-sided comic skit featuring longtime partner Billy Murray, "Casey and Cohen in the Army" (Beacon #2001; 1943). His most famous series was centered around a character named Cohen: "Cohen Gets Married," "Cohen on His Honeymoon," etc., which he inscribed for Victor beginning in 1918, and for Edison Diamond Discs (and Blue Amberols) in 1920. Silver replaced Byron G. Harlan in the Eight Famous Victor Artists in 1918 or 1919. After his recording career ended he continued with nightclub work and on radio. He died in New York. [Walsh 1972/3.]

REV. FRANK HOFFMANN

SILVERTON (LABEL)

SEE DIXI (LABEL)

SILVERTONE (LABEL) (I)

An American record issued by Sears, Roebuck and Co. from ca. 1916 to ca. 1941. Masters were from Columbia at first, then from a variety of labels (Plaza, Paramount, Gennett, etc.). Sears also used the name Silvertone for its radios and phonographs, marketed from 1911. [Rust 1978.]

SILVERTONE (LABEL) (II)

A British label of Cooper Brothers, Ltd. It used matrices of Carl Lindström (London) and Fonotipia, Ltd., from December 1916.

FRANK ANDREWS

SILVERTONE (LABEL) (III)

An eight-inch British label made for Selfridge department stores by the British Homophone Co., Ltd., from its Solex matrices of 1930–1931.

FRANK ANDREWS

SIMEONE, HARRY (9 MAY 1911–)

Harry Simeone was born in Newark, New Jersey. After completing his childhood schooling he went to the Julliard School of Music in New York to refine his piano skills and then began work at CBS Radio where, in 1939, Fred Waring offered him a job as a staff arranger for his group, the Pennsylvanians. After several years of arranging for Waring, Simeone moved to Hollywood where he and his composer

Victor Young worked at the Paramount on Bing Crosby movies.

In 1945 he rejoined Waring as editor for the Shawnee Press publications for seven years until he started with the television show *Voice of Firestone* in 1952 as conductor and choral arranger for the next seven years. He started his own chorale, the Harry Simeone Chorale, and in 1958 he came across an adaptation of a Spanish song "Tabolilleros" by New England organist Katherine Kennicot Davis (1892–1980) and collaborator Henry Onorati. He further adapted it and arranged it with its drum effects for his Chorale album *Sing We Now of Christmas*, giving it the new name of "The Little Drummer Boy." The song was a gold record seller and has become a Christmas standard.

VAL HICKS

SIMON, CARLY (25 JUNE 1945–)

One of the more popular singer/songwriters of the 1970s, Carly Simon — as opposed to Carole King's East Coast R&B leanings and the folk/jazz orientation of Joni Mitchell, two of her notable counterparts — exemplified the polished Los Angeles sound. Simon's pop instincts and rich, expressive voice have enabled her to move into film soundtrack work and adult contemporary playlists when no longer in mainstream fashion.

First recording in the mid-1960s as part of the folk-pop Simon Sisters with her sister Lucy, Carly was signed to Elektra Records as a solo act in 1970 by producer Jac Holzman. Her debut, *Carly Simon* (Elektra #74182; 1971; #30), included the first of many hit singles, "That's the Way I've Always Heard It Should Be" (Elektra #45724; 1971; #10). Her critical and commercial high watermark came with *No Secrets* (Elektra #75049; 1973; #1), driven largely by the success of "You're So Vain" (Elektra #45824; 1972; #1), allegedly written about film star Warren Beatty, and featuring Mick Jagger on background vocals.

Marrying fellow singer/songwriter James Taylor in the mid-1970s, Simon was unable to produce anything quite approaching the quality of *No Secrets*. Nevertheless, she continued issuing solid, if uneven, albums — most notably, *Hotcakes* (Elektra #1002; 1974; #3), *Playing Possum* (Elektra #1033; 1975; #10), and *Boys in the Trees* (Elektra #128; 1978; #10) — which sold moderately well. After her last major hits — "Nobody Does It Better" (Elektra #45413; 1977; #2), from the James Bond film *The Spy Who Loved Me*, and "You Belong to Me" (Elektra #45477; 1978; #6) — Simon has appeared content to cultivate an older audience, releasing, among other things, two albums comprised of pop standards — *Torch* (Warner Bros. #3592; 1981; #50) and *My Romance* (Arista #8582; 1990; #46) — as well as a collection of material identified with the cinema, *Film Noir* (Arista #18984; 1997; #84). Her last charting single was "Coming Around Again" (Arista #9525; 1986; #18), the theme from the film *Heartburn*. She also provided the theme song for the film *Working Girl* (1988), "Let the River Run." She has also devoted an increasing amount of time to writing, no real surprise given the fact that her father helped run the Simon and Schuster publishing house.

FRANK HOFFMANN

SIMON, JOHN (11 AUG 1941–)

Folk and rock producer with a long career, Simon was born in Norwalk, Connecticut, and began playing music at age four. A prodigy pianist, he worked as a jazz player through high school and then while a college student at Princeton. Upon graduation, he took a job as a production trainee at Columbia Records. His first major hit came with "Red Rubber Ball," a number two hit for the folk-rock group the Cyrcle in 1965. Simon oversaw other Columbia artists through the 1960s, including Blood, Sweat and Tears's debut album and Big Brother and the Holding Company's *Cheap Thrills*. But he is perhaps best remembered for his association with the Band, producing their classic first three albums. During the 1970s, he continued to work as a producer and also began issuing his own recordings; he turned to classical composition in the 1980s, but then resurfaced as a singer-songwriter and pop producer in the early 1990s.

CARL BENSON

SIMON, PAUL (13 OCT 1941–)

Paul Simon's recording career has spanned a wide range of styles, from teen idol fare in the late 1950s, to folk-pop minstrelsy in the early 1960s, to continued experimentation with world music as a singer/songwriter. Although enjoying greater critical and commercial success as a member of the seminal folk-rock duo Simon and Garfunkel, his imposing legacy as a songwriter, performer, and studio producer owes much to the decades of solo work.

Born in Newark, New Jersey, and raised in New York City, Simon hooked up with school pal Art Garfunkel to form the group Tom and Jerry. After attempting to make an impact under pseudonyms like True Taylor and Jerry Landis, Simon reverted to his own name and adopted the U.K. as his home base for

a time. He reunited with Garfunkel in 1964; he was back in U.K. when producer Tom Wilson overdubbed electric guitar, bass, and drums on to "The Sound of Silence" (Columbia #43396; 1965; #1), a track from their folk-styled debut album, *Wednesday Morning 3 A.M.* (Columbia #9049; 1964; #30), thereby providing their career breakthrough. His solo U.K. LP, *The Paul Simon Songbook* (Columbia #62579; 1965), provided material for the next couple of Simon and Garfunkel albums.

The legendary duo split up in 1970; however, Simon maintained his career momentum with the release of the eclectic tour de force, *Paul Simon* (Columbia #30750; 1972; #4), which included the Caribbean-tinged singles, "Mother and Child Reunion" (Columbia #45547; 1972; #4) and "Me and Julio Down by the Schoolyard" (Columbia #45585; 1972; #22) and the more pop-oriented *There Goes Rhymin' Simon* (Columbia #32280; 1973; #2), featuring "Kodachrome" (Columbia #45859; 1973; #2) and gospel-inflected "Loves Me Like a Rock" (Columbia #45907; 1973; #2; with the Dixie Hummingbirds). The perfunctory *Paul Simon in Concert/Live Rhymin'* (Columbia #32855; 1974; #33) was followed by the Grammy award-winning *Still Crazy After All These Years* (Columbia #33540; 1975; #1), whose highlights included a duet with Garfunkel, "My Little Town" (Columbia #10230; 1975; #9), and the wry "50 Ways to Leave Your Lover" (Columbia #10270; 1975; #1).

Following a long layoff, *One Trick Pony* (Warner Bros. #3472; 1980; #12) — the soundtrack to his film documentary — and *Hearts and Bones* (Warner Bros. #23942; 1983; #35) seemed out of touch with contemporary music trends such as disco and postpunk. He rebounded, though, with *Graceland* (Warner Bros. #25447; 1986; #3), which was built around African rhythms and musicians (e.g., Ladysmith Black Mambazo). *The Rhythm of the Saints* (Warner Bros. #26098; 1990; #4) took a similar approach, this time drawing inspiration from Brazilian percussion. Never a fast worker, Simon did not produce another studio LP until 1997, a soundtrack to the Broadway musical *Songs from the Capeman* (Warner Bros. #46814; #42), based on the life of Puerto Rican writer Salvador Agron. Simon released a new album, *You're the One* (Warner Bros. #47844), in 2000, his first collection of songs without an overriding theme, but it failed to find much of an audience. This paucity of new work, however, has been supplemented by a steady stream of reissues, including both Simon and Garfunkel and solo material.

SIMON AND GARFUNKEL

American popular singing/guitar duo, consisting of Paul Simon (1941–) and Art Garfunkel (1941–). They

Simon and Garfunkel's 1968 album, *Bookends*. Courtesy Frank Hoffmann

did some early work together, recording as Tom and Jerry and scoring a minor hit in 1958 with Simon's song "Hey Schoolgirl," and then went their separate ways. Teaming again in 1964, they were soon greatly successful with "Sounds of Silence" (Columbia #43396; 1965), and the album of the same name in the following year. Ten other chart albums followed by 1974, most notably *Parsley, Sage, Rosemary and Thyme* (Columbia S #9363; 1966, 1968), and *Bridge Over Troubled Water* (Columbia CS #9914; 1970) which was 87 weeks on the charts and sold 2 million copies. Simon's composition "Mrs. Robinson" was part of the soundtrack for the motion picture *The Graduate* (1968).

The pair split in the 1970s, each pursuing solo careers with great success. *Still Crazy After All These Years* was a Simon chart album of 1975 (Columbia PC #33540). Garfunkel's principal solo success was *Breakaway* (Columbia PC #33700; 1975). There have been periodical reunions of the team for concerts and recordings, including a concert in Central Park (recorded in 1980) and a second reunion tour in 1991.

FRANK HOFFMANN

SIMONE, NINA
(21 FEB 1933–20 APR 2003)

A talented pianist and soulful singer, Simone was born Eunice Kathleen Waymon in Tryon, North Carolina. A precociously talented pianist, Waymon played and sang in church; recognizing her talents,

her parents and neighbors raised money to send her to boarding school to study music, which led to a scholarship to study classical piano at Juilliard in 1950. However, she soon had to leave the school due to lack of funds, and began playing in bars around New York City beginning in the mid-1950s. She developed a unique style that fused her classical, gospel, and jazz influences. She was signed to King Record's Bethlehem subsidary, and in 1958 scored a million-selling record with her version of "I Loves You, Porgy," from *Porgy and Bess*. She moved to the Candix label in 1959, remaining with the label until 1964, and then signed with Phillips. Developing an interest in civil rights, she recorded the anthemic "Mississippi Goddam," which expressed her frustration with being Black in the U.S. She marched with Martin Luther King, Jr., often performing at his rallies, and also befriended Malcolm X. She signed to RCA in 1966, achieving one last classic recording with her "Young, Gifted, and Black," covered by Aretha Franklin, among others; she continued to record for the label through 1974. Citing racism in American society, she left the country in the late 1960s; for the next 25 years she battled personal and financial problems while leading a nomadiclike life, living from time to time in Barbados, Liberia, Switzerland, France, and U.K. She recorded only occasionally, notably making the album Baltimore in 1978 for CTI (#57906). Her autobiography, *I Put a Spell on You*, appeared in 1991, but by the mid-1990s her health was declining; she had to be helped onto the stage to make her final appearances in 2001. She died in Carry-le-Rouet, France.

Various Simone albums have been reissued on CD in their original formats. Simone's Colpix recordings are anthologized on a "Best of" CD (Roulette #98584); a 1965 "Best of" collection of her Phillips recordings has been reissued on CD as well (Polygram #844846). There are many other compilations on a variety of labels.

CARL BENSON

SIMS, ZOOT (29 OCT 1925–23 MAR 1985)

American jazz tenor saxophonist, born John Haley Sims in Inglewood, California. He played professionally as a teen, and at age 18 was performing with Benny Goodman. From 1947 to 1949 he was with Woody Herman. Later he was in Stan Kenton's band and with various ensembles headed by Gerry Mulligan. He continued playing and recording in the U.S. and Europe, taking up the soprano saxophone along with the familiar tenor. *Down Home* (Bethlehem BCP #6051) was a quartet album recorded in 1960 featuring some elegant examples of Sims's mellow extemporization, as in "Avalon" and "Goodnight, Sweetheart." He died in New York.

SIMULATED STEREO

See Reprocessed Stereo

SINATRA, FRANK
(12 DEC 1915–14 MAY 1998)

American popular singer and actor, born Francis Albert Sinatra in Hoboken, New Jersey. With no musical training, he gained acceptance as a radio singer in New York, and was invited to join the Harry James band in 1939. During the next few years, with Tommy Dorsey (1940–1942) and then as a soloist, he rocketed to national fame, becoming an icon in particular for preteen girls who literally swooned at his concerts. He faded in the late 1940s, but returned to public notice with an Academy award-winning film appearance (nonsinging) in *From Here to Eternity* (1953). Then he signed with Capitol Records and began a series of hits, adopting a more swinging style than he had in the 1940s. By 1960 he was again established as the most popular male vocalist and also as a Hollywood actor. Sinatra retired in 1971, but continued performing and recording thereafter. In 1985 he was awarded the Presidential Medal of Freedom. He died in Los Angeles.

Sinatra's first record was a demo made on 3 Feb 1939, "Our Love," with Frank Manne's orchestra; tape copies exist, but the acetate has been lost. His first commercial recording was "From the Bottom of My Heart"/"Melancholy Mood" (Brunswick #8443; 1939), with Harry James. One of his outstanding discs in the James period was "All or Nothing at All" (Columbia #35587; 1939); upon reissue in 1943 it became his first million-selling disc. There were many superb sides made with Tommy Dorsey, but the greatest success was achieved by "I'll Never Smile Again" — sung with the Pied Pipers (Victor #26628; 1940). Later Dorsey hits included "Stardust" — with the Pied Pipers again (1940), "Violets for Your Furs" (Victor #27690; 1941), and "There Are Such Things" — also with the Pied Pipers (Victor #27974; 1942). In 1942 Sinatra also made some records on his own, for Bluebird, one of them the elegant "Lamplighter's Serenade."

Signing with Columbia in 1943, Sinatra immediately enjoyed a chart-topping hit with the reissue of his 1939 recording of "All or Nothing at All. He would go on to have 86 more charting singles with the label through 1952. He also made a number of important V-discs during World War II.

Nelson Riddle wrote outstanding arrangements for Sinatra, among them "I've Got You Under My Skin" (Capitol #W-653; 1956). Sinatra's cool, easy style was exemplified in "Lady Is a Tramp," which he sang in the film *Pal Joey* (1956). "All the Way" (Capitol #3793; 1957) was another outstanding ballad of the time, arranged by Riddle.

Rosemary Cloney and Frank Sinatra at a recording session in 1955. © Bettmann/CORBIS

Later hits included "Strangers in the Night" (Reprise #0470; 1966), winner of four Grammy awards; "Something Stupid" with his daughter Nancy (Reprise #0561; 1967), "My Way" (Reprise #0817; 1969) — the all-time best seller in the U.K., and "New York, New York" (Warner Bros. #49233; 1980). Reprise was his own company, formed in 1961, and sold to Warner Bros. in 1963. Sinatra had 51 solo albums on the charts in 1955–1974, plus many others with such artists as Count Basie, Duke Ellington, Bing Crosby, and Antonio Carlos Jobim. His final chart album was *She Shot Me Down* (Reprise FS #2305; 1981). He made no records after 1986 (a special cut of "The Gentleman Is a Champ" to honor Lew Wasserman of MCA Universal), although he was heard (doing earlier records) on soundtracks in 1988 and 1989. Dozens of CDs have appeared, from EMI and Reprise, documenting a major portion of the Sinatra output.

SINEY, PHILIP (3 APR 1966–)

The only recording engineer still actually working for Decca Records, at company headquarters in Chiswick London, Siney initially pursued an education in electronics engineering, and also received musical training as counter tenor and organist. In 1989 he joined Decca as a location engineer, and went on to receive training as a balance engineer under the tutelage of James Lock, Stan Goodall, and John Dunkerley.

Today, Siney continues to record for Decca, using the classic Decca Tree, three-microphone technique pioneered by Roy Wallace and later refined by Kenneth Wilkinson. At Decca, he regularly works with musical artists such as Flemming, Pavarotti, Scholl, Dutoit, Ashkenazy, Thibaudet, and Chailly, using 24 bit, 96 kHz technology for both stereo and surround mixes. He has worked with recordings that received Grammy awards for best opera (1992 and 2000), and also won the 2002 French Diapason award for a piano album of Fauré's works, performed by Kung Wo Paik.

HOWARD FERSTLER

SINGLETON, SHELBY (16 DEC 1931–)

Producer and label executive. After a stint as sales manager of Mercury Records, Shelby Singleton started producing country acts in the late 1950s. During this time he brought the Big Bopper and Johnny Preston to the label. Later, Singleton worked with Brook Benton and Clyde McPhatter. In 1961 he was given control of Smash, the pop imprint of Mercury Records, and Singleton signed James Brown and Jerry Lee Lewis. Singleton struck out from Mercury in 1967, founding two labels of his own: Plantation and SSS International.

He scored an almost immediate smash country hit with his recording of Jeannie C. Riley's "Harper Valley PTA" (Plantation #3; #1 pop) that year. He later purchased the assets of Sun Records from Sam Phillips.

BRAD HILL

SINGLETON, ZUTTY (14 MAY 1898–14 JULY 1975)

American jazz drummer, born Arthur James Singleton in Bunkie, Louisiana. He played with New Orleans bands as a youth, worked on riverboats and in St. Louis, then moved to Chicago. He became an innovative force in jazz through appearances and recordings with Louis Armstrong's Hot Five (1928), Jelly Roll Morton, and Barney Bigard (1929). His techniques included use of wire brushes, the sock cymbals (later to be the hi hat), ride patterns and offbeat bass accents. In the 1930s he worked with such artists as Sidney Bechet and Roy Eldridge; in the 1940s he recorded with Charlie Parker and Dizzy Gillespie. He remained active later in New York clubs. Singleton died in New York.

Examples of his notable discs are "Muggles" with Armstrong (Okeh #8703; 1928), and "My Little Dixie Home" with Morton (Victor #38601; 1929). He recorded with groups of his own in 1935 and 1940 for Decca; the only 1940 item was "King Porter Stomp"/"Shim-Me-Sha-Wabble" (#18093).

SIRE RECORDS (LABEL)

Since being founded in 1966 by 24-year-old Seymour Stein, with the assistance of producer Richard Gotteher, Sire Records has released a substantial body of trendsetting rock music. The label first achieved success through a distribution arrangement with U.K.'s Blue Horizon, whose roster included Fleetwood Mac and Chicken Shack.

Closely identified with progressive rock in the early 1970s, Sire didn't break into the commercial major leagues until Stein — supported by a distribution pact with Warner Bros. — began signing up-and-coming acts within New York City's punk scene such as the Ramones and Talking Heads around 1976. Following its purchase by Warner in 1980, the label embarked on an ambitious program of expansion, signing Madonna, the Cult, the Pretenders, Echo and the Bunnymen, Lou Reed, Primal Scream, My Bloody Valentine, ex-Talking Heads lead singer David Byrne, Depeche Mode, k.d. lang, Morrissey, Throwing Muses, Belly, theWaterlilies, and Dinosaur, Jr.

In January 1995, Stein moved the Sire imprint to the Elektra Entertainment Group. While established

Sire artists were divided between Warner Bros. and Reprise, new and developing acts — most notably, Aphex Twin, the Waltons, the Rheostatics, and Greenberry Woods — were retained by Sire. Sire left Elektra in 1998, but remain affiliated with the Warner Music Group as a boutique label featuring a diverse artist roster that included Aphex Twin, the Pet Shop Boys, and the Tragically Hip.

Following Warner's acquisition of London Records in December 1999 and the designation of Sire as London's U.S. licensee, Stein's label was renamed London-Sire Records. During the early years of the 21st century, the company was particularly successful with aritsts within the alternative and electronica genres, including Aphex Twin, Guster, Harvey Danger, Morcheeba, Paul Oakenfold, and the Tragically Hip.

SIR HENRI (LABEL)

An American record known by only a few issues, dating from ca. 1910. Material came from Imperial. [Rust 1978.]

SISTER TEAMS IN EARLY RECORDED POPULAR MUSIC

A duo-piano sister team, Jeanne and Irene Douste, recorded one side for Berliner in 1899. Recorded vocal duet performances by sisters apparently began in about 1917, as Fanny and Kitty Watson sang for Okeh and Columbia, continuing until 1920. The Farber Sisters worked for Columbia and Pathé, and the Heart Sisters for Columbia; the Brox Sisters for Victor and Emerson, the Dennis and the MacDowell Sisters for Edison — these among others in the 1920s. Among the most acclaimed of the early popular duos were the Trix Sisters. In the 1930s the Boswell Sisters and the Andrews Sisters were the most famous. Rosa Ponselle's opera career was preceded by vuadeville performances with her sister Carmela, billed as the Italian Girls.

SIX BROWN BROTHERS

A saxophone ensemble, originally the Five Brown Brothers, who recorded ca. 1912 on U.S. Everlasting cylinders. From 1914 to 1920 they worked for Victor, then (1921–1924) for Emerson. Five of them were Browns: Alec, William, Vern, Fred, and Tom; the other, Harry Finkelstein, was not related to them. Others who were in the group at one time or another were Guy Shrigley, James White, and Sunny Clapp. [Rust 1978.]

16 2/3 RPM DISCS

In the 1950s several manufacturers produced discs that rotated at half the speed of the long-playing record, to double the amount of content material. Turntables were marketed with the 16 2/3 speed as well as 33 1/3 and 45 rpm. Sound quality did not prove acceptable for music, but the speed was used for talking books and other literary recordings until the cassette became available.

SKA/BLUEBEAT REVIVAL

The ska/bluebeat revival was a retro movement concerned with recapturing the musical qualities of the 1960s Jamaican genre within a modern social and fashion context. The first wave emerged in the U.K. during the late 1970s. The relocation of Caribbean natives to the London area provided the initial impetus for this revived interest in ska; however, skinheads and punks also became fans of the genre. Many oi (neo-fascist oriented pop style) and punk groups would go on to make ska-styled records by the early 1980s.

The movement extended far beyond mere musical considerations. Like the mods and rockers who had preceded them, ska enthusiasts developed their own fashion statements. Their clothing of choice included black-and-white checkered suits, skinny ties, and porkpie hats. Because the central message of ska revival songs was often one of racial unity, fans tended to exhibit a far greater degree of racial tolerance than was typically found in British society.

Although ska music could be found in major U.K. markets throughout the 1980s, it was no longer a force within the pop music mainstream. The sole exception was the watered-down, albeit highly popular, interpretations of the genre recorded by the likes of UB40.

The second wave, which arose in the late 1980s, featured a large number of American bands, including the Mighty Mighty Bosstones and the Pietasters. Whereas the first wave of ska artists were primarily promoted through televised video clips, the latter day bands found that alternative rock radio stations were very receptive to playing their recordings. As a result, these acts have succeeded in sustaining their careers far beyond mere fad proportions.

FRANK HOFFMANN

SKATING FORCE

The tendency of a spinning disc on an analog record player to draw the cartridge, stylus, and playing end of the pivoting tone arm toward its center. The result will be slightly higher stylus tracking pressure on one side of the groove than the other. Antiskating mechanisms are often used to combat this tendency. A tangential tone arm, which tracks the record by mounting the arm on a sliding mount that does not pivot at all, eliminates skating force. Skating force is a nonissue with digital recordings.

REV. HOWARD FERSTLER

SKILLET LICKERS, THE

The Skillet Lickers — comprised of guitarist/vocalist Riley Puckett, fiddler/banjo player/vocalist Gid Tanner, fiddlers Clayton McMichen, Bert Layne, and Lowe Stokes, banjo player Fate Norris — were one of the top-selling performing and recording acts specializing in old-time country music during the late 1920s and early 1930s. Based in north Georgia, the string band's recorded legacy consisted of 88 sides, 82 of which were issued by the Columbia label between 1926–1931. The vast majority of these recordings consisted of traditional dance songs and fiddle tunes, although a dozen or so were folk-styled ballads and several others qualified as pop fare. The band was also famous for its series of comic skits, most notably "A Corn Likker Still in Georgia," which featured group banter and snippets of songs and tunes. Either Tanner or Puckett were generally given top billing on 78-rpm releases (McMichen was the only other member listed on the record labels).

A chicken farmer throughout his life, Tanner (6 June 1885–13 May 1960) was generally considered more of a showman and comedian than musician. His recording career began in 1924 when an A&R man auditioning Atlanta area talent invited him up to New York; bringing Puckett (ca. 1890–13 July 1946) with him, they cut their first records as a duo, March 7. Most of Tanner's recordings during the 1920s were with the Skillet Lickers, although he occasionally cut sides alone or with Norris and/or his younger brother, Arthur Tanner. Tanner and Puckett would record together extensively in the late 1930s without the other Skillet Lickers.

Musically, the band emphasized harmony fiddling over dance rhythms; a notable exception was "Dixie" (recorded in Atlanta, 29 Mar 1927), the most syncopated selection in their repertoire. The Skillet Lickers often changed the keys of old-time fiddle material not only to accommodate harmony fiddling, but to ensure that Puckett's vocals — considered at the time to be a key factor in their success — would be as rich and mellow as possible. Puckett's unusual single-string bass runs on the guitar were prominently featured in the accompaniment; on the other hand, Norris's banjo part was either so muted or poorly recorded that it is rarely audible. Their better-selling records included "Turkey in the Straw" (Columbia #15084; 1926), "My Carolina Home" (Columbia #15095; 1926), and "John Henry (Steel-Drivin' Man)" (Columbia #15142; 1927).

Tanner and Norris left the band in 1931, with the former continuing to record intermittently over the years. Tanner's recording of "Down Yonder" (Bluebird #5562; 1934), with a later version of the group featuring Tanner's son Gordon on lead fiddle, became a country classic with reputed sales of over a million copies. McMichen formed a more modern-styled band called the Georgia Wildcats; however, the Depression — and poor sales within the record industry — brought a halt to any further recording activity. Their original pressings remain a highly sought-after commodity among collectors. A 16-track CD retrospective, *The Skillet Lickers: Old-Time Fiddle Tunes and Songs from North Georgia* (County #3509; 1996), is a representative sampling of the band's repertoire.

FRANK HOFFMANN

SKYWALKER SOUND

Possibly the best facility of its kind in the world, Skywalker was the brainchild of filmmaker George Lucas in the mid-1970s, and is located in the midst of a 2,600-acre tract in Marin County, about 40 miles north of San Francisco. It is a special-effects, image-manipulation, and movie sound-editing and production facility, as well as a top-quality recording environment for music-only productions of nearly any kind. It offers everything from on-site recording to final soundtrack work, in any format from standard two-channel productions, through Dolby Surround and 5.1-channel Dolby Digital and DTS, on up to eight-channel SDDS. The operation markets its services to first-time directors and independent producers, as well as to established organizations, and it also offers music-production engineers, producers, and performers a recording facility that is second to none. Indeed, the scoring stage has a recording area that measures 60 feet wide by 80 feet long, with 30-foot ceilings, and the area is capable of easily accommodating a 125-piece orchestra. In addition to being responsible for many high-tech motion-picture productions, numerous top-quality sound recordings have been produced in the facility.

HOWARD FERSTLER

SLEDGE, PERCY (25 NOV 1940–)

Sledge will be forever identified with the classic soul ballad, "When a Man Loves a Woman" (Atlantic #2326; 1966), which blended his intense, gospel-inflected vocal with an ethereal organ accompaniment. Success did not come overnight for the singer; he spent the first half of the 1960s performing in the region surrounding his native Alabama. He was a member of the Esquires Combo when he decided to go solo in 1966. Following the release of "When a Man Loves a Woman," which reached number one on both the pop and R&B charts, he scored Top 20 hits with "Warm and Tender Love" (Atlantic #2342; 1966), "It Tears Me Up" (Atlantic #2358; 1966), and "Take Time to Know Her" (Atlantic #2490; 1968).

Sledge's recording career stalled by the late 1960s, but he has continued to tour the U.S., Japan, and the U.K. through the 1990s. The appearance of "When a Man Loves a Woman" in the popular film *Platoon* (1987) spurred a revival of interest in Sledge. That same year the song was re-released in the U.K., where it reached number two on the pop charts. In 1989 he won the Rhythm and Blues Foundation's Career Achievement award.

FRANK HOFFMANN

SLEEVE

The jacket or envelope used for protecting, storing, or marketing a disc recording; also known as a slipcase or record cover. Usually the material is paper or cardboard. Often there is a second envelope inside the sleeve, made of paper or mylar, intended to give the surface additional protection. Sleeves may do more harm than good to their records, however.

See also **Preservation of Sound Recordings**

SLEZAK, LEO
(18 AUG 1873–1 JUNE 1946)

Austrian tenor, born in Mährisch-Schînberg. He sang as a youth in the opera chorus in Brno, then made his debut there as Lohengrin on 17 Mar 1896. From there he went to the Vienna Opera (1901–1926), and sang throughout Europe. His Lohengrin at Covent Garden, 18 May 1900, was greatly acclaimed. Slezak's Metropolitan Opera debut was as Otello on 17 Nov 1909; he remained with the company through 1913. Subsequently he toured Europe and Russia, gave recitals, and made motion pictures. He was known for his sharp sense of humor, exemplified in his famous (perhaps apocryphal) ad lib during a *Lohengrin* performance when the mechanical swan departed the stage without him: "When does the next swan leave?" He died in Egern, Bavaria. His son Walter became a famous movie actor.

Slezak's early records were for Zonophone in Vienna, made in 1901: German versions of "Ah! Dispar, vision" from *Manon* and of "Vesti la giubba"

(#1665, #1667). He also worked for G & T from 1901, producing a large number of songs from a wide repertoire, all in German. Slezak recorded for Pathé in Vienna in 1903–1904, making cylinders and discs. The first two numbers (both reissued by IRCC) were "Auftrittslied des Raoul" from *Huguenots* and "O Mathilde" from *Guillaume Tell* (#19050 and #19051, both sung in German). He did six other arias for Pathé, then worked with Columbia and Odeon in Vienna, Edison in the U.S. (1908–ca.1912), and for Victor. An important Edison Blue Amberol cylinder was "E luce-van le stelle" (#28146; 1912 or 1913). Among the finest tenor records of the acoustic era are Slezak's renditions of "Komm holde Dame" from *Weisse Dame* (G & T #042017; 1903) and "Magische Tîne" from *Kînigin von Saba* (G & T #38002; 1905).

There were five numbers in the Victor 1917 catalog, and two in the 1922 catalog. He continued recording until at least 1921, for Polydor in Germany. His records have been widely reissued by the LP and 78-rpm reissue labels. Many of his G & T records were reissued on Preiser CD #89020 in 1990. [Kaufman 1964.]

SLY AND ROBBIE

Noted Jamaican reggae performers and producers, Sly (Lowell Charles "Sly" Dunbar, b. 10 May 1952) and Robbie (Robert "Robbie" Shakespeare, b. 27 Sep 1953) have sessioned on and produced many recordings from the mid-1970s to today. Drummer Dunbar and bassist Shakespeare first played together in the Jamaican group the Aggrovators, and then the Revolutionaries in the mid-1970s. They became active session musicians in Jamaica around this time, and in 1978 produced Peter Tosh's album *Bush Doctor* under the name Word Sound and Power along with Tosh, among their first production credits. (They would also take the name of the Riddim Boys on many of their productions.) In 1979 they established their own Taxi label, producing several albums for the popular Jamaican group, Black Uhuru, with whom they also toured as performers, through around 1985. In 1980 they signed a distribution deal with Island Records, and Island's chief Chris Blackwell hired them to produce new wave singer Grace Jones.

After breaking with Uhuru, the duo continued to tour under the Taxi Allstars name and produced and sessioned with dozens of artists, both Jamaicans and with major rock stars including Mick Jagger and Bob Dylan, to name just two. From the mid-1980s, they began incorporating electronic drums and other effects into their work, as well as experimenting with the popular dub style (a predecessor of sampling). The duo remained active over the following decades, working in a wide variety of styles from mainstream pop to classic reggae, dub, jazz, and rap. They also partnered with avant-garde producer Bill Laswell in the later 1980s for a series of electronic-experimental albums, and, during the 1990s, Dunbar even ventured into religious recording. In the later 1990s and early 2000s, they have remained hugely prolific.

CARL BENSON

SLY AND THE FAMILY STONE

Sly and the Family Stone helped pioneer one of dominant styles of the 1970s, funk music. Their variant fused the psychedelic rock of the late 1960s with classic soul; in that sense, it differed considerably from the bass-heavy grooves of mainstream funk. As popular on the pop charts as with urban Black youth, the group greatly influenced the careers of later crossover giants such as George Clinton, mastermind of the Parliament/Funkadelic collective, Rick James, and Prince.

The creative core of Sly and the Family Stone, Texas-native Sylvester Stewart, developed an impressive music-business resumé in Sam Francisco during the mid-1960s, excelling as a disc jockey (KSOL, KDIA), songwriter, and record producer for the likes of he Beau Brummels, Bobby Freeman, and the Mojo Men with Autumn Records. His first attempt at heading a group, the Stoners, failed in 1966; however, Sly and the Family Stone — including his brother, guitarist Freddie Stone, sister Rosie Stone, who sang and played keyboards and harmonica, and a cousin, bassist Larry Graham, who would form Graham Central Station in the early 1970s — attracted sufficient local attention in 1967 to garner a contract with Epic Records.

The group's debut LP, *A Whole New Thing* (Epic #30333; 1967) failed to attract much attention. However, the follow-up album, *Dance to the Music* (Epic #26371; 1968; #142), and the exuberant title song (Epic #10256; 1968; #8) elevated them to the forefront of the rock scene. The group maintained its momentum with a steady stream of hit singles — most notably, "Everyday People" (Epic #10407; 1968; #1), "Hot Fun in the Summertime" (Epic #10497; 1969; #2), "Thank You (Falettinme Be Mice Elf Agin)" (Epic #10555; 1970; #1), and "Family Affair" (Epic #10805; 1971; #1) — and albums: *Life* (Epic #26397; 1968; #195), *Stand!* (Epic #26456; 1969; #13), *Greatest Hits* (Epic #30325; 1970; #2), *There's a Riot Goin' On* (Epic #30986; 1971; #1), and *Fresh* (Epic #32134; 1973; #7). The uplifting, anthem-like quality of Sly and the Family Stone's early work gave way to a decidedly more negative, militant tone in *There's a Riot Goin' On*; however, the uniformly high quality of Sly's musical ideas and production work made it the most successful — artistically and commercially — of his albums.

Sly's drug problems in the 1970s led to an increasing inability to meet concert commitments and lackluster studio work. He ceased to perform or record for several years prior to attempting a comeback with the October 1979 release of *Back on the Right Track* (Warner Bros. #3303). Unfortunately, the album lacked strong material and Stone spent much of the 1980s fighting drug convictions. Sly and the Family Stone was inducted into the Rock and Roll Hall of Fame in 1993. Rumors have periodically surfaced since then that the group would soon be releasing new material. In the meantime, their classic recordings have appeared in a host of compilation releases, including *The Collection* (Castle Communications #307; 1991) and *Takin' You Higher — The Best of Sly & the Family Stone* (Sony #471758; 1992; reissued on Epic #477506; 1994).

FRANK HOFFMANN

SMALL, RICHARD (29 MAR 1935–)

A major researcher in audio system theory and design, Small received a bachelor of science degree from the California Institute of Technology in 1956, and went on to obtain an M.S. degree in electrical engineering from the Massachusetts Institute of Technology in 1958. He was employed in electronic circuit design for high-performance analytical instruments at the Bell & Howell Research Center in California from 1958 to 1964, except for a one-year visiting fellowship to the Norwegian Technical University in 1961–1962.

After a working visit to Japan in 1964, Small moved to Australia, and in 1972, following the completion of a program of research into direct-radiator electrodynamic loudspeaker systems, he was awarded the degree of doctor of philosophy by the University of Sydney. He then joined the teaching staff of the School of Electrical Engineering of that university. In 1986 he resigned his position as senior lecturer to return to industry, as head of research at KEF Electronics Limited in Maidstone, Kent, England. In 1993 he returned to the U.S., and he currently holds the position of senior principal engineer with Harman/Becker Automotive Systems in Martinsville, Indiana.

Dr. Small has published dozens of articles and conference papers in AES, Institute of Electrical and Electronics Engineers, and IREE publications, and is well known for mathematically formulating the performance parameters, the Thiele-Small parameters, of all modern loudspeaker systems. He is a senior member of the Institute of Electrical and Electronics Engineers and a member of the Institution of Engineers Australia. He is a fellow of the Audio Engineering Society and a recipient of the Society's Publication award (1976), silver medal (1982), and gold medal (1996). He has served the AES as a member of the Editorial Review Board since 1973, a governor 1989–1991, vice chairman of the Technical Committee on Transducers 1992–1994, and chairman of the Publications Policy Committee since 1992.

See also **Bass Reflex System; Loudspeaker**

HOWARD FERSTLER

SMALLE, ED (2 NOV 1887–23 NOV 1968)

American singer, pianist, arranger, and conductor, born in Roxbury, Massachusetts. He was a highly versatile artist, best known for his singing as soloist and ensemble performer. He recorded for many labels with many groups. In the late 1920s he performed with the Revelers, as pianist and singer. King George invited him to a command performance in 1928. His Leaders Trio recorded for broadcast in U.K., Australia, and Canada. CBS radio featured his Vagabond Glee Club, and in 1935 he was in the motion picture *Radio Nuts*. He made duet records with Billy Murray beginning in 1919 for Victor and Edison Diamond Discs. He and Vernon Dalhart recorded five duets for Edison Diamond Discs in 1924. With Murray's star on the wane, Victor would pair him with Johnny Marvin in the mid-1920s. After an illness Smalle left the mainstream, then returned to local radio in Westerly, Rhode Island, where he died decades later. [Rust 1978; Walsh 1955/5-6, 1969/5.]

REV. FRANK HOFFMANN

SMALL RECORDS (IN THE 78 ERA)

Disc records of lesser diameter than the typical 10-inch size of the 78-rpm era appeared from time to time in the U.S., more commonly in U.K. and Germany. The smallest playable record known was made for Queen Mary's doll house, 1924; it measured one and 5/16 inches. Among the diminutive U.K. and German labels were Baby Odeon, Beka, Broadcast Jr., Crown, Crystalate, Favorite, G & T, Globe, Homo Baby, Homophon, Kiddyphone, Little Marvel, Little Wonder, Marspen, Mimosa, Nicole, Neophone, Odeon, Oliver, Pathé, Phonadisc, and The Bell (some of those labels produced standard-size records as well). In the U.S. the Harper Bubble Books appeared in 1920–1921 and were marketed also in the U.K., as Hodder-Columbia Books that Sing. Little Tots'

Nursery Tunes were published in New York by Plaza Music Co. in 1923–1924. [Andrews 1988/4.]

SMASH RECORDS

Although there had been a small independent label named Smash headquartered in Nashville during the mid-1950s, Smash is best known as a Mercury Records imprint that operated from 1961 until 1970. It was run by former Mercury promotion manager Charlie Fach, and the first 10 releases included Joe Dowell's "Wooden Heart" (#1788; 1961; #1) and Joe Barry's "I'm a Fool to Care" (#1702; 1961; #24). Barry's recording was licensed from Houston-based producer Huey Meaux, and Fach concluded similar deals with other independent producers that brought Bruce Channel, the Angels, and, more controversially, James Brown to the label. Fach also signed the Left Banke, who scored a hit in 1966 with "Walk Away Renee" (#2041; #5); Jerry Lee Lewis, who spectacularly revived his career on Smash in 1968 after a decade in the commercial wilderness; and Roger Miller, who had also been unsuccessful on other labels. In 1970 all the artists on the Smash roster were transferred to the parent Mercury label.

COLIN ESCOTT

SMIRNOV, DMITRI (19 NOV 1882–27 APR 1944)

Russian tenor, born in Moscow. He was with the Bolshoi Theater from 1904, and also the Maryinsky Opera in St. Petersburg. Then he appeared in Paris, and on 30 Dec 1910 at the Metropolitan Opera, as the Duke, remaining through 1912. Then he returned to Europe, singing the Russian repertoire, plus Faust, Don José, Canio, and Rodolfo with great effect. In 1909 he recorded for G & T in Moscow, singing airs from *Rigoletto* ("Parmi veder le lagrime," #022132) and seven other operas. From 1912 to ca. 1922 he worked for HMV. One of his finest discs emerged from that period, "Mi par d'udir ancora" from *Pecheurs du perles* (Victor DB #583; 1921). Smirnov died in Riga, Latvia. [Stratton 1973.]

SMITH, ARTHUR (10 APR 1898–28 FEB 1971)

American country fiddler, born in Bold Springs, Tennessee. He did railroad work, learning country music from his father and playing in his spare time. Then he formed a trio called the Dixieliners in 1932, featuring brothers Sam and Kirk McGee, a string band that performed locally and then advanced to the Grand

Ole Opry. He gained national fame in 1936 with the recording of "There's More Pretty Girls Than One" (Bluebird #6322). Known as the King of Fiddlers, Smith developed a sophisticated variation of the old country fiddle mode that greatly influenced later country and bluegrass artists. His records were mostly Bluebirds, but he also recorded for Capitol, Folkways, and other labels. He retired in the 1950s but made a comeback in the folk music revival of the 1960s. He died in Louisville, Kentucky. He was elected to the Fiddler's Hall of Fame in 1982.

SMITH, BESSIE
(15 APR 1894–26 SEP 1937)

American blues and jazz singer, born in Chattanooga, Tennessee. She performed with touring minstrel shows as a teenager and in Atlanta. Pianist Clarence Williams arranged for her to make records for Columbia, and her first disc established her as a major artist: "Down-hearted Blues" (#A3844). The first important jazz singer, and one of the first to record vocal blues, she is regarded as the greatest classic blues singer, the "Empress of the Blues." Her tours and recordings continued through

Bessie Smith's "Chirpin' the Blues" sheet music cover, c. late '20s. Courtesy David A. Jasen.

1931, when she faded from sight for two years. John Hammond brought her back in 1933 for an important session on Okeh (#8945 and #8949) with Jack Teagarden, Benny Goodman, and other jazz stars; she made no further records. She made public appearances for a few more years. Smith died in Clarksdale, Mississippi, following an automobile accident. Her death has been shrouded in mystery; for years, many claimed she was turned away from a white hospital after the accident and died en route to a segregated facility.

Among Smith's finest solo records were "Back Water Blues" (Columbia #14195; 1927), "After You've Gone" (Columbia #14197; 1927), and "Nobody Knows You When You're Down and Out" (Columbia #14451; 1929). Her skill at jazz improvisation is illustrated in "A Good Man Is Hard to Find" (Columbia #14250; 1927). She also made remarkable duets with Louis Armstrong on cornet, e.g., "St. Louis Blues"/"Cold in Hand Blues" (Columbia #14064; 1925). In "J.C. Holmes Blues" her voice was embellished by Charlie Green's trombone, weaving a background with the Armstrong cornet, both muted (Columbia #14095-D; 1925). A total of 159 recordings are listed in the discography by E. Brooks. Smith was largely responsible for the emergence of Columbia as a race label; she was the best-selling blues artist of the era. [Brooks, E. 1982; Schuller 1968.]

SMITH, HARRY
(29 MAY 1923–11 NOV 1991)

Eccentric record collector and reissue producer. Smith is remembered for compiling the landmark, six-album *Anthology of American Folk Music* set, originally issued by Folkways Records in 1952. Smith was a collector of rare country and jazz 78s; during World War II, when masses of old records were scrapped for their shellac, Smith was able to purchase many unwanted discs from scrap dealers. He approached Folkways' owner Moses Asch with the idea of making this music available. Smith had a unique vision of how to arrange and package the tracks; he did not make distinctions between white and Black performers, but rather organized each two-record set of the three volumes by subject. He also wrote complete notes, giving the original recording information as well as humorous summaries of each song's contents, and illustrated the accompanying booklet with old record advertisements. The idea of reissuing out-of-print 78 recordings on LP was new at the time, and many of the major labels felt it represented piracy of their material (just as they approach sharing of music files on the web today). Asch was successful in defending himself against these charges, and the *Anthology* remained in print for decades. Younger musicians were inspired by these recordings to search out the original performers, many of whom, including Dock Boggs and Mississippi John Hurt, came out of retirement to record and perform again thanks to the *Anthology*. Smith made original recordings during the 1960s of a American Indian peyote ritual in New Mexico, and also recorded the first albums by the avant-garde rock group the Fugs and poet Allen Ginsberg. He also made experimental films. [The *Anthology* was reissued on CD with the original booklet and new, expanded documentation by Smithsonian/Folkways in 1997 (#40090); website: www.harrysmitharchives. com.]

CARL BENSON

SMITH, H. ROYER

Philadelphia music merchant and Victor record dealer. In 1919, after working six years for Lyon and Healy, he bought the Drew Music House, located at 10th and Walnut Streets, and opened his own shop. The H. Royer Smith Co. was the prominent Philadelphia record store of the 78-rpm era. In 1930–1933 the record review monthly *Disques* was issued by Smith; the name changed to *The New Records* in 1933. It was published until 1987, being widely respected and used by librarians and collectors.

SMITH, KATE
(1 MAY 1909–17 JUNE 1986)

American popular singer, born Kathryn Elizabeth Smith in Greenville, Virginia. She sang in church, then went to New York and appeared in several musicals, beginning with *Honeymoon Lane* (1926). She was soon engaged for radio and recording work as well. Smith was one of the first to have a theme song or signature song, "When the Moon Comes Over the Mountain" — it was one of her best records (Victor #25760; 1937). She began to record for Columbia in 1926, doing numbers from *Honeymoon Lane* and stayed with the label (or its subsidiary, Harmony) until 1932. Then she worked for Brunswick, Decca, and Victor through 1939, before returning to Columbia. Her repertoire consisted of love songs and traditional melodies. In 1939 she recorded her greatest hit, "God Bless America," Irving Berlin's national anthem (Victor #26198). Smith continued recording until 1976. She died in Raleigh, North Carolina. [Hayes, R. 1977.]

SMITH, MAMIE
(26 MAY 1883–30 OCT 1946)

American jazz and blues singer, born Mamie Robinson in Cincinnati. As a teen she toured as a dancer, then went to Harlem and established herself as a vocalist. Her record of "That Thing Called Love"/"You Can't Keep a Good Man Down" was the first vocal blues record, and the first record by a Black jazz/blues singer (Okeh/Phonola #4113; 14 Feb 1920). "Crazy Blues," made in her second record session, was a great success (Okeh/Phonola #4169; 10 Aug 1920), selling a million copies in six months. Smith became nationally famous, touring widely and appearing in films through the 1930s. Smith had a fresh approach to singing: "she delivered her songs with a reckless abandon and a wide-open shouting style that was worlds removed from the whimpering balladeers of the day" [Schuller 1968]. She continued to record for Okeh, making many fine discs with her Jazz Hounds ensemble, the membership of which has not been established; trumpeter Johnny Dunn was one player, and Coleman Hawkins was with the group in the early 1920s. Smith remained with Okeh, and that label was a leader in the switch from jazz to blues among the major companies. She died in New York City.

SMITH, PATTI (31 DEC 1946–)

Beat-inspired poet Patti Smith's debut album, *Horses* (Arista #4066; 1975; #47) — with its do-it-yourself (DIY)-inspired blend of raw power and evocative, free-flowing lyrics — helped inspire the 1970s punk explosion. Her refusal to accommodate mainstream musical values throughout her recording career would also prove influential on the later alternative rock movement.

Smith's first foray into recording, the underground single ""Hey Joe"/"Piss Factory" (MER #601; 1974), grew out of her beat poetry readings to guitar accompaniment and associations with rock musicians (e.g., contributing lyrics to Todd Rundgren's 1973 album, *A Wizard/A True Star*). The follow-up LP, *Radio Ethiopa* (Arista #4097; 1976), veered closer to metal than thrash, resulting in lukewarm reviews. *Easter* (Arista #4171; 1978; #20) and *Wave* (Arista #4221; 1979; #18) also bristled with a wired energy, despite the presence of sufficient studio polish to result in charting singles, most notably the Bruce Springsteen-penned "Because the Night" (Arista #0318; 1978; #13).

Smith took an extended sabbatical from recording after marrying ex-MC5 guitarist Fred "Sonic" Smith, returning with the relatively subdued *Dream of Life* (Arista #8453; 1988; #65), which featured the celebratory single, "Power to the People" (Arista #9689; 1988). *Gone Again* (Arista #18747; 1996; #55) and *Peace and Noise* (Arista #18986; 1997) recaptured the intensity of her initial recordings, while exuding a melancholy apparently brought on by the death of her husband. Smith appeared in the late 1990s on a double bill with Bob Dylan, and continued to enjoy a strong cult following. Among other performers, Michael Stipe of R.E.M. has consistently cited her 1970s work as influential on his own songwriting and performing.

FRANK HOFFMANN

SMITH, PINE TOP
(11 JUNE 1904–15 MAR 1929)

American blues singer and pianist, born Clarence Smith in Troy, Alabama. As a teenager he toured as a pianist and dancer, developing a new style that came to be called boogie woogie. His recording of "Pine Top's Boogie Woogie" (Vocalion #1245; 1928) defined the mode and set the standard for others to follow. He also sang effectively on the B side, doing "Pine Top's Blues." Just as his career was blossoming he was killed during a brawl that took place while he was performing in Chicago.

SMITH, WILL (25 SEP 1968–)

Philadelphia native Will Smith (aka the Fresh Prince) first found fame as a comical pop-rapper along with partner D.J. Jazzy Jeff (Jeffrey A. Townes). The duo's crossover success enabled Smith to become the first rap artist to make the transition to television success, a result of his landing the title role in the sitcom *The Fresh Prince of Bel-Air*, which ran six seasons on NBC. A string of film roles (e.g., *Bad Boys*, *Independence Day*, *Men in Black*, *Wild, Wild West, Ali*) followed, which in turn have propelled Smith back to the top of the charts as a solo act.

D.J. Jazzy Jeff and the Fresh Prince's debut album, *Rock the House* (Jive #1026; 1987; #83), attracted considerable attention due to its innovative blend of samples (ranging from James Brown to the *I Dream of Jeannie* theme) and scratching accented by the charismatic wit of Smith's humorous anecdotes. The follow-up, *He's the D.J., I'm the Rapper* (Jive #1091; 1988; #4) — driven by the hits "Parents Just Don't Understand" (Jive #1099; 1988; #12) and "A Nightmare on My Street" (Jive #1124; 1988; #15) — achieved unprecedented crossover popularity, ultimately selling more than two-and-a-half million copies. Subsequent LPs — *And in This Corner* (Jive #1188; 1989; #39; gold record award), *Homebase* (Jive #1392; 1991; #12; platinum record award; included singles "Summertime" [Jive #1465; 1991; #4] and "Ring My Bell" [Jive #42024; 1991; #20]), and *Code Red* (Jive # 41489; 1993) — while selling well, came across as rather silly and contrived.

Although never officially disbanded, the duo hasn't recorded since 1993, apparently due to the demands of Smith's media stardom. His first solo rap recordings — two songs — appeared on the soundtrack, *Men in Black: The Album* (Columbia #68169; 1997). The album, *Big Willie Styles* (Columbia # 68683 1997; #1) — which included the chart-topping single, "Getting' Jiggy Wit It" (Columbia #78804; 1998) — validated Smith's efforts to place his recording career back on the front burner. The film title track, "Wild Wild West" (Overbrook #79157; 1999; #1; featuring Dru Hill and Kool Mo Dee), offered further proof that PG-rated hip-hop possesses considerable sales potential.

FRANK HOFFMANN

SMITH, WILLIE "THE LION,"
(24 SEP 1897–18 APR 1973)

American jazz pianist, born William Henry Joseph Bonaparte Bertholoff in Goshen, New York. He grew up in Newark, New Jersey, and played the piano as a young child. As a teenager he was performing in Harlem, developing the new stride piano style. During World War I he earned his Lion nickname through valor in action. He became famous when he started to record in 1935, beginning with "There's Gonna Be the Devil to Pay" (Decca #7073). His masterful solo series with Commodore in 1939, performing his own compositions "Echoes of Spring" (#521) and "Finger Buster" (#522), with standards like "Stormy Weather" (#519), combined stride with classical elements, counterpoint, and impressionistic harmonies. His peak of popularity was in the late 1940s, when he toured Europe. He died in New York.

SMITH, WILLIE
(15 NOV 1910–7 MAR 1967)

American jazz alto saxophonist, born William McLeish in Charleston, South Carolina. He performed while in college in Nashville, and was heard by Jimmie Lunceford, who invited him to join his band. He was with Lunceford from 1929 to 1942, arranging as well as playing sax and sometimes doing vocals. In the 1940s and 1950s he was with Charlie Spivak, Harry James, and Duke Ellington, and led his own groups. He became recognized as one of the three or four outstanding alto soloists. "Sophisticated Lady," with Lunceford, was a good early example of his art (Decca #129; 1934). "Who's Sorry Now," with Harry James, was an outstanding record of the 1940s (Columbia #36973; 1945). Smith died in Los Angeles.

SMITH REPEATOSTOP CO.

A Chicago firm, active in 1911. It made the Repeatostop device, which either repeated or stopped a disc after it had played one time. R.B. Smith was the inventor, holding U.S. patent #906,319 (filed 16 Sept 1908; granted 8 Dec 1908).

SMITHSONIAN INSTITUTION

The American national museum, founded in 1846, now consisting of several component musuems, most of them in Washington, D.C. The National Museum of American History (NMAH) has a collection of recordings and artifacts pertaining to recorded sound. Included are a Phonautograph; an 1877 Edison tinfoil phonograph; a cylinder ostensibly recorded by Alexander Graham Bell in the Volta Laboratory in 1881; a Berliner photo-engraved record dated 26 July 1887, and a Berliner Gramophone of 1888. The Department of Social and Cultural History of NMAH holds important collections of jazz, popular, blues, and country records dating from 1903; there are more than 1,000 artists represented. Armed Forces Radio and Television Service transcription discs are there, plus the series Hit of the Week Records.

The Department of History of Science in NMAH has Columbia's experimental microgroove recordings of 1943–1946. It also has numerous records of geophysical phenomena, such as radio noise from Jupiter and tapes representing engineering standards. Examples showing the development of audio components are found, including complete phonographs, headphones, tone arms, loudspeakers, receivers, magnetic recording devices, and microphones. Early recordings and early record players are abundant.

In the NMAH Department of National History there is a collection of radio transcription discs from the World War II period. There is also a collection of recordings from political campaigns, from 1896.

The Smithsonian has issued many recordings, including the *Smithsonian Collection of Classic Jazz* (1973), consisting of six 12-inch LPs. This was enlarged and remastered on five CDs in 1989. Individual albums have been released on country, jazz, and swing artists, and for American musicals. *Voices of the Civil Rights Movement: Black American Freedom Songs, 1960–1966* is an important contribution. A re-creation of the Paul Whiteman 1924 concert in Aeolian Hall (which featured the premiere of *Rhapsody in Blue*) was issued on two LPs. Another CD album of special interest is *American Popular Song*, a collection of 110 selections by 62 artist, covering six decades on five compact discs (1988). *Big Band Jazz* won a Grammy in 1984 as the best historical album.

In 1986 the Smithsonian purchased the assets of Folkways Records, establishing Smithsonian Folkways Recordings. The Folkways archives were made part of the Center for Folklife and Cultural Heritage. Subsequently, several other small labels were also incorporated into the archives, including Dyer Bennett, Cook, Fast Folk, Monitor, and Paredon. [Heintze 1985 gives details on audio materials in all Washington institutions.]

SMOOTH JAZZ

The aging of the baby boomers has played a major role in the development of a number of genres, most notably adult contemporary, new age music, and smooth jazz. While jazz has always possessed a softer side, smooth jazz evolved out of the fusion movement of the 1960s and 1970s. From fusion — built on the intermingling of jazz and a wide range of styles, from bossa nova to progressive rock — smooth jazz appropriated rhythmic grooves and instrumental riffing (as opposed to improvisation). The gritty, funkier aspects of many such hybrids, however, have been deemphasized in favor of more polished arrangements. The dance-oriented sensibilities of the generation accustomed to disco and funk undoubtedly contributed to the notion that a steady backbeat could be tamed, thereby functioning as a form of background music. Many smooth jazz recordings possess multilayered textures typically featuring synthesizers, guitars, and horns (saxophones, trumpets, etc.) to create a sound geared more to the subconscious rather than the intellectual domain.

The pop crossover success enjoyed by guitarist George Benson in the mid-1970s — particularly *Breezin'* (Warner Bros. #2919; 1976; #1), *Weekend in L.A.* (Warner Bros. #3139; 1978; #5), and *Give Me the Night* (Warner Bros. #3453; 1980; #3) — provided the template for the newly emerging genre. Kenny G is arguably the style's major star; hit albums such as *Duotones* (Arista #8427; 1986; #6), *Silhouette* (Arista #8457; 1988; #8), and *Breathless* (Arista #18646; 1992; #2) drew legions of new fans to smooth jazz. Other notable artists whose work falls — at least in part — within this field include Fattburger (*Livin' Large*; Shanachie 5012; 1994), Fourplay (*Fourplay*; Warner Bros. #26656; 1991; #97), George Howard (*A Nice Place to Be*; MCA #5855; 1986; #109), and the Yellowjackets (*Mirage a Trois*; Warner Bros. #23813; #145).

FRANK HOFFMANN

SNOOP DOGGY DOGG (20 OCT 1972–)

Snoop Doggy Dogg (aka Calvin Broadus) was a pop-culture celebrity well before the release of his first album, the platinum selling *Doggystyle* (Death Row/Interscope # 50605; 1993). He had already appeared on mentor Dr. Dre's chart-topping album, *The Chronic* (Priority/Interscope #2 57128; 1992), in addition to being arrested in connection with the murder of an alleged Los Angeles gang member. Overnight, he had become a figurehead of the controversial gangsta rap genre, his picture appearing on the covers of mass circulation magazines such as *Newsweek*, *Rolling Stone*, and *Vibe*.

Doggystyle was the fastest-selling debut LP in history, entering the pop album charts at number one and selling almost 1 million units alone in its first week of release. All issues of notoriety aside, the record's success owed much to Dr. Dre's funky production work and Snoop's mesmerizing treatment of both the harsher side of hood life and partying. The commercial rise of rappers 2Pac and the Notorious B.I.G., combined with a weak follow-up album, *The Doggfather* (Death Row/Interscope # 90038; 1996), minus Dr. Dre's studio support, pushed him into the background. Subsequent releases have resurrected his artistic credibility to some degree; however, the appearance of new creative forces — most notably, RZA, Method Man, and other members of the Wu-Tang Clan — have kept him from regaining the rap spotlight. [Graff 1998.]

FRANK HOFFMANN

SNOW, HANK (9 MAY 1914–19 DEC 1999)

Although relatively unknown in the U.S. until 1949, Canadian-born Hank Snow — initially referred to as the "Yodelling Ranger" — was a first-generation disciple of Jimmie Rodgers. Although his hard country singling style fell out of favor in the late 1950s, he enjoyed a number one hit, "Hello Love" (RCA #0215) as late as 1974. An elder statesman of the genre for the last 30 years of his career, Snow enjoyed hit records in the U.S. for five decades (from the 1940s to the 1980s), ranking 21st in success on the country charts through 1988. [Whitburn1996.]

After singing in Nova Scotia clubs during his teens, Snow was given his own radio show on CHNS-Halifax, in 1934. His popularity in that region led to a contract with RCA in 1936. He relocated to the U.S. in the mid-1940s, working on the WWVA *Wheeling Jamboree*, in Hollywood with his performing horse, Shawnee, and KRLD-Dallas. Snow's first appearance on the *Grand Ole Opry*, 7 Jan 1949 — although poorly received — helped break his first nationwide country hit, "Marriage Vow" (RCA #0062; 1949; #10).

Snow's next hit, the self-composed "I'm Movin' On" (RCA #0328; 1950), became one of the most successful country recordings of all-time, remaining number one for 21 weeks (and on the charts for 44 weeks), selling more than 1 million copies. Now an *Opry* regular, his

rich baritone voice, crisp enunciation, and preoccupation with authentic Americana (e.g., trains, Old West bank robberies) made him one of the genre's top stars into the early 1960s. His best-selling recordings included "The Golden Rocket" (RCA #0400; 1950), "Rhumba Boogie" (RCA #0431; 1952), "I Don't Hurt Anymore" (RCA #5698; 1954; gold record, #1 for 20 weeks), "Let Me Go, Lover" (RCA #5960; 1954), and "I've Been Everywhere" (RCA #8072; 1962).

A longtime ambassador for country music, the "Singing Ranger" continued touring intermittently after RCA terminated his recording contract in the early 1980s; Snow's 45 years with the company is believed to be an industry record. He was elected to the Country Music Hall of Fame in 1979.

FRANK HOFFMANN

SNOW, WILLIAM B. (16 MAY 1903–5 OCT 1969)

A pioneer in audio and acoustics, Snow was born in San Francisco and earned B.S. and E.E. degrees from Stanford University. During the Golden Era of sound research between 1923 and 1941, he worked at Bell Laboratories, playing a major role in the advancement of acoustic science. During the war years he was assistant director of the Navy's underwater sound laboratory, at New London, Connecticut. In 1946, he took employment with the Vitro Corp. of America, and became director of physical research and development at the company in 1950. From 1952 to 1960, he ran a consulting practice in Santa Monica, California, and in 1961, he went to work for Bissett-Berman Corp. as head of electro-acoustics. Snow's contributions to audio and the science of recorded sound are manifest, and in 1968 the Audio Engineering Society awarded him its John H. Potts award.

HOWARD FERSTLER

SOBINOV, LEONID (7 JUNE 1872–14 OCT 1934)

Russian tenor, born in Yaroslavl. He studied law in Moscow, graduating in 1894, but also traveled with an Italian opera troupe, and decided to make singing his career. His debut was in 1897 at the Bolshoi, and he remained with that company through his career, singing also at the Maryinsky Theater in St. Petersburg and throughout Europe. He was at La Scala in 1904–1906. His great roles were Lenski in *Eugene Onegin*, Faust, Des Grieux, and Alfredo. Sobinov also excelled in solo recitals (Nicolas Slonimsky was his accompanist during 1918–1919), and was idolized by the public, especially by young girls. He died in Riga.

Sobinov was recorded first by Fred Gaisberg for G & T in St. Petersburg and Moscow in 1901, presenting 26 numbers, mostly Russian opera arias. In 1904 he made another set of G & T discs in St. Petersburg, this time including in the 21 sides a large measure of French/Italian repertoire, sung in Russian. He worked for Pathé also, in 1908, St. Petersburg, offering 10 items on vertical-cut discs. In 1910 he was back with Gaisberg and the Gramophone Co. (in Moscow) for 11 arias, Russian and Western. His last sessions were in 1911, in St. Petersburg and Moscow. Reissues appeared on the Russian Gramplasttrecht label, and later on Melodiya. All the major reissue labels in U.S. and U.K. have covered his repertoire. Among his outstanding records were the arioso of Lenski from *Eugene Onegin* (HMV #2-22649; 1904), "Salut demeure" (#022078; 1904), and "Mein lieber Schwann" (#022137; 1910). [Robertson and Dennis 1978.]

SOCIAL-PROTEST MUSIC

Social-protest songs had existed throughout the 19th century (and much earlier), from labor and abolitionist tunes to farmers' laments and spirituals, and overtly political ballads, but the first recordings were made in the 1920s. While popular (i.e., commercial) music has generally avoided overt political content, particularly of a left-leaning sort, certain musical subcultures have not shied away from complaints and controversial subjects. Blues has inherently dealt with suffering and unrest, although usually in a covert fashion and from a personal perspective. A good selection can be found in the compilation *Hard Times* (Rounder Records #4007). Similarly, old-time music by the late-1920s sometimes included protest and pro-labor/union songs, such as Uncle Dave Macon"'s "Wreck of the Tennessee Gravy Train" and "Buddy, Roll on Down the Line," Bob Miller's "Eleven Cent Cotton and Forty Cent Meat," David McCarn's "Cotton Mill Colic," the Dixon Brothers' "Weave Room Blues," and the Martin Brothers' "The North Carolina Textile Strike." An excellent selection of such early recordings is *Poor Man, Rich Man* (Rounder Records #1026).

More consciously radical rural composers and performers Florence Reese, Ella May Wiggins, Jim Garland, his half-sister Aunt Molly Jackson and sister Sarah Ogan Gunning, Woody Guthrie, particularly in his initial *Dust Bowl Ballads* (RCA, 1940), Agnes "Sis" Cunningham, and John Handcox captured a mix of native radical politics and working-class trials and hardships beginning in the 1930s. Aunt Molly recorded "Kentucky Miner's Wife" (aka "Ragged Hungry Blues") for Columbia Records in 1931, and her Library of Congress recordings were later released (Rounder Records #1002). In the mid-1930s a few

record companies began to emerge that produced songs directly connected with the Communist Party, including the Timely Recording Co., which issued albums by Earl Robinson, the New Singers, and the Manhattan Chorus, soon followed by Keynote Records, which released most of the Almanac Singers sides, including the controversial antiwar album *Songs for John Doe* (1941), as well as Josh White's antisegregationist *Southern Exposure* on Keynote (1941). There were also a few issues of topical song musical shows, such as "Pins and Needles" and "Cabaret TAC," and Lewis Allan's biting antilynching song, "Strange Fruit," as recorded by Billie Holiday for Commodore (1939).

During and soon after World War II the Asch label produced albums of Spanish civil war songs, the pro-union albums *Citizen CIO* and *Roll the Union On*, and much by Woody Guthrie. Following World War II a recorded singing left briefly emerged, led by Charter Record that issued about 10 singles and one album, with Pete Seeger, the People's Songs Chorus, Betty Sanders, and Sir Lancelot. Charter was connected to People's Songs and the Henry Wallace 1948 Progressive Party presidential campaign. The short-lived Hootenanny label issued a series of records in the early 1950s with Laura Duncan, Ernie Lieberman, and the Weavers, including an early version of "We Shall Overcome" by the Jewish Young Folksingers. In 1951 Big Bill Broonzy recorded the hard-hitting "Black, Brown and White" for Mercury. For the remainder of the decade numerous Folkways albums by Pete Seeger, John Greenway, and a few others kept older examples of protest music somewhat available, including the reissue of the Almanac Singers's *Talking Union*, although Seeger's two *Gazette* albums (Folkways #FN2501 and #FN2502) included contemporary examples.

Protest songs made a strong comeback in the 1960s, sparked by the rise of Bob Dylan and the singer-songwriter movement, initially capped by *The Freewhellin' Bob Dylan* (Columbia #CS-8786). In 1962 Sis Cunningham and her husband Gordon Friesen, encouraged by the prolific Malvina Reynolds, launched *Broadside*, a topical songs magazine that issued a series of records distributed by Folkways Records. Beginning with *Broadside Ballads, vol. 1* (Broadside #05301), which included Bob Dylan, the label issued over a dozen albums from 1963 to 1980 with, among others, Pete Seeger, Tom Paxton, Len Chandler, and Phil Ochs. Folkways also released a series of albums relating to the civil rights movement, and soon after Barbara Dane initiated with Paredon Records such titles as *I Hate the Capitalist System* (#01014) and *FTA: Songs of G.I. Resistance* (#01003). Joe Glazer's Collector Records released numerous albums dealing with union/workers' rights and problems. The emergence of folk-rock in the mid-1960s produced a spate of critical songs and albums, particularly Barry McGuire, "Eve of Destruction," and Country Joe and the Fish, "I'm Fixin' to Die Rag." For the remainder of the century a steady steam of protest recordings dealt with civil rights, the women's movement, antiwar and peace issues, labor unions and economic concerns, environmental devastation, and so much more. In addition to the albums of scores of performers, such as Paxton; Bruce "U. Utah" Phillips; Si Kahn; Hazel Dickens; Fred Small; Kim and Reggie Harris; Odetta; Janis Ian; Peter, Paul, and Mary; Joan Baez; Charlie King; Tom Juravich; Holly Near; and so many others, there have been various compilation albums, for example: *Out of the Darkness: Songs for Survival* (Fire on the Mountain #4001), *Swords into Plowshares: Songs of Freedom and Struggle* (Folk Tradition #S005/006), *Don't Mourn — Organize!: Songs of Labor Songwriter Joe Hill* (Smithsonian Folkways SF #40026), *Brown Lung Cotton Mill Blues* (June Appal #006), *Songs for Peace* (Rounder Records #4015), *Reaganomic Blues* (Fuse Music), *Songs of Protest* (Rhino #R2 70734), and *Freedom Is a Constant Struggle: Songs of the Mississippi Civil Rights Movement* (Folk Era #1419CD). Two fascinating collections of new recordings, *Where Have All the Flowers Gone: The Songs of Pete Seeger* (Appleseed #CD-1024) and *The Songs of Phil Ochs* (Sliced Bread Records #CD-SB1176) connect a variety of performers, such as Bruce Springsteen, Ani Difranco, Indigo Girls, Magpie, the Roches, and John Wesley Harding to a somewhat older protest tradition, which continued to be strong and vibrant, including country performers such as Iris DeMent, Hazel Dickens, Steve Earle, and John Prine. [Cohen and Samuelson 1996; Cunningham and Friesen 1999; Goldsmith 1998; Greenway 1953; Malone 2002; Perone 2001; Place and Cohen 2000; Reuss 2000; Robinson 1998.]

RONALD D. COHEN

SOCIET ITALIANA DI FONOTIPIA

An Italian firm, established in Milan in 1904. The original owners were Michaelis, Foa and Co. Ownership passed to Fonotipia London Ltd. in 1906, then to Carl Lindström AG of Berlin, in 1911. The Transoceanic Trading Co., Netherlands, acquired the firm in 1920. It came under control of the Columbia Graphophone Co., Ltd., in 1925, and thence went to EMI, Ltd., in 1931.

Fonotipia was set up to compete with the Gramophone Co. (Italy) Ltd., of which Alfred Michaelis had been general manager. He left in

Italian Fonotipia disc produced c. 1906, distributed in the U.S. by Columbia. Courtesy Kurt Nauck/Nauck's Vintage Records

summer 1904, under disagreable circumstances, and created the Fonotipia rival ca. October 1904, with engineer Dino Foa as his partner. It seems that the new firm was also the Italian agent for F.M. Prescott's Odeon records. Fonotipia's first records, 11 single-sided discs, appeared in 1905. It produced some 360 sides by November 1905. Artists included Alessandro Bonci, Victor Maurel, Giovanni Zenatello, and violinist Jan Kubelik.

See also **Fonotipia Ltd.**

SOCIETY OF MOTION PICTURE AND TELEVISION ENGINEERS (SMPTE)

A professional engineering society that establishes standards for movie production and distribution, including a time-code standard used for audio synchronization.

HOWARD FERSTLER

SOCIETY OF PROFESSIONAL AUDIO RECORDING SERVICES (SPARS)

Founded in 1979, a professional trade organization that unites professional customers with the manufacturers of audio recording equipment and providers of services.

HOWARD FERSTLER

SOCIETY RECORDS

It occurred to Walter Legge, at the Gramophone Co., that a marketable idea in the dismal 1930s would be to issue discs in subscription sets. HMV established various "societies" that involved an advance purchase commitment by the consumer for a series of records of special interest. In 1931 HMV announced the first society set, six albums of songs by Hugo Wolf — sung by Alexander Kipnis, John McCormack, and others — and 500 subscriptions were eventually received. After the Wolf issue appeared in April 1932, a Beethoven/Schnabel set was announced, in 15 albums of six or seven records each. Other society sets that emerged from EMI and its American affiliates included J.S. Bach cello suites (Pablo Casals), "Goldberg Variations" (Wanda Landowska), organ music (Albert Schweitzer), *Art of the Fugue* (Roth Quartet), and *Wohltemperierte Klavier* (Edwin Fischer). Brahms's songs were interpreted by Alexander Kipnis. Delius's works were conducted by Thomas Beecham. The Haydn quartets were played by the Pro Arte Quartet. Landowska also did the Scarlatti sonatas. Glyndeboourne performances of Mozart operas were made, under the direction of Fritz Busch and Beecham. Most of the society releases have been reissued on LP.

SODERO, CESARE
(2 AUG 1886–16 DEC 1947)

Italian conductor, born in Naples. He was a cellist and conductor in Naples from age 15, and conducted widely in Europe while very young. In 1906 he was at the Manhattan Opera as soloist and conductor, and worked also with other companies. Sodero was director of recording and staff conductor for Edison from 1914 to 1929, responsible for more than 11,000 records. He was staff conductor for NBC from 1925 to 1934. From 1942 to 1947, he was a conductor with the Metropolitan Opera.

SOFT MACHINE

Formed in 1966 and taking its name from the title of a William S. Burroughs novel, Soft Machine, in ever-changing incarnations, was a true pioneer of progressive rock and jazz. Evolving out of a group of Canterbury musicians who had played together intermittently since at least 1963, the free-spirited original lineup of Mike Ratledge, Australian Daevid Allen and ex-Wilde Flowers Robert Wyatt and Kevin Ayers are at their melodic best on *Jet-Propelled Photographs* (Charly), a compilation of demos recorded in April 1967; this collection of edgy pop love songs has also been released as *At the Beginning* (Dressed to Kill #380).

By *Volume One* (One Way #22064; 1968) Allen had departed due to visa problems, and on *Volume Two* (One Way #22065; 1969) Hugh Hopper (another former Wilde Flower) had replaced Ayers on bass. *One* and *Two* (available together on Big Beat #920) are characterized by Wyatt's raspy vocals and eccentric, sometimes surreal, lyrics and titles. Soft Machine's inventive musicianship and raw energy as well as Ratledge's compositional skills are highlighted in *Volume Two* as the "Esther's Nose Job" suite builds to a driving crescendo. *Third* (CGK #30339; 1970), considered by some the group's masterpiece, marked Wyatt's last recorded vocals with the group (on "Moon in June"), the notable addition of Elton Dean on saxes, and an almost complete shift to jazz, much of it of the free variety. *Fourth* (One Way #26254; 1971), marking Wyatt's last studio recording with the group (he was also their drummer), and *Fifth* (One Way #26227; 1972) delivers in a similar vein, but in smaller doses than the album side-length pieces of *Third*. *Six* (One Way #26255; 1973), originally an album of live and studio recordings, experiments successfully with minimalism and electronica on the studio cuts. *Six* was Hopper's swan song and introduced composer/keyboardist Karl Jenkins, under whose artistic sway Soft Machine would remain through five more albums, ending with *The Land of Cockayne* (One Way #18936; 1981). The last original member, Ratledge, exited on *Bundles* (See for Miles #283; 1975), which was also notable for the reintroduction of guitar to the lineup after many years' absence, bringing still another change — toward jazz-rock — to the group's direction.

Several compilations and many recordings of early live material, often differing significantly from studio versions, have continued to appear; of the latter, *Peel Sessions* (Dutch East India #8501), assembled from 1969–1971 BBC appearances, is among the best. *Spaced* (Cuneiform Rune #90), recorded to accompany Peter Dockley's 1969 multimedia show of the same title, and replete with tape loops evocative of Burroughs's method of novelistic composition, reveals the group at their most experimental. Soft Machine played several gigs as late as 1984, but by this time they had long since ceased to be, in both personnel and creativity, the same group that had toured with Jimi Hendrix in 1968 or that was charting new directions in both jazz and rock over the next few years.

CRAIG BUNCH

SOFT ROCK AND RELATED STYLES

In a sense, soft rock originated in the late 1950s when pop singers began employing arrangements which incorporated elements of rock 'n' roll. Andy Williams,

Guy Mitchell, and Tab Hunter all achieved notable success aiming their releases at a teen audience. The genre gained more widespread recognition, however, following the rise of folk rock and the singer/songwriter tradition in the mid-1960s. These two styles, both receiving their primary impetus from the Los Angeles recording scene, ushered in a softer form of rock music that made a significant dent in the singles and album charts.

Soft rock had the following identifying features: (1) the rock beat and other abrasive coloring (e.g., intense electric guitar lines, harsh vocalizing) were deemphasized, and (2) song lyrics tended to be upbeat and/or introspective rather than rebellious in nature. The factors guaranteeing its success included the personal music preferences of the power brokers within the music businesses, the efforts of both artists and record company executives to broaden rock's appeal, and the aging of the first generation of rock fans.

The ongoing maturation of the baby boomers — whose concert-going and record-buying habits tended to remain at a much higher level than those of their parents and grandparents — ensured the long-term popularity of the various soft rock styles. Many rock artists employed an increasingly middle-of-the-road approach as their careers evolved in direct response to the perceived shift of their core audience. Chicago, Dr. Hook, and the Doobie Brothers were all examples of artists whose music became softer and acquired greater polish over time. Other soft rock exponents included America, the Association, Bread, the Carpenters, the Cowsills, the 5th Dimension, the Grass Roots, Harpers Bizarre, Loggins and Messina, the Mamas and the Papas, Gary Puckett and the Union Gap, Seals and Crofts, Three Dog Night, and Crosby, Stills, and Nash.

Related styles include:

Middle-of-the-Road (MOR)/Adult Contemporary (AC). While as stylistically varied as soft rock, its practitioners — most notably, Michael Bolton, Rita Coolidge, Tony Orlando and Dawn, John Denver, Barry Manilow, Anne Murray, Olivia Newton-John, Helen Reddy, and B.J. Thomas — tended to employ a more homogenized approach. MOR, or AC — a less prejorative term widely employed by the early 1980s — represented a particular cross section of the radio listening audience which possessed its own clearly defined lifestyle and product loyalties (a vital consideration to brand name advertisers) combined with substantial purchasing power.

Pop Stylists. This subgenre owed more to the Tin Pan Alley tradition than it did to rock music. However, the impact of rock — both in terms of stylistic touches and performing flair — is obvious when those pop singers whose careers began after the mid-1950s are compared with their stylistic ancestors such as Frank Sinatra, Tony Bennett, and Doris Day. Among the leading rock era pop stylists are Engelbert Humperdinck, Tom Jones, Bette Midler, Barbra Streisand, Dionne Warwick, and Andy Williams.

Pop Rock. These artists generally began their careers after the first wave of soft rock in the 1960s. Like such genre trailblazers as the Mamas and the Papas and the Association, rock arrangements are front-and-center. However, pop rockers also exhibit strong MOR leanings. If active in the prerock era, they might well have taken on more characteristics of the pop stylists. The Captain and Tennille, Mariah Carey, Eric Carmen, Kim Carnes, and Fleetwood Mac all belong to this category.

FRANK HOFFMANN

SOLEX (LABEL)

A U.K. record introduced by British Homophone Co. in September 1930. It was a fine grooved disc, eight inches in diameter, said to play as long as a normal 10-inch disc. Matrices were contracted to Selfridge's, who sold them under the label name Silvertone. The eight-inch discs ceased after April 1931. A 10-inch record was introduced in January 1935, but it was only sold for four months. After 1935 there were no further issues. [Andrews 1986/4.]

SOLID STATE

A term applied to various semiconductor devices, e.g., the transistor, to distinguish them from their electron tube counterparts.

SOLO ART (LABEL)

An American record, issued in limited quantities during 1939–1940 by Solo Art Recordings of New York. The producer was Dan Qualey, who recorded the work of jazz pianists he liked best: Albert Ammons, Meade "Lux" Lewis, and Jimmy Yancey. There were about 20–30 issues, on 10-inch and 12-inch records. [Rust 1978.]

SOLOMON, MAYNARD

SEE VANGUARD (LABEL)

SOLOMON, SEYMOUR

SEE VANGUARD (LABEL)

SOLOPHONE CO.

An American firm, located in Harrison, New Jersey. In 1916 it advertised Solophone disc players in three models that sold from $90 to $175.

SOLTI, GEORG, SIR
(21 OCT 1912–5 SEP 1997)

Hungarian/English conductor and pianist, born Gyîrgy Solti in Budapest. He played the piano in public at age 12, and studied at the Liszt Academy (with teachers Ernî Dohnanyi, Béla Bartok, and Zoltan Kodaly). He was accompanist at Salzburg in 1936 and 1937, under Arturo Toscanini, and made his conducting debut in Budapest in 1938. He spent the World War I years in Switzerland, then became conductor of the State Opera in Munich, remaining to 1952. From there he went to Frankfurt, directing symphonic and operatic activity. In 1960, following appearances at the Metropolitan Opera and San Francisco Opera, Solti became director of the Dallas Symphony Orchestra, but after a year went to Covent Garden where he was music director until 1971. He took U.K citizenship and was knighted in 1972. From 1969 to 1990 he was music director of the Chicago Symphony Orchestra, achieving world recognition for himself and the ensemble. The CSO won 20 Grammy awards under Solti's direction. He was also principal conductor of the London Philharmonic Orchestra in 1979–1983. He retired from the Chicago post in 1990, having passed the baton to his chosen heir, Daniel Barenboim. Solti was awarded the National Medal of the Arts in 1993. He died in the Antibes.

Solti's outstanding recordings are numerous. He conducted the *Ring* in the famous John Culshaw recording of 1966 (available on Decca #414 100-2DM15; 1989, 15 discs), and also collaborated with Culshaw in *Salome*. A good selection of Solti's orchestral specialties, most of them with the CSO, appeared on Decca #430 635-2DM12, a 12-disc set (1991). The set includes acclaimed interpretations of Richard Strauss's tone poems, the Brahms Fourth Symphony, Mahler's Fifth Symphony, and Holst's *The Planets*. [Marsh 1984 is a discogrphy of the CSO records.]

SONET (LABEL)

Danish-based jazz/blues label founded in 1951 under the Storyville name. It was renamed Sonet in 1955 when it moved to Stockholm, Sweden, and specialized in licensing U.S. jazz releases for the Scandinavian market. In the 1960s, it began representing U.K. pop labels like Island, and in 1968 opened a U.K. office. Throughout the 1970s and 1980s, it licensed blues and jazz material from small U.S. labels like Rounder and

Flying Fish, and also formed the Kicking Mule label in partnership with blues guitarist Stefan Grossman. It also continued to record European jazz and folk artists, and native Scandinanvian pop and folk acts. In 1990 Sonet's Scandinavian label was sold to PolyGram, while its U.K. division was spun off and renamed Habana Music (no longer active).

CARL BENSON

SONIC YOUTH

Subscribing to the No Wave aesthetics propounded by a small circle of New York City–based artists nominally headed by avant-garde composer/performer Glenn Branca during the early 1980s, Sonic Youth displayed a more pronounced intellectual agenda than most acts arising out of the postpunk movement. The band's genius consisted of the ability to effectively graft melodic hooks onto the chromatic sound collages constituting the core of their recorded output.

Formed in early 1981 by vocalist/lead guitarist Thurston Moore and vocalist/bassist Kim Gordon, Sonic Youth employed a succession of supporting musicians before achieving a semblance of stability (discounting a multitude of side recording projects) with vocalist/guitarist Lee Ranaldo and drummer Steve Shelley. Early releases — the dub-dance styled *Sonic Youth EP* (Neutral #01; 1982; reissued on SST #097; 1987), the cerebral punk showcases *Confusion Is Sex* (Neutral #02; 1983; German LP; reissued on

Sonic Youth album cover. Courtesy Frank Hoffmann

SST #096; 1987) and *Kill Your Idols* (Zensor #10; 1983; German LP), and cassette-only thrashfest, *Sonic Death* (Ecstatic Peace [unnumbered]; 1984; reissued in U.K. on Blast First #32CD; 1988) — featured pro-feminist, socially engaged rhetoric set to abrasive white noise owing much to the garage rock genre of the mid-1960s.

Bad Moon Rising (Homestead #016; 1985) represented a breakthrough of sorts, a collection of gut-wrenching polemics (including references to Charles Manson in "Death Valley '69") that received extensive coverage from the rock press. The band continued to expand their core following through a series of uncompromisingly urbane hardcore statements: *Evol* (SST #059; 1986); *Sister* (SST #134; 1987); the Madonna dance-floor parody, *The Whitey Album* (Capitol #75402; 1988; #63 U.K.; joined forces with the Minutemen's Mike Watt, billed as "Ciccone Youth"); and *Daydream Nation* (Torso #2602339; 1988; #99 U.K.). Signing with a major label, Sonic Youth managed to negotiate a successful merger of high-end production values and counterculture aesthetics in albums like *Goo* (DGC #7599 24297; 1990; #96 U.S., #32 U.K.), *Dirty* (DGC #24485; 1992; #83 U.S., #6 U.K.), *Experimental Jet Set, Trash and No Star* (DGC #24632; 1994; #34 U.S., #10 U.K.), *Washing Machine* (DGC #24925; 1994; #58 U.S., #39 U.K.), and *A Thousand Leaves* (DGC #25203; 1998; #85 U.S., #38 U.K.). Secure in their status as alternative rock icons, they eschewed any chance at commercial success with a release of *Goodbye 20th Century* (Smells Like #04; 1999), comprised of their interpretations of contemporary serious music composers like John Cage, Cornelius Cardew, and Christian Wolff. Entering the new millennium, Sonic Youth appear to have retained the credo characterizing their early years, that of operating within an experimental framework, thereby remaining one step ahead of their constituency.

FRANK HOFFMANN

SONNY AND CHER

Born Salvatore Bono, 16 Feb 1935; Cherilyn Sarkasian LaPier, 20 May 1946. When Flower Power was in bloom in the mid-1960s, Sonny and Cher were America's musical sweethearts. While their ersatz bohemian garb lent them a goofy look, they parlayed Sonny's songwriting and arranging skills and Cher's rich vocals into an act so endearing that two decades later, momentarily reunited, they were emplored to reprise their signature tune, "I Got You Babe" (Atco #6359, 1965) on the *David Letterman* show. (VHI rated it one of rock's "100 Greatest Moments.")

Sonny met Cher while he was working for producer Phil Spector, and she was singing background for the Ronettes. Love ensued, but chart success did not come immediately. They first recorded as Caesar and Cleo for Vault, and later Reprise, but were unsuccessful. However, it took new label Atco and a name change to bring them success, beginning in 1965 with "Baby Don't Go" (1965) and then through a string of hits, culminating in 1967's "The Beat Goes On." After that, the duo unexpectedly dropped from popularity and resorted to working as a lounge act during the early 1970s. However, they made a comeback beginning in 1972, hosting a popular television show through most of the decade, even after their marriage failed. Sonny was a Republican congressman when he died of injuries from a skiing accident at 62; Cher remains a diva of international magnitude — she performed in an over-the-top supposed "farewell concert" in 2003.

See also **Cher**

SONORA (LABEL) (I)

SEE SONORA PHONOGRAPH CO.

SONORA (LABEL) (II)
A Swedish label issued from ca. 1935.

Label issued by the phonograph manufacturer based in New York and Chicago. Courtesy Kurt Nauck/Nauck's Vintage Records

SONORA PHONOGRAPH CO.

A New York firm, successor to Sonora Chime Co., established in 1910. The company issued vertical-cut discs from May 1910, and also made record players for both vertical and lateral-cut discs. Victor sued them for violation, in the record players, of their old Berliner patent #534,543 (covering the groove-driven stylus), and gained an injunction; the injunction was later vacated (and the patent expired in February 1911), but meanwhile Sonora went bankrupt. However, it reorganized, and was again offering the Sonora line of 11 models, at $45–1,000, by 1916. One model player had a "tone modifier" control. Jewel needles were provided. Another dispute with Victor in 1916, over the right to make an enclosed horn machine, was settled with Victor selling Sonora a license to continue.

In March 1921 it was announced, by company president S.E. Brightson, that Sonora records would be launched by the new Sonora Record Corp. Perhaps the most expensive record player of the 78 era, the Bardini, was offered in 1921; it sold for $5,000. Sonora also manufactured player pianos in the 1920s. In January 1922 it constructed the "largest sign in the world" along the New York Central Railroad tracks between Albany and New York City; it was 800 feet long. A Chicago office was operating in 1928, while the executive headquarters remained in New York. The Federal Radio Corp. acquired a controlling interest in Sonora in 1929.

During 1944–1948 a final series of Sonora discs appeared. The firm at that time was named Sonora Record Co., with offices in Chicago and New York. The material offered on the label was popular, country, R&B, jazz, classical, and children's. The successor to that company, Sonora Radio and Television Corp. of Chicago, did not deal in phonograph records.

SONS OF THE PIONEERS

American country group formed in 1933 as the Pioneer Trio. Members were Roy Rogers (then using the name Dick Weston), Bob Nolan, and Tim Spencer. In 1934 fiddler Hugh Farr joined in, and his brother Karl Farr made it a quintet in 1935. Decca recorded the Pioneers from 1934, in their quickly famous renditions of "Tumbling Tumbleweeds" (#46027; 1934), and "Cool Water" (#5939; 1935), both written by Nolan. Many other classics followed, on Decca, then Victor. It was through the work of the ensemble that the romantic cowboy image was widely disseminated, and their harmony singing inspired many imitators.

The Pioneers were a great success in Hollywood, appearing in more than 100 western films. Rogers left the group to concentrate on the movies in 1937; he and the Pioneers made two successful motion pictures together in 1941. There were many changes in membership which complicated the task of the Country Music Hall of Fame when it was deciding whether to induct the group in 1980. It was determined to include six men in the honor, Rogers, Spencer, Nolan, the Farrs, and Lloyd Perryman. Still active in the 1980s, the group retained its basic style and repertoire.

SONY CORP.

A Japanese firm established in 1946 as Tokyo Telecommunications Engineering (current name taken in 1958) in the bombed-out shell of a department store. It made audio components and experimented constantly to find new products and applications. Sony marketed the first Japanese tape recorder in 1950, and the world's first transistor radio in 1955, and went on to miniaturize other components; their pocket radio came out in 1957, gaining great popularity in world markets. Sony transistor television was introduced in 1959, and the solid state video recorder in 1961. Other successful innovations included the desktop electronic calculator (1964), the Trinitron color television tube (1968), and the Walkman (1979). From 300 employees in the early 1950s, the firm went to 4,400 employees in 1961, 22,000 by 1975, and 26,000 by 1980. As of 2002, Sony employed 168,000 people worldwide.

In the audio field, Sony joined with Philips in developing compact disc technology, and has become the market leader in CD players. The firm has invested heavily in DAT and high-definition television. Sony acquired CBS Records from CBS in 1988, for $2 billion, and Columbia Pictures from Coca-Cola in 1989 for $4.9 billion. As of 2002, Sony's principal U.S. businesses include Sony Electronics Inc., Sony Pictures Entertainment, Sony Music Entertainment Inc., and Sony Computer Entertainment America Inc.

SORIA, DARIO
(21 MAY 1912–28 MAR 1980)

Italian/American recording industry executive, born in Rome. He took an economics degree from the University of Rome in 1934. His family fled Italy in 1939 and came to America. Soria worked for the U.S. Office of War Information during World War II, becoming a citizen in 1945. He was head of overseas news broadcasting for CBS (1943–1948). In that period he organized the Cetra-Soria label, drawing on the Cetra matrices, which offered a major catalog of operatic material.

Artists on the Cetra-Soria label included Maria Callas, Cesare Siepi, Ferruccio Tagliavini, and Italo Tajo. Sixteen complete Verdi operas were issued over a seven-year period. In 1953 Soria sold the label to Capitol and assumed leadership of a new EMI American subsidiary which revived the Angel label. He was responsible for elegant packaging as well as high-quality material on Angel until 1961, when he moved to RCA Victor as vice president of the international division. From 1970 he was managing director of the Metropolitan Opera Guild. When he died, in New York, Soria was at work on a planned release of a Metropolitan Opera historic broadcast of *Ballo in maschera*.

SOUL MUSIC RECORDINGS

A term first coined in the 1960s, generally used for the more hard-edged Black performers of the era. The style is based on impassioned expression, and such vocal devices as falsetto, sobs, and shouts. The labels that carried much of the early soul were Atlantic (Ray Charles, Aretha Franklin) and Stax (Otis Redding, Sam and Dave). The term fell into disuse during the disco era.

See also **Rhythm and Blues (R&B) Recordings**

SOUNDBOX

A common designation for the reproducer of an acoustic phonograph; it is usually applied to disc machines. Its parts are the diaphragm, needle arm and screw, spring, cushions, casing, and gasket. It was supplanted in the electric era by the cartridge, or pickup.

SOUND EFFECTS RECORDINGS

Radio programs required the use of simulated sounds to accompany dramatic programs, and these were created in the studio via ingenious means. That task was simplified as phonograph records appeared in the late 1920s. It seems that the earliest specimen was "London Street Sounds," made by Columbia Graphophone Co., Ltd., in 1928. Major labels offered sound effects discs in the 1930s, covering such typical needs as fire engines, crowd noises, storms, and horses. Victor had an elaborate set of records in the 1940 catalog that allowed the user to choose, for example, between a train approaching and passing a point, passing a station, entering a tunnel, coming to a stop, or running at constant speed. Mumbling was available, either by mixed voices or by females alone. The BBC sound effects catalog is now the world's most comprehensive, making 450 effects available on 10 CDs, at a cost in 1990 of 199 pounds. Purchasers will hear the sound of a dental drill (high or low speed), a television

screen being smashed by a cricket ball, birds and sheep on a Welsh hillside, the sounds of a public library in action, bread being sliced, a Rolls Royce door opening and closing, three rams bleating, 40 children on wet gravel, a kiss, a burp, and even a flying saucer taking off. Network Music is another major producer and provider of sound effects recordings, offering a large library of sound effects on 78 CDs.

SOUND FILE

A digital sound file contains one or more sequences of data points that directly or indirectly describes sound in such a way that a suitable program can reconstruct it. Consequently, not only would downloading MP3 data from an internet site be considered a sound file, but commercially produced CD and DVD recordings are sound files, too.

HOWARD FERSTLER

SOUND PRESERVATION AND RESTORATION OF HISTORICAL RECORDINGS

This article has 10 sections:

1. Introduction, Definition of Sound Preservation
2. Formats, especially Obsolete Formats
3. Deterioration of Formats
4. Cleaning and Repairing Formats
5. Playback Equipment
6. Current Standard Preservation Formats (Analog and Digital)
7. Recording Equipment
8. Equalization
9. The Re-recording or Transfer Process
10. Definition of Sound Restoration

1. *Introduction.* is the process of saving and protecting any auditory material, which has significant historical and cultural value from a deteriorating recording medium before the medium becomes unplayable. Sound Preservation is also protecting any articulation made by vocal apparatus (oral histories including radio broadcasts, speeches, interviews, and literature) or any recorded rhythm, melody, or harmony composed to create music (jazz, folk, blues, classical and rock 'n' roll) from injury or destruction. Sound preservation is the professional cleaning and transfer of the original recording to the highest quality technology using the best recording medium available at the time the work has to be done for the sake of saving it for years to come. The resulting sound preservation master should be the fairest representation of the original recording.

Prior to Sound Preservation, archivists should consider a conservation program. Conservation includes assessing a sound collection to establish a condition baseline and/or triggering immediate preservation reformatting if the conditions or the technology indicate such action. Conservation consists of re-housing sound materials into new containers and placing these materials in a monitored temperature (between 65°–75°F) and humidity-controlled (between 40–60% relative humidity (RH)) environment until either a deterioration issue occurs in the collection or before the playback equipment for the sound format becomes obsolete.

Sound preservation is done by sound preservation engineers in specialized commercial sound preservation laboratories or by in-house sound archivists at universities or institutions. The purpose of sound preservation is to preserve the sound of original source material that may be deteriorating. This article focuses on the craft of Sound Preservation. The definition of Sound Restoration can be at the end of the article.

2. *Formats.* The recordings to be preserved can range from wax cylinders, to broadcast transcription discs or acetate disc recordings, to wire, open reel tape that are acetate or polyester base, audio cassettes, belt or band recordings or vinyl recording discs, audio on film or VHS tapes, Digital Audio Tapes (DATs) and mini discs among other formats. These recordings are made of a variety of materials. There have even been recordings made on unusual materials such as x-ray film that needed to be preserved. See DISC for Wax Cylinders, Acetate and Vinyl records, TAPE for various tape formats and see below for a few obsolete belt formats and an obsolete cellulose acetate disc format.

Dictabelt

As stated in a Dictaphone brochure, "Ahead of your time with the Dictaphone Time-Master" was their invitation to prospective buyers and in language that dates the machine: "Thousands of business executives, doctors, lawyers, government men and others whose thoughts are important rely on Time-Masters and Dictabelts as their thoughts thruway." Dictabelt was the medium, or software, as we would call it today, for the famous Dictaphone machine, which was introduced in 1947 by the Dictaphone Corporation. At one time there were tens of thousands of them in the offices of American insurance companies alone. Ten years later Dictaphone would introduce its first magnetic recorder, the Dictet, but the Dictabelt had another decade of life in it, and a few Dictabelts were in service even as late as the 1980's. But by 1979, when Pitney Bowes acquired Dictaphone, they had virtually disappeared. Today it is difficult to find even one.

Dictabelts are composed of a soft cellulose acetate material and contain visible grooves on them. They come in a variety of colors including red, purple and blue.

Magnabelt

In dictation machines, the switch from stylus-and-groove to magnetic belts occurred mainly in the mid 1960's, and magnetic belt dictation machines were being manufactured as late as the mid-1980's by IBM. The new machines were similar in appearance to the older machines, but boasted greater fidelity and the ability to erase and re-use belts. Dictaphone was, of course, a major player in this new technology, which it continued to call the Dictabelt. But Dictaphone had a serious competitor, IBM, whose machines were not compatible with Dictaphone's. There was also a third player, Gray Manufacturing, whose machines were compatible with IBM but not with Dictaphone's. The Gray's were known for their exceptional ruggedness. Lanier Worldwide eventually bought Gray Manufacturing's technologies. Those technologies were sold to companies in Germany.

Magnabelts are quite similar in appearance and operation to the Dictabelt visible belt machines but obviously do not contain grooves. The magnetic belt is made with either acetate or mylar backing.

Dictalog Magnabelt

The Dictalog Magnabelt was manufactured by The Dictaphone Corporation in the 1950s. Only 1,000 of the DL-3A model were made. These machines were used by the U.S. Government in the DEW line radar defense system and by corporations and law firms, who used them for dictating letters because they held twice as much information than the traditional magnetic belts. A well-known sound engineer in the Midwest with extensive experience on this equipment recounted that often a lawyer on a business trip would phone in letters after hours for his secretary to type in the morning. As technology created smaller units that recorded more information these machines became obsolete. However, the belts were sold into the late 1960s.

Dictalog Magnabelts are similar in appearance to Magnabelts but are longer in length than the Magnabelts.

Memovox Disc

The essential technology of a Memovox is stylus-and-groove. An amplified signal was used to drive a stylus that cut analogous grooves into a sixteen-inch cellulose acetate disc. However, Memovox incorporated a lead screw that kept the disc rotating at a constant linear velocity across the stylus. This feature greatly increased the capacity of the medium. The disc is often clear or milky white and the recording plays from inside out.

3. *Deterioration Issues of Formats.* Identifying deterioration issues in the formats is an essential step in sound preservation prior to cleaning so that the engineer does not cause further distress to the format. All formats will collect dirt and debris depending on how they have been stored. Some formats will have developed mold or fungus and others will display other deterioration issues depending on their composition and how they have been stored. The problems can range from tape with sticky shed syndrome or vinegar syndrome, to broken discs, to discs that have lacquer peeling off. There are discs in the collection that could have issues such as palmitic acid and powder residue. Some sound collections can even suffer from biological infestation. Identifying the deterioration issue is key in deciding how the format should be cleaned. Here are some common deterioration issues:

Peeling Lacquer

Moving to first generation or instantaneous discs, these so-called acetates were manufactured with an aluminum, glass or cardboard base. The base was then coated with nitrocellulose lacquer plasticized with castor oil. This was an unstable mixture making these acetates not suitable for long-term storage. Symptoms or problems include continuous shrinking of the lacquer top coating, embrittlement, and irreversible loss of recorded sound because of the loss of the castor oil plasticizer. Since the core does not shrink and the lacquer coating does (or expands under changes in temperature), cracking and peeling of the lacquer coating results.

Palmitic Acid

The production of palmitic acid is caused by the hydrolysis of the castor oil from heat and humidity, which then oozes through the lacquer on a disc. The specks or small mounds on the groove look similar to powder residue but have a more crystallized appearance. Palmitic acid is stubborn to remove and requires extensive hand cleaning.

Powder Residue

Powder residue may appear on lacquer discs as dried white specks or pasty mounds on the grooves. The main symptom is caused by glue from the paper label, which has spread over time onto the recording surface of the disc. Sometimes powder residue is mistaken for mold or palmitic acid.

Vinegar Syndrome

Cellulose acetate reel-to-reel tapes and acetate discs are subject to a slow form of chemical deterioration known as vinegar syndrome. The main symptoms of this problem are a vinegar-like odor and buckling, shrinking, and embrittlement of the tape or cellulose disc. Low temperature storage conditions can aid in slowing down this process. More on Vinegar Syndrome can be found in an article, "Vinegar Syndrome: An Experience with the Silent but Stinky Acetate Tape Killer" published at www.cuttingarchives.com. There is a product by the Image Permanence Institute for measuring the level of acidity. The color on the strip, blue, will change to mustard yellow as it detects high acidity.

Sticky Shed Syndrome

Polyester magnetic tape stock, which came into wide use in the 1960s can develop a condition known as sticky shed syndrome. This problem occurs when oxidation of the tape sticks to the guides and magnetic heads of the playback machine. All polyester based tapes are susceptible to hydrolysis — the absorption of water molecules into the tapes' binder. Over time, particularly for tape stored in moist environments, this accumulation of water molecules causes the binder to become gummy and sticky. Upon playback this tape will stick to the heads and guides of the playback machine and will shed flakes of iron oxide. This causes distortion to the sound of the recording that is called separation or shed loss and can sometimes bring the tape playing on the machine to a grinding halt. It results in very low-level volume, fuzzy sound or inaudible audio.

Tape manufacturers changed the chemistry of their binders in the mid-1970s (approximately 1975) and tapes produced between that time and the mid-1980s are particularly at risk for signs of this sticky shed syndrome.

Mold Growth

Mold is caused by the growth of fungus in elevated temperature or humidity conditions. It can cause serious distortion and physical breakdown in most audio formats, both grooved and magnetic formats alike. The other major agent involved in fungal action is the presence of organic material on the recording medium due to unclean storage areas.

Biological Infestation

On occasion, due to the environment of where the audio materials are stored, the materials will be affected by unusual conditions such as biological infestation. For example, in hot and humid conditions and flood conditions, termites have been known to make their home in open reel tapes. They ate through the reel cardboard boxes and took residence on the tape under the plastic reels.

4. *Cleaning and Repairing Formats.* As stated above, in order to clean and repair the various sound formats, it is important to know the composition of the format and understand the deterioration or problem condition. As a rule of thumb, the formats should be cleaned with the most non-invasive methods as possible. There are times, though, when in order to save the audio from the format, heroic measures might be taken with the approval of the sound collection owner.

Most disc recordings are cleaned with record cleaning solutions, which are usually composed of a degree of dish detergent to many parts distilled water. For more stubborn or complex conditions, for example, acetate reel-to-reel tapes suffering from vinegar syndrome need to be isolated and transferred from all other sound collections especially acetate based recordings and transferred on dedicated playback machines. Polyester based reel-to-reels suffering from sticky shed syndrome either can be baked in a convection oven or undergo treatment in a food dehydrator. In certain cases, commercially manufactured solutions followed by a distilled water washing can be employed.

5. *Playback Equipment.* The sound preservation lab should be equipped with a wide assortment of playback machines. For example, the lab should have a variety of tape playback machines that accommodate various speeds, tracks, and tape sizes. The lab should be equipped with turntables that can accommodate various sized discs and variable disc speeds. It is also important to be equipped with a large array of styli and cartridges. It is important to have a variety of sizes and shape styli. Having the proper phono pre-amp is also an essential part of the playback equipment. A variable e.q. preamplifier can allow the engineer to transfer disc recordings at a pre-Recording Industries Association of America (RIAA) curve setting or a RIAA curve setting depending on when the disc was originally made.

Often, playback equipment is not readily available especially for obsolete audio formats. In those cases, sound labs usually rebuild machines or reverse engineer transfer machines cannibalizing parts from old machines.

Experienced technical engineers should routinely maintain all playback machines.

6. *Current Standard Preservation Formats. (Analog and Digital)* Today some institutions still prefer to preserve their sound collections on ¼-inch open reel analog tape while others choose to digitize their sound collections. Some archivists prefer to have both analog and digital preservation masters and user reference copies on CD-R. The following are typically the standards for both:

One-quarter-inch Open Reel Tape Preservation Master: One each to be a 7.5 ips, full track, 1/4 -inch analog recording made on 1.5 mil polyester audiotape stock. A 1 KHz, 250 nWB/m test tone will be placed at the head of each new preservation recording for reference purposes. This will be the preservation master able to replace the original recording media. This open reel copy shall be made with minimum signal processing so that it will be a fair representation of the original recording.

Digitized Files: Master Files in 96 kHz 24 bit WAV file stored on CD-R, DVD-R, or Removable Hard-Drives depending on size and archivist's needs. Service Files or Reference Copies are made at 44.1 kHz 16 bit WAV and/or mp3 (monaural at a data rate of 128 kbps or stereo at a data rate of 256 kbps). Some archivists request Service Files in streaming audio format. Reference Copies are often made available on CD-R format. The Master and Service Files are usually recorded onto hard disc and can also be FTP'd (File Transfer Protocol) directly to the archivist's secured server. The CD-R stock is normally an archive grade CD made with a phthalocyanine based dye.

7. *Recording Equipment* Quality Assurance starts with the condition of the recording equipment. Analog Tape Decks should be checked by technical engineers for the following: distortion, frequency response, Signal to Noise Ratio, crosstalk, gain difference and phase difference. The machine specifications should be teched out with appropriate calibration tapes. Burned CD-Rs are analyzed by compact disc quality analyzers for any errors. The engineer also A/Bs the original recording to the preservation recording that is being made to assure the fairest representation of the original recording.

8. *Equalization.* For Sound Preservation, the archivist tends to seek a clear and fair representation copy or "forensic" copy not a "restore" copy of their original recordings. The Sound Preservation engineers use selective filtering only in cases where quality or intelligibility of original recording should be improved. The engineers do not apply specific technical applications if it is beyond appropriate filtering and moderate noise reduction without consulting the archivist first.

9. *The Rerecording or Transfer Process.*
   a. inspect the sound format
   b. identify any deterioration issues
   c. clean or repair the format prior to transferring
   d. reference signals are recorded
   e. format is transferred
   f. during transfer the engineer will A/B to compare preservation recording with new recording to ensure the fairest representation
   g. Reference or Service copies are made
   h. Original recording is re-housed

10. *Sound Restoration.* Sound restoration is the process of restoring, renewing, reviving, re-purposing, or re-establishing auditory material as well as the restitution of music or vocals that have been lost. Where sound preservation is a fair representation of the original recording, sound restoration is a recovery of the original recording and even an enhancement to authenticate the original recording. Today with the aid of advanced digital audio software, sound engineers can enhance and work to restore lost audio by removing clicks, pops, tape hiss and surface noise to improve the sound beyond the preservation master.

I would like to thank Alan F. Lewis, AV Archives Consultant of Washington, D.C. for assistance of viewing this from the curatorial standpoint. I would like to thank my colleague, Robert G. Norton who has provided both a keen interest and invaluable expertise in the area of sound preservation. I would also like to thank all of the innovative sound preservation and recording engineers at The Cutting Corporation that I have had the pleasure of working with over the years. I would also like to thank Mary D.L. Cutting and James H. B. Cutting of The Cutting Corporation for their inspiration and leadership. — *Ranjita (Anji) Kalita Cornette*, Director, The Cutting Corporation, Sound Preservation Laboratory, Bethesda, Maryland. For more information, you can email me at cuttingarchives@aol.com, or visit www.cuttingarchives.com.

SOUND RECORDING

The process of registering and reproducing sonic signals. Various means and devices have been applied to this task, beginning with the Phonautograph of 1857, proceeding through cylinder phonographs and disc Gramophones, wire and tape recordings, cassettes, compact discs, and DAT. A description of the way each of those recordings is made is given in the appropriate article.

See **Cylinder; Disc; Recording Practice**

SOUND RECORDING CO., LTD.

A firm established in March 1910 in London to make discs for use with motion picture films. Grammavox was the first label; other labels made later included Champion, Standard, Beacon, Butterfly, Popular, and Stavophone. Imperial was the final label issued, as successor to Popular. The company was absorbed by Crystalate Gramophone Record Manufacturing Co., Ltd., in July 1925.

FRANK ANDREWS

SOUND RECORDINGS AND THE LIBRARY

Guido Biagi, librarian of the Royal Library at Florence, predicted in a talk at the 1904 conference of the American Library Association that "there will be a few readers but an infinite number of hearers, who will listen from their own homes to the spoken paper, to the spoken book. University students will listen to their lectures while they lie in bed, and, as now with us, will not know their professors even by sight. But even if the graphophone does not produce so profound a transformation as to cause the alphabet to become extinct and effect an injury to culture itself ... still, these discs, now so much derided, will form a very large part of the future library" ["Phonographs" 1909].

In the years since his prediction, print has not been replaced by sound recordings, but recordings have become an important part of most libraries.

The first account of sound recordings in an American library was of the piano roll collection in the Evanston (Illinois) Public Library in 1907. Apparently the earliest library to include sound recordings other than piano rolls was the Academy of Sciences at Vienna, which initiated in 1909 its famous phonographic archives.

American libraries soon took interest in recordings, too. The earliest accounts of phonograph records being used in American libraries are sketchy, but it seems that they entered the library early in the 20th century. The Music Teachers National Association reported in 1913 that collections of piano rolls could be found in seven New York libraries, and collections of Gramophone records could be found in seven New York and four California libraries. The Forbes Library of Northampton, Massachusetts, reported in 1912 that it had bought one of the popular Graphophone cylinder machines. One of the first libraries to collect and circulate phonograph records was the St. Paul Library whose collection — for educational purposes only — began in 1914. Obviously the collection was well used, for it reported holdings in 1919 of nearly 600 records which accounted for a circulation of 3,505 for the year. These early accounts point to a growing interest in developing collections of sound recordings. The demands upon public libraries overcame the objections that recordings were fragile and easily damaged, that their sound quality was poor and deteriorated with use, and that they were very expensive for only three minutes of sound.

The earliest documented collection of sound recordings in an academic library was started in 1915 at the University of Wisconsin, in Madison. The earliest detailed information about the beginnings of a record collection in an academic environment refers to a gift from the Antioch College Class of 1928 that provided a fund, a portion of which was "allotted for the purchase of phonograph albums, which would circulate from the college library on the same basis as books" [Lyle 1934]. There were collections of recordings in colleges in that period, but they were generally restricted to students in music appreciation courses. Therefore, the institution of a circulating collection in a college library was innovative, and according to the report, successful. By 1930 the Antioch collection consisted of about 125 albums with a circulation rate of about 400 albums per month.

A review of the status of record collections in U.S. university libraries in the mid-1950s stated that "it is fruitless to look for uniformity in a field so tied up with technological changes and the rapidly fluctuating economy of record production. The administration of record collection will remain one of the frontier areas in librarianship for many years to come" [Duckles 1955]. A survey sent to 500 diverse American libraries in 1960 found that most sound recording collections were less than 15 years old and averaged in size between 100 and 1,000 recordings. [Davis 1960.]

In 1965 a meeting at the Henry Ford Museum in Dearborn, Michigan, by librarians of sound recording collections and private collectors led to the formation of the Association for Recorded Sound Collections (ARSC) in the following year. Other organizations that facilitate dialog among conservators of sound recording collections are the Record Libraries Commission of the International Association of Music Libraries (IAML) founded in 1951 and the International Association of Sound Archives (IASA) founded in 1969. Reports of the work of the Record Libraries Commission, often as summaries of the annual meetings, appear in issues of *Fontes Artis Musicae*. Since its founding, IASA has met annually with IAML, and there is an overlap of membership with the Record Libraries Commission.

In 1974 representatives of Stanford University, Yale University, the New York Public Library, and the Library of Congress met in New York to discuss means of facilitating the cataloging of their sound recording collections. This meeting led to the formation of the Associated Audio Archives (AAA) which was expanded to include the sound archives of Syracuse University and for a time the collection at the University of Toronto. The AAA has produced a set of cataloging rules, a union list of periodicals, and a union list of record manufacturers' catalogs. It developed and tested an innovative technique for cataloging sound recordings using microphotography with computer indexing, and produced the Rigler and Deutsch

Index, which gives access to a majority of the extant 78-rpm recordings.

SOUND RECORDING PERIODICALS

Journal articles about sound recording began to appear in many countries from the 1870s, as news of Thomas Edison's invention spread rapidly around the world. In Russia, in 1878, three articles dealing with the phonograph appeared: "Esche o govoriashchei mashine i fonografe Edissona" (*Svet*, no. 6); "Fonograf" (*Tekhnicheskii sbornik*, nos. 5–6); "Fonograf, govoriashchaia mashina" (*Zhurnal dlia vsekh*, T. 2). In 1894 an article on Thomas Edison appeared in the *Repertorio Colombiano*, from Bogotá, Colombia. By 1902 Russia had a magazine devoted to the Gramophone, *Grammofon i fonograf*. Several other Russian magazines began publication in the next few years, including *Grammofonnyi mir*, *Grammofonnaia zhisn*, and *Novosti grammofona*.

In the U.S., *Phonogram* appeared in 1891 and *The Phonoscope* — "the first independent publication to be devoted primarily to the phonograph field" [Read & Welch 1976] in 1896. *Talking Machine World* (U.S., 1905) was one of the most valuable periodicals for research into the industry. *Phonographische Zeitschrift* was the first German trade journal (1900). *Rivista fonografica italiana* was published in Milan from 1900.

Early recording magazines from England were *Phonogram*, which appeared ca. 1893, *Sound Wave* (1906), and *Talking Machine News* (1906). In France, *Bulletin phonographique et cinématographique* appeared ca. 1899, *Phonociné-gazette* in 1905, and *Musique et instruments* in 1911.

Lists of new records in turn-of-the-century phonograph/Gramophone magazines serve as an interesting chronicle of the entertainment tastes of the times. Many of the early publications contained illustrated interviews with leading personalities. They also offered technical material regarding the history and development of talking machines. In these early magazines, one can trace the rapid growth and expansion of the industry, through articles and reports about record production plants that opened around the world.

A number of more general American periodicals carried information on talking machines. These included *Scientific American* (1845–), *Electrical World* (1885–), *American Machinist* (1877–), *North American Review* (1815–), and the *Journal of the Franklin Institute* (1826–). Similar British periodicals included *Electrician* (1862–), *Electrical Review (1872–)*, *Musical Opinion and Musical Trades Review* (1877–), and *Nature* (1870–). In Germany there were such titles as *Elektrische Nachrichtentechnik* (1924–)

and *Elektrotechnische Zeitschrift* (1880–). Publications from France that presented material on talking machines included: *L'illustration: journal universel* (1843–), *Les inventions illustrées: Sciences, industrie, finance* (1899–), *La nature: revue des sciences et de leurs applications aux arts et à l'industrie* (1873–), *La science et la vie: magazine des sciences et de leurs applications à la vie moderne* (1913–), *La science illustrée* (1887–), and *Science pour tous: revue populaire de vulgarisation scientifique* (1856–).

Russian publications that contained references to early talking machines were: *Zhurnal noveishikh otkrytii i izobretenii* (1896–), *Zapiski russkogo tekhnicheskogo obshchestva* (1867–), *Nauka i zabava* (1893–), *Niva: il. zhurnal lit., politiki i sobr. zhizn'* (1870–), *Ogonek: khudozhestv.-lit. zhurnal* (1899–), *Elektrichestvo* (1880–), *Elektrichestvo i zhisn'* (1910–), *Elektrotekhnik* (1897–), and *Elektrotekhnicheskii vestnik* (1894–).

In the 1920s, sound recording periodicals continued to flourish and proliferate. One early magazine, *Gramophone*, which began in the U.K. in 1923, is still published, and so is *American Record Guide* (1935–). Another early American title, *New Records* (1933), continued publication until 1987. The French magazine, *Musique et instruments*, which underwent various title changes, and which eventually incorporated *Machines parlantes & radio*, began publication in 1911 and continued into the 1980s. As technical advances in sound reproduction increased, more new magazines appeared, recounting developments in sound recording, such as the advent of LPs, 45s, stereo, eight-track tapes, cassettes, CDs, digital audio tapes, etc. Magazines became more specialized to suit the varied needs of record dealers and buyers.

There have been magazines for classical music record collectors, such as: *Fanfare* (U.S.), *Record Collector* (England), *Vocal Art* (U.K.), *Diapason* (France), *Stimmen, die um die Welt gingen ...* (Germany), and *Musica* (Italy), as well as magazines for popular music collectors, such as: *Discoveries* (U.S.), *Goldmine* (U.S.), *Footnote* (later: *New Orleans Music*) (U.K.), *Memory Lane* (U.K.), and *Bulletin du hot club de France* (France). Special interest periodicals have included *The Picture-disk Collector* (Netherlands), *Soundtrack* (Belgium), *Show Music* (U.S.), *Antique Phonograph Monthly* (U.S.), *Jocks* (for disc jockeys; U.K.), *Metal Hammer/Crash* (for heavy metal rock; Germany), *The Beat* (for reggae, Caribbean, African; U.S.), *Latin Beat* (for Latin American, Caribbean; U.S.) and *Sound Choice* (for new age music; U.S.).

For audiophiles, such magazines as *Absolute Sound* (U.S.), *Audio* (U.S.), *Audio Amateur* (U.S.), *Audio Critic* (U.S.), *Stereophile* (U.S.), *Audio* (Germany),

Hi-Fi Stereophonie (Germany), and *High Fidelity* (Denmark) appeared. Other magazines had some technical articles along with extensive record reviews, such as *High Fidelity* (U.S.), *Stereo Review* (U.S.), *Gramophone* (U.K.), *Hi-Fi News* (later: *Hi-fi News & Record Review*) (U.K.), *Diapason/Harmonie* (France), *Fono Forum* (Germany), *Luister* (Netherlands), and *Playback and Fast Forward* (India).

Various association have published their own journals, such as: *ARSC Journal* (Association for Recorded Sound Collections), *B.A.S. Speaker* (Boston Audio Society), *British Institute of Recorded Sound Bulletin* (superseded by *Recorded Sound*), *In the Groove* (Michigan Antique Phonograph Society), *Phonographic Bulletin* (International Association of Sound Archives), and *The Phonographic Record* (Vintage Phonographic Society of New Zealand).

As popular musical styles changed and evolved, sound recording magazines documented the various trends. There were magazines featuring salon dance music, Big Bands, classical, blues, jazz, Latin, rock 'n' roll, disco, calypso, country, rock, heavy metal, reggae, new age, etc.

In the U.S., libraries with substantial collections of sound recording publications include: New York Public Library for the Performing Arts — Rodgers & Hammerstein Archives of Recorded Sound; Library of Congress — Motion Picture, Broadcasting and Recorded Sound Division; Yale University — Historical Sound Recordings Collection; Stanford University — Archive of Recorded Sound; Syracuse University — Belfer Audio Laboratory and Archive.

The list of titles that follows is a preliminary checklist of serial publication in the field of recorded sound. It is international in scope, but emphasizes U.S. periodicals. British and Canadian titles are well represented. Items from other countries are included if they appear in the New York Public Library catalogs or in standard English-language reference works, such as the *Union List of Serials*. The checklist includes house organs of record companies as well as independently produced publications. The periodicals appear in chronological order according to the dates of their first issues. Dates, country of publication, frequency, publisher, title variants, and content annotations are given whenever possible.

Serial Recorded Sound Journals:

1. *Phonogram.* A monthly magazine devoted to the science of sound and recording of speech. 1891–1893. New York, New York. Monthly. "Official organ of the phonograph companies of the United States."

2. *The Phonogram.* A monthly journal devoted to the science of sound and recording of speech. 1893–? London, England. Monthly.

The Phonogram Co., Ltd. Includes articles on the development of the phonograph and how to work it, lists of famous voices recorded by the phonograph, the uses put to the phonograph by actors and actresses, etc.

3. *Billboard.* Monthly (November 1894–May 1900); weekly (June 1900–). Cincinnati, Ohio etc. Title varies: *Billboard Music Week* (v. 73–74, 1961–1962). Material in the earliest years of the publication dealt with theatrical news, including columns highlighting the current theatrical activities and performers from Berlin, London, and Paris. There were also articles on vaudeville, carnivals, fairs, tent shows, and poultry shows; along with skating rink news, film advertisements, film reviews, and some musical news. Articles dealing with sound recordings and record reviews did not appear until the 1930s.

4. *Music, Art and Trade Journal and Talking Machine Review.* 1895–1930. London, England. Earlier title (1895–1925): *Music.* Merged into: *Music Dealer and Radio-Gramophone Review.*

5. *The Phonoscope.* A monthly journal devoted to scientific and amusement inventions appertaining to sound & sight. November 1896–June 1900. New York, New York. Includes illustrated articles on talking machines, inventors, artists, etc. Also mentions recordings of such persons as Sarah Bernhardt, Nellie Melba, Mark Twain, Lillie Langtry, and Ellen Terry. Includes articles on the autograph, zerograph, radiophone, megaphone, and cathoscope; x-rays; automatic slot machines; "picture projecting devices" such as vitascope, phantoscope, eidoloscope, biograph, cinematographe, theatrograph, and kineopticon. Contains brief reviews of films for "screen machines." Includes listings of new records with artist and record company; no record numbers. Listings of the latest popular songs and successes are given as well as listings of new films for projecting devices.

6. *Vsemirnoe tekhnicheskoe obozrenie.* Ezhemesiachnyi politekhnicheskii zhurnal. 1898–1917. St. Petersburg, Russia. Monthly.

7. *Bulletin phonographique et cinématographique.* 1899?–1900? Paris, France. M. Siry, director.

8. *Phonogram.* Printed monthly for those interested in phones, graphs, grams and scopes. "Devoted to the arts of recording and reproducing sound." May 1900–December 1902. New York, New York. Includes gramophone riddles, poems, cartoons, articles dealing with various uses for the phonograph, listings of Edison concert records with label numbers, including spoken word, songs sung in French, Italian, Yiddish, Latin, Swedish, etc., historical articles (example: "The Story of the Phonograph. History: Ancient, Medieval and Modern"), articles on popular theatrical artists.

9. *Canadian Music and Trades Journa.* 1900–? Toronto, Canada. Irregular. Later titles: *Canadian Music Trades Journal* (ca. 1907–1929); *Canadian Music and Radio Trades* (1931).

10. *Phonographische Zeitschrift; Fachblatt für die gesamte Musik-und Sprechmaschinen-Industrie.* 1900–1938. Berlin, Germany. Frequency varies. Organ of Internationaler Verein fur Phonographisches Wissen, Reichsverband des Deutschen Sprechmaschinen-und Schallplatten-Handels, and others. Later titles: *Phonographische und Radio-Zeitschrift; Phonographische, Radio und Musikinstrumenten Zeitschrift.*

11. *Rivista fonografica italiana.* Periodico mensile illustrato. 1900–? Milan, Italy. Monthly.

12. *Grammofon i fonograf.* 1902–1906. St. Petersburg, Russia. Tipografiia N.N. Klobukova. Weekly. Includes listings of newly released recordings, historical surveys of the phonograph/Gramophone industry, illustrated biographical articles of important persons in the Gramophone industry, illustrated articles of early Russian Gramophone apparatus, including factories, libretti of popular recorded songs and arias, illustrated vignettes of well-known artists. Later titles: *Svet i zvuk* ; *Grammofon i fotografiia.*

13. *The Columbia Record.* 1903–? New York, New York. Columbia Phonograph Co. Monthly. Includes news of various early graphophone dealers and stores, technical articles, interviews with performers, brief record reviews, etc.

14. *Edison Amberola Monthly. See Edison Phonograph Monthly.*

15. *Edison Phonograph Monthly.* 1903–? Orange, New Jersey. Monthly. Published for trade use only by the National Phonograph Co. Includes advance listings of new Edison molded records with artists and label numbers, sales information, and lists of U.S. and Canadian jobbers of phonographs and records.

16. *The Talking Machine News.* May 1903–? London, England. Original title: *Talking

Machine News and Record Exchange (nos. 1–2), followed by *Talking Machine New and Cinematograph Chronicle* (nos. 3–29). Subtitles dropped with no. 30 (October 1905). From no. 157 to no. 177? titled *Talking Machine News and Journal of Amusements.* Publication continued into 1930s. Monthly and semimonthly. "The recognized organ of the trade." Includes illustrated articles on popular artists, historical articles, record reviews, technical articles dealing with the upkeep and proper use of talking machines and recordings, and trade articles.

17. *The New Phonogram.* 1904? Orange, New Jersey. Monthly. The National Phonograph Co. Variant title: *The Phonogram.* Includes listings of new Edison records with label numbers, artists and capsule reviews, phonograph cartoons, and poems.

18. *Phono-ciné-gazette.* Revue illustrée des questions intéressant le phonographe, le gramophone. 1905–1908? Paris, France. Bi-monthly. Edmond Benoit Lévy, director. Contains record reviews, concert reviews, listings of spectacles (theater, music hall, etc.), phonograph poems, cartoons, illustrations of artists, theater news, and film news.

19. *Die Sprechmaschine.* Fachzeitschrift für die gesamte Sprechmaschinen-Industrie des In- und Auslandes. 1905–1914. Berlin, Germany. Bi-weekly.

20. *Svet i zvuk.* 1905–1906. St. Petersburg, Russia. Monthly. Formerly: *Grammofon i fonograf.* Includes illustrated technical articles, historical gramophone articles, lyrics of popular arias, and current happenings in the talking machine industry.

21. *The Talking Machine World.* 1905–1934. New York, New York. Later titles: *Talking Machine World & Radio Music Merchant* (from January 1929), *Radio-Music Merchant.*

22. *Sound Wave.* The Gramophone journal. 1906–1941. Finsbury, England. Monthly. Variant title: *The Sound Wave and Talking Machine Record.* Incorporates: *The Phono Trader & Recorder.* Includes articles on popular artists, listings of recordings from various companies such as Gramophone Co., Edison, Sterling, Columbia, Odeon, Zonophone, Beka, Neophone, Imperial, and Edison Bell, giving label numbers, composers and artists; large section of record reviews, technical articles dealing with fine points of recording and playback, articles dealing with novel uses for the phonograph, such as street gospel meet-

ings, the improvement of Jewish synagogue singers, etc.

23. *The Voice of the Victor.* The trade journal of the Victor Talking Machine Co. 1906–1930? Camden, New Jersey. Monthly. Includes industry news, articles dealing with different uses for the Gramophone, listings of new recordings with label numbers, and reviews.

24. *Novosti grammofona* [Gramophone news]. 1907–1908. St. Petersburg, Russia. Monthly. Includes record listings with label numbers, artists and repertoire, illustrated technical articles, illustrated vignettes of artists, texts of recorded songs and arias, etc.

25. *Gramophone & Talking Machine News.* A musical paper for all. 1908?–1928? London, England. Monthly. Includes articles on recording artists, listings of new recordings with company and label numbers, illustrated technical articles, opera synopses, and record reviews.

26. *Ofitsial'nye izvestiia aktsionernogo obshchestva grammofon.* [Gramophone Co. news]. 1908– 1910. Moscow, Russia. Monthly. Continues as *Pishushchii amur i grammofonnye novosti* in 1910. Includes listings of recommended and best new recordings, articles on the Gramophone industry, Zonophone news, small record reviews, articles dealing with Gramophone libraries, Gramophone Co. news from around the world, and humorous Gramophone cartoons.

27. *The Talking Machine News and Journal of Amusements.* 1908?–? London, England. Monthly. Supersedes *The Talking Machine News.* Consecutive numbers are odd-numbered only. Includes illustrated articles on popular artists, record reviews, musical articles, a column written by Mikhail Mordkin titled: "The art of dancing and the talking machine," illustrated technical articles.

28. *Unterricht und Sprechmaschine.* 1908?–1914? Stuttgart, Germany. Publisher: Wilhelm Violet.

29. *Grammofonnyi mir/die Grammophon-Welt* [Gramophone World]. 1910–1917. St. Petersburg, Russia. Monthly. Includes articles in German and Russian, capsule record reviews, technical articles, and illustrated sketches of artists.

30. *Pishushchiiamur i grammofonnye novosti.* 1910–1911. Moscow, Russia. Formerly: *Ofitsial'nye izvestiia aktsionernogo obschestva Grammofon.*

31. *Die Stimme seines Herrn.* 1910–1916. Berlin, Germany. Monthly. Issued by the German

branch of the Gramophone Co. Includes record listings with label numbers, illustrated historical articles, illustrated articles on popular performers, and record reviews.

32. *Grammofonnia zhizn'* [Gramophone Life]. 1911–1912. Moscow, Russia. Bi-weekly. Fabrikant i optovik. Includes listings of new recordings, illustrated technical and historical articles, concert, opera and operetta reviews, illustrated articles about popular artists, and capsule record reviews.

33. *Musique et instruments*. Revue générale de l'industrie et du commerce de la musique des machines parlantes et de la radio. 1911–1984? Paris, France. Weekly, bi-monthly. Auguste Bosc, director. Later title: *Musique et radio*. Absorbed in September 1939: *Machines parlantes & radio*.

34. *Duo-Art Music*. 1913?–1930?. New York, New York: Aeolian Company. Monthly.

35. *Musique-addresses*. Annuaire français de la facture instrumentale, de l'édition musicale et des industries quis'y rattachent. 1913–? Paris, France. Annual. Auguste Bosc, director. Title variant: Annuaire O.G.M.

36. *Muzykal'noe ekho*. 1914. Vilna, Lithuania. Organ of Posviashchennyi grammofonnoi promyshlennosti.

37. *Pishuschii amur*. Zhurnal torgovykh izvestii obschestva "Grammofon." 1914–1916. Petrograd, Russia. Amur Co. Includes copious illustrations of early Russian Gramophone factories and their various operational activities, illustrated articles of popular artists, and listings of new recordings with artists and label numbers. Articles dealing with various uses of the Gramophone include "The Gramophone in the Monastery."

38. *Edison Diamond Points*. 1915–? Orange, New Jersey. Monthly. "Devoted entirely to the Edison Diamond Disc Phonograph and record business. Includes industry articles, music articles, and capsule record reviews.

39. *Along Broadway*. The Edison musical magazine. 1916–? Orange, New Jersey. Monthly. Thomas A. Edison, Inc. Includes illustrated articles on popular artists, musical articles, and record reviews.

40. *The Phonograph*. A musical news weekly. 1916–1978. New York, New York. Weekly. Later titles: *Phonograph and Talking Machine Weekly* (July 1919–5 Sept 5, 1928); *Talking Machine and Radio Weekly* (12 Sep 1928–6 Dec 1933); *Radio Weekly* (13 Dec 1933–26 Apr 1939); *Radio and Television Weekly* (3 May 1939–1978). Includes mainly news of the recording industry.

41. *The Talking Machine Journal*. The national journal of the talking machine industry. 1916–1957. New York, New York City. Monthly. Later titles: *The Talking Machine and Radio Journal*; *Radio & Electric Appliance Journal*; *Radio-Television Journal*; *Radio-Television Journal & The Talking Machine World*; *Radio Journal*; *Radio Television Journal*; *Radio and Appliance Journal*; *RTJ* (*Radio and Television Journal*). Issues for May 1919–June 1923 include listing of "latest record releases." Includes industry news, record statistics (example: "The fastest selling Victor records"), and historical articles.

42. *Victor Educational Bulletin*. 1916–1918. Camden, New Jersey.

43. *The Voice* . The magazine of the Gramophone Co., Ltd. 1916–? Hayes, Middlesex, England. Irregular.

44. *Audio*. 1917–1935. San Francisco, California, New York, New York etc. Suspended publication June 1917–December 1919. Variant titles: *Pacific Radio News* (January 1917–October 1921), *Radio; Audio Engineering*.

45. *The Tonearm*. 1918?–1919? Bridgeport, Connecticut. Monthly. Columbia Phonograph Co., Inc., American Graphophone Co., Columbia Graphophone Manufacturing Co.

46. *Revue des machines parlantes*. 1919–1929. Paris, France. Monthly. Later title: *Machines parlantes et radio*. Edité par L'Office de la Musique.

47. *The Victor Tourist*. 1919?–? For the Victor traveling staff. Camden, New Jersey.

48. *Weekly Bulletin* [Victor]. 1919?–? Camden, New Jersey.

49. *Phono-radio-musique*. Radiophonie, Phonographie, Télévision. 1920?–1937? Paris, France. Monthly. Organe de la Chambre Syndicale de L'Industrie et du Commerce Français des Machines Parlantes. J.M. Gilbert, director.

50. *Record Review* — 1920?–1921? New York, New York. Bi-monthly. Columbia Graphophone Co., Educational Department.

51. *The Total Eclipse*. 1920?–? U.S. Monthly. "Published monthly by the Eclipse Musical Company in the interests of Victor merchants."

52. *Better Selling Bulletin*. 1921?–1923? U.S. Weekly. Later title: *Better Letters Bulletin*. Includes letters to Penn-Victor dealers from the Penn Phonograph Co.

53. *The Gramophone*. 1923–. London, England. Monthly. Title variants: *The Radio Gramophone* (v. 7, no. 84–v. 8, no. 89), *Gramophone*. Includes music articles, listings of recommended recordings, record society articles, and comprehensive record reviews and criticism.

54. *Power*. RCA Victor Service Notes. 1923–1945? Camden, New Jersey. RCA Victor Company, Inc. Irregular.

55. *Elektrische Nachrichtentechnik*. 1924–1943? Berlin, Germany. Monthly? Publisher: K.W. Wagner.

56. *Australasian Phonograph Monthly*. 1925–1927. Sydney, Australia. Publisher: Count L. de Noskowski. Includes articles and record reviews of such labels as Apex, Brunswick, Columbia, HMV, Parlophone, Edison Diamond Discs, and Polydor.

57. *Jahrbuch für Phonotechnik und Phonokunst*. 1925–1927? Berlin, Germany. Variant title: *Internationales Jahrbuch für Phonotechnik und Phonokunst*.

58. *Listener In*. 1925–? Melbourne, Australia. Monthly. Adgar H. Baillie, United Propriety, Ltd. "The wireless journal of Australia."

59. *Radio matériel*. 1925. Paris, France. Monthly. Later title: *Radio et phono matériel*; Revue mensuelle des négociants en T.S.F. et machines parlantes.

60. *Music Lovers' Phonograph Monthly Review*. 1926–1932. Boston, Massachusetts. Monthly. The Phonograph Publishing Co., Inc. "An American magazine for amateurs interested in phonographic music and its development — only American magazine of its kind." Title variant: *The Phonograph Monthly Review* (October 1926–June 1927). Superseded by *Music Lover's Guide*. Includes technical articles with illustrations, articles on recording personalities, the recording industry, comprehensive record reviews, reports from phonograph societies, and listings of new releases with company and label information.

61. *L'édition musicale vivante*; Études critiques de la musique enregistrée: disques, rouleaux perforés, etc. 1927–1933. Paris, France. Monthly. Superseded by *Sélection de la vie artistique* (1934–1935).

62. *The Music Seller Reference Book*. 1927–1936? London, England. Annual. Evan Bros. Ltd. Variant title: *Music Seller and Radio Music Trader*. "Records and music issued." Includes factors (agents) of Gramophone records, addresses of record manufacturers, alphabetical index to separate numbers of operas and oratorios, alphabetical listings of Gramophone records with title, artist, record company and label number, music publisher, addresses of music publishers, list of published sheet music, and classified index of manufacturers and suppliers.

63. *Musique*. Revue d'histoire, de critique, d'esthétique et d'informations musicales. 1927–1930? Paris, France. Monthly. Robert Lyon, director. Marc Pincherle, editor-in-chief. Includes music articles, phonograph articles, book reviews, record reviews, concert reviews, etc.

64. *The Gramophone Review*. 1928–1929. London, England.

65. *Gramophone World and Record Times*. 1928–? London, England.

66. *Le phono*. 1928–? Paris, France. Weekly.

67. *Phono-magazine*. 1928–? Paris, France. Monthly.

68. *Die Tonwiedergabe*. 1928–1938? Vienna, Austria. Fachblatt für Industrie, Handel und Export aller an der Tonwiedergabe Interessierten Kreise.

69. *Grammotechnik*. 1929?–1932? Prague, Czechoslovakia. Verband für Industrie und Handel der Grammophon- und Musikinstrumenten-Branche in der CSSR, Prag.

70. *De gramophoon revue*. 1929–1933. Amsterdam, Netherlands. Monthly. Absorbed by *Schijven schouw*. Published by A.J.G. Strengholt en Allert de Lange. Includes articles on popular recording artists, illustrated technical articles, listings of recordings with label numbers from different companies, and record reviews, both pop and classical.

71. *Kultur und Schallplatte*. 1929–1931? Berlin, Germany. Monthly. "Mitteilungen der Carl Lindström AG, Kulturabteilung." Includes music articles, record releases, and record reviews.

72. *Machines parlantes & radio*. 1929–1939. Continues numbering of *Revue des machines parlantes*. Paris, France. Monthly. Absorbed by: *Musique et instruments*.

73. *Phono-revue*. 1929–? Paris, France. Monthly.

74. *Disques*. 1930–1933. Philadelphia, Pennsylvania. Monthly. Superseded by *The New Records*.

75. *Sprechmaschinen-Radio-Zeitung*. 1930–1932. Berlin, Germany. Variant title: *Radio und Sprechmaschine-Zeitung*. A supplement to *Musik-Instrumenten Zeitung*.

76. *International Record Collector's Club. Bulletin.* 1932–1956. Bridgeport, Connecticut.

77. *Music Lovers' Guide.* 1932–1935. New York, New York. Monthly.

78. *Wurlitzer's Record Notes.* 1932–1935. New York, New York. Monthly.

79. *The Gramophone Record.* 1933–1953? London, England. Monthly. Continues as: *Gramophone Record Review.*

80. *The New Records.* 1933–1987. Philadelphia, Pennsylvania. Monthly. H. Royer Smith Company. Supersedes *Disques.*

81. *Record Review.* 1933–1953. Truro, England. Title varies: *Gramophone Record and Home Musician; Gramophone Record* (1949?–1953), *Gramophone Record Review* (1953).

82. *Recorded Music.* Privately printed in the interests of and dedicated to the gramophoniac at large. 1933–1934. New York, New York. Monthly.

83. *American Record Guide.* 1935–. Milbrook, New York. Bi-monthly. Former titles: *The American Music Lover; The Listener's Record Guide; Music Lovers' Guide.* Absorbed by *The American Tape Guide.*

84. *Disques.* 1935?–1962? Paris, France. Originally a monthly supplement to *Phono-radio-musique*, then became an independent title.

85. *The Monthly Letter.* (E.M.G. Hand-Made Gramophones, Ltd.) 1936–1980. London, England. Monthly.

86. *H.R.S. Society Rag.* 1938–1941? U.S.

87. *Victor Record Review.* May 1938–February 1949. Camden, New Jersey. Monthly. Continued by *RCA Victor Record Review.* Combined with *RCA Victor's In the Groove.*

88. *Gateway to Music, Los Angeles. On the Record.* 1939–1947. U.S. Monthly.

89. *Records.* A monthly review. 1939–1940. New York, New York. Monthly.

90. *The Steinway Review of Permanent Music* (November 1939–January 1942). New York, New York. Monthly. Variant titles: *Review of Permanent Music* (February 1942–December 1949), *Review of Recorded Music* (January 1950–May 1958).

91. *Listen.* Guide to Good Music. 1940–1950? New York, New York. Monthly.

92. *Co-Art Turntable.* 1941–1943. Beverly Hills, California. Monthly.

93. *Cash Box.* 1941–. New York, New York. Weekly. Identifies and lists most popular recordings, from 25 Mar 1950.

94. *International Records Agency. Bulletin.* 1942–1950. Richmond Hill, New York. Bulletin. Modern imported and domestic phonograph records.

95. *The Record Changer.* 1942–1957. New York, New York [varies]. Monthly.

96. *Coda.* 1943–1946. Bridgeport, Connecticut. Monthly. Columbia Records. Superseded by *Columbia's Disc Digest.*

97. *Critique.* A review of gramophone records. 1943–1955. London, England: Gramophone Exchange. Monthly.

98. *The Jazz Record.* 1943–1947. New York, New York. Monthly.

99. *Music Views.* 1943–1959. Hollywood, California. Capitol Records. Variant titles: *Capitol News; Music News; Capitol; News from Hollywood.*

100. *Record Retailing.* 1943–1954. New York, New York. Monthly. Continued by *Record and Sound Retailing.*

101. *The Needle.* Record Collector's Guide. 1944–1945. Jackson Heights, New York. Three per year. Jazz reviews.

102. *Musica e dischi.* 1945–1986. Milan, Italy. Monthly. Variant title (v. 1. no. 1): *Musica; Rassegna della vita musicale italiana.* Superseded by *M & D.*

103. *A.J.Q. Handbook.* (Australian Jazz Quarterly.) 1945–? Melbourne, Australia. Quarterly.

104. *Audio Record.* (Audio Devices, Inc.) 1945–? New York, New York.

105. *Record Review.* 1945–1947. New York, New York. G. Schirmer. Monthly.

106. *Columbia Promotion News.* 1946–1950. Bridgeport, Connecticut. Monthly.

107. *Columbia's Disc Digest.* 1946–1947. Bridgeport, Connecticut. Monthly. Supersedes *Coda.*

108. *Disc.* 1946–?. Mt. Morris, Illinois.

109. *RCA Victor's In the Groove.* 1946–1949? Camden, New Jersey. Monthly.

110. *The Record Collector.* 1946–. Ipswich, Suffolk [etc.] England. Monthly. Includes extensive discographies on early singers. Variant titles: *Bulletin* (v. 1, nos. 1–4), *Record Collector's Bulletin* (v. 1, nos. 5–8).

111. *Record World.* 1946?–1982. New York, New York. Weekly.

112. *Audio.* 1947–. Philadelphia. Monthly. Formerly: *Audio Engineering.*

113. *Disc.* 1947–?. Bristol, England. City of Bristol Gramophone Society.

114. *Swing. Journal.* 1947–. Toyko, Japan. Monthly. Jazz recordings.

115. *The Discophile*. 1948–1958. London, England. Bimonthly. Absorbed (January 1959) by *Matrix*.

116. *Just Records*. (Elaine Music Shop.) 1948–1950? New York, New York. Monthly.

117. *Phonolog Reporter*. 1948–. San Diego, California. Trade Service Publications, Inc. Title varies. Weekly. A loose-leaf service, maintaining a 6,000–page list of 1 million current recordings, classical and popular.

118. *Ceskoslovenská diskografie*; Gramofonové závody. 1949–. Prague, Czechoslovakia.

119. *RCA Victor Picture Record Review*. 1949–1953. Camden, New Jersey. Monthly. Supersedes *RCA Victor Record Review*.

120. *RCA Victor Record Review*. (RCA Victor) v. 1, no. 1, April 1949–v. 1, no. 6, September 1949. Camden, New Jersey. Former title *Victor Record Review*. Superseded by *RCA Victor Picture Record Review*.

121. *Record Letter*. 1949–1950. Kirkland, Washington. Irregular. Superseded by *American Record Letter* and *International Record Letter*.

122. *Record News*. 1949–1951. Brighton, England. Monthly.

123. *Schwann Long Playing Record Catalog*. 1949–1989. Boston, Massachusetts. Monthly [varies]. Title varies: *Schwann Record & Tape Guide* (1971–1984; issued in parts: *Schwann 1 and Schwann 2*), *The New Schwann Record and Tape Guide* (1984), *Super Schwann* (1987, quarterly), *Schwann* (1988–1990, quarterly), *Schwann Compact Disc Catalog* (1985–1989), *Schwann CD* (1989). Cover titles do not always correspond to title-page titles. Superseded by *Opus*, (classical music, quarterly), *Spectrum*, (popular music, quarterly), *In Music* (monthly).

124. *American Record Letter*. 1950–? Kirkland, Washington. Monthly. Supersedes *Record Letter*.

125. *International Record Letter*: A monthly listing of new or unusual records of concert, folk and ethnic music, literary readings, and discs from the theater. October 1950–1952. Kirkland, Washington: B. Richardson [etc.], Monthly. Supersedes *American Record Letter*.

126. *Revue des disques*. 1950–? Brussels, Belgium. Monthly. Superseded by (July 1964) *Revue des disques et de la haute-fidelité*.

127. *Tonband-Aufnahmen*. 1950–1967. Germany. Monthly. Superseded by *Tonband und Schallplatte*.

128. *Almanach du disque*. 1951–1958? Paris, France. Annual.

129. *Disc Collector*. 1951–. Palmer, Michigan. Monthly. Issues 1–11 from the National Hillbilly Record Collectors Exchange.

130. *The Forty-Fiver*. (Le Mire Products.) 1951–1957. New York, New York. Monthly.

131. *High Fidelity and Musical America*. The two periodicals were issued separately as well as bound together. *High Fidelity* was absorbed by *High Fidelity*. 1951–1989. Great Barrington, Massachusetts [etc.]. Monthly. Merged with *Musical America* in 1965 to form *High Stereo Review* in 1989.

132. *Record Year*. A guide to the year's Gramophone records. 1951. London, England. Annual.

133. *Bulletin du Hot Club de France*. 1952?–. Paris, France. Monthly.

134. *Les cahiers du disque*. 1952–1955? Paris, France. I.M.E. Pathé-Marconi. Irregular.

135. *Luister*. 1952–. Amersfoort, Netherlands. Monthly.

136. *Bielefelder Katalog. Katalog der Schallplatten klassischer Musik*. 1953–. Bielefeld, Germany. Semiannual.

137. *Gramophone Classical Catalogue*. 1953–. Harrow, England. General Gramophone Publications, Ltd. Quarterly. Title varies

138. *Harrison Tape Catalog*. 1953–1972. New York, New York. Weiss Publishing Corp. Bimonthly. Title, imprint, and frequency vary. Each issue presented some 20,000 tape titles, covering all formats, including classical and pop. Continued as *Harrison Tape Guide*.

139. *Jazz Discography* (Cassell & Co.) 1953–? London, England.

140. *Journal of the Audio Engineering Society*. 1953–1985. New York, New York. Monthly. Superseded by AES.

141. *Record News*. 1953–1959. London, England. Monthly. Superseded by (April 1958–March 1959) *Record News and Stereo Disc*. Absorbed by *Hi-Fi News*.

142. Revue du son. 1953–. Paris, France. 11 per year. Superseded by *Nouvelle revue du son*.

143. *Schwann Artist Issue*. 1953–1982. Boston, Massachusetts. Formerly: *Schwann Long Playing Record Catalog. Artist Listing: Schwann Catalog. Artist Issue*. Superseded by *The New Schwann Artist Issue*.

144. *Theme*. 1953–1957. North Hollywood, California. Monthly. Formerly: *Record Exchange*.

145. *Vocal Art*. 1953–1971? London, England. Irregular.

146. *Audio League. Report.* 1954–1957. Pleasantville, New York. Irregular.

147. *Broadcast Music, Inc. Record Catalog Supplement.* 1954?–1964? New York, New York. Irregular.

148. *For the Record.* (Book of the Month Club.) 1954–1960. New York, New York. Monthly.

149. *Hi-Fi Music at Home.* 1954–1959. New York, New York. Bi-monthly; Monthly. Absorbed by *High Fidelity.*

150. *Matrix.* Jazz record research magazine. 1954–1975. London, England. Bi-monthly. Absorbed by *The Discophile* in January 1959.

151. *Phono: Internationale Schallplatten-Zeitschrift.* 1954–1966. Vienna, Austria. Quarterly. Incorporated in *Oesterreichischer Musikzeitschrift.*

152. *Record and Sound Retailing.* 1954–1962. New York, New York. M. and N. Harrison. Monthly. Formerly: *Record Retailing.* Superseded by *Home Entertainment Retailing.*

153. *Recordland.* 1954–. Chicago, Illinois.

154. *Audiocraft.* 1955–1958. Great Barrington, Massachusetts. Monthly. Variant title: *Audiocraft for the Hi Fi Hobbyist.* Absorbed by *High Fidelity.*

155. *Better Listening.* 1955–1963? Los Angeles, California. Irregular. Variant title: *Better Listening through High Fidelity.*

156. *Columbia Record Club Magazine.* 1955–1959. New York, New York. Monthly. Superseded by *Columbia Record Club Magazine* (Monophonic), 1959–1967, and *Columbia Record Club Magazine* (Stereo), 1959–1973. Variant title: *Columbia LP Record Club Magazine.*

157. *GTJ & CR News.* (Good Time Jazz Record Company.) 1955–1961. Los Angeles, California. Bi-monthly.

158. *High Fidelity Record Annual.* 1955–1956. Philadelphia, Pennsylvania. Annual. Collection of record reviews from *High Fidelity.* Continued by: *Records in Review.*

159. *Record Research.* 1955–1995. Brooklyn, New York. Bi-monthly with some irregularities. Important articles on early record labels. Extensive label lists.

160. *Records in Review.* 1955–1981. Great Barrington, Massachusetts. Wyeth Press. Annual. Reviews of classical and semiclassical records and tapes from *High Fidelity* magazine.

161. *British Institute of Recorded Sound. Bulletin.* 1956–1960. London, England. Irregular. Superseded by *Recorded Sound.*

162. *Collectors Item.* (New York Gramophone Society.) 1956–1957? New York, New York. Irregular.

163. *Diapason*; la revue du disque microsillon. 1956–1984. Paris, France. Monthly. Superseded by *Diapason-Harmonie.*

164. *Fono Forum*; Zeitschrift für Schallplatte, Musik, HiFi-Technik. 1956–. Bielefeld, Germany. Monthly.

165. *Hi-Fi News.* 1956–1970. London, England. Monthly. Superseded by *HiFi News and Record Review.*

166. *Record Monthly.* (New Zealand Federation of Recorded Music Societies.) 1956–. Christchurch, New Zealand.

167. *Record News.* The magazine for record collectors. 1956–1961. Toronto, Canada. Monthly.

168. *Record Research. Supplement.* 1956-1996. Brooklyn, New York. Irregular. Discographies.

169. *Alta fedeltà.* 1957–. Milan, Italy. Monthly.

170. *High Fidelity Trade News.* 1957–1981? New York, New York. Monthly.

171. *Klassiska skivspegeln.* 1957–1960. Sweden. Superseded by *Skivspegeln.*

172. *Records and Recording.* 1957–1982. London, England. Monthly. Title from February 1967: *Records and Recording and Record Times.* Absorbed by *Music and Musicians.*

173. *Stereo Review's Stereo Buyers Guide.* 1957–. New York, New York. Annual. Former titles: *Stereo Directory* and *Buying Guide.*

174. *Tape Recording and Hi-Fi Magazine.* 1957–1960. London, England. Monthly. Variant titles: *Tape Recording and Reproduction Magazine; Tape Recording & High Fidelity Reproduction Magazine.* Superseded by *Tape Recording Fortnightly.*

175. *Allen's Poop Sheet.* 1958–1975. Higland Park, New Jersey. Irregular.

176. *Audio Cardalog.* 1958–1969? Albany, New York. Monthly.

177. *Il disco.* 1958?–1970. Milan, Italy. Bi-monthly.

178. Farandula. 1958–. San Juan, Puerto Rico. Monthly. Latin American music record reviews and articles.

179. *Great Music.* (Book of-the-Month Club, RCA Victor Society of Great Music.) 1958–1959? New York, New York. Monthly.

180. *Harrison Catalog of Stereophonic Records.* 1958–1959? New York, New York. Monthly. Variant title: *This Month's Records.*

181. *Hi Fi Review.* 1958–1960. Chicago, Illinois. Monthly. Superseded by *Hi Fi/Stereo Review.*

182. *Mezhdunarodnaia kniga. Katalog dolgo-igraiushchie gramplastinok.* 1958–1977? Moscow, USSR. Monthly. Title varies. A catalog of recordings available for purchase outside the USSR, issued in English and Russian. Works are listed by genre, with indexes by composer and artist. There was an earlier series, from 1936.

183. *Modern Hi-Fi.* 1958–1970? New York, New York. Irregular. Superseded by *Modern Hi-Fi & Stero Guide.*

184. *Musica Schallplatte.* 1958–1961. Germany. Bi-monthly. Superseded by *Phonoprisma.*

185. *Philips Music Herald.* 1958–1970? Baarn, Netherlands. Irregular.

186. *Phonoprisma.* 1958–1963. Kassel, Germany. Bärenreiter Verlag. Bi-monthly. Formerly: *Musica Schallplatte.* Issued as a supplement to *Musica (Cassel).*

187. *Record Times.* (EMI, Ltd.) 1958–. London, England.

188. *Recorded Folk Music.* A review of British and Foreign folk music recordings. 1958–. London, England.

189. *Records Magazine.* (Decca Record Co., Ltd.) 1958–1966? London, England. Monthly.

190. *Stereo Review.* 1958–. New York, New York. Monthly. Absorbed by *High Fidelity,* 1989.

191. *Das Ton Magazine.* 1958?–1965? Munich, Germany. Six per year.

192. *Audio Times.* 1959–. New York, New York. Semimonthly.

193. *Blues Research.* 1959–1974? Brooklyn, New York. Irregular.

194. *Discoteca hi fi.* 1959–1960. Milan, Italy. Monthly. Continued by *Discoteca alta fedeltà.*

195. *Das gesprochene Wort.* 1959–1966. Leipzig, Germany. Annual. A section of the national bibliography.

196. *Der Jazz Freund.* 1959?–1982? Menden, Germany. Quarterly.

197. *Music Week.* 1959–. London, England. Weekly. Former titles: *Music and Video Week; Music Week: Record Retailer.*

198. *Musik och ljudteknik.* 1959–1975. Stockholm, Sweden. Irregular. Superseded by *Musiktidningen.*

199. *Der Musikmarkt.* 1959–. Sternberg, Germany. Josef Keller Verlag. Semimonthly.

200. *Records on Review.* A survey of recent record releases. 1959–. U.S.

201. *Studio Sound & Broadcasting Engineering.* 1959–1995. London, England. Monthly. Former titles: *Studio Sound and Broadcasting; Studio Sound.* Incorporates *Sound International.*

202. *Your One-Spot Numerical Reporter.* 1959–? Forest Park, Illinois. Irregular.

203. *Discographical Forum.* A bi-monthly of jazz and blues research. 1960–1982? London, England. Bi-monthly.

204. *Discoteca Fedeltà.* 1960–1978. Milan, Italy. Monthly. Supersedes *Discoteca hi fi.*

205. *Hi-Fi Stereo Review.* 1960–1968. New York, New York. Monthly. Formerly: *Hi Fi Review.* Absorbed by *Stereo Review.*

206. *Hillandale News* (Official Journal of the City of London Phonograph & Gramophone Society). 1960–. London, England. Bi-monthly. Research journal covering all aspects of recorded sound: labels, artists, firms, etc., emphasizing British aspects.

207. *Jazz-Disco.* 1960?–? Malmö, Sweden. Bi-monthly.

208. *Jazz Report.* The record collector's magazine. 1960–1982? Ventura, California. Irregular.

209. *Der Plattenteller.* 1960?–1964. Munich, Germany, Monthly.

210. *Stereo.* 1960–1968. Great Barrington, Massachusetts. Annual; Quarterly.

211. *Tape Recording Fortnightly.* 1960–1961. London, England. Monthly. Formerly: *Tape Recording and Hi-Fi Magazine.* Superseded by *Tape Recording Magazine.*

212. *Audio and Record Review.* 1961–1969. London, England. Monthly. Later titles: *Audio Record Review* (1966–1969), *Record Review.* United with *Hi-Fi News,* in 1970, to form *Hi-Fi News and Record Review.*

213. *Disk.* 1961–? Amersfoort, Netherlands. Monthly.

214. *Recorded Sound.* (Journal of the British Institute of Recorded Sound.) 1961–1984. London, England. Irregular. Supersedes *British Institute of Recorded Sound, London. Bulletin.*

215. *Classical Recordaid.* 1962–1977. Philadelphia, Pennsylvania. Irregular. Began publication in 1943.

216. *Columbia Stereo Tape Club. Magazine.* 1962–1973. New York, New York. Monthly.

217. *Country & Western Roundabout.* 1962–1968. Loughton, England. Irregular.

218. *Gramophone Popular Record Catalogue.* 1962–1987. Harrow, England. General Gramophone Publications, Ltd. Quarterly.

219. *HIP.* The jazz record digest. 1962–1971? U.S.

220. *Harrison Catolog of Stereophonic Tapes.* 1962?–1969. New York, New York. Title varies. Five per year.

221. *Hi-Fi Stereophonie.* 1962–1983. Stuttgart, Germany. Monthly. Merged with *Stereoplay.*

222. *Hillbilly.* 1962–1971? Basel, Switzerland. Quarterly.

223. *Ragtime Review.* 1962–1966. Denver, Colorado. Quarterly.

224. *Reader's Digest Music Guide.* 1962–1964. Pleasantville, New York. Monthly. Superseded by *Music Guide: The magazine of the RCA Victor Record Club*

225. *The Stereophile.* 1962–. Santa Fe, New Mexico. Eight per year.

226. *Tape Recording Magazine.* 1962–1971. London, England. Monthly. Formerly: *Tape Recording Fortnightly.* Superseded by *Sound & Picture Tape Recording.*

227. *Deutsches Rundfunkarchiv, Frankfurt am Main. Hinweisdienst: Musik.* 1963–1964. Frankfurt, Germany. Monthly.

228. *Deutsches Rundfunkarchiv, Frankfurt am Main. Hinweisdienst: Wort.* 1963–1964? Frankfurt, Germany. Monthly.

229. *Home Entertainment Retailing.* 1963–1964? U.S. Irregular. Formerly: *Record and Sound Retailing.*

230. *Paris. Phonothèque Nationale. Bulletin.* 1963–? Paris, France. Irregular.

231. *RPM Music Weekly.* 1963–. Toronto, Canada. Weekly.

232. *Sound Industry Directory.* 1963–. New York, New York. St. Regis Publications. Annual.

233. *Stereo.* 1963–. Japan. Monthly.

234. *Country Corner.* 1964?–1981? Bremen, Germany. Five per year.

235. *Diapason microsillon.* Catalogue général des disques microsillon. Disques classiques. 1964–. Paris, France. Annual.

236. *Disc Collector Newsletter.* 1964–1980. Cheswold, Deleware. Irregular. Superseded by *Disc Collector.*

237. *Le Grand Baton.* (Journal of the Sir Thomas Beecham Society.) 1964?–. Redondo Beach, California. Irregular.

238. *Indiana University. Archives of Folk and Primitive Music. Report.* 1964–1965. Bloomington, Indiana. Three per year. Superseded by *Indiana University. Archives of Traditional Music. Trimester Report.*

239. *Phonolog List of Tapes.* 1964–1989. Los Angeles, California. Trade Services Publications, Inc. [varies]. Quarterly.

240. *Phonolog Tape Parade.* 1964–?. Los Angeles, California. Monthly.

241. *Record Preview.* 1964–. New York, New York. Billboard Publishing Co. Monthly.

242. *Audiofan.* 1965–1967. New York, New York. St. Regis Publications. Monthly. Merged with *Audio* in 1968.

243. *Collector.* 1965–1967? Cosenza, Italy. Bi-monthly.

244. *Federation of British Tape Recordists. Recording News.* 1965–. Essex, England. Bi-monthly. Formerly: *Federation of British Tape Recordists: News and Views.*

245. *Harmonie.* 1965?–1980. Boulogne, France. Monthly. Superseded by *Harmonie hi-fi conseil.*

246. *High Fidelity and Musical America.* 1965–1986. New York, New York. Monthly. Formerly: *High Fidelity.* In 1987, split again into the original magazines *High Fidelity* and *Musical America. High Fidelity* was then absorbed by *Stereo Review* in 1989.

247. *High Fidelity Jahrbuch.* 1965?–1980. Düsseldorf, Germany. Annual. Variant title: *Deutsches High Fidelity Jahrbuch.* Superseded by *HiFi Jahrbuch.*

248. *Indiana University. Archives of Traditional Music. Trimester Report.* 1965–1971. Bloomington, Indiana. Three per year. Formerly: *Indiana. University. Archives of Folk and Primitive Music. Report.*

249. *JEMF Quarterly.* 1965–1985. Los Angeles, California. John Edwards Memorial Foundation. Quarterly. Formerly: *JEMF Newsletter* (1965–1968). Superseded by *American Vernacular Music.*

250. *Music Guide.* (RCA Victor Record Club.) 1965–1966. Indianapolis, Indiana [etc.]. Thirteen per year. Supersedes *Reader's Digest Music Guide.*

251. *The Phonographic Record.* (Journal of the Vintage Phonographic Society of New Zealand.) 1965?–1980? Christchurch, New Zealand. Irregular.

252. *Recording Rights Journal.* (Mechanical Copyright Protection Society.) 1965–1968. London, England. Quarterly.

253. *Schwann's Children's Records.* 1965–1981. Boston, Massachusetts. Annual. Variant titles: *Schwann Children's Record & Tape Catalog; Schwann Children's & Christmas Record & Tape Guide.*

254. *Sir Thomas Beecham Society Newsletter.* 1965-1987. Essex, England. Bi-monthly.

255. *Storyville.* 1965–. London, England. Bi-monthly. Jazz and blues.

256. *Arturo Toscanini Society. Newsletter.* 1966?–? U.S. Irregular.

257. *Discografia internazionale.* 1966–1972. Milan, Italy. Irregular.

258. *Gramofonovy Klub.* 1996? — . Prague, Czechoslovakia. Irregular.

259. *Harrison Catalog of Stereo and Tape Cartridges.* 1966–1969. New York, New York. Bi-monthly.

260. *Hi-Fi Stereo Buyers' Guide.* 1966?–1981. New York, New York. Bi-monthly.

261. *Record Beat.* 1966?–. New York, New York. Record Beat Publishing Co.

262. *Schwann Country and Western Catalog.* 1966–1970? Boston, Massachusetts. Annual.

263. *BN: Blues News.* 1967?–. Helsinki, Finland. Bi-monthly.

264. *db.* The sound engineering magazine. 1967–. U.S. Monthly.

265. *The Discographer.* 1967–1971? Fresno, California. George C. Collings. Irregular.

266. *High Fidelity.* 1967?–. Dragør, Denmark. Monthly.

267. *IAJRC Journal.* (Journal of the International Association of Jazz Record Collectors.) 1967–? Chicago, Illinois. Quarterly.

268. *International Piano Library. Bulletin.* 1967–1971. New York, New York. Quarterly.

269. *RSVP: the magazine for record collectors.* 1967?–? London, England. Monthly.

270. *Record of the Month.* 1967–. London, England. Sinclair's Publications, Ltd. Monthly.

271. *ARSC Bulletin.* (Association for Recorded Sound Collections.) Nos. 1–21, 1968–1989. Silver Spring, Maryland. Annual. Absorbed by *ARSC Journal.*

272. *ARSC Journal.* (Association for Recorded Sound Collections.) 1968–. Silver Spring, Maryland [varies]. Semiannual. An important journal of research in all areas of recorded sound. Includes extensive anno-tated bibliographies of writings in other periodicals. Reviews of books and of sound recordings.

273. *Antique Phonograph Society Newsletter.* 1968-1985. Toronto, Canada. Six per year. Collectors and collecting. Superseded by *Canadian Antique Phonograph Society (Newsletter).*

274. *The Collecta.* 1968–1976? England. Bi-monthly; irregular.

275. *Hi-Fi Sound.* 1968?–1977. London, England. Monthly. Superseded by *Popular Hi-Fi & Sound.*

276. *Kounty Korral Magazine.* 1968–. Västerås, Sweden. Four to six per year. Includes country music record reviews and discographies.

277. *Musica e nastri.* Supplement to *Musicae dischi.* 1968–1970? Milan, Italy.

278. *New Amberola Graphic.* 1968–. St. Johnsbury, Vermont. New Amberola Graphic Phonograph Co. Quarterly. An important journal for collectors, presenting authoritative research about phonographs and Gramophones, as well as recording artists. Illustrations are a useful feature, many of them reproductions from old magazines and sales materials.

279. *Svensk ton pa skiva* [Swedish music on records]. 1968–1981. Stockholm, Sweden. Biennial.

280. *Tonband und Schallplatte.* 1968–1969? Nürnberg, Germany. Monthly. Formerly: *Tonband-Aufnahmen.*

281. *UE-Hi-Fi Vision.* (Unterhaltungs-Elektronik): das schweizer Monatsmagazin für Unterhaltungselektronik und Musik. 1968–. Goldach, Switzerland. Monthly. Formerly: *Unterhaltungs-Elektronik.*

282. *Chi e Dové.* 1969–. Milan, Italy. Annual. Supplement to *Musica e Dischi.*

283. *The Collecta.* 1969?–1976. Watford, Herts., England. Irregular.

284. *Columbia Stereo Tape Cartridge Bulletin.* 1969?–1971? New York, New York. Monthly.

285. *Danske grammofonplader.* 1969–. Copenhagen, Denmark. Nationalmusset, Nationaldiskoteket. Annual. Lists Danish recordings (music of all countries), including cassettes after 1975. Arranged by genre, with artist index.

286. *Discography Series.* 1969–. Utica, New York. Irregular. J.F. Weber, editor and publisher.

287. *Gramophone Spoken Word and Miscellaneous Catalogue.* 1969–. Harrow, Middlesex, England. General Gramophone Publications, Ltd. Annual. Lists discs and tapes of language courses and material in foreign languages, children's material, documentary recordings, instructional recordings, sound effects material, and miscellaneous entertainment items. Indexes of authors, artists, and anthologies.

288. *The Gunn Report.* 1969?–. Benfleet, Essex, England. Bi-monthly; irregular.

289. *The Maestro.* (Journal of the Arturo Toscanini Society.) 1969–1975? Dumas, Texas. Irregular.

290. *Memory Lane.* Britain's no. 1 magazine for nostalgia. 1969–. Hadleigh, Benfleet, Essex, England. Quarterly. Incorporating *The Al Bowlly Circle.*

291. *Record Buyer.* (World Distributors [Manchester], Ltd.) 1969?–. Manchester, England. Monthly.

292. *Record Exchanger.* 1969–1983. Anaheim, California. Art Turco. Irregular. Concerned

with rock music and performers; includes an auction section.

293. *Sound Canada.* 1969–. Toronto, Canada. Monthly. Continues as *Sound & Vision* (1984).

294. *Talking Machine Review International.* 1969–1988. Bournemouth, England. Six per year; irregular. Title varies. Numbers 1–57: *Talking Machine Review.* An important journal dealing with all aspects of recorded sound, with emphasis on label lists and histories of U.K. firms. Outstanding illustrative material was featured, with reproductions from old catalogs and periodicals. Publication ceased with number 75. A continuation began in 1989, *as International Talking Machine Review* (Gillingham, England).

295. *Walrus.* January 1969–December 1969? Philadelphia, Pennsylvania. Bi-weekly. Rock music reviews.

296. *After Beat.* 1970–1972. Daly City, California. Monthly. Big Band discographies and articles.

297. *Audio Amateur.* (E.T. Dell.) 1970–. Swarthmore, Pennsylvania; later Peterborough, New Hampshire. Four to five per year.

298. *Australian Hi-Fi.* 1970?–1975? Narrabeen, Australia. Bi-monthly.

299. *Bomp.* 1970?–1979? Burbank, California. Bi-monthly. Formerly: *Who Put the Bomp.*

300. *Bruno Walter Society & Sound Archive. Information Bulletin.* 1970–? U.S. Irregular.

301. *Hi-Fi News and Record Review.* October 1970–. London, England. Monthly. A merger of *Hi-Fi News* and *Record Review.*

302. *International Federation of Record Libraries. Cahiers.* 1970–? Paris, France. Phonethèque Nationale.

303. *Journal of Country Music.* 1970–. Nashville, Tennessee. Country Music Foundation. Quarterly. Continues numbering of *Country Music Foundation. Newsletter.*

304. *Listening Post.* A selective list of new or recently released recordings published monthly by the Audiovisual Division of Bro-Dart. 1970–1976. U.S. Irregular.

305. *R and B Magazine.* 1970–. Northridge, California. Irregular. Formed by the union of *R and B Collector* and *Quartette.* Rhythm and Blues music history and criticism.

306. *Record Review.* January 1970–September 1970. London, England. Monthly. Formerly: *Audio and Record Review.* United with *Hi-Fi News* in October 1970 to form *Hi-Fi News and Record Review.*

307. *Recording Engineer/Producer.* 1970?–. Overland Park, Kansas. Monthly.

308. *Sound Verdict.* 1970?–1981? London, England. Annual. Index to audio articles and equipment reviews.

309. *Stereo Sound.* 1970?–. Japan. Quarterly.

310. *The Street Singer, and Stars of the Thirties.* 1970?–1974. London, England. Irregular. Absorbed by *Nostalgia Magazine.*

311. *What Hi-Fi?* 1970–. Middlesex, England. Monthly.

312. *Willem Mengelberg Society. Newsletter.* 1970–2000. Wauwatosa, Wisconsin. Irregular.

313. *Arhoolie Occasional.* 1971–1973. U.S. Irregular. Superseded by *The Lightning Express.*

314. *Bim Bam Boom.* 1971–1973. U.S. Irregular.

315. *Commodore.* Light music on 78s. 1971–1974. Kent, England. Quarterly. Superseded by *Vintage Light Music.*

316. *Creative World.* 1971?–1978? U.S. Irregular.

317. *Deltio kritikes diskographias.* 1971–1976? Athens, Greece. Irregular.

318. *Disc.* 1971–1975. England. Weekly. Superseded by *Record Mirror & Disc.*

319. *Index to Record and Tape Reviews.* 1971–1982. San Anselmo, California. Annual. Alternative title: *Record and Tape Reviews Index.*

320. *Modern Hi-Fi & Stereo Guide.* 1971–1974. New York, New York. Formerly: *Modern Hi-Fi.* Superseded by *Modern Hi-Fi and Music.*

321. *Old Time Music.* 1971–. London, England. Quarterly.

322. *Phonogram.* 1971?–1981? Doveton, Australia. Phonograph Society of Australia. Bi-monthly.

323. *Phonograph Record Magazine.* 1971?–1978? Hollywood, California.

324. *Phonographic Bulletin.* 1971–1990. Utrecht, Netherlands [varies]. International Association of Sound Archives. Irregular. Emphasis is on archive organization and on preservation problems.

325. *Popular Hi-Fi.* 1971?–1976?. London, England. Monthly. Variant title: *Popular Hi-Fi & Sound.* Absorbed by *What Hi-Fi?*

326. *Soul Bag.* 1971?–. Paris, France. Comité de Liaison des Amateurs de Rhythm & Blues. Monthly.

327. *Sound and Picture Tape Recording.* 1971–1973. London, England. Monthly. Formerly: *Tape Recording Magazine.* Superseded by *Tape and Hi-Fi Test.*

328. *Stereo Review's Tape Recording & Buying Guide*. 1971–1984. New York, New York. Annual.

329. *Studies in Jazz Discography*. (Institute of Jazz Studies, Rutgers University.) 1971–1973? New Brunswick, New Jersey. Irregular. Continued by *Journal of Jazz Studies*

330. *Suono stereo hi-fi*. 1971?–1980. Rome, Italy. Monthly. Superseded by *Suono*.

331. *Vintage Record Mart*. 1971–1981? Rayleigh, England. Bi-monthly. For collectors of 78 rpm's.

332. *Antique Records*. 1972–. Ditton, England.

333. *Audio-cassette Newsletter*. 1972–. Glendale, California. Cassette Information Services. Quarterly.

334. *B.A.S. Speaker*. (Boston Audio Society.) 1972–. Boston, Massachusetts. Monthly.

335. *Discolandia continental*. 1972–. Mexico. Monthly.

336. *Harrison Tape Guide*. 1972–1976. New York, New York. Bi-monthly. Continues as *Harrison Tape Catalog*.

337. *The Horn Speaker*. 1972–. Canton, Texas. Ten per year.

338. *Jazz Digest*. 1972–1974. Maclean, Virginia. Monthly. Formerly: *HIP-the Jazz Record Digest*.

339. *Micrography*. 1972?–. Amsterdam, Netherlands. Irregular. Jazz and blues discographies on LP.

340. *Music Retailer*. 1972–1979? Chestnut Hill, Massachusetts. Monthly.

341. *RPM: Record Trading Magazine*. 1972–? Poole, Dorset, England. Irregular.

342. *Record Mart*. 1972–1981. Rayleigh, Essex, England. Monthly.

343. *S/N Signals and Noise*. (Newsletter of the New York Audio Society.) 1972–? New York, New York.

344. *Sir Thomas Beecham Society. Bulletin*. 1972–. U.S. Irregular.

345. *Stereo-Video Guide*. 1972–. Toronto, Canada. Six per year.

346. *Stereoplay*. Il piu diffuso mensile di hi-fi, dischi e musica. 1972–. Rome, Italy. Monthly.

347. *Who Put the Bomp*. 1972–1976. Burbank, California. Quarterly. Superseded by *Bomp*.

348. *Whole Lotta Rockin'*. 1972–1976? Rune Halland, Norway. Rock 'n' Roll Society of Scandinavia. Four per year.

349. *Absolute Sound*. The High End Journal. 1973–. Sea Cliff, New York. Bi-monthly. Technical articles and reviews of new equipment in upper price ranges.

350. *Antique Phonograph Monthly*. 1973–1993. Brooklyn, New York. Quarterly. An important collectors' journal, emphasizing material on the cylinder phonograph.

351. *Audiovisione*. 1973–. Rome, Italy.

352. *Bruno Walter Society & Sound Archive. Newsletter*. 1973–1974? U.S. Irregular.

353. *Different Drummer*. The magazine for jazz listeners. 1973–1975. Rochester, New York. Monthly.

354. *Forever*. The first rock 'n' roll collectors' magazine in Japan. 1973?–? Japan. Quarterly?

355. *Hi-Fi Answers*. 1973–1982? London, England. Monthly.

356. *Hi-Fi for Pleasure*. 1973–1980? London, England. Monthly.

357. *HiFi Stereophonie Testjahrbuch*. 1973–1983. Germany. Annual. Superseded by *HiFi Stereophonie Test*.

358. *High Fidelity's Test Reports*. 1973–1981. New York, New York. Annual.

359. *Journal of Jazz Studies*. 1973–1979. New Brunswick, New Jersey. Institute of Jazz Studies. Irregular. Continues as *Studies in Jazz Discography*. Superseded by *Annual Review of Jazz Studies*. Significant research on jazz artists and their recordings. Reprinted by Scarecrow Press, Metuchen, New Jersey.

360. *Media Review Digest*. 1973–1974. U.S. Formerly: *Multi Media Reviews Index*.

361. *Not Fade Away*. 1973–1981. England. Vintage Rock 'n' Roll Appreciation Society. Bi-monthly.

362. *Radio & Records*. 1973–. Los Angeles, California. Weekly.

363. *Record Monthly*. 1973–. Japan. Monthly.

364. *Rumble*. Magazine for collectors of instrumental records. 1973–1977. Rainworth, Mansfield, England. Quarterly.

365. *Sono*. 1973–1978. Montreal, Canada. Irregular.

366. *Stereo*. 1973–. Munich, Germany. Monthly.

367. *Tape and Hi-Fi Test*. 1973–1975. London, England. Monthly. Title variant: *Tape*. Absorbed by *Sound and Picture Tape Recording*.

368. *Aware*. 1974?–? Brooklyn, New York. Bi-monthly. Formerly: *Rock-It-with-Aware*.

369. *Audio Scene Canada*. 1974–1980. Toronto, Canada. Monthly. Superseded by *Audio Video Canada*.

370. *Bielefelder Katalog. Verzeichnis der Jazz Schallplatten*. 1974–1983. Bielefeld, Germany. Continues as *Katalog der Jazzschallplatten*. Continued by *Bielefelder Katalog: Jazz*.

371. *Blues Link.* 1974?–1975. Barnet, Herts., England. Irregular. Absorbed by *Blues World.* Superseded by *Talking Blues.*

372. *Deutsche Bibliographie. Schallplatten-Verzeichnis.* 1974–1977. Bielefeld, Germany. Quarterly with annual index. Continued by *Deutsche Bibliographie. Musiktonträger-Verzeichnis.* Lists all classical and popular recordings issued in the Federal Republic of Germany, with full contents of each disc. Indexes by manufacturer number, title, topic, and artist. A section of the national bibliography.

373. *Filmmusic Notebook.* 1974–1978. Calabasas, California. Irregular.

374. *For the Record. News from the National Academy of Recording Arts and Sciences (NARAS).* 1974–1982? Burbank, California. Irregular.

375. *Goldmine.* The record collector's marketplace. 1974–. Fraser, Michigan. Bi-weekly; varies. All facets of rock music history and discography, with record auction supplement.

376. *Hi-Fi World.* 1974–? Hialeah, Florida. Irregular. Formerly: *The Hi-Fi Newsletter.*

377. *IMDT Newsletter.* (International Institute for Music, Dance and Theatre in the Audio-Visual Media, Vienna.) 1974?–? Vienna, Austria. Irregular.

378. *Klassiek journaal.* 1974?–? Rijswijk, Netherlands. Irregular.

379. *Melting Pot.* (National Association of Discotheque Disc Jockeys.) 1974?–? New York, New York. Irregular.

380. *Music Master.* 1974–. London, England. Annual. Catalogue of recordings currently in print in the U.K. Other publications include: *Music Master CD Index; Music Master Labels List; Music Master Prefix List; Music Master Supplement; Music Master Title Index; Music Master Tracks Catalogue; Music Master Year-book.*

381. *Musician's Guide.* 1974–1978? Boston, Massachusetts. New England Musician's Guide. Monthly.

382. *RTS Music Gazette.* 1974–1994. Costa Mesa, California. Monthly [varies]. Superseded by *Music Gazette.*

383. *Recording Locator.* 1974–? San Jose, California. Quarterly. Deals with recorded religious music.

384. *SMG: A magazine for record collectors.* 1974?–? Rainworth, Mansfield, Notts., England. Monthly. Absorbed by *Hot Buttered Soul* in 1976.

385. *Tape Deck Quarterly.* (FM music program guide.) 1974–1977. South Hampton, New York. Quarterly.

386. *Trouser Press.* 1974?–1984. New York, New York. Monthly. Formerly: *Transoceanic Trouser Press.*

387. *Audio Video Magazine.* 1975–. Paris, France. Monthly. Formerly: *Audio Magazine.*

388. *Australian Hi-Fi Annual.* 1975?–? Australia. Annual.

389. *Band-Amatoren.* 1975–1980? Copenhagen, Denmark. Monthly.

390. *Fritz Reiner Society. Newsletter.* 1975–1982. U.S. Irregular.

391. *Basic Repertoire.* (Stereo Review.) 1975?–1980? Boulder, Colorado. Annual.

392. *Blitz.* The rock and roll magazine for thinking people. 1975–. Los Angeles, California. Bi-monthly.

393. *Diapason. Discopop.* 1975–1977. Paris, France.

394. *Adagio.* 1975?–? Quebec, Canada. Bi-monthly.

395. *Hifi Stereo.* 1975–1981? Paris, France. Eleven per year.

396. *The Horn Speaker.* 1975-2000. Mabank, Texas. Ten per year. Superseded by *The Electronics Collector.*

397. *Canadian LP & Tape Catalog.* 1975–. Ottawa, Canada.

398. *International Musician and Recording World.* 1975–. London, England. Incorporated *One Two Testing Zig Zag.*

399. *Jazz Records.* 1975–1983? Tokyo, Japan. Annual supplement to *Swing Journal.*

400. *Modern Hi-Fi and Music.* 1975–1977. New York, New York. Monthly; bi-monthly. Formerly: *Modern Hi-Fi and Stereo Guide.*

401. *Modern Recording.* 1975–1980. Port Washington, New York. Bi-monthly; monthly. Superseded by *Modern Recording & Music.*

402. *Musik-Informationen.* 1975–1984. Braunschweig, Germany. Monthly. Superseded by *Musik-Info.* Began in 1961.

403. *Nostalgia Magazine.* 1975–? Southgate, England. Incorporating *The Street Singer* and *Stars of the Thirties.*

404. *Paul's Record Magazine.* 1975–? Hartford, Connecticut. Paul Bezanker. Irregular. Features extensive rock discographies.

405. *Recommended Recordings.* 1975–. London, England. Semiannual.

406. *The Record Collector's Journal.* 1975–1976. Covina, California. Monthly. Absorbed by *Goldmine.*

407. *Record Mirror and Disc.* 1975–1976. London, England. Weekly. Formerly: *Disc.* Superseded by *Record Mirror.*

408. *Soundtrack Collector's Newsletter.* 1975. Mechelen, Belgium. Quarterly. Superseded by *Soundtrack! The Collector's Quarterly.*

409. *Stereopus.* 1975–1977. Shalimar, Florida. Quarterly.

410. *Trans-Oceanic Trouser Press.* 1975. New York, New York. Bi-monthly. Superseded by *Trouser Press.*

411. *Vintage Light Music.* 1975–. West Wickham, Kent, England. Quarterly. Formerly: *Commodore:* For the enthusiast of light music on 78s.

412. *Yesterday's Memories.* 1975–1977. New York, New York. Quarterly. Rhythm & blues; rock and roll.

413. *L'anno discografico.* 1976–1979. Rome, Italy. Annual.

414. *Audio & Electronics Digest.* (Society of Audio Consultants.) 1976–1983? Beverly Hills, California. Monthly. Supersedes *Audio Digest and Personal Communications.*

415. *Audiogram.* 1976–1982? Washington, D.C. Irregular.

416. *The Big Beat of the 50's.* 1976?–1982? Australia. Irregular.

417. *Blitz.* 1976?–1979? Dearborn Heights, Michigan. Bi-monthly; irregular. Formerly: *Ballroom Blitz.*

418. *Cadence.* American review of jazz and blues. 1976–. Redwood, New York. Irregular.

419. *Canadian Independent Record Producer Association. Newsletter. (CIRPA).* 1976–. Toronto, Canada. Irregular.

420. *Disco World.* 1976–? Buffalo, New York. Monthly.

421. *Harmonie*; Catalogue général classique. 1976–1979. Boulogne, France. Annual.

422. *Hi-fi conseils.* 1976–1980. Boulogne, France. Ten per year. Superseded by *Harmonie hi-fi conseil.*

423. *Hifi Report.* 1976–1980. Bielefeld, Germany. Annual.

424. *High Fidelity Musica,* Mensile di alta fedeltà, video, attualità e cultura. 1976–. Rome, Italy. Monthly.

425. *High Fidelity's Buying Guide to Speaker Systems.* 1976–1981? Great Barrington, Massachusetts. Annual.

426. *IAR: International Audio Review.* 1976–1980? Berkeley, California. Irregular.

427. *Kastlemusick Exchange.* 1976. Wilmington, Deleware. Monthly. Continued as *Kastlemusick Monthly Bulletin.*

428. *Kastlemusick Monthly Bulletin.* 1976–1983. Wilmington, Delaware. Monthly. Formerly: *Kastlemusick Exchange.*

429. *LARITA.* 1976. Tucson, Arizona. Lewis Audiovisual Research Institute & Teaching Archive.

430. *The Lightning Express*; an occasional newspaper devoted to America's music. 1976–? Berkeley, California. Irregular. Incorporating: *The Arhoolie Occasional.*

431. *Mean Mountain Music.* 1976–? Milwaukee, Wisconsin. Features country, rock and roll artist and label discographies.

432. *Music Week Directory.* 1976–. London, England. Annual. Formerly: *Music and Video Week Directory; Music and Video Week Yearbook; Music Week Industry Year Book.*

433. *New on the Charts.* 1976–1986. New York, New York. Monthly.

434. *Rock & Roll International Magazine.* 1976?–? Ski, Norway.

435. *Rockin '50's.* Dedicated to the true rock 'n' roll era. (Buddy Holly Memorial Society.) 1976–. Lubbock, Texas. Bi-monthly.

436. *The Sensible Sound.* 1976–. Snyder, New York. Quarterly.

437. *Talking Blues.* 1976–1977? London, England. Quarterly. Formerly: *Blues Link.*

438. *Waxpaper.* 1976–1979. Hollywood, California. Warner Bros. Records. Monthly [varies]. Superseded by *Warner World.*

439. *What Hi-Fi?* 1976–1982? London, England. Monthly. Absorbed by *Popular Hi-Fi.*

440. *World Pop News.* 1976–1977? Netherlands. Irregular.

441. *ARSC Newsletter.* (Association for Recorded Sound Collections.) 1977–. Silver Spring, Maryland [varies]. Quarterly.

442. *Anno discografico.* 1977–. Milan, Italy. Monthly.

443. *The Audio Critic.* 1977–. Bronxville, New York. Irregular.

444. *The Audio Scene Canada.* 1977–1981. Toronto, Canada. Monthly.

445. *L'audio glornale.* II mensile professionale del mercato hi-fi e discografico. 1977–. Rome, Italy. Monthly.

446. *Audio Update.* 1977–1981. San Diego, California. Bi-monthly.

447. *BPI Year Book.* (British Phonographic Industry) 1977–. Harrow, England. Annual.

448. *Disc-o-graph.* 1977?–1978? Baltimore, Maryland. Irregular.
449. *Fanfare.* The magazine for serious record collectors. 1977–. Tenafly, New Jersey. Bimonthly. An important source of reviews of new classical recordings.
450. *Gramophone News.* 1977–? San Jose, California. Monthly.
451. *HiFi Stereophonie. Schallplattenkritik.* 1977–1983? Karlsruhe, Germany. Annual.
452. *Inside Stanyan.* (Stanyan Record Co.) 1977–? U.S. Irregular.
453. *Keynote.* A magazine for the arts. 1977–1990. New York, New York. Monthly. Included the WNCN-FM program guide.
454. *The Mix.* The recording industry magazine. 1977–. Emeryville, California. Monthly. Includes descriptions of recording studios, in regional groupings.
455. *Musica.* Bimestrale di informazione musicale e discografica. 1977–. Milan, Italy. Bimonthly.
456. *Musical Heritage Review Magazine.* 1977–. Neptune, New Jersey. Eighteen per year.
457. *NARAS Institute Journal.* (National Academy of Recording Arts and Sciences.) 1977–? Atlanta, Georgia. Semiannual.
458. *Progressive Platter.* 1977?–. Boston, Massachusetts. Irregular.
459. *Record Mirror.* 1977–1985. London, England. Weekly. Formerly: *Record Mirror and Disc.* Superseded by *rm.*
460. *Record Review.* 1977–1984. Los Angeles, California. Bi-monthly.
461. *Recording Industry Index.* 1977–. Cherry Hill, New Jersey. National Association of Recording Merchandisers. Annual.
462. *Rockingchair.* Review newsletter for librarians who buy records. 1977–1982. Philadelphia, Pennsylvania. Monthly.
463. *Sound Advice.* 1977. Los Angeles, California.
464. *Stereoguida.* Il trimestrale hi-fi per non sbagliarel'acquisto. 1977–. Rome, Italy. Quarterly.
465. *Time Barrier Express.* 1977?–1980? Yonkers, New York. Irregular.
466. *Audio.* 1978?–. Stuttgart, Germany. Monthly.
467. *Deutsche Bibliographie. Musiktonträger-Verzeichnis.* 1978–. Frankfurt am Main, Germany. Monthly. Formerly: *Deutsche Bibliographie. Schallplatten-Verzeichnis.*
468. *High Fidelity's Buying Guide to Tape Systems.* 1978–. New York, New York. Annual. Formerly: *Buyer's Guide to the World of Tape.*

469. *International Musician and Recording World.* 1978–1981. U.S. Irregular.
470. *Outlet.* 1978–. Ilford, England. Irregular.
471. *Mr. Audio's Bimonthly.* 1978?–? U.S. Irregular.
472. *Record Digest.* 1978. Prescott, Arizona. Biweekly. Superseded by *Music World & Record Digest.*
473. *Record Finder.* 1978–. U.S. Irregular.
474. *Trouser Press Collectors' Magazine.* 1978?–1980? U.S. Annual.
475. *Australian Sound & Broadcast.* 1979–. Sydney, Australia. Bi-monthly.
476. *Discoveries.* 1979–. U.S. Irregular.
477. *Full Blast.* 1979–. U.S. Irregular. Includes rock music record reviews discographies, and articles.
478. *I.A.S.A. (Australia) Newsletter.* 1979–1986. Australia. Irregular. Variant title: *I.A.S.A. Australian Branch Newsletter.* Superseded by *Australasian Sound Archive.*
479. *Melodiia*: ezhekvartalnyi katalog-biulleten Vsesoiuznoi firmy gramplastinok "Melodiia." 1979–. Moscow, Russia. Six per year.
480. *Music.* Mensile di musica ed alta fedeltà. 1979–. Rome, Italy. Monthly.
481. *Music Hall.* 1979–1980. England. Bi-monthly. Formerly: *Music Hall Records.*
482. *Music World.* 1979–1981? Wollaston, Massachusetts. Irregular. Formerly: *Music World and Record Digest Weekly News.*
483. *Music World & Record Digest.* Mar. 1979. Prescott, Arizona. Weekly. Formerly: *Record Digest.* Superseded by *Music World and Record Digest Weekly News.*
484. *Music World and Record Digest Weekly News.* 1979. Prescott, Arizona. Weekly. Formerly: *Music World & Record Digest.* Superseded by *Music World.*
485. *Overtures.* A magazine devoted to the musical on stage and record. 1979?–1981. Wembley, London, England. Bi-monthly.
486. *Tape Deck.* 1979–. New York, New York. Annual.
487. *Pro Sound News.* 1979?–. Carle Place, New York. Monthly.
488. *Rock & Roll: Musik-Magazine.* 1977–. Oldenburg, Germany. Bi-monthly. Formerly: *Rock.*
489. *Stereo Test Reports.* 1979–. New York, New York. Irregular.
490. *Sound International.* 1979?–? Poole, Dorset, England. Monthly.
491. *Sounds Vintage.* 1979–1983. Billericay, Essex, England. Bi-monthly.

492. *Superstereo Audio Magazine.* 1979–. Milan, Italy. Monthly.

493. *Tarakan Music Letter.* 1979–1985. Port Washington, New York. Five per year, irregular.

494. *Warner World.* 1979–1981? Hollywood, California. Monthly. Formerly: *Waxpaper.*

495. *Audio South Africa.* 1980?–. Johannesburg, South Africa. Bi-monthly.

496. *Audio universal.* 1980?–. Buenos Aires, Argentina. Monthly.

497. *Australasian Sound Archive.* (International Association of Sound Archives) 1980–. Australia. Quarterly. Formerly: *IASA Australian Branch Newsletter.*

498. *Disc'ribe.* A journal of discographical information. 1980–. Los Angeles, California. Irregular.

499. *Early Music Record Services. Monthly Review.* 1980–. Essex, England. Monthly.

500. *The Fortnightly College Radio Report.* 1980-1984. Westfield, Massachusetts. Bi-weekly. Superseded by: *New Fortnightly College Radio Report.*

501. *Guia da audio.* 1980?–. Buenos Aires, Argentina. Annual.

502. *Harmonie hi-fi conseil.* 1980–1981. Paris, France. Monthly. Supersedes *Hi-fi conseils.* Superseded by *Harmonie-opera hi-fi conseil.*

503. *Hi-Fi & Elektronik.* 1980–. Copenhagen, Denmark. Monthly.

504. *Hifi musique.* 1980–? Drogenbos, Belgium. Irregular. Formerly: *Revue des disques et de la haute fidelité.*

505. *High Fidelity's Buying Guide to Stereo Components.* 1980–? New York, New York. Annual.

506. *HiVi.* 198?–. Japan. Monthly. Formerly: *Sound Boy.*

507. *IAR Hotline.* (International Audio Review.) 1980–. Berkeley, California. Irregular.

508. *Library of Congress. National Library Service for the Blind and Physically Handicapped. Instructional Disc Recordings Catalog.* 1980?–. Washington, D.C. Annual.

509. *Modern Recording & Music.* 1980–1986. Port Washington, New York. Monthly. Supersedes *Modern Recording.*

510. *Ovation.* 1980–1990. New York, New York. Monthly. Contains WQXR (New York) Program Guide.

511. *Le petit baton.* 1980–. Redondo Beach, California: The Sir Thomas Beecham Society. Irregular.

512. *Pro Sound.* 198?–. Japan. Bi-monthly. Formerly: *Tape Sound.*

513. *Recordings of Experimental Music.* 1979–1983. Collingswood, New Jersey. Six per year.

514. *Rhythm & News.* 1980–1982. U.S. Superseded by *Whiskey, Women and …*

515. *Soundtrack! The Collector's Quarterly.* 1980–. Mechelen, Belgium. Quarterly. Formerly: *Soundtrack Collector's Newsletter.*

516. *Speaker Builder.* 1980?–. Peterborough, New Hampshire. Quarterly.

517. *Stereo Review Compact Disc Buyers Guide.* 198?– New York, New York. Semiannual.

518. *Suono.* 1980–1985. Rome, Italy. Monthly. Formerly: *Suono stereo hi-fi.*

519. *Vocal Collector's Monthly.* 1980–? New York, New York. Irregular.

520. *L'audio giornale review.* Rivista di elettroacustica ed alta fedeltà. 1981–. Rome, Italy. Monthly.

521. *Audio Review.* 1981–. Rome, Italy. Monthly. Variant title: *Audioreview.*

522. *Audio Video Canada.* 1981–? Toronto, Canada. Monthly. Formerly: *Audio Scene Canada.* Superseded by *Sound Canada.*

523. *Australian Music Directory.* 1981?–? North Melbourne, Vic., Australia. Annual.

524. *Disc Collector.* 1981–. Cheswold, Deleware. Monthly; varies. Formerly: *Disc Collector Newsletter.*

525. *Discophiliac.* A newsletter for serious collectors of classical music. 1981–1984? Garrison, New York. Irregular.

526. *Guide to Recording in the U.K.* (Association of Professional Recording Studios) 1981–. Rickmansworth, England. Annual. Formerly: *Guide to APRS Member Studios.*

527. *Harmonie-opéra hi-fi conseil.* 1981–1982. Paris, France. Monthly. Formerly: *Harmonie hi-fi conseil.* Superseded by *Harmonie panorama musique.*

528. *High Performance Review.* 1981–. Stamford, Connecticut. Quarterly.

529. *RPM Weekly.* 1981-1992? Toronto, Canada. Weekly. Records promotion music charts. Superseded by *RPM Chart Weekly.*

530. *The Record.* 1981–1985. New York, New York. Irregular. Superseded by *Rolling Stone.*

531. *Show Music.* 1981–. Las Vegas, Nevada. Irregular.

532. *Annual Review of Jazz Studies.* 1982–. New Brunswick, New Jersey. Institute of Jazz

Studies. Published by Scarecrow Press, Metuchen, New Jersey. Irregular. Volumes issued in 1982, 1983, 1985, 1988, 1991. Continues as *Journal of Jazz Studies*. A major outlet for scholarly research in jazz.

533. *The Coop.* 1982?–1983? New York, New York. Irregular. Folk music.

534. *Heavy Rock.* 1982?–. Barcelona, Spain. Monthly.

535. *The International Music Review.* 1982–1983. Hialeah, Florida. Irregular.

536. *International Records News.* 1982–? Imola, Italy. Monthly.

537. *Joslin's Jazz Journal.* Dedicated to the glory of record collecting. 1982–. U.S. Quarterly.

538. *Maximum Rock 'n' Roll.* 1982–. Berkeley, California. Six per year.

539. *Record Collector's Monthly.* 1982–. Essex Falls, New Jersey. Monthly.

540. *Resound.* A quarterly of the Archives of Traditional Music. 1982–. Bloomington, Indiana. Indiana University. Quarterly.

541. *Annual Chart Summaries.* 1983–. Cambridge, England. Annual.

542. *Blues & Rhythm, the Gospel Truth.* 1983?–. Cheadle, Cheshire, England. Monthly with some irregularity.

543. *CD Review Digest Annual.* 1983–1988? Voorheesville, New York. Annual.

544. *EAR for Children.* (Evaluation of audio recordings.) 1983–. Roslyn Heights, New York. Sound Advice Enterprises. Quarterly.

545. *Harmonie panorama musique.* 1983–1984. Paris, France. Monthly. Formerly: *Harmonie-opéra-Hi-fi conseil.* Superseded by *Diapason-harmonie.*

546. *HiFi Stereophonie Test.* 1983–1984? Karlsruhe, Germany. Annual. Formerly: *HiFi Stereophonie Testjahrbuch.*

547. *IFPI Newsletter.* (International Federation of Phonogram and Videogram Producers.) 1983–? London, England. Six per year.

548. *IJS Jazz Register and Indexes.* 1983–. New Brunswick, New Jersey. Institute of Jazz Studies, Rutgers University.

549. *Pulse.* (Tower Records) 1983–. West Sacramento, California. MTS. Monthly.

550. *Record & Tape Buyers Guide.* 1983–. Toronto, Canada. Annual.

551. *Rockin' Fifties.* 1983?–. Munich, Germany. Five per year.

552. *Sound & Video Contractor.* 1983–. Overland Park, Kansas. Monthly.

553. *Stimmen die um die Welt gingen.* 1983–. Münster, Germany. Four per year.

Discographies and articles on early opera and operetta singers.

554. *Videolog.* All in one video reporter. 1983?–2001. San Diego, California. Bi-weekly.

555. *Whiskey, Women, and ...* The blues & rhythm jubilee. 1971?–1989? Haverhill, Massachusetts. Irregular. Absorbed by *Rhythm & News.*

556. *Audio.* 1984–. Durango, Colorado. Orion Research Corp. Annual. Formerly: *Audio Reference Guide.*

557. *Digital Audio.* 1984–1985. Peterborough, New Hampshire. Monthly. Superseded by *Digital Audio & Compact Disc Review.* Variant title: *Digital Audio. The Compact Disc Review.*

558. *Fast Folk Musical Magazine.* 1984–. New York, New York. Ten per year. Folk and other popular music articles and record reviews.

559. *Grammy Pulse.* 1984?–1988. Burbank, California. NARAS(National Academy of Arts and Sciences). Bi-monthly. Superseded by *Grammy Magazine.*

560. *Hi-Fi Sound Magazine.* 1984?–. Quebec, Canada. Bi-monthly.

561. *Illustrated Audio Buyers Guide.* 1984–. Shawnee Mission, Kansas. Annual.

562. *Illustrated Audio Equipment Reference Catalog.* 1984–. Shawnee Mission, Kansas. Annual.

563. *In the Groove.* 1984–. Lansing, Michigan. Michigan Antique Phonograph Society. Monthly.

564. *Jazziz.* 1984–. Gainesville, Florida. Bi-monthly.

565. *Journal of the Phonograph Society of New South Wales.* 1984–. Georges Hall, Australia. Quarterly. Title from 1990: *Sound Record.*

566. *The Laser Disc Newsletter.* 1984–. New York, New York. Monthly.

567. *Musik-Info.* 1984–1986. Braunschweig, Germany. Monthly. Superseded by: *Siegert's Fachmagazin für die Unterhaltungs-Gastronomie.*

568. *The New Fortnightly College Radio Report.* 1984–1986. Bristol, Rhode Island. Monthly. Formerly: *The Fortnightly College Radio Report.* Superseded by *The Fortnightly Report.*

569. *Opus.* 1984–1988. Harrisburg, Pennsylvania. Bi-monthly. Incorporated into *Musical America.*

570. *Recording World.* 1984–. New York, New York. Quarterly.

571. *Retro-Rock Review.* 1984–1995. Brooklyn, New York. Quarterly. Superseded by *Retro-Rock.*

572. *Scherzo.* 1984?–. Madrid, Spain. Monthly.

573. *Sound Scrutiny Guides.* 1984–. Middlesex, England.

574. *Stereoplay.* 1984–. Stuttgart, Germany. Monthly. Merged with: *HiFi Stereophonie.*

575. *Canadian Antique Phonograph Society* [newsletter]. 1985–1991. Oshawa, Ontario, Canada. Monthly; slightly irregular. Collectors and collecting. Formerly: *Antique Phonogaph Society* (*Newsletter*). Superseded by *Antique Phonograph News.*

576. *Diapason-Harmonie.* 1985–. Paris, France. Monthly. Formed by the merger of *Diapason* and *Harmonie Panorama Musique.*

577. *Digital Audio & Compact Disc Review.* 1985–1988. Farmingdale, New York. Monthly. Continued by *Digital Audio.* Superseded by *Digital Audio's CD Review.*

578. *Gramophone Compact Disc Digital Audio Guide and Catalogue.* 1985–. Harrow, Middlesex, England. General Gramophone Publications, Ltd. Quarterly. Title varies.

579. *Hifi Heretic.* 1985–1991. Yorba Linda, California. Quarterly.

580. *Juke Blues.* 1985?–. London, England. Quarterly.

581. *The Music Video Leader.* (RCA/Columbia Pictures Home Video) 1985. Burbank, California. Irregular.

582. *Names & Numbers.* 1985–. Amsterdam, Netherlands. Irregular.

583. *The New Schwann Artist Issue.* 1985–. Boston, Massachusetts. Irregular. Formerly: *Schwann Artist Issue.*

584. *Option.* 1985–. Los Angeles, California. Bi-monthly. Covers nonmainstream music.

585. *rm.* 1985–1990. London, England. Weekly. Formerly: *Record Mirror.* In 1990 title changed back again to *Record Mirror.*

586. *Sonics.* 1985–1993. Alexandria NSW, Australia. Bi-monthly. Superseded by *Australian Digital.*

587. *Sound Choice.* 1985–. Ojai, California. Quarterly. Reviews electronic, ethnic, experimental, industrial, jazz, rock, new age, etc. music.

588. *Entertainment Merchandising.* 1986–1988. Duluth, Minnesota. Monthly.

589. *Compact Disc.* 1986–. New York, New York. Quarterly.

590. *Country Sounds.* 1986–1987. Iola, Wisconsin. Monthly.

591. *The Green Compact Disc Catalog.* 1986–1987. Peterborough, New Hampshire. Bi-monthly. Superseded by *The Green CD Guide.*

592. *The Historic Record.* 1986–1991. Ecclesfield, Sheffield, England. Quarterly. Superseded by *The Historic Record & AV Collector.*

593. *Jazz Archivist.* 1986–. New Orleans, Louisiana. Hogan Jazz Archive, Howard-Tilton Memorial Library, Tulane University. Semiannual.

594. *Jocks.* The U.K.'s top selling DJ magazine. 1986–. London, England, Monthly.

595. *Ken's Kompendium of Reviews of Classical Compact Discs.* 1986–1987. Atlanta, Georgia. Quarterly. Superseded by *Ken's Kompendium of Award-Winning Classical CD's.*

596. *M & D.* 1986–. Milan, Italy. Monthly. Formerly: *Musica e dischi.*

597. *Music & Media.* 1986–. Amsterdam, Netherlands. Fifty per year. Formerly: *Eurotipsheet.* Features European top hit record charts.

598. *Needle Time.* 1986?–. Swanage, Dorset, England. Bi-monthly.

599. *Playback and Fast Forward.* 1986–March–April 1993. Bombay, India. Irregular. Superseded by *Audio Video & Broadcasting Studio Systems.*

600. *Pro Sound News (Europe).* 1986–. England. Monthly.

601. *Retro-Rock.* 1986–. Brooklyn, New York. Quarterly. Formerly: *Retro-Rock Review.*

602. *Schwann.* 1986–1990. Boston, Massachusetts. Monthly; quarterly. Formerly: *New Schwann.* Superseded by *In Music Opus, Spectrum.*

603. *Streetsound.* 1986–. Toronto, Canada. Monthly. Popular music of Canada.

604. *BBC Sound Archive. Index.* 1987–. London.

605. *CD classica.* Mensile di musica classica su compact disc. 1987–. Florence, Italy. Monthly.

606. *CD Review Digest.* 1987–1989. Voorheesville, New York. Quarterly. Superseded by *CD Review Digest — Classical* and *CD Review Digest — Jazz, Popular,* etc.

607. *Compact*; La revue du disque laser. 1987–. Paris, France. Monthly.

608. *Cymbiosis.* 1987–. West Covina, California. Bi-monthly.

609. *DJ: Disc Jockey.* 1987?–. London, England. Monthly.

610. *Fairport Fanatics.* 1987?–1988. Baltimore, Maryland. Irregular.

611. *The Fortnightly Report.* 1987–1988. Bristol, Rhode Island. Irregular. Formerly: *New Fortnightly College Radio Report.*

612. *High Fidelity.* 1987–1989. New York, New York. Monthly. Absorbed by *Stereo Review* in 1989.

613. *Home Recording.* 1987–1989. Cupertino, California. Six per year. Superseded by *EQ.*

614. *IPAM Newsletter.* (International Piano Archives at Maryland.) 1987–. College Park, Maryland. Irregular.

615. *Jazzthetik.* 1987–. Münster, Germany. Monthly.

616. *Ken's Kompendium of Award-Winning Classical CD's.* 1987–. Atlanta, Georga. Semiannual. Formerly: *Ken's Kompendium of Reviews of Classical Compact Discs.*

617. *Music-Shop.* 1987–. Munich, Germany. Ten per year.

618. *Notizie dall'archivio sonoro della musica contemporanea.* 1987–. Rome, Italy. Bi-monthly.

619. *Osborne Report of New Releases.* Phoenix, Arizona.1987–1989. U.S. Monthly.

620. *Revista Musical Puertorriqueña.* 1987–. San Juan, Puerto Rico. Instituto de Cultura Puertorriqueña. Semiannual.

621. *Wavelength.* 1987–1993. New York, New York. WNYC Foundation. Monthly. Superseded by *WNYC Program Guide.*

622. *What CD?* 1987?–. Peterborough, New Hampshire. Bi-monthly.

623. *Announced.* This month is classical recordings. 1988–. U.S. Monthly.

624. *Audio Video.* 1988?–. Fairland, South Africa. Eleven per year.

625. *Collector's Noticias.* 1988?–. Rio de Janeiro, Brazil. Bi-monthly.

626. *D & J Mix.* Journal des disc-jockeys. 1988? Symphonien de-Lay, France. Monthly.

627. *Digital Audio Club.* La prima rivista di hi-fi e musica digitale. 1988–. Rome, Italy. Monthly.

628. *Dirty Linen.* 1988–. Baltimore, Maryland. Three per year; bi-monthly. Folk and rock music history and criticism. Formerly: *Fairport Fanatics.*

629. *Discoveries.* 1988–. Port Townsend, Washington. Includes country, jazz, rock and roll, etc., discographies, record reviews, record sales, concert reviews, books, magazines, articles, interviews.

630. *Grammy Magazine.* Official publication of the National Academy of Recording Arts and Sciences, Inc. 1988–2001. Burbank, California. Quarterly. Formerly: *Grammy Pulse.*

631. *Green CD Guide.* January–February 1988–June 1988. Peterborough, New Hampshire. Bi-monthly. Continues as *Green Compact DiscCatalog.* Absorbed by *Digital Audio Yearbook.*

632. *Home & Studio Recording.* 1988–1994. Canoga Park, California. Monthly. Superseded by *Recording.*

633. *Hungaroton.* 1988–. Paris, France. Irregular. Specializing in Hungarian artists and recordings.

634. *Stereo.* 1988–. Rome, Italy.

635. *Audio Carpaetorium.* 1989–. U.S. Irregular.

636. *Audio Week.* 1989–. Washington, D.C. Weekly.

637. *Australian Record & Music Review.* 1989–. Australia. Quarterly.

638. *CD Review.* 1989–1996. Peterborough, New Hampshire. Monthly. Formerly: *Digital Audio's CD Review.*

639. *CD Review Digest — Classical.* 1989–. Peterborough, New Hampshire. Quarterly. Formerly: *CD Review Digest.*

640. *CD Review Digest — Jazz, Popular* etc. 1989–. Peterborough, New Hampshire. Quarterly. Formerly: *CD Review Digest.*

641. *Classical.* 1989–1991. Rahway, New Jersey. Monthly. With WNCN and WQXR program guides as well as updates to the *Stevenson Classical Compact Disc Guide.* Superseded by *Classic CD.*

642. *Digital Audio's CD Review.* v. 5, no. 5, Jan. 1989–v. 5, no. 7, Mar. 1989. Farmingdale, New York. Monthly. Continues as *Digital Audio & Compact Disc Review.* Superseded by *CD Review.*

643. *Ecouter voir.* (Association pour la Cooperation de l'Interprofession Musicale.) 1989–. Paris, France. Quarterly.

644. *Kings Jazz Review.* 1989–1997. East Croydon, Surrey, England. Quarterly.

645. *New Orleans Music.* 1989–. Wheatley, Oxen, England. Bi-monthly. Formerly: *Footnote.*

646. *The Newsletter of the Wilhelm Furtwängler Society of America.* 1989–. Woodside, California. Irregular.

647. *Quarter Notes.* 1989–1992. Cleveland, Ohio. Telarc International Corporation. Three per year.

648. *The Picture-Disk Collector.* 1989–. Roosendal, Netherlands. Quarterly.

649. *Request.* 1989–? Minneapolis, Minnesota. Monthly.

650. *Sound & Vision.* The international record collector for all collectors of records and memorabilia. 1989–. Rome, Italy. Monthly.

651. *Alta Fedelta.* 1990–1996. Milan, Italy. Monthly.

652. *Amadeus*. 1990?–. Barcelona, Spain. Irregular.

653. *The Beat*. 1990–. U.S. Bi-monthly. Includes reviews of African, Brazilian, Caribbean, and reggae recordings.

654. *Chi e Dove*. Annuario dell'industria fonografica e dell'editoria musicale in Italia. 1990?–. Milan, Italy. Annual.

655. *Creativ*. 1990?–1995? Vienna, Austria. Monthly. Reviews of rock music.

656. *Dash World*. 1990?–. Hampshire, England. Sony Broadcast & Communications. Monthly? International recording industry articles.

657. *EQ*. The creative recording magazine. 1990–. U.S. Bi-monthly. Formerly: *Home Recording*.

658. *8-Track Mind Magazine*. 1990?–2000. East Detroit, Michigan. Quarterly.

659. *Entr'acte Muziekjournal*. 1990?–. Amsterdam, Netherlands. Ten per year.

660. *Fonorama*. 1990–. Krakow, Poland. Bi-monthly. Popular music discographies. Collectors and collecting.

661. *Audiophile*. With Hi-Fi Answers. 1990–. England. Monthly.

662. *In Music*. 1990–1991. Boston, Massachusetts. Monthly. Latest new releases. One of the three publications that continued *Schwann CD*.

663. *Je Chante*! 1990–. Paris, France. Irregular. Review of French songs and singers. Includes discographies.

664. *On the Air Magazine*. 1990–1997. Denver, Colorado. Monthly. Includes local radio program guides including WQXR.

665. *Opus*. 1990–. Boston, Massachusetts. Quarterly. Classical music guide. One of the three publications that continued as *Schwann CD*.

666. *Positive Feedback*. 1990?–. Portland, Oregon. Quarterly. Audio equipment articles.

667. *Recollections Jazz Catalogue*. 1990–. Berkeley, California. Irregular. Includes Blue Note labelography and some reprints from *Recollections Quarterly*.

668. *Sonora*. 1990–. Valdarno, Italy. Quarterly. Review of music and other arts. Includes discographies.

669. *Substance*. 1990–. Edinburgh, Scotland. Irregular. Rock music articles and reviews.

670. *Record Mirror*. 1990–. England. Weekly. Formerly: *rm*.

671. *Spectrum*. 1990–. Boston, Massachusetts. Quarterly. Popular music guide. One of the three publications that continued *Schwann CD*.

672. *Turok's Choice*. 1990–. New York, New York. Eleven per year.

673. *A.V. Collector*. An occasional periodical. 1991–. England. Irregular.

674. *The Audiophile Voice*. 1991–. Rye, New York. Five per year. Formerly: *Audiophile Society Journal*.

675. *CD International* (Popular music education). 1991–. Milwaukie, Oregon. Two per year.

676. *Classic CD*. 1991–. Bath, Avon, England. Monthly. Absorbed by *Classical*.

677. *Classical Disc Digest*. 1991?–. Ringwood, New Jersey. Irregular.

678. *Errol Garner Gems*. Journal of the Errol Garner Club. 1991–. Pomona, New York. Irregular.

679. *Fedelta del Suono*. 1991–. Rome, Italy. Monthly. Sound equipment and recordings reviews.

680. *Le Guide Compact Disques*. 1991. Paris, France. Opera International.

681. *Hi-Fi Choice*. 1991–. London, England. Monthly.

682. *Latin Beat*. 1991–. Gardena, California. Monthly. Historical articles, discographies, sound recording reviews, concert and festival notices, of Latin American music and musicians.

683. *Music Box*. 1991–1994. Cincinnati, Ohio. Five or six per year.

684. *Il Pasquino Musicale*. 1991?–. Milan, Italy. Ten per year.

685. *Vibrations*. 1991–. Lausanne, Switzerland. Irregular.

686. *Vitaphone News*. 1991–. Piscataway, New Jersey. Irregular. Early motion pictures.

687. *Antique Phonograph news*. 1992–. Toronto, Canada. Six per year. Formerly: *Canadian Antique Phonograph Society (Newsletter)*.

688. *Audio Video Magazin*. 1992?–. Barcelona, Spain. Eleven per year. Superseded by *Audio Video & Stereofonia*.

689. *Austria Creativ*. 1992–July/August 1994. Vienna, Austria. Ten per year. Superseded by *Creativ*.

690. *BBC Music Magazine*. 1992–. London, England. British Broadcasting Corp. Monthly. Guide to classical music.

691. *Capitolium: Mitteilungen rund um das Sammeln von Schallplatten*. 1992–1997. Lugano, Switzerland. Annual. French and German editions. Collectors and collecting.

692. *Classics*. 1992–1993. Harrow, Middlesex. General Gramophone Publications. Monthly.

693. *Compact Disc Magazine. Edition Classique.* 1992–1994, Troyes, France. Monthly. Formerly: *Compact, la Revue du Disque Laser.*

694. *Dance Music Magazine.* 1992–. Bologna, Italy. Eleven per year.

695. *The Descarga Newsletter.* 1992–1997?. Brooklyn, New York. Irregular. Now continued by web version of newsletter. Latin American music articles and record/video reviews.

696. *Entr'acte muziekjournaal.* 1992–1999. Amsterdam, Netherlands. Ten per year.

697. *Grammy Magazine.* Official publication of the National Academy of Recording Arts and Sciences, Inc. 1992?–2001. Burbank, California. Quarterly.

698. *Hearsay Magazine.* The new magazine for self-recording bands. 1992–. Camberley, Surrey, England. Irregular.

699. *Hi-Fi Video Test.* 1992. Zurich, Switzerland. Ten per year.

700. *The Historic Record & AV Collector.* 1992–. Ecclesfield, Sheffield, England. Quarterly. Formerly: *Historic Record.*

701. *Instant Replay.* 1992?–. Middlesex, England. Sony Consumer Products. Irregular.

702. *Labels.* Le magazine des labels Media 7. 1992?–. Nanterre, France. Irregular.

703. *Nobody Beats the Wiz Beats Magazine.* 1992?–. Toronto, Canada.

704. *Playback.* 1992–. London, England: British National Archive. Three per year.

705. *Pollstar. Record Company Rosters.* 1992–. Fresno, California. Two per year.

706. *Recording Musician.* 1992–1994. Cambridgeshire, Ives, England. Irregular. Superseded by *Sound on Sound.*

707. *Schwann Opus.* 1992–1993–2000. Santa Fe, New Mexico. Quarterly. Formerly: *Opus.*

708. *Schwann Spectrum.* 1992–. Santa Fe, New Mexico. Quarterly. Formerly: *Spectrum.*

709. *Studio Sound and Broadcast Engineering.* 1992–1995. London, England. Monthly. Superseded by *Studio Sound.*

710. *Audio Video & Broadcasting Studio Systems.* 1993–. Bombay, India. Bi-monthly. Formerly: *Playback and Fast Forward.*

711. *Australian Hi-Fi for Sound Advice.* 1993?. Cammeray, N.S.W., Australia. Monthly. Formerly: *Australian Hi-Fi and Music Review.*

712. *B-Side Magazine.* 1993?–. Burlington, New Jersey. Bi-monthly.

713. *Classical Disc Digest.* 1993–. Ringwood, New Jersey. Irregular.

714. *Classical Pulse!* 1993–. West Sacramento, California. Bi-monthly.

715. *Compact Disc Magazine.* Edition Jazz, Blues. 1993–1994. Troyes, France. Monthly.

716. *The Concert Sponsors & Promoters Directory.* Concert sponsors, coffee houses, churches with music ministries, festivals, Bible colleges, concert promoters. 1993?–. Jacksonville, Oregon. Annual.

717. *Digital Audio Broadcasting Newsletter.* 1993–. Grand-Saconnex, Switzerland. European Broadcasting Union. Quarterly. Alternate title: *DAB Newsletter.*

718. *High Test. Das Schweizer Magazin für Audio & Video.* February/March 1993–October/November 1993. Zurich, Switzerland. Bi-monthly.

719. *IASA Journal.* 1993–. Budapest, Hungary: International Association of Sound Archives. Two per year. Formerly: *Phonographic Bulletin.*

720. *Labels.* Le magazine des labels Media 7. 1993–. Nanterre, France. Irregular.

721. *Phonoscopies.* 1993–. Conflans Ste Honorine, France. Quarterly.

722. *RPM Chart Weekly.* 1993–1995. Toronto, Canada. Weekly. Formerly: *RPM Weekly.* Superseded by *RPM.*

723. *Record Collector Rare Record Price Guide.* 1993–. London, England. Record Collector Magazine. Annual.

724. *Scoreboard.* 1993?–. Nashville, Tennessee. Monthly. Gospel music.

725. *Audio Adventure.* 1994–1997. Chevy Chase, Maryland. Bi-monthly.

726. *Auditorium.* 1994–. Rome, Italy. Monthly. Discographies and CD reviews.

727. *Australian Digital.* 1994–. Alexandria NSW, Australia. Irregular. Formerly: *Sonics.*

728. *CD Compact.* 1994?–. Barcelona, Spain. Monthly.

729. *Caustic Truths.* 1994?–. Toronto, Canada. Monthly. Alternative rock music.

730. *Contatto Discografico AWF* (Artists Without Frontiers). 1994–. Rome, Italy. Monthly.

731. *Creativ.* September 1994–May 1995. Vienna, Austria. Monthly. Formerly: *Austria Creativ.* Rock music in Europe.

732. *Futura Musica.* 1994–. Milan, Italy. Monthly. Reviews of CD's and sound systems.

733. *George Birnbaum's Classical CD Scout.* 1994–. New Canaan, Connecticut. Six per year.

734. *Groove.* 1994?–. Frankfurt am Main, Germany. Monthly. Rock music.

735. *Ice: Newsletter.* 1994?–. Santa Monica, California. Monthly. CD newsletter.

736. *Just for the Record.* 1994–. Dover, Kent, England. British Archive of Country Music. Quarterly.

737. *La Lettre du Disque.* 1994?–. Paris, France. Forty-five per year. Popular music radio stations in France.

738. *Live Sound! International.* 1994–. Freport, Illinois. Bi-monthly. Formerly: *Live Sound!*

739. *The Mix.* 1994. Ely, England. Irregular. Continues as *Music Technology.*

740. *Music Gazette.* 1994?–. Las Vegas, Nevada. Monthly. Formerly: *RTS Music Gazette.*

741. *Recording.* 1994–. Canoga Park, Los Angeles, California. Monthly. English and Spanish editions. Formerly: *Home & Studio Recording.*

742. *Scoreboard.* February 1994–No. 10, 1994. Nashville, Tennessee. Ten per year. Superseded by *Gospel Industry Today.* Gospel music and musicians.

743. *Sonero.* 1994–1997. Bradenton Beach, Florida. Three per year; irregular. Popular music of Cuba. Mostly in Spanish; some English.

744. *The Sound Box.* California Antique Phonograph Society. 1994?–. Duarte, California. Bi-monthly. Collectors and collecting.

745. *Sound on Sound.* 1994–. St. Ives, Cambs, England. Irregular. Incorporating *Recording Musician.*

746. *Soundscapes.* 1994?–. Rushcutters Bay, NSW, Australia. Bi-monthly.

747. *Story Untold Music Alliance* [newsletter]. 1994?–. Piscataway, New Jersey. Irregular. Doo-wop music.

748. *Unfiled.* Music under new technology. 1994?–. Surrey, England. Quarterly? Formerly: *Records Quarterly Magazine.*

749. *Victrola and 78 Journal.* 1994?–. Roseville, California. Irregular.

750. *Bossa.* Brazilian jazz world guide. 1995–. Boston, Massachusetts. Monthly. Ten per year.

751. *Caustic Truths!* 1995?–. Toronto, Canada. Monthly. Alternative rock music.

752. *International Classical Record Collector.* 1995–2000. Harrow, Middlesex, England. Gramophone Publications Ltd. Four per year.

Collectors and collecting. Superseded by *Classic Record Collector.*

753. *International Music Connection.* The newsletter of the International Music Collection. 1995?–. London, England: International Music Collection, The British Library National Sound Archive. Irregular.

754. *La Lettre du Disque.* 1995?–. Paris, France. Forty-five per year. Popular music radio stations in France.

755. *Pro Audio Review.* 1995–. Falls Church, Virginia. Bi-monthly; monthly.

756. *RPM.* 1995–. Toronto, Canada. Weekly. Formerly: *RPM Chart Weekly.*

757. *Remembering the Mills Brothers.* 1995–. Ambler, Pennsylvania. Three per year.

758. *Rotations.* 1995–. Woking, Surrey, England. Bi-monthly.

759. *Schwann CD Review Digest. Classical.* 1995–2000? Santa Fe, New Mexico. Quarterly; fourth issue being the annual cumulation.

760. *Schwann CD Review Digest. Rock, Pop, Jazz,* etc. 1995–2000? Santa Fe, New Mexico. Quarterly; fourth issue being the annual cumulation.

761. *Soundscapes.* 1995?–. Rushcutters Bay, NSW, Australia. Bi-monthly.

762. *Stereophile Guide to Home Theater.* 1995–. Santa Fe, New Mexico. Quarterly.

763. *Studio Sound.* 1995–2001. London, England. Monthly. Formerly: *Studio Sound and Broadcast Engineering.*

764. *Swiss Music Info.* 1995–1999. Wabern, Switzerland. Ten per year. Chiefly in German; some French and Italian.

765. *The Tracking Angle.* 1995–. San Jose, California. Bi-monthly.

766. *Victrola and 78 Journal.* 1995–. Roseville, California. Irregular.

767. *Vinyl.* Musique hors bizness. 1995–. Les Essarts-le-Roi, France. Bi-monthly.

768. *AF Digitale.* 1996–. Milan, Italy. Monthly. Formerly: *Alta Fedelta.*

769. *Australian Hi-Fi.* 1996–. St. Leonards, N.S.W., Australia. Twelve per year. Formerly: *Australian Hi-Fi for Sound Advice.*

770. *Le Bulletin de l'Industrie du Disque et des Medias.* 1996?–. Le Chambon-sur-Lignon, France. Semimonthly.

771. *CD Review's Music & the Arts.* 1996–. Peterborough, New Hampshire. Irregular. Formerly: *CD Review.*

772. *Collector's Noticias.* 1996?–. Rio de Janeiro, Brazil. Bi-monthly.

773. *Fi*. The magazine of music and sound. 1996–. San Francisco, California. Ten per year.

774. *Gramofon*. 1996?–. Budapest, Hungary. Monthly?

775. *Gramofonovy Klub*. 1996?–. Prague, Czechoslovakia. Irregular.

776. *Gramophone Explorations*. 1996?–. Harrow, Middlesex, England. Gramophone Publications Ltd. Irregular.

777. *International Music Connection*. The newsletter of the International Music Collection. 1996?–. London, England. British Library National Sound Archive. Irregular.

778. *International Opera Collector*. 1996–1999. Harrow, Middlesex, England. Gramophone Publications Ltd. Quarterly.

779. *InTune*. 1996?–. Hiroshima-shi, Japan. Monthly except August. Chiefly in English; some articles in Japanese.

780. *Positive Feedback*. 1996?–. Portland, Oregon. Quarterly. Audio equipment reviews.

781. *R.E.D. Classical Service*. 1996?–. London, England. Retail Entertainment Data. Monthly. Classical new releases.

782. *Start Up*. 1996?–. La Varenne St-Hilaire, France. Irregular.

783. *The AFIM Music Mix*. News from the Association for Independent Music. 1997–1998. Whitesburg, Kentucky. Monthly. Formerly: *NAIRD Notes* (National Association of Independent Record Distributors and Manufacturers).

784. *Le Bulletin de l'Industrie du Disque et des Medias*. 1997?–. Le Chambon-sur-Lignon, France. Semimonthly.

785. *CRI Currents*. (Composers Recordings, Inc.) 1997–2000. New York, New York. Irregular.

786. *Goldberg*. Early music magazine. 1997–. Pamplona, Spain. Bi-monthly. Text in English and Spanish.

787. *Gramofon*. 1997?–. Budapest, Hungary. Monthly.

788. *Gospel Industry Today*. 1997?–. Nashville, Tennessee. Ten per year. Formerly: *Scoreboard*.

789. *IndieCent*. 1997–1999. Brooklyn, New York. Two per year.

790. *International Piano Quarterly*. 1997–. Sudbury Hill, Harrow, Middlesex, England. Gramophone Publications. Quarterly.

791. *Jazzwise Magazine*. 1997–. London, England. Monthly.

792. *Newsletter. Phonograph Society of South Australia Inc*. 1997?–. Norwood, South Australia. Eleven per year.

793. *Revista Salsa Cubana*. 1997–. Havana, Cuba. Quarterly. Latin music record reviews and historical articles.

794. *Start Up*. 1997?–. La Varenne St-Hilaire, France. Irregular. Popular music recordings.

795. *Tower Records Guide to Classical Music on Video*. 1997–. Berkeley, California. Irregular.

796. *WorldDAB Newsletter*. International news and strategic analysis on digital sound broadcasting. 1997–. Grand-Saconnex, Switzerland. Bi-monthly; irregular. Formerly: *EuroDab Newsletter*.

797. *L'Annee du Disque*. 1998?–. Paris, France. Annual.

798. *Classical Music. The Rough Guide*. 1998?–. London, England and New York, New York. Annual. Formerly: *Rough Guide*: *Classical Music on CD*.

799. *Klassik Heute*. 1998–. Munich, Germany. Monthly.

800. *Music Choice*. 1998. New York, New York. Bi-monthly. Formerly: *Mike*.

801. *R.E.D. Classical Service*. 1998–. London, England. Retail Entertainment Data. Classical music catalogue.

802. *State of Independents*. The newsletter of the Association for Independent Music. March 1998–December 1998. Whitesburg, Kentucky. Six to eight per year. Superseded by *Indie Music World*.

803. *Amadeus*. 1999?–. Barcelona, Spain. Six per year.

804. *Boletin Musica*. 1999–. Havana, Cuba. Three per year. Formerly: *Musica*.

805. *Hard Rock & Metal Hammer*. 1999–. Zug, Germany. Monthly. Formerly: *Metal Hammer/Crash*.

806. *Indie Music World*. 1999–. Whitesburg, Kentucky. Ten per year. Formerly: *AFIM Music Mix and State of Independents*.

807. *On the Record*. International Association of Jazz Record Collectors. 1999–2001. Lady Lake, Florida. Four per year.

808. *R&R Directory*. 1999–. Los Angeles, California. Radio & Records, Inc. Semiannual. Formerly: *R&R Ratings Report & Directory; R&R Program Supplier Guide*.

809. *Songlines*. 1999–. Harrow, England. Gramophone Publications, Ltd. Quarterly. Covers folk, pop and world music.

810. *Classic Record Collector*. 2000–. Harrow, Middlesex, England. Quarterly. Formerly: *International Classical Record Collector*.

811. *The Electronics Collector*. 2000–. Live Oak, Florida. Monthly. Formerly: *Horn Speaker*.
812. *Farandula*. 2000?–. San Juan, Puerto Rico. Monthly. Recording industry articles and record reviews.
813. *International Record Review*. 2000–. London, England. Monthly.
814. *Just for the Record*. 2000?–. Dover, Kent, England: British Archive of Country Music. Quarterly.
815. *Listener: Hi-Fi & Music Review*. 2000?–2002. Greenwich, Connecticut. Bi-monthly.
816. *Revista Salsa Cubana*. 2000?–. Havana, Cuba. Quarterly. Recording industry articles and record reviews.
817. *Schwann Inside Jazz & Classical*. 2000–. Woodland, California. Monthly.
818. *Audio Video & Stereofonia*. 2001–. Barcelona, Spain. Eleven per year. Formerly: *Audio Video Magazine*.
819. *AudioXpress*. 2001–. Peterborough, New Hampshire. Audio Amateur Corp. Irregular. Formed by the union of *Audio Electronics, Glass Audio* and *Speaker Builder*.
820. *Sound & Vision*. 2001–. New York, New York. Ten per year. Formerly: *Stereo Review's Sound & Vision*.
821. *Star-Gennett Foundation. News*. 2001–. Richmond, Indiana. Irregular.
822. *AES News*. Audio Engineering Society Newsletter. 2002?–. New York, New York. Irregular.

This article is a revised, updated, and expanded version of "Sound Recording Periodicals: 1890–1929" (*Performing Arts Resources*, 1989). Information has been gathered from the New York Public Library catalogs, *Union List of Serials, New Serial Titles, Ulrich's Periodicals Directory, Serials Directory* (Ebsco), and various specialized sources. I would like to thank the following individuals and institutions for their kind assistance in the compilation of this listing: Gary-Gabriel Gisondi, Rodgers & Hammerstein Archives of Recorded Sound, New York Public Library (whose publication, "Sound Recordings Periodicals, a Preliminary Union Catalog of Pre-LP-related Holdings in Member Libraries of the Associated Audio Archives" [*ARSC Journal* 10 (19780] was a great source of information; Donald McCormick, Rodgers & Hammerstein Archives of Recorded Sound, New York Public Library; Richard Warren and his staff, Yale University, Historical Sound Recordings Collection; New York Public Library for the Performing Arts; New York Public Library General Research Division and the Annex; Detroit Public Library; National Library of Canada, Music Division; National Archives of Canada, Moving Image and Sound Archives; Vancouver Public Library; National Film & Sound Archive, Canberra, Australia; National Library of Australia; The British Library, National Sound Archive; The British Library, Bibliographical Information Service; Staatliches Institut für Musikforschung Preussischer Kulturbesitz, Berlin; Staatsbibliothek Preussischer Kulturbesitz, Berlin; Phonogrammarchiv der Oesterrichischen Akademie der Wissenschaften, Vienna; Bibliothéque Nationale, Départment de la Phonothéque Nationale et de l'Audio-visuel, Paris; Casalini Libri, Florence; M.E. Saltykov-Shchedrin State Public Library, Leningrad; Lenin State Public Library, Moscow. As the list of titles is no more than a preliminary checklist, additions and corrections from readers are invited.

SARA VELEZ

SOUND REPRODUCTION CO.
A New York firm, located at 56 Liberty St. in 1916. It made the Maestrola disc player, sold for $12.

SOUNDSCAN INC.
SoundScan, Inc. gathers point-of-sale (POS) information from record retailers and reports actual sales of recordings by city, store, chain, artist, and label. The adoption of Uniform Product Code (bar code) by the record industry in 1979 led retailers to keep specific records of sales for inventory management purposes. In 1989 marketing researchers Mike Shalett and Mike Fine formed SoundScan to collect that POS data. By 2001 SoundScan reported sales from over 18,000 retail locations; accounting for over 85 percent of record sales in the U.S. SoundScan data became the basis of *Billboard*'s popularity charts beginning in 1991. In 2000 it began to track internet sales and digital downloads. SoundScan is 60 percent owned by VNU, nv, the Netherlands firm that also owns *Billboard*'s parent company, BPI Communications, AC Neilsen, SRDS, and other data services.

G.P. HULL

SOUNDSTAGING

SEE STEREOPHONIC RECORDING; SWEET SPOT

SOUNDSTREAM
A system of sonic enhancement for acoustic records, invented by Thomas Stockham. Using digital technology, soundstream adds harmonics that were not

produced in the original recording by means of a parallel modern recording of the same work. It reduces surface noise, and brings the singer's voice forward; but also increases the presence of low-pitched rumble. The most notable soundstream recordings are those of Enrico Caruso, issued by RCA.

See also **Sound Preservation and Restoration of Historical Recordings**

SOUNDSTREAM INC.

SEE STOCKHAM, THOMAS

SOUSA, JOHN PHILIP
(6 NOV 1854–6 MAR 1932)

American bandmaster, violinist, and composer, born in Washington, D.C. He studied violin, then the wind instruments, and played with the United States Marine Band at age 13; in 1880 he became its director. He resigned in 1892 to form his own Grand Concert Band, with which he became world famous. The band performed at the Columbian Exposition in Chicago in 1893, and at the Paris Exposition of 1900; it made European tours and a world tour in 1910–1911. Sousa continued band work into the 1920s. His died in Reading, Pennsylvania.

Sousa was a pioneer recording artist with Columbia cylinders from 1890; in the earliest known record sales list there are 59 cylinders by the Marine Band, consisting of 23 marches, five waltzes, nine polkas, and 22 miscellaneous pieces. Only a small complement of the ensemble was involved in the studio recording, as few as 16 or 17 players. Sousa did not participate in recording, being a skeptic about the whole business ("the menace of mechanical music" as he termed it in a magazine article). When his own band began to record, he let other men do the conducting of it, usually Arthur Pryor.

In 1893 the New Jersey Phonograph Co. began to record the new Grand Concert Band, and listed 23 cylinders; however, none has come to light. The band recorded Columbia cylinders from 1895 to 1899, making 52 records. Four undated catalogs of the Chicago Talking Machine Co., issued before 1900, included 29 records by the Sousa Band; one scholar speculates that the recordings date from May 1895 [Smart 1970]. Other labels with Sousa material that were not simply copied from Columbia Records include D.E. Boswell Co., Chicago (eight records), the U-S Phonograph Co., Newark (19 records), Victor (542 sides during 1900–1902), and Edison (36 cylinders in 1909–1910). After 1911 the band became a Victor-exclusive ensemble. There were still 14 titles by the band in the 1940 catalog, including the most enduring of the great

Sousa compositions, "Stars and Stripes Forever" (#20132) and "Washington Post" (#20191).

SOUTH DAKOTA PHONOGRAPH CO.

One of the affiliates of the North American Phonograph Co., established in 1890 in Sioux Falls. Henry Lacey was general manager.

SOUTHERN FOUR

SEE FISK UNIVERSITY JUBILEE QUARTET

SOVEREIGN (LABEL)

A U.K. record, unbreakable and double-sided, offered by British Sonogram, Ltd., in 1907. It was made by the Disc Record Co., Ltd., of Stockport, Cheshire.

SPACED-ARRAY MICROPHONE RECORDING

Sometimes called A-B stereo or difference stereo, uses two spaced-apart microphones to record stereo audio signals. Depending upon the distances between the microphones, the spacing introduces time and phase differences between the signals that results in a realistic, but still somewhat ersatz sense of spaciousness that often works very well in typical home-listening environments. Focus and imaging may be vague, however, unless additional spot microphones are used. The technique is often used to record large orchestral ensembles.

See also **Blumlein Stereo Recording; Coincident Stereo Recording; Microphone**

HOWARD FERSTLER

SPALDING, ALBERT
(15 AUG 1888–26 MAY 1953)

American violinist, born in Chicago. He studied as a child in Florence and Paris, and made his debut in Paris on 6 June 1905, playing the Saint Saëns Third Concerto to great critical acclaim. He played the same concerto in his first "official" U.S. appearance, with the New York Symphony Orchestra on 8 Nov 1908 (he had performed earlier, as a guest soloist at the Metropolitan Opera House, 29 Nov 1908). He toured Europe; served in the U.S. Army during World War I, then concertized extensively and in 1941 he had his own CBS radio program. During World War II Spalding was again in the service, and was for a time head of Radio Rome (for the Allied forces). He was decorated by three governments for his military accomplishments. After five more years of concerts, he retired in 1950, and died in New York.

Spalding was one of several violinists to record for Edison, but the only one with a wide following; he made cylinders in 1909, and Edison Diamond Discs from 1913 to 1929. In 1926 he was briefly with Brunswick. Victor signed him in the 1930s.

The first Edison was a four-minute Amberol cylinder dating from August 1909, the Wieniawski "Polonaise in D-Major" (#177). Later he made a popular cylinder (#3815) and Diamond Disc record (#82536; 1915) of Gounod's "Ave Maria" with soprano Marie Rappold; the disc was used in tone tests. (In 1953 Spalding said of the tone tests that nobody could have distinguished between the live artist and the record; but that on modern records anybody could!) Other singers with whom he collaborated on Edison were Claudia Muzio and Frieda Hempel.

More than 70 Spalding records, concert standards, and arrangements of songs were listed in the 1925 Edison catalog. With Victor he began to deal with the solid repertoire, including the sonatas of Franck, Brahms, Tartini, and Handel. His accompanist of more than 40 years, Andre Benoist, was his partner in those sonatas. A particularly notable disc was the Ludwig Spohr Concert No. 8, with Eugene Ormandy and the Philadelphia Orchestra (#15355–56; album #M-544). [Ferrara 1988/7; Walsh 1954/2–3.]

SPANIER, MUGGSY
(9 NOV 1906–12 FEB 1967)

American jazz cornetist, born Francis Joseph Spanier in Chicago. He played drums as a child, then cornet in school band and then in various Chicago groups. In 1929 he was invited to join the Ted Lewis orchestra, remaining until 1936; then he was with Ben Pollack two years. His subsequent moves were numerous, including time with Bob Crosby, Miff Mole, and Earl Hines. He retired for health reasons in 1964, and died in Sausalito, California.

Spanier's first records were made for Gennett in 1924 with a group he called the Bucktown Five; "Hot Mittens" (#5518) and "Buddy's Habits" (#5418) were the most interesting of the seven sides. In 1939 he recorded again, for Bluebird in four sessions. This time he had his Ragtime Band, and the presentations were in the general style of Bob Crosby's Bobcats, a little out of step with the jazz/swing bands of the period. "Dippermouth Blues" (#B-10506) was an imitation of the King Oliver 1923 disc, and "Livery Stable Blues" (#B-10518) was not unlike the version

by the Original Dixieland Jazz Band (1917). The best two of eight sides made for Decca in 1942, with a large orchestra, were "Chicago"/"Can't We Be Friends?" (#4168). A Riverside LP reissued the Bucktown material (#RLP 1035); a CMS LP (#FL 20009) covered the 1939 records; and Avalon 12 reissued the 1942 material on LP.

SPATIALIZER

Developed by Desper Products, and utilized in some VCRs, televisions, and playback devices to improve the sound of two-channel program sources, it is a spatial enhancement technique that adds matrixing, cross-talk cancellation, and frequency-response manipulations. It is also employed by some motion picture and music recording systems, with the required enhancements applied during the mixing and editing processes. The result in either case simulates a large-stage image up front and phantom-surround effects, doing so without the need of extra channels.

See also **Crosstalk; Q Channel**

HOWARD FERSTLER

SPDIF (SONY/PHILIPS DIGITAL INTERFACE)

A consumer version of the AES3 (old AES/EBU) digital audio interconnection standard based on coaxial cable and RCA connectors.

HOWARD FERSTLER

SPEARS, BRITNEY (2 DEC 1981–)

Attractive, personable, and a born entertainer, it could be argued that Britney Spears was destined to be teen idol material. Certainly the preteen audience in the late 1990s was sufficiently well heeled to provide elbow room for a host of competitors, including Christina Aguilera and Ricky Martin from the Latin music scene, Brandy and Monica (R&B), LeAnn Rimes (country music), Jessica Simpson (Christian contemporary), and 'N Sync (pop-rock). As Spears approaches adulthood, however, it remains to be seen whether she will be able maintain her commercial success à la Michael Jackson or fade into obscurity much like bygone stars David and Shaun Cassidy, Bobby Sherman, Leif Garrett, Tiffany, Debbie Gibson, and the New Kids on the Block.

A veteran of television commercials and the off-Broadway show *Ruthless* (1991) prior to appearing as a regular on *The New Mickey Mouse Club* during the 1993–1994 seasons, Spears's recording career began at age 15 when an audition for Jive Records led to a

Sheet music cover for "… Baby, One More Time," Britney Spear's first major hit. Courtesy David A. Jasen

contract. To record the debut album, Jive — following the formula that had helped lift one of its other acts, the Backstreet Boys, to superstardom — sent her to Stockholm to work with producers Max Martin and Eric Foster White.

Hyped by steady touring — both as an opening act for label-mates 'N Sync and on her own performing to backing tapes at shopping malls — Spears's debut single, "Baby One More Time" (Jive #42525) entered the *Billboard Hot 100* at number one in October 1998. The album of the same name (Jive 41651; 1999) repeated the feat when released the following January. Helped by three more successful singles — "Sometimes" (album cut from Jive #41651; 1999; #21), "(You Drive Me) Crazy" (Jive #42606; 1999; #10), and "From the Bottom of My Broken Heart" (Jive #25013; 2000; #14) — and her provocative blend of suggestive sexuality and youthful innocence, the LP sold more than 13 million copies through 2000, also earning her a Grammy nomination for Best New Artist.

Spears's style combined hip-hop influenced backing tracks with her whitebread voice, repeating an age-old formula of a white artist co-opting a Black style

and achieving great commercial success. Initially, her handlers marketed her as a classic combination of teenage innocence and raw sexuality; but the young star was anxious to establish herself as a "woman" and so the sexual content of her songs and videos was increasingly emphasized.

Spears's follow-up album, *Oops! … I Did It Again* (Jive #41704; 2000), also reached number one, selling in excess of 8 million copies within a year of its release. It also produced a series of hits, including "Lucky" (Zomba #25106; 2000) and "Stronger" (Jive #42762; 2000). She collaborated with her mother on a memoir, *Heart to Heart* (2000), thereby providing an alternative to the legions of knock-off paperbacks attempting to exploit her celebrity. By now a major pop culture phenomenon, she was represented by a flood of import and nonmusical releases in domestic record bins.

Although her third official album, *Britney* (Jive #41776; 2001), strained the credibility of her demure image, it extended her commercial hot streak. Its lead single is "I'm a Slave 4 U" (Jive #25275; 2001), whose phonetic spelling and general sound recalls the mid-1990s work of Prince.

FRANK HOFFMANN

SPECIAL RECORD (LABEL)
A series produced by Columbia/Harmony in the late 1920s especially for use by stage and motion picture theaters; the idea was to promote songs that were popular in the day's performance. Fine artists and a high standard of recording mark the label. [Rust 1978.]

SPECIALTY (LABEL)
Rock/R&B label founded by Los Angeles–based entrepreneur Art Rupe (b. Arthur Goldberg, 5 Sep 1923, in Pittsburgh, Pennsylvania). Rupe came to Los Angeles to attend UCLA, where he met Robert Scherman; the duo set up Atlas Records in 1944 after they graduated. The label lasted only four months, but it managed to make early recordings of Nat King Cole and Frankie Laine. Soon after, Rupe set up Juke Box Records on his own, recording local R&B acts, including Roy Milton and the Sepia Tones. He sold the Juke Box name, although not the masters, to the owner of Sterling Records, Al Middleman, in mid-1946, and restarted under the Specialty Records name. Specialty began with a similar roster of local R&B acts, including Jimmy Liggins and Percy Mayfield. In 1952 Rupe traveled to New Orleans in search of talent, discovering Lloyd Price, who scored a number one R&B hit with "Lawdy, Miss Clawdy" later that year. Soon after, he befriended a Los Angeles bandleader and composer

Robert "Bumps" Blackwell, and hired him to produce sessions for the label. Blackwell went to New Orleans in 1955 where he discovered and produced the first hits of Little Richard. He also oversaw the Soul Stirrers recordings for Specialty. Rupe passed when Blackwell produced a pop session for the Stirrers's lead singer, Sam Cooke, missing out on the monster hit "You Send Me" (it was issued by the smaller, local Keen label instead). Other artists on the label included Joe Liggins and His Honeydrippers, Guitar Slim, Sister Wynona Carr, and John Lee Hooker.

CARL BENSON

SPECTACLE

A combination recorder and reproducer assembly invented by Thomas Edison (U.S. patent #386,974; filled 26 Nov 1887; granted 31 July 1888) with improvements by Ezra Gilliland (U.S. patent #393,640; filed 7 June 1888; granted 27 Nov 1888). The device enabled the user to make a record and then play it back quickly on the same machine, simply by pivoting the spectacle, which held — in a form similar to a pair of eyeglasses — the recorder diaphragm and stylus along with the counterparts of the reproducer. The spectacle was first marketed in Edison's Perfected Phonograph of 1888.

SPECTOR, PHIL (26 DEC 1940–)

Born Harvey Phillip Spector in the Bronx, New York, Spector is among the most influential producers of the rock era. The Spector family relocated to Fairfax, California, in 1953, but Spector's father died soon after. With friends Annette Kleibard and Marshall Leib, Spector formed the teen vocal group the Teddy Bears, who scored a number one hit with Spector's "To Know Him Is to Love Him" (Dore #503) in 1958; the song's title came from the epigraph on Spector's father's tombstone. After working in Los Angeles with producers Lester Sill and Lee Hazelwood, Spector moved to New York to work with songwriters/record producers Mike Leiber and Jerry Stoller, assisting them on various sessions between 1959–1960. In 1961 Spector returned to Los Angeles and partnered with Sills to form the aptly named Philles label.

In the early 1960s, while major record companies churned out disc after disc in hopes of landing a hit, producer Phil Spector had a different approach. At his Philles Records, he would labor over individual releases, overdubbing scores of musicians to create what became known as the Wall of Sound. Spector usually worked out of Goldstar Studios and used a crew of regular backup musicians to give his records their characteristic thunderous sound. The first group Spector recorded at Philles was the Crystals, who had a hit early in 1962 with "There's No Other (Like My Baby)" (Philles #100). The group scored its first number one hit in 1962 with "He's a Rebel" (Philles #106), launching a string of 20 consecutive hits for the Crystals. Other successful acts for Spector included the girl group the Ronettes, and singer Darlene Love. His grandest productions came for the Righteous Brothers ("You've Lost that Lovin' Feelin'" Philles #124; 1964; #1) and the monumental production of "River Deep, Mountain High" for Ike and Tina Turner. However, the later single scored little success at the time, and Spector went into self-imposed retirement, closing Philles soon after.

Spector's work was held in such high regard by the Beatles that, as the group was falling apart, John Lennon approached him about salvaging material recorded during the filming of *Let It Be*. Spector did a characteristic job — much to the chagrin of Paul McCartney, who's "Long and Winding Road," a simple piano ballad, was buried in strings and vocal choruses. Spector then worked with Lennon and Harrison on their initial solo efforts. Lennon, however, began to experience difficulties with the ever-eccentric producer, who ran off with the session tapes for a projected album of rock oldies that the duo was recording in Los Angeles in 1973. The album was eventually completed by Lennon, but by then their creative partnership was over.

Spector formed Warner-Spector records in partnership with the media giant in 1974, both to reissue his earlier recordings and for new releases; for markets outside of the U.S., he partnered with Polydor in the label Phil Spector International. Spector became increasingly reclusive, although he did work on two notable albums toward the end of the 1970s, Leonard Cohen's *Death of a Ladies Man* (1977) and the Ramones's *End of the Century* (1980). After a decade of inactivity, Spector was voted into the Rock and Roll Hall of Fame in 1989. Spector partnered with manager Allen Klein in the early 1990s, and the duo released the boxed set *Back to Mono* (ABKCO #7118), in 1991, making his recordings available for the first time in a well-conceived, documented form. The Spector catalog was sold to EMI in the mid-1990s, it has been re-released by it in various forms since.

Spector's life as a rock legend continued unabated through the 1990s, although he remained in seclusion. Rumors of eccentricity were amply confirmed in 2002 when a woman was found dead at his mansion. Spector's influence is keenly seen in artists as disparate as Bruce Springsteen and the Beach Boys.

REV. CARL BENSON

SPEEDS

A major challenge to all forms of sound recording has been to establish the optimal and agreed-upon speed of the medium as it spins on a turntable, turns on a mandrel, or passes a given point. A speed that is too slow will result in unacceptable distortion products and one that is too quick will use up the recording surface in a short time. Another problem with analog systems is ensuring that the play-back speed is exactly the same as the recording speed. If it is not there will be a change in musical pitch.

Analog discs are supposed to rotate at a constant number of revolutions per minute (rpm). In other words, they operate as constant angular velocity (CAV) systems. There was a fair range of different standardizations among principal manufacturers of discs during the acoustic period. For example, following Victor's lead, most American labels were recording at 78–80 rpm shortly after the turn of the century. However 75 rpm was the norm for Columbia acoustics made in France, Italy, and Spain, and for Odeon acoustics in all countries. Parlophone used 75 rpm for one series, and 80 rpm for another. Victor itself announced in its May 1917 catalog that "all records should be played at a speed of 76"; however, the November 1917 catalog gives the correct speed as 78, suggesting the possibility of a misprint in the May edition.

Other labels showed similar variations from the "standard" 78 rpm. Even the first electric-produced recordings may sometimes be odd. Ault [1987] reports on his study of Columbia set #X198 (1927) of "Les Préludes" by Felix Weingartner and the London Symphony: "The four sides were recorded at four different speeds, the first side at about 74 rpm, with each side a little faster until the last side was at about 77 rpm." Ault [1987] also points out the slow recording speed for the first Bing Crosby record (70 rpm) and the fast speed (83 rpm) of Columbia #50-D of the Original Memphis Five (1924). Variations in speed were even found from one session to another in the same studio.

In modern discographies of old records, the compiler often endeavors to indicate the correct recording (and playback) speed of each disc. John Bolig's *Recordings of Enrico Caruso*, for example, notes all the correct speeds, which range from 75 to 80 rpm. The Phonometer was a 1907 device intended to monitor turntable speed. Eventually, standardization took hold and the 33 1/3–rpm LP microgroove discs and 45 rpm discs that were the mainstay of recorded sound in the home accurately maintained the advertised speeds.

The compact disc operates on a completely different level. The CD requires constant linear velocity (CLV) for its tracking mechanism to maintain a constant tracking speed, meaning a variable angular velocity. Because the CD playback mechanism is digitally controlled, the required speeds can be very accurately maintained. Compact discs rotate from 200 to 500 rpm, as do DVD recordings. Laser discs come in two forms, some having constant linear velocity at from 600 to 1800 rpm, or constant angular velocity at a steady 1800 rpm.

See also **Cylinder; Disc; Surface Speed; Tuning Band**

REV. HOWARD FERSTLER

SPENCER, ELIZABETH (1875–APRIL 1930)

American mezzo-soprano, born Elizabeth Dickerson in Denver, Colorado. She sang in vaudeville and concert, and recorded from 1911 for Edison, who regarded her as his "favorite soprano." She did ballads, some opera ("Hear Me, Norma" on Amberol #629; "My Heart at Thy Sweet Voice," on Diamond Disc #82512), duets (with Charles Harison, Henry Burr, John Young, Walter Van Brunt, and others), and sang with the Homestead Trio (1921–1925), Metropolitan Quartet, and the Edison Mixed Quartet. Her best-selling record was the B side of Diamond Disc #80160 where she sang "On the Banks of the Brandywine," happily combined with Edison's greatest hit, "I'll Take You Home Again, Kathleen," by Van Brunt. Spencer was one of the Edison tone test artists.

In 1917 she turned to Victor and became their exclusive. "A Perfect Day" (#18250) was her first record; her most popular Victor was her last one: "Let the Rest of the World Go By," a duet with Charles Hart (1923). Then she worked for Emerson, Regal, and Banner and returned to Edison in 1921. In 1926 she recorded as one of the Metropolitan Entertainers. Spencer died in Denver. [Walsh 1951/8–9.]

SPENCER, GRACE (1872–1952)

American soprano, one of the earliest recording artists; known as the First Lady of the Phonograph. She recorded five duets with Harry Macdonough in 1900, on Edison brown-wax cylinders, beginning with "Life's Dream Is O'er" (#7559); made a nine-inch Zonophone disc ca. 1900 ("I Will Magnify Thee O God"); and began to record for Victor on 10 July 1901, in Macdonough duets, the first being "When We Are Married" (#V-904). Her first Victor solo, recorded in the same session, and the first by a woman on the label, was "Queen of the Philippine Islands." Spencer had been heard even earlier on Victor, as a member of the Lyric Trio; that group rendered a trio from Verdi's *Attila* on 15 June 1900. [Walsh 1948/4–5.]

SPENCER, LEN
(12 FEB 1867–15 DEC 1914)

American baritone and comedian, born Leonard Garfield Spencer in Washington, D.C. He worked in his father's business school and was attracted by the Columbia "Office Graphophones" there. On an errand to the Columbia establishment, he made some song recordings, and was drawn to a recording career; he became Len Spencer, the singer, and Leonard G. Spencer, the interpreter of famous speeches. He also spoke the announcements on Columbia cylinders and discs. Spencer made more than 50 cylinders for the New Jersey Phonograph Co. by 1893. He made Berliner discs and recorded for Edison. Then he signed an exclusive contract with Columbia in May 1898. Soon he was one of the leading figures in the new industry.

Spencer's repertoire was greatly varied. In 1898 for Columbia brown-wax cylinders he did coon songs and sentimental ballads; he sang duets with Roger Harding, covering a spectrum from "Nearer My God, to Thee" (#8415) to "The Broadway Swell and the Bowery Bum" (#8402). The Spencer Trio was active in the same period.

In 1901 Spencer appeared on Victor discs, in coon and minstrel duets with Vess Ossman. Accompanied by Parke Hunter's banjo, Spencer made his most famous record for Victor on 25 Sep 1903: the comic sketch "Arkansaw Traveler" (#1101). It was still in the catalog in 1922, along with such favorites as "Auction Sale of Household Goods" (#857; 1904) and "Barnyard Serenade" (#4562; 1905). "Arkansaw" had appeared earlier as an Edison cylinder (#8202; 1902); "Barnyard" was also an Edison cylinder (#9191; 1906).

There were also duets with Ada Jones in 1905–1906, Bowery sketches, coon skits, Jewish and Irish routines. Spencer's fine speaking voice was heard in renditions of President McKinley's final speech in 1901, Lincoln's Gettysburg address, and William Jennings Bryan's renowned "Cross of Gold" oration. Jim Walsh cites "Little Arrow and Big Chief Greasepaint" as "one of the funniest things ever cut into wax"; it remained in the Edison catalog until 1929. Spencer's final recording, his only Edison Diamond Disc, was "Uncle Fritz and the Children's Orchestra" (#50196; 1914). He also ran a booking agency in New York, Len Spencer's Lyceum. He died in New York City. [Brooks 1979; Walsh 1947/3–8.]

SPENCER TRIO

A male vocal ensemble that recorded for Columbia cylinders ca. 1897–1898, and for Victor discs in 1903–1904. The membership varied: Len Spencer was always one of the three, with (for Victor) Billy Golden and Steve Porter; or (for Columbia) Billy Golden, Billy Williams, Roger Harding, or Steve Porter. A whistler named Chalfont joined for some records in 1897. "Mocking Bird Medley" (Victor #V-1946; 1903) brought forth whistling by Golden. "Alpine Specialty" was first done for Columbia cylinders, then for Victor discs. [Brooks 1979.]

SPINDLE (I)

The vertical post at the center of a Gramophone turntable. It keeps the disc in position during play, and in certain types of record changer it holds the stack of records to be played, or which have been played. The standard size in the 78 era was 0.25 inches in diameter; this was the size used by Berliner in his original instruments. Other sizes were used, among smaller manufacturers in the early 1900s, notably those based in Chicago: 1/2 inch and even three inches. The RCA 45-rpm record player of 1948 had a 1 3/8 inch spindle to accommodate the little vinyl discs; spindles of that diameter were later available as attachments to LP record players.

See also **Aretino Co., Inc.; United States Talking Machine Co.**

SPINDLE (II)

On a compact disc player, the spindle is the part of the drive that spins the disc.

SPIRIT

Spirit recorded some of the most progressive rock music of the late 1960s. Their albums featured intelligent lyrics, innovative arrangements featuring subtly shifting sound textures, and command of an encyclopedic range of styles, including hard rock, psychedelia, folk-pop, rhythm and blues, and cool jazz. This eclecticism, combined with their reputation for straight-ahead, power rock in concert, undercut efforts to achieve broad-based commercial acceptance.

Spirit was formed in 1967; original members included drummer Ed Cassidy (born in Chicago 4 May 1924) — a veteran jazz drummer who had worked with Woody Herman, Thelonius Monk, Gerry Mulligan, Art Pepper, and Cannonball Adderley — joined stepson Randy California (born Randy Wolfe, then only 14) on lead guitar, guitarist Jay Ferguson, and bassist Mark Andes in 1965 as part of the short-lived folk-rock ensemble, the Red Roosters. Cassidy and California then moved from Los Angeles to New York City for much of 1966, working recording session and with various bands. Later that year they returned to California to form Spirits Rebellious (the band's name was inspired by a Kahlil Gibran book) with a former acquaintance, keyboardist John Locke. Ferguson and Andes, who had formed Western Union in 1966, then joined, and the band decided on a slight name change.

Signed to Lou Adler's Ode label, Spirit released three critically acclaimed albums: *Spirit* (Ode #44004; 1968), *The Family that Plays Together* (Ode #44014; 1969), and *Clear Spirit* (Ode #44016; 1969). In an effort to boost sales, they opted for a greater hard-rock emphasis in *The Twelve Dreams of Dr. Sardonicus* (Epic #30267; 1970). When it failed to out perform its predecessors, Andes and Ferguson left to form Jo Jo Gunne. Cassidy and Locke hooked up with Texans Chris and Al Staehely to produce *Feedback* (Epic #31175; 1971); they then departed, with the Staehelys continuing to tour under the "Spirit" moniker.

In 1974 California — who had done session work in England and produced a solo album — reformed the band with Cassidy. They produced a series of moderate selling LPs for Mercury during the latter 1970s — *Spirit of '76* (Mercury #804; 1975), *Son of Spirit* (Mercury #1053; 1975), *Farther Along* (Mercury #1094; 1976), and *Future Games* (Mercury #1133; 1977) — dominated by California's Jimi Hendrix–inspired ramblings. Andes and Locke briefly returned to the group in the mid-1970s; Andes would then move on to Firefall (Heart in the 1980s), while Ferguson continued his career as a solo artist and producer.

The band continued in various configurations (recording albums for Potato, Rhino, Mercury, I.R.S., and Dolphin) into the early 1990s, always with Cassidy and California at the helm. Any hopes of further reunions were effectively dashed when California drowned off Molokai on 2 Jan 1997 while saving his son's life. The band's music remains widely available, however, with reissues of the most Ode/Epic and Mercury LPs now on CD as well as a compilation featuring the work of the classic lineup, *Time Circle (1968–1972)* (Sony #47363; 1991).

FRANK HOFFMANN

SPIVAK, CHARLIE
(17 FEB 1907–1 MAR 1982)

Russian/American trumpeter, born in Trilsey (some sources give Kiev). Coming early to the U.S., he played with many ensembles, notably Ben Pollack in 1931–1934, the Dorsey Brothers, Jack Teagarden, and Ray Noble. In 1935 he was with Glenn Miller. He was recognized as a melody performer, rather than a jazz improviser, having a particularly lush tone. In the 1940s he led his own band, identifying himself as "the sweetest trumpet in the world." Many agreed, selecting him through the *Metronome* poll as trumpet player of the year in 1940. Willie Smith, alto sax, and Dave Tough, drums, were in the band, and June Hutton was one of the vocalists; a later singer was Irene Daye. His orchestra won the 1944 *Downbeat* poll as the most popular "sweet or dance band." Popularity of the group continued into the late 1940s, after which time Spivak concentrated on smaller combo work. He died in Greenville, South Carolina.

The Spivak orchestra recorded for Okeh in 1941–1942. One of their popular discs was "Star Dreams" (Okeh #6546; 1941). Columbia recorded Spivak's trumpet version of the "Elegy" of Jules Massenet (#36596; 1942).

SPIVEY, VICTORIA
(13 OCT 1906–3 OCT 1976)

Although not the most revered female blues recording artist to emerge in the 1920s, Texas native Victoria Spivey had the distinction of remaining musically active — both as a composer (e.g., "Big Black Limousine," "Mr. Cab") and singer — virtually her entire life. She was a vital force in the 1960s blues revival, creating her own record label, Spivey, which helped revive the careers of many classic blue artists in addition to nurturing new talents, including Olive Brown, Luther Johnson, Lucille Spann, Sugar Blue, and Bob Dylan.

A child singer/actor in vaudeville, Spivey's acidic blues vocals earned her a recording contract with Okeh in 1926. Her debut release, "Black Snake Blues" (Okeh; 1926), a hit in the blues market, was recorded by countless artists over the years. Often backed by legendary musicians such as Louis Armstrong, Lonnie Johnson, and Tempa Red, she produced definitive versions of "T.B. Blues," "Dope Head Blues," and "Murder in the First Degree." While many blues artists were not recruited to cut records after 1929, she developed an aggressive, modern style that kept her in demand as a recording artist during the Depression until 1937.

Spivey was unusual among blues "rediscoveries" in that she actively promoted her own career, rather than being "found" by a record collector or folklorist as many other artists from the 1920s were during the 1950s and 1960s. In 1962 she founded her own record label, also a rare move, and used a young Bob Dylan in several recording sessions as a backup harmonica player. Besides releasing her own material, she recorded other blues survivors, including Alberta Hunter, helping to revitalize their careers. In addition to running Spivey Records during the blues revival, her Greenwich Village folk connections enabled her to perform on many Prestige/Bluesville albums. Following her death, many

LPs containing her work were still in print, including the solo releases *Blues Is Life* (Folkways #3541), *Queen and Her Nights* (Spivey #1006), *Recorded Legacy of the Blues* (Spivey #2001), *Victoria Spivey and Her Blues* (Spivey #1002), and *Victoria Spivey and the Easy Riders Jazz Band* (GHB #17).

FRANK HOFFMANN

SPLICING TAPE

An adhesive tape used in editing recorded tapes; it is not magnetized. Sizes for open-reel tapes and cassettes are available. In studio work a splicing machine applies the tape.

SPLITDORF RADIO CORP.

A Newark, New Jersey, firm, formed as a division of the Splitdorf Bethlehem Electrical Co. in June 1927. Splitdorf had been licensed by RCA and Westinghouse in April 1927. Thomas Edison acquired Splitdorf Radio in December 1928, as a means of access to the radio industry. He renamed the Splitdorf radio as Edison radio, and sold three models in 1929; two of them were radio-phonograph combinations that played Diamond Discs or lateral-cut discs.

SPOKANE PHONOGRAPH CO.

One of the affiliated companies of the North American Phonograph Co., established in 1890 in Spokane Falls, Washington. J.W. Wilson was manager in 1891. Louis Glass was one of the directors; he took the most active role in promoting the firm, in particular his coin-op machines.

SPOKEN WORD RECORDINGS

SEE LITERARY RECORDINGS

SPRING MOTOR RECORD PLAYERS

Because early sources of electrical power were expensive and/or unreliable, most of the pioneer phonograph and Gramophone makers used spring motors to rotate their mandrels and turntables. The first such motor was developed by Edward H. Amet (U.S. patent application filed in 1891) and used on the Edison Class M phonograph of 1894. Frank L. Capps invented a motor with three springs (patented 1896) that was used with the Edison Concert machine of 1899. The motor of J.E. Greenhill was perhaps the first to be used in a phonograph (1893). Henri Lioret

made a talking doll in 1893 with his own spring mechanism. Columbia's first spring motor phonograph was the Type F Graphophone of 1894.

The earliest spring motor for a disc machine was patented buy Levi H. Montross (U.S. #598,529; filed 8 Oct 1896; granted 8 Feb 1898). He sold these in Camden, New Jersey. Eldridge Johnson used the Montross motor in the 200 gramophones he manufactured for the U.S. Gramophone Co. (Berliner's firm) in 1896. He then took an order for another 3,500 machines. An improved governor, invented by Johnson, was used in the Berliner "trademark" model, the Improved Gramophone.

Even after the use of electric power became convenient, spring motors were used to drive portable 78-rpm disc players and cylinder or disc machines used in field recordings. [Koenigsberg 1990; Paul 1991/2.]

SPRINGSTEEN, BRUCE (23 SEP 1949–)

The affection, esteem, and instant recognition behind this automatic greeting from Bruce Springsteen's fans attests to the iconic status of the Freehold, New Jersey, born rocker and hero. "The Boss" took his first steps toward the supernova class of rock by working the Jersey shore club scene hard. Seedy Asbury Park was the mecca around which a sound that melded rock, soul, R&B and something, well, Jerseyish. Springsteen successfully auditioned for legendary producer John Hammond in 1972, and was Hammond's last major signing to Columbia. (This must have appealed to the young singer-songwriter, because Hammond had previously championed Bob Dylan at the label, another controversial signing.) Promoted as a "new Dylan," Springsteen released two albums in 1973, the sparely produced *Greetings from Asbury Park, New Jersey* (Columbia #31903) and the jazz-inflected *The Wild, the Innocent, and the E-Street Shuffle* (Columbia #34432), introducing the world to his backup group, the E Street Band.

Although it only reached number 23 on the *Billboard* charts, 1975's epic shore drama "Born to Run" (Columbia #11209) and the following album of the same name (#33795) made Springsteen an immediate media sensation, with cover appearances on *Time* and *Newsweek* magazines, who proclaimed him the latest "savior of rock 'n' roll." However, difficulties with his then-manager Mike Appel led Springsteen to stay away from the studio for two years; the long-awaited *Darkness at the Edge of Town* (Columbia #35318) marked his return in 1978 with a harder edged sound, reflecting Springsteen's struggle for control of his music. The two-LP concept album, *The River* (Columbia #36854), followed in 1980, produc-

Bruce Springsteen at his home studio in 1994, Los Angeles, California. © Neal Preston/CORBIS

ing Springsteen's first Top 10 single, "Hungry Heart" (Columbia #11391; #5).

Springsteen took a detour in 1982, releasing the acoustic album, *Nebraska* (Columbia #38358), made up of demoes he recorded at home on a four-track cassette machine. The spare production and haunting subject matter made the album a critic's pick, if not a tremendous commercial success. Two years later, however, Springsteen returned to full band recording with a vengeance, releasing *Born in the U.S.A.* (Columbia #38563), which yielded a string of singles during 1984–1985: "Dancing in the Dark" (#04463; #2); "Cover Me" (#04651; #7); "Born in the U.S.A" (#04680; #9); "I'm on Fire" (#04772; #6); "Glory Days" (#04924; #5); "I'm Goin' Down" (#05603; #9); and "My Hometown" (#05728; #8). At this point, Springsteen was again a cultural phenomenon, on the cover of *Time* and *Newsweek*. As always, Bruce's intense, electrifying live performances fueled his fame.

The momentum from the *Born in the U.S.A.* carried over into a three-LP live set (Columbia #65328), drawn on concert recordings made over the decade of 1975–1985, and the darker, more sparely produced follow-up studio album, *Tunnel of Love* (Columbia #40999), reflecting the difficulties Springsteen was experiencing in his first marriage. Nonetheless, the

album produced hits with the first released single, "Brilliant Disguise" (#07595; #5), and the title track (#07663; #9), in 1987.

Springsteen officially dissolved the E Street Band soon after, married backup singer Patti Scialfa, and moved to California. After a period of inactivity, he returned in 1992 with two albums, *Human Touch* and *Lucky Town* (Columbia #53000, #53001), backed by studio musicians. In 1994 the Oscar-winning song "Streets of Philadelphia" (Columbia #77384; #9) appeared, written for the film *Philadelphia*. A year later, another acoustic-folk album in the spirit of *Nebraska* appeared, *The Ghost of Tom Joad* (Columbia #67484). That same year, Columbia issued a *Greatest Hits* package, featuring two new recordings with a reunited E Street Band, heralding things to come. Another compilation followed in 1998, the four-CD set *Tracks* (Columbia #67495), a compilation of outtakes and unused material from throughout his career. That same year, Springsteen was inducted into the Rock and Roll Hall of Fame.

Springsteen began a comeback in 2000 with a tour with the E Street Band, including a live broadcast from New York's Madison Square Garden (released on DVD and CD). He introduced the moving new song, "41 Shots," inspired by the shooting of an unarmed

Black man, Amadou Diallo, by New York City cops. He furthered this approach in 2002 with *The Rising* album (Columbia #86600), introducing a series of reactions to the September 11 terrorist attacks. It was the first studio album by the E Street Band since *Born in the U.S.A.*, and was accompanied by many interviews and a worldwide tour.

BOB SILLERY

SRS (SOUND RETRIEVAL SYSTEM)

Developed by Arnold Klayman and employed in some television sets, desktop personal computers, and stand-alone processors, it adds matrixing and frequency-response manipulations to two-channel, stereophonic program sources (shaping extracted ambiance signals so that they mimic the side- and rear-surround response contouring provided by the pinna of the outer ear), thereby simulating a large-stage effect up front and phantom surround channels, and does so without the need of extra channels.

SST (LABEL)

SST was started in 1980 by Greg Ginn as an outlet for distributing the recordings of his band, Black Flag. Based in Los Angeles, the record company soon became recognized as a guiding force in the newly emerging hardcore music scene. The label's early releases — which focused more on the seven-inch, 45 rpm and 12-inch, 33 1/3 rpm configurations than long-playing albums — consisted largely of talent from the southwestern part of the U.S., including the Minutemen, Saccharine Trust, Overkill, the Meat Puppets, the Stains, Wurm, the Dicks, and the Subhumans.

The addition of St. Paul's Husker Du to SST's roster of artists in 1983 — climaxed by the release of the critically acclaimed double album set, *Zen Arcade* (SST #027; 1984) — represented a quantum leap in prestige for the label. Ambitious bands flocked to the label from around the country. Furthermore, the breakup of Black Flag in 1986 enabled Ginn to concentrate his energies on the development on new projects. New signings during the mid-1980s included St. Vitus, Das Damen, SWA, Angest, Gone, Bad Brains, and the Leaving Trains. At this time, a market strategy seems to have been implemented by company insiders. Bands hovering on the brink of big-time commercial success — most notably, Husker Du and the Meat Puppets — would move on to major labels while SST redoubled its efforts to locate (and sign) talented unknowns performing in hardcore venues nationwide.

SST continued to expand its roster in the late 1980s, releasing material of seminal bands such as Firehose (a more ambient offshoot of the Minutemen) and Sonic Youth, one of the most influential bands of the postpunk era. In the early 1990s, the label released recordings by Pacific grunge pioneers Soundgarden and the Screaming Trees. SST continues to produce records and most of its catalog has been re-released in CD format. [Thompson 2000.]

FRANK HOFFMANN

STACY, JESS [ALEXANDRIA] (11 AUG 1904–5 JAN 1994)

American jazz pianist and Big Band leader, born in Bird's Point, Missouri. He played piano on the riverboats, then in Chicago with various bands from 1926 to 1929. He was acclaimed for his virtuosity, lyricism, and splendid tone. Then he joined Benny Goodman for the first of three partnerships in 1935–1939 (the later associations were 1942–1944 and 1946–1947). Stacy was with Bob Crosby from 1939 to 1942. In four consecutive years, 1940–1943, Stacy was winner of the *Downbeat* poll as most popular jazz pianist. He had his own band in 1945–1946, featuring his wife Lee Wiley as vocalist. After 1960 he was inactive. Stacy made a "comeback" in 1973, recording the sourd track for the film *The Great Gatsby* and performing around the country. He retired again in 1980, and died 14 years later in Los Angeles.

Stacy's greatest records were made as soloist, accompanied by Gene Krupa and a string bass, from 1935 to 1939, and as a sideman with Goodman. Of the solo discs, the standouts are "Barrelhouse" (Parlophone #R-2187; 1935), "Candlelights" (Commodore #517; 1939), and "Ec-Stacy" (Commodore #1503; 1939). His most inspired improvisation on record may be in "Sing, Sing, Sing" with Goodman at the Carnegie Hall concert of 16 Jan 1938 (Columbia SL #160).

STAFFORD, JO (12 NOV 1917–)

American popular vocalist, born in Coalinga, California. She and her sister made youthful appearances on radio as a singing team; then she joined the Pied Pipers and sang with them in the Tommy Dorsey band from 1940. Later she was a soloist with Dorsey, left in 1942 to freelance, and made many radio appearances, notably on *Your Hit Parade*. In 1943 and 1945 she was winner of the *Downbeat* poll as favorite female vocalist. She was married to Paul Weston, and made several entertaining parody records with him. After 1960 she was less active.

With Dorsey there were fine ballad records, notably "He's My Guy" (Victor #27941; 1942). From 1950 to 1957 Stafford had nine chart singles, including "Shrimp Boats" (Columbia #39581; 1951) and "You

Belong to Me" (Columbia #39811; 1952). Among her spoof records were several with Red Ingle, the best being "Tim-Tayshun" (Capitol #412); and several gems with Weston — who masqueraded as Jonathan Edwards — such as "Carioca." Her most popular LP album was *Ski Trails* (Columbia #CL-910; 1956). The "Jonathan Edwards" material is in Columbia album #CL-1024.

STAMPER
The mold part in the disc record-making process that is used to create the final pressing.

See also **Disc**

STANDARD (LABEL)
A record made by the Standard Talking Machine Co. of Chicago from 1903. The discs, surplus items from Columbia, were modified by expansion of their center holes to 9/16 inch. From March 1918 the label was issued by the Consolidated Talking Machine Co. of Chicago. [Rust 1978.]

STANDARD GRAMOPHONE APPLICANCE CO.
A New York firm, located in 1912 at 173 Lafayette St. It advertised the Simplex stop and start attachment for disc players.

STANDARD METAL MANUFACTURING CO.
A New York firm, located in 1907 at 10 Warren St. It made Standard Horns.

STANDARD PLAY
A designation for the 78-rpm disc, in contrast to the 33 1/3-rpm LP microgroove disc.

STANDARD PNEUMATIC ACTION CO.
A New York firm, located in the 1920s at 638 W. 52nd St. Primarily a maker of player piano actions of the inner type, their products were used in over 10 brand-name pianos. One model included a built-in disc phonograph.

STANDARD QUARTETTE
A male vocal group that recorded for Columbia cylinders. They were announced on the records as "gentlemen of color" — "which, if true, would seem to make them the first Black group ever to record." Among their presentations in the 1894–1896 period were "Swing Low," "Nationality Medley," and old-fashioned jubilee songs. [Brooks 1979.]

STANDARD SEQUENCE

SEE MANUAL SEQUENCE

STANDARD TALKING MACHINE CO.
A Chicago firm established in October 1901. It was apparently a branch of the East Liverpool China Co. (established 1901). It sold discs with the label name Standard, and Standard brand talking machines to play them. The discs had 9/16 inch spindle holes, and the record players had spindles to match. Both discs and machines were modified Columbia products. The machines came from the Bridgeport factory, some carrying that information stamped on them. The first to be marketed by Standard, ca. 1903, was identical to the Columbia AU model, with a seven-inch turntable; later there was a similar machine with a 10-inch turntable. In 1913 Standard absorbed the Great Northern Manufacturing Co., formalizing a long association. Standard was succeeded by Consolidated Talking Machine Co. of Chicago; that firm issued 10-inch records with the Standard label in March 1918. [Fabrizio 1980.]

Label from c. 1909 made by this Chicago-based firm. Courtesy Kurt Nauck/Nauck's Vintage Records

STANDING WAVES

Irregularities, often quite audible and unwanted in the bass range, that result when sounds reflected back and forth between the walls of a room interacting with each other and with the direct sounds from the speaker systems (or even musical instruments) that produced them to form alternate reinforcements (peaks) and nulls. The effect is dependent upon the size and shape of the room, and to some extent upon the location of the source. The structural integrity of the walls can also have an effect on the strength of the artifacts. Standing waves can be detrimental to sound reproduction at lower frequencies in small and/or badly proportioned rooms, where their effects are often extreme. In addition to the obvious axial modes that involve opposing walls, the phenomenon also involves tangential and oblique effects that are more difficult to calculate and are thought by some experts to be as negative in impact as the axial modes.

See also **Room Acoustics**

REV. HOWARD FERSTLER

STANFORD ARCHIVE OF RECORDED SOUND (STARS)

The Archive of Recorded Sound, established in 1958 and located at Stanford University, was one of the first major institutional sound collections devoted to the acquisition and preservation of sound recordings. It houses more than 200,000 recordings in formats ranging from wax cylinders to compact discs. Commercial 78-rpm and LP discs, as well as private tape recordings, comprise the majority of the collection. It has worked with other major U.S. sound archives since 1974 to find cooperative solutions to common problems confronting archival sound collections. The Rigler and Deutsch Record Index (RDI), funded by the National Endowment for the Humanities and the Ledler Foundation, was the result of such an effort to provide access to more than 600,000 previously uncataloged items in five major archives in the U.S. Among those who deposit their master recordings on a regular basis at the Archive are the Carmel Bach Festival and the Monterey Jazz Festival. The Archive also maintains an extensive reference collection. It has provided support for the *Encyclopedic Discography of Victor Recordings* (the Victor Project), an ambitious undertaking initiated in 1963 by William R. Moran and the late Ted Fagan. Once completed, it will document in detail all the recording sessions of the Victor Talking Machine Co. (later RCA Victor) from 1900 to 1950. The Archive is a member of the Associated Audio Archives Committee (AAA) of the Association for Recorded Sound Collections (ARSC).

STANLEY, AILEEN (21 MAR 1893–24 MAR 1982)

American vaudeville singer, born Maude Elsie Aileen Muggeridge in Chicago. She and her brother Stanley — whose name she later took for her stage name — were performing in public when she was five years old. Her career went on from there to cover 50 years in the U.S. and the U.K., rising from dingy small-town theaters to private parties in London attended by the Prince of Wales. Stanley was a featured performer in the Keith-Albee circuit, and a radio artist from the early days of the medium, with Rudy Vallee and Paul Whiteman. She appeared in three Broadway musicals, *Silks and Satins* (1920), *Pleasure Bound* (1929), and *Artists and Models of 1930* (1930).

Known as "the Victrola Girl" ("the Gramophone Girl" in the U.K.), Stanley recorded prolifically for Victor/HMV from 1920 (after a few sides for Pathé). "Broadway Blues"/"My Little Bimbo Down on the Bamboo Isle" (from *Silks and Satins*) was her first Victor (#18691; 1920). She also worked for Okeh, Vocalion, Gennett, Edison, and other labels in the 1920s, making a total of 215 recordings. Sales of her discs were reported to have reached 25 million copies.

Aileen Stanley pictured on the sheet music cover for her hit "Ev'rything's Made for Love." Courtesy David A. Jasen

She and Billy Murray made popular duets for Victor, the best being "Any Ice Today, Lady?"/" Whadda You Say We Get Together?" (#20065; 1926). Another was a sensation: "Bridget O'Flynn"/"Who Could Be More Wonderful Than You?" (Victor #20240; 1926). Stanley made few records after 1930, but continued on stage in the U.S. and U.K. Her final disc was "It Looks Like Rain in Cherry Blossom Lane"/"I've Got My Love to Keep Me Warm" (HMV #BD444; 1937). She died in Los Angeles. [Walsh 1963/10–11–12; 1964/1.]

STANLEY, FRANK C. (29 DEC 1868–12 DEC 1910)

American bass singer, born William Stanley Grinsted in Orange, New Jersey. He was one of the most prolific recording artists, with thousands of discs and cylinders on many labels, while also pursuing a career in politics (as an alderman in Newark, New Jersey). He started recording as a banjo player for Edison in 1891, under his real name, inscribing "Lumber Yard Jig" and 11 other numbers. As a singer he was heard in numerous ensembles, among them the Columbia Male Quartet, the Invincible Four, and the Metropolitan Mixed Trio. He made about 70 records for Edison from 1899, beginning with "If You Love as I Love" (#7322). He had many duet partners, including Byron Harlan, Henry Burr, Harry Macdonough, and Corinne Morgan.

In 1906 Stanley initiated a series of duets with Elise Stevenson on Victor and Columbia, then from 1909 on Edison. The two were also members of the Schubert Trio in 1906. Stanley was the first to record songs from *Merry Widow*, with eight Indestructible Cylinders in February 1908.

Stanley was at the peak of his popularity in 1906 when he organized the Peerless Quartet (originally the Columbia Male Quartet) and managed it until his death. His final solo record was "Boy O' Mine" for Edison in October 1910. He died in Newark.

STANLEY BROTHERS (1946–1966)

The Stanley Brothers raised two-part vocal harmonizing to a high art. Although never best-selling artists in the truest sense of the word, their success in popularizing (and preserving) bluegrass — a form grounded in acoustic string instrument renditions of old-time Appalachian folk songs — was surpassed only by the legendary Bill Monroe, whose recording career spanned seven decades. Despite their contributions to this continuously evolving genre, they also provided a clear link with traditional folk material such as "Little Maggie" and "Pretty Polly."

Hailing from Virginia, Carter Glen Stanley (b. 27 Aug 1925) and Ralph Edmond Stanley (b. 25 Feb 1927) formed the Stanley Brothers and the Clinch Mountain Boys in 1946. Shortly thereafter, they began appearing regularly on WCYB radio, in Bristol, Virginia. Securing a recording contract with the Rich-R-Tone label in 1947, the group now modeled itself closely after Monroe; Ralph took up the three-finger banjo technique identified with Earl Scruggs, then a member of Monroe's Bluegrass Boys. Carter, the more musically adventurous of the two, redesigned their sound — due at least in part to economic considerations — to achieve a spare blend of fiddles (often in a twin arrangement), lead guitar, and innovative harmonies.

Their Columbia period, lasting from March 1949 through April 1952, saw them approach a more complete synthesis of the Monroe model with more traditional forms as reflected in songs like "The Fields Have Turned Brown" (1949). It is said that when Columbia signed the brothers, Monroe left the label in protest, claiming they stole his signature sound. After leaving Columbia, the group continued to produce high-quality sides, balancing the classic bluegrass of "How Mountain Girls Can Love" (King; 1958) and "Rank Stranger" (Starday; 1959) with purely religious material, for Mercury, Starday, King, and other labels during the 1950s and 1960s. Their biggest country hit was the novelty, "How Far to Little Rock" (King #5306), a modern-day version of the age-old "Arkansas Traveller" fiddle tune and skit, which reached number 17 in early 1960.

Since Carter's death on 1 Dec 1966, Ralph has attempted to keep the Clinch Mountain Boys sound alive, albeit in an increasingly traditional vein. However, he was responsible for one notable innovation within modern bluegrass, the a cappella gospel quartet, in the early 1970s. Early examples of this approach can be found in "Bright Morning Star" (*Cry from the Cross*; Rebel #1499; 1971) and "Gloryland" (*Something Old — Something New*; Rebel #1503; 1971), both of which are also available on the four-CD box set, *Ralph Stanley and the Clinch Mountain Boys, 1971–1973* (Rebel #4001; 1995). A substantial number of contemporary country artists — including Chris Hillman, Emmylou Harris, Dan Fogelberg, and Ricky Skaggs, a former member of the Clinch Mountain Boys — have paid homage to the Stanley Brothers by reinterpreting their songs. Stanley has continued to record and perform through the 1990s, most recently introducing his son Ralph Stanley III as lead singer and guitarist. His career was given a significant boost when his haunting a cappella performance of the gospel number, "Oh Death," was prominently featured in the hit film, *O Brother Where Art Thou?* (2000) and included on the best-selling soundtrack disc.

FRANK HOFFMANN

STANTON, WALTER O.
(1915–16 APR 2001)

Born in Canton, Ohio, Stanton graduated in 1939 from Wayne State University, with a degree in electrical engineering. In the late 1940s, he invented the easy-to-replace, slide-in phonograph-cartridge stylus, which made it possible for users to replace their own stylus assemblies, thereby helping to revolutionize and expand the nascent hi-fi industry. In 1950 he purchased Pickering and Co., which had been selling his patented stylus, and in 1960 he founded Stanton Magnetics, one of the first American companies that produced truly high-fidelity phonograph cartridges. In later years, he started still another company, branching out into producing headphones and loudspeaker systems. He ran both companies until his retirement in 1998. A former president of the Audio Engineering Society, Stanton was made a fellow in 1959, received a citation from the Society in 1961, and was also instrumental in founding the Institute of High Fidelity.

HOWARD FERSTLER

STAR (LABEL) (I)

A U.K. cylinder record issued from 1904–1907 by the Phonograph Exchange Co., 4 White Lion St., Norwich; and from September 1905 at 73 Farringdon St., London. One of the early issues was of the bells of St. Peter Mancroft Church, in Norwich, recorded in

Philadelphia-based label from c. 1907-09. Courtesy Kurt Nauck/Nauck's Vintage Records

the belfry. An important artist was Maude Dewey, "champion lady whistler of the world," recording bird songs. The Welsh Bethesda choir was also recorded. Most of the repertoire, however, was of the music hall type. [Andrews 1979/10.]

STAR (LABEL) (II)

An American disc record first advertised in March 1907, made by Hawthorne and Sheble. Matrices were from Columbia. Production ceased with the demise of H & S in 1909, but sales continued in U.K. for a time.

STARCK (LABEL)

An American record issued in 1926–1927 by the Starck music stores. There were about 100 items, from Pathé masters. [Rust 1978.]

STARDAY RECORDS (LABEL)

Booking agent Jack Starnes ("Star-") and record distributor Pappy Daily ("day") started Starday in Beaumont, Texas, in June 1953. Don Pierce joined in September, and, as the only full-time partner, was made president. The first hit, Arlie Duff's "Y'All Come" (#104; 1953; #7 C&W) came in late 1953. Starnes signed George Jones in January 1954, and Jones became the label's mainstay (Starnes, though, sold his share of Starday to Pierce and Daily in 1955). In January 1957, Starday began running Mercury Records' country division as a joint venture, Mercury-Starday, and Pierce moved the label to Nashville. When Mercury-Starday dissolved in July 1958, Pierce assumed full ownership of Starday and rebuilt the catalog around old-time and bluegrass artists who had been jettisoned by the major labels. There were a few major hits — including Red Sovine's "Giddyup, Go" (#737; 1965; #1 C&W, #82 pop), Frankie Miller's "Blackland Farmer" (#424; 1961; #16 C&W, #82 pop), Cowboy Copas's "Alabam" (#501; 1960; #1 C#W, #63 pop), and Johnny Bond's "Ten Little Bottles" (#704; 1965; #2 C&W, #43 pop) — but Starday essentially operated as a catalog business. Pierce aggressively marketed via mail order. As the receipts began to diminish, Pierce sold Starday to Lin Broadcasting in 1968 for $2 million. The label was eventually acquired by Nashville-based GML, which revived the Starday imprint, scoring a number one country hit with Red Sovine's "Teddy Bear" in 1976. New product is occasionally issued on Starday, but it remains primarily a reissue label.

COLIN ESCOTT

STARR, KAY (21 JULY 1922–)

Born Katherine LaVerne Starks in Dougherty, Oklahoma, Starr was raised in Dallas where she sang as a teenager on local radio. Starr got her first big break at 15 when bandleader/violinist Joe Venuti heard her Memphis radio program and signed her up to tour with him when she was not in school. She later toured full time with Venuti, Bob Crosby, Glenn Miller, and Charlie Barnet, a thorough grounding in Big Band style. After she collapsed with pneumonia in 1945 and convalesced by refraining from using her voice for six months, she emerged with the deeper, huskier voice that has become her trademark. Starr signed with Capitol in the late 1940s. She recorded country music, jazz, pop, spirituals, Broadway tunes, and rhythm and blues, and had her first big hit with the country song "Bonaparte's Retreat" (Capital #936, 1950). In 1952 she had her biggest hit, "Wheel of Fortune," the number two top-selling single of the year. Starr moved to RCA in 1955, and her "Rock and Roll Waltz" (#6359) hit number one on the charts in 1956. She has always most considered herself a "saloon singer," who told a story with each song, and is recognized for the power and emotion of her singing style. Starr recorded for Capitol again from 1959–1966, and then for ABC/Paramount from 1968–1969. She then retired from performing and recording. With the revival of interest in carbaret singers in the late 1980s, she toured as part of the 3 Girls revue with Margaret Whiting and Helen O'Connell. Starr's *Live at Freddy's* (Baldwin #202) album was released in 1997.

BOB SILERY

STARR, RINGO (7 JULY 1940–)

Born Richard Starkey Jr. in Liverpool, England, Starr is best-known for his association with the Beatles. Fans listening to "Never Without You," Ringo's warm tribute to Beatle bandmate George Harrison on Starr's 2003 *Ringo Rama* (Koch #8429), are delighted that this down-to-earth member of the beloved fab four is surviving and making meaningful music. After all, in the wake of the Beatles's breakup, he was rated the band member least likely to have a solo career. But with his drumming and affable vocals, he has proven them wrong.

In the Beatles, Starr was accused of being a clumsy drummer, but many agreed with bandmate Harrison, who came to his defense, saying "Ringo's the best back-beat in the business." Starr was given the occasional vocal on Beatles albums, such as his country tunes "Act Naturally" (on the 1966 album *"Yesterday" … and Today*) and "Honey Don't" (on 1965's *Beatles '65*). His most famous songs, and his primary vocal contributions

to the Beatles canon, are "Yellow Submarine" (Capital #5715, 1966) and "With a Little Help from My Friends" (*Sgt. Pepper's Lonely Hearts Club Band*, 1967).

Starr was the first Beatle to issue an "official" solo album (Harrison had his electronic music offerings, and Lennon his Plastic Ono Band material, but both were seen as augmenting their work with the Beatles). It was an album of 1930s to 1940s standards, Sentimental Journey (Capitol/Apple #3365), issued in 1970. Quick on its heels, with the help of Nashville producer Pete Drake, Starr released *Beaucoups of Blues* (Capitol/Apple #3368), drawing on his longtime love of country music. During the early 1970s, he had a string of hits, such as "It Don't Come Easy" (Apple #1831; 1971, #4), "You're Sixteen" (Apple #1870; 1973, #1), and "Photograph" (Apple #1865, 1973). The later two songs came from his most successful solo album, *Ringo* (Capitol/Apple #3413), produced by Richard Perry and featuring songs and performances from all three of the other Beatles (although not performing together as a unit). Starr continued to record regularly through the 1970s, with some commercial success, and then more sporadically over the next two decades.

In the 1990s, Starr formed a touring unit with flexible membership, the All-Star Band, mostly of 1960s and 1970s rock veterans performing their "hits." At the same time, he formed a recording partnership with Los Angeles–based producer Mark Hudson, for a series of albums that brought some critical notice, although not much commercial airplay.

BOB SILERY

STARR (LABEL)

An American record issued by the Starr Piano Co., of Richmond, Indiana, in 1916; the name was changed to Gennett in the following year for the U.S. market, but remained Starr in Canada. [Rust 1978.]

STARR PIANO CO.

A firm established in 1872 in Richmond, Indiana, and incorporated in 1878, by James and Benjamin Starr. The first piano was produced in 1873 and was successful; the company was turning out 15 instruments a week by 1884. There was a new incorporation in 1893, with Benjamin Starr as president. Henry Gennett joined the firm that year; when he became president in 1906 the firm had grown to 600 employees. They had made 90,000 pianos by 1912, and were finishing 40 per day. There were more than 30 buildings in the Starr complex in Richmond.

A new structure was built in 1916 for the manufacture of disc records (first advertised in October 1916)

First label produced by the Wisconsin-based firm that was best known for its Gennett label. Courtesy Kurt Nauck/Nauck's Vintage Records

and record players. The records were 10-inch, vertical-cut, playing four to five minutes per side; they sold for $0.65 to $4 each. The long playing time was achieved by fine grooving (150 turns per inch). A new main office was opened in Cincinnati, at 27 W. 4th Ave. West, in October 1916. Starr was the first label name, then — from September 1917 — Gennett. In March 1919 Gennett records were advertised as lateral-cut. There was a New York address for Starr's Gennett Records division, at 9 E. 37th St. Clarence Gennett was treasurer and retail manager at the time, and Henry Gennett the factory manager. R.C. Mayer was head of the recording laboratories, with Fred Myer factory superintendent.

Starr disc players were sold from August 1915, with 11 models available in 1916. Under the Gennett name the company achieved great commercial success (3 million records per year in the mid-1920s) and considerable artistic success. A legal battle with Victor had to be endured for years (1918–1922) over the alleged infringement of Victor's patent for a lateral record-cutting stylus; but in the end Starr was upheld. Starr cut 1,250 masters in 1928, comparing favorably to giant Victor's 1,900. It had a Canadian affiliate, Starr Co. of Canada. W.D. Stevenson, vice president of the Canadian company, was named vice president of the U.S. company in 1925 (the only nonfamily member in a senior position at Starr).

Pianos were not neglected by Starr; there were still 15,000 per year being produced in the mid-1920s. But 35,000 record players were made as well. In March 1926 Starr took on the manufacture of the Portophon

Portable record players, having acquired the patents, machinery, parts, and drawings from the liquidator of the Thomas Manufacturing Co. Then the Depression forced the Gennett label to cease; but the factories continued to make pianos and to press records for other firms. Eventually even the piano manufacture stopped (1949), and finally the Starr property was acquired for salvage by a local businessman who demolished it after 1978. The original 1872 building has been spared. [Klein, A. 1983.]

FRANK ANDREWS

STATE PHONOGRAPH CO. OF ILLINOIS

One of the affiliates of the North American Phonograph Co., established in 1890 in the Home Insurance Building, Chicago. Granger Farwell was president in 1892.

STATLER BROTHERS, THE (1963–2002)

Not really brothers or named Statler, the Statler Brothers have been one of the most popular of the smooth harmony vocal groups in country music for over 30 years.

Originally forming in 1955 as a church-based trio in Staunton, Virginia, around Lew DeWitt, Phil Balsley, and Harold Reid, the group was first called the Kingsmen (not of "Louie Louie" fame; that's another story). In 1960, Harold's younger brother Don joined as lead vocalist, and the group signed on with Johnny Cash's roadshow. Soon after, they changed their name to the Statler Brothers, taking their surname from a Massachusetts-based manufacturer of Kleenex. In 1964 they signed with Columbia Records, and had their first hit with the DeWitt-penned "Flowers on the Wall" a year later. In 1970, they switched to Mercury and had their first solid hit with the crossover success of "Bed of Roses." Many of their 1970s hits were written by the brothers Reid, including 1972's nostalgic "Class of '57," the sentimental tear-jerkers "I'll Go to My Grave Loving You" from 1975, and their first number one single, "Do You Know You Are My Sunshine" from 1978. Recalling their roots as a gospel quartet, they also recorded all-religious albums, including two albums based on the Old and New Testaments released in 1975.

In 1981 the group founded their own "Statler Complex" in their base of Staunton, Virginia, which includes a museum showing their many awards and memorabilia. Around this time, cofounder Lew DeWitt was forced to retire due to continuing problems from Crohn's disease; he died in 1990. His replacement was Jimmy Fortune, who contributed to many of the Statler Brothers' 1980s hits, including "Elizabeth" from 1984, and "My Only Love" and "Too Much on My Heart" from a year later. Although the Statlers fell off the charts in the 1990s, they remained immensely popular. They hosted for many years their own variety show on TNN, which was the top-rated show on the fledgling cable network for seven years; however, when CBS purchased TNN and renamed it the National Network in 1999, the show was canceled. Their brand of smooth, church-oriented harmonies and mixture of sentimental and humorous material made them one of the most popular — and lasting — of all country quartets. However, citing the pressures of continuing to tour, the group announced that 2002 would be their last year as performers.

CARL BENSON

STAX RECORDS (LABEL)

Stax Records, originally known as Satellite until another label with the same name threatened legal action, was created by Jim Stewart and his sister Estelle Axton in the late 1950s. After releasing a few recordings — country, rockabilly, and rhythm and blues — without success, "Cause I Love You" (Satellite; 1960), by Rufus and Carla Thomas, became a regional hit and was picked up for nationwide distribution by Atlantic Records. Carla Thomas would reach the Top 10 with an ethereal, orchestrated follow-up, "Gee Whiz" (Atlantic #2086; 1961; #10), but the Mar-Keys' funky R&B instrumental, "Last Night" (Satellite #107; 1961; #3), provided both a future stylistic direction and expanded version of what would become the company's house band, Booker T. & the MGs. William Bell's "You Don't Miss Your Water (Till Your Well Runs Dry)" (Stax #116; 1962; #95), with its understated eloquence and down-home gospel feel, anticipated other key ingredients of the company's self-proclaimed "Memphis Sound."

By the early 1960s, Stax's chart success served as a magnet for area talent. The label's commercial track record (including subsidiaries such as Volt and Enterprise) during the decade was exceeded only by Tamla-Motown-Gordy conglomerate in Detroit. Leading Stax artists (and their biggest hits) included Booker T. & the MGs — "Green Onions" (Stax #127; 1962; #3) and "Time Is Tight" (Stax #0028; 1969; #6); Otis Redding — "I've Been Loving You Too Long" (Volt #126; 1965; #21) and "(Sittin' On) The Dock of the Bay" (Volt #157; 1968; #1); Sam and Dave — "Soul Man" (Stax #231; 1967; #2) and "I Thank You" (Stax #242; 1968; #9); Johnnie Taylor — "Who's Making Love" (Stax #0009; 1968; #5); and Rufus Thomas — "Walking the Dog" (Stax #140; 1963; #10).

By the 1970s Stax had lost its most promising singer, Otis Redding, in a plane crash, and Booker T. & the MGs — who had provided a spare, rocky-steady backup for many of the label's recordings — had broken up. Nevertheless, the company embarked upon an ambitious plan of expansion, developing comedy and gospel divisions as well as mounting Wattstax, a blend of rock festival and social consciousness. Although the hits continued — most notably, Isaac Hayes's "Theme from Shaft" (Enterprise #9038; 1971; #1) and a string of best-selling LPs, Luther Ingram's "(If Loving You Is Wrong) I Don't Want to Be Right" (KoKo #2111; 1972; #3), and the Staple Singers' "I'll Take You There" (Stax #0125; 1972; #1) and "If You're Ready (Come Go With Me)" (Stax #0179; 1973; #9) — the continued loss of key artists and support personnel, combined with ill-advised financial practices, led to Stax's demise in the mid-1970s.

By the late 1970s the label's classic recordings were being issued by Atlantic and Fantasy (which had obtained rights to the post-1968 catalog). By the 1990s much of the Stax legacy had been reissued on compact disc, including virtually all of the 1960s albums and two exhaustive nine-CD compilations, *The Complete Stax/Volt Singles: 1959–1968* (Atlantic #82218; 1991) and *The Complete Stax/Volt Soul Singles 1968–1971* (Stax #4411; 1991).

FRANK HOFFMANN

STEELY DAN

Lauded throughout the 1970s as the thinking man's rock band, Steely Dan — named after a steam-driven dildo depicted in William Burroughs's beat novel, *Naked Lunch* — had few peers in the production of densely layered, polished progressive rock. Their music — which featured an eclectic blend of contemporary styles accented by jazz-inflected ensemble playing — provided the framework for sardonic commentaries on the moral bankruptcy of American society.

The group evolved out of the songwriting partnership of Bard college alumni, vocalist/keyboardist Donald Fagen and vocalist/bassist Walter Becker, who toured as backing musicians for Jay & the Americans in 1970 prior to landing staff positions at the Los Angeles–based A.B.C.-Dunhill Records. With the support of independent producer Gary Katz, they secured a contract with the label and, augmented in the studio by ex–Holy Modal Rounders guitarist Jeff Baxter, rhythm guitarist Denny Dias, drummer Jim Hodder, and vocalist David Palmer, they recorded *Can't Buy a Thrill* (A.B.C. #758; 1972; #17). The album's success was ensured by the inclusion of the sinuous funk-rock single, "Do It Again" (A.B.C. #11338; 1972; #6).

Follow-up LPs maintained Steely Dan's status as critic's darlings and FM staples; sales, however, relied heavily on the presence of hit singles. Although widely considered to be the group's masterpiece, the bitingly satirical second album, *Countdown to Ecstasy* (A.B.C. #779; 1973; #35), proved to be a commercial disappointment. The popularity of the laid-back love dirge (built around a Horace Silver piano motif), "Rikki Don't Lose that Number" (A.B.C. #11439; 1974; #4), helped propel *Pretzel Logic* (A.B.C. #808; 1974; #8) into the upper reaches of the charts.

The band's decision to function as a studio entity in late 1974 led to the departure of Baxter (to the Doobie Brothers) and Hodder, who were replaced by vocalist/keyboardist Michael McDonald and drummer Jeff Porcaro (who would later help found AOR mainstays Toto). After creatively treading water with *Katy Lied* (A.B.C. #846; 1975; #13), marred by mixing problems, and the incessantly dark *The Royal Scam* (A.B.C. #5161; 1976; #15), Steely Dan — now essentially a duo utilizing a rotating succession of session players — rebounded with a couple of painstakingly crafted works, the lush *Aja* (A.B.C. #1006; 1977; #3) and techno-influenced *Gaucho* (A.B.C. #6102; 1980; #9).

Citing the standard artistic differences mantra, Becker and Fagen dissolved the band. Nevertheless, they maintained a cordial professional relationship, each providing songwriting and production assistance for the other's solo recordings. They revived the group for the 1994 "Alive in America" tour, which was captured in a live album (Giant #24634; #40) the following year. A long-awaited collection of original material, *Two Against Nature* (Giant #24719; 2000; also expanded into a DVD release bearing the same title [Image #8574; 2000]), was stylistically similar to their 1970s' work, albeit somewhat less caustic in tone. The obvious synergy possessed by the duo renders it likely that they'll continue to collaborate as recording artists in the future.

FRANK HOFFMANN

STEERING SYSTEMS

Most visibly employed by Dolby Pro Logic, but also used in some digital and analog music-ambiance systems, steering involves the electronic spatial manipulation of recorded two-channel audio signals. Doing this allows matrixed center-channel or surround-channel signals that would ordinarily only be vaguely imaged to be positively routed to a center channel or surround channel (or channels). Steering thereby strives to simulate multiple independent channels from two-channel sources, and with DSP ambiance systems

it may also strive to simulate a sense of hall space around the listener.

See also **Center Channel; Dolby Pro Logic (DPL); Dolby Surround Sound; DSP (Digital Signal Processing); Phantom Center Image; Stereophonic Recording**

HOWARD FERSTLER

STEGER AND SONS

A Chicago manufacturer of reproducing grand pianos, established in 1879. In addition to player actions, the firm made talking machines beginning in 1919. Models offered in 1920 were in all price ranges, including a "Gothic" at $1,250 and a $60 table model. Tone arms were devised with adjustable pressure for playback of vertical-cut and lateral-cut discs; and advertising stated that "no other phonograph has this pressure adjustment." Location of the company during 1916–1922 was at Wabash Ave. and Jackson Blvd., in its own Steger Building; factories were in Steger, Illinois. In 1923 the firm was at 1541 E. 60th St., on the South Side of the city. The 1929 Chicago directory shows Steger back downtown at 238 S. Wabash Ave. In 1932, the final appearance of a Steger piano firm in the telephone directory, the company name was F.L. Steger, the address was 3317 Hernden.

STEREOPHONIC RECORDING

Usually referred to as stereo, the modern term comes from a Greek word that translates as "solid." It involves the process of recording a sound source so that the result will deliver the impression of a fully developed, three-dimensional soundstage between just two loudspeaker systems. Stereophonic recording is somewhat different from "binaural" recording, which involves headphone reproduction of sounds picked up by a microphone array that simulates the human head. True binaural sound reproduction can deliver a genuine full-dimensional effect, whereas stereophonic sound can only simulate the breadth and depth of the soundstage, and not the acoustics of the original performance space. Both techniques are in contrast to surround-sound recording that involves additional reproduction channels both in front of and adjacent to the listener and extends the three dimensionality clear out into the listening room and expands the size of the listening area accordingly.

Stereo sound reproduction is based on a theory first propounded by Alan D. Blumlein, to the effect that the human hearing mechanism could be imitated by a pair of left-right microphones and just two playback speakers. The stereo effect creates far greater realism than monaural recording, producing an illusion of depth that may be compared to the effect of stereoscopic photography. Stereo works because the brain compares the intensities of incoming sounds and contrasts the input received by each ear. It notes the arrival time from right and left sources, the reverberations, the intensities; and thus is able to determine source direction as well as distance instantaneously (and unconsciously). While the phantom images between the speakers cannot exactly simulate direct sources, the overall effect can be very realistic, at least if the listener occupies a location out in front of and equidistant from each of the speakers.

Early experiments with binaural sound transmission preceded the phonograph; there were such efforts in the U.K. in 1876, by Lord Rayleigh. Silvanus Thompson of Bristol University carried on experiments in 1877–1878. The use of two listening tubes, spaced like human ears, was found to produce a certain localizing ability of the source signals on the part of the listener. Alexander Graham Bell in America was also interested in "stereophonic phenomena" and apparently he was the first to use the term. In Paris, 1881, Clément Ader demonstrated two-channel telephone transmission for a large enthusiastic audience in the Opéra auditorium. Listeners wore headphones. Thomas Edison's second British phonographic patent (#1644; 1878) referred to multiple sound boxes on a single cylinder or disc, probably an effort to secure greater volume in reproduction, rather than a stereo effect. The Columbia Multiplex Grand Graphophone of 1898 utilized the concept.

Real efforts to record stereophonically began with the work of W. Bartlett Jones in the U.S. He patented the idea of putting the left and right sound signals in adjacent grooves of the disc or on opposite sides of the record (U.S. patent #1,855,149). Both methods required two replay styli, and the difficulty of synchronizing these was a serious flaw in the design. (A curiosity in this genre was the perhaps unintentional stereo recording made by Duke Ellington in 1929.) Jones then patented (#1,855,150) a single groove, single stylus system. Simultaneous vertical and lateral modulation of the groove was involved. This idea was not developed commercially at the time.

EMI made experimental 78-rpm stereo discs at the Abbey Road studios in 1933. Pressings of these test discs (one of them Thomas Beecham conducting the Mozart Jupiter Symphony) exist, and are sound effective. Other important research was carried out by Arthur Charles Haddy and colleagues of the Decca Record Co., Ltd., in London. Haddy's work, and that carried on in Germany by Teldec, led to an increased frequency spectrum in stereo playback, and to solving the problems of groove spacing so that space on the disc was not wasted by the dual signals. In the U.S. there was experimental stereo recording in March 1922 in the Philadelphia Academy of Music, as Arthur Charles Keller and a Bell Telephone Laboratories team made records of the Philadelphia Orchestra with two microphones. The output was on two parallel vertically cut tracks in 78-rpm discs. They were demonstrated at the Century of Progress Exposition in Chicago in 1933.

In later analog-disc recordings the twin signals were cut into the same record groove, at an axis of operation of 45/45 degrees. This was also one of the methods Alan Blumlein worked on, and the Blumlein patent applications of 1931 helped to establish all later practice (U.K. #394,325; U.S. #2,095,540). Westrex and Bell Telephone Laboratories received a U.S. patent for the their elaboration of the 45/45 disc technique in 1957. With each sidewall of the disc groove impressed with one program channel, the stereo cartridge distinguishes between them as it picks them up and sends one to each loudspeaker.

RCA initiated commercial recording in stereo in Boston's Symphony Hall on 21–22 Feb 1954, inscribing the Damnation of Faust. They followed that with a recording of the Chicago Symphony Orchestra under Fritz Reiner. These transcriptions did not actually appear in stereo form on discs until a few years later. EMI unveiled its "stereosonic" records in April 1955. Decca's first commercial recording in stereo — using the three-microphone "Decca Tree" assembly — took place in Geneva, with the Orchestre de la Suisse Romande in May 1954. Decca also began to use extra microphones, "outriggers," to capture flanking sounds from the boundaries of the orchestra. Eventually the company recorded the famous Georg Solti Rheingold in 1958 "where a KM-56 Tree captured the main orchestral sound" with a "six-channel unit augmented by a three-input outboard mixer and a single-channel pan-potted amp, a total of just 10 mikes to record what is universally recognized as a landmark achievement in stereo production" [Gray, M. 1986].

In May 1958 the first 45/45 stereo discs were marketed in the U.S. by three independent labels: Audio-Fidelity, Urania, and Counterpoint. That summer RCA and Columbia introduced their discs. The Recording Industry Association of America (RIAA) had finally determined which of the several available systems to endorse, and worldwide mass production followed. Pye issued the first commercial stereo discs in the U.K. in June 1958.

Multichannel optical motion picture recording was first used commercially by Walt Disney studios in *Fantasia* (1940). It had a four-track sound film, derived from eight recording channels. It could best be described in today's terms as surround sound, rather than stereo, since it did not observe the natural sound perspectives of stereo. Cinemascope, developed by Bell Telephone Laboratories and demonstrated in January 1953, was an attempt to created true stereophonic sound on film.

Two-channel tape recording was also produced in the Bell Laboratories. At the New York World's Fair, 1939, demonstration tapes of Vicalloy were successfully displayed. Further important work in stereo tape was carried out by Marvin Camras, with a three-channel wire recorder. Domestic stereo tapes were introduced commercially by EMI in October 1955 — a two-track system, also labeled "stereosonic," with a two-tape set of Nozze di Figaro performed at the Glyndebourne Festival. RCA's four-track system appeared in 1958. For several years the companies produced their releases in both monaural and stereo versions to accommodate users who did not have the new stereo playback equipment. Then compatible systems were developed, with which a stereo disc could be played as if it were only monaural (i.e., without the twin loudspeakers and stereo amplifier). Thus the user without the means or desire to acquire a stereo system could buy stereo records, and the need for manufacturing monaural records evaporated. By the end of the 1960s virtually all commercial recording on disc and tape was stereophonic.

The digital era continued the stereophonic revolution, and because digital systems offer considerably better channel separation than the 45/45 system used to produce the LP record, it was possible for recording engineers to do an even better job of simulating a phantom soundstage between the speakers. Unfortunately, the enhanced separation also required that some tried-and-true practices be modified or even shelved, and so many early CD releases seemed to lack the air and spaciousness of their LP counterparts. Eventually, recording engineers became aware of the requirements of the CD, and many contemporary releases offer up the best stereophonic sound ever produced. [Borwick 1982; Crowhurst 1960; Davis 1958; Ford Autumn 1962; Kogen 1968.]

See also **Hearing; Recording Practice**

REV. HOWARD FERSTLER

STERLING, LOUIS, *SIR* (16 MAY 1879–3 JUNE 1958)

American/U.K. record industry executive. He was born into a family of humble means and had to sell newspapers in New York. But by 1900 he was in the export business; and in 1903 he was in England, working for Gramophone & Typewriter, Ltd., who appointed him manager of the British Zonophone Co., its newly established outlet for its International Zonophone Co. of Germany. Sterling resigned to set up his own Sterling Record Co., Ltd., in December 1904, to make cylinder records. Russell Hunting, director of his recording department, was his partner. On 18 Mar 1905 the firm was renamed the Russell Hunting Record Co., Ltd. It marketed the Sterling Gold Moulded Cylinder record and was appointed as U.K. agent for products of Fonotipia, Ltd. A new company was formed in August 1906, Sterling and Hunting, Ltd.; it took on the Fonotipia agency from 17 Sep 1906, and began to sell Odeon and Fonotipia discs and cylinders made for the Linguaphone Co., Ltd. It also sold the Sterling records made by the Russell Hunting Record Co., Ltd., and marketed by that company until Sterling and Hunting, Ltd., was formed.

Sterling resigned from Sterling and Hunting, Ltd., in April 1908. The Russell Hunting Record Co., Ltd., went into liquidation that year. Sterling set up the new Rena Manufacturing Co., Ltd., with N.D. Rodkinson as his partner, on 12 Nov 1908. Rena sold double-sided discs — the first in the U.K. — from Columbia matrices, plus Rena record players. Sterling was successful with Rena, and was asked to join the Columbia Phonograph Co., General–London, so he closed down his company, letting Columbia have the Rena records business and becoming manager of the Columbia activity on a commission basis. Columbia changed its name to Columbia Graphophone Co. (January 1913), and Sterling became European manager (December 1914). He began a vigorous campaign to record symphonic music and chamber music, repertoires not previously emphasized by the record labels.

Due to World War I, Columbia had to establish itself as a self-sufficient U.K company, and Sterling was instrumental in founding the Columbia Graphophone Co., Ltd., in February 1917 — which became British-owned in April 1923. Sterling was able to take control of the British firm, and then also to gain a controlling interest in the failing American firm, on 31 Mar 1925. The American company had reorganized as the Columbia Phonograph Co., Inc., in February 1924, and that company had passed into the hands of Columbia (International) Ltd., upon its formation by Sterling's Columbia company on 3 Oct 1925.

Sterling had taken an early interest in electrical recording, as witnessed by Columbia's cooperation in the Westminster Abbey effort of November 1920 by Lionel Guest and H.O. Merriman. The new Western Electric system was offered to Victor, which hesitated, and when Sterling got some of the electric masters from Russell Hunting, he went at once to New York, leaving 26 Dec 1924, to obtain the Western Electric license. He had to acquire the Columbia Phonograph Co., Inc. — which had been licensed — to achieve this.

Victor came around, so the two rivals shared the electric system.

The merger of 1931 which created EMI, Ltd., gave Sterling yet another high post — director of the new conglomerate. In June of that year he was knighted, the first person from the record industry to be so honored.

Sterling resigned from EMI before World War II.

FRANK ANDREWS

STERLING (LABEL)

A U.K. cylinder record of the Russell Hunting Record Co., Ltd., Sterling and Hunting, Ltd., and Russell Hunting and Co., issued from June 1905 to February 1909. In 1907, at the peak of the cylinder business in the U.K., Sterling was highly successful; as many as 3 million cylinders were sold in a 12-month period. Issues covered popular music of the day, operatic numbers, Irish and Scottish material. However, there were no new issues after February 1909, the records having been undercut in price by the Edison Bell and Clarion cylinder records. The label was revived briefly in 1909 by James Edward Hough, who purchased the Sterling business after a fire had destroyed the cylinder manufacturing capacity of the Edison Bell plant. [Carter et al. 1975 is a label list.]

FRANK ANDREWS

STERLING AND HUNTING, LTD.

A U.K. firm, formed by the Russell Hunting Record Co., Ltd., on 27 Aug 1906, to be the British sales agency for the Odeon and Fonotipia discs of Fonotipia, Ltd. The new firm also acted as sales agency for the Sterling cylinder records, for the recording and manufacturing company, and for the Sterling-made Linguaphone Language Course cylinders of the International Linguaphone Co., Ltd. Louis Sterling was general manager. The company was successful at first, in large part because of aggressive advertising; one promotional effort sent a balloon flying over London. The company claimed in February 1907 that it had shipped 80,000 records on a single day. Catalogs covered operatic material, popular music of the day, plus Irish and Scottish items. However it was unable to meet the competition — in a period of economic depression — of records coming from Edison Bell and Clarion, selling for 25 percent less than the Sterling. The firm folded by October 1908, and was dissolved 6 Aug 1909. Sterling had already departed and was set up in business as the Rena Manufacturing Co., Ltd.

FRANK ANDREWS

STERLING RECORD CO., LTD.

A U.K. firm established 17 Dec 1904 by Louis Sterling and Russell Hunting, to manufacture and sell phonographs and Gramophones. Charles Stroh, son of the inventor of the Stroh violin, was on the board, and Russell Hunting was director of the recording department. Address was Bishop Road, Cambridge Heath, London.

The firm changed its name on 18 Mar 1905 to Russell Hunting Record Co., Ltd., which stayed in business until 10 Dec 1908.

FRANK ANDREWS

STERLING TRIO

A male vocal group that recorded for many labels from 1916–1920, then exclusively for Victor in 1920–1925. In 1926 it worked for Gennett. Members were Albert Campbell, Henry Burr, and John H. Meyer. (Henry Moeller probably took the place of Burr in 1926.) There were 18 sides in the Victor 1917 catalog, many with geographical themes like "Georgia Moon" (#17927) and "In Florida among the Palms" (#18138). "Down Deep in an Irishman's Heart" was their final Victor effort (#19749; 1925).

STERN, ISAAC
(21 JULY 1920–23 SEP 2001)

Russian/American violinist, born in Kremenetz, Russia. He was taken to the U.S. as a child, studied violin at the San Francisco Conservatory of Music (1928–1931), and made his debut with the San Francisco Symphony Orchestra at age 11. Then he toured Australia and Europe, establishing himself as one of the world's major artists. From 1955 he was part of an important trio, with pianist Eugene Istomin and cellist Leonard Rose. He is also distinguished for his humanitarian activities and for his successful efforts to save Carnegie Hall from destruction.

A Columbia artist for over 50 years, Stern recorded a wide repertoire of solo music, all the major concertos and chamber works — most notably the Beethoven trios — with Istomin and Rose. Among his fine discs are the Brahms sonatas and the sonatas of Debussy and Franck, all with Alexander Zakin; the Sibelius, Brahms, and Bartók (first) concertos with the Philadelphia Orchestra; and the Samuel Barber and Bartók (second) concertos with the New York Philharmonic Orchestra. He inscribed the Copland Sonata, with the composer at the piano.

Isaac Stern won six Grammys, for discs of 1961, 1962, 1964, 1970, 1981, and 1991, along with a Lifetime Achievement award in 1987. In 1995 Sony

Classical launched the reissue of a 44-disc edition of his recordings under the title *Isaac Stern: A Life in Music*. He died in New York City.

STERNO (LABEL) (I)

A U.K. label made for the British Homophone Co., Ltd., by the Gramophone Co., Ltd., some of whose matrices it used — with others specially recorded — in 1926. The disc, named after W.D. Sternberg, founder of British Homophone and the Sterno Manufacturing Co., was 10-inch size; the label was gray, blue, black, and white. The rarity of Sterno discs in U.K. suggests that they were exported to countries where the Homochord label and trademark belonged to others, for these Sternos had equivalent Homochord issues in U.K. No issues have been found later than those of Homochord in December 1926.

FRANK ANDREWS

STERNO (LABEL) (II)

A U.K. label manufactured and sold by British Homophone Co., Ltd., from February 1929 to April 1935. There was a 10-inch disc with a red and gold label, and later a 12-inch disc with a magenta label.

FRANK ANDREWS

STEVENS, CAT (21 JULY 1948–)

Cat Stevens, born Stephen Georgiou in London, crammed two distinctly separate music careers into his first 30 years prior to converting to Islam, adopting the name Yusaf Islam, and retiring from the music business. He is best remembered, however, for his 1970s' incarnation as a singer/songwriter with a gift for socially astute lyrics.

During his early years as a recording artist, Stevens was promoted by the English Decca label as a teen idol. Although a number of his compositions (e.g., "Here Comes My Baby," "First Cut Is the Deepest") were covered by more established stars, he remained relatively unknown stateside in the 1960s. A period spent recovering from tuberculosis in 1968 enabled Stevens, who had been unhappy about Decca's overemphasis on commercial success, to think at length about his future objectives within the music industry.

Following a period of stylistic experimentation, Stevens recorded *Mona Bone Jakon* (A&M #4260; 1970; #63 U.K., #164 U.S.), which featured simple, unadorned acoustic arrangements, thereby focusing on his sensitive vocals and poetic verses. His next two albums — *Tea for the Tillerman* (A&M #4280; 1970; #20 U.K., #8 U.S.) and *Teaser and the Firecat* (A&M

#4313; 1971; #3 U.K., #2 U.S.) — continued in the same vein, making him one of the most successful recording artists of the early 1970s. His singles also sold well (14 entered the *Billboard Hot 100* during the decade), most notably "Peace Train" (A&M #1291; 1971; #7), "Morning Has Broken" (A&M #1335; 1972; #6), "Oh, Very Young" (A&M #1503; 1974; #10), and the Sam Cooke-penned "Another Saturday Night" (A&M #1602; 1974; #6).

He maintained his popularity with the LPs *Catch Bull at Four* (A&M #4365; 1972; #2 U.K., #1 U.S.), *Foreigner* (A&M #4391; 1973; #3 U.K., #3 U.S.), and *Buddah and the Chocolate Box* (A&M #3623; 1974; #3 U.K., #2 U.S.), although the arrangements were seen as increasingly cluttered. His songwriting was also noticeably less inspired in the final releases — *Numbers* (A&M #4555; 1975; #13 U.S.), *Izitso* (A&M #4702; 1977; #18 U.K., #7 U.S.), and *Back to Earth* (A&M #4735; #1978; #33; his only 1970s album not to achieve gold status) — by which time his English audience, in particular, had become largely apathetic. Following his conversion to the Islam faith, Stevens renounced his music career.

FRANK HOFFMANN

STEVENS, ERNEST LINWOOD (15 DEC 1893–6 APR 1981)

American pianist, born in Elizabeth, New Jersey. He started performing publicly in high school. In 1919 Stevens made a test recording for Edison, and was engaged as Edison's personal pianist. He tried out new music and experimented with placement of the piano in recordings. Stevens also made numerous records, as soloist, with his "Recording Orchestra," and with the Ernest L. Stevens Trio, which had a banjo (M. Aron) and saxophone (Charles J. Murray), with various other members (including at one time John Sorin, performing on a Chinese block). Most of his commercial records were made in the experimental studio in West Orange, New Jersey. He retired to private teaching, and had an active studio into the 1980s. Stevens died in Montclair, New Jersey.

The first of his Edison Diamond Discs was "Ma! — Medley Fox Trot" (#50929; 1922). Among his other Diamond Discs of interest were the piano solo "All Over Nothing at All" (#50987; 1922), and "Keep on Building Castles in the Air" (#51016; 1922), with the trio. His first disc with the dance orchestra was "Twilight on the Nile" (#51157; 1923). He used pseudonyms on some records, e.g., Franz Falkenburg and Harry Osborne. The last record by Stevens was "Sun Is at My Window"/"I Loved You Then" (#52526; 1929). [Grable 1979.]

STEVENSON, ELISE
(9 FEB 1878–18 NOV 1967)

U.K. soprano, born Alice C. Stevenson in Liverpool. She was a church and concert singer, with a brief but very active recording career from 1906 to 1911. Her first record was a duet for Victor with tenor Harry Macdonough, "Cross Your Heart" (1906). Later in the same year she did the same song with bass Frank C. Stanley (#4776). Her first solo record was "Last Rose of Summer" for Victor in June 1906. She made 19 other Victor discs to December 1907. She was also heard in the Victor Trinity Choir and the Victor Light Opera Co.

Stevenson made two duets for Edison cylinders in 1909–1910, with Stanley and Macdonough, and took a part in one record by the Manhattan Mixed Trio (with Irving Gillette [Henry Burr] and Stanley). In that month she did a song with the Schubert Trio. She made some Zonophones, then went to Columbia for her best hits, from February 1907, most of them with Stanley, who was also her manager. Her final successful record was a duet with Henry Burr, "Love Is Like a Red Red, Rose" (Columbia #16854; 1911). She then had a baby and gave up her career for motherhood. She died in South Laguna, California.

STEWART, CAL (1856–7 DEC 1919)

American humorist, born in Virginia. He was a favorite recording artist from ca. 1897, beginning with Edison and Berliner, then going to Columbia, Victor, and other labels. He was most famous for his series of monologs and skits about Uncle Josh. The Columbia 14000 series had 32 cylinders about that colorful character (1898–1900), beginning with "Uncle Josh's Arrival in New York." There were 14 Uncle Josh items in the Victor 1902 catalog, and 42 in the Victor 1917 catalog. Edison had 15 records by Stewart in 1898, and 57 by 1912. A special favorite was "Uncle Josh Rides a Bus on Fifth Ave." (Edison #3883; before 1899). Victor records often identified the hero as Uncle Josh Weathersby; but it seems that he was drawn from a creation of Denman Thompson, named Uncle Josh Whitcomb.

Stewart signed an exclusive contract with Columbia in 1903, leading to the rise of imitators on the other labels. By 1906 he had made 37 discs for Columbia; then he was free to return to Victor and Edison in 1907–1908. Edison got an exclusive contract in 1911, but Victor signed Stewart again in 1915, in time for his best-seller "Uncle Josh Buys an Automobile." He continued with Edison, making 14 Diamond discs between 1915 and 1924. In his last year, 1919, Stewart was working for Columbia, recording as many as five monologs per day. He died in Chicago. A number of his records were not issued until after 1925, on Harmony, Diva, Silvertone, and Velvet Tone labels. [Betz 1976; Brooks 1979; Petty 1976; Walsh 1951/1–4, 1952/5.]

STEWART, REX
(22 FEB 1907–7 SEP 1967)

American jazz cornetist, born in Philadelphia. He grew up in Washington, D.C., and was playing on Potomac riverboats in his teens. In New York during the 1920s he was with Fletcher Henderson and McKinney's Cotton Pickers. In the mid-1930s he had his own band, then joined Duke Ellington in 1934, remaining to 1945. Later he toured Europe and Australia. Stewart was also a disc jockey and writer on jazz. He died in Los Angeles.

His first records were noteworthy, made with a pick-up group before he joined Ellington in 1934: "Stingaree"/"Baby, Ain't You Satisfied?" (Vocalion #2880). Stewart's fine recordings include one of his own composition, "Rexatious" with his Fifty-Second Street Stompers (Variety #517; 1936). With Ellington he made the acclaimed "Boy Meets Horn" (another of his own compositions), on Brunswick (#8306; 1938). LP reissues cover all the above titles; the most comprehensive being *Rex Stewart Memorial* (CBS Realm #E-52628).

STEWART, ROD (10 JAN 1945–)

The Rod Stewart story is one of unfulfilled promise. He possesses one of the most expressive voices in rock music history, his hoarse-sounding delivery equally effective negotiating caressing ballads and exuberant rockers. However, he has frequently opted to record material of dubious quality or saddled his delivery with shallow cliches (e.g., sexual posturing in songs like "Hot Legs" and "Do Ya Think I'm Sexy?").

Born Roderick David Stewart in London, Stewart's earliest recordings were made as lead singer for two John Baldry–led bands, the Hoochie Coochie Men (English Decca) and Steampacket (Columbia), between 1964–1967. He had his first taste of rock stardom as the vocalist on the first two albums recorded by the Jeff Beck Group, *Truth* (Epic #26413; 1968; #15) and *Beck-Ola* (Epic #26478; 1969; #15). His fame led to a contract with Mercury in 1969; his joint status as a soloist and group member for two different labels represented a unique arrangement within the rock scene at the time. When the Beck group temporarily disbanded, Stewart continued his dual career until 1975 as a member of the Faces.

Although the Faces releases — most notably — were considered uneven at best, Stewart's early solo albums — *The Rod Stewart Album* (Mercury #61237;

1969; #139); *Gasoline Alley* (Warner Bros. #61264; 1970; #27); *Every Picture Tells a Story* (Mercury #609; 1971; #1), which included "Maggie May" (Mercury #73224; 1971; #1 for five weeks); and *Never a Dull Moment* (Mercury #646; 1972; #2) — all featured sensitive singing, intelligent lyrics, and inspired production values. His switch to Warner Bros., however, found him adopting a more stylized, albeit charismatic, delivery. Nevertheless, his albums — particularly, *A Night on the Town* (Warner Bros. #2938; 1976; #2), including "Tonight's the Night" (Warner Bros. #8262; 1976), which topped the singles chart for eight weeks; *Foot Loose & Fancy Free* (Warner Bros. #3092; 1977; #2); and *Blondes Have More Fun* (Warner Bros. #3261; 1978; #10), featuring the disco-oriented "Do Ya Think I'm Sexy?" (Warner Bros. #8724; 1978; #1 for four weeks) — continued to sell at platinum levels into the early 1980s.

The predictability of his material and approach in subsequent releases caused a drop-off in popularity. Now an entertainment institution, Stewart's recorded output remains highly flawed, despite occasional returns to popularity, most notably *Vagabond Heart* (Warner Bros. #26300; 1991; #10), *Unplugged ... and Seated* (Warner Bros.#45289; 1993; #2), and, "All for Love" (A&M #0476; 1993; with Bryan Adams and Sting), the number one single from the film *The Three Musketeers*. In 2002 Stewart was signed to Clive Davis's J Records label. Davis encouraged him to record an album of standards, *It Had to Be You ... The Great American Songbook* (J #20039), with lush orchestral accompaniments.

FRANK HOFFMANN

STEWART, SLAM
(21 SEP 1914–10 DEC 1987)

American jazz string bassist, born Leroy Stewart in Englewood, New Jersey, on 21 Sep 1914. He studied in Boston and played with various groups there. He was in New York in the 1930s, and teamed with guitarist Slim Gaillard to from Slim and Slam, a novelty/jazz group. Then in the 1940s he performed with Art Tatum, Benny Goodman, and his own trio; and made a fine series of records with Dizzy Gillespie and Charlie Parker. He did important work with Roy Eldridge in the 1950s. During the 1960s he toured Europe. In 1973 he was again with Goodman, in the Rainbow Room, New York. He died in Binghamton, New York.

Slim and Slam had a popular record in "Flat Foot Floogie with a Floy Floy" (Vocalion #4021; 1938). Some of Stewart's finest efforts were heard on the seminal Charlie Parker recordings of 1945, "Hallelujah!" and "Slam Slam Blues" (reissued on Jazztone #J1204), and in Dizzy Gillespie's brilliant "Groovin' High," "Dizzy Atmosphere," and "All the Things You Are" of 1945 (reissued on Savoy MG #12020).

STEWART PHONOGRAPH CORP.

A Chicago firm, established in 1916 at 2815–2853 N. Lincoln Ave. It advertised the Stewart disc player at $6.50, a wind-up table model said to handle any type or make of record. The firm was listed in the 1917 city directory, but did not appear in later directories.

STIFF (LABEL)

The most prominent independent record label identified with the U.K. punk movement, Stiff was notable both as a musical trail-blazer and for the uniformly high quality of its artist roster. The London-based company was established in July 1976 by Dave Robinson and Andrew "Jake" Jakeman, the impetus provided by a 400-pound loan from Lee Brilleaux of the pub-rock band, Dr. Feelgood. Robinson had entered the music business in the 1960s as a tour manager (his client list included Jimi Hendrix) and progressed to ownership of the artist management firm, Famepushers Ltd., in the early 1970s. Jakeman had managed a number of U.K. rock acts, most notably Dr. Feelgood, the Red Hot Chili Peppers, and Chilli Willi.

The label name — designating a "turkey" or "flop" in record industry lingo — exemplified the partners' wry, street-smart approach to marketing contemporary pop music. According to Stiff historian Bert Muirhead, the label's objectives were "to treat musicians as people and not as products; to try to show a profit on each release; to avoid the trap of paying massive advances that can never be recouped; and to release records when they are hot and to work them when they are hot." Stiff's identification with punk came largely because its early releases coincided with that movement. With the exception of the Damned, however, most of the label's early roster — including Nick Lowe, Elvis Costello, Ian Dury, Wreckless Eric, Lene Lovich, Jona Lewie, Graham Parker, and Madness — were too old and too mainstream to be truly categorized as punk or new wave.

After distributing its early singles via mail order and independent retail outlets, Stiff signed a distribution deal with Island (part of the EMI empire) on 11 July 1977. The company's first crisis of note came when Jakeman left in September 1977 for the newly formed Radar Records, taking Costello, Lowe, and the Yachts along with him. Robinson managed to retain the support of investors, largely due to his promotional skills, exceptionally good relations with the press and radio, and ear for talent.

EMI's financial problems caused Stiff to switch distribution to CBS on 9 Oct 1979. Still, the label remained hot well into the 1980s. During its first six years, over 30 percent of the 150 singles released charted (Madness, alone, had 13 consecutive hits), a standard rarely equaled within the music industry in the U.K. or anywhere else. Album releases also sold well, including Elvis Costello's *My Aim Is True* (SEEZ #3; 1977; #10 U.K.), Ian Drury's *New Boots and Panties* (SEEZ #4; 1977; #10 U.K.; 106 weeks on charts) and *Do It Yourself* (SEEZ #14; 1979; #2), and Madness' *One Step Beyond* (SEEZ #17; 1979; #2), *Absolutely* (SEEZ #29; 1980; #2), 7 (SEEZ #39; 1981; #7), and *Complete* (HIT-TV #1; 1982; #1).

In the face of defections to major labels by its best-selling acts the mid-1980s, however, Stiff lost its ability to sign and nurture new talent. The postpunk scene was now dominated by a new galaxy of independent labels such as Beggars Banquet in the U.K. and Sub Pop in the U.S., leaving Stiff little choice but to market its back catalog as nostalgia items.

FRANK HOFFMANN

STIGWOOD, ROBERT (16 APR 1934–)

Born in Adelaide, Australia, Stigwood has worked as a rock manager, producer, and record label owner. Stigwood emigrated to the U.K. in the late 1950s, where he founded a talent agency. One of his early signings was a teen television star named Johnny Leyton, who crossed over briefly to recording success. By the mid-1960s, Stigwood moved into rock management, briefly partnering with Brian Epstein (the Beatles' manager), before forming his own firm. His initial signings included Eric Clapton and the Bee Gees. In the early 1970s, he founded his own record label, RSO (Robert Stigwood Organization), and also moved into movie production, including films such as *Jesus Christ Superstar* (1973) and the Who's *Tommy* (1975). Stigwood's career reached its height in 1977 when he produced *Saturday Night Fever*, featuring his act the Bee Gees prominently on the film's soundtrack. Both film and album were enormous successes, launching the disco era. He followed it a year later with another smash hit, the film *Grease*, which spawned several chart hits for stars Olivia Newton-John and John Travolta.

However, Stigwood's run of success ended abruptly with 1978s' ill-conceived film of *Sergeant Pepper's Lonely Hearts Club Band* as a vehicle for the Bee Gees.

A series of failures followed, and by the mid-1980s he had sold RSO's back catalog and semiretired from the entertainment business. Stigwood returned as a film producer in the 1990s, notably with 1996s' film of the musical *Evita,* and also produced a touring stage version of *Saturday Night Fever* that premiered in 1999.

STILLSON (LABEL)

An American record, issued briefly in 1923 or 1924 from the Gennett studios; it was part of a projected "personal series." The label name was from the orchestra leader Ray Stillson. Only a few were issued, in 1924. [Kendziora 1960/3; Rust 1978.]

STING (2 OCT 1952–)

Feeling stylistically constrained as the frontman for the supergroup Police, Sting (aka Gordon Sumner) has opted for a solo career defined by experimentation across a wide range of genres. His work also demonstrates a literary flair and social commitment while retaining the melodic flair and slick production values that characterized the Police's recordings.

Sting's celebrity status — as reflected by heavy video rotation on MTV and extensive press coverage — helped ensure best-seller status for his ambitious debut release, *The Dream of the Blue Turtles* (A&M #3750; 1985; #2), and its four Top 20 singles. Sting's new band included jazz musicians Kenny Kirkland and Branford Marsalis, an unusual move for a pop-rock musician, showing Sting's interest in jazz rhythms and instrumentation. The work was nominated for an Album of the Year Grammy, while he shared the 1985 Song of the Year Grammy with Mark Knopfler for "Money for Nothing" (Warner Bros. #28950; #1). Most of the jazz and world-beat musicians utilized on his LP accompanied him on a support tour; these concerts were documented on the double live set, *Bring on the Night* (A&M BRIN #1; 1986).

Although extremely active in film acting and pursuing social causes such as Band Aid, Amnesty International, and the Rainforest Foundation, he found time to record another jazz-funk album, *... Nothing Like the Sun* (A&M #6402; 1987; #9). Its dark tone, largely evoked by thickly textured orchestrations, was continued by *The Soul Cages* (A&M #6405; 1991; #2), a stripped-down, folk-oriented affair pervaded by religious references.

Sting's subsequent releases — the triple-platinum *Ten Summoner's Tales* (A&M #0070; 1993; #2), which included the Grammy-winning "If I Ever Lose My Faith in You" (A&M # 0111; 1993; #17); the chart-topping "All for Love" (A&M #0476; 1993; with Bryan Adams and Rod Stewart) from the film *The Three*

Musketeers; *Mercury Falling* (A&M #0483; 1996; #5); and the engaging *Brand New Day* (Interscope #490443; 1999; #9) have been decidedly more upbeat. The first single from the album, "Desert Rose" (Interscope #497321, 2000) failed to see much action until Sting's manager approached Jaguar with the idea of using it in a television commercial for their new model, the S-Type. This was a somewhat controversial move, but it paid off when the song became a major adult contemporary hit and the album, which had previously performed poorly as well, began to sell. The album won two Grammys (Pop Album of the Year and Best Male Pop Vocal Performance for the title song).

FRANK HOFFMANN

STINSON RECORDS (LABEL)

Herbert Harris ran a movie house on 46th Street in New York City in the late 1930s. A member of the Communist Party, he showed Soviet films. When the Soviet Union withdrew from the World's Fair in 1939, Harris was given a stock of Soviet records to sell. These he sold out of his store, the Stinson Trading Co., in Union Square. In January 1943 he signed an agreement with Moses Asch to produce and distribute their records under the joint Asch/Stinson label, but usually one or the other name appeared on the records. Asch/Stinson specialized in folk recordings, but also entered the jazz market, partly through distributing the Signature label in late 1944. Asch supplied the jazz and folk recordings, while Harris controlled distribution until their split in late 1945. They had released significant records by Woody Guthrie, Lead Belly, Josh White, Sonny Terry, Burl Ives, Coleman Hawkins, Mary Lou Williams, and numerous others. Harris continued to issue Asch/Stinson albums after the break, plus new recordings, although for years there would be controversy between Harris and Asch over numerous titles that both claimed (Asch started his own Disc label, then Folkways in 1949). Harris's son Bob became involved with the company in the 1950s, when Kenneth Goldstein began reissuing Asch/Stinson 78s in the new LP format, including the influential *Folksay* series. Into the 1980s Stinson distributed a wide range of folk and jazz artists, including Carlos Montoya, Mugsy Spanier, Patrick Galvin, and Pete Seeger.

RONALD D. COHEN

STITT, SONNY
(2 FEB 1924–22 JULY 1982)

American jazz saxophonist, born Edward Stitt in Boston. He was a Big Band alto saxophone performer in his teens, joining Billy Eckstine in 1945, and the Dizzy Gillespie band in 1946. He led and played with many groups, among them the Miles Davis Quintet. Stitt developed a style drawn from Charlie Parker, but produced more original material when he took up the tenor saxophone around 1950. Two of his important LP albums were *Sonny Stitt Sits in with the Oscar Peterson Trio* (Verve #8344; 1959) and *Stitt Plays Bird* (Atlantic #1418; 1963). He died in Washington, D.C.

STOCK, FREDERICK AUGUST
(11 NOV 1872–20 OCT 1942)

German/American conductor, born in Jülich. He studied in Cologne and played violin in the orchestra there, then was invited by Theodore Thomas to join the Thomas Symphony Orchestra (to become the Chicago Symphony Orchestra in 1912) in 1895 as first violist. He was assistant conductor in 1899, and conductor in 1905, remaining in the post until his death. He promoted contemporary composers, instituted children's concerts, created the Chicago Civic Orchestra (a training ensemble for the CSO), and initiated a recording program. Stock became an American citizen in 1919. He died in Chicago.

Under Stock the CSO was the first major orchestra to make commercial recordings under its regular conductor. Victor recorded the ensemble in New York in May 1916, then in Chicago from 1925, and remained the orchestra's label through the Stock tenure. Interesting items in the 1940 catalog include the J.S. Bach Suite in B-Minor and some of Edward MacDowell's "Woodland Sketches" arranged by Stock for orchestra. A low-price black label set of the Mozart 40th Symphony was offered as album G-3 (for $2.50, while Red Seal albums were selling at $3.50).

STOCKHAM, THOMAS (1933–)

Considered by many to be the father of digital recording, Stockham earned an Sc.D. degree from MIT in 1959 and was appointed assistant professor of electrical engineering at the same school. In 1962 he began experimenting with digital audio tape recordings using a large TX-0 computer and a A/D-D/A converter. (During this time, he also helped fellow MIT professor Amar Bose work on loudspeaker design.) In 1968 he left MIT for the University of Utah, and in 1975 he founded Soundstream, Inc., along with Malcolm Lowe, who had previously helped to found KLH. At this new position, he developed a 16-bit digital audio recorder using a high-speed instrument magnetic tape recorder. Soundstream, located in Salt Lake City, was the first commercial digital recording company in the U.S. Other companies had been experimenting with digital recording since 1971, but Stockham was the first to make a commercial digital recording, using his own Soundstream recorder in 1976 at the Santa Fe Opera.

Using Soundstream technology, the first commercial, digitally mastered LP recording to be released for sale was recorded by Jack Renner, of Telarc in 1978 (Frederick Fennell and the Cleveland Symphonic Winds), and the company released the first compact disc version of this material in the U.S. in 1982. From 1975–1980 Stockham, with the help of scientists such as Jules Bloomenthal, made over 500 digital masters with a completely computerized editing system, and pioneered tapeless hard disc editing. The company sold about 16 of its editing systems at $160,000 each that were used by companies such as Bertelsmann. These machines used a Honeywell 16-track transport and sampled at 50 kHz. Stockham also played a key role in the digital restoration of Enrico Caruso recordings. Soundstream merged with Digital Recording Corporation in 1980 and became DRC/Soundstream.

In 1980, after leaving Soundstream, Stockman became chairman of Electrical and Computer Engineering at the University of Utah. He was named a fellow of the Institute of Electrical and Electronics Engineers, served as president of the Audio Engineering Society (AES) in 1982–1983, and has received numerous awards for his contributions to audio technology, including the Poniatoff gold medal from the Society of Motion Picture and Television Engineers (SMPTE), the gold medal from the AES, and an Emmy in 1988 for the development of tapeless audio recording and editing technology used in television studios. The National Academy of Recording Arts and Sciences (NARAS) awarded him a Grammy in 1994 for his role in pioneering and advancing the era of digital recording. In 1999 the Academy of Motion Picture Arts and Sciences awarded Stockham and Robert B. Ingebretsen a 1998 Scientific and Engineering award for their work in the areas of waveform editing, cross-fades, and cut-and-paste techniques for digital audio editing.

HOWARD FERSTLER

STOCKHAUSEN, KARLHEINZ (22 AUG 1928–)

One of the most important and original composers of the postwar avant-garde, Karlheinz Stockhausen was a pioneer in the fields of electronic music and musique concrète. Initially a serialist in the mold of Webern and Messiaen (with whom he had studied), Stockhausen later began working at the musique concrète studio of French Radio in Paris and the WDR's prestigious Studio for Electronic Music in Cologne (of which he was later appointed director). At the same time, he

pursued studies in phonetics and information theory; these exerted a powerful influence on his work, in his use of aleatory (chance) elements, process-oriented composition, and experiments with language and meaning using cut-up texts. Stockhausen's oeuvre defies easy description, including percussion music, orchestral compositions, works for processed voices, and scoreless compositions (conducted via verbal instructions to the performers). His magnum opus *Licht* is a cycle of seven operas (one for each day of the week) begun in 1977 and remains uncompleted.

DAVE MANDL

STOKES, JONATHAN (10 APR 1964–)

After graduating from the University of East Anglia, with a master's degree in music, Stokes joined Decca in 1987 as an audio editor. Within three years, he had learned enough about recording and recording technology to move on to the location department, where he eventually was promoted to senior engineer, a position that involved responsibility for projects ranging from recording solo recitals to recording grand opera productions, live events, and video productions. In addition to his engineering tasks, Stokes also occasionally worked as a producer, and during his time with Decca, he worked with some of the finest artists in the world, including Bernard Haitink, Cecilia Bartoli, George Solti, Luciano Pavaroti, Placido Domingo, Bryn Terfel, Kiri Te Kanawa, and Al Jarreau, as well as with ensembles such as the Berlin Philharmonic, Vienna Philharmonic, Chicago Symphony Orchestra, Cleveland Orchestra, and the Montreal Symphony, among others.

During his career, Stokes has won a Deutsche Schallplaten award for best opera recording (1994), has won Grammys for Best Engineered Recording twice (in 1992 and 1995), and has had recordings win performance Grammys four times (two in 1995, for Best Choral and Best Solo instrument, plus one in 1996 and one in 2001). He has also won numerous best-recording awards from *Gramophone Magazine*. In November 1997, he left Decca, and with Neil Hutchinson, formed a new recording and mastering facility in London, Classic Sound, built from the ground up to deal with both traditional and the new 5.1-channel formats.

HOWARD FERSTLER

STOKOWSKI, LEOPOLD (18 APR 1882–13 SEP 1977)

U.K./American conductor, born of Polish parents as Antoni Stanislaw Boleslawowich in London. He played violin, piano, and organ as a child, and was the youngest student ever admitted to the Royal College of Music (1895). He was organist of St. James, Piccadilly, and in 1905 at St. Bartholomew's in New York. Stokowski made his debut as a conductor in Paris in 1908, and was heard by representatives of the Cincinnati Symphony Orchestra who were searching for a new conductor. He directed the Cincinnati Symphony from 1909 to 1912, then went to the Philadelphia Orchestra for 25 years, and on to international fame. In 1915 he became an American citizen.

Stokowski was renowned for developing the unique sound of the Philadelphia Orchestra, for his energetic promotion of new compositions (he directed more than 2,000 premieres), and for his flamboyant personality. He appeared in the motion picture *One Hundred Men and a Girl* (1940), and was responsible for the music performed in *Fantasia* (1940). His transcriptions of organ works by J.S. Bach helped to shape the baroque revival that blossomed in the late 1940s. After leaving the Philadelphia Orchestra he formed the All/American Youth Orchestra (1940), and conducted the Houston Symphony Orchestra in 1955–1960. He continued conducting in Europe and America and recording until his death in Nether Wallop, England.

The Victor catalog of 1940 had five pages of Stokowski/Philadelphia Orchestra listings, display-ing the major orchestral repertoire from the 18th to the 20th century. Among the jewels in that array are the Rachmaninoff Second Concerto, performed by the composer (#M-58), the first and fifth symphonies of Shostakovich (#M-192, #M-619), Toccata and Fugue in D Minor of Bach, in Stokowski's resonant transcription (#8697), and brilliant excerpts from Wagner operas. Stokowski's 1965 recording of the Symphony No. 4 by Charles Ives won a Grammy award. (See also the recordings cited in the article on the Philadelphia Orchestra.) The Leopold Stokowski Society was established in 1979 in the U.K.; it has reissued a number of the maestro's recordings under its own label. The latest release is of Sibelius performances, taken from HMV sessions of the 1950s. [Lewis, J. 1977.]

STOLLWERK CHOCOLATE RECORD

A vertical-cut disc issued by Gebrüder Stollwerk AG, a firm that had acquired Edison patents for Germany ca. 1898. Remarkably, the records were made of chocolate, with a foil covering. Other records were also made by Stollwerk, in wax or on a coated, compressed card base. In 1903 the firm produced spring motor disc players.

STORAGE OF RECORDINGS

SEE PRESERVATION OF SOUND RECORDINGS

STRACCIARI, RICCARDO (26 JUNE 1875–10 OCT 1955)

Italian baritone, born in Casalecchio. He studied in Bologna and made his debut there in 1898, as Marcello. From 1904 to 1906 he was with LaScala; in 1905 he sang at Covent Garden. His Metropolitan Opera debut was as Germont on 1 Dec 1906; he remained through 1908 with the company, then went to Europe and South America. The 1917–1918 season found him in Chicago, after which he sang widely in the U.S. and Europe to 1942. He died in Rome.

Figaro in *Barbiere* was Stracciari's most famous role, the "Largo al factotum" recorded acoustically for Columbia in America (#49181; ca. 1917) and again in Milan (#D14652) with about 30 other arias ca. 1925. Other outstanding records include "Lo vedremo" and "O dei verd'anni miei" from *Ernani*, among his earliest discs on the Fonotipia label (#69153, #69154; 1910). His very first disc was "Cruda, funesta smania" from *Lucia* (Fonotipia #39058; 1904). Stracciari starred in two complete opera recordings, *Barbiere di Siviglia* (Columbia #14564/79; 1929) and *Rigoletto* (Columbia GQX #10028/42; 1930). His 78s were made available by all the principal LP reissue labels, and a compact disc of his 1925 Columbia records appeared in 1990 from Preiser (#89003). [Peel and Williams 1985.]

STRACHWITZ, CHRIS

SEE ARHOOLIE RECORDS

STRAIT, GEORGE (18 MAY 1952–)

Born in Poteet, Texas, Strait is one of the great honky-tonk/western swing revivalists, and one of the few new country acts who hasn't strayed too far into pop-rock. The son of a junior high school teacher who also raised cattle on the side, Strait began as most of his generation did playing rock and pop music. After serving in the Army in Hawaii, Strait returned to Dallas and began performing locally with his group, Ace in the Hole, and recorded for the tiny D label (run by legendary promoter Harold "Pappy" Daily) out of Houston. He hit Nashville in the late 1970s, but failed to find a contract until 1981, when he signed with MCA. His first album, *Strait Country* (MCA #31087), established his signature Southwestern sound, scoring a number six hit with his first single, "Unwound." Strait continued to hit it big through the 1980s, covering Bob Wills's classic "Right or Wrong," and Whitey Shafer's "Does Fort Worth Ever Cross Your Mind?" His novelty hit, "All My Ex's Live in Texas," even got some pop radio play.

Beginning in the early 1990s, George recorded more contemporary country material, such as "Ocean Front

Property." He gave an unaffected, straightforward performance in the 1992 film *Pure Country*, which garnered him minor critical praise. His 1995 career retrospective, the four-CD *Strait Out of the Box* (MCA #11263), was a huge seller, and his followup album, *Blue Clear Sky* (MCA #11284), debuted at number one country and number seven on the pop charts, an unusual feat even for a new Nashville artist; the title track was a major hit. He continued to produce big hits through the decade's end, including the amusing "Murder on Music Row," a duet with Alan Jackson. Strait's track record is amazing; only three out of his 61 career singles have failed to chart in the country Top 10.

CARL BENSON

STRAKOSCH, MADAME

A mezzo-soprano who recorded for Bettini. She had 12 cylinders in his 1898 catalog, including "Swanee River," "Home Sweet Home," and "I Dreamt I Dwelled in Marble Halls." It is not impossible that she was Clara Louise Kellogg, the soprano (1842–1916), who had retired in 1887 and married Karl Strakosch.

STRAND QUARTET

SEE CRITERION QUARTET

STREISAND, BARBRA (24 APR 1942–)

American popular singer and actress, born in New York; her given name was spelled in the usual Barbara way, but she later dropped an A. She studied acting, and appeared as a singer in Greenwich Village. At age 20 she made her Broadway debut in the musical *I Can Get It for You Wholesale*. National fame arrived with the show *Funny Girl* (1964), and the film earned her an Academy award in 1968. The cast album won a Grammy. Streisand's hit albums include three named for herself, in 1963 and 1964 (all on Columbia), *People* (Columbia CL #2215; 1964, with her hit song "People" — also a Grammy winner), *Color Me Barbra* (Columbia CL #2478; 1966), and *The Way We Were* (Columbia PC #32801; 1974). Her last great hit album was *Memories* (Columbia TC #37678; 1983). She has had 36 chart albums in all, and eight Grammys.

STRING QUARTET RECORDINGS (HISTORIC)

By about 1910 the major problems of recording strings had been solved, and a few record companies formed quartets that performed arrangements. Already in 1905 an ensemble named the Renard Trio and Quartette had recorded a number of pieces. The American String Quartette played "Solitude of the Shepherdess" on Edison cylinder 10100 in 1909; and the Vienna Instrumental Quartet played "In Vienna — Serenade" and "Tin Soldier" for Edison cylinders in 1910–1911 (#10520, #10304).

Mischa Elman and three artists from the Boston Symphony Orchestra played for Victor, as the Elman String Quartet, placing three numbers in the 1917 catalog: the Theme and Variations from Haydn's Emperor Quartet (#74516), and movements from quartets by Mozart and von Dittersdorf. Several other items by this group were added in the 1922 catalog. There was also the Victor String Quartet, offering three Beethoven movements and several other works in the 1917 catalog. The appearance of the Flonzaley Quartet on Victor, from 1918, marked the beginning of a new era; this was the first recognized string quartet to record. By 1922 it had 14 numbers in the catalog, most of them movements from the quartet literature.

In the 1920s and 1930s other important ensembles began to record for Victor: the Busch Quartet, the Pro Arte Quartet, the Quartetto di Roma, and above all the Budapest Quartet. Columbia had the Roth Quartet, the Lener Quartet, and at times the Budapest Quartet. By the end of the 78 era, most of the important repertoire had been recorded.

STROBOSCOPIC DISC

A special record or printed disc used to check the speed of a turntable. Radial lines on the disc appear to be stationary if the turntable is rotating at true speed. Some commercial discs carrying normal programming have also served as stroboscopics, via an edge marking to assist in turntable speed adjustment; W.D. Sternberg used this device on records issued by British Homophone Co. in 1930 (4 in 1, Plaza, and Sterno labels). The British label Great Scott had strobe marks on the edges of 1934 releases. Decca had a similar marking on certain 1938 discs, and DGG had an edge pattern used, even on LPs, into the mid-1960s.

STROH, JOHN MATTHIAS AUGUSTUS (1828–1914)

German inventor, born in Frankfurt-am-Main. A U.K. post office employee, he made a cylinder phonograph for the chief engineer of the General Post Office and demonstrated it to the Royal Institution on 1 Feb 1878. He then designed various improvements to steady the cylinder movement with counterweights and a clockwork train. His most renowned invention was the Stroh violin. His son Charles was an industry executive, a director with the Russell Hunting Record Co., Ltd., and a manufacturer of the Stroh violin.

STROH VIOLIN

The instrument invented by John Matthias Augustus Stroh for use in acoustic recording, and used widely by the industry for about 10 years from 1904. His son Charles was the first manufacturer. It had the strings of a violin, but instead of a soundbox it had a diaphragm and metal trumpet; these changes presented an amplified, if rather artificial, sound to the recording horn. The first commercial record on which a Stroh violin is heard was Victor #2828, Charles d'Almaine performing "Military Serenade" (23 Apr 1904); the instrument was identified as a "viol-horn." In *TMW* for 1909 there were various advertisements by George Evans, 4 Albany St., Regents Park, London, claiming to be the sole maker of the Stroh violin, as successors to Charles Stroh. [Hoover 1971 has a clear illustration.]

STRONG (LABEL)

An American record issued by the Strong Record Co., Inc., New York, in just a few issues during 1923. The records was advertised as flexible, unbreakable, nonchipable and nonwarping. Material was popular and blues. The firm also offered to make records for clients. Adolf Hawerlander was president of Strong, with Henry Glaue the products manager and A. Lawrence — formerly with Edison — the recorder at the laboratory. Abe Schwartz was the musical director. In December 1923 it was reported that the company had applied for receivership. There was a reorganization and a plan to pay off the creditors, but further information is lacking.

FRANK ANDREWS

STUDER, WILLI
(17 DEC 1912–1 MAR 1996)

Born in Switzerland and a child prodigy and natural entrepreneur, the 19-year-old Studer founded his first company in 1931, building and marketing radio receivers. While the designs were very good, the cost/profit ratio involved put him out of business before the company could become firmly established. After passing an important radio engineering exam, Studer began still another technical-business career in 1948, in Zurich, by building still another electronics equipment factory. The first products were specialized oscilloscopes, but he eventually decided to specialize in audio technology, specifically tape recorders. The experience gained from the adaptation of U.S. tape recorders for the European market helped him to design and build such equipment himself, with extremely high reliability and overall performance quality being the goals. In 1960 he began a cooperating enterprise with EMT Wilhelm Franz GmbH,

which led to a worldwide expansion of Studer/Revox products. Sticking to the concept of quality over quantity, over the years, Studer built his company, now named Revox, into an organization known for superior tape-recording equipment, including the A36 (1956) and A77 (1967) models. In 1978 Studer was awarded an honorary doctorate in technical sciences by the Swiss Federal Institute of Technology in Zurich, and in 1982 the Audio Engineering Society awarded him its highest award, the gold Medal.

HOWARD FERSTLER

STUDER/REVOX

Founded by Wili Studer in 1948, in Zurich, Switzerland, the following year the Studer company produced its first professional-level tape recorder, named the Dynavox. By the early 1950s, Studer had settled on a new brand name for his amateur and professional recording products: Revox. By 1986 the company had 2,000 employees in production centers and subsidiaries in 10 countries, with annual sales reaching 220 million Swiss Francs. In 1990 Studer sold his company to the Swiss Motor Columbus Group, and eventually Studer/Revox joined the Harman International group of businesses. Over the years, the organization has earned a well-deserved reputation as a producer of very high-quality tape-recording equipment, mixers, and recording consoles, as well as some consumer-oriented recording and electronic hardware.

See also **Tape Deck**

HOWARD FERSTLER

STUMPF, CARL
(21 APR 1848–25 DEC 1936)

German psychologist, born in Wiesentheid. He earned a doctorate in 1870, and was a professor at Würzburg in 1873. Later he taught in Prague, Halle, and Munich. In 1893 he established the Psychological Institute at the University of Berlin for research into musical perception. He was also interested in the music of other cultures, which led him to make a cylinder recording of the court orchestra of Siam, as they visited Berlin in 1900. He deposited this and other records in the Berlin Phonogramm-Archiv, established by him in 1905. He died in Berlin.

STYLUS

The jewel or metallic element or needle in a cartridge that tracks the record groove; it is attached by a stylus shank to the magnet in the cartridge. The term needle was applied to this element through the 78 era, when steel needles were the norm. There were sapphire needles and diamond needles, as well as fibers and alloys; they were spherical or conical. The microgroove LP record (1948) required a lightweight tracking device, leading to the various kinds of cartridge and their stylus tips. To avoid surface noise from the groove bottom, styli were often truncated.

Stylus types in use at the end of the LP era (late 1980s) were spherical (conical), suitable to early LP records; elliptical, used with later lighter tone arms; hyperelliptical, with a wider and thinner contact area to improve high-frequency response; and microridge, with the smallest contact area. Diamond styli (1,000-plus hours of playing time) were common, with tips almost invisible to the naked eye. Sapphire tips (about 40 hours of playing time) were a second choice; other materials included tungsten carbide, osmium, and various alloys.

The standard dimensions of styli used on LPs were 0.001 inches (0.6 millimeters) radius and 40–50 degrees included angle. With a 90-degree groove angle, such a tip had an effective radius at the point of contact of 0.0007 inches. Despite close similarity in dimensions, actual standardization of LP styli never occurred. Every manufacturer had slight modifications that made replacement of worn styli a matter of finding specific type numbers in a cross-reference list bearing hundreds of types. [Blacker 1978.]

SUBCODE

Data encoded on a compact disc with miscellaneous inaudible information, e.g., track numbers, copyright, copy inhibit codes.

SUB POP (LABEL)

The Sub Pop label was instrumental in nurturing the grunge movement that first achieved prominence in the late 1980s. During the half decade preceding this revolution, virtually all of the artists identified with the Seattle Sound would record for the label, including Green River — whose *Dry as a Bone* EP (Sub Pop #11) was its first record release — Soundgarden, Mudhoney, Tad, the Walkabouts, and Nirvana.

Sub Pop was formed originally as an audio fanzine in the early 1980s by Bruce Pavitt and Jonathan Poneman. The company's success was due in part to persistent self-promotion and creative marketing decisions. The latter included launching the Sub Pop Singles Club in November 1988; beginning with the then unknown Nirvana ("Love Buzz," #23), a limited edition seven-inch 45 would be issued every two months for the next five years. Later issues included the Smashing Pumpkins, Afghan Whigs, Rapemen, Elastica, Dinosaur Jr., Beat Happening, and Rocket

from the Crypt. Revived in April 1998, the new series would include discs by Luna, Jesus and Mary Chain, and Imperial Teen. The label would also broaden its reach in signing alternative rock talent, eventually recording Oklahoma City's Flaming Lips, San Francisco's Helios Creed, France's Les Thugs, and England's Billy Childish, among others.

Extensive touring by Mudhoney, Soundgarden, and Nirvana brought Sub Pop to the attention of fans in both the U.S. and abroad. Although Nirvana's *Nevermind* (DGC #24425; 1991) reached number one on the pop album charts by virtue of major label promotion and distribution, the group's prior affiliation with Sub Pop enabled the label to reach a wider audience, leading eventually to its partial acquisition by media giant Time Warner. Grunge's inevitable decline in mainstream popularity by the mid-1990s cut into company profits. However, the label continued to acquire an impressive roster of artists throughout the 1990s, including the Poster Children, L7, Hole, and Reverend Horton Heat. [Thompson 2000.]

FRANK HOFFMANN

SUBWOOFER

A loudspeaker system, sometimes of rather large size (although there are also some rather small models that can work surprisingly well), that is dedicated to reproducing only low-bass signals. A subwoofer can be

Infinity PS 12 Subwoofer. Courtesy Harman Kardon International

integrated with an array of smaller satellite speakers, and the result will be large-speaker sound from a small package of speakers that are not visually intrusive. Some subwoofers are able to go deeper and cleaner into the low bass than all but the largest and most expensive full-range systems.

See also **Infinity Loudspeakers; Loudspeaker; NHT Corp.; Room Acoustics; Velodyne Acoustics; Woofer**

HOWARD FERSTLER

SUGAR HILL (LABEL) (I)

The label responsible for bringing rap into the American cultural mainstream, Sugar Hill remained a dominant commercial force well into the 1980s. Prior to the release of "Rapper's Delight" (Sugar Hill; 1979; #4 R&B, #36 pop), recorded by a group of studio rappers named the Sugarhill Gang, rap was disseminated largely on cassettes. As a result of Sugar Hill's success, hip-hop made the transition from New York City street dances to radio airwaves and dance clubs across the nation.

A result of the Charter 11 reorganization of Joe and Sylvia Robinson's All Platinum label, Sugar Hill's early recordings utilized house bands to approximate the breaks hip-hop disc jockeys were using as sound-beds to frame MC raps. The later invention of sampling technology would spell the end for such warm, organic arrangements, resulting in a more synthetic feel.

The company also pioneered artistic statements and social commentary in rap recordings. Before Grandmaster Flash garnered critical raves and crossover sales for the albums *The Adventures of Grandmaster Flash on the Wheels of Steel* (Sugar Hill; 1981) and *The Message* (Sugar Hill #268; #53), the genre functioned almost exclusively to provide Black party music.

Sugar Hill's early success led to many other signings, including Funky 4 + 1, Grandmaster Melle Mel, Spoonie Gee, and the Treacherous 3. Poor sales, however, led to the label's demise in 1985. Its legacy, however, is widely recognized within the hip-hop community; gangsta rappers such as Ice Cube and Dr. Dre as well as more pop-oriented artists (e.g., Busta Rhymes) have sampled classic Sugar Hill tracks. The label's assets were purchased by Rhino Records, who issued *The Sugar Hill Records Story* (#72449; 1997), a five-CD compilation augmented by a 12-inch vinyl disc featuring Grandmaster Flash & the Furious Five's "The Message" and souvenir booklet. It does a thorough job of outlining the company's history.

FRANK HOFFMANN

SUGAR HILL (LABEL) (II)

Country-bluegrass label founded by Barry Poss in 1978. The label had early success with Ricky Skaggs and other progressive bluegrass bands, including Doyle Lawson and Quicksilver, and traditional guitar ace Doc Watson. In 1998, the label was purchased by the Welk Music Group, which had previously purchased Vanguard Records. Dolly Parton also moved to the label that year to return to recording with traditional bluegrass accompaniment. In 2000 the label scored considerable success with Nickel Creek, a young acoustic band who crossed over to success on the country charts. [website: www.sugarhillrecords.com.]

SUMMER, DONNA (31 DEC 1948–)

Donna Summer earned considerable renown as the "Queen of Disco" during the later 1970s; however, few were aware of her ability to interpret a wide range of material, including pop, rock, blues, soul, and gospel. In addition, her talent encompassed acting, songwriting, and record production.

Born Adrian Donna Gaines in Boston, Summer started out singing in European musicals in 1968. Her breakthrough as a recording artist came with a Giorgio Moroder–Pete Bellote production, the erotic "Love to Love You Baby" (Oasis #401; 1975; #2). The record was noteworthy for its half-whispered moaning vocals, simulating the sounds of sexual pleasure, a first for a major pop hit. The background was a generic disco rhythm track. Summer's first albums cashed in on her image as a sultry disco siren: *Love to Love You Baby* (Oasis #5003; 1975; #11; gold record) and *A Love Trilogy* (Oasis #5004; 1976; #21; gold record).

Summer's success could have been limited to this one-hit novelty, but her producers were smart enough to broaden her appeal with slightly weightier songs. While maintaining a disco beat, Summer was allowed to really sing. Many of her songs had simple storylines, albeit packaged in a high-luster production. Her 1970s output moved beyond the topic of sex and love to include a more varied assortment of dance-oriented hits. Her most successful album from this period was *Bad Girls* (Casablanca #7150; 1979; #1; platinum award), which featured the hit singles "Hot Stuff" (Casablanca #978; #1; platinum award), "Bad Girls" (Casablanca #988; #1; platinum award), and "Dim All the Lights" (Casablanca #2201; #2; gold record). Summer also revealed an inclination to try other styles; *I Remember Yesterday* (Casablanca #7056; 1977; #18; gold record) varied the formula with an all-disco side accompanied on the other by a wider selection of material, including the Jimmy Webb classic, "MacArthur Park" (Casablanca #939;

1978; #1). Among her many awards were an Oscar for best movie song in 1978 with "Last Dance" (Casablanca #926; 1978; #3) and three American Music awards that same year (Favorite Female Vocalist — Disco; Favorite LP — Disco for *Live and More*; and Favorite Single — Disco for "Last Dance").

Wishing to make a more dramatic move away from her disco image, Summer signed with Geffen Records in 1980. Since then, her albums — most notably, *The Wanderer* (Geffen #2000; 1980; #13; gold record), *Donna Summer* (Geffen #2005; 1982; #20; gold record), *She Works Hard for the Money* (Mercury #812265; 1983; #9; gold record), and *Cats Without Claws* (Geffen #24040; 1984; #40) — have become increasingly diversified, with a particular emphasis on religious material. She won Grammy awards for Best Inspirational Performance in 1983 and 1984, for "He's a Rebel" and "Forgive Me," respectively.

Following a succession of disappointing LPs, Summer was relatively inactive during the 1990s. Her biggest recording success came with "Carry On," a collaboration with Moroder that won the 1997 Grammy for Best Dance Recording. She has concentrated on songwriting along with husband, Bruce Sudano, particularly for the country market. At the outset of the 21st century they were working on a musical.

FRANK HOFFMANN

SUMMIT (LABEL)

Evolving from the large brass ensemble Summit Brass in the late 1980s, Summit is an internationally distributed label that makes a point of allowing its musicians to get their music to the public, while being treated fairly in the process. The company is committed to state-of-the-art sound, and has released material composed by Daniel Asia, David Sampson, William Goldstein, Joseph Turrin, and Stephen Gryc, among others, and recorded performances by a number of individuals and ensembles, including Robert Sullivan, James Rensink, Pete Barenbregge, Frank Russo, Joseph Alessi, Philip Smith, Robert Hamilton, Seunghee Lee, the Master Chorale of Orange County, the University of Georgia Wind Symphony, and the Boston Brass.

HOWARD FERSTLER

SUN (LABEL) (I)

An American record issued ca. 1907 by Leeds and Catlin.

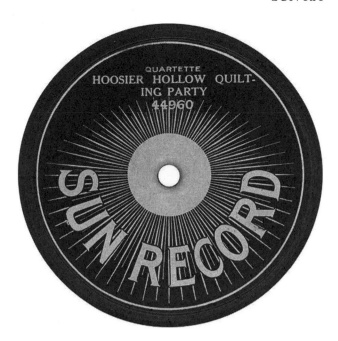

Sun label from c. 1907. Courtesy Kurt Nauck/Nauck's Vintage Records

SUN (LABEL) (II)

A record issued from 1953 to 1959 by Sun Record Co., Inc., 706 Union Ave., Memphis, Tennessee. It was a cradle of the rockabilly style, and was first to record Johnny Cash and Elvis Presley.

See also **Phillips, Sam**

SUNDAZED RECORDS (LABEL)

Sundazed Records was founded by record-store manager Bob Irwin in Coxsackie, New York, in 1989 to reissue American pop and rock music from the 1960s, its first releases putting back into print recordings by the Knickerbockers and the Five Americans. Also working as a freelance reissue producer for Sony's Legacy label, Irwin obtained access to Columbia Records' acts like Bob Dylan and the Byrds and reissued their work on vinyl for the first time in years.

WILLIAM RUHLMANN

SUN RA (22 MAY 1914–30 MAY 1993)

American avant-garde jazz pianist, keyboard player, composer, and band leader, born Herman Poole "Sonny" Blout in Birmingham, Alabama. Sun Ra was one of the pioneering musicians in the free jazz movement who brought polyrhythmic experimentation into the Big Band sound.

Sun Ra was a self-taught pianist who also taught himself how to read music. His early career took off

Later Sun Ra album. Courtesy Frank Hoffmann

after his arrival in Chicago when he joined Fletcher Henderson's big band as pianist and arranger. His work with Henderson lasted from 1946–1947 and it provided him with the experience to form his own band. By the early 1950s he was putting together the core members of what he called the Solar Arkestra, the experimental big band that would become an influential force in experimental jazz. In 1956 Sun Ra started his own record label, Saturn Records, and released the first recordings by the Arkestra, including *Super Sonic Jazz* (Saturn #H70P02160) and *We Travel the Spaceways* (Saturn HK #5445).

By the early 1960s he had firmly adopted the name Sun Ra and told interviewers that he had been born on Saturn. This name change was indicative of the experimental nature of his music. The Arkestra reflected his tastes in Egyptology and space travel as the musicians wore outlandish costumes onstage and created their own instruments with names such as the "space harp" and "space gong." Their performances were multimedia events featuring films, light shows, and avant-garde theatrics. Albums such as *The Magic City* (Saturn LPB #711) and *Live at Montreux* (Inner City IC #1039) were influential on rock performers such as Captain Beefheart, the MC5, Sonic Youth, and the Grateful Dead.

Most of Sun Ra's more well-known recordings for Saturn have been re-released by Evidence including the influential records *Cosmic Tones for Mental Therapy/Art Forms of Dimensions Tomorrow* (Evidence ECD #22036) and *Atlantis* (Evidence ECD #22067).

JOHN ROCCO

SUNRISE (LABEL) (I)

An American record produced by Grey Gull Record Co. ca. 1929; it had a subtitle "The Record of Today." It offered dance music and popular vocals, with some jazz numbers.

SUNRISE (LABEL) (II)

A low-priced RCA record issued in 1933–1934. Material duplicated that of Bluebird, and the price was the same for both labels, $0.35. [Rust 1978.]

SUNSET RECORD (LABEL)

An American record issued by an unidentified company in California between 1924 and 1926. California artists were featured. [Rust 1978.]

SUNSHINE (LABEL) (I)

A paste-over title added to six sides of Nordskog records in 1922 for performances by Kid "Ory' a Jazz Band. The group was identified as Spike's Seven Pods of Pepper Orchestra. "Ory's Creole Trombone" and "Society Blues" were the principal numbers; they were among the first jazz records cut by Black artists. [Rust 1978.]

SUNSHINE (LABEL) (II)

A record issued by the Sunshine Phonograph and Record Co., St. Petersburg, Florida, in early 1925. Masters came from Okeh. [Kendziora 1987/6.]

Shortlived label operated by the black music publishers the Spikes Brothers out of Los Angeles. Courtesy Kurt Nauck/Nauck's Vintage Records

SUPERIOR (LABEL)

A record made by the Starr Piano Co. from December 1930 to June 1932. There were 339 issues, drawing on Gennett material. Vernon Dalhart and Carson Robison were among the better known artists. [Kay 1961; Rust 1978.]

SUPERTONE (LABEL) (I)

A record issued by Brunswick in 1930–1931, using Brunswick masters.

SUPERTONE (LABEL) (II)

Four slightly different labels issued by the Straus and Schram store, Chicago. Material came from Pathé, Grey Gull, Columbia, and Paramount.

SUPERTONE (LABEL) (III)

Two similar labels sold by Sears, Roebuck and Co. by mail order in the 1920s. The first had material from Olympic and Paramount; it was on sale in 1924. The second had material from Gennett, and was sold from 1928 to 1930. [Kendziora 1967/1; Rust 1978.]

SUPERTONE TALKING MACHINE CO.

A New York firm, established in 1916 at 8 W. 20th St. sold the Supertone line of disc players, in three models, ranging from $15 to $100. A report of February 1921 stated that the company was to be reorganized by its creditors.

SUPERVIA, CONCHITA (9 DEC 1895–30 MAR 1936)

Spanish soprano and mezzo-soprano, born in Barcelona. She studied in Barcelona, then traveled to South America and made her debut at the Teatro Colón in Buenos Aires on 1 Oct 1910. She sang in Italy, Havana (1914), Chicago (1915–1916), and from 1924 at LaScala. She died after childbirth in London.

Supervia was a famous Carmen, Rosina, Mignon, and Musetta; she excelled in roles that brought out her vivacious and elegant style. To many hearers that style was marred by an excessive vibrato. She began recording in 1927, for Fonotipia in Italy, Odeon in Spain, and Parlophone in Spain, singing airs from *Italiana in Algeri* as well as her Carmen and Rosina specialties. Those were her labels through her brief recording career, which ceased in 1934. The outstanding numbers were "Una voce poco fa" (Parlophone #R20074; 1929), several *Carmen* pieces also on Parlophone, made in 1931 and 1934, "Connais-tu le pays" (Parlophone #20192; 1930), and Musetta's Waltz (Parlophone #20180; 1932). There were LP versions by all the microgroove reissue labels. Three CDs appeared in 1990, one each from EMI, Preiser, and Club 99; among them they comprise the essential Supervia collection. [Barnes & Girard, 1951.]

SUPRAPHON (LABEL)

A Czech record, issued from the 1950s. In 1991 the American distributor was Koch International.

SUPREME (LABEL)

An American record issued in the late 1920s, one of the low-priced Grey Gull affiliates. Material was dance music and popular vocals. [Rust 1978.]

SUPREMES, THE

A female popular vocal trio established in 1964 by Diana Ross; the other members were Florence Ballard (replaced in 1967 by Cindy Birdsong) and Mary Wilson. The group sang in the new soul music style for Motown records, achieving great success and making 18 chart albums by 1976. *Where Did Our Love Go* (Motown MM #621; 1964) was the most acclaimed, on the charts for about a year. When Ross left in 1970, the Supremes lost their edge and began to decline in popularity.

SURFACE NOISE

The unwanted sound heard in playback of 78-rpm discs, and to a lesser extent in playback of LPs, sometimes caused by mistakes in cutting, mastering, and plating; but especially by abrasives in the shellac compound, and by wear in the grooves and/or playback needle or stylus. Some surface noise can be suppressed as original records are transferred, by means of equalizer and dynamic static filters.

See also **Packburn Audio Noise Suppressor; Sound Preservation and Restoration of Historical Recordings**

SURFACE SPEED

In contrast to turntable rotational speed, this is a measure of the linear velocity of the record surface as it moves beneath the pickup stylus with an LP recording or laser beam with a digital-disc recording. With the LP record, although the angular, rotational velocity remains constant, the linear velocity will obviously decrease as the groove diameter becomes smaller toward the center of the record. This reduction in linear speed can seriously compromise sound quality in the inner-groove area, even if the record/playback system is designed to compensate for the change in linear speed. It was this factor that influenced Thomas Edison to hold to the cylinder record, where surface speed would be constant. Charles Tainter applied for a patent on a device that maintained uniform surface speed on discs in 1887, but he did not follow it with commercial production. Discs issued in the U.K. in 1922–1924, by the World Record Co., did play at constant linear speed. This was achieved by a record controller device, one that was made available for standard Gramophones by Noel Pemberton Billing. Modern digital-disc playback systems of all kinds utilize a variable rotational speed, in order to keep the linear speed constant. (British patents #195,673 and 204,728).

See also **Constant Angular Velocity Discs (CAV); Constant Linear Velocity Discs (CLV); Disc; Speeds; Turntable**

REV. HOWARD FERSTLER

SURF MUSIC

Surfing, which became popular with Hawaiian nobility centuries ago, caught on as a popular recreational activity along the California coast during the post–World War II period. By the early 1960s, surfing had developed into a youth subculture. The surfing lifestyle was widely disseminated by publications such as John Severson's *Surfer Magazine* and a series of excellent film documentaries produced by Bruce Brown, including *Slippery When Wet* (1959), *Barefoot Adventure* (1961), and *Endless Summer*, which documented the mythological worldwide search for the ultimate wave. It encompassed fashion (surfers favored Pendleton shirts, white Levis, baggies, and sun-bleached hair often helped a little by peroxide) and language. Slang surfing terms included "woodie" (a souped-up old wooden-sided station wagon used to haul surfboards), "goofy foot" (a surfer who rode with his right foot forward on the board), and "wipe-out" (resulting when a surfer lost control of the board while fighting to master a wave).

Although he failed to achieve national stardom, guitarist Dick Dale is generally credited with introducing surf music. Backed by the Del-Tones, he developed a strong following in the Southern California area as the "Pied Piper of Balboa," most notably via weekend dances at the Rendezvous Ballroom. The essentially instrumental sound — a visceral stew of wailing saxophones and atmospheric guitar accented by a pounding 12-bar bass beat — attempted to evoke the tremendous sense of power felt through bonding with the forces of nature while surfing.

The Beach Boys almost single-handedly made the surf sound a national sensation through the addition of evocative song lyrics. Brian Wilson's compositional gifts were so fertile that he was able to give a number one hit to the pop duo, Jan and Dean, while keeping his own band supplied with a steady succession of Top 10 material. That gift, "Surf City" (Liberty #55580; 1963), catapulted Jan and Dean past second echelon surf interpreters such as the Surfaris, the Chantays, the Astronauts, the Challengers, the El Caminos, the Fantastic Baggys (featuring P.F. Sloan and Steve Barrie, later to make a name in protest music), and the Marketts. Like the Beach Boys, however, Jan and Dean were savvy enough to avoid too close an identification with the surf sound, mining the car songs genre ("Drag City," Liberty #55641; 1963), new fads such as skateboarding ("Sidewalk Surfin'," Liberty #55724; 1964), and assorted novelty material ("Batman," Liberty #55860; 1966).

At its peak, between 1963 and 1965, surf music was as popular with eastern and midwestern youth as in its native Pacific Coast environment. Bands like the Minneapolis-based Trashmen, Chicago's Rivieras, and New York's Trade Winds all climbed the upper reaches of the singles charts with surf songs. In addition, Hollywood supplied a steady stream of beach movies, most notably American International Pictures. The studio's highly successful titles — including *Beach Party*, *Muscle Beach Party*, *Beach Blanket Bingo*, *How to Stuff a Wild Bikini*, *Bikini Beach*, and *Ski Party* — helped expose many surf acts to a mainstream audience. Other popular surf films included *Surf Party*, *Girls on the Beach*, and *Ride the Wild Surf*.

Surf music gradually lost its momentum in the mid-1960s in the face of changing fashions. The pressing social imperatives of the period (e.g., civil rights, the Vietnam War) rendered the genre irrelevant. It retreated to its former subculture status; however, a small core of cult bands (e.g., Man or Astro-Man, Agent Orange) have continued to produce new music utilizing surf sound conventions into the new millennium.

FRANK HOFFMANN

SURROUND SOUND

This concept goes back to well before the quadraphonic recording era, and also before the period when outfits like Sound Concepts, Audio Pulse, Advent, Acoustic Research, Lexicon, and Yamaha were experimenting with or marketing four-channel surround processors of one sort of another for home-audio use. Indeed, on a commercial level it goes back at least as far as Disney's work on the movie *Fantasia*, released in 1940.

Modern (and successful) surround-sound in home-listening situations is mainly the result of the home-theater boom that began in the late 1980s and continued through the 1990s and into the new century. Mainstream movies had been produced in matrix-surround form since the advent of Dolby Surround (which offered left, center, and right channels, plus one surround channel, embedded into the left and right channels of a stereo mix), and that technology was easily transferred to video-tape copies of movies that were sold or rented to consumers. In order to take advantage of the technology, more and more enthusiasts demanded surround decoders and amplifiers for home use, and manufacturers accommodated them by building hardware that would do the job. Dolby Labs also made its Pro Logic technology available to manufacturers, and this greatly enhanced the separation between channels, particularly the center, left, and right, which was one way that modern surround sound is superior to the old four-channel quadraphonic arrangement. The center channel was not only important for dialog reproduction in movies, but with music reproduction it was found that a genuine center channel improved soundstage realism, particularly when listening from anywhere but the sweet spot.

As the digital audio/video age dawned and home theater became even more popular, outfits like Yamaha, Lexicon, Carver, Pioneer, Sony, Onkyo, Denon, Technics, and quite a few others began to produce very high-quality hardware often at very reasonable prices, and that hardware usually included assorted ambiance modes that allowed two-channel compact disc recordings to decently simulate the surround ambiance of genuine concert halls, nightclubs, etc. Hence, it could be said that home theater helped to usher in the era of surround-sound music playback in the home. Home theater also pretty much forced people who normally would not be concerned with proper speaker positioning for musical playback to rethink the placement of their speakers for a proper soundstage effect. In other words, the location of the television monitor made proper speaker soundstaging more important than ever.

Modern systems have better DSP ambiance simulations than in the past, and the technology that has given us discrete-channel DVD movie surround sound is now giving us multichannel music sound that eclipses the two-channel stereo sound that has existed in commercial form since the 1950s. Indeed, surround sound, at least if we are talking about state-of-the-art, or even reasonably up-scale audio, is the future of home-music sound recording and reproduction.

See also **Ambiance Synthesis; Ambiance Extraction; Dolby Digital; DTS (Digital Theater Systems); DVD-A (DVD-Audio); SACD (Super Audio Compact Disc)**

HOWARD FERSTLER

SUTHERLAND, JOAN (7 NOV 1926–)

Australian soprano, born in Sydney. She made her debut in a concert performance of *Dido and Aeneas* in Sydney in 1947. She went to London in 1951, and appeared at Covent Garden, gaining great praise for her performance as Lucia in 1959. Sutherland sang Lucia at the Metropolitan Opera on 26 Nov 1961, and achieved renown for her coloratura, lyric, dramatic and Wagnerian roles. In 1978 she was made a dame commander of the British Empire.

From 1976–1986, she performed principally with the Australian Opera in Sydney. She gave her farewell performance there in 1990.

Sutherland's recordings span the repertoire. She is featured in complete operas by Bellini, Bizet, Donizetti, Gounod, Meyerbeer, Mozart, Offenbach, Puccini, Rossini, Thomas, Verdi, and Wagner. Her album *Art of the Prima Donna* (London #1214; 1961) won a Grammy for Best Classical Vocal Disc.

SWARF

In the recording process, the material cut or scraped from the surface of a record by the cutting stylus.

SWEET SPOT

The listening position out in front of a stereo pair of speakers that puts each of them the same distance from the listener. The result is an enhanced sense of soundstage realism and imaging from two-channel source material. Sweet-spot listening can even be important for multichannel, surround-sound systems, but it will not be as critical as it is for two-channel set ups.

See also **Dolby Surround Sound; Interaural Crosstalk; Phantom Center Image; Precedence Effect; Stereophonic Recording**

HOWARD FERSTLER

SWINGER

A disc record whose spindle hole is not at the geometric center of the disc circle. In playback a wobbling of pitch results. The same result may occur if a spindle is undersized, allowing loose movement of the disc around it.

SWINGLE SINGERS

A French popular vocal group, highly successful in the 1960s with swinging arrangements of baroque and other classical compositions. They produced the instrumental lines vocally — with varying degrees of pitch accuracy — and added jazz bass and percussion.

The eight members were brought together in Paris in 1962 by Ward Lemar Swingle and Christiane Legrande. They won a Grammy as Best New Artists of 1963, and for their album of that year, *Bach's Greatest Hits* (Philips PHM #200–097), which was on the charts 35 weeks. There were three other Grammys, for *Going Baroque* (Philips PHM #200–133; 1964), *Anyone for Mozart* (Philips PHM #200-149; 1965), and for a rendition of Luciano Berio's *Sinfonia* in 1969. The group disbanded in 1973.

SWISS NATIONAL SOUND ARCHIVE

SEE PHONOTHÈQUE NATIONALE SUISSE

SYLVA, GERTRUDE

A soprano who sang for Bettini cylinders; she had 15 solo arias and songs in the 1897 catalog, plus four numbers with flute and piano; and 13 solos in the 1898 catalog, plus four others with flute. "The Last Rose of Summer" had an accompaniment of piano, violin, and flute.

SYMPHONIC PHONE-NEEDLE CO.

A New York firm that advertised in *TMW* during 1906. It marketed the Symphonic needle, said to play 500–800 times.

SYMPHONOLA

A coin-op produced by Seeburg in the mid-1930s. It operated with a single turntable, which moved to play up to 20 different records.

SYMPHONOLA (LABEL)

An American record distributed by the Larkin Co. department store in Buffalo, New York, ca. 1919–1920. Matrices were from Emerson and Pathé. Most of the output consisted of popular vocal and dance numbers, but there were some sides by Tito Schipa and soprano Yvonne Gall. [Kendziora 1989/9; Rust 1978.]

SYMPOSIUM RECORDS (LABEL)

A U.K. firm founded in 1985, located in East Barnet, Hertfordshire. It offers important compact disc reissues of historical material, originally drawing on early (acoustic-era) recordings and radio broadcasts, but then broadening its reach into the vinyl era of recording. Symposium has developed its own process for remastering early recordings, particularly made in the acoustic era, which it calls the "Authentic Transfer Process." The company has issued early recordings of opera, as well as early instrumental recordings on piano and violin. [website: www.symposiumrecords. co.uk/.]

SYNCHROPHONE LTD.

A U.K. firm that made in 1931 a combination gramophone, radio, and motion picture projector, sold as the Synchrophone. Hans Knudsen, inventor of the machine, had tried to promote it through an earlier firm, Synchrophone Co., Ltd. (1919–1928). Twelve-inch records, with the label name Synchrophone Record, were produced to give sound to the silent films projected. The user was required to start the record and film at the same time, guided by appropriate markings. The company was in liquidation in October 1935. Arthur Woollacott bought the business on 3 Jan 1936 and set up the Synchrophone (1936) Co. It was the earliest label to have a female as recording expert, Ursula Greville. [*TMR* #46 (June 1977) presented an extended advertisement of the firm.]

FRANK ANDREWS

SYRACUSE AUDIO ARCHIVES

SEE BELFER AUDIO LIBRARY AND ARCHIVE

SZELL, GEORGE
(7 JUNE 1897–30 JULY 1970)

Hungarian/American conductor and pianist, born in Budapest. He grew up in Vienna, studied piano and composition there, and made his debut in a concert of his own music at age 11. Five years later he conducted the Vienna Symphony Orchestra; then the Berlin Philharmonic Orchestra. In 1915 he was engaged by Richard Strauss to conduct at the Berlin Staatsoper, and was soon in demand as a conductor of opera and symphony throughout Europe. His American debut was in St. Louis on 24 Jan 1930. From 1942 to 1946 he conducted at the Metropolitan Opera; in 1946 he became an American citizen. In 1946 he was appointed music director of the Cleveland Orchestra, remaining in that post until his death.

Under Szell the Cleveland Orchestra, with a remarkable sound balance that was often likened to chamber music; it came to be regarded as one of the world's greatest ensembles, touring Europe and the Far East. Szell specialized in the Austro-German composers, with relatively little attention to contemporaries other than Bartók. Szell and the Cleveland Orchestra recorded for CBS, Epic, and Angel. The clarity of the orchestra's sound is heard to advantage in the Mozart symphonies, of which numbers 35, 39, 40, and 41 were grouped in Columbia MG #30368, and in Mozart's "Einekleine Nachtmusik" (Columbia MS #7273). Among their outstanding collaborative discs were Mozart's Concertos 21 and 24 with Robert Casadesus (Columbia MS #6695; 1965), the Brahms Violin Concerto with David Oistrakh (Angel #32096; 1970), and the Brahms Double Concerto with Oistrakh and Mstislav Rostropovich (Angel #36032; 1970). CD reissues appeared in 1991 from Sony, covering Haydn (#46332) and Mozart (#46333) material.

SZIGETI, JOSEPH
(5 SEP 1892–19 FEB 1973)

Hungarian/American violinist, born in Budapest. He studied with Jenö Hubay, and performed in public in 1905. He made his London debut in 1907 and remained in the U.K. until 1913. He was in Geneva to 1924, toured in Europe, and appeared in Philadelphia in 1925. World concert tours followed. Szigeti's friendship with Bartók led to his performance, with Benny Goodman (who commissioned the work) and the composer, of the first hearing of "Contrasts" in Carnegie Hall, 1940 (Columbia #70362/3, set X-178). He settled in the U.S. and became a citizen in 1951. After 1960 he was less active, living mostly in Switzerland. He died in Lucerne.

Szigeti's repertoire was extensive, but he was most renowned for his performances of J.S. Bach's uncompanied sonatas and partitas and for his reading of the Beethoven Concerto. His first recording was for the Gramophone Co. in 1908. He did the Prelude from Bach's sixth sonata (#07911), "Zéphire" by Hubay (#07913), and Anton Rubinstein's "Romance" (#07914). In 1926 he became a Columbia exclusive artist, doing the Bach solo works from 1928 to 1932, and the Brahms third sonata with Egon Petri in 1938, among other fine interpretations that were all reissued on two CDs by Biddulph in 1990 (#LAB 005/06). His pianist partners in the Beethoven sonatas included Claudio Arrau. Béla Bartók, and Artur Schnabel. Stern did the Beethoven Concerto with Bruno Walter in 1932 (Columbia #M-177).

SZYMCZYK, BILL (13 FEB 1943–)

Born in Muskegon, Michigan, Szymczyk became a major producer of rock and pop acts during the 1970s. After serving in the Navy in the early 1960s, Szymczyk got a job as an engineer at a small New York studio, where many of the Brill building songwriters cut their demos. He worked as an engineer at New York's Regent Sound from 1965–1967, doing his first production work for rock bassist Harvey Brooks in 1967. A year later, he was hired by ABC/Paramount as a house producer. He first produced B. B. King there, and then signed a new Detroit-based rock group, the James Gang (with lead guitarist Joe Walsh). Szymczyk moved to Los Angeles in 1970, and then a year later relocated to Denver, where he went independent. He had success in the early 1970s with the J. Geil Bands and R.E.O. Speedwagon; but he was best-known for his production work with the Eagles (being brought to the band by Joe Walsh, who had been hired to toughen up their sound), overseeing most of their 1970s-era hits. In the mid-1970s, he took a job with Criterion Sound in Miami, and then in 1976 built his own studio. He continued to produce through the mid-1980s, overseeing albums by Jefferson Starship, the Who, Santana, and Elvin Bishop, but then took some time off. He returned to production work in the 1990s, although with less visibility and success then he had previously enjoyed.

CARL BENSON

T

TAFT, WILLIAM HOWARD (15 SEP 1857–8 MAR 1930)

Twenty-seventh president of the United States (term of office 1909–1913). He is the earliest president whose voice is known to be preserved on record, beginning with campaign speeches of August 1908.

See also **Presidents on Record**

TAGLIAVINI, FERRUCCIO (14 AUG 1913–28 JAN 1995)

Italian tenor, born in Reggio nell' Emilia. He made his debut as Rodolfo in Florence in 1938 and soon gained recognition as one of the leading interpreters of the lyric repertoire. On 10 Jan 1947 he made his Metropolitan Opera debut as Rodolfo, and remained to 1954, returning in 1961–1962. Rossini, Bellini, and Donizetti roles were his specialties. He also sang successfully in concert, applying his bel canto to Italian and French songs. Tagliavini's most popular recording was the complete *Lucia*, with Maria Callas (HMV #5166; 1960). He retired in 1965, and died in his hometown 30 years later. The Bel Canto Society has issued two videos drawn from Tagliavini's appearances on the *Voice of Firestone* television shows of the 1950s (2412, 2413). A CD reissue of a sampler of his recordings from the 1940s through the early 1950s is available on Bongiovanni (#1161); there are also complete operas featuring Tagliavini in the cast among reissue CDs from various labels.

TAINTER, CHARLES SUMNER (25 AUG 1854–20 APR 1940)

British instrument maker and inventor. In 1879 he began working with Alexander Graham Bell in a research facility in Washington, D.C., and in 1881 he was invited by Bell to join him and Chichester Bell in the formation of the Volta Laboratory Association. The purpose of Volta was to carry out acoustical and electrical research. Tainter was probably responsible for the emphasis on developing a talking machine that would improve on Edison's tinfoil phonograph. He applied the principle of engraving into wax as early as 1881, and created a demonstration cylinder that was sealed in the Smithsonian Institution; the record — presenting the voice of Alexander Graham Bell — was apparently played for the first time in public, at the Smithsonian, in 1937; documentation of the event is not positive. Tainter eventually filed, on 27 June 1885, a patent application (U.S. #341,214; granted 4 May 1886) for his method of "recording and reproducing speech and other sounds." His application specified that the recording surface was solid beeswax and paraffin, and that the signal vibrations were inscribed vertically (hill and dale); but the word cylinder did not appear. Another patent application, for a machine with a removable wax-coated cardboard cylinder, was filed on 4 Dec 1885 (U.S. patent #341,288; granted 4 May 1886). The instrument he developed came to be called the Graphophone, giving its name to the new organization established in 1886 by him and the Bells: Volta Graphophone Co.

Tainter's notebooks show diverse experimentation. He worked on a variable-speed turntable to derive constant surface speed in disc recording on lateral-cut records, and on a wax paper strip medium. On 7 July 1887 he filed for a U.S. patent on a foot-treadle Graphophone that turned the cylinder at 200 rpm (#375,579; granted 27 Dec 1887); it used a wax-coated cardboard cylinder, 6-by-1 5/16 inches. Although the treadle feature (an adaptation of the Howe sewing machine) did not succeed commercially with the Graphophone, it was used later in shavers. A coin-op Graphophone was developed and patented in time for exhibition at the World's Columbian Exposition, Chicago, 1893 (U.S. #506,348; filed 27 Apr 1893; granted 10 Oct 1893); it became the Columbia Graphophone Type AS (1897). Tainter received a total of 25 U.S. patents in the phonograph field.

See also **Columbia Record Players**

TAKE

The name given to the smallest identifiable unit of a recording session. In the early period of recording, before the use of magnetic tape to receive the original impression of the signal, a take necessarily included an entire presentation: a song, instrumental composition or discrete movement of a large composition, literary reading, etc. With modern technology, a take may include a minute portion of a presentation, and many takes of the same portion may be made. The best takes are then edited into a satisfactory whole version of the signal presentation, and used to make the negative master. Takes that are not used to make masters are called out-takes.

Record manufacturers sometimes give identification numbers to takes, possibly as parts of matrix numbers. Outtakes are sometimes preserved, and may be used later to make pressings when it is desired to have complete documentation of a performer's work.

See also **Disc; Recording Practice**

TAKOMA RECORDS (LABEL)

Originally founded in 1959 by guitarist John Fahey and music manager ED Denson to issue Fahey's recordings, the label grew to be an important outlet for acoustic guitarists in the 1960s and 1970s, including Fahey, Robbie Basho, and Leo Kottke. Takoma also issued new recordings by rediscovered blues performers, jazz, avant-garde, and country and bluegrass records. In 1978, the label was purchased by Chrysalis Records. Artists issued in the late 1970s and early 1980s included Maria Muldaur, blues guitarist Michael Bloomfield, and the U.K. folk-rock group Steeleye Span. However, by the mid-1980s the label was more or less inactive. In 1995 Takoma's back catalog, along with ED Denson's other label, Kicking Mule, was purchased by Fantasy Records, which has reissued many of its recordings on CD.

CARL BENSON

TALKER

A talking machine (phonograph or Gramophone). The term was widely used in dealer and trade-press jargon during the early years of the industry.

TALKING BOOK

The name given to the recorded version of a book. Originally talking books were discs made for blind persons. They appeared in the U.K. in 1934, made by Decca and EMI for the National Institute for the Blind, using slows speeds, such as 24 rpm. Talking books are circulated in the U.S. by the Library of Congress through a network of local libraries. Cassette tapes replaced the discs in the 1960s, and a wider audience was identified as cassette players became common in automobiles. By the 1980s a large repertoire of fiction and nonfiction works was available on cassette. In most cases long books are abridged on record, but some firms specialize in complete texts. Readings are done by actors who sometimes dramatize fiction material by using different voices for the characters; and many talking books have sound effects and/or background music, simulating radio dramas. "Book-cassettes" marketed by the Brilliance Corp., do not have sound effects or music; they use digital speech compression to achieve a quick reading speed, and use four tracks of a stereo cassette to increase the capacity of their monophonic recordings. The firm Books on Tape advertises itself as having the "world's largest selection of audio books."

See also **Literary Recordings**

TALKING DOLLS

This medium was the earliest format for entertainment records. Thomas Edison's U.S. patent #423,039 (filed 2 July 1889; granted 11 Mar 1890) was for a doll with a cylinder record. The Edison talking doll was shown at the Paris Universal Exposition of 1889 and first sold to the public in April 1890, in New York. The doll was not a commercial success, with only about 500 eventually sold, at $10–25, and many were returned by unsatisfied buyers. Twelve prerecorded records were available.

Emile Berliner's 1889 doll used a disc record; it was also unsuccessful. Maison Jumeau, established 1842, was the most famous doll-maker. The firm produced dolls for a world market, with the most exotic creations emanating from the 1860s through the 1890s, a "golden age" of French doll-making. The dolls were called Poupées (lady-types) and Bébés (child-types). A successful line of the Bébés (at 38 francs), offered in 1896, was fitted with a talking mechanism made by Henri Lioret. [Koenigsberg 1990; Marty 1979 shows three Bébés on p. 74.]

See also **Edison Phonograph Co.**

TALKING HEADS

One of the leading groups spearheading the new-wave movement of the late 1970s, the Talking Heads were instrumental in bringing an intellectual, art-rock sensibility to a genre initially built around the brash, stripped-down energy of punk. Like the more incendiary punk bands, however, they stood in opposition — both in their edgy, eccentric musical arrangements and wry song lyrics — to the corporate rock establishment then dominated by pompous AOR artists such as Foreigner, Journey, and the Doobie Brothers.

Formed May 1975 by vocalist/guitarist David Byrne, vocalist/bassist Tina Weymouth, and drummer Chris Frantz in Manhattan, New York, the Talking Heads were shortly thereafter signed by Sire Records head Seymour Stein, who'd seen them performing at the legendary Bowery club, CGBG's. Following an unsuccessful single release and the addition of guitarist/keyboardist Jerry Harrison, the band's debut album, *Talking Heads '77* (Sire #6306; 1977; #97), was heralded as one of the first masterpieces of the newly emerging punk revolution. The next LP, *More Songs About Buildings and Food* (Sire #6058; 1978; #29), produced by avant-garde artist, Brian Eno, moved the group closer to the commercial mainstream largely due to a funky rhythmic underpinning and Byrne's soulful, albeit idiosyncratic, vocals. Never content to merely tread water, their *Fear of Music* (Sire #6076; 1979; #21), again produced by Eno, featured Third World beats and instrumentation.

Talking Heads reached a creative apex with *Remain in Light* (Sire #6095; 1980; #19), blending punk energy with African polyrhythms and funk phrasing with the assistance of an augmented band featuring Adrian Belew on lead guitar. Sales were considerably enhanced by the MTV-driven success of the single "Once in a Lifetime" (Sire #40649; 1981; #14 U.K.). Following a three-year hiatus from the studio — during which Frantz and Weymouth formed the alternative dance group, the Tom Tom Club, while Byrne explored ethnic music with Eno and composed a stage score, *Songs from "The Catherine Wheel"* (Sire #3645; 1981) — the Talking Heads released *Speaking in Tongues* (Sire #23883; 1983; #15), which included their biggest single, "Burning Down the House" (Sire #29565; 1983; #9). *Stop Making Sense* (Sire #25121; 1984; #41) featured music from a strikingly innovative concert movie directed by Jonathon Demme.

Later works — *Little Creatures* (Sire #25035; 1985; #20), something of a return to the band's stylistic roots; *True Stories* (Sire #25512; 1986; #17), an uneven soundtrack to a Byrne-produced film; and *Naked* (Sire #26654; 1988; #19), an LP long on production values and short on quality song material — suffered from a seeming lack of commitment. Byrne would continue to explore various avant-pop directions, often drawing on international music styles for inspiration. Although an official announcement was not forthcoming until 1991, individual members had long since gone on to solo projects. Harrison, Frantz, and Weymouth would regroup as the Heads in 1996, releasing one album, *No Talking, Just Head* (MCA #11504), built around the contributions of alternative rock stars such as Richard Hell, ex-Blondie Debbie Harry, INXS frontman Michael Hutchence, XTC's Andy Partridge, and Concrete Blonde's Johnette Napolitano.

Frank Hoffmann

TALKING MACHINE

The generic term for the phonograph, and later for the Gramophone, as used in the trade literature and in company names from the early days of the industry into the 1920s. This designation was sometimes abbreviated to "talker."

TALKING MACHINE CO.

See Chicago Talking Machine Co.

TALKING MACHINE JOBBERS' NATIONAL ASSOCIATION

A trade organization formed in September 1907, through a merger of the Eastern and Central States associations. In 1908 the name was changed to the National Association of Talking Machine Jobbers.

TALKING MACHINE WORLD (JOURNAL)

Founded in 1905 by Edward Lyman (known as Colonel E.L.) Bill, this was the major trade journal for the phonograph industry through its folding in late 1929. Universally known as *TMW,* the journal was aimed at phonograph dealers and equipment manufacturers. Bill purchased the *Music Trade Review* in the early part of the 20th century, and transformed it into *TMW* by early 1905. He died in 1916, but the journal was continued under associate editor Raymond Bill and treasurer C.L. Bill, both relatives of the founder. Published in a large, 11 by 15 format on fancy paper, the journal featured many advertisements, and grew from around 100 pages per issue in the mid-1910s to over 200 pages by the mid-1920s. Major labels vied for advertising positions in the journal; Victor held the coveted front cover advertising spot until financial difficulties forced it to give up this position in 1925. It was subsequently purchased by Brunswick. Edison took the back cover. Okeh often purchased two-color (and occasionally even full color) advertisements for its releases. Major phonograph dealers and manufacturers of components advertised regularly. For smaller manufacturers, their ads often are the only record of their activities during this period.

The journal had several regular features. Each issue chronicled developments in major U.S. and U.K. cities. Important artist signings and new releases were noted. Editorials addressing industry problems and concerns give light to everything from the impact of World War I on the nascent industry through difficulties selling recordings. Major new patents were described in detail. And an advance list of new recordings appeared at the back of each issue, although it was limited to labels that advertised in the journal and that had a national presence.

In reaction to the growing influence of radio, the magazine was renamed *Talking Machine World and Radio-Music Merchant* in the later 1920s, and its page length decreased as advertising from record labels, strained by the competition with radio, had to cut back on their budgets. The last known issue appeared in December 1929. Record collectors prize this journal because of its wealth of information on the business and the many fascinating photos and reproductions of early sound-recording equipment. Because it was aimed at the industry and not the general consumer, issues of *TMW* are fairly rare today.

TALK-O-PHONE

A disc record player (sometimes spelled Talkaphone) marketed in the U.K. by the Talkophone Syndicate (established July 1903 in London), and in the U.S. by the Talk-o-Phone Co. of Toledo, Ohio (established 1904). By January 1905 the headquarters was in New York City, and there were branches in Chicago and San Francisco. A.L. Irish was president and treasurer,

C.G. Metzger was vice president, and R.A. Fuller and O.C. Reed were directors.

The price of the American product, shown in an advertisement of 1905 or 1906, was $18–50 for various models. There were also Talk-o-Phone disc records sold in America. Leeds was a label name used. It was claimed that the Toledo firm sold more than 25,000 of the record players in its first year, its factory working double shifts to meet the demand. The Chicago branch moved to larger premises in Steinway Hall on Van Buren St. Talk-o-Phone machines were used as premiums in promotional campaigns of the *Los Angeles Record* and the *San Francisco Call* newspapers.

In fall 1905 litigation ensued, as the Victor Talking Machine Co. alleged infringement of its Berliner patent for the groove-driven reproducer. Then, in November 1905, the Toledo works introduced a new machine which fed the tone arm across the disc by a mechanical feed device beneath the turntable. Reports of great success for the new record player — selling for $1 to $5 — appeared in January 1906.

Nevertheless, the company was reorganized in August 1906 as new capital entered the business; a firm called the Atlantic Phonograph Co. emerged in New York, apparently the heir to the Talk-o-Phone products.

FRANK ANDREWS

TALK-O-PHOTO (LABEL)

A single-sided six-inch record issued by the Talking Photo Corp. of New York in 1919–1920. The discs featured photographs of the recording artists (in the known issues, all were movie stars) on one side and performances by them on the other. Emerson cut the masters. Items listed by Blacker appear to be spoken material, e.g., "How to Become a Star" by David Powell; "My Real Self," by Mae Murray; and "Happiness" by Gloria Swanson. There were 91 records in the series, but only 16 have been identified and just three have been seen and discussed in the literature. Robert B. "Patti" Wheelan was president of Talking Photo Corp. in 1920. [Blacker 1990.]

TALLY, HARRY
(30 JUNE 1866–16 AUG 1939)

American tenor, born in Memphis, Tennessee. The name was also spelled Talley. He was a vaudeville performer, featured on the Orpheum circuit for 25 years.

Tally began recording in 1902 for Columbia, going unidentified on early issues, and remained with the label to 1911. A popular item was the coon song "Love

Me, Phoebe" (#203). He made three Edison cylinders in 1903–1904: "My Little Coney Isle" (#8483; 1903), "There's Music in the Air" (#8518; 1903), and "Seminole" (#8808; 1904), which also appeared later on a Victor disc. His early cylinders were not successful, but he returned to make five popular Edison Diamond Discs, all duets with Harry Mayo; the finest were "At the Ball, That's All" (#50238; 1915) and "Piney Ridge" (#0315; 1915). Tally appeared in Edison tone tests, singing along with these discs. He was also heard on some Zonophone records of 1905.

The first three of his 38 Victor records were made on 1 July 1904. They were "Mandy, Won't You Let Me Be Your Beau?" (#2936), "Seminole" (#937), and "If I Were Only You" (#2938). On 26 July 1907 Tally made his last Victor disc, "Take Me Back to New York Town" (#5230). His popularity was ending by 1917, when there were only two items in the Victor catalog; by 1922 he was not to be found there. He died in Ocean Park, California.

TALMY, SHEL, (c. 1940–)

Talmy is a Chicago-born record producer who made his name working in London with pop artists such as the Kinks and the Who in the mid-1960s. Working initially as a recording engineer for independent Conway Studios in Los Angeles, Talmy traveled to London on vacation in late 1962, carrying several masters with him. Approaching Decca Records, he stretched the truth a bit, claiming to have produced the sides that he had only engineered, and was hired to produce a new pop group, the Bachelors. They immediately scored big in the U.K., and Talmy remained at Decca working with various acts, including Chad and Jeremy and the Kinks. His success with the Kinks's mid-1960s pop hits, such as "You've Really Got Me," brought him to the attention of the Who's manager, Kit Lambert, who hired him to produce "My Generation" and their other tracks recorded in 1965. However, Lambert and Talmy had a falling out over royalties, and Talmy did not work with the group again. Talmy was able to capture the raw energy of the Kinks's and the Who's live sounds, while still giving his records a pop sheen appropriate for radio play. Other Talmy productions include the initial singles recorded by David Jones, later known as David Bowie. Talmy set up his own label, Planet, in 1965, mostly devoted to the group Creation, which he believed would be the next big thing (they never made it); the label was distributed by Phonogram, but only lasted a little over a year before financial problems led to its downfall. In the later 1960s, Talmy worked with folk-rock performers such as Pentangle and Burt Jansch. Talmy remained in the U.K. through the mid-1970s, then returned to the U.S.,

where he has occasionally worked as a producer with various acts, although he has never achieved the same level of success he enjoyed in the mid-1960s.

TAMAGNO, FRANCESCO (28 DEC 1850–31 AUG 1905)

Italian tenor, born in Turin. He worked as a baker and as a locksmith, but also studied at the Turin Conservatory and in 1873 sang in an opera in the Teatro Regio. Rapid success came to him. He performed in several houses and was at La Scala in 1877; he then earned international acclaim in Europe and South America. *Aida*, *Don Carlo*, and *L'africaine* were among his greatest triumphs. In 1887 he created the role of Otello, and took it — with the other Verdi operas — to the stages of the world. He last performed in Naples in 1904 and died in Varese a year later.

Tamagno was signed by G & T in 1903, with the first royalty contract in the industry (10 percent of retail sales and a £2,000 advance, equivalent of U.S. $10,000 at that time). He made 19 records, five in the new 12-inch size. His red label discs cost £1 each (or $5.00 for the American Red Seals), while regular red labels were selling for half that, 10 shillings. Among the most admired of Tamagno's records were the *Otello* death scene (HMV #DS-100) and other numbers from that opera, "Di quella pira" (HMV #52670; 1903), and "Muto asil" from *Guillaume Tell* (HMV #052103; 1905). The 12-inch HMV records of 1904–1905 are considered superior to the 1903 10-inch discs, but Victor released only the 10-inch material in the U.S. All five were carried into the 1922 catalog, but none survived to 1927. Reissues appeared on all the major LP reissue labels, and on CD on Pearl #9846 (complete 1903–1904 recordings), Symposium #1186 (complete recordings), Enterprise #1200 (selected 1903–1905 recordings), and various compilation CDs. [Favia-Artsay & Freestone 1952.]

TANGENTIAL TONE ARM

Also called a linear tracking arm. A type of tone arm that moves straight across a disc record along the disc's radius, rather than in an arc. It is designed to eliminate skating and horizontal tracking error.

TANGERINE DREAM

Considered genre benders — part progressive rock, part avant-garde — during its early years, Tangerine Dream is now viewed as the forefather of electronica, although its recent work has veered dangerously close to the New Age genre. The group has served as a launching pad for the solo careers of many leading experimental synthesizer artists, most notably, Klaus Schulze, Peter Baumann, Michael Hoenig, and leader Edgar Froese.

Tangerine Dream was formed in Berlin in fall 1967 by then-art student Froese, who worked with many different rock and classical musicians prior to the release of the group's debut album, *Electronic Meditation* (Ohr #556004; 1970; reissued February 1996 on Essential #345). Pioneering keyboard-predominated electronic waves of sound, the group issued three more undergound LPs — *Alpha Centauri* (Ohr #556 012; 1971; reissued February 1996 on Essential #346), *Zeit* (Ohr #556 021; 1972; reissued February 1996 on Essential #347), and *Atem* (Ohr #556 031; 1973; reissed February 1996 on Essential #348) — before the increasing appearance of synthesizers in the pop mainstream (e.g., Mike Oldfield's *Tubular Bells*) led to a contract with the Virgin label.

Although Tangerine Dream remained a cult staple in the U.S., its releases — featuring lush synthesizer-derived electronic washes, accented by evocative rhythmic patterns — charted regularly in the U.K. over the next decade, beginning with *Phaedra* (Virgin #13108; 1974; #15), *Rubycon* (Virgin #13166; 1975; #12), the live *Ricochet* (Virgin #2044; 1975; #40), and *Stratosfear* (Virgin #34427; 1976; #39). The next LP, *Sorcerer* (Virgin #2277; 1977; #25), signaled a gradual shift in the direction of movie soundtrack work, including *Thief* (Virgin/Elektra #521; 1981; #43), *Wavelength* (Elektra #81207; 1983), *Risky Business* (Virgin/Elektra #2302; 1983), *Firestarter* (MCA #3233, 1984), *Flashpoint* (Relativity #17141; 1985), *Heartbreakers* (Virgin #212-620; 1985), and *Three O'Clock High* (Relativity #47357; 1987). While continuing to produce high-quality — albeit less innovative — music, largely soundtracks for foreign films, Tangerine Dream has been marketed as a New Age group since the early 1990s.

FRANK HOFFMANN

TAPE

In common audio terminology, a strip of thin plastic, coated with iron oxide or similar substance, that may be magnetized to record sounds. Through the 1950s tapes had an acetate base, and tended to become brittle with age and to break easily. More recent tapes have a polyester base, such as mylar; they do not grow brittle, though their elasticity may be a problem (better tapes are pretensilized to overcome this).

The widely used iron oxide coating was improved upon by Dupont in the late 1960s with the development of chromium dioxide coatings. Better response at high recording levels was achieved in 1978 as 3M introduced pure metal particle (nonoxide iron) tape.

Tape thickness is 1.5 or 1.0 mils (38 or 25.4 micrometers) for the open-reel variety; 0.47 or 0.31 mils for cassette type.

See also **Cassette; Magnetic Recording; Nonmagnetic Tape Recording; Preservation of Sound Recordings**

TAPE COMPOSITION

In electronic music, the composing of music using sounds recorded on segments of magnetic tape. Until the availability of the magnetic tape recorder following World War II, electronic music had only been a live performance medium. The influence of the tape recorder on the very nature and definition of "music" was profound. On one hand it led to the creation of a new kind of music that existed *only* as a recording. On the other, it led to an obsessive quest for new and different electronic music technology and the development of the modern music synthesizer.

The tape recorder transformed the field of electronic music overnight by making it a composer's medium. They sought other sounds, other structures, and other tonalities and worked directly with the raw materials of sound to find them. In the heyday of classic electronic music, nearly every piece of music and every audio effect was somehow dependent on the skills needed to record and edit magnetic tape. Musique concrète — the name given to the music created by the first electronic music studio in Paris — *was* a recording medium, first using acetate discs and then magnetic tape.

The following is a compendium of the classic sound-editing techniques produced using tape recorders and tape editing. Most of these ideas are still relevant even when transcribed to the digital-editing medium.

Tape Splicing. The cutting and splicing of magnetic tape is, in effect, no different from moving sound around in time and space. A given sound that occurred at one time can be moved to another. Every sound has a given length. The mechanics of magnetic tape splicing are simple. Tape is provided on open reels, mounted on a tape recorder, and manually moved across the playback head to locate a precise sound on the tape. The composer's only other tools are a ruler to "measure" time in inches or centimeters of tape, a razor blade, and a *splicing block*. Tape is then cut into segments and spliced to other pieces of tape to form a composition. Splicing could be used in a limited way to change the attack and decay patterns of recorded sounds.

Degeneration of a Recorded Signal. A sound will decay over time when it is played back, re-recorded, and played back over and over again.

Tape Echo, Delay, and Looping. The tape recorder makes possible several basic techniques for repeating sounds that have been popular since the earliest experiments with tape composition. The idea of taking a piece of magnetic audio tape, splicing it end-to-end to form a loop, and then playing it back on a tape recorder so it constantly repeated itself is as old as the field of recorded electronic music and continues to be popular with composers. Unlike echo, during which each repetition of the trigger sound becomes weaker until it diminishes entirely, the sound repeated by a tape loop does not weaken with each repeat.

Echo is the repetition of a single sound that gradually decays in amplitude and clarity with each successive repeat. This was first achieved using tape recorders equipped with three "heads" — the erase, recording, and playback elements across which the reel of tape passed to record, play, and delete sounds. To create echo with a tape recorder, the playback output signal of the machine is fed back into the input, or record head, of the same machine. When this connection is made and the tape recorder is simultaneously recording and playing back, the sound being played is immediately re-recorded by the record head. The distance that the tape must travel from the record head to the playback head determines the length of the delay. Continuing in this manner without interruption creates the echo effect. The signal degrades slightly with each successive playback. The strength or persistence of the echo — how many repeats you hear — is determine by the amplitude of the playback signal being fed back into the recorder.

Echo and reverberation should not be confused. Echo is the periodic repetition of the same sound signal, whereas reverberation is the modulation of single sound signal to produce weaker ghost frequencies, or depth. Reverberation is used, for example, to replicate the ambience of a large room or space.

Tape delay combines the recording and re-recording of a sound using a tape loop or combination of tape recorders. The most interesting approach used two or more widely spaced tape recorders through which a single length of magnetic tape is threaded. A sound was recorded on the first machine and played back on the second, creating a long delay between repeats to form a kind of extended echo effect. If the sounds being repeated are also fed back to the recording head of the first machine, a diminishing effect was created that accumulated on the tape as layers of repeating sounds of various amplitudes.

Tape Reversal — Playing Sounds Backward. The idea of playing recorded sounds in reverse had crude beginnings with the turntablism of primordial musique concrète. With tape composition, the effect came into its own as an essential ingredient of the electronic music repertoire. Tape reverse is created by literally snipping out a length of recorded tape and splicing it back into the reel backward. Or, on a tape recorder that only recorded on one side of the tape, turning the tape over and running it backward passed the playback head.

THOM HOLMES

TAPE DECK

The mechanical element of a tape recorder, nearly always the open-reel design, rather than a cassette version, including its motors, reels, linkages, recording head, erase head, and playback head, but not including the electronic components and electric circuits. It is also known as a tape transport. A deck must be connected to an amplifier in order to drive loudspeakers. The use of separate tape decks arose in the early high-fidelity period (1950s), when users began to demand distinct components in the audio system.

A conventional grading of tape decks assigns them to one of three categories: professional, semiprofessional/audiophile, and consumer. Libraries often use good consumer-grade decks, while sound archives should use only professional or semiprofessional grade. Recording engineers should always opt for professional versions. There is no significant difference in performance between the two better grades, but the professional grade tends to be more rugged and reliable and probably also offers more flexibility. Among the makers of professional-grade tape decks marketed in America are Ampex, 3M, Scully, Crown, Nagra, and Studer. Widely used semiprofessional decks come from Revox, Tandberg, Sony, and TEAC. Sony and TEAC are also major producers of consumer-grade decks.

Over the years refinements in the basic mechanism were offered by various firms. Ampex developed an automatic threader for open-reel tapes. Bell and Howell marketed a "tape inhaler" that pulled the tape to the take-up reel with a vacuum. Sony marketed at one time a tape changer for four open-reel tapes, with a total playing time of 60 hours.

See also **Disc**

REV. HOWARD FERSTLER

TAPE GUIDES

In a tape deck, the rollers or posts that keep the tape in proper position as it moves across the heads.

TAPE LEADER

The section of a tape that precedes the part with the program material. It may be magnetic, carrying technical signals and production information. Or it may be a plain paper or plastic attachment to the magnetized tape, intended merely to aid in the affixing of the tape end to the take-up reel and to protect the recorded portion in storage.

TAPE PACK

The name given to the fully wound tape on its reel, or to the portion of tape that is wound on the reel.

TAPE RECORDING

An audio recording device using magnetic tape as the recording medium. The tape recorder was an outgrowth of earlier sound recording efforts using the technologies of cylinder and disc recording, developed by Thomas Edison and Emile Berliner. The first magnetic sound recorder was actually invented in 1898 by the Danish inventor Valdemar Poulsen, but further technical development of a device that was practical for commercial distribution did not occur until the late 1940s.

Outline of the historical development of the tape recorder:

1857, France — Irish-born E. Leon Scott invented the "Phonautograph," a device capable of inscribing a visual record of sound being directed into a diaphragm. The device used a stylus to record sound on a disc of smoked paper. The Phonautograph had one serious problem: although it could indeed inscribe representations of sound onto paper, it could not reproduce the sound in any way. Twenty years later, in 1877, French physicist Charles Cros conceived of a way to reverse Scott's process so that one might playback the recorded sound. Cros called this device the Paleophone but never succeeded in building a working model.

1876, United States — Edison successfully reproduced recorded sound for the first time. In 1877 he patented his first "talking machine." With this device, a recording of sound was made on a piece of tinfoil wrapped around a rotating brass drum. The recorder consisted of a membrane of parchment stretched over the end of a short brass cylinder. The membrane had attached to it a spring-mounted chisel needle that would vibrate as incoming sound caused the membrane to vibrate. The action of the needle on the piece of revolving tinfoil inscribed a mark that corresponded to the sound. The recording could be reproduced by rotating the cylinder again, but with the needle resting

in the existing cut groove. Edison called this device the "phonograph." Edison also tried wax cylinders as a recording medium. He envisioned the phonograph being used for such practical applications as dictation.

1878, United States — Oberlin Smith, an American engineer, filed a patent caveat, but not a formal patent, for a steel wire recorder. He conceived of it as a way to record telephone conversations. Ten years later, after having never pursued the idea further, he published his theory about magnetic recording in the magazine Electrical World.

1887, United States — Emile Berliner introduced disc recording, solving some of the recording and reproducing problems associated with the cylinder recorder of Edison. His first discs consisted of glass that was coated with a thick fluid of ink or paint. When the disc was rotated by a turntable, a stylus cut into it a spiral groove that corresponded to the sound being picked up by a diaphragm. Berliner called his first machine the "Gramophone" and imagined that it could be used to supply voices for dolls or to reproduce music.

1896, United States — Windup mechanical turntables were introduced to play disc recordings. The disc Gramophone soon gained acceptance. Berliner began to use recording discs from which copies, or imprints, of master recordings could be printed. Gramophone records made available at this time were usually made of thick, brittle shellac, operated at 78 rpm, and had recording on only one side.

1898, Denmark — Valdemar Poulsen of Copenhagen built the first magnetic recorder. It was called the Telegraphone and recorded crosswise (vertically) on a steel piano wire as it was rotated between the poles of an electromagnet. Unlike modern tape recorders, which use iron oxide–coated tape as a medium, the recording medium was an uncoated metal wire. Calling his device an "apparatus for electromagnetically receiving, recording, reproducing, and distributing articulate speech," Poulsen took the 1900 Paris Exposition by storm and won the Grand Prix for scientific invention. He envisioned the device as an office dictation machine. Poulsen had two versions of the Telegraphone. The most widely known was the one that used wire as the recording medium. Because the twisting of the wire caused distortion in the sound, he next tried to use steel tape as a medium. The American Telegraphone Co. was formed around 1900 to produce and sell Poulsen's wire model, which had two spools to transport the wire, a 100-volt motor, and manual rewind. It could record for 30 minutes on a wire moving at seven feet per second. The recorded sound was listened to using earphones, since no practical electrical means (e.g., the vacuum tube) had yet been developed for amplifying sound. The machine was a marketing failure, largely because of the inferior quality of its sound when compared with the Gramophone. ATC ceased operation in 1909. A Dutch firm also licensed to sell the device folded in 1916. Other wire recorders, primarily those made by Air King in Brooklyn, New York, appeared during the 1940s, but were soon superseded by magnetic tape recorders.

1905, United States — By this time, various forms of sound boxes — loudspeakers — had been developed for use with the Gramophone. These ranged from simple diaphragms connected to large horns, to delicately balanced "tone arms" with spring-mounted styli, mica diaphragms, and horns that could be either internally or externally mounted.

1906, United States — Lee De Forest invented the vacuum tube. Sometimes called the thermionic valve, audion, or triode tube, the vacuum tube was capable of controlling electrical current with precision. A vacuum tube could be used for the generation, modulation, amplification, and detection of current and was thus useful for everything from amplifying the sound of Gramophones to detecting radio waves and generating audio signals in tube oscillators.

1912, United States — In an experiment that went largely unnoticed, Lee De Forest succeeded in amplifying the magnetically recorded sound of a Poulsen Telegraphone by using his triode vacuum tube.

1916, United States — E.C. Wente of Western Electric invented the condenser microphone. It was capable of making high-quality, distortionless sound recordings in the frequency ranges associated with speech and orchestral instruments, becoming the industry standard for radio broadcasting and the production of Gramophone records.

1917, United States — G.A. Campbell built an early frequency filter.

1919, United States — A.G. Webster published his paper "Acoustical Impedance and Theory of Horns and Phonograph," which alluded to the possibilities of applying electrical theory to the design of microphones and audio reproducing systems.

Early 1920s, Germany — Kurt Stille, in yet another effort to salvage the Telegraphone, organized the Telegraphie-Patent Syndikat Co. to sell licenses to produce magnetic recorders in Europe. Several firms took part, a number of them using the improved version of the Telegraphone that used steel tape instead of wire. The device was considered for use in the production of sound for movies, and some experimental films using synchronized sound were actually produced in the U.K.

1924, United States — J.P. Maxfield and H.C. Harrison of AT&T successfully built an electrically operated recording and reproducing system using recently developed microphones and vacuum-tube amplifiers. Their system extended the frequency range of prior Gramophone recording systems by more than an octave and with much improved fidelity.

1925, United States — The Maxfield-Harrison recording system was adopted by the recording industry under such brand names as "Orthophonic" (Victor).

Mid-1920s, United States — The AC bias technique for recording sounds was first tried by W.L. Carlson and G.W. Carpenter of the U.S. Navy. They used it to send recorded telegraph messages. Until that time, all attempts at recording had used DC methods. The AC technique eliminated the background noise found in earlier DC recordings and is still the principal method used today.

1929, United States — Special oversized disc recordings were introduced for broadcast use. Called "transcriptions," these ran at 33 1/3 rpm and could carry a 15-minute program on one side of a 16-inch platter. These were the first long-playing records, but they required special playback equipment and were not available to the general public.

1930–1931, United States — Bell Telephone Laboratories undertook a research project in magnetic recording under the guidance of engineer Clarence N. Hickman. He immediately suggested that they use steel tape instead of wire as the recording medium because the greater surface area for recording the magnetic signal didn't require high speeds to maintain fidelity. This meant that they could slow the speed of the recorder from the rate of seven feet per second required for a wire recorder to about nine inches per second. Hickman conceived several applications including a telephone answering machine, a dictation device, and a portable reel-to-reel tape recorder, but none were manufactured.

1932–1935, Germany — Due to Kurt Stille's licensing activity, many varieties of wire and steel-band recorders were being sold in Germany. The Echophone Co. produced a cartridge-loaded unit that simplified operation of the machine. ITT eventually acquired this company, but resold it to the German firm of C. Lorenz Co., which redesigned the recorder and introduced it as the Textophone in 1933. The Nazi party and secret police began to acquire large numbers of such magnetic recording devices.

AEG introduced the Magnetophone in 1935 at the German Annual Radio Exposition in Berlin. This unit employed a coated paper tape instead of steel bands or wire. The supplies themselves cost a mere $.15 per minute of recording time in comparison to the more than $1 cost of using steel tape. This fact, no doubt, contributed to the success of the device at the exposition.

1935, United States — Bell Laboratories, one of the few American firms interested in magnetic recorders, designed the Mirrorphone. This recorder employed steel tape and was used to broadcast weather reports over the phone lines.

1937, United States — The Brush Development Co. introduced the Soundmirror, one of the first commercially available magnetic recorders in the U.S. This steel tape unit could record only one minute of sound. Brush supplied the armed forces with many of these during World War II.

1938, Germany — German engineer Fritz Pfleumer began experimenting with a number of new recording mediums in an attempt to improve on the basic design of magnetic recorders. He tried paper and plastic tapes coated with iron oxide particles as an alternative to wires and steel tapes. The Allgemeine Electrizita~ts Gesellschaft Allgemeine Elektrizit Gesell-Schaft (AEG) became interested in Pfleumer's work and bought all the rights to it. Such early recording tapes used large iron particles as coatings and had the feel of sandpaper. When run through a recorder, the earliest versions immediately clouded the air with residue and dust.

1940–1945, the World War II years — While American firms including General Electric (GE) continued to improve the design of wire recorders for military use, the Germans shifted their attention to tape units. The AEG Magnetophone was further developed, and when the victorious Allies moved into Germany in 1945, they were stunned to find the German tape units to be far superior to wire recorders. By 1945 the Magnetophone had adapted AC bias recordings and coated paper tape, and possessed a surprising frequency response of 10,000 cycles, which was much higher than earlier wire and steel tape units. These German recorders were capable of accurately recording midrange frequencies. The Americans quickly adapted the tape medium. Following the war, the U.S. alien-property custodian held all patents on the AEG Magnetophone and licensed any American company that desired to build it. The only three small companies to earnestly take on the magnetic tape project were Magnecord, Rangertone, and the Ampex Electric Co. The first technical problem that needed to be solved was to replace the low-grade coated paper tape used by the Germans with something more durable and of higher quality.

1947, United States — The Minnesota Mining and Manufacturing Company (3M), introduces the first successful plastic-based recording tape with a magnetic oxide coating. It quickly became an industry standard.

1948, United States — Ampex Corp. manufactured its first professional tape recorder, the model 200.

1949–1950, United States — The first prototype two-channel stereo tape recorders were demonstrated by Magnecord.

1950, United States — A.H. Frisch patented a method for recording sound directly onto magnetic tape without the use of a tape recorder. Using a process called magnetic stenciling, hand-made metal stencils made from paper clips and wire were placed directly on top of the magnetic tape itself. A magnet was passed over this assemblage to imprint a signal pattern onto the tape. The result was played using a tape recorder. Frisch fully developed magnetic stencils, creating electronic music directly onto tape, controlling pitch and modifying amplitude and envelope characteristics using several direct techniques.

1951, France — By this year, Pierre Schaeffer and Jacques Poullin of the Groupe de Recherches Musicales (GRM) had completed three special-purpose tape machine designs to assist them in composing electronic music for magnetic tape. These included the Morphophone, a tape machine with 10 heads for the playback of loops and the creation of echo effects; the Tolana Phonogène, a keyboard-operated version of the Morphophone with 24 preset speeds that could be triggered by the keyboard; and the Sareg Phonogène, a variable-speed version of the Tolana Phonogène tape loop machine.

1963, Netherlands — Philips introduces the compact cassette tape format.

1965, United States — Ford and Mercury introduce the eight-track tape cartridge as a stereo music system option in its luxury cars. It quickly becomes the most widely used commercial tape format. The increasing popularity of the Philips cassette eventually drew interest away from the eight-track format, which was discontinued in 1980.

1978, Japan — Sony introduces the first digital audio recording systems for professional studios.

1980, Japan — The Philips/Sony audio compact disc format was introduced.

First Sony tape recorder, and the first tape recorder made in Japan, introduced in July 1950. Courtesy Sony

1986, Japan — The first Digital Audio Tape (DAT) recorder was introduced by Sony/Philips.

1992, Japan — Philips and Matsushita introduced the Digital Compact Cassette (DCC) recorder/player.

THOM HOLMES

TAPE SPEED

The rate of tape motion, usually stated in inches per second (IPS), of a magnetic tape as it passes the recording or playback head of a tape recorder or tape deck. In the U.S., professional tape speeds have been 30 inches per second (IPS) and 15 IPS. Consumer recording has been at 7 1/2 IPS or 3 3/4 IPS, although 1 7/8 IPS and the higher speeds are sometimes available. In the Philips audiocassette the tape travels at 1 7/8 IPS. Microcassette recorders use a speed of 15/16 IPS.

TAPE TRANSPORT

SEE TAPE DECK

TASCAM

A branch of the Teac Corp., a large manufacturing company located in Japan. In 1969 Teac created a special Audio Systems Corp. branch, with the purpose being to specialize in recording technology for musicians and recording studios. In 1971 the company expanded operations to include an American branch, Teac Audio Systems Corp. of America (hence, TASCAM), with its purpose being to supply products to American recording professionals. TASCAM has become a major supplier of mixing consoles, work stations, studio-grade compact-disc players, recorders, and accessories. The company also owns NemeSys Music Technologies, makers of sampling and music production software. TASCAM products are now marketed worldwide. [website: www.tascam.com.]

HOWARD FERSTLER

TATE, ALFRED O. (1863–6 APR 1945)

An associate of Thomas Edison, born in Petersborough, Ontario. Tate was Edison's personal representative at the convention of the National Phonograph Association in 1893. Tate served as secretary of the Edison Phonograph Works and the Edison Manufacturing Co. In 1887 he became Edison's private secretary. He emerged as a dissident within the Edison circle, and provided his employer with crucial misinformation in the 1888 controversy involving Ezra Gilliland; as a result he came between Edison and his trusted colleague Charles Batchelor. Tate died in Brooklyn, New York. [Welch 1972.]

TATUM, ART (13 OCT 1909–5 NOV 1956)

American jazz pianist, born Arthur Tatum in Toledo, Ohio. He was blind in one eye, and only partly sighted in the other, so he learned music from braille notation. At age 16 he was playing in local clubs, and by 1922 he was in New York, a great success on radio, developing a perfect stride style which he mingled with torrents of notes from his right hand. Tatum was a sensation in New York in 1937 and the U.K. in 1938. In 1943 he formed a trio with Tiny Grimes, guitar, and Slam Stewart, bass; but he was essentially a soloist, one who did not change with style movements in jazz. His prodigious technique prompted many critics to compare him with the great virtuoso pianists like Vladimir Horowitz. At the same time he was criticized for filling every measure with crowds of notes. He did work in a simpler vein during the 1940s. He died in Los Angeles.

Tatum's outstanding records include "Tea for Two" (Brunswick #6553; 1933), "Stormy Weather" (Brunswick #80159; 1937), "Gone with the Wind" (Decca #1603; 1937), and "Lonesome Graveyard" with trumpet counterpoint from Joe Thomas (Decca #8563; 1941). In the 1950s he was with the Norman Granz's Clef and Verve labels, doing splendid numbers like "Ain't Misbehavin'" (#659; 1953). Tatum's output was vast and has been reissued in various formats on LP and CD. Among the notable CD reissues tracing his recording career are *Piano Starts Here* (Columbia/Legacy #64690), anthologizing his first recordings as a leader originally issued on Brunswick; *Classic Piano Solos, 1934–37*, giving 20 of his Decca recordings from this period (GRP #607); *The Complete Capitol Recordings, 1949–52* (#21325); and the massive *Complete Solo Masterpieces*, originally issued on 12 individual Verve albums and later on a seven-CD set from Pablo (#4404), complemented by *The Complete Group Masterpieces*, a six-CD set (#4401); both are drawn on sessions produced by Granz from 1954–1956. There are also various live recordings and V Disc reissues on CD, as well as compilations drawn on the official sessions on various jazz-reissue labels. In 1973 the Tatum album *God Is in the House* (Onyx) won a Grammy award.

TAUBER, RICHARD
(16 MAY 1891–8 JAN 1948)

Austrian/U.K. tenor, born in Linz. He studied in Frankfurt, and made his debut in Chemnitz as Tamino on 2 Mar 1913. He was engaged by the Dresden Opera, but turned to operetta, specializing in Lehar's works and to song recitals. A great success in a New York recital in 1931, he went on to triumphs in the U.K. and Australia. He took British citizenship in 1940. Tauber's final appearance in America was a Carnegie Hall recital on 30 Mar 1947. He died in London.

Tauber began recording for Odeon (Germany) in 1919, with four songs, a German version of "M'appari" and five other arias, plus four selections from Schumann's *Dichterliebe*. Arias from *Mignon* were among the finest of his opera discs (#81938 and #81941). Lenski's aria from *Eugene Onegin* (#80956) and "WinterstÅrme" (#81042) were other outstanding excerpts from opera. Tauber also worked for German Odeon in 1926–1930; Austrian Odeon, 1934–1935; and British Parlophone-Odeon, 1934–1946. A total of 735 sides are known.

Tauber's Lieder performances were covered by Parlophone records, among them elegant songs from Schubert's *Winterreise* (RO #20037/42; 1928). He was also acclaimed for German folk songs, such as those recorded in 1934 (Parlophone RO #20241/46). These and others are on Pearl #9370. For Odeon he made an outstanding "Heidenrîslein" (Schubert; sung in French, #250,849; 1933). Schumann's "Die beiden Grenadiere" has been a favorite with collectors (issued in 1927). Perhaps his most acclaimed discs were "Dein ist mein ganzes Herz" (#0-4949) and "Adieu, mein kleiner Gardeoffizier" (#0-4983).

Operetta remains Tauber's greatest contribution; he recorded the Viennese and Hungarian masterworks for Odeon and Parlophone. A CD from EMI (#69787) offers a fine selection. His opera repertoire is sampled on a Pearl CD (#9327), presenting him in Mozart airs sung in his prime (1922), in addition to Wagner, Verdi, and Puccini. There is more opera on EMI (#69476), but it is less well recorded and edited. [Abell 1969 is a complete discography.]

TAYLOR, CECIL (15 MAR 1929 [SOME SOURCES GIVE 25 MAR]–)

Born Cecil Percival Taylor in Long Island City, New York, Taylor is one of the most innovative and prolific jazz pianists/composers/theorists of the second half of the 20th century, known for his avant-garde style. Taylor was a child prodigy pianist and percussionist, studying classical music, which eventually led to his acceptance at the New York School of Music and Boston's New England Conservatory of Music (1951–1954). By the mid-1950s, he was leading his own small jazz groups in the New York area. Greatly affected by Ornette Coleman's late 1950s experiments with free jazz, Taylor began stretching his own musical style in the early 1960s, forming a lifelong partnership with Jimmy Lyons (1933–1986), an alto saxophonist who shared Taylor's interest in new tonalities and compositional techniques. In 1964, Taylor was among the founders of the Jazz Composers' Guild, which was dedicated to advancing jazz music, and he cut an album with the group's Jazz Composers' Orchestra in 1968. Taylor's first influential solo recordings were made for Blue Note in the mid-1960s, *Unit Structures* (#84237) and *Conquistador!* (#84260); neither album sold well, and Taylor was quickly dropped by the label. Taylor supported himself by working at university jazz departments through much of the 1970s, while his reputation grew in Europe. He had his own, short-lived label beginning in 1973 called Unit Core, and then primarily recorded for European labels like the avant-garde Hat Hut (issuing albums from 1978–1981), Leo (a British label run by a Russian expatriate jazz musician; 1987), and FMP (Free Music Production, a German label associated with the annual Berlin Jazz Festival; 1988–1996). FMP strongly supported Taylor's work, issuing an 11-CD set in 1989 of Taylor's live concert work from Berlin. A popular figure in Europe, Taylor has continued to record and perform through the turn of the 21st century, both with small combos and larger orchestras, although he is less prolific than he was in the 1980s.

CARL BENSON

TAYLOR, CREED (13 MAY 1929–)

Born in White Gate, Virginia, Taylor was one of the most important jazz producers of the 1970s, creating a jazz-rock-pop fusion that was very popular. He attended Duke University where he studied psychology, while leading a dance band (the Five Dukes) on the side playing for parties and at resorts. A talented trumpeter, Taylor continued to work in jazz and dance bands after graduation. In 1954 he joined a small jazz label, Bethlehem, as their A&R chief, and two years later was hired by ABC/Paramount, where he started a jazz label for them called Impulse! in 1960. In 1962 he was hired by MGM, who had just purchased Norman Granz's Verve label, to head their jazz list; he produced Wes Montgomery's popular guitar albums and Stan Getz's Brazilian-jazz fusion recordings at Verve. In 1967 he joined A&M, taking Montgomery with him, and also producing the Brazilian jazz-pop of Antonio Carlos Jobim. In 1970 he formed his own label, CTI, to promote jazz to a wider audience. He often produced theme albums — such as Hubert Laws's jazz reading of Stravinsky's *Rite of Spring* —

packaged in fancy gatefold sleeves, featuring full color artwork. Other artists he nurtured at the label included guitarist George Benson and sax man Stanley Turrentine. He also formed a subsidiary label, Kudu, for more funky R&B–oriented releases. However, Taylor overextended CTI, and it was bankrupt by the early 1980s, when Columbia purchased its back catalog. Taylor started a new CTI in the early 1990s, but by then his style of production was no longer as popular.

CARL BENSON

TAYLOR, JAMES (12 MAR 1948–)

Foremost among the introspective solo singer-songwriters who charted an early 1970s direction away from the band music of the late 1960s was James Taylor. The world-weariness and melancholy of his simple folk-blues guitar and voice seemed the perfect alternative to the excesses of the 1960s, some of which — like heroin — the young Taylor was caught up in.

Born to an academic family in Boston, Massachusetts, and raised in Chapel Hill, North Carolina, Taylor first played as a teenager with the band Flying Machine, featuring longtime associate guitarist Danny Kortchmar, who recorded an unreleased album in 1967. Taylor moved to London in 1968 and was signed to the Beatles' new Apple label, working with producer Peter Asher. (Asher would remain Taylor's producer for many albums to come.) They scored a minor hit with the debut single,

Sheet music cover for James Taylor's first major hit, "Fire and Rain," 1971. Courtesy David A. Jasen

"Carolina on My Mind." Returning to the U.S., Taylor and Asher recorded his breakthrough album, *Sweet Baby James* (Warner #1843), which catapulted him to stardom. Few baby boomers can hear Taylor sing his signature song, "Fire and Rain" (Warner #7423, 1970) from that album without feeling empathy. The subsequent album, *Mud Slim Slim* (Warner #2561), in 1971, contained the number one hit "You've Got a Friend" (Warner #7498) written by Carol King. Taylor's style is understated, personable, and confessional. Taylor backed off from his initial stardom, but continues to release quality material. His 1975 cover of "How Sweet It Is (To Be Loved by You)" (Warner #8109; #50) marked a lightening of his approach. Duets with J.D. Souther on 1981's "Her Town Too" (Columbia #60514; #11) and with Paul Simon and Art Garfunkel on a 1978 cover of Sam Cooke's "Wonderful World" (Columbia #10676; #17) are highlights of his later career. Taylor has continued to release a new album about once every five years since the early 1980s, and he still tours regularly. He was inducted into the Rock and Roll Hall of Fame in 2000.

BOB SILLERY

TAYLOR TRIO

A string trio that recorded for various labels ca. 1904. Membership was not fixed; one group included Alexander Hackel, violin; Albert W. Taylor, cello; and William E. Berge, piano. Alexander Drasein was another violinist, and Oscar W. Friberg another pianist.

TEAC CORP.

SEE TASCAM

TEAGARDEN, JACK (29 AUG 1905–15 JAN 1964)

American jazz trombonist and blues singer, born Weldon Leo Teagarden in Vernon, Texas. He played piano as a young child, then took up the trombone at age 10. After playing in San Antonio, Texas, he went on to New York and Chicago. He joined Ben Pollack's band in 1928, but also played with Red Nichols, Louis Armstrong, Eddie Condon, and others. In 1933 he went to Paul Whiteman's orchestra and was a featured soloist until 1938, when he left to organize his own band. In 1947 he was with the Louis Armstrong All Stars; then he led an all-star ensemble of his own and remained actively performing until his death, in New Orleans.

Teagarden was among the few white musicians to excel in the blues, which he performed with virtuosity (e.g., brilliant trills). He was also a fine jazz vocalist. He began to record in the late 1920s, with Condon, Pollack, Armstrong, and others. "Makin' Friends" with Condon (Okeh #41142; 1928) and "Knockin' a Jug" with Armstrong (Okeh #8703; 1929) are representative of his work in that period. His singing is heard to advantage in "Stars Fell on Alabama" (Brunswick #6993; 1934) and "I Gotta Right to Sing the Blues" (Brunswick #8397; 1939). In 1946 he made some records on a label named for him, Teagarden Presents. Grudge, Jazzology, and Savoy Jazz are among the labels that have issued Teagarden material on CDs. Mosaic 211 presents the complete recordings of Beiderbecke, Teagarden, and Trumbauer made between 1924–1926.

TEBALDI, RENATA (1 FEB 1922–)

Italian soprano, born in Pesaro. She studied at the Parma Conservatory at age 16, and made her debut in *Mefistofele* in Rovigo in 1944. Chosen by Arturo Toscanini to sing at the reopening of La Scala after World War II, she remained with the company, singing also throughout Europe and South America. On 31 Jan 1955 she was heard at the Metropolitan Opera as Desdemona, and appeared regularly there to 1973. Her great roles were Aida, Desdemona, Leonora, Violetta, Mimi, Cio Cio San, Tosca, Eva in *Meistersinger*, and Gioconda. Tebaldi has been acclaimed for the beauty and control of her voice, as well as for her dramatic skills.

Tebaldi has made numerous complete opera sets, all of them remarkable and many definitive. In the Decca LXT series she took part in *Aida, Andrea Chenier, Boheme, Fanciulla del West, Forza del destino, Madama Butterfly, Manon Lescaut, Otello, Tosca, Traviata, Trittico, Trovatore*, and *Turandot*. She recorded *Cavalleria rusticana* and *Turandot* for RCA Victor. Her recital album of 1958 won the Grammy for best classical vocal disc.

TECHNO

Techno — which originated as instrumental-based electronica in 4/4 time centered around hyperactive keyboard riffing and edgy, explosive drumming — drew upon the synthesizer music of 1970s Euro-rock bands such as Kraftwerk, Faust, and Can, and the post-punk industrial dance movement of the 1980s, spearheaded by Cabaret Voltaire, Throbbing Gristle, Ministry, and (primarily) other British artists.

Although first centered in Detroit, the genre was imported by English clubs in the late 1980s. Closely aligned with house music and club raves — i.e., club events incorporating lasers, mammoth sound systems, and countless dancers fueled by the designer drug Ecstasy — techno evolved from the neo-psychedelia of the Manchester-based Stone Roses and Scotland's Primal Scream into a diversity of hyphenated forms in the 1990s, including Ambient Techno and Big Beat.

The ambient school utilized samples of recorded music, nature, and other extraneous noises to create richly textured, synthesizer-driven soundscapes; prime exponents included German classical composer Peter Namlook, England's Aphex Twin, and Australian avant-garde artist Paul Schutze.

Big Beat, sometimes referred to as "Rock Techno," combined pounding rhythms, synthesizer washes, and sampling within a more traditional rock format. This style owed much to the pioneering work of Prodigy, Underworld, and the Chemical Brothers, whose LPs — most notably, *Exit Planet Dust* (AstralWorks #6157; 1995; #9 U.K.), *Dig Your Own Hole* (AstralWorks #6180; 1997; #1 U.K., #14 U.S.), and *Surrender* (AstralWorks #47610; 1999; #1 U.K., #32 U.S.) — were instrumental in making it the best-selling recorded dance music in British history.

FRANK HOFFMANN

TECHNO-POP

Techno-pop, also termed synth-pop or electro-pop, refers to a rock genre built around synthesizers, i.e., computers with musical input (e.g., keyboards)/output (e.g., amplifiers, speakers) devices. While some techno-pop artists have employed synthesizers merely for instrumental coloring (timbre), others applied them to reproduce the full range of ensemble performance from percussive effects to simulations of the human voice. Musicians make frequent use of prerecorded tapes (or digital data stored on various types of computer software) both in the studio and for live shows.

The genre originated through the pioneering efforts of German bands such as Tangerine Dream and Kraftwerk in the early 1970s. While Tangerine Dream was, in the long term, the more influential of the two aggregates — being largely responsible for the rise of new-age space music and the ambient movement — Kraftwerk provided the model for dance-beat style utilized by the first wave of techno-pop artists. The band's "Autobahn" (Vertigo #203) — an early permutation of the then-emerging Euro-disco sound — was a major hit in early 1975. However, Kraftwerk failed to consolidate its success due to a lack of composing talent and the inability of the members to project a telegenic image.

The movement did not reach the mainstream until 1982 when the Human League's "Don't You Want

Me" (A&M #2397) reached the top of the American music charts. The record business was suddenly awash with techno-pop acts, the most successful of whom included the Eurythmics, Soft Cell, Thomas Dolby, Depeche Mode, and A Flock of Seagulls. The ascendency of the genre owed much to (1) the rise of MTV combined with the multimedia savvy of techno-pop performers; (2) advances in electronic equipment that made a wide array of sounds achievable for artists with comparatively limited resources; and (3) the fact that AOR, Top 40, and other radio friendly formats had grown stale.

The competition from other newly emerging post-punk styles in the late 1980s drove techno-pop back underground. It resurfaced into the commercial mainstream as "techno" in late 1996, albeit with more pronounced dance rhythms. Leading acts such as Orbital, Prodigy, Underworld, and the Chemical Brothers remained popular into the 21st century.

FRANK HOFFMANN

TEEN IDOLS

The teen idol phenomenon cut across the entire American popular culture spectrum, embracing the music business, television, radio, Hollywood films, comic books, fan magazines, and general merchandising tie-ins. In all of these media, the formula consisted of selling products associated with photogenic, well-mannered young people (generally ranging in age from early teens to those in their mid-20s) to teenage consumers. The process had the implicit blessing of parents and other authority figures given the alternative: that American youth would fall under the influence of more rebellious cultural icons, including juvenile delinquents feared to inhabit the street corners of every 1950s town and, of course, rock 'n' roll stars.

The first wave of rock 'n' rollers had put both parents and record industry executives on the defensive. The wild performing antics of Black and white musicians alike seemed to hint at a wide array of antisocial behaviors. While Elvis Presley — hep-cat clothes and surly looks, notwithstanding — was soon being portrayed by the media as a likeable mama's boy, the extra-musical escapades of many rock 'n' roll artists soon confirmed the worst fears of adult moralists. Jerry Lee Lewis defiantly defended his marriage to a 13-year-old second cousin, and Chuck Berry was convicted of a violation of the Mann Act for transporting an underaged girl across a state line. Even the Platters, purveyors of smooth group ballads, were embroiled in a sex and drugs scandal. The major record companies, outflanked by smaller independent labels in signing early rock 'n' roll stars, saw an opportunity to create

and promote a new musical trend in which they controlled the talent. This strategy had initially failed when calypso failed to catch on beyond a brief flurry of hits in early 1957. However, with the loss of many early rock stars due to legal problems, military service, religious convictions (Little Richard entered the seminary in 1958), fatal accidents (e.g., Buddy Holly, Ritchie Valens, the Big Bopper, Eddie Cochran), mishaps that disrupted career momentum (e.g., Gene Vincent, Carl Perkins), and the failure to find quality song material for follow-up recordings, the industry-wide push of teen idol surrogates caught on in a big way.

The ingredients of a teen idol recording included an attractive (usually white, conservatively attired, and well-groomed) young media star singing simple lyrics about typically middle-class teen concerns. Given the fact that many idols couldn't really sing, the sugary pop arrangements — exhibiting only a faint suggestion of the big beat — were vital to chart success. Many of the singers were already stars in another medium (usually television or movies), thereby virtually ensuring the success of promotional efforts on the part of the record labels.

Nevertheless, stories of teen idols literally discovered on their front porches (Fabian Forte) abounded in fan publications. If the combined forces of the industry (label promotion, trade ads, and exposure on both radio playlists and *American Bandstand*) were marshaled on behalf of a young performer (no matter how lame), anything was possible. The formula consistently worked from the late 1950s up to the mid-1960s. However, changing cultural mores (e.g., youthful rebellion was seen as more glamorous than wholesome conformity) and the British Invasion (whose artists were often marketed in teen idol fashion) rendered the genre passe. However, teen stars — whether marketed under bubblegum, dance, country, or some other pop music label — have remained a viable commodity up to the present day. [Miller 1980.]

See also **Aguilera, Christina; 'N Sync; Spears, Britney**

FRANK HOFFMANN

TEFIFON

A phonographic device that recorded sound on an endless band of 35 millimeter film — up to 100 feet long — inscribing lateral grooves on the film with a stylus. The film was housed in a cartridge, and played back at 7 1/2 inches per second with a sapphire needle and a crystal pickup. Tefifon was marketed in Germany from about 1950, though the development of it is traced to the 1920s; the main work was carried out by Karl

Daniel (1905–1979) of Cologne, who organized a company to handle it: Tefi-Apparatebau. Because of its long playing time — an hour for a small cartridge, up to four hours for larger cartridges — the device appeared to have a promising future, even in competition with the new LP disc. A catalog was issued in 1954 with 264 prerecorded tapes listed, mostly light music. Inability of the firm to secure the services of major artists, who were under contract to the record labels, prevented the Tefifon from achieving long prosperity, and it passed from the scene ca. 1960. [Czada and Jensen 1983.]

TE KANAWA, KIRI, DAME (6 MAR 1944–)

New Zealand soprano, born in Gisborne. She won a radio prize in Melbourne, and remained there, singing at social functions. Then she gained a study grant to London in 1966, and made her debut as the Countess in *Nozze di Figaro* in 1970; this became one of her finest roles. In 1972 she appeared in San Francisco, and on 9 Feb 1974 at the Metropolitan Opera in an emergency substitution for Teresa Stratas in *Otello*. Verdi and Mozart were her great vehicles, and also her most acclaimed recordings (complete *Nozze di Figaro* [Decca #410-150-2DH3; 1984] and *Simon Boccanegra* [London #2-425628; 1990]). She also made outstanding complete recordings of Puccini's *Manon Lescaut* (London #2-421426-1LH2) and *Rondine* (CBS #2-M2K-37852); and a notable version of the Mahler Fourth Symphony with Georg Solti (Decca #410 188-2DH; 1984). An interesting crossover singer, Te Kanawa has also inscribed an album with Nelson Riddle, *Blue Skies* (London #44666-2), with such numbers as "Here's that Rainy Day" and "How High the Moon."

TELARC (LABEL)

Founded in 1977 by Jack Renner and Robert Woods, two classically trained musicians and former teachers, the goal of these two principals was to fill a niche in the growing audiophile record market by using minimalist recording techniques and little or no postproduction manipulations. The first recordings under the Telarc banner were not digital, but instead were direct-to-disc recordings made with the Cleveland Orchestra and with organist Michael Murray. In 1978 they decided to take the first of many risks that are characteristic of the company's history, by making the first commercial classical recordings in the U.S. in the digital format. Over the years, Telarc has earned a reputation for innovation and production in the area of digital recording techniques, and in 1999 the company began a collaboration with Sony and Philips in the development of their new technology called Direct Stream Digital (DSD). In 2001 the company began distribution of high-definition surround recordings based on the Super Audio Compact Discs (SACD) technology. In 2000 Telarc brought contemporary jazz label Heads Up on board, and the company continues to produce cutting-edge digital recordings. [website: www.telarc.com.]

See also **Stockham, Thomas**

HOWARD FERSTLER

TELDEC (LABEL)

A record belonging to the Time Warner conglomerate, affiliated since January 1988 with its WCI division, marketed and distributed by Warner Classics. Teldec succeeded Telefunken, and continues to specialize in German recordings, its traditional strength since the 1920s. The Esprit line is a low-cost Teldec. Among the artists on recent CDs are the Leipzig Gewandhaus, the Berlin Philharmonic Orchestra, the Mozarteum Orchestra of Salzburg, and the Vienna Concentus Musicus under Nikolaus Harnoncourt. In 2002 Teldec launched the New Line label for world-premier recordings of 20th century works. [website: www.teldec.com]

TELEFUNKEN (LABEL)

A German record made by Telefunkenplatte GmbH, Berlin, from the 1920s. Supraphon was its Czech subsidiary, Ultraphon its French affiliate. Polydor was the related American label in the early LP period, one of the group of 11 labels listed in the first Schwann catalog (1949). The first video/audio discs were demonstrated at the Telefunken building in Berlin on 24 June 1970. Teldec is the current name of the label.

TELEGRAPHONE

The magnetic wire recorder developed by Valdemar Poulsen ca. 1898. It used steel piano wire of 0.01 inch diameter, moving past the recording head at 84 inches (213 centimeters) per second. Poulsen's concept included the possibility of magnetic recording on coated paper strips and even discs, and these alternatives were cited in his British patent #8961 (1899). The telegraphone was patented in the U.S. (#661,619; filed 8 July 1899, granted 13 Nov 1900) and in a dozen other countries. It was demonstrated at the Paris Exposition of 1900 and used to record the voice of Emperor Franz Joseph I in Vienna (the recording still exists, in the Danish Technical Museum, Hellerup). King Edward VII recorded words of appreciation for the invention, and the wire was given to Queen Alexandra, but its whereabouts is unknown.

Despite its early fame, the telegraphone proved unable to compete with the cylinder phonograph because its playback sound was very faint (there were then no adequate means of amplification), its playing time per spool of wire was very brief because of the high speeds required, and the wire tended to tangle in transport to its take-up reel. Later Poulsen and Oscar Pedersen worked out a longer playing wire machine that would run 20 minutes, and some of them were used by the British Post Office and the War Office during World War I, and by the U.S. Navy. But the telegraphone was a commercial failure, and little was heard about it after 1910. [Hoover 1971 has an illustration on p. 124.]

See also **Magnetic Recording**

TELEPHON-FABRIK BERLINER

The J. Berliner Telephon-Fabrik, established in Hanover in 1881 by Joseph Berliner and Emile Berliner. It was there that the first records of the Gramophone Co. of London were pressed.

TELLER, AL[BERT] (1944–)

Born in the Bronx, New York, Teller has held several key positions in the record industry since the early 1970s. He originally studied engineering, then entered Harvard Business School. In 1969 he became assistant to the president for Columbia Records. Except for a brief period at the Playboy label in 1970, he remained at Columbia until 1974. After positions as head of United Artists (1974–1978) and the smaller Windsong label (1978–1981), he returned to become head of Columbia Records (1981–1985). In 1985 he became the head of all of CBS's labels. However, the sale of Columbia to Sony masterminded by Walter Yetnikoff led to Teller's ouster in 1988. Teller and Yetnikoff became archrivals and feuded publicly for years after this split. Teller was quickly hired by MCA, who put him in charge of their label group in 1989. There he was a major champion for alternative rockers Nirvana, and helped build the label into a major powerhouse in popular music. In 1996 he was forced out of MCA, who hired his rival Doug Morris (formerly the head of the Warner Music Group). Teller formed Red Ant Records; that same year, Red Ant was acquired by Alliance Entertainment Group (which owned 15 labels, including Concord Jazz), with the backing of several large investment

funds. Teller was named chairman of the new firm. However, by July 1997, Alliance went bankrupt. In 1999 Teller launched Atomic Pop Records as an internet-based music and video label, with its first major signing being the once notorious gangsta rap group, Public Enemy. A year later, Teller entered into an alliance with Microsoft to offer its products exclusively in Windows format.

Carl Benson

TEMPLEMAN, TED (24 OCT 1944–)

Longtime pop music executive and producer, Templeman was born in Santa Cruz, California. He began his career as the drummer for the group Harper's Bizarre, which had a single hit in 1967 with Paul Simon's "59th Street Bridge Song (Feelin' Groovy)" (Warner #5890; #13). Through the band, he met Warners producer/executive Lenny Waronker, who hired him to play drums and sing on various sessions. In 1971 he brought a demo tape of the group the Doobie Brothers to Waronker and convinced him to sign the group; Templeman coproduced their first album, and continued to oversee their work through the early 1980s, including their late 1970s hits "What a Fool Believes" (on which Templeman played drums), among many others. Templeman also oversaw Doobie vocalist/songwriter Michael McDonald's successful early 1980s solo recordings. Beginning in 1978 Templeman produced Van Halen for Warner, and helped give a pop sheen to their heavy metal songs through their most successful years in the 1980s. Templeman also worked with other Warner acts, including Captain Beefheart and Van Morrison (early 1970s), Nicolette Larsen (1978–1082), and Eric Clapton (1985). Although he remains a staff producer at Warner, Templeman has been less successful and active since the late 1980s.

TEMPTATIONS

American popular vocal group, organized in 1960 from two Detroit-based ensembles, the Primes, a trio including high tenor Eddie Kendricks and baritone Paul Williams, and the Distants, a quintet featuring middle tenor Otis Williams, bass singer Melvin Franklin, and Elbridge Bryant (replaced by gospel-styled tenor David Ruffin in 1964). An audition for Motown led to the formation of the Gordy imprint. Following a number of minor R&B hits in early 1960s, they broke out with a number one hit disc, "My Girl," in 1965 (Gordy #7038).

Referring to themselves as "five lead vocalists" (Rock and Roll Hall of Fame and Museum homepage),

Temptations's "It's Growing" sheet music cover, published by Motown's Jobete Music subsidiary. Courtesy David A. Jasen

the Temptations would enjoy 46 chart songs in the next 15 years. They won two Grammys for "Cloud Nine" (Gordy #7081; 1968), and another for "Papa Was a Rolling Stone" (Gordy #7121; 1972). The most successful of the group's 33 chart albums were two volumes of *Temptations' Greatest Hits* (Gordy #GM919; 1966 and Gordy #GS954; 1970). Despite the departure of Ruffin (1968) and Kendricks (1971) to develop solo careers, the Temptations keep abreast of pop fashions, relying heavily on funk and psychedelic influences beginning in the late 1960s.

The group lost momentum during the disco era, but Ruffin and Kendricks returned to the fold for a reunion LP and lucrative tour in 1982. They have remained a working entity up to the present day — despite the deaths of Paul Williams (1971), Ruffin (1991), Kendricks (1992), and Franklin (1995) — with a line-up featuring Otis Williams.

FRANK HOFFMANN

10CC

The Manchester-based 10cc was rivaled only by singer/songwriter Randy Newman as multilevel humorists — spanning satire, Black comedy, word

play, and nonsense verse — within the rock music scene. 10cc also excelled within the realm of pure music: all members were consummate songwriters and studio producers both inside and outside the band.

10cc was a spin-off of the novelty group, the Hotlegs, famous for the hit, "Neanderthal Man" (Capitol #2886; 1970; #2 U.K., #23 U.S.). Hotlegs personnel — vocalist/guitarist/bassist Eric Stewart, formerly with the Mindbenders; vocalist/guitarist/keyboardist Lol Crème; and vocalist/drummer Kevin Godley — joined forces with ex-Mindbenders vocalist/bassist Graham Gouldman (who'd penned hit songs for the Yardbirds, the Hollies, and Herman's Hermits) in mid-1972. Following several singles — including the U.K. hits, "Donna" (UK/Decca #6; 1972; #2 U.K.) and "Rubber Bullets" (UK/Decca #36; 1973; #1 U.K.) — a debut LP, *10cc* (UK #53105; 1973; #36 U.K.), was released, attracting little attention stateside.

By the time a second album, *Sheet Music* (UK #53207; 1974; #9 U.K., #81 U.S.), appeared, favorable reviews and word-of-mouth regarding the band's rich vocal textures, strong melodic hooks, polished arrangements, and witty song lyrics ensured greater sales. 10cc peaked commercially with *The Original Soundtrack* (Mercury #1029; 1975; #4 U.K., #15 U.S.), driven by the lush ballad, "I'm Not in Love" (Mercury #73678; 1975; #1 U.K., #2 U.S.), which featured hundreds of overdubbed voices intoning wry verses such as "I keep your picture upon the wall/It hides the messy stain that's lying there." The next LP, *How Dare You* (Mercury #1061; 1976; #5 U.K.), sold marginally in the U.S. without the presence of a catchy single.

Godley and Crème — widely acknowledged to be the experimental half of the band — departed to work as a duo, releasing *Consequences* (Mercury #1700; 1977; #52 U.K.). The three-disc set promoted their new "gizmo" guitar device, which provided a range of sonic effects comparable to that achieved by synthesizers. They gained recognition as top-flight video producers in the 1980s, working with the likes of Herbie Hancock and Frankie Goes to Hollywood. Gouldman and Stewart continued at the helm of a less-barbed edition of 10cc, releasing *Deceptive Bends* (Mercury #3702; 1977; #3 U.K., #31 U.S.) — which included the hit "The Things We Do for Love" (Mercury #73875; 1976; #6 U.K., #5 U.S.), *Live and Let Live* (Mercury #28600; 1977; #14 U.K.), *Bloody Tourists* (Mercury #6160; 1978; #3 U.K., #69 U.S.), *Look Hear!* (Warner Bros. #3442; 1980; #35), *Ten Out of 10* (Warner Bros. #7150 048; 1981), and *Window in the Jungle* (Warner Bros. #28; 1983; #70 U.K.) prior to dissolving the band in late 1983.

The four original members reunited in 1991, releasing *Meanwhile* (Polydor #513279; 1992). Despite limited audience interest, Gouldman and Stewart recorded another LP, *Mirror Mirror* (Avex #6; 1995), with distribution limited to the U.K

FRANK HOFFMANN

TENNESSEE PHONOGRAPH CO.

One of the affiliated firms of the North American Phonograph Co., established in 1890 in Nashville; general manager in 1890 was J. Balleran.

TESTAMENT (LABEL)

Blues label founded by Pete Welding in 1963 to issue his own recordings of traditional blues musicians. Welding had been a disc jockey broadcasting folk music and blues on the local educational radio station in Philadelphia in the early 1960s. In 1962 he moved to Chicago, taking some tapes he had made of Philadelphia musicians. Inspired by the Delmark label, he decided to release some of his own recordings, and then began recording local musicians. Testament eventually issued albums by many important players on the scene, including Big Joe Williams, Johnny Young, Robert Nighthawk, Houston Stackhouse, and Otis Spann. The label was active through the mid-1970s. Its back catalog is being reissued on CD by the HighTone label.

CARL BENSON

TETRAZZINI, LUISA
(28 JUNE 1871–28 APR 1940)

Italian soprano, born in Florence. She studied in Florence and made her debut there in *L'africaine* in 1890. She sang in South America and Europe, and in 1904 in San Francisco. Then she went to Covent Garden and the Manhattan Opera (1908-1910), with one season at the Metropolitan Opera after her debut there — to mixed notices — as Lucia on 27 Dec 1911. Tetrazzini appeared later in Chicago, Boston, and Philadelphia; then returned to Italy where she entertained soldiers during World War I. Subsequently she concentrated on recitals, in the U.K. and U.S., until 1931, when she retired to Milan. She died there nine years later.

On 8 Sep 1904 Tetrazzini recorded for the Zonophone label, singing the Mad Scene from *Lucia* first (#10000), and "Caro nome," "Una voce poco fa," Juliette's Waltz, and "Ah, non giunge" from *Sonnambula*. She made many discs for the Gramophone Co. in London from 1907 to 1913, repeating her Zonophone material and adding much of the coloratura repertoire. Her later work was for Victor

Luisa Tetrazzini in the 1917 Victor catalog. Courtesy Jerald Kalstein

in 1911–1920. Among her outstanding discs are "Saper vorreste" from *Ballo in maschera* (Victor #88304; 1911), and the *Lakme* "Bell Song" (Victor #88297, 6340; 1911). She participated in a renowned version of the *Lucia* Sextette, with Enrico Caruso, Pasquale Amato, and Marcel Journet (Victor #96201). Her sisters Eva and Elvira were also recording artists. (The Columbia and Phonadisc issues by "E. Tetrazzini" are by Elvira.) There were numerous LPs released by all the reissue labels. A five-CD set by Pearl (#9220) offers the "complete known recordings." *The Complete Zonophone (1904) and Victor Recordings (1911–20)* are available on a two-CD set from Romophone (#81025). Other CD reissues of selected recordings by the soprano include Phonographe #5099, Minerva #13, Enterprise #1122, and various compilations with other singers. [Richards & Wade 1949 is a discography.]

TEWKSBURY, GEORGE E.

Recording industry executive. He was president of the Kansas Phonograph Co. in 1890, and general manager in 1892–1893. In 1894–1895 he managed the U-S Phonograph Co., Newark, New Jersey. Tewksbury held a basic coin-op patent, U.S. #523,556 (filed 13

Dec 1893; granted 24 July 1894). He became general sales agent for the National Phonograph Co., Thomas Edison's organization (1896–1897), but had a falling out with Edison and died shortly after, afflicted with a form of insanity. He was author of *A Complete Manual of the Edison Phonograph* (1897).

TEXAS PHONOGRAPH CO.

One of the affiliated firms of the North American Phonograph Co., established in Galveston in 1890. H.L. Sellers was president in 1890, and H.E. Landes was president in 1892. General manager was Thomas Coyngton.

TEYTE, MAGGIE, DAME (17 APR 1888–26 MAY 1976)

English soprano, born Maggie Tate in Wolverhampton. She studied in London, then with Jean de Reszke in Paris, changing the spelling of her name to suit French pronunciation. Her debut was as Zerlina at Monte Carlo in 1907. She was greatly successful in song recitals, often accompanied by Debussy at the piano, and became recognized as an outstanding interpreter of French melodie. Teyte continued operatic work as well, at the Opera-Comique in 1908–1910; and in London, Chicago, Boston, etc. Melisande was her favored role. After 1917 she turned more definitely toward a career as recitalist, and remained active through World War II. She died in London.

Her earliest recording was made in 1907 for HMV, "Because" (#3729). She worked for Columbia in 1914–1916, doing mostly English concert numbers. Teyte recorded for Edison Diamond Discs in 1919, presenting some unlikely repertoire; her first piece was "I'se Gwine Back to Dixie" with the Lyric Male Quartet (#82159), which had a solo on the B side, "Ma Curly-Headed Baby." Then she made five other sides, concert songs in English, the last in 1924.

The most important Teyte records were made much later, in the 1940s, when she was "discovered" in America, much to the credit of Joseph Brogan, proprietor of the Gramophone Shop in New York. These records were her true repertoire: French songs, selections from *Pelleas*, and a fine English recital. EMI offered an extensive selection on four LPs (RLS #716) in 1976. The 1930s' era recordings are available on a single CD from Philips/Universal, as part of their Great Singers of the 20th Century series (#467916). A concert recording made when she was over 60 years old is reissued on CD by Video Arts International (#1063). [Tron 1954/11 is a discography.]

THAT GIRL QUARTET

A female vocal group, the "most successful women's recording ensemble"; active from ca. 1910 on many labels. The members were Harriet Keys, Allie Thomas, Presis (or Precis) Thompson, and Helen Summers. They made U-S Everlasting cylinders, then worked for Victor, beginning with "Silver Bell" (#16695; 1911). Edison recorded them also, beginning with "Honeymoon Honey in Bombay" (#10494; 1911). There were six titles in the Victor 1917 catalog, four titles in 1922, but none in 1927. The group may have been the one known as the Savoy Girl Quartet on Columbia records of 1911. [Walsh 1973/1.]

THAU, MARTY (7 DEC 1938–)

New York born Thau has had a long career in the pop music industry, from promoting teen pop and bubblegum in the 1960s to punk and downtown rock in the 1970s. Thau attended NYU and then got hired in the advertisement department of *Billboard*, the music industry journal. On the side, he began managing a down-at-the-heels teen singer, Tony Orlando, although he didn't achieve much success for the future singing star. Through friend Neil Bogart, Thau got a job as a PR man at the small Cameo/Parkway label in 1965, and then two years later became head of promotion for Buddah, where he successfully oversaw the careers of frothy pop acts like the 1910 Fruitgum Co. and disco stars Ohio Express. In 1970 he partnered with Lewis Merenstein to form Inherit Productions; the duo produced Van Morrison's influential *Astral Weeks* and *Moondance* albums, as well as recordings by Mike Bloomfield and John Cale. In 1972 he moved to Paramount Records to head their A&R department, but soon was independently managing a new group, the New York Dolls. Thau got them a record deal with Mercury in 1972, but their first albums failed to sell. However, the Dolls gave him an entree to the downtown/punk scene in New York, and Thau ended up producing demos by the Ramones in 1975. A year later, he formed a new production company, this time with Richard Gottehrer, called Instant Records, producing the first single by Blondie. In 1976 he formed his own label, Red Star, producing the first album by Alan Vega's avant-garde Suicide band. Although he has kept the Red Star label name alive through various reissues on LP and CD, Thau has been less active as a producer over the past 25 years. He continues to be an industry gadfly, writing for the Tres Producers website. [website: http://tres_producers. blogspot.com/.]

THEREMIN

Patented in 1928 by Leo Theremin, and commercially licensed by RCA that same year, the theremin uses an electronic oscillator as a stable reference tone of a very high frequency. It has another electronic oscillator, initially in tune with the reference, which has a variable frequency controlled by the proximity of the hand to a capacitive sensing element, usually an antenna of some sort. The difference between the two frequencies is a pitch in the audible range which is detected and amplified. Move your hand near and away from the sensing element and get musical pitches. The theremin is perhaps the first electronic musical instrument, and is unique in that it is the first musical instrument of any kind that can be played without being touched. It has been used for decades in movie and television soundtracks and rock bands, and has also been played as a serious solo instrument.

HOWARD FERSTLER

THIBAUD, JACQUES
(27 SEP 1880–1 SEP 1953)

French violinist, born in Bordeaux. He took first prize at the Paris Conservatory at age 16, and began to concertize extensively while in his teens. In 1898 he gave 54 recitals in Paris, then played through Europe, and toured in America in 1903. Highly regarded as a soloist, he was perhaps even more noteworthy in chamber music, particularly in the famous trio he formed in 1904 with Alfred Cortot and Pablo Casals. He had another fine collaborator in pianist Marguerite Long. Thibaud's long career ended in an airplane crash in the French Alps.

His earliest records were for Fonotipia around 1905: he began with the *Thais* "Meditation" (#39054) and did five other concert pieces. Later he worked for Pathe, HMV, and others. His greatest records were with the trio, including material by Schumann, Mendelssohn, Schubert, and Beethoven. In 1940 he participated in a superlative recording of the Faure Piano Quartet No. 2, made in Paris with Long, Maurice Vieux (viola), and Pierre Fournier (cello; HMV DB #5103/6). Long and Thibaud recorded Mozart's Violin Sonatas 26 and 34. He and Casals did the Brahms Double Concerto on Victor #8208/11, with Cortot conducting the Barcelona Symphony. An Angel LP, made rather poorly in Japan, reissued a selection of Thibaud's solo work from the 1930s (GR #2079; 1979).

THIELE, ALBERT NEVILLE
(4 DEC 1920–)

One of the most important modern researchers in audio and video system theory and design, including the mathematical profiling of all modern loudspeaker parameters, Thiele was born in Brisbane, Queensland, Australia. He was educated at Milton State School, Brisbane Grammar School, and the Universities of Queensland and Sydney. Interested in the reproduction and transmission of sound as a young man, he decided to study the topic formally and graduated with a bachelor's degree in mechanical and electrical engineering in 1952.

That same year, he joined EMI (Australia) Ltd., and was employed as a design engineer on special projects, including telemetry. After spending several months studying video systems in England, Scandinavia, and the U.S., he returned to Australia and led the design team that developed EMI's earliest Australian television receivers. In 1962 he joined the Australian Broadcasting Commission as a senior engineer, designing and assessing equipment and systems for sound and television broadcasting. In 1978 he was appointed assistant director of engineering for NSW (TV), responsible for engineering of ABC's Gore Hill television studios in Sydney, and in 1980 he was appointed director of engineering development and new systems applications, where he was responsible for the ABC's engineering research and development, and served in this position until his retirement from Gore Hill at the end of 1985.

In 1991 Thiele was appointed honorary visiting fellow at the University of New South Wales, and since 1994 has been honorary professional associate at the University of Sydney, where he teaches loudspeaker design in its graduate audio program. He continues to be a consulting engineer in the fields of audio, radio, television, and electronic filter design.

Thiele has published more than 70 papers on electroacoustics, network theory, testing methods, and sound and vision broadcasting in *Electronic Engineering* (U.K.), *Proc IREE* (Australia), the *Journal of the Audio Engineering Society* (U.S.), and other journals. Some of his papers, notably on loudspeaker design, television testing, and coaxial-cable equalization, have become accepted internationally as references on these topics, including origination of the Thiele-Small parameters for measuring and designing loudspeakers, and the total difference-frequency distortion measurement of audio transmission and recording.

Thiele has lectured extensively throughout the U.S., both at the university level, at Audio Engineering Society, IEE, and Institute of Electrical and Electronics Engineers conventions, and at numerous AES meetings, and in 1994 he was awarded the AES silver medal for pioneering work in loudspeaker simulation. In addition to being a fellow of the AES, and vice president of the international region from 1991 until 1993, and again in 2001, he is a member of the Society of Motion Picture and Television Engineers and a fellow of the Institution of Engineers Australia. He was president of the Institution of Radio and Electronics Engineers Australia from 1986 to 1988, and has been involved internationally in committees of the International Electrotechnical Commission (IEC) and of the Audio Engineering Society, concerned with loudspeaker design and digital audio.

See also **Bass Reflex System; Loudspeaker**

HOWARD FERSTLER

THIELE, BOB
(27 JULY 1922–30 JAN 1996)

American record producer, record company executive, songwriter, born in Brooklyn, New York. Bob Thiele started his first label, Signature Records, at age 17. In 1953 he was hired at Decca's subsidiary, Coral Records, where he signed Buddy Holly and produced numerous pop hits. He left Decca in 1960, briefly joining Dot. He joined ABC Records in 1961, where he took over the jazz subsidiary Impulse!, overseeing sessions by John Coltrane and B.B. King (for ABC/Bluesway), among many others. After leaving Impulse!, Thiele founded a series of small jazz labels, including Flying Dutchman, Blues Time, Dr. Jazz, and finally Red Baron. In 1995 he published his autobiography, *What a Wonderful World*, with Oxford University Press. As a songwriter, he is best known for "What a Wonderful World," recorded by Louis Armstrong.

WILLIAM RUHLMANN

THIELE/SMALL PARAMETERS

SEE LOUDSPEAKER; SMALL, RICHARD; THIELE, ALBERT NEVILLE

THILL, GEORGES
(14 DEC 1887–17 OCT 1984)

French tenor, born in Paris. He was a student of Fernando de Lucia in Naples, and sang at the Opéra-Comique on 15 May 1918 as Don José. His first appearance at the Opéra, in *Thais*, was a great success; he became the leading tenor of the company and remained (with interruption by World War I) until the 1940s. Thill had special acclaim for his roles in *Werther*, *Carmen*, *Faust*, *Turandot*, and Wagnerian works. He was at the Metropolitan Opera in 1930–1932, at La Scala and in Buenos Aires. He died at his home in Draguignan, France.

Thill recorded for Columbia in Paris and Milan during the 1926–1933 period. His major accomplishment was in the complete recording of *Werther*, made in 1931, with Ninon Vallin. The CD reissue of this classic (EMI Références #7-63195; 1990) won the *Gramophone* magazine award as best recording of its type. Other CD reissues include Preiser #89168, Bongiovanni #1145, and a series of CDs on the French Malibran label: #105 (a two-disc set celebrating the centenary of his birth), Sings Massenet (#103), Sings Gounod (#159), Sings Verdi (#164), and Sings Wagner (#168), all drawn from various sources.

THIRD STREAM

A style of composing and performing that blends jazz/popular idioms with the techniques of classical music. The term was first coined in the late 1940s and early 1950s to describe experiments in melding jazz and classical music by bands led by Claude Thornhill and Gil Evans. Gunther Schuller was a famous early experimenter in this style, and composer John Lewis of the Modern Jazz Quartet also took an interest in it.

33 1/3 RPM DISCS

SEE LONG-PLAYING RECORD

THOMAS, JOHN CHARLES
(6 SEP 1891–13 DEC 1960)

American baritone, born in Meyersdale, Pennsylvania. He studied at the Peabody Conservatory in Baltimore, then sang in New York musicals. Turning to the concert stage he found immediate success. He also sang opera in Brussels, Covent Garden, Chicago, and elsewhere; then at the Metropolitan Opera, with a debut on 2 Feb 1934 as Germont, and a stay of 20 years. Thomas retired to California and died in Apple Valley.

His recording career began with Edison Diamond Discs in 1914, but none of the vocal numbers he made were ever issued. His spoken voice was heard on five discs that were released, giving explanatory talks about the artists who performed on the other sides of the discs. In 1916 he was with the Lyric label, making the Forza del destino duet under the name of Enrico Martini, with Mario Chamlee, who appeared as Mario Rodolfi (Lyric #7016A). He moved to Vocalion and made 36 records from 1920 to 1923; those were mostly ballads and light opera numbers. Brunswick recorded Thomas from ca. 1924 to 1929, continuing the concert repertoire. For Victor, from 1931 to 1934, he added several operatic excerpts, from Tannhauser,

Traviata, Herodiade, and Hamlet; but he also sang popular and novelty pieces like "The Green Eyed Dragon" (#1655; 1933). In a final group for Victor, in 1938–1944, there were more opera and concert arias and also a successful series of Broadway musical numbers. He made about 250 records of hymns, for Air Arts, Inc., a firm of which he was half owner. Thomas was seen and heard on three Vitaphone short subjects of 1927, and took part in two complete opera recordings for the Unique Opera label: Barbiere di Siviglia, with Lily Pons and Ezio Pinza (129; 1938), and Traviata, with Vina Bovy and Nino Martini (#285; 1937). A selected reissue of his operatic recordings is available on Nimbus (#7838); pop and light-classical recordings from the 1920s and 1930s are included on the CD *Bluebird of Happiness: Great Original Performances* (Louisiana Red Hot #326). Thomas's papers are housed at the Peabody Institute/Johns Hopkins University Library (http://www.peabody.jhu.edu/lib/jct.html). [Morgan 1979.]

THOMAS MANUFACTURING CO.

A Dayton, Ohio, firm, established in 1903. A catalog of September 1913 (reprinted in *TMR* #54-55) described numerous products: Dayton phonograph motors, Dayton tone arms, and Dayton soundboxes. The Orchestrola and Armoniola disc players were marketed in 1916, in seven models, priced from $15–200. Later Thomas made the Portophon portable machines. When the company failed in 1926, Starr Piano Co. purchased the drawings, patents, machinery, and plant from the liquidator.

FRANK ANDREWS

THOMPSON, HANK (3 SEP 1925–)

American country singer and guitarist, born in Waco, Texas. He taught himself harmonica and guitar as a child, and performed on a Waco radio station before joining the Navy in 1943. After World War II he returned to radio, forming his own group, the Brazos Valley Boys. Capitol Records signed him and he began a fruitful 18-year association; his total record sales came to more than 30 million. He had early hits with compositions of his own, "Humpty Dumpty Heart" and "Today" (1948) and went on to about 70 chart records. His 1952 song "The Wild Side of Life" is considered one of the classic honky-tonk songs, and inspired the famous answer song, "It Wasn't God Who Made Honky Tonk Angels" by Kitty Wells. Among Thomson's later great singles were "I've Run Out of Tomorrows" (Capitol #4085; 1958) and "She's Just a Whole Lot Like You" (Capitol #4386; 1960).

After 1964 Thompson moved to Warner Records, and in 1965 he went to the Dot label, continuing to record there through 1976. His last Top 10 country hits came in 1974 with "The Older the Violin, the Sweeter the Wine" and "Who Left the Door to Heaven Open?" His later recordings suffered from the then-prevalent Nashville-pop style; many were inferior remakes of his original Capitol hits. He recorded a few singles for MCA in 1978–1979, but then did not record again until 1998, when he did an album for Curb Records of duets with new country stars like Vince Gill and Brooks and Dunn (*Real Thing*, #77925), but it failed to sell well. In 2000 he recorded *Seven Decades* for High Tone (#8121), with steel guitarist Lloyd Maines (and father of Natalie Maines of the Dixie Chicks) producing, returning him to his traditional honky-tonk sound.

There are numerous CD compilations of Thompson's recordings throughout his career. For completists, Bear Family offers a 12-CD box set presenting everything Thompson recorded for Capitol between 1947–1964 (#59042). A smaller dose of Thompson's Capitol work is available on the 20-track CD *Vintage* (Capitol #36901), recorded 1947–1961, featuring most of the classic hits.

REV. CARL BENSON

THOMPSON, WILLIAM H. (1873–24 JULY 1945)

American baritone and vaudeville artist, one of the early performers on Edison cylinders. He made about 40 cylinders as a soloist from 1902 to 1911, and also duets with Albert Campbell. The Edison 1902 list included "Sadie, Say You Won't Say Nay" (#8037), plus "In the Moonlight with the Girl You Love" (#8044), and two others. There were further duets on Edison cylinders, with Will Oakland and Albert Campbell, then recordings for U-S Everlasting Records, with Frank Coombs. Thompson cut 14 sides for Victor, in two sessions: 30 Nov 1903 and 21 June 1904. He did not record after 1913. He died in Chicago. [Walsh 1951/5.]

THORBORG, KERSTIN (19 MAY 1896–13 APR 1970)

Swedish contralto, born in Venjan. She studied and made her debut in Stockholm and was with the Royal Opera in 1924–1930. Then she sang in Berlin and Vienna, and at the Metropolitan Opera as Fricka on 21 Dec 1936, remaining until 1950 (except for the 1946–1947 season). She gave many recitals across the U.S. and Canada before retiring to Sweden, where she died in Hedemora.

She began recording for HMV in 1928, with "Mon coeur s'ouvre a ta voix" (#1626-2), and three other arias. For Odeon she sang 22 numbers, mostly in Swedish, in 1928–1933. Columbia recorded her in *Das Lied von der Erde* (#M-300) in 1936. Thorborg was renowned for her Wagnerian roles, which she finally recorded for Victor in 1940–1945. Brangaene's air from *Tristan* was an outstanding example (CS #048862; 1940). Most of the LP reissue labels offered Thorborg material; CD reissues include Preiser #89084. She is also heard on several radio transcriptions from the Metropolitan Opera, including complete versions of *Lohengrin*, *Siegfried*, and *Walkure*. Thorborg was one of those who sang in Arturo Toscanini's acclaimed rendition of Beethoven's Ninth Symphony in 1938, with Jan Peerce and Ezio Pinza (reissued on CD as Symposium #1230). [Frankensten & Bruun 1978 is a discography.]

THORNE, MIKE (25 JAN 1948–)

Born in Sunderland, in the north of England, Thorne was a natural musician and began formal classical piano lessons at the age of 10. Gradually he came to appreciate the music over which he was laboring, and by his midteens he was enthusiastically playing composers such as Schoenberg and Messiaen. While he was a committed musician, Thorne also excelled scholastically, and received his B.A. degree in physics from Oxford University in 1969.

After working as an engineer for a while and then laboring for a time as a writer for *Hi-Fi News and Record Review* (as well as editing the magazine *Studio Sound* and studying composition part-time at London's Guildhall School of Music and Drama), he decided that he would rather make music than write about it, and landed a job with EMI in 1976. After a string of successful recording jobs for the company, including working with the Sex Pistols, Kate Bush, the Buzzcocks, and others, he went on to become staff producer, in 1977, and even did some keyboard work for three albums recorded by the art/punk rock group Wire. In 1979 he left EMI and moved to New York City, where he became an independent producer, dealing with some of the hottest punk and new-wave and dance groups in the business. In 1986 he began his own studio, Stereo Society, which allowed him to solidify his position as one of the most important producers of punk, postpunk, techno-pop, and new wave over the past 20 years. From 1993 until 1996, he was also director of the Synclavier Co., a maker of computerized synthesizers, and since then he has continued with his Stereo Society studio work and also worked as the director of New Music Media Development, a branch of Warner Music International,

between 1994 and 1996. In 1994, Thorne retired from freelance record production, and in 1997 he decided to make his own recordings and develop artists for his web-based Stereo Society label.

HOWARD FERSTLER

THORNHILL, CLAUDE (10 AUG 1909–1 JULY 1965)

American pianist and Big Band leader, born in Terre Haute, Indiana. He studied at the Cincinnati Conservatory and the Curtis Institute of Music, while also playing on a riverboat. He worked for Hal Kemp and settled in New York around 1931. Then he played in Freddy Martin's band, and Paul Whiteman's. Thornhill moved frequently thereafter, performing with Benny Goodman, Leo Reisman, Ray Noble, and Andre Kostelanetz. He had a band briefly in 1937 before moving to Hollywood to freelance there. He started another band in 1940, and reorganized it after military service. In 1941 he hired young arranger Gil Evans, who made some early cool-jazz arrangements for the band during his tenure that lasted through 1945; during this period, Gerry Mulligan also contributed charts. In the 1950s and 1960s he led small groups. Thornhill died in New York.

His 1937 band recorded two sessions, one for Vocalion and one for Brunswick. The 1940 group was with Okeh, then Columbia. "Snowfall" (Columbia #36268; 1941) and "Autumn Nocturne" (Columbia #36435; 1941) were highly popular. In 1946 there was a hit with Fran Warren's vocal of "Sunday Kind of Love" (Columbia #37219). There are numerous CD reissues; *Best of the Big Bands* is a 16-track compilation of his Columbia recordings from 1941–1942 and 1946–1947 (Sony Special Products #28435), and there are various semiofficial reissues on European jazz labels, along with some air check material.

THRASH

Thrash represented a heavy metal–oriented offshoot of the hardcore punk performed by bands like Black Flag, the Minutemen, and Minor Threat. Its raw intensity stuck a responsive chord with alienated working-class youth.

The sound appears to have originated in Metallica's debut LP, *Kill 'Em All* (Megaforce MRI #069; 1983), which featured rock music stripped down to the bare essentials of speed and high volume. By the mid-1980s, groups such as Anthrax, JFA, and W*A*S*P were mining the same vein. During this time, thrash also mutated into a number of other styles, including speed metal (attributed to Megadeth, a band formed by ex-Metallica guitarist Dave Mustaine), death metal (featuring lyrics preoccupied with death and destruction; among the leading exponents were Slayer, Carcass, Napalm Death, Cadaver, and Morbid Angel), and grindcore (death metal crossed with industrial rhythms). [Romanowski and George-Warren 1995.]

FRANK HOFFMANN

THREE KAUFIELDS

A male vocal trio that recorded for Emerson around 1919. Members were Irving Kaufman, Jack Kaufman, and Arthur Fields. Fields and one or the other of the Kaufman brothers also recorded as the Two Kaufields.

THURAS, ALBERT L.

See Loudspeaker

3M

See Minnesota Mining and Manufacturing Co. (3M)

THX

A Lucasfilm Corp. performance certification program for A/V hardware and software. Although the program began with movie theaters (the first film shown in a THX-certified theater was *Return of the Jedi*), it later spread to home-theater equipment and even discs and tapes. THX certification involves quality-control and compatibility standards for hardware and software, but it also involves special emendations to those standards for supposedly enhanced performance, particularly if every component in a home A/V system (players, speakers, processors, amplifiers, and even wires) is so certified.

See also **Dolby Surround Sound; Motion Picture Sound Recording; Surround Sound**

HOWARD FERSTLER

TIBBETT, LAWRENCE (16 NOV 1896–15 JULY 1960)

American baritone, born in Bakersfield, California. His surname was Tibbet, but he gracefully accepted the extra "t" when it appeared as a misprint in an opera program. He was a sheriff's son, and worked as a cowboy. Then he took up Shakespearean acting, served in the Navy during World War I, and became a singer. He made his Metropolitan Opera debut on 24 Jan 1923, and remained with the company to 1950. Tibbett sang

396 times with the Metropolitan in New York and 163 times on tour with them. He portrayed 52 different roles in his lifetime, 48 of them at the Metropolitan. In addition to his star roles as Escamillo, Rigoletto, Scarpia, Ford, Tonio, and Iago, he performed in the premieres of significant American works: *Merry Mount*, *Emperor Jones*, *Peter Ibbetson*, and *King's Henchman*. He made six motion pictures, including *Metropolitan*, *New Moon*, and *Under Your Spell*. In the 1940s he crossed over to the radio program *Your Hit Parade*, giving uneven renditions of such material as "Accentuate the Positive" and "Don't Fence Me In"; unfortunately his magnificent voice had begun to crumble by then.

Tibbett's first records were made in 1927 for Victor: "Believe Me, If All Those Endearing Young Charms" (#1238), "Calm as the Night" (#3043), "Drink to Me Only With Thine Eyes" (#1238) and the "Prologo" from *Pagliacci*. In 1929–1930 he sang arias from *King's Henchman*, and a powerful "Te Deum" from *Tosca* coupled with the "Toreador Song," splendidly demonstrating the smokey resonance of his voice. A fine series of airs from John Stainer's oratorio *The Crucifixion* was made in 1929. "Standin' in the Need of Prayer" from *Emperor Jones* was a remarkable disc of 1934 (#7959). Tibbett also inscribed a Wagnerian set in 1934, excerpts from Act III of *Walkure*, with Leopold Stokowski and the Philadelphia Orchestra. "Without a Song" (#1507; 1931) was a popular light number. From *Porgy and Bess* there were memorable renditions of "It Ain't Necessarily So" (#11878), "I Got Plenty o' Nuttin'" (#11880), and an ineffable duet with Helen Jepson, "Bess, You Is My Woman Now." There are numerous CD reissues of Tippett's work. A CD of his greatest operatic material (*Porgy* included) appeared in 1990 from RCA (#87808); other reissues include Pearl #9307 and #9452, Nimbus #7825 and #7881 (the later includes material from Porgy and Bess and soundtrack material from Tibbett's film appearances), and *Lawrence Tibbett on Stage, 1926–39* (Enterprise #1161). [Bullard and Moran 1977 is a discography.]

TICO (LABEL)

Latin-jazz and salsa label founded by nightclub owner George Goldner in 1948. Goldner ran a successful string of New York clubs catering to Latin music fans, so it was natural that he would begin recording the popular acts who performed there. Early stars including Tito Puente, who remained with the label through 1958 when he signed with major label RCA Victor; however, Puente would return to Tico in the 1960s. Machito, a longtime Latin jazz bandleader, also recorded extensively for the label from its early days. The label's motto was "King of the Cha Cha Mambo," emblazed on the label across the Tico name. Goldner sold Tico in 1957 to Morris Levy along with his rock and R&B labels Rama and Gee, but in a tangled history he somehow continued to issue albums under the Tico name through 1974. At that time, the label's assets were purchased by the New York Latin label Fania Records.

CARL BENSON

TILTON, MARTHA (12 NOV 1918–)

American popular vocalist. She began professionally on radio in Los Angeles in 1935, and joined Jimmy Dorsey for a time in 1936. In 1937 she became a member of Benny Goodman's band, and made the hit record "And the Angels Sing" (Victor #26170). In the 1940s she freelanced and made some fine discs like "I'll Walk Alone" (Capitol #157; 1944) and "Stranger in Town"/"I Should Care" (Capitol #184; 1944). Tilton was on the radio show *Your Hit Parade* in 1947, and in the 1956 film *Benny Goodman Story*. Collectors Choice offers the complete Capitol recordings on *The Liltin' Miss Tilton* (#142). *The Complete Standard Transcriptions* (Soundies #4119) includes 21 radio transcriptions made in 1941, as well as some live recordings from a decade later.

TIM

SEE TRANSIENT INTERMODULATION DISTORTION (TIM)

TIMBRE

The tone color or tone quality of a musical sound. Timbre varies with different patterns of harmonics generated as a tone is produced; it is the principal basis for the audible differences among musical instruments when they play the same pitches. Since many of the harmonics that give specific instruments their identifiable tone color are in the upper range of the audio spectrum, early acoustic recordings (unable to capture that portion of the range) failed to give recognizable representations of numerous instruments, the piano among them. While today's studio recording apparatus is capable of dealing with all timbre problems, some playback equipment may be so poor — e.g., cheap portable cassette players — as to recall the performance limitations of the acoustic era.

TIMELY TUNES (LABEL)

A low-priced label ($.35) introduced by RCA Victor in April 1931, offering dance music and some jazz.

Shortlived RCA budget label from 1931. Courtesy Kurt Nauck/Nauck's Vintage Records

Issues ceased three months later. Most artists appeared under pseudonyms. [Rust 1978.]

TINFOIL PHONOGRAPH

The first cylinder phonograph of Thomas A. Edison, constructed according to his design by John Kruesi and Charles Batchelor between 4–6 Dec 1877. Edison's basic sketch was completed on 29 Nov 1877. "Mary Had a Little Lamb" was the first phrase successfully repeated by the tinfoil phonograph. Edison filed a patent application for the device on 24 Dec 1877, and received U.S. patent #200,521 on 19 Feb 1878. [Koenigsberg 1987].

See also **Cylinder**

TINY TIM (12 APR 1932–30 NOV 1996)

Tiny Tim's strange appearance (long, stringy hair and ill-fitting, hippie clothing) and warbling renditions of Tin Pan Alley chestnuts made him the most popular camp novelty artist of the late 1960s. Born Herbert Khaury, in New York City, he spent many years perfecting his act under pseudonyms such as Darry Dover and Larry Love. By the mid-1960s, he began building a cult audience, singing to his own ukulele accompaniment at adult nightclubs and, by 1968, in rock venues such as the Fillmores East and West. After appearing on *The Tonight Show* (NBC), he became an instant celebrity; he became a frequent guest on the Carson program as well as *Laugh-In*. His marriage to 17-year-old

Victoria May "Miss Vicky" Budinger was broadcast on *The Tonight Show*, 15 Dec 1969, allegedly drawing the widest audience in the show's long history.

Tiny Tim's notoriety earned him a recording contract with the Reprise label. His debut album release, *God Bless Tiny Tim* (Reprise #6292; 1968) reached number seven on the pop charts, fueled by the Top 20 hit, "Tip-Toe Thru' the Tulips with Me" (Reprise #0679; 1968). However, follow-up LP releases did not sell well. Out of the public spotlight by the early 1970s, he continued to perform live, and occasionally appeared on television, most notably the MTV game show, *Lip Service*. He professed that his greatest show business thrill consisted of meeting — and sometimes performing with — many of the crooning era singers (e.g., Nick Lucas, Rudy Vallee) he had modeled himself after.

Tim made a number of "comebacks" through the mid-1990s and continued to record and perform. He died following a Saturday night performance in Minneapolis, suffering a heart attack while singing his signature song, "Tip Toe Through the Tulips."

FRANK HOFFMANN

TITELMAN, RUSS (16 AUG 1944–)

Relatively unknown outside of the record industry, Russ Titelman has nevertheless been highly influential as a songwriter, session musician, and producer. Born in Los Ageles, Titelman started out contributing guitar work and vocals on demos and records (e.g., the Paris Sisters, the Spectors Three) for Phil Spector. In the early 1960s, he became a staff writer for Don Kirshner's Brill Building firm, Aldon Music, collaborating with such notables as Gerry Goffin and Carole King. He went on play guitar on the television program, *Shindig*, in 1965, and found steady work as a songwriter (his credits included "Gone Dead Train," which appeared in the film, *Performance*) and studio musician.

Following his production debut on Little Feat's eponymous album (Warner Bros. #1890; 1970), Titelman was promoted to an A&R executive post. He would continue in that capacity until 1997, working with George Benson, Eric Clapton, Ry Cooder, Rickie Lee Jones, Ladysmith Black Mambazo, Randy Newman, Rufus, Paul Simon, James Taylor, and Steve Winwood, often coproducing with Lenny Waronker. Titelman's trademark was the ability to pack a maximum amount of music into the overall mix while making the result sound natural and effortless. According to Daniel Levitin, "Part of this is engineering, but most of it is arrangement, giving the parts the right room and space within which to breathe."

Titelman has received Grammys for Best Record with Clapton's "Tears in Heaven" (Duck/Reprise #19038; 1992; #2) and Album of the Year with *Unplugged* (Duck/Reprise #45024; 1992; #2). The latter's success provided the impetus for a wave of MTV "unplugged" releases. He presently serves on the board of governors for the New York chapter of NARAS.

FRANK HOFFMANN

TLC

A calculated blend of image and studio production, the Atlanta-based TLC became one of the most successful female recording groups in history during the 1990s. Founded and managed by rhythm and blues singer, Pebbles, the hip-hop trio — consisting of Tionne "T-Boz" Watkins, Lisa "Left-Eye" Lopes, and Rozonda "Chilli" Thomas — exuded a spirited verve that has enabled them to transcend their playful, cartoonish image.

TLC's first album, *Oooooooohhh … On the TLC Tip* (LaFace #26003; 1992; 4 million-seller), owed much of its popularity to the deft use of cutting-edge producers such as L.A. Reid, Babyface, and Daryl Simmons — "Baby-Baby-Baby" (LaFace #24028; 1992; #2; platinum award) — and Dallas Austin — "Hat 2 Da Back" (LaFace #14043; 1993; #30). Another of the LP's tracks, "Ain't 2 Proud 2 Beg" (LaFace #24008; 1992; #6; platinum award), was a studio tour de force, incorporating samples from James Brown's "Escape-ism," Kool & the Gang's "Jungle Boogie," Average White Band's "School Boy Crush," Silver Convention's "Fly, Robin, Fly," and Bob James's "Take Me to the Mardi Gras."

While generally considered less accomplished from an artistic standpoint, the follow-up, *CrazySexyCool* (LaFace #26009; 1994; #1), sold over 10 million copies, driven by the singles "Creep" (LaFace #24082; 1994; #1; platinum award), "Red Light Special" (LaFace #24097; 1995; #2; gold record), "Waterfalls" (LaFace #24107; 1995; #1; platinum award), and "Diggin' on You" (LaFace #24119; 1995; #5; gold record). The third album, *Fanmail* (LaFace #26055; 1999; #1; platinum award) — which included the million-sellers "No Scrubs" (LaFace #24385; 1999; #1) and "Unpretty" (LaFace #24424; 1999; #1) — maintained TLC's commercial momentum. It is unclear whether the group will remain intact following the untimely death of Lopes in early 2002.

FRANK HOFFMANN

TOLLEFSEN TRIO

An instrumental group that recorded for Edison Diamond Discs in 1915. They were Carl Henry

Tollefsen, violin; Augusta Tollefsen, piano; and Michael Penha, cello. One number is listed in Wile and Dethlefson [1990], "Pastel — Menuet" (#80241).

TOMMY BOY MUSIC (LABEL)

Rap/hip-hop label founded by Tom Silverman in 1981, working out of his apartment. His first release was the seminal "Planet Rock" single by Afrika Bambaataa and the Soul Sonic Force; it quickly sold over 600,000 copies, going gold, an incredible feat for a 12-inch single. The label quickly signed other seminal rap/hip-hop acts, including Queen Latifah, Naughty by Nature, De La Soul, and Coolio. In the 1980s, the label expanded into dance music and industrial/electronic bands (Information Society). In 1986, AOL-Time Warner bought a half share in the label, and then purchased the balance of the company five years later. The label was somewhat lost in the larger organization during the 1990s, and Silverman felt a lack of creative freedom there. So, in early 2002 he bought back the label, relaunching it as an independent. [website: http://tommyboy.materialinmotion.com/ customer/home.php.]

TONE ARM

Often written as one word: tonearm. The usually pivoted device in an analog disc record player that holds the cartridge and playback stylus. The stylus tip is propelled across the record surface by the groove wall, and the tone arm moves to accommodate the traverse. In early acoustic systems the hollow tone arm carried the needle/diaphragm vibrations to the horn. In electrical systems the tone arm includes wires that transmits the electrical signals generated by the stylus/cartridge combination to the preamplifier and after "preamplification," to the amplifier. In upscale systems, with upscale cartridge/stylus combinations, normally the downward stylus tracking force is between one and two grams, allowing proper tracking without bringing damaging pressure to bear on the grooves.

The position of the tone arm should ensure that it locates the stylus on a tangent to the record groove. The stylus assembly should always be at a right angle to the groove being tracked. This kind of perfection over the full disc surface is not possible with pivoted arms, since the arm ascribes an arc as the stylus traverses the disc surface. The technical compromise has been to use a bent tone arm: one that keeps the stylus reasonably close to tangent all the way across the disc. Longer arms also help to minimize the problem, but the downside is increased arm mass, which can impact dynamic tracking pressure with even moderately warped recordings. Radial- or linear-tracking arms, which move straight across the disc on a low-friction carriage, have no problems with tangent error. The vertical tracking angle of the stylus has traditionally been about 15 degrees, and good tone arms allow one to adjust the cartridge body for this kind of angle.

A tone arm may be an integral part of the turntable or sold as a separate item that is custom installed on a blank turntable. Separate tone arms can give superior performance but are expensive and may be relatively difficult to install. If this is not done properly the arm may perform worse than integral arms that have been factory installed. The arm must also be free of audible resonances that lead to sympathetic vibrations, and there must be synergy between the arm mass, cartridge mass, and stylus behavior for such vibrations to not be a problem.

The earliest phonograph with a distinct tone arm, as opposed to a stylus/diaphragm attached directly to the horn, was the Echophone invented in 1895. Eldridge Johnson made a key improvement by inventing the tapered tone arm (U.S. patent #814,786; filed 12 Feb 1903; granted 13 Mar 1906), allowing "the sound waves to advance with a regular, steady, and natural increase in their wave fronts in a manner somewhat similar to ordinary musical instruments." The tapered-arm patent was held by Victor, which used it in constant litigation against imitators. The arm was first used on the Victor IV of April 1903. February 1905 advertising from Zonophone announced its "Gibson Patent Tapering Sound Arm."

Major advances in tone arm design followed the research of Percy Wilson in the early 1920s; he attacked the problem of tracking error through mathematical analysis, devising an "overlap and offset" method for achieving the correct tracking angle and overhang. E.G. Lîfgren, H.G. Baerwald, B.B. Bauer, J.D. Seagrave, and J.K. Stevenson wrote significant papers on the same problem of tracking distortion in the 1938–1966 period. Frederick Hunt, although writing primarily on record wear, contributed important findings on tracking force in a 1962 paper. Skating force was effectively addressed by having enough vertical pressure to ensure that the stylus sat firmly anchored in the groove, although other solutions followed once it was seen that low tracking pressures greatly reduced record wear.

The Garrard company introduced articulated tone arms in record changers, to give near-zero lateral tracking angle error, although the downside of this design was increased lateral friction and arm mass. The above-noted radial tone arm, which rides on a straight rail instead of pivoting in an arc from its base at the corner of the turntable, was made commercially viable in the early 1980s, although it had appeared some time before then. It combined low arm mass, straight-line tracking, zero tracking error, and zero skating force. However, in practice it was not judged to be audibly superior to the finest pivoting arms. Also, it was complex and expensive, and the typical short arm length magnified problems with warp wow.

Other features in the latest-generation tone arms included cueing mechanisms, height adjustments, vertical tracking angle adjustments, antiscating compensation, and damping mechanisms. The overall trend in later designs evolved toward lower mass, which allowed for still lower tracking pressures. A problem not fully dealt with at the end of the LP era was the electrostatic attraction of the tone arm by the records in the stack of a record changer, and the fact that the vertical tracking angle would change as the stack piled up. [Kogen 1977; Mitchell 1982.]

See also **Cartridge (II)**

REV. HOWARD FERSTLER

TONE CONTROL

A knob on an audio or audio/video receiver or preamplifier that adjusts the relative balance of treble, midrange, or bass. Most preamp control sections have separate bass and treble tone controls, and some also include a midrange control. In many cases, each channel will have its own set, and some preamplifier units will have switches that allow one to configure different roll-off slopes for each of the tone controls. Some also include a spectral-tilt control that slightly rotates the entire audible spectrum around a specific frequency in the midrange. A tone control can be used to adjust for minor frequency imbalances in a recording (not unusual with older releases), correct for room acoustics problems, or compensate for loudspeaker deficiencies.

See also **Controls; Equalization (EQ)**

TONE TESTS

A puzzling phenomenon of recording history, consisting of recitals sponsored by the Thomas A. Edison Co. to illustrate the quality of Edison Diamond Discs. In those recitals, which were held from 1915 to 1925, singers or instrumentalists would perform a program in partnership with Diamond Disc recordings and would from time to time cease their live performances, allowing the disc to continue the music. A darkened stage permitted the performer to slip away, and the audience would not have been aware of that departure until the lights went back on. The point was to demonstrate that the audience would be unable to distinguish between the live performance and the recorded version. Difficult as it is for those of a later generation to believe that such suspension of disbelief might have occurred on the wide scale that it apparently did, all contemporary reports testify that the illusion was remarkable.

Although special pressings were made of the Diamond Discs used in the tone tests, to minimize the surface noise that plagued regular issues until about 1924, there was no way to improve upon the limited audio frequency range of the acoustic process: about 1,000 to 2,000 or 3,000 Hz.

The earliest test to be reported in the press was held in February 1915 in New York. Participants were Christine Miller, Elizabeth Spencer, Donald Chalmers, and John Young. It was organized by a man named Hallowell, who was succeeded by Verdi E.B. Fuller, a superintendent for Thomas A. Edison, Inc. There was then a test held for a dealers' group in August 1915, followed by a series of national tests. Alice Verlet sang a tone test recital in Orchestra Hall, Chicago; as reported in *TMW* of 15 Dec 1915 there was no claim that the audience was unable to distinguish between voice and machine. But an advertisement in *TMW* on 15 Jan 1916 stated that observers found it "almost impossible" to tell the difference; and by 15 May 1916 the Edison advertisements were saying that audiences found it "impossible" to make the distinction.

Newspaper critics offered glowing praise, in statements that were quoted in Edison promotional material. Among the quotations given in a 1919 publication were: "Impossible to distinguish between the singer's living voice and its re-creation by the musical instrument …" (*Boston Herald*); "No one in the audience … could tell which was the real and which the reproduced" (*Brooklyn Daily Eagle*); "A convincing demonstration of the power of a man to produce tone from an instrument so perfectly as to defy detection when compared side by side with the tone of the original producing artists" (*Musical America*).

Artists who engaged in tone tests included Anna Case, Thomas Chalmers, Arthur Collins, Byron G. Harlan, Frieda Hempel, Mario Laurenti, Margarete Matzenauer, Arthur Middleton, Marie Rappold, Elizabeth Spencer, Maggie Teyte, Jacques Urlus, Alice Verlet, and Giovanni Zenatello. It was during a tone test that Arthur Collins fell into a trap door on the darkened stage, sustaining injuries that affected his career.

Albany, New York, was the site of the largest tone test audience, as 6,000 teachers heard Laurenti sing in the State Armory; they were reportedly unable to detect any difference between disc and the person.

More than 4,000 tests were held by the end of 1920. Overseas tests were reported from Liverpool (England) in 1923, and Melbourne (Australia) in 1924. Mexico City was a site in 1923. The final notice of one of these events appeared in the *TMW* of 15 Aug 1925.

One of the tone test singers may have offered a partial solution to the puzzle of the illusion created by the tone tests, in saying that the performers endeavored to imitate the records. This possibility was explicitly denied in Edison promotional material. Surely there was at least imitation of volume. A remarkable comment by Albert Spalding is more directed toward the persuasiveness of the recordings themselves: he observed that nobody could have distinguished between the live artist and the record, but that on modern records (he was speaking in 1953) anybody could. Frow suggests that the illusion was accomplished because "the world was a simpler place, people were simpler too."

On occasion Brunswick and other labels conducted demonstrations of their products in live/recorded recitals, but it is not reported that they carried out the dramatic lights-out routine of the Edison tests. [Frow 1982.]

TOOLE, FLOYD (19 JUNE 19 1938–)

A major researcher in audio systems and design, Toole was born in Moncton, New Brunswick, Canada, and studied electrical engineering at the University of New Brunswick, receiving a B.Sc. in 1961. He then attended the Imperial College of Science and Technology, University of London, where he received a Ph.D., also in electrical engineering, in 1965. Upon graduation, he joined the National Research Council, in Ottawa, Canada, in the Acoustics and Signal Processing Group. There, he expanded his interests into the complicated interactions of room acoustics and loudspeakers, particularly as they related to the psychoacoustic relationship between what listeners hear and the technical measurements that are used in the design and evaluation of audio products.

The research resulted in improved methods for subjective evaluations and technical measurements. For a paper on this subject he received the Audio Engineering Society (AES) Publications award in 1988. Later work focused on one of the fundamental problems in audio, the perception and measurement of resonances, for which (with Sean Olive) he received the 1990 AES Publications award.

In 1991 he joined Harman International Industries, Inc., in Northridge, California, where he is corporate vice president of acoustical engineering. In 1998 he was appointed to the additional position of senior vice president of acoustical engineering for the Harman Consumer Group.

Dr. Toole has published several papers in the journals of the AES and Acoustical Society of America (ASA), numerous AES preprints, chapters in two audio engineering handbooks, the entry on "Sound-Reproducing Systems" for the 9th edition of McGraw-Hill's *Encyclopedia of Science and Technology*, and dozens of articles in consumer audio publications. He is a fellow of the AES, a member of the ASA, a past president of the AES and, in 1997, he was awarded the AES silver medal award, presented in recognition of outstanding developments in the subjective and objective evaluation of audio devices.

HOWARD FERSTLER

TOPIC RECORDS (LABEL)

Famed British folk label, founded in 1939 as an outgrowth of the Workers' Music Association. Originally associated with union and liberal political groups, the label released early recordings by British folksingers A.L. Lloyd and Ewan MacColl through the 1950s and early 1960s, along with licensed material from U.S. folksingers. During the folk revival of the 1960s, the label grew under the direction of Gerry Sharp, attracting younger performers like the Northumbrian folk instrumental group the High Level Ranters, the vocal harmony group the Watersons, and traditional singers like Jeannie Robertson and Joe Heaney. Many of these recordings were produced by Bill Leader, one of the leading folk producers on the British scene at the time. (Leader took many of his acts with him to his own Leader/Trailer labels in the early 1970s.) In the mid-1970s, following Sharp's death, Tony Engle took charge of the label, and began signing more contemporary acts. A major coup was signing Martin Carthy in 1976 to the label; he had previously recorded for larger labels and had a strong world following. Other 1970s era acts included the Battlefield Band, Dick Gaughan, and Shirley and Dolly Collins. In the late 1970s, Engle partnered with Tony Russell to form String Records for reissues of Western Swing material, but the label was short-lived. During the CD era, Topic has reissued many of its earlier recordings, while continuing to issue new material by a core group of key members of the British folk revival. [website: www.topicrecords.co.uk.]

CARL BENSON

TORMÉ, MEL
(13 SEP 1925–5 JUNE 1999)

American popular singer, born in Chicago. He played piano and drums, and composed, performing as a child in vaudeville and then on radio. After military service in World War II he achieved popularity as a solo singer, nicknamed "Velvet Fog." In later years he developed a jazzy scat style and his greatest successes, capped by a brilliant series of appearances and records with George Shearing in the mid-1980s. "Try a Little Tenderness" (Musicraft #381; 1946) exemplified his "foggy" lyric style; "One for My Baby" (Musicraft #15107; 1947) was his famous dialogue with bartender Joe. "Stranger in Town," one of his two most acclaimed compositions — the other was "The Christmas Song" — was recorded for Capitol (#2529) in 1953. Torme recorded for several labels in his early career, including Capitol (1949–1951), Bethlehem (early to mid-1950s), Verve (1959–1961), Atlantic (1962–1963), and MGM (1964); after that, his style of music went out of favor, and Torme only recorded sporadically until 1982 when he signed with the Concord Jazz label, with which he remained for the rest of his career. His first album for Concord, *An Evening with George Shearing and Mel Torme* (#190), was a Grammy winner. Tormé received another Grammy, as best male jazz vocalist, for a second collaboration with Shearing, the 1983 album *Top Drawer* (Concord #219). (Tormé and Shearing's complete output for Concord Jazz has been reissued on CD in a boxed set [#2144].) Tormé continued to record and tour until suffering a massive stroke in 1996. Three years later, he died in Los Angeles.

There are numerous CD collections of his work. Rhino #71589 is a four-CD set that gives a career overview, minus his later work for Concord; Rhino also issued *At the Movies* (#75841), drawn from his film soundtrack work, mostly from the 1940s. There are numerous other samplers of his work for various labels, including *Spotlight On* (Capitol #89941), drawn from his 1949–1951 recordings for that label; and *Compact Jazz* (Verve #833282), 16 tracks from his years with that label. There are numerous other reissues on nostalgia and jazz labels, both domestic and foreign.

TORRIANI, MADAME

A soprano who recorded for Bettini. In the June 1898 catalog she had 12 numbers, beginning with "Chimes of Normandy" and including arias from five operas; eight of those numbers appeared again in the 1899 catalog.

TORTELIER, PAUL
(24 MAR 1914–18 DEC 1990)

French cellist, born in Paris. He took first prize at the Paris Conservatory at age 16, and made his debut at

17. He was first cellist in the orchestra at Monte Carlo from 1935 to 1937, then played with the Boston Symphony Orchestra in 1937–1939. Tortelier performed widely as a soloist and in chamber ensembles. He lived in Israel in 1955–1956, then joined the faculty of the Paris Conservatory. Tortelier made an acclaimed recording of the Elgar Concerto, with Malcolm Sargent and the London Philharmonic Orchestra (Angel #S-37029), and another of the Brahms Double Concerto with Christian Ferras (Seraphim #S-60048). His Fauré sonatas with Jean Hubeau, and Vivaldi sonatas with Robert Veyron-Lacroix (recorded for Erato) were outstanding, and his *Don Quixote* for HMV with Thomas Beecham was definitive (now on EMI #63106). He continued performing into an advanced age, and died at Manoir de Villarceaux, near Paris.

TOSCANINI, ARTURO
(25 MAR 1867–16 JAN 1957)

Italian conductor and cellist, born in Parma. He entered the Parma Conservatory at age nine, and graduated with a first prize in cello in 1885. He was cellist with an Italian opera troupe in Rio de Janeiro, in 1886, when he had the opportunity to substitute for the regular conductor in a performance of Aida; from then he pursued a conducting career. Back in Italy he conducted the 1892 premiere of *Pagliacci*, and the 1896 premiere of *Boheme*. His genius was recognized by an appointment as chief conductor of La Scala at age 31; a post he held from 1898 to 1903, and again from 1906 to 1908. He was principal conductor at the Metropolitan Opera from 1908 to 1913, and also conducted orchestral concerts in New York. Toscanini returned to La Scala as artistic director in 1921–1929; but he was again invited to the U.S. and conducted the newly merged New York Philharmonic-Symphony Orchestra from 1928 to 1936. Meanwhile, he had been the first non-German to conduct at Bayreuth, in 1930–1931. The NBC Symphony Orchestra was formed for him to conduct in 1937, and he brought it to world stature, remaining with it to 1954, when he retired. When he died in New York, he was widely considered to have been the greatest conductor of his time.

Toscanini's major accomplishments were in performances and recordings of Beethoven, Brahms, Verdi, and Wagner. His repertoire was limited in the moderns, though he did make a definitive disc of Samuel Barber's *Adagio for Strings*. In 1921 he began recording for Victor, with the La Scala Orchestra, doing a miscellaneous group of 10 12-inch and six 10-inch sides. The first item was Ildebrando Pizzetti's

"Quay of the Port of Famagusta" (#64952). There were two Beethoven movements and two Mozart movements; the other material was of a lighter character. Beethoven symphonies were recorded in the 1930s and in the 1950s, seven of them at least twice, giving collectors much ground for comparison and speculation. Toscanini never had a perfect combination of a great orchestra with a great hall to record in; Carnegie Hall and the NBC studio 8H being deficient in spaciousness. He apparently preferred faster tempos as he grew older, though it could be said that he had become more passionate about the scores. Those who wish to examine such questions have the RCA five-CD set (#60324; 1990) which gives all the symphonies in performances from 1939 to 1952. Other definitive Verdi recordings include the RCA CD set #60326 (seven discs), which features *Falstaff* (from radio broadcasts of 1950); *Aida* (from broadcasts of 1949); and the *Requiem* (from a 1951 broadcast, with the Robert Shaw Chorale).

Outstanding interpretations of the Brahms orchestral works were made in the 1940s and 1950s, reissued on an RCA CD set of four discs (#60325; 1990). BMG Classics released his complete Victor recordings on a limited edition, 71-CD set during the 1990s; portions of this material has subsequently appeared on RCA/Red Seal in individual sets under the general title *The Immortal Toscanini*. Even though massive production did not capture all of the maestro's recorded legacy, a large portion of it has been acquired by the Arturo Toscanini Society, founded in 1968, collector of a huge body of material from American and European air shots. There were 800 tapes and 1,000 transcriptions in the Society's library, according to a 1973 account, the last year that the Society issued any material; a British society was founded in 1986 to carry the work forward. Naxos has issued a series of CDs presenting complete concert recordings that were originally broadcast on NBC radio between 1933–1942 as the *Concert Edition* (#110801-844). Collectors Choice has issued a four-CD set of V-Disc recordings made for the armed forces during World War II (#35774). There are many other releases available on a variety of labels.

The largest Toscanini collection is at the New York Public Library, Performing Arts Research Center (Lincoln Center); that collection is "one of the greatest archives ever to document a single career" [McCormick and Winner]. Assembled in the family home at Riverdale, New York, the collection was deposited with the library in 1970. It was not until 1985 that negotiations between the library and the family were completed, and funding was received, from Wanda Toscanini Horowitz, to begin work on processing the archive. It includes such unique items as 4,600 acetate discs of rehearsals and performances; 1,789 test pressings of released performances and 799 test pressings of unreleased performances; and several thousand tape reels of rehearsals, air shots, and concerts. There is also an enormous documentation of published and manuscript material. [Gray 1973 describes the Arturo Toscanini Society; McCormick and Winner 1989 describes the New York archive; its website: http://www.nypl.org/research/lpa/mus/mus.majcoll.html.]

TOUGH, DAVE (26 APR 1908 [SOME SOURCES GIVE 1907]–6 DEC 1948)

American jazz drummer, born in Oak Park, Illinois. In his student days he played with the Austin High School Gang and then with various Chicago groups. In 1927 he went to Europe and freelanced. In the 1930s he was with Benny Goodman occasionally and with Tommy Dorsey for two years. Tough was afflicted with ill health and hardly ever stayed long with one group. His finest period was with Woody Herman in 1944–1945; he took the *Downbeat* award in 1945 and 1946. He died in Newark, New Jersey.

Tough's brilliant work with Herman is heard to advantage in "Caldonia"/"Happiness Is Just a Thing Called Joe" (Columbia #36789; 1945) and "Bijou"/"Put that Ring on My Finger" (Columbia #36861; 1945). Columbia reissued the Herman sessions on LP #6049. In 1947 he made a fine disc of "Stop 'n' Go"/"Pina Colada" with the progressive jazz group of Charlie Ventura (National #9066).

TOUREL, JENNIE (22 JUNE 1900–23 NOV 1973)

Russian-American soprano and mezzo-soprano, born Jennie Davidovich in St. Petersburg. She studied flute and piano, and after the Revolution went to Paris to begin vocal studies. Inspired by her teacher Anna El-Tour, she took a stage name fashioned from hers. In 1930 she made her opera debut in Chicago, singing a role in the American premiere of *Lorenzaccio* by Ernest Moret; in 1931 she made her European opera debut in Paris, and sang in many European houses. Her Metropolitan Opera debut, as Mignon, was on 15 May 1937. She remained in the U.S., taking citizenship in 1946, and sang with the Metropolitan in 1943–1945 and 1946–1947. She portrayed Mignon, Carmen, and Rosina in her last season. Tourel was brilliant in recitals, specializing in Rachmaninoff and other Russian song composers and in the French repertoire. She also taught at the Juilliard School. She died in New York.

Two LP discs from Odyssey (#32880; 1976) cover important material from Tourel's wide repertoire. *Carmen* arias, Debussy songs, and Rossini numbers are included. Missing from that memorial issue were her remarkable Rachmaninoff songs, with Erich Itor-Kahn at the piano, recorded for Columbia (#M-625). Another fine Columbia recording was *Alexander Nevsky* with the Philadelphia Orchestra and Westminster Choir (#M-580). A CD of her work recorded for Decca and related labels, including both popular and light classical material, is available from Philips (#467907); *Jennie Tourel in Opera and Concert, 1944–46* is another sampling, drawn from New York City and San Francisco Opera company appearances; it also includes an interview with Tourel (Eklipse #51). *Live at Alice Tully Hall* is a two-CD set most likely recorded in the 1950s (Vox #5126).

TOURNAPHONE

A German disc player marketed in the U.K. in 1906. Three models are illustrated in Chew [1981], one of them the Baby Tournaphone.

TOUSSAINT, ALLEN (14 JAN 1938–)

New Orleans born pianist/arranger/producer/recording engineer who is famed for his work on numerous R&B and rock sessions of the 1960s. As a teenager, Toussaint began playing with a local doo-wop group, the Falmingos, and by 17 he was sessioning for Smiley Lewis, Earl King, and Fats Domino. In 1957 he was befriended by Dave Bartholomew, Domino's producer, leading to a job as a staff musician for RCA a year later; he recorded a solo album in 1958, *The Wild Sounds of New Orleans* (RCA #1767), billed as Al Tousan. In 1960, he was hired by local businessman Joe Banashak to oversee his Minit label; there, Toussaint produced, arranged, and performed on recordings by Irma Thomas, Aaron Neville, Jesse Hill, Lee Dorsey, and Ernie K-Doe, among others, through 1963, when he was drafted into the Army. After his release in 1965, he returned to New Orleans and performing and producing, partnering with local producer Marshall Sehorn to form Sansu Enterprises, a record label and production company. Sansu's houseband became known as the Meters, and they scored several hits during the late 1960s and early 1970s. In 1971 Toussaint released his first solo album since his debut on Sire Records, and then cut three albums for Reprise from 1972–1975. Also in 1972, with Sehorn, he opened his own studio, Sea-Saint, which became a favorite for local acts and visiting performers like Paul Simon and Paul McCartney when they were looking for a New

Orleans sound. He continued to produce through the 1970s, notably overseeing Dr. John's hit "Right Place, Wrong Time" and Labelle's "Lady Marmalade." In 1978 he made another solo album. Toussaint remained active over the next 20 years in his studio. In 1996 Toussaint started a new label, NYNO, issuing another solo album, and in 1998 he was inducted into the Rock and Roll Hall of Fame in the nonperformer category.

CARL BENSON

TOY RECORDS

Small discs (usually five to seven inches in diameter) intended for children, often sold with small record players. Thomas Edison held a patent for toy and doll cylinder phonographs (U.S. #423,039; filed 2 July 1889; granted 11 Mar 1890), but exploited only the doll. Emile Berliner marketed toy Gramophones in 1889 in Germany, with five-inch "plates." In view of the repertoire on those plates, it may be that the product was miniature in size but not necessarily for children. In December 1900 the Consolidated Talking Machine Co., immediate predecessor of Victor, advertised a Toy Gram-O-Phone for $3, with six records and 100 needles included.

After World War I there were several sets of toy records, in the U.S. Mother Goose Records were distributed by Emerson Phonograph Co. in 1920. Harper Brothers issued Bubble Books in 1919. Both the Emerson and the Harper releases were combinations of children's books with small discs.

In U.K. there were numerous examples in the 1920s. The Bob-o-Link Talking Book was offered from 1922. Other labels in the field included Little Marvel, Kiddyphone, Mimosa, Victory, Broadcast Junior, HMV (Nursery Series), Homo Baby, Savana, Pigmy Gramophone, and the Bell. J.E. Hough offered the Bell, whose matrices were used to press under other labels as well, namely Marspen, Savana, Boots the Chemists, the Little Briton, John Bull Record, the Dinky, and the Fairy.

The smallest discs (diameter 1 5/16 inches) were the HMV records made for the Queen Mary's Doll House Gramophone, shown at the Wembley Empire Exhibition in 1924.

Little Tots' Nursery Tunes records appeared in 1923, with releases in the U.K. and U.S. HMV presented a series of seven-inch records of children's material in 1924, featuring Auntie and Uncle characters. Another seven-inch children's issue in U.K. was on the Goodson label in 1930. In the same year Crystalate offered a Nursery Rhymes series. Other nursery rhymes were issued on the Durium label in 1932. Kid-Kord was another seven-inch label of 1932.

LP toy records appeared from Oriole Records, Ltd., in about 1951. Others came from the Children's Record Co., London (the Cricket label), Selcol Products, Ltd. (Gala Nursery Records), Lumar, Ltd., of Swansea, Wales (Kiddietunes — Extra Long Play), and Pickwick International, Inc. (G.B.), Ltd. (Happy Time Records).

Many small records were not intended for children, but carried regular repertoire; both adult and children's small discs are discussed in Andrews [1988/4]. [Haines 1973, with reader comments in *TMR* #24 (October 1973), pp. 255–256.]

See also **Berliner (Label); Children's Records**

FRANK ANDREWS

TRACK

The path on a magnetic tape that is used for recording and playback. Full track means that the entire width of the tape is used; dual track means that half the width of the tape is used for each continuous signal. An eight-track tape employs eight side-by-side tracks, representing four separate stereo programs of two channels each, or two programs of four channels each.

See also **Multitrack Recording**

TRACKING

The movement of the needle or stylus as it follows the undulations of a record groove. Failure of the stylus to follow the groove variations closely results in the distortion known as tracking error.

See also **Tracking Force**

TRACKING ERROR

In disc playback, a failure in tracking. Ideally the stylus movement should trace a perfect radius from its axis at each point on the disc groove to the center hole. However, the radius is closest to perfect only as the stylus approaches the inner rim, farthest from its starting point at the outside of the record. Thus the stylus is not always equally able to follow the groove undulations perfectly, with tracking error as the distortion that results. To overcome this problem the pickup may be designed with an angle of twist, such as 14.5 degrees.

TRACKING FORCE

In a disc player, the pressure exerted by the pickup or cartridge on the stylus. A low tracking force is advantageous in terms of disc wear, but too little tracking force will allow the stylus to bounce in the groove — that leads to disc wear too, and to distortion. Modern LP cartridges track at two grams or less. The Shure V-15 tracks at about one gram (optimum value).

TRADITION RECORDS

Patrick Clancy (1923–1998), with the assistance of his brothers Tom and Liam, and the economic support of Diane Hamilton, a member of the Guggenheim family and active in the Country Dance and Song Society, initiated Tradition Records in 1956 in New York City. Kenneth Goldstein was instrumental in recording and producing many of the early albums. They quickly recorded and released Isla Cameron, *Through Bushes and Briars*, *Odetta Sings Ballads & Blues* (1956) and *Odetta at the Gate of Horn* (1957), Paul Clayton, *Whaling and Sailing Songs* (1956), the Clancy Brothers and Tommy Makem, *Rising of the Moon* and *Come Fill Your Glass With Us* (both 1959), and others by Ewan MacColl and Peggy Seeger, Oscar Brand, Carolyn Hester, Seamus Ennis, A.L. Lloyd, Ed McCurdy, Mary O'Hara, and Lightnin' Hopkins. During 1960–1961,Charlie Rothschild took over the business side of Tradition, while Patrick Clancy continued to oversee production. Having issued over 45 albums, Clancy sold the company to Bernard Solomon at Everest Records in 1966. Everest/Tradition continued to release the older albums, and in addition issued a steady stream of jazz reissues, including Louis Armstrong, Teddy Wilson, Pete Fountain, James P. Johnson, Meade Lux Lewis, Jelly Roll Morton, and various compilation albums, such as *Best of the Blues Tradition*, *Music for the Jet Set*, *Banjo Jamboree*, and the like. Everest, now Legacy International, licensed the masters to Rykodisc in the mid-1990s, which released much of the label on CDs, while Legacy International also continued to issue various Tradition albums into 2002.

RONALD D. COHEN

TRAFFIC

Beginning as an eclectic pop band with strong psychedelic leanings, Traffic increasingly moved toward jazz-influenced arrangements featuring extended instrumental jamming. Steve Winwood, whose intensely soulful vocals had recently turned the Spencer Davis Group into a hit-making entity, invited woodwinds specialist Chris Wood, drummer Jim Capaldi, and guitarist Dave Mason to a countryside cottage to write material and rehearse. The resulting album, *Mr. Fantasy* (United Artists #6651; 1968), contained two Top 10 British singles, and became an FM-radio staple stateside. The artistic conflicts between Mason's pop songcraft and Winwood's jazz leanings was reflected in the stylistically divergent selections comprising *Traffic* (United Artists #6676; 1968).

Following a patchwork farewell LP in 1969 titled *Last Exit* (United Artists #6702), Winwood joined forces Cream alumni Eric Clapton and Ginger Baker and Rick Grech (formerly of Family) to form the supergroup Blind Faith. After one album and a tour, followed by the brief stint with Ginger Baker's Air Force, Winwood reunited with Wood and Capaldi to record, *John Barleycorn Must Die* (United Artists #5504; 1970), Traffic's most commercially successful release, reaching number five on the pop album charts. The group's lineup was expanded to include Grech, Mason, and percussionists Reebop Kwaku Baah and Jim Gordon for the live recording, *Welcome to the Canteen* (United Artists #5550; 1971). Gordon and Grech departed after the release of the gold album, *The Low Spark of High-Heeled Boys* (Island #9306; 1971). Its laid-back, improvisational mode was continued in *Shoot Out at the Fantasy Factory* (Island #9323; 1973), which included Muscle Shoals session players bassist David Hood and drummer Roger Hawkins. Yet another Muscle Shoals musician, keyboardist Barry Beckett, was added on the live album *Traffic on the Road* (Island #9323; 1973).

After *When the Eagle Flies* (Asylum #1020; 1974), which featured the Traffic's original trio plus bassist Rosco Gee, Winwood and Capaldi concentrated on solo careers. By the 1990s, Wood, Grech, and Kwaku Baah were dead, but Winwood and Capaldi recorded one more album together under the group name, *Far from Home* (1994). Previously, Winwood made a pop career comeback in 1986–1988 with a number of top pop hits.

FRANK HOFFMANN

TRANCE

Trance is a broad designation for various permutations of electronically generated dance music characterized by repeated crescendos featuring Doppler effects, sequencer riffs, and propulsive bass and drum patterns. It is built primarily on three prior traditions: synthesizer-driven postpunk industrial music, Detroit-based techno disco, and early 1970s psychedelia.

Closely related to ambient, techno, and house, the genre originated in Germany during the late 1980s. Its earliest manifestation was marked by the merging of TB 303 synthesizers with mainstream dance material. Augmented by widespread use of the methamphetamine drug Ecstasy, trance spread to Goa and Thailand in the early 1990s, and then to the European club scene, most notably in the U.K., Holland, and Italy.

From the outset, trance has continued to evolve, providing the impetus for a considerable number of subgenres, including hard trance, acid trance, trancecore (heavily influenced by 1980s hardcore), psychedelic trance, and progressive trance. The artists and disc jockey producers most instrumental in shaping the style have included Paul Oakenfold, BT, Sash, Robert Miles, DJ Taucher, Paul Van Dyk, Tall Paul, Vincent de Moor, Ferry Corsten, Astral Matrix, Juno Reactor, and William Orbit.

FRANK HOFFMANN

TRANSATLANTIC (LABEL)

British folk-pop label of the 1960s and 1970s, founded in the early 1960s by businessman/entrepreneur Nathan ("Nat") Joseph. The label was similar to the U.S. Vanguard label (which licensed some Transatlantic recordings for sale in the U.S.) in that it grew significantly during the 1960s folk revival by signing contemporary acts such as the folk-rock-jazz group Pentangle (released in the U.S. by Reprise), the unaccompanied harmony singers the Young Tradition, and guitarists Bert Jansch and John Renbourn. In 1963 Transatlantic entered into a licensing arrangement with Folkways Records to issue its more popular albums in the U.K. on the budget XTRA label; Transatlantic also distributed Folkways's other releases in the U.K., as well as folk albums from Prestige. Producer Bill Leader oversaw most of Transatlantic's recordings, often working in Nic Kinsey's Livingston Studio (located in what was once an old chapel in suburban Barnet). Leader entered into an arrangement with Transatlantic in 1972 to start his own labels, Leader (for older, traditional acts) and Trailer (for young revivalists). Among his signings were singer/guitarists Dick Gaughan and Nic Jones and Irish revival group the Boys of the Lough. In 1977 Joseph sold the company, which was relaunched as Logo/Transatlantic, but it folded by the early 1980s. The back catalog has changed hands several times, until 1996 when it was purchased by Castle Communications, itself now a subsidiary of the Sanctuary Records Group. Various Transatlantic albums have been reissued on CD by Castle.

CARL BENSON

TRANSCRIPTION DISCS

Large diameter (between 16 and 20 inches) acetate, later vinyl, discs used in film recording and in radio in the 1930s. A vertical-cut disc came from Bell

Telephone Laboratories, playing at 33 1/3 rpm, with 200 grooves to the inch; it had a thin wax cover on an aluminum backing, with gold sputtering. Playback discs were translucent acetate, later vinyl.

See also **Disc; Instantaneous Recordings; Radio Program Recordings**

TRANSDUCER

Any device that converts one form of energy into another. In an electrical audio recording system such conversions occur as input signals (mechanical energy) which are changed to electrical energy by the microphone, then back to mechanical energy by the cutting head as it creates the groove pattern. The sequence is reversed in playback.

See also **Disc; Mechanical Electrical Analogies; Microphone**

TRANSIENT INTERMODULATION DISTORTION (TIM)

The type of distortion in playback of an audio system that follows sudden overloads of the amplifier, too quick for the compensating negative feedback to counteract it. A loud sforzando in a musical work, like those in Haydn's "Surprise Symphony," is a typical cause. The result is a ringing effect or, in piano recording, a ping sound.

See also **Transient Response**

TRANSIENT RESPONSE

In audio playback, the reaction of the system to a sudden change in amplitude of the signal, or of its frequency. Poor transient response, often caused by loudspeaker inadequacy, brings a boom in the bass or an edgy sound at the top of the spectrum.

See also **Transient Intermodulation Distortion (TIM)**

TRANSISTOR

A semiconductor device that can amplify or (with power gain) switch electrical signals. Transistors generally replaced vacuum tubes in audio systems during the 1960s.

TRANSPORT

The element in a CD player that spins the disc while isolating it from vibration.

TRAUBEL, HELEN (20 JUNE 1899–28 JULY 1972)

American soprano, born in St. Louis, Missouri. She studied singing as a child, and made a concert debut with the St. Louis Symphony Orchestra on 13 Dec 1923, performing in Mahler's Fourth Symphony. She continued singing and studying locally, and then sang at the Metropolitan Opera in a minor role on 12 May 1937. After singing her first major part, as Sieglinde on 28 Dec 1939, she was quickly identified as the prime American Wagnerian soprano. She was Kirsten Flagstad's successor as BrÅnnhilde, Elsa, Isolde, and the other Wagner heroines. She was also outstanding as the Marschallin, and occasionally ventured into the Italian repertoire with fine results. An early operatic crossover singer, she enjoyed working in New York nightclubs; objections from the Metropolitan management in 1953 led her to quit the opera company and remain with the popular idiom. Traubel then performed on Broadway, in films and on television. She died in Santa Monica, California.

Her records were for Victor (1940 and 1947) and Columbia (1945–1949). Traubel's remarkable Isolde is illustrated in Columbia MM #573 (1945), including the Narrative and the Liebestod, and in the 1947 duet with Torsten Ralf (Columbia X #286). Perhaps her greatest discs were the Act I duets from *Walkure* and the Dawn Duet from *Gîtterdammerung* with Lauritz Melchior, under Arturo Toscanini (Victor LM #2452; 1941). This material has been reissued unofficially on various European labels, with varying sound quality; the best available is the official version, part of RCA Red Seal's Toscanini reissue program (#60304). Sony's two-CD set, *Helen Traubel and Lauritz Melchior Sing Wagner* (#60896), is drawn from late 1940s recordings of the duo; despite its name — an obvious attempt to confuse consumers who might think they're getting the Victor Wagner material — they do not sing together. Various Traubel solo Victor recordings are anthologized on Preiser #89120. Enterprise #10 presents radio transcriptions, including some pop songs, from 1937–1941, and Eklipse 56 presents 1947–1951 concert recordings.

TRAVIS, MERLE (29 NOV 1917–20 OCT 1983)

American country singer and guitarist, born in Rosewood, Kentucky. He learned banjo first, and transferred some of the technique to the guitar (thumb picking on top of the melody line). He played on Indiana radio, then on WLW in Cincinnati. Fame arrived with a move to California in 1944, as he signed with Capitol Records and made discs of some of his own compositions: "No Vacancy" (Capitol #258; 1946), "Divorce Me C.O.D." (Capitol #290; 1946), "So Round, So Firm, So Fully Packed" (Capitol #349; 1946), and above all "Sixteen Tons" (in Capitol album #50; 1947). A later composition, "Smoke, Smoke, Smoke that Cigarette," was made into a hit record by Tex Williams. Travis was elected to the Country Music Hall of Fame in 1977. He died in Tahlequah, Oklahoma.

There are various CD reissues of Travis's classic work, on Capitol, Bear Family, Rounder, and other labels.

TRAVIS, RANDY (4 MAY 4 1959–)

Randy Travis was an instrumental figure in country music's transition from crossover ambitions to hard-country retrenchment. Along with George Strait, he was the genre's dominant male vocalist prior to the hegemony of neotraditionalist "hat acts" in the early 1990s, whose style he'd played a major role in nurturing.

Born Randy Traywick in Marshville, North Carolina, his father — a farmer and construction company entrepreneur who greatly admired classic honky-tonk singers like Hank Williams, George Jones, and Lefty Frizzell — encouraged him to learn guitar as an eight-year-old. By the end of the 1960s, he had teamed with brother Ricky to perform at area venues as the Traywick Brothers. Running away to nearby Charlotte at 16 after his brother was incarcerated, he won a talent contest at Country City U.S.A. The bar's owner, Lib Hatcher, immediately hired him as a performer, cook, and dishwasher. She also became his legal guardian when a judge pronounced him one transgression short of a long jail term.

As his manager, Hatcher helped Travis sign with the Paula label in 1978. Two singles — including "She's My Woman" (Paula #431; #91 C&W — issued in 1979) flirted with the country charts. The couple (who would marry in May 1991) relocated to Nashville in 1982, where she managed the Nashville Palace. As the resident performer there, Travis made a recording, the independently released *Randy Ray Live*, sold largely at the nightclub.

The publicity ensuing from the album and his live shows lead to a record contract with Warner Bros. in 1985. His first release with them, "On the Other Hand" (#28962; 1985), did not sell particularly well; however, when reissued following the Top 10 success of "1982" (Warner Bros. #28828; 1985), it rose to number one. His first LP for the label, *Storms of Life* (Warner Bros. #25435; 1986), achieved triple platinum sales. The follow-up, *Always & Forever* (Warner Bros. #25568; 1987), went quadruple platinum and helped earn Travis the Country Music Association's Male Vocalist of the Year award for 1987. It also contained "Forever and Ever, Amen" (Warner Bros. #28384; 1987), the first of Travis's seven straight number one country singles, followed by "I Won't Need You Anymore" (Warner Bros. #28246; 1987), "Too Gone Too Long" (Warner Bros. #28286; 1987), "I Told You So" (Warner Bros. #28256; 1987), "I Told You So" (Warner Bros. #27969; 1988), "Honky Tonk Moon" (Warner Bros. #27833; 1988), and "Deeper than the Holler" (Warner #27689; 1988). Although his first nine Warner Bros. albums all achieved platinum or gold status, his aching vocals and bedrock country arrangements have not translated to a wider pop audience.

Although eclipsed commercially by rock-influenced artists such as Garth Brooks, Travis remained an important country artist in the 1990s. He switched labels, signing with the newly formed DreamWorks, in 1997. *Inspirational Journey* (Warner Bros. # 47893, 2000), a collection of traditional and contemporary religious material, represented a stylistic change of pace typifying country artists who have achieved institutional status.

FRANK HOFFMANN

TREMONT (LABEL)

An American record of the mid-1920s, produced by the American Record Manufacturing Co., of Framingham, Massachusetts. Masters were from Cameo. [Rust 1978.]

TRIANGLE (LABEL)

An American record made by Bridgeport Die and Machine Co. from September 1922 to 1925. Paramount and Emerson provided most of the masters. The price was $.50. [Rust 1978.]

TRIO DE LUTECE

An instrumental ensemble that recorded for Columbia in 1916. Members were George Barrere, flute; Carlos Salzedo, harp; and Paul Kefer, cello. "Chant sans paroles" of Tchaikovsky and "Serenade" by Widor were played on #2684.

TRISTANO, LENNIE
(19 MAR 1919–18 NOV 1978)

American jazz pianist, born Leonard Joseph Tristano in Chicago. He became blind in childhood, but went ahead with his planned career, studying at the American Conservatory of Music in Chicago (B.Mus., 1943). He was highly praised for his club performances. In 1946–1947 he made trio recordings for the small jazz label, Keynote (reissued on Mercury #830921). In 1949 he made a fine LP for Capitol, *Crosscurrents* (#11060), one of the first freely improvised sessions on record and a classic in the jazz world; oddly, it's not yet available on CD. A 1955 Atlantic record, *Lennie Tristano*, offered group recordings and some fine Tristano solos; among the most enduring are "These Foolish Things" and "You Go to My Head." "Turkish Mambo" demonstrated his skill with rhythmic complexities. (Both of his mid-1950s Atlantic albums are available on a single CD from Rhino #71595.) Tristano ceased recording much after the early 1960s; and he ceased performing altogether in the U.S. in 1968, although he continued to teach jazz piano until his death in New York a decade later.

TRITON PHONOGRAPH CO.

A New York firm, established in 1913. In 1916, five models of the Triton disc player were marketed, selling for $10 to $50.

TRIX, HELEN, CA. (1892–18 NOV 1951)

American vaudeville singer, born in Newmanstown, Pennsylvania, date uncertain. She recorded early for Edison cylinders, with six solos and an ensemble number in 1906–1907, the first being "Is Your Mother In, Molly Malone?" in Irish dialect (#9365; 1906). Her biggest hit for Edison was "The Bird on Nellie's Hat" (#9450; 1907); it was also recorded for Victor in 1907. In the 1920s she and her sisters Josephine and Alma performed on stage together as the Trix Sisters, gaining acclaim in the U.K. and the U.S. She made records for HMV in the early 1920s, and later made electrics for Columbia in the U.K. She remained active until after World War II. Trix died in New York. [Brooks 1990; Walsh 1954/4–5.]

TROCADERO ORCHESTRA

A London hotel ensemble that recorded for the Gramophone Co. in 1898 and 1899, producing some of the earliest dance music on record. They also played marches and selections from opera, beginning with "Hip Hip Hurrah March." The Trocadero recordings of "La Marseillaise" and of the Austrian and Prussian national anthems (all in September 1898) appear to be the earliest disc recordings of that genre.

TROJAN (LABEL)

U.K.-based reggae label active from 1969–1976. The label was named for Jamaican soundman/producer Duke Reid, and initially served as the British agent for recordings made by him on his Treasure Island label. The label was coowned by Lee Gopthal, who had previously run the British Pyramid label, and Chris Blackwell (founder/director of Island Records), and was initially distributed by Island. The label had initial success with Jimmy Cliff, and then expanded with other popular reggae artists. Another Jamaican producer Lee "Scratch" Perry was brought on board who had his own Upset label; several of his recordings, billed as by the Upsetters, featured a then-unknown singer and group Bob Marley and the Wailers. However, Blackwell split from the business in 1972 (taking Marley with him to Island), and Gopthal took the label to a new partner/distributor, B&C. He also formed a subsidiary label, Big Shot, for party records (mostly slightly risqué spoken material). When B&C went bankrupt in 1975, it took Trojan with it; Trojan's assets were subsequently sold to Saga Records, who then sold it in the early 1990s to Receiver Records. Both focused on reissuing the Trojan back catalog and did not sign new acts to the label. [website: www. trojanrecords.com.]

CARL BENSON

TROMBONE RECORDINGS (HISTORIC)

Early trombone cylinders were made for Edison in 1898–1903, by Nicholas Scholl and Leo A. Zimmerman. "Five Hundred Thousand Devils" (by Scholl; #5600) was the first of the group of 10 items. Zimmerman also played on Columbia cylinders ca. 1900, and did a solo with Gilmore's Band in 1903. He recorded for Electric cylinders and Odeon Records when Sousa's Band visited the U.K. in the first decade of the century. Because of the British brass band movement, many trombone works were recorded in the U.K.: solos, duets, and combinations with cornets. An unnamed artist performed six solos for Berliner discs in October 1898, beginning with "Rocked in the Cradle of the Deep."

The lack of an interesting repertoire has inhibited the appearance of international concert artists on the trombone. However, the instrument is vital in jazz and swing music, beginning with early Dixieland style. It was Eddie Edwards who was heard on the first jazz record to be issued, by the Original Dixieland Jazz Band. Miff Mole played with the Original Memphis Five in the 1920s; Bill Rank was with Bix Beiderbecke and Frank Trumbauer. Kid Ory was a skillful handler of the instrument's brazen sound. Jack Teagarden was the principal virtuoso of the 1930s.

Great trombonists of the swing era included Tommy Dorsey, who developed a uniquely dulcet legato;

J.C. Higginbotham, Bill Harris, and J.J. Johnson. Glenn Miller was a trombonist, and so was Will Bradley. Other featured trombone artists in the Big Bands included Benny Morton (Count Basie), Ray Coniff (Bunny Berigan), and Pee Wee Hunt (Glen Gray).

TRUETONE NEEDLES
A brand of needle produced by the New York Disc Needle Co. In 1916 they advertised a variety of needles, categorized as loud, extra loud, opera, medium tone, and soft tone.

TRUMBAUER, FRANKIE (30 MAY 1901–11 JUNE 1956)
American jazz saxophonist, born in Carbondale, Illinois. After military service in World War I he went to Chicago and played with various groups. In 1925–1926 he had his own band in St. Louis, Missouri, with Bix Beiderbecke; the two of them went on to Paul Whiteman's orchestra in 1927. Trumbauer, Beiderbecke, and guitarist Eddie Lang made an important group of Okeh recordings, including "Wringin' and Twistin'" (Okeh #40916). Trumbauer also recorded with his own band, with varying personnel, but featuring Beiderbecke; Jimmy Dorsey, Adrian Rollini, Jack Teagarden, Matty Malneck, and Eddie Lang are among the men heard on Okeh discs made in 1927–1930. Smith Ballew and Johnny Mercer did some of the vocals. "Trumbology" (Okeh #40871; 1927), "Singin' the Blues" (Okeh #40772; 1927), and "I'm Coming, Virginia"/"Way Down Yonder in New Orleans" (Okeh #40843; 1927) were among the best of the records. Trumbauer left the music field in 1940 for aviation; he was a test pilot in World War II. He died in Kansas City, Missouri. There are numerous CD reissues of his work, both under his own name and with others. *1927–1946: His Best Recordings* gives a good overview (Best of Jazz #4069); the Classics label has reissued his complete recordings in chronological order through 1936, and Mosaic has issued a seven-CD boxed set of *The Complete OKeh & Brunswick Recordings of Bix Beiderbecke, Frank Trumbauer, and Jack Teagarden 1924–1936* (#211) drawing on various sources.

TRUMPET RECORDINGS (HISTORIC)
It was the cornet that was used in early recordings, and sometimes the bugle, rather than the trumpet. The cornet and trumpet are very similar, but the cornet, with a slightly more conical bore, is easier to play and gives a more mellow tone. Emil Cassi, of Theodore Roosevelt's Rough Riders, did offer some bugle calls on the trumpet (according to Koenigsberg [1987]) on an Edison cylinder made before May 1899. In Dixieland jazz groups, cornets were typically present. In the mid-1920s the trumpet took the place of the cornet in jazz and dance ensembles, thanks to the genius of Louis Armstrong and his very successful recordings. Recordings of 1927–1929 illustrate the change over, as major groups turned to the trumpet sound and distinguished performers appeared. The California Ramblers had Chelsea Quealey; Red Nichols played trumpet with Miff Mole and His Molers; Manny Klein was with Jack Teagarden, and Gene Prince with Andy Kirk. King Oliver, famous as a cornetist, played trumpet in 1929 recordings. There were three trumpets in the Fletcher Henderson band of 1927, setting the pattern for the Big Bands of the 1930s. Edna White was a noted soloist of the 1920s, but not a member of a Big Band.

Those bands had many outstanding trumpeters, among them several future band leaders. Charley Teagarden was with Paul Whiteman; Buck Clayton was with Count Basie; Bunny Berigan and Charlie Spivak were with Tommy Dorsey; Cootie Williams and Rex Stewart were with Duke Ellington. Benny Goodman had Harry James and Ziggy Elman. Jimmie Lunceford had Sy Oliver. Other soloists who emerged in the late 1940s and 1950s include Roy Eldridge, Charlie Shavers, Maynard Ferguson, Miles Davis (who dominated the 1960s as well), Chet Baker, and Dizzy Gillespie.

On the classical side there have been a number of prominent soloists, despite the paucity of repertoire. Among the more prolific recording artists are Maurice Andre, Gerard Schwarz, and Thomas Stevens. Wynton Marsalis is the most renowned crossover trumpeter, with important recordings in the classical and popular catalogs.

TUBA RECORDINGS (HISTORIC)
This instrument is heard to best advantage in the band or orchestra, rather than as a solo performer; indeed there is virtually no concert literature for it. An unidentified artist played "Rocked in the Cradle of the Deep" on a Columbia cylinder ca. 1900 (#29200) with a piano accompaniment. There were several LP records by classical tuba players, such as Harvey Phillips and Roger Bobo. Ralph Vaughan Williams wrote a concerto for the instrument, performed on an RCA LP (#3281) by John Fletcher. "Tubby the Tuba" was a children's disc by Danny Kaye, recorded later by Carol Channing. Musical satirist Martin Mull achieved a novelty hit in 1973 with his "Dueling Tubas" (Capricorn #0117), a take-off on the then-popular instrumental hit "Dueling Banjos" (from the film *Deliverance*).

TUBB, ERNEST (9 FEB 1914–6 SEP 1984)

American country singer, songwriter, and guitarist, born in Crisp, Texas. He developed a distinctive deep drawling vocal tone and gained success on several radio stations in Texas. He appeared at the Grand Ole Opry from 1942, becoming a regular performer there, then formed a group called the Texas Troubadours and toured with them. A honky-tonk variant of country music emerged from their work. Tubb performed at Carnegie Hall in 1947, in the first country program to be presented in that auditorium. He had a record shop in Nashville, and broadcast a program from there called *Midnight Jamboree*. The young Elvis Presley was among the singers presented. Tubb was one of the great names in country music for a half century. He used an electric guitar, and he fostered the use of the term "country" in place of the derogatory "hillbilly." He was elected to the Country Music Hall of Fame in 1965. He died in Nashville.

Tubb's recordings were consistent hits from the 1940s until the 1980s. An early chart song was a duet with Red Foley, "Goodnight, Irene" (Decca #6255; 1950). Among his 35 *Cash Box* country single chart numbers in 1958–1982, perhaps the most appreciated were "I Cried a Tear" (Decca #30872; 1959), "Next Time" (Decca #30952; 1959), and "Thanks a Lot" (Decca #31526; 1963). He had several successful duet discs with Loretta Lynn, the most popular being "Mr. and Mrs. Used to Be" (Decca #31643; 1964). Most of his career was with Decca, but he made some 1979 discs for the Cachet label.

TUCKER, RICHARD (28 AUG 1913–8 JAN 1975)

American tenor, born Reuben Ticker in Brooklyn. As a child he sang in the synagogue and on radio. In 1943 he made his opera debut with the Salmaggi Co. in New York, as Alfredo. He joined the Metropolitan Opera on 25 Jan 1945, as Enzo, and stayed 30 years as one of the tenor mainstays of the company. He excelled in the Verdi and Puccini roles. In 1947 Tucker made his European debut in Verona, in a performance with Maria Callas, making her Italian debut. He was heard subsequently in Covent Garden, La Scala, Vienna, etc. He died in Kalamazoo, Michigan.

The Tucker recorded legacy is strongest in the complete opera sets he made for Columbia and Victor. *Forza del destino* was among his finest, recorded in 1955 with Callas (HMV #5120) and again in 1965 with Shirley Verrett for Victor (#5527/30). His other complete opera sets were of *Aida*, *Boheme*, *Cavalleria rusticana*, *Cosi fan tutte*, *Lucia*, *Madama Butterfly*, *Pagliacci*, *Rigoletto*, *Traviata*, and *Trovatore*. Much of this material is available on CD.

TUCKER, SOPHIE (13 JAN 1884–9 FEB 1966)

Russian vaudeville performer and popular singer, known as the "Last of the Red Hot Mamas." She was born Sonia Kalish-Abuza on a train between Russia and Poland. Tucker was brought to America at age three, and did her first work as a waitress in her father's restaurant in Hartford, Connecticut. She went to New York and got various singing jobs in vaudeville and burlesque. She was in the *Ziegfeld Follies of 1909*, but did not attract much notice.

Her earliest records were six Edison cylinders made in 1910, among them "My Husband's in the City" (#10366) and "That Loving Soul Kiss" (#10493). She was a "coon shouter" in the early days, with suggestive lyrics; later she sang in a cabaret style. offering more sophisticated material. She had her own group, Five Kings of Syncopation, in the early 1920s, and made some records with them for Arto and Okeh. "After You've Gone" (Okeh #40837; 1927) was accompanied by Miff Mole's Molers. Her all-time favorite disc was "Some of These Days," recorded with Ted Lewis in 1926 (Columbia #826-D); recorded again for Victor in 1929 (#22049). "There'll Be Some Changes Made" (Okeh #40921) was another great success. Tucker was a popular motion picture actress from 1929 to 1945, and she had star billing in several Broadway revues. As her voice faded in the 1950s and 1960s she developed a quiet talking style of presentation. CD reissues of her classic 1920s era recordings are available on Pearl (#7807), Parade/Koch (#2031), and many other nostalgia-jazz labels.

TUCKER, TANYA (10 OCT 1958–)

Born in Seminole, Texas, and raised in Phoenix, Arizona, the very young Tucker was encouraged to sing country music by her father. When Tanya reached nine years old, he financed a trip to Nashville. After several unsuccessful attempts, her demo tape landed in the hands of producer Billy Sherrill, who signed her at age 13 to Epic. She immediately hit with the slightly suggestive "Delta Dawn" and "Would You Lay with Me (in a Field of Stone)." By the end of the 1970s as she reached her late teen years, Tucker's career took a detour into an ill-advised attempt to crossover into pop/rock with the album, *T.N.T.* (she appeared on the cover decked out in leather, in an attempt to give her a more "mature" image). The early 1980s brought duets with her then-husband Glen Campbell in a more mainstream country style. After struggling to find a style, she returned in the mid-1980s to traditional country and honky-tonk sounds. During the early 1990s, she had several hits, including the sassy anthem, "It's a

Little Too Late." The later 1990s were more difficult for Tucker on the charts, but her touring activity went unabated. Her last chart single to date was 1997's "Little Things," a Top 10 country hit. That same year, she published her autobiography, *Nickel Dreams*, which was a bestseller. In 2002, she released her 31st album on her own Liberty Home label, but it failed to attract much attention.

CARL BENSON

TUNER

In a radio receiver, the device that selectively converts radio signals to audio signals. It is often a separate component in an audio system, used with an audio amplifier.

TUNING BAND

On certain early discs, a band that followed the program material; it reproduced a fixed pitch, for the purpose of setting the correct turntable speed. A 1904 G & T record, #053048 (a song by Giordano sung by a soprano named Frascani) and a 1909 Gramophone Concert Record, #GC-37851 ("Ave Maria" for cello and piano) had such bands, termed "key-notes" by G & T. Fonotipia copied the device, but gave it up following protests from the Gramophone Co. (Italy), Ltd.

TURNER, ALAN

British baritone. He sang with various opera companies in the U.K. and in Chicago and Philadelphia. Turner made many opera and operetta recordings for Edison, Victor, Gramophone Co., Odeon, Edison Bell, Marathon, Operaphone, Pathé, and others. He organized his own Alan Turner Opera Co. and toured widely in the 1930s. His Edison cylinders were "In Happy Moments" (#9291; 1906), "Queen of the Earth" (#9876; 1908), and "Goodbye, Sweetheart, Goodbye" (#9843; 1908). In 1906 he made four records for G & T, including the "Toreador Song" (#3-2455) and the *Pagliacci* "Prologo" (#02081). He also performed in the Gramophone Co.'s 1908 recording of Gilbert and Sullivan's *H.M.S. Pinafore*, singing the role of Sir Joseph Porter; this was the first nearly complete recording of a Gilbert and Sullivan operetta made on disc, and was presented on 14 10-inch and four 12-inch discs. He was pictured in the 1915 *Victor Book of the Opera* clad as Count di Luna, and a number from *Trovatore* was among the 25 listings for him in the 1922 Victor catalog; he disappeared quickly with the arrival of electrical recording — there was no sign of him in the Victor 1927 catalog.

TURNER, "BIG" JOE
(18 MAY 1911–14 NOV 1985)

One of the leading shout blues interpreters of the 1930s and 1940s, Big Joe Turner — he was six feet, two inches in height, and weighed 300 pounds — would later find a new audience as a rock 'n' roll trailblazer. Taken in its entirety, his career represented a synthesis of most major 20th- century styles, including gospel, blues, swing, rhythm and blues, jazz, and rock 'n' roll.

Turner grew up in Kansas City, Missouri, absorbing gospel singing in church, and folk, blues, and pop songs from local performers and sound recordings. In addition to selling papers and junk as a youth, he earned money singing with a blind guitarist in the streets. By the late 1930s, he had become a highly regarded blues singer, though limited to performing in run-down bars and theaters in the Midwest. He was also garnering attention as a songwriter; his compositions included "Cherry Red," "Hold 'Em Pete," "Lucille," "Piney Brown Blues," and "Sun Risin' Blues." His earliest known recordings — done in a boogie-woogie style that was back in vogue following his success at the 23 Dec 1938 Carnegie Hall "Spirituals to Swing" concert — were made for Vocalion on 30 Dec 1938 with pianist Pete Johnson: "Goin Away Blues" and "Roll 'Em Pete." The duo worked together at Café Society and Café Society Uptown in New York City for the next five years as well as recording for Decca in 1940.

Turner continued to make records for the label's Race and Sepia series for the next four years, both solo and with Willie "The Lion" Smith, Art Tatum, Sam Price, and the Freddie Slack Trio. Turner cut 11 singles for National Records between 1945–1947, but with limited success. He spent the next few years recording for a wide variety of companies — including Freedom, MGM, Down Beat/Swingtime, Modern/RPM, Aladdin, Rouge, Imperial, and DooTone — but making little impact due to declining interest in the blues.

Sensing his potential as an updated R&B belter, Atlantic Records added him to their roster in 1951. Now referred to as the "Boss of the Blues," Turner enjoyed his greatest success as a recording artist with hits such as "Chains of Love" (Atlantic #939; 1951; #2 R&B, #30 pop), "The Chill Is On" (Atlantic #949; 1951; #3 R&B), "Sweet Sixteen" (Atlantic #960; 1952; #3 R&B), "Don't You Cry" (Atlantic #970; 1952; #5 R&B), "Honey Hush" (Atlantic #1001; 1953; #1 R&B, #23 pop), "Shake, Rattle, and Roll" (Atlantic #1026; 1954; #1 R&B, #22 pop), "Flip Flop and Fly" (Atlantic #1053; 1955; #2 R&B), "Hide and Seek" (Atlantic #1069; 1955; #3 R&B), and "Corrine Corrina" (Atlantic #1088; 1956; #2 R&B, #41 pop). When the singles stopped charting after 1958, he shifted his focus to albums, proving equally adept at classic blues, jazz, and R&B-inflected rock 'n' roll. Notable releases included *The Boss of the Blues* (Atlantic #1234; 1956), *Joe Turner* (Atlantic #8005; 1957), *Rockin' the Blues* (Atlantic #8023; 1958), *Big Joe Is Here* (Atlantic #8033; 1959), and *Big Joe Rides Again* (Atlantic #1322; 1960).

Turner continued to record up to his death for many labels, including Arhoolie, United Artists, MCA, Black and Blue, Big Town, Spivey, Muse, Savoy, and Pablo. Many of his classic recordings have been reissued on compilations such as *His Greatest* Recordings (Atco #376; 1971), The *Big Joe Turner Anthology* (Rhino #71550; 1994), and *Volume 1: I've Been to Kansas City* (Decca/MCA #42351).

FRANK HOFFMANN

TURNER, EVA, DAME
(10 MAR 1892–16 JUNE 1990)

British soprano, born in Oldham. She sang in the chorus of the Carl Rosa Opera Co., then had solo roles and was heard by someone who arranged for an audition with Arturo Toscanini in Milan. As a result she was engaged at La Scala for Wagnerian roles, and began an international career. Turandot became the role most associated with her, and also Aida — performed with great success in Chicago in 1928–1930 — but she retained her Wagner connections, doing an acclaimed *Tristan* under Albert Coates in London in 1937. Turner died in London.

She recorded exclusively for Columbia, making 30 sides in Italy (1927–1928), and London (1928, 1933, 1938). Turner's finest records include "In questa reggia" from *Turandot* (Columbia #D1619, replaced by #D1631; in the U.S., #D12588; 1928) and "Ritorna vincitor" (Columbia #D1578; in the U.S., #D12587; 1928), and "Oh patria mia" (Columbia #L1976; in the U.S., #D16404; 1927). All were reissued by Columbia on LP. There are various CD reissues, including the three-CD *Complete Recordings* (Pearl #0094), *Opera Arias and Songs* (EMI #69791), and *Milan Recordings 1936–28/Broadcast 1938/Serenade to Music (1938)* (Claremont #78-50-66), drawn from radio broadcast and film soundtrack sources. [Richards 1957 is a discography.]

TURNER, IKE (5 NOV 1931–)

Although generally mentioned in relation to his one-time wife, Tina, Ike was one of the early pioneers of rock 'n' roll in his own right. His talents — which spanned many aspects of the music industry — also play a key role in furthering the careers of many other Black artists.

Turner formed a band while still in high school, the Top Hatters. Later known as the Kings of Rhythm, they worked the small clubs throughout the Mississippi delta. He secured a recording session at Sam Phillips's legendary Sun Studios in Memphis; his band cut the R&B chart-topper, "Rocket 88," there cited by many experts as the earliest rock 'n' roll recording. Due to obscure contractual considerations, however, Chess (who licensed the recording from Phillips) gave label credit to saxophonist Jackie Brenston and the Delta Cats, thereby denying Turner a notable footnote in pop-music history. He also alleged that the company paid him only $40 for writing, producing, and recording the disc.

Turner continued as a highly regarded session guitarist, producer, and talent scout during the 1950s. His collaborations with the likes of Johnny Ace, Bobby "Blue" Band, Roscoe Gordon, Howlin' Wolf, B.B. King, and Otis Rush were released on Chess, Modern, and RPM. By the mid-1950s, he was a high-profile club attraction based in St. Louis, Missouri. One night in 1956, Annie Mae Bullock — who'd moved from Knoxville, Tennessee, to St. Louis to try to build a career as a vocalist — was given a chance to sing with his band during a club date. Impressed with her performance, Turner asked her to join the group; they were married in 1958.

The couple's recording breakthrough came unexpectedly in 1959 when a singer tapped to record Ike's composition, "A Fool in Love," failed to appear for the scheduled session. Tina (her adopted stage name) was substituted and the track (Sue #730) reached number two on the R&B charts (#27 pop) the following year. As a result, Ike decided to focus the act on Tina, bringing in a female backing group (the Ikettes), and working out arrangements and choreography to take advantage of her dynamic voice and stage presence. They recorded a long string of R&B hits for a variety of labels — including Kent, Loma, Modern, Philles, Warner Bros., Innis, Blue Thumb, Minit, and Liberty — in the 1960s, though few performed well on the pop charts. Producer Phil Spector had been particularly interested in packaging the duo for a wider audience, but the commercial failure of his reputed masterpiece, "River Deep, Mountain High" (Philles #131; 1966; #88 pop) — though it did reach number one in the U.K — reputedly led to his decision to retire from the music business.

The late 1960s, however, brought a change of fortune as roots-based sounds once again began dominating mainstream pop. The Turners received invaluable exposure by touring with the Rolling Stones and performing on major television programs and Las Vegas venues. Tina's energetic dancing (complemented by the backup singers, known as the Ikettes), along with her legendary legs, helped the duo gain a large audience. Among their best-selling singles were "I Want to Take You Higher" (Liberty #56177; 1970; #34), John Forgerty's "Proud Mary" (Liberty #56216; 1971; #4), and "Nutbush City Limits" (United Artists #298; 1973). Their albums also regularly made the charts, most notably *Outta Season* (Blue Thumb #5; 1969), *In Person* (Minit #24018; 1969), *River Deep-Mountain High* (A&M #4178; 1969; recorded 1966), *Come Together* (Liberty #7637; 1970), *Workin' Together* (Liberty #7650; 1970), *Live at Carnegie Hall/What You Hear Is What You Get* (United Artists #9953; 1971), *'Nuff Said* (United Artists #5530; 1971), *Feel Good* (United Artists #5598; 1972), and *Nutbush City Limits* (United Artists #180; 1973).

Despite their commercial success, the couple's marriage was in trouble. Tina ultimately decided to leave the act in Dallas during a 1975 tour; she obtained a divorce the following year. While she went on to both commercial and artistic success as a solo performer in the 1980s, Ike found nothing but problems. Not only did his recording activities fail to go anywhere, but he was dogged by a string of drug and other personal problems. The one bright spot has been the public's continued interest in the classic work of the Ike and Tina Turner Revue, which has led to the release of many recorded anthologies as well as original albums such as *Dance* (Collectibles #5759; 1996), *Don't Play Me Cheap* (Collectibles #5763; 1996), *Dynamite* (Collectibles #5298; 1994), and *It's Gonna Work Out Fine* (Collectibles #5137; 1994).

See also **Turner, Tina**

FRANK HOFFMANN

TURNER, TINA (26 NOV. 1939–)

Born Annie Mae Bullock in Nutbush, Tennessee, Tina Turner first drew attention as the charismatic lead singer/dancer in the Ike and Tina Turner revue. After divorcing Ike in the mid-1970s and falling from the public eye (besides a memorable apperance as the Acid Queen in the Ken Russell film of the Who's *Tommy*), Tina enjoyed a remarkable career turnaround during the 1980s, beginning with her *Private Dancer* album (Capitol #512330; 1984), which spawned several hits, including the title track and "What's Love Gotta Do With It?" In 1985, she starred opposite Mel Gibson in the film *Mad Max: Beyond Thunderdome*, contributing the hit title song, "We Don't Need Another Hero." However, after that her career declined in the U.S., although she remained a major concert draw through the 1990s, particularly in Europe. She

continued to release albums about every four to five years through the decade, garnering respectable sales if not marketable hits.

See also **Turner, Ike**

FRANK HOFFMANN AND CARL BENSON

TURNTABLE

The platter or platform on which analog record discs are rotated in recording or playback. By extension the term is applied to the complete assembly: platter, spindle, driving components, and motor. An ideal turntable has a constant and accurate speed of rotation, without rumble, and without effects from outside vibrations or feedback. These desired conditions were hardly to be found in the early turntables of Emile Berliner, operated by hand cranking, or later models with treadle power. Spring motor phonographs ran more dependably, and finally electric power made constant speed possible.

Three types of operation are found: a belt drive, in which a resilient belt connects the motor to the turntable platter; an idler-wheel drive, where the motor drives the inner rim of the platter via a rubber-covered outrigger wheel; and a direct drive, in which a slow-speed motor is directly coupled to the platter's center shaft. Any of these three can give satisfactory results, although direct drive has been preferred in professional work for its simplicity and durability. (Interestingly, although there was no motor but the human engine involved, Berliner record players can be classed as both belt driven and direct; some had a belt to carry the cranking energy to the platter, some had the crank attached to the platter.)

Heavy turntables (about eight pounds) offer greater stability and are used in studio work, but they require a stronger motor than consumer turntables (weighing about four pounds, or less). Some consumer designs,

Panasonic SL-BD22K turntable. Courtesy Panasonic, Inc.

such as the classic model produced by Acoustic Research in the 1960s and 1970s, used a fairly lightweight platter, driven by a moderately powerful motor. Felt covering was used on turntable platters in the 1890s. The first advertising for velvet-covered turntables appeared in 1921. Mats produced for turntables in the modern era emphasized antistatic qualities and nonconductivity.

In the best LP turntables, beginning in the 1960s with the above-noted Acoustic Research player, and exemplified later on by the Linn product line and Yamaha PF-800, there was a suspended subchassis isolation system, to prevent any unwanted feed through from the mounting shelf or floor. Many turntables also feature a fine-tuning speed control, a built-in strobe light, and strobe markings on the edge of the platter. [LONG 1988.]

See also **Cartridge (II); Flutter; Pitch (I); Record Changer; Tone Arm; WOW**

REV. HOWARD FERSTLER

TURNTABLISM

Turntablism is the use of the turntable as a musical instrument. A vital and broadening disc jockey performance culture has emerged during the past 30 years. Since about 1977, when Grand Wizard Theodore invented the "scratch" technique, turntablism has been at the center of several musical idioms, most notably hip-hop, techno, electronica, and other kinds of House or dance music. Each style has its own use of the turntable. What they have in common is an affinity for active sound mixing as a performance element and the application of electronic effects and synthesizer modules to broaden the sound spectrum of the turntable.

In 1936 Varèse had experimented with turntables that could play in reverse and had variably adjustable speeds. In John Cage's apocryphal credo on experimental music written in 1937, he mentioned turntables as one of several electrical instruments that would help usher in a new era in the history of music. Recordings of music on 78-rpm discs were widely available at the time and provided the only practical means for making sound recordings until the availability of the tape recorder by about 1950. Cage composed a piece for prerecorded discs called *Imaginary Landscape No. 1* in 1939 for which test records were played at the same time and their speeds variably adjusted according to Cage's instructions. In 1948 Pierre Schaeffer completed his first work of musique concrète — the *Études de bruits* — using turntable technology to collect, playback, and record the final version of the piece.

A repertoire of disc jockey skills has evolved. Scratching is the manual reversal of the spin of a record to run the needle backward over the sound in a quick, rhythmic swipe. The manipulation of beats is another intrinsic characteristic of turntablism. A spinning record is itself a loop, especially when the needle is made to hug a groove rather than move ahead with the natural spiral of the track. Beat juggling uses either two identical turntable recordings or one disc and a digital sampler to repeat the same sounds as a "breakbeat." Digital looping and delay are also common to beat manipulation. These techniques are for the turntablist what finger exercises are for the piano player.

The omnipresence of turntable music in today's culture has been likened to an earlier generation that grew up emulating rock and roll artists. "Today's new guitar is the turntable," remarked contemporary turntablist Christian Marclay (b. 1955) (Christian Marclay, interview with Mike Doherty, *Eye*, 30 Nov 2000, http://www.eye.net/eye/issue/issue_11.30.00/ music/marclay.html, [11 July 2001]). These artists use the turntable the same way that another musician might work with the piano or a saxophone. They view their instrument as a resource for new musical possibilities.

Like the pioneering composers before them, a new generation of turntablists has clearly reclaimed the record player as an instrument for musical expression and performance.

THOM HOLMES

TURTLES, THE

The Turtles illustrated the dilemma facing most rock acts at a time when commercial viability was tied to maintaining an ongoing string of hit singles. Despite a strong melodic sense and two of the finest pop singers of that era, Mark Volman and Howard Kaylan (born Kaplan), the band felt compelled to continually shift stylistic gears in order to retain an audience. The pressures generated by such compromises appears to have played as much of a role as their widely known legal disputes with the White Whale label over finances in the group's demise.

The nucleus of the Turtles — Volman, Kaylan, Al Nichol, and Chuck Portz — began performing together while still attending high school in southern Los Angeles. While attending local colleges, they added drummer Don Murray to the lineup. Known as the Crossfires in 1964–1965, the band's sound was modeled after their idols, the Beatles. A series of weekend engagements with Manhattan Beach's Rebellaire Club resulted in owner Reb Foster's offer to manage them. One of his first moves was to secure a recording contract with the newly formed White Whale label. The debut album, *It Ain't Me Babe* (White Whale #7111; 1965), had a pronounced folk-rock feel, with two protest numbers — the title track by Bob Dylan (White

Whale #222; 1965; #8) and "Let Me Be" (White Whale #224; 1965; #29) — doing well on the singles charts.

As folk-rock faded, the Turtles turned increasingly to pop-rock featuring noncontroversial lyrics. Hit songs included one of the most perfectly constructed rock recordings ever, "Happy Together" (White Whale #244; 1967; #1), as well as "She's Rather Be With Me" (White Whale #249; 1967; #3), "You Know What I Mean" (White Whale #254; 1967; #12), "She's My Girl" (White Whale #260; 1967; #14), "Elenore" (White Whale #276; 1968; #6), and "You Showed Me" (White Whale #292; 1969). "Elenore" represented the high point of the band's aesthetic disillusionment. Written as a sarcastic satire of pop songs, with overly sentimental, stilted Tin Pan Alley–styled verses, its commercial success confounded group members. Their albums — most notably, *Happy Together* (White Whale #7114; 1967), *The Turtles! Golden Hits* (White Whale #7115; 1967), *The Turtles Present the Battle of the Bands* (White Whale #7118; 1968), *Turtle Soup* (White Whale #7124; 1969), *The Trutle! More Golden Hits* (White Whale #7127; 1970) — also sold well throughout the later half of the 1960s.

Unhappy with the direction their music had taken and hopelessly entangled in litigation over financial issues with White Whale, the group disbanded in 1970. Interested in exploring a more satirical bent, Volman and Kaylan joined Frank Zappa's Mothers of Invention. Their vocals rendered Zappa's work more musically accessible than any other phase of his career. They then formed the duo Phlorescent Leech and Eddie (later Flo and Eddie), releasing a long string of albums that expanded the boundaries of humor within a progressive rock format. The duo's creative energies spanned a wide range of activities, including live performing, journalism, and radio work. They also took an increased interest in the Turtles's legacy, working with Rhino Records to release anthologies of both classic tracks and rare materials: *The Turtles — 1968* (Rhino #901; 1978), *20 Greatest Hits* (Rhino #5160; 1984), *Chalon Road* (Rhino #70155; 1987), *Shell Shock* (Rhino #70158; 1987), and *Turtle Wax; The Best of the Turtles, Volume 2* (Rhino #70159; 1988), as well as the original LPs. The company also produced a video documentary of the band's career, *Happy Together* (#976000; 2000), in the DVD format.

FRANK HOFFMANN

TWAIN, SHANIA (28 AUG 1965–)
Born Eileen Edwards in the backwoods of Ontario in the small town of Timmins, Twain began singing and performing locally as a teenager. She trained as a Broadway style singer/dancer/performer in Toronto,

and began performing at the resort town of Deerhurst after both her mother and stepfather were tragically killed in an automobile accident. She moved to Nashville in 1991 seeking a record deal, and was quickly signed to Mercury Records, hitting it big with her first single, "Whose Bed Have Your Boots Been Under." Her self-title debut album (Mercury #514422), produced by Robert "Mutt" Lange, who also cowrote many of the songs, featured more hits, including "Any Man of Mine" and "(If You're Not in It for Love) I'm Out of Here." The album eventually went nine times platinum, and remained on the charts for nearly 200 weeks.

Lange and Twain returned in 1997 with *Come on Over* (Mercury #536003), which produced many more hits, including the ballads "You're Still the One" and "From This Moment," to the spunky "That Don't Impress Me Much," "Don't Be Stupid," and "Man! I Feel Like a Woman." This latter song was used in an advertising campaign by Revlon featuring Twain. The album broke all records, selling over 18 million copies through 2002, spawning eight hit singles, and becoming by *Billboard*'s estimation the best-selling recording by a female artist of all time, in any genre.

After a break to have a child, Twain returned in late 2002 with the album *Up* (Mercury #170314). In an unusual move, the CD was released in three versions: American buyers received two CDs, one mixed for the country market, the other for pop; Europeans received a unique mix of their own, plus the pop mix. The album's first single, "I'm Gonna Getcha," was an immediate number one hit on country and pop charts, boding well for Twain's continued success.

CARL BENSON

TWEAKING
A method of suppressing resonances and vibrations in audio playback by the placement of dampers under components. The dampers, made of various kinds of absorbent materials, are sometimes called isolation feet. Good results have been reported with such feet positioned beneath a turntable. [Whyte 1989.]

TWEETER
A high frequency (treble) loudspeaker.

TWENTIETH CENTURY GRAPHOPHONE
Columbia's 1905 model BC and the 1906 model BCG were identified as Twentieth Century machines.

See also **Columbia Record Players**

TWIN DOUBLE SIDED DISC RECORD (LABEL)

A British record, often referred to as the Twin, sold from June 1908. It was made by the Gramophone Co., Ltd., from its own matrices and those of its sister companies. They were the firm's first double-sided discs in the U.K. (there were already double-sided Gramophone concert records on sale in Europe), sold behind the facade of "The Twin Record Co.," a subdivision of Gramophone Co. with its own headquarters office (later registered in 1910 as a private limited company, with all shares held by the parent company).

Twin discs had their own single-face number series, quite separate from Gramophone Concert discs, and from Zonophone single-sided discs (which had an "X" prefixed single-face numbers in repertoire blocks). The British Zonophone Co. had been set up earlier by G & T to handle U.K. issues of Zonophone Records and machines from the G & T German subsidiary, International Zonophone Co. (In 1910 British Zonophone also became an independent private limited company, as a subsidiary of the Gramophone Co., Ltd.) The two labels came together in May 1911, the Zonophones having been sold under British Zonophone since February 1904 and the Twin since June 1908. The new label of the combined catalogs was "Zonophone Record — The Twin." It bore the twin cherubs design, a registered trademark. The Twin label was used in India after World War I, by the Gramophone Co. India, Ltd.

FRANK ANDREWS

TWITTY, CONWAY
(1 SEP 1933–5 JUNE 1993)

American country and rock singer, born Harold Lloyd Jenkins in Friars Point, Mississippi. He took his stage name from the names of two southern towns. He performed with a group he formed at age 10, then was in military service from 1954 to 1956. In 1958 he signed with Mercury Records and made a hit with "I Need Your Lovin'" (#71086; 1957). "It's Only Make Believe" (#12677; 1958; #1) was his first chart song on the MGM label, which recorded him until 1961. Twitty was a rock star, but he departed from that style as the hits tapered off in the 1960s; by 1965 he had become a country singer. Together with his new group, the Lonely Blue Boys, he was a great success in the 1970s, with more than 40 country chart singles, many of which reached number one. His duets with Loretta Lynn were particularly popular, e.g., "As Soon as I Hang Up the Phone" (MCA #40251; 1974) and Grammy winner "After the Fire Is Gone" (Decca #32776; 1971). MCA was his label through the 1970s; in the 1980s he was with Elektra. He died in Nashville, Tennessee.

TWO KAUFIELDS

SEE THREE KAUFIELDS

2 LIVE CREW

Formed in 1985 in Miami, Florida. Luke Skywalker (born Luther Campbell, 22 Dec 1960), Fresh Kid Ice (born Christopher Wong-Won, 29 May [year not given], Trinidad), Brother Marquis (born Mark Ross, 2 April [year not given], New York), Mr. Mixx (born David Hobbs, 29 September [year and city of birth not given], California. If the Rolling Stones are the Bad Boys of Rock, then what is 2 Live Crew? *Really* Bad. Formed in California in the early 1980s, the group moved to Miami in 1985 following the success of their single "Revleation" in Florida; it was released on the small California Makola label. They hooked up with local promoter Luther Campbell (aka Luke Skywalker), who then became a member of the group, taking it in a new direction, away from social commentary to more sexually oriented lyrics. After releasing their debut album in 1986 on their own XR label, Campbell signed a deal with Atlantic for his own Luke label. In 1987, 2 Live Crew was the first act to issue simultaneously "dirty" and "clean" versions of an album (*Move Somethin'*; Luke 101/Atlantic #91649). The rap group best known for its explicit lyrics toiled away in relative obscurity until a Broward County, Florida, court in 1990 declared 2 Live Crew's 1989 release, *As Nasty as They Wanna Be* (Luke/Atlantic #91651), obscene. The album reached number 29 on the pop charts; a single, "Me So Horny" (Effect #127; vinyl single), topped at number 26. The group put a parental warning sticker on the package and released an edited version *As Clean as They Wanna Be* (Luke/Atlantic #91652), which did not do nearly as well. In May 1992, the 11th U.S. Circuit Court of Appeals reversed the ruling; the U.S. Supreme Court later refused to hear an appeal.

Campbell formed a new lineup for the group in 1994, but quickly ran into legal trouble when they were sued in 1994 by the publisher of the Roy Orbison hit "Oh, Pretty Woman," who had refused to give a license to 2 Live Crew for their version. The suit was overturned by a court, which ruled Crew's version a parody. In 1995 Luke Records went bankrupt, and Campbell signed with Joe Weinberger's Lil' Joe label. (Weinberger had previously been Campbell's business partner, making the entire deal somewhat suspicious.) Group members formed a new 2 Live Crew without Campbell in 1996, recording one album in 1998, while Campbell continued on his own. However, neither group nor Campbell on achieved much chart success.

BOB SILLERY

Two Live Crew provocative cover for *As Nasty As They Wanna Be* album. Courtesy Frank Hoffmann

TYNER, MCCOY (11 DEC 1938–)

Pianist McCoy Tyner was an integral part of John Coltrane's historic quartet in the 1960s and has recorded a large number of important albums as a leader. He was born in Philadelphia and started taking classical piano lessons when he was 13. He met Coltrane while both were still in Philadelphia, and he would become a member of Coltrane's landmark quartet in the late 1950s. Coltrane released *My Favorite Things* (Atlantic #1419; 1960), on which Tyner's use of fourths and fifths in his left hand and pentatonic patterns in his right hand helped transform the title cut into a ground-breaking modal experiment. Tyner was present on one of Coltrane's masterpieces, *Live at Birdland* (Impulse #50; 1963), which features outstanding versions of "Afro Blue" and "Alabama." Tyner was with Coltrane as he moved further away from tonality on the free jazz anthem, *Ascension* (Impulse #95; 1965).

Tyner's first release as a leader, *Inception* (Impulse #18; 1962), demonstrates his remarkable bebop chops, and his wonderful arranging skills are heard on "There Is No Greater Love." *The Real McCoy* (Blue Note #84264; 1967), which features Joe Henderson, is considered by many to be his finest album as a leader. Two of his many wonderful compositions, "Passion Dance" and "Blues on the Corner" were debuted here. Tyner has recorded well over 40 albums as a leader. Some of his other finer releases include *Expansions* (Blue Note #84338; 1967), *Supertrios* (Milestones #55003; 1977), *Quartets 4X4* (Milestones #55007; 1980), and *New York Reunion* (Chesky JD #51; 1991).

GARTH ALPER

U

U2

Undeniably the most consistently popular rock band of the postpunk era, U2 — much like the Beatles and other classic 1960s artists — have remained committed to musical experimentation. As a result, they defy easy categorization; radio formats embracing their recordings include AOR, modern rock (alternative), adult contemporary (easy listening), and contemporary hits radio (Top 40).

Formed in Dublin, Ireland, in 1977, the band — consisting of vocalist Bono Vox (r.n. Paul Hewson), guitarist/keyboardist The Edge (r.n. David Evans), bassist Adam Clayton, and drummer Larry Mullen — produced a couple of successful recordings for the Irish market, the EP *U2: Three* (CBS #7951; 1979) and colored (both yellow and orange versions) single "Another Day" (CBS #8306; 1980), which led to an Island contract featuring international distribution. Their debut album, *Boy* (Island #9646; 1980; #63), produced by the highly regarded Steve Lillywhite, received extensive praise from the rock press. The follow-up LP, *October* (Island #9680; 1981) further refined the group's strikingly original formula: politically charged lyrics passionately delivered by Bono, accented by The Edge's jagged guitar riffing, and anchored by a economically driving rhythm section.

U2 appeared destined to remain a cult favorite until the release of *War* (Island #90067; 1983; #12), aided by the extensive MTV rotation of the videos for "New Year's Day" (Island #99915; 1953; #53), composed in tribute to Lech Walesa's Polish Solidarity Union, the martially stirring "Sunday Bloody Sunday," and "Two Hearts Beat as One" (Island #99861; 1983). After creatively treading water with the dynamic in concert outing, *Under a Blood Red Sky* (Island #90127; 1983; #28), *The Unforgettable Fire* (Island #90231; 1984; #12), featuring Brian Eno's ambient-tinged production work, elevated the band into the superstar ranks. Another stopgap release, the partially live mini-LP *Wide Awake in America* (Island #90279; 1985; #37), was followed by arguably one of the greatest rock albums ever, *The Joshua Tree* (Island #90581; 1987; #1). Highlighted by the singles "With or Without You" (Island #99469; 1987; #1), "I Still Haven't Found What I'm Looking For" (Island #99430; 1987; #1), and "Where the Streets Have No Name" (Island #99408; 1987; #13), the work deftly ran the gamut of emotions, from exultant anthems to spiritual introspection. *Rattle and Hum* (Island #91003; 1988; #1) — the live/studio hybrid soundtrack to a rockumentary of the same name — was a commercial hit, although panned by many critics for failing to break new artistic ground.

U2 responded by incorporating pronounced dance elements into both *Achtung Baby* (Island #10347; 1991; #1) and *Zooropa* (Island #518047; 1993; #1). Following an interlude devoted to the composition and recording of film music — most notably the single from *Batman Forever*, "Hold Me, Thrill Me, Kiss Me, Kill Me" (Island #87131; 1995; #16) — the band's obsession with kitschy mainstream music culminated with the uneven *Pop* (Island #210; 1997; #1). Recent years have revealed U2 to be in a holding pattern, releasing occasional singles, remixes, and compilations amid various collaborations with other artists.

FRANK HOFFMANN

UB40

The multiracial, English band, UB40 — the first important exponent of reggae to hail from outside Jamaica — rose to popularity in the midst of the ska/bluebeat revival in the U.K. Although they did not address the topical concerns of West Indies reggae artists (e.g., Rastafarianism, ganja rituals, European colonialism), their songs exhibited a strong sociopolitical bent, addressing, among other issues, the U.K.'s unemployment problems (the band's name itself was inspired by an English unemployment form), nuclear war, and the repressive policies of former U.K. Prime Minister Margaret Thatcher.

UB40's key members — lead vocalist/guitarist Ali Campbell and lead guitarist/singer Robin Campbell — were sons of Ian Campbell, a Scottish folk interpreter popular during the early 1960s. Formed in early 1979, the band — ranging in size from eight to 12 members over the years, including core members Astro, vocals/trumpet; Michael Virtue, keyboards; Earl Ralconer, bass; Brian Travers, saxophone; Jim Brown, drums; and Norman Hassan, percussion — became a fixture on the U.K. charts with the release of the album, *Signing Off* (Graduate #2; 1980; #2 U.K.). UB40's popularity spread to much of Europe in the early 1980s on the strength of LPs combining a punk attitude with augmented brass arrangements replicating an authentic R&B feel.

Until the band signed with A&M Records in 1983, their recordings had only been available in the U.S. as imports. Pushing Ali's wholesome good looks and reggae-pop treatments of rock classics such as Sonny and Cher's "I Got You Babe" (A&M #2758; 1985; #28; w/Chrissie Hynde), Neil Diamond's "Red Red Wine" (A&M #2600; 1983; #34), the Temptations' "The Way You Do the Things You Do" (Virgin #98978; 1990; #6), Al Green's "Here I Am" (Virgin #99141; 1991; #7), and Elvis Presley's "(I Can't Help) Falling in Love with You" (Virgin #12653; 1993; #1 U.K., #1 U.S.) via video clips geared toward cable television and dance clubs, UB40 achieved considerable success in the U.S. with the following albums: *Labour of Love* (A&M #4980; 1983; #14; consisted entirely of cover versions), *Geffery Morgan* (A&M #5033; 1984; #60), *Little Baggariddim* (A&M #5090; 1985; #40), *Rat in the Kitchen* (A&M #5137; 1986; #53), *CCCP: Live in Moscow* (A&M #5168;

1987; #121), *UB40* (A&M #5213; 1988; #44), *Labour of Love II* (Virgin #91324; 1990; #30; another collection of covers), and *Promises and Lies* (Virgin #88229; 1993; #6).

Ali's departure in 1995 for a solo career disrupted UB40's creative and commercial momentum. With his return to the fold in 1997, the band picked up where they left off, placing recordings high on the U.K. charts — e.g., *Guns in the Ghetto* (DEP International #16; 1997; #7 U.K.) and *Labour of Love III* (DEP International #18; 1998; #8 U.K.) — albeit enjoying less success stateside.

FRANK HOFFMANN

ULTONA

The reproducer marketed by the Brunswick-Balke-Collender Co. in 1916. It could play vertical-cut or lateral-cut discs.

UNITED (LABEL)

An American record issued ca. 1911 to ca. 1913 by the United Talking Machine Co. of Chicago, a division of the Great Northern Manufacturing Co. The material consisted of Columbia overstock, modified with larger spindle holes (1 1/2 inches) and pasteover labels. Playback required access to a machine made by the Great Northern Manufacturing Co. When United Talking Machine was succeeded by the Consolidated Talking Machine Co., sometime before March 1918, the United label was continued by Consolidated. [Rust 1978.]

UNITED HEBREW DISK RECORDS

An American label issued by the United Hebrew Disk and Cylinder Co. of New York. Advertising appeared from January to November 1905. Pierre Long was manager of the firm.

FRANK ANDREWS

UNITED HOT CLUBS OF AMERICA (UHCA)

A record issued by the Commodore Music Shop in New York from 1936 to ca. 1941. It was a reissue label for jazz classics that were no longer available through normal channels. Rust has accounted for 86 sides in all. [Rust 1978.]

UHCA, jazz reissue label operated by the Commodore Record Shop during the mid-'30s. Courtesy Kurt Nauck/Nauck's Vintage Records

UNITED STATES GRAMOPHONE CO.

The second American firm established by Emile Berliner, succeeding his American Gramophone Co. in April 1893. Located at 1410 Pennsylvania Ave., Washington, D.C., the firm marketed Gramophones as well as one-sided seven-inch discs with the Berliner label. The machines produced included hand-driven models and battery-operated models; about 1,000 were sold in 1894. In fall 1894 a factory and salesroom opened in Baltimore. The Berliner Gramophone Co. took over both manufacturing and sales of all products (except for the District of Columbia region). United States Gramophone Co. continued to hold the Berliner patents. [Wile 1979/2.]

UNITED STATES MARINE BAND

One of the principal musical ensembles of the 19th century, greatly acclaimed under the direction of John Philip Sousa. The band was one of the leading groups on early records, beginning with work for Columbia cylinders in 1890. (Only a small number of the musicians — as few as a dozen of them — actually made the studio recordings.) When Sousa resigned in 1892, Francesco Fanciulli succeeded him and directed the record sessions until 1897; William H. Santelmann followed Fanciulli. On Columbia the band had a wide repertoire apart from marches: two-steps, polkas, waltzes, ballads, hymns, etc. Berliner recorded the Marine Band in September 1899, as they rendered "You Got to Play Ragtime." From 1909 the band was

1895 record catalog from the United States Gramophone Co. From the Collections of the Library of Congress

also heard on Edison cylinders (20 numbers by 1912), Edison Diamond Discs (11 sides by 1925), and then on Victor discs, from 1906 to 1927. There were 13 sides in the Victor 1917 catalog, directed by Santelmann; one of them the "Maple Leaf Rag." [Hoover 1971, p. 73, shows about 14 members of the band, identified as "Sousa's Band," in the studio in 1891.]

UNITED STATES PHONOGRAPH CO.

SEE CYLINDER

UNITED STATES RECORD MANUFACTURING CO.

A firm established in 1920 in Long Island City, New York, where its factory was located, with offices in New York. Victor H. Emerson was president. It was announced in March 1921 that the company was prepared to press 10-inch discs in substantial quantities and to supply stock matrices for the presses of others. Thomas H. McClain, an engineer formerly with Thomas Edison, supervised the factory. A label named H.I.T.S. was advertised by the firm in September 1921.

FRANK ANDREWS

UNITED STATES TALKING MACHINE CO. (I)

A Chicago firm active in 1897. It sold a finger-wound disc player at a cost of $3, and records for it (disguised Berliner discs). Joseph N. Brown was the inventor of the machine (U.S. patent #653,654, filed 22 Apr 1897; granted 17 July 1900), which had a wooden tone arm, steel needle, and gutta percha listening tubes. Despite its low selling price, and a manufacturing cost of only 12 1/2 cents per unit, the device was a market failure and remainders were sold off at $.98 each. [Koenigsberg 1990.]

UNITED STATES TALKING MACHINE CO. (II)

A Newark, New Jersey, firm established in 1916. It advertised in that year a line of Ideal disc players, in eight models, selling from $12 to $85.

UNITED TALKING MACHINE CO.

A Chicago firm, established in 1911 as a division of the Great Northern Manufacturing Co. Record players were sold under the Symphony name, and discs had the United label. The players had 1 1/2 inch spindles, to accommodate the extra large spindle holes that were cut into the discs (which were Columbia overstock records, relabeled by United). The firm seems to have been absorbed by the Consolidated Talking Machine Co. sometime before March 1918. [Fabrizio 1980.]

UNIVERSAL MUSIC GROUP

The Universal Music Group (UMG) was formed in 1996 as a successor to MCA Music Entertainment. Two years later, UMG's owner, Seagram, purchased PolyGram and combined it with its other music holdings. In 1999 a number of both UMG's and PolyGram's less-profitable labels were either combined or closed, including the venerable A&M label, alarming industry watchers who felt new artists would have less chance to be signed. In 2000 Seagram sold its share of MCA, Inc., to French media giant Vivendi. UMG has continued to expand, expanding PolyGram's previous 60 percent holding in Def Jam Records to full ownership, forming Universal Music Enterprises (UME) for catalog and special market recordings, and establishing Universal Music Publishing as a successor to the earlier MCA Music Publishing.

UNIVERSAL PHONOGRAPH CO.

A New York firm. The January 1899 issue of *Phonoscope* advertised its records as guaranteed to be original, and invited clients to "come and take the records off the rack as they are being made." Material included "catchy music" as well as selections from "works of Wagner, Meyerbeer, etc." George Rosey and his orchestra and Albert Campbell were artists identified in the promotion copy. Joseph W. Stern & Co. was proprietor, and Mitchell Marks was manager.

UNIVERSAL QUARTET

A male vocal ensemble who recorded for Zonophone around 1905. Tentative identification of the membership, by Walsh, mentions Geoffrey O'Hara, tenor; Reinald Werrenrath, baritone; and Walter MacPherson, bass. [Walsh 1962/10.]

UNIVERSAL TALKING MACHINE CO.

A firm which Frank Seaman took part in establishing on 10 Feb 1898, with Orville La Dow as president. The purpose of Universal was to make machines for Seaman's National Gramophone Co. Seaman was sole sales agent for Berliner Gramophones and discs, and the Berliner Gramophone Co. objected to Seaman's attempts to handle alternative cheaper machines. As a consequence, Seaman took part in organizing the National Gramophone Corp. on 10 Mar 1899, as sales outlet for the Universal Talking Machine Co. machines (called Zonophones) as soon as they would be in production. The first products were in fact unauthorized disguised Berliner items, a situation that led to a break between Berliner and Seaman. After litigation brought by the Graphophone interests over alleged infringements by Seaman of the Bell-Tainter patent for incising in wax, there was a consent agreement allowing Columbia to use the Zonophone line of players. Universal held a sheriff's sale of patents and equipment on 28 Oct 1901. Then the Zonophone business was reorganized under control of a new company founded for the purpose on 19 Dec 1901, the Universal Talking Machine Manufacturing Co. (The continuing Universal Talking Machine Co. acted as sales representative for some time.) Failure of the National Gramophone Corp. followed, but Seaman maintained his rights as sole sales agent for the Berliner Gramophone Co. The original Universal Talking Machine Co. kept its corporate existence to 6 June 1903, when its share of stock was acquired by G & T, along with the shares of stock of Universal Talking Machine Manufacturing Co. and that of the American and German International Zonophone Co. In September 1903 G & T sold the Universal assets to Victor.

As a Victor subsidiary the Universal firm continued to produce the Zonophone line of discs and players. In 1908 it offered five discs by Luisa Tetrazzini, in nine-inch size for $.75, and in 11-inch size for $1.25. The address of the UTMMC was given in a July 1911 advertisement as 4th and Race Streets, Philadelphia. Columbia successfully litigated UTMMC out of business in 1912, on grounds of patent infringement, as it had never been licensed by Columbia. All masters and factory stock of American-made Zonophone records had to be destroyed by court order.

The American company was not related to the British Universal Talking Machine Co., Ltd.

FRANK ANDREWS

UNIVERSAL TALKING MACHINE CO., LTD.

A U.K. firm, not related to the American company of like name, registered on 9 Nov 1907 in London. It was a successor to the Gramophone branch of Aldridge, Salmon and Co., Ltd. U.K. Gramophones were sold. The firm wound up operations on 5 May 1908, then reorganized and continued in business under the same name. E.J. Sabine and Thomas F. Bragg were among the directors, while controlling interest was held by Aldridge, Salmon and Co., Ltd. A record with the Elephone label was issued from November 1908. Liquidation came on 6 June 1909. The Universal name was used for a time in 1910 by William Andrew Barraud, before he gave his company his own name. [Andrews 1990/6.]

UNIVERSAL TALKING MACHINE MANUFACTURING CO.

SEE UNIVERSAL TALKING MACHINE CO.

UP-TO-DATE (LABEL)

A rare American record of ca. 1924, apparently related to the Blu-Disc. Record #2019 was a vocal by Florence Bristol accompanied by Duke Ellington. [Rust 1978.]

URLUS, JACQUES (9 JAN 1867–6 JULY 1935)

German tenor, born near Aachen. His family moved to the Netherlands when he was 10 years old. He studied engineering, then voice, and sang in a minor operatic role in 1894, with the National Opera at Amsterdam. He continued with the company until 1899, becoming a leading tenor, then sang in Leipzig from 1900 to 1915. Urlus became known as one of the finest Wagner tenors, performing at Bayreuth (1911–1914) and singing Tristan with great success at Covent Garden in 1910. He was the leading heldentenor at the Metropolitan Opera in 1913–1917. He sang through Europe, and retired after a final performance in Amsterdam in 1932. Urlus died in Noordwijk, Netherlands, during surgery.

Pathé cylinders and discs of 1903, sung in Dutch, marked the beginning of his recording career. He did 15 Wagner numbers, plus tenor arias by Mascagni, Leoncavallo, Verdi, Gounod, Bizet, and Meyerbeer. In 1907 he recorded in Leipzig for Grammophon, beginning with a German version of "O paradiso" (#3-42898). He recorded a total of 76 numbers for Gramophone Co. labels, the last being in 1912. Thereafter he sang for Edison Diamond Discs from 1914 to 1925, doing 30 solos and three duets with Marie Rappold.

Urlus recorded in 1923 for Deutsche Grammophon, on the Musica or Polydor labels (11 items); for Odeon, in Germany, in 1924 (17 items). His final recording session was on 25 Jan 1927. Several of his great Wagner arias were reissued by the Club 99 on LP (1962), including "Winterstürme" from Walküre, and "Preislied" from Meistersinger. CD reissues include Preiser #89502 and Marston #52301-02, a two-CD set reissuing all of his Edison recordings made between 1913–1917.

U-S EVERLASTING RECORD

SEE CYLINDER

U.S. PHONOGRAPH CO.

SEE CYLINDER

U-S PHONOGRAPH CO.

SEE CYLINDER

V

VAGUET, ALBERT (1865–?)

French tenor, one of the most prolific to record acoustic operatic discs, as well as French song records. He recorded for Pathé cylinders and discs from 1902 to 1919, and again in 1927–1928, creating over 300 recordings. While most of his output was from French composers, he also dealt with Italian opera and even some Wagner, but he sang everything in French.

VALENS, RITCHIE
(13 MAY 1941–3 FEB 1959)

The importance of Valens's short-lived career is largely symbolic in nature; he was the first Latin recording artist to have an impact on the rock-era charts. In his wake would follow Dave "Baby" Cortez, Chris Montex, Sunny and the Sunglows, the Premiers, Cannibal and the Headhunters, and many others.

Born Richard Stephen Valenzuela in Pacoima (outside Los Angeles), California, Valens learned to play guitar as a youth and formed a band, the Silhouettes, while in high school. He signed a contract with Del-Fi Records in spring 1958, and just missed the Top 40 in the fall with "Come On, Let's Go" (Del-Fi #4106). He followed with a double-sided hit, "Donna"/"La Bamba" (Del-Fi #4110; 1958–1959), reaching numbers two and 22, respectively, on the *Billboard Hot 100* chart. Ironically, the latter track, based on a traditional Mexican wedding song, has proven to be his most popular recording (a 1987 biopic based on his life, and featuring the music of Los Lobos, was titled *La Bamba*).

Valens was in great demand as a performer, appearing on national television programs and package tours. On 3 Feb 1959, a small plane carrying Valens, Buddy Holly, and the Big Bopper (aka J.P. Richardson) crashed near Clear Lake, Iowa, immediately following a concert. A distinctive vocalist — equally capable of addressing romantic ballads and energetic rock materials — and solid guitar accompanist, he remained largely forgotten by the public at large until the release of *La Bamba*. His studio recordings, which essentially fit on one compact disc, have been released in many editions since his death.

FRANK HOFFMANN

VALESCABECKER, DORA

A violinist who made 16 cylinders for Bettini in 1898, beginning with a mazurka by Wieniawski. She was the first woman to record the violin.

VALIQUET, LOUIS P. (C.1878–1925)

Inventor of several important audio components, holder of 33 U.S. patents filed from 1897 to 1909. His research formed the basis for products of the Universal Talking Machine Co. (for which he was factory superintendent) and the National Gramophone Corp. His patent #651,904 (filed 21 Apr 1899; granted 19 June 1900) was for the machine that was marketed as the Zonophone by Frank Seaman from May 1900. He developed a horn-support device, needed in the days of large, heavy horns (U.S. patent #705,165; filed 19 Mar 1902; granted 22 July 1902). Another major invention was the disc turntable with a spring-loaded pin for securing the record (U.S. patent #780,246; filed 27 Mar 1902; granted 17 Jan 1905); it was used in 1,900 models of the Zonophone even before the patent application had been filed. Other Valiquet patents were for a coin-op, a case, soundboxes, and a motor. [Koenigsberg 1990.]

VALLEE, RUDY
(28 JULY 1901–3 JULY 1986)

American popular singer and orchestra leader, born Herbert Pryor Vallee in Island Pond, Vermont. He attended Yale University, graduating in 1927; established and toured with his Yale Collegians band. He led groups in Boston and New York, with a repertoire of college songs and novelties. He became popular as Rudy Vallee and his Connecticut Yankees, and gained national attention on a weekly radio show from 1929. Vallee appeared on Broadway and in films. After service in World War II he gradually

Rudy Vallee publicity photo from the early '30s. Courtesy David A. Jasen

changed from music to comedy and serious acting. He died in Los Angeles.

A number of well-received records were made for Victor between 1929 and 1936, among them the orchestra's theme song, "My Time Is Your Time" (Victor #21924; 1929), "I'm Just a Vagabond Lover" (Victor #20967; 1929), and "Betty Coed" (Victor #22473; 1930). The Bluebird label carried a hit, "Whiffenpoof Song," with chorus by the Gentlemen Songsters (#7135; 1937). His material has been widely reissued, first on LP and more recently on CD, primarily on budget nostalgia labels.

VALLIN, NINON
(8 SEP 1886–22 NOV 1961)

French soprano, born in Montalieu. She studied in Lyon, then sang in Paris and made her opera debut there at the Opera-Comique, as Micaela, on 14 Oct 1912. She remained with the company to 1916, greatly popular as Manon and Mimi. Vallin was at La Scala in 1917, and performed throughout Europe and in Buenos Aires. Late in her career she appeared in America — Chicago and Washington, D.C., but not at the Metropolitan Opera. Vallin taught at the Montevideo Conservatory of Music from 1953–1957, and then retired to Lyons, where she died.

Vallin recorded extensively for Pathé (after two sides for HMV in 1913), covering the French repertoire and certain Italian arias. Her first Pathé records were duets from *Manon*. Her most renowned discs were the complete set of *Werther* with Georges Thill (Columbia LFX #151/165; 1931), which was reissued on CD in 1990 and recognized by *Gramophone* as historical album of the year. She also did a *Louise* album for Columbia ca. 1935 (RFX #47/54), and a *Tosca* set for Odeon (#123810/16) ca. 1932. *Canciones, Lieder, and Peruvian Folk Songs* (Video Arts International #1127) offers a selection of material of unknown recording date. [Barnes 1953.]

VAN BRUNT, WALTER
(22 APR 1892–11 APR 1971)

American tenor and comic singer, born in Brooklyn, New York; widely known by the stage name Walter Scanlan (a name he adopted during World War I when anti-German feelings were particularly strong). He played piano and sang in church, while collecting phonograph records and trying to sing like Billy Murray. In 1907 he began to record for the Indestructible label, then went to Edison — where he became the inventor's favorite tenor and maker of the most popular Edison Diamond Disc, "I'll Take You Home Again, Kathleen" (#80160; 1914). There were four Edison cylinders before 1912, and many more as an exclusive Edison artist in 1914–1918. He made 66 solo Edisons as Van Brunt, and 70 solos as Scanlan, plus 43 duet and ensemble records. During 1919–1920 he was with Emerson, then he returned to Edison. Before signing as exclusive with Edison, Van Brunt also recorded for Victor (from 1909), beginning with "Summer Reminds Me of You" (#16304). "When I Dream in the Gloaming with You" was his first Victor hit (#16363; 1909). There were 15 items in the Victor 1917 catalog. He made duets with Ada Jones, and apparently substituted for Billy Murray when that worthy failed to appear at record sessions with the American Quartet. Finally, he had Murray as his own duet partner, on eight Edison Diamond Discs (beginning with "My Blackbirds Are Bluebirds Now" (#52422; 1928) and on the last Victors he made: "Oh Baby! What a Night" (#22040; 1929) and "In Old Tia Juana" (Matrix #53510, not released).

One of Van Brunt's popular Irish numbers was "Wearin' o' the Green," made for Edison in 1923. He also did tone tests in 1924. And he made Jewish dialect records. After the demise of Edison, Van Brunt recorded for Banner, Crown, Cameo, and other labels; and was a regular radio performer in the 1930s with Billy Murray, Marcella Shields, and others. He died in Ohio. [Corenthal 1984 lists dialect material; Walsh 1951/11–12; 1952/1–2.]

VANCE, CLARICE
(14 MAY 1875–24 AUG 1961)

American vaudeville artist, born in Louisville, Kentucky. She specialized in Black dialect numbers, becoming known as "the Southern Singer." Vance made two Edison cylinders in 1905: "Mariar" (#9051) and "Save Your Money, Cause de Winter Am Coming On" (#9214). Then she went to Victor in 1906, singing "If Anybody Wants to Meet a Jonah Shake Hands with Me" (#4931) and nine other sides by 1907. Her Victor hit was "I'm Wise" (#5253; 1907). Vance quit recording but remained on stage to ca. 1917. She died in Napa, California. [Walsh 1963/4–5.]

VANDROSS, LUTHER (20 APR 1951–)

Vandross enjoyed a very successful career as a session singer and in recording commercials prior to becoming one of the preeminent R&B stylists of his generation, widely known for his impeccable phrasing and vocal control. Born in New York City, he began playing piano at age three. One of his compositions, "Everybody Rejoice (A Brand New Day)," was included in the Broadway musical, *The Wiz*, in 1972. During the 1970s, he became a fixture on ad jingles, from the U.S. Army to Burger King spots.

Vandross's entrée to the pop music industry came when a friend, guitarist Carlos Alomar, introduced him to David Bowie. He contributed a song, "Fascination," and sing on Bowie's highly successful LP, *Young Americans* (RCA #10998; 1975), later touring with him as well. While continuing to sing jingles and cutting two obscure albums under the name Luther, he quickly became one of the busiest backing vocalists and arrangers around, recording with Bette Midler, Ringo Starr, Carly Simon, Donna Summer, Barbra Streisand, Chaka Khan, Chic, and Change.

With several labels expressing an interest in Vandross as a solo artist, he produced two demos, "Never Too Much" and "A House Is Not a Home." As a result, Epic Records signed him in 1981, granting him full creative control. Beginning with *Never Too Much* (Epic #37451; 1981; #1 R&B), he released a long string of platinum-selling albums, including *Forever, For Always, For Love* (Epic #38235; 1982), *Busy Body* (Epic #39196; 1983), *The Night I Fell in Love* (Epic #39882; 1985), *Give Me the Reason* (Epic #40415; 1986), *Any Love* (Epic #44308; 1988), *The Best of Luther Vandross … The Best of Love* (Epic #45320; 1989), and *Power of Love* (Epic #46789; 1991). Although his singles have had limited crossover appeal, they have consistently reached the R&B Top 10. Despite the demands ensuing from pop stardom, he has continued to write and produce for other artists into the 21st century, most notably Aretha Franklin, Cheryl Lynn, Dionne Warwick, Teddy Pendergrass, and Whitney Houston. Furthermore, he made his acting debut in Robert Townsend's 1993 film, *Meteor Man*. [George-Warren and Romanowski 2001.]

FRANK HOFFMANN

VAN DYKE, ERNEST
(2 APR 1861–31 AUG 1923)

Belgian tenor, born Ernest Van Dijck in Antwerp. After study in Louvain and Brussels, he made his opera debut in the French premiere of *Lohengrin* (Paris) on 3 May 1887, then went to the Vienna Opera from 1888 to 1898, also appearing in Bayreuth as Parsifal in 1888. From 1898 to 1902 he sang Wagner roles at the Metropolitan Opera, then returned to the European stage until 1906, when he retired and taught singing. Van Dyck died in Berlaer-lez-Lierre, Belgium.

He made Bettini cylinders in 1898, early Wagner vocal records; there were five items, including two songs and numbers from *Rheingold*, *Walkure*, and *Tannhauser*. Van Dyck recorded later on Pathé cylinders in London, recording five songs and three arias, two from Wagner. In 1905 he made two sides for Fonotipia in Paris, then sang an aria from *Werther* for Homophone in 1906. IRCC reissued the *Walkure* "Spring Song" and "Stances d'ossian" from *Werther* (5007). [Dennis 1950/2.]

Grey Gull budget label from the late '20s. Courtesy Kurt Nauck/ Nauck's Vintage Records

VAN DYKE (LABEL)

An American record, one of the Grey Gull family, issued from 1929 to 1930. It was a low-cost ($.35) product, carrying dance music and popular vocals. Van Dyke was a successful record, even exported to the U.K. for sale in chain stores. [Rust 1978.]

VAN EPS, FRED
(30 DEC 1878–22 NOV 1960)

American banjoist; his name spelled at first Van Epps, then with one "p." He learned to play by listening to Vess Ossman on wax cylinders, and later had the satisfaction of remaking nearly all the Ossman records for Victor. He was a great success as soloist (George Gershwin was one of his accompanists), and with ensembles of his own devising, the Van Eps Trio (he and his brother William on banjos, with Felix Arndt at the piano — later replaced by Frank E. Banta; the second banjo later replaced by drummer Eddie King, who was in turn replaced by saxophonist Nathan Glantz) and the Van Eps Quartet (Joe Green, xylophonist, joining the trio).

Van Eps made his first Edison record in 1901: "Concert Waltz" (#7888). In 1910 he began with Victor ("The Burglar Buck") and with Columbia. He also did some work for Pathé, using the pseudonym Edward Boynton. Van Eps was with the Record Makers ensemble, and then with Eight Famous Victor Artists. His period of greatest success was 1913–1922 with the trio, performing dance and ragtime pieces for Victor, Edison, etc. He gave up recording for Victor in 1922; in that year he had 18 solo sides in the Victor catalog. The last of his dozen Edison Diamond Discs was made in 1926: "Dinah"/"I'm Sitting on Top of the World" (#51703).

Van Eps had many children who became well-known musicians. His son Fred was a guitarist with several leading bands in the 1930s, and his son George was a well-known jazz guitarist, who is credited with introducing the seven-string guitar to jazz. His son Robert was a Hollywood composer and arranger, who worked on the *Wizard of Oz*, among other films. [Walsh 1956/1–4.]

VAN GELDER, RUDY (2 NOV 1924–)

Noted jazz recording engineer, Van Gelder was a professional optometrist who, in the early 1950s, became interested in recording jazz music. In the late 1940s, he built a studio in the living room of his parent's home in Hackensack, New Jersey, and in 1953 began to record for the Blue Note label. By the mid-1950s, he was also overseeing most jazz sessions for Prestige. (Thelonious Monk named one of his pieces, "Hackensack," after the location of Van Gelder's studios.) In 1959, Van Gelder moved to a professional studio in Englewood Cliffs, New Jersey, and continued to record for Prestige and Blue Note along with a variety of small jazz labels, notably Impulse and CTI, through the early 1970s. Van Gelder was known for his crisp, unadorned recording style and for creating a relaxed atmosphere where musicians could be creative. Beginning in 1999, Blue Note began a "RVG Editions" reissue series, inviting Van Gelder to remaster his original recordings in 24-bit format for CD.

CARL BENSON

VANGUARD (LABEL)

Seymour Solomon and his younger brother Maynard founded Vanguard records and the affiliated Bach Guild in June 1950. Julliard school graduate Seymour was a violinist as well as classical music reviewer and radio commentator, while Maynard, a recent graduate of Brooklyn College, preferred pre–Civil War abolitionist novels along with classical music. Borrowing $10,000 from their father (with an additional $13,000 two years later), they opened a small office at 80 East 11th St. in New York City and launched their ambitious company; they took full advantage of the length and fidelity possibilities of the new 10-inch and 12-inch 33 1/3-rpm records. Starting with five Bach cantatas, they soon had a commercial success with a recording of the vocal/orchestral music of Gustav Mahler released in February 1951. The next year they indicated

Vanguard label, c. mid-'60s. Courtesy Frank Hoffmann

their interest in folk music with *Music of Poland*, soon followed by *Russian Folk Songs* and at least two by blues and gospel singer Brother John Seller. John Hammond produced the Jazz Showcase series from 1953–1958, furthering expanding Vanguard's musical range, which also recorded the Newport Jazz Festival for a few years. The Solomon brothers always stressed the highest quality in recording and manufacturing, often using large ballrooms as recording studios along with their own equipment and engineers.

Vanguard took a new turn with the release in 1957 of *The Weavers at Carnegie Hall*, recorded during the Weavers' reunion Christmas concert in 1955, indicating Maynard's growing interest in folk music, quickly followed by albums by Paul Robeson, Cisco Houston, Odetta, Ramblin' Jack Elliott, the Rooftop Singers, and numerous others. With *Joan Baez*, appearing in October 1960, Vanguard signaled its vital role in the quickly developing folk music revival; Baez would continue to record diverse albums for the company until 1972, although Vanguard would issue retrospective albums for many more years. It also began recording the Newport Folk Festival in 1959, with multiple albums from the 1963 and 1964 festivals, but only one from 1965 as folk music became overshadowed by folk rock and rock music. The Solomons kept pace with the changing market by signing Country Joe and the Fish — Country Joe McDonald thought the company's slogan might no longer be appropriate, "Recordings for the Connoisseur" — Chicago blues performers Jimmy Cotton, Junior Wells, Buddy Guy, and others, many produced by Samuel Charters. In the

1970s the company explored new approaches with Oregon, Alisha, the electronic sound of dance club singles, jazz-fusion, and Detroit rock.

In 1986 the Solomons sold Vanguard to the Welk Music Group, which reissued older artists on the new CD format and produce new albums by Alison Brown, the Dillards, and Livingston Taylor. In 1990 Seymour Solomon reacquired Vanguard's classical catalog, some of which has been reissued on his Vanguard Classics label. The Welk Group continued to issue albums in three series: Vanguard Sessions, Generations, and the Jazz Showcase. Maynard Solomon retired from the music business to write biographies of Beethoven and Mozart. For many decades Vanguard remained as one of the most important, and versatile, of the independent labels. [Cohen, 1989; website: www.vanguardrecords.com.]

RONALD D. COHEN

VAN HALEN

In 1974, after playing the local Los Angeles circuit for two years as Mammoth, the brothers Van Halen, Edward (guitar) and Alex (drums), recruited Michael Anthony (bass), and David Lee Roth (vocals) to join the group and were soon on their way to becoming one of the most successful bands to emerge from the 1970s. After discovering that another band had the rights to the name Mammoth, the group was renamed Van Halen; rejecting the name Rat Salade. While continuing to play local gigs and rock clubs, the group received their first big break in 1977 when Kiss bassist Gene Simmons discovered them at a local club and financed a recording session for the band. Van Halen was signed to Warner Bros.

Van Halen's debut album, which many fans still consider their best, *Van Halen* (WB #3075) was released in 1978 including the hit singles "Running with the Devil," "Jamie's Cryin'," and a cover of the Kinks' "You Really Got Me," as well as the often imitated but never duplicated "Eruption," the classic Edward Van Halen guitar solo that soars high into the sonic stratosphere, ripping up the fretboard with the finger tapping/hammer-on pull-off technique and tremolo dive-bombs made famous and conventionalized by Edward. Six months later the album *Van Halen* was certified platinum.

During the next few years, the "Ultimate Party Band" released several multiplatinum albums including *Van Halen II* (WB #3312), *Women and Children First* (WB #3415-2), *Fair Warning* (WB #3540), and *Diver Down* (WB #3677) until New Year's Day 1984 when the band released *1984* (WB #23985) bringing them to Top 40 radio and MTV via the mega-hits "Jump," "Panama," and "Hot for Teacher." In 1985, after taking time off to record his successful solo album *Crazy from the Heat* (WB #2522292), David Lee Roth left the band in a much-publicized split.

Van Halen quickly replaced Roth with Sammy Hagar ("I Can't Drive 55" on VOA GEF #24043). Though there was much speculation on whether Hagar would succeed in the footsteps of "Diamond Dave," fans answered by making 1986's *5150* (WB #35394) Van Halen's most popular album to date. Hagar's tenure with the band outlasted Roth's and fostered several more albums; including *OU812* (WB $25732), *For Unlawful Carnal Knowledge* (WB #26594), and *Live: Right Here Right Now* (WB #45198); until 1995's *Balance* (WB #45760), the last album with Hagar on vocals.

Soon after Hagar's departure, Roth returned for a highly anticipated reunion that spawned two new songs for the greatest hits (*Best of Van Halen Vol. 1*; WB #46332-2) release and an appearance on the "MTV Music Awards" show. While fans returned to the argument of best front-man, Dave or Sammy, Gary Cherone (formerly of Extreme, "Hole Hearted," "More than Words" on Pornograffitti AM #75021-5313-1) was recruited as the third lead singer of Van Halen. The much-anticipated album of the new line-up, appropriately titled *Van Halen III* (WB #46662), was released in the spring of 1998. Although the album debuted high on the charts, it was thought of as a disappointment by fans and critics.

Fans are still waiting for the band to return with a new album with Dave.

JAMES L. VAN ROEKEL

VANITY RECORD LABELS

In a sense, vanity labels — record imprints existing primarily as a status symbol or source of ego gratification — existed back in the early years of record sound history. In isolated instances, entrepreneurial recording stars such as Henry Burr (Par-O-Ket) created their own labels, primarily as a means of maximizing earnings and creative control.

It was rare for such companies to become major entities; Frank Sinatra's Reprise was a notable exception, achieving corporate dimensions shortly after its inception. On the other hand, rock icons with an eye sharply focused by the bottom line like Frank Zappa (Bizarre/Straight, followed by many other labels) and the Grateful Dead (Grateful Dead) built labels initially supported by cash infusions from major companies into large-scale enterprises encompassing mail order retailing, philanthropic programs, and countless other activities.

By the late 1960s, the vanity imprints became a bargaining chip enabling the majors to hold on to their most prized artists, generally progressive rock groups possessing sufficient talent and economic savvy to acquire control over virtually all career facets, from songwriting, recording, and touring to souvenir merchandizing. The pivotal development was Capitol's agreement to market all of the Beatles releases — and those of promising new artists discovered and nurtured by the group — on the Apple label.

Because record companies were amenable to giving top-earning artists any perk unlikely to compromise their earning power (e.g., greater creative freedom, optimum royalty arrangements, designer subsidiary for releases) during a period of unrivaled economic growth, other superstar acts — most notably, the Beach Boys (Brother), the Rolling Stones (Rolling Stones), the Moody Blues (Threshold), the Jefferson Airplane/Starship (Grunt), Todd Rundgren (Bearsville), Led Zeppelin (Swan Song), and Elton John (Rocket) — insisted on similar treatment. Many of these labels faded from view once the artists in question ceased to be top-grossing entities. Nevertheless, the practice of instituting vanity labels continues to the present day, albeit on a smaller scale, with artists such as Madonna (Maverick).

FRANK HOFFMANN

VANNI, ROBERTO
(21 AUG 1861–25 SEP 1941)

Italian tenor, born in Livorno. He was popular in many Italian cities, and sang in *Manon* and *Carmen* in Madrid. He performed opposite Adelina Patti in Buenos Aires and Chicago, and appeared in supporting roles at the Metropolitan Opera from 1894 to 1903; he also continued singing in South America and Europe. He retired to Italy in 1935 and died in Milan.

Vanni is of interest in recording history because he recorded four arias for Bettini in 1899, from *Otello*, *Trovatore*, *Lucia*, and *Martha*.

VARÈSE, EDGARD [EDGAR]
(22 DEC 1883–6 NOV 1965)

American composer of French extraction. Most of his works were composed in the 1920s for winds, brass, and percussion; his final works are classics of electro-acoustic music.

Varèse conceived of his music as "spatial — as bodies of intelligent sounds moving freely in space," anticipating stereo panning. His unfinished work *Espace*, begun in the late 1920s, called for simultaneous broadcasts by performers worldwide. During the 1930s Varèse unsuccessfully sought industrial and institutional funding to develop electronic instruments (as early as 1917 Varèse desired "instruments obedient to my thought" to contribute "a whole new world of unsuspected sounds"). The rejections led to a period of near-silence from 1936 to 1954.

An anonymous gift of an Ampex tape recorder in 1953 led to new compositions for tape. *Déserts*, for 20 instrumentalists and tape, featured "interludes" made of processed factory sounds and percussion. The work's 1954 premiere was the first stereo live broadcast in France.

Varèse's last completed work was *Poème Electronique*, created for the 1958 Worlds Fair in Brussels. Premiered in the Philips Pavilion designed by Le Corbusier, *Poème Electronique* used processed percussion and pitched instruments, bells, sirens, electronic tones, machine sounds, and voices. The sounds were routed to various configurations of over 400 speakers by a separate "control tape" (anticipating MIDI controllers). Varèse later remarked, "for the first time I heard my music literally projected into space." Over six months, Varèse's music was heard by 15,000 visitors daily. (The building was unfortunately later demolished.)

In the 1960s Varèse's work was recorded by Pierre Boulez and by Robert Craft. Frank Zappa also championed his work. In 1998 Riccardo Chailly recorded all of Varèse's completed work, along with reconstructions by Varèse expert Chou Wen-Chung and a newly remastered *Poème Electronique*, for *The Complete Works* (London #460208).

KEVIN HOLM-HUDSON

VAN ROOY, ANTON
(1 JAN 1870–28 NOV 1932)
Dutch bass-baritone, born in Rotterdam. He studied in Frankfurt, and after an audition with Cosima Wagner was engaged to sing Wotan at Bayreuth (1897). Subsequently he became one of the leading Wagnerian baritones, singing in leading houses of Europe and at the Metropolitan Opera from 1898 to 1908. He then sang in Frankfurt until retirement in 1914. Van Rooy died in Monaco.

All but one of his few recordings were Wagnerian. For HMV in London, 1902, he sang "Wotan's Farewell" and four other Wagner airs. In the U.S. in 1903, he recorded for Columbia "Nach Frankreich zogen zwei Grenadier" by Robert Schumann (reissued on the Sony CD *The 1903 Grand Opera Series*; #62334). He made four Edison cylinders in 1906, the "Toreador Song" plus the "Evening Star" and "Oh kehr zurück" from *Tannhäuser*, and "Wie oft in Meeres tiefen Schlund" from *Fliegende Holländer*. In 1906–1907 he was with Columbia in the U.S., for "Toreador Song" again and five Wagner numbers. IRCC and Historic Record Society reissued three of

his records on 78 rpm; and Top Artists Platters included one aria on their LP, *Twenty Great Wagnerian Singers* (#322). On CD, besides the Sony reissue noted above, four Wagnerian selections and one traditional German folk song are available on *The Harold Wayne Collection, Vol. 8* (Symposium #1100).

VARIETY (LABEL) (I)
An American record issued in 1927, having about 100 releases, all from Cameo matrices.

VARIETY (LABEL) (II)
A record produced by the publisher/agent Irving Mills in 1937. Good material was recorded by Cab Calloway, Charlie Barnet, and other jazz groups. [Rust 1978.]

VARIGROOVE RECORDING
The method of making a disc record which allows the lateral movement of the cutting stylus to determine the spacing between adjacent grooves. Thus the louder signals will have wider spaced grooves than the quieter signals. This practice permits a longer playing time for a given disc diameter.

VARSITY (LABEL)
A record issued by the United States Record Corp., New York, from 1939 to 1940; Eli Oberstein was the owner. Good jazz material was featured, including

Label issued by Eli Oberstein in the late '30s. Courtesy Kurt Nauck/Nauck's Vintage Records

Harry James, Jack Teagarden, and Frank Trumbauer; Buddy Clark was one of the vocalists. Their discs sold for $.35. When the label folded in 1940, the matrices went to Musicraft. In 1948 the label name was revived for LP issues by Varsity Records of New York, again with Oberstein as president. Varsity was absorbed by the Record Corp. of America in 1953. [Rust 1978.]

VASSAR GIRLS QUARTET

A female singing group that appeared on Edison cylinder (#9460; 1907) performing "Kentucky Babe." Members were Katherine Armstrong, Lovira Taft (or Tait), Florence Fiske, and E. Eleanor Patterson.

VAUGHAN, SARAH
(27 MAR 1924–3 APR 1990)

American popular singer, born in Newark, New Jersey. As a teenager she won an amateur contest in New York's Apollo Theatre and got a job with Earl Hines as singer/pianist. She later worked with Billy Eckstine and John Kirby, but essentially pursued a solo career after 1946. She and Ella Fitzgerald were probably the most influential and admired female vocalists of the 1940s and 1950s, regarded as successors to Billie Holiday. Vaughan made a preliminary session for the small Continental label in 1944, and then recorded for Musicraft from 1946–1948, launching her careeer. In 1949 she moved to major label Columbia, remaining there until 1953, when she moved to Mercury (for pop recordings) and its jazz subsidiary, EmArcy. Her great popularity came in the mid-1950s, when she earned the nickname "Divine Sarah" and sold more than 3 million records in one six-month period. Among her 15 chart singles in 1955–1960, "Misty" (Mercury #71477; 1959) and "Eternally" (Mercury #71562; 1960) are the most memorable examples of her dulcet ballad style.

In 1960 Vaughan moved to Roulette Records, remaining there for four years, then returning to Mercury through 1967. However, jazz singing was falling out of popularity with rock dominating the charts, so Vaughan did not record again until 1971, when she appeared on the jazz-specialty Mainsatream label (through 1974) and then moved to Norman Granz's Pablo Records (1977–1982). Her 1982 CBS album, *Gershwin Live* (#37277), recorded with conductor Michael Tilson Thomas, won a Grammy for Best Female Jazz Vocal. Her recording career waned after the early 1980s, but she continued to be a world-renowned performer until shortly before her death. She died from lung cancer in Los Angeles.

Vaughan's recording legacy is well-represented on CD. Her Musicraft material has appeared on various European jazz-specialty labels (including Pair,

Sarah Vaughan reissue album. Courtesy Frank Hoffmann

Discovery, Jazz Factory, and other labels); *In Hi Fi* (Columbia/Legacy #65117) reissues one of her best Columbia albums of the 1949–1953 period, featuring Miles Davis among other jazz musicians backing her (a previous two-LP overview of her Columbia material is not currently available on CD); her 1950s-era Mercury/EmArcy material is available both on CD reissues of the original albums as well as various anthologies, notably *The Definitive* (Verve #589949), which draws on this material along with some tracks cut for Roulette; two albums from Roulette with arrangements by Benny Carter are anthologized by Capitol (#28640), while her complete Roulette sessions have been reissued on a eight-CD boxed set by Mosaic (#214); and her Pablo material has been reissued in its original LP format on CD.

V-DISCS

Records produced during and after World War II by the U.S. War Department for distribution to military personnel. The earliest issues appeared in October 1943, the final ones in May 1949. V-Discs were made of unbreakable vinyl, in 12-inch size; the pressing was done by Victor and CBS. By means of tight grooving (136/inch) a playing time of up to 6 1/2 minutes was achieved, allowing more than one piece to appear on each side. Leading popular and classical artists donated their time for original recordings, and others were heard from contributed matrices. Often the performer would introduce a disc with some spoken lines, in the manner of the old announcements on acoustic discs and cylinders. It is interesting that many of the V-Discs were made during the recording ban ordered by the American Federation of Musicians, the only instrumental commercial records officially created during that period. More than 8 million V-Discs were distributed, and all the matrices were publicly destroyed when the project terminated. [Sears 1980.]

VEEJAY

A television or music video equivalent of the disc jockey: the person who announces the numbers. The first veejay was Cathy McGowan in the U.K., who announced the ITV pop program *Ready! Steady! Go!* in the 1960s.

VEE-JAY RECORDS

According to Old Town Records executive Sam Weiss: "Vee-Jay came the closest to being the number one black-owned pop label. ... They penetrated the white market like a cannonball going through butter. Had they overcome the family and financial problems that ultimately destroyed them, they would have become as big as Motown."

Vee-Jay was founded by disc jockey Vivian Carter and her husband, Jimmy Bracken ("Vee" and "Jay," respectively), in Gary, Indiana, in 1953, in order to provide an outlet for the kind of Black rhythm and blues that was still hard to find on records. The label's first two singles — Jimmy Reed's "High and Lonesome"/"Roll and Rhumba" (Vee-Jay #100; 1953) and the Spaniels's "Baby It's You"/"Bounce" (Vee-Jay $101; 1953; #10 R&B; the A side was the first song recorded by the company) — sold well, enabling Vee-Jay to adopt a more ambitious recording agenda. In addition to Reed and the Spaniels, the label found success in the 1950s with R&B acts such as the El Dorados, Jerry Butler, the Dells, Dee Clark, the Magnificents, John Lee Hooker, and Wade Flemons.

By 1955 Vee-Jay was successful enough to have established its own house band for use in the studio; key members included Lefty Bates on guitar, Quinn B. Wilson on bass, Paul Gusman and Vernel Fournier in drums, Horace Palm on piano, Red Holloway, Lucias Washington, and McKinley Easton on sax, Harlen Floyd on trombone, arrangers Von Freeman and Riley Hampton, and bandleader Al Smith. In 1957, the label began issuing albums and founded its first subsidiary, Falcon, in order to garner a greatly broadcast share (the threat of a lawsuit from a Southern label led Vee-Jay to rename the label Abner, named for executive Ewart Abner; another subsidiary, Tollie, would be created in the early 1960s). In 1958 the company formed a jazz department (signees would include Eddie

Harris, Bill Henderson, Lee Morgan, Wynton Kelly, and Wayne Shorter), and substantially expanded its slate of gospel releases the following year, the first group of LPs featuring the Staple Singers, Swan Silvertones, Five Blind Boys, and Highway QC's.

By 1960 Vee-Jay had its own headquarters building at 1449 Michigan Ave., Chicago, and had adopted its distinctive label design: a rainbow-colored band around a black and silver background that featured an inset red and white oval logo. In an attempt to garner a greater share of the mainstream pop market, the company issued Jerry Butler's "Moon River" (Vee-Jay #405; 1961; #11 pop, #14 R&B, #3 easy listening), the first time it scored on three national charts simultaneously.

Vee-Jay was recognized as a major force within the record industry by early 1963, having scored number one hits with Gene Chandler's "Duke of Earl" (Vee-Jay #416; 1961) and the Four Seasons's "Sherry" (Vee-Jay #456; 1962), "Big Girls Don't Cry" (Vee-Jay #465), and "Walk Like a Man" (Vee-Jay #485; 1963). Furthermore, they were given U.S. distribution rights to EMI artists Frank Ifield and the Beatles. Ifield's "I Remember You" (Vee-Jay #457; 1962) reached number five, but a succession of releases by the soon-to-be famous Fab Four all flopped.

By late 1963, however, the label was threatened by a rash of lawsuits, many of which were instigated by artists such as the Four Seasons due to poor bookkeeping practices and the failure to keep up with royalty payments. Ultimately, the loss of its leading artists — and the failure to find new talent at the height of the British Invasion — caused Vee-Jay to close its offices and file for bankruptcy in May 1966. Beginning in the early 1990s, the company's classic material was being reissued by the New York–based Vee-Jay Limited Partnership.

FRANK HOFFMANN

VELODYNE ACOUSTICS

One of the premier manufacturers of subwoofers in the U.S., the company was started in 1983 by David Hall, and has expanded to become dominant in its field. Velodyne's first product was the ULD-18 subwoofer, followed shortly later by the smaller and lower-priced ULD-15. Because of their remarkable and revolutionary servo-controlled amp/driver systems, these two systems demonstrated the lowest distortion and deepest extension of any bass-reproducing systems of the era. Subsequent models from the company continue to set standard for superior low-frequency performance in subwoofer systems.

HOWARD FERSTLER

VELVET FACE EDISON BELL CELEBRITY RECORD (LABEL)

A U.K. 10-inch and 12-inch record issued by J.E. Hough, Ltd., from 1910 to 1915. The same firm had released its first Velvet Face Edison Bell disc in December 1910.

FRANK ANDREWS

VELVET TONE (LABEL)

SEE MARCONI VELVET TONE (LABEL)

VELVET TONE (LABEL)

A Columbia low-cost disc issued from 1925 to 1932. About 1,500 releases were made, nearly all duplicated on the Harmony label, offering popular and dance material with some blues and race records. [Rust 1978.]

VENET, NIK (3 DEC 1936–)

Born Nikolas Kostantinos Venetoulis in Baltimore, Maryland, Venet was playing in a local jazz band during his teen years. While visiting Shreveport, Louisiana, in 1957, Venet met a local guitarist named Jimmy Burton who was playing with a local singer, Dale Hawkins. Venet was asked to engineer an impromptu session, and the result was the hit record "Suzie Q" (Checker #863; #27), a rockabilly classic. Venet was bitten by the recording bug, and worked his way to Los Angeles, where he was hired by a small jazz label, World Pacific. There he oversaw a wide range of recordings, from Chet Baker's moody jazz to comedy by Lord Buckley and world music by Indian sitarist Ravi Shankar. In 1960, he was hired by Capitol, and scored his first hit as a producer a year later with the Lettermen on "When I Fall in Love." In 1962 Venet was assigned to a new local group that was signed by the label, the Beach Boys, and he produced their first hits including, "Surfin'," "Surfin' Safari," and "Surfin' U.S.A." Venet's biggest mid-1960s hitmaker was Glen Campbell, who scored a number of hits with pop songs "Gentle on My Mind," "By the Time I Get to Phoenix," and "Wichita Lineman." Venet also produced the local folk-pop trio the Stone Poneys, featuring young Linda Ronstadt as their lead vocalist, overseeing their 1967 hit, "Different Drum," and Ronstandt's first solo recordings. Venet continued to work with other folk-pop singer/songwriters, notably Fred Neil in the later 1960s and, after leaving Capitol to go independent, John Stewart in the mid-1970s. After that, he was less active on the pop scene.

CARL BENSON

VENETIAN INSTRUMENTAL TRIO

An ensemble that recorded two numbers for Edison cylinders in 1909. The members were Eugene Jaudas, violin; Eugene C. Rose, flute; and Charles Schuetze, harp. The numbers offered by this probably unique combination of instruments were "Moszkowski's Serenade" (#10152) and "Song of the Mermaids" (#10027). In 1913 the group made an Edison Diamond Disc of "Dear Heart" (#50061; previously issued anonymously on #50005). It would seem that "Serenade" (#80006 and #80012; ca. 1913) was by the same artists. And they may have been three of the four members of an ensemble that made a dozen other Edison Diamond Discs in 1912–1913; that group was identified only as violin, flute, harp, and cello.

VENTED BAFFLE

SEE BASS REFLEX SYSTEM

VENTURES, THE

The most successful American instrumental group during the rock era, the Ventures led the way in establishing the guitar-based sound dominating popular music from 1960 onward. Their distinctive sound — pulsing drums and metallic, twanging guitars — spanned a wide range of material (e.g., calypso, blues, Latin, psychedelia, folk rock, Merseybeat), surviving many changes in public taste. Many genres — most notably, surf music, the British Invasion, power pop, and alternative rock — have been influenced by the band.

Based in Seattle, the Ventures's first release, "Walk Don't Run" (Dolton #25), reached number two on the pop charts in August 1960. They had 14 hits in all during the 1960s, including the Top 10 recordings "Walk Don't Run '64" (Dolton 96; 1964) and "Hawaii Five-O" (Liberty #56068; 1969). In 1965 the band issued one of the most popular instructional records ever, *Play Guitar with the Ventures* (Dolton #16501). The Ventures — which included founding members Bob Bogle (guitar, bass) and Don Wilson (guitar) — continued to tour extensively through the 1990s, long after the hits stopped coming. [George-Warren and Romanowski 1995]

FRANK HOFFMANN

VENUTI, JOE (16 SEP 1898–14 AUG 1978)

Italian/American jazz violinist, born in Lecco, Italy (some sources say he was born in Philadelphia, with his family emigrating shortly before his birth from Lecco). Venuti studied classical violin; then he turned to the popular styles, playing in a combo with guitarist Eddie Lang. They were successful in New York, and both were with Paul Whiteman in 1929–1930. Venuti free-lanced in the 1930s, at times leading a Big Band, later smaller groups through the mid-1940s. He worked the West Coast lounge circuit during the 1960s, primarily out of his new home of Seattle. During the late 1960s early 1970s jazz revival, Venuti returned to active concertizing and recording in a variety of contexts, showing the same vigor and sense of humor that marked his earlier playing. He died in Seattle.

Venuti and Lang recorded first for Columbia in 1926, doing "Black and Blue Bottom"/"Stringing the Blues" (#914-D). They were joined by Adrian Rollini, bass saxophone, and pianist Arthur Schutt for four Okeh sides in 1927, performing under the name the Blue Four. Various other players would record with Venuti and Lang under this name in the future; Jimmy Dorsey was one of the Blue Four who recorded "Blue Room" for Okeh in 1928 (#41144). A group called the Blue Six — including Benny Goodman, Bud Freeman, and Rollini — did a sparkling "Sweet Lorraine" in 1933 (Columbia #CB-708). His 1970s-era recordings appeared on a variety of labels, including Chiaroscuro, Vanguard, and Concord Jazz. CD reissues of his work with Venuti have appeared on numerous labels. A good overview of his early career is *Violin Jazz, 1927–34* (Yazoo #1062); for the true fan, Mosaic offers an eight-CD set (*The Classic Columbia and Okeh Joe Venuti and Eddie Lang Sessions*; #213) that encompasses everything Venuti and Lang recorded during this period in various small groups and big bands, although not their nonjazz recordings. Much of Venuti's 1970s output, originally on LP, has been reissued in the same format on CD.

VERTICAL CUT

The name given to a recording process (also known as hill and dale) that utilizes a vertical modulation or pattern made in the spiraling groove on a cylinder or disc. Vibrations are cut into the medium perpendicularly to the surface. This was the method of the Thomas Edison phonographs. Both lateral-cut and vertical-cut recordings were made in the Volta Laboratories in the early 1880s. First used on commercial discs by Neophone Co., Ltd., in 1904, it was popularized by Pathé from 1906. Vertical cut was never as popular as the lateral-cut method, although Edison preferred it, making vertical-cut cylinders and Diamond Discs until 1929, at which time he also made some lateral records.

See also **Lateral Recording**

VERVE (LABEL)

An American record issued by Norman Granz in Los Angeles from 1956 to 1960. The label was formed by Granz as a consolidation of his Clef, Down Home, and Norgran labels. Jazz, pop, folk, comedy, and gospel material was offered. Ella Fitzgerald was the first star performer, achieving great acclaim for her "songbooks" series. Ricky Nelson made his first records for Verve. Despite the success of Verve, Granz decided to sell out to MGM in December 1960. Creed Taylor was recording director from 1961 to 1967, and continued the popularity of the label with recordings by such luminaries as Count Basie, Duke Ellington, Bill Evans, Stan Getz, Johnny Hodges, Antonio Carlos Jobim, and Oscar Peterson.

On 5 May 1972, MGM sold all its record labels to Polydor, which concentrated on reissues in Europe and Japan. Beginning in the early 1980s, Polydor (and its corporate successors, Polygram, MCA, and finally the Universal Music Group) began reissuing Verve material aggressively in the U.S. in boxed sets and on individual CDs, as well as signing new jazz acts. The Verve back catalog remains one of the most important repositories of 1950s' and 1960s' jazz. In 1999 the owners of the Verve catalog, Universal Music Group, placed all of their jazz labels under the umbrella of the Verve Music Group, including GRP, Impulse!, and Blue Thumb, as well as the jazz catalogs of several other Universal-owned labels, including Commodore, Chess, Decca, Brunswick, Argo, Cadet, Dot, Coral, Decca, ABC-Paramount, A&M, Mercury, Philips, and Polydor. [Ruppli 1986.]

VICTOR CAFE

A restaurant located in the Italian section of Philadelphia (1303 Dickinson St.), opened in 1933 by John Di Stefano, a former Victor record dealer. He played opera records during meals, attracting a distinguished clientele of recording artists from the Victor studios in neighboring Camden, New Jersey: Giovanni Martinelli, Giuseppe De Luca, Titta Ruffo, Beniamino Gigli, Ezio Pinza, and many others. Upon the death of Di Stefano in 1954, the business was continued by his son Henry (who died in 1986). Another son, Armand, also contributed an hour of weekly operatic records — from the family collection of 30,000 discs — to a Philadelphia radio station until his death in 1989. The custom of having waiters and waitresses sing operatic numbers created a delightful atmosphere in the establishment. Mario Lanza was one of those earnest vocalists. [A photo of the Cafe is in *TWR* #17 (August 1972).]

VICTOR LADIES QUARTET

A female vocal ensemble that recorded briefly for Victor ca. 1915, and was quickly set aside (no records in the 1917 catalog). Members were probably

Elizabeth Wheeler, Olive Kline, Elsie Baker, and Marguerite Dunlap. [Walsh 1961/10.]

VICTOR LIGHT OPERA CO.

An ensemble created ca. 1909 to record operettas and Broadway musicals. By the time of the 1917 catalog it was named the Victor Opera Co. A long list of excerpts appeared in that catalog, from nearly 80 stage works, some grand operas among them. Membership varied, but included at one time or another many of the leading Victor artists, e.g., Reinald Werrenrath, S.H. Dudley, Elsie Baker, John Bieling, Steve Porter, Elise Stevenson, Harry Macdonough, Ada Jones, Billy Murray, Olive Kline, and William F. Hooley. Members of the Lyric and Orpheus Quartets, and of the Revelers, were often the basis for the company's recordings. The group was still in the catalog in 1940 (as the Victor Light Opera Co. again), but with a reduced list of discs.

VICTOR MALE QUARTET

See Orpheus Quartet

VICTOR MINSTRELS

A house group formed to make Victor records, known also as the Victor Minstrel Co. It was active from ca. 1903 to ca. 1909. Members included, at various times, Len Spencer and the Hayden Quartet. After a long hiatus, the group — or the concept — was restored with a disc by the Victor Minstrels in January 1929, named "Minstrel Show of 1929" (#35961). Singers included Billy Murray, Monroe Silver, and James Stanley. Frank Crumit joined in on the flip side. There were no further releases.

See also **Minstrel Recordings**

VICTOR OPERA CO.

See Victor Light Opera Co.

VICTOR OPERA SEXTET

A house group formed to make operatic ensemble discs for Victor in 1915. Members were Olive Kline, Marguerite Dunlap, Lambert Murphy, Harry Macdonough, and Reinald Werrenrath. They sang the *Lucia* Sextet (#70036); also available on a double-sided record with the *Rigoletto* Quartet (#55066; a low-cost bargain, at $1.25 for the double, compared to the several $5 and $7 versions with Enrico Caruso et al.).

VICTOR ORCHESTRA

A house ensemble formed in 1906 to record orchestral works for Victor. Walter B. Rogers conducted and played cornet. Other members were Charles D'Almaine, first violin; Louis Christie, clarinet; Darius Lyons, flute; Emil Keneke, cornet; Herman Conrad, bass; O. Edward Wardwell, trombone; Frank Reschke, violin and saxophone; Walter Pryor, cornet; A. Levy, clarinet; Arthur Trepte, oboe; Theodore Levy, violin; S.O. Pryor, percussion, and C.H.H. Booth, organ. They recorded movements from Beethoven's Fifth Symphony and Dvorak's New World Symphony (#35275), the *Egmont Overture* (#35493), and a few other symphonic masterworks; but most of their extensive list was made up of light classics and arrangements.

The Victor Concert Orchestra coexisted with this group, and was presumably similar in membership, as it was in repertoire. By the time of the 1927 catalog, the Victor Orchestra had been renamed the Victor Symphony Orchestra (the Concert Orchestra was connected to it by a "see also" reference), and there was also a Victor Salon Orchestra, with Nathaniel Shilkret directing. In the 1938 catalog Shilkret conducted the Victor Symphony Orchestra on both black label — where all the above ensembles had been kept — and on a Red Seal album of John Alden Carpenter's *Skyscrapers* (#M-130). Claude Lapham directed the Victor Symphony on a second Red Seal, doing a work of his own, *Mihara Yama* (#11895). In the 1940 catalog the Symphony Orchestra had three Red Seal items; and the Victor Salon Group and Orchestra was well represented on Red Seal, directed by Shilkret, with various George Gershwin medley records, plus other Broadway musical "gems."

VICTOR RECORD SOCIETY

An organization established in 1937 by Thomas F. Joyce, as a promotion for Victor records. A small record player attachment for a radio was offered to members at $14.95, and the concept proved attractive enough to draw 150,000 members, who agreed to buy a specified number of discs. A boost to lagging sales resulted, especially in the popular record area.

VICTOR SALON ORCHESTRA

See Victor Orchestra

VICTOR SYMPHONY ORCHESTRA

See Victor Orchestra

VICTOR TALKING MACHINE CO.

This article has nine sections: 1. The first decade of Victor; 2. The 1910s; 3. The 1920s; 4. RCA and the 1930s; 5. The 1940s; 6. Engineering innovations; 7. Studios; 8. Artists and repertoire; 9. Victor officials.

1. *The First Decade of Victor.* The fledgling disc industry was in a state of confusion in 1900. Eldridge R. Johnson was a machinist providing Gramophones for Emile Berliner, the first producer of commercial disc records. Johnson began to make records himself in January 1900. He released his first commercial records a few months later, with gold print on black paper labels (Berliner discs had no labels), seven inches in diameter. Those discs bore the label name Improved Gram-O-Phone Record. They sold for $.50. The first recording, listed as number A-1 in Johnson's matrix log, was a recitation by George Broderick of Eugene Field's poem "Departure.

In summer 1900 Johnson and Leon F. Douglass formed the Consolidated Talking Machine Co. to market Johnson's machines and records, and to utilize his improved recording process. There were daily recording sessions, and a few discs were pressed from material recorded in Europe by Fred Gaisberg and Belford Royal for the Gramophone Co., Ltd. In fall 1900 five models of disc players were advertised, not from Consolidated but from Eldridge R. Johnson: a Toy ($3), Type A ($12), Type B ($18), Type C ($25), and Type D ($6).

The company name was changed to Eldridge Johnson, Manufacturing Machinist to avoid a name conflict with Berliner's holding company, Consolidated Talking Machine Co. of America.

In January 1901 the first 10-inch discs were made. Johnson issued them at first (3–10 January) with the label name Victor Ten Inch Record; then as Victor Monarch Record. The cost was $1. Following a court order of 1 Mar 1901, restraining Johnson from using the term Gramophone for his products, he changed the label name of the seven-inch disc to Improved Record. (That court ruling was reversed on appeal in June 1901, then restored on 22 July 1902. At that point Johnson chose to settle out of court with the instigator, Frank Seaman, rather than prolong the legal proceedings.) Yet another label name was introduced on 12 Mar 1901, as Johnson registered the trademark Victor Record for the seven-inch discs. A report of September 1901 showed that the previous 12 months had been successful for the Johnson firm, with a profit of $180,000.

Berliner and Johnson agreed to pool their patent, trademark, and manufacturing interests, and incorporated the Victor Talking Machine Co. on 3 Oct 1901. It was organized on 5 Oct 1901 with Eldridge Johnson, president; Leon F. Douglass, vice president and general manager; Thomas S. Parvin, treasurer; A.C. Middleton,

Early Victor Record label, 1912. Courtesy David A. Jasen

secretary; and Horace Pettit, general counsel. Berliner received 40 percent of Victor's stock but did not participate actively in the company. Terms of the incorporation included the issue of 20,000 shares of common, and 5,000 shares of 7 percent preferred (stock). The Consolidated Talking Machine Co. of America (Berliner's firm) received 8,000 shares of common for the Berliner patents, and paid $50,000 for 500 shares of preferred with a bonus of 1,000 additional shares of common. This provided the new company with much needed working capital. Johnson received 10,000 shares of common and 3,000 shares of preferred for his plant, his patents, and his ongoing business. The remaining 1,000 shares of common and 1,500 shares of preferred went into the company's treasury. A contract was drawn up with the Gramophone Co. which gave them an option on three times their purchases for the previous year up to 50 percent of the company's capacity. They agreed to contribute up to $10,000 a year to the expense of the company's experimental laboratories, to provide a 25 percent profit over costs, to protect the company's patents, trademark, etc., and to promote the sale of the product in Europe, in U.K. colonies and possessions, and in Russia and Japan. [Aldridge 1964]. Thus the partnership between Victor and the Gramophone Co. was established, a relationship that was to continue until 1953.

When the Victor Talking Machine Co. was established, Johnson's records and instruments had already been accepted and sold by influential music stores, such as Wurlitzer, Lyon and Healy, and Sherman Clay. A large manufacturing complex was soon developed around Johnson's machine shop in Camden, New Jersey, across the Delaware River from Philadelphia.

Executive offices were at 114 N. Front St.; instruments were assembled in a four-story factory at 120 N. Front St., using cabinets purchased from Sheip Manufacturing Co. Philadelphia was the site of the recording studio (10th and Lombard Streets), and a sales office (Girard Building, on 12th St.). Records were pressed by the Duranoid Co. until Victor's pressing facility was built at 23 Market St., Camden, in 1902. (From 1907 all pressing was done in Camden.) One-half of Victor's instrument production was purchased by the Gramophone Co., Ltd., for sale in Europe and the U.K. (excepting Canada where Berliner Gramophone of Montreal had rights).

Nipper appeared for the first time on Victor record labels in January 1902. On 18 Jan 1902 Johnson and Douglass personally bought the Globe Record Co. from the Burt Co., and sold it on 15 Feb 1902 to the American Graphophone Co. These transactions formed part of a negotiation with the Columbia interests, ending patent litigations between the firms, and leading to a cross-licensing agreement that gave them control of the major industry patents. By the end of 1902, Victor had produced about 2 million records. Some 2,000 discs a day were coming from Camden, utilizing Johnson's new multiple stamper system.

In Europe the Gramophone Co. and others were releasing recordings of classical music by operatic artists such as Feodor Chaliapin and the new sensation, Enrico Caruso. The records had special red labels and sold at higher prices than nonclassical records. In the U.S. most of the early recorded material consisted of popular songs, comic songs and recitations, and band music. Victor did have a little classical material in 1900, by George Broderick (opera arias in English), Rosalia Chalia, and Emilio de Gogorza. But the great advance came with the first Red Seal records, announced in March 1903. That was the 5000 series, 25 imports (including Enrico Caruso's Milan recordings) from the Gramophone Co., selling for $2.50 each.

Victor made its own first Red Seal recording on 30 Apr 1903 in room 826 at Carnegie Hall with Australian mezzo-soprano Ada Crossley singing "Caro Mio Ben" on a 10-inch Monarch (#81001). Louise Homer, Johanna Gadski, and Antonio Scotti also recorded in room 826, as did Caruso on 1 Feb 1904, after he was signed to an exclusive contract by Victor. Other celebrities to sing on early Red Seals included Zélie de Lussan, Emma Eames, Marcel Journet, and Marcella Sembrich. Victor developed a strong hold on the operatic field that it never relinquished. Mauve-colored Victor "Melba" Records — a special label for the diva — were offered in March 1904, and Victor "Patti" Records (Red Seal) appeared in December 1905. Those were premium discs; the Patti items sold for $5.

One of Johnson's articles of faith was in the power of advertising. The F. Wallis Armstrong advertising agency handled Victor promotions to 1925, emphasizing the notions of product quality, the pleasure of Gramophone ownership, and the greatness of Victor artists. In good times or hard times, Victor advertising was ubiquitous in newspapers and national magazines. Profits were substantial in the early years: 1902 — $151,000; 1903 — $495,000; 1904 (the year of a disruptive fire in the Camden complex) — $424,00; 1905 — $607,000. More than 3.5 million records were sold by the end of 1905.

A permanent matrix numbering system was introduced in April 1903. In that year there was a new label line as well, the De Luxe series. On 11 March a 14-inch De Luxe, changed soon to the De Luxe Special Record, was announced; it ran 60 rpm and sold for $2. A 12-inch De Luxe (black label) appeared in fall 1903 for $1.50, and a 12-inch De Luxe (Red Seal) for $3.

The first Red Seal duet was extremely popular: "Solenne in quest' ora" from *Forza del destino*, sung by Caruso and Antonio Scotti (#89001; March 1906). And the first recording of the *Rigoletto* Quartet was a great hit, selling for $4. It presented Caruso, Bessie Abott, Louise Homer, and Scotti (#96000; February 1907).

Eldridge Johnson continued to improve the instrument line. The tapered tone arm and goose neck were introduced in 1903. The recording laboratory was managed by Calvin G. Child. Harry O. Sooy was the chief recordist; he was later joined by his brothers Raymond A. and Charles E. Sooy. Arthur Pryor was the first musical director, succeeded shortly by Walter Bowman Rogers. As Douglass left his post of general manager because of illness, Louis Geissler succeeded him in 1906, remaining to 1918 (Geissler was then a director until 1921). A trade publication, *The Voice of the Victor*, was introduced for dealers in April 1906 to keep them informed about new records, sales methods, and artist tours. The Victor dealers formed the National Association of Talking Machine Jobbers.

In 1906 Victor introduced a new phonograph with the horn enclosed within its cabinet. It was the Victrola, styled at first the Victor-Victrola, priced at $200. It was a success in many console and table models, setting the industry standard. A less-inspired invention was also introduced in 1906, the Auxetophone. On 1 Sept 1906, Victor bought the 8,000 shares of its stock that Berliner's firm had acquired in the Victor incorporation.

Victor's Red Seal classical records were single-sided until 1923. But to match Columbia's double-sided discs (introduced in 1904) Victor began its 16000 popular series of double-sided records in September 1908. They sold for $.75 (10-inch) and $1.25 (12-inch), while single-faced records were selling for $.60 and $1.

At the end of its first decade, Victor was in an excellent position. More than 35 million records had been

Advertisement for various Victrola models made by the Victor Talking Machine Co. Courtesy David A. Jasen

sold, and the phonographs (606,596 sold through 1910) had gained acceptance as the finest made.

See also **Disc**

2. *The 1910s.* The Camden complex continued to grow in response to the volume of sales. In 1911, 124,000 phonographs were sold. External horn instruments accounted for 25 percent of sales, Victrola table models 42 percent, and console Victrolas 33 percent of sales in 1911. In April 1911 an educational department was established, under the direction of Frances E. Clark, to develop an interest in music among school children.

Additions to Victor's artist roster from 1910 to 1913 included George M. Cohan, Al Jolson, John McCormack, Mischa Elman, Fritz Kreisler, Alma Gluck, Victor Herbert, Jan Paderewski, Jan Kubelik, Giovanni Martinelli, and the Flonzaley Quartet. Amelita Galli-Curci began recording for Victor in October 1916. There were around 600 titles in the Red Seal catalog in 1912. In 1916 Calvin Child became head of Victor's artist department and Josef Pasternack became musical director. In February 1917 Charles Sooy was able to successfully capture the Original Dixieland Jazz Band's new music on wax.

The *Victor Book of the Opera*, edited by Samuel H. Rous, appeared in the first of many editions in 1912, offering opera plots along with photos and promotions

of Victor artists, for $.75. No fewer than six *Lucia* Mad Scenes were noted in the book.

Victor's instrument production was severely curtailed by the company's effort to supply material for World War I, as skilled workers of the cabinet factory made aircraft assemblies, rifle stock, and detonator cases. Recording artists appeared at war bond rallies, and their recordings helped boost morale. A new label design, the so-called Wing label, was introduced in 1914.

During 1917–1934, the Victor name was replaced by Victrola on Red Seal issues.

There were 6,043 licensed Victor dealers in 1916, and 103 distributors. A "Tungs-tone Stylus" was marketed, as an alternative to steel needles. The Camden plant had its greatest period of investment from 1912 to 1917.

After satisfactory recordings were made by Pasternack and the 51 musicians of the Victor Symphony Orchestra, the Boston Symphony under Karl Muck and the Philadelphia Orchestra under Leopold Stokowski were brought to Camden to make their initial recordings. As the studio in Building 15 could not accommodate the large orchestras, the recordings were made in an auditorium in the new executive office building. The Trinity Baptist Church building located three blocks from the plant complex was purchased and used as a studio for the recording of large groups. Jascha Heifetz began recording for Victor in November 1917. Normal production in

Instructions from Victor on how to play records on its Victrolas. From an early Victor catalog. Courtesy Jerald Kalstein

1155

Camden after the war was reached in October 1919 and instrument sales reached 560,000 in 1920.

The Red Seal roster was the monumental achievement of the firm. In the 1917 catalog, celebrities not mentioned above included sopranos Lucrezia Bori, Emma Calvé Emmy Destinn, Geraldine Farrar, Johanna Gadski, Maria Galvany, Alma Gluck, Frieda Hempel, and Alice Nielsen. Contraltos included Clara Butt, Julia Culp, Jeanne Gerville-Réache, Margarete Matzenauer, and Ernestine Schumann-Heink. Leading tenors were Fernando de Lucia, Francesco Marconi, Riccardo Martin, Giovanni Martinelli, Leo Slezak, Francesco Tamagno, and Evan Williams. Baritones included Mario Ancona, Mattia Battistini, Giuseppe de Luca, Maurice Renaud, Titta Ruffo, and Mario Sammarco. Pol Planáon was a leading bass. Instrumental stars included Jan Kubelik, Ignace Paderewski, and Efrem Zimbalist.

On black label records there were acclaimed artists as well, of which only a few will be mentioned: Henry Burr, Eddie Cantor, Billy Golden, Al Jolson, Harry Lauder, and Reinald Werrenrath. More than 205 million Victor records had been sold by the end of 1919.

3. *The 1920s*. Sergei Rachmaninoff and Paul Whiteman became Victor artists in 1920. Caruso made his last recordings in Camden on 16 Sep 1920. His death in August 1921 ended the career of the single artist who contributed most to the success of Victor and the early phonograph industry. Victor's instrument sales dropped in 1921 as Brunswick and Sonora offered the flat-top cabinets that were preferred by the public. Phonograph sales were greatly eroded by the increasing popularity of radio as a form of home entertainment. By the fall of 1924 Victor halted instrument production and budgeted $5 million for a massive sales campaign. N.W. Ayer was engaged as advertising agent, replacing Armstrong.

The phonograph industry had been doing little to improve its product. James Owens and Albertis Hewitt had conducted electrical recording experiments at Victor as early as 1913, but their approach was strictly trial and error. Early in 1924 Victor had rejected an offer made by Bell Telephone Laboratories to witness a demonstration of a new electrical recording process and improved acoustical playback equipment. But by December 1924 Victor arranged to have a demonstration for its technical staff in Camden. Victor and Columbia obtained rights to use the new recording and reproduction systems. In March 1925 the studio in Camden began making electrical recordings for Victor's classical and popular catalogs. The New York studio made its first electrical recordings on 31 July 1925, in a process that Victor named "Orthophonic Recording." In a short time 10,000 Credenza Orthophonic Victrolas were built, hand-wound acoustic taking machines with reentrant horns. The new products were introduced to the public on 2 Nov 1925, and by the end of 1926 there were 43 new Victrola models. Included in the new line were models with a radio chassis and electrical playback apparatus made by RCA. An "Electrola" line had electric amplification. The electrically recorded discs had a new scroll design on their labels. Public acceptance of the new records and instruments was satisfying, and by the end of 1926 the working loss of $6.5 million incurred in 1925 had been recovered. Great hit records emerged from the electrical process, including J.S. Bach's "Toccata and Fugue in D-Minor" in a brilliant transcription for the Philadelphia Orchestra.

Eldridge Johnson sold his interest in Victor in December 1926 to bankers Speyer and Co. and J. & W. Seligman of New York, for an estimated $30 million. Johnson's inventiveness and business sense had developed the wheezy instrument and noisy discs of the 1890s into a product line that through 1929 resulted in the manufacture of nearly 8 million instruments and more than one-half billion records.

E.E. Shumaker, former purchasing agent and director of the company, became the new Victor president. Many new dance bands and popular groups were Victor artists during the late 1920s, including the Coon-Sanders Orchestra, Jan Garber, Ray Noble, Fred Waring, and Ted Weems. Jazz artists included Duke Ellington, Jean Goldkette, Jelly Roll Morton, Bennie Moten, Ben Pollack, and Fats Waller.

Nathaniel Shilkret was the principal conductor of the Victor Orchestra and accompanist of popular vocalists. Field recordings were made with portable electrical recording equipment during the summers of 1927 and 1928 in Virginia, Tennessee, North Carolina, and Georgia. Jimmie Rodgers and the Carter Family were among the artists discovered in these sessions.

New Red Seal performers of the 1920s included Marian Anderson, Pablo Casals, Richard Crooks, Vladimir Horowitz, Wanda Landowska, Lauritz Melchior, Yehudi Menuhin, Ezio Pinza, Rosa Ponselle, Sergei Rachmaninoff, Elisabeth Rethberg, Paul Robeson, Tito Schipa, and Lawrence Tibbett. Toscanini made records with the New York Philharmonic Symphony Orchestra, and Serge Koussevitzky recorded with the Boston Symphony Orchestra.

Another instrument advance came in March 1927, with the first record changer. The early version played either 10-inch or 12-inch records, while a later model (November 1928) could mix the two sizes.

In 1929 RCA (Radio Corp. of America) acquired Victor Talking Machine Co. Victor, in its 28-year existence, had made a major impact on home entertainment. It was an industry pioneer in the use of the advertising media. It provided jobs for 10,000 workers, and at least 30 investors in the company received investment returns of more than $1 million each. By the end of 1929, record sales had reached around 600 million. Some $700 million in total sales had been posted. About 8,130,000 instruments had been made.

4. *RCA and the 1930s.* When the Victor Talking Machine Co. was bought by RCA (Radio Corp. of America) on 4 Jan 1929, 60 percent of RCA was owned by the General Electric Co. (GE) and 40 percent by Westinghouse Electric and Manufacturing Co. (Westinghouse). Victor became the Victor Division, along with the Radiola Division, of the new Radio-Victor Co. (a sales organization). The Audio Vision Appliance Co. was the manufacturer for both divisions. This company was created by GE and Westinghouse to operate the large Victor plant in Camden, but beginning in 1931 all of these activities were brought together in the RCA Victor Co., Inc. That name appeared on record labels. Then, by a consent decree of 13 Nov 1932, RCA became independent of GE and Westinghouse. In 1935 RCA Victor and RCA Radiotron merged to form the RCA Manufacturing Co., Inc., and that name was given on record labels. In 1942, that company was merged with the parent corporation, RCA, and the responsibility for manufacturing given to its RCA Victor Division. In 1954 RCA Victor and the RCA Home Instruments Division were merged into RCA Consumer Products. In 1969 RCA Victor became a part of the National Broadcasting Company (NBC).

This outline of the placement of RCA Victor in the hierarchy of RCA does not tell the whole story. RCA Victor had three units: Home Instruments, the Advanced Technology Laboratories, and the David Sarnoff Research Center (known as "The Labs") in Princeton, New Jersey. Home Instruments had the responsibility for the development, design, manufacture, and sales of the record players and radio-phonograph combinations. The role of what was first known as Advanced Development, then Applied Research, and finally as Advanced Technology Laboratories, was largely informal, voluntary, and self-directing. Since the beginning of RCA in 1919, this engineering adjunct was attached to one division and then to another. It was a place where first evaluations could be made of new technologies and proposed new products. "The Labs" supported RCA Victor with pure and practical research in all areas, particularly in the design of recording studios, acoustics, monitoring speakers, and sound compensation.

The acquisition of Victor cost RCA $150 million, but the value received was enormous. A prize item gained was the His Master's Voice (Nipper) trademark, with its heritage of customer loyalty and confidence. Another valuable item in the package was the extensive Victor phonographic and record business,

which had earned more than 25 percent in average annual dividends for 20 years. There were more than 1,000 artists in the Victor catalog. And there was a sales and distribution network unequaled in the industry. A third significant item was the Camden manufacturing complex, one of the largest in the nation, with 16 buildings and more than 10,000 employees. Camden was immediately pressed into radio manufacture, to meet the ever increasing demand, while continuing to produce records. It had 160 swing leaf record presses on the fifth floor of Building 13. Those presses, dating from 1912, were used by RCA Victor until 1977 when they were replaced by 49 Alpha 12-inch automatics that provided somewhat more than the 75 million yearly production of the manual presses. The matrix department — with its plating tanks, inspection, packing, and shipping units — was in the same building.

Along with the Camden complex came full ownership of Victor of Canada, 67 percent of Victor of Japan, 50 percent interest in the Gramophone Co. Ltd., of Britain, and companies in Argentina, Brazil, and Chile.

The U.S. national economy was at its lowest point in 1931 and 1932, giving RCA its only deficit years. The radio business remained profitable, leading to demands within the firm that the phonographic products be eliminated. Yet radio stations and broadcast networks were dependent on records for program material. The technology developed for Vitaphone discs in the 1920s was applied to the transcription of continuing radio shows and commercials. These were "transcribed" on 16-inch plastic lacquers in studios in Chicago and New York. The lacquer was immediately heavily plated to produce a copper master that was used for pressing a few (never more than 50) approval copies. When approval was given, the lacquer was given normal matrix processing in the plant and pressings were made. These 33 1/3 rpm, narrow (2.5 mil) groove "Thesaurus" records on 16-inch plastic (Vitrolac) discs served the radio broadcast industry for more than 30 years.

Between radio applications and jukebox sales, the record industry had enough business to survive the early years of the Depression. The 50,000 jukeboxes in operation in 1930 accounted for about half of the 6 million records sold in that year. At the same time, Victor's recording facilities and manufacturing plant were held in readiness, and had some opportunities to bring some profits. In 1934 the Duo Jr. record player was sold for plug-in use with a radio; a second version had a lighter weight crystal pick-up, a smaller turntable, and a lower price. That was the machine used in 1937 to promote membership in the Victor Record Society.

During the 1930s popular records outsold Red Seals by a ratio of three to one. An advance for the Red Seals was made with the formation of the NBC Symphony Orchestra for Arturo Toscanini in 1937.

Toscanini's weekly broadcasts created an audience for classical music and an increase in classical record sales. In the period 1932–1938, industry-wide record production increased by 661 percent; Victor's production increased 440 percent.

Artists who made thier first Victor records in the 1930s included E. Power Biggs, Jussi Bjîrling, the Boston Pops Orchestra, Budapest Quartet, Nelson Eddy, Kirsten Flagstad, José Iturbi, Helen Jepson, Lotte Lehmann, Lily Pons, Artur Rubinstein, Artur Schnabel, Rudolf Serkin, and John Charles Thomas. *See also* **Disc**

5. *The 1940s.* During 1939–1945, RCA Victor was engaged in a variety of activities related to the war effort. At the same time research continued in phonographic products, among them the vinyl disc (introduced in 1945). And record sales climbed in both popular and classical categories. A large percentage of the internationally acclaimed classical soloists and orchestras were under contract. Alexander Kipnis, Andrés Segovia, and Helen Traubel made their first appearances on Victor. Red Seals were sold for $1, black label discs for $.75 and $.50, and Bluebird (a pop label introduced in 1933) records for $.35. Bluebird carried important material by Shep Fields, Earl Hines, Vincent Lopez, Freddy Martin, Glenn Miller, Artie Shaw, Fats Waller, and many others. Big Bands heard on regular Victor black label discs included Sammy Kaye, Wayne King, and Tommy Dorsey. Benny Goodman's Victor releases defined the swing era. Duke Ellington's Victors of 1940–1942 display his band at its creative peak.

In 1943 record labels showed a change from RCA Manufacturing Co., Inc., to RCA Victor Division of Radio Corp. of America. From January 1946 the label name was RCA Victor.

The seven-inch vinyl record, with a narrow groove for a light-weight crystal high-fidelity pickup, was introduced in 1949 with a speedy record changer. Critical analysis had established that a record speed of 45 rpm was required for good performance of a seven-inch record. The next objective was to have the 33 1/3-rpm long-play RCA Victor record with a three-speed record changer available within one year. In the light of Columbia's acclaimed 33 1/3 microgroove LP disc (1948), the technical wisdom and the commercial expediency of the 45 was widely doubted, but by February of 1951 the small disc had found universal acceptance for popular music, and billions were sold in the next 30 years.

6. *Engineering innovations.* With the introduction of its 33 1/3-rpm LP in 1950, RCA Victor was able to compete effectively with other LP labels in the classical field. The next technical advance in the industry was stereophonic recording. In 1954 John F. Pfeiffer of RCA Victor's New York recording studio worked with Fritz Reiner and the Chicago Symphony Orchestra (in Orchestra Hall, Chicago) to capture Strauss' *Also Sprach Zarathustra* and *Ein Heldenleben* in stereo. By today's standards, the setup in Orchestra Hall was primitive: 30 ips two-track tape, two Neumann M-50 omni microphones positioned 12 feet high and 24 feet apart with the orchestra between them. But the recordings are superb.

Stereo tape recordings spurred activity to develop stereo disc records. H.E. Roys, chief engineer of RCA Victor and chairman of the Electronic Industries Association (EIA) committee on the phonograph, was heavily involved in the establishment of worldwide industry standards for full stereo records before major producers placed them on sale in 1958. It took more than statesmanship to accomplish this. The "more" ingredient was the analytical skill that had established 45 rpm as the correct speed of a seven-inch record with 5 1/2 minutes playing time and less than 10 percent tracing distortion. In 1957 Roys asked Murlan S. Corrington of the Advanced Development Section of Home Instruments to make a comparative analysis of the 45-45 degree and the vertical-lateral proposals for stereo discs. Corrington reported on 27 Jan 1958 to the EIA committee on recording. His conclusions served as the basis for the choice of the 45–45 degree system and its standardization by the record industry.

In 1961 an electronic processor was sold that reproduced monaural records in stereo. The RCA New Orthacoustic Response Curve was adopted by the record and broadcast industries in June 1953. From 1953 to 1956 the Indianapolis plant installed 12 seven-inch automatic presses, adding an annual production potential of 32 million to the 18 million of the 46 seven-inch manual presses.

By 1977 the record plant in Indianapolis had reached a production capacity of 165 million discs a year, of which 90 million were 45s. There were three other U.S. plants, with a further capacity of 32 million discs. International plants, in Argentina, Australia, Brazil, Canada, Chile, the U.K., Greece, Italy, Mexico, and Spain had about 200 presses and a 45-million production capacity. Thus the total RCA Victor capacity was 224 million records per annum. A fully automatic plant completely dedicated to tape duplication and cassette loading was opened in 1984 in Weaverville, North Carolina.

Abraham M. Max, manager of the chemical and physical laboratory, RCA Victor Records Engineering (1944–1972) and research director of the American Electroplating Society, applied and adapted state-of-the-art processes to change the plating time of a record stamper, which had been as long as 60 hours, to one hour, and to increase the life of a Red Seal stamper from 100 to 2,500 records. For other pressings from unfilled compounds, 10,000 records per stamper was not uncommon.

RCA Victor sealed records in shrink-wrap beginning in 1964 and thereby participated in a bold change in product marketing. Other innovations did not fare as well, e.g., four-channel sound. Near success was achieved even though the technology applied proved to be overextended. However, there was no great demand in the marketplace for something beyond stereo. The 1973 Dynaflex record was designed to have laminar flow of the compound in the press and to have a positive profile to achieve performance goals through the conformity of flexibility rather than the precision of rigidity. Record plant production facilities and personnel were not yet ready for this approach.

7. *Studios*. In the 1930s a converted livery stable with a colorful equestrian-motif entrance on 155 W. 24th Street in New York City became the flagship of RCA Victor recording studios. It housed studios A, B, and C. Studio C was in constant use as a storage room and after 1940 as a reverberation chamber. The first original cast recording of *Hello Dolly!* was one of many Broadway shows recorded in Studio A, which was used for recording Big Bands. Smaller ensembles, vocalists, and commercials were accommodated in Studio B. Victor had been scoring soundtracks for movies and re-recording from film soundtrack to disc since doing the Paramount picture *Leatherneck* in 1929. RCA Photophone had a studio on Lexington Ave. where the first continuing radio shows were recorded on film phonographs. Then the "soundtrack" recording was taken to the 24th St. studios and there transcribed onto a lacquer. This operation gave origin to the name "transcriptions" for those recordings. At the studios, the lacquer was processed for approval copies and passed on to the plant for the completion of matrixing and for final pressing as 16-inch 33 1/3-rpm "transcriptions" with the Thesaurus trademark. Radio shows were also transcribed in the Chicago studios. Although original recording on film persisted until the coming of stereo in 1958, a groove cut by a recording lathe was the predominant recording method until magnetic tape replaced it after World War II.

The first tape machines used in the studios were the RT-11s of the RCA Broadcast Division. They were replaced by the Ampex two-track 201s and subsequently by multitrack models.

John E. Volkmann, head of the wartime government sound department at RCA, envisioned the recording studio as an integrated acoustical unit. After the war he set about translating his concept into RCA recording studios, large-scale auditoriums, and projection of sound for large gatherings of people. The 1962 grand opera RCA studio in Rome embodied the concept. That studio featured a built-in speaker system. The two 50-cubic-foot enclosures were protrusions from a brick wall. The speakers with 24-inch woofers and appropriate size mid-range units and tweeters were nearly transparent aurally inasmuch as there were hardly any of the usual speaker-induced artifacts.

In time the studio 24th St. in New York, headed by Al Pulley, became overburdened and overcrowded with equipment. In 1969 RCA Victor launched the "Queen Mary" of studios at 1133 Avenue of the Americas, New York. Studio A, designed to be world class and number one, had size, variable ceiling height, variable acoustics, sonic insulation, and an integrated control room. The five other studios and supporting functional areas were similar in refinements. When Leonard Bernstein brought the company of *West Side Story* to Studio A for its first cast recording, John Volkmann and RCA Victor knew that their objective for Studio A had been achieved.

The Chicago studio had noteworthy accomplishments of its own. It was located during the 1930s in the Merchandise Mart — near NBC for "transcriptions." It moved to Lake Shore Drive in 1940 and handled a flow of recording engagements for such artists as Glenn Miller, Duke Ellington, and Tommy Dorsey. A new studio was opened on Wacker Drive, designed by Volkmann with the characteristics of New York's Studio A. The Hollywood studio moved in 1950 from above the record plant on Olive Ave. to a Volkmann-designed studio in the RCA building at 6363 Sunset Boulevard. It became the recording home for Henry Mancini, Hugo Montenegro, other Hollywood bands and motion picture stars, and any number of popular groups. Country and western recording, developed by A&R man Steve Sholes, outgrew the Quonset-hut studio in Nashville, and a new recording center was built. Managed by Chet Atkins, it became the home base for legendary artists.

Studio adequacy in the U.S. is augmented by the existence of concert halls, civic centers, and opera houses. Commercial recording takes place in such halls as the Academy of Music in Philadelphia, Orchestra Hall in Chicago, Carnegie Hall in New York, the Opera House in Pittsburgh, and many others. RCA Victor executed a landmark recording event on location on 13 Jan 1973. Studio manager Larry Schnapf of New York headed a team that recorded Elvis Presley's *Aloha from Hawaii* live at the Honolulu International Center. Audio feed for satellite television, four-channel sound records, stereo records, regular television, radio, and for the public address system covering the live audience was carried out in an exemplary manner.

8. *Artists and Repertoire*. Victor dominated the classical field, and from the 1940s it also held a high place in popular genres. It was the leading producer of country and western hits between 1944 and 1988, with

1,935 chart records. Million-selling albums included *The Sound of Music* (three years on the charts) and *Hello Dolly!* (on the charts longer than any other album). Perry Como, Tommy Dorsey, and Artie Shaw were among the stellar performers of the 1940s. John Denver and Elvis Presley were among the later pop artists. Henry Mancini received 20 Grammy awards. Between 1958 and 1978, 113 of the 134 Grammys received by the 10 top winners went to RCA Victor artists. RCA Victor artists won a larger percentage of awards and chart appearances than the RCA Victor percentage of total record sales would indicate.

The Victor name, its trademark, its artists, its catalog, its studios, its RCA Music Services, its manufacturing business, and its heritage became a part of Bertelsmann AG on 15 Apr 1986.

9. *Victor Officials.*

Presidents

Eldridge R.Johnson, 1901–1925
Edward E. Shumaker, 1926–1928
Edward Wallenstein, 1932–1938
Frank B. White, 1938–1949
James Murray, 1949–1956
George Marek, 1956–1968
Norman Rascusin, 1968–1973
Kenneth Glancy, 1973–1975
Rocco Laginastra, 1975–1978
Robert Summer, 1978–1986

Chief Engineers

Hill Reiskind, 1942–1956
H.E. Roys, 1956–1966
Warren Rex Isom, 1966–1976
James Frische, 1976–1980
Dave Mishra, 1980–1984

Musical Directors

Arthur Pryor, Walter Rogers, Josef Pasternack, Rosario Bourdon, Nathaniel Shilkret, Edward King, Cliff Cairns, Roy Shields.

EDGAR HUTTO, JR. (SECTIONS 1–3)
WARREN REX ISOM (SECTIONS 4–9)

[Aldridge 1964; Baumbach 1981; Fagan 1983; Isom 1977; Rust 1970; Sherman 1987; Smart 1977; Voice 1986. Several articles in *Hobbies* (by Stephen Fassett or Jim Walsh) are useful: a listing of the 5000 series, pressed in the U.S. from G & T masters in 1903, appeared in April, May, and June 1947, and in March 1955. The first domestic Red Seals (2000 series) were listed in May 1942. The 76000 series of 12-inch singles-sided Red Seals appeared in April 1942. Black labels of the 5000 series were listed in July and December 1941, April 1942, July 1943, May 1945, and March 1946. The 10-inch 91000 series (G & T, 1902–1903) was listed in July 1941. The 12-inch 92000 series by G & T (1906–1908) was listed in November 1941. In December 1941 the G & T 94000 and 95000 series were listed (including the Melba, Tamagno, and Patti material). The Victor catalog of February 1901 was listed and discussed in January, February, and March 1968; the October 1901 catalog was listed in April 1968; the August 1902 catalog in May 1968. Notable releases from the catalogs of 1902–1905 were discussed in December 1949. Victor record sales of 1901–1942 were listed by year in June 1971 (the same data are in Sherman 1987). *Hobbies* of October, November, December 1968, and February, March, April 1969, explained "How to Tell When Victor Records Were Made."]

VICTOR VAUDEVILLE CO.

A group formed around 1908 to make comedy records for Victor. Members were Byron Harlan, Billy Murray, and Steve Porter. The 1917 catalog had one record by the group, identified as the Vaudeville Quartet: "Lucia Sextet Burlesque" (#17119). Record #35609 (1917) was listed in catalogs as a Victor Vaudeville Co. release, but it was in fact by the Peerless Quartet: "Court Scene in Carolina"/"Darktown Campmeetin' Experiences."

VICTORY (LABEL) (I)

A U.K. record issued by Blum and Co., Ltd., from September 1912. They were actually relabeled Stella records, identified first as Victory Gramophone Records, then as Victory Records. Material included military band numbers, popular material, and some items by Billy Williams. In June 1913 it was announced that Victory Records would henceforth be sold as Diploma Records. [Andrews 1988/10.]

VICTORY (LABEL) (II)

A seven-inch disc issued in U.K. by Crystalate Gramophone Record Manufacturing Co., Ltd., from 1928 to 1931. It was billed as a long-playing record, as it had approximately the playing time of a standard 10-inch disc.

VICTROLA

A tradename registered by the Victor Talking Machine Co., filed 1 Dec 1905 (registration #50,081/2), for a disc record player; it became the most popular and famous disc phonograph in the industry. Distinctive features of the instrument were the enclosure of all mechanical parts and the horn within a cabinet, a door on the front of the cabinet that could be opened or closed to control the volume, and storage space for records inside the cabinet. Eldridge Johnson held the patent covering these features, U.S. #856,704 (filed 8 Dec 1904; granted 11 June 1907), although in 1927 John Bailey Browning received credit for prior conception of the Victrola.

The Victrola (derivation of the name is uncertain) was announced to the trade on 7 Aug 1906. Advertising in 1906 identified the machine as a "Victor-Victrola," but the name was simplified to Victrola in 1907; it was also known as "Victrola the Sixteenth" or Model XVI. Table models were available from 1911, with sales rivaling those of the floor models. Either a spring motor or (from August 1913) AC (mains) electric power was offered.

Prices presented a wide range of choice. The open-top table models cost $15 (Victrola IV) and $25 (Victrola VI). Table models with lids cost $40 (Victrola VIII) or $50 (Victrola IX). Consoles varied greatly in size, record storage capacity, and finish. They cost from $75 (Victrola X) to $400 (the highest price for a Victrola XVIII).

By 1910 some 40,000 Victrola consoles had been sold. The table model quickly reached 50,000 sales in its first year, 1911. Thereafter the annual sales for each model were in six figures. In 1920 the console Victrola had its peak sales, 333,889; there were 212,363 table Victrolas sold that year. However, the arrival of the radio brought about a slump from 1922. Production was halted in 1924, but resumed in the next year with the introduction of the Orthophonic Victrola.

Electrical recording created the need for an appropriate record player, since the new electric discs reproduced with excessive volume and stridency on the regular Victrolas. In June 1925 Victor announced its plan for a solution, a completely new machine (and set up a half-price sales campaign to move the older stock). On "Victor Day," 2 Nov 1925 there were nationwide demonstrations by dealers of the new Credenza model ($275–405) of the Orthophonic Victrola — sales were strong from the outset: 42,446 before the end of 1925, and 260,436 in 1927.

Technically, the novelties in the Orthophonic were its pleated aluminum diaphragm (in place of the mica disc of the standard Victrola), a stylus assembly in ball bearings, and a folded exponential horn. Response was from about 100 Hz in the bass to about 5,000 Hz in the treble.

Varieties of the Orthophonic were numerous. The most expensive was the electric Borgia II model, at $1,000. It was housed in a double cabinet, with a radio in one of them (the Radiola 28); and the records could be played through the radio amplifier for complete volume control. There were spring motor machines also, and table models as well as elaborate consoles. Victor's all electric instrument was known as the Electrola-Victrola; it competed with the Brunswick Panatrope,

made from the same RCA components. Victor's first record changer was introduced in 1927, the Automatic Orthophonic; it was the first changer to reach a mass market. Model 955, with a radio and record changer in its grand walnut cabinet, was "Victor's pride and joy in 1927, and is unquestionably the most impressive instrument they ever built" [Baumbach 1981]. It sold for $1,550. With the creation of these combination radio-phonographs, run by electric power, and complete with disc changers, Victor established the format of the record player that was to remain the norm until the high-fidelity era of the 1950s and the move toward separate components. [Baumbach 1981 describes and illustrates all models of the Victrola through 1929; Hoover 1971 has illustrations of table model IV (p. 50) and of the Automatic Orthophonic Victrola of 1927 (pp. 82–83).]

VIDEO RECORDING

The storage and reproduction of visual images were perfected by the Ampex Corp. in the U.S. in 1956 and offered commercially for professional studio use in 1957. The Ampex system was in tape format, using two-inch-wide tapes running at 15 inches per second. Video disc recording was first accomplished by Telefunken and Decca in 1966, using a microgroove record with 25 grooves in the space of a typical LP record groove. Signals were vertically inscribed and frequency modulated. The pickup sensed changes in pressure. In a demonstration at the AEG Telefunken building in Berlin, 24 June 1970, the discs were of thin flexible plastic foil, with a playing time of five minutes. They revolved at television picture frame rates: 1,500 rpm (in Europe; the American speed was 1,800 rpm). This was basically a mechanical system.

An optical video disc system was launched by Philips in 1978 and named the laser disc. In this process a laser beam traces a spiraling track of depressions or pits in a highly reflective aluminum layer on a vinyl disc. The spot of reflected light activates a photodiode to produce the electric signal that is then processed to reproduce a color picture and audio signal in a conventional television set. From this technology the compact (audio) disc (CD) emerged. The format was not initially successful, because it was more expensive and less flexible than the popular videotape formats (VHS and Beta), which also allowed home recording. In the late 1990s, the DVD, a CD-sized video disc, took its place, and has since become equally popular as videotape for home rentals, thanks to the low cost of DVD players and new recording technologies that allow for home recording on some machines.

HOWARD FERSTLER

VIENNA INSTRUMENTAL QUARTETTE

A piano and string ensemble, also known as the Vienna Quartette, that recorded for Edison cylinders in 1910–1911. Members were Jacques Grunberg, piano; Licco Liggy, violin; Otto Krist, cello; and Ludwig Schonberger, viola. Their numbers were "In Vienna — Serenade" (#10520) and "Tin Soldier" (#10304).

VIG, BUTCH (8 DEC 1957–)

Born Bryan Vigorson in Viroqua, Wisconsin, Vig was a well-known producer of alternative rock in the 1990s who has gone on to a career as a performer with his band, Garbage. Playing piano and drums as a child, Vig spent two years in college before dropping out to perform with a local band, Spooner. With bandmate guitarist Steve Marker, Vig purchased his first recording equipment, and produced the band's three albums. By the late 1980s, he had established his own studio, Smart Studios, in Madison, Wisconsin, recording local indie acts. His work drew the attention of a new band out of Seattle, Nirvana, and they recorded their 1991 debut album, *Nevermind*, at his studios; Smashing Pumpkins also cut their debut, 1992's *Gish*, there, making Vig the hot producer of the moment. In 1994 he formed Garbage with old friend Marker, enlisting vocalist Shirley Manson, a Scottish singer who had performed with the group Angelfish. The band's great success in the later 1990s led Vig to curtail his production work and focus on his burgeoning career.

CARL BENSON

VILLCHUR, EDGAR M. (28 MAY 1917–)

After earning an M.S.Ed. degree from the City College of New York in 1939, Villchur served as a captain in the Army Air Corps during World War II, specializing in electronics. After some postwar courses and self-study, he became a teacher of acoustics and sound reproduction at New York University. During this time he was also writing articles on sound reproduction for *Saturday Review*, *Audio Magazine*, the *Journal of the Audio Engineering Society*, and other periodicals. In 1957 he published *The Handbook of Sound Reproduction*, and in 1965 he published *The Reproduction of Sound*.

In 1953 Villchur developed and built a prototype acoustic-suspension woofer system. To supply the restoring force to the woofer cone, the acoustic-suspension design substitutes the elastic body of air in a sealed speaker cabinet for the usual mechanical suspension. Since the elastic cushion of air is essentially linear for these small pressure changes, harmonic distortion for this type system is much less than for a system with an all-mechanical restoring force. He applied for and received a patent for acoustic-suspension loudspeaker.

In 1954 Villchur and former student Henry Kloss founded Acoustic Research, Inc. (AR) with Villchur as president. (Kloss left AR in 1957 to form his own company, KLH, which manufactured acoustic-suspension loudspeakers under license from Acoustic Research.) Villchur went on to develop the dome tweeter (first used in the 1958 AR-3 speaker system) and an award-winning turntable.

Although the primary purpose of the acoustic-suspension system was to reduce bass distortion, the necessary reduction in cabinet size was at least as important in creating public acceptance, and by 1966 AR had approximately 32 percent of the domestic speaker market. The AR-3, with an acoustic-suspension woofer, dome tweeter, and dome midrange, is part of the Smithsonian Institution's Museum of American History exhibit on the history of sound reproduction.

In 1967 Villchur sold AR to Teledyne, Inc., and left to establish the Foundation for Hearing Aid Research, a nonprofit laboratory. Since that time he has worked as a visiting scientist at the Massachusetts Institute of Technology and the Albert Einstein School of Medicine. He has pioneered the use of multichannel compression in hearing aids. His latest book, *Acoustics for Audiologists*, was published in 2000.

See also **Loudspeaker**

HOWARD FERSTLER

VIM (LABEL)

A Chicago record, issued by the Vim Co., with material of uncertain origin. Rust reports he has seen only one release, a banjo solo by Vess Ossman. The date is suggested as sometime in "the first decade of the century." [Rust 1978.]

VINCENT VOICE LIBRARY

A unit of the Michigan State University Library, East Lansing, Michigan. G. Robert Vincent was an early documentary recording enthusiast, making wax-cylinder recordings of Theodore Roosevelt in 1912; subsequently he was employed by Edison Laboratories and became a specialist in preserving and restoring early recordings. In 1962, he was named assistant director of Michigan State University's library and the director of the National Voice Library (as it was then known); it was renamed in his honor on his retirement in 1973. Dr. Maurice Crane headed the collection from 1974 through mid-2000, at which point the collection was made part of the library's Digital and Multimedia Center.

Documentary and historical recordings are collected, currently consisting of speeches, performances, lectures, interviews, and broadcasts made by over 50,000 people "from all walks of life." The colleciton is broken down into over 900 subsections, containing over 7,000 individual recordings. A printed catalog of the collection — all of which is in tape format (as of 2002, the collection was in the process of being digitized) — was published in 1975 by G.K. Hall (Boston). The collection is searchable through the electronic online catalog maintained by the MSU library system. [website: www.lib.msu.edu/vincent/index.html]

VINYL

The compound used in making disc records, replacing shellac gradually in the 1940s and then totally with the advent of the LP record. Union Carbide developed a vinyl resin in the 1930s (Vinylite) that was compatible with production equipment of the time, so that factories set up to make shellac records could make vinyl records as well, or change over completely. Western Electric used vinyl for radio transcriptions, and Muzak used it for its music services. RCA made vinyl (Victrolac) radio transcriptions, and then the unbreakable V-Discs during World War II. In 1944 RCA issued a few Red Seal records on transparent cherry-red vinyl. Cosmo Records made the first major seller on vinyl, a children's item named "Tubby the Tuba." Red vinyl was also used for the RCA 45-rpm record, and for the Columbia microgroove LP of 1948.

The basic vinyl material is polyvinyl chloride (PVC). It is produced by cracking the hydrocarbons in petroleum products to derive vinyl monomer, which is the PVC raw material. Coal and agricultural products are alternative sources for the monomer. LP discs were compression molded of vinyl chloride vinyl acetate copolymer. Injection molding of seven-inch 45-rpm discs used modified polystyrenes.

Important factors in the vinyl disc manufacturing process include careful selection of the resins and stabilizers in the compound, use of carbon black with ideal particle size and distribution, selection of fillers, and blending of special additives. [Isom 1977; Khanna 1977.]

VIOLA (LABEL)

A rare American record issued by the Southern California Phonograph Co., Los Angeles, ca. 1921. Evidently the discs were distributed as incentives toward the purchase of the firm's Viola Phonograph. Matrices came from Olympic, Black Swan, and other labels. [Rust 1978.]

VIOLANO

SEE MILLS NOVELTY CO.

VIOLIN RECORDINGS (HISTORIC)

The instrument, or its functional imitation, the Stroh violin, was heard on many early discs and cylinders. There were about 50 solo numbers in the Edison output by 1905, beginning with performances by Fred Hager in 1898 ("Annie Laurie" was his initial offering, on #6700). Two artists made Bettini cylinders in 1898: Henri Marteau (four numbers) and Dora Valesca Becker, the first female violinist on record (14 numbers). Another 1898 performer was T. Herbert Reed, on cylinders of Reed, Dawson and Co., which claimed "the only successful violin records." Other very early violinists included Charles D'Almaine, on Columbia in 1899–1900, Edison in 1899, and Victor 1900–1907; and J. Scott Skinner, one of the persons recorded by Fred Gaisberg in his Glasgow expedition for the new Gramophone Co. in September 1899, later an Edison artist. Other Edison cylinder violinists were Eugene Jaudas, on Edison from 1905; Leopold Moeslein, on Edison from 1906; and William Craig, on Edison from 1910. Edison also recorded nine pieces for violin (Jaudas) and flute (Eugene C. Rose), during 1903–1905.

It was the Gramophone Co. that sought the leading concert artists of Europe. Important violinists who recorded for HMV were, by year:

1901 — Paul Viardot
1902 — Jan Kubelik
1903 — Franz Drdla, Joseph Joachim, Ferenc von Vecsey
1904 — Willy Burmeister, Pablo de Sarasate, Mary Hall, Fritz Kreisler, Maud Powell
1905 — Jacques Thibaud
1906 — Mischa Elman
1908 — Joseph Szigeti.

An EMI LP of 1989 (#761062) included material by these violinists, plus Eugäne Ysaye, who recorded ca. 1912. Victor had about 200 titles listed in its 1917 catalog, including Gramophone Co. material. Most of those discs were arrangements, but Maud Powell did play a movement from the Mendelssohn Concerto (Victor #74026, from HMV #85040). In the 1930s a more substantial repertoire was available. Fritz Kreisler recorded the Beethoven, Brahms, and Mendelssohn concertos. Mischa Elman and Jascha Heifetz performed major concertos, and Heifetz also did sonatas by Fauré, Mozart, and Richard Strauss. Yehudi Menuhin offered some uncommon material, such as the Elgar and Schumann concertos and the J.S. Bach unaccompanied sonatas. Albert Spalding, who had recorded for Edison in 1909–1924, moved over to Victor in the 1930s and contributed some important repertoire by Tartini, Handel, Franck, and Brahms; he also made his acclaimed record of the Ludwig Spohr concerto with Eugene Ormandy and the Philadelphia Orchestra.

The outstanding historical release of violin performers was issued by Pearl in 1991: *The Recorded Violin* (BVA #1) on six CDs. It covered artists who recorded from the early acoustic days to the 1930s, presenting them in birth order: Joachim (born 1831) to Ida Haendel (born 1923). There are many other historic violin reissues on various CDs devoted either to individual artists or to overviews of individual labels.

VIRGIN RECORDS (LABEL)

Founded in 1973 by record-store owner Richard Branson, Virgin had a major success from the start with its first album release, *Tubular Bells* by Mike Oldfield (V #2001), which immediately sold over five million copies. In 1977 the label moved into punk music with the signing of the Sex Pistols and soon after XTC. In the early 1980s, the label moved into mainstream pop-rock with the success of Human League, Culture Club, and Simple Minds. In 1984 Virgin purchased the back catalog of Charisma Records, inheriting artist Phil Collins for the U.K. market. By the end of the decade, the Virgin America subsidiary was established, with notable signings including rocker Lenny Kravitz. In 1992 Branson sold his record business to EMI. During the 1990s, EMI made major deals with big name acts, including the Rolling Stones and Janet Jackson, and the ill-fated signing of Mariah Carey, who was paid a hefty sum by the label to break her contract after her initial album for the company bombed. [website: www.virginrecords.com.]

VITAGRAPH CO.

A firm established in 1899 by James Stuart Blackton, Albert E. Smith, and W.T. Rock. Blackton bought an Edison Kinetoscope movie projector, and Smith adapted it to make films as well as show them. The firm made low-budget motion pictures in New York and became an important part of the new industry. By 1913 it was making five-reel pictures with a variety of subjects. In 1914 it was located in Brooklyn, with branches in Chicago, London, Paris, and Berlin; there was also a New York City office. On 7 Feb 1914 the Vitagraph Theatre opened, with music by a Wurlitzer "orchestra."

Vitagraph was renamed VLSE in 1917, having bought out a consortium, and continued successfully until 1925; Warner Bros. acquired the firm at that time.

VITANOLA TALKING MACHINE CO.

A Chicago firm active ca. 1916–1920 and 1922–1925. It marketed the Vitanola disc player, in eight models, selling for $25–250. Though lavish advertising continued, the firm announced bankruptcy in 1920. By 1922 it had reorganized and was back in business, moving in October to Saginaw, Michigan. Advertising continued to 1925.

VITAPHONE (LABEL) (I)

A disc issued by the American Talking Machine Co., a licensee of American Graphophone Co., in 1898–1900. The records were of various colors, including red, green, and black. As the firm ceased operations in 1900, the Vitaphone label died with it. Later (ca. 1902–1903) there was a seven-inch issue named American Vitaphone Record.

VITAPHONE (LABEL) (II)

An American record issued by the Vitaphone Co. of Plainfield, New Jersey, from ca. 1912–1917. The label was styled Music Master Vitaphone Record; it was purple, and pressed by American Graphophone Co.

VITAPHONE CO.

A New Jersey firm, incorporated 1 Mar 1907 in Plainfield. It produced the Vitaphone disc player in ca. 1912, capable of handling lateral-cut records (Victor and Columbia), Edison Diamond Discs, and Pathé vertical-cut records. It had a wooden tone arm, and a diaphragm located at the horn, activated by the vibrations sent along a cord from the tone arm. This novel approach was patented by Clinton B. Repp (U.S. #1,003,655; filed 24 June 1909; granted 19 Sep 1911). Vitaphones were sold as external horn table models at $17.50, enclosed horn table models at $25, and console models up to $175 for the Vitaphone Grand. Vitaphone label records were also produced.

H.N. McMenimen was general manager from August 1912. *TMW* reported the firm was bankrupt in June 1917. [Fabrizio 1976.]

VITAPHONE CORP.

A New York firm, established 20 Apr 1926 as a joint venture of Warner Bros. and Western Electric. The purpose was to make disc records that would provide sound for motion pictures. This was one of the two active approaches to the making of talking pictures, the other being the optical soundtrack. While the optical soundtrack became the norm eventually, in the late

1920s both systems were competing for attention in the film industry, which was of course dealing only with silents at the time. For a year the Vitaphone work was carried on in the Manhattan Opera House, then from 1927 in Hollywood.

Vitaphone is of special interest in the history of sound recording not only for its technology, which soon took second place and was forgotten in a few years, but for the content of its productions, many of which were made by outstanding musical artists. The most famous of the 400-plus Vitaphone films was *The Jazz Singer* of 1927, with Al Jolson, the first commercial talking picture to achieve national success.

Discs used in the Vitaphone system were shellac, but with less of the usual abrasive filler, so that the surfaces were smoother and quieter. The disadvantage was rapid wear of the discs, which had to be replaced frequently in the projection room. Records played from inside to outside, probably to give the projectionist a better chance of seeing the needle come to the end of its playing surface, thus allowing a timely transfer to the next disc. Diameter was 16 inches, and speed was 33 1/3 rpm (the same as the later commercial LP record). Synchronization between film and records was accomplished through manual placement of the needle at the starting point in the center of the disc when a cue flashed on the screen; although this seems a risky method, synchronization did not prove to be a problem in practice. Projection of the sound was from behind and below the theater screen, using four long horns (12–14 feet).

Despite the success of the Vitaphone short subjects, Warner discontinued making them in 1930, as the advantages of soundtracks became more apparent. [Taylor 1985.]

See also **Motion Picture Sound Recording**

VIVATONAL

The Columbia counterpart of the Victor Orthophonic record player, introduced in 1925. There was major advertising in 1927, which claimed a frequency range exceeding that of any "ordinary" player, but the instrument did not succeed in its competition with Victor.

VOCALION (LABEL) (I)

An American record marketed by the Aeolian Co., New York, from May 1918 (as Aeolian-Vocalion). From 1921 to 1927 the name was simply Vocalion. They were vertical-cut discs (until 1920, then lateral), single- or double-sided at first, in 10- or 12-inch sizes. Brunswick acquired the label from Aeolian in 1924,

Vocalion label. Courtesy David A. Jasen

retaining control until 1931, when American Record Corp. absorbed it. In 1938 CBS bought it from ARC.

A small but respectable roster of classical artists was assembled for the label, including John Charles Thomas, Marguerite d'Alvarez, and Florence Easton; but it was the jazz and popular realm that brought the label to great prominence. The Original Dixieland Jazz Band recorded for Vocalion in 1917, not long after they made the first jazz recordings for Victor and Columbia. At one time or another, Vocalion recorded Bunny Berigan, Cab Calloway, the Dorsey Brothers Orchestra, Cliff Edwards, Erskine Hawkins, Fletcher Henderson, Earl Hines, Billie Holiday, the Louisiana Rhythm Kings, Wingy Manone, Jelly Roll Morton, King Oliver, Adrian Rollini, Joe Venuti, and Cootie Williams. Jack Kapp was responsible for much of the label's success; he became manager in February 1928. Columbia acquired the label in 1940, and changed the name to Okeh (reviving that label that had been silent for five years) in the same year.

An LP Vocalion was issued in 1949, with Decca as the parent label. The label name has continued into the CD era, a Decca subsidiary distributed by MCA.

VOCALION (LABEL) (II)

A U.K. label issued from 1920 by the Aeolian Co., Ltd.; at first styled the Aeolian-Vocalion label. In January 1925 the Aeolian Co., Ltd., sold its record business to a newly incorporated entity, the Vocalion Gramophone Co., Ltd. Vocalion records continued to appear from this source into 1927, then the label was terminated. In 1932 the Crystalate Gramophone Record Manufacturing Co., Ltd., bought the business of the Vocalion Gramophone Record Co., Ltd., and proceeded to form a new Vocalion Gramophone Co., Ltd., the prior firm being in liquidation. Then in March 1937 Decca Record Co., Ltd., acquired the record interests of Crystalate; and in 1951 the label was brought back once more. Like the American Vocalion label, the U.K. record was distinguished for its jazz and popular artists, many taken from the U.S. masters. Vocalion remains an active label, distributed in the U.S. by MCA.

From 1963 to 1968 there was another Vocalion and a Vocalion Pop label, from Vogue Records, Ltd., in U.K.; those were 45s.

VOECKS, KEVIN (19 SEP 1956–)

Currently director of research and technology at the Revel division of Madrigal Audio Laboratories, a Harman International company, Voecks has a background that includes a mixture of engineering, manufacturing, and retailing high-end audio equipment that dates back to his time in high school, when he imported and sold high-end audio from his parent's home. In 1975, while attending Worcester Polytechnic Institute, one of the few schools to offer specialization in audio engineering at the time, Voecks founded Natural Sound, a high-end audio store in Framingham, Massachusetts. He later sold the operation, and then began Symdex, a small high-end company specializing in the production of upscale loudspeaker systems.

In 1979 Voecks moved on to join Mirage Loudspeakers as chief engineer, with the job of designing all of their models, and in 1985 he went to work for Snell Acoustics, also as chief engineer, shortly after Peter Snell's untimely death. While at Snell, he designed the entire Snell speaker line for many years, making good use of the Canadian National Research Council's famed loudspeaker research facilities, headed at that time by Floyd Toole. In January 1996, Dr. Sidney Harman announced the formation of Revel Loudspeakers within the Harman International group, with Voecks signing on as chief engineer. In that position, he continues to have responsibility for all technical details with the company's very high-end line of loudspeaker systems.

HOWARD FERSTLER

VOGUE (LABEL) (I)

An American record issued from the Vogue Recording Co., Detroit, from May 1946. Tom Saffady was president of the firm. Vogue was the most famous of the picture discs, pressed on vinyl surfaces over an aluminum core, with the illustration sealed inside the vinyl coating. Surfaces were quiet and durability was good. Among the artists signed by Vogue were Phil Spitalny and his "all-girl" orchestra; Art Kassel, Charlie Shavers, Shep Fields, Frankie Masters, Clyde McCoy, and Joan Edwards. There are 98 records listed in Lindsay [1989].

Vogue discs sold for $1.05, while standard Victors and Deccas were selling for $.50. After an initial flurry of sales and several good critical reviews, business began to slip. By 1947 the firm ceased making new releases. Advertisements for liquidation of remaining stock appeared in July, and in August bankruptcy proceedings began.

The pictures were "multi-colored, almost cartoon-like representations of the song title" — "they were garish, obvious, and often downright silly" [Brooks]. Despite the novelty of the illustrations and the high quality of much recorded material, there was never a hit record on Vogue. It remains unique in recording history, the only label to have illustrated its entire output. [Brooks 1977/7; Lindsay 1989 (a label list).]

VOGUE (LABEL) (II)

A record initiated in France in 1948, which licensed jazz material from the U.S. A U.K. subsidiary, Vogue Records, Ltd., was founded in 1951. Vogue discs included material by Sidney Bechet, Earl Hines, Thelonious Monk, Josh White, and Mahalia Jackson. Vogue came under control of Pye of Cambridge in 1965. Vogue-Coral discs were issued, via Coral of the U.S., which was Decca-owned. Coral rights passed to U.K. Decca in early 1956, and the Vogue label returned again — then changed to Vocalion in March 1963. Vocalion has remained a Decca subsidiary.

FRANK ANDREWS

VOICEWRITER

The tradename of Edison dictating cylinder machines, made by the Voicewriter Division of Thomas A. Edison, Inc. It succeeded the Ediphone, which succeeded the original Edison Business Phonograph. When Edison ceased all other record production on 1 Nov 1929, dictation cylinders were continued. Production went on after a merger in 1956 with McGraw Electric Co.

VOIGT, PAUL GUSTAVUS ADOLPHUS HELMUTH (9 DEC 1901–9 FEB 1981)

Voigt was an English/Canadian electronics engineer who developed electromechanical recording and reproductions systems, amplifiers, and loudspeakers. Born in Forest Hill, London, Voigt had an early interest in the application of valve amplifiers. After graduating with a B.Sc. from University College, London, he was employed by J.E. Hough, Edison Bell Works. He became interested in the mechanical (and later electrical) side of recording and developed principles and equipment, in particular capacitor microphones for in-house and commercial purposes. When the Edison Bell Co. closed in 1933, Voigt founded his own company, Voigt Patents, Ltd., concentrating on loudspeakers for theaters and developing horn loudspeakers for domestic use and Gramophone pick-ups. In 1950 he immigrated to Toronto, Canada, and taught electronics; from 1960 to 1969 he was employed by the Radio Regulations Laboratory in Ottawa. After retirement he worked with theoretical cosmology and fundamental interactions. He died in Brighton, Ontario, Canada.

GEORGE BROCK-NANNESTAD

VOLT (LABEL)
A subsidiary of the STAX label.

VOLTA GRAPHOPHONE CO.
An organization established in Washington, D.C., in January 1886 (incorporated on 3 Feb 1886) by Alexander Graham Bell, Chichester Bell, and Charles Sumner Tainter. It was a successor to the Volta Laboratory Association, established by the same men in 1881. Acoustic and electrical research was the object of the Volta Laboratory, and the Graphophone their principal product — which gave its name to the new company. Volta Graphophone Co. held the key Bell-Tainter patents, which it licensed to the new American Graphophone Co., established on 28 Mar 1887.

VOLTA LABORATORY ASSOCIATION
A group organized in Washington, D.C., on 8 Oct 1881 by Alexander Graham Bell, Chichester Bell, and Charles Sumner Tainter; location was first at 1325 L St., then 1221 Connecticut Ave. The purpose of the association was to carry on electrical and acoustic research. An early emphasis on the telephone was shifted to phonographic research, probably because of the interests of Tainter. Having developed and filed for a patent on the wax surface principle of the Graphophone, the association endeavored in vain to bring Thomas Edison into the enterprise (Tainter spent two months in New York trying to stimulate the interest of Edison and Edward H. Johnson), then went ahead with the project independently. The Volta Graphophone Co. was established on 2 Feb 1886 to carry on with development. [Wile 1990/2.]

VOLUME
The intensity of an audio signal, the function of the amplitude of the sound wave. It is expressed in decibels relative to a standard reference volume.

See also **Amplitude; Level**

VOLUME CONTROL
Early playback systems had no means of adjusting the intensity of the output signal, other than to change needles; there were needles that gave degrees of louder to softer output. In 1916 Pathé advertised an "exclusive on Pathéphone": a "tone control' knob on the side of the cabinet to adjust volume. Sonora had a comparable "tone modifier," and the Aeolian Graduola, marketed in 1920, had the same function, although advertising copy clouded its purpose.

VON KARAJAN, HERBERT
SEE KARAJAN, HERBERT VON

VORSETZER
The Welte-Mignon "push-up" attachment for the making of reproducing piano rolls.

VOX (LABEL) (I)
A German record issued by the Deutsche Schallplatten und Sprechmaschinen AG, Berlin, from 1921 to 1929. The disc, with a triangular label, enjoyed great success in the mid-1920s, and the firm opened an American office in New York, the Vox Corporation of America (1923). Gramophones were also manufactured. In the economic crisis of 1929, the firm collapsed. The Vox rights were taken over by the Kristall Schallplatten GmbH. [Sieben 1985.]

VOX (LABEL) (II)
An early American LP label, one of the 11 listed in the first edition of the Schwann catalog, October 1949. (It had begun with some 78-rpm issues in 1945.) Main offices were in New York. It was available in the U.K. from 1951.

Vox was founded by George H. de Mendelssohn-Bartholdy (1912–1988), who was indirectly related to the famous composer. Born in Budapest, Hungary, he studied piano there and for a while in the early 1930s in Paris; by the end of the 1930s, he was living in New York. After serving in Wolrd War II, he formed Vox Productions to market European recordings by then little-known (in the U.S.) conductors and performers. He entered into a licensing deal with French Polydor, and was among the first to issue LP records in 1949. One of the interesting early issues was the Igor Stravinsky *Concerto in D for Violin and Orchestra*, with the composer conducting (VLP #6340). A low-cost line of albums, "Vox Boxes," was popular in the 1950s through the 1980s; the name has been carried over to CDs, each "box" carrying two or three budget-priced CDs. In 1965 Vox introduced a further budget line, Turnabout, and then a year later a midpriced line, Candide.

In 1978 Mendelssohn sold the company to Ira Moss of the Moss Music Group. Mendelssohn formed a new label, Pantheon, sold through a distributor of remaindered books and records, but it folded after a short period. Moss introduced themed collections under the Vox Cameo Classics label as yet another way of repackaging catalog material. In 1988 Moss Music Group was sold to SPJ Music. [website: www.voxcd.com.]

REVISED BY CARL BENSON

VULCAN RECORD CO.

A New York firm incorporated in June 1921. Fred Hedinger was general manager and secretary. Sets of three "indestructible" 10-inch discs in a Junior Operetta Series appeared from August 1923, packed in containers costing $2.50. The content was fairytales set to music by Charles A. Prince, sung and played by well-known artists. Announcements continued through November 1923.

FRANK ANDREWS

VU METER (VOLUME UNIT METER)

The standard unit of measurement in a recording system is the volume unit. Jointly developed by Bell Labs, CBS, and NBC, and put into use in May 1939. A VU meter, whose response is supposed to be closely related to the perceived loudness and dynamics of the audio signal, will register zero level on its scale when the potential corresponding to one milliwatt in 600 ohms (0.775 volts) is applied. The dynamic characteristics of a proper VU meter are such that it reaches 99 percent of its 0-dB maximum in 0.3 second if a steady sine wave of 0 dBm is applied to it. Obviously, the traditional VU meter has an inherent weakness: it will not respond quickly enough to measure certain transient program material. Due to the requirements of digital recording systems, it has been replaced or augmented in some instances by peak program indicators that allow the recording engineer to be guaranteed of no signal clipping. The use of peak indicators increases the chance of background noise becoming audible, however, and in many cases the standard VU meter still has operational advantages.

HOWARD FERSTLER

W

WAGNER, "HERR"

A German tenor who sang five numbers for Edison cylinders (#4401-#4405), all recorded before March 1888. Four were songs, and one was an aria,: the *Tannhäuser* Evening Star.

WAGNER, ROGER (FRANCIS) (16 JAN 1914–1989)

This French-born organist and conductor was born in Le Puy. He came to the U.S. as a child, and as a young man, studied the priesthood in Santa Barbara, California, then returned to France for organ studies with Marcel Dupre. He returned to Los Angeles in 1937 as organist and choirmaster at St. Joseph's Church. In later years, he took classes and seminars at UCLA and USC in philosophy and French literature. He also studied conducting with Otto Klemperer and Bruno Walter and orchestration and composition with Lucien Caillet at the University of Southern California.

In 1946 Roger Wagner formed his own chorale for recording, concretizing and touring in the U.S., Canada, and South America. Martin Bernheimer (*LA Times* music critic) used the terms "tonal opulence, flexibility and precision" in describing the Roger Wagner Chorale. Wagner did this for almost 20 years until 1965 when he founded the Los Angeles Master Chorale and Symphonia Orchestra from which he retired in 1985 and was named conductor laureate. He earned a musical doctorate at the University of Montreal. He taught many graduate level choral courses and published numerous choral arrangements.

Through the years, his chorale recorded several albums including the appropriately titled *Virtuoso!* and the lushly melodic *Songs of Victor Herbert.*

VAL HICKS

WAGONER, PORTER (12 AUG 1927–)

American country singer, songwriter, and record producer, born in West Plains, Missouri. He began performing on radio in 1950, and then on television on Red Foley's *Ozark Jubilee* program. From 1955 he recorded for Victor, and had 52 solo chart songs by 1979. He also recorded successfully with Dolly Parton (22 chart records); he wrote many of her songs and also produced her early recordings. Among Wagoner's most important discs were "Satisfied Mind" (Victor #6105; 1955) and "Cold Hard Facts of Life" (Victor #9067; 1967). The Parton duets included "Just Someone I Used to Know" (Victor #0267; 1969) and "Please Don't Stop Loving Me" (Victor #10010; 1974). Wagoner was dropped by RCA in 1981. Although Wagoner remains active as a performer, particularly on the *Grand Ole Opry*, he has rarely recorded since the mid-1970s, often simply doing new (and weaker) versions of his original hits. He returned to recording new material in 2000 on the small Nashville-based Shellpint label, releasing new CDs in 2000 and 2002. RCA has issued two compilation CDs, *The Essential* (#66934) and *The Essential Porter Wagoner and Dolly Parton* (#66958) that give the major hits, and for the Wagonerites there is also a 112-track set on Bear Family covering his entire RCA career (#15499; four CDs).

WALCHA, HELMUT
(27 OCT 1907–11 AUG 1991)

German organist, born in Leipzig. He lost his eyesight at age 19, but persisted in his career as a church organist. He was assistant organist at the Thomaskirche in Leipzig, then organist in Frankfurt. Walcha became a professor of music in the Leipzig Hochschule für Musik in 1938, and remained until his retirement in 1972. After World War II he recorded extensively for the Archiv label; his *Kunst der Fuge* of J.S. Bach was Archiv's first stereo offering (#2708002). He recorded the complete Bach organ works on 16 LPs (Archiv #413125; reissued on CD in a boxed set, Universal #463712, and in a two-disc reduction as Polygram #453064). He died in Frankfurt am Main.

WALDEN, NARADA MICHAEL
(23 APR 1952–)

Born in Kalamazoo, Michigan, Walden is best-known for his mid-1980s production work with pop artists Whitney Houston and Aretha Franklin. Walden was originally a jazz-fusion drummer, working with John McLaughlin and Jeff Beck, before settling in the San Francisco Bay area in the late 1970s, where he began working as a producer. Arista label head Clive Davis heard his work, and invited him to work with a new artist he was cultivating, Whitney Houston, in the mid-1980s; the result was a string of major hits from 1986–1991. Davis also hired him to help revive Aretha Franklin's career. In 1985 Walden opened his own recording studio, Tarpan Studios, which has become his center of operations. In addition to his production work, Walden has recorded as a solo artist for Atlantic Records, beginning in 1976, initially in the jazz-fusion style and then in a more pop-R&B mold. He has been less active since the early 1990s, releasing his last solo album to date in 1995, *Sending Love to Everyone*.

WALKMAN®

Small, portable cassette player, developed by Sony Electronics, and first marketed in 1979 under the name the "Soundabout." By the end of the 20th century, over 100 million Walkman-type players had been sold by Sony alone, and countless other manufacturers had copied the original machine. The Walkman® revolutionized portable music listening in much the same way that the earlier Boombox had done. But now, thanks to small headphones that offered excellent fidelity, the listener could enjoy music without disturbing his or her surroundings. Later Walkman-style

First Sony Walkman, model TPS-L-2, introduced in July 1979. Courtesy Sony

machines were developed to play MiniDiscs, CDs, MP3s, and other audio file formats.

CARL BENSON

WALLER, FATS
(21 MAY 1904–15 DEC 1943)

American jazz pianist and organist, born Thomas Waller in New York. He studied violin and piano, but learned primarily from imitating piano rolls. At 14 he was organist for a Harlem theater. He took lessons from James P. Johnson, and then from Leopold Godowsky. In 1929 he wrote a Broadway revue, *Hot Chocolates*, including the hit song "Ain't Misbehavin'." He also composed "Honeysuckle Rose." Waller had a brilliant stride piano style, mingled with his happy sense of humor, well suited to parody vocals on popular tunes. He toured widely in the 1930s, including Europe, made motion pictures in Hollywood, and had a Big Band for a time. Organ playing was not neglected either; he had a radio program devoted to it, and he played organ at New York theaters in the 1920s. He died on a train arriving at Kansas City on 15 Dec 1943.

Waller recorded incessantly, from 1922 for Okeh, with "Muscle Shoals Blues"/"Birmingham Blues" (#4757); thereafter for Victor and Bluebird. He also made piano rolls for QRS; e.g., "I've Got to Cool My Doggies Now" (#2149; 1922). "Ain't Misbehavin'" was made in 1929 (Victor #22092), and "Honeysuckle Rose" in 1934 (Victor #24826). Later hits included "Fractious Fingering" (Victor #25652; 1936) and "Yacht Club Swing" — used as his theme song (Bluebird #10035; 1938). Waller's vocalization was exemplified in "A-Tisket, A-Tasket" (HMV #BD-5398; 1938) and "Sheik of Araby" (Victor #25847; 1938). "Your Feets Too Big" (Bluebird #10500; 1939) illustrated his comedic approach. "Don't Try Your Jive on Me" had Waller at the organ and singing (HMV #BD-5415; 1938). The elaborated stride style is heard to advantage in several of his compositions recorded in 1929, such as "My Feelin's are Hurt"/"Smashing Thirds" (Victor #38613; 1929). There were numerous LP albums, both originals and reissues. As with most early jazz figures, there are numerous CD reissues of Waller's work, many on European-based jazz labels, some with less-than-optimal sound quality. Over the years, RCA has reissued Waller's recordings in a bewildering array of discs, including everything from his "complete" recordings through various "greatest hits" packages. Biograph has reissued Waller's piano roll recordings on CD. [Davies & Cooke 1953.]

WALLERSTEIN, EDWARD
(9 DEC 1891– 8 SEP 1970)

American record industry executive. He was with Brunswick from 1925, serving as eastern manager of the music division to 1930, then as sales manager. He left Brunswick in 1932 to head RCA Victor Records. He addressed the economic problems of the times with a number of successful initiatives, including renewed publication of the Victor catalogs and promotion of a turntable that would play through a radio. The turntable, named Duo Junior, proved very popular, although it sold for $16.50, a stiff price during the Depression. Wallerstein left Victor in 1938 to become president of the newly organized Columbia Recording Co., just acquired by CBS from American Record Corp. Indeed it was Wallerstein who had recommended to William S. Paley, CBS president, the purchase and rehabilitation of the Columbia label. Wallerstein unveiled the new LP microgroove record at a press conference in 1948.

After 12 years at Columbia, during which the label prospered and he became chairman of the board as well as president, Wallerstein retired in 1951. He then served as a consultant to Jack Kapp and in 1959 was vice president of the Belock Instrument Corp., makers of Everest Records. He died in Ft. Lauderdale, Florida.

WALSH, ARTHUR
(26 FEB 1896–13 DEC 1947)

American record industry executive, U.S. senator, and violinist, born in Newark, New Jersey. He recorded for Edison from 1916, and participated in tone tests. From 1924 to 1931 he was an executive with Thomas A. Edison, Inc., rising to general manager of the phonograph division, and then executive vice president of the company. He concluded his career with a successful run for the U.S. Senate, where he served from 1943 to 1947. Walsh died in South Orange, New Jersey.

WALSH, JIM (20 JULY 1903–24 DEC 1990)

Historian of the record industry, born Ulysses Walsh in Richmond, Virginia. He wrote a column in the monthly magazine *Hobbies*, "Favorite Pioneer Recording Artists," from January 1942 to May 1985. In his writings Walsh relied on an extensive personal communication with the artists and their families, producing accurate documentation that was infused with the human side of each performer. A chronological list of those articles to 1977 appeared in *NAG* #27 and *RR* #159–160, with an alphabetical index to the 1942–1982 articles in *NAG* #44.

Walsh wrote also for other journals, and contributed to *Edison Blue Amberol Recordings* by Ron Dethlefson (1981). His collection of records and materials was donated to the Library of Congress. He was posthumously honored with a Lifetime Achievement award by the Association of Recorded Sound Collections in 1991.

WALSH, LINCOLN
(3 NOV 1903–17 NOV 1971)

Educated at Stevens Institute of Technology, and earning an M.E. from that institute in 1926, Walsh also studied at Columbia University and Brooklyn College. Prior to World War II, he founded the Brook Amplifier Co., and during the war itself he worked with Rudy Bozak at the Dinion Coil Co. in Caldonia, New York, developing power supplies for radar use. After the war, he worked with Bozak to develop some of the first Bozak speaker systems, and later he designed a single-driver speaker, the Walsh Driver, that has been utilized in some Ohm Corp. loudspeakers for many years. Walsh was an early member of the Audio Engineering Society, and was also a member of the IRE and AIEE (these later merged to become the Institute of Electrical and Electronics Engineers).

HOWARD FERSTLER

WALTER, BRUNO
(15 SEP 1876–17 FEB 1962)

German/American conductor, born Bruno Walter Schlesinger in Berlin. After study in Berlin, he went to Cologne at age 17 as an opera coach. At 18 he was assistant conductor, under Gustav Mahler, at the Hamburg State Theater. He was then Mahler's assistant at the Vienna Opera, in 1901–1913. During the 1920s he became internationally famous, directing the Berlin Philharmonic Orchestra, the New York Philharmonic, and the Leipzig Gewandhaus. He was a guest conductor in Europe and the U.S. in the 1930s, then a resident in France during World War II. In the late 1940s he conducted at the Metropolitan Opera, and led the NBC Orchestra. He was appointed conductor of the New York Philharmonic in 1947, remaining to 1949. Walter retired to California in 1960, and died in Beverly Hills.

Known as a master of the Viennese school, and of Mahler, Walter inscribed some splendid recordings of those works. He directed the New York Philharmonic-Symphony Orchestra in major concertos: Beethoven's Violin Concerto with Joseph Szigeti (Columbia #M-177), the Beethoven Emperor Concerto with the Vienna Philharmonic Orchestra and Walter Gieseking (Columbia #M-243), and also with the New York Philharmonic-Symphony Orchestra and Rudolf Serkin (Columbia #M-500). He recorded the Beethoven Eroica, Fifth, and Eighth Symphonies, also with the New York orchestra. In the album of the Fifth Symphony (#498) there is a side on which he is heard rehearsing the orchestra. Walter's recording of the Mahler *Lied von der Erde* brought attention of a wide audience to that work, and to its composer (Columbia #M-300; 1936); it was performed with the Vienna Philharmonic Orchestra, assisted by singers Charles Kullman and Kerstin Thorborg. Compact disc reissues of his Beethoven symphonies are available, and of the Mahler *Lied*, plus Walter's renditions of Mahler's Symphonies Nos. 1, 2, 5, and 9; all from CBS.

WAND (LABEL)

SEE SCEPTER/WAND (LABELS)

WAR

Although early frontman Eric Burdon did not last past War's debut album in 1970, War remained one of the few successful interracial funk acts well into the 1980s. Although the group did not record any new material for roughly a decade beginning in the mid-1980s, the band — whose work had been covered or sampled by many R&B and alternative rock artists, including Janet Jackson, TLC, Korn, and Smash Mouth — was still releasing albums at the outset of the 21st century.

The band, originally billed as Eric Burdon and War, consisted of a Los Angeles–area aggregate formerly known as Nite Shift, the former Animals vocalist, and Danish harmonica player, Lee Oskar. Following several hits featuring Burdon's keening vocals — *Eric Burdon Declares "War"* (MGM #4663; 1970; #18), *The Black-Man's Burdon* (MGM #4710; 1970; #82), and the million-selling single "Spill the Wine" (MGM #14118; 1970; #3) — the members of War decided to operate as a separate act, signing with United Artists. Emphasizing its strong rhythmic underpinning and first-rate songwriting skills, the band released a string of trailblazing recordings, including the gold singles "Slippin' Into Darkness" (United Artists #50867; 1972; #16), "The War Is a Ghetto" (United Artists #50975; 1972; #7), "The Cisco Kid" (United Artists #163; 1973; #2), "Why Can't We Be Friends?" (United Artists #629; 1975; #6), and "Summer" (United Artists #834; 1976; #7), and the albums *All Day Music* (United Artists #5546; 1971; #16; gold record), *The War Is a Ghetto* (United Artists #5652; 1972; #1; gold record), *Deliver the Word* (United Artists #128; 1973; #6; gold record), *War Live!* (United Artists #193; 1974; #13; gold record), and *Why Can't We Be Friends?* (United Artists #441; 1975; #8; gold record).

Beset by changing fashions (most notably, the rise of disco), personnel changes, and varying label support — Blue Note, MCA, RCA, Priority, Lax, Virgin, and Avenue have all released new material by the band since 1977 — War has failed recently to match the commercial success they enjoyed in the early 1970s. Nevertheless, the band — now dominated by keyboardist/vocalist Leroy Jordan and producer Jerry Goldstein — has continued to produce engaging work, ranging from film soundtrack and jazz experiments in the late 1970s to the eclectic *Peace Sign* (Avenue #76024; 1994) and Hispanic-influenced *Coleccion Latina* (Avenue #72866 1997), both of which featuring guest contributions from the likes of Oskar and guitarist José Feliciano. A competing version of War — featuring four original members of the band — began recording as Guerra ("war" in Spanish) and, later, Same Ole Band, in the late 1990s.

FRANK HOFFMANN

WARING, FRED
(9 JUNE 1900–29 JULY 1984)

American orchestra leader, born Fred Malcolm Waring in Tyrone, Pennsylvania. He learned the banjo and played in a four-man banjo "orchestra" in his teens, and continued music-making while an engineering student at Pennsylvania State University. (Later his technical knowledge helped him to gain a lucrative patent, for the Waring Blender.) He formed a larger orchestra and glee club — the Pennsylvanians — and gained engagements on college campuses. The group was a great success on a tour to France. The glee club was a hit everywhere, with its romantic arrangements and clear diction contrasted with hummed passages. In 1933 he was engaged for a radio program sponsored by Old Gold cigarettes (one of the group's favorite songs was "A Cigarette, Sweet Music, and You"). Other tunes associated with the ensemble included several theme songs, "Sleep" (Victor #19172; 1923), "I Hear Music," and "Breezin' Along with the Breeze." "Dancing in the Dark" was a memorable arrangement (Victor #22708; 1931).

The Waring orchestra and chorale appeared on numerous radio programs and toured widely, maintaining a high level of popularity, and had a television show in the early years of the medium. They made 145 Victor records, and also worked for Decca and Reprise. Because they declined to make records at all for a nine-year period, 1923–1932, many of their popular renditions were not preserved. Waring died in Danville, Pennsylvania. [Gottlieb 1972.]

Sheet music cover for "Dreary Weather" featuring photos of Fred and Tom Waring. Courtesy David A. Jasen

WARNER BROS. (LABEL)

Warner Bros. Records was founded in 1958 as a subsidiary of the Warner Bros. film company, and originally headed by ex-Capitol Records employee Jim Conklin. It was originally limited to issue soundtracks from Warner's films and television programs. In 1960 Warner jumped into the pop market by signing the Everly Brothers. Popular 1960s acts included comedy stars Bob Newhart, Allan Sherman, and Bill Cosby, along with folk stars Peter, Paul, and Mary. In 1963 Frank Sinatra's Reprise label was purchased, bringing noted executive Mo Ostin to Warner, where he would remain until 1998; besides its U.S. acts, Reprise licensed U.K. recordings from Pye Records, including hits by the Kinks and Petula Clark. In 1967 Seven Arts purchased Warner Bros. and the label was renamed Warner Bros.–7 Arts; the Atlantic label was also purchased by the new company. Two years later, the Kinney Corp. purchased the firm, and the label returned to its Warner Bros. name; Elektra was added to the music division, now known as WEA. Noted Warner Bros. acts of the late 1960s to 1970s include the Grateful Dead, who remained with the label through the mid-1970s, James Taylor, and Little Feat. Signings in the 1980s included Paul Simon, Prince, who formed his own Paisley Park label (he later feuded with the label because Warners refused to release as much material as he recorded), and R.E.M. Also, in 1980, Warner absorbed Sire Records, which had great success through the 1990s with major star Madonna (eventually, she was given her own Warner label, Maverick). In 1990, Warner Communications merged with Time, Inc. to form Time-Warner; subsequently, in 2000, America Online purchased the conglomerate and renamed it AOL/Time Warner. After the AOL purchase, Warner Bros. Records long-time executives Mo Ostin and Lenny Waronker left the firm to run Dreamworks Records. [website: www.wbr.com.]

CARL BENSON

WARNER BRUNSWICK LTD.

With Brunswick discs', of British Brunswick, Ltd., demise in the U.K., the Hollywood film-maker Warner Bros. (which had purchased the Brunswick Radio

Corp.) resuscitated the Brunswick label in the U.K. Warner Brunswick, Ltd., was formed with £40,000 capital on 11 Oct 1930, with the registered trademark of Brunswick acquired for the U.K. The new firm took over the Panatrope trademark as well and serviced those machines. A factory was at Shepherds Bush, London. Chappell Piano Co., Ltd. of Bond St. was contracted to be the first distributors of Brunswick discs, all of them by American Brunswick artists but pressed in London. In December 1930 the first catalog of those discs appeared, offering 10-inch records at three shillings each.

In April 1931 Warner Brunswick, Ltd., introduced Panachord discs to the U.K. market, with many masters from the U.S. Melotone label; the Panachord price was two shillings (reduced to 1s 6d in July). Chappell was the sole concessionaire. By September 1931 the business had achieved success, employing hundreds of U.K. workmen at the factory, which covered hundreds of acres. There were studios in London, Milan, Buenos Aires, Sydney, Chicago, Los Angeles, and New York. Radios were also made at the London factory. All European business was transferred from London to the New York office.

Although U.K. radio stations were not allowed to advertise, Warner Brunswick did broadcast commercials, beamed to U.K. through Radio Paris. English recorded discs were introduced on the Brunswick and Panachord labels just before Decca Record Co., Ltd., purchased the business and share capital of Warner Brunswick, the parent company having already disposed of its end to the American Record Corp., which then formed the Brunswick Record Corp. (The British Crystalate Gramophone Record Manufacturing Co., Ltd., had a third share in American Record Corp.) The sale was reported in the first week of May 1932. Decca continued the record names, but added "Made by Decca" to the labels. Pressing was transferred to the Decca factory at New Malden. Warner Brunswick, Ltd., disappeared with the company's change of name to Brunswick, Ltd., in July 1933.

FRANK ANDREWS

WARONKER, LENNY (3 OCT 1941–)

Producer and label executive. Waronker was born to the music business; his father, Si[mon] Waronker, cofounded Liberty Records in 1955. After working his way up the corporate ladder, Lenny Waronker was hired in the A&R department of Reprise Records (a division of Warner Records) in 1966, and became head of A&R in 1971. At Warner/Reprise he signed his childhood friend Randy Newman, and later Little Feat, Rod Stewart, Curtis Mayfield, the Doobie Brothers,

Maria Muldaur, and Rickie Lee Jones. Neil Young released the album *After the Gold Rush* in 1970 for Warner/Reprise during Waronker's tenure. In 1989 Lenny Waronker became president of Warner Records and signed Elvis Costello. Waronker retired from Warner soon after mentor Mo Ostin left the company in the wake of its purchased by AOL in 2000. The two reemerged as coheads of SKG/Dreamworks.

BRAD HILL

WARWICK, DIONNE (12 DEC 1940–)

American popular singer, born Dionne Warwicke in East Orange, New Jersey. She began singing with her sister and a cousin, doing gospel songs, then worked in New York. She impressed composer Burt Bacharach and producer Hal David, and got a recording contract with Scepter, staying with the label from 1962 to 1971. Warwick became a sophisticated soul singer, thriving on songs written for her by Bacharach, such as "Walk on By" (Scepter #1274; 1964) and "I'll Never Fall in Love Again" (Scepter #12273; 1969). She won a Grammy for the latter record, and another for "Do You Know the Way to San Jose?" (Scepter #12216; 1968). The hit album, *Dionne* (Arista #AB4230; 1979), on the charts 40 weeks, included the popular singles "Deja Vu" (Arista #0459) and "I'll Never Love This Way Again" (Arista #0419). Her last chart album was *How Many Times Can We Say Goodbye?* (Arista #AL8 8104; 1983). Warwick had 44 chart singles and 33 chart albums.

WAS, DON (13 SEP 1952–)

Born Donald Fagenson in Detroit, Michigan, Was became a well-known rock-pop performer/producer in the 1980s. Partnering with fellow Detroiter David Was (born as David Weiss), the duo became known as Was (Not Was), issuing their first self-produced single in 1981. This led to a contract with Island, earning them a following in the U.K. In 1988 they scored their biggest U.S. hit, "Walk the Dinsoaur" from the album *What Up, Dog* (Chrysallis #21664). Was became an in-demand producer, working with Bob Dylan, the B-52s, and Bonnie Raitt (overseeing her early 1990s' comeback recordings). He has won two Grammys, in 1989 for Raitt's *Nick of Time* album and then in 1994, garnering the Producer of the Year honor. His last major producer was 1994's *Voodoo Lounge* by the Rolling Stones. However, Was fell out of favor as a pop-producer by the late 1990s.

CARL BENSON

WASHINGTON, DINAH
(29 AUG 1924–14 DEC 1963)

Born Ruth Lee Jones in Tuscaloosa, Alabama, Washington was a versatile and gifted vocalist, recording jazz, blues, and R&B, as well as middle of the road pop.

Raised in Chicago, Washington was heard working in local clubs by bandleader/vibe player Lionel Hampton, who hired her as a vocalist in 1943; working with members of Hampton's band, she also made her first solo recordings that year for the small Keynote label, which were produced by jazz enthusiast/critic Leonard Feather. Washington remained with Hampton's band until 1946, and signed with EmArcy/Mercury, recording R&B. She scored significant hits on the R&B charts through the 1950s, and then in 1959 crossed over into pop success with "What a Diff'rence a Day Makes" (Mercury #71435; 1959), that caused critics to accuse her of selling out to a commercial style backed by lush orchestration. Yet even in her mainstream pop efforts, she retained a tough, unsentimental viewpoint, with a high-pitched voice and crystal-clear phrasing. "This Bitter Earth" (Mercury #71635; 1960) and "September in the Rain" (Mercury #71876; 1961) are examples of hits that did not compromise her gritty, bluesy style. Her 1960 duet with Brook Benton on "Baby (You've Got What It Takes)" (Mercury #71629) was a major hit. She moved to Roulette in 1962, continuing in the lush, mainstream style. She lead a turbulent life, with seven marriages, and died of an accidental overdose of diet pills and alcohol. She remains a major influence on most Black female singers, especially in R&B and soul.

Many of Washington's original Mercury albums are available on CD reissue, and her complete Mercury recordings from 1946–1961 are available on seven three-CD sets. There are numerous compilation albums as well of this material. Her later Roulette recordings are anthologized on *The Best of* (Roulette/Capitol #99114).

BOB SILLERY

WASHINGTON, GROVER JR.
(12 DEC 1943–17 DEC 1999)

Born in Buffalo, New York, Washington was one of the most successful saxophonists on record from the early 1970s through his death. His father was a saxophonist, and taught him the basics of the instruments. Washington first toured as a backing musician with the pop vocal group the Four Clefs from 1959–1963, and then freelanced until 1965, when he enlisted in the Army. After his discharge, he moved to Philadelphia in 1967, where he worked as a sessionman. Combining light R&B with jazz stylings, Washington was a pioneer of what would later be known as "smooth jazz." His first success came with his solo album, *Inner City Blues* (Kudu #03; 1971), produced by Creed Taylor, and it led to a series of highly successful instrumental albums through the 1970s. Washington's sound was set and varied little through his career, retaining a pleasant mix of jazzy elements with mainstream R&B accompaniment; most of his albums reached number one or at least the Top 5 position on the jazz charts through the early 1980s, and he had several Top 10 R&B hits. In 1980 Washington moved to Electra, and then in mid-decade to Columbia. He died suddenly of a heart attack while taping a television appearance in New York City.

WATERS, ETHEL
(31 OCT 1896–1 SEP 1977)

American blues singer, born Ethel Howard in Chester, Pennsylvania. She made an unfortunate decision to marry at age 13, then had to work as a laundress in Philadelphia, while breaking into vaudeville. She attracted attention and made some records in 1921. "New York Glide"/"At the New Jump Steady Ball" was on the Cardinal label (#2036), and "Oh Daddy"/"Down Home Blues" was on Black Swan (#2010). She was paid $100 for the Black Swan effort, which turned out to be a big enough hit to help save the new company from ruin. A few months later Waters had a Black Swan contract that made her "the highest paid colored recording star in the country" [Dixon & Godrich 1970] with the stipulation that she would not marry again. She continued to work for the label until its demise in 1923, then went to Paramount, Vocalion, and Columbia. She gathered her own groups of sidemen, including distinguished artists like Tommy Dorsey, Jimmy Dorsey, Benny Goodman, Adrian Rollini, Eddie Lang, and Joe Venuti. "When Your Lover Has Gone" (Columbia #2409; 1931), which had Tommy Dorsey, Goodman, Venuti, and Lang backing her up. Waters sang a fine "Stormy Weather" for Brunswick in 1933 (#6564).

She was in many Broadway musicals, most notably in *Cabin in the Sky*, with an all-Black cast (1940), and made a brilliant record of its hit song, "Taking a Chance on Love" (Liberty Music Shop #L-310; 1940). She became a serious stage actress, and then a partner to Billy Graham in his evangelistic travels. Waters died in New York. Classics has reissued her complete recordings in chronological order from 1926–1940 on a series of CDs, and there are various other compilations available on a variety of jazz-reissue labels.

WATERS, MUDDY
(4 APR 1915–30 APR 1983)

American blues singer, born McKinley Morganfield in Rolling Fork, Mississippi. He was reared on a plantation by his grandmother, learning to sing and play harmonica and guitar, and acquiring his nickname. Alan and John Lomax recorded him in 1941 for the Archive of Folk Song at the Library of Congress, doing "Country Blue"/"I Be's Troubled" (Archive of American Folk Song #18); the complete recordings later appeared on LP and CD by MCA/Chess. He was successful thereafter in Chicago and nationally, singing blues in his own rough manner. He signed with Aristocrat in 1947, the predecessor of Chess Records, and formed a long relationship with label owners Leonard and Phil Chess, remaining with the label through 1972. He took up the electric guitar, requiring louder singing, and visited U.K. in 1958 with great effect. U.K. blues-revivalists were early Waters fans, including young Mick Jagger and Keith Richard, who named their band, the Rolling Stones, in his honor. A magazine took the same name, and Bob Dylan later composed a song further playing off Waters's famous lyric, "Like a Rolling Stone." Eric Clapton in his Yardbirds days was another Waters's enthusiast. Although Waters did not break through to a rock audience in as big a way as other blues veterans, such as B.B. King, his career was helped by all of this exposure. By the mid-1970s, Waters became a revered elder statesmen of the blues-rock movement, giving a memorable performance at The Band's famous Last Waltz concert (immortalized on the film and recording made of the event). Slowed by a stroke in 1970, Waters had to perform sitting down, but was no less powerful in his delivery. After becoming less active in the later 1970s as a performer, Waters died in Downers Grove, Illinois.

Waters commercial recording career began in 1947 when he made his earliest discs, using his electric guitar. "Walkin' Blues" (Chess #1426; 1950) was a success, and "Louisiana Blues" — with harmonica player Little Walter — was another (Chess #1441; 1950). His more advanced and raucous manner was demonstrated in "Tiger in Your Tank" (Chess #1765; 1960). Five of his records won Grammys. Only one LP album reached the charts, *Electric Mud* (Cadet Concept LPS @214; 1968). In 1969 Chess paired him with young Chicago blues revivalists Paul Butterfield and Michael Bloomfield on *Fathers and Sons* (expanded CD version, #112648), and, in another attempt to broaden his audience, released *The London Muddy Waters Sessions* (#60013; reissued on CD as #9298) in 1971 featuring U.K. blues-rock musicians including Stevie Winwood in a rather ragged session. In 1977 Johnny Winter produced his triumphant return, *Hard Again* (Blue Sky/Columbia #34449), and it was followed by two more albums.

Muddy Waters album cover from the early '70s. Courtesy Frank Hoffmann

Waters work is well-represented on CD. MCA/Chess has issued various compilations, notably the three-CD Chess Box (#80002), which offers a healthy selection of his recordings for the label made between 1947–1972. His Blue Sky albums of the 1970s are available on CD in their original release format.

WATERSON, HENRY
(CA. 1871–10 AUG 1933)

American record industry executive, founder of the Little Wonder and Cameo labels. He was also a force in music publishing, as co-founder of the firm Waterson, Berlin and Snyder. He died in Saratoga, New York.

WATSON, DOC (2 MAR 1923–)

Born Arthel Lane Watson in Deep Gap, North Carolina, Watson is a talented guitarist, whose smooth-voiced singing has won him a wide following in folk, bluegrass, and to some extent country circles. Coming from a musical family and blind from birth, Doc early on showed capabilities on a number of instruments. Inspired by his idol Merle Travis, he began playing fiddle tunes and elaborate melody fills on the guitar. By the late 1950s, he was working in a local band playing electric lead guitar on rockabilly, country, and pop songs.

Folklorist Ralph Rinzler discovered Watson while recording old-time banjo player Clarence "Tom" Ashley. Watson was brought North, and soon began

Doc and Merle Watson album from the late '60s. Courtesy Frank Hoffmann

performing and recording with his son, Merle (8 Feb 1949–23 Oct 1985), on second guitar. He became a major star on the folk-revival circuit, signed to Vanguard Records. Watson's big break came when he was included on the sessions for *Will the Circle Be Unbroken?*, the Nitty Gritty Dirt Band's homage to country music legends released in 1971. Watson's vocals were prominently featured, as well as his legendary flatpicking. He was immediately signed to the Poppy label (a part of United Artists). In the 1980s, he signed with Flying Fish Records, a folk/bluegrass label, and in the 1990s to Sugar Hill Records. He has been awarded five Grammys, twice for Best Ethnic or Traditional Recording (1973, 1974), twice for Best Folk Album (1986, 1990), and once for Best Country Instrumental Performance (1979).

Although Watson remains active as a performer, the death of his son Merle from a farm accident in the mid-1980s devastated him and he went into semiretirement. He has continued to perform, often with Merle's son Richard as an accompanist.

CARL BENSON

WATT

The unit of electrical power measurement. In an audio system wattage is a consideration with regard to an amplifier (indicating the amount of work it can perform, primarily in the driving of loudspeakers) and to loudspeakers (referring to a speaker's efficiency in converting electrical power into acoustic power).

WAX

One of the earliest and most-used materials for records, both cylinder and disc. Initially, waxes were carnauba (brittle yellow), from Brazilian palm leaves, or a mineral derived from brown coal.

See also **Cylinder; Disc**

WEATHER REPORT

Weather Report was the antithesis of the 1970s' jazz fusion style. Core members include Josef Zawinul, keyboards and synthesizers, and Wayne Shorter, saxophone; they incorporated rock, classical, and Third World ethnic influences within a harmonic and improvisational jazz framework, enabling the group to achieve a mainstream commercial success that eluded most of its peers. The recordings resulting from this collaboration possessed an orchestral grandeur that would greatly influence later jazz developments, most notably the European ambient labels like ECM and the lite jazz of Kenny G, Dave Grusin, and others.

Zawinul, an Austrian native, and Shorter first worked together in the Miles Davis aggregate responsible for the landmark LPs, *In a Silent Way* (Columbia #9857; 1968) and *Bitches Brew* (Columbia #40577; 1969). In 1970 Shorter left Davis (with whom he had worked since 1964) and Zawinul departed the Cannonball Adderley Quintet, after serving nine years as electric pianist and composer, to form Weather Report, along with Czech bassist Miroslav Vitous, drummer Alphonse Mouzon, and Brazilian Airto Moreira on percussion. The latter three musicians would all move on in the early 1970s to be replaced by a rapid succession of jazz performers.

The group's eponymous debut (Columbia #30661; 1971; #191) established the mold for emerging fusion movement, balancing richly textured instrumental pieces calculated to appeal to a progressive rock audience with adventurous arrangements and first-rate ensemble playing. The follow-up albums — *I Sing the Body Electric* (Columbia #31352; 1092; #147), the B side excerpted from a Tokyo performance released on two discs in Japan; the funk-influenced *Streetnighter* (Columbia #32210; 1973; #85), the first work to feature Zawinul's synthesizer leads; and *Mysterious Traveller* (Columbia #32494; 1974; #46), whose preoccupation with dance-floor rhythms reflected the increasing industry profile of disco music within the music industry — solidified Weather Report's position as taste-makers within the jazz fraternity.

The addition of bassist Jaco Pasorius in 1976 ushered in the group's most popular phase. *Heavy Weather* (Columbia #34418; 1977; #30; gold record), which featured the radio hit, "Birdland," *Mr. Gone* (ARC #35358; 1978; #52), and *8:30* (ARC #36030; 1979; #47), with three of four sides culled from live 1979 dates, sold particularly well. By 1987, however, the group had lost its creative momentum, and the decision was made to disband. Although the former members have embarked on other projects (Pastorius died of a drug overdose in 1987), compilations and reissues of the original albums on CD continue to sell well.

FRANK HOFFMANN

WEAVERS

American folk singing group, established in 1948 by Pete Seeger. The other members were Lee Hays, Ronnie Gilbert (the only female), and Fred Hellerman. Performing at the Village Vanguard in Greenwich Village from December 1949, they were soon successful in combining folk harmonies with current pop styles, and were an important influence in the folk song revival of the 1950s. Among their early recorded hits were "Goodnight Irene" (Decca #27077; 1950) "So Long" (Decca #27376; 1951), and "On Top of Old Smokey" (Decca #27515; 1951). The Weavers were world favorites in a few years, but suffered from congressional investigations into alleged Communist sympathies and were blacklisted. Seeger departed in 1958; a grand farewell reunion appearance at Carnegie Hall in 1980 was presented on radio and PBS-TV with the title *Wasn't that a Time*.

WEBB, CHICK
(10 FEB 1909–16 JUNE 1939)

American jazz drummer and Big Band leader, born William Webb in Baltimore. He taught himself drumming as a child, and went to New York in about 1925, setting up his own band. By 1928 he had found success, and was engaged at the Savoy Ballroom, where he remained through the 1930s. The band was one of the finest of the era, with strong arrangements by Edgar Sampson, and the imaginative driving performances of Webb, "the finest big-band drummer of his time" [Schuller 1989]. When 16-year-old Ella Fitzgerald joined the ensemble in 1935, the style changed from hot to mild swing, with a novelty element, to a more commercially acceptable but much less interesting mode. Webb died in Baltimore; Fitzgerald briefly took over running the band, but World War II and her own lack of experience managing such a large group led it to fold in 1942.

Webb's early records, "Dog Bottom" and "Jungle Mama," made for Brunswick in 1929, already show his great abilities; and the 1931 "Heebie Jeebies," arranged by Benny Carter — who was with the band a short time — is a tour de force (Vocalion #1607). Other outstanding work included "Stompin' at the Savoy" in a potent Sampson arrangement (Columbia #2926D; 1934) and Sampson's "Let's Get Together

Early '60s lineup of the Weavers featuring Erik Darling on banjo. Courtesy Vanguard Records

(Columbia #CB-741; 1934). After 1935 most of the records featured Ella Fitzgerald, but on the flip side of her great nonsense hit "A-Tisket, A-Tasket" (Decca #1840; 1938) there was still a fine drumming display by Webb in "Liza." Fitzgerald herself developed gradually from an indifferent vocalist to an outstanding jazz stylist, but not until a decade after Webb's death.

The French Classics labed has issued two individual CDs tracking Webb's band recordings, without vocalist Fitzgerald, in chronological order, *1929–1934* (Classics #502) and *1935–38* (Classics #517; some tracks feature the young vocalist Louis Jordan, who would score big with his jump band in the postwar years). Separately, Classics has issued the orchestra's recordings that emphasize Fitzgerald's vocals in a series devoted to her work in chronological order. For a general overview of the band's best work, *Stompin' at the Savoy* (ASV/Living Era #5416) gives 25 prime tracks, including Fitzgerald's breakthrough hit on "A-Tisket, A Tasket."

WEBER, HENRI

A baritone who recorded extensively for Pathé cylinders in Paris, during 1897–1900. He made at least 42 records by 1900, and another nine in 1902. Columbia also recorded him, with 17 cylinders in 1902–1903, and Edison made three records in Paris in 1905. Weber was one of the very earliest to record operatic arias, offering first "De l'art splendeur" from *Benvenuto Cellini* by Diaz (#0020), followed by 14 other arias, mostly from French composers. He was apparently the first baritone to inscribe the "Toreador Song" (#0308).

In 1904 Weber began to record for G & T in Paris, with about 60 French songs and a few arias. His final effort was under the pseudonym D'Haller, in a chorale number made on 1 Sep 1911. His G & T work was not transferred to American Victor.

WEBSTER, ARTHUR G.

SEE LOUDSPEAKER

WEBSTER, BEN
(27 MAR 1909–20 SEP 1973)

American jazz saxophonist, born in Kansas City, Missouri. He studied violin and piano, and played during silent movies in Amarillo, Texas. Then he joined various groups, and learned tenor saxophone, which became his specialty. He had a distinctive human-like tone, particularly effective in ballads. In the 1930s he worked with Bennie Moten, Andy Kirk, Fletcher Henderson, Benny Carter, Cab Calloway, Roy Eldridge, Duke Ellington, and Teddy Wilson; in 1940 he joined the Ellington band, staying until 1943, and returned to him in 1948–1949. Later he freelanced widely across the U.S. Webster settled in the Netherlands in 1964, then moved to Copenhagen, performing extensively in many European locales. He died in Amsterdam.

Webster was heard in solo work on Victor discs made in 1931 by Blanche Calloway and her Joy Boys, and later with many of the ensembles cited above. His first major solo in ballad tempo was "Dream Lullaby" with Benny Carter (Vocalion #2898; 1934). Webster's earliest solo on a Duke Ellington record was in "Truckin'" (Brunswick #7514; 1935). His later work with Ellington included outstanding presentations in "Mauve" (Standard Radio Transcription #P-132; 1941; not issued on 78 rpm), and "What Am I Here For?" (Victor #20-1598; 1942). Though slow numbers were best for Webster, he turned in some fine upbeat renditions, such as "This Can't Be Love" with the Oscar Peterson Trio.

Webster signed with EmArcy, the Mercury jazz subsidiary, in the early 1950s while living in Los Angeles (his complete recordings for the label have been reissued on EmArcy #824836). In 1953 he signed with Norman Granz's Clef/Verve labels, remaining with Verve through 1960 (many of his original Verve LPs have been reissued on CD). From the mid-1960s, he recorded primarily in Europe for a variety of labels, notably Black Lion. [Evensmo 1978.]

WEEMS, TED (26 SEP 1901–6 MAY 1963)

American Big Band leader, among the favorites of the late 1920s and 1930s. He was born in Pitcairn, Pennsylvania, and played violin as a youth. He switched to trombone while attending the University of Pennsylvania, forming his first band with his brother Art. His recordings began with Victor in 1923, going to 1933; he also worked for Columbia in 1934 and for Decca in 1936–1940. His group performed in a swing/jazz style, marked by technical perfection and originality. Weems was fortunate in having a number of fine vocalists, including Dusty Rhoades, Parker Gibbs, Arthur Jarrett, and Elmo Tanner — who was best known as a whistler — and Perry Como, in his first recordings (1936–1942). Among the fine Weems recordings were "Am I a Passing Fancy?" sung by Jarrett (Victor #22038; 1929), "One of Us Was Wrong" sung by Tanner (Victor #22877; 1931), and "T'ain't So" featuring Tanner. Tanner whistled while Como sang on several sides, including "Simple and Sweet" (Decca #2019; 1938), and Tanner whistled solo on "Heartaches" (Decca #2020; 1938). Weems died in Tulsa, Oklahoma. A nice selection of his more jazz-oriented 1926–1929 Victor recordings are gathered on *Marvelous!* (ASV/Living Era #5029), with a similar survey available from Retrieval (#79034). Collector's Choice #174 recorded 25 of his hits from the Victor era through 1933. Other than radio airchecks from the 1940s, his later more popular recordings are not available currently on CD, perhaps because the sweeter style of this material is less popular among jazz listeners today.

WEINRICH, CARL
(2 JULY 1904–13 MAY 1991)

American organist, born in Paterson, New Jersey. He studied at New York University and at the Curtis Institute in Philadelphia, and had instruction from Marcel Dupré and Lynwood Farnam. When the latter died suddenly, Weinrich succeeded him as organist at the Church of the Holy Communion, New York. He gave important recitals in New York and on tour, playing J.S. Bach. Weinrich taught at several universities, and directed music at Princeton's Chapel from 1943 to 1973. He died in Princeton, New Jersey.

The Weinrich recordings, made on the Praetorius organ of Westminster Choir College in Princeton, were landmarks in establishing the clean sound of the baroque organ in American consciousness. Well recorded by the new Musicraft label from 1937, Weinrich produced definitive versions of the Bach Trio Sonatas, earning great success (Musicraft #1040-1 and #1041-2). He then did the Bach Chorale Preludes in a five-disc album (Musicraft #MC-22), and the great "Toccata and Fugue in D-Minor" (Musicraft #1116), plus other preludes and fugues.

Little of Weinrich's work is available on CD. One exception is a 1937 recording featuring Weinrich on organ playng Bach's *St. Matthew Passion*, conducted by Serge Koussevitzky, featuring the Harvard Glee Club, originally issued on 78 by RCA Victor in three large albums and now available on a three-CD set (Rockport #5012-14). Weinrich's papers are held in the Westminster Choir College/Rider University Library. [website: http://library.rider.edu/talbott/specialcollections.html#weinrich.]

WEINSTOCK, BOB (2 OCT 1928–)

American record company executive, record producer, born in New York. Bob Weinstock founded Prestige Records in New York in 1949. The jazz label recorded such performers as Miles Davis, John Coltrane, Thelonious Monk, and Sonny Rollins. Weinstock produced many of the recordings, but also employed noted jazz recording engineer Rudy van Gelder and others to handle his sessions. Weinstock

licensed European recordings and, in the early 1960s, added a folk-music subsidiary. He sold Prestige to Fantasy Records in 1971.

WILLIAM RUHLMANN

WEISSMANN, FRIEDER
(23 JAN 1895– 1984)

German conductor, born in Frankfurt am Main. One of the most prolific conductors on disc, he once estimated his output at around 4,000 records. He directed house orchestras for Odeon in the 1920s, and was the first conductor to inscribe all nine Beethoven symphonies. In the mid-1940s he conducted operas for Victor. A two-disc LP album of extracts from his 1926–1933 work was issued by Ritornello Records in 1983 (#1001) and reissued under the same catalog number on two CDs by Diska Archivia.

WELK, LAWRENCE
(11 MAR 1903–17 MAY 1992)

American dance-band leader and accordionist, born in Strasburg, North Dakota. He led local groups, performing polkas and other ethnic dance music, and had some radio time in the late 1920s in South Dakota. He enlarged the ensemble into a dance orchestra, achieving an airy sound referred to as "Champagne Music," and was successful in several Midwest cities. His orchestra recorded for Gennett in 1928, and made three sides for Lyric in 1931, disguised as Paul's Novelty Orchestra. Welk settled in Chicago's Aragon and Trianon ballrooms in the late 1930s, and made records for Vocalion. His great success came with television, on which he displayed a beguiling showmanship. His program was one of the most popular in the 1950s and 1960s, with music, comedy, and dancing. The polka remained his signature mode, heard on many of his best-selling records: "Beer Barrel Polka" (Vocalion #4788; 1939), "Clarinet Polka" (Decca #3726; 1941), and "Pennsylvania Polka" (Decca #4309; 1942). Among his later chart singles were "Calcutta" (Dot #16161; 1960) and "Baby Elephant Walk" (Dot #16365; 1962) — both were also the titles of successful LP albums. There were 31 chart albums between 1955 and 1974, notably *Moon River* (Dot #3412; 1961) and *Wonderful, Wonderful* (Dot #3552; 1963). He died in Santa Monica, California.

WELK MUSIC GROUP

A music publishing, record, and video producing company, originally founded by Lawrence Welk to administer his music copyrights. The company expanded into country-music recordings with its purchase of Vanguard Records in 1986, followed by Sugar Hill Records in 1998. The company is currently headed by Welk's son Larry Welk.

WELLS, JOHN BARNES (17 OCT 1880–8 AUG 1935)

American concert tenor, born in Ashley, Pennsylvania. He was a church singer, then made his concert debut in New York in 1915. Before that event he was already recording for Edison, and had a popular Amberol of "Good Night, Dear" (#187; 1909). His first and most enduring disc for Victor was "Sweet Genevieve" with the Hayden Quartet, made in 1910. Another great success was the 1913 Victor of "The Rosary." Wells recorded also for U-S Everlasting cylinders, and made a duet with Grace Kerns for Regal. His last discs were for Aeolian-Vocalion in 1919, except for some special pressings by Columbia for Psi Upsilon fraternity, in which he was one of the quartet. He also sang for a time with the Stellar Quartet. Wells died in Roxbury, New York.

WELLS, KITTY (30 AUG 1919–)

American country singer and songwriter, born Muriel Ellen Deason in Nashville. She sang on Nashville radio with her sister, and then teamed with (and married) singer Johnny Wright. Wells and Wright appeared on the *Louisiana Hayride* show from 1947 to 1952. Wells was heard on the *Grand Ole Opry* from 1952. She recorded for Decca from 1952, and made 55 chart singles in the next 20 years. Her breakthrough hit was "It Wasn't God Who Made Honky-Tonk Angels" (Decca #28232; 1952), an "answer song" to Hank Thompson's hit, "Wild Side of Life." The song proved to Nashville that female vocalists could do equally well with songs of heartbreak and honky-tonking as men did. Through the 1950s and 1960s, Wells scored major hits on solo recordings ("I Can't Stop Loving You," "Mommy for a Day," "Heartbreak U.S.A."), and on duets with Red Foley ("One by One," "As Long as I Live"). Although less active as a recording artist by the early 1970s, Wells continued to perform and tour. In 1976 Wells was elected to the Country Music Hall of Fame and won a Grammy Lifetime Achievement award in 1991, only the third country performer to be so honored, and the first woman.

CD reissues of Wells's recordings include *Country Music Hall of Fame* (MCA #10081), which reissues Decca recordings cut between 1952–1965, including all of her hits in the heartache genre; and *The Queen of Country* (Bear Family #15638), a four-CD set featuring all of her RCA and Decca material recorded between 1949–1958.

REV. CARL BENSON

WELLS, MARY (13 MAY 1943–26 JULY 1992)

On the strength of her cool, but sexy vocals, Mary Wells became Motown Records' first star. Born in Detroit, she auditioned for Berry Gordy, Jr., trying to place one of her songs with his client Jackie Wilson. Gordy signed her as a singer; the song "Bye Bye Baby" (Motown #1003; 1961) was released as her debut single. Smokey Robinson provided understated production work for a string of hits: "The One Who Really Loves You" (Motown #1024; 1962), "You Beat Me to the Punch" (Motown #1032; 1962), "Two Lovers" (Motown #1035; 1962), "Laughing Boy" (Motown #1039; 1963), "You Lost the Sweetest Boy"/"What's Easy for Two Is So Hard for One" (Motown #1048; 1963), and "My Guy" (Motown #1059; 1964; #1).

At the peak of her success, Wells sued Motown, arguing that the recording contract she signed at 17 was invalid. She received a lucrative offer from 20th Century-Fox, along with promises that she'd be provided opportunities to appear in films. However, the label failed to deliver hits or acting roles. Following unsuccessful stints with Atco and Jubilee, she retired from the music business until a revived interest in the classic Motown Sound in the late 1980s led to a demand for concert appearances. After recording the LP *Keeping My Mind on Love*, Wells was diagnosed as having cancer of the larynx. Lacking health insurance, record industry associates provided financial support prior to her death. [Romanowski and George-Warren 1995.]

WILLIAM RUHLMANN

WERRENRATH, REINALD (7 AUG 1883– 12 SEP 1953)

American baritone, born in Brooklyn. He was highly versatile, singing in opera (Metropolitan Opera debut on 19 Feb 1919 as Silvio, with Enrico Caruso, remaining with the company through 1921), concert (more than 3,500 appearances), and the recording studio. His first recording was with the Criterion Quartet, for Edison in 1903, issued in 1905: "Little Tommy Went A-Fishing" (Edison #8866). Werrenrath's first solo record was "My Dear" (Edison #9604; 1907). He began with Victor in 1909, singing "Danny Deever" (#31738), and was an immediate success. He was with the Victor Opera Co., the Orpheus Quartet, and the Lyric Quartet. He began on black label Victors (about 65 items in the 1917 catalog), then was heard on both black label and Red Seal. A fine version of the Rigoletto Quartet was made with John McCormack and Lucrezia Bori (#89080; 1914); it sold for $4 (later the price dropped to $2). Werrenrath's last concert was at Carnegie Hall on 23 Oct 1952. He died in Plattsburg, New York. [Walsh 1948/8.]

WEST, DOTTIE (11 OCT 1932–4 SEP 1991)

American country singer, born Dorothy Marie Marsh in McMinnville, Tennessee. She had a successful single in 1963, "Let Me of at the Corner" (Victor #8225), then found sudden stardom in 1964, interpreting a song cowritten with her husband, Bill West: "Here Comes My Baby" (Victor #8374; it recieved a Grammy, and remained 27 weeks on the charts). There was another hit single in 1964: "In Its Own Little Way"/"Didn't I?" (Victor #8467). Fifty chart singles followed by 1982, in addition to studio collaborations with Jimmy Dean, Don Gibson, Jim Reeves, and Kenny Rogers. West died in an automobile accident in Nashville en route to perform at the Grand Ole Opry.

WEST COAST PHONOGRAPH CO.

One of the affiliates of the North American Phonograph Co., established in Portland, Oregon, in 1890. Louis Glass was director.

WESTERN ELECTRIC CO.

A firm established in 1869 by Enos Barton and Elisha Gray, manufacturer of the equipment used by the Bell Telephone Co., and controlled by Bell after 1882. It has remained in the Bell family, currently as a subsidiary of American Telephone and Telegraph Co. (AT&T). In the 1920s at Western Electric, J.P. Maxfield and H.C. Harrison made important experiments in electrical recording, and developed the major system used by Victor and Columbia. A steel-tape magnetic recorder was developed by Western Electric in 1940.

WESTERN PENNSYLVANIA PHONOGRAPH CO.

A Pittsburgh firm, one of the affiliates of the North American Phonograph Co., established in 1890 at 146 Fifth Ave. George B. Motheral was president in 1892.

WESTERN PHONOGRAPH CO.

A Chicago firm. In 1896 it manufactured a coin-op, using the spring motor of Edward Amet, attached to an Edison top.

WESTMINSTER (LABEL)

An American independent record, issued from 1949. James Grayson and two partners set it up, utilizing the new technology of recording on a magnetic tape and cutting LP masters from it. Many of the tapes were brought from Vienna. The high quality of the recordings and of the artists brought great success to Westminster, which had 500 items in the catalog by the end of 1954, and 1,000 items five years later. The first releases in the U.K. were in 1953, handled by Nixa. Hermann Scherchen, Paul Badura-Skoda, Jorg Demus, Fernando Valenti, and Antonio Janigro — fresh names on the American scene — dominated the lists. Baroque music was a specialty, as with most of the classical LP labels, but there were also important performances of Mahler, Gliere, and other (up to that time) neglected modern masters. The label survived into the mid-1970s, but has not reappeared in CD format.

WESTPORT (LABEL)

A U.K. record of 1922–1924, sold in the Curry's stores. It was produced by Edison Bell Consolidated Phonograph Co., Ltd., with some masters from Gennett. Artists were given pseudonyms. The label is also found as a paste-over on Imperial records of the Crystalate Gramophone Record Manuafacturing Co., Ltd.

FRANK ANDREWS

WEXLER, JERRY (10 JAN 1917–)

American record producer, record company executive, born in New York. In the late 1940s and early 1950s, Jerry Wexler was a reporter for *Billboard*, where he coined the term "rhythm and blues." In 1953, he went to work as a producer at Atlantic Records. He remained there 22 years, producing such artists as Ray Charles and Aretha Franklin. In 1975, he became a freelancer, handling sessions by Dire Straits and Bob Dylan among many others.

WILLIAM RUHLMANN

WHARFEDALE

Founded in 1932, by Gilbert Briggs, in Yorkshire, England, Wharfedale has become one of the more venerable institutions in home audio. In 1933 Briggs set up a small factory in Bradford, England, in order to build the company's increasingly popular loudspeaker drive units. From this time, Wharfedale went from strength to strength, and, following a move to a larger factory, production reached 9,000 speakers in the year of 1939. Production levels grew dramatically after the war, with loudspeakers being shipped across the world, and in 1956 Wharfedale formed its own subsidiary company in the U.S. The following year, the company opened a massive new automated cabinet factory in Bradford. In 1958 Briggs, by then over 68 years old, sold the company to the Rank Organization, a major U.K. industrial group which also owned the audio electronics company Leak and also Heco, a German loudspeaker company. Rank made major investments in R&D and in marketing and distribution, and Wharfedale pioneered technological developments such as the first use of ceramic magnets. By 1988 the company was listed on the London Stock Exchange, and in 1992 it changed its name to the Verity Group and purchased a number of other companies including Mission, Cyrus, and Quad Premier Musical Instruments. The then managing director of Wharfedale led a management buyout and formed a new company, the International Audio Group, which incorporated Wharfedale loudspeakers, Quad audio electronics, Leak high-end audio electronics, and Airedale loudspeakers. In 2001 Wharfedale had its sales, marketing, and design departments headquartered in Huntingdon, England, with a new production and distribution facility in Bradford, only a few miles away from the site of the original factory of 1933.[website: www.wharfedale.co.uk.]

HOWARD FERSTLER

WHEELER, ELIZABETH (20 JULY 1875–AFTER 1961), AND WILLIAM WHEELER (13 JULY 1879–NOV 1916)

An American singing duo, "the most successful husband and wife duet pair in the history of the phonograph" [Walsh]. She was born Bess Nicholson in Kokomo, Indiana, on 20 July 1875; he was born in Shawano, Wisconsin, on 13 July 1879. They married in 1904, and performed widely, doing standard ballads, light opera, and hymns. Elizabeth made some solo cylinders for Leeds & Catlin, Edison, and others, and then the two began their duet recordings in 1910, for Victor. "Beautiful Isle of Somewhere" was an early hit (#16700; 1910), though it did not reach the 1917 Victor catalog, where there were 17 other titles by the pair. Their final Victor recording was the most popular one, "What a Friend We Have in Jesus" (#18287; 1917). The Wheelers also made disc records for Leeds & Catlin, on the Imperial, Concert, and Nassau labels.

Elizabeth made many solo Victors, beginning in 1909; she sang ballads and children's songs, and also "Elizabeth's Prayer" from *Tannhäuser* (#35096). William did some solo work for Pathé. They did not record after the acoustic period, and "What a Friend" was the only one of their titles to reach the 1927 Victor catalog. William Wheeler died in November 1916. [Walsh 1961/8–9.]

WHISTLING RECORDINGS

This was a popular type of record in the early days, both for bird imitations and for musical material. The Victor 1917 catalog had about 55 items, most of them by Guido Gialdini. John Yorke AtLee was apparently the earliest whistler to record, making Columbia cylinders from 1889 to 1897, and also Berliner discs. Another pioneer whistler on disc was Frank Lawton, who was heard on 11 seven-inch Berliner records of October/November 1898, commencing with "Il bacio" (#9261-X).

Edison cylinders presented 23 whistling numbers by 1912, including works by two of the most famous artists, AtLee and Joe Belmont, and a less familiar female whistler, Nina Angela. Other artists included Albert Whelan, "The Australian Entertainer," who often whistled his music hall signature tune ("The Jolly Brothers Waltz") at the start and end of his records; Margaret McKee, on Victor; and Maude Dewey, "champion lady whistler of the world" according to advertising of Star cylinders (1904–1907).

The most famous whistling record was "Whistling Coon," written and performed by George W. Johnson in 1890–1891 for many cylinder labels. "Whistling Girl" was another Johnson number.

In the 1920s whistling records disappeared from the catalogs, except for occasional novelty numbers like "Whistler and His Dog" (done for Victor by Pryor's Band, #19869). Elmo Tanner revived interest in the art during the 1930s, performing with the Wayne King and Ted Weems orchestras. Hoagy Carmichael whistled and sang some of his own compositions for Decca, e.g., "Stardust"/"Hong Kong Blues" (#18395; 1942). Fred Lowery, "The Blind Whistler," made several Columbia discs with the Horace Heidt band in 1940–1941, including "Indian Love Call" (#36200) and "William Tell Overture" (#35234). Ronnie Ronalde performed for Columbia in U.K. after World War II. Bing Crosby sometimes whistled briefly on his records.

See also **Animal Imitations**

WHITE, BARRY [EUGENE] (12 SEP 1944–)

With his heavy-breathing vocals and lush orchestrations, White trod a fine line between soulfulness and easy-listening. Yet singles such as "Can't Get Enough of Your Love, Babe" (20th Century #2120, 1974; #1 pop/R&B) and "You're My First, My Last, My Everything" (20th Century #2133, date 1974; #2 pop, #1 R&B) achieved infectiousness by blending a driving rhythm track with an appealing willingness to come close to a parody of soul. He cut his teeth musically as an organist for a local church in Galveston, Texas. In 1966, as an A&R man at Mustang Records (owned by producer Bob Keene), White teamed up with three female singers to form the Love Unlimited Orchestra, who had a hit with "Walking in the Rain with the One I Love" (1972) Love Unlimited later had an instrumental hit with "Love's Theme" (20th Century #2069; 1973), which highlighted his skill as a producer. In 1973 to 1974 alone, White wrote, produced, or performed on records that had sales totaling more than $16 million. White had a string of hits through the later 1970s, culminating with his last major pop hit, "It's Ecstasy (When You Lay Down Next to Me)" (20th Century #2350, #4 pop, #1 R&B). However, by the late 1970s, White's appeal began to wane, though he had a minor hit in 1979 with a cover of Billy Joel's "I Love You Just the Way You Are." White enjoyed somewhat of a career boost in the early 1990s when his earlier hits were prominently featured as background music on the hit television series, *Allie McBeal*, as well as his "appearances" on the animated show, *The Simpons*. He scored a number one R&B, number 18 pop hit with his comeback song, "Practice What You Preach" in 1994 (A&M #0778), from the multiplatinum *The Icon Is Love* (A&M #540280) album. White is said to have sold over 100 million albums worldwide.

BOB SILLERY

WHITE, EDNA [CHANDLER] (1892–1992)

American trumpeter, with a long career onstage and as a soloist with bands and orchestras. She had a vaudeville act with her second husband, and in the 1930s also sang in musicals. White was a prodigy, noticed by Frank Damrosch, who invited her to study at the Institute of Musical Arts (later the Juilliard School), where she graduated at age 15; she then toured the vaudeville circuit with a female ensemble (two trumpets, two trombones). The opening ceremony in March 1915 of the first transcontinental telephone transmission (Brooklyn to San Francisco) was enlivened by her performance of "Silver Threads among the Gold." In the 1930s she was on the radio, and on 9 Feb 1949 she gave a recital at Carnegie Hall. White retired in 1957, although she continued to mentor young trumpeters and was occasionally interviewed in the popular press and for trumpet-oriented publications.

White began to record with the Edna White Trumpet Quartet in 1918, for Columbia, doing first "Just a Baby's Prayer at Twilight" (#A-2538). She continued with Columbia to 1921. Her first Edison discs (15 Dec 1920) were "The Debutante" (#80650) and "Recollections of 1861–1865" (#80613). She made eight more Edisons, the final one in September

1926: "Sweet Genevieve" (#52036). During this period, she was married to vocalist Torcum Bezazian, who appeared on some of her recordings and toured with her on the vaudeville circuit. In 1980 Merritt Sound Recordings of Buffalo, New York, issued the cassette *Life with My Trumpet*, featuring some of her early recordings and White reminiscing about her career, recorded at that time (a copy is held by the Library of Congress). [Wile 1977/3.]

WHITE, JOE (14 OCT 1891–28 FEB 1959)

American tenor, born Joseph Malachy White in New York. He was a boy soprano in church work, then served in World War I. He sang in minstrel troupes, and then in 1925–1930 on radio. The novelty of wearing a mask while he performed brought him national attention, and the sobriquet of "silver-masked tenor." White recorded for Edison and Columbia, in 1917, and then for Victor in 1925–1929. He also appeared on U.K. HMV and Zonophone issues. Irish numbers were his specialty, e.g., "Kathleen Mavourneen"/"The Harp that Once through Tara's Halls" (Victor #19916; 1925). White died in New York.

Joe White's son Robert White is also a recording artist and teacher. He is a popular concert tenor, specializing in folk songs, oratorio, and ballads. He is known for presentations of the John McCormack repertoire (favorites of his father) in concert and on record. *Memories: Tribute to John McCormack* (RCA #5400) incorporates some of that material. As of 2002, White was teaching voice at the Juilliard School, giving recitals, and recording for Hyperion Records.[Walsh 1973/3.]

FRANK ANDREWS

WHITE, JOSH (11 FEB 1915–5 SEP 1969)

American blues, folk, gospel singer, and guitarist, born Joshua Daniel White in Greenville, South Carolina. He was a street singer as a child, then teamed with Blind Joe Taggart at age 13. The two made a Paramount record, with White playing guitar and singing, "There's a Hand Writing on the Wall" (#12717; 1928). He recorded later for many labels, and by age 25 was nationally recognized. He formed a group, the Carolinians, for some records, and he used the nom du disque Pinewood Tom on others. On Vocalion he was Tippy Barton. He performed at the White House, and gradually moved to a more sophisticated style quite removed from his roots. White died in Manhasset, New York.

"Crying Blues" was among White's most popular discs of the 1930s; it appeared as Melotone #12727, Perfect #0234, Romeo #5240, Oriole #8240, and

Banner #32794. "Southern Exposure" (Keynote #514; 1941) exemplified his social protest songs of the 1940s. During the later 1940s through the 1950s, White was a popular figure in America and Europe during the folk-blues revival; he recorded for several labels, including Folkways, Elektra, Tradition, and ABC. One of his last popular records was "House of the Rising Sun" (ABC #124; 1957). White continued to tour through the 1960s, but recorded less frequently in the U.S. His son Josh White, Jr., has been a popular performer on the folk circuit since the 1970s.

Document Records has issued White's complete early recordings, made from 1928–1947, in chronological order on seven CDs, tracing his career from his blues-oriented performances to his more popular-folk material. His late 1940s-era Folkways's recordings are anthologized on Free and Equal Blues (Smithsonian/Folkways #40081). Two mid-1950s Elektra albums, *Josh at Midnight/Ballads* and *Blues*, are reissued on Collectables #7463 and are typical of his later style.

REV. CARL BENSON

WHITE NOISE

Broad-band noise having constant energy per unit of frequency, as opposed to pink noise, which has constant energy per octave. White noise can sometimes be used for testing audio equipment and can also be used for rapidly setting up levels in a surround system by ear or meter.

HOWARD FERSTLER

WHITEMAN, PAUL
(28 MAR 1890–29 DEC 1967)

American violist and Big Band leader, born in Denver. He played viola in the symphony orchestras of Denver (1907–1913) and then San Francisco, and during World War I he directed a Navy band. After his military service he organized a dance band in San Francisco, and was in New York by 1920, making a sensational hit record of "Whispering"/"Japanese Sandman" (Victor #18690; 1920) that sold a million copies. A stream of Victor records followed, with many successes; the most popular was "Three O'Clock in the Morning" (Victor #18940; 1922).

In Whiteman's most famous concert, 12 Feb 1924 at Aeolian Hall, New York, the premiere of *Rhapsody in Blue* was performed, with George Gershwin at the piano. Whiteman and Gershwin recorded the work on 10 June (Victor #55225).

Whiteman, not a jazz musician, was nicknamed the King of Jazz. His orchestra was really a swinging dance band, but many notable jazz artists were featured at different times, including Matty Malneck, Tommy Dorsey, Jimmy Dorsey, Bix Beiderbecke, Frankie Trumbauer, Eddie Lang, Miff Mole, Red Nichols, Bunny Berigan, Jack Teagarden, Joe Venuti, and Wingy Manone. Trumpeter Henry Busse and pianist Ferde Grofé started with Whiteman in 1919. Bing Crosby made early records with the orchestra, as one of the Rhythm Boys, including his first solo disc in 1927. Charles Harrison, Lewis James, Wilfred Glenn, Elliott Shaw, Mildred Bailey, Johnny Mercer, Paul Robeson, Joan Edwards, Lee Wiley, the Modernaires, and Red McKenzie were among the vocalists heard on Whiteman records. There were outstanding arrangers in Lennie Hayton, Grofé, and Bill Challis, who wrote complex scores for the 19 or 20 players who made up the typical forces. Altogether Whiteman recorded more than 600 sides, bringing jazz and swing together in a manner that was delightful to the public and that opened the door for the great hot bands of the 1930s. There were radio shows and motion pictures through the 1940s, after which Whiteman was less active. He died in Doylestown, Pennsylvania.

There are numerous reissues of Whiteman's classic recordings available. *Bix and Bing* (ASV/Living Era #5005) is a particularly fine selection of 1927–1929 Victor and Columbia recordings featuring the legendary trumpeter and the soon-to-be legendary crooner. Pearl/Flapper #9178 gives a more representative career overview of the early band, from the early 1920s through the beginnings of the Swing Era; this CD also includes an abbreviated version of George Gershwin's "Rhapsody in Blue," which Whiteman commissioned and popularized. The same 1927 recording is featured on *Greatest Hits* (Collectors Choice Music #61), which anthologizes his biggest sellers recorded for Victor from 1920–1928. (A follow-up anthology on the same label of Whiteman's Columbia recordings suffers from a poor selection of material.) [Rust. 1982]

WHITING, MARGARET (22 JULY 1924–)

American popular vocalist, born in Detroit. She sang on Hollywood radio with Johnny Mercer in 1941, and made appearances on *Your Hit Parade*. Her first hit record was "That Old Black Magic" (Capitol #126; 1943) with Freddie Slack, followed by a fine "Silver Wings in the Moonlight" (Capitol #146; 1944) also with Slack. "My Ideal" (Capitol #134; 1943) and "Moonlight in Vermont" (Capitol #182; 1944) both with Billy Butterfield, were much acclaimed. Whiting made popular recordings for Capitol of the great ballads of the 1940s. A particularly noteworthy side was "Baby, It's Cold Outside" with Mercer (Capitol #57-567; 1949). She brought out some fine LP albums, especially the *Jerome Kern Song Book* (Verve #V-3039), including the little known gem, "Let's Begin." By the later 1950s she was less active both live and on record. However, like many singers of her generation, she made a comeback in the late 1970s to early 1980s, recording three CDs for Audiophile between 1980–1985. She continued to make occasional appearances at cabarets and nightclubs through the 1990s. *Spotlight on Margaret Whiting* (Capitol #29395) anthologizes her recordings for that label from the late 1940s to early 1950s; Collectors Choice Music has issued a two-CD set of all her chart hits for Capitol (#132). Her later Audiophile albums have been reissued on CD, often with additional "bonus" tracks from the same sessions.

WHITLOCK, BILLY
(18 JULY 1874–26 JAN 1951)

U.K. music hall artist, born Frederick Penna in Cheltenham. His activities included work with the Stanley Operatic Co. in India, touring four years; ice skating at championship rank; theatrical promotion, and film performances. He was also recording expert for Favorite Records in London for a period. He played the xylophone and bells, and did comic numbers, being one of the earliest to do "laughing songs." He made thousands of records, usually writing his own material, for many U.K. labels, with numerous American reissues by Columbia and Vocalion. His recordings were also issued under many pseudonyms, both male and female, under English and foreign names, e.g., Dudley Roy and Madame Paula. His first cylinders were for Edison Bell in 1904, starting with "The Laughing Friar" (#5740). He continued recording to 1926, then was inactive until the 1950s — his return occasioned by the 1949 Decca reissue disc (London label in the U.S.) of Whitlock's 1904 instrumental "Scotch Hot." Renamed "Hop Scotch Polka," it was re-recorded by Whitlock and became a best seller. Thus Whitlock, who had become an impoverished night watchman, had some brightness for his last years. He died in London. [Andrews 1976; Rust 1979b; Walsh 1950/2.]

WHITNEY, EDWIN MORSE
(17 MAR 1877–5 JUNE 1957)

American actor and tenor, born in Parma Center, New York. He sang in the Whitney Brothers Quartet (the other members were Alvin, William, and Yale Whitney), then became a radio actor; in 1928 he was program director for NBC. All his records were made in 1908–1910, for Victor. A hardy best seller was "Darky and the Boys" (Victor #5636), his first solo monologue. "Old Folks at Home" was the best of the quartet records (Victor #16454; released in 1912); it remained in the catalog, with another nine sides, to 1922, but all the Whitney discs were gone by 1927. Edwin Whitney died in New York.

WHITSIT, PERRY B.

American record jobber, whose business was located in Columbus, Ohio, in 1913. He was active in the National Association of Talking Machine Jobbers, being its secretary in 1909 and 1913, and president in 1909.

WHO

Innovative U.K. rock group formed in London in 1964 as the High Numbers. The original members included Peter Dennis Blandford Townshend (guitar and vocal), Roger Harry Daltrey (vocal), John Alec Entwistle (bass, French horn, vocal), and Doug Sandon, who was soon replaced by the considerably more proficient Keith Moon (drums). They first attracted attention with "I Can't Explain" (Decca #31725; 1965; #8 U.K., #93 U.S.) and the teen anthem (Decca #31877; 1965; #2 U.K., #74 U.S.). Following a number of flawed masterpieces (e.g., the miniopera "A Quick One" from *Happy Jack* [Decca #74892; 1966; #4 U.K., #67 U.S.] and Townshend's rock opera, *Tommy* [Decca #7205; 1969; #4]) — Who was one of the earliest attempts to merge rock dynamics with large-scale compositions and to achieve international acclaim. The band's next album, *Live at Leeds* (Decca #79175; 1970; #4) — an exercise in stripped down aggression — is widely considered to be one of the finest live rock recordings ever. *Who's Next* (Decca #79182; 1971; #4) may well represent the pinnacle of the Who's artistry, combining synthesizer textures with a organically seamless set of pop compositions.

From this point onward, the band found it hard to surpass their already impressive legacy. *Quadrophenia* (MCA #10004; 1973; #3) came across as an uneven reprise of *Tommy*, while the balance of 1970s' releases were divided between compilations of older material and tentative efforts at finding new stylistic directions. Moon's death in 1978 spelled the end of the Who as a vital concert unit, although the group soldiered on (despite prematurely calling it a day in 1983), touring intermittently and recording a series of uninspired — albeit best-selling — albums. Daltrey, a talented stage and film actor, Entwistle (who died in 2002), and Townshend all devoted an increasingly greater amount of time to their respective solo recordings. By the

1990s, the band's output was limited largely to CD reissues and compilations punctuated by occasional tours catering to nostalgic fans.

FRANK HOFFMANN

WHYTE, BERT (1920–31 MAR 1994)

Born in Belfast, Northern Ireland, Whyte came to the U.S. in 1924, and ended up working as an assistant to the director of the British Ministry of War Transport, prior to the U.S. entering World War II. When the war began, he joined the Army and served in the medical corps. In 1949 he went to work for Concord Radio, in Chicago, moved on to Magnecord, and then ended up working for Loew's/MGM in New York. During this time, he learned a great deal about recording techniques and recording technology.

Shortly later, along with Harry Belock, Whyte founded Everest Records, where he served as recording director and engineer and the director of classical artists and repertoire. During this time he also pioneered the use of 35-mm magnetic film for multitrack stereo recording. In addition, Everest got the jump on some of the larger recording companies and recorded some fine European orchestras in stereo, releasing the material on 7.5-inch reel-to-reel tapes, well before the stereophonic LP had appeared. Whyte's technical talents were well enough known by them for him to also be hired by RCA, where in 1951 he made the first modern classical stereo recordings with Leopold Stokowsky and the first Big Band stereo recordings with Benny Goodman, Woody Herman, and Stan Kenton.

Whyte made additional stereo recordings with major symphony orchestras in the U.S. and Europe, and during that time he refined a three-microphone technique that allowed everything to be picked up in complete balance, with a minimum of mixing artifacts. In addition to his recording and consulting work, he wrote magazine articles for *Radio/TV News*, and in 1953 he became an associate editor of *Audio Magazine*, where he also served as a reviewer and critic. It is in that capacity that he was known to most audio enthusiasts, and he remained with the magazine into the 1990s.

In the 1970s, while continuing with his magazine writing, Whyte served as a consultant for a number of hi-fi equipment manufacturers and recording companies, he supervised regular and direct-to-disc releases recorded on the Crystal Clear label, and recorded a number of Fiedler/Boston Pops and Vergil Fox organ performances that are now available on the Bainbridge and Laserlight labels.

HOWARD FERSTLER

WIDMANN, EUGENE A. (CA. 1877–3 FEB 1938)

American record industry executive, born in New York. He was president of Pathé Frères Phonograph Co., the American branch of the firm, 1912–1923, and for a time also chairman of the board. Later he headed Widmann & Co., a firm of investment brokers. He died in Brooklyn.

WIEDOEFT, RUDY (3 JAN 1893–18 FEB 1940)

American saxophonist and clarinetist, born in Detroit. He was the first recognized saxophone virtuoso, concertizing and recording extensively in the 1920s. He added five keys to the saxophone to improve range and tone. Wiedoeft was heard on Edison Diamond Discs, beginning with "Valse Erica" (#50462; 1917) and "Saxophone Sobs" (#50454; 1917) and on Victor records, beginning with "Saxophobia"/"Valse Erica" (#18728; 1921). He had eight sides in the 1927 Victor catalog, and four remained in 1938, but they were deleted two years later. His Edison output included nine solos, two items with the Wiedoeft-Wadsworth Quartet (who were Wheeler Wadsworth, saxophone; J. Russell Robinson and Harry Akst, pianos; and Wiedoeft), four with Rudy Wiedoeft's Palace Trio, and three with Rudy Wiedoeft's Californians. The final Edison was made on 12 June 1922, with the Californians: "Rose of Bombay" (#51020). The Trio also recorded for Victor and Okeh in 1920–1921. The Californians appeared also on Vocalion. Wiedoeft died in Flushing, New York. *Kreisler of the Saxophone* (Clarinet Classics #0018) offers solos recorded by Wiedoeft in the 1920s.

WILDLIFE SOUNDS ON RECORDS

Ludwig Koch made the first wildlife recording in 1889 of an Indian thrush called a shama, and continued recording into the 1940s. Bird records were in demand in the early days of the recording industry; the Victor 1917 catalog had 40 titles with bird sounds. The first commercial disc of wildlife sounds was issued by Beka (Berlin) ca. 1910, presenting material gathered by Koch. By 1968 there were 341 recordings tabulated by Jeffrey Boswall at the BBC, who estimated that he had found about 8 percent of the total issues. Records of captive birds were issued from 1910, the first being HMV #9439, a "unique bird record made by a captive nightingale." The proliferation of bird sound records was more or less summarized in a 1966 set of EMI seven-inch records, *Bird Recognition: An Aural Index*; the discs presented the complete vocabularies of selected species.

Apart from birds, which obviously have the most potential for interesting records, there have been extensive field expeditions to inscribe the voices of mammals and amphibians, and to catch the ambient sounds of natural settings.

When Koch fled Germany (leaving his large collection of records) to the U.K. in 1936, he was backed in the development of a new collection of sounds. Eventually he built up a substantial library, which was acquired by the BBC Sound Archives; holdings of the BBC were already inclusive of 3,000 species in 1972, on about 15,000 recordings. The U.K. remains the center of interest in wildlife recording. The Wildlife Sound Recording Society was established there in 1968 to foster recording and broadcasting, and to share information. Another active entity is the Swedish Broadcasting Corp.

The British Library of Wildlife Sounds was officially opened in London on 2 July 1969, as part of the British Institute of Recorded Sound (now the National Sound Archive). Within five years the sounds of some 700 species of animal had been collected. In the U.S., the Laboratory of Ornithology at Cornell University, Ithaca, New York, is a major archive.

Folkways Records had a long tradition of issuing sounds of nature. Label owner Moses Asch produced *Sounds of American Tropical Rain Forest* (Folkways #06120) in 1952 for the Museum of Natural History in New York City, and two years later *Sounds of Animals* (#6124). *Sounds of North American Frogs* was originally issued in 1957, and developed a cult following among progressive music listeners; it was reissued on CD in 1998 for a new audience (Smithsonian/Folkways #45060). Folkways also issued sounds of sea animals, birds, and insects.

Occasionally, wildlife recordings have gained cult followings. In 1971 Dr. Roger Payne released an album of his recordings under the name, *Songs of the Humpback Whale,* after Judy Collins had used a small portion of it as background to her recording of the traditional sea shantey, "Farewell to Tarwathhie" the year before. The record became popular among New Age listeners. [Discographies of the U.K. holdings cited above appeared in various issues of *Recorded Sound* magazine; several are listed in #85, p. 40. *Recorded Sound* #34 (April 1969) was devoted to articles on wildlife sounds and the collections of them. Books on the topic include Bondesen 1977; Simms 1979; Margoschis 1977; Thielcke 1976.]

See also **Animal Imitations**

WILEY, LEE (9 OCT 1915–11 DEC 1975)

American popular vocalist, born in Port Gibson, Oklahoma. After study in Tulsa, she moved to New York and sang in clubs and on radio. She was with the Leo Reisman band from 1931 to 1933; later she sang with Paul Whiteman, the Casa Loma Orchestra, and others. An important early record was "A Hundred Years from Today" with the Casa Loma Orchestra (Brunswick #6775; 1934). She married Jess Stacy and sang with his group in the mid-1940s. Wiley offered a loose swing style that was well suited to the ballads of the era. One of her best singles was "It's Only a Paper Moon" with Stacy (Victor #20-1708; 1946). She is also credited as the first artist to record 78 "albums" (four discs containing eight songs) for Columbia, dedicated to the work of individual composers including Vincent Youmans, Irving Berlin, Cole Porter, George Gershwin, Harold Arlen, and Rodgers and Hart. These were called "songbooks," and were reissued on 10-inch LPs by the label in the early 1950s. The songbook concept was further developed in the mid-1950s by producer Norman Granz, working with singers like Ella Fitzgerald. During the 1950s, Wiley continued to record jazz and popular material, often with studio band accompanists, but then mysteriously retired in 1957, making only one further recording before she had a triumphant comeback appearance at the New York Jazz Festival in 1972. She died three years later in New York.

Vintage Jazz 1023 reissues Wiley's complete early recordings, made between 1931–1937, when she was primarily doing pop material. Some of her classic songbooks are also available on CD, including *Sings the Songs of George & Ira Gershwin & Cole Porter* (Audiophile #1) and *Sings the Songs of Rodgers & Hart and Harold Arlen* (Audiophile #10). Selections from her final two albums before her retirement, recorded for RCA in 1956–1957, have been reissued on a Bluebird CD (*As Times Goes By*, #3138).

WILLIAMS, ANDY (3 DEC 1930–)

American popular singer, born Andrew Williams in Wall Lake, Iowa. He began singing on local radio as a child, then appeared with the Williams Brothers Quartet, gaining success in various American and European cities. Williams pursued a solo career from 1954, was acclaimed on television, and hosted *The Andy Williams Show* from 1959. His singing style was in the easy ballad manner. The earliest of his 46 chart singles was "Canadian Sunset" (Cadence #1297; 1956); the same title was used for a 1965 Columbia album (CL #2324). Williams had two highly successful albums in 1962: *Moon River and Other Great Movie Themes* (Columbia CL #1809), 107 weeks on the charts; and *Warm and Willing* (Columbia CL #1879), 25 weeks. Other notable albums of the 1960s included *Days of Wine and Roses* (Columbia CL

#2015; 1963) and *Call Me Irresponsible and Other Academy Award Winners* (Columbia CL #2171; 1964). There were 37 chart albums, the last in 1975.

WILLIAMS, BERT (12 NOV 1874–4 MAR 1922)

Singer and comedian, born Egbert Austin Williams in the Bahamas. His family moved to California when he was a child, and he left home at 17 to join a traveling minstrel troupe, Seig's Mastodon Minstrels. They toured mining and lumber camps. He made his way to New York, and formed a successful vaudeville duo with George W. Walker. They appeared successfully in the operetta *Gold Bug*, and did blackface routines (though Williams was Black) in many other shows. Walker retired, but Williams went on to the Ziegfeld Follies in 1910–1919, breaking the color barrier there. A sensation in the U.K. in *Dahomey* (1903), Williams gave a command performance for Edward VII at Buckingham Palace. He died in New York.

His first records were cylinders for the Universal Phonograph Co. of New York in 1897. He made discs for Victor in 1901, after which he made no records until 1906 when Columbia signed him exclusively. He stayed with Columbia until his death. Williams and Walker made their first Victor on 11 Oct 1901, "I Don't Like that Face You Wear" (#V-987). "If You Love Your Baby" was Williams's first solo Victor, made on the same day; there were other duets and solos made then, too. Popular as they were, the duo did not last long in the Victor catalog, there being no listings for either of them in 1917.

The first Columbia was a 10-inch disc, "Nobody" (#3423; 1906). A great hit was "Let It Alone," made in 1906 and released on two sizes of cylinder and on disc. After dropping Williams from the catalog, Columbia brought him back in 1940 with some reissues of 1919 and 1920 songs.

Williams had a recitative style of singing, and a raspy voice well suited to his broad material. "One of the finest talking machine records ever made" [Walsh] was "You Can't Do Nothin' till Martin Gets Here" (Columbia #A-6216; 1913?). Document Records had reissued Williams's complete recordings in chronological order, but only his final recordings, made between 1915–1921, are currently available from the label on CD (#5661). [Walsh 1950/9–10–11.]

WILLIAMS, BILLY (1854–1910)

American vaudeville and minstrel artist; he should not be confused with the Australian artist of the same name. He was performing from the 1860s, and made records as early as 1892, for the New Jersey Phonograph Co. He recorded with the Spencer Trio in 1894–1897.

WILLIAMS, BILLY (1877–9 MAR 1915)

Australian comedian and music hall artist, born in Melbourne; he should not be confused with the American artist of the same name. He transferred to England in 1899, and quickly made his place on the stage, one of the star performers of his time, although his career was cut off by his untimely death. His first record was a great success, issued on more than 25 labels: "John, John, Go and Put Your Trousers On" (Edison two-minute cylinder #13539; 1906). John, it may be noted, was wearing kilts. There are 148 titles in the discography by Frank Andrews and Ernie Bayly, the last being made in May or June 1914: "There's Life in the Old Dog Yet" (Regal #G6783). Among his other hit records were "I Must Go Home Tonight" (Homophone Record #555; 1909) and "Where Does Daddy Go When He Goes Out?" (Columbia Rena Record #1978; 1912). His famous song "When Father Papered the Parlour" is still heard in sing-alongs in the U.K. [Andrews& Bayly 1982 is a complete discography.]

WILLIAMS, COOTIE (24 JULY 1910 [SOME SOURCES GIVE 10 JULY 1911]–15 SEP 1985)

American jazz trumpeter, born Charles Melvin Williams in Mobile, Alabama. He was self-taught on the trumpet, and at age 14 was touring with a band that included Lester Young. He went to New York in 1928, made recordings with James P. Johnson, and joined various bands. From 1929 to 1940 he was in the Duke Ellington band, and played solos in hundreds of compositions. He also had his own band, in 1941–1948, which had Charlie Parker and Bud Powell as members; then he led a small rhythm and blues group in the 1950s. In 1962 Williams returned to Duke Ellington, staying until the late 1970s. He died in New York.

Williams developed a swing style with remarkable shadings and a way of handling all modes and situations. Among the sides with Ellington two stand out: "Echoes of the Jungle" (Victor #22743; 1931), and "Concerto for Cootie" — which Ellington wrote to observe the return of Williams to the flock in 1940 — (Victor #26598; 1940). With words added, the Concerto became the great ballad "Do Nothing till You Hear from Me." "Harlem Air Shaft" was another outstanding record (Victor #26731; 1940). In the 1950s Williams released fine LP albums, especially *Porgy and Bess Revisited* (Warner #1260; 1958). Cootie's 1930–1940s' era recordings are reissued on a series of CDs, in chronological order, from the Classics label. *Cootie Williams in Hi-Fi* (RCA #51718) reissues a mid-1950s album of the same name, along with 11 singles Williams recorded for the label during that period, all with Big Band accompaniment.

WILLIAMS, EVAN
(7 SEP 1867–24 MAY 1918)

American tenor, born in Mineral Ridge, Ohio. He sang in a church choir while working in a coal mine, studied in Cleveland and New York, and did church work in Brooklyn. He drew inspiration from a visit to Wales (he was of Welsh parentage), and became a leading concert singer after 1906, making many fine recordings. His earliest discs were made for G & T in 1906, the first being "Abide with Me" (#3-2485). Altogether he made 79 sides for HMV. Williams recorded six numbers for Pathé in London in 1911.

Williams was a Victor regular from 1906 to 1917, singing ballads, songs, and some oratorio and opera arias. He made 135 Victor sides, of which about 80 were in the Victor 1917 catalog, and his records were said to have sold more copies than any other singer except Enrico Caruso and John McCormack. "Sound an Alarm" from *Judas Maccabaeus* is one of the acoustic tenor discs most favored by collectors (Victor #74131, 6321). Other popular Victors were "Holy City"/"Face to Face" (#6312) and "Just A-Wearyin' for You"/"Perfect Day" (#857); these were in the 1927 catalog, but were deleted in the 1930s. [Lewis, G. 1978.]

WILLIAMS, HANK
(17 SEP 1923–1 JAN 1953)

Born King Hiram Hank Williams, in rural Mount Olive, Alabama, Williams was America's greatest honky-tonk singer/songwriter, whose unaffected singing style and bluesy songs were tinged with a rough sense of humor revolutionized country music after World War II. Williams's family relocated to metropolitan Greenville when he was around 10 years old, and then, around 1937, the family relocated to Montgomery where Williams made his first public appearance, leading to a regular spot on local radio. He formed his first band, the Drifting Cowboys, a name that he would use for his backup band throughout his career. He also composed "Six More Miles (to the Graveyard)," a blues that for the first time showed his unique sense of gallow's humor.

The war years were spent in Mobile, Alabama, shipyards, with a return to music with a new band, featuring a young female singer, Audrey Sheppard Guy, who was to become his first wife (and mother of Hank Williams Jr.). Williams signed with Nashville publisher Fred Rose in 1946, who became the mastermind behind his successful career. After a brief stint with the small Sterling label, Williams signed with MGM in 1947, charting with his first release, the bluesy and ballsy "Move It On Over," and his first honky-tonk anthem, "Honky Tonkin'." In August 1948 Williams

Hank Williams cover. Courtesy Frank Hoffmann.

was invited to join the prestigious *Louisiana Hayride* radio program, which spread his sound throughout the Southwest, and helped propel his cover of the 1920s' novelty number "Lovesick Blues" into a number one country hit in 1949. An invitation to join the Grand Ole Opry followed, elevating Williams to the heights of country stardom.

Suffering from a painful, chronic back problem, William became increasingly dependent on alcohol and painkillers. By mid-1952, hard drinking and drug use caught up with the star. He was expelled from the Opry and his marriage ended in divorce. He died in the back of a car on the way to a performance on New Year's Day 1953. As often happens, his death propelled his final recordings, "Your Cheatin' Heart" and the novelty "Kaw-Liga," to the top of the country charts.

Williams's recordings have been issued on CD in a variety of formats. *The Complete Hank Williams* (Mercury #536077) is a 10-CD, 224-track compilation of "all" of Williams's studio recordings and demos, but it doesn't include some live and other material available on other Mercury/Polydor releases. For more general introductions, *40 Greatest Hits* (Polydor #233; 2 CDs) or *The Original Singles Collection … Plus* (Polydor #194; 3 CDs) give good career overviews. *The Health and Happiness Shows* (Polydor #862) reissues radio shows prepared for broadcast in the early 1950s. *Rare Demos: First to Last* (Country Music Foundation #067) reissued Hank performing just with his own guitar accompaniment.

CARL BENSON

WILLIAMS, HANK, JR. (26 MAY 1949–)

Born Randall Hank Williams, in Shreveport, Louisiana, Williams has toiled in the shadow of his famous father for many years, often suffering in more ways than one from the comparison. Williams's early career was shaped by his manipulative mother, Audrey, who hoped to make him a junior version of his famous father. Hank's old record label, MGM, participated in her plan by having the younger Williams record near carbon-copy renditions of his father's songs. However, by the late 1960s, Williams was bridling at his mother's management of his career and the limitations of being a Hank Sr. clone. He had a number of hits in which he commented on his strange situation, including 1966s' "Standing in the Shadows (of a Very Famous Man)." He also began to write songs in a plain-spoken, straightforward style, and befriended the Nashville outlaws, including Willie Nelson and Waylon Jenningss. In 1974, Williams left Nashville to live in Alabama, recording his breakthrough album, *Hank Williams Jr. and Friends* (MGM #5009; reissued Universal #543370), featuring country-rockers like Charlie Daniels and Chuck Leavell. The album shocked his record label while it announced his new freedom from the slick Nashyille sound.

In 1977 Williams transformation was completed when he switched from his father's label to Warner Bros. Williams had a series of hits there, particularly in the late 1970s and early 1980s, starting with 1978's "I Fought the Law" capped by 1981's "All My Rowdy Friends." However, by the late 1980s, the hits had slowed and Williams seemed to be searching for a new direction. In 1990, following the discovery of an unissued acetate featuring his father singing a previously unknown composition, "There's a Tear in My Beer," Williams made a new version in which he sang the song as a duet with his father. Williams's later 1990s work was neither commercially nor artistically successful. In the late 1990s, he began recording for Curb records. In 2003 he performed with rapper Kid Rock in a joint concert broadcast by Country Music Television. Many of Williams's albums have been reissued on CD. For overviews, *Living Proof* (Mercury #320) traces his MGM recording career from 1964 to 1975, and *The Bocephus Box 2000* (Curb/Carbicorn #77940) covers 1979–1999.

CARL BENSON

WILLIAMS, J. MAYO (1894–2 JAN 1980)

Noted Black record producer and musician, Williams oversaw major recordings by blues and jazz musicians in Chicago from the early 1920s through the 1940s. Born in Monmouth, Illinois, Williams was a talented athlete as a teen, and he entered Brown University on a sports scholarship. After graduating in 1921, he settled in Chicago, where he began working as a sports writer. Noting the growing interest in blues, he approached Paramount Records looking for a job in mid-1922, and was hired as a freelance producer to recruit artists in Chicago. Williams quickly discovered a series of female blues artists, first Ida Cox, and then, late in 1923, his major discovery, Ma Rainey, who became the first big seller in the genre. He also recorded the first major male blues artist, "Papa" Charlie Jackson, another hitmaker for the label. Williams remained at Paramount through 1928, also helping to run the short-lived Black Patti label during 1927. He then moved to Vocalion, continuing to record blues and jazz musicians, including boogie woogie pianist Pine Top Smith. In 1931, with the record business hurting from the Depression, Williams temporarily left the field, only to return three years later when he was hired by Jack Kapp to work for the new Decca label. For Decca, Williams produced small band swing music with the Harlem Hamfats and Louis Jordan's Tympany Five, as well as smooth vocalists the Ink Spots. Williams left Decca in 1946, and was involved with several smaller labels through the 1950s.

CARL BENSON

WILLIAMS, MARY LOU (8 MAY 1910–13 MAY 1981)

American jazz pianist and arranger, born Mary Elfrieda Scruggs in Atlanta. She played piano as a child and joined various groups, one led by John Williams,

Record issued by Mary Lou Williams on her own Mary label in 1974. Courtesy David A. Jasen

who became her husband. They both joined the Andy Kirk band in 1929, where she did the arrangements, remaining until 1942. She then freelanced as a pianist and arranger, active into the 1970s, widely regarded as the leading female jazz artist. Williams taught at Duke University from 1977, and died in Durham, North Carolina.

She composed *Zodiac Suite* and made a successful recording of it (Asch #620, #621; 1945); the work was performed in Carnegie Hall by the New York Philharmonic Orchestra. Another fine disc was her "Waltz Boogie" (Victor #20-2025; 1946). She continued to record through the early 1950s, when a religious conversion led her to retire from music-making for the next decade and a half. She returned in the 1970s, beginning with *From the Heart* (Chiaroscuro #103; 1970). Williams formed her own label, Mary, in the mid-1970s to issue her own recordings.

Williams's *Zodiac Suite* recording from 1945 is reissued on Smithsonian/Folkways #40810. Classics has issued there CDs giving her complete recordings, in chronological order, from 1944–1951. *Zoning* (Smithsonian/Folkways #40811) reissued a 1970s era album originally issued by Williams on her Mary label.

REV. CARL BENSON

WILLS, BOB (6 MAY 1905–13 MAY 1975)

American country singer and fiddler, born near Kosse, Texas. He played with several groups in the 1920s, then organized his Texas Playboys in 1934, gaining much attention regionally. The group's lead singer, Tommy Duncan, offered smooth, popish vocals, while Wills's shouted encouragement of the band members gave the performances great energy. The group relocated to California in 1942, and toured extensively. After World War II, Duncan left the band but Wills soldiered on with various singers, although the craze for his style of music was fading. Wills and Duncan reunited for some final recordings in the early 1960s, and then Wills made a few solo recordings on the fiddle in the mid-1960s. Wills was elected to the Country Music Hall of Fame in 1968. He was brought out of retirement in 1973 by fan Merle Haggard, who reunited alumni of various Wills's bands for a final session. He died in Fort Worth, Texas.

Wills signed with Columbia/Okeh in 1935 and immediately began producing hits. Among his hit records, "Steel Guitar Rag" was an early standout (Okeh #03394; 1936), and "New San Antonio Rose" was the most popular of all (Okeh #05694; 1940). After the war, Wills recorded for MGM, continuing to produce hits through the early 1950s. In the early 1960s, he recorded two albums for Liberty with

Bob Wills reissue album. Courtesy Frank Hoffmann

Tommy Duncan; "Image of Me" from these sessions was his last chart hit (Liberty #55264; 1960). His last full album was made in 1973, *For the Last Time* (Liberty #A216; reissued on CD as Capitol #28331); on the night before the final session for this album, Wills suffered a stroke and the band completed the album without him.

Wills's popularity has only increased with the western swing revival of the past quarter decade. There are numerous CDs available anthologizing his work. *Anthology, 1935–73*, is a good introduction to his complete recording career (Rhino #70744). His Columbia, MGM, and Liberty recordings are also available on various CDs produced officially by these labels (or the companies that own their back catalogs) as well as in various semiofficial (mostly European) reissues. Rhino has issued 10 CDs of radio transcriptions made by the band, that Wills made for the Tiffany Music Co., a firm he coowned, in 1946–1947; many went unbroadcast at the time and were only discovered years later.

REV. CARL BENSON

WILLS, NAT (11 JULY 1873–9 DEC 1917)

American vaudeville artist, known as the Happy Tramp, born in Fredericksburg, Virginia. He first performed at Ford's Theatre in Washington, D.C. He recorded for Victor and Columbia, making an early hit with "No News, or What Killed the Dog" (Victor #5612; Columbia #A1765); he had 12 items in the 1917 Victor catalog, and was listed until 1927. His first

Edison record was "Down in Jungle Town" (#10178; 1909). The final record Wills made for Victor, in February 1917, was "Automobile Parody" (#35601), and ironically he died 10 months later of carbon monoxide fumes. [Walsh 1951/6.]

WILSON, BRIAN (20 JUNE 1942–)

American songwriter, musician, singer, producer, born in Hawthorne, California. Brian Wilson formed the Beach Boys in 1961 and wrote, arranged, and produced the bulk of their material during their first five years, including numerous hits. He also produced singles by other artists, including the Honeys (a female vocal trio featuring his wife, Marilyn) and Glen Campbell. His production style was very much influenced by Phil Spector, and he used the same Goldstar Studio and many of the same studio musicians that Spector employed during the 1960s. All of the backing tracks for his Beach Boys' hits were recorded "live" without overdubbing; vocals were subsequently added. Wilson only worked in mono, because of deafness in one ear. He was less involved with the Beach Boys after the late 1960s due to psychological problems from which he eventually recovered. In 1988 he launched a solo career that found him increasingly active and by the early 2000s he was touring regularly.

WILLIAM RUHLMANN

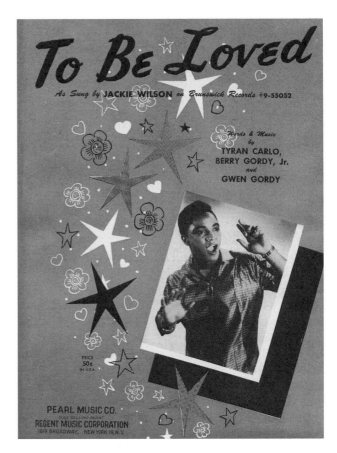

Sheet music cover for "To Be Loved" by Jackie Wilson, late '50s. Courtesy David A. Jasen

WILSON, JACKIE
(9 JUNE 1934–21 JAN 1984)

Jackie Wilson rivaled James Brown as one of the most dynamic performers of his generation, exuding a sexy athleticism capable of working his audience into a frenzy. He was also one of the most versatile vocalists in the rock era, ranging from the soulful, gritty style of a Wilson Pickett to the smooth, gospel-inflected pop associated with Sam Cooke and Clyde McPhatter.

Born and raised in a blue-collar section of Detroit, Wilson began his career as a boxer, winning his Golden Gloves weight division in the late 1940s. After high school, he began singing in local nightclubs. In 1953 Wilson joined Billy Ward and His Dominoes as a replacement for McPhatter, who'd departed to found the Drifters. During his tenure the group recorded "St. Therese of the Roses" (Decca #29933; 1956), which reached number 13 on the pop charts.

Wilson went solo in late 1956, signing with Brunswick Records. Between 1957–1972 he recorded 49 charting singles, including the Top 10 hits "Lonely Teardrops" (Brunswick #55105; 1958), "Night" (Brunswick #55166; 1960), "Alone at Last" (Brunswick #55170; 1960), "My Empty Arms" (Brunswick #55201;

1961), "Baby Workout" (Brunswick #55239; 1963), and "(Your Love Keeps Lifting Me) Higher and Higher" (Brunswick #55336; 1967). When record sales dropped off, he was relegated to playing the oldies circuit. On 25 Sep 1975, as part of the Dick Clark revue at the Latin Casino in Cherry Hill, New Jersey, he suffered a major heart attack while singing "Lonely Teardrops." Emerging from a coma with considerable brain damage, he never performed again. He was inducted into the Rock and Roll Hall of Fame in 1987.

FRANK HOFFMANN

WILSON, NANCY (20 FEB 1937–)

American popular singer, born in Chillicothe, Ohio. She sang in clubs and on television in Columbus, Ohio, made a tour with Rusty Bryant's band, and went on to acclaimed performances in New York as a jazz and rhythm and blues singer. Her 1964 record, "How Glad I Am" (Capitol #5198) put her name on the charts for 14 weeks and won her a Grammy. "Face It, Girl, It's Over" was another of her seven chart singles (Capitol #2136; 1968). Wilson made 22 solo chart albums, notably *Hollywood — My Way* (Capitol #2712; 1963), 30 weeks on the charts, and *Yesterday's Love Songs — Today's Blues* (Capitol #2012; 1964). She was a skilled ensemble vocalist as well as soloist, making notable albums with George Shearing in 1961 and with Cannonball Adderley in 1962. Wilson remained with Capitol through 1984, then moved to Columbia. Her last hit album was *The Two of Us*, with Ramsey Lewis (Columbia #39326; 1984). In 2000 she signed with Telarc Jazz. Many of her original albums remain available on CD, as do various collections of her hits.

WILSON, TEDDY
(24 NOV 1912–31 JULY 1986)

American jazz pianist, born Theodore Shaw Wilson in Austin, Texas. In college in Alabama he majored in music, then went to Detroit and Toledo, Ohio, where he worked with various groups. Moving to Chicago he performed with Louis Armstrong and Jimmie Noone; then he worked with Benny Carter in New York. Wilson accompanied Billie Holiday on records, and was with the Benny Goodman band from 1936 to 1939, when he formed his own band and later a sextet. Producer John Hammond also used Wilson as the primary accompanist for Billie Holiday's classic late 1930s-early 1940s sessions. After another period with Goodman he freelanced, toured in Europe, and taught at the Juilliard School. Wilson continued to record and perform through the rest of his life, with little change in his style or repertory. He died in New Britain, Connecticut.

Wilson's playing was often referred to as "impeccable," his contributions to any ensemble being invariably imaginative, tasteful, and supportive. He employed unusual chord formations and ingenious counterpoint, developing an airy relaxed texture. Among his finest recordings were "Don't Blame Me" (Brunswick #8025; 1937), "Smoke Gets in Your Eyes" (Columbia #36631; 1941), and "I Know that You Know" (Columbia #36633; 1941). In 1937 and 1938 Wilson won the *Downbeat* poll as favorite pianist, and in 1939 he won the *Metronome* poll.

There are many CD reissues of Wilson as bandleader, soloist, and, of course, as a member of the Goodman band and as an accompanist to Billie Holiday.

WILSON, TOM (25 MAR 1931–6 SEP 1978)

A noted pop producer of the 1960s, Wilson is known for his work with Simon and Garfunkel, Bob Dylan, the Animals, Frank Zappa, and the Velvet Underground. Born Thomas Blanchard Wilson, Jr., in Waco, Texas, the Black Wilson attended Harvard where he first heard and fell in love with jazz music. On graduation, he was hired

by Savoy records, and then worked briefly for United Artists and Audio Fidelity, producing albums for jazz musicians John Coltrane, Sun Ra, and Cecil Taylor, among others. Wilson joined Columbia in 1963 in their pop department as a staff producer. Assigned to work with Bob Dylan, Wilson oversaw Dylan's transformation from folk-protest singer to surrealist rock poet, producing the classic albums *Another Side of Bob Dylan* and *Highway 61 Revisited*. Wilson also oversaw the debut album by the folk-protest duo, Simon and Garfunkel, adding drums to their subdued recording of "Sounds of Silence," and transforming it into a hit. That success led him to be hired by MGM in 1965 to head the pop department of their Verve label and bring younger acts to the label. He signed Frank Zappa's Mothers of Invention to the label, overseeing its initial albums, as well as the first recording by the New York avant-garde rock band the Velvet Underground; his biggest pop success at MGM came with the U.K. group the Animals. Wilson was less active as a producer after the early 1970s, turning his attention to various business ventures, including New York's Record Plant Studio, which he cofounded in 1968 with his engineer Gary Kellgren and additional partner Chris Stone; it became the premier recording studio in the city by the late 1970s, with a second, successful branch in Los Angeles. Wilson died in Los Angeles after suffering a heart attack.

WINAMP

Winamp is one of the most popular software devices for playing back MP3 files on an Apple Mac or PC. It was one of the first to appear, which gave it an instant foothold. It has retained this by being very small — both in terms of the size of the installation software and also the space it occupies on screen. At the same time Winamp has incorporated extra functionality and hi-fi-like components such as graphic equalizers. Produced by Nullsoft in Arizona, it is one of many success stories from comparatively tiny companies that have driven the multimedia development of worldwide operating systems such as Microsoft Windows and driven acceptance of the MP3 music file format. Founded in 1995 by Justin Frankel, Nullsoft and Winamp were sold to AOL Time Warner in 1999. Winamp now coexists with the company's other, complementary creation Shoutcase, a system for receiving streaming, radio-style internet transmissions.

IAN PEEL

WINDHAM HILL (LABEL)

SEE ACKERMAN, WILLIAM

WINEY, JAMES

See Loudspeaker; Magnepan Loudspeakers

WINNER (LABEL)

A U.K. record from J.E. Hough, Ltd., latterly Edison Bell, Ltd., issued from 1912 to 1933. The label name was variously The Winner, Winner, Edison Bell Winner Record, and Edison Bell Winner. The discs were nominally issued by the Winner Record Co., a syndicate controlled by Hough. A final series of Winner records was issued by the Decca Record Co., Ltd. [Andrews 1984/12.]

WINTER, PAUL (31 AUG 1939–)

Although he first became famous as a jazz musician, Paul Winter's most enduring legacy will be his formative influence on the New Age genre. His recordings display a strong eclectic bent, blending classical, jazz, and world-music elements with environmental subject matter.

Winter, a soprano saxophonist, launched a jazz ensemble comprised of college students in the Chicago area in the early 1960s. His group, the Paul Winter Sextet, recorded many albums for Columbia during the 1960s; the most popular title, *Jazz Meets the Bossa Nova* (Columbia #8725; 1962; #109), was a rather derivative fusion of Latin and cool jazz elements, based on the work of Stan Getz and Charlie Byrd, among others.

In 1967, he formed the Paul Winter Consort — built around virtuoso musicians including guitarist Oscar Castro-Neves, keyboardist/songwriter Paul Halley, and cellist Eugene Friesen — a vehicle for expressing his interest in cultural unity and environmental harmony. Their recordings evolved from the densely layered arrangements of ancient and modern instruments in the George Martin–produced *Icarus* (Epic #31643; 1968; reissued on CD by Living Music #0004; 1986) to *Common Ground* (A&M #3344; 1978), which intermingled the sounds of animals and nature with the rhythmic compositions based on international folk music themes.

Winter's world music interests represent a political statement for the artist; *Earthbeat* (Living Music #0015; 1987), a collaboration with the Moscow-based Dimitri Potrovsky Singers comprised largely of traditional Russian songs, released during the militant posturing of the Reagan administration, is a case in point. Although *Canyon* (Living Music #0006; 1986; #138) — a collection of musical scenes from the Grand Canyon — is the only consort work to enter the *Billboard 200*, Winter's albums — including *Callings* (Living Music #0001), *Missa Gaia/Earth Mass* (Living Music #0002), *Sun Singer* (Living Music #0003), *Concert for the Earth* (Living Earth #0005), and *Wintersong* (Living Music #0012; 1986) — remain consistent sellers within the New Age market.

FRANK HOFFMANN

WINTERTHALER, HUGO (15 AUG 1909– 17 SEP 1973)

Orchestral arranger and recording artist Winterthaler was a popular producer of easy-listening instrumental music in the 1950s and 1960s. He studied music at the New England Conservatory and, on graduation, taught music until he began working in the mid-1930s as a professional Big Band arranger. His work arranging for singer Dinah Shore landed him a job as a music director at the new MGM label in 1948. In 1950 he moved to RCA Victor, where he became a popular recording artist leading studio orchestras as well as an arranger for singers like Perry Como. His biggest hit came in 1956 with "Canadian Sunset," featuring pianist Eddie Heywood. Winterthaler remained at Victor until 1963 when he moved to Kapp, where he remained through the mid-1960s when he began working as a Broadway arranger. During the "lounge music" revival of the 1990s, many of Winterthaler's recordings received renewed attention. He died in Greenwich, Connecticut.

WINWOOD, STEVE (12 MAY 1948–)

The man who was once described by Al Kooper as "the finest white blues singer I have ever heard" was proving that very point at the age of 16 as vocalist for the Spencer Davis Group. Hits like the 1967 "Gimme Some Lovin'" sound uncannily Black: sort of like "Sam & Dave Go to London." Winwood brought his soulful vocals and insistent organ riffs to his own group, Traffic, and later to the short-lived supergroup Blind Faith, with Ginger Baker and Eric Clapton. Winwood went into a bit of a hiatus in the late 1970s, but the 1981 hit album *Arc of the Diver* (Island #9576) brought him back, with a Top 10 single, "When You See a Chance" (Island #49656; #7). In 1985 his most popular album, the triple-platinum *Back in the High Life* (Island #9844), with its single, "Higher Love" (Island #28710), brought him all the way back to the top of the charts. His last major hit came with new label Virgin on "Roll With It" (Virgin #99326; 1988; #1 pop/adult contemporary). After that, Winwood faded from the charts. In 1994 Winwood joined ex-band mate Jim Capaldi in a Traffic reunion. He brought Brazilian music into his mix with *About Time* (Sci Fidelity 1; 2003).

BOB SILLERY

WISCONSIN PHONOGRAPH CO.
An affiliated firm of the North American Phonograph Co., located in Milwaukee, in 1890. W.S. Burnet was superintendent in 1890, and John H. Frank was president.

WISE (LABEL)
An American record of ca. 1926, issued by the Wise Co., New York. Masters came from Emerson and several of the Grey Gull labels. [Kendziora 1988/6.]

WISSERT, JOE
Born Joseph Wissert in Philadelphia, Pennsylvania, Wissert began his career working with teen pop acts in the 1960s and then moved on to considerable success producing R&B and mainstream pop through the 1970s. After taking third place as a dancer on Dick Clark's *American Bandstand*, the teen approached Clark for guidance in getting into the record business. Clark directed him to the local Cameo/Parkway label, where he began engineering pop acts, including the Orlons and Dovells. Moving to Los Angeles in the mid-1960s, he was hired by the Koppelman-Rubin production company, producing a new group for them, the Turtles, overseeing their major hits beginning with "Happy Together" (1967). He also worked with another Koppelman-Rubin client, the Lovin' Spoonful, on their *Everything Playing* album in 1968. He was hired as a staff producer by Warner Bros. in 1970, initially working with singer/songwriter Gordon Lightfoot, but then was assigned to a new R&B group, Earth, Wind, and Fire, producing their major hits at Warner and then at Columbia through 1976. Having gone independent, Wissert continued to score in the mainstream pop arena, overseeing major hits from Helen Reddy and Boz Scaggs in the mid- to late 1970s. His last major production work in the U.S. came in the early 1980s with the J. Geils Band, and then in 1985 he moved to Australia, where he worked for seven years. On his return to Los Angeles, Wissert tried to reestablish himself as a producer, but has mostly worked with local groups through the 1990s.

CARL BENSON

WOLFMAN JACK
(21 JAN 1938–6 JULY 1995)
Radio and television personality. Probably America's most famous disc jockey in the 1960s, Wolfman Jack gained a huge audience through the dual forces of personality and megawattage. Born Robert Weston Smith in Brooklyn, Wolfman Jack was a protégé of Nashville disc jockey John Richbourg, who gave him his initial break by recommending him to a small Virginia-based station that focused on a Black audience. His croaking vocal tones gave him his distinctive moniker. Broadcasting his wild-man persona beginning in 1960 from Mexico-based XERF-AM, a 250,000-watt station just across the U.S. border, the Wolfman played rock and roll, ethnic R&B, and southern blues to most of North America. He took over Tijuana's XERB in 1966, sending tapes of his show across the border. In 1970 he began a 16-year association with U.S. Armed Forces Radio, becoming a favorite of servicemen everywhere. In 1972, the Guess Who honored him with the song, "Clap for the Wolfman." During the 1970s Wolfman Jack also shifted to television, hosting "The Midnight Special" on NBC for over eight years. During this time he continued work in radio, in both New York (WNEW-FM starting in 1973) and Los Angeles (KRTH starting in 1976). A small role in the 1973 film *American Graffitti* helped spread his legend and made him among the most famous disc jockeys in America. During the 1980s and 1990s, Wolfman made thousands of personal appearances in live and televised shows, hosted the *Rock 'n' Roll Palace* on the Nashville Network, and producing a weekly radio show from a Planet Hollywood restaurant in Washington, D.C. He died shortly after the publication of his autobiography in 1995.

BRAD HILL

WOLVERINES
A jazz group of the 1920s, also known as the Wolverine Orchestra, featuring Bix Beiderbecke, cornet. They recorded for Gennett in 1924, making 18 sides. "Fidgety Feet" (#5408) was Beiderbecke's first recording. "Tiger Rag" and "Sensation" were among the other important numbers by the group.

WONDER, STEVIE (16 MAY 1950–)
American soul singer, instrumentalist, and composer, born Steveland Judkins or Steveland Morris in Saginaw, Michigan. Blind from birth, he sang and played harmonica as a child. When Berry Gordy heard him perform, he gave the youngster a Motown contract and named him Little Stevie Wonder. In 1963 Wonder made a hit single, "Fingertips (Part 2)" (Tamla #54080). He remained with the Tamla label, developing a complex style that incorporated gospel, rock, jazz, African, and Latino idioms into songs of protest. By 1972, when he toured with the Rolling Stones, he was widely acclaimed by white audiences. He took over the production of his records, composed the

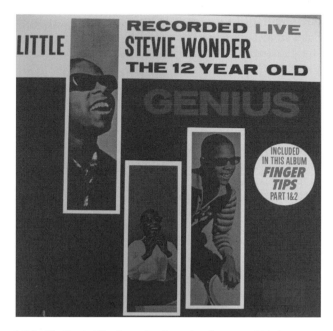

Mid-'60s Stevie Wonder collection when he was still being promoted as a young harmonica virtuoso. Courtesy Frank Hoffmann

songs, and played most of the instruments. *Talking Book* (Tamla #T319L) was a sensation in 1972, on the charts 57 weeks. In the next year he issued *Innerversions* (Tamla #T326L), which won five Grammys as well as pioneered the use of the synthesizer as a solo instrument; his follow-up, *Fulfillingness First Finale* (Tamla #8019; 1974; #1), also garnered five Grammys. Wonder's most popular album was *Songs in the Key of Life* (Tamla #T13-340C2; 1976; #1), which spent 90 weeks on the pop charts. Following several years of inactivity, he garnered raves in some quarters for the soundtrack to the film *Jungle Fever* (Motown MOTD #6291; 1991). His accomplishments would also place him on the cover the September 1991 issue of *Down Beat*. Although popular with record consumers, the bulk of his 1980s' and 1990s' work has been uneven, lacking the innovative spirit of his earlier recordings.

REV. FRANK HOFFMANN

WONDER (LABEL)

An American record issued by the Wonder Talking Machine Co., New York, known only from a printed catalog of ca. 1898. "The contents tally exactly with those of the Berliner catalog of the same presumed date" [Rust]. It may be that the records were given to purchasers of the Wonder disc player, also produced by the firm. A player of that name was still being sold by a company of that name according to a 1916 trade directory; there were five models, all priced under $20.

In March 1922 the Wonder Phonograph Co., incorporated in Delaware, succeeded the Wonder Talking Machine Co. [Paul 1991/1; Rust 1978.]

WOODS, ROBERT (7 JULY 1947–)

Born in Chillicothe, Ohio, Woods earned a B.M.E. from Otterbein College, studied voice at Oberlin College, and did extensive postgraduate work at Kent State University. He was a student at Tanglewood in the early 1970s, as well as at the Blossom Festival School (Cleveland Orchestra equivalent). Woods is currently president of Telarc Records, and in that position has won 10 Grammys as Classical Producer of the Year, as well as many other nominations. In addition to having produced a few hundred recordings, he has also been the guiding force behind Telarc's evolution from its original roots as a classical label into the genres of jazz, crossover, blues, and instrumental pop. While limiting his producing activities in recent years, Woods still enjoys the "hands-on" part of the business whenever possible and is at home producing a wide variety of musical genres. He has also served time on the National Endowment of the Arts recording panel.

HOWARD FERSTLER

WOODWIND RECORDINGS (HISTORIC)

While never so prestigious as vocalists, violinists, or pianists, woodwind performers were still remarkably active in the earliest days of recorded sound. Commercial woodwind recordings of the acoustical era, though restricted in repertoire, document the outstanding artistry of notable virtuosi as well as the often unappreciated skills of many now long-forgotten flutists, clarinetists, oboists, and bassoonists. The electrical era brought a dramatic increase in the variety of recorded woodwind repertoire and the number of recorded virtuosi. By the mid-1920s contemporary composers were beginning to devote more attention to wind instruments, and through the recording of this new music important interpretations were preserved. Later, the LP inspired an explosion of recordings by woodwind soloists and ensembles, presenting an array of works ranging from rediscovered Renaissance dances to aggressive avant-garde experiments.

While the majority of today's classical woodwind artists are concert or orchestral performers, in the first two decades of the 20th century many were members of professional bands that were already recording actively at the time. Musicians from the ensembles of John Philip Sousa, Arthur Pryor, Patrick S. Gilmore, and others recorded prolifically as soloists, with and without the accompaniment of the bands themselves, and often supplemented these activities by working as studio musicians. But apart from these featured band performers, woodwind soloists were something of a rarity in American concert life. Even principal players from the established orchestras seldom had the opportunity of being heard in solo concert performances, or of recording extensively. This situation changed slowly when major American orchestras began recruiting their principal woodwind players from France and Belgium, a procedure that brought musicians like Marcel Tabuteau, Georges Barräre, Gustave Langenus, and Georges Laurent to this country. The influence of these virtuosi on playing styles, repertoire, and public opinion would prove significant.

It is therefore disappointing that some of the most important of these woodwind virtuosi left a recorded legacy scarcely representative of their contemporary reputations, primarily because of restraints placed upon the recorded repertoire at the time. This was particularly true during the acoustical era. Music not usually associated with woodwinds was frequently arranged for their use, possibly in an effort to make these still-unusual instruments more accessible to the general public. Early recordings of woodwinds present a mixture of popular songs, well-known operatic arias, a few traditional instrumental showpieces, and familiar light classics. It was not until these instruments began to gain some individual stature that an indigenous woodwind repertoire began to appear extensively on record.

Popular songs, from familiar ballads and folk tunes to current stage successes, were especially common on pre-1900 woodwind recordings. Clarinet selections from the 1897 Columbia catalog, played by William Tuson, included "Comin' thro' the Rye," "Sally in Our Alley," and Foster's "Massa's in de Cold, Cold Ground." While there were many unadorned renditions of such songs, more often elaborate variations were added to enliven performances. A similar treatment befell operatic themes and medleys. Recordings by the U.K. clarinetist Charles Draper, listed in the Edison Bell catalog for 1903, included selections from *Rigoletto* and *Fra Diavolo*, while a rare 1902 recording for G & T by the Spanish-born clarinetist Manuel Gomez offered a set of variations on "Caro nome."

Of a more purely instrumental nature were the many ostentatious works designed to display virtuosic agility. Julius Benedict's "Carnival of Venice," for example, was a favorite of virtually every instrumentalist in search of a reputation. While this type of music was frequently deplored, it was heavily recorded — often, ironically, by some of its principal critics. Closely related to these technical marvels were pieces which exploited particular instrumental eccentricities. Piccolos were thought to be especially well suited to

bird imitations, often in polka form. George Schweinfest, perhaps the earliest piccolist on record (for Edison cylinders in 1889), has 22 titles listed in Columbia's 1897 catalog, among which were nine "bird polkas." Much of this avian repertoire was composed by E. Damaré, a French piccolist who recorded 12 of his own works for Bettini, listed in the latter's June 1901 catalog. The flute was assigned a similar pastoral role, albeit a slightly more dignified one, illustrated particularly well in the innumerable obbligati it provided for singers. Certain of those were recorded with pronounced frequency: "Charmant oiseaux" from David's *La Perle du Brésil*, the Mad Scene from *Lucia di Lammermoor*, Henry Bishop's "Lo, Here the Gentle Lark," and several other titles featured not only famous sopranos, but some of the most noted flutists of the day.

Less fortunate in its extramusical associations was the bassoon, which was regarded almost wholly as a novelty in the acoustical era. It was usually relegated, often in combination with the piccolo, to descriptive works like "The Nightingale and the Frog," or "The Elephant and the Fly," or to purely comic orchestral effects.

A very large percentage of the woodwinds' early recorded repertoire was drawn from salon music, including minor works of well-known composers (two venerable examples are Mendelssohn's "Spring Song" and Beethoven's "Minuet in G"), and major works of forgotten composers: "Serenade" by Anton Titl (1809–1882), "The Herd Girl's Dream" by August Labitzky (1832–1903), and a long list of others, all ubiquitous fixtures in record catalogs between 1905 and 1935. Such works were particularly popular when arranged for small groups — flute and clarinet duets, or mixed trios of flute, violin, and harp, or flute, cello, and harp. Every label seems to have had such an ensemble. Victor's Neapolitan Trio (flute, violin, and harp) began recording around 1911, reaching its peak in 1923 with 34 titles in print, and continued to record electrically. Columbia's house trio, usually composed of George Stehl [or Stell] (violin), Marshall Lufsky (flute), and Charles Schuetze (harp), pursued the same repertoire. That type of music lingered for many years before its eventual dismissal from the repertoire. As late as 1940 Victor's Red Seal catalog included "The Aeolians," a quartet of flute, violin, cello, and harp playing, among other things, MacDowell's "To a Wild Rose," and Rimsky-Korsakov's "Flight of the Bumblebee."

Serious music for woodwinds was slow to appear on record. German performers of the early electrical recording era did show a preference for baroque and classical music. The 1926–1927 Polydor catalog listed performances by the Leipzig Gewandhaus Quintet of works by Klughardt, Beethoven, Reicha, and Mozart. French performers had a predilection for the latest

French compositions. Soloists and ensembles such as the Trio d'Anches, the Quintette Instrumentale (both of Paris), and the Société Taffanel commissioned and recorded modern works by many important 20th-century composers. In the U.S., the growth of a distinctive, modern repertoire for woodwinds only began developing in the 1930s. Pioneering labels like New Music Quarterly Recordings featured such works, often performed by the composers or by the groups that had commissioned or premiered them. Concurrently, the major international labels began "modern music" series.

Flutists active at the turn of the century often recorded on the piccolo because of its piercing sound and its popularity as a band instrument. George Schweinfest has been mentioned. Eugene Rose, a flutist in Sousa's Band in 1900–1901, made cylinders for Edison in 1889, along with two other flutists, Carl Wehner and Gustav Gast. Many players recorded acoustically on both piccolo and flute — Frank Badollet (1870–?) of the United States Marine Band, and two members of Sousa's Band, Darius Lyons (1870–?) and Marshall Lufsky (1878–1948). Other flutists came to the recording studio from orchestral careers. Clement Barone (1876–1934) became a Victor studio flutist in 1910 after seven years with the Philharmonia Orchestra. His recordings include flute and piccolo solos, dozens of titles with the Neapolitan Trio and Florentine Quartet, and obbligati for numerous sopranos. Albert Fransella (1866–1934), a Belgian whose performing career was primarily in the U.K., was at different times a member of the Scottish, Crystal Palace, Royal Philharmonic, and Queen's Hall orchestras. His earliest recordings were Berliners made in 1898 and 1899 — flute and piccolo solos, and several selections by the "Fransella Flute Quartet." He later provided recorded obbligati for Nellie Melba and Ruth Vincent, and made several flute and piccolo recordings of popular material issued by English Columbia in 1911.

During the acoustical period, few flutists had performing careers completely independent of orchestras or bands. One or two did appear as concert artists, often in association with singers, particularly sopranos. John Lemmone (1862–1950), a self-taught Australian flutist who was for many years obbligatist and concert manager for Melba, recorded several colorful works with descriptive titles and picturesque musical effects for Victor. His 1910 recording of "By the Brook" (#70023) has a piano accompaniment by Melba herself. John Amadio of New Zealand (1884–1964), who also performed frequently as an obbligatist for numerous sopranos, possessed an amazing technical ability that was amply illustrated by his "Carnival of Venice," Paganini's "Witches' Dance," and other virtuosic works recorded for HMV.

Since the later half of the 19th century, the influence of French flutists has been acknowledged throughout the world. It is significant that the first major reissues of historical flute recordings presented performances by six French flutists: Gaubert, Hennebains, Barrâre, Laurent, Moyse, and Le Roy. It is unfortunate that of these six men, only the latter two recorded extensively. Philippe Gaubert (1879–1941), also renowned as a composer and conductor, recorded two obbligati for Melba in 1904 and seven short selections, including two of his own works, for the French Gramophone Co. in 1918–1920. Adolphe Hennebains (1862–1914), flutist at the Paris Opéra (1891–1914), recorded an assortment of short works by Chopin, Godard, Pessard, Massenet, and others in 1907 and 1908, also for the French Gramophone Co. Georges Barrâre (1876–1944) and Georges Laurent (1886–1964) were influential concert and orchestral performers in America, but their recording careers were sporadic. Barrâre's first American solo recordings, made for Columbia in 1913 and 1915, were of the light salon pieces so favored by the public. His later electrical recordings emphasized the baroque and contemporary literature that he himself preferred, but his discs were unfortunately few in number. Laurent, for many years principal flutist of the Boston Symphony, recorded only a handful of titles as a soloist — primarily the works of J.S. Bach and a few modern composers, such as Howard Hanson and Roy Harris.

Marcel Moyse (1889–1984) and René Le Roy (1898–1985), both of whom began recording in the early electrical period, are more fully represented on disc. Le Roy's first recordings were probably the J.S. Bach sonatas recorded by the National Gramophone Society in 1928. In the course of his career he recorded many of the works dedicated to him, such as Honegger's *Danse de la chàvre*. Moyse was probably the best-known flute virtuoso of the 78 era. A host of notable French flutists followed Moyse, the most prominent being Jean-Pierre Rampal.

Most of the American flutists who recorded electrically or on LP were students of these influential Frenchmen. William Kincaid (1895–1967), pupil of Barrâre and for nearly 40 years the first flutist of the Philadelphia Orchestra, recorded as a soloist with that orchestra. John Wummer (1899–1977), another Barrâre student, recorded extensively for Columbia, performing works by Debussy, Foote, Handel, Bach, and others. An Irish virtuoso, James Galway (b. 1939), is the most internationally famous flutist of recent times.

The clarinet ("clarionet" is some older record catalogs) was heard on Edison cylinders in 1889; Henry Giese was the artist. Like the piccolo, it was popular as a band instrument, and many of the clarinetists recording at the turn of the century were band players.

William Tuson, of Sousa's and Gilmore's bands, had an active studio career for 10 years. Louis H. Christie, a Victor studio performer, made many early solo recordings for that company. In the U.S., however, the major orchestral clarinetists were poorly represented on record until the electrical era. Gustave Langenus (1883–1957), an important performer and a principal of the New York Symphony and New York Philharmonic, appears to have made virtually no recordings outside those made by the orchestras. He is said to have recorded at least one selection for his own Celesta label, established in 1926, but it is not known whether the recording was actually released.

Certain woodwind instruments have exhibited pronounced national ties. For many years France had a monopoly on flutists, and was also considered by many to be the source of the best oboe and clarinet players. However, as French and French-trained musicians wandered about Europe in pursuit of performing opportunities, their influence began to spread. the U.K., in particular, had a long succession of fine clarinetists. The Gomez brothers, Manuel (1859–1922) and Francisco (1866–1938), though born in Spain and educated in France, spent most of their lives in the U.K. where they were well-known performers. Both recorded; Francisco made at least one Berliner in 1899, and Manuel made a handful of G & Ts (later issued on Zonophone) in London in 1902. Charles Draper (1869–1952), a noted orchestral player and one of the cofounders of the New Symphony Orchestra of London, probably recorded first for the Gramophone Co. in London in 1901. The Edison Bell catalog of 1903 also lists many recordings by him, including one of the earliest recorded performances of the Weber *Concertino* (an even earlier recording of this work played by Henri Paradis [1861–1940] appeared in the June 1901 Bettini catalog). Draper had a lengthy career, and later went on to record major works such as Brahms's Clarinet Quintet, released by Columbia in 1929.

Electrical recordings reflected the continuing French and U.K. domination of the instrument. Frederick Thurston (1901–1953), particularly well known as a soloist with the BBC Symphony Orchestra (1930–1946) recorded primarily in the 1930s and 1940s, performing several of the U.K. compositions he had premiered, such as the Bliss Clarinet Quintet in 1944. Reginald Kell (1906–1981), who is considered to have revolutionized clarinet playing, recorded extensively from both the standard and 20th-century repertoire. Kell's successors in the U.K. include Jack Brymer (b. 1915), Thea King (b. 1925), and Gervase de Peyer (b. 1926). In France, Gaston Hamelin (1884–1951) made the first recording of the Debussy *Premiäre rapsodie* for clarinet in Paris in 1933. Louis

Cahuzac (1880–1960), who had begun recording for Pathé in about 1904, continued to record into the 1950s. At age 78 he recorded Hindemith's Clarinet Concerto for the Angel label with the Philadelphia Orchestra, the composer conducting.

The discs of Benny Goodman are among the outstanding American recordings from the electrical period. Goodman and Josef Szigeti commissioned Béla Bartok's *Contrasts* and recorded the work for Columbia on 13 May 1940, with Bartok at the piano. Later releases by Goodman include other works written for him, such as Copland's *Clarinet Concerto*, and selections from the standard solo repertoire.

The double-reed instruments were never as well-represented on record as flute or clarinet in the acoustical era. The earliest oboe recordings were probably made in France, or at least by French oboists, who were considered the finest in the world at the time. The noted instructor at the Paris Conservatory, Georges Gillet (1854–1934) recorded in the first decade of this century for French Odeon. One of his pupils, Louis Gaudard, is said to have recorded prior to 1900, though none of these recordings have been documented. Gaudard did appear in the Edison Bell catalog for 1903, and by 1906 he had made several discs for the English Neophone Co., including the "Pastorale" from the overture to Rossini's *William Tell*. Other oboists appearing on record before 1910 were less well known, and may simply have been versatile reed players "doubling" on the instrument. B. Sylvester, who used the pseudonym "Orpheus" and recorded for Edison Bell in about 1903, performed a repertoire of Irish songs on both the oboe and the musette (bagpipe). Acoustical recordings of the English horn are even fewer, although some outstanding examples, usually solos from the operatic or orchestral literature, do exist — for example, the solo that precedes Gertrude Fîrstel's "Frau Holda kam" from *Tannhauser*, recorded in Bayreuth in summer 1904 (G & T #43576).

Many European oboists moved to America. Marcel Tabuteau (1887–1966), a pupil of Gillet, came in 1905 to join the New York Symphony Orchestra under Damrosch. His subsequent career included 40 years as principal oboist of the Philadelphia Orchestra. While he is heard in many recordings by that orchestra, his solo recordings are fewer than his reputation should have demanded. They include Bach's Brandenburg Concertos, recorded for Victor, and major works by Handel and Mozart issued on Columbia LPs. Bruno Labate (1883–1943), soloist with the New York Philharmonic from 1919 to 1943, began recording acoustically for Pathé, and continued recording throughout his career, performing works like Loeffler's Two Rhapsodies (Schirmer Set #10; 1941).

Leon Goossens was the first virtuoso oboist of international reputation. Many of his pupils, among them Evelyn Rothwell (b. 1911), have had active recording careers as well.

American oboists, many of them students of Tabuteau or Labate, began to assume equal stature with their European counterparts in the late 1940s and early 1950s. Among those whose recordings have been particularly outstanding are John de Lancie, Robert Bloom, Harold Gomberg (1916–1985) and Ralph Gomberg (b. 1921).

The bassoon was generally the most neglected of the woodwinds on early recordings, treated more as a sound effect than as a musical instrument. A mysterious "Mr. Cooper" who recorded for Berliner in London in 1898 may be the earliest bassoonist to have recorded solos — his selections included several popular songs and a theme with variations from *Don Pasquale*. Frederick James (1860–1920), who played in the Queen's Hall Orchestra, London Symphony Orchestra, and at Covent Garden, was also recording early in the century, with six titles in the Edison Bell catalog for 1903. But solo bassoon recordings were to remain few in number for many years. From 1915 to 1921, Victor offered only one solo bassoon recording, in addition to the brief examples of the instrument provided in their educational catalog. Several outstanding players did much to improve the bassoon's status on record in the electrical era. Archie Camden (1888–1979), a prominent English bassoonist, inscribed a diverse repertoire of solo and chamber music. His recording of the Mozart Bassoon Concerto, made for English Columbia in 1926, is the earliest made of that work. In France, bassoonist Fernand Oubradous (b. 1903) actively promoted chamber music through his recording and conducting activities. He began to record in the late 1920s, playing both the standard classical works and contemporary French material. Later European and U.K. bassoonists include Maurice Allard (b. 1923), who recorded into the LP era, and Wilfred and Cecil James, respectively son and grandson of Frederick James.

The growing importance of the bassoon in chamber music has contributed to its renaissance on LP. Many of the bassoonists in the U.S. have played with woodwind quintets while pursuing solo and orchestral careers. Leonard Sharrow (b. 1915), who has recorded works ranging from the Mozart Bassoon Concerto to the Hindemith Bassoon Sonata, was also a member of the American Woodwind Quintet. Arthur Weisberg (b. 1931) and Sol Schoenbach (b. 1915) are also chamber players.

Acoustical recordings of woodwind ensembles were even fewer than those of the individual instruments. In the acoustical period, duets were favored, using two matched instruments (piccolo duets were quite common) or two different ones. Flute and clarinet were frequently paired, though more unusual combinations were heard, such as the flute and saxophone duets recorded for Victor in 1900 by Frank Badollet and Jean-Baptiste Moermans. American concert reviews reveal that even in the 1930s larger woodwind ensembles were regarded as oddities, or charming 18th-century anachronisms. While many ensembles were successful in concert, few recorded with any regularity. The Barräre Ensemble, Barräre Little Symphony, and Trio de Lutäce, all woodwind and mixed ensembles founded by flutist Georges Barräre, recorded for Columbia between 1915 and 1922, but played only arrangements of popular light pieces. In 1927 recordings by the London Flute Quartet included selections like "The Flight of the Bumblebee" and "Carnival of Venice."

Woodwind ensembles were heard to greater advantage in the electrical era. German quintets were especially active. The 1926–1927 Polydor catalog alone lists performances by the Berlin Opera Wind Sextet, the Dresden State Opera Orchestra Wind Quintet, and the Leipzig Gewandhaus Quintet. The Leipzig repertoire includes, along with classical serenades and divertimenti, Hindemith's *Kleine Kammermusik* op. 24, no. 2. The number of professional quintets and other small groups increased throughout the 1930s, with radio further encouraging the growth of chamber performance. In France, one of the most active woodwind groups was the Trio d'Anches de Paris, founded in 1927 by the bassoonist Oubradous. It emphasized the modern French composers, such as Darius Milhaud, Jean Rivier, Georges Auric, and Henry Barraud. Other notable French ensembles included the Société des Instruments à Vent de Paris, and flutist René Le Roy's Quintette Instrumental de Paris (flute, strings, and harp), which was active from 1922 to 1939, and recorded for HMV in the mid-1930s.

In the U.S., the formation of more or less permanent ensembles for the performance of woodwind music did not take place until the 1940s. The New York Woodwind Quintet was founded in 1949, the Boston Symphony Woodwind Quintet in 1954, and the Philadelphia Woodwind Quintet in 1950. These ensembles and others have made enormous contributions to the recorded repertoire, particularly in contemporary music. There are some striking parallels between the development of a discrete, sophisticated literature for woodwinds and the recorded history of the instruments themselves. The growth of woodwind music in the 20th century, achieved through the revival of older works and the creation of new ones, has been supported by the opportunities for presenting that literature through recordings. At the same time, the existence of a more suitable and varied repertoire has encouraged an increase in both live and recorded performing activity.

Two LP reissues by Pearl are of special importance: *The Great Flautists, Vol. I* (#GEMM 284; 1985) and *Vol. 2* (#GEMM 302; 1986). [Dorgeuille 1986; Langwill 1965; Weston 1971, 1977.]

See also **Clarinet Recordings (Historic)**

SUSAN NELSON

WOOFER

The loudspeaker driver in a speaker system that handles the bass-frequency range. In a three- or four-way system, the woofer will probably cover the range between a lower cut-off point of 20 to 60 Hz on up to anywhere between 130 to 600 Hz, before the midrange driver begins to cut in. In a two-way system, the woofer may also handle a substantial percentage of the midrange, all the way up to 2, 3, or even 4 kHz, before the tweeter gradually cuts in.

See also **Subwoofer**

HOWARD FERSTLER

WORK, JOHN W.
(15 JUNE 1901–17 MAY 1967)

Composer, educator, musicologist. An extensively educated music scholar with a specialty in Black folk songs, Work held teaching and administrative positions at Fisk University, from which he graduated with a history degree in 1923. He directed Fisk's music department from 1951 to 1957, and retired in 1966. Work's interest in Black folk music led him to create choral arrangements of spirituals, but his formal choral compositions generally do not include folk elements. In 1946 Work composed the cantata "The Singers," which won first prize in a contest sponsored by the Fellowship of American Composers. Work's *American Negro Songs and Spirituals,* published in 1940, remains a seminal collection book. Work made several "field trips" in the 1930s and 1940s to record traditional singers, and accompanied Alan Lomax on the trip that led to the discovery of blues singer Muddy Waters.

BRAD HILL

WORLD BROADCASTING SYSTEM INC.

A New York firm, which issued, for radio stations only, a series of "World Program Service" transcription discs, from 1933 to 1963. [Kressley 1968 is a label list and history.]

WORLD PHONOGRAPH CO.

A Chicago firm, maker of the World record player in 1919–1920. It went bankrupt in October 1920.

WORLD RECORD CO., LTD.

A U.K. firm, active in 1922–1924, with showrooms in Piccadilly, London. The main product was a Gramophone and a disc (World Record) designed to operate at a constant groove speed (outside RPM reduced, inside RPM increased). Use of this system, an invention of Pemberton Billing, provided three to five times the playing time per record of ordinary discs. Billing demonstrated his discs and machine controller in New York in 1923, having obtained rights in the U.S. Vistaphone Co. in 1922. World Record Co. was also set up in Australia in 1922–1925. The promise of this method was not fully exploited, however, as the firm sold its business to the Vocalion Gramophone Co., Ltd., in 1925, which company began issuing Vocalion Long Playing Records made under Billing's patents. Production ceased in late 1925. The World Record Co., Ltd., retained its corporate existence, but not with records or machines.

FRANK ANDREWS

WORLD'S COLUMBIAN EXPOSITION, CHICAGO, 1893

At this great world's fair there were important musical exhibits. Fifty-eight firms exhibited pianos and organs, but the only player piano seems to have been the Hupfeld Self Playing Piano, a "push-up" player attachment. Thomas Edison had an exhibit in the Electricity Building, including his Household Phonograph.

WORLD'S FAIRS

See PANAMA PACIFIC EXPOSITION, SAN FRANCISCO, 1915; PARIS EXPOSITION, 1889; ST. LOUIS EXPOSITION, 1904; WORLD'S COLUMBIAN EXPOSITION, CHICAGO, 1893

WORLD'S GREATEST MUSIC/WORLD'S GREATEST OPERA (LABELS)

Records issued in the U.S. in 1938–1940 by the Publishers Service Co., a subsidiary of the *New York Post.* For the World's Greatest Music label, the discs were pressed by RCA Victor, using Victor artists (not identified on the records), and sold at bargain prices to newspaper purchasers. Many of the performances were by members of the Philadelphia Orchestra,

Late '30s label marketed by the *New York Post* to its readers. Courtesy Kurt Nauck/Nauck's Vintage Records

playing in the Academy of Music. In 1940 the related World's Greatest Opera label was formed. Among the anonymous artists were Rose Bampton, Mack Harrell, Eleanor Steber, Norman Cordon, and Leonard Warren, with 12 operas issued. [Gray 1975.]

WOW
A fluctuation in pitch (frequency) that results when a phonograph turntable does not rotate at constant speed, or when the disc is not fully stabilized on the turntable. In a tape player there is wow when the tape slips somewhere in the transport system, usually at the capstan.

WURLITZER (RUDOLPH) CO.
A music instrument manufacturing firm, established in 1861 in Cincinnati, Ohio, by Rudolph Wurlitzer. At first it made drums and bugles for use in the Civil War, then other band instruments. It was soon the largest retailer of its kind. In 1890 the firm incorporated as the Rudolph Wurlitzer Co., Inc.

Wurlitzer made pianos, electric pianos, coin-op instruments, automatic piano roll changers, and other automatic musical devices. By September 1904 the firm had become an official jobber for Edision products. Before 1913 the firm was located at 122 E. Fourth St., Cincinnati, and after 1913 at 982 Fourth St. It was active in furnishing theater instruments. An advertisement in *Billboard*, September 1913, claimed that "thirty-three motion picture theatres in twenty-five cities installed Wurlitzer music during August alone." The reference was to the "One-Man Orchestra," a photoplayer. The company had 20 branches, including one at 115–119 W. 40th St., New York.

In the late 1920s there were also Wurlitzer coin-op phonographs, and then the fully developed jukebox of the 1930s. About 750,000 jukeboxes were made up to 1974, when production ceased. [Hoover 1971, cover, shows jukebox model #1015, 1946.]

See also **Motion Picture Music**

WYNETTE, TAMMY
(5 MAY 1942–6 APR 1998)
Born Virginia Wynette Pugh, near Tupelo, Mississippi, Wynette was raised by her grandparents. She showed a talent for music early on, learning to play several instruments as well as singing. She joined her mother in Birmingham, Alabama, during her teen years, working as a beautician during the day and club singer at nights. Wynette came to Nashville in the mid-1960s in search of a career, auditioning for several labels while working as a singer and song plugger. Producer Billy Sherrill signed her to Epic in 1966, where she had an immediate hit "Your Good Girl's Gonna Go Bad" (Epic #10134; 1967) Wynette followed with a series of hits, including "I Don't Wanna Play House" (Epic #10211; 1967) and "D-I-V-O-R-C-E" (Epic #10315; 1968)and the classic "Stand by Your Man" (Epic #10398; 1968) the song most closely associated with her.

Also in 1968, Wynette began a seven-year stormy marriage with hard-drinkin' country star George Jones. The duo often recorded together, including an album of duets from 1972 (with a hit in 1973 with "We're Gonna Hold On" [Epic #11031]) and again in 1976, hitting it big with "Golden Ring" (Epic #50264) and "Near You" (Epic #50314; even though they divorced in 1975); they reteamed in 1980, scoring a hit with "Two-Story House" (Epic #50849). Meanwhile, Tammy continued to record through the 1970s, scoring major hits through the middle of the decade, including in 1972 "Bedtime Story" (Epic #10818) and "My Man (Understands)" (Epic #10909) and "Kids Say the Darndest Things"(Epic #10969) in 1973; "Another Lonely Song" (Epic #11079; 1974), and her last solo number one country hit, "You and Me" (Epic #50264) from 1976. Many of these songs were cowritten by producer Sherrill, and were carefully crafted to fit Wynette's image.

By the early to mid-1980s, Wynette's career was in the doldrums. The increasingly pop orientation of Sherrill's production was ill-suited to her basically honky-tonk style. An attempt to remake her for the new country generation in 1987 on her album *Higher*

Ground (Epic #40832), produced by Steve Buckingham and featuring a duet with Ricky Skaggs, was a critical, if not financial, success. Wynette even dipped to self-parody, recording with the U.K.-based technorock group KLF, scoring a U.K. hit in 1992 with "Justified and Ancient." At the end of 1993, Wynette was hospitalized suffering from a serious infection; she recovered, but was in a weakened condition. In 1994, she reunited with George Jones for an album (*One*; MCA #11248) and tour, but her physical condition was obviously precarious. Wynette died of a blood clot four years later in her Nashville home.

CARL BENSON

WYOMING PHONOGRAPH CO.
A firm affiliated with the North American Phonograph Co., established in 1890 in Cheyenne, in business at least to 1893. E.L. Lindsay was manager in 1890.

X

XTC

Although rarely able to rise above cult status stateside, XTC were extremely popular in their native England during the early years of the post-punk era. Hurt by their aversion to live performing, the band's recorded work — featuring a gift for infectious melodies, tight song arrangements eschewing extended solos, and quirky, rapid-fire rhythms and instrumental flourishes revealing a pronounced punk influence — has frequently been compared with the Beatles.

Formed in Swindon, England, in 1976, XTC — originally comprised of guitarist/singer/composer Andy Partridge, bassist Colin Moulding, drummer Terry Chambers, and keyboardist Barry Andrews — earned a contract with Virgin Records in short order based on their gift for pop songcraft, frequently laced with wit and incisive social commentary. The decided power-pop leanings of the band's early albums — *White Music* (Virgin #2095; 1978; #34 U.K.), *Go 2* (Virgin #2108; 1978; #21 U.K.), *Drums and Wires* (Virgin #13131; 1979; #34 U.K., #176 U.S.), *Black Sea* (Virgin #13147; 1980; #16 U.K., #41 U.S.), and *English Settlement* (Epic #37943; 1982; #5 U.K., #48 U.S.) — caused them to be largely overlooked by the rock press, then infatuated with the punk revolution.

As Partridge exercised greater control over XTC in the mid-1980s, the music in the LPs *Mummer* (Geffen #4027; 1983; #51 U.K., #145 U.S.), *Big Express* (Geffen #24053; 1984; #38 U.K., #178 U.S.), and the Todd Rundgren–produced *Skylarking* (Geffen #24117; 1986; #90 U.K., #70 U.S.; latter pressings included the controversial underground hit, "Dear God") took on a more reflective, complex tone. In

keeping with Partridge's notoriously eccentric outlook, the band's alter ego, the Dukes of Stratosphear, released two tributes to 1960s' psychedelia, the EP *25 O'Clock* (Virgin #C 1; 1985), which outsold *The Big Express*, and *Psonic Psunspot* (Geffen #2440; 1987).

Despite various extramusical problems (e.g., litigation against a former manager in the late 1980s, a recording strike against Geffen during much of the 1990s), XTC has continued to release engagingly eclectic albums. *Oranges & Lemons* (Geffen #24218; 1989; #44) was named the top college-radio LP of 1989, while *Nonsuch* (Geffen #24474; 1992; #97) also reached number one on the college charts. Newly signed to the indie Indie label, TVT, the band released material stockpiled during the decade as two LPs, *Apple Venus Volume I* (TVT #3250; 1999; #42 U.K.), which featured acoustic material set off by lush orchestrations, and the more typical *Wasp Star (Apple Venus Volume 2)* (TVT #3260; 2000).

Frank Hoffmannn

X-Y STEREO RECORDING

See Coincident Stereo Recording

XYLOPHONE RECORDINGS (HISTORIC)

Charles P. Lowe appears to have been the earliest person to record the instrument, on cylinders that were listed in the 1893 catalog of the New Jersey Phonograph

Co., and others for Columbia and Edison before 1900. In Europe, early recordings of the xylophone were made for the Gramophone Co. by M. Raphael (a polka, in July 1899) and Mlle. Borde (six sides in July 1900). Marches, polkas, and waltzes were the principal repertoire of the pioneer performers, but there was also a record about air travel, apparently the first song of that genre: "Come Take a Trip in My Airship," played by Albert Benzler (Edison #8931; 1905; sung a year earlier for Victor by Billy Murray).) The Edison artists — Lowe, Benzler, Charles Daab, and J. Frank Hopkins — compiled about 60 numbers before 1900. Victor had 37 xylophone items listed in its 1917 catalog, most by W. H. Reitz, who also played the bells. There were no xylophone records in the 1927 catalog, but four were listed in 1938.

As the xylophone declined in public interest during the 1920s, the vibraphone was introduced into jazz performance. While the instruments are similar, the xylophone has wooden bars while the vibraphone has metal bars; and the vibraphone has electric controls that allow it to produce vibrato. Lionel Hampton was the first jazzman to give identity to the vibraphone, with Benny Goodman's Quartet in 1936–1940. Prominent xylophonists who followed him include Milt Jackson (of the Modern Jazz Quartet) and Gary Burton.

Y

YALE COLLECTION OF HISTORICAL SOUND RECORDINGS

One of the principal archives of its kind, established as a department of the Yale University Libraries in 1961 with an initial deposit of about 20,000 recordings by Mrs. and Mrs. Laurence C. Witten II. Many other individuals and organizations have since contributed records and documentation to the collection, which numbered over 160,000 recordings in various formats as of 2002. Composer recordings are a major concentration; another focus is on early singers. Jazz collecting has been emphasized in recent years. There are important holdings also in musical theater, poetry, and drama. [Blair 1989; Moore 1964; website: www.library.yale.edu/musiclib/collections.htm#hsr.]

YAMAHA CORP.

Founded by Torakusu Yamaha as Nippon Gakki, Ltd., in 1887, Yamaha has grown from a company that specialized in the making of excellent pianos and organs to the world's larger producer of musical instruments. The company is also a leading producer of recording and playback hardware, and of products as diverse as semiconductors, specialty metals, machine tools, motorcycles, golf clubs, industrial robots, furniture, and even bathtubs. The company now owns 44 subsidiaries and representative offices in overseas markets, in addition to numerous related companies in Japan. Yamaha Music Corp., founded in 1966, has generated a wide range of music activity throughout global society, including Yamaha music schools and the Junior Original Concert.

In 1986 the audio-products division introduced the first DSP ambiance synthesizer to home audio, and since then the company and its subsidiaries, including Yamaha Corp. of America, established in 1960, have been a dominant force in the world consumer-audio marketplace, producing both affordable and state-of-the-art surround-sound receivers, CD players, cassette and hard-drive CD recorders, and even video projectors, a well as highly regarded professional recording equipment available from the company's pro group. [website: www.yamaha.com.]

HOWARD FERSTLER

YANKOVIC, WEIRD AL

SEE COMEDY RECORDINGS

YARDBIRDS

The Yardbirds are generally considered to be one of the most influential bands in rock history. They anticipated progressive rock by experimenting with an eclectic array of musical styles and helped usher in a new virtuosity, particularly for the electric guitar. They were at the forefront of virtually every notable technical innovation for that instrument during the mid-1960s, including feedback, fuzztone, and modal playing. Nevertheless, the Yardbirds remain best known for extramusical developments: the presence of three of England's greatest rock guitarists — Eric Clapton, Jeff Beck, and Jimmy Page — within the band at one time or another, and the evolution of Page's New Yardbirds into the leading heavy-metal act of the 1970s, Led Zeppelin.

Formed in 1963, the London-based Yardbirds — whose original members included lead singer/harmonica player Keith Relf, drummer Jim McCarty, bassist Paul Samwell-Smith, rhythm guitarist Chris Dreja, and lead guitarist Eric Clapton — built a reputation as a blues-revival band before recording the albums *Five Live Yardbirds* (British Columbia #1677; 1964; reissued in U.S. as bootleg and as CD on Charly #182; 1989) and *Sonny Boy Williamson and the Yardbirds* (Mercury #61071; 1965; reissued as CD by Repertoire #4776; 1999). Clapton departed after the session that produced "For Your Love" (Epic #9790; 1965; #6) — notable for its innovative harpsichord and bongos arrangement — convinced that the band was becoming too commercial. With Beck on lead guitar, the Yardbirds reached their creative and commercial peak on *For Your Love* (Epic #26167; 1965; #96), *Having a Rave Up with the Yardbirds* (Epic #26177; 1965; #53), and *Over Under Sideways Down* (Epic #26210; 1966; #52).

In mid-1966, Samwell-Smith left the band; his replacement, the session veteran Page, sometimes would play second lead guitar, the most notable example being "Happenings Ten Years Time Ago" (Epic #10094; 1966; #30), which featured one of the most dynamic double guitar solos in rock history. However, Beck departed for a solo career in October 1966; the sole album produced by the remaining quartet, *Little Games* (Epic #26313; 1967; #80), featured bland material and stilted arrangements in an attempt to move into the commercial mainstream.

The band dissolved in mid-1968 with Page and Dreja then forming the New Yardbirds, the precursor to Led Zeppelin. Beck, McCarty, Dreja, and Samwell-Smith joined with guitarist Rory Gallagher and keyboardist Max Middleton to record two LPs in the mid-1980s. The Yardbirds' classic recordings, as well as previously unreleased live material and studio out-takes, have continued to be issued in countless retrospectives over the years.

FRANK HOFFMANN

YAW, ELLEN BEACH
(14 SEP 1868–9 SEP 1947)

American soprano, born in Boston. She made her opera debut in London in 1895, and sang at Carnegie Hall in 1896, acclaimed for her remarkable range, from G below middle C to the highest F on the piano. Yaw sang Lucia in Rome in 1907 and at the Metropolitan Opera in the 1907–1908 season. Her first records were made in 1900 for the Gramophone

Co.: the Queen of the Night aria (#3095) and seven others. She recorded four published sides for Victor (1907) and made one Edison Diamond Disc, "Annie Laurie" (#82049; 1913). Yaw also worked for Keen-O-Phone, whose 1914 catalog included her *Mignon* Polonaise (#50001), "Annie Laurie" (#50003) and a song of her own, "Skylark" (#50002). The "Annie Laurie" also appeared as Rex #1054, and on the Rishell label. In the Victor 1917 catalog, Yaw was represented on Red Seal by two of the 1907 recordings: the Bell Song from *Lakme* (#74090) and the "Nightingale's Song" from *Noces de Jeannette* (#74092). She was not in the 1927 catalog. She made some private recordings in 1937 for HMV and in 1941 for Co-Art. IRCC #3082 has "Skylark" and the *Mignon* aria from the Keen-O-Phone material. Yaw died in West Covina, California. [Altamirano 1955.]

YAZOO RECORDS

SEE PERLS, NICK

YEARWOOD, TRISHA (19 SEP 1964–)

The daughter of a small-town banker father and schoolteacher mother, Yearwood was born in Monticello, Georgia. She came to Nashville in 1984 to pursue a music/business degree at Belmont College. She interned at the publicity department at MTM Records, and began doing demo and studio work, where she met another young unknown, Garth Brooks. She was signed to a solo deal in 1991, producing the megahit "She's in Love with the Boy," an uptempo ballad. Pop music agent Ken Kragen, who had overseen Kenny Roger's career, took Yearwood under his professional wing in 1992. Kragen signed her up to a high-visibility contract with Revlon to promote her own perfume, and oversaw the making of her second album. Surprisingly, although the album was well received critically, Yearwood did not achieve the same chart success she had originally, and was in danger of becoming a one-hit wonder. However, despite this slight career detour, Yearwood proved her staying power as a country hitmaker through the 1990s. Major hits include her 1994 "XXXs and OOOs (An American Girl)" and 1998 "I'll Still Love You More." In 1997 she got into something of a mud fight with fellow singer LeAnn Rimes when both recorded Diane Warren's "How Can I Live Without You"; eventually, Rimes had the bigger hit. Yearwood continued to score hits through the end of the decade.

CARL BENSON

Shortlived dance label of the mid-'20s. Courtesy Kurt Nauck/Nauck's Vintage Records

YERKES DANCE RECORDS (LABEL)

An American record issued briefly in 1924 by the Yerkes Recording Laboratories of New York. The founder was Harry A. Yerkes, a successful dance band leader, most prominently as director of the S.S. Flotilla Orchestra. [Kendziora 1982/10; Rust 1978.]

YES

The group epitomized 1970s' progressive rock, featuring meticulously crafted, extended compositions, elaborate thematic concepts reinforced by Roger Dean's fantasy LP cover art, and virtuoso instrumental work. Plagued by constant personnel shifts, legal bickering, and a stylistically dated sound from the late 1970s onward, their legacy is based largely on the ambitious, albeit self-indulgent, early albums.

Formed in London in mid-1968, Yes — originally consisting of lead singer Jon Anderson, bassist Chris Squire, drummer Bill Bruford, guitarist Peter Banks, and keyboardist Tony Kaye — signed with Atlantic, releasing a workmanlike eponymous debut (Atlantic #8243; 1969) and follow-up, *Time and a Word* (Atlantic #8273; 1970; #45 U.K.) that only hinted at the more baroque efforts to come. With the addition of innovative guitarist Steve Howe (replacing Banks, who helped form the jam band Flash) for *The Yes Album* (Atlantic #8283; 1971; #40 U.S., #7 U.K.) and keyboardist Rick Wakeman (following the departure of Kaye) prior to the release of *Fragile* (Atlantic #7211; 1971; #4 U.S., #7 U.K.), the group's signature

sound — the rich, swirling instrumental interplay punctuated by Anderson's high-pitched vocals — reached fruition. The band's commercial breakthrough was assisted by the extensive radio play of the U.S. single "Roundabout/Long Distance Runaround" (Atlantic #2854; 1972; #13), culled from the latter LP.

Yes hit its creative peak with *Close to the Edge* (Atlantic #7244; 1972; #3 U.S., #4 U.K.), featuring the atmospheric title track (which comprised all of side A); the sprawling three-disc live set, *Yessongs* (Atlantic #100; 1973; #12 U.S., #1 U.K.), which now included drummer Alan White; the conceptual double album, *Tales from Topographic Oceans* (Atlantic #2908; 1973; #6 U.S., #1 U.K.), widely criticized for the allegedly aimless improvising of its extended pieces; and impressionistic *Relayer* (Atlantic #18122; 1974; #5 U.S., #4 U.K.), built around the multitracked synthesizer lines contributed by Patrick Moraz, who had been recruited when Wakeman left for a solo career.

Following a hiatus in which group members worked on solo albums, Wakeman returned for the stripped-down *Going for the One* (Atlantic #19106; 1977; #8 U.S., #1 U.K.), released at the height of the U.K. punk revolution. *Tormato* (Atlantic #19202; 1978) and *Drama* (Atlantic #16109; 1980; #18 U.S., #2 U.K.) — the latter featuring two ex-Buggles members, vocalist Trevor Horn and keyboardist Geoff Downes, who replaced Anderson and Wakeman, respectively — revealed the band to be at a creative impasse. Yes revamped their lineup in 1983, adding South African guitarist/songwriter Trevor Rabin to the core of Anderson, Kaye, Squire, and White. The resulting release, *90125* (Atco #90125; 1983; #5 U.S., #16 U.K.), was a major hit with the MTV generation, driven by the chart-topping single, "Owner of a Lonely Heart" (Atco #99817; 1983; #1 U.S., #28 U.K.).

Yes split into two camps during the late 1980s, one including Squire, White, Kaye, and Rabin, the other consisting of Anderson, Bruford, Wakeman, and Howe. The Squire faction won rights to the name in 1989, requiring the latter combination to release an album under the moniker *Anderson, Bruford, Wakeman, Howe* (Arista #90126; #30 U.S., #14 U.K.). The two groups went on to settle their differences, combining forces to release the moribund *Union* (Arista #8643; 1991; #15 U.S., #7 U.K.). The subsequent works, featuring a rotating cast of musicians, revealed Yes to be a creatively bankrupt entity content to trade on past glories.

FRANK HOFFMANN

YETNIKOFF, WALTER (AUG 1933–)

Irascible had of Columbia Records from 1975–1990, Yetnikoff built the label into a major presence in the pop music world, and oversaw its sale to Japanese consumer electronics giant Sony in 1988. Born in Brooklyn, Yetnikoff's father was an immigrant house painter. He worked his way through college and law school, joining Columbia Records in 1961 as an accountant. He became known as a talented artist negotiator at the label, and worked his way steadily up the ranks. In 1975 he replaced Clive Davis at the label as its president, after Davis was embroiled in controversy over alleged illegalities involving fraudulent payments. Yetnikoff quickly befriended Columbia star acts, including Barbra Streisand, Bruce Springsteen, Billy Joel, George Michaels, and Michael Jackson, and brought the Rolling Stones to the label in the early 1980s. However, Yetnikoff often battled with his staff and his bosses, first with CBS head Thomas Wyman and then, when the company was sold to businessman Lawrence Tisch in 1986, Yetnikoff publicly criticized Tisch for his tight-fisted approach to the business. He convinced Tisch to allow him to open negotiations with Sony to buy the label, a deal that was consummated in 1989. At about the same time, he brought on board as his lieutenant talent agent Tommy Mottola. Ironically, within a year Mottola had replaced Yetnikoff as head of the label. At this point Yetnikoff's famous temper, and ties to record promoter/alleged mobster Joseph Isgro, had sullied his reputation. Also, he badly mishandled a deal in which he encouraged Sony to hire the Hollywood producers Jon Peters and Peter Guber, which enflamed rival studio Warner Bros., who still held the duo's contract. The upshot was costly to Sony, and Guber and Peters proved to be inept at managing the studio. Meanwhile, Yetnikoff publicly admitted to problems with substance abuse, entering a clinic for treatment of alcoholism in 1987. In 1996 Yetnikoff returned to the business, opening Vel Vel Records in an attempt to return to the pop music business, but the label was sold three years later to the distributor/record producer Koch International.

CARL BENSON

YOAKAM, DWIGHT (23 OCT 1956–)

Born in Pikeville, Kentucky, Yoakam has helped revive the pure-country sound created by Buck Owens and Merle Haggard in the Bakersfield, California, region in the late 1950s through the mid-1960s. Yoakam's father was serving in the military in Kentucky when he was born, but the family relocated to Cincinnati when Dwight was two. After completing high school and spending a couple of years as a philosophy major at Ohio State, Yoakam moved to Los Angeles. There he became a fixture in the local punk-rock scene; his retro looks and sound seemed to fit in better with a punk sensibility than it did in the day's middle-of-the-road country. The height of Yoakam's chart success in country and pop arenas came in the late 1980s, with songs like "Little Sister" and "Streets of Bakersfield," a duet with Buck Owens that brought him his first number one country tune in 1988. That same year, "I Sang Dixie" followed at the top of the charts. He had a major hit with his cover of "Suspicious Minds" in 1992, originally recorded by Elvis Presley, which Yoakam recut for the film *Honeymoon in Vegas*. Yoakam's last major country hit came in 1993 with "Ain't that Lonely Yet." Six years later, he had a fluke minor pop hit with a cover of Queen's "Crazy Little Thing Called Love," after recording it for a Gap khaki advertisement.

CARL BENSON

YOUNG, FARON
(25 FEB 1932–2 DEC 1996)

Fashions have come and gone during Young's lengthy career, but he remained faithful to his traditional country roots. Born in Shreveport, Louisiana, he practiced guitar chords while tending the family cows on a farm outside of town. Forming his first band at school, he was hired by radio station KWKH. Webb Pierce was sufficiently impressed to hire him as a featured vocalist; they appeared regularly on the popular radio show the *Louisiana Hayride* in 1951.

Young first recorded with Tillman Franks and His Rainbow Boys for Gotham in 1951. After going solo in 1952, he was invited to join the Grand Ole Opry. Now signed to record for Capitol Records, he had his first hit with "Goin' Steady" (Capitol #2299; 1953), a song pitched directly to the teen market. He was a fixture on the country charts for the next four decades, appearing there 88 times through 1988, including the number one singles "Live Fast, Love Hard, Die Young" (Capitol #3056; 1955), "Alone With You" (Capitol #3982; 1958), "Country Girl" (Capitol #4233; 1959), "Hello Walls" (Capitol #4533; 1961), and "It's Four in the Morning" (Mercury #73250; 1971).

Young appeared regularly in films, mostly low-budget productions such as *Stampede*, *Daniel Boone*, *Raiders of Old California*, *Country Music Holiday*, *Road to Nashville*, and *That's Country*. The picture *Hidden Guns* (1956) provided him with his nickname, "The Young Sheriff," and band name, "His Country Deputies." A prosperous businessman, he at one time owned a booking agency, a music publishing form, the Faron Young Executive Building near Music Row, and the magazine *Music City News* (which he also founded). Less active in the 1980s and 1990s, Young took his own life after several years of suffering from emphysema and cancer.

FRANK HOFFMANN

YOUNG, LESTER
(27 AUG 1909–15 MAR 1959)

American saxophonist, born in Woodville, Mississippi. His family settled in New Orleans, where his father taught him several instruments. He played drums in a touring band, then teamed with Art Bronson's Bostonians, taking up the tenor saxophone. Young gained recognition in Minneapolis clubs (the city was his family home from 1919), and in 1933 with Bennie Moten's band in Kansas City, Missouri. He left Kansas City in 1934 with Count Basie, then shifted to Fletcher Henderson — replacing Coleman Hawkins — and rejoined Basie in 1936. He made an important series of appearances with Billie Holiday, led his own band, saw military service, and became famous after World War II in the Jazz at the Philharmonic events staged by Norman Granz. He was a freelancer, struggling with poor health the rest of his life, gradually gaining the status of prime performer on his instrument, "the most influential artist after Armstrong and before Charlie Parker" [Schuller 1989]. His last major engagements were in Paris, and he died shortly after, in New York.

Young was heard on eight sides of the Kansas City Six, notably on his cheap metal clarinet in "I Want a Little Girl" (Commodore #509), illustrating a tender lyrical style, contrasting with the percussive tendency of Hawkins. In a 1939 session for Columbia, with Glenn Hardman and His Hammond Five, Young was featured on sax and clarinet. "Lester Leaps In" was done in 1939 (Vocalion #5118) with the Kansas City Seven for the Keynote label, offering a loose and biting line. Young was with King Cole in 1942, recording a remarkable "Body and Soul" (Philo #1000) and an inspired "These Foolish Things" (Philo/Aladdin #142) that kept the spirit of the melody without sounding it. Records made immediately after Young's military service show signs of decline in his powers, but in 1950–1951 he was superbly supported by pianist John Lewis in some sides of great brilliance, e.g., "Let's Fall in Love"; and there was another resurgence with the Oscar Peterson Trio in 1952, notably in "I Can't Get Started" — all these on the Verve label, and reissued on CD.

Young's CD discography is large, consisting of many reissues of his original 78s and LPs in various formats, from complete sets for the true fan to overviews for the casual listener. There are also many "semiofficial" reissues, mostly on European jazz labels, that vary in sound quality and selection from just barely passable to excellent. In the LP days, Columbia issued a series of two-LP sets somewhat misleadingly titled *The Lester Young Story*; Young never recorded as a leader for this label, so these sets collect all of his sideman work, but that's not necessarily a bad thing as it includes his great sessions with Count Basie and his famous accompaniments for Billie

Holiday. (Although not available from Columbia in this format on CD, the Young material can be found on Columbia reissues of Basie's and Holiday's work.) *The Complete Savoy Recordings* (Savoy Jazz #17122) is a two-CD compilation of all 46 tunes recorded by Young for that label between 1945–1949. *The Complete Lester Young Studio Sessions on Verve* is an eight-CD set containing all of his recordings for Norman Granz's Verve and associated labels from 1946–1959 (Verve #547087) is for the diehard Young fan; most of this material is also available in compilations and/or reissues of the original albums.

YOUNG, NEIL (12 NOV 1945–)

Neil Young is one of the great talents, albeit highly idiosyncratic, within the rock music scene. An accomplishment composer and sensitive song interpreter, his material often seemed ill-suited to his singing capabilities, reducing his vocals to an off-key whine. A lyrical, intense guitar player, his extended pieces could sometimes meander aimlessly. Nevertheless, it could be argued that the refusal to be predictable, even to the point of undercutting his commercial potential, has been a major factor in his retaining a substantial following since the 1960s.

Born in Toronto, Young's earliest recordings — *Buffalo Springfield* (Atco #200; 1967; #80), *Buffalo Springfield Again* (Atco #226; 1967; #44), and *Last Time Around* (Atco #256; 1968; #42) — were as a member of the short-lived folk-rock group, Buffalo Springfield. His early solo releases — *Neil Young* (Reprise #6317; 1969), *Everybody Knows This Is*

Neil Young's second album. Courtesy Frank Hoffmann

Nowhere (Reprise #6349; 1969; #34), *After the Gold Rush* (Reprise #6383; 1970; #8), and *Harvest* (Reprise #2032; 1972; #1) — combined a profound melodic gift, augmented by evocative lyrics and tight ensemble playing. Young's career — which peaked commercially with the number one single, "Heart of Gold" (Reprise #1065; 1972) — was assisted by his brief association with the supergroup, Crosby, Stills, and Nash. Two best-selling LPS — *Déjà Vu* (Atlantic #7200; 1970; #1) and the live *4 Way Street* (Atlantic #902; 1971; #1) — resulted from this collaboration and, while Young remained cool to later reunions, he did contribute to *American Dream* (Atlantic #81888; 1988; #16).

Beginning with his tentative experimental film soundtrack, *Journey Through the Past* (Warner Bros. #6480; 1972; #45), Young seemed committed to producing an uncompromising body of recorded work, the expectations of his audience be damned. His albums have revealed a passing interest in a wide range of styles, including techno (*Trans* [Geffen #2018; 1983; #19]), country (*Old Ways* [Geffen #24068; 1985; #75]), rhythm and blues (*This Note's For You* [Reprise #25719; 1988; #61]), rockabilly (*Everybody's Rockin'* [Geffen #4013; 1983; #46]), and white noise (*Arc/Weld* [Reprise #26746; 1991; #154]). But far more disconcerting than Young's stylistic hop-scotching has been his tendency to veer between perfunctory studio exercises to inspired masterpieces; for instance, the dissonant formalism of *On the Beach* (Reprise #2180; 1974; #16) was succeeded by the harrowing tension of *Tonight's the Night* (Reprise #2221; 1975; #25), the bland, folk-pop of *Comes a Time* (Reprise #2266; 1978; #7), and the revivalist rock of *Rust Never Sleeps* (Reprise #2295; 1979; #8).

One of the few 1960s generation musicians to have openly espoused the work of postpunk bands and rappers alike, Young was inducted into the Rock and Roll Hall of Fame in 1995. Still a force in the marketplace — his collaboration with alternative rockers Pearl Jam, *Mirror Ball* (Reprise #45934; 1995), reached number five on the pop albums chart — Young appears capable of producing vital recordings well into the 21st century.

FRANK HOFFMANN

Z

ZAENTZ, SAUL (21 FEB 1921–)

Perhaps best known as an independent movie producer — three of his films, *One Flew Over the Cuckoo's Nest* (1975), *Amadeus* (1984), and *The English Patient* (1996), won the Academy award for Best Picture — Saul Zaentz has also found commercial and artistic success heading the Berkeley-based Fantasy Records. Many rock fans remember his legal efforts to halt distribution of John Fogerty's diatribe regarding Fantasy's tight-fisted fiscal practices, "Zanz Kant Danz," from the LP *Centerfield* (Warner Bros. #25203; 1985; #1).

Born in Passaic, New Jersey, Zaentz was active in record distribution following World War II. In 1955, following a brief stint with Norman Granz's jazz recording enterprises, he began working for Fantasy, the label that first recorded cool jazz pianist Dave Brubeck, satirical comedian Lenny Bruce, and roots rock band Creedence Clearwater Revival. With the support of an investment group, he purchased the company in 1967. Hit recordings by Creedence and other pop-oriented artists such as Vince Guaraldi — whose biggest success came with "Cast Your Fate to the Wind" (Fantasy #563; 1962; #22) — enabled Fantasy to become the largest jazz label worldwide by the 1970s. Its roster has included the Blackbyrds, Freddie Hubbard, Wes Montgomery, and Merle Saunders, among others, as well as the back catalogs of legendary labels such as Prestige.

See also **Creedence Clearwater Revival; Fantasy Records (Label)**

FRANK HOFFMANN

ZAPPA, FRANK
(21 DEC 1940–4 DEC 1993)

Born Francis Vincent Zappa, Jr., in Baltimore, Zappa had a long career as a composer, performer, and record label executive who often fought the music industry. Zappa's father worked for the government as a scientist, but played guitar as a hobby. When Frank was 10, the family moved to Southern California, settling in Lancaster. As a teenager, Zappa learned to play many different instruments, as well as developing a love for a wide variety of music, from 1950s doo-wop to the avant-garde experimentations of Edgard Varèse. Between 1960–1964, Zappa composed film soundtracks for low-budget movies, wrote pop songs (co-composing "Memories of El Monte" with Ray Collins for the vocal group, the Penguins), and worked as a studio musician. In 1964 he joined the Soul Giants, a local blues-rock band, which he took over as leader and rechristened the Mothers. Heard by pop producer Tom Wilson, who was then working for Verve Records, the group was signed to a contract and recorded their first album, which was released in 1965. Zappa proved to be a prolific, and wide-ranging, composer/record producer; in 1967 he produced with the Mothers the albums *Absolutely Free* (Verve #65013), featuring tape montage and other avant-garde techniques linking its satiric songs, and the Beatles' satire, *We're Only in It for the Money* (featuring its famous cover parodying *Sergeant Pepper*'s; Verve #65045), and in 1968 followed with two spinoff projects, *Lumpy Gravy* (Verve #68741; featuring a 50-piece orchestra) and the doo-wop homage, *Cruising with Reuben and the Jets* (Verve #65055). In 1968 Zappa signed a

Frank Zappa in the control room of his home studio, 1988. © Lynn Goldsmith/CORBIS

dealer with Warner/Reprise to create his own labels, Bizarre and Straight, recording early work by Alice Cooper, the all-girl rock group the G.T.O.s, and seminal avant-garde rocker Captain Beefheart (a longtime Zappa associate and friend). Briefly disbanding the Mothers in 1970, Zappa produced the symphonic soundtrack for his film *200 Motels* (United Artists #[2]9956) and *Hot Rats* (Bizarre #6356), a jazz-rock collaboration with French violinist Jean-Luc Ponty. (Zappa also composed and produced the music for Ponty's first solo album at the same time.)

Zappa's work through the 1970s varied in quality, although not in quantity, as he continued to be a prolific recording artist with both various versions of the Mothers and as a "solo" artist. He also produced other acts, including Grand Funk Railroad. In 1979 Zappa formed a new label, the self-named Zappa Records, distributed by Mercury, but his controversial material soon lead to Mercury ending the deal. In 1981 Zappa returned with his own Barking Pumpkin Records, distributed by Columbia/CBS. A year later, he had a major pop hit with his satiric "Valley Girl" (Barking Pumpkin #02972), featuring his daughter, Moon Unit, speaking in the popular Southern California slang. Meanwhile, Zappa's reputation as a composer continued

to grow; in 1984 Pierre Boulez released an album of Zappa's compositions, *Boulez Conducts Zappa: The Perfect Stranger* (Angel #38170), which reached number seven on the classical charts. In 1985, angered by the growing demands for labeling of pop records by groups like the Parents Music Resource Center, Zappa testified before Congress on behalf of freedom of expression. He also made a licensing deal with Rykodisc to re-release his back catalog on CD.

In 1991 it was announced that Zappa was suffering from cancer. Still composing, primarily using electronic equipment, Zappa continued to release new compositions nearly to the end of his life. He died in his Los Angeles home.

CARL BENSON

ZARVAH ART (LABEL)
An American record of 1922, the name derived from the names of its founders, Zarh Myron Bickford and Vahdah Olcott-Bickford, its home being in the Zarvah Art Record Co. of New York. The two Bickfords played a guitar-mandolin duet on one of the few sides issued. [Rust 1978.]

ZENATELLO, GIOVANNI
(22 FEB 1876– 11 FEB 1949)

Italian tenor, born in Verona. He began as a baritone, singing Silvio in his 1898 debut. After further study he made a second debut, also in *Pagliacci*, this time as Canio (Naples, 1901). He created the role of Pinkerton at La Scala on 17 Feb 1904, and sang Enzo in *Gioconda* for his American debut in New York in 1907. Zenatello did not appear with the Metropolitan Opera, but sang with the Boston Opera in 1909–1914, with the Chicago Opera, and then on extended world tours. He retired in 1928, and settled with his wife, soprano Maria Gay, to teach in New York, where he died.

Zenatello was a prolific maker of phonograph discs, commencing with nine G & T sides in Milan in 1903, including the "Improvviso" from *Andrea Chenier* (#52702), "Salve dimora" ("Salut demeure") from *Faust* (#52703), and "Donna non vidi mai" from *Manon Lescaut* (#52721). He went to the Fonotipia label from 1905 to 1911, and turned out about 100 records from the Italian/French repertoire; among them were two sides from *Madama Butterfly*, some seven years after the premiere. An outstanding disc from this series was "Sulla tomba," the *Lucia* duet, with Maria Barrientos (#39825).

In the U.S. Zenatello worked with Columbia from 1912, and made Edison Diamond Discs from 1921 to 1922, starting with the tomb duet from *Aida*, with Maria Rappold (#83035). Then he recorded in Europe again, for HMV, doing one of his famous roles, Otello. His last discs were for Victor in 1928–1930. Zenatello was one of the few opera singers who recorded a duet with his wife (Maria Gay): "Ai nostri monti" (Columbia #A5370). LP reissues were extensive, from IRCC, Rococo, Eterna, and Belcanto Disc; among the CD reissues are a sampler/overview (Preisser #89038) and *The Collected Recordings* on Pearl (two four-CD sets, #9073, #9074) [Hutchinson 1962.]

ZIMBALIST, EFREM
(21 APR 1889–22 FEB 1985)

Russian/American violinist, born in Rostov-on-the-Don. He took a gold medal at the St. Petersburg Conservatory, as a student of Leopold Auer. After European concertizing in his teens, he emigrated to the U.S. in 1911. He performed with the Boston Symphony Orchestra on 27 Oct 1911, and then with many orchestras and in recital. His second wife was Mary Louise Curtis Bok, founder of the Curtis Institute of Music in Philadelphia, which Zimbalist directed from 1941 to 1968. He retired to Reno, Nevada, where he died. His son, Efrem Zimbalist, Jr., became a noted film actor.

Zimbalist recorded prolifically. There were 20 solos in the Victor 1917 catalog, and duets with Alma Gluck (his first wife) and Fritz Kreisler. The Kreisler duet was the first recording of J.S. Bach's Concerto for Two Violins (Victor #76028/29). In his records Zimbalist did not exploit the great repertoire of the instrument, but focused on arrangements, such as "Old Black Joe" (Victor #64640) and César Cui's "Orientale." His recordings were deleted from the catalog after the 1920s. On CD, Pearl 32 offers a selection of Zimbalist's classic recordings, and Doremi 7739 offers *Plays Brahms*, including the Concerto in D Major, Op. 77, and Sonata for Violin & Piano No. 3 in D minor, Op. 108.

ZINES

The earliest fanzines were independent publications mimeographed by passionate science fiction fans. Their circulation within that subculture began around 1930. Sometimes the writers critiqued SF, but they were more likely to go off on weird tangents, a tendency that holds true in zines today.

The first rock zines were the product of young science fiction readers who understood the mechanics of self-publishing, and sought to apply their skills to analyzing contemporary pop. Paul Williams's somewhat academic *Crawdaddy* (launched February 1966) just predates Greg Shaw's more fannish *Mojo-Navigator*, which with its base in the Haight-Ashbury proved an important document of the San Francisco psychedelic scene. Another emerging late 1960s media outlet was the underground paper which, in addition to political and satiric content, typically included music reviews.

Prezine, pop coverage was limited to publicist-driven promotional material in teen magazines like *Tiger Beat* and *Dig,* or short blurbs in adult titles like *Playboy* and *Esquire*. With their lengthy, thoughtful record reviews that treated popular records as art deserving serious consideration, zines helped establish a critical language. Soon *Rolling Stone, Circus,* and *Creem* were adapting fannish passions to more professional publishing ventures.

By the early 1970s, rock criticism was attracting smart, daring writers, some of whom developed personality cults similar to those of the rock stars they chronicled. Richard Meltzer's compulsive self-analysis and Lester Bangs's Romilar-fueled diatribes frequently drew attention away from their excellent analytical work. Small magazines like Greg Shaw's historically minded *Bomp*, Los Angeles's proto-punk *Back Door Man*, and the long-lived *Zig Zag* in the U.K. were sought out by music fiends desperate for intelligent, informed criticism and access to the growing number of self-released records.

The punk scene spawned many zines, which helped spread the do-it-yourself philosophy and propagated the raw graphic style — partly derived from earlier Situationist and Lettrist small press publications — which would become synonymous with the movement. Influential titles included *Slash*, *Search and Destroy*, *Punk*, *Sniffin' Glue,* and *Maximum RocknRoll.*

By the turn of the 1990s, the zine scene was thriving. Mike Gunderloy's science fiction fan newsletter *Factsheet 5* had evolved into a huge compendium of reviews and contact addresses. Publications occupied more eclectic zones, with straight music titles giving way to cultural journals heavily salted with personal, highly confessional writing ("per-zines") and, all too often, stories about serial killers. Important zines of this period include *Forced Exposure, Breakfast Without Meat, Answer Me!, Bananafish,* and *Rollerderby.* There remained a strong market for collector-style music magazines like *Kicks, Unhinged,* and *Ugly Things,* with their focus on rootsy obscurities.

Zining has always been heavily influenced by the available technology. In the late 1960s, underground papers thrived due to offset printing, which was cheaper and less messy than mimeography, and allowed for large, fast print runs. But the technological leap that would have the greatest impact on zining was the ubiquity of the photocopy machine, which from the late 1970s became the instrument of tens of thousands of self-publishers. Home computers freed zinesters from their dependence on blue line paper and rubber cement, and eventually the internet made physical printing unnecessary. And while there remain a small number of excellent zines committed to publishing on paper today, there are far more that maintain a presence on the web.

KIM COOPER

ZITHER RECORDINGS (HISTORIC)

This instrument was heard on very early records: there were 14 cylinders by Bettini in 1898, all by a Professor D. Wormser. The same artist made six records for Edison in 1899–1902, and about 20 Columbia cylinders ca. 1899. Sometime after 1908 he began to work for Victor; there were eight records in the 1917 Victor catalog. Zither music was made up of arrangements, with much of the Wormser repertoire drawn from German folksongs. The zither category was dropped from Victor catalogs in the 1920s. A revival of interest in the instrument occurred after its featured appearance in the motion picture *Third Man* (1949), with Anton Karas performing "The Harry Lime Theme" and other numbers; Decca recorded two LP albums by Karas (#LF 1053 and #LF 1145).

ZIV [FREDERIC W.] CO.

An American firm, located in Cincinnati, producer or syndicator of about 7,050 radio programs plus many television programs. Transcriptions of certain series are of interest to collectors, e.g., those that covered Wayne King, Guy Lombardo, and Freddy Martin. Extensive lists of the titles were compiled by David Kressley [1983].

ZOBEL O.J.

SEE LOUDSPEAKER

ZOMBA

Music publishing and recording group founded by Clive Calder in the mid-1970s. It is best known for its Jive Records label, begun in 1981 to release rap recordings, but which in the mid-1990s scored major success with teen pop stars Britney Spears and boy bands the Backstreet Boys and 'N Sync, and grew to be the largest independent label in the U.S. In 1991 Bertelsmann Music Group purchased 25 percent of Zomba's music publishing holdings, and five years later 20 percent of its recording labels. Under the deal, Calder received options that effectively forced Bertelsmann to purchase the balance of the company by the end of 2002; the deal was finalized in late September. At the time, it was announced that Calder would remain as an "advisor," but as of late November, Calder had resigned from the company, as did his chief A&R staff, but BMG was in talks trying to hold on to these executives. At the same time, the Backstreet Boys sued Zomba, claiming the label failed to pay a promised $5 million advance and canceled their fourth album, instead focusing on lead singer's Nick Carter's career.

CARL BENSON

ZONOPHONE

A disc record player made by the Universal Talking Machine Co. and marketed for $25 by the National Gramophone Co. from October 1898; Frank Seaman was associated with the former company and the founder of the latter. The machine was merely a Berliner Gramophone, and indeed the first advertising referred to it as the "Improved Gramophone (Zon-O-Phone)." Eldridge Johnson had been the developer of the Improved Gramophone, based on the original machines of Emile Berliner, and Seaman had been a successful authorized promoter of it for Berliner Gramophone Co. But the new name for the product brought conflicts between Seaman and Berliner (and Johnson). In June 1900 Berliner stopped doing business with Seaman, but

Seaman obtained a court injunction that actually prevented Berliner from selling Berliner products — as Seaman had the exclusive sales contract for all the U.S. except the Washington, D.C., area. This dispute was complicated by an earlier action (October 1898) brought against Seaman by the Columbia (Graphophone) interests for infringement of their patents. During the ensuing litigation, the Universal Co. was tooling up to manufacture genuine Zonophone machines, and the National Gramophone Co. business in Berliner products was acquired by a new firm, the National Gramophone Corp., established March 1889, with Seaman as treasurer. Modifications were introduced, so that differences could be noted between the Zonophone and its parent Gramophone; for example the winding crank was moved to rotate parallel to the side of the machine, instead of parallel to the surface. Nevertheless, the court order did materialize, and both Seaman and the National Gramophone Corp. were enjoined in May 1900 from producing or selling any more talking machines, under any name whatsoever. A consent agreement between National Gramophone Corp./Universal Talking Machine Co. and Columbia Phonograph Co., General, gave Columbia an entry into the disc and disc player market by use of the Zonophone line.

When the National Gramophone Corp. failed in 1901, a new manufacturer of the Zonophones was established by the name of Universal Talking Machine Manufacturing Co., the original Universal firm becoming the temporary sales outlet. Zonophones were exported to Europe, and the International Zonophone Co. was founded in New York and Berlin in spring 1901 to control the business. In June 1903 the Gramophone and Typewriter Co., Ltd., purchased the two Universal companies and the majority of stock shares in International Zonophone. In Europe Zonophone machines remained on the market. They continued to be available in the U.S. as well, but from September 1903 under the Victor Talking Machine Co. — which was sold to the American end of the Zonophone business by G & T. Because the Universal Talking Machine Manufacturing Co. had not been licensed by Columbia, that firm brought a successful action against it for patent infringement, and the Zonophone business in America was terminated by court order in 1912. The European Zonophone business continued.

FRANK ANDREWS

ZONOPHONE (LABEL) (ALSO WRITTEN AS ZON-O-PHONE; LATER STYLED ZONOPHONE RECORD)

An American record produced by the Universal Talking Machine Co. (established 10 Feb 1898). It was marketed by the National Gramophone Corp., in

which Frank Seaman had a strong commitment, once Seaman had ceased ordering Gramophones from the Berliner Gramophone Co., Berliner retaliated by refusing to deliver discs to Seaman's agency. The earliest discs suitable for the new Zonophone machines were modified "Berliners" which were either copied or had a hole drilled through near their centers to locate on the peg in the first Zonophone turntables, as an antiskid device.

Actual manufacture of the discs may have been done at the Yonkers, New York, factory of the Universal Talking Machine Co., with materials provided by the Burt Co. or the Auburn Button Works. Records with the Zonophone name went on sale in spring 1900, in seven-inch size, single-faced, through the National Gramophone Corp. But on 5 May 1900 the company was enjoined by a U.S. court, following an action brought by the Columbia interests, its machines and discs deemed in infringement of Columbia patents. However, two weeks later both National Gramophone Corp. and the manufacturing arm, Universal Talking Machine Co., were licensed by the Columbia interests to make and sell the Zonophone products.

One year later, a nine-inch diameter "Superba" disc was introduced — later described as the "Concert" size record. The seven-inch disc, designated the "Parlour" size, was also marketed. Selections from both sizes were exported to Europe for inclusion in the catalogs of the International Zonophone Co. and its agencies. But in the very month that International Zonophone issued its first lists, September 1901, National Gramophone Corp. went into liquidation. There was a reorganization of the Zonophone business in New York, after which the discs underwent a change. They were then made of a brown material, with paper labels (following the example of the International Zonophone discs), and were styled as a Universal Zonophone Record. Further changes ensued after Victor acquired the American end of the Zonophone businesses from their new (June 1903) owners: The Gramophone and Typewriter Co., Ltd. The seven- and nine-inch discs were terminated and in September 1903 new sizes appeared: 10-inch, 11-inch, and 12-inch. The new discs were of black material with labels printed gold on green or gold on black, and became double-sided before Universal Talking Machine Manufacturing Co. was court-ordered out of business in 1912. That action followed from the claim of patent infringement by the Columbia interests.

In European countries, from September 1901, Zonophone Records — and labels with local translations of the name — began coming from the Berlin presses. Agents were appointed in many countries, who arranged the contracting of artists and then for advertising and sales in their respective territories.

1217

Where no agencies were contracted, International Zonophone dealt with dealers directly and arranged for its own recordings through representatives.

Zonophone Records had different price categories in the seven-inch and 10-inch sizes. Label colors were black, orange, or blue, according to celebrity status of the artists. In Italy there was a dark blue Disco Reale, but it is uncertain whether that line was out before or after the Gramophone and Typewriter Co. took control of International Zonophone (June 1903). In 1902 double-sided Zonophone discs were produced for Casa Edison, a South American agency — they were the first double-sided discs to be marketed.

Under Gramophone and Typewriter, International Zonophone was used to produce cheaper records than the regular G & T lines. Green labels were substituted for black, and the higher-priced labels were gradually phased out. Double-sided Zonophone Records were sold on the continent before they were sold in the U.K., where Zonophone remained single-faced until May 1911. At that time the Zonophone catalog was merged with that of the Twin Record Co., Ltd. (a Gramophone Co. subsidiary), and nearly all Zonophones became coupled as "Zonophone Record — The Twin." Exceptions were the Zonophone Grand Opera Records, which remained single until 1913. Zonophone Records persisted in the U.K. (the name simplified to Zonophone in 1926) until December 1932, when the catalog was merged with Regal to become "Regal-Zonophone." Regal-Zonophone continued to 1949.

Two price wars in Europe brought the introduction of the brown-label Zonophone Record (September 1909) and the cheap lilac label (September 1913). In many countries Zonophone Records were converted into green-label HMV discs from ca. 1911. Zonophones had separate catalogs in various parts of the U.K.

In America, Zonophone's early repertoire was simply taken over from Berliner discs. Later material was comparable to other cheaper American labels, mostly dance and popular vocals. Material on the British Zonophone records came from Victor masters (including jazz and dance music, plus country music) and from recording in Europe. The most famous Zonophone records were made by the Italian branch, in 1903: 10 numbers by the young Enrico Caruso. [Andrews 1989.]

FRANK ANDREWS

ZONOPHONE QUARTET

SEE RAMBLER MINSTREL CO.

ZORN, JOHN (12 SEP 1953–)

John Zorn is — with the possible exception of Bill Laswell — the most prolific avant-garde composer/musician active today; his recordings span musique concrete, free jazz, fusion, bebop, hardcore, film soundtrack compositions, world music, and the European classical tradition. In order to document the full breadth of his eclectic experiments, Zorn has recorded for a wide range of independent and European labels as well as Elektra/Nonesuch, issuing albums both as a solo artist and under various group configurations. His collaborators read like a who's who of cutting-edge art music, jazz, and rock, including Laswell, Derek Bailey, George Lewis, Bill Frisell, Vernon Reid, Fred Frith, Wayne Horovitz, Bobby Previte, Albert Collins, Yamatsuka Eye, and the Kronos Quartet.

Born in Brooklyn, Zorn had developed a highly personalized approach to composition and improvisation prior to emerging as a creative force on New York's Lower East Side in the mid-1970s. While mining the free-jazz genre, he recorded his first solo albums — including *School* (1978), *Pool* (Parachute #0011/12; 1980), and *Archery* (Parachute #0017/18; 1981), reissued as part of the seven-CD set, *The Parachute Years* (Tzadik #7607; 1995) — all of which were initially limited to the European market. Zorn's first major label release, *The Big Gundown* (Elektra/Nonesuch #979139; 1986) — a skewed take on Ennio Marricone's cinema compositions — represented an early manifestation of his lifelong fascination with television and film.

While issuing stylistically diverse solo albums at a dizzying pace — *News for Lulu* (Hat Art #6005; 1987), a bebop tribute, was followed three months later by *Spillane* (Elektra/Nonesuch #979172; 1986), which featured conflicting fragments of sound spliced together — he became increasingly involved in a seemingly endless array of side projects. Naked City explored postpunk styles such as grindcore; beginning with *Naked City* (Elektra/Nonesuch #979238; 1990), the band issued six LPs through 1994. Painkiller veered even closer to speed metal with *Guts of a Virgin* (Earache #045; 1991) and *Buried Secrets* (Earache #062; 1992). Masada and Bar Kokhba, two units devoted to Yiddish/Middle Eastern music, produced more than a dozen albums between 1995–2000. Other platforms have included his Spy vs. Spy band, dedicated to reinterpreting Ornette Coleman's work within a postmodern rock context, East Asian bar bands, and deconstruction of classical music formats such as the string quartet and piano concerto

FRANK HOFFMANN

Bibliography and Key to Citations

This bibliography includes works cited in brackets at the end of articles as well as general resources in the field of recorded sound.

When an author has multiple citations for the same year, original bracketed citations are included at the end of bibliography entries. Serial columns in periodicals list the month of publication after the year, so that [Andrews 1978/3] refers to Frank Andrews column in *Talking Machine Review International* in March of 1978, while [Andrews 1978/4] refers to his review in April.

In other cases where sources could be misidentified, original bracketed citations are similarly included at end of bibliography entries.

The bibliography has been revised and updated for this second edition by Bruce Hall.

Abell, G.O., L.E. Abell, and James F.E. Dennis. "Richard Tauber." *Record Collector* 18-8/12 (Oct.–Dec. 1969): 171–272; 19-3/4 (June 1970): 81–86.

Adamson, P.G. "Berliner Labels." *Talking Machine Review International* 24 (Oct. 1973): 247–254.

———. "Berliner and 7-inch G & T Records." *Talking Machine Review International* 65/66 (1983): 1793–1794. A commentary on Rust 1981.

Adrian, Karlo, and Arthur Badrock. *Edison Bell Winner Records*. Rev. ed. Bournemouth, England: Talking Machine Review, 1989. 9 parts in 1 vol.; unpaged. (1st ed. 1974)

Aeppli, Felix. *Heart of Stone; The Definitive Rolling Stones Discography, 1962–1983*. Ann Arbor, Mich.: Pierian Press, 1985. 575 p.

Aldridge, Benjamin L. *The Victor Talking Machine Company*. Camden, N.J.: RCA Sales Corp., 1964. 120 p. Reprinted in Fagan & Moran 1983.

Allen, Walter C. *King Joe Oliver*. Stanhope, N.J.: Author, 1955; London: Sidgwick & Jackson, 1959. 224 p.

———. *Hendersonia: The Music of Fletcher Henderson and His Musicians; A Bio-discography*. Highland Park, N.J.: Author, 1973. 651 p.

———, ed. *Studies in Jazz Discography. I. Proceedings of the First and Second Annual Conferences on Discographical Research, 1968–1969, and of the Conference on the Preservation and Extension of the Jazz Heritage, 1969*. New Brunswick, N.J.: Rutgers University, Institute of Jazz Studies, 1971. 112 p.

Albert, George and Frank Hoffmann. *The Cash Box Black Contemporary Charts, 1960–1984*. Metuchen, NJ: Scarecrow Press, 1986.

Altamirano, Antonio. "Ellen Beach Yaw." *Record Collector* 10-7 (Dec. 1955): 149–161.

Andrews, Frank. "The 'Jumbo' Story As I See It." *Hillandale News* 61 (June 1971): 21–22. [Andrews 1971/1]

———. "Toward the Complete Documentation of All So-Called 78 RPM Records." *Talking Machine Review International* 12 (Oct. 1971): 108–110. [Andrews 1971/2]

———. "Record Research No. 5." *Talking Machine Review International* 16 (June 1972): 108–210.

———. "Lambert in Britain." *Talking Machine Review International* 27 (Apr. 1974): 70–91; 29 (Aug. 1974): 152. [Andrews 1974/4]

———. "Guiniphones." *Hillandale News* 80 (Oct. 1974): 233–235. [Andrews 1974/5]

———. "The International Indestructible Cylinder Records." *Talking Machine Review International* 30 (Oct. 1974): 190–196. [Andrews 1974/10]

———. "The North American Phonograph Company." *Talking Machine Review International* 38 (Feb. 1976): 571–582. [Andrews 1976/2]

———. "A Fonotipia Fragmentia." *Talking Machine Review International* 40, 41, 42, 44, 45, 48, 49b (1976–1977). Serialized in seven parts. [Andrews 1976/5]

———. "Some Errors in the Society's Cylinder Catalogues." *Hillandale News* 90 (June 1976): 508–509. [Andrews 1976/6]

———. "The Columbia Bubble Books." *Hillandale News* 92 (Oct. 1976): 46–49. [Andrews 1976/10]

———. "Minstrels, Minstrel Shows, and Early Recordings." *Talking Machine Review International* 47 (1977): 1,063–1,066, 1,071–1,076. [Andrews 1977/1]

———. "The Recordings of 1907 in Britain." *Hillandale News* 98 (Oct. 1977): 239–241. [Andrews 1977/10]

———. "Neophone." *Talking Machine Review International* 51 (Apr. 1978): 1,304–1,313; 52/53 (June–Aug. 1978): 1,333–1,339; 54/55 (Oct.–Dec. 1978): 1,397–1,400. [Andrews 1978/3]

———. "EdisoniaEdison Bell." *Talking Machine Review International* 51 (Apr. 1978): 1,301–1,302. [Andrews 1978/4]

———. "Star Records." *Talking Machine Review International* 60/61 (Oct.–Dec. 1979): 1,617–1,622; 68 (June 1984): 1,873–1,874. [Andrews 1979/10]

———. "A Further Look at the International Zonophone Company, May 1901 to June 1903." *Talking Machine Review International* 62 (1980); 1,691–1,696; 63/64 (1981): 1,717–1,725; 65/66 (Feb. 1983): 1,811–1,818. [Andrews 1980/2]

———. "From Orchestrelle to Vocalion; An Account of the Aeolian Companies and Their Involvement with Talking Machines." *Hillandale News* 116 (Oct. 1980): 99–106; 117 (Nov. 1980): 120–155. [Andrews 1980/10]

———. "British Brunswick; The History of Brunswick Cliftophone, Brunswick Cliftophone Ltd., and Brunswick in the 1920s." *Hillandale News* 122 (Oct. 1981): 265–273. [Andrews 1981/1]

———. "Broadcast: The Story of a Record." *Hillandale News* 129 (Dec. 1982): 126–131; 130 (Feb. 1983): 148–149. [Andrews 1982/12]

———. "The History of the Crystalate Companies in the Recording Industry, 1901–1937." *Hillandale News* 134 (Oct. 1983): 259–290; 135 (Dec. 1983): 291–297; 136 (Feb. 1984): 317–324. [Andrews 1983/10]

———. "Duo-Trac." *Hillandale News* 137 (Apr. 1984): 16–23. [Andrews 1984/4]

———. "Genuine Edison Bell Records." *Hillandale News* 141 (Dec. 1984): 125–130; 142 (Mar. 1985): 159–164; 143 (Apr. 1985): 179–184; 145 (Aug. 1985): 233–242. [Andrews 1978/12]

———. "Imperial Records." *Talking Machine Review International* 69 (Dec. 1984): 1,908–1,912. [Andrews 1984/12]

———. *Columbia Ten-Inch Records Issued 1904 to 1930.* London: City of London Phonograph and Gramophone Society, 1985. Unpaged. Lists U.K. issues of the various Columbia labels. [Andrews 1985/1]

———. "The Birth of Electrical Recording." *Hillandale News* 144 (1985): 199–202. [Andrews 1985/6]

———. "Homophone in Britain." *Hillandale News* 147 (Dec. 1985): 284–290; 148 (Dec. 1986): 312–317; 149 (Apr. 1986): 5–8; 150 (June 1986): 32–35. [Andrews 1985/12; 1986/4]

———. *The Edison Phonograph; The British Connection.* Rugby, England: City of London Phonograph and Gramophone Society, 1986. 140 p.

———. "The Coming and Demise of the Marathon Records and Machines." *Talking Machine Review International* 72 (Apr. 1987): 2,081–2,105. [Andrews 1987/4]

———. "The His Master's Voice Record Catalogues." *Hillandale News* 158 (Oct. 1987): 255–261; 159 (Dec. 1987): 284–291; 160 (Feb. 1988): 320–329. [Andrews 1987/10]

———. "John Bull Records and Ercophone Gramophones." *Talking Machine Review International* 73 (Feb. 1988): 2,139–2,150. [Andrews 1988/2]

———. "The Under-Twenty-Fives; A History of British Disc Records of Less than 25 cm (10 Inch) Diameter." *Hillandale News* 161 (Apr. 1988): 6–11; 162 (June 1988): 40–46. [Andrews 1988/4]

———. "Joseph Leonard Blum and His Gramophone Records." *Talking Machine Review International* 75 (Autumn 1988): 2,182–2,196. [Andrews 1988/10]

———. "The Zonophone Record and Its Associated Labels in Britain" *Hillandale News* 166 (Feb. 1989): 150–156; 167/168 (June 1989): 206–211. Corrections by Andrews in *Hillandale News* 170 (Oct. 1989): 276.

———. "Nipper's Uncle; William Barraud and His Disc Records." *Hillandale News* 174 (June 1990): 37–42; 175 (Aug. 1990): 67–72; 176 (Oct. 1990): 112–116; 177 (Dec. 1990): 134–138.

———. "Records in Store." *Hillandale News* 181 (Aug. 1991): 268–276.

Andrews, Frank, and Ernie Bayly. *Billy Williams Records: A Study in Discography.* Bournemouth, England: Talking Machine Review, 1982. 72 p.

Annand, H. H. *The Complete Catalogue of the United States Everlasting Indestructible Cylinders, 1905–1913.* London: City of London Phonograph and Gramophone Society, 1966. 38 p.

———. *Block Catalogue of the Cylinder Records Issued by the U.S. Phonograph Company, 1890–1896.* Hillingdon, Middlesex, England, 1970.

———. *The Catalogue of the United States Everlasting Indestructible Cylinders, 1980–1913.* 2nd ed. Bournemouth, England: Talking Machine Review International, 1973. 36 p.

Aranza, Jacob. *Backward Masking Unmasked.* Shreveport, La.: Huntington House, 1984. 115 p.

Arfanis, Stathis A., and Nick Nickson. 1990. *The Complete Discography of Dimitri Mitropoulos.* Athens: IRINNA, 1990. 111 p.

Association for Recorded Sound Collections. *Preliminary Directory of Sound Recordings Collections in the United States and Canada.* New York: New York Public Library, 1967. 157 p.

———. *Audio Preservation: A Planning Study; Final Performance Report.* Rockville, Md.: Association for Recorded Sound Collections, Associated Audio Archives Committee, 1988. 2 vols., looseleaf.

Atchison, Glenn. "The Musical Theatre in Canadaon Stage and on Record." In Hummel 1984, pp. xxxiv–xl.

Audio Key: The Canadian Record & Tape Guide. Winnipeg: Audio Key, 1985 (annual).

Ault, Bob. "CBS and the Columbia Phonograph Company." *Antiques and Collecting Hobbies* (Nov. 1986): 53–56.

———. "A Few Observations on the Art of Playing Old Records." *Antiques and Collecting Hobbies* (Feb. 1987): 48–50.

The Australian Music Industry; An Economic Evaluation. Music Board of the Australian Council. Sidney: The Board, 1987. 298 p.

Bachman, W. S., B. B. Bauer, and P. C. Goldmark. "Disk Recording and Reproduction." *IRE Proceedings* 50 (May 1962): 738–744. Reprinted in Roys 1978.

Backensto, Woody. "Red Nichols Memorial Issue." *Record Research* 96/97 (Apr. 1969): 2–18.

Backus, John. *The Acoustical Foundations of Music.* New York: Norton, 1969. 312 p.

Badmaieff, Alexis, and Don Davis. *How to Build Speaker Enclosures.* Indianapolis: Sams, 1966. 144 p.

Badrock, Arthur. *Dominion Records: A Catalogue and History.* Bournemouth, England: Talking Machine Review, 1976. 31 p.

———. "Unravelling Ariel." *Talking Machine Review International* 75 (Autumn 1988): 2,197–2,199.

Badrock, Arthur, and Frank Andrews. *The Complete Regal Catalogue.* Malvern, England: City of London Phonograph and Gramophone Society, 1991. 358 p.

Badrock, Arthur, and Derek Spruce. "Aco." *R.S.V.P.* 2 (June 1965) to 15 (Aug. 1966); 17 (Oct. 1966) to 25 (June 1967); 27 (Aug. 1967) to 31 (Dec. 1967); 34 (Mar. 1968); 35 (Apr. 1968), 40 (Sept. 1968) to 42 (Nov. 1968). Additions and corrections in 43 (Dec. 1968), 47 (Apr. 1969), 52 (Jan.–Feb. 1970).

Bahr, Edward. *Trombone Euphonium Discography.* Stevens Point, Wis.: Index House, 1988. 502 p.

Bailey, A. R. "A Non-Resonant Loudspeaker Enclosure." *Wireless World* (Oct. 1965): 483–486.

Baker, Darrell, and Larry F. Kiner. *The Sir Harry Lauder Discography.* Metuchen, N.J.: Scarecrow Press, 1990. 198 p.

Barnes, Harold. "Ninon Vallin." *Record Collector* 8-3 (Mar. 1953): 52–65.

Barnes, Harold, and Victor Girard. "Conchita Supervia." *Record Collector* 6-3 (Mar. 1951): 51, 54–71; 8-2 (Feb. 1953): 41–44.

Barnes, Ken. "Record Cleaning." *Antique Phonograph Monthly* 2-10 (Dec. 1974): 3, 8; 3-1 (Jan. 1975): 5–7.

———. "The Bristophone: An 'L' of a Reproducer." *Antique Phonograph Monthly* 3-3 (Mar. 1975): 3–5.

Barr, Stephen C. "Gull(s) of My Dreams." *New Amberola Graphic* 39 (Winter 1982): 3–12.

———. "Ring Out Wild Bells! A Study of Bell Records." *New Amberola Graphic* 46 (Autumn 1983): 3–7.

Basart, Ann P. *The Sound of the Fortepiano; A Discography of Recordings on Early Pianos.* Berkeley, Calif.: Fallen Leaf Press, 1985. 472 p.

Batten, Joseph. *Joe Batten's Book; The Story of Sound Recording.* Foreword by Compton Mackenzie. London: Rockliff, 1956. 201 p.

Bauer, Benjamin B. "Tracking Angle in Phonograph Pickups." *Electronics* 18 (Mar. 1945): 110–115. Reprinted in Roys 1978.

———. "Vertical Tracking Improvements in Stereo Recording." *Audio* (Feb. 1963): 19–22. Reprinted in Roys 1978.

Bauer, Benjamin B., Daniel W. Gravereaux, and Arthur J. Gust. "A Compatible Stereo-Quadraphonic (SQ) Record System." *Journal of the Audio Engineering Society* 19-8 (1971): 638–646. Reprinted in Roys 1978.

Bauer, Robert. *The New Catalogue of Historical Records, 1898–1908-09.* 2nd ed. London: Sidgwick and Jackson, 1947. 494 p. (1st ed. 1937) Reprinted by Sidgwick and Jackson, 1970.

Baumbach, Robert W. *Look for the Dog; An Illustrated Guide to Victor Talking Machines, 1901–1929.* Woodland Hills, Calif.: Stationery X-Press, 1981. 326 p.

Bayly, Ernie. "The Decca Portable." *Talking Machine Review International* 26 (Feb. 1974): 596–597. [Bayly 1974/2]

———. "Small Records." *Talking Machine Review International* 28 (June 1974): 116–119. [Bayly 1974/6]

———. "Double Sided Records." *Talking Machine Review International* 38 (Feb. 1976): 596–597.

———. "Zonophone Pseudonyms." *Talking Machine Review International* 43 (Dec. 1976): 857–858. [Bayly 1976/12]

———. "DeWolf Hopper." *Talking Machine Review International* 70 (Dec. 1985): 1,966, 1,979.

———. "5-Inch Berliner." *Hillandale News* 163 (Aug. 1988): 71.

Bebb, Richard. "The Actor Then and Now." *Recorded Sound* 47 (July 1972): 85–93; 48 (Oct. 1972): 115–124.

Bennett, Bill. "Capitol, 1942 to 1949 and Beyond." *Record Research* 183/184 (July 1981): 11; 185/186 (Oct. 1981): 12; 187/188 (Dec. 1981): 12; 189/190 (Mar.–Apr. 1982): 11; 191/192 (July 1982): 12, 14; 193/194 (Oct. 1982): 10; 197/198 (Mar.–Apr. 1983): 11; 199/200 (June 1983): 13.

———. "Capitol 15000 Series 78 RPM, Oct. 1947 to Mar. 1949." *Record Research* 227/228 (Mar. 1987): 1–2; 229/230 (June 1987): 10; 231/232 (Oct. 1987): 10; 233/234 (Feb. 1988): 9; 239/240 (Apr. 1989): 8; 241/242 (Sept.–Oct. 1989): 24; 243/244 (May–June 1990): 23; 245/246 (Jan. 1991): 23.

Bennett, John. "Fonotipia Catalogue." *Hobbies* (Feb. 1954): 25–27.

Bennett John R. *Voices of the Past.* et al. Lingfield, Surrey, England: Oakwood Press, 1955–1970. Facsimile typescript listings of vocal records on labels issued by the Gramophone Co. and affiliates. Coverage by volume (full titles of the volumes are in Rust 1980):

1. HMV English catalogues, 1898–1925 (1955);
2. HMV Italian catalogues, 1898–1925 (1958);
3. Dischi Fonotipia (1964?);
4. International red label catalogues (1961);
5. HMV black label catalogues, D and E series (1960);
6. International red label catalogues (1963);
7. German catalogues (1967);
8. Columbia catalogue of English celebrity issues (1972);
9. French catalogues (1971?);
10. Plum label C series;
11. Russian catalogues, 1899–1915 (1977);
12. (Vol. LP1) Columbia blue and green labels, 1952–1962 (1975);
13. (Vol. LP2) HMV red label, 1952–1962 (1975);
14. (Vol. LP3) HMV plum label, 1952–1962 (1975).

———. *Melodiya; A Soviet Russian L.P. Discography.* Westport, Conn.: Greenwood Press, 1981. 832 p.

Benson, Joe. *Uncle Joe's Record Guide: The Rolling Stones.* Glendale, Calif.: J. Benson Unlimited, 1987. 124 p.

Berger, Karol. "The Yale Collection of Historical Sound Recordings." *Association for Recorded Sound Collections Journal* 6-1 (1974): 13–25.

Berger, Monroe, Edward Berger, and James Patrick. *Benny Carter: A Life in American Music.* Metuchen, N.J.: Scarecrow Press, 1982. 877 p.

Bergman, Billy. *Hot Sauces: Latin and Caribbean Pop.* NY: Quill, 1985.

Berliner, Oliver. "Wags and Tales that Started a Revolution." *Audio* (Dec. 1977): 36–40.

Betrock, Alan. *Girl Groups: The Story of a Sound.* New York: Delilah Books, 1982. 175 p.

Bettini Catalog for June 1898; *Bettini Catalog for April 1900*; *Bettini Catalog for June 1901.* Stanford, Calif.: Stanford University Archive of Recorded Sound, 1965. (Reprint Series, 1)

Betz, Peter. "Uncle Josh before Cal Stewart." *Talking Machine Review International* 41 (Aug. 1976): 726–728.

———. "John Kreusi [sic]: The Man Who 'Made This'." *Hillandale News* 177 (Dec. 1990): 131–133.

Bianco, David. *Heat Wave: The Motown Fact Book.* Ann Arbor, Mich.: Pierian Press, 1988. 524 p.

Biel, Michael. "For the Record." *Association for Recorded Sound Collections Journal* 14-1 (1982): 97–113. [1982/1]

———. "For the Record." *Association for Recorded Sound Collections Journal* 14-3 (1982): 101–111. [1982/2]

Blacker, George. "Disco-ing" columns. *Record Research*, 1955–1990. Cited by date only.

———."How to Play Old Records on New Equipment." *High Fidelity* (Apr. 1973): 48–57.

———. "The Pennsylvania Vertical Group Preliminary Report." *Record Research* 131 (Jan. 1975): 1, 6; 132 (Apr. 1975): 5–6; 133 (June 1975): 5–6. Considers relationships among vertical-cut labels Domestic, Keen-O-Phone, McKinley, Phono-Cut, Rex, and Rishell.

———. "Playing Oldies the New Way." *Antique Phonograph Monthly* 3-7 (Aug.–Sept. 1975): 3–6. [Blacker 1975/8]

———. "The Data Sheet Again!" *Record Research* 139/140 (May–June 1976): 12. [Blacker 1976/5]

———. "Some Pointed Remarks about Styli." *Record Research* 159/160 (Dec. 1978): 2.

———. "Parade of Champions, 1925 to 1930, 1500 to 16133." *Record Research* 169/170 (Jan. 1980): 2–16; 171/172 (Mar. 1980): 6–6; 173/174 (June 1980): 8, 24; 175/176 (Sept. 1980): 12; 179/180 (Feb. 1981): 11. [Blacker 1980/1]

———. "Further Remarks on Electronic Cylinder Playback." *Record Research* 175/176 (Sept. 1980): 2. [Blacker 1980/9]

———. "Some Comments on the Edison Kinetophone Cylinders of 1912." *Antique Phonograph Monthly* 6-10 (1981): 3–7.

———. "Cylindrography or Cylindrographically Yours." *Record Research* 179/180 (Feb. 1981): 2, 23. [Blacker 1981/2]

———. "Little Wonder Records." *Record Research* 197/198 (Mar.–Apr. 1983): 1–2; 199/200 (June 1983): 8; 201/202 (Sept. 1983): 12; 203/204 (Dec. 1983): 7; 205/206 (Mar. 1984): 10–11; 207/208 (June 1984): 10; 209/210 (Oct. 1984): 11; 211/212 (Feb. 1985): 10; 213/214 (May 1985): 12; 215/216 (July 1985):10; 217/218 (Oct. 1985): 11; 219/220 (Jan. 1986): 14; 221/222 (Apr. 1986): 12.

———. *The Columbia Master Book Discography.* Westport, Conn: Greenwood Press, 1990.

———. *Little Wonder Records: A History and Discography.* St. Johnsbury, Vt.: New Amberoea Phonograph Co., 1999.

———. "The English Singers and Roycroft Revisited." *Record Research* 209/210 (Oct. 1984): 3–4; 211/212 (Feb. 1985): 4–5, 11.

———. "Beginning of the Emerson Dynasty." *Record Research* 239/240 (Apr. 1989): 1–2; 241/242 (Oct.–Nov. 1989): 2; 243/244 (May–June 1990): 5; 245/246 (Jan. 1991): 6; 247/248 (Sept. 1991): 6.

———. "Talk-O-Photo." *Record Research* 243/244 (May–June 1990): 4; 247/248 (Sept. 1991): 5.

Blackmer, David E. "A Wide Dynamic Range Noise Reduction System." *db* (Aug.–Sept. 1972): 54–56.

Blair, Linda W. "The Yale Collection of Historical Sound Recordings" *Association for Recorded Sound Collections Journal* 20-2 (Feb. 1989): 167–176.

Bloesch, David. "Artur Schnabel: A Discography." *Association for Recorded Sound Collections Journal* 18-1/3 (1986): 33–143.

Blyth, Alan. *Opera on Record.* London: Hutchinson, 1979, 1984. 2 vols.

———. *Song on Record.* New York: Cambridge University Press, 1986, 1988. 2 vols.

Bolig, John. *The Recordings of Enrico Caruso.* Dover, Del.: Delaware State Museum, 1973. 88 p.

Bond, Johnny. *The Recordings of Jimmie Rodgers; An Annotated Discography.* Los Angeles: John Edwards Memorial Foundation, University of California, 1978. 76 p. (JEMF Special Series, 11)

Bondesen, Poul. *North American Bird Songs: A World of Music.* Klampenborg, Denmark: Scandinavian Science Press, 1977. 254 p.

Boots, Robert C. *Military Music Holdings at the United States Army Military History Institute.* Carlisle Barracks, Penn.: U.S. Army Military History Institute, Audio Visual Archives, 1981. 391 p.

Bordman, Gerald. *American Musical Theatre A* Chronicle. New York: Oxford University Press, 1978. 749 p. (3rd ed. 2001)

Borwick, John. "The Diamond Stylus Company." *Gramophone* (July 1975): 258.

———. "Dual Gebrüder Steidinger." *Gramophone* (Apr. 1976): 1,693.

———. *The Gramophone Guide to Hi-Fi.* London: David & Charles, 1982. 256 p.

———. *Sound Recording Practice.* 4th ed. New York: Oxford University Press, 1994. 557 p. (1st ed. 1976) [Borwick 1987/1]

———. "A Music-lover's Guide to CD and Hi-Fi." *Gramophone* (Mar.–Aug. 1987). A series of six articles. [Borwick 1987/3]

———. *Loudspeaker and Headphone Handbook.* London: Butterworths, 1988. 573 p. (3rd ed., Oxford: Focal Press, 2001)

———. "The British Library National Sound Archive." *Gramophone* (July 1989): 251–252. [Borwick 1989/7]

———. "JVC, Japan." *Gramophone* (Oct. 1989): 787–788. [Borwick 1989/10]

———. "Microphone Balance." *Gramophone* (May 1990): 2,094.

Bott, Michael F. "Riccardo Martin." *Record Collector* 26-1 2 (May 1980): 5–42.

Bowman, Rob. *Soulsville U.S.A.: The Story of Stax Records.* New York: Schirmer Books, 1997.

Bridges, Glenn. *Pioneers in Brass.* Detroit: Sherwood, 1968. 129 p.

Brooks, Edward. *The Bessie Smith Companion; A Critical and Detailed Appreciation of the Recordings.* New York: Da Capo Press, 1982. 229 p.

Brooks, Tim. "Columbia Acoustic Matrix Series; Preliminary Research." *Record Research* 133 (June 1975): 1–8; 134 (Aug. 1975): 3–4; 135/136 (Nov.–Dec. 1975): 8–12.

———. "Vogue, the Picture Record." *Record Research* 148 (July 1977): 1–8; 151/152 (Jan. 1978): 4–10; 153/154 (Apr. 1978): 10; 159/160 (Dec. 1978): 10; 161/162 (Feb.–Mar. 1979): 3.

———. "Columbia Records in the 1890s: Founding the Record Industry." *Association for Recorded Sound Collections Journal* 10-1 (1978): 5–36.

———. "A Directory to Columbia Recording Artists of the 1890s." *Association for Recorded Sound Collections Journal* 11-2/3 (1979): 102–138.

———. "Current Bibliography." *Association for Recorded Sound Collections Journal* 10-2/3 (1979). Continuing series. [Brooks 1979/1]

———. "The Artifacts of Recording History: Creators, Users, Losers, Keepers." *Association for Recorded Sound Collections Journal* 11-1 (1979): 18–28. [Brooks 1979/2]

———. "ARSC; Association for Recorded Sound Collections— An Unusual Organization." *Goldmine* (Feb. 1983): 22–23.

———. "A Survey of Record Collectors' Societies." *Association for Recorded Sound Collections Journal* 16-3 (1984): 17–36.

———. "One-Hit Wonders of the Acoustic Era (... And a Few Beyond)." *Antique Phonograph Monthly* 9-2 (1990): 8–11.

———. *Lost Sounds: Blacks and the Birth of the Recording Industry, 1890–1919.* Urbana: Univ. of Illinois Press, 2004.

Brown, Alan. "The Kinetophonograph." *Talking Machine Review International* 40 (June 1976): 716–719.

Brown, Denis. *Sarah Vaughan; A Discography.* Westport, Conn.: Greenwood Press, 1991. 192 p.

Brown, Jake. *Suge Knight: The Rise, and Fall, and Rise of Death Row Records.* New York: Amber Books, 2001. 206 p.

Brown, Scott, and Robert Hilbert. *The Life and Music of James P. Johnson.* Metuchen, N.J.: Scarecrow Press, 1986. 503 p.

Brownstein, Mark. "One Disc at a Time: Moldy Discs." *CD-ROM Enduser* (Feb. 1990): 29.

Bruun, C.L., and J. Gray. "A Bibliography of Discographies." *Recorded Sound* 1-7 (1962): 206–213.

Bruyninckx, Walter. *60 Years of Recorded Jazz.* Mechelen, Belgium: Author, 1980. 36 vols.

Bryan, Martin F. "Columbia BC Half-Foot-Long Records." *New Amberola Graphic* 41 (Summer 1982): 3–9.

———. "Orlando R. Marsh, Forgotten Pioneer." *New Amberola Graphic* 71 (Jan. 1990): 3–14. Supplemented in *New Amberola Graphic* 72 (Spring 1990): 3–5.

Bryan, Martin F., and William R. Bryant. *Oxford and Silvertone Records, 1911–1918.* St. Johnsbury, Vt.: New Amberola Phonograph Co., 1975. 56 p.

Bryant, E.T. *Collecting Gramophone Records*. New York: Focal Press, 1962. Reprint Westport, Conn.: Greenwood Press, 1978. 153 p.

Bryant, E.T., and Guy Marco. *Music Librarianship: A Practical Guide*. 2nd ed. Metuchen, N.J.: Scarecrow Press, 1985. 449 p. (1st ed. 1959)

Bullard, Thomas R., and William R. Moran. "Lawrence Tibbett." *Record Collector* 23-11/12 (Aug. 1977): 242–287; 24-1/2 (Jan. 1978): 36–46.

Bullock, Robert M., III, and Peter E. Hillman. "A Transmission Line Woofer Model." Paper read at the 81st Conference of the Audio Engineering Society, Nov. 1986.

Bunnett, Rexton S. "The British Musical." In Hummel 1984, xix–xxvi.

Burlingame, Roger. "Emile Berliner." *Dictionary of American Biography*. Supplement 1, 1944, pp. 75–76.

Burros, Harold. "Frida Leider." *Record Collector* 1-5 (Sept. 1946): 50–53. Burros also wrote the discography in *Playing My Part*, by Frida Leider (New York: Da Capo Press, 1978).

Burt, Leah. "Chemical Technology in the Edison Recording Industry." *Journal of the Audio Engineering Society* 25-10 11 (Sept.–Oct. 1977): 717–717.

Buth, Olga. "Scores and Recordings." *Library Trends* 23 (Jan. 1975): 427–450.

Capes, S.J. "Early Pianoforte Records." *British Institute of Recorded Sound*. Bulletin 3 (Winter 1956): 13–19.

Carolan, Nicholas. *A Short Discography of Irish Folk Music*. Dublin: Folk Music Society of Ireland, 1987. 40 p.

Carreck, J.N. "Early Organ Recordings." *Hillandale News* 1 (Oct. 1960): 4, 8.

———. "Obituary: Dr. Ludwig Koch, Sound Recording Pioneer, 1881–1974." *Hillandale News* 79 (Aug. 1974): 223–224.

Carter, Sydney H. *Edison Two-Minute Cylinder Records: The Complete Catalogue of the Edison Gold Moulded Two-Minute Cylinder Records, 1901–12*. Abbots Close, Worthing, England: Author, 1965? 156 p.

———. *Edison Amberol Cylinder Records ... Foreign Issues, 1908–12*. Abbots Close, Worthing, England: Author, 1965? 39 p.

———. *A Catalogue of Clarion and Ebonoid Records*. Bournemouth, England: Talking Machine Review, 1977. 70, 27 p.

———. "Air-Pressure Operated Amplifying Gramophone." *Hillandale News* 94 (Dec. 1977): 98–101. [Carter 1977/12]

———. *Blue Amberol Cylinders: A Catalogue*. Bournemouth, England: Talking Machine Review, 1978. 130 p.

Carter, Sydney H., Frank Andrews, and Leonard L. Watts. *Sterling*. Bournemouth, England: Talking Machine Review, 1975. 108 p. Contents: "A Catalogue of Sterling Cylinder Records," by Sydney H. Carter; "A History of Their Manufacture," by Frank Andrews; "Sterling Cylinders on Pathé Discs," by Len Watts.

Caruso, Enrico, Jr., and Andrew Farkas. *Enrico Caruso: My Father and My Family*. Amadeus, Oreg.: Amadeus Press, 1990. 850 p. Includes a discography by William R. Moran.

Castleman, Harry, and Walter Podrazik. *All Together Now. The First Complete Beatles Discography, 1961–1975*. Ann Arbor, Mich.: Pierian Press, 1976. 387 p. Two supplementary volumes were issued by the same authors and publisher: *The Beatles Again* (1977; 280 p.) and *The End of the Beatles?* (1985; 553 p.).

Catalogue of Twelve-Inch Monarch Records in March 1904 Gramophone Co., Ltd. London: Gramophone & Typewriter, Ltd., 1904. Reprint Bournemouth, England: Talking Machine Review, 1972. 35 p.

Catalogue of Nicole Records, Season 1905–1906. London: Nicole, 1905. Reprint Bournemouth, England: Talking Machine Review, 1971. 25 p.

Celletti, Rodolfo. *Le grandi voci*. Rome: Istituto per la Collaborazione Culturale, 1964. 1,044 columns.

A Century of Pop Music. Menomonee Falls, Wisconsin: Record Research, 1999, 242 p.

Chambers, Iain. *Urban Rhythms: Pop Music and Popular Culture*. London: Macmillan, 1985. 272 p.

Charosh, Paul. *Berliner Gramophone Records*. Westport, Conn.: Greenwood Press, 1995. 290 p.

Charters, Samuel B. "Sears Roebuck Sells the Country Blues." *Record Research* 27 (Mar.–Apr. 1960): 3, 20.

———. "Liner Notes." *Vanguard Collector's Edition* 163: 66-2 (1997).

Chew, V.K. *Talking Machines*. 2nd ed. London: Her Majesty's Stationery Office, 1981. 80 p. (1st ed. 1967)

———. "Disc Tinfoil Phonograph." *Hillandale News* 124 (Feb. 1982): 328–329.

Clifford, Mike. *The Harmony Illustrated Encyclopedia of Country Music*. New York: Harmony Books, 1988.

Clough, Francis F., and G.J. Cuming. *The World's Encyclopedia of Recorded Music*. London: Sidgwick & Jackson, 1952. 890 p. First supplement (Apr. 1950–May June 1951) bound in Second supplement (1951–1952), 1952. 262 p. Third supplement (1953–1955), 1957. 564 p. Reprint Westport, Conn.: Greenwood Press, 1970. 3 vols. Usually cited as WERM.

———. "Discography." In *Minor Recollections* by Otto Klemperer, translated from the German by J. Maxwell Brownjohn (London: Dobson, 1964; 124 p.), pp. 103–117.

———. "Myra Hess Discography." *Sound* 24 (Oct. 1966): 104–106.

Cluley, Leonard, E., and Pamela N. Engelbrecht, *Dictionary Catalog of the G. Robert Vincent Voice Library at Michigan State University*. Boston: G.K. Hall, 1975. 677 p. [Vincent 1975].

Cohen, Abraham B. *Hi-Fi Loudspeakers and Enclosures*. 2nd ed. Rochelle Park, N.J.: Hayden Book Co., 1968. 438 p.

Cohen, Norm. "Record Reviews." *Journal of American Folklore* 102 (Apr.–June 1989): 195–198.

Cohen, Ronald, and Dave Samuelson. *Songs for Political Action: Folk Music, Topical Songs, and the American Left, 1926–1953*. Hamburg, Germany: Bear Family Records BCD 15720-JL, 1996.

Cohodas, Nadine. *Spinning Blues Into Gold: The Chess Brothers and the Legendary Chess Records*. New York: St. Martin's Press, 2000. 358 p.

Cole, Roger. "The Aeolian Company." *Hillandale News* 57 (Oct. 1970): 161–165.

Collier, James Lincoln. *Louis Armstrong, An American Genius*. New York: Oxford University Press, 1983. 383 p.

Collins, William J., and James F.E. Dennis. 1979. "Giovanni Martinelli." *Record Collector* 25-7/8/9 (Oct. 1979): 149–215; 25-10/11/12 (Feb. 1980): 221–255; 26-9/10 (May 1981): 237–239.

Connor, Russell D. *Benny Goodman: Listen to His Legacy*. Metuchen, N.J.: Scarecrow Press, 1988. 409 p.

Cooper, David E. *International Bibliography of Discographies: Classical Music, and Jazz and Blues, 1962–1972*. Littleton, Colo.: Libraries Unlimited, 1975. 272 p.

Cooper, Reg. "Independent Record Companies." *Talking Maching Review International* 62 (1980): 1,669–1,671.

Copeland, George A. "Understanding the Edison Reproducer." *New Amberola Graphic* 73 (July 1990): 10–14.

Copeland, Peter C. "Playback." *Hillandale News* 172 (Feb. 1990): 336. Comments on this article were made in a letter to *Hillandale News* 174 (June 1990): 52.

Corenthal, Michael G. *Cohen on the Telephone; A History of Jewish Recorded Humor and Popular Music, 1892–1942.* Milwaukee, Wis.: Yesterday's Memories, 1984. 108 p.

———. *Iconography of Recorded Sound, 1886–1986.* Milwaukee, Wis.: Yesterday's Memories, 1986. 243 p.

Cott, Jonathan. *Conversations with Glenn Gould.* Boston: Little, Brown, 1984. Discography pp. 139–150.

Cotter, Dave. "Flexo, San Francisco's Obscure Record Company." *Record Research* 118 (Oct. 1972): 1, 4–7.

———. "National Music Lovers." *New Amberola Graphic* 1-25 (Fall 1975–Apr. 1988). Series of brief articles.

Creighton, James. *Discopaedia of the Violin, 1889–1971.* Toronto: University of Toronto Press, 1974. 987 p.

Cros, Charles. "Comptes rendus des séances de l'Académie des Sciences ... 3 decembre 1877." Paper deposited with the *Académie* on 30 Apr 1877.

Croucher, Trevor. *Early Music Discography: From Plainsong to the Sons of Bach.* Phoenix, Ariz.: Oryx, 1981. 2 vols.

Crowhurst, Norman. *The Stereo High Fidelity Handbook.* New York: Crown, 1960. 183 p.

Crutchfield, Will. "Brahms by Those Who Knew Him." *Opus* 2-5 (Aug. 1956): 12–21, 60.

Culshaw, John. *Ring Resounding; The Recording in Stereo of Der Ring des Nibelungen.* London: Secker & Warburg, 1967. 284 p.

———. *Reflections on Wagner's Ring.* London: Secker & Warburg, 1976. 105 p.

———. *Putting the Record Straight.* New York: Viking, 1981. 362 p.

Cunningham, Agnes "Sis," and Gordon Friesen. *Red Dust and Broadsides: A Joint Autobiography.* Amherst: University of Massachusetts Press, 1999. 371 p.

Curry, Edgar L. *Vogue: The Picture Record.* Everett, Wash.: Author, 1990. 92 p.

Cuscuna, Michael, and Michel Ruppli. *The Blue Note Label: A Discography.* Westport, Conn.: Greenwood Press, 1988. 544 p.

Czada, Peter, and Frans Jansen. "Tefifon." *Hillandale News* 130 (Feb. 1983): 169–171.

Dales, J.S. "Edison Dictation Cylinders." *Talking Machine Review International* 62 (1980): 1,675.

Danca, Vince. *Bunny Berigan: A Bio-discography.* Rockford, Ill.: Author, 1978. 66 p.

D'Andrea, Renzo. *Tito Schipa nella vita, nell'arte, nel suo tempo.* Fasano di Puglia, Italy: Schena, 1981. 246 p. Discography by Daniele Rubboli, pp. 225–240.

Dangarfield, Jim. "Nina Koshetz." *Sound Record* 7-4 (June 1991): 154–155.

Daniels, William R. *The American 45 and 78 RPM Record Dating Guide, 1940–1959.* Westport, Conn.: Greenwood Press, 1985. 157 p.

Dannen, Frederick. *Hit Men; Power Brokers and Fast Money inside the Music Business.* New York: Times Books, 1990. 387 p.

Darrell, R.D. *The Gramophone Shop Encyclopedia of Recorded Music.* Edited by Robert H. Reid. New York: Crown, 1948. 3rd ed. 639 p. Reprint Westport, Conn.: Greenwood Press, 1970. (1st ed., compiled by R.D. Darrell, New York: Gramophone Shop, 1936) 574 p.

Davies, John R.T., and Roy Cooke. *The Music of Fats Waller.* 2nd ed. London: Century Press, 1953. 40 p. (1st ed. 1950)

Davies, John R.T., and Laurie Wright. *Morton's Music.* 2nd ed. Chigwell, Essex, England: Storyville Publications, 1968. 40 p.

Davis C.C., and J.G. Frayne. "The Westrex Stereo Disk System." *IRE Proceedings* 46 (1958): 1,685–1,693. Reprinted in Roys 1978.

Davis, Chester K. "Record Collections, 1960; *LJ*'s Survey of Fact and Opinion." *Library Journal* 85 (Oct. 1, 1960): 3,375–3,380.

Davis, Lenwood G. *A Paul Robeson Research Guide; A Selected, Annotated Bibliography.* Westport, Conn.: Greenwood Press, 1983. 879 p. Discography, pp. 771–795.

Day, Rebecca. "Where's the Rot?" *Stereo Review* 54-4 (Apr. 1989): 23–24.

Deakins, Duane D. *Comprehensive Cylinder Record Index.* Stockton, Calif.: Author, 1956–1961. Five parts in one volume. Contents in Rust 1980, p. 92.

Dearling, Robert, and Celia Dearling. *The Guinness Book of Recorded Sound.* With assistance from Brian Rust. Enfield, Middlesex, England: Guinness Books, 1984. 225 p.

Debenham, Warren. *Laughter on Record: A Comedy Discography.* Metuchen, N.J.: Scarecrow Press, 1988. 387 p.

Debus, Allen. "Bert Williams on Record." *Hillandale News* 154 (Feb. 1987): 154–157.

De Cock, Alfred. "Maurice Renaud." *Record Collector* 11-4/5 (Apr.–May 1957): 74–119; 11-7 (July 1957): 166–167; 12-1/2 (Jan.–Feb. 1958): 37. [De Cock 1957]

Delalande, Jacques, and Tully Potter. "The Busch Brothers: A Discography." *Recorded Sound* 86 (1984): 29–90.

Delaunay, Charles, and George Avakian. *New Hot Discography.* 4th ed. New York: Criterion Books, 1948. 608 p. (1st ed., *Hot Discography*, Paris: Hot Club de France, 1936)

De Lerma, Dominique René. "Philosophy and Practice of Phonorecord Classification at Indiana University." *Library Resources and Technical Services* 13 (Winter 1969): 86–98.

Denisoff, Serge R. *Solid Gold; The Popular Record Industry.* New Brunswick, N.J.: Transaction Books, 1975. 504 p.

———. *Tarnished Gold; The Record Industry Revisited.* New Brunswick, N.J.: Transaction Books, 1986. 487 p.

Dennis, James F.E. "Dating by Labels." *Record Collector* 1 (Aug. 1946): 22–23.

———. "Jean De Reszke." *Record Collector* 5-1 (Jan. 1950): 3, 6–11. [Dennis 1950/1]

———. "Ernest Van Dyck." *Record Collector* 5-2 (Feb. 1950): 27–32. [Dennis 1950/2]

———. "Sigrid Onegin." *Record Collector* 5-10 (Oct. 1950): 223–231; 5-12 (Dec. 1950): 280–281; 12-8/9 (Nov. 1959): 200. [Dennis 1950/10]

———. "Edouard De Reszke." *Record Collector* 6-5 (May 1951): 99–106. [Dennis 1951/5]

———. "Lillian Nordica." *Record Collector* 6-9 (Sept. 1951): 195–206. [Dennis 1951/9]

———. "Kirsten Flagstad." *Record Collector* 7-8 (Aug. 1952): 172–190.

———. "Mattia Battistini." *Record Collector* 8-11/12 (Nov.–Dec. 1953): 244–265. [Dennis 1953/11]

———. "Helge Rosvaenge." *Record Collector* 23-5/6 (Sept. 1976): 99, 140; 25-5/6 (Aug. 1979): 120–122.

Dennis, James F.E., Alfred Frankenstein, and Boris Semeonoff. "Friedrich Schorr." *Record Collector* 19-11/12 (Apr. 1971): 243–284; 20-3 (Oct. 1971): 71.

Dennis, James F.E., and John Stratton. "Lili Lehmann." *Record Collector* 26-7/8 (Feb. 1981): 150–190; 26-9/10 (May 1981): 199–214. [Dennis 1981/2]

Dennis, Pamela, and James F.E. Dennis. "Jacques Urlus." *Record Collector* 26-11/12 (Sept. 1981).

Dethlefson, Ronald. *Edison Blue Amberol Recordings.* Brooklyn: APM Press, 1980–1981. 2 vols.

———. "Dubbing De-Mystified." *Antique Phonograph Monthly* 7-2 (1983): 3–5.

Dethlefson, Ronald, and Raymond R. Wile. *Edison Disc Artists and Records, 1910–1929*. Brooklyn: APM Press, 1985. 177 p. Revised edition entered at Wile 1990/4.

De Veaux, Scott. "Bebop and the Recording Industry: The 1942 AFM Recording Ban Reconsidered." *Journal of the American Musicological Society* 51-1 (Spring 1988): 126–165.

Dezettel, Louis M. *Record Changers: How They Work*. Indianapolis: Sams, 1968. 144 p.

Di Cave, Luciano. "Lina Pagliughi." *Record Collector* 21-5/6 (Oct. 1973): 99–125.

Dickason, Vance. *The Loudspeaker Design Cookbook*. 3rd ed. Francestown, NH: Marshall Jones Co., 1987. 75 p.

Directory of Member Archives. Compiled by Grace Koch. 2nd ed. Milton Keynes, England: International Association of Sound Archives, 1982. 174 p. (1st ed. 1978)

Dixon, Robert M.W., and John Godrich. *Recording the Blues*. London: Studio Vista, 1970. 85 p.

Docks, L.R. *American Premium Record Guide*. Florence, Ala.: Books Americana, 1980. 737 p. Includes 500 label illustrations.

Doran, James M. *Erroll Garner; The Most Happy Piano*. Metuchen, N.J.: Scarecrow Press, 1985. 500 p.

Dorgeuille, Claude. *The French Flute School, 1860–1950*. 2nd ed. London: Tony Bingham, 1986. 138 p.

Drummond, H.J. "The Seven Zonophone Records." *Gramophone* (Sept. 1969): 140–143.

Dubal, David. *The Art of the Piano*. New York: Summit Books, 1989. 476 p.

Duckenfield, Bridget. "Sir Landon Ronald and the Gramophone." *Hillandale News* 177 (Dec. 1990): 139–142.

Duckles, Vincent. "Musical Scores and Recordings." *Library Trends* 4 (1955–1956): 164–173.

Dyment, Christopher. "The Recordings of Karl Muck; Some Unresolved Problems." *Association for Recorded Sound Collections Journal* 9-1 (1977): 66–68. Followed by a discography by Dyment and Jim Cartwright, pp. 69–77.

———. "Misunderstanding Toscanini." *Association for Recorded Sound Collections Journal* 18-1/3 (1986): 144–171a.

Eargle, John E. "Loudspeakers." *Journal of the Audio Engineering Society* 10-11 (1977): 685–688.

Edison Phonograph. New York: North American Phonograph Co., 1893. Unpaged. Reprint Brooklyn: Allen Koenigsberg, 1974.

Edison Coin-Slot Phonographs. Orange, N.J.: National Phonograph Co., 1906. 20 p. Reprint Brooklyn: Allen Koenigsberg, 1974.

Edwards, Ernie, George Hall, and Bill Korst. *Big Bands Discography*. Whittier, Calif.: Erngeobil, 1965–1969. 7 vols. Contents in Cooper 1975.

Einstein, Edwin K., Jr. "Zinka Milanov: A Complete Discography." *Le grand baton* (May 1968): 7–16.

Eke, Bernard T. "Alma Gluck." *Record Collector* 1-8 (Dec. 1946): 81–88; 6-2 (Feb. 1951): 27, 33–45; 6-3 (Mar. 1951): 53.

Elste, Martin R.O. "100 Jahre Schallaufzeichnung: Eine Chronologie." *Fonoforum* 5 (May 1977): 434–447.

Enderman, Hans. "Original Dixieland Jazz Band and Its Recreations." *Micrography* 77 (May 1989): 4–10.

Englund, Björn. *Durium; Hit of the Week*. Stockholm: Nationalfonotekets, 1967. 14 p.

———. "Scandinavian Record Labels, No. 2: Grand." *Talking Machine Review International* 4 (June 1970): 101.

———. "Sixty-Five Years of Deutsche Grammophon Gesellschaft, 1898–1963." *Hillandale News* 63 (Oct. 1971): 49–59. Condensed translation of a booklet issued by DGG in 1963.

Evans, H. "A Hot Performer." *Hillandale News* 168 (June 1989): 214–215. Describes the hot air motor of 1910.

Evans, Roy. "More for Less." *Record Research* 165/166 (Aug. 1979): 14; 167/168 (Oct. 1979): 14.

Evensmo, Jan. *The Guitars of Charlie Christian, Robert Normann, Oscar Aleman*. Hosle, Norway: Author, 1976. Unpaged.

———. *The Tenor Saxophone of Ben Webster, 1931–1943*. Hosle, Norway: Author, 1978. 52 p.

Fabrizio, T.C. "Disc Records of the Talking Machine Companies of Chicago." *Talking Machine Review International* 20/21 (Feb.–Apr. 1973): 118–120.

———. "Survey of American Talking Machines Employing Unusual Methods of Reproduction." *Talking Machine Review International* 42 (Oct. 1976): 787–791.

———. "The Chicago Companies." *Talking Machine Review International* 48 (1977): 1,085–1,089.

———. "The Twilight of the O'Neill-James and Aretino Companies of Chicago, 1910–1914." *Talking Machine Review International* 56/57 (Feb.–Apr. 1979): 1,480–1,481.

———. "The Disc Records of Turn-of-the-Century Chicago and the Companies which Sold Them." *Association for Recorded Sound Collections Journal* 12-1/2 (1980): 18–25.

Fagan, Ted. "Pre-LP Recordings of RCA at 33 1/3 RPM, 1931 to 1934." *Association for Recorded Sound Collections Journal* 13-1 (1981): 20–42; 14-3 (1982): 41–61; 15-1 (1983): 25–68.

Fagan, Ted, and William R. Moran. *The Encyclopedic Discography of Victor Recordings*. Westport, Conn.: Greenwood Press, 1983, 1986. 2 vols. Vol. 1 includes a reprint of Aldridge 1964.

Farkas, Andrew. *Opera and Concert Singers; An Annotated International Bibliography of Books and Pamphlets*. New York: Garland, 1985. 363 p. Includes comments by William R. Moran on the discographical components of many biographies.

Farmer, John. "The Reproducing Piano." *Recorded Sound* 25 (Jan. 1967): 131–134; 26 (Apr. 1967): 172–180; 28 (Oct. 1967): 249–254.

Favia-Artsay, Aida. "Frances Alda." *Record Collector* 6-10 (Oct. 1951): 219–233.

———. "The Speeds of DeLuca's Acoustical Victors." *Hobbies* (Feb. 1955): 24–25. [Favia-Artsay 1955/2]

———. "Bettini Catalogs." *Hobbies* (Dec. 1955): 26–27; (Feb. 1956): 28–31; (Mar. 1956): 26–29, 35. Contents of Bettini catalogs of May 1897, June 1898, and 1899. [Favia-Artsay 1955/12]

———. *Caruso on Records: Pitch, Speed, and Comments*. Valhalla, N.Y.: The Historic Record, 1965. 218 p.

Favia-Artsay, Aida, and Gordon Whelan. "Amelita Galli-Curci." *Record Collector* 4-10 (Oct. 1949): 162–179.

Favia-Artsay, Aida, and John Freestone. "Francesco Tamagno." *Record Collector* 7-2 (Feb. 1952): 26, 29–39.

Federal Cylinder Project. U.S. Library of Congress. Washington, D.C.: Government Printing Office, 1984. Vol. 1, Vol. 8. Vol. 8 includes a list of 101 cylinders made at the World's Columbian Exposition, Chicago, 1893.

Feinstein, Robert. "Caruso and Bettini: The Eternal Youths." *Antique Phonograph Monthly* 8-2 (1985): 5.

Fellers, Frederick P. *The Metropolitan Opera on Record; A Discography of the Commercial Recordings* Westport, Conn.: Greenwood Press, 1984. 101 p.

Fellers, Frederick P., and Betty Meyers. *Discographies of Commercial Recordings of the Cleveland Orchestra (1924–1977) and the Cincinnati Symphony Orchestra (1917–1977)*. Westport, Conn.: Greenwood Press, 1978. 224 p.

Fenton, Alasdair. "Where Have All the Big Bands Gone?" *Talking Machine Review International* 11 (Aug. 1971): 67–70.

Ferrara, D.E. "The Legacy of Early Recordings by Pupils of Liszt." *Piano Quarterly* 23 (1975): 42–44.

———. "Virginia Rea (A.K.A. Olive Palmer)." *New Amberola Graphic* 63 (Jan. 1988): 10–11. [Ferrara 1988/1]

———. "A Spalding Centenary." *New Amberola Graphic* 65 (July 1988): 12–15. [Ferrara 1988/7]

Ferrara, Dennis E. "Charles W. Harrison; An Edison Retrospect." *New Amberola Graphic* 77 (July 1991): 4–6. [Ferrara 1991/7]

Ferstler, Howard. *High Definition Compact Disc Recordings.* Jefferson, N.C.: McFarland, 1994. 258 p.

———. *High Fidelity Audio/Video Systems: A Critical Guide for Owners.* Jefferson, N.C.: McFarland, 1991. 253 p.

———. *The Home Theater Companion.* New York: Schirmer Books, 1997. 437 p.

———. *The Digital Audio Music List.* Madison, Wisc.: A-R Editions, 1999. 463 p.

Fewkes, Jesse W. "A Contribution to Passamaquoddy Folklore." *Journal of American Folklore* 3 (1890): 257–280. [Fewkes 1890/1]

———. "On the Use of the Phonograph among Zuni Indians." *American Naturalist* 24 (1890): 687–691. [Fewkes 1890/2]

Field, Mike. "The Bell-Tainter Graphophone." *Hillandale News* 161 (Apr. 1988): 12–15.

Fitterling, Thomas. *Thelonious Monk: Sein Leben, seine Musik, seine Schallplatten.* Waakirchen, Germany: OREOS, 1987. 175 p.

Flemming, Bill, comp. *Directory of Australian Music Organizations.* Rev. ed. Sydney: Australia Music Center, 1985. 67 p. (1st ed. 1978)

Flower, John. *Moonlight Serenade; A Bio-Discography of the Glenn Miller Civilian Band.* New Rochelle, N.Y.: Arlington House, 1972. 554 p.

Foerster, Try, ed. *Elvis Just for You: A Special Goldmine Anthology.* Iola, Wis.: Krause Publications, 1987. 128 p.

Foote, Robert. "The Labels of the U.S. Black and Silver Columbia Records of 1902–1908." *Talking Machine Review International* 4 (June 1970): 97–99.

Ford, Peter. "History of Sound Recording." *Recorded Sound* 1-7 (Summer 1962): 221–229; "The Age of Empiricism" 1-8 (Autumn 1962): 266–276; "The Evolution of the Microphone, and Electrical Disc Recording" 1-10/11 (Apr.–July 1963): 115–223; "The Evolution of Magnetic Recording" 1-12 (Oct. 1963): 146–154; "Motion Picture and Television Sound Recording" 2-1 (Jan. 1964): 181–188.

Foreman, Lewis. *Systematic Discography.* Hamden, Conn.: Linnet Books, 1974. 144 p.

Francis, John W.N. "The Gilbert & Sullivan Operettas on 78s." *Association for Recorded Sound Collections Journal* 20-1 (Spring 1989): 24–81.

Frankenstein, Alfred, D. Brew, Tom Kaufman, and James F. E. Dennis. "Maria Ivoguen." *Record Collector* 20-5 (Jan. 1972): 98–119; 20–12 (Dec. 1972): 283–284.

Frankenstein, Alfred, and Carl Bruun. "Kerstin Thorberg." *Record Collector* 24-9 10 (Oct. 1978): 196–215.

Frankenstein, Alfred, and James F. E. Dennis. "Alexander Kipnis." *Record Collector* 22-3/4 (July 1974): 51–79; 23-7/8 (Dec. 1976): 166–171.

———. "Jarmila Novotna." *Record Collector* 25-5/6 (Aug. 1979): 101–140.

Frederick, H.A. "Recent Fundamental Advances in Mechanical Records on 'Wax'." *Society of Motion Picture Engineers Journal* 18 (Feb. 1932): 141–152. Reprinted in Roys 1978.

Frow, George. "Some Notes on the World Record, and Its Inventor Noel Pemberton Billing." *Hillandale News* 54 (Apr. 1970): 69–71.

———. *The Edison Disc Phonographs and the Diamond Discs: A History with Illustrations.* Sevenoaks, England: Author, 1982. 286 p.

Frow, George L., and Al Sefl. *Edison Cylinder Phonographs, 1877–1929.* West Orange, N.J.: Edison National Historical Site, 1978. 207 p.

Gaeddert, Barbara Knisely. *The Classification and Cataloging of Sound Recordings: An Annotated Bibliography.* Ann Arbor, Mich.: Music Library Association, 1977. 32 p.

Gaisberg, Frederick W. *The Music Goes Round.* New York: Macmillan, 1943. 273 p. British edition titled *Music on Record.*

Galo, Gary. "Transmission Line Loudspeakers. Part I: Theory." *Speaker Builder* (Feb. 1982).

———. "Caruso: The 'Unpublished' Recordings of ARM4-0302 and the Question of Authenticity." *Antique Phonograph Monthly* 7-9 (1984): 6–8.

———. Review of "The Bayer Complete Caruso" sound recording. *Association for Recorded Sound Collections Journal* 21-2 (1990): 283–289.

———. Review of "The Complete Caruso" and "The Caruso Edition, I, II" sound recordings. *Association for Recorded Sound Collections Journal* 22-1 (Spring 1991): 118–125.

Gambaccini, Paul. *Paul McCartney in His Own Words.* New York: Flash Books, 1976. 111 p.

Garlick, Lewis. "The Graphic Arts and the Record Industry." *Journal of the Audio Engineering Society* 25-10/11 (Sept.–Oct. 1977): 779–784.

Garrod, Charles. *Larry Clinton and His Orchestra.* Zephyrhills, Fla.: Joyce Record Club, 1984. 30 p. [Garrod 1984/1]

———. *Stan Kenton and His Orchestra (1940–1951).* Zephyrhills, Fla.: Joyce Record Club, 1984. 64 p. [Garrod 1984/2]

———. *Stan Kenton and His Orchestra (1952–1959).* Zephyrhills, Fla.: Joyce Record Club, 1984. 64 p. [Garrod 1984/3]

———. *Claude Thornhill and His Orchestra.* Zephyrhills, Fla.: Joyce Record Club, 1985. 35 p.

———. *Woody Herman,* Vol. 1 (1936–1947). Zephyrhills, Fla.: Joyce Record Club, 1985. 60 p. [Garrod 1985/1]

———. *Harry James and His Orchestra (1937–1945).* Zephyrhills, Fla.: Joyce Record Club, 1985. 66 p. [Garrod 1985/2]

———. *Harry James and His Orchestra (1946–1954).* Zephyrhills, Fla.: Joyce Record Club, 1985. 70 p. [Garrod 1985/3]

———. *Harry James and His Orchestra (1955–1982).* Zephyrhills, Fla.: Joyce Record Club, 1985. 65 p. [Garrod 1985/4]

———. *Woody Herman,* Vol. 2 (1948–1957). Zephyrhills, Fla.: Joyce Record Club, 1986. 64 p.

———. *Charlie Spivak and His Orchestra.* Zephyrhills, Fla.: Joyce Record Club, 1986. 38 p. [Garrod 1986/4]

———. *Jimmy Dorsey and His Orchestra.* Rev. ed. Zephyrhills, Fla.: Joyce Record Club, 1988. 65 p.

———. *Tommy Dorsey and His Orchestra (1928–1945).* Rev. ed. Zephyrhills, Fla.: Joyce Record Club, 1988. 93 p. [Garrod 1988/1]

———. *Tommy Dorsey and His Orchestra (1946–1956).* Rev. ed. Zephyrhills, Fla.: Joyce Record Club, 1988. 80 p. [Garrod 1988/3]

———. *Woody Herman,* Vol. 3 (1958–1987). Zephyrhills, Fla.: Joyce Record Club, 1988. 57 p. [Garrod 1988/4]

————. *Dick Jurgens and His Orchestra.* Zephyrhills, Fla.: Joyce Record Club, 1988. 35 p. [Garrod 1988/5]

————. *Sammy Kaye and His Orchestra.* Zephyrhills, Fla.: Joyce Record Club, 1988. 71 p. [Garrod 1988/6]

————. *Eddy Duchin and His Orchestra.* Zephyrhills, Fla.: Joyce Record Club, 1989. 28 p.

————. *Shep Fields and His Orchestra.* Zephyrhills, Fla.: Joyce Record Club, 1989. 36 p. [Garrod 1989/1]

————. *Spike Jones and the City Slickers.* Zephyrhills, Fla.: Joyce Record Club, 1989. 39 p. [Garrod 1989/2]

Garrod, Charles, and Bill Korst. *Charlie Barnet and His Orchestra.* Zephyrhills, Fla.: Joyce Record Club, 1984. 79 p.

————. *Gene Krupa and His Orchestra (1935–1946).* Zephyrhills, Fla.: Joyce Record Club, 1984. 51 p. [Garrod and Korst 1984/4]

————. *Gene Krupa and His Orchestra (1947–1973).* Zephyrhills, Fla.: Joyce Record Club, 1984. 63 p. [Garrod and Korst 1984/5]

————. *Kay Kyser and His Orchestra.* Zephyrhills, Fla.: Joyce Record Club, 1986. 51 p. [Garrod and Korst 1986/2]

————. *Artie Shaw and His Orchestra.* Zephyrhills, Fla.: Joyce Record Club, 1986. 64 p. [Garrod and Korst 1986/3]

————. *Nat King Cole: His Voice and Piano.* Zephyrhills, Fla.: Joyce Record Club, 1987. 70 p.

————. *Bob Crosby and His Orchestra.* Zephyrhills, Fla.: Joyce Record Club, 1987. 59 p. [Garrod and Korst 1987/1]

————. *Glen Gray and the Casa Loma Orchestra.* Zephyrhills, Fla.: Joyce Record Club, 1987. 45 p. [Garrod and Korst 1987/2]

Gart, Galen. *ARLD; The American Record Label Directory and Dating Guide, 1940–1959.* Milford, N.H.: Big Nickel Publications, 1989. 259 p.

Geduld, Harry M. *The Birth of the Talkies: From Edison to Jolson.* Bloomington, Ind.: Indiana University Press, 1975. 337 p.

Gelatt, Roland. *The Fabulous Phonograph, 1877–1977.* 2nd rev. ed. New York: Macmillan, 1977. 349 p. (1st ed. 1955)

Geller, Sidney B. *Care and Handling of Computer Magnetic Storage Media.* Washington, D.C.: National Bureau of Standards, 1983. 128 p. (NBS Special Publication, 500-101; SuDoc #C 13.10:500-101).

George, Nelson. *The Death of Rhythm and Blues.* New York: E.P. Dutton, 1989.

Gibson, Gerald. "Preservation and conservation of Sound Recordings." In *Conserving and Preserving Library Materials in Nonbook Formats,* edited by Kathryn Luther Henderson and William T. Henderson. Urbana, Ill.: University of Illinois, Graduate School of Library and Information Science, 1991, pp. 27–44. (Allerton Park Institute series, 30.)

Giese, Hannes. *Art Blakey: Sein Leben, seine Musik, seine Schallplatten.* Schaftlach, Germany: OREOS, 1990. 217 p.

Gillett, Charlie. *The Sound of the City: The Rise of Rock and Roll.* New York: Outerbridge & Dienstfrey, 1970.

Ginell, Gary. *The Decca Hillbilly Discography, 1927–1945.* Westport, Conn.: Greenwood Press, 1989. 402 p.

Girard, Victor, and Harold M. Barnes. *Vertical Cut Cylinders and Discs: A Catalogue of All "Hill-and-dale" Recordings of Serious Worth Made and Issued between 1887–1932 Circa.* London: British Institute of Recorded Sound, 1971. 196 p.

Glazer, Joe. *Labor's Troubadour.* Urbana: University of Illinois Press, 2001. 299 p.

Goddard, Steve. "The Beatles Sessions, CDs, VHS and FDS." *Discoveries* 2-3 (Mar. 1989): 34–35.

Godrich, John, and Rober M.W. Dixon. *Blues and Gospel Records, 1902–1942.* Rev. ed. London: Storyville Publications, 1969. 912 p. issue (4th ed. 1997).

Goldmark, Peter, Rene Snepvangers, and William S. Bachman. "The Columbia Long-Playing Microgroove Recording System." *IRE Proceedings* 37-8 (1949): 923–927. Reprinted in Roys 1978.

Goldsmith, Peter. *Making People's Music: Moe Asch and Folkways Records.* Washington, D.C.: Smithsonian Institution Press, 1998. 468 p.

Goldstein, Kenneth. "A Future Folklorist in the Record Business." In *Transforming Tradition: Folk Music Revivals Examined,* edited by Neil V. Rosenberg. Urbana: University of Illinois Press, 1993, pp. 107–121.

Goslin, John G. "Revolving Thoughts." *Talking Machine Review International* 65-2 (1983): 1,778.

Gottlieb, R.E.M. "Waring's Pennsylvanians." *Record Research* 116 (May 1972): 3–8; 119/120 (Dec. 1972–Jan. 1973): 8–9; 121 (Mar. 1973): 8–9; 122 (June 1973): 4–5.

Grable, Ronald J. "Mr. Edison's Right Hand Man: Ernest L. Stevens." *Record Research* 161 162 (Feb.–Mar. 1979): 4–5; 163/164 (May–June 1979): 10–11.

Grainger, Percy. "Collecting with the Phonograph." *Journal of the Folk-Song Society* 12 (May 1908): 147–169.

Gray, Judith A., ed. *The Federal Cylinder Project.* Vol. 3: Great Basin Plateau Indian Catalog, Northwest Coast Arctic Indian Catalog. Washington, D.C.: American Folklife Center, Library of Congress, 1988.

Gray, Judith A., and Edwin J. Schupman, Jr., eds. *The Federal Cylinder Project.* Vol. 5: California Indian Catalogue, Middle and South American Indian Catalogue, Southwestern Indian Catalogue-I. Washington, D.C.: American Folklife Center, Library of Congress, 1990.

Gray, Michael H. "The Arturo Toscanini Society." *Association for Recorded Sound Collections Journal* 5-1 (1973): 26–29.

————. "The 'World's Greatest Music' and 'World's Greatest Opera' Records: A Discography." *Association for Recorded Sound Collections Journal* 7-1/2 (1975): 33–55.

————. *Beecham; A Centenary Discography.* New York: Holmes & Meier, 1979. 129 p.

————. *Popular Music.* New York: Bowker, 1983. 205 p. (Bibliography of Discographies series, 3)

————. "The Birth of Decca Stereo." *Association for Recorded Sound Collections Journal* 18-1/3 (1986): 4–19.

————. *Classical Music Discographies, 1976–1988.* New York: Greenwood, 1989. 334 p. Continues from Gray and Gibson 1977.

Gray, Michael H., and Gerald D. Gibson. *Bibliography of Discographies.* Vol. 1: Classical Music, 1925–1975. New York: Bowker, 1977. 164 p. Continued in Gray 1989.

Green, Stanley. *Encyclopedia of the Musical Theatre.* New York: Dodd, Mead, 1976. 492 p. Reprint New York: Da Capo Press, 1980.

————. *Broadway Musicals, Show by Show.* London: Faber, 1987. 361 p. (Originally published: Milwaukee, Wis.: H. Leonard Books, 1985.)

Greenfield, Edward, Robert Layton, and Ivan March. *The New Penguin Guide to Compact Discs and Cassettes.* Harmondsworth, England: Penguin Books, 1989. 1,366 p.

Greenfield, Mark, and Tony Middleton. *Dinah Shore; An Exploratory Discography.* London: Authors, 1982. 24 p.

Greenway, John. *American Folk Songs of Protest.* Philadelphia: University of Pennsylvania Press, 1953. 348 p.

Griffin, Marie P. "Preservation of Rare and Unique Materials at the Institute of Jazz Studies." *Association for Recorded Sound Collections Journal* 17-1/3 (1985): 11–17.

Griffiths, Peter H. "Composers' Recordings of Their Own Music." *Audiovisual Librarian* 3-2 (Autumn 1976): 48–55.

Gronow, Pekka. "American Columbia Finnish Language 3000 Series." *Record Research* 101 (Oct. 1969): 8–9; 102 (Nov. 1969): 10.

———. *American Columbia Scandinavian E and F Series.* Helsinki: Finnish Institute of Recorded Sound, 1974. 113 p.

———. *The Columbia 33000-F Irish Series; A Numerical Listing.* Los Angeles: John Edwards Memorial Foundation, University of California at Los Angeles, 1979. 78 p. (JEMF Special Series, 10)

———. "Sources for the History of the Record Industry." *Phonographic Bulletin* 34 (Nov. 1982): 50–54.

———. "Early Gramophone Periodicals in Russia." *Talking Machine Review International* 65/66 (Feb. 1983): 1,784–1,785.

Gronow, Pekka, and Ilpo Saunio. *An International History of the Recording Industry.* London: Casell, 1998. 230 p.

Guralnick, Peter. *Feel like Going Home: Portraits in Blues and Rock 'n' Roll.* New York: Outerbridge & Dienstfrey, 1971. 260 p.

———. *Lost Highway: Journeys and Arrivals of American Muscians.* Boston: Godine, 1979. 364 p.

———. *The Listener's Guide to the Blues.* New York: Facts on File, 1982. 134 p.

———. *Searching for Robert Johnson.* New York: Dutton, 1989. 83 p.

———. *Last Train to Memphis: The Rise of Elvis Presley.* Boston: Little, Brown, and Co., 1994. 560 p.

———. *Careless Love: The Unmaking of Elvis Presley.* Boston: Little, Brown, 1999. 767 p.

———. *Sweet Soul Music: Rhythm and Blues and the Southern Dream of Freedom.* Boston: Little, Brown, 1999. (First Published 1986)

Guy, P.J. "Disc Recording and Reproduction." In *Encyclopedia of High Fidelity*, Vol. 3. New York and London: Focal Press, 1964. 232 p.

Haggin, B.H. *Music on Records.* 4th ed. New York: Oxford University Press, 1946. 279 p. (1st ed. 1938)

Haines, D.E. "The British 'Toy' Gramophone Records of the 1920s." *Talking Machine Review International* 20 21 (Feb.–Apr. 1973): 111–118.

Halban, Desi, and Arthur E. Knight. "Selma Kurz." *Record Collector* 13-3 (May 1960): 51–56; 17-1/3 (Oct. 1968): 46.

Hall, David. *The Record Book.* New York: Smith and Durrell, 1940. 771 p. Subsequent editions: *The Record Book; International Edition*, by David Hall (New York: Smith and Durrell, 1948), 1,394 p.; *Records: 1950 Edition*, by David Hall (New York: Knopf, 1950), 524 + 20 p. ; *The Disc Book*, by David Hall and Abner Levin (New York: Long Player Publications, 1955), 471 p. + unpaged addenda and index.

———. "The Rodgers and Hammerstein Archives of Recorded Sound: History and Current Operation." *Association for Recorded Sound Collections Journal* 6-2 (1974): 17–31.

———. "An Era's End." *Association for Recorded Sound Collections Journal* 12-1/2 (1980): 2–5.

———. "The Mapleson Cylinder Project." *Association for Recorded Sound Collections Journal* 13-3 (1981): 5–20.

———. "A Provisional Mapleson Cylinder Chronology." *Association for Recorded Sound Collections Journal* 13-3 (1981): 14–20. [Hall 1981/2]

———. "A Mapleson Afterword." *Association for Recorded Sound Collections Journal* 14-1 (1982): 5–10. [Hall 1982/1]

———. "The Mapleson Cylinder Project." *Recorded Sound* 82 (July 1982): 39–60; 83 (Jan. 1983): 21–56. [Hall 1982/7]

———. "New Music Quarterly Recordings—A Discography." *Association for Recorded Sound Collections Journal* 16-1/2 (1984): 10–27. [Hall 1984/1]

———. "Recordings: Live at the Met, 1901–1903." *Ovation* (Oct. 1984): 26–33; (Nov. 1984): 19–21, 34. [Hall 1984/10]

———. "Discography: A Chronological Survey." In *Modern* 1989, pp. 173–184.

Hall, George. *Jan Savitt and His Orchestra.* Zephyrhills, Fla.: Joyce Record Club, 1985. 32 p.

Hamilton, Chris. "Hines—Not 57 Varieties." *Hillandale News* 150 (June 1986): 46–49.

Hamilton, David. *Listener's Guide to the Great Instrumentalists.* New York: Facts on File, 1982. 137 p.

———. Review of "The Metropolitan Opera on Record" by Frederick P. Fellers. *Association for Recorded Sound Collections Journal* 16-3 (1984): 57–62.

Hammond, John, with Irving Townsend. *John Hammond on Record: An Autobiography.* New York: Ridge Press; 1977. 416 p.

Hanna, John. "The Gramophone Company, 1898–1925." *Journal of the Phonograph Society of New South Wales* 6-4 (July 1990): 6–11. Continues in the *Sound Record* (new name of the journal), 7-1 (Sept. 1990): 16–19 (covering 1925–1952).

Hansen, Hans. *Lauritz Melchior: A Discography.* Rev. ed. Copenhagen: Nationaldiskoteket, 1972. 40 p. (1st ed. 1965)

Harman, Carter. "Composers Recordings, Inc." *Association for Recorded Sound Collections Journal* 6-1 (1974): 26–29.

Harris, Harmony Steve. *Jazz on Compact Disc: A Critical Guide to the Best Recordings.* New York: Harmony Books, 1987. 176 p.

Harrison, Max, et al. *Modern Jazz; The Essential Records.* London: Aquarius Books, 1975. 131 p.

Harrison, Max, Charles Fox, and Eric Thacker. *The Essential Jazz Records. Vol. 1: Ragtime to Swing.* Westport, Conn.: Greenwood Press, 1984. 595 p.

Hart, Mary L., Brenda M. Eagles, and Lisa N. Woworth . *The Blues: A Bibliographical Guide.* New York: Garland, 1989. 636 p.

Hart, Philip. "Towards a Reiner Discography." *Association for Recorded Sound Collections Journal* 19-1 (1987): 63–70.

Hartel, Harold H. "The H3 Chrono-Matrix File." *Record Research* 175/176 (Sept. 1980): 5–10. A series that had reached 36 parts, with 247/248 (Sept. 1991). It is a chronological list of the jazz, blues, and gospel recordings that appeared in Rust 1961 (1969 ed.) and Godrich 1969. Artist, matrix, label number, title, and references are given for each disc. The time period covered is Feb. 1922 to Aug. 1933 (as of *Record Research* 247/248).

Harvey, Hugh H. "Nellie Melba." *Record Collector* 4-12 (Dec. 1949): 202–215.

Harvith, John, and Susan Edwards Harvith, ed. *Edison, Musicians, and the Phonograph.* Westport, Conn.: Greenwood Press, 1987. 478 p.

Hasse, John Edward. *Ragtime: Its History, Composers, and Music.* New York: Schirmer Books, 1985. 460 p.

Hayes, Cedric J. "Imperial Matrix Listing (IM 1 to IM 2000)." *Record Research* 235/236 (June 1988): 8; 237/238 (Nov. 1988): 8; 239/240 (Apr. 1989): 8; 241/242 (Oct.–Nov. 1989): 9; 243/244 (May–June 1990): 9; 245/246 (Jan. 1991): 9; 247/248 (Sept. 1991): 10. A continuing series that extends Rotante 1985.

Hayes, Jim. "Sherlock Holmes? No, It's 'Shellac Hayes'." *Talking Machine Review International* 10 (June 1971): 42, 44–45.

Hayes, Jim G. *Panachord and Rex.* Liverpool: Author, 1974. 23 p.

Hayes, Richard K. *Kate Smith Discography.* Cranston, R.I.: Author, 1977.

Hazelcorn, Howard. *A Collector's Guide to the Columbia Spring-Wound Cylinder Graphophone.* Brooklyn: Antique Phonograph Monthly, 1976. 36 p. (APM Monographs series, 2.)

Hedberg, Tom. "Rescuing the Voices of the Dead—A Laser-Read Sound Reproducing System." *Antique Phonograph Monthly* 5-8 (1978): 7–8.

Heintze, James R. *Scholars Guide to Washington, D.C., for Audio Resources.* Washington, D.C.: Smithsonian Institution Press, 1985. 395 p.

Helmbrecht, Arthur J., Jr. *Fritz Reiner: The Comprehensive Discography of His Recordings.* Novelty, Ohio: Fritz Reiner Society, 1978. 79 p. Supplement, Apr. 1981, 9 p.; and Addenda, Apr. 1991, 4 p. (Madison, N.J.: Author, 1981).

Helmholtz, Hermann L. *On the Sensations of Tone as a Physiological Basis for the Theory of Music.* Reprint of the 2nd English ed., trans. and rev. by Alexander J. Ellis, based on the 4th German ed. (1887); with a new introduction by Henry Margenau. New York: Dover, 1954. 576 p.

Hemphill, Paul H. *The Nashville Sound.* New York: Simon & Schuster, 1970. 289 p.

Henriksen, Henry. "Gennett Research." *Record Research* 94 (Dec. 1968): 3–5.

———. "Herschel Gold Seal." *Record Research* 131 (Jan. 1975): 1, 5.

———. "Autograph." *Record Research* 153 154 (Apr. 1978): 4–7.

———. "Black Patti." *Record Research* 165/166 (Aug. 1979): 4–8; 167/168 (Oct. 1979): 4–8; 171/172 (Mar. 1980): 4–5, 24; 173/174 (June 1980): 9; 177/178 (Nov. 1980): 8; 181/182 (Apr. 1981): 10; 183/184 (July 1981): 9; 185/186 (Oct. 1981): 8; 187/188 (Dec 1981): 8. At this point a label list begins: 189/190 (Mar.–Apr. 1982): 8; 191/192 (July 1982): 8; 193/194 (Oct. 1982): 9; 195/196 (Jan. 1983): 13; 197/198 (Mar.–Apr. 1983): 9.

Henrysson, Harald, and Jack W. Porter. *A Jussi Björling Phonography.* Stockholm: Svenskt Musikhistoriskt Arkiv, 1984. 269 p.

Henstock, Michael. *Fernando De Lucia.* London: Duckworth, 1991. 505 p. Discography, pp. 437–482.

Hernon, Michael. *French Horn Discography.* Westport, Conn.: Greenwood Press, 1986. 292 p.

Hervingham-Root, Laurie. "David Bispham: Quaker Baritone." *Talking Machine Review International* 7 (Dec. 1970): 197–199. Continued in *Talking Machine Review International* 8, 9, 10, 12, 13, and 14.

Hervingham-Root, Laurie, and James F. E. Dennis. "Pol Plançon." *Record Collector* 8-7/8 (July–Aug. 1953): 148–191; 8-10 (Oct. 1953): 236–237; 10-12 (Nov. 1956): 277; 12-7 (Oct. 1959): 165.

Herzhaft, Jerard. *Encyclopedia of the Blues.* Translated by Brigitte Debord. 2nd Ed. Faytteville, AR: Uarkansas Press, 1997.

Heyworth, Peter. *Otto Klemperer: His Life and Times.* Cambridge, England: Cambridge University Press, 1983. Discography by Michael H. Gray, pp. 444–452.

Hillman, Peter E. "Symmetrical Speaker System with Dual Transmission Lines." *Speaker Builder* (Sept. 1989): 10.

Hinze, Michael. "Medallion Revisited." *Record Research* 144/145 (Mar. 1977): 12–13.

Hirsch, Julian. "Feelin' Groovy; Head to Head Lab and Listening Tests of Five Leading Phono Cartridges." *Stereo Review* (Jan. 1988): 74–79.

Hirshey, Gerri. *Nowhere to Run: The Story of Soul Music.* New York: Da Capo Press, 1994.

H. Wiley Hitchcock, and Stanley Sadie, ed., *New Grove Dictionary of American Music.* London: Macmillan, 1986. 4 vols.

Hoffmann, Frank. *The Development of Library Collections of Sound Recordings.* New York: Dekker, 1979. 169 p.

———. *The Literature of Rock, 1954–1978.* Metuchen, N.J.: Scarecrow Press, 1981. 349 p. Continued by Hoffmann, Cooper, and Hoffmann 1986/2.

Hoffmann, Frank, and Lee Ann Hoffmann. *The Cash Box Singles Charts, 1950–1981.* Metuchen, N.J.: Scarecrow Press, 1983. 876 p.

Hoffmann, Frank, B. Lee Cooper, and Lee Ann Hoffman. *The Literature of Rock II* Metuchen, N.J.: Scarecrow Press, 1986. 2 vols. Continues from Hoffmann 1981. [Hoffmann, Cooper, and Hoffmann 1986/2]

Hoffmann, Frank, and George Albert. *The Cash Box Country Singles Charts, 1958–1982.* Metuchen, N.J.: Scarecrow Press, 1984. 605 p.

———. *The Cash Box Black Contemporary Album Charts, 1975–1987.* Metuchen, N.J.: Scarecrow Press, 1989. 249 p. [Hoffmann and Albert 1989/1]

———. *The Cash Box Country Album Charts, 1964–1988.* Metuchen, N.J.: Scarecrow Press, 1989. 300 p. [Hoffmann and Albert 1989/2]

Hoffmann, Frank, George Albert, and Lee Ann Hoffmann. *The Cash Box Black Contemporary Singles Charts, 1960–1984.* Metuchen, N.J.: Scarecrow Press, 1986. 704 p. [Hoffmann, Albert, and Hoffmann 1986/1]

———. *The Cash Box Album Charts, 1975–1985.* Metuchen, N.J.: Scarecrow Press, 1987. 556 p.

———. *The Cash Box Album Charts, 1955–1974.* Metuchen, N.J.: Scarecrow Press, 1988. 528 p.

Hogarth, Will H. "Nellie Melba." *Record Collector* 27-3/4 (Mar. 1982): 72–87.

Hogarth, Will, and R. T. See. "Marjorie Lawrence Discography." *Record Collector* 32-1/2 (Jan. 1987): 7–18; 33-11/12 (Nov. 1988): 300–303.

Hoggard, Stuart. *Bob Dylan: An Illustrated Discography.* Oxford, England: Transmedia Express, 1978. 108, 23 p.

Holcman, Jan. "The Honor Roll of Recorded Chopin, 1906–1960." *Saturday Review* (27 Feb. 1960): 44–45, 61–62.

———. "Liszt: Piano Recordings." *Music Magazine* (Nov. 1961): 14–16, 48. [Holcman 1961/11]

———. "Liszt in the Records of His Pupils." *Saturday Review* (23 Dec. 1961): 45–46, 57. [Holcman 1961/12]

———. "Liszt Records: Part Two." *Music Magazine* (Dec. 1961): 24–25, 60. [Holcman 1961/12]

———. "Debussy on Disc: 1912–1962." *Saturday Review* (Aug. 25, 1962): 34–35.

Holzman, Jac, and Gavan Daws. *Follow the Music: The Life and Times of Elektra Records in the Great Years of American Pop Culture.* Santa Monica, Calif.: First Media Books, 1998. 441 p.

Holdridge, Lawrence F. "Charles Hackett." *Record Collector* 22-8/9 (Feb. 1975): 171–214; 22-10/11 (Apr. 1975): 257.

Holmes, John L. *Conductors on Record.* London: Gollancz; Westport, Conn.: Greenwood Press, 1982. 734 p.

Hoover, Cynthia A. *Music Machines American Style; A Catalog of the Exhibition.* Washington, D.C.: Smithsonian Institution Press, 1971. 140, 15 p.

Horn, Geoffrey. "Geoffrey Horn Visits Celestion." *Gramophone* 66 (Nov. 1988): 896–898.

Hounsome, Terry, and Tim Chambre. *Rock Record.* 3rd ed. New York: Facts on File, 1981. 526 p. (Published in Britain as *New Rock Record*, 1981. 1st ed. titled *Rockmaster*, 1978; revised as *Rock Record*, 1979.)

Hume, Martha. *You're So Cold I'm Turnin' Blue.* New York: Viking, 1982. 202 p.

Hummel, David. *Collector's Guide to the American Musical Theatre.* Metuchen, N.J.: Scarecrow Press, 1984. 2 vols.

Humphreys, Ivor. "ARCAM." *Gramophone* (Oct. 1990): 857–862.

Hunt, John. *The Furtwängler Sound.* 2nd ed. London: Furtwängler Society, 1985. Apparently superseded by a later edition, cited in *Gramophone* (May 1990): 1,935.

———. *From Adam to Webern: The Recordings of Von Karajan.* London: Author, 1987. 130 p. (Bound with *Philharmonia Orchestra: Complete Discography 1945–1987,* by Stephen J. Pettitt.)

Hurd, Daniel. "35 Shades of Black: The Johnny Cash Story." *Discoveries* (Aug. 1990): 94–97. Includes a discography of LPs.

Hurst, P.G. *The Golden Age Recorded.* 2nd ed. Lingfield, Surrey, England: Oakwood, 1963. 187 p. (1st ed. 1947)

Hutchinson, Tom. "Alessandro Bonci." *Record Collector* 11-7 (July 1957): 148–162; 11-9/10 (Sept.–Oct. 1957): 234–235; 12-4/5 (Feb.–Mar. 1959): 108, 116; 18-1/2 (Oct. 1968): 47.

———. "Tito Schipa." *Record Collector* 13-4/5 (June–July 1960): 75–109.

Hutchinson, Tom, and Clifford Williams. "Giovanni Zenatello." *Record Collector* 14-5/6 (1961): 100–143; 14-7/8 (1961): 170–171. Copies seen did not have dates.

International Piano Archives at Maryland. *Catalog of the Reproducing Piano Roll Collection.* College Park, Md.: Author, 1983. 281 p.

Isom, Warren Rex. "How to Prevent and Cure Record Warping." *High Fidelity* 22 (Sept. 1972): 50–53.

———. "Evolution of the Disc Talking Machine." *Journal of the Audio Engineering Society* 25-10/11 (Sept.–Oct. 1977): 718–723.

Isom Warren Rex, ed. "The Phonograph and Sound Recording after One Hundred Years." *Journal of the Audio Engineering Society* 25 (Oct.–Nov. 1977). Centennial issue of the journal. Individual articles cited separately in this Bibliography are Burt 1977, Khanna 1977, Kogen 1977, and Olson, H. 1977.

Jackson, John. *Big Beat Heat: Alan Freed and the Early Years of Rock and Roll.* New York: Schirmer Books, 1994. 400 p.

———. *American Bandstand: Dick Clark and the Making of a Rock 'n' Roll Empire.* New York: Oxford University Press, 1998. 336 p.

Jackson, Paul T. *Collectors' Contact Guide.* Rev. ed. Springield, Ill.: Recorded Sound Research, 1975. 58 p. (1st ed. 1973)

Jansen, F.A. "Non-Magnetic Sound Recording on Tape." *Hillandale News* 133 (Aug. 1983): 239–241.

Jasen, David. "Zez Confrey, Creator of the Novelty Rag; Preparatory Research." *Record Research* 111 (July 1971): 5, 10.

———. *Recorded Ragtime, 1897–1958.* Hamden, Conn.: Archon Books, 1973. 155 p.

Jasen, David, and Gene Jones, *Spreadin' Rhythm Around: Black Popular Songwriters,* 1880–1930. New York: Schirmer Books, 1998, 435 p.

———. *That American Rag: The Story of Ragtime from Coast to Coast.* New York: Schirmer Books, 1999, 336 p.

———. *Black Bottom Stomp: Eight Masters of Ragtime and Early Jazz.* New York: Routledge, 2001. 272 p.

Jefferson, Alan. *Lotte Lehmann, 1888–1976.* London: Julia MacRae Books, 1988. 333 p. Discography on pp. 243–322.

Jepsen, Jorgen Grunnet. *A Discography of Stan Kenton.* Brande, Denmark: Debut Records, 1962. 2 vols.

———. *Jazz Records 1942–1962.* Holte, Denmark: Knudsen, 1963–1969. 12 vols.

———. *A Discography of Dizzy Gillespie, 1937–1952.* Copenhagen: Karl Knudsen, 1969. 39 p.

———. *A Discography of Dizzy Gillespie, 1953–1968.* Copenhagen: Karl Knudsen, 1969. 30 p.

———. *A Discography of John Coltrane.* Rev. ed. Copenhagen: Karl Knudsen, 1969. 35 p.

Jewell, Brian. *Veteran Talking Machines.* Tunbridge Wells, England: Midas, 1977. 128 p.

Johnson, Colin. "The Oldest Person to Record?" *Hillandale News* 130 (Feb. 1983): 167.

Johnston, Brian Fawcett. *Count John McCormack.* Bournemouth, England: Talking Machine Review, 1988. 57 p. Errata noted in *Hillandale News* 165 (Dec. 1988): 126–127.

Jorgensen, Finn. *The Complete Handbook of Magnetic Recording.* 3rd ed. Blue Ridge Summit, Penn.: Tab Books, 1988. 740 p.

Kalil Ford, ed. *Magnetic Tape Recording for the Eighties.* Washington, D.C.: National Aeronautics and Space Administration, 1982. 170 p. (NASA Reference Publications 1075)

Kallman, Helmut, Gilles Potvin, and Kenneth Winters, eds. "A & M Records of Canada, Ltd." (p. 1); "Ed Archambault, Inc." (p. 27); "Arc Records" (p. 30); "Beaver Records, Ltd." (p. 70); "Berliner Gramophone Company" (p. 80); "Bernadol Music Limited" (p. 79); "Boot Records, Ltd." (p. 99); "Brunswick" (p. 126); "Canada Baroque Records. Ltd." (p. 137); "Canadian Academy of Recording Arts and Sciences" (p. 140); "Canadian Recording Industry Association" (p. 154); "Canadian Talent Library" (p. 155); "Canadian Vitaphone Company" (p. 155); "CAPAC" (pp. 156–157); "Capitol Records-EMI of Canada, Ltd." (p. 157); "CBC Recordings" (p. 167); "CBS Records Canada, Ltd." (pp. 169–170); "Compo Company, Ltd." (p. 212); "CRTC" (p. 246); "Gamma Records, Ltd." (pp. 364–365); "GRT of Canada, Ltd." (p. 395); "Hallmark Recordings, Ltd." (p. 406); "Juno Awards" (p. 487); "Kébec-Disk, Inc." (p. 492); "London Records of Canada (1967), Ltd." (p. 561); "Pathé Frères" (p. 729); "Polydor, Ltd." (p. 769); "Quality Records, Ltd." (p. 784); "RCA Limited" (p. 795); "Recorded Sound" (pp. 796–800); "Rococo Records" (p. 816); "Rodeo Records, Ltd." (pp. 816–817); "Sparton of Canada, Ltd." (p. 888); "Starr" (p. 891); "Gordon V. Thompson, Ltd." (p. 914); "True North Records" (p. 936); "Waterloo Music Company, Ltd." (p. 988). *Encyclopedia of Music in Canada.* Toronto: University of Toronto Press, 1981. 1,108 p. French version: Montreal: Fides, 1982.

Kaplan, ed. *Variety's Directory of Major Show Business Awards.* Mike 2nd ed. New York: Bowker, 1989. 750 p. (1st ed. 1985)

Kastlemusick Directory for Collectors of Recordings. 1981–1982 ed. Wilmington, Del.: Kastlemusick, 1981. 84 p. (1st ed. 1977)

Kaufman, Tom, and James F. E. Dennis. "Leo Slezak." *Record Collector* 15-9/10 (1964): 195–235.

Kay, George W. "Those Fabulous Gennetts." *Record Changer* 12 (June 1953): 4–13.

———. "The Superior Catalog." *Record Research* 37 (Aug. 1961): 1–4; 38 (Oct. 1961): 10–11; 41 (Feb. 1962): 11; 42 (Mar.–Apr. 1962): 2, 20.

Kelly, Alan. *His Master's Voice: La voce del padrone: The Italian Catalogue ... 1898 to 1929* Westport, Conn.: Greenwood Press, 1988. 462 p.

———. *His Master's Voice: La voix de son maitre; The French Catalogue ... 1898–1929* Westport, Conn.: Greenwood Press, 1990. 679 p.

———. *His Master's Voice / Die Stimme Seines Herrn: The German Catalog ... 1898 to 1929.* Westport, Conn.: Greenwood Press, 1994.

———. *His Master's Voice / De Stem Von Zign meester: The Dutch Catalog ... 1900 to 1929.* Westport, Conn.: Greenwood Press, 1997.

Kelly, Alan, John F. Perkins, and John Ward. "Selma Kurz: A Discography." *Recorded Sound* 73 (Jan. 1979): 2–5.

Kelly, Alan, and Vladimir Gurvich. "Discography." In *Chaliapin: A Critical Biography,* by Victor Borovsky. New York: Knopf, 1988, pp. 541–587.

Kendziora, Carl. "Behind the Cobwebs" columns. *Record Research* 1949–1986. Cited by date only.

———. "Problems of Dating Recorded Performances." In Allen 1971, pp. 8–18.

Kennedy, Michael. *Barbirolli, Conductor Laureate.* London: Hart-Davis, 1973. 416 p. Reprint New York: Da Capo Press, 1982. Discography on pp. 341–402.

Kenyon, Percy, Clifford Williams, and William R. Moran. "Pasquale Amato." *Record Collector* 21-1/2 (Mar. 1973): 3–47; 21-5/6 (Oct. 1973): 128–132.

Khanna, S. K. "Vinyl Compound for the Phonographic Industry." *Journal of the Audio Engineering Society* 25-10/11 (Sept.–Oct. 1977): 724–728.

Kincaid, Bradley [Sound recording]. Bluebonnet BL 105, BL 107. (1964) Program notes contributed by D.K. Wilgus.

Kiner, Larry F. *The Al Jolson Discography.* Westport, Conn.: Greenwood Press, 1983. 194 p.

———. *The Rudy Vallee Discography.* Westport, Conn.: Greenwood Press, 1985. 190 p.

———. *The Cliff Edwards Discography.* Westport, Conn.: Greenwood Press, 1987. 260 p.

Kinkle, Roger D. *The Complete Encyclopedia of Popular Music and Jazz, 1900–1950.* New Rochelle, N.Y.: Arlington House, 1974. 4 vols.

Kirvine, John. *Jukebox Saturday Night.* London: New English Library, Times-Mirror, 1977. 160 p.

Klee, Joe. "From the Golden Age of Opera Recordings." *Antique Phonograph Monthly* 7-1 (1981): 8–9.

———. "From the Golden Age: Caruso Reissues." *Antique Phonograph Monthly* 7-6 (1983): 6–7.

———. "From the Golden Age ... Caruso on Compact Disc." *Antique Phonograph Monthly* 8-6 (1987): 15–16.

———. "In the Beginning ... From Berliner to World War I." *Antique Phonograph Monthly* 9-3 (1990): 13–15.

Klein, Andrew. "A History of the Starr Piano Factory." *Talking Machine Review International* 65/66 (Feb. 1983): 1,787–1,789, 1,818.

Klein, Larry. "Amplifier Damping Factor: How Important Is It?" *Radio Electronics* 60-1 (Jan. 1989): 78–79.

Kline, Pete. "The Capitol Years" *Discoveries* 2-7 (July 1989): 18–21. Discography of Frank Sinatra's Capitol records, 1953–1962.

Klinger, Bill. "The Short-Lived Harris Everlasting Record." *Antique Phonograph Monthly* 10-1 (1991): 3–4.

Knight, Arthur E. "Roland Hayes." *Record Collector* 10-2 (July 1955): 27–45; 12-3/4 (Feb.–Mar. 1959): 116; 12-8/9 (Nov.–Dec. 1959): 215.

Knight, G.A. "Factors Relating to the Long Term Storage of Magnetic Tape." *Phonographic Bulletin* 18 (July 1977): 16–35.

Koeningsberg, Allen. "In the Pink: A Lambert Discography." *Antique Phonograph Monthly* 6-8 (1980): 4–10; 6-9 (1980): 8–9.

———. *Edison Cylinder Records, 1889–1912; With an Illustrated History of the Phonograph.* 2nd ed. Brooklyn: APM Press, 1987. 42 + 172 p. (1st ed. 1969)

———. *The Patent History of the Phonograph, 1877–1912.* Brooklyn: APM Press, 1990. 72 + 87 p.

Kogen, James H. "Gramophone Record Reproduction: Development, Performance and Potential of the Stereo Pickup." *Proceedings of the IEEE* (Aug. 1968): 116–118.

———. "Record Changers, Turntables, and Tone Arms—A Brief Technical History." *Journal of the Audio Engineering Society* 25-10/11 (Sept.–Oct. 1977): 749–758.

Korenhof, Paul. "Maria Callas discographie." *Luister* 302 (Nov. 1977): 197–122.

Koster, Piet, and Dick M. Bakker. *Charlie Parker Discography.* Amsterdam: Micrography, 1974–1976. 4 vols. Covers 1940–1955.

Koster, Piet, and Chris Sellars. *Dizzy Gillespie,* Volume I, 1937–1953. Amsterdam: Micrography, 1985. 68 p.

Kressley, David. "Catalog of World Transcriptions (1933–1963)." *Record Research* 89 (Mar. 1968): 1–8; 90 (May 1968): 6–7; 91 (July 1968): 5; 92 (Sept. 1968): 5; 93 (Nov. 1968): 8–10; 94 (Dec. 1968): 7; 98 (May 1969): 7–9.

———. "The Frederic W. Ziv Company." *Record Research* 201/202 (Sept. 1983): 4–6 on Wayne King.; 203/204 (Dec. 1983): 1–2; 205/206 (Mar. 1984): 8; 207/208 (June 1984): 8; 209/210 (Oct. 1984): 9; 211/212 (Feb. 1985): 11.

Kunstadt, Len. "The Lucille Hegamin Story." *Record Research* 40 (Jan. 1962): 3, 19.

———. "The Labels behind Black Swan." *Record Research* 229/230 (June 1987): 1, 4–5. Continues a compilation that began in *Record Research* 221/222 under Carl Kendziora's name. The Kendziora articles were reprinted from *Record Changer,* but the Kunstadt continuation is new material.

———. "Unmasking the Associated's." *Record Research* 235/236 (June 1988): 1, 4; 237/238 (Nov. 1988): 1, 4; 239/240 (Apr. 1989): 5–9; 241/242 (Oct.–Nov. 1989): 6.

Kweskin, Jim. "Woody Guthrie." *Record Research* 161/162 (Feb.–Mar. 1979): 13; 163/164 (May–June 1979): 13.

Lambert, M.J. "Decca Records, 1929–1980." *Hillandale News* 130 (Feb. 1983): 156–161; 131 (Apr. 1983): 176–181.

Lambert, Ruth L. "Needle Tins." *Talking Machine Review International* 70 (Dec. 1985): 1,945–1,947, 1,997–1,999.

Lane, Michael R. "Equalization and Equalizers." *Association for Recorded Sound Collections Journal* 14-2 (1982): 29–36.

———. "Sonic Restoration of Historical Recordings." *Audio* (June 1991): 35–44; (July 1991): 26–37.

Lane, Michael, and Richard C. Burns. "On 'Fifty Questions on Audio Restoration and Transfer Technology'." *Association for Recorded Sound Collections Journal* 16-3 (1984): 5–11. A response to Owen 1983. Owen replied; then Lane and Owen had further comments in *Association for Recorded Sound Collections Journal* 17 (1985): 1–3.

Langwill, Lyndesay. *The Bassoon and Contrabassoon.* New York: Norton, 1965. 269 p. Discography on pp. 223–258.

Laubich, Arnold, and Ray Spencer. *Art Tatum; A Guide to His Recorded Music.* Metuchen, N.J.: Scarecrow Press, 1982. 359 p.

Lawrence, A. F. R., and Steve Smolian. "Emma Eames." *American Record Guide* 29 (1962): 210.

Leder, Jan. *Women in Jazz: A Discography of Instrumentalists, 1913–1968.* Westport, Conn.: Greenwood Press, 1985. 310 p.

Lee, Dorothy Sara. *Native North American Music and Oral Data: A Catalogue of Sound Recordings, 1893–1976.* Bloomington, Ind.: Indiana University Press, 1979. 479 p.

Lenoir, Abbe. "Procédé d'enregistrement et de reproduction des phénomènes perçus par l'ovie." *Semaine du clergé* (Oct. 10, 1877).

Léon, J. A., and Alusio R. Guimaraes. "Bidu Sayao." *Record Collector* 13-6 (Aug. 1960): 123–133; 16-2 (Sept. 1964): 46–47.

Leonard, William Torbert. *Masquerade in Black.* Metuchen, N.J.: Scarecrow Press, 1986. 431 p.

Levarie, Siegmund. "Noise." *Critical Inquiry* 4-1 (Autumn 1977): 21–31.

Levarie, Siegmund, and Ernst Levy. *Tone: A Study in Musical Acoustics.* 2nd ed. Kent, Ohio: Kent State University Press, 1980. 248 p. Reprint Westport, Conn.: Greenwood Press, 1981. (1st ed. 1968)

————. *Musical Morphology: A Discourse and a Dictionary.* Kent, Ohio: Kent State University Press, 1983. 344 p.

Lewine, Richard, and Alfred Simon. *Songs of the Theater.* New York: H.W. Wilson, 1984. 897 p. Replaces their *Songs of the American Theater* and *Encyclopedia of Theater Music.*

Lewis, Gareth H. "Evan Williams." *Record Collector* 24-11/12 (Dec. 1978): 242–277.

Lewis, John Sam. "Fritz Kreisler: The First Hundred Years (1987–1975)." *Record Research* 139/140 (May–June 1976): 8–10.

————. "Stokowski: The Centenary." *Record Research* 149/150 (Oct. 1977): 4–5, 12.

————. "Early Violinists." *Record Research* 167 168 (Oct. 1979): 12.

————. "First Lady of the Keyboard: Wanda Landowska." *Record Research* 163/164 (May 1979): 9; 165/166 (Aug. 1979): 13.

————. "The Beecham Celebration." *Record Research* 171/172 (Mar. 1980): 12; 173/174 (June 1980): 12; 175/176 (Sept. 1980): 11.

————. "Jan Kubelik and Jacques Thibaud." *Record Research* 179/180 (Feb. 1981): 9, 23 about Kubelik.; *Record Research* 181/182 (Apr. 1981): 11, 24 about Thibaud..

————. "The Violinists: Samuel Gardner." *Record Research* 213/214 (May 1985): 11–12.

————. "Efrem Zimbalist (1889–1985)." *Record Research* 221/222 (Apr. 1986): 8–9; 223/224 (Aug. 1986): 9; 225/226 (Nov. 1986): 2.

————. "The Pupils of Franz Liszt." *Record Research* 235/236 (June 1988): 5; 237/238 (Nov. 1988): 5; 239/240 (Apr. 1989): 7; 241/242 (Oct.–Nov. 1989): 8.

Lewis, Ted. "Our Society." *Hillandale News* 18 (Apr. 1964): 24–25. About the City of London Phonograph and Gramophone Society.

Lieb, Sandra R. *Mother of the Blues: A Study of Ma Rainey.* Amherst, Mass.: University of Massachusetts Press, 1983. 226 p.

Liliedahl, Karleric. "Swedish Record Labels: Dacapo." *Talking Machine Review International* 10 (June 1971): 35–36.

————. *Dixi-Silverton.* Trelleborg, Sweden: Author, 1973. 93 p.

————. *Comprehensive Discography of Swedish Acoustic Recordings, 1903–1928.* Stockholm: Arkivet för Ljud och Bild, 1987. 800 p. Lists 10,000 titles on 52 labels; excluding Gramophone Co.

Lindsay, Joe. "Vogue, the Original Picture Disc Label." *Discoveries* 2-3 (Mar. 1989): 24–27.

Lindsay, Joe, Peter Bukoski, and Marc Grobman. *Picture Discs of the World: Price Guide and International Reference Book.* Scottsdale, Ariz.: Biodisc, 1990. 205 p.

Linkwitz, Siegfried H. "Active Crossover Networks for Noncoincident Drivers." *Journal of the Audio Engineering Society* 1-2 (1976).

Litchfield, Jack. *Canadian Jazz Discography: 1916–1980.* Toronto: University of Toronto Press, 1982. 945 p.

Little, Donald C. "Discography of Tuba Solo Literature." *NACWPI Journal* 26 (Winter 1977–1978): 43–44.

Long, Edward M. "SME V Tonearm and Talisman Virtuoso DTi Cartridge." *Audio* (June 1986): 88–96.

————. "Mats & Clamps by the Numbers." *Audio* (Apr. 1988): 45–52. Discusses mats for turntables.

Lonstein, Albert L. *The Revised Compleat [sic] Sinatra.* Ellenville, N.Y.: S.M. Lonstein, 1979. 702 p.

Lorcey, Jacques. *Maria Callas: d'art et d'amour.* Rev. ed. Paris: Editions PAC, 1983. 615p. Discography on pp. 537–585 609–612. (1st ed. 1977)

Lorenz, Kenneth M. *Two-Minute Brown Wax and XP Cylinder Records of the Columbia Phonograph Company: Numerical Catalog, August 1896-ca. March 1909.* Wilmington, Del.: Kastlemusick, 1981. 75 p.

Lowery, Alvin L. *Lowery's International Trumpet Discography.* Baltimore: Camden House, 1990. 2 vols.

Lumpe, Ernst A. "Pseudonymous Performers on Early LP Records: Rumors, Facts, and Finds." *Association for Recorded Sound Collections Journal* 21-2 (Fall 1990): 226–231.

Lustig, Larry, and Clifford Williams. "Giuseppe Anselmi." *Record Collector* 32-3/4/5 (Apr. 1987): 51–85.

Lyle, G. R., and Rose Krauskopf. "Phonograph Collection in Antioch College Library." *Library Journal* 59 (15 Mar. 1934): 266–267.

Lynch, Richard Chigley. *Broadway on Record; A Directory of New York Cast Recordings of Musical Shows, 1931–1986.* Westport, Conn.: Greenwood Press, 1987. 357 p.

MacDonald, J. Fred. *Don't Touch that Dial: Radio Programming in American Life, 1920–1960.* Chicago: Nelson-Hall, 1982. 412 p.

MacKenzie, John R., and John Godrich. "The Broadway Race Series." *Matrix* 48 (Aug. 1963): 3–13.

Magnusson, Tor. "The Gene Austin Recordings." *Skivsamlaren* 15 (Feb. 1983): 1–82.

Malone, Bill C. *Country Music U.S.A.; A Fifty-Year History.* Rev. ed. Austin, Tex.: University of Texas Press, 1985. 562 p. (1st ed. 1968)

————. *Don't Get Above Your Raisin': Country Music and the Southern Working Class.* Urbana: University of Illinois Press, 2002. 392 p.

Manildi, Donald. "The Rubinstein Discography." *Le grand baton* 20-56 (Dec. 1983): 56–100.

Mann, Alfred, ed. *Modern Music Librarianship: Essays in Honor of Ruth Watanabe.* Stuyvesant, N.Y.: Pendragron Press, 1989. 252 p. (Festschrift Series, 8).

Manzo, J. R. "A Lambert Sampler." *New Amberola Graphic* 32 (Spring 1980): 4–7.

Marco, Guy A. "Bibliographic Control of Sound Recordings: An International View." *Audiovisual Librarian* 15 (Feb. 1989): 19–24.

Margoschis, Richard M. *Recording Natural History Sounds.* Barnet, England: Print & Press Services, 1977. 110 p.

Marsh, Dave. *The Heart of Rock & Soul: The 1001 Greatest Singles Ever Made.* New York: New American Library, 1989. 717 p. (reissued NY: Da Capo Press, 1999)

————. *Louie Louie: The History and Mythology of the World's Most Famous Rock 'n' Roll Song.* New York: Hyperion, 1993. 245 p. (reissued Ann Arbor, MI: U of Michigan Press, 2004)

————. *Bruce Springsteen: Two Hearts, The Definitive Biography, 1972–2003.* New York: Routledge, 2004. 696 p.

Marsh, Dave, and John Swenson, eds. *The New Rolling Stone Record Guide.* Rev., updated ed. New York: Random House/Rolling Stone Press, 1983. 648 p. (1st ed. 1979).

Marsh, Robert C. "Solti in Chicago: A Critical Discography." *Harmonie-panorama-musique, new series* 20-46 (Oct. 1984): 26–29, 35.

Martel, Joseph. "Roger Harding—A Forgotten Recording Pioneer." *New Amberola Graphic* 65 (July 1988): 3–8.

Martland, Peter. "Colonel Gouraud's Present." *Hillandale News* 162 (June 1988): 30–32.

——. "Theodore Birnbaum." *Hillandale News* 168 (June 1989): 225.

Marty, Daniel. *Illustrated History of Talking Machines.* New York: Dorset Press, 1979. 193 p. Originally in French: *Histoire illustrée du phonographe.* Lausanne: Edita-Vilo, 1979.

Mason, David. "Aviation on Records." *Talking Machine Review International* 68 (June 1984): 1,843–1,848.

Masters, Ian. "The Demon Room." *Stereo Review* (Apr. 1990): 23–25.

——. "The Basics." *Stereo Review* (Jan. 1990–Feb. 1991). A series covering various components of the home audio system.

Mathews, Emrys G. *John McCormack: Centenary Discography, 1904–1942.* Llandeilo, Wales: Author, 1986. 72 p.

Matthews, Denis. "Cadenzas in Piano Concertos." *Recorded Sound* 68 (Oct. 1977): 723–727.

Mauerer, Hans J. *Sidney Bechet Discography.* Rev. ed. Copenhagen: Knudsen, 1970. 86 p.

Mawhinney, Paul C. *Music Master: The 45 RPM Record Directory; 35 Years of Recorded Music, 1947 to 1982.* Allison Park, Penn.: Record-Rama, 1983. 2 vols.

McCarthy, Albert J. "Discography." In *Big Bill Blues, William Broonzy's Story as Told to Yannick Bruynoghe.* New York: Oak Publications, 1964, pp. 153–173.

McCormick, Don, and Seth Winner. "The Toscanini Legacy." *Association for Recorded Sound Collection Journal* 20-2 (1989): 182–190.

McCoy, William, and Mitchell McGeary. *Every Little Thing: The Definitive Guide to Beatles Recording Variations, Rare Mixes & Other Musical Oddities, 1958–1986.* Ann Arbor, Mich.: Popular Culture, 1990. 368 p.

McCulloh, Judith. *Ethnic Recordings in America—A Neglected Heritage.* Washington, D.C.: Library of Congress, 1982. 269 p.

McDonough, Jack. *San Francisco Rock: The Illustrated History of San Francisco Rock Music.* Introduction by Paul Kantner. San Francisco: Chronicle Books, 1985

McKee, Elwood. "ARSC AAA: Fifteen Years of Cooperative Research." *Association for Recorded Sound Collection Journal* 20-1 (Spring 1989): 3–13.

McPherson, J., and William R. Moran. "Ernestine Schumann-Heink." *Record Collector* 17-5/6 (June 1967): 98–144; 17-7 (Aug. 1967): 154–159; 20-6/7 (May 1972): 165; 25-3/4 (June 1979): 75–77.

——. "Jeanne Gerville-Réache." *Record Collector* 21-3/4 (July 1973): 51–79; 21-7/8 (Dec. 1973): 190–191.

McWilliams, A.A. "Tape Recording and Reproduction." *Encyclopedia of High Fidelity*, Vol. 4. New York and London: Focal Press, 1964. 287 p.

McWilliams, Jerrry. *The Preservation and Restoration of Sound Recordings.* Nashville, Tenn.: American Association for State and Local History, 1979. 138 p.

——. "Sound Recordings." In *Conservation in the Library: A Handbook of Use and Care of Traditional and Nontraditional Materials*, edited by Susan G. Swartzburg. Westport, Conn.: Greenwood Press, 1983, pp. 163–184.

Melville-Mason, Graham. "Re-scoring for Recording." In *Phonographs and Gramophones,* Edinburgh: Royal Scottish Museum, 1977, pp. 95–96.

Merriman, H. O. "Sound Recording by Electricity, 1919–1924." *Talking Machine Review International* 40 (June 1976): 666–681.

Methuen-Campbell, James. *Chopin Playing: From the Composer to the Present Day.* New York: Taplinger, 1981. 289 p.

——. "Early Soviet Pianists and Their Recordings." *Recorded Sound* 83 (Jan. 1983): 1–16.

——. *Catalogue of Recordings by Classical Pianists. Vol. 1. Pianists Born before 1872.* Chipping Norton, England: Disco Epsom, 1984. 66 p.

Migliorini, Louis, and James F. E. Dennis. "Olive Fremstad." *Record Collector* 7-3 (Mar. 1952): 51–65.

——. "Emma Eames." *Record Collector* 8-4 (Apr. 1953): 74–96.

Migliorini, Louis, and Nicholas Ridley. "Johanna Gadski." *Record Collector* 11-9/10 (Sept.–Oct. 1957): 196–231; 11-11/12 (Nov.–Dec. 1957): 257–285; 12-1/2 (Jan.–Feb. 1958): 36.

Miller Jim. *Almost Grown: The Rise of Radio.* London: Heinemann, 1999.

Miller, Jim, ed. *The Rolling Stone Illustrated History of Rock and Roll.* Rev. and updated. New York: Rolling Stone, c1980.

Miller, Philip L. "In Memory of the Carnegie Set." *Association for Recorded Sound Collections Journal* 4 (1972): 21–28.

——. "Margarete Matzenauer." *Record Collector* 23-1/2 (Jan. 1976): 3–47.

Mitchell, Peter W. "Which Tracks Best, a Pivoted or a Radial Tonearm." *Audio* (June 1982): 25–29.

Mitchell, Ray. "Panachord Label." *Matrix* 68 (Dec. 1966) through 91 (Feb. 1971). A series listing issues of 1931–1939.

Montgomery, Michael. "Piano Rollography of Adrian Rollini." *Record Research* 135/136 (Nov.–Dec. 1975): 5–7.

——. "Eubie Blake Piano Rollography." *Record Research* 159/160 (Dec. 1978): 4–5.

Moogk, Edward B. *Roll Back the Years: History of Canadian Recorded Sound and Its Legacy: Genesis to 1930.* Ottawa: National Library of Canada, 1975. 443 p.; phonodisc in pocket. Parker 1988 is a title index to Canadian works cited.

Moon, Robert, and Micheal Gray. *Full Frequency Stereophonic Sound. A Discography and History of Early London Decca Stereo Classical Instrumental and Chamber Music Recordings (1956–1963) on Records and Compact Discs.* San Francisco: Robert Moon, 1990. 83 p.

Moore, Jerrold N. "Yale University Historical Sound Recordings Program: Its Purpose and Scope." *Recorded Sound* 16 (Oct. 1964): 270–279.

——. *A Voice in Time: The Gramophone of Fred Gaisberg, 1873–1951.* London: Hamilton, 1976. 248 p.

Moran, William R. "Geraldine Farrar." *Record Collector* 13-9/10 (1960–1961): 194–240; 13-11/12 (Apr. 1961): 279–280; 14-7/8 (1961): 172–174; 20-6/7 (May 1972): 163–164.

——. "Discography." In *Yankee Diva: Lillian Nordica and the Golden Days of Opera*, by Ira Glackens. New York: Coleridge Press, 1963, pp. 285–300.

——. "Mario Ancona." *Record Collector* 16-5/6 (Apr. 1965): 100–139; 16-7/8 (Sept. 1965): 188; 20-6/7 (May 1972): 164.

——. "Bettini Cylinders." *Record Collector* 16-7/8 (Sept. 1965): 148–185.

——. "Discography." In *Forty Years of Song*, by Emma Albani. New York: Arno Press, 1977, pp. i–v.

——. "The Recordings of Emma Calvé." In *My Life*, by Emma Calvé. New York: Arno Press, 1977, pp. i–viii.

——. "The Recordings of Emma Eames." In *Some Memories and Reflections*, by Emma Eames. New York: Arno Press, 1977, pp. 313–320.

——. "The Recordings of Olive Fremstad." In *The Rainbow Bridge*, by Mary Watkins Cushing. New York: Arno Press, 1977, pp. i–iv.

———. "The Recordings of Sir Charles Santley." In *Reminiscences of My Life*, by Charles Santley. New York: Arno Press, 1977, pp. i–ii.

———. "The Recordings of Ernestine Schumann-Heink." In *Schumann-Heink, the Last of the Titans*, by Mary Lawton. New York: Arno, 1977, pp. 339–428.

———. "The Recordings of Francesco Tamagno." In *Tamagno*, by Mario Corsi. New York: Arno Press, 1977, pp. 215–218.

———. "Discography." In *Mattia Battistini: il re dei baritoni*, by Francesco Palmegiani. New York: Arno Press, 1977, unpaged.

———. "Discography." In *The Glory Road*, by Lawrence Tibbett. New York: Arno Press, 1977, pp. i–xxii.

———. "Discography." In *Nellie Melba, A Contemporary Review*. Westport, Conn.: Greenwood Press, 1984, pp. 447–472.

———. "Discography." In *Titta Ruffo: An Anthology*. Westport, Conn.: Greenwood Press, 1984, pp. 251–269.

Morby, Paul. "Aureliano Pertile." *Record Collector* 7-11 (Nov. 1952): 244–260; 7-12 (Dec. 1952): 267–277; 8-1 (Jan. 1953): 37–41; 10-12 (Nov. 1956): 277.

Morgan, Charles I. "John Charles Thomas." *Record Collector* 25-1/2 (Mar. 1979): 5–31.

Morgenstern, Dan. "A New Standard For Reissues." *Downbeat* (Dec. 1983).

Morin, Philippe. *Conversations avec Pablo Casals*. Paris: A. Michel, 1982. 455 p. Discography on pp. 417–444.

Morritt, Robert D. "Carson J. Robison." *New Ambrola Graphic* 29 (Summer 1979): 4–8.

Moses, Julian Morton. *Collector's Guide to American Recordings, 1895–1925*. New York: American Record Collectors' Exchange, 1949. 200 p. Reprint New York: Dover, 1977.

Mulholland, Pauline. *The Music Recording Industry in Australia*. Fitzroy, Victoria, Australia: Victorian Commercial Teachers Association and Victoria Education Department, 1989. 27 p.

Music Recording Industry in Australia, The. Industries Assistance Commission. Canberra: The Commission, 1978. 79 p.

Musical Instruments at the World's Columbian Exposition. Chicago: Presto Co., 1895. 328 p.

Myers, Kurth, ed. *Index to Record Reviews: Based on Material Originally Published in Notes, the Quarterly Journal of the Music Library Association, between 1949 and 1977*. Boston: G.K. Hall, 1978–1980. 5 vols. Supplements 1985, 1989. Supersedes *Record Ratings*. New York: Crown, 1956.

Narvaez, Peter. "A Tribute: Kenneth S. Goldstein, Record Producer." *Journal of American Folklore* 109 (Fall 1996): 450–463.

Newsom, Iris, ed. *Wonderful Inventions: Motion Pictures, Broadcasting, and Recorded Sound at the Library of Congress*. With an introduction by Erik Barnouw. Washington, D.C.: Library of Congress, 1985. 384 p.; two 12-inch LP records included. A collection of articles, including three of interest to sound recording: "A Sound Idea: Music for Animated Films," by Jon Newsom; "Emile Berliner and Nineteenth-century Disc Recording, " by James R. Smart; and "Cartoons for the Record: The Jack Kapp Collection," by Samuel Brylawski.

Newville. Leslie J. "Development of the Phonograph at Alexander Graham Bell's Volta Laboratory." In *Contributions from the Museum of History and Technology*. Washington, D.C.: Smithsonian Institution, 1959, pp. 69–79.

Nolden, Rainer. *Count Basie: Sein Leben, seine Musik, seine Schallplatten*. Schaftlach, Germany: OREOS, 1990. 184 p.

Novitsky, Ed. "The Mercury 5000 Series." *Record Research* 233/234 (Feb. 1988): 4–5; 235/236 (June 1988): 9; 237/238 (Nov. 1988): 9; 239/240 (Apr. 1989): 9; 241/242 (Oct.–Nov. 1989): 9; 243/244 (May–June 1990): 9; 245/246 (Jan. 1991): 9; 247/248 (Sept. 1991): 9. The 5000 series appeared in 1946–1952.

O'Brien, Ed, and Scott P. Sayers. *Sinatra: The Man and His Music—The Recording Artistry of Francis Albert Sinatra, 1939–1992*. Austin, Tex.: TSD Press, 1992. 303 p.

O'Dair, Barbara. *The Rolling Stone Book of Women in Rock: Trouble Girls*. New York: Random House, 1997. 608 p.

Odell, L Brevoort. "The Edison Diamond Disc Phonograph— Perfect Fidelity 60 Years Ago!" *Association for Recorded Sound Collections Journal* 6 (1974): 3–12.

Oja, Carol J. ed. *American Music Recordings: A Discography of 20th-Century U.S. Composers*. Brooklyn: Institute for the Study of American Music, 1982. 368 p.

Olcott, Evan. "Audio Reversal in Popular Culture." Retrieved from www.triplo.com, Dec. 13, 2001.

Olson, Harry. *Elements of Acoustical Engineering*. 2nd ed. New York: Van Nostrand, 1947. 539 p.

———. "The RCA Victor Dynagroove System." *Journal of the Audio Engineering Society* 12-2 (1964): 98–114. Reprinted in Roys 1978.

———. "Microphones for Recording." *Journal of the Audio Engineering Society* 25-10/11 (Oct.–Nov. 1977): 676–684.

Olson, Harry, John Preston, and Everett G. May. "Recent Developments in Direct-Radiator High-Fidelity Loudspeakers." *Journal of the Audio Engineering Society* 2 (October 1954): 219.

Olson, Robert C. "The Grey Gull 4000 Series." *New Amberola Graphic* 56 (Spring 1986): 3–10.

Oprisko, Peter Paul. "Frank Sinatra 7-inch Collectibles." *Discoveries* (Sept. 1990): 24–32.

Ord-Hume, Arthur W. J. G. *Pianola: The History of the Self-Playing Piano*. London: Allen & Unwin, 1984. 394 p.

Owen, H. G. "Elisabeth Schumann." *Record Collector* 7-10 (Oct. 1952): 220–239.

Owen, H. G., and William R. Moran. "Marcella Sembrich." *Record Collector* 18-5/6 (May 1969): 99–138; 20-6/7 (May 1972): 165.

Owen, Tom. "Electrical Reproduction of Acoustically Recorded Discs and Cylinders." *Association for Recorded Sound Collections Journal* 14-1 (1982): 11–18.

———. "Fifty Questions on Audio Restoration and Transfer Technology." *Association for Recorded Sound Collections Journal* 15-2/3 (1983): 38–45. Comments noted at Lane and Burns 1984.

Palmer, Robert, and Mary Shanahan. *The Rolling Stones*. Garden City, N.Y.: Rolling Stones Press, Doubleday, 1983. 253 p.

Palmieri, Robert. *Sergei Vasil'evich Rachmaninoff; A Guide to Research*. New York: Garland, 1985. 335 p. (Garland Composer Resource Manuals, 3) Discography on pp. 93–118.

Park, Bill. "Lily Pons." *Record Collector* 13-11/12 (Apr. 1960): 243–271, 283.

———. "Discography." In *Ponselle, a Singer's Life*, by Rosa Ponselle and James A. Drake. Garden City, N.Y.: Doubleday, 1982, pp. 248–307.

Parker, C. P., and David Emerson. "Title Index to Canadian Works Listed in Edward B. Moogk's Roll Back the Years ..." Ottawa: Canadian Association of Music Libraries, 1988. 13 p.

Paul, George. "The Kalamazoo Duplex." *New Amberola Graphic* 48 (Spring 1984): 6–7.

———. "The Metaphone Echophone." *New Amberola Graphic* 51 (Winter 1985): 4.

———. "Phonograph Forum." *New Amberola Graphic* 66 (Oct. 1988): 6–7.

———. "Step on It! Dance on It! A Wonder Record Surfaces." *Antique Phonograph Monthly* 10-1 (1991): 5.

———. "The First Spring-Motor Gram-O-Phone." *New Amberola Graphic* 77 (July 1991): 3.

Pavarotti, Luciano. *Pavarotti: My Own Story.* Garden City, N.Y.: Doubleday, 1981. 316 p. Discography on pp. 291–308.

Pearmain, M. D. J., and R. P. Seemungal. "Miliza Korjus." *Record Collector* 16-2 (Sept. 1964): 28–45; 16-7/8 (Sept. 1965): 188–189.

Peel, Tom, and Cliff Williams. "Riccardo Stracciari." *Record Collector* 30-1/2 (Feb. 1985): 39–53; 31-8/10 (Sept. 1986): 239.

Peel, Tom, and John Holohan. "Beniamino Gigli." *Record Collector* 35-8/9/10 (Aug.–Oct. 1990): 191–240.

Perkins, John F., and Alan Kelly. "The Gramophone & Typewriter Ltd. Records of Camille Saint-Saens (1835–1921)." *Recorded Sound* 79 (Jan. 1981): 25–27.

Perone, James. *Songs of the Vietnam Conflict.* Westport, Conn.: Greenwood Press, 2001. 168 p.

Petersen, Phillip. "The Origin of the I.C.S. Language Cylinders." *Antique Phonograph Monthly* 1-4 (Apr. 1973): 3–4.

———. "Amberol: A Word Study." *Talking Machine Review International* 33 (Apr. 1975): 316–322.

Petts, Leonard. "A Host of Angels." *Talking Machine Review International* 23 (Aug. 1973): 210–211. Descriptions and illustrations of labels with the Angel trademark.

———. *The Story of "Nipper" and the "His Master's Voice" Picture Painted by Francis Barraud.* Introduction by Frank Andrews. 2nd ed. Bournemouth, England: Talking Machine Review, 1983. 68 p.

Petts, Leonard. "Berliner's Compact Disc." *Hillandale News* 165 (Dec. 1988): 114–119.

Petty, John A. "A Look at a Phenomenal Recording Schedule: Cal Stewart's 1919 Columbia Matrices." *New Amberola Graphic* 16 (Winter 1976): 3–5.

———. "Kalamazoo Discs." *New Amberola Graphic* 48 (Spring 1984): 10–11.

———. "Busy Bee Labels." *Hillandale News* 163 (Aug. 1988): 68–70.

Phillips, Ronald. "Mattia Battistini." *Record Collector* 2-9 (Sept. 1947): 129–133; 3 (May 1948): 73.

"Phonographs in Libraries." *Library Journal* 34 (July 1909): 324.

Pickett, A. G., and M. M. Lemcoe. *Preservation and Storage of Sound Recordings.* Washington, D.C.: Library of Congress, 1959. 74 p.

Pinne, Peter. "Australian Theatre on Disc." In Hummel 1984, pp. xxvii–xxxiii.

Pinta, Emil R. *A Chronologic Jan Peerce Discography, 1932–1980.* Worthington, Ohio: Author, 1987. 29 p.

Pitts, Michael R. *Radio Soundtracks: A Reference Guide.* 2nd ed. Metuchen, N.J.: Scarecrow Press, 1986. 349 p.

———. *Kate Smith, A Bio-bibliography.* Westport, Conn.: Greenwood Press, 1988. 320 p.

Place, Jeff, and Ronald D. Cohen. *The Best of Broadside, 1962–1988: Anthems of the American Underground from the Pages of Broadside Magazine.* Smithsonian Folkways Records SFW CD 40130, 2000.

Pohlmann, Ken C. *The Compact Disc; A Handbook of Theory and Use.* Madison, Wis.: A-R Editions, 1989. 288 p.

Polic, Edward F. *The Glenn Miller Army Air Force Band.* Metuchen, N.J.: Scarecrow Press, 1989. 2 vols.

Poole, Louis. "Louise Homer." *Record Collector* 2-7 (July 1947): 96–98.

Popa, Jay. *Cab Calloway and His Orchestra, 1925–1958.* Revised by Charles Garrod. Zephyrhills, Fla.: Joyce Record Club, 1987. 38 p. (1st published 1976)

Porter, Bob. "National Records." *Record Research* 149/150 (Oct. 1977): 8–9; 151/152 (Jan. 1978): 15; 153/154 (Apr. 1978): 11–12; 155/156 (July 1978): 13, 16. [Porter 1978/7]

———. "Majestic Masters Listing." *Record Research* 157/158 (Sept. 1978): 8–9; 159/160 (Dec. 1978): 12; 161/162 (Feb.–Mar. 1979): 12; 163/164 (May–June 1979): 12; 165/166 (Aug. 1979): 12; 167/168 (Oct. 1979): 9. [Porter 1978/12]

———. "List of Signature Masters." *Record Research* 171/172 (Mar. 1980): 11; 173/174 (June 1980): 11; 177/178 (Nov. 1980): 14; 179/180 (Feb. 1981): 12; 181/182 (Apr. 1981): 9.

Porterfield, Nolan. *Jimmie Rodgers: The Life and Times of America's Blue Yodeler.* Champaign: University of Illinois Press, 1992. 460 p.

Potter, Tully. *Adolf Busch: The Life of an Honest Man.* Billericay, Essex, England: Author, 1985. Vol. 1. Discography on pp. 59–135.

Potterton, Robert, and James F. E. Dennis. "Zélie de Lussan." *Record Collector* 17-8 (Dec. 1967): 171–182.

Poundstone, William. *Big Secrets.* New York: William Morrow & Company, 1983. 228 p.

Powell, James R., Jr. "Audiophile's Guide to Phonorecord Playback Equalizer Settings." *Association for Recorded Sound Collections Journal* 20-1 (Spring 1989): 14–23.

Proceedings of the 1890 Convention of Local Phonograph Companies. Introduction by Raymond R. Wile. Reprint ed. Nashville, Tenn.: Country Music Foundation Press, 1974. 210 p.

Proudfoot, Christopher. *Collecting Phonographs and Gramophones.* New York: Mayflower Books; London: Studio Vista, 1980. 119 p.

Randel, Don Michael, ed. *The New Harvard Dictionary of Music.* Cambridge, Mass.: Harvard University Press, 1986. 942 p.

Raymond, Jack. "A Numerical Listing of Liberty Music Shop Records." *Record Research* 181/182 (Apr. 1981): 8; continued by Len Kunstadt: 185/186 (Oct. 1981): 9; 187/188 (Dec. 1981): 9; 189/190 (Mar.–Apr. 1982): 10; 191/192 (July 1982): 10; 195/196 (Jan. 1983): 12; 197/198 (Mar.–Apr. 1983): 8; 201/202 (Sept. 1983): 11; 203–204 (Dec. 1983): 9; 205/206 (Mar. 1984): 12; 207/208 (June 1984): 11; 209/210 (Oct. 1984): 12; 215/216 (July 1985): 11; 217/218 (Oct. 1985): 2; 219/220 (Jan. 1986): 5; 221/222 (Apr. 1986): 4; 227/228 (Mar. 1987): 10; 229/230 (June 1987): 14; 231/232 (Oct. 1987): 12; 233/234 (Feb. 1988): 6.

———. *Show Music on Record from the 1890s to the 1980s.* New York: Ungar, 1982. 253 p.

Read, Oliver, and Walter L. Welch. *From Tin Foil to Stereo: Evolution of the Phonograph.* 2nd ed. Indianapolis, H.W. Sams, 1976. 550 p. (1st ed. 1959)

Record Tape Collector's Directory. 2nd ed. Santa Monica, Calif.: Rare Record Tape Collector's Directory, 1978. 47 p. (1st ed. 1976)

Reed, Peter Hugh. "Frieda Hempel." *Record Collector* 10-3 (Aug. 1955): 51–71.

Reid, Gordon. "CEDAR." *Hillandale News* 172 (Feb. 1990): 314–319.

Reinhard, Kurt. "The Berlin Phonogramm-Archiv." *Recorded Sound* 1-2 (June 1961): 44–45.

Reiss, Eric. *The Compleat Talking Machine: A Guide to the Restoration of Antique Phonographs.* Vestal, N.Y.: Vestal Press, 1986. 184 p.

Rektorys, Artus, and James F. E. Dennis. "Emmy Destinn." *Record Collector* 20-1/2 (July 1971): 3–47; 20-4 (Dec. 1971): 93–94.

Renton, Arthur. "Toti dal Monte." *Record Collector* 4-9 (Sept. 1949): 142, 147–150.

Reuss, Richard A., and JoAnne Reuss. *American Folk Music and Left-Wing Politics, 1927–1957*. Lanham, Md.: Scarecrow Press, 2000. 297 p.

Richards, John B. "Elisabeth Rethberg." *Record Collector* 3-2 (Feb. 1948): 26–30; 3-4 (Apr. 1948): 51–56; 4-11 (Nov. 1949): 192–196; 5-1 (Jan. 1950): 11–16; 8-1 (Jan. 1953): 4–19. [Richards 1948/2]

———. "Lucrezia Bori." *Record Collector* 3-10 (Oct. 1948): 161–166; 4-1 (Jan. 1949): 2–12; 4-5 (May 1949): 98–99; 9-5 (1954): 104–123; 21-7 8 (Dec. 1973): 147–168. [Richards 1948/10]

———. "Elisabeth Rethberg." *Hobbies* (Mar. 1950): 18–19; (Apr. 1950): 18; (May 1950): 18–19.

———. "Eva Turner." *Record Collector* 11-2/3 (Feb.–Mar. 1957): 28–57, 71; 11-8 (Aug. 1957): 183–184; 11-9/10 (Sept.–Oct. 1957): 231–233.

———. "Hipolito Lazaro." *Record Collector* 16-3/4 (Nov.–Dec. 1964): 52–94; 16-9/10 (Jan. 1966): 226–228; 18-11/12 (Dec. 1969): 280–281.

———. "Gemma Bellincioni." *Record Collector* 16-9/10 (Jan. 1966): 196–219; 18-5/6 (May 1969): 139–140.

———. "Claudia Muzio." *Record Collector* 17-9/10 (Feb. 1968): 197–237; 17-11 (Apr. 1968): 256–263; 28-5/6 (Oct. 1983): 120–128.

———. "Lucrezia Bori." *Record Collector* 21-7/8 (Dec. 1973): 147–168.

Richards, John B., and Phillip Wade. "Luisa Tetrazzini." *Record Collector* 4-8 (Aug. 1949): 122–139.

Richards. John B., and J. P. Kenyon. "Ezio Pinza." *Record Collector* 26-3/4 (Aug. 1980): 51–95; 26-5/6 (Dec. 1980): 101–137.

Ridley, Nicholas A. "Emma Albani." *Record Collector* 12-4/5 (Feb.–Mar. 1959): 76–101; 12-8/9 (Nov.–Dec. 1959): 197–198; 14-9/10 (1961): 236.

Riemens, Leo. "Julia Culp." *Record Collector* 2-7 (July 1947): 100–104.

———. "Irene Abendroth." *Record Collector* 6-4 (Apr. 1951): 75–85.

Riggs, Quentin. "The Revelers." *Talking Machine Review International* 6 (Oct. 1970): 158–163.

Roach, Helen. "Two Women of Caedmon." *Association for Recorded Sound Collections Journal* 19-1 (May 1988): 21–24.

Robertson, Alex. "Canadian Gennett and Starr-Gennett 9000 Numerical." *Record Research* 195/196 (Jan. 1983): 1–7; 197/198 (Mar.–Apr. 1983): 7; 199/200 (June 1983): 10–11; 201/202 (Sept. 1983): 10; 203/204 (Dec. 1983): 4.

———. "The Rare Canadian Aurora Label from Victor Masters." *Record Research* 219/220 (Jan. 1986): 1, 3–8.

Robertson, John, and James F. E. Dennis. "Leonid Sobinoff." *Record Collector* 24-7/8 (Sept. 1978): 147–190.

Robinson, Earl, and Eric A. Gordon. *Ballad of an American: The Autobiography of Earl Robinson*. Lanham, Md.: Scarecrow Press, 1998. 477 p.

Romanowski, Patricia and Holly George Warren, eds. *The Rolling Stone Encyclopedia of Rock*. New York: Rolling Stone Press/Simon and Schuster, 2001, 1136 p.

Ronin, Ro. *Have Gun, Will Travel: The Spectacular Rise and Violent Fall of Death Row Records*. New York: Main Street Books, 1999. 372 p.

Rose, Al. *Eubie Blake*. New York: Schirmer, 1979. 214 p. Discography on pp. 174–188.

Rosenberg, Kenyon C. *A Basic Classical and Operatic Recordings Collection for Libraries*. Metuchen, N.J.: Scarecrow Press, 1987. 255 p.

———. *A Basic Classical and Operatic Recordings Collection on Compact Discs for Libraries*. Metuchen, N.J.: Scarecrow Press, 1990. 395 p.

Rosenberg, Kenyon C., and Paul T. Feinstein. *Dictionary of Library and Educational Technology*. 2nd ed. Littleton, Colo.: Libraries Unlimited, 1983. 185 p. (1st ed. 1976: *Media Equipment: A Guide and Dictionary*, by Kenyon C. Rosenberg and John S. Deskey.)

Rosenberg, Neil V. *Bill Monroe and His Blue Grass Boys: An Illustrated Discography*. Nashville, Tenn.: Country Music Foundation Press, 1974. 120 p.

Rotante, Anthony. "The 'King' of R&B Labels." *Record Research* 22 (Apr.–May 1959), Continued in nos. 24, 25, 27, 29, 30, 87, 90, 91, 92, 93, 94, and 98 (1969). A serial label list, with background on the firm in issue 87. Title varies.

———. "Bluesville." *Record Research* 73 (Jan. 1966): 5.

———. "Federal; The Federal 12000 Series." *Record Research* 111 (July 1971), Continued in nos. 113, 114, 115, 116, 117, 119, 120, 121, 122 (June 1973).

———. "De Luxe 6000 Series." *Record Research* 124 (Nov. 1973): 10; 125/126 (Feb. 1974): 14.

———. "Maurice Chevalier on Pathé Salabert Labels." *Record Research* 135/136 (Nov.–Dec. 1975): 4.

———. "Edith Piaf: The Early Years, Polydor Records 1936–1944." *Record Research* 199/200 (June 1983): 4; 201/202 (Sept. 1983): 10; 203/204 (Dec. 1983): 8.

———. "Imperial." *Record Research* 215/216 (July 1985): 1, 3–4; 217/218 (Oct. 1985): 6–7; 219/220 (Jan. 1986): 12; 221/222 (Apr. 1986): 10–11; 223/224 (Aug. 1986): 12; 225/226 (Nov. 1986): 10; 227/228 (Mar. 1987): 8; 229/230 (June 1987): 11; 231/232 (Oct. 1987): 8–9; 233/234 (Feb. 1988): 10–11. Continues as Hayes, C. 1988.

Royal Scottish Museum. *Phonograph and Gramophone Symposium, 2 July 1977*. Edinburgh: The Museum, 1977. 142 p.

Roys, Henry Edward, ed. *Disc Recording and Reproduction*. Stroudsburg, Penn.: Dowden, Hutchenson and Ross, 1978. 394 p. Consists of 42 papers, reprinted from technical journals.

Rules for Archival Cataloging of Sound Recordings. Association for Recorded Sound Collections, Associated Audio Archives Committee. Silver Spring, Md.: The Association, 1978. 72 p.

Ruppli, Michel. *Atlantic Records: A Discography*. Westport, Conn.: Greenwood Press, 1979. 4 vols.

———. *Charles Mingus Discography*. Frankfurt: Norbert Ruecker, 1981. 47 p. (Jazz Index Reference Series, 1)

———. *The Chess Labels: A Discography*. Westport, Conn.: Greenwood Press, 1983. 2 vols.

———. *The Clef Verve Labels: A Discography*. Westport, Conn.: Greenwood Press, 1986. 2 vols.

Ruppli, Michel, and Bob Porter. *The Prestige Label: A Discography*. Westport, Conn.: Greenwood Press, 1980. 378 p.

———. *The Savoy Label: A Discography*. Westport, Conn.: Greenwood Press, 1980. 443 p.

Rust, Brian. *The Victor Master Book, II (1925–1936)*. Stanhope, N.J.: Allen, 1970. 776 p. Covers Victor black label issues and Bluebird issues of 1933–1936. Vol. 1 was not published.

———. *The Complete Entertainment Discography, 1897–1942*. 2nd ed. New York: Da Capo Press, 1989. 794 p.

An updated and expanded reprint of the 1st ed. (New Rochelle, N.Y.: Arlington House, 1973).

———. *The American Dance Band Discography, 1917–1942.* New Rochelle, N.Y.: Arlington House, 1975. 2 vols. A series of additions and corrections has been appearing in issues of *Record Research* since 157/158 (Sept. 1978).

———. *The American Record Label Book.* New Rochelle, N.Y.: Arlington House, 1978. 336 p.

———. *British Music Hall on Record.* Harrow, England: General Gramophone Publications, 1979a. 301 p.

———. *Discography of Historical Records on Cylinders and 78s.* Westport, Conn.: Greenwood Press, 1979b. 327 p.

———. *Brian Rust's Guide to Discography.* Westport, Conn.: Greenwood Press, 1980. 133 p.

———. "(British) Berliner, G & T and Zonophone 7-inch Records." *Talking Machine Review International* 63/64 (Autumn 1981): 1,726–1,758. Adamson 1983 has useful comments on this list.

———. *Jazz Records, 1897–1942.* 5th ed. Chigwell, England: Storyville, 1982. 2 vols. (1st ed. 1961)

Rust, Brian, and Rex Bunnett. *London Musical Shows on Record, 1897–1976.* Rev. ed. London: British Institute of Recorded Sound, 1977. 672 p. (1st ed. 1958, with Supplement 1959.) A revised edition is Seeley 1989.

Rust, Brian, and Sandy Forber. *British Dance Bands on Record, 1911 to 1945, and Supplement.* Harrow, England: General Gramophone Publications, 1989. 1,496 p. A reprint of the original (1986) edition, with a 72 p. supplement.

Sackville-West, Edward, and Desmond Shaw-Taylor. *The Record Guide.* London: Colins, 1951. 763 p.

Salewicz, Chris. *McCartney.* New York: St. Martin's, 1986. 263 p.

Samuels, Jon. "A Complete Discography of the Recordings of Emanuel Feuermann." *Association for Recorded Sound Collections Journal* 12-1/2 (1980): 33–77.

———. "A Complete Discography of the Recordings of the Flonzaley Quartet." *Association for Recorded Sound Collections Journal* 19-1 (1987): 25–62.

Sanders, Alan. *Sir Adrian Boult: A Discography.* Harrow, England: General Gramophone Publications, 1981. 37 p.

———. *Walter Legge: A Discography.* Westport, Conn.: Greenwood Press, 1984. 452 p.

Sarnoff, David. *Edison (1847–1931).* New York: Newcomen Society, 1948. 24 p.

Schuller, Gunther. *Early Jazz; Its Roots and Musical Development.* New York: Oxford University Press, 1968. 401 p. (History of Jazz series, 1).

———. *The Swing Era; The Development of Jazz, 1930–1945.* New York: Oxford University Press, 1989. 919 p. (History of Jazz series, 2).

Schwartz, Leonard. "The Coon-Sanders Orchestra." *Talking Machine Review International* 69 (Dec. 1984): 1,898–1,902.

Schwarzkopf, Elisabeth. *On and Off the Record: A Memoir of Walter Legge.* New York: Scribner's Sons, 1982. 292 p.

Scott, Michael. *The Record of Singing to 1914.* London: Duckworth, 1978. 243 p. Issued with the EMI record series, *The Record of Singing* (EMI #RLS 724). Continued by Scott 1979.

———. *The Record of Singing: Volume Two, 1914–1925.* London: Duckworth; New York: Holmes & Meier, 1979. 262 p. Continues Scott 1977.

———. *The Great Caruso.* New York: Knopf, 1988. 322 p. "A Chronology of Caruso's Appearances," by Thomas G. Kaufman, pp. 201–264; "A Caruso Discography," by John R. Bolig, pp. 265–293.

Sears, Richard S. *V-Discs: A History and Discography.* Westport, Conn.: Greenwood Press, 1980. 1,166 p. (ARSC Reference Series). 1st Supplement, 1986 (272 p.).

Seeliger, Ronald, and Bill Park. "Tiana Lemnitz." *Record Collector* 15-2 (1963): 28–43.

Seeger, Anthony, and Louise S. Spear. *Early Field Recordings; A Catalogue of Cylinder Collections at the Indiana University Archives of Traditional Music.* Bloomington, Ind.: Indiana University Press, 1987. 198 p.

Seeley, Robert, and Rex Bunnett. *London Musical Shows on Record, 1889–1989.* Harrow, England: General Gramophone Publications, 1989. 457 p. A revision of Rust 1979a.

Segond, André. *Renata Tebaldi.* Lyon, France: Laffont, 1981. 260 p. Discography on pp. 237–253.

Semeonoff, Boris, and Alan Kelly. "New Complete Discography of Feodor Chaliapin." *Record Collector* 20-8/9 10 (Aug. 1972): 171–230.

Seymour, Henry. *The Reproduction of Sound.* London: W. B. Tattersall, 1918. 324 p.

Shaman, William. "The Operatic Vitaphone Shorts." *Association for Recorded Sound Collections Journal* 22-1 (Spring 1991): 35–94.

Shaw, Arnold. *The Rockin' 50s.* New York: Hawthorne, 1974. 296 p. Reprint New York: Da Capo Press, 1987.

———. *Honkers and Shoulers: The Golden Years of Rhythm and Blues.* New York: Macmillan, 1978.

Shawe-Taylor, Desmond, and E. Hughes. "Arthur Nikisch." *Recorded Sound* 4 (Oct. 1961): 114–115.

Sheridan, Chris. *Count Basie: A Bio-Discography.* Westport, Conn.: Greenwood Press, 1986. 1,350 p.

Sherman, Michael. "The First Commercial Berliner Records Made in America." *Antique Phonograph Monthly* 9-3 (1990): 3–7.

Sherman, Michael W. *The Paper Dog; An Illustrated Guide to 78 RPM Victor Record Labels, 1900–1958.* Brooklyn: APM Press, 1987. 43 p.

Shipton, Alyn. *Groovin' High: The Life of Dizzy Gillespie.* New York: Oxford University Press, 1999. 422 p.

Shipway, E. L. M. "Getting the Best Results from 78 RPM Records in 1984." *Talking Machine Review International* 65/66 (Feb. 1983): 1,888–1,889.

Sieben, Hansfried. "Vox and Successor." *Talking Machine Review International* 70 (Dec. 1985): 2,000–2,001.

Simms, Eric. *Wildlife Sounds and Their Recording.* London: Elek, 1979. 144 p.

Simon, George T. *The Big Bands.* Rev. ed. New York: Macmillan, 1974. 584 p. (1st ed. 1967)

Sitsky, Larry. *Busoni and the Piano.* Westport, Conn.: Greenwood Press, 1985. 409 p. Discography on pp. 326–333.

———. *The Classical Reproducing Roll: A Catalogue-Index.* Westport, Conn.: Greenwood Press, 1990. 2 vols.

Slide, Anthony. *Great Radio Personalities in Historic Photographs.* New York: Dover, 1982. 117 p.

Slonimsky, Nicholas. *Baker's Biographical Dictionary of Musicians.* 8th ed. New York: Schirmer, 1992. 2115 p.

Small, Richard H. "Closed-Box Loudspeaker Systems." *Journal of the Audio Engineering Society* (Dec. 1972): 798–808; (Jan.–Feb. 1973): 11–18.

Smart, James R. *The Sousa Band: A Discography.* Washington, D.C.: Library of Congress, 1970. 123 p.

———. *Radio Broadcasts in the Library of Congress, 1924–1941: A Catalog of Recordings.* Washington, D.C.: Library of Congress, 1982. 149 + 14 p.

————. "Carl Engel and the Library of Congress's First Acquisitions of Recordings." *Association for Recorded Sound Collections Journal* 15-2 3 (1983): 6–18.

Smart, James R., and Jon W. Newsom. *"A Wonderful Invention": A Brief History of the Phonograph from Tinfoil to the LP.* Washington, D.C.: Library of Congress, 1977. 40 p.

Smiraglia, Richard P. *Music Cataloging.* Englewood, Colo.: Libraries Unlimited, 1989. 222 p.

Smith, John L. *The Johnny Cash Discography.* Westport, Conn.: Greenwood Press, 1985. 203 p.

Smithson, Roger. *The Recordings of Edwin Fischer.* Rev. ed. London: Author, 1990. 25 p. (1st ed. 1983)

Smolian, Steven. *Handbook of Film, Theatre and Television Music on Records, 1948–1969.* New York: Record Undertaker, 1970. 2 vols. in 1; 64 p.

————. "Four Decades of the Budapest Quartet." *American Record Guide* 37 (Dec. 1970): 220–224.

————. "Standards for the Review of Discographic Works." *Association for Recorded Sound Collections Journal* 7-3 (1976): 47–55.

————. "Preservation, Deterioration and Restoration of Recording Tape." *Association for Recorded Sound Collections Journal* 19-2/3 (1987): 37–53.

Soames, Victoria, ed. *The Clarinet Historical Recordings,* Volume I. Clarinet Classics CC #0005, 1993.

————. *The Clarinet Historical Recordings,* Volume II. Clarinet Classics CC #0010, 1994.

Southall, Brian. *Abbey Road: The Story of the World's Most Famous Recording Studios.* Cambridge, England: Patrick Stephens, 1982. 217 p.

Special Collections in the Library of Congress; A Selective Guide. Washington, D.C.: Library of Congress, 1980. 464 p.

Spottswood, Richard K. *Ethnic Music on Records: A Discography of Ethnic Recordings Produced in the United States, 1893–1942.* Urbana, Ill. : University of Illinois Press, 1991. 7 vols.

Stambler, Irwin. *Encyclopedia of Pop, Rock and Soul.* 2nd ed. New York: St. Martin's, 1989. 881 p. (1st ed. 1974)

Stambler, Irwin, and Grelun Landon. *Encyclopedia of Folk, Country and Western Music.* 2nd ed. New York: St. Martin's, 1983. 396 p. (1st ed. 1969)

Stanford, Stan, ed. *The Acoustic Era Clarinet Recordings, 1898–1918.* Stan Stanford, 1998.

Stark, Craig. "Dolby S: A New Standard for Cassette Recording?" *Stereo Review* (May 1990): 78–79.

Steane, J. B. *The Grand Tradition: Seventy Years of Singing on Record.* London: Duckworth, 1974. 628 p.

Steane, John. "Discography." In *My Life,* by Tito Gobbi. London: Macdonald and James, 1979, pp. 201–210.

Stephenson, Tom. "The Impressive Dominion Autophone." *Hillandale News* 135 (Dec. 1983): 288–289.

Sterling, Christopher H., and John M. Kittross. *Stay Tuned: A Concise History of American Broadcasting.* Belmont, Calif.: Wadsworth, 1978. 562 p.

Stevens, S. S., and Fred Warshofsky. *Sound and Hearing.* 2nd ed. New York: Time-Life Books, 1969. 200 p.

Stevenson, Gordon. "Discography: Scientific, Analytical, Historical and Systematic." *Library Trends* 21-1 (July 1972): 101–135.

Stover, Suzanne. "The 'Fair Use' of Sound Recordings: A Summary of Existing Practices and Concerns." *Association for Recorded Sound Collections Journal* 21-2 (1990): 232–240.

Stratton, John. "The Recordings of Jean de Reszke." *Recorded Sound* 27 (July 1967): 209–213.

————. "Dmitri Smirnov." *Record Collector* 14-11/12 (July 1973): 244–247.

————. "Florence Eaton." *Record Collector* 21-9/10 (Jan. 1974): 195–239; 21-11/12 (Mar. 1974): 256.

Stroff, Stephen. "Django's Dream; The Life of Django Reinhardt." *Antiques and Collecting Hobbies* (May 1988); (June 1988): 57–59. [Stroff 1988/5]

————. "Young Jussi Björling." *Antiques and Collecting Hobbies* (Oct. 1988): 59–64.

————. "Gennett Records; the Label that Changed History." *Antiques and Collecting Hobbies* (June 1989): 66.

Summers, Harrison B. *A Thirty-Year History of Programs Carried on National Radio Networks in the United States, 1926–1956.* Columbus, Ohio: Department of Speech, The Ohio State University, 1958. 228 p. Reprints New York: Arno Press, 1971; Salem, N.H.: Ayer, 1986.

Sunier, John. "A History of Binaural Sound." *Audio* (Mar. 1986): 36–44.

Sutton, Allan. *A. K. A.; Pseudonyms on American Records, 1900–1932.* Baltimore: Author, 1991. 16 p.

Swartz, Jon D., and Robert C. Reinehr. *Handbook of Old-Time Radio: A Comprehensive Guide to Golden Age Radio Listening and Collecting.* Metuchen, N.J.: Scarecrow Press, 1993.

Swartzburg, Susan G. *Preserving Library Materials.* 2nd ed. Metuchen, N.J.: Scarecrow Press, 1991. 503 p. (1st ed. 1980)

Taylor, George. "Dating Gramophone Co. London Recordings, 1908–1925." *Hillandale News* 132 (June 1983): 204–206.

————. "Vitaphone." *Hillandale News* 144 (June 1985): 218–222; 146 (Oct. 1985): 257–260; 149 (Apr. 1986): 19–22.

————. "Opera on Bettini." *Hillandale News* 155 (Apr. 1987): 174–185.

————. "The Mapleson Cylinders." *Hillandale News* 157 (Aug. 1987): 228–236.

————. "The Recorded Legacy of Jean de Reszke." *Record Collector* 33-1/2 (Jan. 1988): 22–25.

————. "Berliner at the Opera." *Hillandale News* 173 (Apr. 1990): 2–4. Comments by P.G. Adamson in *Hillandale News* 174 (June 1990): 36.

Tesoriero, Michael. "Beniamino Giglithe One and Only." *Journal of the Phonograph Society of New South Wales* 6-3 (Apr. 1990): 20–26; 6-4 (July 1990): 21–29.

Thielcke, Gerhard. *Bird Sounds.* Ann Arbor, Mich.: University of Michigan Press, 1976. 190 p.

Thiele, A. N. "Loudspeakers in Vented Boxes." *Journal of the Audio Engineering Society* (May 1971): 382–392; (June 1971): 471 483.

Thorgerson, Storm, and Roger Dean. *Album Cover Album.* New York: A & W Visual Library, 1977. 160 p.

Thorgerson, Storm, Roger Dean, and David Howells. *Album Cover Album: The Second Volume* New York: A & W Visual Library, 1982. 159 p.

Thorin, Suzanne E., and Carole Vidali Franklin. *The Acquisition and Cataloging of Music and Sound Recordings: A Glossary.* Washington, D.C.: Music Library Association, 1984. 40 p. (Technical Reports series, 11).

Timner, W. E. *Ellingtonia: The Recorded Music of Duke Ellington and His Sidemen.* 3rd ed. Metuchen, N.J.: Scarecrow Press, 1988. 554 p.

Toborg, D. "Tex Ritter Collection." *Record Research* 108 (Dec. 1970): 139–140; (May–June 1976). A series of label lists that appeared in most issues of *Record Research* in the period shown.

————. "Tex Ritter: The Complete Capitol Discography." *Record Research* 163/164 (May–June 1979): 217–218; (Oct. 1985). A series of listings that appeared in most issues of *Record Research* in the period shown.

Treichel, James. *Woody Herman's Second Herd, 1947–1949.* Zephyrhills, Fla.: Joyce Record Club, 1978. 56 p.

Tremaine, Howard M., ed. *Audio Cyclopedia.* 3rd ed. Indianapolis: Sams, 1977. 1,757 p. (1st ed. 1959)

Tron, David. "Recordings of Maggie Teyte." In *Star on the Door,* by Maggie Teyte. New York: Arno Press, 1977, pp. 188–192.

Tron, David, and James F. E. Dennis. "Maggie Teyte." *Record Collector* 9-6 (Nov. 1954): 128–138; 9-11 12 (Apr.–May 1955): 270–271.

Tuddenham, Adrian, and Peter Copeland. "Record Processing for Improved Sound." *Hillandale News* 162 (June 1988): 34–39; 163 (Aug. 1988): 72–77; 164 (Oct. 1988): 89–97.

Tudor, Dean. *Popular Music; An Annotated Guide to Recordings.* Littleton, Colo.: Libraries Unlimited, 1983. 647 p. Supersedes Tudor's 1979 books *Jazz, Black Music, Grass Roots Music,* and *Contemporary Pop Music.*

Turner, Patricia. *Dictionary of Afro-American Performers.* New York: Garland, 1990. 433 p.

Turner, Rufus P., and Stan Gibilisco. *The Illustrated Dictionary of Electronics.* 6th ed. Blue Ridge Summit, Penn.: Tab Books, 1994. 760 p. (1st ed. 1985)

Usill, Harley. "A History of Argo." *Recorded Sound* 78 (July 1980): 31–44.

Vaché, Warren W. *This Horn for Hire; The Life and Career of Pee Wee Erwin.* Metuchen, N.J.: Scarecrow Press, 1987. 441 p.

Villchur. Edgar M. *The Reproduction of Sound in High Fidelity and Stereo Phonographs.* New York: Dover, 1965. 92 p.

Villetard, Jean François. "Coleman Hawkins, 1922–1944." In *Micrography,* Amsterdam: 1984. 80 p. Continued by "Coleman Hawkins, 1945–1957" (1985; 80 p.) and "Coleman Hawkins, 1958–1969" (1987; 80 p.).

Von Békésy, Georg. *Experiments in Hearing.* New York: McGraw-Hill, 1960. 745 p. Reprint Huntington, N.Y.: Robert E. Krieger, 1980.

Vreede, Max E. *Paramount 12000–13000.* London: Storyville Publications, 1971. Unpaged.

Wachhorst, Wyn. *Thomas Alva Edison: An American Myth.* Boston: Massachusetts Institute of Technology Press, 1981. 328 p.

Wade, Graham. *Segovia, a Celebration of the Man and His Music.* London: Allison & Busby; New York: Schocken Books, 1983. 153 p. Discography on pp. 121–132.

Wallman, James. "The Berne Convention and Recent Changes in U.S. Copyright Law." *Cum notis variorum* 132 (May 1989): 8–10.

Walsh, Jim. "Favorite Pioneer Recording Artists" columns. *Hobbies,* 1942-1985. Cited by date only.

Waltrip, Bob. "Function and Restoration of Edison Rice Paper Diaphragms." *New Amberola Graphic* 73 (July 1990): 9–10.

Want, John. "The Great Beka Expedition, 1905–06." *Talking Machine Review International* 41 (Aug. 1976): 729–733.

Ward, Alan. *A Manual of Sound Archive Administration.* Aldershot, England; Brookfield, Vermont: Gower, 1990. 288 p.

Ward, Andrew. *Dark Midnight When I Rise: The Story of the Jubilee Singers Who Introduced the World to the Music of Black America.* New York: Farrar Straus & Giroux, 2000. 493 p.

Warner, Larry. "Researching the Pre-LP Original Cast Recording." In Hummel 1984, pp. xli–xliv.

Warren, Richard, Jr. "A Preliminary Bibliography of Published Basic Source Materials and Guides to Dates of Recording for Pre-LP Classical Music and Spoken Word Sound Recordings." *Association for Recorded Sound Collections Journal* 10-2/3 (1979): 163–166.

Waters, Howard J. "The Hit-of-the-Week Record; A History and Discography." *Record Research* 26 (Jan.–Feb. 1960): 2–18.

Watts, Len, and Frank Andrews. "The Vertical-Cut Disc Record." *Hillandale News* 108 (June 1979): 249–255.

———. "Pathé Records in Britain." *Hillandale News* 170 (Oct. 1989): 258–263; 171 (Dec. 1989): 289–295; 172 (Feb. 1990): 320–325; 173 (Apr. 1990): 8–11.

Weerasinghe, Lalia, ed. *Directory of Recorded Sound Resources in the United Kingdom.* London: British Library, 1989. 173 p.

Welch, Walter L. *Charles Batchelor: Edison's Chief Partner.* Syracuse, N.Y.: Syracuse University Press, 1972. 128 p.

Weston, Pamela. *Clarinet Virtuosi of the Past.* London: Hale, 1971. 292 p.

———. *More Clarinet Virtuosi of the Past.* London: Author, 1977. 392 p.

Whisler, John A. *Elvis Presley: Reference Guide and Discography.* Metuchen, N.J.: Scarecrow Press, 1981. 265 p.

Whitaker, Donald W. "Brass Recordings." *Instrumentalist* 20 (June 1966): 73–78.

Whitburn, Joel. *The Billboard Book of Top 40 Country Hits.* New York: Billboard Books, 1996.

———. *The Billboard Book of Top 40 Albums.* 3rd ed. New York: Billboard Books, 1995, 400 p.

———. *The Billboard Book of Top 40 Hits,* 8th ed. New York: Billboard Books, 2004.

———. *Top Pop Singles, 1955–2002.* Menomonee Falls, Wisconsin: Record Research, 2003. 998 p.

———. *Top R&B Albums: 1965–1998.* Menomonee Falls, Wisconsin: Record Research, 1990. 347 p.

———. *Top R&B Singles, 1942–1999.* Menomonee Falls, Wisconsin: Record Research, 2000. 667 p.

White, Charles. The Life and Times of Little Richard: The Quasar of Rock, New York: Harmony Books, 1984.

White, Don, and William Hogarth. "Florence Austral." *Record Collector* 14-1/2 (1962): 4–29; 14-7/8 (1962): 168–169.

White, Glenn D. *The Audio Dictionary.* Seattle: University of Washington Press, 1987. 291 p.

Whittington, Jennifer. *Literary Recordings: A Checklist of the Archive of Recorded Poetry and Literature in the Library of Congress.* Rev. ed. Washington, D.C.: Library of Congress, 1981. 299 p. (1st ed. 1966)

Whyte, Bert. "Shure Things." *Audio* (Apr. 1986): 26–27. [Whyte 1986/4]

———. "Fingering Prints." *Audio* (Aug. 1986): 16–18. [Whyte 1986/8]

———. "Put on Your Happy Feet." *Audio* (July 1989): 36–40. Discusses tweaking.

Wile, Ray. "The First Electrics." *Record Research* 85 (Aug. 1967): 5.

———. "The Edison Long-playing Record: Complete List of Issued and Unissued Masters." *Record Research* 88 (Jan. 1968): 8; 90 (May 1968): 9.

———. "How Well Did Edison Records Sell?" *Association for Recorded Sound Collections Journal* 3-2/3 (1971): 59–78. [Wile 1971/1]

———. "The First Martinelli Recordings." *Association for Recorded Sound Collections Journal* 3-2/3 (Fall 1971): 25–45. [Wile 1971/2]

———. "The Edison Discs of Frieda Hempel." *Association for Recorded Sound Collections Journal* 3-2/3 (Fall 1971): 47–51. [Wile 1971/3]

———. "The Edison Recordings of Gladys Rice." *Record Research* 143 (Dec. 1976): 5–7.

————. "Edisonia Local Phonograph Companies (1890–1893)." *Record Research* 115 (Feb. 1972): 8; 116 (May 1972): 9; 117 (Aug. 1972): 10.

————. "The Rise and Fall of the Edison Speaking Phonograph Company, 1877–1880." *Association for Recorded Sound Collections Journal* 7-3 (1976): 4–31, with 9 plates.

————. "The Edison Recordings of Edna White, Trumpet." *Record Research* 144/145 (Mar. 1977): 5. [Wile 1977/3]

————. *Edison Disc Recordings*. Philadelphia: Eastern National Park and Monument Association, 1978. 427 p.

————. "The Edison Recordings of Anna Case." *Association for Recorded Sound Collections Journal* 10-2/3 (1979): 167–184. [Wile 1979/1]

————. "Berliner Sales Figures." *Association for Recorded Sound Collections Journal* 11-2/3 (1979): 139–143. [Wile 1979/2]

————. "The Edison Invention of the Phonograph." *Association for Recorded Sound Collections Journal* 14-2 (1982): 5–28.

————. "Record Piracy." *Association for Recorded Sound Collections Journal* 17-1/3 (1985): 18–40. [Wile 1985/1]

————. "The Last Years of Edison Recording Activities Day by Day, January 1928 to October 1929." *Record Research* 213/214 (May 1985): 1, 3–10; 215/216 (July 1985): 8–9; 217/218 (Oct. 1985): 1, 12–13; 219/220 (Jan. 1986): 13; 223/224 (Aug. 1986): 10–11. [Wile 1985/2]

————. "Jack Fell Down and Broke His Crown: The Fate of the Edison Phonograph Toy Manufacturing Company." *Association for Recorded Sound Collections Journal* 19-2/3 (Feb. 1989): 5–36.

————. "Etching the Human Voice: The Berliner Invention of the Gramophone." *Association for Recorded Sound Collections Journal* 21-1 (Spring 1990): 2–22. [Wile 1990/1]

————. "The Development of Sound Recording at the Volta Laboratory." *Association for Recorded Sound Collections Journal* 21-2 (Fall 1990): 208–225. [Wile 1990/2]

————. "From the Edison Vault: Edison Blue Amberol 28100 Series." *New Amberola Graphic* 74 (Oct. 1990): 3–13. Lists 189 records in the "Concert" or "Grand Opera" series. [Wile 1990/3]

————. "Edison and Growing Hostilities." *Association for Recorded Sound Collections Journal* 22-1 (Spring 1991): 8–34.

Wile, Raymond R., and Ronald Dethlefson. *Edison Disc Artists and Records, 1910–1929.* 2nd ed. Brooklyn: APM Press, 1990. 187 p. (1st ed., see Dethlefson and Wile 1985) [Wile 1990/4]

Williams, Clifford, and Edward Hain. "Giuseppe De Luca." *Record Collector* 11-6 (June 1957): 124–140; 11-7 (July 1957): 184–185; 12-8 9 (Nov.–Dec. 1959): 199.

Williams, C., and T. Hutchinson. "Giacomo Lauri-Volpi." *Record Collector* 11-11/12 (Nov.–Dec. 1957): 233–272; 12-1/2 (Jan.–Feb. 1958): 34–35; 12-3 (Mar. 1958): 66–67; 12-4/5 (Feb.–Mar. 1959): 108; 20-8 10 (Aug. 1972): 239.

Williams, Clifford, and William R. Moran. "Adelina Patti." *Record Collector* 10-8/9 (July–Aug. 1956): 168–196.

Williams, Clifford, and John B. Richards. "Celestina Boninsegna." *Record Collector* 12-1/2 (Jan.–Feb. 1958): 4–33; 12-8/9 (Nov.–Dec. 1959): 200 (by Rodolfo Celletti); 12-10/11 (Dec. 1959): 257–258 (by C. de Villiers); 12-12 (Feb. 1958): 267–283 (by William R. Moran).

Williams, Frederick P. "The Times as Reflected in the Victor Black Label Military Band Recordings from 1900 to 1927." *Association for Recorded Sound Collections Journal* 4-1/2/3 (1972): 33–46; 8-1 (1976): 4–14; 13-3 (1981): 21–59.

————. "Eugene Ormandy Meets the Dorsey Brothers." *New Amberola Graphic* 52 (Spring 1985): 4–6.

Williamson, B.A. "Electrical Reproduction of Acoustical Records." *Talking Machine Review International* 10 (June 1971): 45, 48.

Wilson, Percy. *The Gramophone Handbook.* London: Methuen, 1957. 227 p.

Wodehouse, Artis Stiffey. "Early Recorded Pianists: A Bibliography." Ph.D. dissertation, Stanford University, 1977. 221 p.

Wolf, Robert. "Mengelberg Recordings: A Discography." *Le grand baton* (Aug.–Nov. 1971): 40–54.

Wolfe, Charles. *A Good-Natured Riot: The Birth of the Grand Ole Opry.* Nashville, Tenn.: University of Tennessee Press, Country Music Foundation, 1999. 312 p.

Wölfer, Jürgen. *Dizzy Gillespie; Sein Leben, seine Musik, seine Schallplatten.* Waakirchen, Germany: OREOS, 1987. 195 p.

Woods, Robin. "Report on National Program Archives." *Association for Recorded Sound Collections Journal* 2-2/3 (Spring–Summer 1970): 3–21.

World Wide Record Collectors' Directory. Los Angeles: Hollywood Premium Record Guide, 1970. 46 p. (Possibly a revision of *World Wide Collectors' Directory,* by Will Roy Hearne, 1957.)

Worth, Paul W., and Jim Cartwright. *John McCormack: A Comprehensive Discography.* Westport, Conn.: Greenwood Press, 1986. 185 p.

Yankovsky, M.O. "Nikolai Figner." Translated by John W. Robertson; revised and edited by Boris Semeonoff. *Record Collector* 35-1/2 (Jan.–Feb. 1990): 3–21.

Young, Edward D. "Serge Koussevitzky: A Complete Discography." *Association for Recorded Sound Collections Journal* 21-1 (Spring 1990): 45–129; 21-2 (Fall 1990): 241–265.

Young, Jordon R. *Spike Jones and His City Slickers.* Beverly Hills, Calif.: Moonstone Press, 1984. 192 p. Includes a 35-page discography.

Contributors

Dr. Garth Alper is an Associate Professor in Jazz Piano and Coordinator of the Music Media Division at the University of Louisiana, Lafayette. An active composer and arranger, he performs regularly with the Garth Alper Trio.

Frank Andrews is an English collector and writer who has authored more than 100 articles about acoustic-era labels and phonograph history, including histories of Aeolian-Vocalion, Edison Bell, Imperial, Zonophone, and Homophone. He served as Contributing Editor for the first edition of the *Encyclopedia of Recorded Sound*.

Rev. Claude G. Arnold, C.S.B., is an Associate Professor, Department of English, St. Michael's College, University of Toronto.

William Ashbrook is a contributing editor for *Opera Quarterly*. He is Distinguished Professor Emeritus, Indiana State University, Terre Haute, Indiana.

Carl Benson is the editor of *The Bob Dylan Companion* and writes on pop, rock, and folk music and music history.

Garrett Bowles, Music Librarian, University of California at San Diego, is the former President of the Association for Recorded Sound Collections.

George Brock-Nannestad, who was with the School of Conservation of the Royal Danish Academy of Fine Arts, Copenhagen, Denmark, for 7 years specializes in early sound recording technology.

Tim Brooks, Vice President, Research, USA Cable Network, New York is Past President, Association for Recorded Sound Collections, and contributing editor to its journal. He is the author of *Complete Directory to Prime Time Network TV Shows* and numerous articles.

E. T. Bryant was a City Librarian in England. His memory is honored annually through the E. T. Bryant Prize given by the IAML and the Music Libraries Trust for a significant contribution to the literature of music librarianship by a library and information science student. It recognizes the enormous contribution that Bryant made to the field of professional music librarianship.

Craig Bunch, Library Coordinator, Coldspring Independent School District, has contributed articles on the arts to *The St. James Encyclopedia of Popular Culture* and *The Dictionary of American History*.

Richard C. Burns, Audio Engineer, Packburn Electronics, Inc., Dewitt, New York was formerly an audio engineer, Syracuse University School of Music and producer of Overtone Records in the 1950s.

John Case is the owner of Priority/Anomaly Records in Fort Worth, Texas.

Ronald Cohen is Professor of History at Indiana University, Norhtwest. He is the author of many books including *Rainbow Quest: The Folk Music Revival and American Society, 1940–1970*, and recently edited *Alan Lomax: Selected Writings, 1934–1997*.

Kim Cooper is founder and co-edits *Scram*, the fanzine that is devoted to pop music obscurities. She co-edited the collection Bubblegum *Music Is the Naked Truth* and has a new collection, *Lost in the Grooves*, forthcoming from Routledge.

B. Lee Cooper, Provost and Vice President for Academic Affairs, Newman University, Wichita, Kansas, is the author of numerous scholarly articles and monographs relating to popular music recordings.

Ranjita (Anji) Kalita Cornette has over fifteen years of experience with sound engineering and preservation. She is Director of the Sound Preservation Laboratory at the Cutting Corporation in Bethesda, Maryland (www.cuttingarchives.com). Her work and staff were featured in the documentary *Save Our History Save Our Sounds*.

Martin Elste, Curator, Musikinstrumenten-Museum, Staatliches Institut für Musikforschung PK, Berlin, is the author of, among many other books and articles, *Kleines Tonträger-Lexikon*, *Modern Harpsichord Music: A Discography*, and *Meilensteine der Bach-Interpretation 1750–2000* which won the ARSC Award for Excellence in Historical Recorded Sound Research, 2001. Having been a record reviewer for *Die Zeit*, *Fono Forum*, *Klassik heute*, and *Fanfare*, he has served on the panel of the German Record Critics' Award since 1983 and was elected its President in 2000.

Colin Escott writes on rock, rhythm & blues, country music, and much more. The author and co-author of over a dozen books and annotator of more than 500 recordings, he has published groundbreaking research on Sun Records, Carl Perkins, Jerry Lee Lewis, Hank Williams, and others. Routledge recently published his book *Roadkill on the Three-Chord Highway*.

Howard Ferstler, formerly Librarian for Florida State University, is the author of *High Fidelity Audio-Video Systems*, *High Definition Compact Disc Recordings*, *The Home Theater Companion*, and *The Digital Audio Music List*.

Paul Fischer, Associate Professor of Recording Industry at Middle Tennessee State University, studies the origins and development of recording technologies and the careers of inventors. He writes on the application of literacy and cultural theory to popular culture and American popular music, among other subjects.

Doug Gelbert, in addition to writing on issues relating to popular music, is the author of a series of guides on hiking.

Gerald D. Gibson is Head, Curatorial Section, Motion Picture, Broadcasting and Recorded Sound Division, Library of Congress, Washington, D.C., and Past President of the Association for Recorded Sound Collections.

Michael H. Gray, Researcher, Voice of America, Washington, D.C. is Past President, Association for Recorded Sound.

Bruce D. Hall is a Music Coordinator/Reference Librarian of the Newton Gresham Library at Sam Houston State University, Texas.

Val Hicks is a retired music educator, vocal arranger, song writer, music historian, and veteran member (52 years) of the Barbershop Quartet Society, the SPEBSQSA. Dr. Hicks just completed a book entitled *The Six Roots of Barbershop Harmony*.

Brad Hill is a writer, musician, and computer expert. He has worked in the online field since 1992 and is the bestselling author of many books including *MIDI for Musicians*, *The Digital Songstream*, and numerous columns on digital technology and music. His website is www.bradhill.com.

Frank Hoffmann is a Professor of Library Science at Sam Houston State University in Huntsville, Texas. He has written over 35 books and many articles, including *Popular American Recording Pioneers: 1895–1925* with Tim Gracyk and CHOICE book award winner *The Literature of Rock* with B. Lee Cooper.

Thom Holmes, software designer, composer and performer of electronic music, has been active in the field of electronic music for over thirty years. He recently published a second edition of *Electronic and Experimental Music*. His website is www.thomholmes.com.

Kevin Holm-Hudson is a Professor of Music Theory at the University of Kentucky. He recently edited the anthology *Progressive Rock Reconsidered*.

Geoffrey Hull is Professor of Recording Industry and coordinator of the music business program at Middle Tennessee State University.

Edgar Hutto, Jr. was formerly Principal Member, Advanced Technology Laboratories, Radio Corporation of America (RCA).

Warren Rex Isom (1910–2003) was formerly Chief Engineer, RCA Records and Engineer, RCA Applied Research.

Paul T. Jackson is the initiator, a founding member, former VP, and Contributing Editor of ARSC. A retired librarian, he is the owner of Trescott Research, which does information and library development consulting. He is also a writer and editor of the Plateau Area Writers' Association's Quarterly; a choral musician and timpanist for Renton Community Concert Band; and President and timpanist for the Gateway Concert Band; all in Washington State.

Allen Koenigsberg teaches Ancient History and Classics at Brooklyn College in NYC and is the author of *Edison Cylinder Records, 1889–1912* and *The Patent History of the Phonograph*. For many years, he was the Editor and Publisher of *The Antique Phonograph Monthly*. His research website is located at www.phonobooks.com.

Dave Mandl is a writer and photographer. His weekly radio show "World of Echo" can be heard on WFMU in New York and Resonance FM in London.

Martin Manning, Research Librarian for the U.S. Department of State in Washington, D.C., has degrees from Boston College (B.S.) and Catholic University of America (M.S.L.S.). He has been a federal librarian and archivist for thirty years and he has contributed to several reference books. His book, *Historical Dictionary of American Propaganda*, will be published by Greenwood at the end of 2004.

R. Dale McIntosh is Associate Professor and Chair, arts in education, at the University of Victoria,

Victoria, British Columbia. Formerly, he was director of Performing Arts for the Province of Alberta.

Christopher Meeder teaches Jazz at Rutgers University, Newark in addition to being a jazz musician. He is the author of the forthcoming *Jazz: The Basics*.

Chuck Miller is the author of *Warman's American Records*, soon to come out in a second edition, as well as writing extensively on music and animation.

Kurt Nauck is the owner of Nauck's Vintage Records in Spring, Texas (www.78rpm.com), and author of the *American Record Label Image Encyclopedia*.

Susan Nelson teaches Instrumental Music at Bemidji State University, Bemidji, Minnesota, where she has also worked as a music librarian.

Richard C. Norton is the editor of the field-defining three volume set, *A Chronology of American Musical Theater*, among other publications.

Robert J. O'Brien is Professor of English at West Virginia Wesleyan College, in Buckhannon, West Virginia. A long-time member of the Association of Recorded Sound Collections, he has an extensive collection of literary recordings, especially of Shakespeare's works, and has delivered many presentations on recordings of Shakespeare.

Ian Peel, producer and writer, has contributed to the *Virgin Encyclopedia of Popular Music*, the *New Grove Dictionary of Music and Musicians*, and other reference works in addition to being the author of *Music & The Internet (Future, 1995), The Unknown Paul McCartney (Reynolds & Hearn, 2003)*, and numerous reviews and interviews.

Steven Permut is Senior Music Cataloger, Library of Congress, Washington, D.C. Formerly, he had worked as Music Cataloger and Reference Librarian at the University of Maryland.

Jeffrey Place is Archivist, Ralph Rinzler Archives, Center for Folklife Programs and Cultural Studies, Smithsonian Institution, Washington, D.C. He is the producer and annotater of over two dozen recordings of American music for the Smithsonian.

Robert C. Reinehr is Professor of Psychology, Southwestern University, Georgetown, Texas, and the co-author of *Handbook of Old-Time Radio: A Comprehensive Guide to Golden Age Radio Listening and Collecting* with Jon D. Swartz.

John Rocco is editor of *The Doors Companion, The Nirvana Companion, Dead Reckonings: The Life and Times of the Grateful Dead,* and *The Beastie Boys Companion.* He is Assistant Professor of the Humanities at Maritime College of the State University of New York.

William Ruhlmann, music critic for All Music Guide and author of hundreds of articles and liner notes, is author of the forthcoming *Breaking Records* (Routledge, 2004).

Brian Rust is an independent scholar and collector who lives in England. He formerly served as a librarian at the BBC Gramophone Library.

Henry Sapoznik, the award-winning author of *The Compleat Klezmer* and *Klezmer! Jewish Music from the Old World to Our World,* is the producer of Sony Legacy's historic reissue of klezmer titles and of the Yiddish Radio project in addition to being a Grammy-nominated producer–performer.

William Schurk is Sound Recordings Archivist, Jerome Library, Bowling Green State University, Bowling Green, Ohio.

Julia Scott is a journalist in San Francisco. She teaches at DeAnza College.

Gerald Seaman is Professor of Music, University of Auckland, Auckland, New Zealand.

Bob Sillery has written and edited on music and science for various trade magazines.

James Smart is a former Reference Librarian, Music Division, Library of Congress.

Stan Stanford is professor of music at Portland State University in Oregon where he teaches clarinet and music history. He is a collector of wind-up phonographs and early recorded sound. His website is www.clarphon.com .

Ron Streicher is Proprietor of Pacific Audio-Visual Enterprises, Pasadena, California, and current President of the Audio Engineering Society. During the summer, he also is the Director of Audio Production for the Aspen Music Festival and School. His book, *The New Stereo Soundbook*, has become a reference standard of the audio industry.

Jon D. Swartz is a psychologist and formerly Associate Dean for Libraries and Learning Resources and Professor of Education and Psychology at Southwestern University, Georgetown, Texas. He is the co-author of *Handbook of Old-Time Radio: A Comprehensive Guide to Golden Age Radio Listening and Collecting* with Robert C. Reinehr.

Susan Garretson Swartzburg (1938–1996) was Preservation Specialist and Assistant Librarian for Collection Management, Rutgers University Libraries, New Brunswick, New Jersey.

James L. Van Roekel, Director of Academic Instructional Technology and Distance Learning at Sam Houston State University, is a part-time musician, audio engineer, and sound designer.

Sara Velez is Librarian, Rodgers & Hammerstein Archives of Recorded Sound, New York Public Library.

Dario Western writes on British popular music. He lives in Australia.

Index

Note: **Bold** page numbers refer to main headings in the encyclopedia.